★★★

hotel oleggio

P9-CSG-372

Tel. 0039/321/93301
Booking: 0039/321/94890 - Fax 0039/321/93377
E Mail: holeggio@starnova.it
Internet: www.saritel.it/TPHOTEL

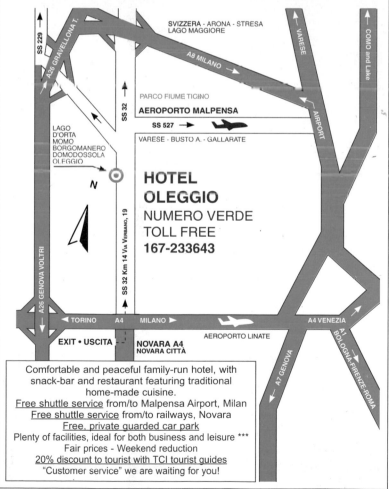

★ ★ ★ ★
Mare Pineta
International Campground - Bungalows - Apartments

LIDO DEGLI ESTENSI - FERRARA - ADRIA RIVIERA

International Campground
MARE PINETA

44024 Lido degli Estensi
Comacchio (FE)
Tel. +39 533 330194-330110
Telex +39 533 511498
Fax +39 533 330052
Tel. +39 544 971753-33937 (wintertime)
Fax +39 544 30388 (wintertime)

By the sea ◆
Natural pinewood ◆
In the center of the town ◆
Four swimming pools ◆
Sports tournaments ◆
Recreational activities ◆
Water sports ◆
Campers with 6, 4 and 2 beds ◆
Caravans with 4 beds ◆
Bungalows and apartments ◆
Organized excursions ◆

✦ THE HERITAGE GUIDE ✦

ITALY

A complete guide to 1,000 towns and cities

and their landmarks, with 80 regional tours

Touring Club of Italy

Touring Club of Italy

President and Chairman: *Giancarlo Lunati*

Chief Executive Officer: *Armando Peres*

Managing Directors: *Adriano Agnati* and *Radames Trotta*

Editorial Director: *Marco Ausenda*

Coordination: *Michele D'Innella*

Managing Editor: *Anna Ferrari-Bravo*

Senior Editor: *Marcella Borghi*
with the assistance of *Viviana Arrigoni* and *Guglielmo Martinello*

General Consultant: *Gianni Bagioli*

Jacket Layout: *Federica Neeff*

Map Design: *Cartographic Division – Touring Club of Italy*

Translation, adaptation, and editing: *Antony Shugaar*

Copy Editor: *Derek Allen*

Layout: *Giovanni Filippi*

Drawings: *Antonello* and *Chiara Vincenti*

Picture credits:

Cover: *Michelangelo's David* by Bullaty Lomeo/Image Bank
Foreword: *photos* by Tony Nicolini/Archivio T.C.I.; Image Bank/Grant Faint

Typesetting: *Centro Grafico Ambrosiano - San Donato Milanese*
Printed by: *G. Canale & C. - Borgaro Torinese (Torino)*

© 1999 Touring Editore s.r.l. - Milano
Code L2A
ISBN 88-365-1522-3
Printed in October 1998

Foreword

Florence: Duomo

ITALY, part of "The Heritage Guide" series, is a guide to the treasures of Italy, its regions and its cities, its landscapes and its natural heritage. It may not have everything, but it has all you will need to travel well in Italy: routes through the loveliest and best-known areas, a chapter on the regions of Italy, a section listing cities, towns, villages, and archeological sites, in alphabetical order, and a section in the back of the book with a wealth of practical suggestions, hints, and listings, with hotels and restaurants. Thanks to the historical and artistic descriptions, on the one hand, and the practical hints and suggestions on the other, the rich array of maps and city atlases, and the bountiful illustrations, we hope that this guidebook truly will prove to be an indispensable tool for getting the most out of travelling in Italy.

TCI's criteria in the ranking and classification of monuments and artworks have been recognized by the Italian government, and TCI is the only institution to compile a complete catalogue of Italian treasures.

It is our hope that foreigners in Italy, touring the many places and seeing the many things described here, may perceive the complex intertwining of past and present, history, art, and lifestyle, which are so much a part of the Italian experience.

Reggio di Calabria: Bronze of Riace

Contents

How to Use this Guidebook

We have attempted to use the original Italian names of all places, monuments, buildings, and other references where possible. This is for a number of reasons: the traveller is thus made to feel more at home with the names he or she is likely to encounter in Italy on signs and printed matter. Note also that maps in this book for the most part carry the Italian version of all names. Thus, we refer to Livorno and S. Pietro, rather than to Leghorn and the cathedral of St. Peter's. On first mention, we have tried to indicate both the Italian and the English equivalent; we have renewed this dual citation when it is the first mention in a specific section of text. With regard to Italian names, one of the most common abbreviations found is "S." for "saint". Note that "S." may actually be an abbreviation for four different forms of the word "saint" – "San", "Sant'", "Santo", and "Santa". Many other terms, while generally explained, should be familiar: "museo" is a museum, "biblioteca" is a library, "torre" is a tower, "giardino" is a garden, "pinacoteca" is an art gallery, and so on.

Excursions. This guidebook opens with 80 excursions, extending from the Alps to the islands. Each excursion is a specific route through an area, carefully selected and laid out by experts; each one covers an area in Italy which is noteworthy either for its artistic heritage, or for its landscape.

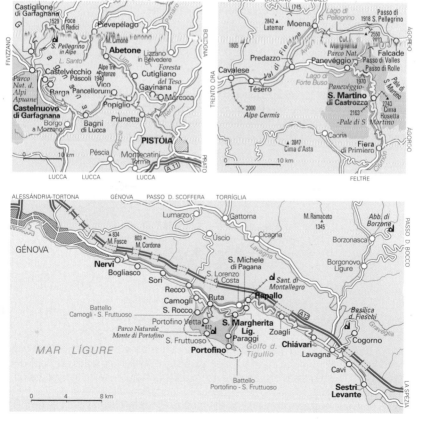

Italy and its Regions. The remarkable variety of Italy's twenty regions is described in as many brief introductory profiles. Arranged in alphabetical order, these profiles "photograph" the geographic, historical, and artistic characteristics of each region.

Italy A to Z. The chapter of individual geographic entries is arranged in alphabetical order, and comprises cities and towns, landmarks, and individual monuments that are not located in population centers; for instance: Fossano (Abbazia di, Abbey of), or S. Clemente a Casauria (Abbazia di, Abbey of).

Each place is provided with a succint description, and most are given a short historical profile as well. Differences in typography (names shown in **bold** or in *italics*) larger or smaller type size, and one or two asterisks (*) (**) indicate the importance of each monument, museum, or other site. Written descriptions are accompanied by drawings that help the reader to visualize works of art or architecture which should not be missed.

Useful information for prospective visitors, hours, and scheduled closings are indicated in *italics* directly following the name of the monument or museum; we provide information up-to-date as of the writing of this book. Let the reader beware that some subsequent changes may have been made in hours or schedules.

 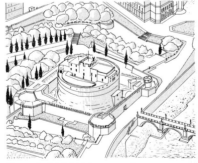

Venice: Ponte di Rialto *Rome: Castel S. Angelo*

Italy: Instructions for Use. This chapter contains all the information you will need to organize your tour, in order to see all the most interesting sights, and to avoid snags. From the addresses of embassies to tips on how to use public transportation, from shopping suggestions to descriptions of the cuisine, from hints on the best times of year to visit specific places to the most noteworthy cultural and folk events.

Information for Travellers. A compendium of useful addresses, hotels and restaurants which suggests – town by town, site by site – a selection of the finest hospitality facilities. Specific criteria are described on page 419.

Notice regarding telephone numbers. As of the 18th December 1998, each location's telephone code must also be dialled for local calls and are listed next to the symbol ☎ in the section Information for Travellers, page 419. For those calling from abroad, the local code (including the 0) must be dialled after international code for Italy, followed by the subscriber's number.

Maps and Plans. Excursions: illustrated in territorial maps, the 80 introductory routes cover the entire Italian peninsula, and are numbered progressively. In order to identify an area immediatly, the number is indicated both in the specific maps and in the overall map, where each excursion in indicated by an inset.
City plans. You will find monuments, train stations, and other useful infrastructure indicated in the following manner:
- if there is only one map of the city, such as "Como" for instance, the text describing that city will include the map coordinates, in the form of a letter and a number. For example: "Broletto (A–B2)";
- if there is more than one map of the same city, the indication of the map coordinates will be preceded by a Roman numeral identifying the specific map, such as in "Rome", for instance, "St. Peter's Square (I, E2)";
- the notation *(off map)* indicates that the specific monument or location is not shown on the map.

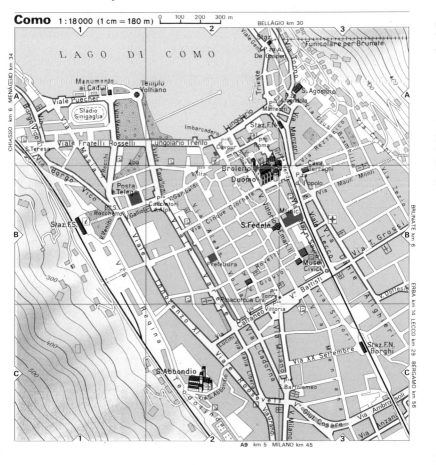

Excursion Key Map

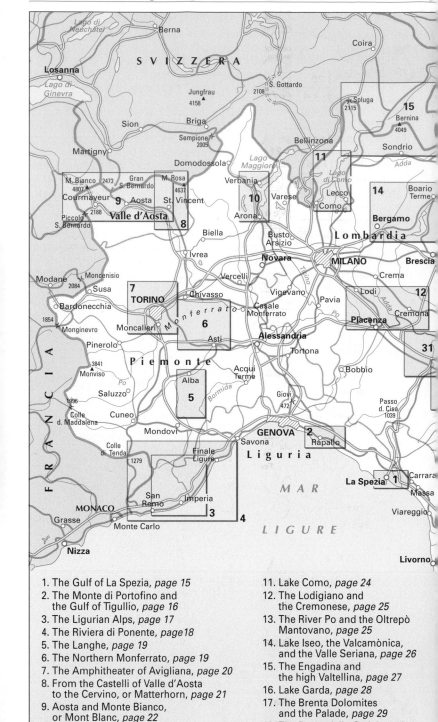

Excursion Key Map

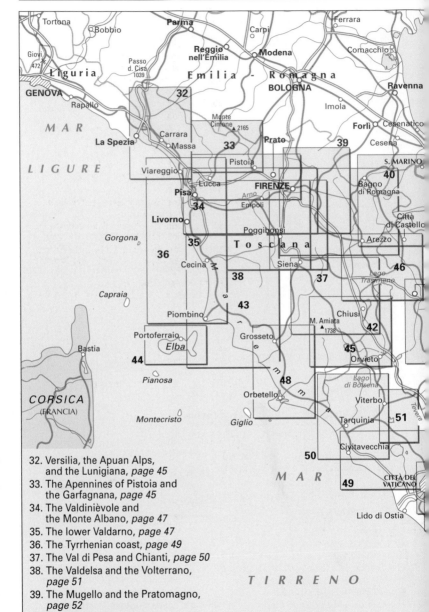

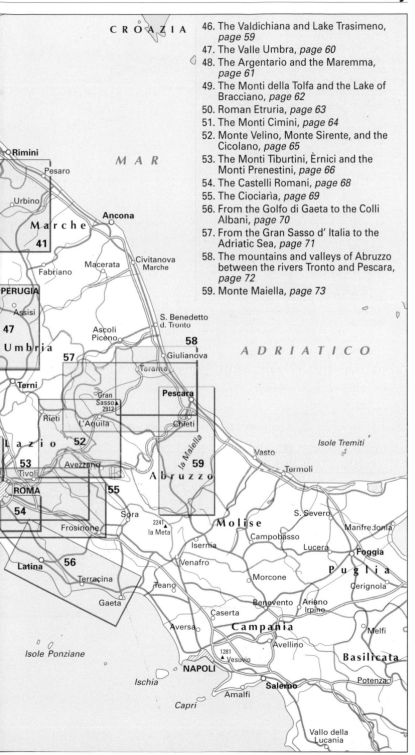

Excursion Key Map

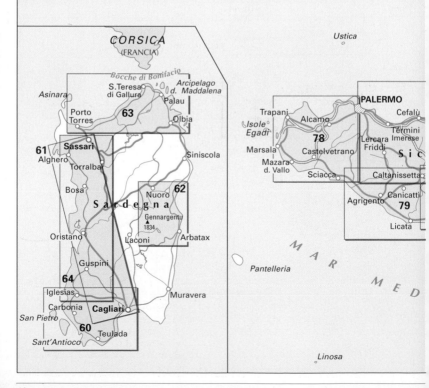

Southern Italy

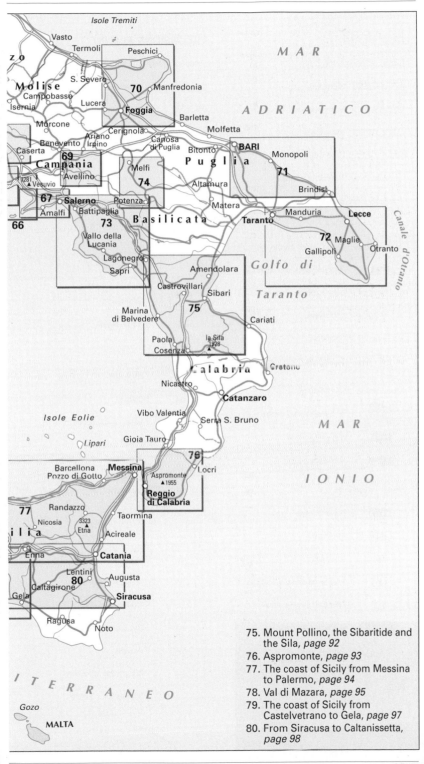

Conventional Signs Used in the Maps

CITY PLANS

Lines of communications

	Highways
	Highways and throughfares
	Main roads
	Other roads
	Pedestrian ramps
	Secondary roads
	Trails
	Roads under construction
	Railroad lines and stations
PORTO DI MARE Ⓜ	Subway lines stations
	Cableways
	Chairlifts
	Cable cars

Monuments and buildings

	of exceptional interest
	quite interesting
	interesting

Other indications

	Public offices
	Churches
	Hospitals
	Tourist information offices
	Principal parking areas
	Gardens and parks
	Contour map showing elevation and grade
	Arcades

EXCURSIONS PLANS

Lines of communications

	Excursion, with direction followed
	Detour from the route
A1	Highway, with route number
	Main roads
	Other roads
	Cableways and chairlifts
	Shipping lines

Towns and cities

O	Places to see along the excursion
	Urban area
O	Other places

Symbols

	Churches
	Castles
	Villas, monumental palaces
	Monuments
::: ⋏	Ruins
	Prehistoric remains (Nuraghi, etc.)
	Caves
*	Waterfalls, natural curiosities
	Mountain huts
	Mountain passes
·	Mountain peaks
347	Elevations
	Airports
⊕	Geographic directions
	Borders of countries

Excursions

The Gulf of La Spezia   1

La Spezia - Portovènere - Lérici - Ameglia - Luni - Sarzana - La Spezia (107 km.)

A mix of nature's bounty and strategic planning, with olive groves, jutting cliffs, and a historic naval base: in this distant corner of eastern Liguria the interaction between man and earth, sea, and plants has always smacked of the presence of the navy, a navy that has left visible marks in its wake, so to speak. In terms of the geography of the Ligurian littoral, the deep cleft of the Gulf of Spezia is unique along the entire arc of that coastline: it flows inland for better than 13 km., stretching nearly 9 km. across at the mouth, lying open to southern breezes. Like extended pincers of the Apennine range, the two mountainous arms that stretch out on either side of La Spezia to enfold and shelter the waters of the gulf — one running southeast as far as the promontory of Montemarcello, the other southwest to the promontory of Portovènere, with the islands of Palmaria and Tino extending the pincer's grasp out into the waters of the Ligurian Sea — remained under uninterrupted Ligurian rule until the fall of the Genoan Republic. The living forms of this world — grapevines, olive groves, farmers and fishermen — are at the heart of this route. North lies the coastline of the Cinque Terre, south is the Valle della Magra and the Luni littoral; they meet at the foot of the promontory of Montemarcello, where Punta Bianca joins two worlds. To the west, the jagged Ligurian coast, with crashing waves and drifting spray; to the east, the crescent-shaped Tuscan dunes, the sea lapping gently at the sandy beaches, the black line of pine forests, and in the distance, the white line of the Apuan Alps, mountains rich in marble.

The route. Leave La Spezia via the state road 530, following the promontories and inlets of the gulf; at a distance of 13.5 km. to the SW, you will reach Portovènere. As you head back to La Spezia, the road that climbs up from the Arsenale leads on to Riomaggiore and Manarola, in the Cinque Terre, with magnificent and varied views along the coastline of the Mar Ligure, or Ligurian Sea, as far as the Punta del Mesco. Return once again to La Spezia, and this time, you will follow the eastern shore of the gulf as far as Lérici. From here it is another 4.5 km. to Tellaro. From Lérici the route continues along a road with panoramic views, midway up the slope, amidst pine woods and olive groves, to Montemarcello. The scenery changes as you descend from Montemarcello to Ameglia: before you stretches the green land of Versilia, at the foot of the craggy peaks of the Apuan Alps. Cross the river Magra to reach Marinella di Sarzana, Luni, and Sarzana; from here, you will drive up the narrow little valley between Romito and Pùgliola, to return to the gulf of La Spezia, along a route with panoramic views.

Halting places of interest. Portovènere*, with its compact colorful rows of tall houses perched over the waves, and the ancient fortified coast town is one of Liguria's most charming spots; note the enchanting church of S. Pietro. **Riomaggiore**, easternmost of the Cinque Terre, boasts lovely and cleverly built houses, high on the steep slopes of the valley of a covered mountain stream; you can reach **Manarola** by following a walkway carved into the rock high over the waves (Via dell'Amore). **San Terenzo**: Villa Magni was the last residence of the poet, P.B. Shelley. **Lérici**, with its looming castle, was built in the 13th c. by Pisa as a military counterweight to the fortress of Portovènere; the coast route through **Fiascherino** leads to the almost intact coastal village of **Tellaro** (you can also go by boat), perched on a rocky spur. **Montemarcello** towers 266 m. over the sea. Walk to Punta Corvo, with its vast panoramic view. **Ameglia** is a hill town of high narrow houses, topped by a castle. **Luni**: archeological excavations and a museum of the ancient Roman town, which once thrived on shipping marble; it was stranded by a receding sea. **Sarzana** is a city with a long and complex history, studded with monuments including a Romanesque-Gothic cathedral which dates back to the 13th century.

The Monte di Portofino and the Gulf of Tigullio 2

Nervi - Camogli - Santa Margherita - Portofino - Rapallo - Chiàvari - Sestri Levante (63 km.)
When you think of the word "riviera," this elegant section of the Riviera di Levante is probably what comes to mind: once a watering hole of high society, now a popular resort area; lovely by nature and tirelessly improved upon by man. They've been seen a thousand times, yet they never grow old — sun, sea, palm trees, colorful houses, jagged rocks, dishes laden with seafood. Generations of the leisured class have planted exotic plants, such as the "pitòsforo," or butterbush, and bougainvilleas, growing in pink and mauve patches on walls. The olive tree is a symbol of the Mediterranean landscape, but it was introduced to these dizzying terraced slopes 300 years ago; just 150 years ago, odd to say, the farmers here planted "grapevines beneath the olive trees, and between the rows of vines, they would plant wheat and rye..." (D. Bertolotti, 1838). In the sweeping views you must visualize the sweat and back-breaking fatigue of generations of farmers; in the glittering waves, danger to sailors, even death. Only then can you appreciate the the votive offerings in local churches. Seaside villas are girt with medieval towers and a vast array of eclectic styles; a few are authentic "magnificent" homes of Genoan nobles. There are also turn-of-the-century hotels and many noteworthy monuments: consider the 13th-c. basilica, S. Salvatore dei Fieschi. Portofino, Camogli, and Chiàvari are jewels of Ligurian history; the Monte di Portofino is a splendid piece of Ligurian/Mediterranean nature.

The route. The stretch of the Riviera di Levante, along which runs the route recommended here and shown on the map, has heavy traffic in summer and on the weekends. Beginning from Genoa, you will take the Via Aurelia (state road 1), which offers many spectacular vistas. The name of this road (from Caius Aurelius Cotta, consul in 241 B.C.) originally described the ancient Roman road, which however only ran as far north as Vada Volterrana or Pisa; the Ligurian coastal road was first completed around 1830. You will leave the Via Aurelia, for the first time, at Recco, to reach Camogli, and then you will return to the Via Aurelia at Ruta (from here, you can take detours to the viewpoint of San Rocco and, along a private toll road, to Portofino Vetta); you will leave the Via Aurelia a second time, just past the tunnel of Ruta, to drive down to Santa Margherita Ligure, Portofino, and Rapallo. Follow the state road 227, a splendid coast road, from Santa Margherita Ligure to Portofino (built in 1878); though in the holiday seasons, you may encounter long delays (better to take a motorcoach or a boat). The route runs back along the Via Aurelia, from Rapallo as far as Sestri Levante.

Halting places of interest. Nervi*, a famed resort town with an enchanting marina, waterfront promenade, and the Serra-Gropallo park. **Camogli***: this ancient fishing village has tall, colorful houses, facing the sunny waterfront; on the second Sunday in May, the chararteristic annual Fish Festival takes place here. **Portofino Vetta**, fine panoramic view (416 m.), center of many paths running through the natural park of the Monte di Portofino. **San Lorenzo della Costa**: in the parish church, exquisite late-15th-c. Flemish triptych. **Santa Margherita Ligure***: straddling two inlets, this little seaside resort town still has the dignified elegance of the 19th c., when it was developed; it is surrounded by villas with parks. **Paraggi**, a small cluster of houses, once inhabited by fishermen and millers, who ran its 20 mills; note the landscape around the inlet. **Portofino****: the tall houses overlooking the little marina are no longer inhabited by sailors and fishermen, but by celebrities and society folk; by boat or on foot, along a path, you can reach **San Fruttuoso di Capodimonte***, a remarkable little village. **Monte di Portofino***, a unique promontory on the Ligurian coast, is crisscrossed by trails through the Mediterranean maquis, or underbrush, with fine views of jagged coastline. **San Michele di Pagana**, with colorful houses lining the beach; in the parish church, note canvas by A. Van Dyck. **Rapallo**, is an elegant resort town, which has expanded in recent years, though the waterfront is still intact. **Chiàvari** is an historical little town with a lively center lined with low porticoes and digni-fied 19th-c. architecture; at a distance of 4.5 km, across the river Entella, note the 13th c. **Basilica dei Fieschi***, one of the most important Romanesque-Gothic buildings in Liguria. **Sestri Levante**: the promontory shelters the delightful hidden inlet to the south known as the Baia del Silenzio, an important holiday resort.

The Ligurian Alps 3

Albenga - Garessio - Ponte di Nava - Viozene - Mònesi - Colle di Nava - Imperia (147 km.)
Coastline and countryside, followed by Alpine sweep, the realm of generations of mountain shep-herds. Though it does not appear to the eye, the Sella d'Altare, west and high above Savona, sepa-rates Apennines from Alps, as the ancient Roman historian Strabo first noted. The route recom-mended here runs through the hinterland of the Riviera di Ponente, and then cuts across a patch of Piedmont; it is a course run from the sea to a remarkable sort of Alpine universe, and then back down to the sea, up high valleys and over passes where salt caravans once jolted along the moun-tain trade routes. The landscape changes as you approach the mountains: kitchen gardens, olive groves, the greenhouses of the great "flower industry" of the Riviera di Ponente; the tortuous course of the Valle del Neva and its "borghi" lost in time; the wild high valley of the river Tànaro; larch trees and green pastures in the Ùpega basin; beech trees and stands of pine, with spectacular panoramic views from the ridge separating Mònesi and Nava; fields of lavender bloom from May to June on the Colle di Nava and outlying slopes; there are chestnut woods in the Valle dell'Arroscia. We end with the olive trees that infinitely dot the hills of Imperia, their leaves rustling at the sight of the glittering sea below. As you pass from the high valley of the Tànaro to the river Arroscia, you may note borrowed styles, distinctly non-Ligurian: Alpine houses, with more wood than is common in Liguria and rooves of overlapping slabs of stone, known here as "ciappe."

The route. Beginning in Albenga, you will take the state road 582, following the Val Neva, dri-ving over the Colle S. Bernardo (957 m.), and then driving down to Garessio, in the Tànaro valley, in Piedmont. Turning on to the state road 28, which runs up the Tànaro, you will pass through Ormea, and then Ponte di Nava; from here, a local road runs through the wild Valle del Negrone, and on to Mònesi, a Ligurian sum-mer resort and center for winter sports. Crossing over the crest between the rivers Tanarello and Arroscia, at Nava you return to the state road 28; this road, after passing the Colle di Nava (941 m.), leads to Pieve di Teco. On your way back to the coast, we recommend the detour that runs up to the Colle S. Bartolomeo (620 m.), along the watershed between the rivers Arroscia and Impero. Following the valley of the Impero, again along the state road 28, you will drive down to Imperia.

Halting places of interest. Albenga*, an ancient village with an inland main square, is noteworthy in general; note numerous monuments. **Zuccarello** is a walled village, with a street lined by medieval porticoes. **Castelvecchio di Rocca Barbena** is another walled village with narrow streets, typically Ligurian houses, and, in its midst, a castle perched on a giant mass of rock; from the **Colle S. Bernardo** is a fine view of sea and the Isola Gallinara. **Garessio** is a spa, while **Ormea** is a resort town with a medieval center. **Ùpega** has rustic mountain houses, each fronted by a broad balcony. From **Mònesi**, take a chairlift up to Monte Saccarello (2,070 m.), to gaze out over the Alpi Marittime. **Colle di Nava**, a wide hollow of meadows, a pass linking the valleys of Tànaro and Arroscia. **Pieve di Teco** is a nearly intact 14th-c. Ligurian village; note the 15th c. frescoes in the church of S. Maria della Ripa. **Colle S. Bartolomeo** has a splendid view of the Alpi Liguri (Ligurian Alps). **Pontedassio** has a Museo Storico degli Spaghetti, on the history of pasta.

Spotorno - Albenga - Imperia - Taggia - San Remo - Ventimiglia - Ponte San Luigi (112 km.)
Landscape and climate shift considerably as you follow this stretch of Ligurian riviera; Bordighera is considerably south of Genoa. Contrary to common belief, the "tall palm trees" were introduced much earlier than the 19th c., when the English first discovered this part of Italy; Leandro Alberti wrote about them in 1550, describing the vegetation as "lovely to behold and fragrant as well," adding that there are "delightful gardens, in which to rest and banish all melancholy." And the description holds true. If you expect this coast road to offer a continual view of the sea, "as it murmurs and whitens the length of the shore" (Tasso), consider instead that the sight, smell, and sound of the sea can be had only on beaches and waterfront promenades. This road offers only a few fine views, from the capes and points, chiefly (Noli, Mele, Cervo, Berta, for example). Along the so-called "Riviera dei Fiori," or Riviera of Flowers, in the westernmost section of the route, there is a profusion of greenhouses. There are many places to stop and enjoy the sights and works of art, but they must be sought out with patience and skill.

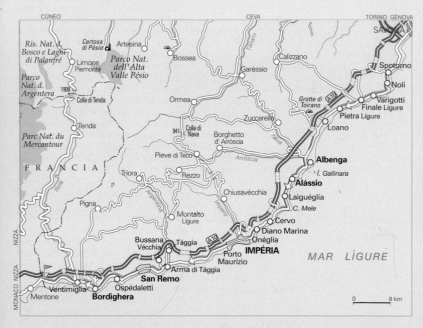

The route. The route to be followed is quite simple: it corresponds to the state road 1, the Via Aurelia (which you can take from Spotorno, after exiting the Autostrada A10), all the way to the French border. The road follows the coast the whole way; only in the last stretch, after Mòrtola, does it split into a high and a low road. As the road runs through the many beach resorts, traffic slows, and is often routed through less interesting outskirts. Handsome beachfronts, old streets of unmistakably Ligurian flavor, and excellent architecture can be found all over this coastline: park your car and seek them out.

Halting places of interest. Noli*, an ancient village beneath the fortified Castello Ursino. **Varigotti**, with singular terrace-roof Ligurian houses. **Finale Ligure**: note the 15th-c. town walls at Finalborgo, the innermost, historical section of town. **Loano**, with the renowned **caverns of Toirano***. **Albenga*** is the centerpiece of this route, in terms of atmosphere and ancient monuments; note the Museo Navale Romano. **Alassio***, an extensive and elegant beachside resort; take a boat to the **Isola Gallinara**. **Laigueglia**, with the nearby **Colla Micheri** (162 m.; 3 km. away), a perfect little village with olive groves. **Cervo***, an intact Ligurian fishing village. **Imperia**: Oneglia and Porto Maurizio, two towns with two ports, flank the city. **Taggia***, a well preserved ancient village, dotted with lovely sights; note paintings by L. Brea in S. Domenico. **Bussana Vecchia**, partly destroyed by an earthquake in 1887, is now an art "colony." **San Remo***: the Pigna, the medieval center of town with steep narrow streets, overlooks the 19th-c. resort town, now a modern city. **Bordighera***, an elegant sunny town shaded by palm trees; note petroglyphs in the Museo Bicknell. **Ventimiglia** still has a medieval air; to the east, Roman archeological excavations. **Mòrtola Inferiore** boasts the celebrated Giardini Hanbury, a botanical garden on the steep slopes. The **Balzi Rossi***, or red cliffs, tower over the sea; note caverns inhabited by early humans in the Paleolithic; also note the small museum.

The Langhe 5

Bra - Cherasco - La Morra - Monforte - Dogliani - Murazzano - Bossolasco - Alba (101 km.)
Two etymologies provide two hints regarding the nature of this area. "Langa," the singular of Langhe, means, in local dialect, the narrow ridge of a chain of hills. Following the "langa" means staying in the highlands, avoiding the valleys, and in fact this route offers fine views of vineyards and castles, perched on the higher hills. The other etymology is for truffle, or "tartufo." It originally comes from Latin; Petronius Arbiter speaks of "territubera," while in rustic dialect, the term was "territufer." In any case, the meaning is "tuber of the earth." Alba, where the route comes to an end, has a famed annual truffle fair; there are also excellent mushrooms (*porcini*, or boletus mushrooms, and *ovoli*, or royal agaric), vegetables, fruit, rabbits, pheasants, and partridges. Hilly landscapes and excellent food and wine, therefore, can be derived from these two etymologies. The wines are classic Piedmontese varieties; grape harvest, gathering mushrooms, and tours of the autumn colors are popular pastimes here.

The route. Beginning in Bra, you will head south along a regional road that crosses the river Stura di Demonte, passing through Cherasco, and then reaching Narzole. Here, you will drive down to cross the river Tànaro and then back up to La Morra. Then you will continue along hilltop ridges, "per langa," as the expression goes, southward, passing through Monforte d'Alba, Dogliani, Belvedere Langhe (literally, "fine view of the Langhe"), and Murazzano. From this last town, the general direction of the route changes, heading north. With a fine view of the Valle del Belbo, you will head over the Passo della Bòssola, and through the towns of Bossolasco (known as the "pearl of the Langhe") and Serravalle Langhe. A bit further on, at the fork in the road at Pedaggera, take a left onto the road that leads to Serralunga d'Alba. After following this road as far as Gallo d'Alba, you will turn right and drive to Grinzane Cavour; then, from Diano d'Alba, drive down toward the river Tànaro and the city of Alba.

Halting places of interest. Bra is a handsome town full of Baroque architecture, and was once known as "Brayda." **Cherasco** boasts an improbable Visconti castle, dowry for the Visconti bride of Louis d'Orléans (1387), and used as a pretext a century later when Louis XII of France laid claim to the duchy of Milan. **La Morra**, a medieval hilltop village; fine view. Along the road to Grinzane Cavour, note the former Abbey of the Annunziata, with private wine cellar and museum. **Barolo**: in the Castello Falletti, note the Museo della Civiltà Contadina, featuring exhibits of peasant life. **Dogliani** is a wine-making town with a high medieval section; take a detour down to the river Tànaro, and then to **Carrù**, with a Baroque parish church by F. Gallo, and then to **Bastìa Mondovì**, where you can see late-Gothic frescoes in the church of S. Fiorenzo. **Murazzano**, is a resort with excellent views. **Bossolasco** (see Dogliani), is another resort; view from central square. **Serralunga d'Alba** is a hilltop town, with the elegant Castello Falletti di Barolo. **Grinzane Cavour**: fine wines, a regional wine-cellar in the Castello Cavour, residence of Camillo Cavour, the 19th-c. statesman who united Italy. **Alba** is a little town with medieval architecture, towers and tower-houses; sections strongly redolent of the 19th c. It is renowned for its white truffles and its wines.

The Northern Monferrato 6

Asti - Moncalvo - Santuario di Crea - S. Maria di Vezzolano - Cortazzone - Asti (119 km.)
In the heart of the Middle Ages, a "Codex Astensis" praises the excellence of the local wines; in the 13th-c. another manuscript praises the wines of Monferrato, a highland over the Po, at the foot of the Ligurian Apennines, north of the Langhe, and mingling with it. This is the northern Monferrato, high in elevation, stretching north from Asti and the Turin-Piacenza highway running through it to the Po, arching between Moncalieri and Valenza. These highlands are dotted with vineyards facing the sun, towns perched on ridges and peaks, and views that change with each curve in the road. And then there are the castles...

The route. The route recommended here is circular, beginning from and returning to Asti. You will follow the state road 457 as it climbs over the ridge separating the rivers Tànaro and Po, following the course of the river Versa for a stretch, passing through Calliano and Moncalvo. Further along, just before you reach the banks of the river Stura, at La Madonnina, you will take a left along a road that leads to the Santuario di Crea; then, through Serralunga di Crea, you will reach the state road 590 (which runs up the valley of the Stura), turning off to enter Murisengo. Further along, a detour to the left will take you to Montiglio, once again in the valley of the river Versa. As you continue NW, you will reach Cocconato, a village with a splendid vantage point; from here, you will drive down to the state road 458, following it for a short stretch, toward Chivasso, and then you will turn left, passing through Albugnano and reaching the Abbey of Vezzolano. The next segment of the route leads from Albugnano south to Castelnuovo Don Bosco and the village of Colle Don Bosco (8 km. further south). As you take secondary roads over small rises, heading SE, you will reach first Cortazzone, then Baldichieri d'Asti, not far from the state road 10, Padana Inferiore; you can take this road back into Asti.

Halting places of interest. Moncalvo: home to the 17th-c. painter G. Caccia; from the tower in Piazza Carlo Alberto, fine 360-degree view of Monferrato, the Po, and the Alps. Santuario di Crea, a 16th-c. religious sanctuary, with 23 chapels scattered in the woods. Murisengo, with a fine 17th-c. castle and a Piedmontese-Rococo parish church. Montiglio, with a noted series of 14th-c. frescoes, in the park of the castle. Cocconato, a hilltop town with a 15th-c. Gothic town hall; also noted for its fine food. S. Maria di Vezzolano** (open daily, closed Mon.), noteworthy Romanesque-Gothic abbey, said to have been founded by Charlemagne but in fact built in the 13th c. Castelnuovo Don Bosco: birthplace of a noted Italian man of the cloth, Don Bosco. Cortazzone, boasts a handsome Romanesque church, S. Secondo, perched on a hilltop outside of town. Asti*: a town of red brick and yellow tufa, medieval architecture, farmers and vintners.

The Amphitheater of Avigliana   7

Turin - Giaveno - Sacra di S. Michele - Avigliana - Viù - Lanzo Torinese - Turin (151 km.)
Leaving aside Turin's "collina," which overlooks town from across the Po, there are mountains close to Turin to the west as well. The route recommended here explores, along unusual routes, the landscape of the Alpine ridges, in a farflung range of mountains, valleys, and hills, from the Chisola to the Stura. There are views of placid foothills; the hills in the three concentric belts of the morainic amphitheater of Rìvoli, where glaciers once carved out vast hollows, now blue with the lakes of Avigliana; the harsh, stern mountains of the narrow pass of the Valle di Susa; occasionally, a forested wilderness. We advise how best to reach panoramic overlooks that show the geography of this area. Monuments and architectural flavors are as interesting as the nature here: Avigliana, the Sacra di S. Michele, and S. Antonio di Ranverso are three notable sites from the Piedmontese Middle Ages. These are lands with old legends, preserved and perhaps engendered by Alpine isolation: the devil cheated out of a soul by the astute stratagem of a peasant of Lanzo, and the lovely Alda, who hurled herself from high atop a crag to defend her virtue from lusting soldiery, and was held up by angels (Alda jumped a second time, to show off to her friends, and this time the angels let her fall).

The route. You will drive out of Turin heading SW, toward Orbassano and Piossasco. A modern detour allows you to avoid the two small towns, joining up with the state road 589 near the fork that leads to Cumiana. From here, continue north along a scenic road that runs over a mountain ridge — Colletta (621 m.) — passing from the Valle della Chisola to the Valle del Sangone, entering the plain of Giaveno. A steep and winding road will then take you on to the Colle Braida (1,007 m.), and to the Sacra di S. Michele (962 m.), overlooking the Valle di Susa. You can then drive down another stretch of scenic road to the two lakes and the town of Avigliana. Follow the road for Rìvoli for a while, running over morainic hills on the right side of the lower Susa valley, as far as Buttigliera Alta; there, a left will take you to S. Antonio di Ranverso. A short stretch of the state road 25 in the Valle di Susa, heading west, will take you to the fork in the road, near Avigliana, that runs over the river Dora Riparia and climbs up to Almese. Continue north from Almese, and you will climb over the Colle del Lis (1,311 m.), between the valleys of the Susa and the Stura di Viù (one of the Valli di Lanzo). Follow the wooded lower valley of Viù down to Lanzo Torinese. You can drive back to Turin on either the right or left bank of the river Stura di Lanzo; on the right bank, you will drive past the Parco Regionale La Mandria, a regional park, and pass by Venarìa, while on the left bank you will go past Cirié and Caselle Torinese.

Halting places of interest. Piossasco: in the quarter of San Vito, note the Romanesque parish church and three hilltop castles. **Giaveno** is a resort and a manufacturing town; from the **Alpe Colombino** (1,240 m., 10 km. west), enjoy the view of the morainic arena of Rìvoli. **Sacra di S. Michele***: this renowned abbey, also known as the "Abbazia della Chiusa", is one of the masterpieces of medieval architecture in Piedmont, the high point of the route. **Avigliana** has a handsome medieval center; in the morainic hollow, note two lovely little lakes now part of a national park. **S. Antonio di Ranverso***, a fine example of medieval architecture in Piedmont, with clear French-Gothic influence. **Lanzo Torinese** is a thriving little manufacturing town, with a medieval center of narrow lanes and arches.

Around the 14th-c. Ponte del Diavolo hovers a legend that it was built in one night by Satan, who was cheated of the soul promised in exchange. **Cirié**, an industrial town at the mouth of the Lanzo valleys, has a notable Duomo. **Venarìa Reale**, once a Savoy hunting lodge, is now an industrial town in the orbit of Turin.

From the Castelli of Valle d'Aosta to the Cervino, or Matterhorn 8

Pont-Saint-Martin - Issogne - Verrès - Saint-Vincent - Châtillon - Breuil-Cervinia (66 km.)
Around 1750, a physician of Berne, Johannes Georg Zimmermann, wrote that, when standing before mountains, "the imagination soars to greater heights." In the face of the "grandeur of nature, amid vast masses of ice, when dangling over bottomless chasms or wandering past thundering torrents and through deep forests," the mind "begins to ponder the nullity of human strength." It is hard to say whether any of us now alive would be able to summon such pre-Romantic lyric vision, but this may be as close as we get: the sight of the Matterhorn (called the Cervino in Italy). This is the destination of the route. The Cervino was first climbed, up the Swiss side, on 14 July 1865, by the English mountaineer Edward Whymper, with a party of six (four died on the way down). On the Val d'Aosta side, on the same day, the abbot Aimé Gorret, Jean Antoine Carrel, and Jean Baptiste Bich were just beneath the peak, which they attained, a close second, on the 17th. Along this route, for a number of reasons, getting there is as enthralling as actually arriving: the stern Alpine landscape of the lower Valle d'Aosta and the feudal, late-Gothic atmosphere of the castles; lastly, as if you were climbing a staircase, from lake to lake, through meadows, past villages, through the lovely Valtournenche.

The route. The beginning of this route is the Quincinetto exit from the Autostrada to Aosta. You thus turn from the right bank of the river Dora Baltea and you take the state road 26 toward Pont-Saint-Martin, Bard, Verrès — from here, there is a short detour to Issogne, on the far side of the valley — and Saint-Vincent. Once you have reached Châtillon, you will take the state road 406 through the Valtournenche, a tributary valley on the left of the Valle d'Aosta, following it for 27 km., climbing all the way up to the hollow of Breuil-Cervinia.

Halting places of interest. Carema, last town

of the Canavese, surrounded by steep slopes dotted with vineyards (fine red Nebbiolo). **Pont-Saint-Martin**: the bridge over the Lys is Roman (1st c. B.C.), as is the stretch of road just beyond **Donnas**, with an arch cut into the rock. **Bard**, locked in a narrow gorge, over which towers a spectacular fortress, was rebuilt in the 19th-c. **Verrès**, with the square 14th c. Castello degli Challand, atop a lofty crag. **Issogne** (see Verrès): the 15th-c. castle may be the loveliest in all Valle d'Aosta. **Montjovet**: looming over the town are the ruins of the town's castle. **Saint-Vincent**, an elegant spa resort which hosts one of Italy four municipal casino; its popularity dates back to 1770, when an abbot discovered the curative properties of the springs. **Châtillon** is a market and manufacturing town at the mouth of the Valtournenche. On a rocky crag overlooking the river Dora stands the 14th-c. **Castello di Ussel**. **Valtournenche** is perched high in the valley of the same name; you can descend to the **Gouffre des Busserailles**, an "orrido" or gorge of the river Marmore. **Breuil-Cervinia***, renowned mountain resort, surrounding by high rocky peaks sheated in ice; fine view of the Matterhorn (in Italian: Cervino). Take a cableway up to the **Plateau Rosà*** (3,480 m.) and to the **Cresta del Furggen**** (3,488 m.), on the Swiss-Italian border.

Aosta and Monte Bianco, or Mont Blanc 9

Châtillon - Fénis - Nus - Aosta - Pré-Saint-Didier - Courmayeur - Entrèves (71 km.)
In the region of Valle d'Aosta the landscape, both natural and human, varies widely. Let us leave for another visit the 14 tributary valleys that lead up to the ridges of the Pennine and Graian Alps and the Gran Paradiso massif. The main valley, watered by the Dora Baltea, ranges from a valley floor, at Pont-Saint-Martin, just over 300 m., to the 1,000 m. of Pré-Saint-Didier. On either side, ranks of mountains are dotted with fields, vineyards, and warehouses; then there are tiny villages, perched high on mountain slopes, with no apparent means of reaching them. There are patches of high mountain meadows, set amidst forests, naked boulders, little waterfalls that freeze solid in winter, and ice raking the sky. Castles and once-mighty ruins line the valley and rise on dizzying ridges, guardians of an ancient and violent history. Trade between France and Italy continues to flow through this valley, along with hikers, mountaineers, and skiers. Mont Blanc, or Monte Bianco, towers at the end of this route; scaled for the first time on 8 August 1786, it can be reached by a cableway.
The route. This route hooks up with the preceding one. The route follows the state road 26, from Châtillon, up the Valle d'Aosta; except for one short detour — just before Nus, to Fénis — you will stay on this route as far as Pré-Saint-Didier. From there you will be following the state road 26 *dir*, which runs through Courmayeur and Entrèves. Just past this latter town, you will find the entrance of the Mont Blanc (Monte Bianco) tunnel. The state road runs parallel to the Autostrada A5, with the intense traffic from the Mont Blanc tunnel.

Halting places of interest. Chambave is a small town surrounded by vineyards. Just north, on the road to Saint-Denis, note the ruins of the **Castello di Cly**, atop a panoramic crag. The 14th-c. Castello di **Fénis** is certainly the most intact of Valle d'Aosta's castles. Further on, at **Nus**, the 13th-c. Castello di Pilato; another 14th-c. castle stands at **Quart** (2 km. along the road that runs off to the right of the quarter of Villair). **Aosta***, with its walls virtually intact, the Collegiata di S. Orso with its Romanesque cloister, its odd mountain-urban air, is a city of remarkable artistic, architectural, and historical value. **Sarre**: the castle, rebuilt in the 18th-c., has remarkable interiors; another castle, at **Saint-Pierre**, has a museum of natural science. **La Salle** has vineyards that climb up to elevations of 1,000 m., and produces fine white wines. **Pré-Saint-Didier**: from the hot springs, renowned among the ancient Romans, you can walk down to the "orrido," or dramatic steep gorge, of the Dora di Verney. **Courmayeur***:

the oldest and best known ski resort in the Italian Alps, is also a capital of mountaineering; the peak of Mont Blanc is 9 km. from town, as the crow flies; excursions first took place in the 19th c. **Entrèves**: from La Palud take a cableway up to the Punta Helbronner (3,642 m.), and then up over the dizzying rock spires of Mont Blanc, to Chamonix (France).

Lake Maggiore and Lake Orta   10

Arona - Mottarone - Orta San Giulio - Omegna - Baveno - Stresa - Arona (104 km.)

One somewhat excitable geographer wrote of these lakes that they are "isolated depressions and valleys, in which the rushing waters of land and sky finally find peace, unable to thunder off elsewhere." These lakes are of glacial origin. The Lago d'Orta comes from the glacier of Òssola or or the river Toce. The little lake of Mergozzo was separated from Lago Maggiore a thousand or more years ago. The remarkable views should be understood in the context of a climate that allowed the introduction of exotic species, of mountains rearing straight up from the lake shore, and distant snow-capped peaks, of a history of churches, castles, and sanctuaries, surrounded by tight little villages. In recent centuries, noble villas and thrusting middle-class hotels have been built up along the lakefront. Literary travellers have provided descriptions; the Isole Borromee — perhaps the jewel of this route — are called "art playing with nature" (J. Cambry, 1788); while E. Quinet (1832) said that they "resemble a creation of Ariosto. They have the same inventive grace as the Orlando Furioso, with an added pinch of the savage...."

The route. The hilly and mountainous area overlooking the western shore of the Lago Maggiore, from Arona to the river Toce, is called the Vergante. From Arona you climb up to the plaza of the S. Carlone and, driving through the Vergante, you will pass through Dagnente, Ghevio, Massino Visconti, and Gignese, and then you will drive up to the Mottarone (private road). This is the watershed between the lakes of Maggiore and Orta; you will drive down to Lago d'Orta, passing through Armeno and reaching the eastern shore at Orta San Giulio. Along the state road 229, you will follow this shore of the lake as far as Omegna, and then you will drive down the valley of the river Toce, to Gravellona. Drive around Monte Orfano and, after passing through the town of Mergozzo, you will drive around the little lake of Mergozzo; after crossing the river Toce, you will find yourself on the shores of Lago Maggiore at Feriolo. Then you can drive back to Arona, on the state road 33, enjoying the varied landscapes of Baveno, Stresa, Delgirate, and Mèina. During the fine season, this road is often plagued by heavy traffic.

Halting places of interest. In the old part of **Arona** there is still a flavor of the ancient lakefront marketplace; note the nearby gigantic 17th-c. statue of St. Charles Borromeo, the "S. Carlone." **Massino Visconti** has a castle that was the origin of the Visconti, lords of Lombardy until the mid-15th c. **Carpugnino** has a handsome Romanesque-Gothic parish church, S. Donato. **Gignese** (see Stresa): this town produced many master umbrella-makers, who emigrated throughout Europe; now there is a Museo dell'Ombrello e del Parasole (Museum of Umbrellas and Parasols). **Alpino**: 1,500 species and varieties of Alpine plants and medicinal herbs, in the Giardino Alpinia. **Mottarone**, with the 1,491-m. peak looming above the road; when the sky is clear, the view is spectacular: Monte Rosa and all the western Alps, seven lakes, and the Po valley. **Orta San Giulio** has ancient houses, loggias, Baroque facades, and lovely narrow lanes. Behind it is the **Sacro Monte d'Orta**, a hilltop series of spectacular chapels; take a boat to the **Isola di S. Giulio***, with its fine Romanesque basilica. **Omegna**, at the northern tip of the Lago d'Orta, is a manufacturing town with medieval and Renaissance structures. **Mergozzo**: a high road above the isolated little lake leads to Montòrfano, with the Romanesque church of S. Giovanni. **Baveno**: aristocratic homes and gardens overlook Lake Maggiore from the southern shore of the Golfo Borromeo. **Stresa***, an exclusive lake-side resort, with a strong Belle Epoque flavor; from here you can take a boat to the renowned **Isole Borromee*** three small islands called Isola Bella, Isola dei Pescatori and Isola Madre. **Belgirate**: distinctive houses, with porticoes and loggias, in the upper, older part of town.

Lake Como

Lecco - Onno - Asso - Bellagio - Como - Gravedona - Còlico - Varenna - Lecco (183 km.)

The magnolia tree, with its dense shadow of glistening leaves, the delicate wisteria, clinging to a gaze-bo, dark cypresses standing against the bright sky or the soft light colors of the mountain slopes, aza-leas, rhododendrons, and, in the words of Stendhal "groves of stunningly green chestnuts, bathing their branches in the lapping waves"; 16th-c. villas, late-Baroque and Neoclassical estates, parks built and defended over the centuries; venerable lakefront towns, their houses clustered together, with the whisper of the lapping wavelets; Romanesque parish churches made of grey stone. The blend of nat-ural beauty and historical heritage is perfectly balanced here; joined to the gentle climate, the "man-made" landscape attains something close to perfection. From the shore roads and from the lakefront promenades, shaded by ancient trees, you can always see the opposite banks; thus, each place you visit, you will first see, from across a silvery sheet of lakewater. And this preliminary view joins the preconceptions provided by literature and fame. Indeed, sometimes the view is even superfluous. For example, one morning in 1865, H.A. Taine, the French critic and historian, boarded a steamboat in Como. The white boat with black smokestack and thundering wheels took him for a tour of the lake, and the French writer spent the entire day amidst the red velvet of the salon, reading, researching, and writing about Venice. He emerged on deck only in the evening, but later wrote of the trip: "All day long, thoughtlessly, effortlessly, we sailed across a goblet of light...."

The route. Starting out from Lecco, you will cross the river Adda and then take the state road 583, which runs along the western shore of the branch of the lake identified with the great Italian author, Alessandro Manzoni, until you reach the village of Onno. This is where you start on a road that enters the Valbrona — with a steep climb and fine views of the Grigne moun-tains beyond the lake and, high above, the Corni di Canzo — and then descends to Asso. From Asso, you will take a scenic road that runs up the Valassina — or high valley of the river Lambro — as far as the Passo del Ghisallo, (754 m.), a name that is tinged with heroism for fans of mountain bicycle racing; you will then drive down to Bellagio. From this central point of the three branches of Lake Como, you will take the state road 583, following the eastern, or "inland" shore of the Como branch of the lake. From Como, the route continues up the western shore, following the Via Regina (state road 340), which is splendidly scenic (after Cernobbio and as far as Torriggia, the new road rides high above the lakeshore villages; elsewhere, the road hugs the shore, sometimes running through the villages), back to the central basin of the lake and then up to the northern branch. When you reach the

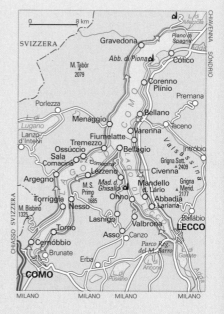

northern tip of the lake, you will cross the river Mera, drive across the so-called Piano di Spagna and cross the river Adda. On your way back to Lecco along the eastern shore of the lake, you can choose — at least as far as Abbadia Lariana — between the old and scenic road, running along next to the lake, and the new, faster road, the state road 36, which runs through many long tunnels. This entire route has heavy traffic on weekends.

Halting places of interest. Lasnigo: along the climb from Asso to the Ghisallo, note the Romanesque church of S. Alessandro, with its handsome 12th-c. campanile and late-15th-c. Lombard frescoes. **Passo del Ghisallo**, with the little church of the Madonna del Ghisallo, patron saint of bicyclists; splendid views of Lake Como during the descent to Civenna. **Civenna** offers another spectacular view from the tree-lined plaza of the Belvedere Grigne. **Bellagio*** is well located, at the juncture of the three basins of Lake Como; it has an old center with narrow lanes, hotel parks, and noble villas. **Torno** has two centers: one down near the marina, and another up toward the church of S. Giovanni; the 16th-c. Villa Pliniana graces the view from the far bank. **Como***: in this "city of silk," exquisite relics of the age of the communes and of the Lombard Renaissance stand side-by-side with notable buildings from the early 20th c. **Cernobbio**, practically a residential suburb of Como, has grand vil-las and a fine lakefront promenade; from the sanctuary atop **Monte Bisbino**, panoramic view of the lake, the plains, and the Alps. **Sala Comacina**: take a boat to the Isola Comacina, the only island in the lake. **Ossuccio**: the church of S. Maria Maddalena, has an impressive late-Gothic bell tower. **Tremezzo**: note the early 18th-c **Villa Carlotta***, with its azaleas and rhododendrons blooming in

April and May. **Gravedona**: fine views of this lovely town, and the church of S. Maria del Tiglio, a major work of Lombard Romanesque. **Còlico**: follow the shore of the lacustrine gulf, called the Lago di Piona; a short detour takes you to the **Abbazia di Piona**, an ancient monastery (note 13th-c. cloister). **Corenno Plinio**: this village is clustered and perched on a lakefront crag. **Bellano**, a pleasant health resort which boasts the renowned gorge of the Pioverna stream. **Varenna**: note the lakefront promenade and the stairs leading up between houses, with fine views of the old center. **Fiumelatte**, named for the river that tumbles down, from spring to fall, white with foam; it is only 250 m. in length.

The Lodigiano and the Cremonese   12

Lodi - Sant'Angelo Lodigiano - Casalpusterlengo - Pizzighettone - Cremona (89 km.)
The 15th-c. Bolognese architect A. Fieravanti (who later went to Moscow to build cathedrals in the Kremlin) worked on the irrigation and reclamation of southern Lombardy for the duke F. Sforza (1460). He noted that this area is not blessed by nature, and that hard work and organization was needed to make it the rich agricultural region that it has since become. This route invites the traveller to note the way that humans have changed this landscape, sunny in summer, foggy in winter, vast, flat, and abundant. The nuanced riverside views of the last part of the route are dotted with distinctive Lombard features: farming, churches, town squares, castles, and cities — such as Lodi and Cremona — that form part of this agrarian world with its long and venerable history.

The route. Beginning in Lodi, you head west, to Lodi Vecchio. From here, the general direction of this route is south at first, and then east. After crossing over the superhighway (*autostrada*) and the river Lambro, you will reach Sant'Angelo Lodigiano. You will then follow the river Lambro through the hills of San Colombano al Lambro; to the south of town, you will take a left onto the state road 234, which leads through Casalpusterlengo and Codogno, to the river Adda and to Pizzighettone. Just beyond this town, you will leave the state road, taking a road to the right through the territory of the Parco dell'Adda Sud, and on to Crotta d'Adda. You will then cross back over the river, passing through Meleti and Castelnuovo Bocca d'Adda, before reaching the Po, at the bridge of San Nazzaro. Take the state road 10 — Padana Inferiore — past Monticelli d'Ongina and back over the Po; you will finally reach Cremona, where the route ends.

Halting places of interest. Lodi* is a distinctly medieval Po valley town, picturesque and monumental; in the Renaissance Santuario dell'Incoronata, four exquisite panels by Bergognone; in the Romanesque Duomo, note the relief from the wealthy old town of "Laus Pompeia," attacked and leveled by Milan in 1158. **Lodi Vecchio** has an isolated Romanesque-Gothic basilica (S. Bassiano), with notable frescoes. **Sant'Angelo Lodigiano**: the restored castle has fine collections of art. **San Colombano al Lambro** is an ancient farming village at the foot of a hill studded with grapevines. **Casalpusterlengo** still has a few traces of its rural origins and a large town tower, a relic of the feudal castle. **Codogno**, now a modern manufacturing town, has fine paintings in the 16th-c. parish church. **Pizzighettone** is surrounded by the bastions of its venerable fortifications, defending the bridges across the river Adda. **Cremona***, a modern bustling city, has a splendid monumental center, with much surviving intact from the Middle Ages.

The River Po and the Oltrepò Mantovano   13

Mantua - Sabbioneta - Guastalla - Suzzara - San Benedetto Po - Mantua (135 km.)
Stands of tall poplars, irrigation canals, and embankments bordering the fields, a landscape of care-

fully tended, low-lying farmland: Sabbioneta is just 25 m. above sea level; San Benedetto Po, 19. The immense volume of silt borne by the river continually raises its waters; near Pavia the Po is already higher than the surrounding farmland. Reclamation, drainage, and construction of earthen banks along the Po began in the early Middle Ages, and continue today. The embankments tower as high as 10 m. (villages lie at their base); climb the banks, or cross a bridge, and you will note that vast expanses of land lie within the embankments, sometimes dry in the hot Po Valley summers, sometimes wreathed in heavy fog or blanketed with snow, and sometimes drowned by a flooded river (high-water season in May-

June and October-November; low-water in January-February and August-September). The two art centers along this route — aside from the point of departure and terminus, Mantua — are San Benedetto Po and Sabbioneta, representing two different phases in the construction of this riverine realm: Benedictine monks undertook the first drainage and reclamation, beginning in 1007; while Sabbioneta was one of the "little capitals" of the Gonzaga during the Renaissance, with a sophisticated princely court and remarkable architectural treasures.

The route. You will leave Mantua along the state road 420, which runs straight SW. After crossing the river Oglio near Gazzuolo, you will run through a number of small towns before reaching Sabbioneta. From there, the route continues south, heading toward the Po; once you reach the state road 358, turn toward Viadana. Remaining on the left bank of the river Po, you will pass through Pomponesco, Correggio Verde, and over the bridge to Guastalla, in Emilia. Take the state road 62 toward Mantua, cross through Luzzara and, as you return to Lombardy, you will pass through Suzzara, in the Oltrepò Mantovano. From here you will continue east, over the Autostrada A 22 (Modena-Brenner Pass), and through Pegognaga and then San Benedetto Po. With the last section of this route, you will first turn west, up the course of the river Po, through Portiolo and Motteggiana, and then onto the state road 62, to cross the Po a second time, on the bridge of Borgoforte, to return to Mantua.

Halting places of interest. Mantua**: this city's superb architecture is matched by the charm of its silent streets. It was the birthplace of Vergil. It is surrounded by three lakes, formed by the river Mincio as it flows past the city. **Villa Pasquali** is a small town whose spectacular parish church is one of the most significant creations of the late Baroque in the Mantua region, both in terms of size and inventiveness. **Sabbioneta*** is a fortified, complete, unchanging "ideal city" of the 16th-c., the dream of a Gonzaga prince, splendid and perfectly useless. **Viadana**: the relics of extensive settlements of stilt-dwellings, dating from the Bronze Age, discovered in 1885, are on display in an 18th-c. palazzo. **Pomponesco** has a large, late-Renaissance porticoed square. **Guastalla** still has a few relics of its past as a "minor Gonzaga capital"; note the monument to Ferrante I Gonzaga (Leone Leoni, 1564), the Palazzo Ducale, and the Cattedrale, both 16th-c. Nearby, **Gualtieri** has a handsome porticoed square and the 16th-c. Palazzo Bentivoglio. **Luzzara** has Palazzo della Macina, a Gonzaga residence. Outside town, toward **Suzzara**, a former convent now houses a museum of primitive art. Suzzara: the Galleria d'Arte Contemporanea features the artworks awarded the "Premio Suzzara" (1948 to the early 1970s). **Pegognaga** has a handsome Romanesque church, S. Lorenzo. **San Benedetto Po** dates back to the foundation of the Benedictine abbey of Polirone; church, re-built by G. romano in 1539-47, refectory, and three cloisters, all dating back to the 15th-c, survive. **Motteggiana**: the **Corte Ghirardina***, a 15th-c. country home, possibly by L. Fancelli, is an interesting blend of palazzo-court-villa-castle.

Lake Iseo, the Valcamònica, and the Valle Seriana   14

Sàrnico - Lóvere - Pisogne - Darfo - Breno - Capo di Ponte - Boario Terme - Passo della Presolana - Clusone - Albino - Bergamo (166 km.)

The lake, the petroglyphic "stories" carved into rocks, the hardworking people of the foothills, and fine paintings: there are numerous attractions in the course of this route. The traveller is free to choose those found most attractive. Writing about the Lago d'Iseo in the early 19th-c., one author cited the "beaches crowded with olive groves" and the "theatrical savagery of certain points, which contrast so well with the glittering shoreline" ... This region was also the birthplace of Italian industry: the low and middle Valcamònica, watered by the river Oglio, are stern pre-Alpine valleys; the slopes are dotted with vineyards and chestnut groves, while the valley floors feature farmland and factories. All around are iron mines; in this region, the highest point, physically, is the Passo della Presolana, with a fine distant view. The artistic high points are Capo di Ponte, with prehistoric petroglyphs, and the gallery of Lóvere, with Venetian paintings.

The route. The route recommended and shown on the map begins at Sàrnico, where the river Oglio

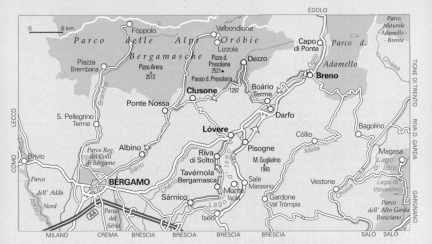

flows out of the Lago d'Iseo; for the first section it follows the western — or Bergamasque — shore of the lake, along the state road 469. You will stop at Tavèrnola Bergamasca for a tour of Monte Isola. From Lóvere, at the northernmost tip of the Lago d'Iseo, you will cross the Oglio to the far bank, at Pisogne. The lower stretch of the Valcamònica, which opens out here, is traversed by two roads, on opposite sides of the river: from Pisogne you can get on the easternmost of the two and drive up the valley, through Darfo and Breno, as far as Capo di Ponte (state road 42). You will then double back to Breno, following the road on the right bank of the river Oglio as far as Boario Terme, where you will enter the Valle di Scalve (state road 294); after reaching Dezzo di Scalve you will take the road that — after crossing over the Passo della Presolana (1,297 m.) — drops down to Clusone (648 m.). The last segment of the route runs down through the Valle Seriana, through Ponte Nossa and Albino, to Bergamo.

Halting places of interest. Sàrnico is a summer resort, with some medieval architecture in the town center **Tavèrnola Bergamasca** is an old harbor, from the days when there were no coast roads. There are houses with loggias and fine frescoes, including a youthful effort by Romanino, in the church of S. Pietro. Steamers will take you out to Sensole, on **Monte Isola**; walking tours of the island. **Lóvere**, overlooking a lovely lakefront, has noteworthy medieval architecture. Do not miss the Galleria dell'Accademia Tadini. **Pisogne**: note the frescoes by Romanino in the 15th-c. church of the Madonna della Neve. **Breno**: again, note frescoes by Romanino, in the former church of S. Antonio and in the town parish church. **Capo di Ponte** boasts more than a hundred boulders with petro-glyphs, or rock-carvings, in the 30 hectares of the Parco Nazionale delle Incisioni Rupestri di Naquane*; do not miss the Romanesque church of S. Salvatore and, in the village of Cemmo, the 11th-c. parish church of S. Siro. **Boario Terme**, an important spa resort since the 19th-c; as you drive up the Val di Scalve, beyond Àngolo Terme, the "Via Mala" — an old mountain road, which you can take, though you may prefer the more modern detour — penetrates into the deep gorge of the Dezzo. **Clusone** has a handsome old town center, in a tranquil setting. A Triumph of Death and a Danse Macabre are frescoed (1485) on the walls of the Oratorio dei Disciplini. **Albino**: this was an early manufacturing center; note the paintings by G.B. Moroni, who was born here, in the church of S. Giuliano and the Santuario della Madonna del Pianto.

The Engadina and the High Valtellina   15

Còlico - Chiavenna - Sankt Moritz - Passo del Bernina - Livigno - Bormio (160 km.)

In the heart of the mountain fastness, the Alpine range extends endlessly; quite as impressive as the length of this great mountain range — running from the Colle di Cadibona all the way to Ausburg and Vienna, sloping down to the Danube — is, so to speak, its "breadth": about 150 km. across, on a line with Mont Blanc, and more than 330 km., on a line between Verona and Ausburg. Since Italy's northern border, as is well known, runs nearly unfailingly along the high crest of the Alps, save for in the Canton Ticino, the steeper and short slopes, facing south, are part of the Italian landscape; every stream here runs down to the river Po and to the Adige. The route suggested here, which runs across the Swiss border, allows you to enjoy views of the far side of the watershed, to the other edge of the Rhaetian Alps, and, in particular, to the north slope of one of the most notable Alpine moun-tain groups, the Bernina, a mighty colossus of rock and ice, with the highest summit (4,049 m., there-fore constituting the last 4,000 to the east of the Simplon), and watered by torrents and rivers whose waters will flow all the way through Europe, to the Black Sea. The names of the valleys through which you will travel or which you will cross are evocative of so many different faces of the Alpine world: Val di Chiavenna, Val Bregaglia, Engadina (the first syllable is merely the Romanche version of the name of the river Inn, the tributary of the Danube that runs through the Engadina), Val Bernina, Val Poschiavina, Val di Livigno (a little patch of Italy just jutting over the watershed), Val Viola, and Valtellina. Along the way, there are a few artistic landmarks but the enjoyment of this route comes chiefly from the variations of landscape through which you will move, as you head over passes and drive down into valleys; note another feature of this route: cableways take you quickly up to high altitudes and spectacular views.

The route. The route recommended here winds along mountain roads and crosses passes that should not be attempted during the winter months. Beginning in Còlico, on the northern end of Lake Como, you cross the river Adda and, following the state road 36, you will reach Chiavenna. From here, climbing the Val Bregaglia along the state road 37 and entering Switzerland on the N. 3 road, you will reach the Passo Maloja, which takes you into the Alta Engadina, down which you can reach as far as Sankt Moritz. Just outside of town, near Celerina, is the fork from which the N. 29 road runs to Pontresina and then on to the Passo del Bernina (2,323 m.). Just 3 km. beyond the pass, as you descend into the Val Poschiavina (basin of the river Adda), you will take a left onto the road that runs into Italy at the Forcola di Livigno (2,315 m.), passing through the town of the same name (Valle dello Spöl, a tributary of the river Inn). At Livigno the route continues along the state road 301, which runs up the east slope of the valley, and over the Passo d'Eira (2,208 m.), and then the Passo di Foscagno (2,291 m.; customs checkpoint; Livigno is a free-trade zone) and finally, through the wooded Val Viola, down to Bormio, in the Alta Valtellina.

Halting places of interest. Còlico, overlooking the water, with a 19th-c. landing embarcadero, offers a last glimpse of Lake Como. **Chiavenna** is well located, with fine views, excellent landscape, historic heritage, and much art (church of S. Lorenzo, Baptistery, and treasure). **Casaccia**: at the first ramps of the steep climb up to the Passo Maloja, note the path to the gorge and waterfall of Orlegna. **Passo Maloja**, with a fine view of the Val Bregaglia; in the small town, note the house of the artist Segantini and a castle dating from 1885. **Silvaplana**: from nearby Surlej you can take a cableway up to Piz Corvatsch (3,303 m.), amidst glaciers; there is a spectacular view of the Engadine Alps. **Sankt Moritz***: note the spectacular landscape of this world-famous ski resort; also, visit the Museo Engadinese and the Museo Segantini, with work by the Tridentine artist who painted in the Engadina late in life. **Pontresina** lies surrounded by a great Alpine arc. On your way up to the Passo del Bernina you will pass by the base-stations of two high cableways: one leads to the Diavolezza (2,973 m.), a remarkable high-elevation viewpoint overlooking the glacier of Morteratsch, the Bernina, and the Piz Palù; the other runs up to the Piz Lagalb (2,959 m.), with an equally fine view of the Bernina group. **Livigno** lies on the broad valley floor; its houses were all once made of wood, widely separated for fear of fires. The old part of **Bormio** is still a typical Alpine village; in the Torre degli Alberti, in 1496, Ludovico Sforza "the Moor" and Beatrice d'Este lived here for awhile.

Lake Garda   16

Salò - Tremòsine - Riva del Garda - Malcésine - Peschiera del Garda - Sirmione (134 km.)
To quote a 17th-c. author: "delightful gardens, full of lemon trees, orange trees, and cedars, lush and flowering throughout the year, offer an exceedingly agreeable view, amidst laurel and myrtle, in a temperate and fragrant climate." He was describing the microclimate of Italy's largest lake, a piece of the Mediterranean amidst the Alps: the cypress became common here under Venetian administration, the grape vine dates back to remotest times, the olive tree may have been introduced by the Etruscans, but the Austrians developed it as a business. The mulberry has long vanished. Citrus trees

were first grown by Franciscan brothers under Venetian rule; there are ruins of ancient winter greenhouses on the terraced slopes. Under Austrian rule, many towns without roads were served by a steamer called the "Archduke Ranieri"; on the Lombard side, a coastal road was not built until 1931. This route runs through a varied succession of landscapes: steep slopes and villas below, then even steeper rocks; the breathtaking view from the highlands of Tremòsine, overlooking Monte Baldo; the colors of Venetian architecture, venerable little ports along the east shore; vast views, more like an arm of the sea than a lake, lie beyond Punta di S. Vigilio. Last comes Sirmione, frequented and described by Catullus: "Paene insularum, Sirmio, insularumque ocelle," the "delight of peninsulas and islands."

The route. From Salò you will follow the Lombard shore of Lake Garda, on the state road 45 bis, or Gardesana Occidentale. Once you have passed through Gargnano, you will take the road that climbs up to the highland of Tremòsine, and then drops back down to Limone sul Garda. From here, again along the shore, you will drive on to Riva del Garda and Tórbole, at the lake's northern tip. The route then runs the length of the eastern, Venetian shore on the state road 249, as far as Peschiera del Garda. Then you will take the state road 11 west, turning right at the fork for Sirmione and its peninsula, the final point along the route. Throughout this route traffic will be heavy, especially during the summer months.

Halting places of interest. Salò*, with a handsome historical center, lies in an inlet, amidst green hills: the beauty of the site is the reason for its renown. **Gardone Riviera***: a lovely lakefront promenade embellishes this exclusive resort; also worthy of attention is the remarkable Vittoriale, home of the early-20th-c. poet Gabriele D'Annunzio. **Maderno** lies on the delta of the river Toscolano; note the Romanesque church of S. Andrea. **Pieve**, center of the township of Tremòsine, has a remarkable overlook; to reach it you must take a detour up a twisting mountain road, into the gorge of the river Brasa. **Limone sul Garda**, set amidst abandoned olive, cedar, and lemon groves, has handsome homes in the old center, at the end of the lakefront promenade. **Riva del Garda**: this little town is a perfect combination of Alpine, Tridentine, and Venetian flavors (for a few brief decades, in the 15th-c., it was ruled by the Serenissima). **Tórbole** has an enchanting lakefront. "Marmitte dei Giganti," notable geological formations, line the road to Nago and from Nago to Arco. **Malcésine**: the most remarkable features of this old town are the Palazzo dei Capitani del Lago and the Castello; you can also take a cableway up to Tratto Spino (1,780 m.), on the crest of the Monte Baldo, with a two-fold vista of Lake Garda and the Adige valley. **Torri del Benaco**: a Scaliger castle dominates this lovely little village. **Punta di S. Vigilio***, amidst olive and cypress trees, deserves its reputation as the most romantic place on the lake. **Garda**: again, an enchanting lakefront, lined with handsome old houses. **Bardolino** lies amidst vineyards whose grapes are used to produce the wine of the same name; in the town, note the Romanesque church of S. Severo and the little church of S. Zeno, surrounded by small handsome houses. **Lazise** has a nearly intact ring of medieval walls. In the lovely panorama of the broad basin of the southern lake, note the enchanting — though often overcrowded — setting of the marina. **Peschiera del Garda** was a Venetian outpost fortress, the stronghold of the Austrian Quadrilateral: the town's military function can be seen in the fortifications that surround the strongly Venetian center, where the river Mincio flows into Lake Garda. **Sirmione***: the spectacular medieval walls of the Rocca Scaligera, the remarkably twisting streets of the "borgo," and the fine views of the lake are all well known, printed on too many postcards, perhaps, but still eminently enjoyable. The celebrated, so-called Grottoes of Catullus are actually the ruins of the largest ancient Roman villa from imperial times surviving in northern Italy.

The Brenta Dolomites and the Palade   17

Riva del Garda - Ponte Arche - Stènico - Tione di Trento - Madonna di Campiglio - Malè - Fondo - Passo delle Palade - Merano (162 km.)
There is an odd similarity in the history of the two towns on either end of this route, Riva del Garda and Merano; both were "patches of southern sun" for the Austro-Hungarian empire and its client states. There, however, the similarities end. Riva del Garda is dotted with olive trees, lemon groves, and cypresses, and overlooks a glittering blue lake; Merano blooms with apple trees against a backdrop of snow-

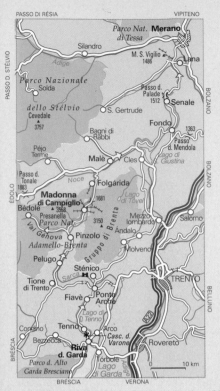

caps and crags. Moreover, these two extremes are just the beginning and end of a startling array of mountain landscapes, following a route that links Trentino with Alto Adige: chestnut groves and stands of beech trees line the turquoise waters of the Lago di Tenno; in the Val Rendena, beneath slopes dark with conifer forests, delicate green fields of good earth — one etymology holds that the name "Rendena" means "land of generous yields." Then there is the broad and sunny Anaunia, or Val di Non, where hidden torrents rush through deep gorges. The high notes of this symphony of landscapes, at any rate, come from the two mountain groups on either side of the Val Rendena. They differ even in their component rock: the Adamello-Presanella, crystalline, to the west, the limestone Dolomiti di Brenta (Brenta Dolomites), to the east. The latter can be seen from Madonna di Campiglio; while the former can be viewed from a detour to Val Genova. These are exquisitely Alpine mountains, with high ridges looming well above tortuous glaciers, jagged rock arenas, titanic stairways of seracs, little lakes, unannounced waterfalls thundering in the silence; the Adamello (3,539 m.; the highest peak) stands to the left of the valley; the Presanella (3,558 m.) stands to the right. The valley itself forms part of the Parco Naturale Adamello-Brenta: this is a haven for ermines, marmots, martens, and grouse. Overhead soars the golden eagle, and moving timidly through the forests are the last brown bears of the Alps. Here, we have spoken almost exclusively of nature; in the Val Rendena you can admire a number of paintings by the Baschenis family, a 15th-c. dynasty of artists from Averara near Bergamo.

The route. From Riva del Garda, the state road 421 leads north through Tenno, Vigo Lomaso, and Ponte Arche in the Sarca valley; from here, a 5-km. detour leads to Stènico. Follow the state road 237 along the river, pushing into the Giudicarie; from Tione di Trento, you will take the state road 239 up the Val Rendena. At Carisolo, you can turn off from the main road along a detour into the verdant Val Genova, as far as Pian di Bédole (19.5 km.). Then, after returning to the state road 239, you will follow the Valle di Campiglio as far as Madonna di Campiglio and the high pass of Campo Carlo Magno (1,681 m.). Follow the Val Meledrio down into the Val di Sole, at Dimaro. Then you will follow that valley, and its continuation, the Val Anaunia, through Malè, Ponte Mostizzolo, and — to the north of the Lago di S. Giustina — Revò. You will then reach Fondo, at the beginning of the state road 238; this road runs up the valley of the river Novella, reaching the Passo delle Palade/Gampenpass (1,512 m.), and then drops down the Adige valley to Lana and then to Merano.

Halting places of interest. Riva del Garda*: this little town is a blend of Alpine, Tridentine, and Venetian flavors; at the start of the road to Tenno, note the **waterfall of Varone**, where the water plunges 80 m. into a narrow gorge. **Tenno:** the old village lies in the shadow of a castle; from the church of S. Lorenzo (with 14th-/16th-c. frescoes) fine view of the plain between Riva and Arco. **Lago di Tenno:** a small tree-lined island lies amidst calm waters. **Fiavè**, a panoramic resort; during the Bronze Age, a large settlement of lake-dwellings was built here. **Stènico:** the castle is one of the oldest in Trentino, with sections from the 13th c. **Pelugo:** the church of S.Antonio has exterior frescoes by D. Baschenis (1493). **Pinzolo** has a "Danza Macabra," or 'dance of death,' by S. Baschenis (1539) on the side of S. Vigilio, a small cemetery church; inside, is another fresco by the same artist. **Val Genova***, mantled with woods, is a majestic landscape that leads up to the Adamello and the Presanella: 4.5 km. from **Carisolo**, note the waterfall of Nardis* with a sheer drop of over 100 m., 19.5 km. away is Pian di Bédole (1,578 m.) in an amphitheater of rock and ice. **Madonna di Campiglio*** is an elegant mountain resort, with skiing and mountain climbing; take a cableway up to the **Monte Spinale** (2,104 m.), with breathtaking view of the Brenta group; another fine view from the Grostè (2,348 m.), accessible by cableway from **Campo Carlo Magno**, a mile or so further along. **Malè**, main centre of the Val di Sole, boasts much old architecture; note the remarkable Cappella di S.Valentino, next to the parish church. **Senale** (see Fondo): situated in a lonely valley, this village is called Unsere Liebe Frau im Walde in German, after the ancient hospice of S. Maria in Silva; you reach it by leaving the Palade road just before the pass. **Lana:** the houses are scattered amongst the vineyards and apple orchards; note the carved gilt 16th-c. altar in the parish church of Lana di Sotto, or Niederlana; fine view of the Valle dell'Adige, as far as the Dolomites, can be had by taking a cableway up to the **Monte S. Vigilio/Vigiljoch** (1,486 m.). **Merano/Meran**:** the ancient center is typical of Alto-Adige; hotels, parks, and promenades, all with a flavor of Mitteleuropa.

Spondigna - Solda - Trafoi - Passo dello Stelvio - Giogo di S. Maria - Santa Maria in Val Monastero - Màlles Venosta - Resia (110 km.)

The first to reach the peak of the Ortles (3,905 m.) was Joseph Pichler, known as Passeyer Josele, a hunter of chamois from Sluderno, in Val Venosta, in September 1804; the local peasants said that he couldn't have made the climb without the help of the devil. As you drive up the 48 hairpin turns of the Stelvio road, at each turn a little higher with respect to the glaciers on the Ortles, you can lazily imagine the sensations of that first climb. The road climbs to an elevation of 2,758 m. — at Rocca Bianca, one of the finest viewpoints, you pass an obelisk commemorating the climber — and was built for military reasons, with no help from the devil, between 1820 and 1825, at the orders of the emperor Francis I, father of Marie Louise, the second wife of Napoleon. The road was meant to link the Val Venosta of the southern Tyrol with the Valtellina and Lombardy, which had just been recovered from the wreckage of Francis's son-in-law's enormous empire. Stagecoaches passed here in the summer; the rocks and ice echoed with the bells and snapping whips. In winter, sleighs whisked past on the snow. After 1859, the pass marked the border between Austria and Italy for 60 years. Aside from the Stelvio, the rest of this route has all the allure of high-mountain landscapes: the Val di Solda, with its glittering icy peaks, high above the meadows of the valley floor; the Val Monastero, eastern corner of the Grisons; the vast green expanses and lakes on the way up to the Passo di Resia and the source of the river Adige (in Val di Solda and Val di Trafoi you are in the Parco Nazionale dello Stelvio). All this of course is expected, given the location of the tour; perhaps more surprising is the art, especially the Carolingian paintings of Màlles and Müstair and the medieval frescoes of Tubre and Monte Maria.

The route. Beginning in Spondigna, in the Val Venosta, this route runs along a stretch of the road through the Stelvio pass, and then runs up the Val di Solda as far as Solda. After returning to Gomagoi, you will keep driving up the challenging series of hairpin turns to the Passo dello Stelvio (2,758 m.). On the way down the Lombard slopes, you will be following the road that turns right onto Swiss territory, over the Col of S. Maria (2,498 m.), dropping down into the Val Monastero/Münstertal. This valley, which is a collateral to the Val Venosta, leads you back onto Italian soil just a little way before Tubre. Further along, past Glorenza, and at Sluderno, you will join up with the state road 40, which runs upstream along the river Adige. Just beyond Màlles Venosta, at Burgusio, there is a short detour (1.5 km.) up to the Abbey of Monte Maria. Then, as you follow the state road 40, along the shores of the two manmade lakes of Muta and Resia, you reach Resia, not very far from the Austrian border, where this route finally comes to an end. As is the case with other roads leading through high mountain passes in the Alps a trip along the Stelvio is really advisable only during summer months.

Halting places of interest. Solda/Sulden, resort famed for the skiing and mountain climbing; take a cableway up to the **Rifugio Città di Milano** (2,573 m.), an Alpine hut with a fine view of the glaciers of the Ortles-Cevedale group. **Trafoi**: take a cableway up to the **Rifugio Forcola** (2,153 m.), an Alpine hut, with another view of the Ortles; from the town, walk (2 km.) to the **Santuario della Madonna delle Tre Fontane** (1,605 m.), with many votive offerings. **Passo dello Stelvio/ Stilfser Joch** (2,758 m.): the surrounding National Park extends into the Ortles-Cevedale group and along the Valtellina and Valvenosta; take a cableway up to the Nuovo Albergo Pirovano, and another up to the **Rifugio Livrio** (3,174 m.), an Alpine hut in a high mountain setting surrounded by glaciers. **Müstair** (Monastero), in the Val Monastero, Switzerland, descends from an abbey founded in Carolingian times, the Abbazia di S. Giovanni Battista: note the museum and fine frescoes in the church. **Tubre/Taufers im Münstertal**, on the Swiss border, with frescoes from the early-13th c. and others from 1370, in the church of S. Giovanni. **Glorenza/Glurns***, enclosed by sober, intact 16th-c. walls. **Sluderno/ Schluderns**: armory, art, and furnishings in the towering Castel Coira, 13th/16th c. **Màlles Venosta/Mals im Vinschgau**: the village is studded with towers, campaniles, and structures of great antiquity; note the exceedingly rare Carolingian frescoes in the little church of S. Benedetto. **Abbazia di Monte Maria/Kloster Marienberg**

founded in the 13th-c, a luminous white building with Gothic cloister dating back to the 16th-c, set in the spruce forest on the mountainside, with 12th-c. frescoes in the crypt. **Curòn Venosta/Graun in Vinschgau**: the 14th-c. campanile of the old town rises from the waters of the manmade **lake of Resia**, which flooded the village in 1950; in the new church, altarpieces from the old one.

The Grande Strada delle Dolomiti   19

Bolzano - Passo di Costalunga - Vigo di Fassa - Canazei - Passo Pordoi - Passo di Falzàrego - Cortina d'Ampezzo (109 km.)

The road here was built between 1895 and 1909, during the reign of the Austro-Hungarian emperor Francis Joseph; note the Belle-Epoque hotels along the road. Back then, people traveled these mountain roads in open buses called "torpedoni"; against the great clouds of white powder kicked up they wore dusters, helmets with earflaps, and goggles, cheerfully turning in every direction to see the spectacular Dolomites. This route has few rivals on earth, and is spectacular for the skyline and for the steep climbs. Consider these vertical distances: from Bolzano to the Passo di Costalunga (1,745 m.), from the Val di Fassa to the Pordoi (904 m.), from the Val Cordévole to the Passo di Falzàrego (691 m.); a total of 3,074 m. The descents are considerable as well: from Pordoi to Arabba, 638 m. in less than 10 km. And you can see, or take pictures of many peaks of the Dolomites along the road: the Catinaccio, the Latemar, the Sassolungo, the Sella, the Marmolada, the Sorapiss, the Antelao, the Pelmo, the Civetta, the Nuvolau, the Tofane, and the Cristallo. If you take the cableway up to the Sass Pordoi (2,950 m.), the entire vast mountainscape lies before you, beneath the bright sky, as if in a geographic model, all the way to the arc of the Alps.

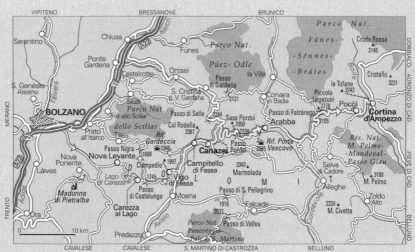

The route. Just east of Bolzano you leave the road over the Brènnero, or Brenner Pass, entering the gorge of the Val d'Ega and climbing up to the Passo di Costalunga (1,745 m.), the first of the Dolomite passes aong the route. A first 18-km. detour leads from Ponte Nova, via Rionero, to the Santuario della Madonna di Pietralba. From the Passo di Costalunga you drive down into the Val di Fassa, through which runs the river Avisio, driving up this valley as far as Canazei, where a road runs 12 km. up to the Lago di Fedaia, a mountain lake at the base of the Marmolada. From Canazei you will make your way up to the Passo Pordoi (2,239 m.), the highest pass on this road, the watershed between the basins of the rivers Adige and Piave. During the ensuing descent you will cross the Livinallongo, the high course of the mountain stream Cordévole, as far as Cernadoi, where you begin to climb up again, toward the third Dolomite pass, the Falzàrego (2,105 m.). The final stretch of this route is downhill, alongside the slopes of the Tofane, into the hollow of Cortina d'Ampezzo.

Halting places of interest. Santuario della Madonna di Pietralba/Maria Weissenstein, a traditional destination for pilgrims of Alto Adige, this sanctuary dates back to the 17th-c, and is set amidst spruce trees and Alpine views. **Nova Levante/Welschnofen:** a ski resort amidst the craggy Dolomites. **Lago di Carezza/Karersee***: the bright blue waters, with hints of cobalt, reflect the dense, dark stands of fir trees, white slides of gravel, and ridges of the Latemar; this is the first "picture-perfect" setting in the Dolomites along this route, well known, and still heartbreakingly lovely. At the **Passo Nigra/Nigersattel** (1,690 m.) between Carezza al Lago and the Passo di Costalunga, a road runs off to the left, beneath the Catinaccio; the pass at the end of the detour is 6 km. away; on the way back there are fine views of the Latemar. **Passo di Costalunga/Karerpass** 1,745 m.; this marks the boundary between Alto Adige and Trentino. **Vigo di Fassa** is a mountain resort town, with winter sports; in the section of San Giovanni, note the 15th-c. Gothic church of San Giovanni, with a slender bell tower and fine frescoes; take the cableway up to the meadows of **Ciampedìe** (1,997 m.), with panoramic views of the Catinaccio, the Pale di S. Martino, the Latemar, and the Marmolada group. **Rifugio Gardeccia** 1,948 m., in the high valley of Vaiolét, with a view of the jagged rocks of Larsec; you can walk or, in summer, there is a minibus from Pozza di Fassa or from the fork in the road between Pera di Fassa and Mazzin; continue on foot for an hour to reach the **Rifugio Vaiolét** (2,243 m.), an Alpine hut situated in the heart of the Catinaccio beneath the celebrated Torri del Vaiolét. **Campitello di Fassa**, renowned winter sports centre, take the cableway up to the **Col Rodella*** (see Canazei) 2,387 m., an astonishing overlook with a far-reaching view of the Dolomites. **Canazei**, a resort with skiing and mountain climbing; follow the high Valle dell'Avisio to the **lake of Fedaia**, and from there take a cableway up to the glacier of the Marmolada. **Passo Pordoi** (2,239 m.) is the highest point along the Grande Strada delle Dolomiti; this marks the shift of watershed from Adige to Piave; take a cableway up to the **Sass Pordoi*** (2,950 m.), where the 360-degree view is one of the most breathtaking in all the Dolomites. **Arabba** (see Pieve di Livinallongo), in the Val Cordévole, is the first location in the Cadore in the route; take a cableway up to the Porta Vescovo (2,550 m.), a balcony overlooking the icy slopes of the Marmolada. **Passo di Falzàrego** 2,477 m.: the Swiss stone pine dots the high meadows; take a cableway up to the **Piccolo Lagazuoi** (2,746 m.), with another panoramic view of the Dolomites. **Pocòl**: the nearby viewpoint offers a fine view of the fabulous mountainous hollow of Cortina d'Ampezzo; at sunset, before stretching shadows swallow them in darkness, the mountains glow in nuanced shades from pink to violet. **Cortina d'Ampezzo**:** set in a spectacular location, this world-renowned resort is justly famous.

The Val Gardena and the circuit around Mount Sella   20

Bolzano - Siusi - Castelrotto - Ortisei - Passo di Sella - Passo Pordoi - La Villa - San Cassiano - Corvara in Badia - Passo di Gardena (119 km.)

The Sella group (3,152 m.) is a magnet to mountaineers, and its architecture is described in terms more typical of military architecture: bastions, curtain walls, towers...Straight and sheer, the mountain appears at the head of four valleys (Fassa, Gardena, Badia, Livinallongo); the color of the rock changes by the hour, as clouds hide the sun or reflections reverberate from the snow that drifts onto the "cenge," or high ledges, that dot the cliff face — this is the classic image of the Dolomites. It is ringed by roads that, from valley to valley, run over four famous passes: Pordoi, Campolongo, Gardena, and Sella; the "Giro del Sella," along these passes, is as classic a climb in the Dolomites as the Grande Strada (and coincides with that route, briefly, over the Pordoi pass). In these passes, each year, you will see young men in colorful tops, pedalling furiously, followed by small armies of technicians, journalists, and publicity vehicles: on walls and bare rock you will see painted messages of encouragement, as if meant as captions to the spectacular views. In the "magic ring" of the passes, in this route, you begin with the Val Gardena, taking it from Bolzano along a route that soon leaves the Val d'Isarco and runs up to the Alpe di Siusi. When Montaigne passed through here, in the valleys, he had his secretary note: "beyond the first mountains, we could see other, taller mountains, cultivated and inhabited, and we learned that still further up there were vast lovely meadowlands that provide fodder for the cities beneath, as well as rich farmers and handsome homes." Between the Passo di Campolongo and the Passo Gardena, the route wanders through meadows and forests, in the high Val Badia and the Valle di S. Cassiano.

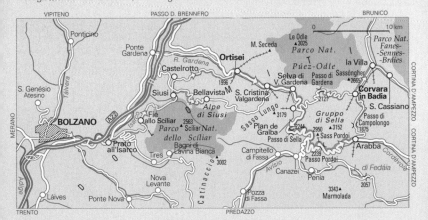

The route. After leaving Bolzano and taking the state road toward the Brenner via Bressanone, at Prato all'Isarco you will turn off toward the Alpe di Siusi, along a road that runs through the towns of Fiè allo Sciliar/Völs am Schlern, Siusi, and Castelrotto; you will then drive down into the Val Gardena/Grödner Tal, to Ortisei or to Sankt Ulrich. The road then climbs up along the loveliest part of this valley, then more steeply up to the Passo di Sella (2,214 m.), the first of the four Dolomite passes that ring the mountain group, or massif, of the Sella. On the drive down from the high pass, you will come to the fork leading off to the Passo Pordoi (2,239 m.), after which, at the highest elevation in the whole trip, you drop down into the Livinallongo, i.e., the high valley of the river Cordévole, at Arabba. From here, you return to the climb up over the Passo di Campolongo (1,875 m.) and you enter into the Val Badia; after you pass Corvara, you will follow this valley as far as La Villa. At this point, you will take the road up to the Passo di Valparola, which runs into the Valle di S. Cassiano, a valley that we recommend exploring, as far as the town of San Cassiano (beginning in Corvara, this detour is 8 km. long). After returning to Corvara in Badia, you will begin the climb up to the last pass on this route, the Passo di Gardena (2,121 m.). At Plan de Gralba, there is a fork for either Selva di Val Gardena or the Passo di Sella and the Val di Fassa; this joins the last link to the first in this chain around the group of the Sella, which is called the "Sella Ronda," or Round Saddle, literally, in Ladin, the Rhaeto-Romanic dialect of the southern Tyrol.

Halting places of interest. Siusi/Seis, a resort surrounded by pine forests; about 10 km. to the east is the **Alpe di Siusi/Seiser Alm***, rolling and serene. **Castelrotto/Kastelruth** is another highland resort. **Ortisei/Sankt Ulrich***, a famed ski resort, is the capital of the Val Gardena; the Museo della Valle in Cësa di Ladins is noteworthy in terms of the history of local wood-carving. **Plan de Gralba/ Kreuzboden**: a cableway runs up to the Rifugio Piz Sella (2,240 m.), beneath the Sassolungo, with a fine view of the high Val Gardena, the Sella, and the Odle. **Passo di Sella**: a rather tortuous yet spectacular pass which links the Val Gardena and the Val di Fassa; certainly one of the most celebrated passes in the Dolomites. **Passo Pordoi:** in a harsh and grandiose setting, you cross the watershed between Adige and Piave. **Corvara in Badia/Corvara** is a resort with winter sports; in the Gothic parish church, note the 15th-c. frescoes. **La Villa/Stern**, another ski resort, lies in a broad hollow at the foot of the Sassongher. **San Cassiano/Sankt Kassian** is the chief town of the idyllic valley of S. Cassiano, which runs into the Val Badia. **Passo di Gardena/Grödnerjoch**: like the other high passes of the "Sella Ronda," it offers remarkable variants on the landscapes and panoramas of the Dolomites.

The Pale di S. Martino and the Val di Fiemme 21

Fiera di Primiero - San Martino di Castrozza - Passo di Vàlles - Falcade - Passo di S. Pellegrino - Moena - Cavalese (87 km.)

The taste for exploring mountains, of course, is historically a fairly recent development. The value of nature as anything which goes beyond the merely utilitarian, as a master which is to be feared or even hated, the mountain as something akin to a sublime experience — all these aspects are part and parcel of a mentality and attitude that dates from the late-18th-c., when the Enlightenment was in the throes of yelding to early Romanticism, the age in which men and women first began to climb mountains for anything other than personal profit. Of this route through the Dolomites, an ancient traveler would undoubtedly have noted the importance of the mines (long since abandoned) of Fiera di Primiero, the amount of fine wood to be cut in the spruce forest of Paneveggio, in the high Val Travignolo, the hay of the Val di Fiemme, and the annual tribute that the high valleys paid to the bishop-prince in the plains below; certainly, it is possible our ancient traveler might not even have mentioned the Pale; the Camaldolites, who made their way up to San Martino di Castrozza centuries ago, were interested only in finding solitude and something resembling a certain closeness to God. These historical "interferences" certainly add an extra dimension to this rapid mountain foray from the high Cismon to the middle Avisio, two Tridentine valleys that are tributaries, respectively, of the Piave and the Adige, through the three passes of Rolle (1,970 m.), Vàlles (2,033 m.), and S. Pellegrino (1,918 m.); nowadays, most people would seem to agree however, that the objective and the chief point of interest certainly remains the group of the Pale di S. Martino — the highest point being the Cima di Vezzana (3,192 m.), while the sharp triangular pinnacle of the Cimon della Pala (3,185 m.) dominates the landscape of San Martino — with sheer unbroken walls, perpendicular bastions, deep fissures and crannies, and the broad hidden uplands, inconceivable when viewed from the valley below, entirely made of rock, blanketed in snow, pocked with pools of fresh water that springs from the rock, and with patches of glacier in the rough rolling surface. The alternatives among which you are forced choose, between the Passo di Rolle and the Passo di Vàlles, feature a descent into a forest of towering Norway spruce trees, as far as Paneveggio, and Alpine silence amidst the rock arena of the Pale, from the Baita Segantini (an Alpine hut).

The route. From Fiera di Primiero you climb up through the Val Cismon to the hollow of San Martino di Castrozza and then on to the Passo di Rolle (1,970 m.). After descending for a certain distance through the Val Travignolo, you will take a right along the road over the Passo di Vàlles (2,033 m.). Between these two passes, however, there is an alternate route: just prior to reaching the Passo di Rolle you can take a right onto a secondary road that climbs up to the Baita Segantini, an Alpine hut, at the foot of the looming Cimon della Pala; you will then drive down into the Val Venegia; in time, you will reach the road through the Passo di Vàlles, mentioned above. From the Passo di Vàlles you can descend to Falcade, in the river basin of the Cordévole, and then climb right back up to the Passo di S. Pellegrino (1,918 m.) which opens into the Valle di S. Pellegrino, a tributary of the Val di Fiemme. And it is through the Val di Fiemme that the last section of this route runs, down from Moena to Predazzo and to Cavalese.

Halting places of interest. Fiera di Primiero, resort, with skiing and mountain-climbing, once a mining town; in the Gothic church of S. Maria Assunta, note the old altar of the miners. **San Martino di Castrozza***, a famed mountain resort; take the chairlift up to the Col Verde (1,965 m.), then a cableway to the **Cima Rosetta** (2,609 m.), at the edge of the rock upland of the Pale di S. Martino. **Forest of Paneveggio**: this is the largest forest in the Italian Alps; you pass through it on the route from the Passo di Rolle to the Passo di Vàlles. **Falcade** is a scattered town in the Valle del Biois; the first little community you reach, as you descend from the **Passo di Vàlles***, just beyond the fork for the Passo di S. Pellegrino, is Falcade Alto, within sight of the Civetta. **Passo di S. Pellegrino** 1,918 m., between the Valle del Biois and the Val di Fassa; take a cableway up to the Col Margherita (2,511 m.), fine view; just beyond the pass, a detour takes you through the larch forest to the lake of S. Pellegrino. **Moena** is a noted ski resort; note the little ancient church of S. Volfango. **Predazzo** is another ski resort; there is a museum of geology and paleontology. **Tésero** (see Cavalese), with frescoes on houses and churches; note the frescoes on the little church of S. Rocco, including one that deplores working on Sunday. **Cavalese** is the chief town of the Valle di Fiemme; art collection in the Palazzo della Magnifica Comunità medieval in origin, the Palazzo retains a strong 16th-c. appearance; take a cableway up to the **Alpe Cermìs** (2,000 m.), in the chain of the Lagorai; fine view.

Lake Misurina and the High Pusterìa   22

Cortina d'Ampezzo - Passo Tre Croci - Lago di Misurina - Dobbiaco - Lago di Bràies - Lago di Anterselva - Brùnico (79 km.)

A lake, a sheer rock face, idyllic nature, and a lethal challenge. Every mountain has a personality all its own; these are features of the Dolomites. A little, brilliant lake, a flat narrow lakeshore, fragrant with the aroma of spruce trees, the gaze hemmed in by a round arena of ridges high above the treetops — an overall sense of tranquil serenity. When faced with a bare rock face, a climber coolly calculates the grip, the route, the ledges, the transits, balancing difficulty against strength (anyone else simply gazes in astonishment, admiration, and perhaps a little fear). Lakes and rock faces are the protagonists of a number of the episodes of this route through the inexhaustible Dolomites, which runs from Cortina d'Ampezzo to Brùnico, from the hollow of Cadore, in the shadows of the Tofane and the Cristallo to the broad, open, green Pusterìa, over the Passo Tre Croci and the Valle di Landro. Among the lakes of the Dolomites, it seems that the smaller they are, the greater their fame, aside from the really small ones — the lake of Landro, almost dry now; Dobbiaco, surrounded by a sparse woods; Anterselva/Antholzersee, with green waters; a good example however is the Lake of Misurina, surrounded by such peaks as the Sorapiss, the Cadini, the Marmarole; another is the Lake of Bràies/Pragser Wildsee, reflecting the Croda del Becco in solitary splendor. As for the rock face, the Rifugio Auronzo, an Alpine hut, faces the Tre Cime di Lavaredo, one of the greatest challenges in climbing in the Dolomites; even if you are not about to climb it, with rope, pitons, and crampons, and are only gazing up from below, it is a daunting sight.

The route. From Cortina d'Ampezzo, the road to the Passo Tre Croci (1,805 m.) leads into the high valley of Ansiei and to the lake of Misurina. A bit further along, note a detour onto a private toll road, which takes you 7.5 km. to the Rifugio Auronzo, an Alpine hut (2,320 m.), at the base of the Tre Cime di Lavaredo. On your way back from this side-trip, you will enter Alto Adige; following the state road 51 through the Val di Landro, you will descend to the hollow of Dobbiaco, in Pusterìa. The second part of the route follows this mountain valley, with the flow of the river Rienza. Still, the route splits off from the river twice; once, after Villabassa, up to the lake of Bràies, and once, about 6 km. past Monguelfo, to detour into the side valley of Anterselva, toward the Alpine watershed, all the way up to the lake of Anterselva (17.5 km.). The route then continues into Pusterìa, ending at Brùnico.

Halting places of interest. Rifugio Lorenzi

(2,948 m.): from the road to the Passo Tre Croci via the Cristallo chairlift at Som Forca (2,230 m.), then take a long-distance cableway to the Forcella Staunies (2,989 m.); the Alpine hut is nearby; spectacular view of the Dolomites and the Alps. **Lago di Misurina*** 1,745 m.: the peaks surrounding the hollow in which the lake lies form one of the classic settings in the Dolomites; a walk around the lake takes 40 minutes. **Rifugio Auronzo** 2,320 m.: it is surrounded by the legendary, mighty **Tre Cime di Lavaredo**; you can proceed to the Rifugio Lavaredo and then, on foot, to the Forcella Lavaredo (45 minutes), with a notable view of the Tre Cime. **Lago di Landro/Dürrensee** 1,403 m.: just beyond, on the right, a view of the Tre Cime di Lavaredo. Dobbiaco/Toblach: in the ancient center of the renowned mountain resort, with its strong flavor of the Alto Adige; note the Baroque parish church and the castle. **Lago di Bràies/Pragserwildsee*** 1,493 m.: this is another of the motionless lakes of the Dolomites; it reflects the dark green fir trees and luminous rocks of the Croda del Becco and the Sasso del Signore; in one hour you can walk around it. **Lago di Anterselva/Antholzersee** 1,642 m.: the dark green waters of this lake, surrounded by woods, is the destination of the detour from Valdàora to the Alpine watershed, along the tranquil valley of Anterselva, with a fine view of the Vedrette di Ries. **Brùnico/Bruneck:** an old road, typical of Alto-Adige, lies at the heart of the little town; nete the castle, dating back to the 13th c, and the nearby war cemetery; in the quarter of **Teodone/Dietenheim**, note the Museo degli Usi e Costumi della Provincia Bolzanina, focusing on local folkways.

The highlands of Trentino and Asiago 23

Rovereto - Folgarìa - Serrada - Tonezza del Cimone - Arsiero - Caltrano - Asiago - Passo di Vézzena - Lavarone - Trent (158 km.)

A little museum in Roana, in Val d'Assa, just a few km. from Asiago, on the highland of the Sette Comuni, is devoted to the "Cimbrian tradition." The Cimbrians, as you may remember from schooldays, were a tribe swept away by complex migratory patterns in the ancient world. They lived in what is now Schleswig, between the Baltic and the North Sea; they moved with the neighboring Teutons of Holstein into Gaul, and then broke off, in an attempt to settle in the Alps. They entered Italy over the Norico pass, defeating the Romans in the Valle dell'Adige, and then pouring into ancient "Venetia," until Marius defeated them at "Campi Raudii," near *Vercellae* (Vercelli), in 102 B.C. On the highland of the Sette Comuni and other nearby highlands, northern tribes did settle (M.R. Stern speaks of "strange and ancient languages") but only the scholars of the Renaissance truly thought they were the Cimbri; in fact, Germans colonized this area in the high Middle Ages. In this mountain region, between the Adige, the plains, and the large oxbow curve of the Brenta as it runs through the Valsugana, the highlands of Folgarìa, Tonezza, Sette Comuni, and Lavarone, to name them in the order this route takes them, wandering from Veneto to Trentino. All share the same lovely landscape, with rolling pasturage, immense forests, high terraces, hills, dales, silhouettes of nearby mountains, spruce trees and beech groves, dizzying views from the ridges overlooking broad valleys, and the clear signs of centuries of back-breaking labor (before resorts and ski slopes). Then came WWI, and the violence here was unthinkable: Austrian offensives were met by Italian counterattacks; ancient Asiago was wiped away, and shells and bombs were so scattered through the valleys that some mountain folk made a precarious, risky living for decades,

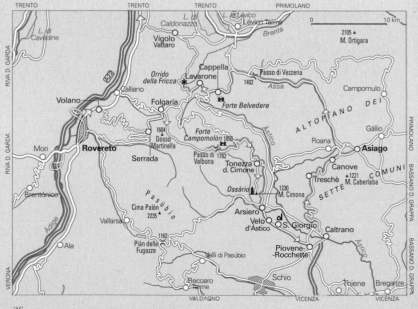

collecting them up carefully by hand and selling them to other people to be utilized as scrap metal.

The route. Climbing up from Rovereto through the Val Lagarina toward Trento, you will soon leave the state road 12, at Calliano, and turn onto the state road 350, which runs up to the upland of Folgaria, where a 5-km. detour will take you to Serrada. From Folgaria you will be following a route through the mountains, along secondary roads; after you cross the Passo della Vena (1,546 m.), you will descend to the upland of Tonezza del Cimone (side-trip to the Ossuary on the peak of Monte Cimone) and to the Val d'Àstico, a valley over Vicenza. In the Val d'Àstico you will pass through Arsiero, Velo d'Àstico, Piovene and, on the opposite slope, Caltrano. From here, you will be driving uphill again, reaching the upland of the Sette Comuni and Asiago. From Asiago, the state road 349, along the mountain river Assa, runs up to the Passo di Vézzena (1,402 m.), and then on to the upland of Lavarone. To the west, at the crossroads of Carbonare, you will be taking the road toward the high pass of the Fricca, which overlooks the Valsugana and then continues, via Vigolo Vattaro, on to Trent.

Halting places of interest. Rovereto: the city, typically Tridentine, with patches of Venetian flavor, is dominated by the great castle erected by the Castelbarco family in the 14th-c, which houses the Museo Storico Italiano della Guerra, or museum of the history of war; another museum boasts works by the Futurist Fortunato Depero, who was born here. **Volano:** this village has the small church of S. Rocco, with frescoes by local, 15th-c. artists. **Serrada:** take a long-distance cableway to the Dosso della Martinella (1,604 m.), with a fine view of the lower Trentino and the Pasubio. **Tonezza del Cimone**, winter-sport resort; detour of 4.5 km. to the Piazzale degli Alpini (1,109 m.), then a 15-min. walk takes you to the Ossario (Ossuary) atop **Monte Cimone** (1,230 m.). **Velo d'Àstico:** in the village of San Giorgio, a Romanesque-Gothic parish church with 12th-c. frescoes. **Asiago**, center of the uplands of the Sette Comuni, resort town; you can tour the astrophysics observatory; 360-degree view of the upland can be had by taking the chairlift up to Monte Caberlaba (1,221 m.). **Forte Belvedere**, an intact stronghold of the Austrian defenses during WWI (known in Italy as "The War of 1915-18"); to get there, you take a walk from the village of Cappella, on the Lavarone upland. **Orrido della Fricca*:** it offers a spectacular view of jagged rocks, worn by water, along the route, after Carbonare.

The Colli Euganei   24

Padua - Teòlo - Montagnana - Este - Monsélice - Arquà Petrarca - Battaglia Terme - Valsanzibio - Àbano Terme (118 km.)

The Colli Euganei rise up from the flat Venetian plain in the form of regular green cones; the Monte Venda (601 m.) is the tallest among them. On the southern slopes, there are many Mediterranean details; elsewhere, you will be able to find a wide variety of trees such as chestnut, hornbeam, manna-ash, and durmast; here and there you will come across orchards and vegetable gardens, vineyards and olive groves. The region had volcanic origins. History has scattered the landscape with jewels: hermitages of the 12th c., cunningly arranged with spectacular views, medieval castles, villas, gardens, and parks of the Venetian nobility. The waters here have curative properties, as the Romans has already known many centuries beforehand; over time, it was forgotten, but by the 13th c., the city of Padua was passing new

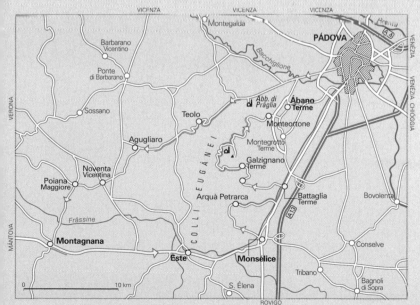

laws regulating the use of these waters. The route begins just entering the northern foothills, up to Teòlo, then it runs west and south around them, passing through the historic cities of the Paduan area — Montagnana, Este, Monsélice — and returns to the beginning, entering the famous locations of the highlands: Arquà, Valsanzibio, the hermitages of Monte Rua.

The route. Beginning in Padua you will take a road heading SW, past the turnoff for Àbano Terme, and up into the Colli Euganei and on to Teòlo. Driving down from the hills onto the plains, you will then continue through Vò and Agugliaro, to Noventa Vicentina; from here, you will continue through Poiana Maggiore and on to Montagnana. Turning east here, on the state road 10, you will drive through first Este and then Monsélice. From there, following secondary roads, you will drive back up into the Colli Euganei to see Arquà Petrarca. Once you are back in the lowlands, you will drive for a short stretch along the state road Monsélice-Padova, as far as Battaglia Terme. At this point, you will take one last drive through the hills, up through Valsanzibio and Galzignano Terme, to the Hermitage of Monte Rua. On your way down from here, you will pass through Torreglia and Monteortone, ending the route at Àbano Terme.

Halting places of interest. Abbazia di Praglia**: a boulevard lined with plane trees leads to the solemn Benedictine monastery founded in the 12th-c century and almost totally re-built in the 15th-16th-c, with church and four cloisters. **Teòlo** is believed to be the birthplace of the Roman historian Livy; fine view from the 13th-c parish church of S. Giustina at the highest point in town; from the square in front of the church, a road enters the Parco Lieta Carraresi, a nature reserve with excellent scenery and views. **Noventa Vicentina**: Villa Barbarigo, at the center of a small town that grew up around it, is now the town hall; in the parish church note a canvas by Tiepolo. **Poiana Maggiore**: of the three villas that belonged to the Pojana family, one was designed and built by A. Palladio. **Montagnana***: girt with intact medieval walls, among the finest in Europe; in the Duomo, note paintings, one by P. Veronese; Palazzo Pisani, just outside of town, is by A. Palladio. **Este***: still intact are the walls of the Castello Carrarese around the holiday home of the Mocenigo family (note museum on Venetia prior to the Romans); canvas by Tiepolo, among others, in the Duomo. **Monsélice***: along the walk on this flinty hill are the Castello, the Duomo Vecchio, the Santuario delle Sette Chiese, the Villa Duodo, and fascinating views of the plains. **Arquà Petrarca:** here the great 14th-c. poet Petrarch lived in old age and died; his tomb is in the church courtyard. **Battaglia Terme:** Stendhal frequented this thermal spa; around it are the Villa Selvatico Capodilista high on the Colle di S. Elena and, along the road to Padua, the Villa Cataio. **Valsanzibio** (see Arquà Petrarca), with the Italian-style garden of the Villa Barbarigo. **Eremo di Rua**: this hermitage is inhabited by Camaldolite monks, who live in cloistered seclusion; the setting is green and silent, the view extends to the hills, the plain, the Alps, and Venice. **Monteortone***: this 15th-c. sanctuary is supposedly the site of a miracle. **Àbano Terme***: the large Venetian "ville d'eaux" is typical of the turn of the 20th c.

The Brenta plain and the Marca Trevigiana   25

Padua - Stra - Mira - Mestre - Treviso - Castelfranco Veneto - Cittadella - Piazzola sul Brenta - Vicenza (130 km.)

"Beyond the handsome fields that extended on either side, we would pass through merry little villages, and at every hour we saw noble homes, many of them quite splendid, belonging to the powerful of Venice, who come to spend the summer and part of the fall here...." This is the Riviera del Brenta, the first section of this route; Leandro Fernandez de Moratin, a Spanish traveller, saw it "from the boat that leaves Venice two times every day," as described in his "El Viaje de Italia," 1793-96. Even if you leave aside the cities, with their universal culture of art, architectural style, and atmosphere — Padua and Vicenza at either end and Treviso in the middle are exquisite — a great deal can be learned from the Venetian countryside: from the fragments of rough, combattive medieval culture, pre-Venetian, and the "culture of the villa" from the 16th to the 18th c. — the nobility was moving inland, farming, living in the pleasant countryside, studying, socializing, or simply whiling away the newly civilized rustic day. This route joins the two eras: the former can be found in the Castello di Castelfranco Veneto and the menacing walls of Cittadella, the latter along the Riviera del Brenta and on the Terraglio (the road from Mestre and Treviso), in Villa Foscari alla Malcontenta, Villa Emo a Fanzolo, or Villa Contarini a Piazzola. As Andrea Palladio put it: "The true gentleman will draw great benefit and consolation from the 'case di villa,' or country home..."; today those gifts can be had by the unassuming tourist as well.

The route. Starting out from Padua, Stra marks the point at which, on the state road 11, you reach the Riviera del Brenta, following it as far as Villa Foscari, the Malcontenta, not far from the lagoon. A stretch of the state road 309 toward Mestre will take you to the Padua-Trieste Autostrada; a quick jog along this highway ring-road, around Mestre, will avoid the crowded trek through the city of Mestre. You will leave the Autostrada at the exit of Mestre Est, on a line with the state road 13, known as the Terraglio, which you will then follow to Treviso. You will then continue west along the state road 53 Treviso-Vicenza as far as Castelfranco Veneto and Cittadella, except for the detour to Villa Emo (5 km. from Vedelago). At Cittadella you will take the state road 47 toward Padua, following it until you reach the turnoff for Piazzola sul Brenta. Lastly, you will head for Vicenza, via Piazzola sul Brenta, Camisano Vicentino, and Torri di Quartesolo.

Halting places of interest. Stra: Villa Pisani, with its palatial interiors, fresco by Tiepolo, park, and

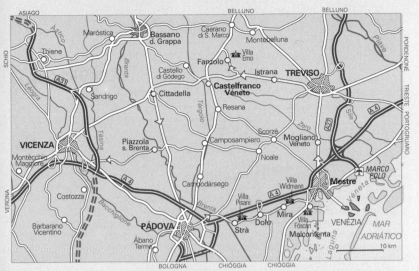

labyrinth, is the sumptuous introduction to this trip along the Riviera del Brenta. **Dolo** main centre of the Riviera in the 18th-c: near the surviving fragments of the 16th-c. locks, note the old plaque with inscribed boat tolls. **Mira**: go see Villa Widmann, a fine piece of Venetian rococo dating back to 1719. **Malcontenta** is the name of the place, as well as of the Villa Foscari, both built by Palladio, at the end of the Riviera del Brenta, near the lagoon. **Treviso*** is an alluring city with fine art and architecture; here the setting counts as much as monuments, canvases, and collections. **Istrana** (see Treviso) boasts the 18th-c. Villa Lattes with noteworthy artwork. Villa Emo di **Fanzolo** (see Castelfranco Veneto): you will pass through Vedelago to reach this Palladian villa. **Castelfranco Veneto:** this dignified little Venetian town is the birthplace of Giorgione; you can tour his home and, in the Duomo, you can admire a celebrated altarpiece. **Cittadella** still has intact its elliptical ring of walls. **Piazzola sul Brenta**: note the spectacular Villa Contarini and its vast grounds.

Monte Grappa, the hills of Asolo, and the Strada del Vino Bianco 26

Maròstica - Bassano del Grappa - Monte Grappa - Possagno - Àsolo - Masèr - Valdobbiàdene - San Pietro di Feletto - Conegliano (132 km.)

It is difficult to weigh the places you will see along this tour, where the Veneto rises up into hill country: Àsolo della Regina, the creation of Paolo Veronese and Andrea Palladio in Villa Barbaro at Masèr, Possagno where the birthplace of Antonio Canova and the museum of his remarkable sculpture give you a sense of his creative process, the lovely medieval atmosphere of Maròstica, or the river Brenta rushing past the piers of the covered wooden bridge of Bassano. Àsolo is certainly the most renowned; Caterina Cornaro, queen of Cyprus, held court here after her abdication in 1489, with twelve hand-maidens, eighty servants, a dwarf named Zavir, and as guests, her cousin the Venetian scholar and prelate Pietro Bembo — who as a young man courted Lucrezia Borgia, and at 69 was made cardinal by Pope Paul III — and the three ladies and gentlemen who for three days discussed love in Bembo's "Asolani." In truth, Àsolo is one of those places that fame, descriptions, and visitors are unable to wear out: there is always a detail, a color, a slow summer sunset over a valley in which lights twinkle on one after another in 16th-c. villas, the shiver of the unexpected. And yet it may be bested, in the final analysis, by the hillside villages with taverns and trattorias, with tables set out of doors under the spreading branches of the plane trees, along the Strada del Vino Bianco, or Road of White Wine, toward Conegliano — the specific places to stop are up to the driver, the mood, and the temptation of Cartizze, a fine Venetian white wine. In the end, it is the landscape as a whole, the intertwining confusion and the mingling of art and nature, the rustic and refined, or, to take a verse by Pietro Bembo, with "...the aroma from far away, the cool, and the hour / of the green fields...."

The route. From Maròstica, the starting point of this route, less than 30 km. north of Vicenza, you will soon reach Bassano del Grappa. You will then drive up to the Monte Grappa (1,775 m.) along the "Strada Cadorna," or state road 141, and then you will drive down along the "Strada Giardino," through Campo Croce and Semonzo. The road running along at the base of the hills, which you will join soon thereafter, runs to Possagno. Take another secondary road to Àsolo. After you drive down from the hill of Àsolo, at the crossroads of Casella you will continue NE along the route via Masèr, Cornuda, Ponte sul Piave di Vidòr, and Valdobbiàdene; from the last of these places, you can take a 12-km. detour along a scenic road up to Pianezze (1,095 m.). After you return to Valdobbiàdene you can take the Strada del Vino Bianco (Road of White Wine; marked as such), which runs through a countryside of hilltop vineyards, through Soligo, Solighetto, Refrontole, and San Pietro di Feletto, ending at Conegliano.

Halting places of interest. Maròstica: the fortified "borgo," with two castles, and walls running up the hill, offers a rare, dreamy image of the Middle Ages. **Bassano del Grappa*:** in this compact old city, with fascinating architecture, note the renowned wooden covered bridge which was built to plans drawn up by Andrea Palladio in 1569; the town holds other attractions as well. **Cima Grappa*** 1,775 m. is a site of broad vistas and grim memories of the months of 1917-18, the end of WWI, when the mountain was a hard-defended anchor of the Italian line. **Possagno** is the birthplace of the 18th-c. sculptor, Antonio Canova; note the home and the Neoclassical Temple that he built, and in which he is buried. **Àsolo*:** landscape, architecture, and the legacy of illustrious visitors all form part of the charm of this intact old town. **Masèr:** Andrea Palladio built a villa here for the brothers Barbaro; it is considered one of the Renaissance architect's finest works, and is frescoed by Paolo Veronese. **Pianezze;** you go through Valdobbiàdene to get up here; take a chairlift to the crest of the Monte Barbaria (1,464 m.), with a panoramic vista. **Solighetto:** in the 18th-c. Villa Brandolin, there is a small museum devoted to the great soprano, Toti Dal Monte. **San Pietro di Feletto**: note the millennium-old parish church of S. Pietro, on a hill with a view. **Conegliano:** the old, high part of town is distinctly Venetian; Cima da Conegliano lived in a house here, and there is an altarpiece by him in the Duomo.

The coastal strip of Friùli-Venezia Giulia — 27

Portogruaro - Cervignano del Friùli - Palmanova - Grado - Monfalcone - Trieste (131 km.)
"Glad view, cheering, and lovely appearance / Such is the sea when, tranquil and calm / It murmurs, whitening, up to the shore." These words are from the pen of Torquato Tasso, "Il Mondo Creato." The "lieta vista" appears roughly midway through the route and especially in the last section, along the luminous shore of the Gulf of Trieste. The route, which runs from Portogruaro along the littoral, may seem distant from the sea (in atmosphere, culture, and history, if not in actual miles) when it runs through the vineyards and intensive farming of the Friulian plain or past the grassy bastions of the Venetian citadel of Palmanova. In reality, the ties to the sea are close and fertile: note the landscape of the lagoon of Grado — silent motionless sheets of water, reflecting the flight of aquatic birds and a fringe of pinasters on the horizon — and the all-encompassing relationship between sea, people, and history. Beginning with Portogruaro itself, an ancient market town, greeting boats and goods; then Aquileia, where the cypress adorns the ruins of the Roman city, another fine river harbor; not to mention the cosmopolitan reach of Trieste.

The route. The starting point is Portogruaro in the province of Venice; from here, we would recommend two interesting excursions: the first, 2 km. to the south, is to Concordia Sagittaria; the second, 10 km. to the north, leads to Sesto al Règhena where you can tour the abbey of S. Maria in Sylvis. From Portogruaro you can then take the state road 14 toward Venezia Giulia to Trieste, as far as Cervignano del Friùli. Here you will turn onto the state road 352, for a northward detour, as far as Palmanova. On your way back, you will continue past Cervignano, still on the state road 352, toward Aquileia and, across the lagoon, to Grado. Following this road across the island of Grado and through the reclaimed land on either side of the mouth of the river Isonzo, you will reach Monfalcone. Last comes Trieste, along the state road 14 which here hugs the coast of the Golfo di Trieste.

Halting places of interest. Portogruaro, small town on the river Lemene, with strong 15th-/16th-

Venetian influence, largely intact; at **Concordia Sagittaria**, note the solitary ruins of the late-Roman/high-medieval settlement (cathedral, baptistery, excavations); at **Sesto al Règhena**, note the Romanesque-Byzantine abbey of S. Maria in Sylvis, with frescoes dating from the 12th-13th-c above the entrance and in the vestibule. **Latisana**: in the Duomo of this little town on the river Tagliamento is an altar piece by P. Veronese. **Palmanova**, with a radial plan, is a star-shaped fortress with bastions, ramparts, and embankments, truly a city-cum-citadel; the Venetians built it (1593) to protect their open eastern frontier; take an 8-km. detour from Cervignano del Friùli. **Aquileia***: Roman ruins, museums, and the basilica with its early-Christian mosaics are all eloquent commemorations of the centuries of late-antiquity and the high Middle Ages when this was a prosperous and powerful center of a vast region. **Grado***, with its medieval center of narrow lanes and "campielli" and its early-Christian churches. **San Giovanni di Duino**, with the Bocche del Timavo, where the waters of this river return to the light of day, after their long passage underneath the Carso, or Karst. **Duino**: in this former fishing village, note two castles of local siegneurs, with the legend of the ill-fated Dama Bianca, who was turned to stone; also, literary history tells us that Dante Alighieri spent much time pondering, seated on the rocks overlooking the sea, and that Rainer Maria Rilke took inspiration here for his "Duino Elegies." **Sistiana:** beach resort, in a small rocky inlet, surrounded by woods. **Castello di Miramare**: this castle stands between the waters of the gulf of Trieste and the dark holm-oaks, fir trees, and cypresses inland, a Romantic and princely Hapsburg residence.

The Strada Romea 28

Ravenna - Comacchio - Abbazia di Pomposa - Mésola - Chioggia - Mestre (158 km.)
The state road 309, or Strada Romea, between Mestre and Ravenna, follows one of the routes used by "Romei," or pilgrims headed for Rome. The route is not haunted by these phantoms, however; rather it wanders among images of reclaimed farmland and untouched wetlands. In the late-17th c., one traveller was moved by the fertility of the newly drained Ravenna territory, "once so sterile and waterlogged"

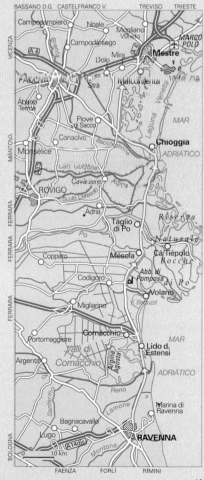

(Misson); modern sensibilities are different, and the terms "marsh" or "wetlands" have lost their negative connotations. There are rivers (Reno, Po, Adige, Brenta) and branches of the sea as well, and everywhere, signs of the impetuous modifications made by man: dry land where once was water. The changes in the littoral can be seen on the map: Ravenna once sat between lagoons and the harbor of the Roman fleet; where ships once rode at anchor, fields now sprout green. In Etruscan times, for instance, the waves of the Adriatic broke against sandy dunes at a point midway between Pomposa and Codigoro (now Taglio di Po). Today, the lighthouse of Bocca del Po di Pila is 25 km. eastward, while the estuaries of Comacchio stretched some 20 km. inland. The Valli di Comacchio and the Po delta are joined, of course, by the Laguna Veneta, or Venetian Lagoon, another realm of water and land, "nature" preserved by the wisdom of the Serenissima, a world of colors that change with the sky. The architecture of Comacchio, Pomposa, Mésola, Chioggia, or La Malcontenta is all worth seeing, whether monumental or minute, all part of the landscape in which it is immersed.

The route. You will head north out of Ravenna along the state road 309, or Strada Romea, which runs through the pine forest of S. Vitale. At Porto Garibaldi you will turn left, heading inland, for a tour of Comacchio; from here, an 18-km. detour along the road to Alfonsine runs over the embankment, or Argine Agosta. Then you will head back toward the coast, and back onto the Strada Romea for a short stretch; then, at the turnoff for San Giuseppe, you will follow secondary roads, to Borgo Manara, Valle Bertuzzi, Lido di Volano, Volano, and then to the Abbey of Pomposa. Here, you are back on the Strada Romea, heading north, leaving it only for two short detours: the first leads to the nature reserve of the Gran Bosco della Mésola (from a crossroads 7 km. from Pomposa);

the second runs to Ca' Tiepolo from Taglio di Po, with a 12-km. drive along the course of the Po di Venezia. After touring Chioggia, you will get back onto the Strada Romea, including the stretch that runs around the Venetian Lagoon, as far as Mestre.

Halting places of interest. Comacchio was once surrounded by "valli," or water barriers, has now been thoroughly reclaimed, crisscrossed by canals, unassuming yet charming; the remarkable landscape can be seen by following the embankment, or Argine Agosta, along the road to Alfonsine. **Volano** is a village on the banks of the Po di Volano, a branch of the Po, whose delta is a nature reserve. **Abbazia di Pomposa**:** the bell tower dates from the year 1000; it rears up to mark the site of the abbey, solitary on the vast plain; a notable achievement of Romanesque architecture and art; note the precious series of frescoes in the refectory of the Monastery. **Riserva Naturale Bosco della Mésola**, a nature reserve, was once part of a vast Este hunting park; you can tour it now only on foot or by bicycle. **Mésola** is a 16th-c. Este hunting lodge. **Ca' Tiepolo**: on the island of the Donzella, this is the seat of the township of Porto Tolle; you get there by following the Po di Venezia, a branch of the Po, with privileged views of the endless universe of nuanced space and water textures of the Po delta. **Chioggia*** is a town wedged into the southern edge of the Laguna Veneta, or Venetian Lagoon, with the houses, "calli," or lanes, canals, colors, and sounds of a working-class Venice, as Carlo Goldoni must have known it in the 18th c. La **Malcontenta** or Villa Foscari built around 1555 for the Foscari brothers, by Andrea Palladio, lies just a few hundred meters from the Strada Romea (right at the fork for Fusina). **Mestre:** Piazza Ferretto, the Duomo, the Torre dell'Orologio, and a few other fragments of ancient architecture show that this town is more than just a manufacturing outpost of Venice and a bedroom community for those who have moved away from the Serenissima.

Eastern Romagna 29

Rimini - Santarcàngelo di Romagna - San Leo - San Marino - Montefiore Conca - Saludecio - San Giovanni in Marignano - Cattolica (128 km.)

The remarkable Sigismondo Malatesta, an accomplished soldier and ruler of Rimini, summoned Leon Battista Alberti to transform a Gothic church into a classical "temple," a mausoleum for himself and his third wife, Isotta degli Atti, ("O lovely sweet light, proud soul," as he described her in his poetry; he murdered his previous two wives, poisoning one, strangling the other); we see him depicted by Piero della Francesca, kneeling between two greyhounds. This route passes almost entirely through lands of his family, in a distant corner of Romagna, bordering the Marche, here and there venturing into that region (Valle della Marecchia, and then up into the lovely green hills of the Valle del Conca). Amidst the lands and forts of the Malatesta family, however, the route passes through two other major landmarks: one is San Leo, high overlooking a tributary of the Marecchia; Federico da Montefeltro ordered the fort built by F. di Giorgio Martini in the 15th c. The other is San Marino, with its rocky ridge of Monte Titano, crowned with fortifications. Why this little medieval town, no different from many others, should have survived as a sovereign state, is a strange twist of history.

The route. You leave Rimini along the state road 9, a part of the Via Emilia, and you come fairly quickly to Santarcàngelo di Romagna; you will then continue south along the road that hugs the north bank of the Marecchia; at Ponte Verucchio you will cross the river, then drive up to Verucchio (296 m.). After that little sidetrip, take the state road 258 toward Novafeltria, turning off at the fork, just after Pietracuta, where the scenic route leads up to the peak upon which San Leo is nestled (583 m.). Returning along the same route for a stretch, after Pietracuta, you will take the road that runs via Torello up to San Marino (381 m.). Drive back down from San Marino, leaving this diminutive republic, heading south; you will reach the valley floor at Mercatino Conca. Now, staying on secondary roads, you will follow the course of the river Conca, toward the sea; then, you will come to the fork where a road splits off toward the hills along the valley's southern slopes, leading to Montefiore Conca (385 m.). Passing through San Felice, you return along a lengthy stretch of panoramic road, down toward the Conca valley floor, reaching it at Morciano di Romagna. A last climb takes you up through more hill country to Saludecio. The return to the coast follows another scenic route, at first, via Santa Maria del Monte, and via San Giovanni in Marignano. The route comes to an end at Cattolica.

Halting places of interest. Rimini* is a city of manifold attractions; the beach is only the best known of those attractions, not necessarily the most interesting. **Santarcàngelo di Romagna:** this little farming town has an old section, perched on a hill, with twisting streets; the fortress dates from the 15th c; the "grottoes" are remarkable underground warehouses, whose remote origins are swathed in debate;

and there is a museum devoted to the folkways of Romagna. **Verucchio:** the hills that form bookends for the "borgo" were onced topped by menacing forts; one survives, rebuilt in the 15th c. by Sigismondo Malatesta; the Museo Archeologico is notable for its collections of artifacts from the Villanovan culture, centered here in the early-Iron Age. **San Leo*:** this town is inaccessible, or practically so, on its limestone crag; the rustic parish church and the Duomo are Romanesque, while the renowned fort has the severe 15th-c. perspective and volume given it by Fdi Giorgio Martini; after Rimini, this is the artistic focus of the route. **San Marino*:** leave the capital town of the tiny republic, a lofty village straddling the crown of the Monte Titano, and follow the ridge for a pleasant stroll to the Guaita, the Cesta, and the Montale, three impressive towers. **Montefiore Conca** surveys the valley from atop a hill, with a ring of walls enclosing the old section, in the shadow of a 14th-c. fortress, built by the Malatesta (note detached frescoes of figures from the past, and battles). **Saludecio**, is a medieval "borgo," enclosed by walls and tapering in plan along the hill road, with terracotta buildings, note the neoclassical parish church of S. Biagio. **San Giovanni in Marignano:** you can still see the straight-edged 14th-c. layout; in the Biblioteca, note the archeological finds from imperial Rome. **Cattolica** is a fishing town and a beach resort; the old part sits on a terrace, 1 km. inland, on what was once the shoreline.

The hill country between Parma and Reggio 30

Parma - Sala Baganza - Torrechiara - Traversétolo - Ciano d'Enza - Canossa - Quattro Castella - Reggio nell'Emilia (87 km.)

The Via Emilia is a single straight road, centuries old, linking Parma and Reggio nell'Emilia (cities located in different states until 1859); the land this road runs through is relatively homogeneous, in terms of dialect, accent, and cordial hospitality. Outside of the cities — with their many relics of long and illustrious histories, with perfect settings and remarkable monuments — everything is farmland, the pride of the plains of northern Italy. The broad sweeping landscape is sealed off to the south, however, by broad rolling verdant hills, climbing up to the Apennines, flanking the long river valleys. This route runs among these hills. The landscape varies widely; it rolls by peacefully, at times solitary and even harsh, invariably abounding in harmonies of color, ranging from tender greens and electric greens in the spring time, sere burnt yellows in the full heat of summer, under a dizzying blue sky, or the majestic array of autumn, with the red and antique-gold leaves of chestnut trees withering, preparing for winter. This place is packed with history, which tangles and catches at the castle towers, just as valley-bound fog wraiths and snags at the wizened branches of brier bushes and leafless trees on winter mornings. There are stout castles: Torrechiara, Rocca dei Rossi, Montechiarùgolo dei Sanvitale, Rossena, Canossa (stronghold of the powerful countess of Tuscany, Matilda, the "gran contessa,") a castle built a thousand years earlier by a certain Azzo of Longobard descent. Quattro Castella owes its name to four fortresses that once surrounded it, overlooking the forests beneath from atop four different peaks: Monte Vetro, Monte Bianello, Monte Lucio, and Monte Zane (one survives; the three others lie in ruins). Many local place names seem like a list from the counter of an Italian delicatessen: Felino, synonymous with exquisite salami; Langhirano (on the river Parma, which is slightly neglected in this route) is known for the excellence of its prosciutto, rivalled perhaps only by that of Parma. Mentioning them, however, may help to transport all these castles and the ruins and memories of such castles out of their romantic haze, and present them as genuine military tools, designed to hold sway and defend this land, made fruitful by backbreaking labor.

The route. You will leave Parma, heading SW along the state road 62 via Fornovo di Taro, Berceto, and the Passo della Cisa, leaving that road just prior to reaching Collecchio (8 km.), at the turnoff for Sala Baganza; stay on this route, along secondary roads, through Sala Baganza, Felino, Pilastro, and Torrechiara. You will return to the crossroads of Pilastro after touring Torrechiara, and from there you will continue eastward, crossing the river Parma, and then the river Enza, just past Traversétolo, where a 7.5-km. detour north leads you to Montechiarùgolo. Before you enter San Polo d'Enza you will cross the state road 513, where you will turn right toward Ciano d'Enza. From here, you will stick to the scenic route through the hills, on to the castles of Rossena and Canossa; then, via the church

of Grassano, you will return to San Polo d'Enza. In the last part of this route, heading toward Reggio nell'Emilia, the scenic road runs via San Polo d'Enza, Quattro Castella, and Scandiano, at the base of the hills and the edge of the plains; you will turn into the plains when you reach the turnoff for state road 63 which will take you into Reggio nell'Emilia.

Halting places of interest. S. Biagio di Talignano is a Romanesque parish church, which can be reached from Sala Baganza along a detour of 3 km. through the Parco Regionale dei Boschi di Carrega, a regional park. Castello di **Torrechiara*** is a 15th-c. castle, one of the largest and best preserved in the region; note the renowned Camera d'Oro, or Room of Gold, with its rare cycle of frescoes dealing with profane subjects, attributed to Benedetto Bembo (1463). Villa Magnani is located in **Corte di Traversétolo**, and boasts a notable collection of paintings. From Traversétolo, you will then continue on to **Montechiarùgolo** with its Rocca, or fortress, with notable frescoes on the interior. **Castello di Rossena** is a 13th-c. fortress set high atop a crag, with fine views. **Castello di Canossa** stands on a white rock base in a stern panorama of badlands: note its remarkable history, the view, the ruins, and a small museum. **Quattro Castella:** these four fortresses were an outpost of Canossa, though only the Bianello survives (privately owned); in town, there is a 16th-c. palazzo and a parish church of Romanesque origins.

A tour through Verdi's homeland and along the river Po   31

Fidenza - Fontanellato - Soragna - Busseto - Roccabianca - Colorno - Parma (97 km.)
Perhaps the true sites of Verdi's past are the boards and the backdrops of the stages, the "mystic gulf" of the orchestra pit, the seats, the boxes of the theaters, or La Scala where the composer's first work, "Oberto," was presented when he was 26; the Queen's Theater of London, where "I Masnadieri" was acclaimed; the theater of the Khedive in Cairo, where "Aïda" was produced; the Teatro La Fenice of Venice, the S. Carlo of Naples, the Argentina or the Apollo in Rome; Florence's La Pergola or the Opéra in Paris. Or perhaps we should travel, in our imagination, to other lands, historical times, and settings: those evoked by the props, the Babylon of the "Nabucco," Paris of "La Traviata," the grim Hapsburg Spain of "Don Carlos," the bittersweet England of "Falstaff," which the maestro composed at 69 ("I am just writing for my own enjoyment," he would say). But if we are going to tour the land of his youth, where he returned as a grown man, then we will visit the plains between Parma and the Po, farmland, a handsome countryside with distinct seasons, silence and snow, trees like shadows in the fall mists, as the swifts dart back and forth in the sunset, cities, towns, and villages with rich aromatic cooking and a tradition of "bel canto." Those towns are three, to be exact: Verdi's birthplace, Róncole; Busseto, the dignified little town where he learned music and forged his destiny; and Sant'Agata: the maestro, already successful, bought a house and land there, encouraged by his second wife, Giuseppina Strepponi, an opera singer. In the route that

we recommend, these places are parentheses along the way: do not miss the three portals of the facade of Fidenza's Duomo, a high masterpiece of Po Valley Romanesque. Then there is the blend of Middle Ages and Renaissance in the castles of Fontanellato and Soragna. Lastly, there is the magic landscape of the Po, glimpsed through the trees, or from secluded roads along the banks.

The route. From Fidenza, you will head east for 12.5 km. along the Via Emilia, as far as Castelguelfo; then you will turn NW along secondary roads, passing through Fontanellato, Soragna, Róncole Verdi. From here, along state road 588 toward Cremona, you will reach Villa Verdi, which requires a slight detour, just past the bridge over the Ongina. Just north of Villa Verdi, you will get back on to the state road, heading for Zibello and, with a route that follows the course of the river Po, you will drive through Roccabianca and on to Colorno. The straight state road 343 leads to Parma, which marks the end of this route.

Halting places of interest. Fidenza: the Duomo is one of the finest Romanesque monuments in the Po Valley. **Fontanellato:** note the Rocca, or fort, with frescoes by Parmigianino; it stands, pale red and battlemented, facing the broad square of a farming village. **Soragna:** another farming village, another Rocca, the sumptuous princely home of the Meli Lupi family. **Róncole Verdi** has the birthplace of Giuseppe Verdi, a modest enough place, and, in the church of S. Michele, the organ on which Verdi first practiced music. **Busseto:** the cult of Verdi does not interfere with the history and dignity of what was once the capital of the little state of the house of Pallavicino; there is a museum in the Villa Pallavicino; in the church of S. Maria degli Angeli, note the Lament for The Death of Christ terracotta group by G. Mazzoni (1476-77). **Villa Verdi** a Sant'Agata: the maestro spent his summers here, composing opera; you can tour his living quarters. **Roccabianca:** the Po flows by, slow and majestic, just a few hundred meters away; the 15th-c. Rocca, or fort, was by P.M. Rossi, built for his beloved, Bianca Pellegrini, hence the name Rocca-Bianca. **Colorno:** restoration has helped to recover some of the charm and allure of the ducal palazzo and estate, hunting grounds and holiday spot of the dukes of Parma, upon which many architects worked for long years.

Viareggio - Camaiore - Pietrasanta - Castelnuovo di Garfagnana - Forte dei Marmi - Massa - Carrara - Fosdinovo - Sarzana - Pontrèmoli (180 km.)

The glittering blue sea spreading out below the jagged Apuan mountains, studded with white fragments of marble amidst high-elevation forests: this is the setting of a small but ancient principality that once lay along the boundary between Tuscany and Liguria. Between the rivers Magra and Serchio, low sand dunes run up to stands of pinasters and holm-oaks. Versilia runs from the lake of Massaciùccoli to the mouth of the Cinquale, stretching inland to the Apuan crest. In the mid-19th c., the first bathing establishments were built, precursors to today's resorts. The swimsuits were far more ample and clumsy then, but the light, the air, and the sparkling water were the same as today. Rising sharply behind green hills, the high Apuans are riven with "canali," as the natives call the narrow and jagged high valleys. They are also a treasure trove of fine marble. Once this was the principality of Massa and Carrara, named for its two capital towns. From the 15th c. until the unification of Italy (1861), these two cities feuded, proud of their marble, mountains, and seacoast. The route ends with the Lunigiana, a land of nuanced and melancholy charm. Watered by the river Magra, Lunigiana is a blend of Tuscany, Liguria, and Emilia. This farmland set among terraced mountain slopes and chestnut groves was once so poor that there was only one alternative to eating chestnuts and the occasional bowl of polenta: to emigrate, sailing toward distant shores.

The route. Starting from Viareggio, you drive directly to Camaiore; returning along the same road, you turn at Pianore toward Pietrasanta. Here, you get on to the Via Aurelia (running inland, instead of along the coast, as is usual). At Querceta you turn off — this is part of the route — and drive over the Apuans, passing through Seravezza and the Cipollaio tunnel to Castelnuovo di Garfagnana. Take the same route back to Querceta, and continue to the coast, at Forte dei Marmi. You will then follow the coast north, to Marina di Massa. The route then heads inland, passing through Massa, then over the hills to Carrara; the panoramic route of the Spolverina (state road 446 d) running over the pass of the Foce, at an elevation of 560 m., and from Fosdinovo drops down into Liguria just out side of Sarzana. Lastly, state road 62 of the Cisa takes you through the Magra (or Lunigiana) valley, to the town of Pontrèmoli.

Halting places of interest. Viareggio*, with its broad beaches, pine groves, and maritime air, has been a prominent beach resort for the past century-and-a-half, as well as a social and cultural watering spot. **Camaiore** boasts a Romanesque collegiate church and a backdrop of lovely hills. **Pietrasanta** is a town of marble carvers and sculptors, with handsome monuments lining the Piazza del Duomo. **Castelnuovo di Garfagnana** proudly surveys a green expanse of mountains; here two great Italian poets ruled as governors for the Este family: Ludovico Ariosto and Fulvio Testi. **Forte dei Marmi***, set amidst the Mediterranean maquis and pine groves, is the most elegantly exclusive beach in Versilia. **Massa:** the medieval village clusters around the old fortress; beneath it, the 15th-c. town features the princely palace of the Cybo-Malaspina family, facing a square dotted with orange trees. **Carrara** is a venerable capital of the marble trade (spectacular quarries at Colonnata, 8.5 km. to the east), renowned as well for its rebellious and anarchic history. **Fosdinovo:** Dante is said to have looked out from the castle of the Malaspina over the Gulf of La Spezia. **Sarzana** is a town with an intricate history, its buildings a blend of Ligurian and Tuscan style: in particular, its 13th-c. cathedral. **Santo Stefano di Magra**, a Ligurian village, still boasts earmarks of a fortified medieval "borgo." **Villafranca in Lunigiana** features an Ethnographic Museum, which documents local culture. **Pontrèmoli** is a town with an ancient flavor; on the Piagnaro hill, the castle houses the remarkable museum, with its collection of local stelae-statues and other items of archeological interest.

The Apennines of Pistoia and the Garfagnana   33

Pistoia - Abetone - Foce delle Radici - Castelnuovo di Garfagnana - Pistoia (190 km.)

"...while the Apuan peaks / are shrouded with a sunlit vermilion mist, / and the rays glitter against the distant / glass panes of Tiglio; / come to this new fountain, with / ewers balanced on your heads, shining like a mirror, / delicately balanced, o maidens / of Castelvecchio..." (Pascoli, "La Fonte di

Castelvecchio"). While he was teaching Latin and Greek in the towns of Matera, Massa, and Livorno, Professor Giovanni Pascoli often submitted Latin poetry to competitions held in Amsterdam, and more than once he was awarded first place; with his winnings, the great Romagnolo poet was able to purchase himself a home in this land on the far side of the Apennines, in the Garfagnana, at Castelvecchio di Barga. The tour of Pascoli's home is a literary parenthesis in this route, which is chiefly focused on mountain landscape, hill country, valleys, and the Apennines. High elevations, forests, endless vistas, air fragrant with mountain balsam: the many and steep climbs and descents only contribute to the excitement of this route. In the first leg, on the Pistoia slopes of the Apennines, for example, you begin close to sea level, then you cross the Passo di Oppio at 821 m., at La Lima you are at 454 m., at Abetone at 1,388 m. During all these climbs, you have passed from one valley to another, and though you have never left Tuscany, you have driven some distance alongside the course of the river Reno, which then runs down to the Adriatic through the plains of Romagna; the Reno, and its valley, are adjacent to other tributaries bound for the Tyrrhenian Sea, in the intricate mountain topography over Pistoia. The eye wanders over remarkable craggy silhouettes, amidst the green of alders, beech, white and red-deal trees. After Abetone you head down the Modena slopes as far as Pievepèlago, and the climbs and descents continue: after going over two high passes, the mouths of the Radici and the Terrarossa, you enter the Valle del Serchio — Garfagnana, part of Tuscany but for three centuries ruled by the Este family, dukes of Ferrara, later reduced only to Modena and Reggio Emilia. You can make out the rolling crests of the Apennine watershed and the sere, jagged peaks of the Apuans. The circle is closed as you follow the valley of the river Lima, a tributary of the Serchio, running through steep gorges.

The route. Leaving Pistoia along the Via di Porta al Borgo and heading north along the state road 66,

you will drive through Le Piastre and Pontepetri, and over the Oppio pass, and then on to San Marcello Pistoiese and the small town of La Lima. Here you turn right on the state road 12 toward the Abetone pass, and from there down to Pievepèlago, onto the state road 324, and past the Foce delle Radici, 1,529 m., Foce di Terrarossa, 1,441 m., and Castiglione di Garfagnana, finally dropping down to Castelnuovo di Garfagnana. You will drive along the Serchio valley and after Ponte di Campia, then on through Castelvecchio Pascoli, Ponte di Catagnana, Barga. From there you will return to the road along the river's left bank, and, at Ponte a Serraglio, you will rejoin the state road 12 running back to Abetone. This will take you to the fork in the road at La Lima. For a short distance, you will be back on the same road you took earlier, though heading for San Marcello Pistoiese, but you will soon turn right onto the state road 633, through Prunetta (958 m.), and on to Le Piastre. You will return to Pistoia the way you left it.

Halting places of interest. Maresca is a resort at the edge of the Teso forest, and can be reached via a slight detour just after the Passo di Oppio. **Gavinana**: in a small Museum, you can see documents regarding the battle of 1530 between the Florentines under Francesco Ferrucci (who was slaughtered by the Calabrian soldier, Fabrizio Maramaldo, even though he was wounded and a prisoner) and the imperial troops of the Prince of Orange; the Florentine defeat marked the end of the republic and the return of the Medici to Florence. **Cutigliano** can be reached via a 1.5-km detour from Casotti, on the road to Abetone, after La Lima; a cableway takes you up to the 1,715-m. crest of the Apennines, between Libro Aperto and the Corno alle Scale; panoramic view. **Abetone**, 1,388 m., is a noted ski resort near a large forest; fine views from the Rifugio Selletta, a mountain hut at an elevation of 1,711 m. (take a chairlift up) and from Monte Gòmito at 1,892 m. (another cableway up). **Pievepèlago** is a resort town in the Modenese valley of the Scoltenna; take an 11.5-km. road up to the little Lago Santo (1,501 m.) at the foot of Monte Giovo. **Foce delle Radici** (1,529 m.) is a pass between Emilia and Tuscany; fine view. At San Pellegrino in Alpe, via a 2.5-km. detour, you have a vista that reaches to the sea. Also note the little Museo Etnografico. **Castiglione di Garfagnana** lies within the walls of a 14th-c. Lucchese fortress, in the 15th-c church of S. Michele, note the Madonna by Giuliano di Simone (1389) and the 15th-c. wooden crucifix. **Castelnuovo di Garfagnana**: from 1522-25 the great epic poet Ludovico Ariosto lived, as governor, in the 12th-c. fortress here. **Castelvecchio Pascoli**: the house that belonged to Giovanni Pascoli, a great 19th-c. Italian poet, is outside the town, among the houses of Carpona. **Barga**: the Romanesque Duomo stands on the high meadow of the Arringo, towering over the ancient village, with a panoramic view over valley and mountains. **Bagni di Lucca** is a spa with a venerable reputation, founded by Elisa Baciocchi, sister of Napoleon and princess of Lucca; as the 19th c. wore on, an elect international clientele would come here to "take the waters," including celebrated authors, in 1840 the first casino to be built in Europe was established here. **Vico Pancellorum** is a secluded village high in the valley of the Lima, at the end of a 2.5-km. detour, a few km. past Fabbriche and just before Popiglio. **Popiglio**: note the ancient towers in the village's skyline, and the medieval parish church of the Assunta.

Lucca - Montecatini Terme - Pistoia - Vinci - Prato - Florence (134 km.)

The Nièvole is a brief mountain stream that runs from the Apennines down to sink away into the Padule di Fucecchio, but the Valdinièvole (or Nièvole Valley) is a world to itself: a high hilltop meadowland, fading into hillocks topped by cypresses, chestnut trees, grape vines, light-colored expanses of olive trees, and, in the valleys, fields dense with flowers. The Valdinièvole includes the valleys of the Pescia and the Pescia di Collodi, as well as Montecatini Terme and the town of Pescia. The route runs from west to east. The Florentine author of "Pinocchio," Carlo Lorenzini, took his pen name from the town of Collodi, where he spent part of his childhood. We may suppose that this was the landscape in which Pinocchio "rolled his eyes around to see, amidst the dark green of the trees, a white speck in the distance: a little house as white as snow," the house of the "little girl with light-blue hair." At any rate, the town of Collodi perennially celebrates the little boy carved of wood. Monte Albano is a forest-covered chain of hills, running NW to SE, between Montecatini Terme and the Arno, sealing off to the south the plain of Pistoia and Prato. And these two cities, with their remarkable ancient quarters, certainly offer the artistic highlights of this route: in Pistoia, the silver altar frontal of S. Jacopo (mentioned by Dante); in Prato, Donatello's dancing cherubs on the pulpit of the Sacro Cingolo, to mention only two.

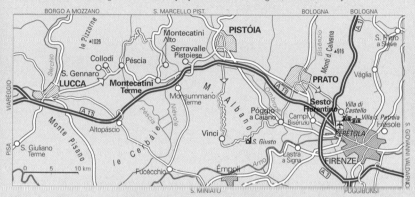

The route. From Lucca, you head east toward Pescia, along the state road 435. From Pescia, you will drive north along the river Pescia, then east through Vellano and Marliana, in a wide arc over the hills (this area is known as the "Switzerland of Pescia") that ends at Montecatini Terme. Continuing east, you will reach first Serravalle Pistoiese, then Pistoia itself. Exiting the city southward, along the road to Émpoli, you climb over Monte Albano and reach Vinci. The next leg of the trip runs NE over secondary roads: through Vitolini and Carmignano to Poggio a Caiano. Finally, you will reach Prato. From here, after a detour to the church of S. Giovanni Battista at the motorway interchange of Florence North, or Firenze Nord, you will return to Florence through Sesto Fiorentino.

Halting places of interest. San Gennaro can be reached by taking a detour from the state road 435, about 12 km. from Lucca; it boasts a remarkable Romanesque church. **Collodi** requires another detour, soon after, from the state road 435; it is notable for the Parco di Pinocchio and the garden of Villa Garzoni. **Pescia:** in the church of S. Francesco, note panel by Bonaventura Berlinghieri (1235); flowers are grown intensively. **Montecatini Alto** has medieval sections; to get here, you must detour 2 km. from the road; noteworthy view. **Montecatini Terme*:** parks, Art-Nouveau (or "liberty," in Italian), and the high-society elegance of a spa town. **Serravalle Pistoiese** has ruins of medieval fortifications; in the former Romanesque church of S. Michele, 14th-c. Florentine frescoes. **Pistoia*:** this city rivals Lucca and Florence, both in the history of art and of politics; you can spend more than one intensely interesting day examining art, collections, monuments, and the ancient city itself. **Vinci** has a 13th-c. castle, with a museum devoted to Leonardo da Vinci, continue along till you come to the Romanesque parish church of San Giusto, on the ridge of Monte Albano. **Poggio a Caiano** features a Medici villa by Giuliano da Sangallo. **Prato*:** it is best known as a thriving wool-manufacturing town, but the old section, enclosed by 14th-c. hexagonal walls, has a venerable air and great monuments of Italian art. **Chiesa di S. Giovanni Battista**, near a major highway interchange, the Firenze Nord, a masterpiece of modern architecture, by Giovanni Michelucci (1960-64). **Sesto Fiorentino:** note the Museo delle Porcellane di Doccia, or museum of shower tiles, and, in the outlying neighborhood of Quinto, the Etruscan tomb of Montagnola; continue along through the outskirts of Florence, and stop by the Medici villas of Castello and Petraia.

The lower Valdarno 35

Pisa - Vicopisano - San Miniato - Fucecchio - Vinci - Signa - Florence (128 km.)

Although the Arno's flow, from Florence to Pisa and on to the sea, is anything but straightforward, it does tend ever westward; this route runs through the Arno Valley, upstream from Pisa and Florence, and almost entirely forsakes the two more common roads on either bank of the river, in favor of less well known routes, looking down on the winding Arno from the high roads. This route heads north over the Monte Pisano, then south through the Valdera and over the hills between Palaia and San Miniato, and lastly north, through Cerreto Guidi and Vinci, over the Monte Albano. The valley shows the hand of man nearly everywhere, thriving and prosperous; this route offers remarkable vistas, exquisite art and architecture, and lovely stretches of scenery. Let us mention two, which formed subjects for two lost masterpieces of Tuscan art. At Càscina, the Florentines, who had pushed thus far in their war against Pisa, risked it all on a toss of the dice (and won) on 28 July 1364, battling fiercely against the 800 men-at-arms under the Pisan commander-general, Giovanni Acuto (the Italian version of the name of the English soldier John Hawkwood, who fought for Florence as well; note the funerary monument painted by Paolo Uccello in S. Maria del Fiore). When commemorating this past glory of Florence, at one point, the Gonfaloniere, Pier Soderini commissioned Michelangelo to paint a fresco of the event. Michelangelo "filled the painting with nude men, who were cooling off from the summer heat in the river Arno, at the very moment that the battle began in the field" (Vasari): that work is now lost, as is its companion piece, the Battle of Anghiari, by Leonardo da Vinci — they both could be seen once in Palazzo Vecchio. Drive on through olive groves and vineyards to the town of Vinci, where the great artist was born, an "illegitimate son" (according to the town records) of a notary and property owner in Anchiano, and a certain Caterina, who later married Attaccabriga di Pietro del Vacca.

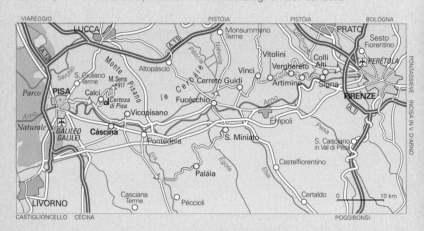

The route. Heading east out of Pisa (from Via Garibaldi, along the Arno's right bank) you will drive directly to Calci, and then south. At Caprona, north of the Arno, you will turn left along the road to Florence, until you hit the turnoff to Vicopisano. You will cross the Arno and drive through the Era valley, past Ponsacco. At Capànnoli, you will turn, cross the Era, and take secondary roads to San Miniato, past Villa Saletta, Palàia, Chiecinella, and La Serra. Driving down from the hilltop town of San Miniato, you will head north, crossing the Arno again, past Fucécchio. You will take the state road 436 for a short way, and then turn right at Le Corti. Secondary roads, some of them panoramic, take you through Cerreto Guidi, Vinci, Vitolini, Verghereto, and Artimino; you will rejoin the Arno at Signa. You will finally reach Florence, on the right bank of the Arno, through Colli Alti, along the state road 66 from Pistoia. This route follows some very small roads; keep an eye out for roadsigns and use your map.

Halting places of interest. Calci: the Certosa, or Charter House, of Pisa is here, as is an 11th-c. parish church; take a 12-km. detour over the Monte Serra to the highest peak on the Monte Pisano (917 m.): there is an immense vista, with the sea, the Apuans, Valdarno, and the Apennines. **Càscina:** you take a 3-km. detour from Lugnano to get here; note the 14th-c. frescoes in the Oratorio di S. Giovanni and the Romanesque parish church of S. Maria. **Vicopisano:** note the maze of medieval lanes, a Pisan Romanesque parish church, and the ruins of the fortifications restored by Brunelleschi, following the Florentine conquest of 1407. **Palaia:** note the parish church in the old section of town and the church of S. Martino just outside of town, both dating from the 13th c. **San Miniato** has very fine monuments and collections of art; note the views and medieval sections of town. A theater festival takes place in the piazza at the end of July, and there is a national market exhibition of white truffles in November. **Fucecchio** stands on the outlying ridges of the Monte Albano; the Collegiata di S. Giovanni Battista is at the top of a stairway (note the view from a square to the left). **Cerreto Guidi:** a splendid stairway by Bernardo Buontalenti leads up to the Medici villa in 1576, Paolo Giordano Orsini strangled his wife Isabella here. **Vinci:** Leonardo da Vinci took his name from this village, although he was probably born in Anchiano; note the Museo Vinciano in the Castello. **Artimino**, amid olive groves and vineyards; facing the town is the Medici villa, La Ferdinanda. **Signa** is a town in which straw and terracotta objects are manufactured; in the upper part of town, note the 15th century baptismal font and frescoes depicting the life of S. Giovanna in the parish church of S. Giovanni Battista.

Viareggio - Pisa - Tirrenia - Livorno - Bólgheri - Suvereto - Populonia - Piombino (146 km.)

"...si dice in galea o nave o altra fusta, quando fussino stati alcuno giorno senza vedere terra..."; this is an old sea chantey, from the second half of the 15th c., and it translates roughly: "they say in ships or galleys, or any other vessel, when they have gone several days without sighting land..." At the end of each verse, the chantey returns to call on the help of the Lord and the saints, naming a patron saint or a sanctuary, with specific references to stretches of shoreline or points on the coast. This "pilot's book" of the Catholic faith describes — for the short stretch that corresponds to the beginning of this route along the coastline of northern Tuscany, between Viareggio and Livorno — the Volto Santo Lucchese, San Ranieri, Santa Maria del Ponte Nuovo, and San Piero a Grado (Pisan), Santa Giulia and Montenero (Livornese). Here is a typical verse: "Die' n'aì (meaning "God help us") e Santa Maria delle Grazie di Monte Nero di Livorno..." The ancient mariner's chantey, clearly, reflects the route that we are suggesting here: the lovely thing about driving along the coastline, for that matter, is the continual series of glimpses it offers of the sea, parallel to the glimpses of land that so comforted ancient sailors in their terror. Even if we leave aside the marvels of Pisa, among the charms of this route are the alternating distance and approach to the sea, long beaches and a jagged coastline, little coves with crashing waves and gurgling undertow, and, far above, the Mediterranean underbrush, known as "macchia," or "maquis," pine trees, holm-oaks, ash trees, elms, the northwest wind, or "maestrale," fragrant with resins and sap, clouds scudding across the windy sky, the "flocks of black birds" that flap their way "through the vespertine sky" (there are many verses by Nobel laureate G. Carducci, that seem to describe this region): in this exchange between earth and sea along the coast, the most beautiful section lies between Antignano and Cècina. And if you look inland instead of out to sea, what draws nearer and further away is the outline of hills and blue hazy mountains; you will see grapevines and olive groves, cypresses, Etruscan ruins, hilltop towns with noteworthy views. Lastly, as you move as much as a degree of latitude south, the climate becomes slightly milder in winter. The last stretch of road, where you begin to see Elba, is the coast of the Maremma, and specifically the so-called Pisan Maremma: from here you can take a lovely inland detour.

The route. Leaving Viareggio along the Viale dei Tigli, you will drive through the Pineta di Levante, a great pine forest. After Torre del Lago Puccini, take the Via Aurelia (state road 1) to Pisa. Leaving Pisa along the Lungarni, or riverfront boulevards, of the river's left bank, you will reach Marina di Pisa; from here, follow the coast road (state road 224) to Livorno. Take the Viale Italia out of Livorno, along the coast as far as Antignano, where you will rejoin the Aurelia, and take it to San Vincenzo. Here, the Aurelia runs inland; continue along the coast road, which then cuts across the promontory and runs to Piombino. There is a detour through the Maremma, which cuts off from the Aurelia at the fork for Castagneto Carducci. Climbing and descending along secondary roads, you will drive past Castagneto Carducci, Sassetta, Suvereto, Cafaggio, Campiglia Marittima, and Venturina. Here, after a brief jog to the right along the Aurelia, at Caldana, you take the road to La Torraccia, on the coast south of San Vincenzo, back on the main route. You will then reach Piombino, after a short detour to Baratti and Populonia. This entire detour, which requires you to keep a sharp eye on roadsigns and map, lengthens the drive by 44 km.

Halting places of interest. Torre del Lago Puccini, near the Lago di Massaciùccoli, with the stately home and the tomb of Giacomo Puccini. **Pisa****: with its Baptistery, Cathedral, Cemetery, and famous leaning bell tower, the Campo dei Miracoli, or Piazza del Duomo, a broad meadow, is certainly one of the most famous places on earth; this is the greatest glory of this ancient Tuscan city, on the banks of the river Arno, a powerful maritime republic of bygone centuries. Still, Pisa has much more to offer; every visit results in many new discoveries. **San Piero a Grado***: this 11th-c. Pisan church, whith early 14th-c frescoes can be reached by taking a detour from the road linking Pisa with Marina di Pisa. **Livorno:** this harbor city is a thriving port with venerable

old sections; this was the first outlet to the sea of the Tuscan grand-duchy; from Antignano you will drive up to the Santuario di Montenero (collection of votive offerings from those who survived perils of land and sea). **Castiglioncello:** this quietly elegant beach resort stands on a promontory, dense with pine trees and holm-oaks, nearby are inlets and little beaches. **Rosignano Marittimo:** detour from Rosignano Solvay, 2 km. inland; the old town stands on a scenic rise. **Marina di Cècina:** take a 2.5-km. detour; the beach is on the other side of the pine forest. **Bólgheri:** in order to get here, you must leave the Via Aurelia at the 18th-c. octagonal chapel of San Guido, driving a little less than 5 km. along cypress-lined boulevards described by 1906 Nobel laureate and poet, Giosuè Carducci, truly a lovely sight (as a child, Carducci lived in a house in town here). In the variant that we recommend for the last part of this route: **Castagneto Carducci,** a hillside resort area; the poet lived here as a youth. **Suvereto** (see Campiglia Marittima) may take its name from the groves of cork-trees that once surrounded it; note the Romanesque church of S. Giusto, and the 13th-c. Palazzo Comunale. **Campiglia Marittima,** for the most part, still has a medieval appearance; on the Venturina road, note the cemetery, with the parish church of S. Giovanni (note the late-12th-c. carving on the architrave over the portal). **Baratti:** on the bayshore, note the Etruscan necropolis. **Populonia** still has its 14th-c. "borgo," unchanged by time, perched on the promontory; this was the powerful Etruscan town of "Pupluna", note the small Muses Collezione Gasparri, which contains finds from the Etruscan necropolis.

The Val di Pesa and Chianti 37

Florence - Poggibonsi - Siena - Castelnuovo Berardenga - Greve in Chianti - Florence (184 km.)

In 1838, Baron Bettino Ricasoli, 29, later the absolute ruler of Tuscany and prime minister of the Kingdom of Italy, took up residence in his castle at Brolio, in Chianti, to devote himself to farming; he wrote that "agriculture in Tuscany takes heart and it takes brains, it is almost a calling." One of the results of that "calling" was Chianti, a wine that had existed since 1716 — along with the now less famous Pomino, Carmignano, and Valdarno — but which Ricasoli made both great and renowned. In the route recommended here, Chianti comes in the later part, though all of the landscape is enchanting. From Florence you continue on to the Val di Pesa, with its venerable tradition as an aristocratic holiday spot; you drive through this valley for some way, then you climb through hills in the Valdelsa (the Pesa and the Elsa flow into the lower Arno, from the left bank); after Siena, you return to Florence, with a pause in the land of Chianti. Experts distinguish an aroma of violet in this wine; it is made with Sangiovese grapes, from 75 to 90 percent, while the rest is a blend of black Canaiolo grapes, Tuscan Trebbiano grapes, and Malvasia del Chianti. In the landscape, which varies from grim to lovely, with an endless combination of villas, holm-oaks, farm houses, scrub brush, villages, towers, steep hills, winding roads, parish churches, venerable oak trees, cypresses, and olive trees, you will often see vineyards as well, occupying only the sites that receive plenty of sun, with the finest soils. Save for the secluded Certosa del Galluzzo, with paintings by Pontormo, the turreted skyline of Monteriggioni and, of course, Siena, this tour is of lesser sites, with nature domesticated, and the brilliant clear light, the clear distilled magic essence of Tuscany.

The route. Leaving Florence from the Porta Romana (left bank of the Arno) along the Via Senese, and taking the Cassia (state road 2), through San Casciano in Val di Pesa and Poggibonsi, you will reach Siena. From there, leaving by the Porta Pispini along the road to Arezzo, you will drive about 15 km. and then turn left to climb up to Castelnuovo Berardenga. This is the beginning of Chianti, where, partly along state roads 484 and then 408, you will drive through Castello di Brolio, Gaiole in Chianti, and Badia a Coltibuono. From here, you will proceed west to Radda in Chianti and, on the state road 429, to Castellina in Chianti. The next leg, heading north, runs along the state road 222, to Greve in Chianti (midway, detour to the right to Làmole). Beyond is the fork for Impruneta, after Strada. From Impruneta you will return to Florence, driving down from the hills south of the city.

Halting places of interest. Certosa del Galluzzo*: church, cloisters, monks' cells, and paintings by Pontormo. To get here, turn off the Via Cassia at Galluzzo and drive for 1 km., past cypresses and olive trees. **San Casciano in Val di Pesa:** note the Crucifix by Simone Martini at

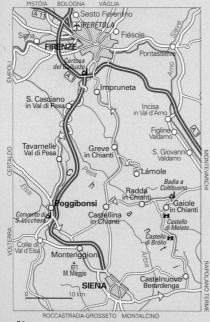

the church of Misericordia. **Poggibonsi** is a thriving modern town; 1.5 km. south, note the convent of S. Lucchese amid the olive groves. **Monteriggioni*** was a Siennese outpost; Dante's description — "di torri si corona," meaning "crowned with towers" — still applies. **Siena****: in the history of Italy, this is Florence's great rival; in terms of painting, sculpture, and city design, Siena expresses a second, world-class Tuscan culture. It is said that the Siennese speak the best Italian. **Castello di Brolio**: built in the 12th c. by the Ricasoli family, it was later restored in 1860. **Gaiole in Chianti** lies amid hills covered with vineyards; note the Romanesque parish church of S. Maria a Spaltenna; the Castello di Meleto, a fortified medieval farm, just 2.5 km. away; and you can see the Romanesque church, all that survives of the nearby **Badia a Coltibuono** (5 km. north). **Radda in Chianti** has an elongated elliptical layout, a relic of the Middle Ages. **Castellina in Chianti** has stood on its hilltop since the Renaissance; it lies between the valleys of Arbia, Elsa, and Pesa and has retained much of its Renaissance atmosphere. Note the 14th-c. fortress. **Greve in Chianti** (see Impruneta) has a porticoed asymmetrical plaza; note the terraces. From here, a 6-km. detour takes you to **Làmole**; note the Villa di Vignamaggio, birthplace of the woman who sat for Leonardo's Mona Lisa (La Gioconda). **Impruneta**, on the Florentine hills, is known for its venerable October fair, its pottery kilns (here, Brunelleschi fired the bricks used to build the cupola of S. Maria del Fiore), and the basilica of S. Maria.

The Valdelsa and the Volterrano 38

Florence - Émpoli - Certaldo - Volterra - San Gimignano - Colle di Val d'Elsa (147 km.)
The literary references here are of the highest quality: Certaldo was the birthplace of the 14th-c. author Boccaccio, and here he returned as a bitter old man, to die and be buried and when he returned, he said: "comincianmi già i grossi panni a piacere e le contadine vivande" — "I am happy to wear rough clothing and eat peasant food." Certaldo lies in the Valdelsa. The river Elsa which runs through it flows down from the Montagnola, a small mountain west of Siena; it then flows into the Arno near Émpoli. This valley road, which once ran high on the hillcrests before the malarial riverside plain was reclaimed, was the route of "Romei," pilgrims bound for Rome; it was a main leg of the Via Francigena, a heavily used route in medieval Europe. That may explain the ferocity with which Florentines and Siennese fought over it (the Florentines triumphed in the late-14th c.). The route runs from Florence and enters and runs up the Valdelsa after descending the Arno; it is perhaps at its most intensely Tuscan when it leaves that valley, at Certaldo, and then twists west into valleys and over hills, before ending, once again near the Elsa. Along this route, you pass through two exquisitely Tuscan places, different in surroundings and atmosphere: Volterra, with Etruscan and medieval heritages, stern, a clear light silhouetting surrealistic hills, with clayey slopes torn away in desolate washes, and the chasms of the Balze. San Gimignano is immersed in a landscape with all the gentle lines and delicate colors of Siena's finest painters.

The route. You leave Florence from Piazza Gaddi, along the Via Bronzino (left bank of the Arno), and follow the road to Pisa (state road 67), along the Arno, through Émpoli, to Ponte a Elsa. Here, you take the state road 429 toward Siena, which runs along the Elsa to Certaldo. Turning right, you will follow a road west to Gambassi Terme, Il Castagno, Vicarello, and lastly Volterra. Heading east from Volterra on the state road 68, you reach Castel San Gimignano, where you turn left to then take a twisting but panoramic road all the way to San Gimignano. You will continue east, hitting the Valdelsa (Elsa valley) at Poggibonsi. After a short drive along the Cassia toward Siena, you will take a right at the fork for Colle di Val d'Elsa, and this will take take you to the end of the route.

Halting places of interest. Badia di S. Salvatore a Sèttimo: restored following damage inflicted during WWII, this abbey is enclosed by crenelated walls: you must turn off, just outside of Florence, just after the Autostrada. **Lastra a Signa** (see Signa) still has part of the old walls; nearby, at Gangalandi, note the 11th-c. parish church of S. Martino, with 13th-c. paintings and frescoes. **Montelupo Fiorentino**; note the Museo Archeologico e della Ceramica, in Palazzo del Podestà. **Émpoli:** Palazzo Ghibellino witnessed a council that met to decide the fate of Florence, after its disastrous defeat at the 13th-c. battle of Montaperti ; note frescoes by Masolino da Panicale in the Museo della Collegiata and in the church of S. Stefano; note local glass-making industry. **Oratorio della Madonna della Tosse:** 2-km. detour from Granaiolo; note chapel that once contained frescoes by Benozzo Gozzoli (1484), now in Castelfiorentino. **Castelfiorentino:** in the old town center, note the lavish Baroque churches, with 14th-/15th-c. artwork. The Raccolta

Comunale d'Arte has the two series of frescoes by B.Gozzoli. **Certaldo:** strongly medieval in flavor; note Boccaccio's house, rebuilt, set high on the hill. **Montaione** is an ancient village with a view; it can be reached by a 3-km. detour, at a fork just past Gambassi Terme; another 4.5 km. (from a crossroads just before Montaione) takes you to the convent of S. Vivaldo (404 m.), with 20 chapels containing Della Robbia terracottas; it is in the forest of Boscolazzeroni, a nature reserve. **Volterra*** is a windswept hill-top town, sternly alluring; the atmosphere is medieval, with towers and grey buildings. Relics of the Etruscan origins can be seen at the Museo Guarnacci. **San Gimignano**** is a perfect intact town of medieval Tuscany; gates, houses, squares, and roads, as well as the 14 surviving towers; works by great artists in the churches and in the Pinacoteca. In particular, in the Collegiata, major works by Giuliano and Benedetto da Maiano, Bartolo di Fredi, and Jacopo della Quercia. **Colle di Val d'Elsa:** you may reach the old "borgo" by taking the Via del Castello, up high. Note the birthplace of Arnolfo di Cambio, born here in 1232; an exhibit on his work is located in the Palazzo Pretorio.

The Mugello and the Pratomagno 39

Florence - Pratolino - Borgo San Lorenzo - Vallombrosa - San Giovanni Valdarno - Florence (195 km.)

The Mugello, north of Florence, is an exceedingly green hollow, an ancient lakebed, through which the river Sieve runs, a tributary of the upper Arno (this provides much of the Arno's water; in Florence a rhyming proverb goes:"Arno non cresce se Sieve non mesce," meaning"Arno won't grow if the Sieve does-n't flow"; when the Sieve does flow excessively, flooding ensues, sometimes with disastrous results, as in 1966). The Pratomagno is a long mountain ridge, running crosswise between Florence and Arezzo; around it, the Arno runs in a great oxbow curve. The highest elevation — the Croce di Pratomagno — stands 1,592 m. above sea level; one slopes overlooks the Casentino, the other faces Valdarno di Sopra. The two slopes are linked by the Passo della Consuma. The ridges are expanses of meadow, as one might expect from the name (Pratomagno means "great meadow"). On the side facing Florence is the dense forest of Vallombrosa; the lower slopes are covered with olive trees, vineyards, and fields, especially toward the Valdarno — this is the slope along which this route runs — while in the Casentino, chest-nut trees grow at elevations of close to a thousand meters. Along the road, you will see sites associated with great Tuscan artists. In Vespignano, a section of Vicchio, in Mugello, a certain Bondone "a man who worked the land," had a son named Ambrogiotto, or Giotto, for short; near here, the great 13th-c. artist Cimabue discovered him, as a young boy, while on a "flat clean slab or rock, with a slightly pointed stone," he was sketching one of the sheep he was guarding, "without having been in any way taught, save by the instincts of nature" (Vasari). Fra' Angelico was born in nearby Vicchio. Tommaso di Ser Giovanni di Mone, better known as Masaccio, son of a notary, came into the world in San Giovanni Valdarno; during Vasari's lifetime, it was said that one could still see "a number of drawings done by him in his youth" in the area.

The route. You will leave Florence heading north, through the Porta S. Gallo; take the state road 65 Della Futa, climbing to Pratolino. Take a right off this road, toward the Convent of Monte Senario, and then rejoin the road at Vaglia; follow it past Cafaggiolo, and then take the road through the hills that runs past Galliano, Sant'Agata (341 m.), and Scarperìa. Drive down to San Piero a Sieve, where you will join the state road 551, which runs down along the left bank of the Sieve. Take this road through Mugello, past Vicchio, to Dicomano, and continue along the state road 67 along the Sieve to an intersection just past Scopeti. Here, you can turn off along a panoram-ic road that runs through Pomino. At Borselli, you will rejoin the road that runs from Pontassieve to the Consuma pass (1,060 m.). Just before Con-suma, you take a right along a local road through the forest to Vallombrosa (958 m.). Dropping down into the upper Arno valley, the road runs along the slopes of the Pratomagno, through Reggello (390 m.), Pian di Scó, and Loro Ciuf-fenna (330 m.). After a loop through Anciolina, San Giustino Valdarno, and Gròpina — a recommended detour (37Km. see below) — you will drive down to cross the Arno between Terranuova Bracciolini and Montevarchi. You will return to Florence along the state road 69, through San Giovanni Valdarno; at Incisa, you will take the highway for the last dozen km.

Halting places of interest. Pratolino: Villa Demidoff with its immense grounds was one of the homes that Francesco I de' Medici gave to the lovely and restless Venetian noblewoman Bianca Capello, his lover and later his wife. **Monte Senario**: from the 12th-c. convent at 815 m., a notable view; a liqueur is made here called "Gemma di Abete." **Cafaggiolo**: the Renaissance architect Michelozzo transformed an old fortress into a villa for Cosimo de' Medici; note nearby The Castello di Trebbio, built by Michelozzo for Cosimo il Vecchio. **Sant'Agata** has a Romanesque parish church. **Scarperìa**: the craft of fashioning fine knives and cutting implements has been practiced here for generations. **Convento del Bosco ai Frati**: in the church, note the wooden Crucifix believed to be by Donatello; you get here by taking a 3-km. detour from a fork just before San Piero a Sieve. **Borgo San Lorenzo** is the main town of the Mugello, with a Romanesque church, S. Lorenzo dating back to 1263; its facade was re-built using original materials in 1922. **Vespignano**: you can visit what is believed to be the birthplace of Giotto. **Vicchio** has a small Museo dell'Angelico, devoted to Fra' Angelico, who was born here. **San Godenzo**, an ancient Benedictine abbey, is at the end of a 10-km. detour from Dicomano from the road up to the Passo del Muraglione. **Vallombrosa**: the landscape, with famed woods of fir trees, is stupendous. The abbey was founded in 1051; a detour takes you through the forest and on up to Monte Secchieta (1,449 m.), 10 km. away; vista. **Cascia**, with the Romanesque parish church of S. Pietro, can be reached from Reggello, with a short detour along the road to Figline Valdarno. The former **Badia di Soffena**, a 14th-c. abbey, has notable frescoes; nearby is the town of Castelfranco di Sopra. **Loro Ciuffenna:** you can extend the route from here by taking a panoramic detour of 37 km., up to the village of Anciolina (933 m.), at the foot of Monte Lori, one of the peaks of the Pratomagno; you then descend to San Giustino Valdarno and you return to Loro Ciuffenna via Gròpina, with its Romanesque church of S. Pietro. **San Giovanni Valdarno:** it is said that the old center of town was designed by Arnolfo di Cambio; in the Museo della Basilica are noteworthy artworks, including an altarpiece by Fra' Angelico, formerly in the convent of Montecarlo.

The Casentino   40

Florence - Consuma - Camàldoli - La Verna - Arezzo (180 km.)
Mastro Adamo Guidi was a counterfeiter of Florentine coins. Burned at the stake for this crime, he later appeared in Dante's "Divine Comedy", punished in the "Inferno" by a burning unslakable thirst, and tormented by visions of the sparkling streams of his homeland. Mountain streams and brooks indeed water these slopes (Pratomagno to the west, Alpi di Serra and Alpi di Catenaia to the east), running down eventually to the Arno. The landscape of the Casentino is framed by mountains of sandstone and limestone, with squat ridges and low peaks (Falterona, 1,654 m.), snowcapped for much of the year. Their slopes are covered with emerald meadows, and dark dense stands of fir trees, and forests of ash, holm-oaks, oak trees, and chestnut trees on the slopes; in the valleys grow fields of wheat, orchards, tobacco, hemp, and — dotting the land — mulberries, olive groves, and vineyards. Woodcutters and shepherds once predominated here, following their flocks down to the Maremma in winter. This is a land of ancient churches, castles, and silent hermitages: Vallombrosa, Camàldoli, and La Verna.

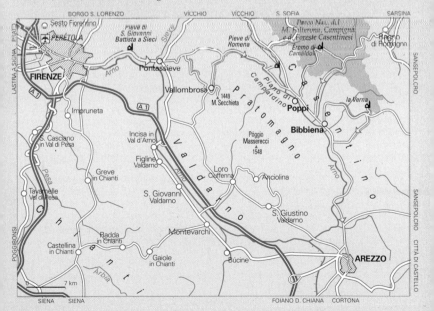

The route. From Florence, you will drive along the Arno to Pontassieve (state road 69 toward Arezzo). You then turn on to the state road 70, which, after crossing the Consuma pass (1,060 m.), descends along another stretch of the Arno valley (the Casentino, through which the river runs before doubling back in an oxbow around Pratomagno).You then arrive at Poppi. Here, you turn on to a secondary road that twists up to the Hermitage (1,104 m.) and the monastery of Camàldoli. From there, you drive down to the Arno via Serravalle and the state road 71, until you reach Bibbiena. Here, the state road 208 takes you back up to La Verna (1,128 m.). Then drive back down the road to Chitignano, which will take you once again to the Arno at Ràssina. From here, the state road 71 continues to Arezzo.

Halting places of interest. Le **Sieci** boasts the Romanesque parish church of S. Giovanni Battista a Rèmole, some 12 km. outside Florence, on the road to Pontassieve. **Vallombrosa:** the landscape of the fir forest, the more-than-900-year old convent; take a 10-km. detour through the forest, up to the Monte Secchieta (1,449 m.); fine view. **Pieve di Romena*** is the most interesting parish church in the Casentino (10th/12th c.); take a short detour past the ruins of the Castello di Romena, descending from Consuma to Poppi. **Piano di Campaldino**: where the road from Stia intersects with this route, note the column commemorating the great battle of Campaldino (11 June 1289), in which the 24-year-old Dante Alighieri fought. **Poppi:** turn off at Ponte a Poppi; in the 13th-/14th-c. Castello (note artwork) you can sense the power of the Conti Guidi, a noble ruling family. **Hermitage and Monastery of Camàldoli:** the hermitage is at an elevation of 1,104 m.; the monastery at 816 m.; both stand in a dense fir grove. The monastery was founded by Saint Romualdo and is nearly 1,000 years old. **Bibbiena** is the largest town in the Casentino, with an old center, high on the hill: note panel by Arcangelo di Cola in the church of Ss. Ippolito e Donato, and the intense Tuscan vista, from the terrace of Piazza Tarlati; Palazzo Dovizi belonged to a cardinal, known as the Bibbiena, a friend of Raphael and a noted playwright. **La Verna*:** a limestone peak, a forest, and a convent founded by St. Francis of Assisi.

San Marino, the Montefeltro, and the Apennines of Tuscany and Romagna

Pesaro - Cattolica - San Marino - San Leo - Carpegna - Sansepolcro - La Verna (225 km.)
Around the yellow and green hills, with red towers adorning their crowns, a network of history weaves the pattern of two family names, Malatesta and Montefeltro. They were both strivers after power and, in the Renaissance, canny commissioners of artwork. Both are believed to have originated in Montefeltro, the land of mountains, forests, and castles between Romagna and Marche: the Malatesta possessed the Billi and the Penna (two ranges that combine in the name Pennabilli), the "mala testa," or evil head, belonged to the founder of the dynasty, Verucchio; in time they ruled Fano, Pesaro, Rimini, and other parts of Romagna. The Montefeltro were descendants of the Conti di Carpegna, and by the end of the 12th c. they had occupied San Leo. The name Montefeltro came from that place's Latin name, "Mons Feretri." The final destiny of this family was to rule Urbino, however. Verucchio, Pennabilli, Carpegna (and you can add the enduring republic of San Marino): the route runs through this region, climbing from Pesaro to high Apennine passes. From there, the Tiber valley (Val Tiberina) opens out: landscape, color, and light such as in the Baptism of Christ, which Piero della Francesca painted for the priory of S. Giovanni Battista in Sansepolcro (the painting is now in London). As you reach the end of the route, you will see other remarkable places: Anghiari, where a great battle took place in 1440 (Machiavelli says that there was only one death in this battle, and that by accident; the mercenaries were far too professional to hurt each other); Caprese, birthplace of Michelangelo Buonarroti; La Verna, site of early Franciscan occupation, "in the harsh rock between Tiber and Arno" (Dante).

The route. Starting in Pesaro, you follow the Adriatic coast to Cattolica. Cutting inland along the valley of the Conca, you pass through San Giovanni in Marignano, Morciano di Romagna, and Montescudo. Drive up the eastern slope of San Marino. You will then drive northward down to Verucchio. From here, follow the state road 258 toward Novafeltria, following for some way the Marécchia valley; at Villanova, turn off for San Leo (589 m.). You will continue southward, across the Montefeltro, through Madonna di Pugliano, Villagrande (915 m.), and Caturchio, to Carpegna; from there, NW to Pennabilli (629 m.). Driving downhill, just past Pennabilli, you will reach the state road 258. This road will take you back up the Marécchia valley, and over the Apennine crest through the Viamaggio pass (983 m.). From here, drive down through the Tiberina valley, to Sansepolcro. The Ruga valley will take you directly across the valley to Anghiari. From here, you will climb to Caprese Michelangelo (469 m.). Continue north, along a road that intersects with the route from Pieve Santo Stefano up to La Verna, the end of the route.

Halting places of interest. Pesaro: behind the Marina, with its fanciful Art-Nouveau Villetta Ruggeri, the historical center features an exquisite art gallery, with works by Giovanni Bellini, among others. **Gradara:** take a 5-km. detour from Casteldimezzo inland; the fortress of the medieval "borgo" witnessed the love (and tragic murders) of Paolo and Francesca, real-life characters described in Dante's Inferno. **Gabicce Monte** 144 m. has a remarkable view of the sea, and the endless series of beaches of the Romagna. **San Marino***, cheerful and crowded in the summer, is the oldest republic in Europe; of the three fortresses, the Cesta boasts the finest vista. **Verucchio**, original home of the powerful family of the Malatesta, has an impressive Rocca, or fortress, and a Museo Archeologico in the former convent of S. Agostino. **San Leo*:** the fort atop the steep crag was the creation of the great Renaissance architect, Francesco di Giorgio Martini. **Carpegna**: the impressive Palazzo Carpegna stands in the center of town, a resort with fine views; a 3-km. side trip takes you up to the Cippo, in the forest of Monte Carpegna. **Pennabilli:** from the two rocky crags, the two castles of the Penna and the Billi once glared at one

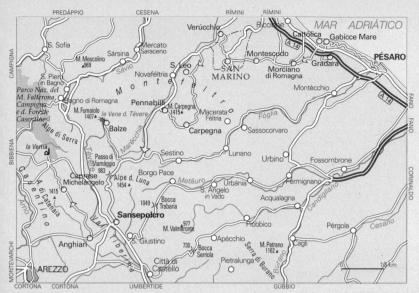

another; on one now stand the ruins of a Malatesta fortress; on the other is the medieval heart of the town. **Vene del Tevere:** (these are the two sources of the river Tiber, at an elevation of less than 1,300 m., under the peak of Monte Fumaiolo (1,407 m.); to get here, take a 17-km. detour, taking a right turn from a fork in the road, 8 km. past Badia Tedalda, via the resort area of Balze (1,090 m.), along the road to the Passo dell'Incisa. **Sansepolcro:** note the fragments of medieval construction, and a predominantly Renaissance architecture; there are a number of celebrated paintings by Piero della Francesca, who was born here, in the Museo Civico. **Anghiari:** medieval roads, squares, and homes lie within the ring of old city walls; in the Renaissance Palazzo Taglieschi is the Museo delle Arti e Tradizioni Popolari dell'Alta Valle del Tevere, devoted to the folkways and crafts of the upper Tiber valley. **Caprese Michelangelo:** the great Renaissance artist was born here, in the Casa del Podestà, now a Museo Michelangiolesco. **La Verna*** (1,129 m.). this mountain is sheer on three sides, crowded round with a fir and beech forest; the renowned Franciscan convent stands just beneath the peak.

From the Siennese Crete to the Valdichiana 42

Siena - Monte Oliveto Maggiore - Montalcino - Pienza - Chiusi - Città della Pieve (147 km.)

In the springtime, the landscape to the SE of Siena becomes green with clover and early wheat; in other seasons, the sere bareness of this land is dramatically evident, amidst an almost treeless landscape: these are the Siennese "Crete," easily eroded hillocks, with deceptively gentle silhouettes, rutted by washouts of clay. Other colors appear between the rivers Ombrone and Orcia and the Valdichiana, later along the route. The Ombrone rises in Chianti and flows down to the Tyrrhenian across the plain of Grosseto; the Orcia pours down from the Monte Cetona, south of Chiusi, and into the Ombrone some distance west: here the rivers flow erratically among gentle peaceful hills. Cypresses stand around the secluded monastery of Monte Oliveto Maggiore, olive trees alternate with vineyards on hilltops; downhill, little towns stand as they have for centuries, stranded by long-vanished ebb tides of history. Montalcino still remembers how the white-spotted banner of the Siennese Republic fluttered high over the town for four years, after the surrender in 1555 following a siege, starvation, and disease: 650 families survived the siege. Pienza, solitary and silent, stands as a visible dream of Humanistic perfection. Montepulciano is an alternation of Renaissance spaces and palazzi with far more ancient and venerable views. As you reach the former Etruscan town of Chiusi, you are venturing into the Valdichiana: there is a topographic map drawn by Leonardo da Vinci (1502-1503), with shaded mountains, the round, grey-blue lake of Trasimeno, and even larger and elongated, the ancient marsh of the Chiana plain; Chiusi marks the southern edge of this expanse. This route comes to an end with a jog into Umbria: Città della Pieve is your first taste of the region, a

cluster of red brick between the green slopes, distant mountain outlines and the blue of the sky.

The route. Take Porta Pispini out of Siena, toward Arezzo and Perugia. At Taverne d'Arbia take the state road 438, toward Asciano, via Le Crete. A small road leads up to the abbey of Monte Oliveto Maggiore, and then down to Buonconvento. Continue for a very brief jog along the Cassia (state road 2), then cut off to the right along a small road that leads to Montalcino (from here, detour to S. Àntimo; km 10) and back to the Cassia at Torrenieri. Take the Cassia to San Quìrico d'Orcia, and then take state road 146 east to Pienza, Montepulciano, Chianciano Terme, and Chiusi, until you reach the intersection with the state road 71, which you take toward Orvieto, winding up at Città della Pieve.

Halting places of interest. Asciano is a medieval "borgo"; adjacent to the Romanesque Collegiata is the Museo d'Arte Sacra; less than a km. from the hill of Monteapertaccio, the Guelphs of Florence were defeated by the Ghibellines of Siena, led by Provenzano Salvani and Farinata degli Uberti (this was the battle of Montaperti, 4 September 1260; described by Dante in his Inferno). **Monte Oliveto Maggiore*:** this noted Benedictine abbey, secluded amidst cypresses on a hilltop, was founded in 1313 by Bernardo Tolomei; in the cloister, note frescoes by Signorelli and Sodoma. **Buonconvento:** girt by a ring of medieval walls, this town has noteworthy artworks in its Museo d'Arte Sacra. **Montalcino:** the fine red Brunello produced here is considered by many to be Italy's best wine; the fortress was the last bastion of Siennese independence; at a distance of 8 km. is the solitary Romanesque abbey of S. Àntimo, said to have been founded by Charlemagne at the end of the 8th c. **San Quìrico d'Orcia:** note the Romanesque Collegiata. **Pienza**:** here the Renaissance architect Bernardo Rossellino interpreted the scholarly concepts of Enea Silvio (or Aeneus Silvius) Piccolomini, Pope Pius II, in renovating the village in which the pope was born; no other place in Europe came so close to attaining the status of "ideal city" dreamed of by the 15th-c. Humanists. **Montepulciano**:** the architecture of the Renaissance, which is set amidst the medieval buildings of this ridge-top village between Chiana and Orcia, is by Michelozzo, Vignola, and Antonio da Sangallo the Elder (who also built the lovely, solitary, classical church of S. Biagio). **Chianciano Terme*:** this renowned spa stands on foothills; the old town is secluded. **Chiusi:** originally an Etruscan town; note the artworks in the Museo and the necropolis in the nearby countryside. **Città della Pieve:** the Renaissance artist Perugino was born here, and the countryside reappears in much of his work (paintings by him are in the Cattedrale, and in the church of S. Maria dei Bianchi, and other churches).

The Colline Metallifere and the Coastline of Grosseto 43

Volterra - Massa Marittima - Grosseto - Castiglione della Pescaia - Piombino (189 km.)
You can see the Cima delle Cornate on your left, as you drive from Larderello to Massa Marittima; it stands on the border between the provinces of Siena and Grosseto, rising to an altitude of 1,060 m., high above the smaller hills; geographers consider it to be the nucleus of the "anti-Apennines," also known as the Colline Metallifere ("metal-bearing hills"). Minerals, mining, the "bowels of the earth": these are the threads that tie together this route, running from Volterra south, first of all through the Colline Metallifere. In Volterra you will see workshops, walls, and sometimes entire streets covered with the white dust of alabaster (in ancient Latin and Greek, "alabastros" meant a small ointment jar; there has been much discussion as to whether the jar gave the name to the stone, or vice versa; in any case, there are two varieties of alabaster, the calcareous variety, and the dusty, gypsum variety, such as is found in the Volterra region); the Saline, which give their name to the industrial part of Volterra, are mines with alternating strata of salt, clay, and gypsum; the boric acid of the "lagoni" of Montecèrboli and the hot "soffioni" bubbling through those bodies of mineral water made the fortune of François de Larderel, a French aristocratic ruined by the Revolution, once a travelling vendor of ribbons and fabrics from Livorno, who established a hot-springs spa here; the prosperity of Massa Marittima during the Middle Ages, apparent from the many monuments, was produced by veins of copper and silver; also found in the region are various pyrites, blende, galena, lignite, quartzite, and alumite. Mineral collectors crowd the annual mineral fair; Gavorrano, surrounded by iron mines, is known for its yellow pyrite crystals. The mineral-rich region borders on the Maremma, dominated by Massa Marittima. There is a bitter old saying: "Va a Massa, guardala e passa," meaning "Go to Massa, look but don't stay"; the proverb refers to the centuries of abandonment and neglect, the swirling lethal marsh air of the Maremma, where malaria reigned until the Tuscan archdukes began to make reforms and projects of reclamation in the 18th c. This is now a popular vacation spot, though some people still remember how school teachers used to administer a dose of quinine to each pupil every morning, to ward off malaria. Pineta marks the end of this trip, with fragrant aromas of the maquis and the broad gulf of Follonica (midway between Grosseto and Piombino), coming after a visit to the Etruscan ruins of Vetulonia, hearkening back to the Etruscan Volterra, where this trip started.

The route. From Volterra you will drive down to Saline di Volterra. There, you turn left on to the state road 439, to Pomarance (just beyond, at Croce Bulera, you can turn off along a secondary road to San Dalmazio and the Rocca di Sillano, a fortress). At Montecèrboli, a turnoff on the left takes you to Larderello, and then runs back to the state road further south. After reaching Massa Marittima, drive back along the same route briefly, then take a secondary road off the state road, through Bellavista and Perolla, to intersect with the Aurelia (state road 1) at Stazione di Gavorrano. Take the Aurelia to Grosseto. The second half of this route takes you from Grosseto along the state road 322, which, running largely along the coast, goes from Castiglione della Pescaia to Follònica. Here, take the Aurelia; turn off just Vignale, and you will soon be at Piombino.

Halting places of interest. Volterra*: the charm of this town emanates from the vast landscape that can be seen from the hills between the rivers Cècina and Era, and the stern medieval urban layout; the notable urns of the Museo Guarnacci will take you on a trip through the "Etruscan underworld." Note the alabaster craftsmen here. **Rocca di Sillano:** the ruins of this fortress (530 m.) dominates the view along the road after Pomarance: you will climb up from San Dalmazio, with the last stretch on foot, over mule tracks. **Larderello:** jets of stream rise here, with cooling towers breaking the horizon; the commercial exploitation of the "soffioni," first undertaken by a certain Larderel who gave his name to the place, has been going on since 1818; the parish church of the residential area is by the 20th-c. architect Giovanni Michelucci. **Massa Maríttima*:** medieval transformations made the structure of the city still more complex, and the square, with the Romanesque-Gothic cathedral, is certainly the finest feature of the town; in the

landscape of the surrounding Maremma, there is a history of mining; the sea is far off. **Vetulonia** (5 km. away from the Aurelia; turn off at I Grilli): this medieval town occupies the acropolis of the Etruscan town; the necropolis is scattered over the countryside. **Montepescali** (see Grosseto), with a castle on a hill covered with olive groves, is known as the "balcony of the Maremma" for the fine views; a 3.3 km. detour will take you here from Braccagni. **Grosseto** is the prime market place of the reclaimed Maremma and is renowned as an agricultural centre; the modern city surrounds the small historic nucleus, and the hexagonal enclosure of bastions and walls has been transformed into boulevards and gardens. **Castiglione della Pescaia:** near the beach is a pine forest, while the town is marked by walls and towers; in the canal-harbor there are more pleasure boats than fishing boats nowadays. **Punta Ala*,** at the end of a 9 km. detour from Pian d'Alma, is an exclusive beachfront residential area, amidst the Mediterranean vegetation. **Follònica** is a beach resort and a manufacturing town, with beaches and pine forest overlooking the gulf. **Piombino** is a city of iron mills and a port; from a terrace overlooking the sea you can glimpse Elba and the Tuscan archipelago, as well as the marina.

The Island of Elba 44

Portoferraio - Marciana - Marina di Campo - Porto Azzurro - Cavo - Portoferraio (130 km.)
It is said that Elba is a precious stone that fell into the sea, when one of Aphrodite's necklaces broke; it is an island with coves, bays, promontories, reefs, and crescent-shaped beaches — the 118 km. of coastline is four times the extent one would expect of an island this size — steep slopes dotted with olive and almond trees, silent lofty villages, holm-oaks, and sunny vineyards, producing sweet wines, palm trees, agave plants, eucalyptus trees, and cork-oaks. On the eastern beaches, the sand of the beaches is mixed with pyrite, and a rusty iron-red dominates in the rocks. The Greek name was "Aethalia," which means "place of soot," because of the smoke from the ironworks here; "Ilva," the Roman name, refers to the early lords of the island, the Ligurian Ilvates. Porto Argoo (so-called because Jason, sailing the Argo, landed here during one of his quests), now called Portoferraio, was many centuries ago the main town of Elba; another name it once bore is that of Cosmopoli. Here is what happened: Cosimo I de' Medici had defended the entire Piombino territory against the wrath of the Barbary pirate and admiral Khair-ed-Din, known also as Barbarossa, or Redbeard. Cosimo then persuaded the Holy Roman Emperor Charles V to let him protect, and rule, the mainland and islands of this patch of what he considered maritime Tuscany, sweetening the pot with a loan of 200,000 ducats. Later, Charles's only son and heir Philip II bestowed Piombino and most of Elba to the Appiani family, leaving Cosimo with Portoferraio. Here, on the site of a modest village, the architect Giovambattista Bellucci had built a city and fortress for the Medici (1548-59): an efficacious piece of military architecture, but also the translation into concrete form of the last tattered dreams of the "ideal city" of the Renaissance. This relic of utopian ambitions, epitomized in the name Cosmopoli, can still be seen.

The route. This detailed exploration of the island starts from Portoferraio, where the car ferry docks. First, take a quick drive to Capo d'Ènfola, then you will double back almost all the way to Portoferraio before taking the northern coast road, along the water or over hills, around the western half of Elba: Procchio, Marciana Marina, Poggio, and Marciana. After rounding Punta Nera you will follow the southern coast to Fetovaia, Càvoli, Lacona (one detour takes you to the peninsula of Lacona; further on anoth-

er one leads to Capolìveri and Morcone), and Porto Azzurro. The tour of the eastern half of the island is completed by driving from Porto Azzurro to Rio nell'Elba, Rio Marina, and Cavo — near the northernmost point. Returning along the same road, after Rio Marina but before Rio nell'Elba, take a right on to a secondary road which takes you back to Portoferraio.

Halting places of interest. Portoferraio: note the strategic position guarding the little bay, the dignified architecture, and the late-Renaissance city layout, the creation of Cosimo I de' Medici; the town also contains the Foresiana art Gallery boasting works from the 16th-19th-c, and an archeological museum with local pieces. **Capo d'Ènfola:** note the clear waters, abounding in fish, around the promontory. **Villa di Napoleone**: take a detour from the fork of Bivio Boni; this was Napoleon's summer home. **Marciana** is a village on the slopes of Monte Capanne, 1,018 m., (you can reach the peak by cableway and walking trails); on Monte Giove (a bit of a hike is required) note the Santuario della Madonna del Monte. **San Piero in Campo**: take a detour just before Marina di Campo; this village dating back to Roman times lies at the foot of an old fort. **Penisola di Lacona**: this peninsula can be reached by a detour from a fork near the Golfo della Stella; forest landscape and beaches of exceedingly fine sand. **Capolìveri**: there is a spectacular view from the "borgo," which can be reached from a turnoff just before Porto Azzurro; note the secluded beaches of Morcone. **Porto Azzurro**: the Spanish built the fortress (now a prison) which looms over the town and the little gulf; from the road to Rio, you can detour to the Santuario di Monserrato (also founded by the Spanish, and dedicated to the Virgin of Monserrat, near Barcelona). **Rio nell'Elba** is a mining town in iron country. **Rio Marina** has a small Mining Museum in town hall. **Cavo**: note the ruins of a Roman villa on the promontory of Capo Castello.

Monte Amiata and the Valle del Paglia 45

Chiusi - Radicòfani - Monte Amiata - Acquapendente - Orvieto (150 km.)

Here, on the Monte Amiata, they call it "latte di luna," or "milk of the moon": it is fossil dust, or organic silica, formed by the deposit of countless myriads of diatom algae; it is found in the area around Santa Fiora and is used in the manufacture of dynamite, filters, and insulation. Among the resources of the mountain, it is less well known than cinnabar, from which mercury is obtained; the Etruscans used it as a dye. As for Monte Amiata itself, the tallest peak in Tuscany south of the river Arno, and the star of this route, it is an isolated cone, mantled on its upper slopes by beech and chestnut forests; on the north slope, a patch of snow endures through spring; in May the mountain explodes in blooming snowdrops (*Galanthus nivalis*), violets (*Viola odorata*), and broom (*Cytisus scoparia*); the crystal clear springs that run off this mountain provide the water that is drunk in the areas around Siena, Grosseto, Viterbo, and in the Maremma. Midway up the slopes, where grain, grapes, and olives are grown, the towns ring the mountain like a wreath: you will be exploring them, their dark clustered houses, their narrow steep lanes, the castles, the walls, the abbeys, and the air of the Middle Ages. Before you reach the Monte Amiata, from Chiusi in Valdichiana, you will join the Via Cassia beneath Radicòfani on its basalt crag. After the circuit around the Monte Amiata, you will enter the Valle del Paglia (a tributary of the Tiber that flows down from the mountain); the route, which thus far has remained in Tuscany, proceeds downriver, jogging into Lazio for a short distance, running through Acquapendente, and then enters Umbria. From crag to crag: the second major crag in this tour is the flat and isolated plateau of tufa upon which stands Orvieto; at its base you will find the river Paglia again.

The route. Drive west from Chiusi along the state road 146, and at Querce al Pino you will turn left on to state road 478 for Sarteano and Radicòfani. From here, take a small road that runs to Abbadia San Salvatore via Le Chiavi and Zaccaria. Here you will turn off to drive counterclockwise around Monte Amiata, via Seggiano, Castel del Piano, Arcidosso, Santa Fiora, and Piancastagnaio. Then drive south along the Paglia valley, until you hit the Cassia (state road 2). Take this, still south, to Acquapendente. Take a left just beyond Acquapendente onto a secondary road that leads to Orvieto, via Castel Viscardo.

Halting places of interest. Chiusi: the Etruscan origins and heritage (see the Museum) are not the only attractions. **Sarteano** lies in the shadow of a 15th-c. castle, and is renowned as a holiday and spa resort. **Radicòfani:** medieval houses with rustication, along narrow lanes; Montaigne and Chateaubriand stayed at La Posta, an old hotel here. **Abbadia San Salvatore:** the medieval village is virtually intact; all around are dense chestnut groves. A road runs nearly to the peak of Monte Amiata (stopping at 1,651 m.), and you can walk on up to enjoy the immense vista from the peak (1,738 m.); nearby is the largest mercury mine on earth. **Arcidosso** is a resort with a well-preserved medieval center. **Santa Fiora:** the town has a medieval air; note the remains of the castle and the Romanesque parish church. **Acquapendente :** note the relics in the mortuary chapel of the cathedral. **Castel Viscardo** is a hill resort with great views; the castle dates from the 15th c. **Orvieto**:** perched atop a tufa plateau, this town is deserving of its renown; the Duomo, by Lorenzo Maitani, is one of the most exquisite pieces of Gothic architecture in Italy.

The Valdichiana and Lake Trasimeno 46

Arezzo - Lucignano - Cortona - Castiglione del Lago - Perugia (168 km.)

Every village and town is perched on a hill, overlooking the plain, like some broad green sea, and across that plain to the opposite shore of hills and highlands. The Valdichiana, indeed, is a great rift running north-south across Tuscany, between Arezzo and Chiusi and, following the collapse of the Roman reclamation project in the Middle Ages, was immersed in swamps, marshes, and shallow lakes, until the beginning of the 19th c. All around, the background color is provided by the leaves of the olive trees that shade houses, villages, walls, towers, and castles. The idea behind this route is simple: from Arezzo it runs south, first along the western hills, with Monte San Savino and Lucignano, then on the other side of the valley, with fine views of Cortona, proud on its high perch, with medieval keeps, Etruscan artifacts, and remarkable art (note the 15th c. clarity of the church of the Madonna del Calcinaio, by Francesco di Giorgio Martini). Breaking away from the Chiana, you enter Umbria. Gentle slopes, bedecked with olive groves and vineyards, surround the silence and reeds of Lake Trasimeno; the three islands, Polvese, Maggiore, Minore, stand quietly enveloped in turquoise light. You travel almost all the way around the lake, then other hilltop roads take you to lovely Perugia, star-shaped, with long arms of walls and houses reaching out across the hillcrest ridges. Throughout this trip, history is found at every stop, on every hillside. History is present, in sinister garb, at the Magione, on a rise between Lake Trasimeno and Perugia: in the Magione, or Castle of the Knights of Malta, then held by the cardinal Giambattista Orsini, in September of 1502, a number of local lords angry at and fearful of Cesare Borgia, the Valentino, son of pope Alexander VI and brother of Lucrezia, assembled to conspire. Within three months, Borgia had destroyed the conspiracy, and four of them — Vitellozzo Vitelli, Oliverotto da Fermo, Paolo and Francesco Orsini — had been killed in Senigallia with what Machiavelli enthusiastically described as a "rare and wondrous deed" (they were simply poisoned after being invited to dinner). The Cardinal Orsini, meanwhile, was dying — or being killed — in Rome's Castel Sant'Angelo.

The route. You will leave Arezzo heading for Siena; cross the Valdichiana (state road 73) and, at its western edge, climb up to Monte San Savino. A small road takes you to Lucignano and Foiano della Chiana. From here, you will drive back up the Valdichiana along the 327, turning right, after 4 km., on to the road that crosses the valley and intersects the state road 71 at Castiglion Fiorentino.

Take this road toward Rome beyond Castiglione del Lago (on Lake Trasimeno), turning off to the left to skirt the southern and eastern shores of the lake, as far as Passignano sul Trasimeno. Doubling back, via Magione, you will arrive in Perugia. A number of sidetrips, beginning with the climb up to Cortona, are indicated at the respective halts.

Halting places of interest. Monte San Savino: this is the feudal holding of the Dal Monte family (pope Julius III was a Dal Monte), a medieval town now rich in Renaissance art. **Lucignano** is a medieval village with a remarkable layout; nearby is the Renaissance sanctuary of the Madonna delle Querce. **Foiano della Chiana:** this thriving hilltop town has old churches and small 16th-c. palazzi; note the panel by Luca Signorelli in the Collegiata di S. Martino. **Castiglion Fiorentino:** amid the walls of this medieval town, you can still see the keep of the castle, now the Pinacoteca Comunale, with a notable collection of fine art; further along, to the left of the Valdichiana road, note the large castle of Montecchio Vesponi. **Cortona*:** you take a fork at Camucìa; landscape, history, and Etruscan relics, medieval townscape, and artworks (by Pietro Lorenzetti, Luca Signorelli, and Fra' Angelico) make this the jewel of the route, one of Italy's artistic capitals; take a small detour to Madonna del Calcinaio, and note the Etruscan hypogeum of Tanella di Pitagora; a detour from the road to Città di Castello takes you to the Convento delle Celle. **Castiglione del Lago:** the old town sits amidst olive trees on a promontory overlooking Lake Trasimeno. **Castel Rigone:** take a 6-km. detour from a fork at San Vito; the Santuario della Madonna dei Miracoli is one of the masterpieces of the Umbrian Renaissance. **Passignano sul Trasimeno:** also perched on a lakefront promontory, this town has an old center of steep little lanes; on the nearby Isola Maggiore, note the 14th-c Gothic church of S. Michele Arcangelo with a crucifix by Bartolomeo Caporali. **Corciano** is a turreted medieval village, the last detour on the road from Magione to Perugia.

The Valle Umbra 47

Perugia - Assisi - Spello - Foligno - Spoleto - Montefalco - Perugia (153 km.)
When Marco Boschini used the Italian term for "picturesque" in the title of his book "Carta del Navegar Pitoresco," it simply meant "of or about painting." In time, it came to indicate a wealth of nuance, and then to describe a style of painting devote to secluded and evocative landscapes. Nowadays it means: "visually charming," "quaint," "graphic," or "vivid." However commonplace the term has become, it may fairly be applied to the Valle Umbra, or Umbrian Valley, watered by the rivers Ose, Topino, Chiona, Clitunno, and Teverone, ringed by hills, farmland, maple trees, vineyards, silvery olive groves, and towns such as Perugia, Assisi, Spello, Trevi, Spoleto, Montefalco, and Bevagna. The "visually charming" and "quaint" are unquestionable; as for the "graphic" and "vivid," they apply to the overall panorama, made up of such elements as lovely patches of landscape; remarkable art, ancient and modern,; poplars and willows reflected in the clear rippling chilly waters of the Fonti del Clitunno; the wooded Monteluco behind grey Spoleto with its ancient stones; the dreamy medieval air of Bevagna; the glittering color of paintings by Pinturicchio, at Spello, or in the Collegio del Cambio in Perugia; the frescoes by Giotto at Assisi; the pink stones of Assisi, seen from the Monte Subasio; the reliefs and statuettes by the Pisano family, around the Fontana Maggiore of Perugia, with the white-and-red marble flanks of the cathedral, the Etruscan and Roman fragments, part of an architecture that blends perfectly with the landscape, with masterpieces of fine art side-by-side with jewels of the applied arts. Everywhere is power and restraint. It is not often that Italy, as rich as she is, showers so lavish and enchanting a treasure on so small a space.

The route. The first part is notably straightforward: you take the state road 147 from Perugia to Assisi; then, heading south, you will pass through Spello and Foligno, following the state road 3 Flaminia as far as Spoleto. The drive back will follow the other, western side of the Valle Umbra. On secondary roads, through Bruna and Madonna della Stella, you will reach Montefalco, continuing on to Bevagna via Pietrauta, and then, remaining on secondary roads, you will reach Bettona; from there, you will return to Perugia, via Torgiano and the Osteria dei Cipressi. It is advisable to pay close attention to the road signs and to your road map, especially in the second part of the route, from Spoleto to Perugia.

Halting places of interest. Assisi** overlooks much of the Valle Umbra: it has relics of its Roman past and of its medieval existence, but it is quintessentially a Franciscan town; in the basilica of St. Francis, one of Christendom's holy places, note the frescoes of Giotto; plan on spending an intense and fascinating day here. Four km. away is the Eremo delle Carceri, a hermitage in a stand of holm-oaks and oak trees: Francis and his brothers "incarcerated" themselves in prayer here. **S. Maria degli Angeli**: this 16th-c. church was built on the site where St. Francis lived and died, and is one of the most important sanctuaries in Italy. **Spello***: a medieval town, with twisting lanes, churches, old houses, and palazzi, luminous orchards and gardens; note the frescoes by Pinturicchio in the Baglioni Chapel in S. Maria Maggiore. **Foligno:** the old center of the town lies in the plazas near the Duomo; a little less central is the Romanesque church of S. Maria Infraportas; 6 km. away is the secluded abbey of Sassovivo. **Trevi:** you take a 3-km. detour from the Via Flaminia; the town has an ancient air and excellent views: medieval churches and an art gallery in the former convent; note the Renaissance Madonna delle Lacrime, 1 km. away. **Fonti del Clitunno:** these freshwater springs feed a small lake, surrounded by poplars and willows. **Spoleto****, grey on a hill topped by a strong fortress; the Duomo and other monuments stands in medieval surroundings. **Monteluco**: 8-km. detour from Spoleto; a hilltop town, surrounded by holm-oaks and once the home of hermits and anchorites; high up is a convent, with fine view. **Castel Ritaldi** is a village with a 13th-c. castle, at the end of a short detour from Bruna. **Madonna della Stella** is a large sanctuary, by a grove of holm-oaks and cypresses; take a 2-km. detour from Mercatello. **Chiesa di S. Fortunato**: this church has frescoes by Benozzo Gozzoli; to get here, turn right at crossroads 1 km. before Montefalco. **Montefalco***: the nickname "ringhiera dell'Umbria," or "balcony of Umbria," nicely describes its location and views. **Bevagna:** the square is the epitome of an intact medieval scene. **Bettona** is a village atop an olive-clad hill, with a banner by Perugino, set in the 13th-c. church of S. Maria Maggiore.

The Argentario and the Maremma   48

Grosseto - Argentario - Capalbio - Magliano in Toscana - Grosseto (172)
This is an exploration of the Maremma, along the coast, or inland, beginning in Grosseto and returning to Grosseto. You immediately sense the sea. Stretching from the mouth of the Ombrone and extending to Talamone, the coastline of the Monti dell'Uccellina comprises the Parco Naturale della Maremma; the shore is jagged and wild, the hills are covered with dense Mediterranean underbrush, the solitary towers are old watch posts, built to alert the inhabitants to pirate raids. You must apply to visit the park; further along, however, the so-called Via Aurelia Etrusca runs along the shore of a gulf, with the promontory of the Argentario in the background. In the lagoons of Orbetello, sheets of water separate the necks that link the Argentario to the mainland; this was once an island. More than 150 species of bird have been sighted here. Travel around the promontory via a road which gives views both of rocks, inlets, and little harbors, and views of the islands of the Giglio and Giannutri. Claudius Rutilius Namatianus sailed these waters, on his way home to Gaul, from Rome, a few years after the sack of Alaric, in 417; his little poem ("De Reditu Suo") tells of his homeward journey; a few verses seem like snapshots. About the promontory, he wrote: "the Argentario plunges down into the midst of the waves, laying a two-fold yoke around bright-blue bays" ("Tenditur in medias mons Argentarius undas / ancipitique iugo caerula curva premit"); of Porto Ercole at sunset: "the light breeze follows gently upon the declining day" ("vergentem sequitur mollior aura diem"); and at Cosa, "the shadow of the pines wavers at the edge of the waves" ("pineaque extremis fluctuat umbra fretis"). The coastal route ends at the fork for Capalbio.
Heading inland, on the way back, you go past Capalbio, Magliano in Toscana, and Istia d'Ombrone; it is hard to imagine these lands when they were malarial swamps, before their reclamation. Now they are farmland, forests, or wild grass, with colors ranging from green to reddish brown and ocher; along the embankments, amidst the old red farmhouses, there is a reigning silence and brightness of light that make this land unique.

The route. Except for the detours mentioned at each point in the various stops, you will be following the Via Aurelia, from Grosseto toward Rome, as far as Albinia, where you will turn onto the road that leads to Porto Santo Stefano via the Tómbolo della Giannella. You will drive around the Monte Argentario, going through Porto Ercole, Orbetello, and lastly Orbetello Scalo, where you will rejoin the Via Aurelia. Along that road you will continue until you reach the turnoff for Capalbio, to the left. After reaching Capalbio you will head north on secondary roads until you hook up with the state road 74 (Magliano in Toscana-Impostino-Cantoniera dell'Aurelia). Two km. north you will leave the Via Aurelia at a turnoff to the right, which

will take you to Istia d'Ombrone and then to Roselle. After reaching the ruins of Roselle a little further NE, you will return to Grosseto along the state road 223.

Halting places of interest. Marina di Alberese: take a 14-km. detour from Rispèscia; fine view of the Uccellina coast. **Monti dell'Uccellina:** these are within the Parco Naturale della Maremma, a great nature reserve; the visitor center is at Alberese, not far from the Via Aurelia. **Talamone:** the old part is a port-side village, overlooking the bay; take a 5-km. detour from Fonteblanda. **Porto Santo Stefano** in an ancient town, elegant and popular, on an inlet of the Argentario. **Porto Ercole** is a harbor town with a large citadel and three old Spanish forts. **Orbetello** occupies a remarkable site between the two lagoons. **Ansedonia** overlooks the sea from atop a promontory; high up are the Roman ruins of Cosa. Take a 3-km. detour from the Via Aurelia; nearby is the Tagliata Etrusca, a piece of ancient Roman engineering designed to keep the port free of sand. **Capalbio:** this medieval hilltop village is now an exclusive resort of Italy's rich and powerful, the parish church of S. Nicola contains Roman relics and frescoes from the 15th-16th c. **Magliano in Toscana:** medieval in appearance, it stands on an olive-bedecked hill in the Maremma landscape. **Istia d'Ombrone** is an old village on a riverside rise. Rovine di **Roselle:** these are ruins of what was long ago one of the main towns of northern Etruria settentrionale; notable Etruscan and Roman ruins have been found.

The Monti della Tolfa and the Lake of Bracciano   49

Rome - Cervèteri - Civitavecchia - Tolfa - Bracciano - Rome (194 km.)

In the Roman "campagna," or countryside, the days of shepherds wearing fleecy vests and leaning on knobby sticks are long past; also long vanished are the skittish, unshod ponies of the "butteri," mounted cowherds of this region, wearing leather chaps and a rifle slung around the neck; no longer do the "seasonal" workers sleep in a circle in the fields. Still, you may glimpse fragments of that lost world now and again: the gritty farmhouse, perhaps, or a stand of pinasters, an ancient clump of ruins, or the gentle curve of the meadowland. Starting from and returning to Rome, this route runs through four different landscapes, redolent with nature and history. The first follows the crescent-shaped Tyrrhenian coastline, as far as Capo Linaro and Civitavecchia. You will follow the Via Aurelia, as you head toward the first encounter with the ancient Etruscans: Cervèteri, withdrawn from the shore, with its burial grounds of rounded hillocks, tufted with grass, humping across the countryside around the medieval "borgo," and the ancient ports along the seacoast. After Civitavecchia and its harbor ("interior medias sinus invitatus in aedes / instabilem fixis aera nescit aquis"; as an ancient poet, Rutilius Namatianus, described it, when the port was known as "Centumcellae": "the inner gulf, invited amongst the houses, ignores the skittish winds with its steady waters"), the route turns inland, and the second landscape is that of the Monti della Tolfa. In the seaside maquis, or in amongst the inland forests, you may still chance upon a wolf, lone descendants of the wolves that were forced down out of the Apennines by the icy winter of 1956. Geologists will find ores such as blende, galena, pyrite, alumite, kaolin, and cinnabar, all of which prompted ancient mining operations here. The third landscape surrounds the Lake of Bracciano: looking down from the high ridge, you will see the lake at the bottom of its funnel-shaped depression, houses crowded along the banks amidst clumps of alders, willows, and poplars; perched on poles, improbable seagulls watch as coots dive into the tranquil waters. Sometimes a sharp-taloned kite will soar overhead. Last comes the solitary landscape of long-lost Veio, and the rustic promenade across fields to the ruins of the temple of the Vulcan Apollo (the statue is now in Rome, in the Museo Etrusco of Villa Giulia).

The route. You will start out from Rome, heading west along the Via Aurelia (state road 1), all the way to Civitavecchia; on your right, after Borgo Vaccina, note the short detour (3.5 km.) that takes you to Cervèteri, one of the prime destinations on this route. Once you have passed through Civitavecchia, exit through Porta Tarquinia and take the scenic route to Bracciano; this road first runs up the western slopes of the Monti della Tolfa, passing through Allumiere and Tolfa, and then beginning the long descent toward the Lago di Bracciano, passing through Manziana on the way. From the town of Bracciano, the route turns north, making a nearly complete clockwise circuit around the lake, and passing through Trevignano Romano, Anguillara Sabazia, and Vigna di Valle. Then, moving away from the lakeshore drive, you will take the state road 493 Via Claudia Braccianese, returning toward Rome until you hit the state road 2 Via Cassia. From that crossroads, a detour to the north climbs for 2 km. up to the town of Isola Farnese, high overlooking the ruins of Veio. Again, take the state road 2 and then the state road 3 Via Flaminia back into Rome, crossing the Tiber on the Ponte Flaminio, or Flaminian Bridge.

Halting places of interest. Cervèteri*: the stern medieval center of town, high on a tufa spur, stands on the site of the Etruscan town of "Kysry," a wealthy trading port and sea power; in the Castello, note the Museo Nazionale Cerite. Nearby, in the empty landscape of pinasters and cypresses, is a necropolis, with circular barrow tombs. **Santa Severa:** south of the distinctive castle here, archeologists have excavated "Pyrgi," the largest port-of-call of ancient "Caere" (antiquarium). **Santa Marinella:** beach resort; note the Castello Odescalchi, set amidst pine trees near the little marina of "Punicum," another port-of-call of ancient "Caere." **Civitavecchia:** Michelangelo built the eight-sided keep of the high fort that bears his name; this city is now Lazio's most important port. In the Museo Nazionale Archeologico, note materials from earliest times to the Roman empire; the nearby Terme Taurine are the baths of a huge Roman villa, owned by the emperor. **Allumiere** lies on the slopes of the Monte Le Grazie; as the town's name indicates, this was once a quarry for rock alum, used in dyeing wool. **Tolfa** gave its name to the surrounding mountain group; the papal state mined iron ore here for three centuries. The shafts are abandoned now. **Bracciano:** vast view of the Lago di Bracciano from the stern 15th-c. Castello Orsini-Odescalchi, with fine furnishings. **Trevignano Romano** is a village founded in the remote past on the northern lakeshore; the Museo Archeologico houses material from the necropolises of an Etruscan-Roman center. **Anguillara Sabazia** stands on a point of the shore of Lake Bracciano; it is one of the 13 castles that Pope Paul II seized in the 15th c. from the Anguillara family during a 12-day war. **Vigna di Valle:** alongside airplanes of every era, this Italian air force museum, the Museo Storico dell'Aeronautica Militare, has exhibits on the history of flight and the polar expeditions of the dirigibles Norge and Italia. **Isola Farnese:** this "borgo" stands high on a crag over two gorges; around it are scattered the ruins of Etruscan Veio in a lovely setting.

Roman Etruria 50

Viterbo - Vetralla - Tuscania - Ischia di Castro - Vulci - Tarquinia (111 km.)
Roman Etruria coincided with what is now northern Lazio, or southern Etruria, amongst the Monti Volsini, the Monti Cimini, the Monti Sabatini, and the Tyrrhenian coastline. This route runs through the NW section, at the edge of the Maremma along the seaside. There are four noteworthy Etruscan sites, illustrious and timeworn: Norchia, Tuscania, Vulci, and Tarquinia. At Norchia, which may have been called "Orcla" by the Etruscans, the air is remote, surreal, among the architectural facades of the cliffside tombs, long ago plundered, and the medieval ruins of the town. At Tuscania, rather than the much faded Etruscan memories, it is the two early Romanesque churches that attract the eye: these are prototypes of the glorious Italian architecture that blends the Mediterranean style with northern European rigor, creating something uniquely independent, complete unto itself. The beautiful landscape of Vulci, not far from the sea — on a tufa highland on the right bank of the river Fiora — was the site of a heartbreaking act of plunder. In 1828, Luciano Bonaparte, the grasping younger brother of Napoleon, and the papal prince of nearby Canino, excavated in the Etruscan necropolis here, and in four months carried off 2,000 vases. Others followed in the treasure hunt, opening 6,000 tombs, and destroying everything which was not immediately salable, including countless priceless terracottas. Of Tarquinia, and its tomb-paintings, little needs to be said, so great are their fame. Perhaps the native Tarquinian V. Cardarelli said it best: "Here laughed the Etruscan, one day, reclining with his eyes leveled at the harbor. His pupils took in the infinite silent splendor of the lush young land, of which he had so gaily drunk the mysteries...."
The route. From Viterbo you will follow the Via Cassia (state road 2) toward Rome as far as Vetralla; from here, a 14-km. detour takes you to Norchia. Just prior to entering Vetralla, another road leads north, through rolling countryside, to Tuscania and, still further north, to Piansano and Valentano. From here, you will head SW toward the Tyrrhenian coastline, running through Ischia di Castro — and from here you can venture into the forest of Lamone as far as the ruins of Castro (10 km.) — Pianiano, and the archeological site of Vulci, in a countryside frequented for the most part by agricultural machinery and little else, and mantled in long expanses of wheat and other grains. Near Montalto di Castro you can join up with the Via Aurelia (state road 1), following it back toward Rome until you reach the intersection for Tarquinia.

this village, partly medieval in appearance, is a point of departure for visiting **Norchia***, whose Etruscan necropolis features tombs carved out of the tufa, with architectural facades. **Tuscania*:** within the medieval walls of this town is a secluded atmosphere; the town was rebuilt after the earthquake of 1971; on a hillside outside of town, note the churches of S. Pietro and S. Maria Maggiore, masterpieces of Italian architecture of the high Middle Ages. **Valentano**, on the lip of the crater hollow of Làtera, with hues of emerald in spring, sere and yellow in summer; note the vista, which extends beyond the great round hollow of Làtera, the lake of Bolsena and, in the distance, Monte Amiata. **Ischia di Castro** is a medieval "borgo" on a tufa-stone crag, with the Palazzo Ducale by Sangallo. Note Etruscan artifacts from Castro in the Museo Civico. **Farnese**, where medieval buildings and Renaissance palazzi stand side-by-side; note the gilded wooden tabernacle in the parish church of S. Salvatore. **Rovine di Castro**: "Qui fu Castro" — Here stood Castro — is inscribed upon a solitary column on a great mass of tufa-stone; the city, once capital of the Farnese duchy of Castro and Ronciglione, was leveled in 1649. **Vulci**: architecture and landscape are very old friends here, as you may note from the bridge, which re-uses fragments of earlier Etruscan and Roman structure; also note the Abbadia, which houses the Museo Nazionale di Vulci, originally a medieval castle, the ruins of the long-vanished Etrusco-Roman town, the vast Etruscan necropolises in the surrounding territory. **Montalto di Castro**, a "borgo" on the edge of the Maremma, a site noted for the as yet to be completed power station. **Tarquinia***: in this ancient hilltop city, note the 14th-c. Palazzo Vitelleschi, with the Museo Nazionale Tarquiniense; separately, note the Romanseque church of S. Maria di Castello, and, east of town, the Necropolis of Monterozzi, with outstanding tomb paintings.

The Monti Cimini 51

Viterbo - Bomarzo - Cìvita Castellana - Caprarola - Viterbo (111 km.)

The ambiguous term, "mannerism," was first used by L. Lanzi in the late-18th c. to designate a 16th-c. style in the fine arts, "characterized by a complex system of perspective, elongation of forms, strained gestures or poses of figures, and intense, often strident color." It tended to include the bizarre, the capricious, the fantastic, and a tormented restlessness; anticlassical art, if you will, self-referential rather than an "imitation of nature," and popular with aristocratic patrons, who were learned, jaded, and obsessed with a dream of "artificial" beauty. This style is found in this route in three exemplary sites: Bagnaia, Bomarzo, and Caprarola. At Bagnaia, Cardinal Gambara had the architect Vignola create, for what is now Villa Lante, an Italian-style garden replete with ornate fountains (it appears that work was halted by a visit from St. Charles Borromeo, who was auditing for Pope Pius V the lavish spending of cardinals). Bomarzo, more than the other two places, is disquieting, causing intellectual shivers with its Parco dei Mostri, or Park of Monsters, dreamed up by Vicino Orsini and recently rediscovered with the advent of a new attitude toward mannerism. At Caprarola, it was again Vignola who

transformed an old fort, built by Sangallo, into the Palazzo Farnese, with a round central courtyard and a profusion of virtuoso decorations, inside and out. And the surrounding countryside, dominated by the Monti Cimini, through which the route runs, SE of Viterbo, is gently rolling, with extinct volcanoes, sere landscapes, steep bluffs, high tufa cliffs, and dense forests of oak and chestnut, beneath the beech groves atop the Monte Cimino, overlooking the solitary Lago di Vico, ancient boundary of the Roman realm.

The route. Viale Trieste, which takes you east out of Viterbo, turns into the state road 204, runs through Bagnaia, and then turns toward Orte. After the detour (3 km.) toward Vitorchiano, at the intersection with the road toward Bomarzo (3-km. detour), you will turn right toward Soriano nel Cimino; from there, along secondary roads, you will head SE, running past the Monte Cimino and through Canepina, Vallerano, Vignanello, and

Corchiano. From Civita Castellana a 6-km. detour will allow you to tour "Falerii Novi," while the main route runs west, beyond Castel Sant'Elia, to Nepi and, with a short jog along the Via Cassia (state road 2), to Sutri. Then you will head north, and, after Ronciglione, you will follow the Via Cimina along the eastern rim of the crater which forms the lake of Vico, with fine views of the lake and of the conical Monte Venere, with a steep descent down to Caprarola on the right (3.5 km.). Through the Monti Cimini you will reach San Martino al Cimino; from here, you can quickly return to Viterbo.

Halting places of interest. S. Maria della Quercia*: the sanctuary, a lovely piece of Renaissance architecture, appears at the end of a long avenue, with a Della Robbia terracotta portal; the nearby museum houses a collection of ex-voto offering dating from 1490-1730. **Bagnaia**: the medieval section lies on a rocky promontory between two rushing streams; the 16th-c. addition lies uphill, and culminates in the Villa Lante, designed by the Vignola, with the fountains and streams in the garden. **Vitorchiano**: this largely intact medieval village has houses overlooking a precipice; the 14th-c church of S. Maria has beeen largely re-built. **Bomarzo:** dominating the old village is the 16th-c. Palazzo Orsini; in the surrounding area, the Parco dei Mostri, the enigmatic creation of Vicino Orsini, a soldier and man of letters of the late-16th c. **Soriano nel Cimino:** There are two major attractions in this medieval town — the Castello Orsini and the Mannerist Papacqua fountain in the Palazzo Chigi-Albani. **Monte Cimino**: among the beeches that cover the mountain, there is a 250-ton trachyte boulder that will rock back and forth if you pull on a lever; it is called the Sasso Menicante, "naturae miraculum" according to Pliny the Elder. **Canepina** lies among groves of chestnut and hazelnut trees, with the parish church of S. Maria Assunta by Sangallo. **Vallerano** has a 17th-c. sanctuary dedicated to a miracle of the Virgin Mary. **Vignanello**, a town that produces flavorful wines, with a view of the Tiber valley, lies beneath Palazzo Ruspoli re-built in 16th-c. **Corchiano**: note the 15th-c. frescoes in the church of S. Biagio. **Civita Castellana:** the Cosmatesque portico of the Duomo is the most renowned monument of the town, but hardly the only one: in the fortress by Sangallo is a notable archeological museum, and nearby are the ruins of the Roman **"Falerii Novi"***. **Castel Sant'Elia** (see Nepi): pilgrimages are made to the nearby sanctuary of S. Maria ad Rupes, carved out of the rock; tourists instead visit the Romanesque Basilica di S. Elia. **Nepi:** 16th-c. walls enclose the village, extending along a tufa ridge, dating back to the Middle Ages and the Renaissance. **Sutri:** here too the village is built on tufa stone, along with the Etruscan, Roman, and medieval monuments; dark holm-oaks stand around the amphitheater; the shrine to the Madonna del Parto dates back into the mists of time. **Ronciglione:** the streets and aristocratic 16th-/18th-c. palazzi of this town overlook the lake of Vico; note the close-set medieval "borgo." **Caprarola:** the Renaissance village lies at the base of the five-sided Palazzo Farnese (note the circular courtyard), built by the Vignola for the nephew of Pope Paul III late-16th-c., frescoes recall the splendor of this powerful family. **San Martino al Cimino**: medieval walls enclose the 17th-c. town and the 13th-c. abbey of S. Martino, built by the Cistercians of Pontigny.

Monte Velino, Monte Sirente, and the Cicolano   52

Rieti - L'Aquila - Avezzano - Lago del Salto - Rieti (212 km.)

From Rieti to the Piana del Fùcino, round trip: varied mountainous landscapes, contrasting between narrow passes — the gorges of the Velino on the Via Salaria, the cliffs of the Valle del Salto — and vast horizons — the basin of Aquila, the "plain" of Rocca di Mezzo, the meadows of the Fùcino. Midway through this route, the city of L'Aquila, with its art treasures (though elsewhere in the route, you will find castles, ancient ruins, and Romanesque churches). The names in the title of this route refer to three different worlds, as it were. The river Velino rises in a corner of Lazio wedged between Umbria, Marche, and Abruzzo. Velino is also the name of a mountain in Abruzzo (2,487 m. tall; on clear winter days, you can see both seas, Tyrrhenian and Adriatic, from the peak); like the Monte Sirente (2,349 m.), it is located between L'Aquila and the Piana del Fùcino. As you pass through the "plain" of Rocca di Mezzo, the Velino is to the west, the Sirente is to the east (the "plain," or "piano," is a major feature, a large karstic hollow, lined with meadowland, and surrounded by peaks towering hundreds of meters overhead; the runoff water disappears into karstic sinkholes). Lastly, the Cicolano is an area of Lazio, SE of Rieti, that comprises the middle and high valley of the river Salto, which flows down to Rieti. This route, then, runs through Lazio and Abruzzo; the regional border lies between Antrodoco and the Sella di Corno, as you climb into Abruzzo, and after Magliano de' Marsi, as you leave it. In the division of Italy into north, central, and south, Abruzzo is technically part of central Italy, extending as it does NE of Lazio. Historically, however, it has been part of the "southern realm" since the 12th c. The regional boundary is a major one, therefore.

The route. The road from Rieti, in Lazio, to L'Aquila, in Abruzzo, is the Via Salaria (state road 4), running first through Cittaducale and Antrodoco, and then, just past the gorges of the river Velino, on the left, it shifts to the Via Sabina (state road 17), which runs over the Sella di Corno (1,005 m.). From L'Aquila you will continue along the state road 5 *bis* over the upland of Rocca di Cambio (1,433 m.). The descent runs through Celano, the Piana del Fùcino, and Avezzano; from here, a 10-km. detour will take you to the archeological excavations of "Alba Fucens." For the return to Rieti, you will leave Avezzano and head for Cappelle (intersection, where you will turn right onto the state road 578), Magliano de' Marsi, with a segment of road 7 km. long, to the church of S. Maria in Valle Porclaneta,

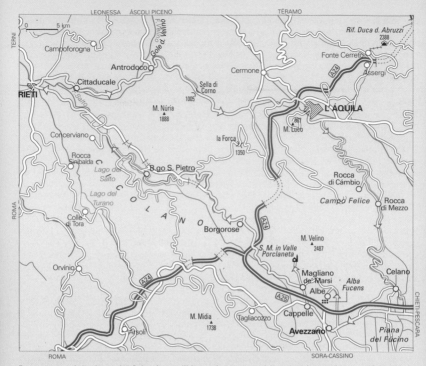

Borgorose, and the Lago del Salto (you will leave the state road, hugging the north coast of the lake). You will then return to Rieti along the Valle del Salto.

Halting places of interest. Rieti, along the river Velino and at the edge of a broad green valley, within sight of Monte Terminillo, preserves intact the structure and monuments of the town center of the Middle Ages. **Cittaducale**, founded in the 14th c., under Angevin rule, has a regular layout; note original towers and intact sections of the walls. **S. Maria Extra Moenia**, a Romanesque church with, adjacent, the hexagonal baptistery of S. Giovanni with frescoes from the 15th-16th-c. **Antrodoco:** "Interocrium," or amidst the mountains, is the ancient name, certainly applicable still. **Gole del Velino*:** these jagged wild gorges still have, midway along, the boulder of the Orso, carved out vertically by the Romans for some 30 m. **L'Aquila*** is a mountain town that savors of ancient history, crowded with monuments, artwork, and startling mountain vistas; it is the largest city in Abruzzo. **Celano:** the old village lies in the shadow of the stern Castello Piccolomini; narrow, jagged, and deep are the Gole, or Gorges, of Celano nearby. **Rocca di Cambio** is the highest town in Abruzzo, beloved by skiers. **Rocca di Mezzo**: this resort has a fine little religious museum, with sacred objects and wooden statues. **Avezzano:** rebuilt after the earthquake of 1915 and again after WWII, this city lies on the western edge of the Piana del Fùcino; near the "borgo" of Albe, note the little Romanesque church of S. Pietro and the archeological digs of the ancient Roman "Alba Fucens." **S. Maria in Valle Porclaneta*** has a secluded 11th-c Romanesque church on the mountain slope, with an exquisitely detailed interior. **Lago del Salto:** this man-made hydroelectric basin was built in 1938, submerging Borgo San Pietro; the new town looks down on the lake from above the road.

The Monti Tiburtini, Èrnici and the Monti Prenestini   53

Rome - Tìvoli - Subiaco - Fiuggi - Palestrina - Rome (202 km.)
Over mountains and through valleys to the east of Rome: the Monti Tiburtini line the left bank of the river Aniene, from the point where the river, on its way down, turns sharply from NW to SW, down to where they sink into hills on the plain downstream from Tìvoli; the highest point is the Monte dell'Ara Salere (795 m.). As you head back up the Aniene, you will see them on the right. Beyond that sharp turn, the river borders the Monti Simbruini: this is Subiaco. The Monti Èrnici, which you will cross as you leave the Valle dell'Aniene, crossing the uplands of Arcinazzo and then heading down to Fiuggi, are much taller (Pizzo Deta, 2,041 m.). They stretch from west to east as far as Sora in the Valle del Liri, north of the broad cut of the river Sacco. The Monti Prenestini, lastly, stretch from north to south, between the basins of the rivers Aniene and Sacco, behind Palestrina; with Monte Guadagnolo, they reach an altitude of 1,218 m. The landscape is still that of the Apennines: sere hills, clustered villages, here and there dark stretches of woods. You begin with Villa Adriana, or Hadrian's

Villa, with its giant cypresses and endless fields of ruins, then Tivoli with the sound of water amidst the crags; on the way back, at Palestrina, note the terraces of the Roman sanctuary, where the oracles foretold destinies; in the middle, Subiaco, where the Benedictines founded a world of medieval monasteries. The composer Hector Berlioz came up here, in 1832, when he was staying in Villa Medici after winning the "Prix de Rome"; he wrote about "the cavern where St. Benedict lived, where the rosebush he planted still flourishes" and "the cell of Blessed Lorenzo, sheltered by a rock wall which is made golden by the sun," and lastly, the "great groves of dark-leaved chestnut trees, with ruins where, in the evening, every so often a human shadow will appear for a moment and then disappear without a sound... shepherds, perhaps, or brigands...."

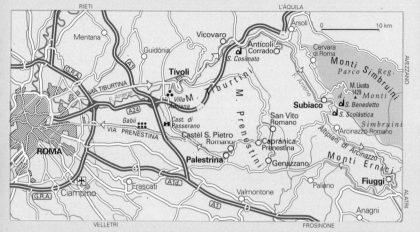

The route. The Via Tiburtina (state road 5; in the city of Rome it begins at the arches of S. Viviana) leads along the river Aniene to Tivoli and to Vicovaro. You will turn off it after the intersection of Anticoli Corrado, the destination of a short detour (3 km., to the right), along a road that continues along the river Aniene, running up to Subiaco and then over the uplands of Arcinazzo (841 m.), to the spa of Fiuggi on the southern slopes of the Monti Ernici. On the return to Rome, the route follows a circuit through the Monti Prenestini, along secondary roads with scenic stretches, through Genazzano, then to San Vito Romano, Capranica Prenestina, and Palestrina. From here the Via Prenestina runs through Santa Maria di Cavamonte and the ruins of Gabii back to Rome.

Halting places of interest. Villa Adriana**: a mirror of ancient style, physical catalogue of culture, repository of souvenirs from the travels of the emperor Hadrian, who devoted long years to its construction; they are now some of the most significant and varied ruins of antiquity. **Tivoli***, overlooking the Roman countryside ("campagna"), was an aristocratic watering hole, surrounded by jagged rocks, lush greenery, a circular Temple of Vesta, villas, gardens, parks, waterfalls, and fountains. **Vicovaro**, atop a hill on the Aniene's right bank, features ruined walls and a 15th-c. eight-sided church, S. Giacomo. **S. Cosimato** is a Franciscan hermitage set amidst cypresses and pines; it stands high atop a crag overlooking the Aniene, on the ruins of a Roman villa. **Anticoli Corrado** (see Vicovaro): this village, with medieval relics scattered here and there, is renowned for the beauty of its women and its 120 years of popularity with artists, note the fountain in the Medieval borgo. **Subiaco*:** this small, intensely medieval town, set amidst mountains dense with woods, is redolent with the heritage and memory of St. Benedict of Norcia (or Nursia), his brother monks, and the monastic world they created; the monasteries of S. Scolastica and the Sacro Speco stand in seclusion in the narrow Aniene valley; NE of Subiaco you can climb **Monte Livata** (1,324 m.), a popular resort both for skiing and summering. **Fiuggi*** was already famous for its mineral waters in ancient times, one of the finest spas in Italy; the greenery of Fiuggi Fonte (or, springs of Fiuggi) contrasts with the medieval flavor of Fiuggi Città (or, town of Fiuggi). **Genazzano**, on the slope of an isolated hill, boasts the Santuario della Madonna del Buon Consiglio, Gothic houses, and the Castello Colonna, stronghold of the famed family; in the ruins of the nymphaeum, strewn across the fields, it is said that Ovid was smitten with the love that ultimately caused Augustus to exile him to the Black Sea, where he died: in reality they are the ruins of a Renaissance building. **San Vito Romano**: this "borgo," or village, lies snug at the feet of the castle known as Palazzo Tresoldi. **Castel San Pietro Romano** is a country village lodged on the site of the ancient acropolis of "Præneste"; atop the hill, note the ruins of the Rocca dei Colonna, the Colonna family stronghold, and the immense vista of the Colli Albani and the Valle del Sacco. **Palestrina*:** the medieval city merges, in the most remarkable way, with the Roman sanctuary of Fortuna Primigenia; up in the 17th-c Palazzo Barberini is the Museo Archeologico Prenestino. The medieval **Castello di Passerano** stands in an inspired setting (go through Santa Maria di Cavamonte, turning off for 4 km. along the road to Tivoli). **"Gabii":** the ruins of this Latin city stand on the right side of the Via Prenestina; note the cella of the temple of Juno Gabina, from the time of the Republic.

Rome - Frascati - Velletri - Albano Laziale - Marino - Rome (117 km.)

"In the morning and evening," wrote Goethe, "a little fog descends upon Rome. On the hills outside of town, however, at Albano, Castel Gandolfo, and Frascati, where I spent three days last week, the air is always clear and pure." He visited the hills more than once; of one stay, with a marvelous December sunshine, he wrote: "Aside from the evergreens, a number of oak trees are still dense with leaves; likewise the young chestnut trees, through their leaves have yellowed. The landscape has hues of remarkable beauty..." The geography of the Colli Albani can best be glimpsed from an airplane; or else from a topographical map, perhaps an old-fashioned, patiently sketched one. In origin, they are a large volcanic system, with a clearly defined crater area, some 30 km. across, broken only to the SW, ripped apart by the eruptions that tore open the lesser craters that are now the lakes of Albano, Nemi, and Ariccia — though the latter is now a dry bed. In the center are Monte Cavo (949 m.) and Monte Faete (956 m.). The chestnuts and oaks mentioned by Goethe are largely found in the central region, while on the gentle outer slopes are olive groves and vineyards, famed for the "vini dei castelli," or "castle wines." About these wines, Leo XIII (pope from 1878 to 1903) wrote: "exilarant animos, curasque resolvunt," i.e., "they cheer the soul and wipe away cares." The villages and small towns on the slopes are the Castelli Romani, or Roman Castles, properly speaking, 13 in number (Frascati, Grottaferrata, Marino, Castel Gandolfo, Albano, Ariccia, Genzano, Nemi, Rocca di Papa, Rocca Priora, Monte Còmpatri, Monte Porzio Catone, and Colonna), and called "castles" because noble Roman families and popes owned fortified country houses there. As times became easier, the fortified manors made way for open villas; popes and nobles spent their holidays here, just as the ancient Romans had done (Cicero had a villa at "Tusculum," Domitian built one at Castel Gandolfo, the site of ancient "Alba Longa"). "In the evening — wrote Goethe, from Frascati, in late September — by moonlight, we walk around admiring the villas, sketching the most interesting features, even in the dark..."

The route. The Via Tuscolana — which you can reach from central Rome by exiting through the Porta S. Giovanni and following a short stretch of the Via Appia Nuova — leads to Frascati (there are also a number of other routes to Frascati). From Frascati, the first section of the painstaking exploration of the Castelli Romani suggested here involves, in order: a drive to Monte Porzio Catone; a tour of the ruins of Tusculum (with a detour from the main route between Monte Porzio Catone and Grottaferrata); a tour of Grottaferrata; a lovely scenic road from Grottaferrata to Rocca di Papa and a drive up Monte Cavo (949 m.; 5.5 km. from Rocca di Papa). After descending from Monte Cavo you will take the Via dei Laghi (literally, "lake route"; state road 217), following it — except for a brief detour to Nemi — as far as Velletri. From Velletri, on your way back to Rome along the Via Appia (state road 7), you will pass through Genzano, Ariccia, and Albano Laziale. You climb from here up to Castel Gandolfo, and then on the way back down, you will take a drive around the Lago Albano, counterclockwise, with a detour up to Marino. Then back downhill from Marino to the Lago Albano and, once you have completed the drive around the lake, you will see a tunnel on your right; this takes you onto the Via Appia (state road 7), which leads back into Rome.

Halting places of interest. **Frascati:** this is the most popular of the Castelli Romani; sumptuous villas have been built here since ancient Roman times. **Monte Porzio Catone** is a 16th-c. village built on a hill blanketed with olive groves. **"Tusculum"*:** the ruins of this Latin city can be reached by making a 2-km. detour from the route to Grottaferrata; note the remains of the ampitheater, the theater, the forum and the so called Villa di Tiberio. **Grottaferrata:** the venerable abbey, fortified with walls and moats, is a monastery founded in 1004 by S. Nilo, or St. Niles. **Rocca di Papa** has a medieval uphill section and a modern, prosperous section, with gardens; continue along your route, through the woods, and above the Lago Albano you will find the **Santuario della Madonna del Tufo**, built around a boulder frescoed by A. Romano. **Monte Cavo*:** with good weather, you can see forever across the Colli Albani, glimpsing Rome, the Tyrrhenian Sea, the Circeo, Monte Terminillo, and the Gran Sasso d'Italia. **Nemi:** the town overlooks the lake, deep blue at the bottom of the crater. **Velletri** lies perched on a spur of the southern slopes of the Colli Albani, amidst expanses of grapevines. **Genzano di Roma** fans out across the outer slope of the crater of the lake of Nemi; a road along the north bank of the lake takes you to the Museo Nemorense, or Museum of Nemi. All that survives of the famous late-imperial Roman ships of Nemi are models and fragments. **Ariccia:** the central square, with fountain and the round church of S. Maria dell'Assunzione, was designed by G. L.

Bernini. **Albano Laziale:** it is said that the tombs of the Horatii, early Roman heroes, and their Curiatii opponents, are here; in reality it is an anonymous late-Republic Roman tomb. **Castel Gandolfo** looks out from the rim of the crater of the Lago Albano; the 17th-c. summer residence of the pope is in Piazza Plebiscito. **Marino:** "Mole stat sua" is the motto inscribed on the hèraldic column of Palazzo Colonna, in the center of the "borgo," high above the lake, atop a peperino spur.

The Ciociarìa   55

Rome - Palestrina - Segni - Anagni - Alatri - Frosinone (136 km.)

The Ciociarìa extends along the river Sacco between the Monti Èrnici and the Monti Lepini. The towns through which this route runs — Segni, Anagni, Ferentino, and Alatri — will surprise you with their intense character: all of them are pre-Roman, and seem like a rustic symphony. There are the sharp high notes of cathedrals, town walls, and palazzi, the basso continuo of the lesser architecture, all harmonizing fluently with the surrounding countryside. The land takes its name from Cicero — though the name Ciociarìa only appears in the 18th c. — who described it as "aspera et montuosa et fidelis et simplex et fautrix suorum" (harsh, mountainous, faithful, simple, caring for its own). No traveller can hope to verify all those qualities in a single quick visit, but one can make comparisons with the land described by A. Baldini, in the 1920s: "harsh lands — again, the adjective used first by Cicero — perched on steep mountain slopes, black with storms"; "where the stone of the palazzi and the plaster of the more rustic walls easily turn dark as pitch with time" along with the "burnt autumnal color of dead leaves, spread across the roofs by wandering lichens." Amidst all this darkness, one has luminous views "between one wall and another, or beneath the arches of these steep streets," of distant valleys and mountains," "of bright red geraniums," "of green pergolas behind the houses." Baldini found the men "sun-darkened, hirsute, and grim," while the women he hailed as having "the faces of madonnas, framed by raven hair," and "a most particularly graceful way of walking" caused by the custom of "carrying heavy, sometimes immensely heavy objects balanced on their heads, climbing and descending constantly along these steep stone walkways...": yellowed photographs of an Italy long lost.

The route. Aside from the Autostrada, the route from Rome to Frosinone runs along the Via Casilina (state road 6), which begins in the city in Piazza di Porta Maggiore. The route turns off from this route three times, all the same. In fact, just after Stazione di Palestrina, you will take a left onto the detour that runs to Palestrina itself; from this town, you will return to the Via Casilina along the secondary road that rejoins it at Valmontone. You will branch off from the Via Casilina a second time at the turnoff for Colleferro: take secondary roads along the route that leads first south to Colleferro and Segni, and then north across the river Sacco, the Sacco valley, and the Via Casilina, to climb up to Anagni. From Anagni you will drive right back onto the Via Casilina, leaving it one last time at the fork for Ferentino. From Ferentino you will take a scenic road to Alatri; from here a detour will take you 13.5 km. north to Collepardo and to the Certosa di Trisulti. Lastly you will reach Frosinone from the north, along the state road 155.

Halting places of interest. **Palestrina*:** the Roman sanctuary of Fortuna Primigenia, perched high on the slope, constitutes the backdrop of the medieval town; even higher, in Palazzo Barberini, note the Museo Archeologico Prenestino. **Valmontone,** is partly medieval, and sits high on a tufa rise at the confluence of two valleys; note the 17th-c. Palazzo Doria and the nearby Collegiata dell'Assunta, re-built in 1685-89. **Segni** lies dark amidst the chestnut groves, staggered down the slope of a spur of the Monti Lepini, with stretches of complex walls, and the renowned Porta Saracena, or Saracen Gate. In the lofty acropolis is a 13th-c. church occupying the cella of an ancient temple. **Anagni*** sits high atop a spur overlooking the Valle del Sacco; one part of the town has a strongly medieval air, particularly intense in the "Quartiere dei Caetani," with the palazzo of Boniface VIII (Caetani) — supposedly the site of a slap in the papal face, inflicted by soldiers of Philip IV, the Fair, of France. Also note the Romanesque cathedral, with 13th-c. frescoes in the crypt. **Ferentino*:** pre-Roman walls hold up the old acropolis and the Duomo that occupies its "platea," or plaza; the town is a trove of ancient and medieval structures. Note S. Maria Maggiore, a Cistercian Gothic church. **Alatri***, this little medieval city stands on a hill blanketed with olive groves; note the Duomo in the silent tree-lined "piazzale" atop the hill, as well as 2 km. of intact polygonal walls. Continue on to **Collepardo**, with the nearby Grotta dei Bambocci, full of stalactites and stalagmites; also, note the **Certosa di Trisulti**, an old charterhouse, founded in the 13th-c and restored in the 18th-c, with an ancient apothecary shop and a building in which the zealot pope, Innocent III, may have written his manifesto, "De comtemptu mundi," or "Misery of the Condition of Man." **Frosinone**, chief town of the Ciociaria, is mostly modern; the old quarter high on the hill overlooks the Piana del Sacco.

From the Golfo di Gaeta to the Colli Albani   56

Gaeta - Terracina - Circeo - Fossanova - Sezze - Cori - Velletri (183 km.)
Gaeta, overlooking the blue crescent of the gulf as far as the Circeo, the Agro Pontino, olive groves, limestone landscapes, and the "borghi" of the Monti Lepini. "Gaeta is a fortress, not unlike Gibraltar: an exceedingly well fortified peninsula, capable of becoming more so," wrote Montesquieu, a clear-eyed travel writer. In 1848 the pope, the grand-duke of Tuscany, and the king of Naples took refuge in Gaeta from the rising tide of European revolt. The Circeo takes its name from the Latin "circus," for the shape of the promontory. Though some, including Dante, have linked the name to Homer's Circe, all reference to the Odyssey is spurious. Midway along the coast, however, in the Grotta di Tiberio, near Sperlonga, in the late Fifties fragments of statuary were found that in time proved to be part of four Hellenistic groups: Ulysses and Diomedes plundering the Palladium of Troy; Ulysses with the corpse of Achilles; the blinding of Polyphemus, or Cyclops; and the snakelike Scylla plucking sailors from the vessel of Ulysses (these statues now occupy a museum of their own). The Agro Pontino was once a miserable swamp where, as Horace wrote: "mali culices ranaeque palustres avertunt somnos" ("savage mosquitoes and marsh frogs drive away sleep"); it has since been drained and entirely reclaimed. The Monti Lepini — Monte Semprevisa is 1,536 m. tall — form a backdrop for the plain, distant from the sea; it is in this mountain range that the true surprises of this route may be found: the little towns perched on the slopes were fortresses of the ancient Volsci, before Roman supremacy; cyclopean stones and stern medieval walls clash in surprising contrast.

The route. The first part of this route is primarily a coastal road: from Gaeta you will follow a lovely shore road till just past Sperlonga; there you will turn inland, at a fork in the road near the lake of San Puoto, and on to Fondi. From Fondi, you head back to the sea, at Terracina, following the Via Appia (state road 7); here you return to the coast road. This road, including a scenic section with spectacular views, runs behind the promontory of the Circeo; a brief turnoff allows you to visit San Felice al Circeo. At the fork leading to Sabaudia, you will break away from the Tyrrhenian coastline, and, with a road that runs through the park of the Circeo and the reclaimed Pontine plain, you will reach the Abbey of Fossanova and, a bit further on, Priverno. This marks the beginning of a different section of the route, which follows the edge of the Monti Lepini, frequently climbing up to pass through old villages that look down on what was once a marshy and malarial plain. As you follow small roads, turnoffs, and detours, you will pass through Sezze, the abbey of Valvisciolo, Sermoneta, Norma, and the ruins of Ninfa and Cori. As you pass through the village of Giulianello, the route approaches the Colli Albani, ending in Velletri, at the base of these hills.

Halting places of interest. **Gaeta:** of particular note is the older section of town, on a peninsula, separated from the mainland by the Monte Orlando (171 m.); atop the hill is a Roman mausoleum, and a remarkable view. **Grotta di Tiberio***: the Grotto of Tiberius, once part of the emperor's villa, lies just past Torre Capovento, and just before **Sperlonga**, with its white medieval houses huddled on the promontory; note the Hellenistic marble carvings with the myths of Ulysses, found here but now in the nearby Museo Archeologico Nazionale. **Fondi**, near the lake, amidst citrus trees, has Roman walls and layout, as well as the Gothic cathedral of S. Pietro, a castle, and the Palazzo del Principe, a mix of Angevin and Catalonian styles. **Terracina**, on the Golfo di Gaeta: the center was originally the Roman Forum; the Duomo, rich in art treasures, stands on the site of the chief temple; you can climb up through olive groves to see the ruins of the temple of Jove Anxur . **San Felice Circeo:** the elegant beach, the caverns, the spectacular views, and the road high over the sea, out to the Faro di Torre Cervia, a lighthouse; on your way to **Sabaudia**, you will pass through the 16th-c. Torre Paola, near the Roman emissary of the Lago di Sabaudia. Sabaudia, set amidst lagoons, is one of the better-designed building complexes of the great reclamation project of the Agro Pontino. **Abbazia di Fossanova**:** this was the earliest abbey built in Italy in the Cistercian Gothic style; St. Thomas Aquinas died here. **Priverno** is the first village along the route to date its origins back to ancient times; it looks purely medieval now, and is secluded in the hills, aloof from what was once a malarial plain. **Sezze** is clustered at the base of a hill; climb up to see the megalithic walls and the Duomo that took so long to build. On Good Friday, note the procession of the Passion of Christ. **Abbazia di Valvisciolo:** this abbey stands amidst olive and eucalyptus groves; it was built in the 8th c. by Greek marks; the church and cloister are from the 13th c. **Sermoneta:** another medieval village proudly surveying the plain: powerful and grim, the Castello dei Caetani, built in the first half of the 13th-c, in turn surveys it. **Norma**, firmly saddling a ridge of the Monti Lepini, is strongly medieval, but is best known for the nearby ruins of ancient "Norba" (see Norma). The medieval **ruins of Ninfa*** are reflected in an evocative little lake; in the surrounding nature preserve nest a remarkable array of birds. **Cori** is profoundly medieval, and is surrounded by fragments by a ring of three walls; from its perch on the slope of the Lepini, it overlooks the Pontine plain and the Circeo. The remarkably ancient **Velletri** stands on a ridge of Monte Artemisio, on the vine-bedecked southern slopes of the Colli Albani; Octavian lived here as a child, before becoming Augustus, the first Roman emperor.

From the Gran Sasso d'Italia to the Adriatic Sea 57

L'Aquila - Campotosto - Isola del Gran Sasso d'Italia - Atri - Pineto (132 km.)
At the Passo delle Capannelle (1,299 m.) you are on the watershed between Aterno and Vomano, two rivers that "envelop" the massif of the Gran Sasso d'Italia, both flowing down to the Adriatic. All around is quiet seclusion. You make your way up here, on the way from L'Aquila to the Adriatic Sea, winding amidst white badlands, along jagged, forest-covered slopes. You also pass by the ruins of "Amiternum," city of the Sabines; Vergil depicted the Amiternini fighting at Turnus's side against Aeneas. The line of descent is along the Valle del Vomano, but it makes detours and circles so that you have spectacular views of the Gran Sasso d'Italia: at Campotosto, alongside the great manmade lake with jagged shores, you see the Gran Sasso to the NW, at an angle; at Prati di Tivo, the two peaks of the Corno Grande and the Corno Piccolo stand out clear, harsh, and naked, looking like peaks of the Dolomites, above rolling meadows and steep pastures gouged with gulleys; at Isola del Gran Sasso d'Italia, in the valley of the Mavone, near the Vomano, you can see the peaks glow again just after sunset when the weather is good. As you get closer to the Adriatic, amid the gently rolling hills, you head up to Atri, a two-fold balcony: on the one side you bid farewell to the distant mountain, high over the rows of hills; on the other you greet the approaching sea, vast and fresh, with a long coastline. In the city of Atri, you can see the work of the leading Abruzzese painter, Andrea De Litio. Almost nothing is known of his life, and his work is found almost exclusively here; he is believed to have worked around 1450, and is thought to have been influenced by the work of Piero della Francesca; his work can be seen in the choir of the cathedral.

The route. You leave L'Aquila heading NW along the state road 80, which runs over the Passo delle

Capannelle (1,299 m.) and down into the Valle del Vomano. On your way down, at a roadside house (or "cantoniera"), you will see a road running off to the left; this road is largely scenic, and leads (18 km.) to Campotosto, on the shore of the manmade lake of the same name. Continue back along the state road 80, passing by an optional detour on the right (16 km.) to Pietracamela and Prati di Tivo. Near Montorio al Vomano, you can turn south onto the state road 491, which leads — after Tossicìa and a short jaunt to the Santuario di S. Gabriele dell'Addolorata — to the Isola del Gran Sasso d'Italia, in Valle del Mavone. Driving downhill from here along the valley, you pass an optional 7-km. detour on your right to Castelli, and you then reach the junction with the state road 150, which you will then take down toward the Adriatic Sea. We recommend two short detours on the left: the first, toward Guardia Vomano, where you can see the church of S. Clemente al Vomano, and a second detour, to the church of S. Maria di Propezzano. From the crossroads for the latter detour, the state road 553 leads in the opposite direction through the hills to Atri; from here, you drive on down to Pineto, on the Adriatic coast.

Halting places of interest. San Vittorino: beneath the Romanesque church of S. Michele, at the center of town, is a catacomb with the supposed remains of a Christian martyr, Vittorino; at the foot of the hill are the ruins of ancient Sabine and Roman "Amiternum," birthplace of Sallust. **Campotosto** is a summer resort near a manmade lake formed by damming the Rio Fùcino; the lake reflects the peaks of the Gran Sasso d'Italia. **Pietracamela**, another resort town on the slopes of the Gran Sasso d'Italia, is downhill from Prati di Tivo. From there, you can take a chairlift up to the Madonnina del Gran Sasso (remarkable view of the peaks of the Gran Sasso d'Italia and of the Monti della Laga). **Montorio al Vomano:** the modern section lies on the main road, while the medieval section is high on a hill; note the large 18th-c. wooden altars in the parish church. **Tossicìa:** note venerable houses and a portal by A. Lombardo (1471) on the church of S. Antonio Abate. **Santuario di S. Gabriele dell'Addolorata:** the remains of a 19th-c. saint — the patron saint of Abruzzo — are buried here. **Isola del Gran Sasso d'Italia** stands on a ridge of the north slope of the great massif; the windows of the old houses bear sententious Latin mottos. **Castelli:** the production of fine ceramics here dates from the 13th c.; the local museum has a ceramics collection and a reproduction of a 16th-c. artisan's workshop. **S. Giovanni al Mavone** is a Romanesque church frescoed in the apse and crypt. **S. Maria di Ronzano** is a 12th-c. church with original frescoes. **S. Clemente al Vomano*** is partly Romanesque, with noteworthy ciborium a certain Maestro Ruggero and his son Roberto. **S. Maria di Propezzano*** is another Romanesque church, built between the 12th-14 c, which commemorates a long-ago apparition of the Virgin Mary; note the 15th-c frescoes inside the church. **Atri** looks out from atop a lush spur, to the blue of the Adriatic in the distance; in the celebrated 13th-c. Cattedrale, note the 15th-c. frescoes by A. De Litio (15th c.); situated in the piazza is the Teatro comunale, a reduced version of the Scala opera house in Milan; also note the Museo Diocesano, through the adjacent cloister. **Pineto** (see Atri): a pine grove adorns this beach resort, near the mouth of the river Vomano.

The mountains and valleys of Abruzzo between the rivers Tronto and Pescara   58

Giulianova - Civitella del Tronto - Teramo - Penne - Pescara (168 km.)
"Behind the Gran Sasso the setting sun filled the whole springtime sky with a brilliant pinkish light: and, since the moist fields and the river waters and the waters of the sea and the ponds during the day had emitted much vapor, houses and sails and poles and trees and every single thing appeared tinged with pink; as the shapes acquired a sort of transparency, the sharpness of outline began to waver, almost fluttering in that bath of rosy light": this is a glimpse of the Abruzzo coast from "Le Novelle della Pescara" by Gabriele D'Annunzio. The Gran Sasso invariably rules the horizon throughout this route: through valleys and over hills, along winding secluded roads, down the rolling ridges that drop away to the sea from the high mountains of the Monti della Laga and the Gran Sasso d'Italia: this is seaside Abruzzo, east of the Apennine ridges. The rows of hills are divided by rivers that run, more-or-less parallel, down to the Adriatic, as if so many tines raking the length of the beach. The north-south stretch that you will cover is crossed by the rivers Tronto (bordering the Marche), Vibrata, Salinello, Tordino (the valley of Teramo, Vomano (pouring into the sea between Roseto degli Abruzzi and Pineto), Piomba (this river, with the Fino and the Tavo, empties 8 km. from the sea into an exceedingly short river, the Saline), and — last on this route — Pescara. You head inland just south of the first river, and you will cross the valleys of all the others. Crests, isolated hills, clayey badlands, gravel washes, rows of tremulous poplars, olive groves, the evergreen holm-oaks high on the crags: this road runs through ever-new landscapes, surprising at every turn; the clouds are swept inland by the offshore breeze; even the sky and the light are different. Running alongside the Pescara, you return to the sea coast, described by the native Pescarese G. D'Annunzio, as extending "in an almost virginal serenity, along the shore that arcs slightly toward the south, in its splendor displaying the bright color of a Persian turquoise. Here and there, where currents surge, there are twisting patches of darker hue...."

The route. From Giulianova you head north on the state road 16 along the Adriatic coastline, and,

after crossing the river Salinello, you cut away from the coastline, to the left; should you choose to drive along the coast a little further, on the other hand, in just 3 km. you will be in Tortoreto Lido, the coastal offshoot of the inland town of Tortoreto. First you drive up the left bank of the river Salinello, then you continue along secondary roads as far as Civitella del Tronto. From here, you drive down to reach the state road 81, which you will take southward. After you pass Campovalano (there is a 1-km. detour here to the church of S. Pietro) and the fork where another, 3-km. detour leads off to the left to Campli, the road reaches Teramo, crossing the river Tordino and then runs up over the hills that divide this valley from the valley of the river Vomano; continuing over ridges and hilltops, the road crosses the rivers Piomba, Fino, and Baricello, and then heads uphill to Penne. Here, you will leave the state road, and continue downhill SE to Loreto Aprutino and the floor of the Tavo valley. Then you drive up a stretch of the left bank of the Tavo river, until you hit the state road 81 again. This road, running SE, past spectacular views, runs along the hill on which Pianella stands; here you leave the main road, just outside of Pianella, for a secondary road that runs 7 km. up to Moscufo. Back on the main road, you cross over the Bologna-Taranto highway and then you take the state road 602 to Pescara.

Halting places of interest. Giulianova sits atop a low hill to the north of the river Tordino: there is a 15th-c. octagonal Duomo and a gallery, chiefly devoted to 19th-c. Neapolitan painting; downhill, on the Adriatic coast, extends **Giulianova Lido**, a fishing town and resort. **Tortoreto Lido**: you can swim amidst abundant verdant nature, at the foot of gently rolling hills. **Tortoreto** is a secluded hilltop village; note the 16th-c. frescoes in the church of S. Maria della Misericordia. **Civitella del Tronto** is a small town straddling a slope, with a slight, late-Renaissance flavor; from the high Fortezza, or fortress, which endured four sieges, you have a vista ranging from the mountains to the sea. **S. Pietro**: take a short detour immediately after Campovalano, and visit the 13th-c. church next to the ruins of a 12th-c. Benedictine convent. **Campli**: extending across a natural terrace, this little city has medieval and Renaissance architecture and an archeological museum located on the site of a former convent; note artifacts from necropolis of Campovalano. **Teramo:** most of the city is modern, except for where it dates back to Roman and medieval times; in the Cattedrale note the frontal by Nicola da Guardiagrele and a polyptych by Jacobello del Fiore, both from the 15th c. **Penne** stands on two hills with medieval views and ancient churches; outside of town, on a wooded hill, S. Maria in Colleromano still harbors relics of its 14th-c. foundation. **Loreto Aprutino:** the ceramics of Castelli and other towns of the territory are found in the Galleria Acerbo; south of town, note the church of S. Maria in Piano, with remarkable 14th-c. frescoes. **Pianella:** on a hill outside of town, note the Romanesque church of S. Maria Maggiore, with 12th-c. pulpit and 12th-/15th-c. frescoes. **Moscufo**: near the town, on an olive-clad hill with spectacular views, the 12th-c. church of S. Maria del Lago, with an exquisite pulpit (1159) and 12th-/14th-c. frescoes. **Pescara:** the canal-port, crowded with fishing boats — actually the mouth of the river Pescara — divides the thriving Adriatic town in two; with the pine forest made famous by D'Annunzio to the south, and the long seafront promenade to the north. The Museo delle Genti d'Abruzzo, opened in 1991, is devoted to the folkways and history of this region, and occupies a former Bourbon dynasty prison. In the birthplace of Gabriele D'Annunzio you will see memorabilia of Italy's so-called "vate," or bard. A renowed international jazz festival take place in the town during the month of July.

Monte Maiella 59

Pescara - Chieti - Guardiagrele - Pescocostanzo - Sulmona - Caramànico Terme - Pescara (237 km.)

When the town of L'Aquila dared to raise its head in rebellion, in 1528, Philbert de Châlons, prince of Orange and viceroy of Naples (French-born but, to repay a slight offered him by Francis I, a turncoat and renegade, in the service of the Holy Roman Emperor, Charles V), sallied furiously forth with his Lansquenet troops. He sacked the town, fined it 100,000 ducats, and set an additional annual tribute toward the construction of a grim castle. He then turned his troops back to Naples; on the way back he lost 500 of his precious German mercenaries in a sudden March blizzard in the Piano delle Cinquemiglia, which stretches south from Sulmona to Isernia. Given the circumstances, the loss of seasoned troops meant more than did the usual chance passerby swept away by a flurry of snow; the emperor ordered five strong towers to be built, as shelter for lost wayfarers; they are long gone. Stark, deserted, and with only the 19th-c. road as a mark of man, this mountainous highland is now highly valued for its vast ski slopes and lush lonely meadows in summer. You will pass through it as

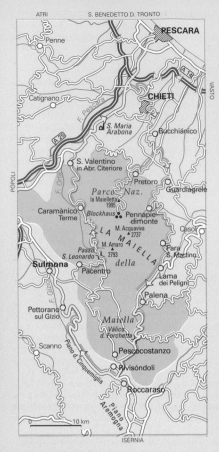

you begin to return northward on the circuit of the Maiella. The slopes of this mountain bristle with beech trees and holm-oaks and, higher up, with pine trees; the meadows blossom with flowers in spring; and the mountainside yawns with deep, wild gulleys, eroding away into the limestone. Second only to the Gran Sasso d'Italia, this is the most notable mountain group in the central Apennines, running roughly north-south, from Chieti to Sulmona. The valleys of the river Pescara and its tributary, the Orta, bound it to the north and west; then come a series of karstic plains. To the south and SE is the valley of the Aventino, which flows into the Sangro; to the east it is lined by low foothills that level away down to the Adriatic Sea. The highest peak, Monte Amaro, stands 2,793 m. tall. After the thrills and views of the mountain, you will pass by the two cities of Chieti and Sulmona, the Cistercian church of S. Maria Arabona (it is incomplete) and the lovely town of Guardiagrele, home of the most celebrated goldsmith of Abruzzo, Ghiberti's student Nicola di Andrea Gallucci, known as Nicola da Guardiagrele.

The route. This tour of the Maiella runs first along the base of the eastern slope, overlooking the Adriatic, and then over the western slope. Beginning in Pescara, you take the state road 5 for a short stretch up the valley of the river Pescara, as far as the fork, marked for Chieti. After you pass through Chieti, you will take the state road 81, which runs through valleys and over highlands. At the fork of Ponte di Alento keep to left, following the old road, which runs up to Bucchiànico and over the Colle Spaccato until it intersects with the state road 263; turn right onto this road, to take the longest detour in this route (this 32-km. detour runs just after the bridge over the state road 81, along the road to Pretoro and the Passo Lanciano, 1,306 m.) all the way up to the Blockhaus (2,142 m.) on the high slopes of the Maiella). Just past the fork where the old road joins the modern state road 81, take a right onto the road to Guardiagrele, and once past that town, you will be back on the state road 263. In succession, you will pass through Pennapiedimonte and Fara San Martino, and then the road runs into the state road 84, which runs SW up to the pass of the Forchetta (1,270 m.). Further along, off to the right, there are two short detours to Pescocostanzo and Rivisóndoli, while if you turn left at the crossroads of the state road 17, you will reach Roccaraso in just 2 km. The route then proceeds in the opposite direction on the state road 17, crossing the Piano delle Cinquemiglia, and running through Pettorano sul Gizio and on to Sulmona. Now you must take the state road 487, which runs over the western slopes of the Maiella, over the Passo San Leonardo (1,282 m.). Then you will follow the river Orta down to Caramànico Terme and to the valley of the river Pescara. Here the state road 487 comes to an end, intersecting the state road 5; this road will take you back to Pescara, on the Adriatic coast, where you started out; on the right, a short jaunt up to Manoppello Scalo will take you to the church of S. Maria Arabona.

Halting places of interest. Pescara: modern, active, lively, this city extends along the river Pescara and the canal/port that forms its outlet into the sea: to the south are the Museo delle Genti d'Abruzzo, the birthplace of G. D'Annunzio, and a lovely pine grove; to the north is the Museo Ittico (or Museum of Ichthyology) and a long beachfront boulevard. **Chieti** closely follows the contours of the hillside, high over the Pescara river valley; the town's backbone is Corso Marrucino. The archaic severity of the Warrior of Capestrano (6th-c B.C.) can be admired in the excellent Museo Archeologico Nazionale, the 15th-c. eight-sided church of S. Maria Tricalle stands outside of town, along the road from Pescara. **Bucchiànico**: spread out on an upland, with fine churches, this town has a notable piece of folk tradition, the "Sagra dei Banderesi" honoring St. Urban (22-25 May). **Blockhaus** has a spectacular view from the ridge between the Maielletta and Monte Acquaviva (2,737 m.). **Guardiagrele** has a venerable crafts tradition of goldwork and wrought iron; adjacent to the 11th-c Romanesque church of S. Maria Maggiore, the Museo d'Arte Sacra has a processional cross by Nicola da Guardiagrele. **Pennapiedimonte** is a little town with steep stairways and an 18th-c. white parish church. **Fara San Martino**, on a terrace on the east slope of the Maiella, was founded in Lombard times, and rebuilt after WWII; note painting in parish church by T. da Varallo. **Lama dei Peligni**: take a cableway up to the Grotta del Cavallone, copied onto a backdrop of the famous production of a tragedy by G. D'Annunzio. **Palena** is an old village with lovely bits of architecture, rebuilt after being devastated by heavy fighting in 1943; note the 16th-c wooden statue of the Madonna in the Chiesa del Rosario. **Pescocostanzo***: this ancient village, with a notable 11th-c basilica, rebuilt in the 15th-c and enlarged in 1558, overlooks the highland of Quarto Grande; for centuries, it has produced fine lace, and is also a renowned winter skiing resort. **Rivisóndoli** is a resort on a spur overlooking the highland. **Roccaraso:** people come here to summer and to ski (highland of Aremogna). **Pettorano sul Gizio**: note the fine old rustic architecture. **Sulmona:** set against the mountains girding the Valle Peligna, this town with its ancient air demands a leisurely tour, to admire individual monuments (note the Cattedrale and the Annunziata) and the surprising elegance of the town itself. **Pacentro** is a village on the slopes of the mountains of Morrone; note the 14th-c. towers of the Castello dei Cantelmo. **Caramànico Terme** is a spa; the old town has medieval walls and gates, a castle, and notable churches. **San Valentino in Abruzzo Citeriore** has a parish church by L. Vanvitelli. **S. Maria Arabona** is a Cistercian Gothic abbey church (13th c.), with frescoes by A. da Atri.

The Iglesiente   60

Cagliari - Santa Margherita - Sant'Antìoco - Iglesias - Cagliari (192 km.)

In 1832, at the beginning of a tour of the East, Lamartine landed in the Gulf of Palmas (between the island of S. Antìoco and the coast of the Sulcis) and described a beach "at the far end of the gulf," in all likelihood, the littoral strip of the Stagno di S. Caterina: white sand, large thistles, little clumps of aloe vera, and, in his words: "little herds of wild horses roaming free through the heath, galloping up to investigate us, sniffing at the air and then, with a wild neighing, tearing off again like flocks of crows; a mile away are grey, bare mountains, with patches of dried-out plants on their slopes; a sky you might expect to see in Africa arches over the limestone peaks; an immense silence hangs over the countryside...." This handsome description may serve as an introduction to this first Sardinian route, more than half of it is coastline, and all of it encompasses vast landscapes, sweeping horizons, with the colors of the sea, cliffs, shoals, and rocks of every mineral family. Let the sea not distract the traveller from the history that came from that sea: Cagliari, originally "Kàralis," which is now a large town, like "Nora" and "Bithia," along the coast of the great southern gulf of Sardinia, were all cities founded by Phoenicians. "Nora," on a spit of land jutting out into the sea, was the first city on Sardinia, according to classical lore, and was founded by Phoenicians from the Iberian peninsula; like the other Phoenician colonies, it was absorbed by Carthage, itself a Phoenician colony. "Bithia" was first discovered in 1835, by A. La Marmora, and as late as the reign of Marcus Aurelius, was administered by "sufeti," or Punic magistrates. On the western coast of the Iglesiente, Sant'Antìoco stands on the island of the same name; it occupies the site of one of the earliest Phoenician cities on Sardinia, "Sulcis." During Carthaginian times, it was a major mining center in the Sulcis-Iglesiente area.

The route. You will leave Cagliari heading west, and you will drive along the western coast of the Gulf of Cagliari, at first along the state road 195 — at Pula there is a turn-off for a 3-km. detour to

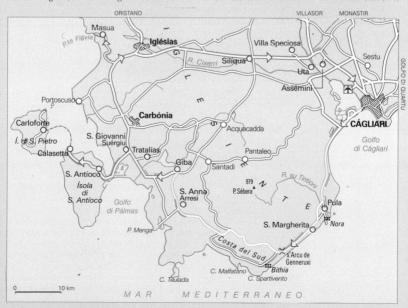

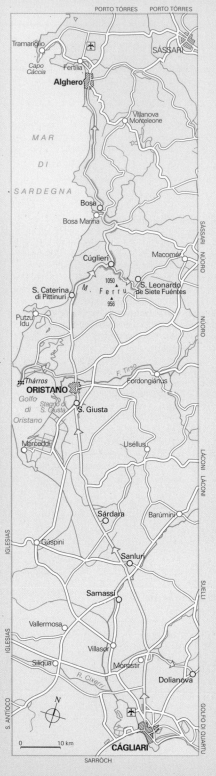

"Nora" — then, after s'Arcu de Genneruxi, where this road runs inland, along a rough road that offers fine views and vistas as it runs across the Costa del Sud (Southern Coast), past the detour to the left toward "Bithia." After rejoining the state road 195 to the SW of Teulada, you will drive through Sant'Anna Arresi and Giba past the detour toward Tratalìas (4 km.) and then on to San Giovanni Suergiu, a town from which the state road 126 runs toward the island of S. Antìoco (11 km.) and the nearby island of S. Pietro. From San Giovanni Suergiu you will again follow the state road 126 north, as far as Iglesias (a handsome side-trim of 12 km. leads to the sea near Masùa), while the state road 130, built for fast driving, will take you back to Cagliari by way of Siliqua, Villa Speciosa — from here it is just a 2.5-km. detour to Uta — and Assèmini.

Halting places of interest. Cagliari*, clustered around the Pisan-Spanish castle, "Su Casteddu," is the chief town of Sardinia. **"Nora"*** was a Phoenician city that later became Roman; it is still being excavated, and certain parts are now under the waves. **"Bithia"** is another city of Phoenician origin, extending out along a small promontory. **Tratalìas**: this village on the edge of the reclaimed marshes of Sulcis has a 13th-c. Romanesque church, S. Maria di Monserrato. **Sant'Antìoco** is the chief town of the island of the same name, which was known as "Sulcis" in Phoenician times; note the Museo Archeologico and relics of sacrifices. **Carloforte** is the chief town of the nearby island of S. Pietro; settled by exiled Ligurians, from Tunisia, in the 18th c. **Carbonia** was a mining town built in the Thirties; most mining has stopped among the bare mountains. **Masùa** with a handsome and dramatic port, lies between crags and grottoes. **Iglesias**, in the heart of the mining region, still has medieval details; note the Museo mineralogics, which boasts a vast collection of minerals. **Siliqua** has traditional houses in the old center; to the south are the ruins of the Castello di Acquafredda. **Villa Speciosa** has a Romanesque church, S. Platano (12th c.). **Uta**, too, has a 12th-c. Romanesque church. **Assèmini** is known for the cross-shaped Oratory of S. Giovanni, in Byzantine style.

From Cagliari to Alghero through the Campidani   61

Cagliari - Sanluri - Oristano - Bosa - Alghero (202 km.)

Sparse trees, prickly-pear bushes, vast horizons: the hill of Monastir, some twenty km. north of Cagliari, offers a vantage point from which to appreciate the size of the Campidani, a broad plain in southern Sardinia. One historian wrote that the view helped him understand the seeds of war between Rome and Carthage, when the fault lines of history and geography became evident before his eyes: it was over the harvests of this vast fertile plain that two great ancient powers of the hungry Mediterranean fought to the death. The Campidani was an historic breadbasket of the region; it was created by the ancient Carthaginians, who chopped down dense forests; as late as the 18th c., by the records of the port of Marseilles, this made Sardinia the fifth-largest producer and exporter of wheat and other crops. After crossing the Campidani — note the reclaimed land around Arborèa — you will reach the sea, replete with history and bordered by fragmentary relics of ancient peoples, come from afar. In the Gulf of Oristano, set on the slender peninsula of Capo S. Marco, is "Tharros," founded by the Phoenicians around 800 B.C., and later used by the Carthaginians as a stopover base on the route to "Massalia" (Marseilles). The sea becomes a succession of little "calette," or coves, and rocks at Santa Caterina di Pittinuri; nearby are the insubstantial ruins of "Cornus," probably a Carthaginian settlement. From Bosa, a town on an estuary, you can sail down to the sea along the river Temo: coral-diving and fine goldwork are pursued here. Then you drive along a seashore with vivid pink sunsets, a jagged coast-line, attractive little beaches, and, at last, Alghero, standing out sharp against the bright waters of the roadstead behind, perched on its small promontory: a fortress with the population and facilities of a town — "Bonita, por mi fé y bien assentada" (Lovely, in faith, and well built) was the imperial opin-ion of Charles V, according to local lore — and the Catalonian architecture and language left by mid-13th-c. Iberian colonists.

The route. You will leave Cagliari heading north; the first leg of the route then runs through the Campidani, largely coinciding with the route of the state road 131 (the Strada Carlo Felice), from which short detours will take you to Dolianova (13.5 km.) and Samassi (6 km.). Once you have dri-ven through Sanluri and Sàrdara, you will be on the plain of Oristano, driving along the shores of the vast pond of S. Giusta; also note the church of S. Giusta. While an enjoyable detour (21 km.) along the NW coast of the gulf of Oristano leads to "Tharros," from Oristano the route follows the state road 292 north, as far as Santa Caterina di Pittinuri along the coast, then cuts inland toward Cùglieri (a detour to San Leonardo de Siete Fuentes is 15 km. long), splitting off from the state road at Suni, toward Bosa. From Bosa, last of all, the coast road runs through Sa Mesa de s'Attentu, lead-ing to Alghero.

Halting places of interest. **Dolianova** has a Romanesque church, S. Pantaleo, note the remains of frescoes from the 12th-13th c in the apse. **Samassi** has another Romanesque church, S. Gemiliano. **Sanluri:** in the middle of this farming village is a 13th-c. castle which also houses the Museo "Duca d'Aosta" with relics dating back to the Risorgimento and the two World Wars. **Sàrdara** boasts the 14th-c. church of S. Gregorio and, to the north, the "nuraghic" well-temple of S. Anastasia. **S. Giusta*** is a large Romanesque church near the vast pond of the same name. **Oristano** is a thriving mod-ern town, with few traces of its medieval past. **"Tharros"*** was a Phoenician city, later Carthaginian and then Roman, now partly underwater and partly on a peninsula near Capo S. Marco. **Santa Caterina di Pittinuri** is a beach resort with limestone rocks and, nearby, the archeological sites of Columbaris and "Cornus." **Cùglieri**, at the base of the Montiferru, is where you turn off for the detour to **San Leonardo de Siete Fuentes**, a rustic village with 7 therapeutic springs, amidst holm-oaks, oaks, and elms. **Bosa** is a little town on the north bank of the estuary of the river Temo, beneath the walls of the Castello di Serravalle; on the other bank is the church of S. Pietro Extra Muros (11th c.). To the west, the port and beach of Bosa Marina. **Alghero*:** 16th-c. bastions gird the old town, Catalonian in style, set on a promontory overlooking the brilliant roadstead; across the gulf is **Capo Caccia***.

The Gulf of Orosei, the Ogliastra, and the Gennargentu   62

Nùoro - Dorgali - Lanusei - Fonni - Orgòsolo - Nùoro (206 km.)

The area overlooking the northern section of the Gulf of Orosei, around Dorgali, and all the way north along the coast to Siniscola and Posada, constitutes the Baronia, a name that dates from the 14th c. The author S. Satta describes spring there: "what sweet aromas amidst the reed beds, in the scrub alive with wild hares and partridges, when the bright sunlight revived the dead and aban-doned wood of the low-lying vineyards." As you think back on this route, you will certainly remem-ber the coastline, the blue sea, the rosemary growing against the blinding white limestone of Cala Gonone, the Grotta del Bue Marino; perhaps you will also think of the low circular stone walls of the prehistoric huts, or "nuraghi" (large, tower-shaped prehistoric stone structures peculiar to Sardinia) of the village of Serra Òrrios, with the sound of wind tossing the olive branches; or the Grotta di Ispinigoli, a great cavern with a deep shaft called the Abisso delle Vergini. Carthaginian jewelry found at the bottom of the shaft, now in the Museo di Dorgali, lends some credibility to the legend of bloodcurdling virgin-sacrifices. The Ogliastra is another broad plain of eastern Sardinia. A landscape of rocks, harsh but varied, and dotted with pasturage, vineyards, ancient olive groves; you cross the Ogliastra between Tortolì and Lanusei, after fine panoramic views from the high ridge road over the hills. The region may take its name from the little island off S. Maria Navarrese: Isola dell'Ogliastra, or Agugliastra, with reddish boulders of porphyry in the turquoise sea. A timeless scene, with a sense of how it must have looked to the ancient inhabitants. The last leg of this route, on the way back to Nùoro, runs through mountains: you climb to the slopes of the Gennargentu "where amidst white granite the oaks and the dark ilex toss their leaves" (Cardarelli); then you run through the Barbàgia di Ollolai, a stern archaic landscape peopled by shepherds.

The route. Beginning from Nùoro, this route heads predominantly SE toward Oliena, and then east — note the brief detour on the right (2 km.) to the springs of Su Gologone and the other, on the left, to Serra Òrrios. Once you reach Dorgali — detours along the way will take you to the cave of Ispinigoli and to Cala Gonone — then you will head south along the state road 125, which climbs over the pass of Genna Silana (1,017 m.) and over five other lower passes before reaching Baunei; a short distance further along, you will head down to the sea at Santa Maria Navarrese. After returning to the main road further south, you will reach Tortolì; from here, you may choose to drive to the seacoast again at Àrbatax (4.5 km.), or you may head inland, crossing the Ogliastra on the state road 198 as far as Lanusei. The route back to Nùoro (state road 389) runs across the plain of the Alto Flumendosa and over the Arcu Correboi (1,246 m.) and the Pass of Caravai (1,118 m.), reaching Fonni on the northern slopes of the Gennargentu, and finally descending to Mamoiada. Here you will head east toward Orgòsolo; and from there, you will drive back to your starting point at Nùoro along a road through the valley of the Rio de Locoe, or river Cedrino.

Halting places of interest. Nùoro: a typical inland Sardinian town, birthplace of 1926 Nobel laureate Grazia Deledda. **Oliena** is an old town with traditional houses lining long, narrow, twisting lanes, at the base of the limestone mountain, the Sopramonte; costumes are worn for the feast of S. Lussorio, on 21 August. **Su Gologone** is a karstic stream, the most important in Sardinia, in an idyllic patch of landscape. **Serra Òrrios*** is a village of "nuraghe," amidst olive and mastic trees. **Grotta di Ispinigoli**: this cave runs for 10 km., one of Italy's largest; one of the stalagmites is 38 meters high. **Dorgali** is a village sheltered by Monte Bàrdia; from the nearby fishing village of Cala Gonone, on the Gulf of Orosei, you can take a boat to the Grotta del Bue Marino (or Grotto of the Monk Seal, an animal which perhaps was once found here). **Santa Maria Navarrese**: sand, shoals, islets, and a venerable old wild olive tree by the church, which may have been built in the 11th c., supposedly in thanks for the survival of a shipwrecked princess; note the 17th-c Spanish tower situated on the coast. **Àrbatax** has red porphyry cliffs. **Lanusei** is the capital of Ogliastra. **Fonni** is the highest village in Sardinia (1,000 m.), with skiing in winter. **Mamoiada** lies secluded in an oak and chestnut forest. **Orgòsolo** is a harsh town of shepherds by the Sopramonte, with fine views. To celebrate Assumption Day on the 15th August, a procession is hold with knights in costume.

From the Golfo dell'Asinara to the Costa Smeralda   63

Porto Torres - Santa Teresa Gallura - La Maddalena - Olbia (193 km.)
The Isola di S. Stefano is one of the seven main islands — the other six being La Maddalena, Caprera, Spargi, Budelli, Razzoli, and S. Maria — in the archipelago that lies just off the NE coast of the Gallura. It is wedged between Palau on the coast and the island of La Maddalena; the channels that separate it from the two shores are only a few hundred meters across. In February of 1793, the 500 soldiers of the kingdom of Sardinia who were garrisoning the island of La Maddalena saw 23 vessels emerge from the sound of Bonifacio, beyond the Bocche di Bonifacio, landing cannon and soldiers on S. Stefano. The purpose and consequences of this expedition are still matters for historical study; it was commanded by a Corsican, C. Cesari, while the artillery — two cannons and a mortar — was commanded by a 23-year-old Corsican captain, Napoleon Bonaparte. Bonaparte began to bombard La Maddalena (a shell is still on display in the mayor's office), but his Provençal marines mutinied when ordered to land. A disgusted Bonaparte hastily departed for Toulon. The remarkable archipelago where this minor chapter of history unfolded, overlooking steep jagged rocks, tufts of maquis, inlets, narrow beaches, and sheer rock walls and shoals churning white amidst the cobalt water and the strong winds of the Bocche di Bonifacio, lies halfway along this route on the northern coast of Sardinia. Before you reach here, you will have seen the broad gulf of the Asinara, the fortifications of Castelsardo, the red cliffs of the Costa Paradiso, the cluster pines and granite of Capo Testa. It ends with exclusive resort areas amidst the promontories and inlets of the Costa Smeralda, with their "Neomediterranean" architecture, wild nature, and rich guests.

The route. Beginning in Porto Torres you will drive along the state road 200, following the arc of the Golfo dell'Asinara all the way to Castelsardo; on the right a short but scenic detour (7 km.) runs up to the church of Nostra Signora de Tergu. Further along, you will drive across the coastal plain of the river Coghinas, remaining a certain distance from the shore, amidst highlands, maquis, and rocks,

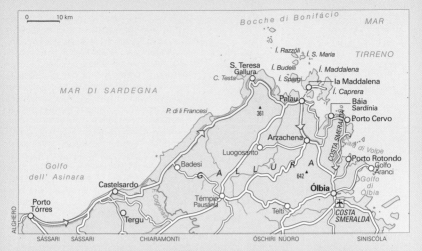

until you come even with Vignola Mare. The next stretch of road enjoys a succession of spectacular sea views, with coastal overlooks from the Punta di li Francesi all the way to Capo Testa; then, along the state roads 133 bis and 133, you will continue from Santa Teresa Gallura to Palau, where you can take boats to the islands of La Maddalena and Caprera. From Palau the route runs inland through Arzachena; just past Arzachena and Mulino di Arzachena, you will turn off from the road that runs directly to Olbia and turn toward Baia Sardinia, completing the tour of the promontory that extends northward; to the west is the Gulf of Arzachena, to the east is the Costa Smeralda (short detours lead to exclusive beach resorts). At the end of the inlet of Porto di Cugnana, the road turns inland once again, to Olbia.

Halting places of interest. Porto Torres is a port and industrial town on the Golfo dell'Asinara, with the 11th-c. Basilica di S. Gavino, and Roman ruins. **Nostra Signora de Tergu** is a 13th-c. Romanesque church which originally belonged to a Benedictine monastery. **Castelsardo:** set on a promontory, surrounded by old walls, this village is crisscrossed with narrow lanes and steep stairs; the castle houses a museum which displays examples of local crafts. **Santa Teresa Gallura** is a fishing village and a resort town, on a deep inlet facing the windy Bocche di Bonifacio; to the west, note the granite promontory of Capo Testa. **Palau** is a beach town and landing point for ships heading for **La Maddalena:** the handsome town is the only one on the island. You can set out for boat trips through the sunny archipelago; note Caprera, where Garibaldi died. **Baia Sardinia** is a fine beach area. **Porto Cervo:** the luxurious village and marina are the best-known resort of the Costa Smeralda. **Cala di Volpe** is an inlet in a glorious setting. **Porto Rotondo** has a famed beach in a cozy little bay. Olbia is a port at the end of the Gulf of **Olbia**, with a Romanesque church, S. Simplicio.

Western Sardinia from Sassari to Iglesias   64

Sassari - Macomèr - Abbasanta - Oristano - Gùspini - Iglesias (224 km.)

Many varied images are caught in the mind's eye after this long tour of the island from north to south: the rolling plain of the Logudoro with Pisan-Romanesque churches, the bare basaltic upland of the Campeda, the broad valley of the river Tirso, with endless vistas, the tree-shaded Campidani, with ponds and the waves of the Gulf of Oristano, the farms and eucalyptus trees of the reclaimed plain of Arborèa, the sere highlands of the Iglesiente — mining country dotted with the dense foliage of cork-oaks and the skeletal remains of a vanishing industry. The "nuraghe" (a large, tower-shaped prehistoric stone structure) is a leit-motif throughout much of the trip: there are about 7,500 nuraghes on the island, which comes out to one every 4 sq. km. (though in places like the meadows of Màrghine, NE of Macomèr, or in the Trexenta, east of Sanluri, the density is twice that). The best-known, the Nuraghe Santu Antine, lies near the beginning of this route. The word "nuraghe" comes from the proto-Sardinian term "nur," meaning both concave and convex. The nuraghe is, indeed, both. A tapered tower of stones stacked without mortar, topped by a terrace with parapet, it has a circular inner chamber — or more than one, stacked — covered by a false vault (the Greek "thòlos"), with a spiral stairway inside the thick wall. Nuraghes range in height from 10 to 20 m., in diameter from 8 to 12 m. The nuraghic culture dates from 1800 B.C. until the end of the 6th c. B.C.; patches survived inland until well after the Roman conquest. Over time, multiple nuraghes were built, complex structures with secondary towers, keeps, and curtain walls: built to withstand assault. Castles, in other words, comparable with those of the Middle Ages, with the same prehistoric social functions.

The route. Running from north to south, this route basically follows two state roads: the state road 131 Carlo Felice, one of the island's most important arteries, from Sassari to Oristano, and the state road 126, from Oristano to Iglesias. You leave Sassari, heading south, and pass, on your left, the state

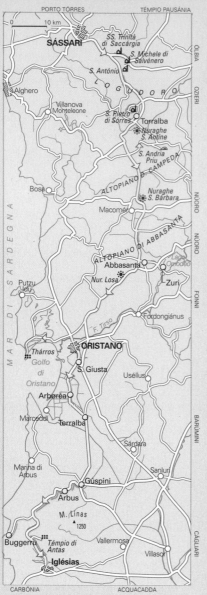

road 597 to Olbia — you may take a detour here, to see the Romanesque churches of SS. Trinità di Saccargia, S. Michele di Salvènero, and S. Antonio di Salvènero — which takes you through Torralba; near here, you should note the church of S. Pietro di Sorres and the Nuraghe Santu Antine (there are two detours leading to them, respectively 10 and 4 km. long). After Bonorva, where you can take a detour to the necropolis of S. Andrea Priu (9.5 km.), the state road 131 Carlo Felice curves around past Macomèr and heads down toward Abbasanta, with the renowned Nuraghe Losa and the Lago Omodeo, at a distance of 11 km. from the town. From Oristano you may choose to take the detour to "Tharros" (21 km.) or else, just past Santa Giusta, you may take the state road 126, which runs through Arborèa, Terralba, and Gùspini, climbing up to the Arcu Genna Bogai (549 m.). There are two other detours here: one to the right to Buggerru (15.5 km.) and the other to the left to the temple of Antas (2 km.). At the bottom of the descent is Iglesias.

Halting places of interest. **SS. Trinità di Saccargia*** is one of the most outstanding Romanesque monuments on the island; note the bell tower and the series of 13th-c frescoes in the apse. **S. Michele di Salvènero** is another 12th-c. church, **S. Antonio di Salvènero** is a 13th-c. one. **S. Pietro di Sorres*** is an isolated Romanesque basilica on a rise. **Nuraghe Santu Antine***: the central tower is the largest of all of Sardinia's nuraghes. **Necropoli di S. Andrea Priu** a hypgaeum of 20 cliff-side tombs. **Nuraghe Santa Barbara** has a four-tower bastion around the central structure. **Nuraghe Losa*** has a central tower that once stood three stories tall. **Lago Omodeo** is a manmade basin formed by the river Tirso, which submerged the village of Zuri (the new village, on the west shore, has a Gothic-Romanesque church, S. Pietro). **"Tharros"***: near the rocky Capo S. Marco and partly under the waves is a city founded by the Phoenicians, and later occupied by Carthaginians and then Romans. **Oristano**: note the medieval architecture in this provincial capital; note the Duomo, whose 18th-c appearance belies its 13th-c origins. **S. Giusta***: overlooking the immense pond is a 12th-c. Romanesque church. **Gùspini** is a mining village with many olive groves; to the NW is the mine of Montevecchio (lead and zinc).

Buggerru (see Iglesias) is a mining village high over the sea, in a deep inlet. **Tempio di Antas**: note the ruins of this Roman temple, dedicated to a syncretic god, Sardus Pater Babi. **Iglesias** is the center of the mining region; note the Castello di Salvaterra and the 14th-c. Cattedrale.

Phlegrean Fields and the Island of Ischia 65

Naples - Cuma - Baia - Pozzuoli - Pròcida - Ischia (71 km.)

"The purity and clarity of that water," wrote the 16th-c. Neapolitan historian, Camillo Porzio, about the Gulf of Naples, "seems to those who see it to be like quicksilver." The western shores of the gulf in question are the subject of this route, along with the incredible sideshow of the Phlegrean Fields, in which the phenomena of volcanic activity do some of their less spectacular "numbers". There is the enchanting landscape and there are geological oddities; alongside them, the third attraction for curious sightseers, is the aura of classical antiquity, which is so much more intense and evident to the senses here than anywhere else in southern Italy. A brief and far from exhaustive listing of classical sites along this route follows: at Nisida, Marcus Brutus, assassin of Julius Caesar, venturing off to the fatal battle of Philippi, where he was defeated by Augustus and Mark Antony, bade a last farewell to his wife Portia, daughter of Cato; in the harbor of Pozzuoli, St. Paul debarked; Vergil set the entrance to the Underworld at the Lake of Averno; Liternum was the site of the country estate to which Publius Cornelius Scipio, Africanus Major, the greatest Roman general before Caesar, retired, disgusted with politics; in Cumae the Sibyl made her prophecies; the Lake of Miseno was said to be the Stygian swamp across which Charon ferried lost souls; Capo Miseno, according to the ancient historian Strabo, was the land of the Lestrigons, giants who hurled great boulders at the ships of Ulysses; the Gulf of Baiae was without equal on earth, in the opinion of the poet Horace (an opinion shared by those who had villas here, among them Marius, Crassus, Caesar, Nero, Pompey, and Varro); in the Lago Lucrino a certain Sergius Orata harvested oysters, while on the banks the architect Cyrus built for Cicero the Cumanum, with a portico extending out into the lake waters; the island of Ischia was also known as Ænaria, and was renowned for its climate and its health-giving waters, as much in Roman times as it is today: in Forìo, back then, it was customary to try to see the "green ray" at sunset.

The route. There are two "classic" routes to Pozzuoli: one is the coast road that runs around the promontory of Posillipo (following Via Caracciolo and then Via Mergellina); the other follows the Via Domiziana (state road 7 *quater*), inland (from Piazza Sannazaro through the tunnel). From Pozzuoli you will continue along the Via Domiziana until you reach a fork 5 km. after the junction between Via Domiziana and the Autostrada; here you will take a right onto a road that runs near the Lago di Patria. Another road leads to the ruins of Liternum and then back to the Via Domiziana, which you will follow south to the turnoff for Cuma. Then you will follow secondary roads around the peninsula that encloses, on the west, the Golfo di Napoli, or Gulf of Naples, passing through Cuma, past the Lago di Fusaro, Torregàveta, Monte di Pròcida, Bàcoli, Bàia, and finally returning to Pozzuoli. Ferryboats, which will take cars, leave for Pròcida and Ischia from the harbor of Pozzuoli (similar ferryboats sail from Naples harbor as well). The circuit of the Isola d'Ischia covers a total of 31 km.

Halting places of interest. Naples**: the capital of the south welcomes the tourist with open arms in piazza del Plebiscito. **Marechiaro**: this village of fishermen and famous trattorias, with the "fenesta" from a classic song by Salvatore Di Giacomo; it lies at the end of a detour from the crossroads of the Capo. **Nìsida**: you reach the little island, originally an ancient volcanic crater of almost circular shape, by driving along the embankment, turning off from the coast road just past the promontory of Posillipo. **Pozzuoli**: set adjacent to the luminous waters of the gulf are the Roman monuments of the Serapaeum and the amphitheater, while the Rione Terra is perched high on a promontory; nearby, note the surprising volcanic phenomena of the **Solfatara**** (you pass by here if you take the Via Domiziana) and the dark waters of the **Lago d'Averno***, a great crater with woods on its steep slopes (fine view to be had, a bit further along). **Liternum**: the ruins of the little Roman town lie at the edge of the Lago di Patria. **Cuma*:** classical ruins and memories are to be found in this great archeological field, where a Greek colony was founded, conveying the alphabet in due time to the rest of the Italian peninsula; also note the cave of the Sibylla Cumana, or Sybil of Cumae, a sanctuary venerated in ancient times. **Bàcoli**: fishing village, with the Roman ruins of the Cento Camerelle and the Piscina Mirabile. **Miseno**: this small village is located on the cape of the same name; a short detour from Bàcoli passes over the dam between the coastal lagoon and the ancient port of Miseno; these two features together made this a major Roman naval base. **Bàia*:** in the archeological park note the spectacular Roman ruins, probably part of the Palatium, or palace, of the emperors. **Pròcida** presents a brightly colored composition of Mediterranean architecture. **Ischia***: you will land at Ischia Porto (the fishing village of Ischia Ponte, with a bridge built in the style of Aragon linking it to the islet of the Castello, is a couple of km. east); the tour of the island, involving steep climbs, seascapes with craggy coastlines, green vineyards, citrus groves, and pine woods, takes you, among other places, to: **Casamicciola Terme**, destroyed by a violent earthquake at the end of the 19th century; **Lacco Ameno**, a hot springs, with the reef of the Fungo just off the little beach; **Forìo**, a dazzling white town on a promontory, and renowned for its wines; **Sant'Angelo***, a fishing village, at the base of a small peninsula (to get there, you must turn off the main ring road); **Barano d'Ischia**, located in a pleasant site, from which you may venture down to the long beach of **Lido dei Maronti**.

Naples to Sorrento and to Capri 66

Naples - Ercolano (Herculaneum) - Vesuvio - Pompeii - Sorrento - Capri (54 km.)

It began with "a cloud, remarkable in size and appearance," as Pliny the Younger was to write to Tacitus, describing the eruption of 24 August of A.D. 79, and the death of his uncle, Pliny the Elder, who sailed from Capo Miseno to assist the fleeing population; its shape "most closely resembled that of a pine tree. It rose straight up as if borne upon a high trunk, and then opened out into numerous branches... here it was bright white, there it was mottled and dirty, where earth and ashes had been carried aloft." For many of the residents of Herculaneum, Stàbia, and Pompeii, that was the last thing they ever saw. At the end of this route through another half of the coastline of the Gulf of Naples, a traveller may be tempted to try to rank the remarkable impressions and sights: what ranks first? The dead cities, slain by a volcano, the inimitable island of Capri, the relaxed beauty of Sorrento amid its citrus groves, or the lunar landscape of the crater of Vesuvius? Certainly, there are plenty of powerful impressions here.

The route. The first leg of this route, to Ercolano, or Herculaneum, will follow the state road 18 (from Piazza del Municipio along Via Nuova della Marina along the port); expect heavy traffic. From Ercolano a scenic road climbs up the slopes of Vesuvio, or Vesuvius; on the way down, you will head directly for the toll booth and on-ramp at Torre del Greco for the Autostrada for Salerno, which will take you along a ring road to Castellammare di Stàbia. You will then continue on to Sorrento via Vico Equense and Meta. At Sorrento you can take a ferry to Capri; only from November to February can you take your car to the island with you. In the other months, only residents, with a few other special categories are allowed to drive.

Halting places of interest. Naples**: Palazzo S. Giacomo and the Maschio Angioino overlook the bustling port; **Portici**, and its Railway Museum of Pietrarsa remind visitors that one of the first railway lines linking this town to Naples was built here. **Ercolano, or Herculaneum****: all that you see of this small ancient town, with its charming location, once the exclusive holiday resort of the wealthy and powerful of imperial Rome, was excavated from a dense, compact slab of lava and mud, from 12 to 25 m. high. **Vesuvio***, or Vesuvius, seen from the west: if you turn off from the main route, following the slopes of Mt. Vesuvius, you will climb up to the lower station of the chair lift, passing by the observatory on your way (the upper station lies at an elevation of 1,158 m.; from there you can walk up to the great tear in the earth, the now deceptively tranquil crater), or else to the 1,017 m. of the northern slope of the terminal cone. **Torre del Greco:** here, craftsmen fashion exquisite work from coral and mother-of-pearl; you can see their creations in the Museo del Corallo. **Torre Annunziata:** one of the Neapolitan pasta capitals. **Pompei, or Pompeii: the excavations**** have unearthed at least three-fifths of the city that was buried by the eruption of Vesuvius in A.D. 79 (the town probably had a population of about 30,000); nowhere is the voyage backwards in time so entrancing. **Castellammare di Stàbia:** note the excavations of the Roman villas of long-vanished Stabiae; also, the antiquarium. **Monte Faìto** (1131 m.): beech trees, conifers, chestnuts, and cedars crowd its slopes; the view of the Sorrento peninsula and of the gulf is particularly fine from the "belvedere*," or viewpoint; you drive up from Castellammare di Stàbia and then you drive down to **Vico Equense** with its 14th century Cathedral, the total variant is 30 km. **Sorrento*** lies on a tufa terrace, high over the sea, amidst gardens and the dark, shiny green leaves of the citrus groves; the exuberant style of the applied arts of the 17th and 18th c. can be enjoyed in the Museo Correale di Terranova. **Isola di (Island of) Capri****: the colors of the sea, sky, rocks, and vegetation, the craggy Faraglioni, vineyards, gardens, and breezes: you could easily to stay here a lifetime, or thereabouts. The emperor Tiberius was neither the first nor the last to be captivated by the place. You land at **Marina Grande**; to reach the celestially blue transparency of the **Grotta Azzurra***, or Blue Grotto, a marine cave half-filled with sea water, you take a boat; you can take a cableway up to the main town, also called **Capri**, with its little Mediterranean piazzetta, at once simple and sophisticated: from here, you can walk to see a number of fine sites: the Certosa di S. Giacomo; the Belvedere Cannone, with its view; the ruins of Tiberius's Villa Iovis; the Arco Naturale, a natural arch; the Belvedere di Tragara; and **Marina Piccola**. The town of **Anacapri*** is white, suspended in the lush greenery; it is located on the western side of the island: you should tour the Villa S. Michele, once owned by a Swedish author, Axel Munthe; the best view is to be had by taking a chairlift to the peak of Monte Solaro (589 m.).

Amalfi Coast 67

Sorrento - Positano - Amalfi - Ravello - Vietri sul mare - Salerno (90 km.)

The coastline faces south here, overlooking sea and bright sunshine; the Monti Lattari plunge sharply down, a rocky bastion broken only by harsh deep valleys, with citrus and olive groves and vegetable gardens on rocky terraces, held up by small, rocky walls created by the back-breaking labor of generations; elsewhere, all you can see is Mediterranean underbrush and stones. The houses all cluster around the mouths of the deep valleys: the steep slopes determine the architectural style, which stacks volume, stairways, and rooves, crisscrossed by intricate lanes, refreshingly shady after the inexorable sunlight that is reflected by the sea and the whitewashed walls. For the entire 10th c. and much of the 11th c., Amalfi grew quickly and extensively, taking Pisa's place in Mediterranean trade — a place that would later belong to Genoa. Amalfi had trading colonies in Naples, Messina, Palermo, in the ports of Puglia, and, outside of Italy, in Durazzo, Tunis, Tripoli, Alexandria, Acre, Antioch, and of course, in the great metropolis of this time, Consantinople. Along with wealth, Amalfi took from the Byzantines and the Muslims a cultural influence that can be seen in the art. The little state of Amalfi, the first of Italy's "maritime republics," included the stretch of coastline from Positano to Cetara, with the islands of Li Galli and Capri; inland, it stretched to Tramonti and, over the crest of the Monti Lattari, it included Gragnano and Lettere. The end came late in the 11th c., as the Normans pushed north, allying themselves with the Pisan fleet in order to rid themselves of the pushy maritime merchants of Amalfi. The sun still shines down on the coastline, the sea breezes still brush the aromatic scrub, or maquis, and in the little cloister bedecked with intertwined arches, the palm trees still cast their shade over the "Paradiso."

The route. This route runs from Sorrento west along the Via Capo; soon, you will take a turn onto Via Nastro Verde, cutting across the promontory, passing Sant'Agata sui Due Golfi, and hugging the southern coast of the peninsula as far as Salerno. Aside from the various detours indicated in the next section of this route, there are two main side-trips that will enrich your enjoyment. First, just after you set out, you will follow secondary scenic roads along the tip of the peninsula, passing through Massa Lubrense and Tèrmini, and hooking back up with the main route just past Sant'Agata sui due Golfi. The second side-trip turns off at Atrani, climbing up to Ravello, and then on over the high pass, or Valico di Chiunzi (656 m.) in the Monti Lattari, and then back down to Maiori along the Valle di Tramonti.

Halting places of interest. Sorrento*: the sea of the Sirens (and some attribute the name to the mythological creatures), the tufa crags and cliffs, the orange orchards and olive groves that so enchanted the 16th-c. poet Torquato Tasso; collections of objects and the applied arts in the aristocrat palazzo of collectors at the Museo Correale di Terranova; an initial variant on the route offers spectacular views from 18 km. of secondary roads; you will pass through **Massa Lubrense** (120 m.), a lovely vacation spot on a rolling verdant plateau (you can make your way down to the village, the marina, and the beach of **Marina della Lobra**) and Tèrmini 330 m., a secluded village (by mule-track, 45 minutes to the Punta della Campanella, facing Capri). **Sant'Agata sui Due Golfi** (394 m.): the name of this little holiday town refers to the two gulfs of Naples and Salerno. **Positano***: the mountain spurs, covered by terraced white houses, run down to the harbor of the old fishing village, long since become an elegant resort. **Grotta di Smeraldo***: the Emerald Grotto, with its surreal green lighting, is located between Praiano and **Conca dei Marini**. **Agèrola** (630 m.), this highland of the Monti Lattari features resort spots amidst meadows and chestnut groves; fine views of the Amalfi coast, Capri, and the Gulf of Salerno can be enjoyed from the vantage point of San Lazzaro; 18-km. detour from Vèttica Minore. **Amalfi***, white, stacked in terraces on the steep slopes over the sea: touches of exotic architecture in the Duomo, with its bronze doors from Constantinople (1066), the intertwined arches in the cloister of the Paradiso — all these things are relics of ancient maritime explorations, trade with the east, the commerce and glory of the republic of Amalfi of the 10th and 11th c. **Atrani** is magnificently situated in an inlet, between high rock walls; the church of S. Salvatore di Bireto, where the doges of Amalfi were elected, has bronze doors from Constantinople (1087). **Ravello*** (350 m.): the site is perched on cliffs and crags, the roads are rustic at best, the landscape is colorful, and there are simple treasures to be found here, despite the fame and renown. To mention the finest aspects: note the Arab-style ancient architecture and the exotic plants of the garden of Villa Rufolo, the bronze doors by Barisano da Trani in the Duomo, the vista of sea, mountains, and coastline from the high terraced land between the valleys of the Dragone and the Reginna in the Cimbrone overlook. **Minori**, a beachfront town, formerly an arsenale of the republic of Amalfi; note the ruins of a Roman villa. **Maiori:** spreading out like an amphitheater in its inlet, at the foot of the majolica dome of the church of S. Maria a Mare; museum. **Cava de' Tirreni**, containing beautiful ancient village. **Abbazia della Trinità di Cava**: a 7-km. detour from **Vietri sul Mare**, famed for its majolica, will take you to this abbey, founded in the year 1101 and almost completely re-builtin the 18th-c; the church dates from the 18th c., the Benedictine monastery includes a fine little 13th-c. cloister and a museum. **Salerno*:** two rare and exquisite artworks are in the Museo del Duomo: a 12th-c. ivory frontal and a 13th-c. illuminated "Exultet"; the Duomo itself is one of the most notable monuments in southern Italy, in terms of architecture, history, and artwork; the seafront is lined with palm trees, and is bathed in the light of the gulf.

Terra di Lavoro and the highlands of Roccamonfina   68

Caserta - Santa Maria Capua Vètere - Capua - Sessa Aurunca - Teàno (72 km.)

The name in Italian — Terra di Lavoro — and the appearance of the landscape, would seem to suggest, as the origin of the term, "Land of Labor," from the great and fruitful work of a people of tireless farmers. Not so: the original Terra Leboriae refers to the Leborini, the original inhabitants of this area. Nowadays, the term Terra di Lavoro describes the territory of the province of Caserta between the elevations of Monte Massico and the northern rim of the Phlegrean Fields; in bygone times, the name described a larger portion of Campania. What the 16th-c. Neapolitan historian Camillo Porzio once wrote is still true: this territory is "superior to all other lands on earth in fertility and quality and any other thing that can delight or help the human race, rich and abundant. The cities that you will see there — Caserta, Santa Maria Capua Vètere, and Capua — cast bright lights on the history of the region from ancient times, as well as on the history of the entire south of Italy, while the artwork found here (to mention only a few items, the archaic "mothers" of the Museo Campano in Capua; frescoes, with their Byzantine iconography, painted by local artists in the second half of the

11th c., on the walls of the Benedictine basilica of Sant'Angelo in Formis; and the 18th-c. palace, or Reggia di Caserta) stands out in the body of Italian art. As for the mountain of Roccamonfina, it is a volcano, extinct since antiquity; upon its slopes, softened by the passage of thousands of years, olive trees and vineyards yield to thick dark chestnut groves as you climb: amid the branches and shadows, you will find a classic literary idyll, as is so often the case in southern Italy.

The route. You will leave Caserta along Viale Douhet, with the Reggia, or palace, on your right, and then continue along to Santa Maria Capua Vètere; from here, you will head north to Sant'Angelo in Formis, crossing the river Volturno, and, via Triflisco, reaching Capua, entering town from the west along the Via Appia (state road

7) and the bridge over the Volturno. You will leave Capua as you entered it, but immediately afterward, you will turn off the Via Appia onto the road that runs inland toward the Piana di Carìnola, via Brezza, and Sant'Andrea. From Carìnola you will continue on, reaching the Via Appia and following it for a short distance until you reach the turnoff for nearby Sessa Aurunca. Continuing along this road, you will then climb up to Roccamonfina (612 m.) and then head down, east, via Filorsi, Preta, and Tuoro, until you reach Teàno.

Halting places of interest. Caserta*: the Reggia, or palace, and the grounds are the masterpiece of the Neapolitan architect Luigi Vanvitelli, who expressed in stone and brick the ambitions of the first Bourbon king of Naples, probably inspired in turn by his great-grandfather, Louis XIV, the Sun-King: the facade of the building extends nearly 250 m., the grounds cover 120 hectares; the city grew up around the Royal Palace here. **Casertavecchia***: the crowning jewel of this still-intact medieval town, overlooking the plain from high atop a hill, is the 12th-c. cathedral, a rich composite of styles ranging from the Romanesque to Sicilian-Arabic and Benedictine; 10-km. detour before leaving Caserta. **Santa Maria Capua Vètere** is the town known as Capua to classical antiquity; Roman ruins survive: note the Campanian amphitheater and the Mithraeum. **Sant'Angelo in Formis***: this basilica from the year 1000 is adorned with remarkable frescoes of the same period. **Capua:** in ancient times, this was Casilinum; it stands in a curve of the river Volturno, enclosed in 16th-c. bastions; in the Museo Campano note the 200 "madri," archaic votive statues; over the river stretches a Roman bridge. **Carìnola**, with its ruined castle, Romanesque cathedral, and 15th-c. Catalonian-Gothic houses. **Sessa Aurunca:** before you enter this small town, take the country road to see the **Roman bridge of the Aurunci***, rearing high against the surrounding landscape, with 21 arches; the village occupies the site of the ancient town of Suessa, of which ruins can still be seen; note the pulpit supported by carved lions and the paschal candelabrum* in the Romanesque Duomo. **Roccamonfina:** this resort town lies amidst chestnut groves on the slopes of an extinct volcano; at a distance of 2.5 km. is S. Maria dei Làttani, a 15th-c. sanctuary. **Teàno:** note the 12th-c. Duomo and the ruins of the Roman theater.

Among the mountains of Irpinia 69

Avellino - Bagnoli Irpino - Mirabella Eclano - Avellino (148 km.)

This is a land with scars, where the wounds have healed slowly, where the terrible scars in the architectural and artistic heritage are unmistakable, in some cases irreparable. The earthquake that struck here, in the darkness of an early autumn evening — 23 November 1980 at 7:35 pm — lasted for one long, seemingly endless minute. When seen on a geographic map, the area hit by the earthquake stretches parallel with the overall orientation of the Italian peninsula, elongated, and including Naples, Benevento, the Vùlture, Potenza, and the Vallo di Diano. The epicenter, which is to say the area of the most violent, wracking lurches and jolts, lay straddling the high valleys of the rivers Òfanto (flowing into the Adriatic just west of Barletta) and Sele (emptying into the Tyrrhenian sea, through the plains north of Paestum), bounded by Sant'Angelo dei Lombardi and Laviano. There were 3,000 dead, 10,000 injured, some 70 towns and villages wholly destroyed or badly damaged. The enormous quantity of energy that was unleashed in the space of a minute was measured as a 6.4 quake on the Richter scale. The route through the Irpino mountains recommended here runs entirely through the greenery of mighty and solitary forests, gently rolling landscapes, mountains, hills, the high valleys of gathering streams, the Apennine courses of the rivers Sàbato, Calore, Òfanto, and Sele. The earthquake has not damaged the patterns of nature, only the information-rich landscape of man; among the areas hardest hit is a diffuse "agrarian" architectural heritage, a body of structures of venerable age and an artistic fabric — not masterpieces perhaps, but eminently worthy — that had long been neglected and ignored, until the earthquake came, swept much of it away, and finally revealed its true worth.

The route. You will leave Avellino on the Autostrada toward Salerno, exiting at Serino. A scenic road, the state road 574, leads up through the Piano di Verteglia (1,230 m.) and the Passo Cruci (980 m.) to Montella in the high valley of the river Calore. The state road 368 then takes you to Bagnoli Irpino. You will then climb up to the Lago di Laceno and to Piano Laceno (1,053 m.) and, along the scenic route running over the northern slopes of Monte Calvello and Monte Oppido, you will reach the turnoff for Caposele. The ensuing landmarks will be Caposele, Materdòmini, and Lioni in the high valley of the Òfanto. Now you are on the state road 7 Appia, but you will soon leave that road to drive up to Sant'Angelo dei Lombardi. From here, the state road 425 will take you in turn to the state road

303, which runs over the ridge separating the valleys of the rivers Frédane and the river Ufita. From the Passo di Mirabella you will continue to Grottaminarda; from there you will return to Avellino on the Autostrada from Puglia. This route is fairly intricate; we would recommend studying a road map carefully before setting out.

Halting places of interest. Avellino is a modern city located in a verdant hollow of the Valle del Sàbato, in a mountainous setting; note the Museo Diocesano and the Museo Irpino. **Atripalda:** remains of the Sarnites and Roman Abellinum. **Serino:** summer excursions and winter ski-ing. **Monte Terminio** (1783 m.) is a nature reserve amidst spectacular forests; it extends on the left of the route, and is accessible from Serino. **Bagnoli Irpino** is a resort at the head of the Valle del Calore. **Caposele:** above the town are the intake and pumping stations for the great Pugliese aqueduct. **Materdòmini** is a resort town, set amidst oak groves, with the Santuario di S. Gerardo at Maiella, destination of pilgrimages. **S. Guglielmo al Goleto** is a ruined abbey containing the remains of the chiesa grande and the chiesa piccola, founded in the 12th c. by Saint Guglielmo di Vercelli; this requires a short detour from the state road 7, after Lioni. **Sant'Angelo dei Lombardi:** take a short detour; at the head of the Valle dell'Ófanto, this town was devastated by the earthquake of 1980; the 16 th-c Cattedrale with its late Renaissance portal, was only partly destroyed; the "Lombardi" were, of course, the Longobards, who founded the town. **Aeclanum** was originally a Samnite town, and later a Roman town: the archeological excavations are just a short way west of the Passo di Mirabella. **Mirabella Eclano:** you will take a 2.5 km. detour from the Passo di Mirabella; a carved and painted wooden 12th-c. Crucifix can be seen in the church of Matrice; on a Saturday in September, during the "Festa del Carro," a 25-m.-tall obelisk is transported into town from a hill, with a statue of Our Lady of Sorrows. **Grottaminarda** is a hilltop farming town, with the 18th-c church of S. Maria Maggiore by Vanvitelli. Basilica dell'Annunciata: founded in early times, the oldest medieval church in Irpinia was partly carved out of the tufa, near a catacomb; this may have been the headquarters of the earliest bishops of Avellino; 7-km. detour, exiting the Autostrada at Avellino Est, then along the state road toward Grottaminarda until you reach **Prata di Principato Ultra**, noted for its Basilica dell'Annunziata, where a further stretch on secondary roads is necessary.

The Gargano and the Tavoliere   70

Foggia - Manfredonia - Monte Sant'Angelo - Vieste - Pèschici - Rodi Gargànico - San Giovanni rotondo - San Severo - Lucera - Troia - Foggia (309 km.)
The Tavoliere is the broadest plain in the entire Italian peninsula, occupying 3,000 sq. km., one percent of the nation's surface. In ancient times, this was seabed; in centuries gone by it was winter pasturage, where nomadic sheep herders would lead their flocks; in Foggia there was a "dogana della mena delle pecore," or shepherds' customs station (it was established in 1447 by Alphonse of Aragon, and it provided the royal coffers with an endless stream of cash; it was abolished after Italian unification); today this is farmland, where grain, forage, vineyards, and fruit orchards grow. It is true that the eye sees only an endless tableland here, but that is not the origin of the name, which refers to the *Tabulae Censuariae*, the register in which the immense landholdings of the government in this territory were recorded. At a distance, it is surrounded by the outcroppings and spurs of the Samnite Apennines, the rim of the Murgia highlands, and the Gargano. It is from the last elevations of the Apennines as they sink into the plain that Lucera and Troia look out over the Tavoliere from the west: Lucera, where Frederick II gathered the troublesome Saracens of Sicily, a reserve for recruits to his loyal and much feared royal guard; Troia, with its Romanesque cathedral, an outstanding example of the architectural style of the Pugliese Middle Ages, veined with Byzantine and Muslim styles. The Gargano, on the other hand, is the other landscape of this route, which follows virtually the entire Gargano coastline before crossing it. The great karstic limestone massif, with rounded mountaintops, rises from the plain in two successive terraces; extending out into the Adriatic, it plunges sheer into the sea with high, steep coasts, broken here and there by small beaches. At the base of this massif on the southern side are the churches of the Siponto, a region strangled by malarial swamps and earthquakes; on high is the Santuario dell'Arcangelo Michele in Monte Sant'Angelo, dedicated to the Archangel Michael, perched atop a high ridge. The coastline has been a relatively recent discovery here; for many years the peninsula was secluded, trapped between the sea and the marshlands of the Tavoliere: today people are drawn here by the shoals and the sands, the olive groves and pine forests, the bright southern light, inland near the scattered remains of the forest that once extended where now only underbrush and pasturage are seen, where white rocks jut out of the arid soil.

The route. You will leave Foggia on the Via San Lazaro and the state road 89, heading for Manfredonia. Continuing along the same road, you will begin the circuit around the Gargano, but at Mattinata you will turn off onto a twisting, scenic coastal route, that runs around the promontory, via Vieste, Pèschici, and Rodi Garganico. About 5 km. further on, you will turn left onto the road that runs via Ischitella to Vico del Gargano, where you can turn off onto the scenic road that cuts across the peninsula, from north to south, through the Foresta Umbra, to Monte Sant'Angelo. Retracing your route for a short distance, you will then head west on the state road 272, which will take you to San Giovanni Rotondo and San Marco in Lamis. From here, secondary roads will take you to Rignano Garganico, and then on down to the Tavoliere, north of Foggia, to Lucera (the landmarks along this route are

Ponte Villanova, Masseria Monaco Cappelli, Stazione di Rignano Garganico, and Pàlmori). From Lucera to Troia you will follow the state road 160; from Troia you will return to Foggia along the state road 546.

Halting places of interest. Foggia, at the heart of the Tavoliere, is a thoroughly modern town: the Romanesque cathedral was heavily restored in the 18th c.; in the Museo Comunale and the Pinacoteca Comunali, there are also exhibits concerning the Foggia-born composer, Umberto Giordano. **S. Leonardo di Siponto***: note the 12th-c. church, formerly an abbey of the Knights Templar, with its splendid portal decorated with 13th-c reliefs. **S. Maria di Siponto****: note the 11th-c. Romanesque cathedral, once part of the long-vanished town. **Manfredonia**: the castle (like the city, founded and built by Manfredi, or Manfred, the natural son of the emperor Frederick II), facing the waterfront, is the site of the Museo Nazionale Archeologico del Gargano.

Monte Sant'Angelo*: in the grotto here, the Archangel Michael was purportedly seen in an apparition in the late-5th c.; at that time, the Longobards were particularly devoted to Michael, as a national saint; the sanctuary and town grew together, through the faith of the pilgrims; the so-called tomb of the Longobard king Rotari is actually a later baptistery, in all likelihood; note the Museo Tancredi, with the arts and folkways of the Gargano. **Vieste:** note the old town, with stepped lanes amid white houses joined by arches; note the view of the coastline and sea from the castle. **Pèschici:** high on the coast of the Gargano, perched upon a crag, overlooking the beach below. **Rodi Gargànico:** set on a promontory on the north coast of the Gargano; twenty nautical miles away are the **Tremiti islands**, with their clear waters, rocky coasts, and aromatic vegetation, the maquis. **Vico del Gargano:** the Trappeto Maratea is an old mill used for producing oil. **Foresta Umbra*** is a vast forest of beech trees, pines, maples, and hornbeams, in the recently established **Parco Nazionale del Gargano. San Giovanni Rotondo:** site of pilgrimages commemorating the Christian virtues of Padre Pio da Pietrelcina. **San Marco in Lamis**, dominated by the like named convent founded by the Lombards. **San Severo:** site of medieval churches and widely renowned for the production of white wines. **Lucera*:** this little town is dense with history, from Roman times, up through the remarkable reigns of Frederick II and of the Anjou: the castle that overlooks the plain was enlarged by Charles I d'Anjou with a vast ring of towers and walls; the 14th-c. Duomo is also Angevin; the Museo Civico Giuseppe Fiorelli has exhibits chiefly of archeology. **Troia:** the rose window and bronze doors by Oderisio da Benevento embellish the cathedral, a sterling example of the Pugliese Romanesque; Museo Diocesano and Museo Civico; note the proto-Romanesque church of S. Basilio.

Trulli and Grottoes 71

Bari - Castellana Grotte - Alberobello - Fasano - Brindisi (146 km.)
The Adriatic coast, which you will be following in part along this route, often forms a last little rocky cliffline, in the succession of terraces of "rocky Puglia," as the Murge hills are often called. The "trullo," a remarkable type of dwelling found here (more about "i trulli" below, in due time), gives its name to another part of the Murge, the SE sector (Murgia dei Trulli). This rolling highland, dark green with crops, drops away toward the Adriatic coastline like a steep rampart, between Mola di Bari and Ostuni, covered with white houses; toward the Gulf of Taranto, on the other hand, it slopes gently in a succession of terraces. The two sections of the Murge differ in terms of agriculture and in terms of population, which is scattered throughout the countryside further south. And there are three notable grottoes or caverns. At Polignano a Mare, the Grotta Palazzese encloses waters of an intense blue-green; it yawns open, with many other marine grottoes, in the steep cliff-face, which has been burrowed out by the tireless sea waves. The Grotta di Putignano is a karstic cavity, a treasure chest of alabaster some 20 m. tall, covered with pink mineral encrustations. The most notable grottoes, or caves, however, are the Grotte di Castellana, first explored by a group of local youths in the 18th c. They extend for a good 2 km., some 50 m. under the surface of the earth; stalactites and stalagmites dangle and jut, stirring the imagination of cave-explorers, and prompting fanciful names such as: Ciclopi (Cyclops), Angelo (Angel), Civetta (Owl), Presepe (Crèche), Serpente (Serpent), Altare (Altar), Duomo di Milano (Cathedral of Milan), and Torre di Pisa (Leaning Tower of Pisa); at the end of this succession of caverns and formations, you encounter the crystalline whiteness of the Grotta Bianca, which has been described as "the world's most beautiful cave." Along the road, there are olive groves and almond groves everywhere, and more than half of the route runs along the seashore. Toward the

end of the route, you will be retracing the steps of Horace, in the voyage he describes in his fifth Satire. Egnazia was the final stage of this trip: "Gnatia lymphis iratis exstructa," he wrote: "The construction of Gnatia having angered the waters," with reference to the aridity of the region. Lastly, Horace described "Brundisium longae finis chartaeque viaeque," calling Brindisi the "end of the journey and of the paper," meaning that his poem ended with the great historic port town, terminus of the Appian Way.

The route. After leaving Bari along the Lungomare Nazario Sauro, you will drive along the Adriatic coast on the state road 16 as far as Polignano a Mare. A scenic road then leads inland to Castellana Grotte. Soon after, at Putignano, the state road 172 will take you on to Alberobello and Locorotondo. Then you will head back to the sea along the route Fasano Torre Canne. You will continue on to Brindisi on the recently built beach road (state road 379), turning off from it in the stretch between Villanova and Torresabina, to head inland to Ostuni and Carovigno.

Halting places of interest. Bari: the historical centre of this regional capital contains two Romanesque churches, S. Sabino e S. Nicola. **Mola di Bari:** set on a promontory, with a 13th-c cathedral renovated in the Renaissance style by architects from Dalmatia; note the fishing harbor and the Angevin castle, erected in 1278. **Polignano a Mare:** overlooking the Adriatic Sea from its jagged cliffs; the light and colors in the Grotta Palazzese are a pale blue: it is the best known grotto in this stretch of coastline, and you can tour it by boat. **Conversano:** on a detour from the main route between Castellana Grotte and Polignano a Mare, with its Duomo, other venerable old churches, and a vista of the coastline from the square in front of the castle. **Grotte di Castellana**:** carved out by an ancient underground river, this is the largest complex of caves in Italy. **Putignano,** a resort in the Murgia range; in town, note the church of Madre di S. Pietro; 1 km. away is the **grotto,** with pink alabastrine encrustations. **Alberobello*:** the "trulli," round whitewashed houses, with conical grey limestone rooves, line the long steep twisting streets, creating a remarkable townscape. **Martina Franca*:** take a 6-km. detour from **Locorotondo*,** which offers fine views of the **valley of Itria,** scattered with "trulli"; the city stands on the highest elevation of the southern Murgia range, and has vigorous architecture and a fine Baroque flavor. **Fasano:** resort on a spur of the Murgia range; all around, amidst the Mediterranean vegetation are bright white "trulli" and exotic animals. **Egnazia:** the necropolis, the musem, and the ruins of ancient Gnatia can all be reached via an 11-km. detour, climbing north along the coast, from Torre Canne. **Ostuni** glitters white amidst the olive trees on the hills of the Murgia; note the medieval borgs, illuminated at night. **Carovigno,** with a 15th-c. castle and the walls of the Messapic town Carbina. **Brindisi:** two Roman columns mark the end of the Via Appia, or Appian Way, on the shore of the peninsula where the modern city stands between two inlets that constitute an excellent natural harbor; note the Museo Archeologico Francesco Ribezza and, at a distance of 2 km., the 13th-c. church of **S. Maria del Casale,** the most outstanding monument in the city.

Salento   72

Lecce - Ótranto - Marina di Leuca - Gallìpoli - Taranto (240 km.)
The castle of Ótranto is pentagonal, with three round towers; this menacing military construction was erected by Ferdinand of Aragon at the end of the 15th c., it has nothing to do with Walpole's "The Castle of Otranto", the horrifying first work in a literary genre. Here, indeed, in the Salento, everything is so sunny and free of dark shadows. This is the extreme tip of the easternmost peninsula of the larger Italian peninsula surrounded by the waters of the Adriatic, which begins at the channel of Ótranto — about 40 nautical miles between the Italian and Albanian shores — and the waters of the enveloping Ionian sea. The coast is jagged, in places lined with pine groves; it drops away sheer

into the crashing waves, the limestone cliffs studded with marine caves in which humans once lived, in the Paleolithic; the gently rolling reddish land supports olive groves and vineyards, amid the jutting white rocks. This route runs from Lecce to Taranto, around the cape of Santa Maria di Leuca — *lapygium promontorium* — almost invariably hugging the coast, but we have mentioned Ótranto first of all because, in the past, when Puglia was broken up into three parts, the Salento peninsula was part of what was then called the Terra d'Ótranto. This comprised the modern-day provinces of Taranto, Lecce, and Brindisi, but the peninsula nowadays corresponds to the province of Lecce alone. The capital of this province is Lecce, alluring for its remarkable architecture. Paul Bourget saw it in 1890, and wrote about it in his "Sensations d'Italie," admitting that in Lecce he had discovered new meanings for the terms Baroque and Rococo, which were then mere pejoratives, not yet accorded the dignity of artistic styles: "Lecce showed me that these words could also be synonymous with a light-fingered fancy, mad elegance, felicitous grace"; the city proved to be a "single furor of caprice," even more so in that "its chiseled brightness emanates an almost Eastern light," while "the air is slightly stirred by the breeze that swells the sails of the ships in "Embarquement pour Cythère," reminiscent of the great and melancholy Watteau."

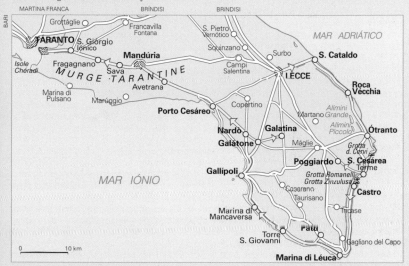

The route. You will leave Lecce along the Via del Mare, reaching the coast at San Cataldo. Here you will take the coast route south, along the state road 611 (as far as Ótranto) and the state road 173, as far as Capo Santa Maria di Leuca. A bit further on, at Leuca, you will turn inland to Patù, and from there you will drive back down to the sea at Torre San Gregorio on the Golfo di Taranto. You will then continue along the coast road as far as Santa Maria al Bagno There is a stretch inland along secondary roads, with the landmarks of Nardò, Galatone, Galatina, and Leverano; then you return to the coast at Porto Cesáreo. Take the Via Salentina (state road 174), directly behind Porto Cesáreo, and you will reach Manduria on the range of the Murge Tarantine. Then, for one last time, you will reach the coast at Campomarino, continuing along the coast road as far as Taranto.

Halting places of interest. Lecce**: this town, capital of the Salento, should be toured carefully, unhurriedly, and patiently; and not only for the celebrated, flamboyant Baroque architecture of the churches, palazzi, piazzas, and streets. **San Cataldo**, main beach of the province's capital. **Roca Vecchia**: the ruins of the castle on the cliffs were once a Messapic city. **Ótranto**: an enormous and famous 12th-c. mosaic covers the floor of the cathedral*; in the town, mostly enclosed within walls, note also the Aragonese castle and the Byzantine-style church of S. Pietro. **Santa Cesàrea Terme:** the springs pour forth out of caverns in the cliffs and then drop sheer away into the sea. **Poggiardo:** a 20-km detour from Santa Cesàrea Terme: in a museum you can see the medieval frescoes detached from the crypt of S. Maria; at a distance of 1.5 km, note the crypt of S. Stefano, with remains of frescoes dating back to 12th-15th-c. **Grotta Zinzulusa*:** this cavern is outstanding among the caves in the cliffs around Ótranto, in terms of encrustations, underground fauna, and prehistoric finds. **Castro** stands high among the olive groves, with its ancient cathedral, 16th-c. walls, and vast view of sea and coast; beneath it is the little port of Castro Marina. **Marina di Leuca:** the lighthouse, the Santuario di Finibus Terrae, the caverns in the cliffs, and the waves of the Ionian sea: this is the far tip of the Salento peninsula. **Patù** (see Marina di Leuca): the Centopietre is a great Messapic or medieval megalithic construction at the edge of town, facing the little Romanesque church of S. Giovanni. Usentum: scanty ruins of the Roman port can be seen in the inlet of Marina San Giovanni; a little further along, the islet of Pazzi, inhabited in prehistoric times. **Gallìpoli*:** the medieval "borgo," with white terraced houses, stands on an islet, linked by a bridge to the modern part of town, on a peninsula, jutting into the sea. **Galàtone** (see Galatina), interesting examples of Lecce style Baroque. **Galatina:**

Stories of the Virgin Mary, painted according to an apocryphal Gospel, and other 15th-c. frescoes, cover the interior of the church of S. Caterina. **Nardò**, rivalled Lecce as the most important cultural and artistic city in the Salento province during the 17th century. **Porto Cesàreo**, situated along part of the coast which is to become a marine park. **Manduria:** in the this little town in the range of the Murge Tarantine, note the ancient Duomo, the medieval ghetto, the Baroque Palazzo Imperiali, the Messapic walls, and the remarkable Fonte Pliniano. **Taranto***, whose splendid past is hinted at in the golden jewels contained in the Museo Archeologico Nazionale.

Cilento and the Vallo di Diano 73

Salerno - Paestum - Palinuro - Maratea - Sala Consilina - Potenza (330 km.)
"The air was delicately scented by the remarkably large and lovely violet. At last, we glimpsed the sublime and powerful rows of columns hemming in the horizon, in the midst of a desolate wasteland." These are the words of a letter to a friend by the English poet Percy Bysshe Shelley, who saw Paestum in February 1819. "Between one column and the next in this temple — it is called the Temple of Ceres — you can see in one direction the sea, toward which the gentle slope of the hill on which it stands runs down, and in the other direction you can see the vast amphitheatre of the Apennines, dark-colored, purplish mountains with diadems of snow, over which sail thick and leaden cloudbanks." The Greeks of Sybaris sailed across the Mediterranean to found this city, calling it Poseidonia, after their sea god; the Lucanians who later descended from the Apennines to take the city for themselves gave it its modern name. Here Shelley was unable to enjoy the excitement of the sacred dances performed by girls depicted on the metopes of the Heraion of the river Sele; he did not see the diver portrayed on a tomb slab: neither of these artworks, now in the museum, had yet been unearthed. Beyond Paestum, along the route, one is astonished by the nature of the coast of the Cilento, the crags, the cliffs, the inlets, and the glittering light that flashes off the sea, losing itself among the fluttering leaves of the olive groves. Watchtowers are relics of the centuries of Saracen pirate raids, little harbors are reminiscent of the trade in grain, wine, and olive oil, a trade once carried on by the sailor-monks of the abbey of Cava de' Tirreni. Midway up the Cilento coast is another Greek city, Elea (or *Velia* as it was written by Pliny), renowned for the school of philosophy that was begun here by the Ionian Xenophanes of Colophon and continued by Parmenides and Zeno (the latter known for his elegant logical paradoxes, such as that of Achilles being unable to outrun the tortoise; less well known for his participation in an unsuccessful conspiracy against the tyrant Nearchus. When Nearchus interrogated the philosopher, he bit his own tongue off, so as not to betray his fellow-conspirators, and spit it in the tyrant's face. As a result, the tyrant had him crushed to death under a mill stone). Velia, like Paestum, was attacked by the Lucanians, but it withstood the siege. After completing this tour, you will return north along the Vallo di Diano, the highland that separates the Apennine ridge of the Maddalena from the mountains of the Cilento, and then you will head east to Potenza, where you can admire the artifacts of the Lucanians, Italic descendents of the ancient Samnites, in the Museo Archeologico.

The route. Leaving Salerno along the Lungomare Marconi, you will be following the Tyrrhenian coastline, all the way to the southermost point on this route, Praia a Mare (to be precise, the littoral of the Piana del Sele as far as Paestum; from Paestum a secondary road to Agròpoli; from there, the state road 267 along the coastline of the Cilento, continuing on through Ascea, Pisciotta, and Palinuro; the state road 562 from Palinuro all the way to the junction, on the Golfo di Policastro, with the state road 18, along which you will continue). From Praia a Mare, heading back north again, you will retrace the same route for a short stint, and after the bridge over the river Castrocucco, you will turn off onto the road for Lagonegro, taking the Autostrada north at the Lagonegro-Maratea interchange. Then you will leave the Autostrada at the Padula-Buonabitàcolo interchange, following the state road through the Vallo di Diano, as far as Sala Consilina; from here, secondary roads will take you to Teggiano on the western side of the Vallo, or great end moraine; then on to Polla, and then into the Valle del Tanagro, to Pertosa and to Auletta. Finally, at the interchange of Buccino, you will reach the Autostrada that runs to Potenza (the stretch not on Autostrada between the interchanges of Padula-Buonabitàcolo and Buccino allow you to tour the Certosa di Padula and the Grotte di Pertosa, as well as making other stops mentioned below).

Halting places of interest. Salerno*: set between the hills and the coastline of the gulf, its seafront dotted with palm trees; this town boasts the medieval Duomo built by Robert Guiscard, one of the most important monuments in southern Italy; there are a few precious works of art in the Museo del

Duomo, and archeological collections in the Museo Provinciale. **Santuario di Hera Argiva**: take a 2-km. detour from Torre Kernoi, after the river Sele; it is said to have been founded by Jason; among the ruins, not particularly impressive to see nowadays, were found the archaic Greek sculptures (metopes) now in Paestum. **Paestum****: the ancient Doric columns of the three temples of Greek Poseidonia, the pentagonal walls that mark the perimeter of the vanished city, the excavations, the Museo with the metopes from the Santuario di Hera Argiva, and painted Greek and Lucanian slabs: this is one of Italy's leading archeological sites, justly famous. **Agròpoli:** from the ruins of the Byzantine castle in the old town, perched high over the sea, you can enjoy the vista of the Gulf of Salerno, as far as Capri. **Santa Maria di Castellabate**, whose waters are protected by an underwater park. **Scavi di Velia:** this town, founded as a Phocaean Greek colony, was the town of Elea of the subtle philosophers Xenophanes, Parmenides, and Zeno; the ruins are scattered across the plain and the acropolis. **Palinuro:** located in an inlet at the foot of the promontory; by boat, you can go to the Grotta Azzurra, or Blue Grotto, in 10 minutes, to enjoy the amazingly blue light and water. **Marina di Camerota**, at the beginning of the Golfo di Policastro, with the Calabrian coast in the background. **Sapri**, with its annual commemoration of the landing of the three hundred. **Maratea**, medieval "borgo" perched on a rock, and bathing spots lining the coast; among the numerous grottoes, note the grotto of Marina di Maratea with its stalactites and stalagmites. **Praia a Mare:** uphill from the beach resort is the Santuario della Madonna della Grotta; you can take a boat to the island of Dino, about 1.5 km. offshore. **Lagonegro:** this village stands on a slope of the Monte Sirino, set in a ring of mountains. It is said that the woman who inspired Leonardo da Vinci's Mona Lisa lain to rest in the ancient panish church. **Padula:** downhill from the town is the immense Baroque charterhouse, or Certosa di S. Lorenzo, site of the Museo Archeologico della Lucania Occidentale. **Teggiano:** the layout of this medieval town stands high on a secluded hilltop; note the Roman and medieval marble carvings in the former church of S. Pietro. **Sala Consilina**, whose historical centre overlooks the rampants of Diano. **Polla**: note the 16th- and 17th-c. paintings and the carved choir chancel of the convent church of S. Antonio, in the high part of town; from the square in front of the church, fine view of the entire Vallo di Diano. **Grotta di Pertosa***: once the channel of an underground river, this cavern extends its heavily encrusted walls, with galleries, lakelets, and halls, for more than 2 km. **Potenza:** a modern city stands around the medieval center, high atop a ridge, at an elevation of 816 m.; note the Museo Archeologico Nazionale.

Mountains of Northern Basilicata 74

Potenza - Monticchio - Melfi - Venosa - Potenza (186 km.)

As a child, the Roman poet Horace is said to have escaped from his nurse, and wandered through the mountain forests until, exhausted, he fell asleep; the tale goes that he was protected by mysterious doves, who covered him with branches of laurel and myrtle, "ut tuto ab atris corpore viperis / dormirem et ursis" (so that he could sleep, his little body safe from black vipers and bears); this remarkable event astounded the woodsmen who later found him. The mountain upon which the infant Horace had his adventure was the Vùlture, an ancient volcano with harsh landscapes, covered with forests of beech trees, oaks, chesnuts, lindens, maples, hornbeams, elms, ashes, poplars, and alders — the high point in terms of views of this route over the Ofanto and the Bradano. The birthplace of Horace, of course, is nearby Venosa, or Venusia, once a Roman military colony, and now part of the Basilicata on the border with Puglia; the poet was born here and completed his youthful studies, under a tutor named Flavius, who taught "magni pueri magnis e centurionibus orti," or "big boys, the sons of big centurions" (later his father took Horace to study with the best masters in Rome). In the other cities and sites along this route — including Melfi, the Castello di Lagopésole, Venosa with the Abbazia della Trinità, Acerenza with its large cathedral with French-style ambulatory around the presbytery — what prevails is the air of medieval history, of the Normans, Swabians, and Angevins, with the great shadow of Frederick II looming over all: Lagopésole, made of reddish limestone, is the largest and the last of this emperor's castles; from another, Norman castle, in Melfi — Frederick had restored Melfi's walls — he decreed his "Constitutiones Augustales," which his jurists, including the renowned Pier delle Vigne, had developed to regulate feudal law.

The route. You will leave Potenza, heading north along the state road 93 as far as Rionero in Vùlture. This marks the beginnning of the circuit around Monte Vùlture (on state roads 167, 401, and 303), heading for Monticchio, Melfi, and Rapolla. At Rapolla you will rejoin the state road 93, taking it toward Lavello, but turning off shortly at a crossroads, and taking the road to Venosa. From Venosa, you will head south along twisting, scenic

secondary roads, to Maschito, Forenza, and Acerenza, and then onto the state road 169. Along this road, through Pietragalla, you will reach the crossroads of San Nicola, where once again you will turn onto the state road 93, which will take you back along your tracks to Potenza.

Halting places of interest. Potenza occupies the crest of a hill in the high valley of the river Basento; the Museo Archeologico Nazionale is devoted to the ancient inhabitants of Lucania, as Basilicata was once called. **Castello di Lagopésole***, is a monumental residence and stronghold, begun by the emperor Frederick II eight years before his death, and never finished during his lifetime. **Atella**: this village was founded in the 14th c., and still has fragments and details from that period; it is said that Giovanna I, queen of Naples, was held prisoner in the Benedictine monastery. **Monte Vùlture** is an extinct volcano: you can drive up to an elevation of 1,245 m. with a scenic road, 5.5 km. from **Rionero in Vùlture**, a town alive with history, situated between two hills, or you can take a cableway from the lakes of Monticchio to an elevation of 1,214 m. **Laghi di Monticchio***: the larger of these lakes is on the left of the road, the smaller is to the right; their green waters lie in the crater of a volcano, amidst dense stands of poplars and black alders. **Melfi:** this town lies at the foot of the large old castle, and is enclosed by ancient walls, relics of the time when this was the residence of Norman kings and, later, of the emperor Frederick the Swabian; note the renowned sarcophagus of Rapolla in the Museo Nazionale Archeologico. **Rapolla** lies on mountain slopes, with a 13th-c Gothic cathedral whose magnificent portal dates back to 1253 and the Norman church of S. Lucia, with a clear Byzantine influence. At a distance of 6 km. is **Barile**, a village of Albanian traditions (settlers from Scùtari and Croya, fleeing the Turks, arrived here around 1460). **Venosa***: in the image of this city, birthplace of Horace (the so-called Casa del Poeta, or House of the Poet, is actually a tepidarium from Roman baths) the monuments of the Middle Ages and the Renaisssance, especially the abbey of the Trinità, predominate over the Roman ruins. **Maschito**: beginning in 1467, this town was repopulated by Albanian refugees. Some still speak the dialect. In the Palazzo Comunale is a remarkable collection of paintings by the local artist Mario Cangianelli. **Forenza**, is a delightfully situated holiday resort. **Acerenza**, overlooking the high valley of the river Bràdano, has a magnificent large Romanesque cathedral with bell tower, whose origins go back to the 11th-c; re-built in the 16th-c, the crypt contains restored frescoes. **Pietragalla**, with old dungeons dug out of the tuff.

Mount Pollino, the Sibaritide, and the Sila 75

Lagonegro - Sìbari - Rossano - Camigliatello Silano - Cosenza (261 km.)
This Calabrian symphony develops through three movements, as it were. The first is the Pollino, a vast massif, the southern terminus of thé Lucanian Apennines, largely stretching east to west, as if it were a barrier warning away would-be visitors to the region; geographers tell us that this is the southernmost Apennine group to show the marks of glacial activity, and for those who love nature, this is a harsh, powerful, solitary mountain, dotted with secluded and intact settings. This route runs across the southern slopes of it; it would be wise to base excursions out of Morano Calabro and Castrovìllari; from the geodetic beacon of the highest peak — Monte Pollino, known also as the Telegrafo (2,248 m.) — you can see the regions of Calabria and the Basilicata, the Tyrrhenian and the Ionian seas. The second phase takes us back to classical antiquity. Sybaris was an Achaean colony, wealthy from its silver mines (in what is now San Marco Argentano), a city of refined living, with probably the worst reputation of all of Magna Grecia, probably because it was defeated in war. The army of Crotone, in a campaign lasting 70 days, stormed the city, sacked it and plundered it, and then destroyed it entirely (510 B.C.). According to tradition, they then shifted the course of the river Crati to submerge the ruins. The search for the actual site of the city empassioned scholars and put archeologists to stern task for many years: now you can see and explore it. It was only discovered several decades ago, in a landscape altered by reclamation: 500 hectares of rolling plains, straddling the modern course of the river Crati about 4 km. from its mouth, where it empties into the gulf of Taranto. The third movement in the symphony involves a drive across the Sila. This area has been compared countless times to Switzerland, and with good reason! The first mention we are able to find was in the travel journal of the Marquis Adolphe de Custine, who ventured off the beaten track in Italy. Writing in 1812, he said that the Sila forest: "occupies a great expanse of mountainous terrain, its chestnut groves shade meadows and brooks, and the villages all show a freshness that makes it hard to believe that these Swiss scenes are located on the same latitude as Sicily [note: the Marquis errs here; the island is at least a degree further south]. This lovely forest is now a haven for the wealthy invalids of Cosenza and the poor brigands of all the Calabrias... I crossed it without incident, charmed by the pureness of the air and the beauty of the vegetation." Evocative words indeed.

The route. The first stretch of this route runs along the Salerno-Reggio Calabria Autostrada; you will leave the highway at the Morano-Castrovìllari exit. Take the ring road, and then the state road 19 to Morano and Castrovìllari. From here, you will proceed to Sìbari in the Piana del Crati, in part along secondary roads, driving down from Cassano to the Ionian Sea. Take the recently built coastal road, which runs some distance from the sea (state road 106 r); at Sìbari take the turnoff for Corigliano Calabro, which is an uphill drive; then take the old state road 106 as far as the Rossano turnoff. This little city marks the beginning of the last mountain route, running along the state road 177 through the Sila Greca, and reaching the highland of the Sila Grande at Camigliatello Silano (1,272 m.). You

will then continue along the western edge of the highland, finally taking the highway down to Cosenza.

Halting places of interest. Lagonegro, in a ring of mountains, on a slope of the Monte Sirino; at a distance of 2 km. in the Valle del Noce is a zoological park. **Morano Calabro** is scattered over a morainic hill, with lovely geometric buildings. **Castrovìllari,** at the base of the Monte Pollino (Parco Nazionale), with a 15th-c. castle in the old section, the church of S. Maria di Castello on a hill, and, on the Corso, or main boulevard, the Museo Civico. **Cassano allo Ionio,** dominates the plain of the river Crati; note the Museo Diocesano. **Sìbari:** the Museo della Sibaritide is found in the reclaimed village that bears the name of the ancient Greek colony; the archeological digs of Sybaris, Thurii, and Copia are further along, on the right of the road. **S. Maria del Patire*** is the solitary church of a long-vanished Basilian monastery founded in 1101-05; note in the interior the valuable mosaic floor with animal relief carvings of the 12th-c. Take a 7.5-km. detour through the woods after **Corigliano Calabro,** with notable view. **Rossano** overlooks the Ionian Sea from the furthest spur of the Sila Greca: the Byzantine church of S. Marco dates from the 11th c.; in the Museo Diocesano is the exquisite and rare Codex Purpureus. **Longobucco** is a village overlooking the wild gorges of the Trionto; artworks and fine furnishings are found in the churches and in the Museo Parrocchiale; wool, silk, and linen are hand-woven here. **Camigliatello Silano** is a resort area amid the woods of the Sila; you can take a cableway up to the **Monte Curcio** (1,760 m.); fine view. **Cosenza:** at the confluence of the rivers Busento and Crati, amid the highlands, with the dense old section at the base of the Colle Pancrazio and a Norman castle; in the Gothic Duomo is the 13th-c. tomb of Isabella of Aragon, queen of France.

Aspromonte

Reggio di Calabria - Gambàrie - Locri - Palmi - Reggio di Calabria (285 km.)

Although in Italian the "aspro," might seem to mean "harsh," the name actually comes from the Greek word *aspròs,* or "white." A cluster of gently rounded dome shapes (Montalto, 1,955 m.) stands at the center of a starburst-shaped plateau, whose spurs run down to the three coasts along the extremity of the peninsula. Even at considerable elevations, you can sense the cool air of the Tyrrhenian and or Ionian sea. Oaks and holm-oaks blanket the slopes of the mountain; higher up, pine trees and beeches are found; always, through the straight trunks of the trees, you can glimpse the sparking blue of the sea. The expanse of the Aspromonte is crossed by this route from south to north in the high sections, and from north to south along the coastline. We have already referred to the mountain; the other landscape, vineyard-bedecked hills with chestnut forests, huge hundred-year-old olive trees looking down on little harbors, the arid river beds, flowering with oleanders — all are surprising, "exotic" even to those from other parts of Italy. Here, for instance, are the impressions of the Parisian author Paul-Louis Courier who, as a soldier with a copy of Homer in his rucksack, marched through Calabria with Napoleon Bonaparte's expedition of 1805, which put Joseph Bonaparte on the throne of the Two Sicilies. From Reggio di Calabria Courier wrote, ("we are triumphant and on the move constantly, and we have stopped only here, where the land came to an end") in a letter to a lady back home: "the cities are in no way notable, at least to my eyes; but the countryside is remarkable. How can I describe it? It resembles nothing I have seen so far. Let us not even consider the orange groves and stands of lemon trees; there are so many other trees and exotic plants, which spring up in great profusion under the bright sunlight; or you may find the same species found in France, but growing larger and lusher here, giving the landscape an entirely different appearance. And when you see the crags, crowned everywhere with myrtle and aloe and palm trees in great ravines, you might think you were on the banks of the Ganges or Nile, except that there are no pyramids, nor elephants; instead there are water buffaloes, looking quite at home amidst the African plants; likewise the color of the inhabitants is not of our world...."

The route. You will leave Reggio di Calabria heading south, along Via Galilei, following the coast road (state road 106) as far as Mèlito di Porto Salvo. You will continue north along the state road 183 which climbs up the Aspromonte, and then you will cross over the pass of the Sella Entrata (1,408 m.), go through Gambàrie, and reach the Brandano turnoff. Here you will take the road that runs through Delianuova, Scido, and Santa Cristina d'Aspromonte, running over the watershed at Piano Zillastro (1,057 m.), and then descending to Platì and on to the Ionian coast along the Careri river valley. You will pass through Bovalino Marina, hugging the coast as far as Locri. Now you will begin climbing again, crossing the peninsula from the Ionian Sea to the Tyrrhenian Sea, first of all

on the state road 111 on the route through Gerace, over the Passo di Ropolà (465 m.) and the Passo del Mercante (952 m.), and Taurianova; just past this last town, you will take the road for Palmi. From Palmi you will return to Reggio di Calabria along the Costa Viola, on the state road 18, and after Villa San Giovanni, by Autostrada.

Halting places of interest. Reggio di Calabria: there is a fine view of both the strait and the Sicilian coast from the seafront promenade, along the elongated checkerboard of the city; note the bronze statues of Riace, rare Greek originals from the 5th c.B.C., in the Museo Nazionale. **Pentedàttolo*:** this village is perched atop a sandstone crag with five pinnacles (named after the Greeek *pentedàktylos*, meaning five fingers); an 11-km. detour starts 5 km. past Saline Ioniche. **Mèlito di Porto Salvo**,

where Garibaldi twice disembarked, renowned for its production of bergamot and hand made pipes. **Montalto:** a 13-km. detour starts about 4 km. past the Sella Entrata; this is the highest peak of the Aspromonte. **Gambàrie**, mountain holiday resort in the midst of green forests. **Cippo Garibaldi:** this stele marks the site on which the general who united Italy was wounded during a battle between his troops and the royalist soldiers commanded by General Pallavicini, on 29 August 1862; take a 1.5-km. detour from the village of De Leo. **Delianuova**, a resort amidst the olive groves; note the fine old artwork in the parish church. **Locri:** the museum and the excavations of the Greek colony of Locri Epizefiri can be found at Torre di Gerace, just outside of modern Locri. **Gerace** is a medieval town high on a crag overlooking the Ionian Sea, with a grand Byzantine-Norman-Swabian cathedral, the largest sacred monument in Calabria. **Palmi** overlooks the Marina and the Costa Viola from its high terrace; note the remarkable view all the way to Mt. Etna and the Aeolian Islands from **Monte Sant'Elia** (see Palmi), which you can reach via a 1.5-km. detour, from the state road toward Reggio. **Bagnara Calabra:** a fine sandy beach, and a town set between two rocky spurs. **Scilla:** a crag overlooking the sea, a castle, a lighthouse, and the Homeric reference to Scylla, the sea monster foiled by cunning Ulysses.

The coast of Sicily from Messina to Palermo   77

Messina - Milazzo - Cefalù - Palermo (371 km.)

The Tyrrhenian shoreline is the entrance to Sicily; here the island gives a first taste, a sampling, of many, if not all, its delights, evoking the counterpoint of literary accounts and recollections. Let's consider the plants: the ubiquitous prickly pear, or Indian fig, a harsh and bizarre piece of vegetal architecture, comes from Mexico, and has been here only since the 17th c.; in origin, the Mediterranean landscape of this ancient, timeless island, is that of grains, olive trees, and vineyards. The orange tree, on the other hand, enclosed with its dark-green foliage in secluded seafront gardens, dates from the Arab occupation: "Rejoice in the oranges that you have plucked," advises a poem of those centuries, "to have them is to have happiness. / All hail the pretty cheeks of the branch; all hail the glittering stars of the tree! / You might think that the heavens had rained down pure gold, and that the earth had then moulded that gold into glowing spheres." One of the first places you will encounter is Tindari, profoundly Greek in nature: the features of the island immediately remind the traveller of that other Mediterranean people, who sailed forth from their cramped archipelago in search of boundless horizons; a few lines of the poet Salvatore Quasimodo (Nobel laureate, 1959), were not long ago more famous than the place itself: "Tindari, mite ti so / fra larghi colli pensile sull'acque / dell'isole dolci del dio..." which translates as "Tindari, I know you are gentle, lying between broad hills, floating over the waters, of the gentle waters of the god..." Cefalù adds two more pieces to the game-board: the composite culture — Romanesque-Byzantine-Arab-Norman — of the cathedral, with its hieratic mosaics, and the sharp-eyed 15th-c. art of Antonello da Messina, painter of a portrait of a man with a distracting smile ("The interplay of resemblance is a delicate and exceedingly sensitive matter in Sicily, a form of research... Who does the unknown man of the Museo Mandralisca resemble?" — Leonardo Sciascia). Lastly, as you approach Palermo, you can explore the villas of Bagheria, the images of an aristocratic life of the past, "Gattopardi," or Leopards, as in the novel by Tomasi di Lampedusa, and viceroys; the surrealistic sculptures of Villa Palagonia, then as much as today, a must for sightseers. Goethe, a traveller who was also a contemporary of the man who ordered the creation of this villa, vents a page of spleen to it: to stroll amongst those "aberrations" gives one the "unpleasant sensation" of receiving "painful blows of madness."

The route. The coastal state road 113 runs parallel with the Autostrada. You will take the Autostrada for the first leg of the route, until you reach the Milazzo-Isole Eolie exit; then you will continue to Milazzo. On your way back, you will take the state road, following it all the way to Cefalù. Here you

will be leaving the coast to take a broad circuit through the Madonie, in part on secondary roads, on a route that runs through Cefalù, Castelbuono, Portella del Bafurco, the fork of Geraci, Petralìa Soprana and Petralìa Sottana, Polìzzi Generosa, and Collesano. You will return to the coast at Campofelice di Roccella, and a bit further along you will get on the Autostrada (Buonfornello interchange) that leads to Palermo. You will have to leave the Autostrada again, however, first to tour Tèrmini Imerese (exit of the same name) and again to take the scenic route to Capo Zafferano and Capo Mongerbino, and to tour Solunto and Bagherìa (Casteldaccia exit, get back on at the Bagherìa exit).

Halting places of interest. Messina*: this town overlooks the strait, with a modern appearance, the result of bombing and earthquakes; the famed astronomical clock of the Duomo, the Museo Regionale (among other things, note the polyptych by Antonello da Messina and canvases by Caravaggio), and the church of the SS. Annunziata dei Catalani are of interest. **Milazzo:** the walls of the old section of this strategically important town enclose the Renaissance style 17th-c. Duomo and the castle; at a distance of 6 km., from the lighthouse at the tip of the narrow peninsula, you will have a fine view from Mt. Etna to the Isole Eolie, or Aeolian Islands. **Villa Romana di San Biagio:** the ruins of this Roman villa, with mosaic floors, are uphill from San Biagio, an outlying quarter of Castroreale Terme. **Tìndari:** you will turn off the state road briefly at Locanda; alongside the ruins of Tyndaris, with Greek theater of the 2nd-3rd c. B.C. and basilica, there is a sanctuary on the site of the acropolis and a fine view of the coast. **Sant'Agata Militello:** beautiful beaches aside, the Museo Etno-Antropologico dedicated to the farming civilization of the Nèbrodi is worthy of attention. **S. Stefano di Camastra,** one of the most famous centers of ceramics production in Sicily. **Mistretta:** you will take a 17-km. detour after Santo Stefano di Camastra, on the Monti Nèbrodi; note an altarpiece by Antonello Gagini in the Chiesa Madre; also note other important churches, buildings, and artworks. **Cefalù*,** at the foot of a massive hill-sized boulder, has a superb Norman cathedral with renowned mosaics and fine works, in the Museo Mandralisca, at a distance of 15 km., note the Santuario di Gibilmanna. **Castelbuono,** is a small resort town in the Madonie; the Matrice Vecchia is a 14th-c. church; in the 14th-c castle, note the Museo Civico and the Cappella di S. Anna with stuccoes by Giuseppe and Giacomo Serpotta. **Petralìa Sottana** is a little resort town in the Madonie; here and uphill from here, in **Petralìa Soprana**, there are noteworthy artworks and architectural details in the churches; fine view of the Madonie, Monti Nèbrodi, and Mt. Etna from the Baroque church of S. Maria di Loreto. **Polìzzi Generosa** is yet another little resort town in the Madonie: note the Flemish triptych in the style of Memling in the church known as the Chiesa Madre. **Collesano** lies at the base of the Madonie, with the 16th-c. church of Matrice and fine artworks. **Ruins of Imera,** a Greek colony of Zancle (Messina); note the antiquarium; you will take a detour, continuing along the state road 113 beyond the interchange for the Autostrada at Buonfornello. **Tèrmini Imerese** has Roman ruins in the Villa Palmeri, the public gardens; at a distance of 10 km., note **Càccamo** (a name taken either from the Greek *kakkabe*, "partridge," or from the Punic *caccabe*, "horse's head," or from the Latin *cacabus*, "boiler"), with a large bastioned castle. **Solunto:** the Hellenistic-Roman ruins of this city founded by the Phoenicians stand on a spur of the Monte Catalfano, within sight of the sea. **Bagherìa:** among the aristocratic villas of this seaside town surrounded by citrus groves and vineyards, of particular architectural note are the Villa Valguarnera and the Villa Palagonia, with its odd statuettes.

Val di Mazara 78

Palermo - Álcamo - Trapani - Castelvetrano (194 km.)
The Arabs first set foot in Sicily in A.D. 827 at Mazara del Vallo, 205 years after the Hegira, and 116 years after Muslim troops invaded Europe across the Strait of Gibraltar; the conquest of the Byzantine-ruled island took some 75 years (the Norman warrior, Count Roger I of Altavilla, began his attack 234 years after the Saracens first landed, and finally expelled them from Sicily after thirty years of

fighting, in 1091). Under Arab rule, the great island was divided into the three "valli" of Mazara, Demone, and Noto. The Val di Mazara comprised the western end of the island; its boundary was a line drawn from a point on the northern coast between Tèrmini Imerese and Cefalù and Licata, on the southern coast. This route explores the westernmost section of the "vallo." There are three locations in the early section of this route that provide splendid instances of Sicily's originality: Monreale, Segesta, and Érice. In the first of the three, Arab-style stalactites hang down from the cross-vault of the Duomo amidst the glittering gold of the Byzantine style mosaics executed by Sicilian and Venetian master craftsmen; in Segesta the Doric enclosure of the temple of the Elimi features odd, unfluted columns, without any sign of the traditional cella; in upper Érice you are surrounded by a medieval atmosphere. This route passes through areas that figured in the saga of Garibaldi's unification of Italy: Marsala, where Garibaldi's army of Red Shirts landed; Calatafimi, where they fought their first battle; Álcamo and Partinico, through which the tiny army of liberation passed on its way to Palermo to face the 20,000 soldiers under Generale Lanza (Álcamo: The evocative palm fronds spread over the walls of the gardens here; every house has the appearance of a monastery; a pair of dark eyes flashes down from a high balcony; you stop, you look up, and the lovely apparition has vanished...," Giuseppe Cesare Abba, a soldier under Garibaldi). At Mazara in the narrow lanes of the old center, there is still a flavor of the Arab city; you can hear Arabic spoken by the Algerian and Moroccan sailors who work on the huge fishing fleet.

The route. In order to drive up to Monreale you will leave Palermo along Corso Calatafimi. From Monreale you will continue toward Partinico (state road 186), and from there you will head down to the Golfo di Castellammare, following the coast until you reach the turnoff for the road up to Álcamo. From here, the state road 113 will take you to Calatafimi. You retrace your route to tour Segesta, and then you take the entrance to the Autostrada toward Trapani. From the Trapani exit you will climb up to Érice, continuing on into the town of Trapani, and following the coast road to Marsala. With the state road 115 you will reach Mazara del Vallo; finally, you will take the Autostrada to Castelvetrano.

Halting places of interest. Monreale*: the Norman Duomo, covered with spectacular mosaics, and with a 12th-c. cloister with slender twin columns, is one of the finest medieval monuments in all Italy; at a distance of 10 km. is **San Martino alle Scale** (see Monreale), a resort set amidst pine groves, near a Benedictine abbey. **Álcamo**: this town features classic 14th-c. architecture and layout, with remarkable artworks in the old churches (note the S. Oliva by Antonello Gagini in the 18th-c. church of S. Oliva). **Calatafimi**, set on a ridge amongst hills, at the foot of the ruins of a castle; an Ossuary commemorating a battle in Garibaldi's Sicilian campaign (15 May 1860) stands on a rise at a distance of 4.5 km. **Segesta*:** take a short detour off the road between Calatafimi and the highway entrance; secluded on a high crag is the Doric temple of the ancient city of the Elimi, higher up is a Hellenistic theater, overlooking the distant sea; fine view. **Érice*** stands, medieval and silent in the triangle of walls that enclose it, atop a crag: of particular note in the charming setting are the 14th-c. church of Matrice and its campanile; also note the Annunciation by Antonello Gagini in the Museo Comunale, views of the sea and of the Isole Égadi from the outer roads; detour of 8 km., on the way to Trapani. **Trapani**, extending over a promontory, boasts the 18th-c. Santuario dell'Annunziata and the impressive Museo Regionale Pepoli (among the items on display are a painting by Titian and a beautiful statue of S. Giacomo by Gagini). **Mozia*:** you can take a boat out to the excavations and the museum of the ancient Phoenician city, on the island of San Pantaleo; detour for boat slip after San Leonardo. **Marsala:** the main square has Baroque monuments (note the Museo degli Arazzi Fiamminghi adjacent to the cathedral, with Flemish tapestries bestowed by Philip II of Spain); to the west of town, near the sea, note the Roman *insula* and the Punic *liburna* (in the Museo di Capo Lilibeo). **Mazara del Vallo:** this is an exceedingly active fishing port; in the intricate, Arab-built old town, note the cathedral (with Transfiguration, by Antonino Gagini, the little Norman church of S. Nicolò Regale, and the Museo Civico). **Rocche di Cusa**: take a 13-km. detour after Mazara del Vallo, passing through **Campobello di Mazara**; there are tufa quarries, and through the vegetation you can see the cuts where the stones of the temples of Selinunte were extracted. **Castelvetrano**, on a terrace over the coast, with a John the Baptist by Antonello Gagini in the church of S. Giovanni, along with other artworks and examples of sacred architecture; at a distance of 3.5 km to the west, note the 12th-c. Norman church of **SS. Trinità di Delia.**

The coast of Sicily from Castelvetrano to Gela

Castelvetrano - Sciacca - Agrigento - Gela (208 km.)

In 1875 Ernest Renan, professor of Hebrew at the Collège de France, was invited to Palermo to attend a scientific conference; among those present were Prince Umberto di Savoia, or Humbert of Savoy, the heir apparent to the Italian crown, and Ruggero Bonghi, minister of public education. Bonghi asked Renan to join the national commission on antiquities in a tour of "all the major ruins of Sicily," a tour to decide where archeological excavations should be concentrated. Renan accepted, and the scholars and scientists boarded the Archimede, a steamer that carried them from Trapani to Syracuse. Along the way, Renan and the others landed at Selinunte and travelled inland to Agrigento, the two most important stops on this route along the southern coast of Sicily, from Castelvetrano to Gela. We can only give you an impression of the Sicily that greeted their eyes in that long-ago year. At Selinunte "a fierce harsh sun (even though it was September), a land dried out by five months of heat, pierced only by a delightful little double white lily." Of the temples and their Doric capitals, he ventured: "in no other place can you so clearly see, step by step, the progress of these divine curves that so nearly reach perfection... Here is the miracle that only the Greeks managed to achieve: to find an ideal and, having found it, stick to it." Concerning a trip inland toward the sulfur-mining area, he wrote: "we saw Africa stretching before us on that day, in a range of hills burnt by sulfureous fumes, without trees, without greenery, without water." At Porto Empedocle Renan landed "under a portico decorated with statues of King Victor Emmanuel and Empedocles"; the name of Empedocles "is scattered through the public places as widely as is that of Garibaldi". The "rude journée" of tours also included a "cordial banquet offered by the people of Agrigento in the very midst of the ruins."

The route. Between Castelvetrano and Sciacca there are two roads, the state roads 115 and 188 bis: you will be taking the second one, built more recently, faster and further inland (on your way back from the detour to Selinunte you will find the interchange for state road 188 bis on your right, just past the junction with the state road 115). From Sciacca you will continue along a scenic secondary road to Caltabellotta, inland, then returning south to the sea, until you hit the state road 115 which, with the occasional detour, you will follow along the coast, though not actually on the water, through Porto Empedocle and Licata as far as Gela.

Halting places of interest. Castelvetrano: amidst olive groves and vineyards, this little town on a natural terrace boasts fine artworks set in its venerable old churches, and a noteworthy Museo Civico; at a distance of 3.5 km., note the Norman church of **SS. Trinità di Delia. Selinunte*:** you will take a 14-km. detour just after Castelvetrano; the columns of the Doric temples and the ruins of the acropolis, overlooking the sea, stand in an alluring coastal setting; the Greek colony of Megara Hyblaea was the westernmost of Sicily. **Menfi** is a village founded in the 17th c., with an orderly checkerboard layout; its blind alleys and courtyards however, still

breathe the air of the long-ago Arab domination. **Sciacca:** the Steripinto, a remarkable 15th-c. construction, was the "testa della corsa," or finish line for the races run with riderless Berber horses; high atop **Monte San Calogero** 388 m., at a distance of 7 km., note the pine grove, the sanctuary, and the "stufe vaporose" (caves with steam vapors), and the fine view. **Caltabellotta**, with its intense island atmosphere, extends over three rocky hills: venerable old churches with artworks, excellent view from the ruins of the castle. **Eraclea Minoa:** the ruins of this Greek city founded by the inhabitants of Selinunte and by Spartan settlers stands on the bare upland of Capobianco, high overlooking the sea; you will take a 4-km. detour just after the bridge over the river Plàtani. **Agrigento**:** the city extends over a spur dominating the Valle dei Templi, or Valley of the Temples, where an archeological walking tour leads you in succession to the Hellenistic-Roman quarter, to the church of S. Nicola, the Museo Archeologico Regionale, and lastly, the renowned Doric temples of Olympian Jove (Giove Olimpico), Hercules (Ercole), Concord (Concordia), and Juno (Giunone), exquisite relics of the Greek colony, scattered over a beautiful landscape. **Licata:** archeological finds from all over the territory in the Museo Civico, fine view from the **Castel S. Angelo. Gela*:** the city is modern in appearance although its origins can be traced back to a flourishing Greek colony founded in 689 B.C.; the relics of classical times are concentrated in the Museo Regionale Archeologico and the fortifications of Capo Soprano.

Siracusa - Palazzolo Acrèide - Caltagirone - Enna - Caltanissetta (203 km.)

Myths chase each other through the landscape of Trinacria, the ancient name for Sicily. The site where Pluto abducted the young girl Kore (or, variously, Persephone or Proserpina), daughter of Zeus and Demetra, as she sat amidst a company of nymphs, braiding garlands of flowers, lies in the heart of the island. Vincent Vivant, the Baron Denon, secretary of the French embassy to Naples, travelling through Sicily in 1788, expected in vain to see, in the area around Castro Giovanni (now Enna), "the plentiful waters form placid lakes, whose cool shores were always enameled with the delicate blooms of the plains," the "delightful" countryside where, for six months of every year, Artemis and Athena were said to have come to live. All the same, the Lago di Pergusa — the divine abduction supposedly occured here — still opens its bright blue eye beneath the towering bastions of the city walls of Enna. This route, which begins in Siracusa, leads to Enna, and then continues on to Caltanissetta (not far from the hills where sulphur was mined for eight decades, with a terrible toll in human health and life, until recent years), and then runs up over the ridges of the Monti Iblei, limestone plateaus broken only by the "cave," or gorges, narrow, deep, with sheer rock walls, dug out by rushing streams and mountain rivers. The road then passes over the terraces and rounded peaks of the Monti Erei, watershed between the Mar d'Africa, to the south, and the Ionian Sea, to the east. In various spots, you may explore specific sites or themes: at Pantàlica, the cliffside necropolis; the ruins of Akrai near Palazzolo Acreide; the 18th-c. architectural inventions of Caltagirone. Lastly, at the Casale di Piazza Armerina, you will see other myths depicted in the mosaic floors of the Roman villa: the struggle between Eros and Pan, Hercules, Ulysses and the Cyclops, Daphne, Endymion awaiting Selene, Arione riding a dolphin and playing a lyre.

The route. To reach the state road 124 that leads to Palazzolo Acreide via Floridia, you will leave Siracusa along Viale Paolo Orsi. You will continue along this same state road through Buccheri, Vizzini, Grammichele, Caltagirone, and San Michele di Ganzarìa. A little further along, at the Gigliotto crossroads, you will join the road from Gela (state road 117 bis), which will take you to Piazza Armerina and then on to Enna. About 12 km. past Piazza Armerina you will take a left through the Portella Grottacalda and then right at the Ramata crossroads, reaching Enna after driving past the Lago di Pergusa. From Enna you will take the Autostrada to Caltanissetta.

Halting places of interest. Siracusa**: in a hard-bitten defense of the town against a besieging force, Archimedes used an ingenious array of mirrors to focus the bright sunlight on the Roman ships commanded by Marcello, setting fire to the fleet, supposedly in the port between the island of Ortigia and the immense Greek colonial city on the coast; the ancient sites range from the Fonte Aretusa to the Castello Eurialo, alongside the well known monuments, the Galleria Regionale of Palazzo Bellomo (with the renowned Annunciation by Antonello da Messina), the archeological finds in the Museo Regionale, and the sun-bathed landscape — all offer material for patient, unforgettable explorations. **Necropolis of Pantàlica*:** you will take a 26-km. detour, turning off at a "cantoniera," or roadman's house, about 14 km. past Solarino, passing through Ferla; there are 5,000 tombs from the long-vanished, indigenous town of Hybla, carved into the rock walls rising sheer over the rivers Anapo and Calcinara. **Palazzolo Acreide*:** the archeological area of the Greek town of Akrai, founded by Siracusa in 664 B.C., lies on the Acremonte, a hill alongside the little 18th-c. town located in the Monti Iblei. **Grammichele:** the orderly late-17th-c. layout of this town extends from the perfect hexagon of the central square. **Caltagirone:** the "queen of the mountains," as the town is known, has an 18th-c. appearance and extends over three hilltops; the Palazzetto della Corte Capitaniale was built by

Antonuzzo and Gian Domenico Gagini, while the Gesù and S. Giacomo are Baroque churches; you can reach S. Maria del Monte by climbing up a stairway decorated with majolica tiles; there is a centuries-old local crafts tradition of ceramics. The Museo Regionale della Ceramica documents the history of Sicilian ceramics in general, dating back to prehistoric times. **Piazza Armerina*:** picturesque town located in the heart of Sicily; in the Baroque Duomo note an exquisite 15th-c. panel Crucifix. **Villa Romana del Casale****: at a distance of 5.5 km. from Piazza Armerina; the ruins give some indication of the manifold and vast complexity and luxury of a late-imperial country residence; the mosaic floors are astonishing, both in their expanse and in the variety of depictions. The **Lago di Pergusa** summons up images of the myth of Persephone - Prosperina stolen away by Hades; today a motor racing track encircles the lake. **Enna***, "belvedere," or vantage point, of Sicily, this town overlooks the Valle del Dittàimo from a lofty natural terrace; note the Museo Alessi and the Byzantine-Norman-Swabian Castello di Lombardia. **Caltanissetta**, a modern city set amidst the hills of Sicily's mining region; the Museo Civico, with archeological finds, and the Museo Minerario, or mining museum.

Italy and its Regions

An extraordinary variety of climate and land can be found in the 1,300-kilometer length (808 miles) of the boot-shaped peninsula that stretches out into the Mediterranean Sea, between Greece and Spain. Only a quarter of Italy's total surface area (301,270 square kilometers, equal to 139,087 square miles) is occupied by plains; more than 7,500 km. (4,660 mi.) of Italian coastline is pounded by the gentle waves of the coastal seas: Mar Ligure, Mar Tirreno, Mar Jonio, and Mar Adriatico (Ligurian Sea, Tyrhennian Sea, Ionian Sea, and the Adriatic Sea).

To the north the barrier of the Alps, a mountain chain that includes the tallest peak in Europe, Mont Blanc (4,807 m.), protects the peninsula from sudden changes in weather, as well as providing an immense reserve of hydroelectric power. The product of more recent geological formation, and with lower altitudes, the mountains of the Apennines extend from Genoa to Sicily (interrupted only by the Strait of Messina) and form the backbone of the entire country. From Naples to Sicily, the volcanoes are the warning lights of a land that still experiences eruptions and earthquakes.

Over 54 percent of the Italian population, which is now 56,411,290, is urban; the largest cities are in the north and in central Italy.

A referendum vote determined, in June 1946, that Italy become a Republic; its new Constitution, in January 1948, decreed that it be a Parliamentary Republic, run by a President, who has a seven-year term, and by two parliamentary bodies — Chamber of Deputies and Senate — whose members are chosen through general elections.

The Italian political system is unusual, neither unitary, nor federal, with political power wielded both by the Italian State and by the twenty-one regions; five of those regions (the border regions plus the two island regions) have special autonomy.

Regional sentiment runs quite strong in all of Italy, the heritage of Italy's history of division into a multitude of independent states, often warring one against another. The former capitals of these numerous states still have distinct identities; by and large we can sum them up as follows: bureaucratic and administrative activity in Rome, business and finance in Milan, intellectual activity in Florence, Bologna, and Padua. In the other major cities, Turin, Genoa, Naples, and Palermo, manufacturing and service industries coexist.

The transformation of the economy, from agrarian to industrial, which began at the end of the Second World War, is further shifting toward service industries. Among the unresolved economic problems that still challenge the country is the difference of living standards between north and south, a particularly stubborn problem, and unemployment among the young.

Abruzzo

With a surface area of 10,794 sq. km., Abruzzo has a population of 1,243,690, with a population density of 115 persons per sq. km., some 40 percent that of the Italian national average. The territory lies almost entirely along the Adriatic side of the peninsula, and extends some 130 kilometers along the coast, between the mouths of the rivers Tronto and Trigno (with Ortona and Pescara as the main ports). Part of the central Apennines, the mountains — the largest and most complex group in peninsular Italy — appear as an array of massifs, separated by hollows and high valleys, in three distinct lines parallel to the Adriatic Sea: in the easternmost line are the largest massifs (Monti della Laga, the Gran Sasso d'Italia, Mt. Maiella); towering over 2,000 meters are the chains in the middle line, with the Monte Velino and Monte Sirente; the westernmost peaks, lowest and most broken up, include the Monti Simbruini, Monti Èrnici, and Monti della Meta, looming over Lazio. Stunning landscapes of harsh limestone are broken by the occasional vast "conca," or valley (those of L'Aquila, Sulmona, and Fùcino) and by the "piani" (flat uplands ringed by mountains, such as Rocca di Mezzo and Cinquemiglia). There are many karstic phenomena, with dolinas, caverns, and sinkholes. The economy is primarily agrarian: wheat (especially in the Fùcino valley), market gardens, especially along the coast, grape vines, olive groves and fruit orchards, and, in the valley around L'Aquila, saffron; sheep herding is in decline, though the nomadic herding traditions were once very important here. Note the divisions in the labor force: 12 percent agriculture, 28.4 percent industry, and 59.6 percent in service industries (national data, respectively, 9, 32, 59 percent). Industry is concentrated along the lower course of the river Pescara (Chieti Scalo-Pescara). Much of the service industry revolves around mountain and ski resorts, and especially beach resorts. L'Aquila is the regional capital; the provincial capitals are Chieti, Pescara, and Teramo.

History. Bellicose Italic tribes — the Picenti, Pretuzi, Marrucini, Peligni, Vestini, Marsi, and Equi — withstood Roman conquest, like the Samnites of nearby Molise (turn of the 3rd c. B.C.) and took part in the rebellion of 90 B.C. (Social Wars). The name first appeared, in the form "Aprutium," indicating the area around Teramo, when the Longobards included it in the region around the duchy of Spoleto. Pope Adrian IV, in the 12th c., gave it in fief to William I, the Bad, king of Sicily, but the Normans gained a foothold in the Molise; thus Abruzzo became part of the long-lasting "regno meridionale," or "southern kingdom," until it became part of Italy in 1860 (geographically, the entire region is actually north of Rome). There is some debate as to whether the foundation of L'Aquila should be attributed to Frederick II or Pope Gregory IX, though the latter seems more likely. Near Tagliacozzo (1268) Conradin, the last Swabian, was defeated and captured, due to the growing strength of the Anjou dynasty. In the wars that followed the murder (1345) of Andrew of Hungary, husband of Jane I queen of Naples, Abruzzo was split up into quarrelsome factions. At the turn of the 15th c., the attempt of the condottiere Braccio da Montone to establish a kingdom in central Italy ended with his defeat and death under the walls of L'Aquila (1424). The "southern kingdom" then fell to Aragon (1442); to the Spanish, following "Italian Wars" against the French; the Austrians for a short interval following the War of Spanish Succession (early-18th c.); and lastly the house of Bourbon, from 1735 until Italian Unity (under Napoleonic rule, when under Joaquim Murat the secretary of public education was the poet Dante Gabriele Rossetti of Vasto, later an exile in London).

Art. Dating back to the Italic culture is the renowned warrior of Capestrano, in the Museo Archeologico Nazionale in Chieti; Roman ruins are found in Chieti, Teramo, "Amiternum," and "Alba Fucens." An intense and original artistic period ran from the 11th to the 14th c.; during this time, with a mixture of styles, among the projects built were the cathedrals of Atri, Teramo, and Chieti; the abbeys of S. Clemente a Casàuria, S. Maria Arabona, and S. Giovanni in Venere; and other notable churches, such as S. Pietro presso "Alba Fucens," S. Pelino in Corfinio, S. Giusta in Bazzano, S. Maria in Valle Porclaneta; distinctive architectural features include rectangular facades with straight tops, such as that found in S. Maria di Collemaggio at L'Aquila, and, in the decoration, the carved ambo. Sulmona and Guardiagrele were major centers for goldsmiths until the 16th c. Andrea De Litio (15th c.), who painted the frescoes in the cathedral of Atri, was the greatest Abruzzese painter. After marginal participation in the Renaissance (among the scattered examples, note the Palazzo dell'Annunziata in Sulmona, the facade of the church of S. Bernardino in L'Aquila, where the Tuscan-style sculptor Silvestro dall'Aquila worked), the Baroque style of Naples and Rome prevailed. The painting of the 19th c. includes work by Francesco Paolo Michetti, and the brothers Giuseppe, Filippo, and Francesco Paolo Palizzi.

Alto Adige / Südtirol

This is a semi-independent province, with its capital at Bolzano, of the specially chartered region of Trentino-Alto Adige, established in 1948. This is a land of two tongues (Italian and German), while a few valleys are Ladino in culture. This province covers the southern slopes of the "Alpi Atesine," comprising the basin of the river Adige as far as the Alpine watershed, including the northernmost point in all Italy (Vetta d'Italia; 2,912 m.). Primarily mountainous, it includes notable Dolomitic groups (Sella, Scìliar, Sassolungo, Odle, Puez, Catinaccio-Latemar, Tre Cime di Lavaredo). The landscape is famous: steep slopes and sheer faces give way to great gentle hollows and rolling high meadows (Merano, Bressanone, Vipiteno), high pastures (Renon, Alpe di Siusi), and high massifs looming over fir woods or harsh rock slides, mirrored in calm clear little lakes (Carezza, Bràies).

The landscape dictates the economy: agriculture dominates, especially fruit orchards (more than a third of Italy's apples grow here) and vineyards; livestock; lumber; with most industry in Bolzano (wood carving flourishes in Val Gardena); tourism (summer resorts, mountain climbing, hiking, winter sports).

History. In Roman times, this province was split up into the regions of Venetia, Rhaetia, and Noricum. When the Baiuvari, following the death of Theodoric, invaded the land that took their name (Bavaria), they also poured into modern Tyrol and, on the Italian side of the Alpine watershed, into the valleys of the Isarco and the Pusteria. A number of other historical episodes enhanced the German flavor of this region. Conrad II, in 1027, created the episcopal principality of Bressanone; the counts of Venosta gradually accumulated power among the secular feudal lords, and from 1140 on, they added Tyrol to their title, ruling from a castle above Merano. The country passed, through various bloodties, to the counts of Gorizia, and then to the Hapsburgs

(1363), who in time brought this with them into their empire. The vicissitudes of the Napoleonic Wars upon the House of Austria led to the secularization of the episcopal principality (1803) and to its annexation as part of Austria, while the Tyrol (including the modern-day province of Bolzano) was made part of Bavaria (Treaty of Pressburg, 1805). The brief annexation to Bavaria, a French ally, was marked by the insurrection (1809) led by Andreas Hofer, a patriot of the Val Passiria, who was later shot by a firing squad in Mantua, and is still considered a Tyrolian national hero. The territory then fell under Austrian rule, following the overthrow of Napoleon, and was incorporated into the province of Innsbruck; then it became part of Italy, at the end of WWI (1918), along with Trentino; the belief that the boundary along the Alpine watershed would simplify things failed to take into account the problems posed by the presence of different language groups.

Art. This land on the boundary between two universes — Latin and Germanic — has an exquisite artistic heritage: frescoes of the High Middle Ages, in S. Procolo at Naturno, and of Carolingian times in S. Benedetto at Màlles; then Romanesque sculpture in Castel Tirolo (see Merano) and the frescoes of Monte Maria di Burgusio (see Màlles Venosta), Castel Appiano, and S. Giovanni in Bressanone.

The Gothic style looked outside of Italy for its inspiration, as one can see in the cathedrals of Bolzano and Merano, the many churches with the high spires of their bell towers and their steep roofs, the castles, the "chivalric" paintings of Castel Ròncolo, the frescoes of the cloister of Bressanone, and the common tradition of carved and painted altars (though Bolzano vaunts its frescoes by Giotto).

Bound up between Italian and German traditions, the greatest artist this land produced was the late-15th-c. painter and sculptor Michael Pacher. This two-fold aspect reappears in the Renaissance and the Baroque of the cathedral of Bressanone and the abbey of Novacella.

Basilicata

This is one of the smallest Italian regions (surface area 9,992 sq. km., roughly a 30th of Italy's total territory), and is the 3rd from the last in population (605,940 inhabitants; population density 60 persons per sq. km.,). Bordered by Puglia, Campania, and Calabria, it overlooks the Ionian Sea, the Gulf of Taranto, and has a small stretch of Tyrrhenian coastline in the Gulf of Policastro. Largely mountainous (flatlands amount to 8 percent), the Basilicata has a number of high peaks to the west, a continuation of the ranges of Campania, while in the center there are mountains no taller than 2,000 meters (Volturino, 1,836 m.) and to the south, higher mountains (Sirino, 2,005 m., Pollino, 2,267 m.); the ancient former volcano of the Vùlture (1,326 m.), in the northern part of the region, rises with a green mantle of grapevines and olive groves; above them are chestnut woods, and higher still, turkey oaks and beech trees. In the eastern section, clay, marls, sandy lowlands run down — crisscrossed by the broad valleys of the rivers Sinni, Agri, Basento, and Bràdano — toward the uniform sand beaches of the Ionian Sea. The labor force is divided thus: 21.62 percent in farming, 26.63 percent in industry, 51.75 percent in service industries (national data, respectively, 9, 32, 59 percent). This indicates the importance of agriculture, though yields are still relatively low, up from traditional levels. Grains, sugar beets, potatoes, vegetables on the valley floors, olives, grapes, and — a recent innovation along the Ionian coast, fruit orchards — make up the agricultural landscape. Traditional processing of agricultural products has been joined, in recent decades, by other more industrial activites in Potenza and Matera, along the Ionian coast, and — most recently — in Melfi, as well as the older and better known chemical and machine-tool industries of the Valle del Basento between Ferrandina and Pisticci, the result of hydrocarbon deposits. There are fine crafts products (hand-woven cloth, terracotta, carved woods), though this sector is declining. Tourism, and especially beach resorts, has been encouraged by improvements in transportation (Ionian coast road, Basento highway) and by reclamation. Coastal and low-valley areas have been developed, while the old mountain towns are suffering; the reverse of what happened when the coastal cities of Magna Graecia were abandoned dozens of centuries ago, due to flooding, malaria, pirate raids. Potenza is the regional capital, while the second provincial capital is Matera.

History. The Ionian coast was first settled by Greek colonists in the 8th and 7th c. B.C., with the foundation of the cities of Metapontos and Siris, later Eraclea. Emerging from the hinterland, the Lucani ousted the Hellenic peoples in the 6th c. B.C. Under the Roman empire (the Lucani allied with Rome in 298 B.C., but the area had to be reconquered following the great battle with the troops of the king Pyrrhus, who attained one of his proverbial victories on the river Siris in 280 B.C.), this territory was part of the Regio Lucania et Bruttii, and with the decline of the empire, and the spread of malaria, the region declined. The Longobards joined part of this region to the Duchy of Benevento, and it was then almost entirely incorporated (847) in the principality of Salerno. Byzantine rule (9th/10th c.) was restored (the name of the Byzantine governor, "basilikos," is the source of the name Basilicata). The castle of Melfi, the first Norman stronghold, witnessed great moments of Norman and Swabian history: the coronation of Robert Guiscard (1059); feudal homage paid to the new king, Roger II (1129); and the promulgation by Frederick II of Swabia of the "Constitutiones regni," basis of the southern kingdom. But in this new southern kingdom, with its capital first in Palermo, later in Naples, the Basilicata was on the outskirts, ruled by high-handed

barons. For seven centuries, under Normans, Swabians, Anjou, Aragon, French, Spanish, and the Bourbons, the Basilicata felt only distant shocks and echoes. It joined the Kingdom of Italy in 1860.

Art. Basilicata has yielded an abundance of archeological material from early times and classical antiquity; much of this material can be seen in the museums of Potenza, Matera, Melfi, Metaponto, and the Siritide; there are few surviving monuments from Greek settlement (the "Tavole Palatine" and other relics in Metaponto) or Roman times (amphitheater of Venosa). In the Middle Ages, certainly a livelier time for art and architecture, the region borrowed shapes and styles from Puglia, Campania, Sicily, and even from France. In the Romanesque period (11th/13th c.) the two most notable monuments follow the French style: the abbey of the Ss. Trinità in Venosa and the Cathedral of Acerenza; the Duomo di Matera is Pugliese in style, while there is clear Sicilian influence in the campanile of the Duomo di Melfi; there are other French references in the Castello di Lagopésole, the hunting lodge of Frederick II. Among the Gothic monuments (13th/14th c.) note the cathedral of Rapolla, the Duomo di Atella, the campanile of the Cathedral of Irsina, the church of S. Giovanni in Matera. There is not much Renaissance art and architecture, though there is some Venetian art: by Bartolomeo Vivarini in Matera, by Cima da Conegliano in Migliònico. During the Baroque period, all art was Neapolitan in style.

Calabria

With a surface area of 15,080 sq. km., equal to roughly 1/20th of Italy's territory (the population is 2,037,686, with a population density of 135 per sq. km.), Calabria consitutes the southernmost extremity of the Italian peninsula, and is itself a long peninsula jutting between the Tyrrhenian and Ionian seas. Narrow plains cover less than 9 percent of the total surface area (plains of Sìbari, Sant'Eufemia, and Gioia), while the rest is mountainous. The mountains have an odd shape: rounded or flattened ridges, dramatic valleys cutting sharply into the slopes, and at the valley bottoms, broad "fiumare," cobble-strewn riverbeds that flood crazily from time to time, but are usually dry, blooming with oleanders. To the north, the mountains of Calabria join with the main peninsular mountain range (group of Monte Pollino; 2,267 m.), from which the Catena Costiera (coastal range) extends southward along the Tyrrhenian, ranging in altitude from 1,300 to 1,500 meters. To the east, riven by the course of the river Crati, rise the wooded highlands of the Sila, with a high point in the Monte Botte Donato (1,928 m.), the heart of the regional mountain range. To the south of the isthmus between the two gulfs of Sant'Eufemia and Squillace, the elevations continue with the range of the Serre (1,000-1,400 m.), linked to the massif of the Aspromonte (Montalto, 1,955 m.), the last mountain in the peninsula. The statistics concerning the division of labor show that the region still has a considerable number of agricultural workers, the highest in Italy (21.77 percent), and the lowest percentage of industrial workers (18 percent), while service industries claims a slightly higher percentage (60.13 percent) than the national average (national data, respectively, 9, 32, 59 percent). Calabria has the highest rate of unemployment in Italy (one person out of work for every three jobholders) as well as the lowest per capita income; more people emigrated during the 1960s than from any other region. Agriculture is hindered by the mountainous terrain; it should come as no surprise that the best yields are found along the coasts or in the flatlands; among the crops are citrus fruits, especially bergamot, olive groves, grains, vegetables and fruit, grapevines, chestnuts, figs (Cosenza); recently, greenhouse flowers and plants have become a popular crop. Forestry — of particular importance in the Sila area — offers lumber for building. The effort to industrialize, encouraged by the government, has had uneven results; the leading industrial town is Crotone, while others are Vibo Valèntia Marina, Catanzaro Marina, Lamezia, and Praia a Mare (a steelmill planned for Gioia Tauro has been replaced by a power plant). One major local activity is the production of citrus extracts and the distillation of essence of bergamot and jasmine, found in the area around the Strait. Swordfish offers renowned fishing, though this area produces only 1.7 percent of Italy's fish. Among the crafts industries are ceramics, carved wood, tapestries, carpets, blankets, and handwoven cloth. Recently tourism has been growing, especially along the spectacular beaches; it has been encouraged by improvements in the road sys-

tems. The regional capital is Catanzaro, while the provincial capitals are Reggio di Calabria, Cosenza, and the two new ones, Crotone and Vibo Valèntia.

History. In antiquity, this region was part of Magna Graecia, and Greek colonists founded Sìbari, Crotone, Caulonia (Monasterace Marina), Locri Epizephyri, Medna (near Nicòtera), Ipponio (Vibo Valèntia), and Rhegion (Reggio). Roman consuls celebrated their triumph over Lucania and Bruzio — Bruzio was the ancient name of Calabria — in 273-272 B.C.; the conquest had been the result of the help given by the locals to Pyrrhus, king of Epirus, who passed into Italy to support the Greeks of Tarentum (Taranto), but it was only consolidated following the Second Punic War, when the Bruzi sided with Hannibal. In the division of Italy under Augustus, this area formed part of the Regio Lucania et Bruttii. The territorial unity was broken by the Longobards who brought the area around Cosenza into the duchy of Benevento, then (847) into the principality of Salerno; the rest of the region remained under Byzantine rule, the "thema di Calabria" (this land was given this name in the second half of the 7th c. or the beginning of the 8th c.). In the first half of the 9th c., the Arabs occupied much of the coastline and raided the interior, but then under Nicephorus II Phocas the Byzantines regained control over the region (9th/10th c.): the Byzantine imprint can still be seen. The Norman conquest took place in the 11th c.; thus the region became part of the larger body of the "southern kingdom," with which it became a pawn of larger forces (the chronology runs as follows: after the Normans, the Swabians from 1194, the Anjou from 1266, the house of Aragon from 1442, Spanish viceroys in Naples from the 16th c. on, and the house of Bourbon from 1735 on). Isolation, the subalternate status, and feudal barony weighed on the region. Only Cosenza enjoyed prosperity and a certain autonomy, in the 14th c., with a further cultural flourishing later on (16th c.) when Bernardino Telesio founded an academy in his city. Tommaso Campanella, author of the City of the Sun, a utopian description of an ideal state, was born in Calabria. In 1799, Cardinal Fabrizio Ruffo, from San Lucido, vicar general of the ousted king of Naples, led Calabria in rebellion, and with his bands of "Sanfedisti," took Naples, setting up the Repubblica Partenopea; in the decade of Napoleonic rule (1806-1815), with Joseph Bonaparte ruling in Naples, followed by Joaquim Murat, the region's border-state status (Sicily remained under Bourbon rule, with British protection) encouraged pro-Bourbon brigandage; in the Castello di Pizzo, on 31 October 1815, a firing squad of Bourbon troops shot Murat, who had unwisely landed in the hopes of leading an impossible popular uprising; during the Restoration, there was a spread of revolutionary "Carboneria," but the revolution — announced by Mazzini — failed to materialize when the Venetian brothers Attilio and Emilio Bandiera landed, in the company of a few supporters; they were soon captured and shot, near Cosenza. In 1848 a peasant uprising took place, but the Bourbon regime collapsed just twelve years later, when Garibaldi and his troops moved through Calabria toward Naples; the region joined Italy in 1860.

Art. The archeological treasures of the museum of Reggio di Calabria — where the celebrated bronzes of Riace are on display — as well as the lesser collections of Sibari, Crotone, Catanzaro, Locri, Vibo Valèntia, and Cosenza, all document the ancient artistic culture of the region; excavations still under way have unearthed considerable sections of ancient Greek Locri; a Doric column from the sanctuary of Hera Lacinia still stands by the sea at Capo Colonna, near Crotone; ruins of Greek Sybaris and Roman Copia can be seen in the plain of Crati, Greek walls can be seen at Vibo Valèntia and along the seafront, at Reggio. Ruins of Roman baths (Reggio), theaters (Gioiosa Ionica), and bridges are also present. Peculiar to the region and linked to the long dependency on Byzantium are the exquisite Byzantine relics: the purple evangelary of Rossano (6th c.) certainly comes from the Greek East; Byzantine architecture can be found in buildings from the 9th/12th c., such as the baptistery of Santa Severina, the domed church of the Cattolica at Stilo, and the church of S. Marco at Rossano; elsewhere Byzantine elements coexist with other Romanesque features, as in the Roccelletta near Squillace, in the cathedrals of Gerace and Tropea. Gothic churches — the style first appeared in this region at the turn of the 13th c. — are numerous; among them note the cathedral of Cosenza and S. Maria di Altomonte. The style of the Renaissance, rather than in such buildings as S. Michele in Vibo Valèntia, can be seen in paintings such as those by Antonello da Messina in Reggio and by Bartolomeo Vivarini in Morano Calabro, and in sculptures from the Neapolitan school or by the Palermitan sculptor Antonello Gagini. In the 17th/18th c., a great many churches, monasteries (Certosa di Serra San Bruno), and baronial palaces were built, following disastrous earthquakes, largely in the Neapolitan-inspired Baroque style. Neapolitan painting of the 17th c. featured work by the vigorous Calabrian artist Mattia Preti, from Taverna; Futurism boasted the work of the painter and sculptor Umberto Boccioni, from Reggio.

Campania

Occupying less than 1/20th of Italy's territory (area 13,595 sq. km.) and, in population, second only to Lombardy (pop. 5,589,587, nearly a quarter of which is in the regional capital, Naples), Campania has one of the highest population densities of all the regions of Italy (411 inhabitants per sq. km.). Its Tyrrhenian coastline extends from the river Garigliano to the Gulf of Policastro, bounded inland by a line separating it from Lazio, Molise, Puglia, and Basilicata. Inland from the largely level coastal strip, which is broken here and there by volcanic features (Monte Roccamonfina, 1,005 m., Phlegraean Fields, Mt. Vesuvius) and mountains of sedimentary origin (Monti Lattari, 1,443 m. on the Sorrento peninsula) is the mountainous hinterland, complex in structure, broken up into chaotic massifs (Monte Miletto, 2,050 m. and the group of the Matese, Monte Taburno, 1,394 m., and the group of the Picentini, 1,089 m., Monti Alburni, 1,742 m., Monte Cervati, 1,898 m. in the Cilento area), separated by interior watercourses (Benevento, Avellino) that create a complex hydrographic system. Among the main rivers are the Tyrrhenian Garigliano, Volturno, and Sele, whose courses are only partly in Campania; pleasant agricultural areas in the provinces of Benevento and Avellino belong to the Adriatic watershed, with the waters of the rivers Fortore, Cervaro, and Ofanto. The landscape is varied, especially around the gulf of Naples and the gulf of Salerno: the alternation of plain, hill, and mountain, jagged coastline, a flourishing vegetation, luminous sea, and the islands of Capri, Ischia, and Pròcida create views, dramatic expanses, settings that are always equal to their celebrated reputations. The economic and social structure, as seen in the breakdown of the labor force (11.58 percent in farming, 24 percent in manufacturing, 64.42 percent in service industries, as compared with national data, respectively, of 9, 32, 59 percent) shows the importance of farming in this region (the percentage is 3.5 times that of Lombardy, for example) and the minor role of manufacturing. It should be noted moreover that Campania is the region with the third-highest level of unemployment, after Calabria and Sicily. In the area of farming, the renowned fertility of the land of Campania is concentrated in zones with ancient agrarian traditions, such as the Terra di Lavoro and the Agro Sarnese-Nocerino, where fruit and vegetables are the chief crops (the tomato is king); there are also areas which have been more recently reclaimed, such as the plains of the Sele and the lower Volturno-Garigliano; here vegetable gardens alternate with wheat and other grains; other level inland plains, such as the Valle Caudina and the Vallo di Diano have much lower yields. There are grapevines on the volcanic slopes, citrus orchards and olive groves in the Sorrento peninsula and at Bàcoli, walnut trees in the Sorrento

peninsula, hazelnuts in the areas around Avellino and Nola, elsewhere peach, apple, and apricot orchards; hemp is grown at Aversa (a declining crop), tobacco in the area around Caserta, Benevento, and Salerno. Statistics show that the region has solid standing in the national agricultural market: first place in the production of almonds (43 percent of the Italian total) and potatoes (24.6 percent), second place in the production of peaches (27 percent). Manufacturing is concentrated in Naples and Salerno; the Italian government's efforts to encourage southern economic development in past decades has led to the construction of enormous steelmills in Bagnoli and Torre Annunziata, machine-tool plants in Pozzuoli, and car and airplane factories in Pomigliano d'Arco and Avellino; all these plants are experiencing economic difficulties. Among the distinctive craft industries are that of leather and fine leather goods, in Naples; processing of coral and mother-of-pearl in Torre del Greco; inlays in Sorrento; and ceramics in Vietri. Naples is a major business and commercial center, a major Mediterranean port, especially for passenger traffic, even though it is only the third largest port on the peninsular Tyrrhenian coast and ninth-largest in Italy in terms of volume of goods. In terms of art, archeology, natural attractions, and lovely vacation spots, the region contains some of the most celebrated and popular tourist spots in Italy, and even in Europe. Naples, third-largest Italian city in terms of population, is the regional capital; the other provincial capitals are Avellino, Benevento, Caserta, and Salerno.

History. Greek colonists settled on the coasts of Campania beginning in the 8th c. B.C. at Cumae, the first city of Magna Graecia, Parthenope later "Neapolis" (Naples), Posidonia (Paestum), Elea (Velia), and elsewhere. In the fertile plains of the hinterland, the Etruscans pushed southward, and in the 6th c. B.C. founded Capua; from the mountain ridges the Samnites looked grimly down; Capua yielded to Roman rule in 330 B.C. in order to have protection from the Samnites, and the defense of Campania was the prime motive behind the "Samnite Wars" and the Romanization of the region. "Campania Felix" was a choice resort for Roman emperors, due to the natural beauty of the area. Augustus made it part of Latium; Diocletian separated it again. Territorial unity broke down under Longobard rule: much of the hiterland came under the duchy of Benevento (A.D. 570), which later absorbed Salerno as well; in 846 Salerno established itself as an independent principality, and another Longobard principality formed at Capua in A.D. 900, extended its control over Benevento. Byzantine rule meanwhile survived in the duchy of Naples, though the territory was increasingly detached from the metropolis, while Amalfi, having broken free from Longobard rule, was prospering from maritime trade, enjoying a splendid period as a "maritime republic" (9th/11th c.). A duke of Naples, in recognition of the assistance given against the Longobards, ceded (1030) to the Norman Rainulfo Drengot the county of Aversa, the first Italian territory held by those warriors; next came the eleven brothers of the Altavilla family; in the course of just a few decades during the turbulent high Middle Ages, during that family and the Normans in general became lords of Campania (Capua 1062, Salerno 1070, Amalfi 1137, Naples 1139) and all of southern Italy. The history of Campania mingled from then on with that of the "southern kingdom" (successively: Kingdom of Sicily, Kingdom of Naples, and the Kingdom of the Two Sicilies). Rule fell to a succession of Normans, Swabians (from the end of the 12th c.) Anjou (from the second half of the 13th c.) who made Naples the capital of the kingdom, and Aragon (from 1442). The "crisis of Italian liberty," with the easy triumph of Charles VIII of France (1494) and the Franco-Spanish War led to a long period of Spanish rule (1503-1734), during which a viceroy governed in Naples. After the kingdom was assigned to Charles of Bourbon, great-grandson of the Sun King and the son of a Farnese lady, the period of Bourbon rule — save for the intervals of the Parthenopean Revolutionary Republic, 1799, and the Napoleonic viceroys Joseph Bonaparte and Joaquim Murat, 1806-1815 — lasted from 1734 until the triumphant entrance into Naples of Giuseppe Garibaldi, 7 September 1860, confirming shortly thereafter by plebiscite the union of the region with the Kingdom of Sardinia. The establishment of the kingdom of Italy worsened social problems in the south. The capitalist-oriented economy of the new state replaced the more modest self-sufficient economy of the Bourbon reign, thus resulting in a disequilibrium which, to this very day, lies at the very heart of the so called "questione meridionale" (question of the Southern Italy).

Art. Classical antiquity offers unique testimonials in Campania, such as the archeological sites of Paestum, Cumae, Pompeii, Herculaneum, the Roman amphitheaters of Pozzuoli and Santa Maria Capua Vètere, the ruins of the imperial palace at Baiae, the Arch of Triumph of Benevento, the villas of Capri, the bridge of Sessa Aurunca, and the artworks in various museums, foremost among them the museum of Naples, certainly one of the leading archeological museums on earth. There are monuments of early Christian art, such as the baptistery of S. Giovanni in Fonte and the catacombs of S. Gennaro in Naples and S. Maria Maggiore in Nocera, and the basilicas of Cimitile; dating from the era of Longobard rule, there are traces in Capua and Benevento (S. Sofia). A remarkable period of creativity began in the 11th c., continuing until the 13th c.: it produced churches and cathedrals at Sessa Aurunca, Capua, Sant'Angelo in Formis, Caserta Vecchia, Salerno, Amalfi, and Ravello, in which we find an artistic culture that blends classical, Byzantine, Lombard, and Arabo-Norman styles, with notable sculpture in the pulpits, ambos, and bronze doors. A precious document of Byzantine-Cassinese art is the series of frescoes on the walls of the church of Sant'Angelo in Formis. In the 13th c. the house of Anjou summoned French architects, who brought with them the Gothic style; likewise the house of Aragon summoned Catalonian master builders. Naples became the capital of this southern kingdom, thus acquiring the artistic supremacy that it maintained thereafter. Outside of Naples, examples of Catalonian Gothic architecture can be found in Capua and Cariñola. Renaissance and Baroque in this region were but a modest reflection of the work being done in the capital; the Palazzo Reale di Caserta, the only original monument built in the provinces, is a major work of Italian 18th-c. architecture.

Emilia-Romagna

Italy's sixth-largest region, Emilia-Romagna occupies just over a thirteenth of the country's area, or 22,123 sq. km. Placing eighth in population, with 3,899,170 inhabitants, Emilia-Romagna has a population density of 178 per sq. km. It extends south from the Po, to the high crest of the Apennines, and as far as Cattolica on the Adriatic coast. The SE section is Romagna; the name once indicated the distinction between Byzantine, or Roman, territory, from the land of the Longobards. The Via Emilia runs with considerable precision along the natural boundary between plains and greater elevations. The plains are alluvial, fed by Apennine torrents. On the northern coast of this region, the so-called Valli di Comacchio are shallow lagoon areas, long-ago deltas of the Po, abounding in fish.

The northern slopes of the Apennines form a mountainous and hilly area, some 40 km. in width, crisscrossed by spurs and ridges, largely between 1,000 and 2,000 m. in height (the highest point is Monte Cimone, 2,165 m.).

Only in southern Italy is there a higher proportion of farmers (nearly 10 percent here); and yet in Emilia-Romagna, agriculture is almost an industry, run with modern efficiency. This region leads the nation in production of soft wheat, sugar beets, peaches, and wine (15 percent of the Italian total). Thriving livestock production yields fine cheeses and salami (the name Bologna says it all). The coastlines are rich in fish.

Industry is rich and varied, here. The knitwear of Carpi, the ceramic tiles of Sassuolo, the ceramics of Faenza, and Ferrari in Maranello. Ravenna is a busy port city. Tourists are drawn chiefly by the beach resorts of Romagna's coast, though art, spas, and the mountains are also attractions. Bologna is the regional capital, while the other eight provinces are those of Ferrara, Forlì-Cesena, Modena, Parma, Piacenza, Ravenna, Reggio nell'Emilia, and Rimini.

History. The order established by the Etruscans in this region (7th/6th c. B.C.; foundation of Marzabotto, Felsina or Bologna, Spina where they traded with the Greeks) was overthrown by the Celtic invasion (5th/4th c. B.C.); Roman settlement dates from after the Second Punic War, when the Via Emilia was built (191-187 B.C.), between Rimini and Piacenza (it took its name from the consul Marcus Æmilius Lepidus, giving its name to the region, and uniting it, acting as its spinal cord). With the decline of the empire, Ravenna became the capital of the Western Empire (from A.D. 402), then the capital of Theodoric, and finally of Byzantine Italy; the rest of the region was invaded by Longobards in 568. With the dissolution of the Marca degli Attoni di Canossa, which included Reggio, Parma, Modena, and Ferrara (with Mantua and Brescia), after the death of the countess Matilda of Tuscany (1155), there was more room for the formation of independent communal governments, as in the rest of the Po Valley. Significant events of Italian history occurred here during the Middle Ages: the humiliation of Henry IV at Canossa (1077); the diet of Roncaglia summoned by Frederick I Barbarossa (1158), where he reaffirmed imperial rights, and rejected the independence of the communal governments

(Bologna, Piacenza, Modena, and Reggio later formed part of the Lombard League); the battle of Fossalta (1249) in which Bolognese and Romagnoli of the second Lombard League defeated the imperial army and captured king Enzo, the son of Frederick II. The era of seigneurial rule saw the Visconti victorious at Piacenza and Parma, the Este ruling first at Ferrara and later in Modena and Reggio, the Pepoli, followed by the Bentivoglio in Bologna. Other minor seigneuries split up Romagna among them, and in the fight for supremacy, which involved Florence, Venice, and the Papal State, the Church prevailed (acquiring Bologna, 1506, and the duchy of Ferrara, 1598, as well), so that in the second half of the 16th c., after the treaty of Cateau-Cambrésis, which marked the end of the Wars of Italy between France and Spain, the political order of the region stablized, with duchies alongside the Church: Parma and Piacenza under the Farnese (this was the family of Pope Paul III; the duchy later fell to a branch of the house of Bourbon), Modena and Reggio under the Este. This tidy arrangement collapsed during the period of the French Revolution and Empire, but it was established once again following the Restoration, with this variation: the duchy of Parma and Piacenza was assigned for life to Maria Luisa of Austria, the second wife of Napoleon Bonaparte. With the defeat of Austria by the Franco-Piedmontese army in the second war of Italian independence, the region, unified under the provisional dictatorship of Luigi Carlo Farini, joined the kingdom of Italy under Vittorio Emanuele II (1860) by plebiscite.

Art. At Marzabotto an Etruscan city has been unearthed, while the materials of the necropolis of the vanished Etruscan town of Spina can be seen in Ferrara; Rimini has the most notable Roman ruins (Arco di Augusto). Ravenna, late-Roman and Byzantine, has celebrated early-Christian and Byzantine monuments and mosaics (5th/6th c.). The cathedrals of Modena, Parma, Piacenza, and Ferrara are outstanding examples of Po Valley Romanesque; during the same period, the sculptor Wiligelmo was at work in Modena; while the sculptor and architect Benedetto Antelami was at work in Parma. Among the heritage of Italian Gothic, we should mention, in Piacenza, the Gotico or Palazzo del Comune, in Bologna, the churches of S. Francesco and S. Petronio; the school of Bolognese art of the 14th c. (Vitale da Bologna and others), one of the great moments of Italian art. With its 15th-c. painters Cosmè Tura, Francesco del Cossa, and Ercole de Roberti, and the architect Biagio Rossetti, (note the Addizione Erculea, a rare piece of urban planning), Ferrara holds a distinguished place in the early Italian Renaissance. In the 15th c., and during the Renaissance, the artistic heritage was enriched by Tuscan architects at Rimini (the Tempio Malatestiano by Leon Battista Alberti), Cesena (the Biblioteca, or library), Faenza (the Duomo), Bologna (Palazzo Bevilacqua);

also in Bologna, the sculpture of the Siennese Jacopo della Quercia, and, later, the painting of Lorenzo Costa and Francesco Raibolini (known as the Francia), and the sculpture of Niccolò dell'Arca; at Parma, the painting of Correggio, known as the greatest artist of Emilia, and Parmigianino. At the end of the 16th c. and in the 17th c., Bologna with the Carracci, Guido Reni, Guercino (from Cento) and others, developed another school of painting in the context of post-Renaissance and Baroque art. Later notable painters from Emilia-Romagna include the 19th-c. landscape artist Antonio Fontanesi (from Reggio), the "macchiaiolo" Silvestro Lega (from Modigliana), and in the 20th c. the Ferrarese artists Gaetano Previati, Giovanni Boldini, and Filippo De Pisis, and the Bolognese artist Giorgio Morandi. The poetics of Metaphysical Art ("pittura metafisica") developed in Ferrara from the meeting of De Chirico, Savinio, Carrà, and De Pisis (1916-17).

Friùli - Venezia Giulia

The area of this region is 7,846 sq. km., equal to slightly more than 2.5 percent of Italy's territory; the population is 1,193,520, with a population density of 152 per sq. km. Easternmost tip of continental Italy, it occupies the land stretching from the course of the river Tagliamento and the river Livenza, to the west, to that of the Isonzo, in the east, as well as small patches of land on the left bank of the Isonzo downstream from Gorizia and the coast of the Gulf of Trieste, with the city of Trieste, Muggia and a strip of the Carso inland. Following the natural course of the waters upstream, you will pass from the coastal lagoons between the Tagliamento and Monfalcone, to the plains, to the morainic amphitheater of the Tagliamento, to the Alpine foothills (Prealpi Carniche: Monte Cavallo, Altopiano del Cansiglio) and, to the north of the course of the Tagliamento and the Fella, its tributary, to the Alps, culminating in the straight wall of the Carnian Alps, from the pass of Monte Croce di Comèlico to Tarvisio, none too high (maximum elevation, 2,780 meters, Monte Coglians) but daunting, with mighty peaks and spires. The Carso, a limestone tableland, extends eastward from the middle and lower course of the Isonzo: it features karstic phenomena (caverns, subterranean rivers, etc.).

The current distribution of employment of the labor force (5.18 percent in farming, the lowest percentage after Lombardy, 31.53 percent in industry, roughly the national average, 63.29 percent in service industries) is an indication of the recent industrial transformation of the agrarian Friùli. Dating from the 19th c. is the shipbuilding tradition of Monfalcone; note the postwar "boom" in applicance manufacturing in Pordenone; of particular note is the fine "prosciutto" of San Daniele. Trieste is a city with economic problems due to its isolated location; all the same, it is the third-largest Italian port, and the largest on the Adriatic coastline. Note the beach resorts (Lignano Sabbiadoro, Grado, the Triestine coastline). Friùli-Venezia Giulia has been a region with special autonomy since 1963; Trieste is the regional capital; Gorizia, Pordenone, and Udine are the other provincial capitals.

History. Friùli comes from "Forum Iulii," ancient name of Cividale, founded by Julius Caesar; the name of the "Gens Julia" appears elsewhere, as in the "Alpes Iuliae," which gave the region its name — Venezia Giulia — in 1863; the two parts of the modern region had different historical experiences, at least in certain centuries. Romanized in the 2nd/1st B.C., these areas were part of the X Regio Augustea "Venetia et Histria," in which Aquileia, a Roman colony founded in 181 B.C., a great port, was the main town. Following the tumultuous end of the Roman Empire, the Longobards entered Italy over the Julian Alps and founded their first duchy in Cividale, causing the split whereby land-bound "Venetia" remained under the rule of the duchy of Friùli (Cividale) while maritime "Venetia" fell under Byzantine rule (Grado). All the same, episcopal authority was growing, particularly that of the Patriarch of Aquileia. From the 11th c. on, the patriarchate, which joined Friùli and Istria, was the leading ecclesiastical principality in northern Italy. The easternmost territories were ruled by the counts of Gorizia, German feudal lords (from the 11th c. to the 15th c.). The "patria del Friùli" ("patria," from patriarchate) fell under Venetian rule in 1420, while the domain of the counts of Gorizia came under the rule of the House of Austria which, in order to hamper Venice and its sway in the "Golfo" (the Adriatic Sea), encouraged the development of Trieste as a harbor and trading center (made a free port in 1719). Friùli too became Austrian, along with the Veneto, or Venetia. The division between the two regions was renewed when Friùli alone, with Veneto, joined the Kingdom of Italy, 1866. Venezia Giulia (Gorizia, Trieste, and Istria) became Italian at the end of WWI (1918); the modern-day provinces of Trieste and Gorizia are what remain; most of it went to Yugoslavia at the end of WWII, and is now under the sovereignty of Slovenia and Croatia, although there are still Slavic minorities in Italy, and Italian minorities across the border.

Let no one forget the catastrophe of 1976 in Friùli: earthquake and aftershocks killed more than a thousand people, and badly damaged towns and villages in the basin of the Tagliamento; even after the reconstruction, there was permanent damage to the natural setting and art of places like Gemona and Venzone.

Art. Roman ruins can be seen in Trieste (the theater), Concordia Sagittaria near Portogruaro, and especially at Aquileia, a major archeological site of late-Latinity; there are early-Christian buildings from the Hexarchy in Grado (S. Eufemia, Baptistery); Cividale del Friùli, with its Tempietto Longobardo and the sculptures in the Museo Cristiano del Duomo, offers a rare glimpse of art from the Longobard period. The time of the patriarchate is documented by the Basilica of Aquileia, a Romanesque-Gothic monument with early-Christian mosaic floors. The rebuilt cathedrals of Gemona and Venzone are Gothic. This was an "artistic province" of Venice from the 15th c. on, as you can clearly see in Pordenone, in Palmanova, a 16th-c. citadel, in the 18th-c. villa of Passariano, and especially in the central square of Udine (where Tiepolo worked). The Borgo Teresiano of Trieste is an interesting piece of urban planning under an "enlightened dictator."

Lazio (Latium)

The total area of this region is 17,203 sq. km.; the population is 5,031,230 (with population density of 299 per sq. km.); half of the population lives in the city of Rome. From the coast of the Tyrrhenian Sea, between the mouth of the river Chiarone, just south of the Argentario, and the river Garigliano — dotted with the ports of Civitavecchia, eleventh-largest in Italy in terms of volume of goods, fifth-largest on the peninsular Tyrrhenian coastline; Fiumicino, Anzio, Terracina, and Gaeta — the region stretches inland, over hills and mountains, with irregular borders. The tallest mountains, rising to altitudes of between 1,000 and 2,000 meters, are mostly limestone, jagged in shape, bare, with karstic phenomena; belonging to the ranges of the Apennines (Appennino) and the Subappennino, pushing into the ranges of Abruzzo (Monti Reatini, with Mt. Terminillo, 2,216 m.) and the upper reaches of the river Tronto. More verdant and varied are the Monti Sabini, Monti Prenestini, Monti Simbruini, and Monti Ernici: sometimes plunging down to the plains, like the Monti Tiburtini and the Monti Lepini, often surrounded by gentle, lower mountains and hills, the slopes blanketed with grapevines, olive groves, and fields of grain, as in the middle valley of the Aniene, in the Monti Prenestini, and in the western Sabina. Between Orvieto and Rome extend three of the region's four volcanic complexes (Monti Volsini, 639 m.; Monti Cimini, 1,053 m.; Monti Sabatini, 612 m.), while the fourth, the Colli Albani (948 m.) lies south of the capital; crater structures surround the green banks of the lakes of Bolsena, Vico, Bracciano, Albano, and Nemi. Running through the region from the north to the center is the Tiber, Italy's third-longest river, into which flows the river Aniene, its second tributary after the Nera, inside Rome near the Ponte Salario (Salarian Bridge).

The percentages of the labor force require interpretation: agriculture 5.3 percent, industry 19.8 percent, and service industries 74.9 percent (national data, respectively, 9, 32, 59 percent). The numbers of workers in the service industries can be explained by the presence of the national bureaucracy in Rome; setting that aside, farming actually prevails over manufacturing. Land use includes grains and wheat (with low yields, except for the Agro Pontino), market gardens, with greenhouses as well (Campagna Romana, Agro Pontino, Viterbese), fruit orchards, olive groves on the southern slopes, vineyards (with celebrated wines, in the Castelli Romani and the area of Montefiascone, and between Terracina and Formia). Manufacturing, mostly recent, is concentrated around Rome, in the valleys of the Sacco and the Liri, in the area around Latina. Rome is first in the service industries serving tourists, including the pilgrims to the Eternal City. Rome is the capital of the Italian republic, as well as the region of Lazio and the province of Rome; the other provincial capitals are Frosinone, Latina, Rieti, Viterbo.

History. This region's history is largely a reflection of the history of Rome. Before the rise of Rome, which was complete in this region by the 4th c. B.C., modern-day Lazio was inhabited by Etruscans, on the right bank of the Tiber, by Latins, organized in a league of cities around the religious center of "Alba Longa," on the river's left bank, and by the Ernici, Equi, and Volsci in the valleys of the Liri and the Sacco. With the decline of the Roman empire began the long process of the formation of the temporal power of the church, with struggles between Byzantines (the duchy of Rome, after the "Gothic war") and Longobards (the "donation of Sutri" in 728, by Liutprand, created the core of the "estate of St. Peter"), and then with the complex relations with the Holy Roman Empire (the emperors came to Rome fully armed for their coronations: the first was Charlemagne in A.D. 800; the last of them, Frederick III of Hapsburg, in 1452), all of it fundamental to the shape of European, and world, history. In regional terms, we may mention the foundation of the monastery of Montecassino by Benedetto da Norcia (St. Benedict of Nursia, 6th c.), the presence of a Saracen camp at the mouth of the river Garigliano (870-910) with extensive raiding, and

the centuries of conflict and strife between forces surrounding, supporting, and opposed to the popes: the Roman Commune (12th c.) which strove mightily to subjugate the surrounding countryside; the free cities of Viterbo, Corneto (now Tarquinia), Tivoli, Velletri, Terracina, and Anagni; the great families who renewed in feudal forms their ancient power, assembling huge landholdings. From these families descended the barons who lorded it over Rome when the popes were in Avignon (1309-77), even though Cardinal Albornoz (1353-77) worked to restore papal authority while biding their return. It was only with the end of the destabilizing effects of the Western Schism (1378-1449), with the gradual subjugation of the noble familes of the Caetani, Colonna, Orsini, and Savelli, and the crisis of the "wars of Italy" (16th c.), that regional history begins to blend with the relatively quiet history (aside from the Napoleonic period) of the larger Papal State, until the union with the Kingdom of Italy in 1870.

Art. The presence of the huge art capital of Rome was a fundamental factor in the development of the region, though there is a rich and splendid array of art "extra muros," a few notable points of which we shall mention here.

Balancing the Etruscan relics of northern Lazio (ruins of Veio and necropolises of Tarquinia and Cervèteri) are, in southern Lazio, the acropolises and the polygonal pre-Roman walls of Norma, Ferentino, and Alatri. Of Roman art, there are relics — from the Republic — in Palestrina, Tivoli, Terracina, and Cori, and — from the Empire — in Hadrian's Villa near Tivoli, and at Ostia, Albano, Anzio, and Gaeta. A major portion of the Italian architectural heritage is constituted by such medieval religious monuments as S. Pietro and S. Maria Maggiore in Tuscania, S. Flaviano in Montefiascone, S. Maria di Castello in Tarquinia, S. Elia near Nepi, and the Duomo of Anagni, all of which can be considered Romanesque; closely allied with the architecture of Rome of the same period are the Duomo of Terracina and the Duomo of Civita Castellana, as well as the cloister of S. Scolastica at Subiaco. The 13th-c. abbeys of Fossanova and Casamari belong to the Cistercian monastic Gothic tradition, serving as inspiration for the churches of Ferentino and Priverno and the abbey of Valvisciolo. Likewise Gothic are the Palazzo dei Papi at Viterbo and the buildings of the Sacro Speco in Subiaco. Roman "marmorari," or marble workers, scattered mosaic floors, ambos, ciboria, and portals everywhere, signs of a remarkable phase of art. As ties became closer with Rome, architecture produced the 15th-c. church of S. Maria della Quercia at Viterbo, Palazzo Vitelleschi at Tarquinia, hovering between Gothic and Renaissance, the Castello Orsini-Odescalchi at Bracciano, the fortresses of Ostia, Nettuno, and Civita Castellana. The painters Lorenzo da Viterbo and Antoniazzo Romano worked in this region during the 15th c. From the 16th c. on, Roman commissions prevailed: such is the case with Palazzo Farnese at Caprarola (Vignola), Villa d'Este at Tivoli (Pirro Ligorio), Villa Lante at Bagnaia (Vignola), the fortress of Civitavecchia, designed by Bramante, Antonio da Sangallo the Younger, and Michelangelo, and the villas built over three centuries in the aristocratic holiday spots, especially at Frascati. The Neapolitan style inspired the Baroque reconstructions of the abbey of Montecassino; Bernini worked at Ariccia; Sabaudia, a city built in the 1930s, is considered a fine piece of urban planning.

Liguria

This region covers the Tyrrhenian slopes of the Maritime Alps and the Ligurian Apennines, which are joined at the Colle di Cadibona, forming a great arch around the gulf of Genova, extending from the river Roia in the west to the Magra in the east. Liguria is Italy's third-smallest region, just 5415 sq. km; 40 percent of the population of 1,668,078 lives in Genoa; the population density (317 per sq. km) is almost twice the Italian average. Spurs of the Alps and Apennines reach down to the sea, crowding the coastal strip. Liguria is wholly mountainous or hilly, and one of the region's charms is certainly the close encounter of mountain and sea. Genoa splits the arch of coastline into the two parts (Riviera di Levante and Riviera di Ponente, literally, east and west shores), long and widely renowned. In a sense, this is a "postindustrial" region. Although the mild weather favors agriculture, there is almost no land for it. Thus, fruit and vegetable gardens, flowers and ornamental plants, grapes, and olives are grown along this coast.
Genoa is a port city with problems, but it still takes with Marseille the lion's share of Mediterranean shipping; rival ports include Savona and La Spezia, which is also a naval base. Manufacturing is concentrated in Genoa, the gulf of La Spezia, and the territory of Savona and Vado. Shipbuilding and other mechanical industries prevail. Tourism is a major industry here.
Genoa is the regional capital; provincial capitals are Savona, Imperia, and La Spezia.

History. The pre-Indo-European population of the Liguri gave this region its name, though they occupied a larger territory. Romans arrived in the 1st c. B.C. Longobards and Franks moved in during the high Middle Ages, and the area was split into marches and counties.
Genoa's naval, mercantile, and colonial might — it was one of Italy's four historic "maritime republics" — developed from the 11th c. on; Genoan hegemony was complete by the end of the 14th c. Wars followed with Venice, for supremacy at sea, and with the French and Spanish, who subjugated Genoa. The great admiral Andrea Doria regained Genoan independence (1528). The small but wealthy Republic of Genoa fell to Napoleon (1805), and was later ceded to the Savoy. Ligurians such as Garibaldi and Mazzini played major roles in the Risorgimento.

Art. The earliest architecture of note is Roman (Ventimiglia, Luni) and early Christian (Albenga). The most significant periods in artistic terms were Romanesque and Gothic and, later, the late 16th c. and the Baroque period. Lombard, French, Pisan, and Byzantine influence is found in the architecture; noteworthy work is found in Genoa, Noli, Albenga, and the abbeys of San Fruttuoso di Capodimonte and San Salvatore di Lavagna. Sculpture and paintings abound, throughout the region in the 14th and 15th c.; in Genoa during the 16th c.

Lombardy

This region occupies the central portion of the Po Valley and the Alps. Lake Maggiore with the river Ticino, to the west, and Lake Garda with the river Mincio to the east, and the Po to the south, are only approximate guides to its borders: other pieces of Lombardy are the Lomellina, the Oltrepò Pavese, and the Oltrepò Mantovano; only the Valtellina extends to the Alpine watershed. The rest of

Lombardy's (which is also to say, Italy's) northern border lies alongside Switzerland's Ticino canton, which pushes well south, coming close to Como.

In terms of area, with 23,834 sq. km, Lombardy makes up a twelfth of Italy; it is the fourth-largest region. Of the region's 8,831,264 inhabitants (population density of 375 per sq. km, making this Italy's most populous and second-most densely populated region), just under half live in the province of Milan, and about a sixth live in Milan proper.

Lombardy is divided into three natural areas: mountain, plains, and hills. The highest peak is the Piz Bernina, 4,049 m., though several other peaks and massifs tower nearly as high. The gently rolling hills, separated by small plains, are dotted with sparkling little lakes (Brianza, Varesotto). Midway between mountains and hill country, however, in the Prealpe, or Alpine foothills, stands the limestone group of the Grigne, while the lake region of Maggiore, Lugano, Como, Iseo, and Garda is justly renowned for its landscape.

The plains were formed by the many tributaries of the great river Po. Lombardy produces a quarter of Italy's GDP and 30 percent of its exports. Agriculture is particularly prosperous here, enjoying the benefits of an abundant supply of water and centuries of diligent irrigation. Among the chief crops are rice (Lomellina), and feed; the latter supports livestock, which in turn yields dairy products (Lodi, Melzo, Codogno, Soresina, to name a few areas). Wine is produced in Valtellina, the Oltrepò Pavese, Franciacorta, and the morainic hills around Mantua.

Light and heavy industry flourishes in Milan, Monza, Brescia, Pavia, Varese, Como, Busto Arsizio, Legnano, Gallarate, in the Brianza, and Vigevano. Aside from steel, chemicals, machining, and printing, the region produces textiles, furniture, and leather. Lombardy leads Italy in the service industries. Tourism prevails on the lakes, on the ski slopes, and in the many fine museums of cities large and small.

History. Milan already existed (founded probably by the Galli Insubri in the early 4th c. B.C.), when the Romans arrived in what is now Lombardy. By the late 3rd c. A.D., Milan was briefly the capital of the western Empire.

The Longobards established their capital at Pavia, giving their name to the region. By the time the Franks supplanted the Longobards (774), feudal government prevailed.

The government of the Communes — warlike and prosperous — began in the 11th c.; later Italian history has exalted the Lombard League, in which the armies of the Communes united to defeat the Holy Roman Emperor Frederick Barbarossa at Legnano. Milan's predominance swelled with the Visconti and later the Sforza (14th/15th c.). The great dukedom thus created was gradually eroded as Venice, Switzerland, and the Savoy of Piedmont rose in power.

As Italy fell under foreign domination in the 16th c., French and Spanish monarchs quibbled over the tastiest morsel, the dukedom of Milan. The Spanish Habsburgs won, only to be replaced by Austrian Habsburgs in 1714. Lombardy was part of the Cisalpine Republic and later, the Kingdom of Italy, under Napoleon. Then the Austrians returned in 1814, remaining until the Risorgimento expelled them in 1859.

Art. Little survives from Roman times (chiefly at Milan, Brescia, and Sirmione) or of early-Christian architecture (note Milan's S. Lorenzo). Construction thrived here from the High Middle Ages onward, and Lombardy was, in a sense, the cradle of Romanesque architecture, between the 8th and 12th c. Intensely concerned with the technical problem of roofing broad spaces, this school applied the vault to increasingly impressive structures. Monuments, religious and civil, are found in cities (Milan, Pavia, Como, Cremona, Brescia, and others) and scattered throughout Lombardy (S. Pietro at Civate, S. Vincenzo at Galliano, S. Tommaso at Almenno San Salvatore, Ss. Pietro e Paolo at Agliate, and others).

Gothic architecture, from the 13th to the 15th c., made use of the pointed arch, the oval cross-arch, and brick masonry (although the Milan cathedral, built late, in 1386, took its inspiration from non-Italian Gothic). Renaissance architecture here adopted Tuscan innovations with decorative fillips and a lively sense of color and composition (Certosa di Pavia, Colleoni chapel in Bergamo). The strong Renaissance flavor seen in many famed Lombard monuments came from elsewhere: Leon Battista Alberti in Mantua, Donato Bramante in Milan, and later Giulio Romano, also in Mantua.

A Lombard style of painting matured in the 15th c. Major names are V. Foppa, the Bergognone, and B. Luini; their tradition was greatly influenced by the presence and work of Leonardo da Vinci. Bergamo and Brescia, in the cultural orbit of Venice, developed schools of their own (note Savoldo, Romanino, and Moretto). Art and architecture thrived from the second half of the 16th c. on, with the patronage of two Borromeo cardinals.

The great artist Michelangelo Merisi, named Caravaggio after his birthplace, studied here but spent most of his life further south.

The Neoclassical style abounds, in country villas and in the palazzi of Milan. Both Milan and Lombardy were prominent in the development of 19th-c. Italian art and of Futurism and other modern movements.

Museums here boast a remarkable collection of work, much of it not Lombard. Suffice it to mention Michelangelo's Pietà Rondanini, and the galleries of Brera, in Milano, and the Accademia Carrara, in Bergamo.

Marche

The area, 9,694 sq. km, amounts to just over 3 percent of Italy's territory; the population (1,427,666) is slightly below (147 persons per sq. km) the average density of Italy. Its coast stretches along the

Adriatic, from the river Foglia to the Tronto, lying along the eastern slopes of the Apennines. It is mountainous and hilly; with a series of rib-like elevations running from watershed to coast, growing progressively higher toward the south, culminating in the Sibillini (Monte Vettore, 2,476 m.), now part of a national park.

The hill country is 25-30 km. in width, and reaches to the sea; there is almost no plain. Vines and olive groves mark the landscape; fishing is a major activity here (third, after Sicily and Puglia). There is a major paper industry (Fabriano) here, and musical instruments are made in Castelfidardo, Camerano, and elsewhere. Ceramics have been made for centuries, especially in Urbino and Pesaro.

Splendid beaches attract tourists, as do mountains and ski slopes. The art of Urbino brings visitors from all over the world. The capital of the region is Ancona; the four other provincial capitals are Ascoli Piceno, Macerata, Pesaro, and Urbino.

History. The river Esino, which flows into the sea to the east of Falconara Marittima, once divided the northern lands, occupied by Gauls, from the southern lands of the Piceni, who had been Roman allies since 299 B.C. Romanization began in the 3rd c. B.C. The Longobards settled to the south of Ancona, while the Byzantines controlled the north (namely the maritime Pentapolis: Rimini, Pesaro, Fano, Senigallia, Ancona), which the Franks later handed over to the Church (752). The term "marca," which, later, in the plural ("marche") gave the region its name, first appears in the 10th c., indicating imperial influence and sovereignty: Marca di Camerino, Marca di Fermo (including Ancona and its territory). Among the communal governments that were established, foremost was Ancona; among the seigneurial families that arose from the 13th c. on, let us mention the Montefeltro in Urbino, the Cagli, the Fossombrone, the Da Varano in Camerino, the Malatesta from Pesaro at Osimo. The Church was active in establishing rule over this region, with cardinal Albornoz in the period of Avignonese rule (14th c.); following the short-lived reigns of Francesco Sforza (1433-44) and Cesare Borgia, the Valentino (early-16th c.), the Church took the entire area, occupying Ancona (1532) and the Duchy of Urbino (1631). Suspended during Napoleonic rule, papal government was definitively overthrown in 1860, when the Marche became part of the Kingdom of Italy.

Art. Roman ruins can be seen in Ascoli, Fermo, Urbisaglia, "Helvia Ricina," and "Faleria"; the arches of Augustus in Fano and Trajan in Ancona are almost perfectly intact. In Romanesque architecture (11th/13th c.), Lombard features merged with Byzantine style; noteworthy churches include: S. Maria in Portonovo near Ancona, S. Maria at Pie' di Chienti, S. Vittore delle Chiuse, S. Claudio al Chienti, S. Maria di Rambona, S. Ciriaco in Ancona, the cathedral and parish church at San Leo; the baptistery of Ascoli. In the Gothic period (13th/15th c.) Venetian influence grew; note S. Francesco at Ascoli, S. Nicola at Tolentino, and G. Orsini. Certainly the high point was the Renaissance, first at the court of Urbino and the Palazzo Ducale, a major crossroads in Italian art history; later in the less well known Basilica della Santa Casa at Loreto. Among the artists who worked in the two places: the architects L. Laurana, F di Giorgio Martini, B. Pontelli, the Sangallos; the sculptor A. Sansovino; and the painters P. della Francesca, M. da Forlì, L. Signorelli, the Vivarini.

Other construction worthy of note was done in Pesaro, Jesi, and San Leo. Although the local school of painting that formed in the early 15th c. (G. da Fabriano the Salimbeni) blended early with its Umbrian counterpart, such Venetian artists worked here as C. Crivelli, Giovanni Bellini, L. Lotto, and Titian. Unquestionably, this region's greatest gifts to Italian art were its two native sons, Bramante and Raphael. The Renaissance was also the finest period of Marche majolica, from Castel Durante (now Urbania), Urbino, and Pesaro. After the Renaissance and on through the Baroque period, Roman influence predominated here. In literature, the great poet, Giacomo Leopardi, was from Recanati.

Molise

It is the second-smallest Italian region, in size and in population (surface are, 4,438 sq. km.; population 327,893, with a population density of 75 inhabitants per sq. km.). Its territory lies between the Trigno, the middle course of the river Sangro, the upper Volturno, the peaks of the Matese, and the middle course of the river Fortore. This is mountainous land, running up to the crest of the Apennine ranges of the Mainarde and the Matese (2,050 m.), and in part including the Monti del Sannio, then sloping along hills down to the Adriatic coast, along which it extends for some 35 km., between the mouths of the rivers Trigno and Saccione, where Tèrmoli is the only port. Not all the rivers flow into the Adriatic (along with the rivers mentioned, the Biferno and Fortore do; the Fortore empties along the Pugliese coast), since the plain of Venafro and the valley of Isernia, which lie between the Mainarde and the Matese, on the other side of the Apennine watershed, are watered by the river Volturno (which flows into the Tyrrhenian Sea), and by its tributary, the Sordo. The composition of the labor force (19.8 percent in farming, the third-highest level in Italy; 25.9 percent in industry; 54.3 percent in service industries), when compared with the average Italian figures (respectively 9, 32, and 59 percent) shows that this is a largely agrarian region: intensive agriculture in the plains and chief valleys, which are nonetheless none too productive; goats and sheep are grazed as well. In terms of manufacturing, it is characterized by small companies, with such old traditions as knife-making in Campobasso and Frosolone and bell-casting in Agnone. Historically, it was a single region with Abruzzo until 1963; the regional capital is Campobasso; another provincial capital is Isernia.

History. In antiquity, this region has much in common with Abruzzo; the Longobards joined it with the Duchy of Benevento, establishing the Gastaldato di Bojano, which under the Normans became "Comitatus Molisii" (the name may come from one of the leading families). In the context of the southern kingdom, which Molise followed, it was joined to the Terra di Lavoro by Frederick II (1221); then, in the 15th c., to the Capitanata, until 1807, when, under the reign of Joseph Bonaparte, it was made a province, with capital at Campobasso.

Art. There are relics of Samnite and Roman culture at Pietrabbondante, Larino, Sepino, and Venafro. Following the classical age, Molisan art went much the same route as Abruzzese art. Of particular note, from the Middle Ages, are the 9th-c. frescoes in the crypt of S. Lorenzo in S. Vincenzo al Volturno, the Badia di S. Maria di Canneto, and the cathe-

drals of Tèrmoli and Larino. The styles of Naples and Rome prevailed during the Baroque period.

Piedmont

Italy's westernmost region, Piedmont occupies the inner slopes of the western section of the broad arch of the Alps (Maritime, Cotian, Graian, and Pennine Alps); in the east, Piedmont covers the western portion of the Po Valley, as far as Lake Maggiore and the river Ticino. With an area of sq. km. 25,399, it is Italy's second-largest region. The population is 4,290,412, a quarter of that residing in the city of Turin; population density is 168 per sq. km. Piedmont has three natural zones: mountain, plains, and hills. There are several major Alpine massifs (Monviso, Gran Paradiso, Monte Rosa); the plains extends along the left bank of the river Po; hill country extends south of the Po, including Turin, the Monferrato and Langhe areas, and, north of the river, a number of morainic formations (Rivoli and the Serra di Ivrea). The landscape is dotted with lakes (Maggiore, Orta, the lakes of the Canavese, and others).

This region has a history of manufacturing, encouraged by the abundant supply of water. Automobiles and office machinery are the main historical fields of development (Fiat and Olivetti), though the textiles industry has long flourished here (wool in the area around Biella, cotton and synthetics elsewhere). Chemicals, paper mills, tanneries, glass manufacturing, apparel and fashion, sweets, and foods are also important in Piedmont. Silver (Vercelli) and gold (Valenza) are worked by craftsmen. Agriculture flourishes, especially rice, wines, and dairy products. Resorts dot the Alpine slopes and the lovely lakes and hill country.

The capital is Turin; provincial capitals are Alessandria, Asti, Biella, Cuneo, Novara, Verbano-Cusio-Ossola, and Vercelli.

History. The lands that are now called Piedmont (the name "Pedemontium," or foothills, dates from the mid-12th c. to indicate a scanty stretch of flat country to the south-west of Turin between the Po and Sangone rivers) did not fall under Roman rule until the beginning of the Empire. Later, Longobards and Franks ruled, and Piedmont was split up into dukedoms, counties, and marches. Ivrea and Turin vied for supremacy; the Savoy of Turin finally prevailed, only to be dominated by forces from beyond the Alps. Together with the Communes, the marches of Saluzzo and Monferrato began to assert themselves from the 12th-c. onwards. Still, the Savoy gradually extended their sway over a greater territory, till 1743, when Piedmont attained its modern size. Napoleon made it part of his empire and it was then to become the heart of the kingdom of Sardinia. In the 19th c., the minister to the Savoy court, Camillo Benso, Count of Cavour, worked to unify Italy. After the Risorgimento, Turin was Italy's first capital, until 1865.

Art. Relics of Roman times survive in Turin (Porta Palatina) and Susa (Arch of Augustus). The most notable periods of artistic endeavor in this region were the 11th/15th c. (Romanesque and Gothic art) and the 17th/18th c. (Baroque). Romanesque bell towers and other relics are common; among surviving medieval monuments, we should mention the abbeys of Vezzolano and Staffarda and the Sacra di S. Michele, as well as the Gothic church of S. Andrea in Vercelli and the church of S. Antonio in Ranverso. During the Renaissance, a lively school of painters flourished in Vercelli. The court of Savoy set praiseworthy architects to work in Turin, from the late-16th-c. on; supreme among them G. Guarini and F. Juvarra. The region also boasts impressive museums; of special note, the Museo Egizio, or Egyptian Museum of Turin.

Puglia

Occupying roughly 1/15th of Italy's territory (surface area, 19,347 sq. km.), Puglia ranks seventh in population among the Italian regions (3,986,430 inhabitants; population density 206 persons per sq. km.). Extending from the river Fortore in the north, along the Adriatic and the Ionian seas, it lies in the extreme SE part of the Italian peninsula. Geologically, limestone predominates, as do all the physical characteristics that go with it; this distinguishes Puglia from the surrounding regions; it is largely flat in topography. Here are some of the salient features: vast plains such as the Tavoliere and the peninsula of the Salento; flat or terraced uplands sloping downward from north to south (Monte Calvo in the Gargano rises to an elevation of 1,055 m., in the Murge the altitudes range from 700 m. to 300 m.; in the Serre Salentine the elevations are no higher than 200 m.); there is little surface water, save for the rivers Fortore and Ofanto; there are common karstic phenomena (dolina, "puli," grottoes), especially in the uplands of the Murge and in a few steep areas of the coastline. The coastline extends for more than 800 km., towering steeply around the Gargano, elsewhere varying between rocky and sandy and low. The economy is defined by the labor force: 16.86 percent in farming — in absolute numbers, the largest in Italy — 24.85 percent in industry, and 58.26 percent in service industries (national data, respectively, 9, 32, 59 percent). Farming in this region is of particular importance: Puglia produces 56 percent of Italy's table grapes, 54 percent of the olive harvest, 19 percent of the durum wheat harvest (for pasta), and 28 percent of the lettuce crop; also, there are vegetables in general, almonds, figs, wine grapes, and tobacco (Lecce). Puglia is second in fishing, following Sicily, and producing 16 percent of Italy's total fish harvest. Industry is largely devoted to processing agricultural products; the chemicals and steel plants developed by the Italian state (at Taranto, Brindisi, Bari, and Barletta) are undergoing notorious problems. In terms of volume, Taranto is the fourth-largest port in Italy, and Brindisi is a major harbor for passenger ships to Greece; Bari has ties with many Mediterranean and Asian countries. Tourism is attracted to the beaches, especially on the Gargano, to the area of the "trulli," and to the towns of historic and artistic importance. The capital of the region is Bari, second-largest city in Southern Italy; the other provincial capitals are Brindisi, Foggia, Lecce, and Taranto.

History. The Apuli, as the Romans called the earliest inhabitants of the easternmost Italian coasts, were peoples of Illyrian origin, who had sailed across the Adriatic Sea from its eastern shores. Taranto (Tarentum), a Greek colony founded at the end of the 8th c. B.C., was one of the wealthiest and most powerful cities in Magna Graecia, and ruled Gallipoli and Otranto; it had to struggle mightily against the cities of the original Messapic inhabitants. Rome conquered Taranto, in 272 B.C., establishing its rule over the territory; a supremacy that did not waver even with Rome's defeat at Canae by Hannibal in the Punic Wars (216 B.C.). Puglia was linked with Rome by the Via Appia, or Appian Way, which terminated at the port of Brindisi (Brundisium), gateway to the eastern Mediterranean. With the fall of the empire, this region was soon contested (6th c.) by Byzantines and Longobards, then harried by Arab sea raiders, who occupied Bari (A.D. 840) making it the center of an emirate. The Byzantines, who had managed to hold onto the Salento, re-established their rule for another couple of centuries. In the 11th c. the coastal cities revived (Trani, Barletta, Molfetta, Bari) through commercial ties with Amalfi, the Dalmatian coast, and the ports of the Levant. It is traditionally stated that the first Normans in Puglia were pilgrims to the sanctuary of the Archangel Michael at Monte Sant'Angelo: soon however the region had become part of the Norman monarchy in southern Italy. Trade developed with the East, and Puglia was a natural stepping-off point for the Crusades, and for trade with the Holy Land. Under the Swabians, and especially under Frederick II (late-13th c.), Puglia enjoyed a golden age of wealth and artistic splendor. The southern kingdom declined, and Puglia with it, under the houses of Anjou (beginning in 1266), and Aragon (from 1442). Sea trade passed into the hands of the Venetians, Turkish fleets terrorized the coastal towns (sacking and occupying Otranto, 1480). Decline continued, exacerbated by famines, malaria, and huge landholders, under the Spanish (1503-1707), who beat the French in the fight for dominion in southern Italy (this was the period of the "duel of Barletta," 1503). With the arrival of the Bourbon dynasty (from 1734) there were glimmers of enlightened reform, and the so-called "French decade" (1806-1815) seemed to promise a bright future, but Puglia fell back into stagnation with the Bourbon restoration. When Garibaldi's troops overthrew the Kingdom of the Two Sicilies, almost all of the 278,000 votes in the great plebiscite (1860) were in favor of Italian unity.

Art. This region abounds in prehistoric (dolmens, menhirs) and early historical monuments, up until the colonization and cultural influence of the Greeks, who left their mark in the form of the extensive ceramic furnishings of the necropolises, now found in the museums of Taranto, Bari, Lecce, and other smaller centers. Noteworthy archeological complexes are found in Canne della Battaglia and Egnazia. Roman ruins can be found all over; note the monumental columns believed to mark the terminus of the Appian Way in Brindisi and the amphitheaters of Lecce and Lucera. The region displayed its originality beginning in the 11th c. and continuing until the 14th c.: this was principally the period of Pugliese Romanesque, an illustrious chapter of Italian art. The cathedrals feature elements of Latin Christianity (for example, the galleries) in S. Nicola di Bari, the archetype of the style, in the cathedral in the same city and in the cathedrals in the cathedrals of Trani, Barletta, Molfetta, Bitonto, Ruvo di Puglia, and Bitetto;

the Roman basilican scheme in the cathedrals of Taranto and Otranto; an imprint of Eastern Byzantine Christianity can be seen in the Capitanata, with the cathedrals of Troia and Foggia, S. Maria Maggiore in Monte Sant'Angelo, S. Maria and S. Leonardo in Siponto, near Manfredonia; all of this holy architecture is enriched with vigorous sculpture in bishop's thrones, ambos, bronze doors, and portals, in which the Romanesque intertwines with the classical, traces of Byzantine, and even Arabian styles. Pointed-arch architecture reached Puglia from France and from the Holy Land as early as the 12th c., as you can see in the church of Ss. Nicolò e Cataldo in Lecce; during the 13th c. it was used in numerous castles (Bari, Gioia del Colle, Lucera, and, particularly brilliant and enigmatic, Castel del Monte), although the architecture of churches, with a few exceptions, such as the cathedral of Lucera and the church of S. Caterina in Galatina, remained largely faithful to the local Romanesque tradition. With the decline of creative independence in the 14th c., the region proved indifferent to the Renaissance style, though paintings were imported from Venice. In Baroque times, in Lecce in particular but also elsewhere in the region, there developed a new architecture, in churches and palazzi, notable for the exuberant and fanciful decoration; it may have developed as a result of the easy-to-work local stone. At the same time, in many places, including Bari, Bitonto, Conversano, Gravina, Lecce, and Gallìpoli, a new school of painting sprang up, borrowing from the Neapolitan style, but original in its own manner. Interesting Pugliese artists developed in the 19th c., largely working elsewhere, among them Gioacchino Toma, Michele De Napoli, and Saverio Altamura, members of the Macchiaioli group, and Giuseppe De Nittis, who enjoyed fame in Paris.

Sardinia (Sardegna)

This is the second-largest island in the Mediterranean Sea (after Sicily), and is the third-largest Italian region, with a population density just slightly above the national average (area 24,090 sq. km.; population, 1,637,705, equivalent to a population density of 68 per sq. km.). Relatively compact in shape (a rectangle with its long sides running north-south, and with roughly 1,900 km. of mostly rocky coast, some of it jagged and rocky, some dotted with inlets or broad scimitar-shaped bays) this island lies at a considerable distance from the ports of the Italian peninsula (125 nautical miles from Civitavecchia to Olbia, 250 from Genoa to Porto Torres, 267 from Naples to Cagliari). With isolated massifs, narrow uplands, modest hills, the Sardinian mountainscape is split in two by the plains of Campidani, which extend from the Gulf of Cagliari to the Gulf of Oristano. The largest mountainous area lies between the northern coast and the extreme SE corner, with Monte Limbara (1,359 m.), the range of the Gocèano (Monte Rasu, 1,259 m.), the massif of Gennargentu, which has the highest elevation on the island in Punta La Marmora (1,834 m.); the smaller mountain range is in the Iglesiente, to the SW, with Monte Linas (1,236 m.). The rough landscape is dotted with rocks and infrequent scrub. The percentages of the labor force (farming, 14 percent; industry, 23 percent; service industries, 63 percent, as against the national data, respectively, 9, 32, 59 percent) and an unemployment rate of close to 20 percent, as compared with a national average of 11 percent, are the results of an economy in which, in farming, a major role is played by sheep-herding on none-too-rich permanent grazing lands (with a high percentage of stands of cork oak in the roughly 400,000 hectares of forests); mining, of considerable historic importance, is declining (zinc and lead in the Iglesiente; fossil fuels in the Sulcis; non-metal-bearing minerals, such as barite, fluorite, kaolin, and talc) while even manufacturing, though recent in origin (petrochemicals at Cagliari and Porto Torres; plastics at Porto Torres and Ottana; chemicals and manmade fibers at Sant'Antìoco, Assèmini, and Ottana; paper at Àrbatax; aluminum and cement at Portovesme), is encountering difficulties. With the growing refinement of the products, crafts industries have been thriving (fabrics, embroideries, leather, wrought iron, and ceramics). Also increasing is summer tourism, especially in the beach resorts. This is a region with special autonomy; the regional capital is Cagliari, the other provincial capitals are Nùoro, Oristano, and Sassari.

History. The island's long prehistory culminates in the culture of the "nuraghes." The Phoenician presence along the coasts was replaced and reinforced by the Carthaginians (7th c. B.C.), and then by the Romans, who took the island as their own between the first and second Punic Wars (3rd c. B.C.). With the decline of the Western Empire, Vandals invaded the island (mid-5th c.), but the Eastern Empire retook the island, and repelled the attempted Longobard conquest. Too distant from Byzantium, Sardinia lived in autonomy, with the four kingdoms of Cagliari, Torres, Arborèa, and Gallura. The intervention of the joint fleets of Pisa and Genoa came in reaction to an attempted conquest by the Arabs, around 1015, who had been raiding the Sardinian coasts sporadically from the 8th c. on. From that point onward, the two maritime republics occupied the island (Pisa held the northern and western sections, while Genoa held the southern and eastern areas), taking a rich harvest of minerals, wheat, livestock, cheese, hides, salt, honey, and coral. The investiture of James of Aragon with Sardinia by Pope Boniface VIII to (1297) preceded the seizing of the island by the house of Aragon (1323-26) and 150 years of violence, rebellion, and plunder, during which Doria and Malaspina, the township of Sassari, and the judges of Arborèa resisted their rule. The unification of the kingdoms of Castille and Aragon made the Sardinians subjects of Spain; Spanish rule, through a viceroy, ended at the turn of the 18th c., with the War of the Spanish Succession, between Bourbons and

Hapsburgs. The Treaty of Utrecht (1713) gave the island to Charles of Austria, who had conquered it, but the final arrangements were made, following an attempted reconquest by Cardinal Alberoni, minister of Spain, at the Congress of London a few years later (1718): Vittorio Amedeo II di Savoia (Victor Amadeus II of Savoy) was forced to exchange his new crown as king of Sicily for that of king of Sardinia. The House of Savoy, which bore the title until proclaimed Kings of Italy, governed the island with a viceroy, and resided here after they were driven out of Turin, from 1799 until the fall of Napoleon and the Restoration.

Art. The most significant of the unusual aspects of this island is constituted by the monuments of prehistory and proto-history, with the megalithic "tombe dei giganti," or tombs of the giants, the "domus de janas" (literally, houses of witches, sepulchers from the nuragic age, carved into the rock), "nuraghes" (there are 7,000), nuragic bronze figurines in the Museo Archeologico Nazionale in Cagliari. The second rare aspect of this area are the mosaics and archeological digs from Phoenician and Phoenicio-Punic settlements, such as Monte Sirai, "Tharros" and "Nora." Besides the two last sites mentioned, which later became Roman, there are other Roman relics, at Porto Torres and Cagliari. The third artistic singularity is consituted by the Romanesque churches, with Pisan or Lombard influence (11th/13th c.): S. Gavino at Porto Torres, S. Maria del Regno in Àrdara and S. Antioco in Bisarcio, SS. Trinità di Saccargia, S. Pietro di Sorres, S. Giusta near Oristano, S. Maria di Monserrato at Tratalias, S. Nicola in Ottana. Note the significant medieval military architecture of the towers of Cagliari and Oristano, the castle of Serravalle at Bosa. With the conquest by the house of Aragon, Sardinia entered into the artistic circle of Spain, so that you will find another remarkable feature: Catalonian-Gothic churches (the Cathedral of Alghero, the Purissima and S. Domenico in Cagliari) and a school of local painters, active during the 15th and 16th c., also of Catalonian derivation. From the 17th c. on, perhaps the most notable production was in the area of folk art, which is still producing a strong crafts tradition.

Sicily (Sicilia)

This is the largest island in the Mediterranean Sea, and the largest Italian region, occupying with its 25,708 sq. km. a little less than a twelfth of national territory; it is third in population, after Lombardy and Campania (population 4,961,383, with a population density of 192 persons per sq. km.). Set in the heart of the Mediterranean, separated from the southern extremitiy of the Italian peninsula by the narrow Strait of Messina, triangular in shape (the name of the island in classical times, Trinacria, meant in ancient Greek, "three heads"), this island is primarily hilly and mountainous. The orography is fairly complex: the only true mountain chain is in the north, with the Peloritani (Pizzo di Polo, 1,286 m.) similar to the mountains of Calabria, the Nèbrodi or Caronie, with rounded mountain tops rising above 1,500 m. (Monte Soro, 1,847 m.), and the group of the Madonìe, at the heart of which lies a karstic upland, topped by peaks less than 2,000 m. tall (Pizzo Carbonara, 1,977 m.). In the western section of the island are isolated or clustered peaks (inland: Monte Cammarata, 1,579 m. and the Rocca Busambra, 1,615 m.), while others flank the Tyrrhenian, such as the Monti della Conca d'Oro and Monte San Giuliano (Erice). In the south are the sulfur uplands, with clay, gypsum, and sulfur deposits. The SE corner of the island is occupied by the Monti Iblei (Monte Lauro, 986 m.). On the Ionian coast, note the great volcanic massif of Mt. Etna (at 3,343 m., the tallest peak on the island); while there are smaller volcanic groups on the lesser islands: Stròmboli, Vulcano (active), Ustica, and Pantellerìa. The plains are narrow and restricted to the coastal areas; the only relatively large plain is the alluvial plain of Catania.

Farming, until a few decades ago, was the chief economic activity; now manufacturing outpaces it. The employment breakdown is as follows: agriculture, 14.71 percent, industry, 20.57 percent, service industries, 64.72 percent (national data, respectively, 9, 32, 59 percent); but the island of Sicily is second only to Calabria in unemployment. Orchards abound in the coastal areas, while garden markets and greenhouses are the leading sectors of agriculture; grain, cereal, and wheat crops are extensive in the interior and along the southern coast, but it is a far cry from the times when the island was the great "breadbasket" of a far-less populous Mediterranean. The citrus fruit production of this island yields 63 percent of the national product; only slightly behind Veneto and Emilia Romagna, Sicily is one of the largest producers of grapes, and hence wine (14 percent of the Italian total). It leads Italy

in fishing, with 21.5 percent of total production. With the end of sulfur mining, the same area developed the extraction of potassium salts, while oil has been found in the areas around Ragusa and Gela. There is massive production of table salt, both from rock salt deposits, and from sea salt (Trapani, Augusta). The surge of industrialization has led to the construction of factories and plants at Augusta-Siracusa, Gela, Porto Empèdocle, and Milazzo, with other plants at Isola delle Femmine, Catania, Ragusa, Fiumefreddo di Sicilia, and Tèrmini Imerese. In terms of volume, Augusta is Italy's second-largest port; other Sicilian ports — Milazzo, Gela, and Palermo — are in the top 20. Messina is the focal point for rail and auto transport, with its ferries to the mainland. Sicilian crafts industries include a remarkable array of products: the "pupi," or puppets, of Palermo, painted wood, musical instruments, embroidery, ceramics. Tourists have been visiting places like Taormina, Siracusa, Agrigento, and Palermo since the 18th c.; new attractions focus on sun, sea, the southern vegetation of the northern and eastern coasts, and the smaller neighboring islands.

Since 26 February 1948, the island of Sicily has been a region with special autonomy; the regional capital is Palermo, while the other provincial capitals are Agrigento, Caltanissetta, Catania, Enna, Messina, Ragusa, Siracusa, and Trapani.

History. The aboriginal people of the island (Siculi and Sicani) moved inland when Greek colonists appeared on the coast, deciding to settle instead of just trading. After Nàxos, the earliest Greek city on the island (735 B.C.), came Siracusa, Leontinoi (Lentini), Megara Iblea, Catania, Zancle (Messina), Imera, Selinunte, Agrigento, and Gela. In the westernmost corner of the island, the Carthaginians settled, heirs to the Phoenicians, at Mozia, Panormo (Palermo), and Solunto. The duel between Greeks and Carthaginians for possession of the island continued with varying results, until the Roman conquest. One of the most powerful of the Greek cities was Siracusa, which was victorious in the naval battle of Imera (480 B.C.) against the Carthaginians, defeating the Etruscans in the waters off Cumae in 476, and in 415-413 withstanding the attack of the Athenians. Rome fought Carthage in the First Punic War (264-241 B.C.) basically for the possession of Sicily. The Romans won, and in 212 B.C. took Siracusa, in a siege in which Archimedes displayed his genius as a builder of military engines (he was then killed in the sacking of the city). With the fall of the Roman Empire, Vandals and Goths came and went; the Byzantines then took control in 535, remaining for three centuries; it took the Arabs 75 years to conquer Sicily (826-962). The Normans took the island with Roger I (1061-1091), and last came the Swabians, in particular with Frederick II (first half of the 12th c.); prosperous chapters in Sicilian history. When the island fell under Anjou rule with the rest of the kingdom, following the death of Manfred in the battle Benevento (1266), their "mala signoria" led to the explosion of the revolt of the "Sicilian Vespers" (1282), when the Sicilians gave themselves to Pedro of Aragon, husband of Constance, who was the daughter of Manfred. The region thus entered the Iberian realm, at first part of Aragon, and later a Spanish dominion for three centuries (1415-1712) with its own viceroy. As a result of the "War of the Spanish Succession," the island for a decade was ruled by Vittorio Amedeo II (making the Savoy a royal house for the first time), then briefly by the Austrians, and lastly by the house of Bourbon, who ruled from Naples (taking refuge in Palermo, with the protection of the British fleet, during the Napoleonic period). Garibaldi and his troops landed at Marsala on 11 May 1860 and ousted the Bourbon army from the island in just ten weeks.

Art. Sicily was a province of ancient Greek art: remarkable work can be seen in the museums of Palermo (with the archaic metopes from Selinunte), Siracusa, Agrigento, and Gela; excavations and conservation of all sorts have helped to preserve the trove of monuments, including, among other things, the theater, the temple of Athena, the prisons and the castle of Eurialo at Siracusa, the Doric temples at the foot of modern Agrigento, the walls of Gela, the ruins of Selinunte, the temple of Segesta, the ruins of Akrai at Palazzolo Acreide, and the ruins of Eraclea Minoa and other cities. There are also significant Roman ruins, including the amphitheater of Siracusa, the theater of Taormina, the excavations of Tindari and Solunto, the Villa of Piazza Armerina with its remarkable mosaic floors, and the recently discovered mosaics near Eloro and at Patti Marina. Under Norman rule (11th/12th c.) a body of architecture developed, with strains of Latin, Byzantine, and Arab cultures and work by masters from various places, including the church of the Martorana and the Cappella Palatina, lined with Byzantine mosaics, the cathedral, S. Giovanni degli Eremiti, the Arab-style buildings of the Zisa and the Cuba in Palermo, the Duomo of Monreale and the Duomo of Cefalù, likewise glittering with mosaics, the Duomo of Messina, and other buildings. Then the Gothic style appears in the 13th-c. imperial castles of Siracusa (Castel Maniace) and Catania (Castello Ursino), and in the 14th c. in various baronial palaces, such as the Steri and Palazzo Sclafani in Palermo, and others still in Taormina, Siracusa, and elsewhere. In the 15th c., political ties with the Iberian peninsula encouraged the use of the flamboyant style of Catalonian Gothic, originally developed by the architect Matteo Carnelivari in Palermo in Palazzo Abatellis and in the church of S. Maria della Catena. In Messina Antonello was beginning to work; after travelling to Venice (where he was known as Antonello da Messina) he established himself as a major figure in Italian painting. The Renaissance style was timidly copied by painters of the Messinese school; more notable work was done by sculptors, such as the Dalmatian Francesco Laurana and Domenico Gagini, from Bissone, founder of a family that produced remarkable work in the island; then, in the 16th c., numerous artists linked to Roman and Tuscan Mannerism came to Sicily. In the Baroque era (17th/18th c.) Sicily experienced a new and rich artistic flowering: the basic appearance of Palermo is Baroque, as is the Piazza del Duomo (cathedral square) of Siracusa, the urban grid and the architecture of the reconstruction of Catania, Ragusa, Noto, Còmiso, Scicli, and other towns, following the earthquake of 1693; in the 17th c., in Messina, the architect Guarino Guarini, from Modena, had worked, producing architecture of European renown; the Palermitan architect Giovanni Battista Vaccarini worked in Catania, the Siracusan Rosario Gagliardi worked in Ragusa; the local master of stucco Giacomo Serpotta worked in Palermo. Giovanni Battista Filippo Basile was an interesting Palermitan architect working in the 19th c.; his son Ernesto was the founder of the Sicilian "Liberty" school, the Italian version of Art Nouveau. Note the 20th-c. Sicilian painter Renato Guttuso, from Bagheria, who developed in the Roman school of painting.

Tuscany (Toscana)

In size, 22,992 sq. km., this is the fifth-largest Italian region, extending over 1/13th of Italy's territory; it has a population of 3,510,114, with a population density of 153 per sq. km.. Occupying a section of Central Italy from the arc of the Apennine watershed, which veers closer to the Adriatic than to the Tyrrhenian (diverging in several places from the border), to the Tyrrhenian coastline, from the beaches of Luni all the way to the Argentario. This region is largely hilly and mountainous, with two distinct areas: the Apennines, and the "Antiappennino." In the Apennines, basins run lengthwise between the watershed range (from the Cisa pass to the Alpe della Luna) and the secondary ranges that run parallel: among these basins are the Mugello, the Casentino, and the Alta Val Tiberina (upper Tiber valley). Running to the west of the broad Garfagnana, parallel with the Tyrrhenian coastline, is the jagged ridge of the Apuan Alps. The mountains to the south of the Arno have the conventional name of the Antiappennino Toscano, varied in origin and appearance; note the Tuscan uplands between the rivers Arno and Ombrone, fragmented into isolated mid-sized mountains (Colline Metallifere); a number of coastal peaks (Monti dell'Uccellina); Mt. Amiata (1,738 m.). Among the plains are the Valdarno Inferiore (lower Arno valley), the basins running between ranges, the Maremma, and the coastal strip. In this coastal strip, long straight beaches (Versilia) alternate with sweeping curved beaches, and sharp promontories (promontory of Piombino). Between the Tyrrhenian coast and Corsica lie the scattered islands of the Tuscan Archipelago (Arcipelago Toscano), jagged and entrancing (the largest is the Isle of Elba). The Tuscan countryside, well known from books and paintings, features a fertile landscape, neat farmlands, farmhouses surrounded by cypresses and haystacks, grazing oxen with long horns: an agrarian wonderland. Statistics give a good idea of the changing social structure: the percentage of farmers (5.51 percent) is sharply below the national average (9 percent); those working in manufacturing is a bit higher (34.69 percent as compared with 32 percent), and those in service industries is roughly equivalent (59.78 percent as compared with 59 percent). Farming is a centuries-old tradition, with renowned specialites: the vineyards of Chianti and Montepulciano, for example; the olive groves of the area around Lucca, and the greenhouse flowers of the Pistoia area. The region ranks third in Italy — after Liguria and Trentino — in forested area (38.7 percent, largely deciduous trees and chestnut woods). Minerals are extracted extensively (though mining is showing signs of decline): iron from Elba, pyrite and mercury from Mt. Amiata, rock salt from the area around Volterra, lignite from the upper Valdarno, marble from the Apuan mountains, and borax-laden geysers (used in the production of geothermal power) at Larderello and the Mt. Amiata. Industry is vast and diversified, with local traditions, such as the metallurgy of Piombino, the shipyards of Livorno, Marina di Carrara, and Viareggio, caustic soda at Rosignano Solvay, glass in the upper Valdarno, Empoli, Pisa, and Livorno, ceramics in Sesto Fiorentino, Florence, and Montelupo, and the woolmills of Prato. Among the crafts industries, note art, decorations, and silver in Florence, goldwork in Arezzo, alabaster in Volterra, and wrought iron in Siena and Pienza. In terms of volume of goods handled, Livorno is Italy's eighth-largest port, the second-largest on the peninsular Tyrrhenian coast. For tourists, the range of attractions is vast: cities with incredible treasuries of art, beaches, thermal springs, mountain resorts. The regional capital is Florence, while the other nine provincial capitals are Arezzo, Grosseto, Livorno, Lucca, Massa, Pisa, Pistoia, Prato, and Siena.

History. "Extending over land and sea was the power of the Tuscans prior to the dominion of the Romans," wrote Livy. This was the Etruscan region (this, and more), "a sort of painting of stupendous beauty," according to Pliny the Younger (the Etruscan period extended from the 8th c. B.C. to the Roman takeover, in the 4th/3rd c B.C.). A second major period of history, which left a deep mark on the region's appearance, was that of communal government, beginning in the 11th c., when the Tuscan cities teemed with trade, cultural ferment, social activity, and varied manufacturing; they soon lorded it over the surrounding countryside, and before long were struggling for predominance: Lucca, Pisa, Pistoia, Siena, Arezzo, and Florence, to say nothing of the smaller contenders. The emergence of Florence, a great Italian power, and, in financial and commercial terms, a European player, as the political ruler of the region was not a rapid process, and met numerous obstacles from the 14th c. onward; in any case during the Middle Ages Tuscany, under Florence, acquired Pistoia, Arezzo, Pisa, and their territory. In the wake of the "wars of Italy" between France and the Holy Roman Empire, Florence and its state were ruled by the Medici, now princes, who conquered the Republic of Siena (1555-59), rising with Cosimo I to the standing of grand dukes of Tuscany (1569). In 1737, with the extinction of the Medici, the title and lands passed to Francesco Stefano duke of Lorraine (Lorena; husband of Maria Theresa of Hapsburg, and thus emperor) and his successors. Lucca was excluded from the great regional state (until 1847), as was Massa-Carrara, under the seigneury of the Cybo Malaspina and later the D'Este, and a few other fragmentary territories. The first six decades of the 19th c. witnessed the spectacular institutional transformations under Napoleon (with his sister, Elisa Bonaparte Baciocchi, grand duchess of Tuscany), the restoration of the Lorraine, and the role played in the creation of a unified Italian state: the last grand duke, Leopoldo II, left Florence after the demonstrations of 27 April 1859; in March 1860 a plebiscite vote led to Tuscany's annexation to the kingdom of Italy.

Art. There are Etruscan relics everywhere in the region: Fièsole, Cortona, Chiusi, Volterra, Populonia, Vetulonia, and Sovana, gates, walls, temples, necropolises chiefly. Less common are Roman ruins: the walls of Cosa, the earliest Roman monument in Etruria, ruins of Roman baths in Pisa, amphitheaters at Luni (under the administration of Liguria), Lucca, and Arezzo, theater and baths at Volterra, with the more significant antiquities at Fièsole (temple, theater, baths). With the 11th c., "Tuscan art" proper first appears; between the 14th c. and the turn of the 16th c., Tuscan painting, sculpture, and architecture were to create one of the most remarkable bodies of work in the world of art. The seeds lie in the Romanesque architecture (with classical accents) that develops in Florence (S. Miniato) and Pisa (Duomo). The Pisan style, echoed and enriched in Lucca, was to spread to Pistoia, Prato, Volterra, and Carrara. Civil and religious buildings erected in Florence and Siena in the 13th c. and 14th c. offer a particular modulation, a certain clarity of Gothic line, a simple and majestic solemnity. The intense construction of the two centuries in question changed the architectural face of cities such as Pistoia, Pisa, San Gimignano, Volterra, and Cortona. From Pisa, with Nicola and Giovanni Pisano, a new school of sculpture spread to Florence, where Arnolfo di Cambio, Andrea Pisano, and Andrea Orcagna worked; to Siena, with Tino da Camaino, and elsewhere. Painting, like trade and politics, had two major centers in the 13th and 14th c.: Florence, with Cimabue, Giotto, and the followers of Giotto; and Siena with Duccio di Buoninsegna, Simone Martini, and Ambrogio and Pietro Lorenzetti. In the 15th c., Florence was the leading center; the Renaissance is a Florentine artistic creation; let us mention just the three Florentine artists who are said to have given "new form" (Vasari) to the main arts: Filippo Brunelleschi, Masaccio, and Donatello. There was a complex and dynamic relationship with the surrounding region; influences spread and mingle, Florentine and Tuscan artists corresponded and moved from place to place; the provinces produced renowned artists: J. della Quercia, F. di Giorgio Martini, B. Peruzzi (Siennese); P. della Francesca from Sansepolcro, L. Signorelli from Cortona, M. Civitali from Lucca; Florentines worked throughout the region, creating a Renaissance style, single and coherent, though veined with subtle variations, that is now the face of Tuscany: Bernardo Rossellino, architect of Pienza, Michelozzo and Antonio da Sangallo at Montepulciano, Benedetto da Maiano at Arezzo; Giuliano da Sangallo and Filippo Lippi at Prato, Benozzo Gozzoli at Pisa and San Gimignano... Leonardo da Vinci and Michelangelo Buonarroti were Florentines by culture and Tuscans by birth, and Raphael too spent time in Florence. At the turn of the 16th c., however, leadership in Italian art shifted to Rome. Tuscan art, from then on, was to become separate, though still of excellent quality, confident in style, preserving the dignity and spirit of this region. To mention names means risking a partial representation. Still, consider Pontormo, Cellini, and the style of Mannerism, the dignified clarity of Neoclassicism, the painting of the Macchiaioli, modern Tuscan masters (the painters O. Rosai, from Florence, and Amedeo Modigliani, from Livorno; the sculptor Lorenzo Viani from Viareggio; the architect Giovanni Michelucci, from Pistoia).

Trentino

This is a semi-independent province, with its capital at Trent, of the specially chartered region of Trentino-Alto Adige, established in 1948. The area is 6,123 sq. km, with a population of 447,556, and a density of 65 inhabitants per sq. km. The territory lies along the middle Adige valley, and includes the valleys of the various tributaries and the high course of the river Sarca, the Chiese, the Brenta, and the Cismon. It is bounded to the NW by the chain of mountains that run from the Cevedale to the Adige, to the west by the Adamello group, and to the east by the Dolomites.

This is a land of mountains and forests (which cover more than half its area), with a wide range of landscapes: pre-Alpine, Dolomitic, and Alpine, with high meadows (Folgaria, Lavarone), small mountain lakes (Molveno, Toblino, Caldonazzo, Lèvico, and Tovel), and the northern basin of Lake Garda, a sunny corner of the Mediterranean.

Most workers are farmers or in the service industries, especially tourism. Timber, livestock, orchards and vineyards, on the one hand, and mountain resorts, climbing, and winter sports, on the other, make up this province's prime resources.

History. What is now Trentino was settled by the Romans between the 3rd and 2nd c. B.C. The Holy Roman Emperor Conrad II, concerned that the passage between Germany and Italy over the Brenner Pass be held by allies, established the ecclesiastical principality of Trent (1027; along with that of Bressanone). Not all the 51 bishop-princes who ruled the territory until 1803 were German (under the Italian Cristoforo Madruzzo, in 1545, the famous Council of Trent was inaugurated in the cathedral of Trent). An imperial holding, coveted by the Hapsburgs (they had influence and power here from 1363 on as counts of the Tyrol; then, in 1511 Maximilian of Hapsburg imposed a sort of protectorate over the ecclesiastical principality), it was directly ruled by Austria following the Napoleonic wars, until the end of WWI, when Italian troops entered Trent on 3 November 1918.

Art. Romanesque architecture and sculpture show Lombard influence; note the cathedral of Trent. Gothic churches (Cavalese, Cles) castles, and paintings, were produced through the end of the 15th c. (frescoes in the castle of Avio, Torre dell'Aquila in Trent, and Trent cathedral). The Renaissance first appears here in the Magno Palazzo in the Castello del Buonconsiglio at Trent (1528); the Dossi and the Guardi had links with this area.

Umbria

The total surface area of this region is 8,546 sq. km., less than 3 percent of Italy's national territory; it is the fourth from the last in population (804,054); population density is 95 persons per sq. km., less than half the Italian average. It is surrounded by Tuscany, the Marche, and Lazio, the only region in peninsular Italy to have no coastline; it is largely hilly or mountainous, and uniform in topography. The highest features, rarely taller than 1,500 m., are part of the main range of the Apennines, in the section known as the "tratto umbro-marchigiano," which extends to the east of the region (the highest peaks are in the SE, toward the Monti Sibillini and the Monte Terminillo); in the rest of the region, small rolling mountains slope away to the west. Between mountains or hills stretch out large basins, flat or sloping slightly, one-time lakes long since filled with alluvial material: the Valle Umbra, running between Perugia and Spoleto, the Val Tiberina, through which the Tiber flows, the plains of Gubbio, Norcia, and Terni. The landscape abounds in water: springs, such as the Sorgenti del Clitunno, the waterfalls of the Màrmore, the lakes of Trasimeno and Piediluco. Economic transformations, which have shaken this largely agricultural area in recent years, have led to distribution of the labor

force along the Italian average: 8.52 percent in farming, 32.13 in industry, 59.35 in service industries (national data, are, respectively, 9, 32, and 59 percent). Grapevines and olive groves dot the landscape; grapes and wine particularly in the area around Orvieto; olive groves in the land around lake Trasimeno and between Assisi and Terni. In the modern array of industrial activities, note the steel-making and machine industries of the Terni area, powered by the hydroelectric plants running on the rivers Velino and Nera. There is an age-old tradition of ceramics in the towns of Deruta, Gubbio, Gualdo Tadino, Perugia, and Orvieto. Perugia is the regional capital, while the second province is that of Terni.

History. First of all there were the Umbri, powerful warriors, who lived along the left bank of the Tiber, and then the Etruscans, who lived along the right bank; both were subjugated by the Romans in 295 B.C. Later came the Longobards in the duchy of Spoleto (6th/8th c.), and last were the communal governments of the cities, in the 11th and 12th c., foremost among them Perugia. Alongside the saints (Benedict of Nursia and Francis of Assisi), local history is filled with adventuresome condottieri: the Piccinino family, Malatesta Baglioni, Gattamelata da Narni, and Braccio da Montone. The Roman Catholic church struggled from the 8th to the 16th c. to control this region, and succeeded only when the local seigneuries died out: the Trinci in Foligno, the Atti in Todi, the Monaldeschi in Orvieto, and the Baglioni in Perugia. The Papal State survived longer, following the period of Napoleonic rule. In 1859 the Perugians rebelled, and Pius IX sent 2,000 Swiss soldiers to take the city, which they brutally sacked: these were the "massacres of Perugia"; the following year, Italian troops took the city, under the general Manfredo Fanti.

Art. Etruscan ruins can be found in Perugia (Arco d'Augusto, Ipogeo dei Volumni), Orvieto, Bettona (the walls), and Todi; there are Roman ruins in Assisi (Temple of Minerva, amphitheater), Spoleto (Arco di Druso, amphitheater, theater, Ponte Sanguinario), Spello (the walls and gates), and Gubbio (theater), not to mention the archeological sites of "Carsulae" and "Ocriculum." Among the exquisite early-Christian buildings are S. Salvatore in Spoleto, the Tempietto del Clitunno, and S. Angelo in Perugia. Building flourished after the 12th c.; among the Romanesque churches, based on the Lombard style, are the Duomo and the church of S. Gregorio in Spoleto, the Duomo of Assisi, S. Silvestro and S. Michele in Bevagna, and other churches in towns, villages, and countryside. The architectural style of almost all the towns in Umbria dates from the Gothic period: in Assisi, note the two stacked churches of S. Francesco — where Cimabue, Giotto, Simone Martini, and Pietro Lorenzetti worked, among others — and the church of S. Chiara were built; Orvieto had the Siennese architect Maitani build its Duomo; alongside the cathedrals note the secular public buildings: the Palazzo dei Priori in Perugia, the Palazzo dei Consoli in Gubbio, the Palazzo del Popolo in Orvieto, and others in Todi and Città di Castello. Though few in number, the examples of Renaissance architecture are notable: the Oratorio di S. Bernardino, with its sculpture, in Perugia, the Palazzo Ducale in Gubbio, and S. Maria della Consolazione and Todi. Tuscan artists came to work in Umbria (Benozzo Gozzoli in Montefalco, Filippo Lippi in Spoleto, and Luca Signorelli in Orvieto, to name only a few) but Umbrian painting began to take shape as well, with a number of "centers" (Gubbio, Foligno, Spoleto, and Perugia); foremost however were Pinturicchio (from Perugia) and Perugino (from Città della Pieve), teacher of Raphael.

Valle d'Aosta / Vallée d'Aoste

This is a section of the Alpine arc, tucked away in the northwesternmost corner of Italy, with some of the tallest mountains in Europe. Its area (3,262 sq. km.), one percent of Italy's surface area, makes it the smallest of Italy's twenty regions. Valle d'Aosta is also the least populous region (115,397 inhabitants) and the lowest in population density (36 inhabitants per sq. km.).

The central topographic axis is the valley of the Dora Baltea (a northern tributary of the Po, its confluence just downstream of Chivasso), running west-to-east; into this valley angle the valleys of a number of smaller tributaries. Chief among these smaller valleys are the Valle del Gran San Bernardo, Valtelline, Valtournenche, Valle di Challand-Ayas, Valle del Lys; on the southern side: Valle di La Thuile, Valgrisenche, Val di Rhêmes, Valsavarenche, Valle di Cogne, and Valle di Champorcher. Among the major peaks: Mont Blanc, 4,807 m., the Matterhorn (called Cervino by the Italians), 4,478 m., and Monte Rosa, 4,637 m., all to the north; the Gran Paradiso, 4,061 m., to the south. Mountainous massifs with vast glaciers, high passes in use since ancient times (complemented nowadays by the Mont Blanc and the Gran San Bernardo tunnels), Alpine hollows, forests, the exquisite wildlife and plantlife of the Alps, Roman and medieval monuments, castle after castle, a robust country architecture — all these are the finest features of this great valley; here history, landscape, and nature intertwine. During the summer, the valley is thronged; among the numerous resorts, there are such venerable names as Courmayeur at the foot of Mont Blanc, Breuil-Cervinia in the shadow of the Matterhorn, Gressoney, Brusson, Champoluc, Valtournenche, Cogne, and La Thuile. Many of these resorts, especially those at the head of the valley, are also popular with skiers, winter and summer; the facilities and slopes are often first-rate. For mountain climbers and hikers, there are numerous huts and bivouacs; Alpine guides can be found in any mountain village here. Gressoney and Champoluc are base camps for ascents of Monte Rosa, Breuil-Cervinia for scaling the Matterhorn, Courmayeur for climbers heading up the Mont Blanc group; Cogne is an ideal point of departure for hikers in the Parco Nazionale del Gran Paradiso. Among the resort towns, Saint-Vincent is particularly well-known, the site of many different annual events and home to a major casino. The valley has a considerable industry; encouraged by the autonomous regional government, recent economic development has integrated mountain agriculture with crafts and service industries, further driven by tourism.

The Valle d'Aosta is a special autonomous region, governed by a Consiglio di Valle with extensive administrative jurisdiction; it is officially bilingual (Italian and French); the capital is Aosta.

Veneto (Venetia)

With an area of 18,364 sq. km, this region makes up 6 percent of Italy's territory; in terms of population (4,363,157) and density (239 inhabitants per sq. km) it ranks fifth. It extends from the Alpine watershed to the Adriatic Sea: it covers the northeastern section of the Po Valley (bounded by Lake Garda and the river Mincio, to the west, by the Po, to the south, and by the rivers Livenza and Tagliamento, to the east) and part of the eastern Alps. There are, thus, two natural zones: plains and mountains. The alluvial plain is flanked, at the coast, by the Venetian lagoon and by the northern portion of the Po delta.

Upon that plain, between Verona and Padua, the Monti Bèrici and the Colli Euganei stand out. At the north of the plain begin the Prealpi, or Alpine foothills, limestone formations that extend from Lake Garda to Friùli, rising to elevations of between 1,500 and 2,000 m. These massifs and highlands are covered with meadows and forests; they are separated from the Alps by long east-west depressions and are crisscrossed with river valleys.

The Alpine section of Veneto includes the high basin of the river Piave, the spectacular views and peaks of the Dolomites, and a length of the watershed, in the Carnian Alps.

The past fifty years have seen the Veneto undergo economic transformation more radical and thorough than anywhere else in Italy, a country that has itself experienced startling changes. Once predominantly a farming region, Veneto is now devoted chiefly to manufacturing and service industries.

Agriculture still flourishes here (Veneto leads Italy in the production of wine grapes and corn, and it is second in production of wine, sugar beets, and beef). Heavy industry is concentrated on the edge of the Lagoon; wool is produced in the area around Vicenza. Some areas have traditional industries: glass in Murano, eyeglasses and lenses in Cadore, gold in Vicenza, ceramics in Bassano, Nove, and Este. Venice is still a busy port, the Adriatic's second largest.

Tourism and resorts are big business here, both mountains, beaches, and hot springs, and, of course, artistic capitals such as Venice — with all the problems that this entails.

The regional capital is Venice, while the six other provincial capitals are Belluno, Padua, Rovigo, Treviso, Verona, and Vicenza.

History. There is an ancient date, as precise as it is mythical: the foundation of Padua by the Trojan, Antenor, in 1184 B.C.; it is believed that paleo-Venetian settlements date from the 10th c. B.C., between the rivers Adige and Livenza, and that the culture of the ancient Venetians developed from there. Romanization dates from the 3rd and 2nd c. B.C.; according to the Augustan census, Padua was the second-wealthiest city in Italy, following Rome. At the end of the period of great tribal migrations, the arrival of the Longobards triggered the separation of hinterland and lagoon, where refugees from earlier invasions had already found safe haven. The hinterland, or "terraferma," fell to the Longobards, Franks, and then the Holy Roman Empire, while the "estuary" was Byzantine and was later ruled by the Serenissima, or Venetian Republic. As the Republic consolidated, it took back the "terraferma." Inland, Veneto, or Venetia participated in the history of the Po Valley, with the formation of communal government in the cities (11th/12th c.), followed by the rise to power of feudal seigneurial families (13th/14th c.): the Della Scala in Verona (the most expansionistic, halted by a coalition of Venice, Florence, and Milan, 1336-39), the Carraresi in Padua, the Da Camino in Treviso, and the D'Este, who moved from Este to Ferrara. Venice, meanwhile, was enjoying centuries of dazzling power: political, mercantile, and maritime power, more Mediterranean than Italian. Venice's first great conquest outside of the lagoon was Treviso (1339); the "politics of the terraferma" and the struggle with the Visconti, who had invaded the Veneto, led to the "inland dominion" (turn of the 15th c.; see also Venice), which also included, besides what is now Veneto, or Venetia, the Friùli and eastern Lombardy, as far as the river Adda. Following the critical war of the League of Cambrai (1509), in which Venice came a hair's-breadth from catastrophe, the unified government of Venice lasted until the fall of the Republic (1796) and Bonaparte's annexation to Austria (Treaty of Campo Formio, 1797). Save for the Napoleonic reconquest (1805-1815), Venetia remained Austrian until annexation to the Kingdom of Italy (1866), as the political outcome of the Third War of Independence.

Art. The Arena of Verona is the chief Roman monument in northern Italy. During the Middle Ages, Veneto, which is part of the Po Valley, shared its artistic culture, while Venice adhered to its own: thus, S. Zeno in Verona is Lombard in character, while St. Mark's, in Venice is Byzantine.

On the mainland, construction was thriving during the 13th and 14th c.; Romaneseque, Gothic, and Po Valley brick structures: note the churches of S. Antonio in Padua, S. Anastasia in Verona, S. Lorenzo in Vicenza, the Castelvecchio of Verona, the Palazzo della Ragione in Padua, the Palazzo dei Trecento in Treviso, and the walls around Montagnana, Cittadella, and Castelfranco Veneto. Venice, in the meanwhile, was developing its own highly original Gothic, with that complex of structures, space, shapes, and colors that was so fitting to the Rialto islands, where architecture — it has been said — appears as the resonance of color between the infinity of sea and sky (Palazzo Ducale, Ca' d'Oro, the churches of the Frari and S. Zanipolo).

Giotto painted in Padua in the 14th c. (Scrovegni chapel); in the 15th c., Padua was the source in northern Italy of Renaissance influence. The Florentine Donatello worked here, as did A. Mantegna, a native. During the same century, the magnificent era of great Venetian painting was beginning, one of the highest moments in Italian, and world, art: Gentile and Giovani Bellini, V. Carpaccio, Tintoretto, Cima da Conegliano, Giorgione (from Castelfranco), Tiziano (from Pieve di Cadore), and P. Veronese.

Even in Renaissance form, Venetian architecture maintained its original "flavor of the lagoon," both in such churches as S. Maria dei Miracoli and S. Zaccaria and in private homes. The austere 16th-c. architecture of J. Sansovino (Libreria Marciana) fit in equally well with that unique atmosphere, as did the spirit of the Paduan Andrea Palladio (churches of S. Giorgio and Redentore), who also shaped the appearance of Vicenza and the Veneto countryside, dotted with Palladian villas.

The culture of Venice continued to find glorious echoes in the "terraferma." Baroque architecture was perfectly tailored to Venice by B. Longhena: the Salute, Ca' Pesaro, and the luminous color of 18th-c. painting is unequalled (Piazzetta, Giambattista and Giandomenico Tiepolo, Guardi, Canaletto). Pietro Longhi, with his "brilliant and bizarre spirit" (in the words of Longhi's son), depicted the same Venetian life described by Carlo Goldoni. In later years, illustrious Venetians worked outside of the city of canals: the architect and engraver G.B. Piranesi; the sculptor Antonio Canova, and, in the 20th c., the sculptor Arturo Martini.

Italy A to Z

Aeolian Islands / Isole Eolie

pop. 12,642, Sicily, province of Messina.

This **archipelago** comprises 7 islands: the three largest islands — *Vulcano, Lìpari*, and *Salina* — are quite close, while *Fìlicudi* and *Alicudi* lie to the west; *Panarea* and *Strómboli*, to the north.

Lìpari, with steep coastline, is surrounded by stacks (columns of rock isolated from shore by wave action) and shoals; it is the largest island in the archipelago; the steep island culminates in the Monte Chìrica (602 m.) and Monte S. Angelo (594 m.).

The lovely little town of **Lìpari** lies at the center of the archipelago, with the port and beach of *Marina Lunga* to the north, and the hydrofoil landing and *Marina Corta* to the south.

The 16th-c. Spanish bastions of the **Castello*** include medieval towers and curtain walls (13th c.), as well as an older Greek tower (4th/3rd c. B.C.); these walls stand on the site of the old acropolis. Until the 18th c., the entire town lay within their perimeter.

In the *archeological zone* the digs (explanatory maps) have uncovered layers of buildings that range from the oval huts of the early (17th/15th c. B.C.) to the mid-(14th/13th c. B.C.) Bronze Age, ruins of early-Iron Age huts (11th/9th c. B.C.), up to ruins of Hellenistic constructions.

Note the **Museo Eoliano*** *(open, 9-2; holidays 9-1)*, which offers a remarkable picture of the unbroken human presence on these islands through the Neolithic.

Surrounding areas. From **Canneto**, a little village on an inlet on the eastern coast, 3.5 km. to the north, you can reach the enormous obsidian lava flow (30 min.) of the **Forgia Vecchia***, the *pumice quarries** and another obsidian lava flow of the *Rocche Rosse**.

Vulcano. The two picturesque inlets of *Porto Ponente* and *Porto Levante* open out onto the short isthmus linking Vulcano and Vulcanello. At Porto Levante, natural hot sulphur springs boil into the clear waters of the sea.

There is a fine view* from **Vulcanello** (123 m.), the little volcanic cone that forms the northernmost tip of the island; we know it was formed in 183 B.C.
South of the isthmus you climb up (40 min.) to the **main crater** of Vulcano (391 m.), an enormous funnel 500 m. across; there is a spectacular *view*** of the archipelago, the Sicilian coast, and Mt. Etna.

Salina. This is the second-largest island, as well as the tallest (Fossa delle Felci, 962 m.).

Santa Marina Salina is at an elevation of 25 m., midway along the eastern coast, on the beach; at a distance of 2.2 km., at *Lingua* is the lagoon that gave the island its modern name; in ancient times it was called Didyme (twin), for its two peaks.

Panarea. A *prehistoric village** *(custodian)*, with oval huts (18th/13th c. B.C.) on the promontory of Milazzo is the most interesting point on the island, which has three small villages —*Iditella, San Pietro*, and *Drauto* — amongst the olive groves on the eastern slopes of the Timpone del Corvo (420 m.).

Strómboli. The white Mediterranean houses, set amidst green palm trees, olive groves, and citrus orchards, of the three quarters of Piscità, Ficogrande, San Vincenzo, which make up the town of **Strómboli** (43 m.), lie on the island's NE coast; Strómboli is a single, huge volcanic cone, harsh and alluring, secluded in its stretch of sea.

The **crater of the volcano*** *(3 hours; you should be accompanied by an authorized guide)* opens out at an elevation of 750 m., with a flared basin that spews forth the products of eruptions on the steep slope of the Sciara del Fuoco; the best point of view can be had from the observation platform of *Punta Labronzo*.
You can get a fine view of the *Sciara del Fuoco** from below *(by boat, 25 min.)*: lava, blocks of stone, and lapilli drop down to the sea from the crater, during eruptions, whistling as they plunge down, and spouting up columns of steam and water as they hit.

Filicudi. The steep cone of the mountain of Filicudi (773 m.) is covered with bare rocks; in ancient times, it was called Phoenicusa, for the many ferns that grow here.
At *Capo Graziano* note the Bronze Age *prehistoric village (custodian)*, with oval huts (18th/13th c. B.C.).

Alicudi. In ancient times this island was called Ericusa for the "erica," or heather, that covered it. The houses are scattered between the beach and the slopes of the Timpone della Montagnola (675 m.). Lobsters are trapped and sold here.

Agrigento**

elev. 230 m., pop. 55,440, Sicily, provincial capital.
The main reason for going to Agrigento is certainly to see the amazing array of ancient Greek ruins in the old city; nowhere else on earth, not even in Greece, will you see so many sacred buildings in one place. The Greek colony here was founded in 581 B.C. by settlers from nearby Gela and by other settlers, from Rhodes and from Crete. In the century that followed, the philosopher Empedocles lived and worked here.

Historical note. Modern-day Agrigento is composed of a city with a strong medieval flavor; it occupies the western hill which, until a century ago, was separated by a depression from the Rupe Atenea to the east. The depression was filled in and now Piazza Vittorio Emanuele and Piazza Aldo Moro stand on the site; here the 19th-c. town grew. On the plain that runs down from the Rupe Atenea, where the acropolis probably stood, toward the sea, the ancient city once stood; it is now suffering from encroaching and uncontrolled development.

Places of interest. Via Atenea. The crowded and lovely medieval section of Agrigento is

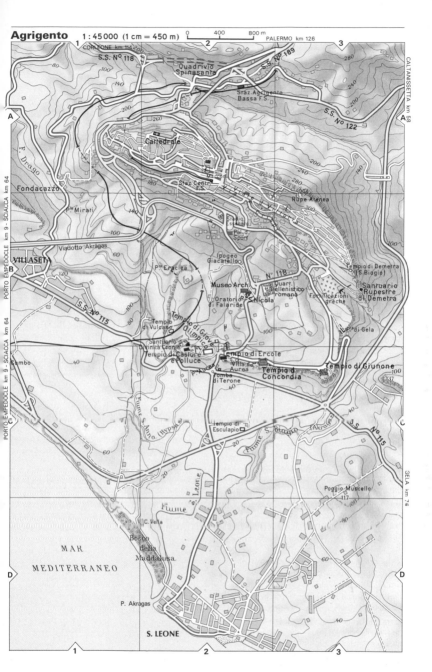

crossed by the winding Via Atenea, the main thoroughfare, running from Piazza Aldo Moro, at the boundary of the new addition (near *Piazza Marconi, A2*), to Piazza Pirandello.

S. Spirito* is a late-13th-c. abbey, heavily rebuilt; the stuccoes on the interior *(custodian at n. 2, opposite)* are attributed to Serpotta; in the former monastery, note the cloister and various remarkable pieces of medieval architecture.

Duomo* *(A2)*. This cathedral has a complex history, ranging from the 11th to the 17th c.; note

the architectural details and the artworks. Also note the acoustic phenomenon whereby, from the cornice of the apse, it is possible to hear a person whisper at the entrance of the church.

Città Antica. From *Piazza Marconi (A2)*, if you follow the first stretch of the state road 118 *(Via Crispi)* and then drive down into the *Valle dei Templi* (Valley of the Temples), you will reach the large plaza (parking area) facing the enclosure of the Temple of Olympian Jove; then you should continue east, passing the three main temples and returning to the state road 118: this route is the **archeological tour****.

Quartiere Ellenistico-Romano* *(B2-3; open, 9-an hour before sunset; closed holidays)*. More than any other, this site offers a sense of just what the ancient city looked like at its foundation (4th to 2nd c. B.C.) and on until the fall of the Roman empire; the area was crossed by 4 parallel roads *(cardines)* which connected with the decumanus (now the state road at this juncture); the road is lined with homes and shops.

S. Nicola*. The 13th-c. Gothic-Romanesque church of S. Nicola shows Cistercian construction; the site it occupies has seen a Greek, a Hellenistic, and a Roman sanctuary, monasteries, and a Norman church. Note the famous **sarcophagus*** engraved with the myth of Phaedrus (2nd-/3rd-c. A.D.). Fine view* of the temples from the square in front of the church.

Oratorio di Falaride* *(B2)*. This little temple represents the Hellenistic phase of the sanctuary, on the site now occupied by the church of S. Nicola.

Museo Archeologico Regionale** *(B2; open, 9-1 and 3-6)*. This fine archeological museum is located behind the church; it has collections from the city of Agrigento itself, as well as from the various ancient sites in the provinces of Agrigento and Caltanissetta. Of particular note is the **telamon*** (human figure used as a column) from the Temple of Olympian Jove, *artifacts** from the excavations of the Roman-Hellenistic quarter, a marble *Ephebe** (a beardless youth), dating from about 470 B.C. circa, and a red-figured krater* with a scene of Amazon warriors in combat (5th c. B.C.).

Tempio di Giove Olimpico* *(B-C2)*. This temple to Olympian Jove, built after a victory over Carthage at Imera (480 B.C.), was destroyed by earthquakes; you can still see the vast perimeter, heaped with rubble; it did not have the normal circuit of columns. Rather, the outer wall was punctuated by half-columns alternating with telamons (human figures used as columns). This is therefore a pseudo-peripteral temple.

The area to the west of the temple *(B-C2)* is dense with ruins of sacred buildings: the numerous altars, the bases of the temples, the sacred enclosures, and the "favissae" (dedicatory ditches) all dating from the 6th/5th c. B.C. were part of a *sanctuary of the chthonic deities** (Demetra and Persephone). At the center of this area stand four columns with a fragmentary trabeation from the *Temple of Castor and Pollux** (5th c. B.C.; the trabeation dates from Hellenistic-Roman times). This notable group of columns is one of the best-known sights of Agrigento; the other temples are arrayed further east along the rocky ridge.

Tempio di Ercole* *(C2)*. Eight columns standing in a heap of rubble belong to the *Temple of Hercules*, a six-column peripteral temple from the late-6th c. B.C., perhaps the earliest Doric temple in Agrigento.

Tempio della Concordia** *(C2-3)*. The 6th-c. A.D. transformation of this ancient temple into a Christian church probably helped to ensure its survival. It may have been dedicated to the Dioscuri (Castor and Pollux, sons of Zeus and Leda, brothers of Helen); the six-column peripteros, built

Agrigento: Tempio della Concordia

around the middle of the 5th c. B.C., is intact in its majestic proportions. This is considered to be one of the most perfect works of Greek architecture (the arcades cut into the side walls of the cella date from the adaptation of temple as church).

Tempio di Giunone** *(C3)*. Now a distinctive feature of this lovely landscape, the *Temple of Juno* *(C3)* stands alone at the edge of the rocky terrace; it had a six-column peripteros, much like the Temple of Concordia, from the same period.

Alberobello

elev. 428 m., pop. 10,655, Puglia, province of Bari. A forest of grey conical roofs top the massive round buildings of this town. Called "trulli," there are about a thousand of these strange round homes in Alberobello; the town's architecture is as unique as it is ancient.

Places of interest. The **monumental section*** comprises the *quarters of Monti* and *Aia Piccola*, with the "trulli" aligned along steep and winding lanes. Looking in through the front doors, you can see the interior structures of these remarkable

Alberobello: "trulli"

homes (*you should have little difficulty in touring one*): a central chamber communicates through archways with the kitchen and the other rooms. The most complete and the tallest "trullo" is the *Trullo Sovrano*, 2 stories tall, in a little square behind the church known as the Chiesa Madre.

Alghero

pop. 39,026; Sardinia, province of Sassari. Charles V landed here in October of 1541, while sailing with 40 galleys to take Algiers; reviewing the crowd from the balcony of Palazzo De Ferrera — it is said — he declared, "Estode todos caballeros," let all of you be knights. The city (whose name means "place of much algae") was at that time securely fortified; it stands on the promontory that seals off the enchanting bay, extending from the island's western coast. In the 14th c., the house of Aragon settled a colony of Catalonians here (the language is still spoken, and the architecture shows Catalonian influence), after deporting the entire native population on accusations of treason. The city has been growing throughout this century, only in part because of its popularity as a resort.

Places of interest. **Mura Catalane**. The Catalonian walls still enclose the entire historical city center; they are dotted with towers and offer pleasant places to stroll. Overlooking the harbor is the *Fort of Maddalena*, rebuilt in the 18th c. Behind it is the *Porta a Mare*, a gate leading into the old town. At the NW point of the walls is a tower called the *Torre della Polveriera*, at the SW point is the octagonal and slightly Gothic *Torre di S. Giacomo*, and at the SE point is the **Torre dello Sperone**, which dates from 1364. Overlooking the new town are the 16th-c. *Torre di S. Giovanni*, and the 14th-c. *Porta a Terra*.

Cattedrale*. The Catalonian late-Gothic style of the original 16th-c. church of *S. Maria* can be seen in the apse, campanile, aisles, cupola, and in some chapels.

S. Francesco. First built in the 14th c. and rebuilt in the 16th c., this church has a number of impressive statues of Christ.

Amalfi*

elev. 6 m., pop. 5,699, Campania, province of Salerno. This one-time Maritime Republic wrote a major chapter in the history of Europe, with Pisa, Genoa, and Venice. Along the splendid coastline extends the blindingly white town, with its intricate narrow lanes, some of them roofed over.

Places of interest. By the seaside is the **Piazza Flavio Gioia** (named for the man said to have invented the compass). Nearby, with two aisles crowned with Gothic arches, are the remains of the *Arsenale della Repubblica*.

The **Duomo***, high atop a stairway, dates from the 9th c., and was rebuilt in Sicilian Arab-Norman style in 1203, and again in the 18th c.; the facade was redone in the 19th c.; the handsome campanile*, with little towers and interwoven Arab-style arches high atop it, dates from 1180-1276; beneath the Gothic atrium, the central portal features an exquisite bronze door*, cast in Constantinople (circa 1066). In the presbytery,

Amalfi: Duomo

note two candelabra and two mosaic ambos (12th/13th c.); in the crypt, with the supposed relics of the apostle Andrew, statues by M. Naccherino and Pietro Bernini; alongside the left aisle is the Cappella del Crocifisso, with fragments of the 13th-c. church.

You can enter the renowned **Chiostro del Paradiso*** (*open, 9-7*) from the far left end of the atrium of the Duomo: this cloister served as the burial place of the noble and illustrious citizens of Amalfi.

Anagni

elev. 424 m.; pop. 19,314; Lazio, province of Frosinone. Tradition has it that the god Saturn founded this ancient city, perched high atop a ridge overlooking the valley of the river Sacco. Later, it became a sort of papal capital. Here, a supporter of a French king (Philip IV) slapped a pope (Boniface VIII), who later died of mortification; here a pope, Alexander III, excommunicated — with bell, book, and candle — a Holy Roman Emperor, Frederick I.

Places of interest. **Casa Barnekow**. Best known of the many medieval-style houses of Anagni, it actually dates from the 16th c. The name was given by a Swedish nobleman who bought it in the mid-19th c., decorating it with frescoes and plaques. Facing it is the Romanesque campanile of the church of **S. Andrea**; inside, note the fine 14th-c. triptych.

Piazza Cavour. Created around 1560, this handsome square overlooks, like a broad balcony, the city center and the distant valley of the Sacco; note the elegant church of *S. Maria di Loreto* (1750).

Palazzo Comunale. This 12th-c. building has a Lombard-Romanesque appearance. On the ground floor, a majestic vault leads to the square behind, where markets were held and justice was once meted out.

Cattedrale**. One of the most important and influential pieces of Romanesque architecture in Lazio, built between 1072 and 1104 and renovated in the 13th c. with Gothic accents, this cathedral stands along high above the town. In the magnificent and lively left side, the Gothic chapel of the Caetani (1292) thrusts forth, beside a loggia topped by a statue of Boniface VIII Caetani. Note the baptistery and apses, and the 12th-c. campanile.

Inside, note the Cosmatesque floors (1231). In the *presbytery*, a handsome ciborium* above the altar, a tortile paschal candelabrum*, and the bishop's seat at the end of the apse, are all by P.Vassalletto (1267). In the left nave, note the Gothic *Caetani* chapel. The **crypt**** has fine frescoes* done between 1231 and 1255 by Benedictine painters. Also note the *Cappella di S. Tommaso Becket* (St. Thomas a Becket), perhaps originally a Roman Mithreum.

Adjacent to the Cathedral is a **museum** (*open by request, contact the parish priest, 9-12 and 3-7; winter until 5*), with a rich treasury, partly comprising objects donated by Pope Boniface VIII (13th c.); a section features ancient and medieval marble carvings.

Palazzo di Bonifacio VIII. Built by Pope Gregory IX, it passed into the hands of the Caetani family in 1295. Note the loggia and mullioned windows on the front, and the high arched buttresses in the back. **Inside** (*open, by request*) are numerous halls, some frescoed; in one of these, the famed Slap of Anagni took place, when Sciarra Colonna, a supporter of the French king, Philip the Fair, struck the pope, Boniface VIII, so roundly despised by Dante. Note the *Museum* (*open 9-12, 3-6*), with archeological exhibits and documentation on the history and monuments of Anagni. Not far away is **Palazzo Traietto**, once the home of Boniface VIII.

Ancona

pop. 101,285; Marche, capital of the region. This active and courageous town (badly damaged by bombs in WWII and an earthquake in the Seventies) extends like an amphitheater, westward, on outcroppings of the Cònero (Goethe wrote that, from Piazza Da Sangallo, beneath the citadel, you can see the "loveliest sunsets on earth"), and has two parts: the old section, beneath the Basilica di S. Ciriaco, a landmark for sailors; and the modern section, spilling over to the eastern shore. As the Colle Guasco had eroded, the emperor Trajan sent his architect, Apollodorus of Damascus, to build a mole and a new port.

Historical note. Ancona is now a city with two separate parts: the old historical and monumental center, with its medieval lanes, ramps, and stairs, perched on the Colle Guasco, atop which the Greek acropolis once stood (now the Romanesque cathedral of S. Ciriaco); and the modern grid of the section built since the late-18th c. The chief relics of the Roman city are the amphitheater and Trajan's arch, overlooking the port. After the western Roman empire fell, Ancona became part of Byzantium's maritime Pentapolis; Charlemagne made a gift of Ancona to the Church. Rebuilt after the ravages of the Saracens in A.D. 848, the city traded with Dalmatia and the Levant from the 10th to the 15th c., constantly warring with Venetian fleets and imperial German armies, and with the local rival towns of Òsimo, Macerata, and Jesi, and the Malatesta family. Wealth from trading allowed Ancona to build two new sets of walls in the 13th and 14th c., completing the church of S. Ciriaco and building the churches of S. Maria della Piazza, S. Francesco delle Scale, and S. Agostino, as well as the Palazzo del Governo, Palazzo degli Anziani, and Palazzo del Senato. Ancona might have grown to be a great maritime power, had it not stood in the shadows

of Venice and the papacy; in 1532 it fell to Pope Clement VII, who built the Cittadella on the Colle Astagno. Ancona grew over the next few centuries of papal rule, along the coast, to Porta Pia and the Mole Vanvitelliana. Only after Italian unification in 1861 did the town grow west and east, to the train station and Piazza Cavour.

Places of interest. Mole Vanvitelliana. Pentagonal in shape, this fortress-hospital was begun in 1733 by L. Vanvitelli. Nearby, in Via XXIX Settembre, is the late-Baroque *Porta Pia* (1789).

S. Agostino. This former church still has a fine Venetian Gothic portal*, begun by G. Orsini da Sebenico (1460-75), and completed by M. di Giovanni da Milano and G. Veneziano (1494).

Piazza della Repubblica. At the heart of Ancona, it opens out over the port between the 16th-c. church of the *SS. Sacramento* and the *Teatro delle Muse* (1826). Corso Garibaldi, Ancona's main street, leads to the vast Piazza Cavour.

Viale della Vittoria. From Largo XXIV Maggio, this boulevard crosses Ancona, almost reaching the sea, and ending at the **Monumento ai Caduti**, commemorating the WWI dead, by G. Cirilli (1923-33), where steps descend to the sea.

Via della Loggia. At the beginning of this road are the *Palazzo Giovannelli Benincasa* (ca. 1450) and the **Loggia dei Mercanti***, with a lovely Venetian Gothic facade, by G. Orsini da Sebenico (1451-59), restored by P.Tibaldi; the huge interior hall is by Tibaldi, as are the statues (some are by G.Varlè). Further along is the 13th-c. Romanesque church of **S. Maria della Piazza***; note the facade*, with several orders of blind arcades (1210-25), and large portal. Under the church (*visible through slabs of glass in the floor*) are remains of the 5th- and 6th-c. churches that once stood here; note mosaic fragments.

Piazza del Plebiscito. Elongated plaza with an 18th-c. statue of Pope Clement XII, and on one side, flanked by a 16th-c. tower, the handsome **Palazzo del Governo**, now the Prefettura, or Prefecture, designed by F. di Giorgio Martini (1484); a late-15th-c. Renaissance arch leads into the fine courtyard. At the end of the square, a spectacular stairway leads up to the church of **S. Domenico** (1771-88), built on the site of a 13th-c. church, and damaged by earthquake in 1930, by bombs in 1944, and again by earthquake in 1972. Inside, statues and medallions by G.Varlè, and fine paintings by artists such as Titian (1558) and Guercino (1662). Nearby, at the mouth of Via Matteotti, the *Arco Ferretti*, a city gate built in 1221 on the old walls of the 9th c. In Corso Mazzini, the **Fontana del Calamo**, a fountain designed by P.Tibaldi (1560), and in Piazza Roma, the *Fontana dei Cavalli* (1758), designed by L. Daretti, with sculpture by G.Varlè.

Pinacoteca Civica "Francesco Podesti" and the Galleria d'Arte Moderna. *Open 9-7, Sun. 9-1; closed Mon*. Located at n. 17 in Via Pizzecolli, in the 16th-c. *Palazzo Bosdari*. The collection includes works by C. Crivelli, Titian, L. Lotto, A. del Sarto, S. del Piombo, N. di Bicci, Pomarancio, and Guercino, and, among the modern artists, M. Campigli, B. Cassinari, C. Levi, F. Menzio, V. Guidi, and L. Veronesi.

S. Francesco delle Scale. Set high atop a stairway, this church overlooks Piazza S. Francesco d'Assisi. Rebuilt in the 18th c., it has a huge Venetian Gothic portal* by G. Orsini da Sebenico (1454); inside, work by L. Lotto, A. Lilli, and P. Tibaldi.

Piazza Stracca. With a panoramic view of the port, this square is flanked by the Neoclassical *church of Gesù* (1743), by L.Vanvitelli, and by the 13th-c. **Palazzo degli Anziani**: note the rear, with Gothic-Romanesque elements and 15th-c. windows. Next is Palazzo Ferretti, which houses the Museo Archeologico.

Museo Archeologico Nazionale delle Marche*. *Open, 8:30-1:30.* Located in the 16th-c. *Palazzo Ferretti*, in Via Ferretti, 6, the museum features materials that include: tomb furnishings; magnificent red-and-black Attic vases*; a 5th-c. B.C. "dinos" on a bronze tripod from Amándola*; splendid Etruscan bronzes*; Hellenistic and Roman items that range from fine gold and silver to household implements; a group of gold-plated bronzes (two women and two men on horseback), found at Cartoceto di Pérgola in 1946.

Piazza del Senato. The 13th-c. two-story **Palazzo del Senato** stands here, facing the 18th-c. church of *Ss. Pellegrino e Filippo Neri*; note 13th-c. Byzantine-style Crucifix.

Anfiteatro Romano. This Roman amphitheater seated 8,000 (93 m. long; 74 m. wide). You can see the main entrance to the amphitheater, and in the square, stretches of Roman wall and a vault.

Colle Guasco. At the end of Via Giovanni XXIII, or by stairway, you reach this hilltop overlooking the port; here stands the cathedral of S. Ciriaco; fine view in all directions*.

S. Ciriaco**. This is the pride of Ancona, and certainly one of the most interesting medieval churches in the Marche. Built from the 11th to the 13th c. in Romanesque style with some Byzantine influence and a few Gothic features. Note the 13th-c. dome and, in the white-and-pink *facade*, the impressive Gothic portal*, with reliefs.

Museo Diocesano. To the left of S. Ciriaco, this religious museum features fragments of architecture and sculpture from old and ancient churches in the local area; note the 4th-c. sarcophagus of Flavius Gorgonius*.

Ancona: S. Ciriaco

Arco di Traiano*. Trajan's Arch overlooks the port, at the foot of the Colle Guasco; the architect was Apollodorus of Damascus (A.D. 115), and the arch was built to commemorate the construction of the wharf. Not far off is the *Arco Clementino*, honoring Pope Clement XII, designed by L. Vanvitelli (1738).

Aosta / Aoste*

elev. 583 m.; pop. 36,095; Valle d'Aosta, regional capital. All around rises a majestic mountain landscape; on the outskirts of town are the marks of recent development, the product of intense traffic bound for mountain resorts and for the ski slopes of the high valley, and — more importantly — for France and Switzerland. The latter, international traffic has grown greatly since the completion of the Mont Blanc (Monte Bianco in Italian) and the Great St. Bernard (Gran S. Bernardo in Italian) tunnels. Further growth has come about through the city's status as capital of this autonomous region. From the outskirts, we proceed to the city's ancient heart, amidst the timeworn stones of the "Rome of the Alps," the ancient "Augusta Praetoria." Here too we find remarkable relics of the Middle Ages, a "borderland" school of art, and the stern, tranquil atmosphere of a mountain town.

Historical note. Aosta was founded during the reign of Augustus, in 25 B.C. The city's layout still basically reflects the original Roman grid, rectangular, enclosed by walls, with a checkerboard pattern of cross-streets. The main street of the Roman "camp" — the "decumanus maximus"   followed the route of the Little Saint Bernard, as can still be clearly seen. In the twilight of the Carolingian Empire, Aosta fell to the kingdom of Burgundy (A.D. 888); in 1025 the Burgundian king ceded Aosta to his chief adviser, Umberto Biancamano, founder of the Savoy dynasty. A few years later (1033), the great bishop of the city, Anselmo d'Aosta (St. Anselm), was born there; Aosta had converted to Christianity in the 5th c.; Anselm later became archbishop of Canterbury, a saint, and a Doctor of the Church. The materials of the Roman walls — a good portion of which has survived, and can be easily seen — and of some of Aosta's 18 proud towers were re-used to build castles; an excellent example is the Torre Bramafam. This tower belonged to the family of the Challand, viscounts of Aosta (and representatives of the counts of Savoy; the bonds between Savoy and Aosta, both city and valley, were always strong). In 1295 the Challand renounced their title of viscounts of the city, allowing Aosta a certain degree of self-government, and a council. Roman monuments aside, history has given the urban grid three distinct focal points, in terms of both art and setting. They are: Piazza Chanoux, the very core of Aosta; the cathedral, which stands near the site of the Roman forum; and — "extra muros," or "without the walls," toward the river Buthier, and perhaps on the site of Aosta's first cathedral, stands the collegiate church, or Collegiata di S. Orso. The third, S. Orso, is an exquisite medieval complex, with a late-15th c. priory facing it across a small square. The priory was built at the orders of the prior, Giorgio di Challand, who also built the castle of Issogne. The original Roman grid has even influenced the most recent additions to the city.

Getting around. The historical center of Aosta, and especially the central area from the Arco di Augusto to the Piazza della Repubblica, is closed to private automobile traffic. The route suggested here and marked on the map is a walking tour.

Places of interest. Arco di Augusto**. Located outside the walls, this Roman arch was built at the time of the founding of the city (25 B.C.), and was dedicated to Caesar Augustus. It has a single fornix, or vault, framed by Corinthian pilasters. The Crucifix under the arch is a copy of a 14th-c. original set there in the 15th c., and is now in the Museo della Cattedrale. From the square, fine panoramic view of the surrounding mountains. Not far off, beyond the river Buthier, is a single-span *Roman bridge*; it once spanned a mountain torrent, which shifted its course in the 13th c.

S. Orso*. The largest medieval complex in Aosta, in a secluded corner of town, dominated by a Romanesque *bell tower** (1131), with a centuries-old linden tree. Note the Collegiata (collegiate church); and the Priorato (Priory). The *Collegiata*, founded in early times (994-1025), was rebuilt more than once, most recently in the 15th c. The facade has a pointed-arch portal. The interior is Gothic, with handsome cross-vaults and frescoes from the late-15th c.; fragments of older frescoes (11th c.) in the high areas of the nave, can be seen in the attic (*enquire in sacristy*). In the presbytery, carved wooden chancel* from the early-16th c. Note the 11th-c. crypt, with five little aisles. The Tesoro, or Treasure (*open by request*) has a rich collection of precious medieval objects. From the right aisle (or from a passageway on the right of the church) you can enter the Romanesque *cloister*** (12th c.; arches and vaults date from the 15th c.), set on slender columns with intricate carved capitals.

Priorato di S. Orso. This picturesque priory was built between 1494 and 1506. It has elegant crossed terra-cotta windows and an octagonal tower.

S. Lorenzo. A passageway behind the church of S. Lorenzo, facing S. Orso, leads to the remains of an early-Christian complex from the 5th c., which have been roofed over.

Porta Pretoria*. This gate formed part of the ancient city walls (1st c. B.C.). It is made of enormous square-hewn blocks, forming a double curtain wall with three fornices, or vaults (buried about 2.5 m. deep by the rising level of the streets). To the left, note the massive Torre dei Signori di Quart.

Parco Archeologico del Teatro Romano*. *Open, in summer, 9:30-12 and 2:30-18:30; in winter, until 4:30*. The ruins of this Roman theater include a stretch of the tall facade wall (22 m.) with several rows of windows, and the lower section of the "cavea" and the "scaena." To the north of the theater, in the courtyard of the *convent of S. Caterina*, dating from the 13th c. (*open by request*), you can see ruins of the *Roman Amphitheater*.

Terme Pubbliche Romane. Situated in an area behind the Municipio, or town hall, these Roman baths include apsidal areas, a *"calidarium"*, and a *"tepidarium."*

Piazza della Cattedrale. This square occupies in part the old site of the Roman Forum, remains of which can be seen (*custodian on the site*) in the enclosure alongside the Cathedral: beneath the level of the street you can see the left side of the podium of a temple; you can descend into the **cryptoporticus**, which rans around three

Aosta: Teatro Romano

sides of the Forum, part of which was under the church (*excavations now underway*).

Cattedrale*. Surviving from the original Romanesque version of this cathedral (11th/12th c.) are two apsidal bell towers; the rest of the church was rebuilt repeatedly from the 15th c. on. The facade dates from 1526. The interior is Gothic: note the 15th-c. stained glass; the mosaic floor of the presbytery (12th/13th c.), the Gothic wooden choir* (ca. 1469); the funerary monument to Count Tommaso II of Savoy (14th/15th c.), in the apse.

In the arches of the apses, where you can also see the remains of one of the five Romanesque apses, under glass, is the **Museo del Tesoro** (*open, weekdays only in summer, 10-12 and 3-5; holidays year round, 3-5:45*) with collections of architectural fragments and works of art from the Cathedral and other structures, including an ivory diptych depicting the emperor Honorius (406), reliquaries (silver reliquary of S. Grato, 15th c.), a 15th-c. wooden altar frontal, with 20 carved panels, a 14th-c. Crucifix that once stood beneath the Arco di Augusto, sculptures in stone and wood, goldwork, glass, enamel, and so on. From the side-aisle you can enter the cloister* (1460; closed; *visible only in part and only from a gate in Via St-Bernard-de-Menthon*).

Museo Archeologico Regionale. In Piazza Roncas, near the Ex Convento della Visitazione, this regional archeological museum has a collection ranging from the Neolithic to Roman times, from digs in surrounding areas.

Other monuments. Mura, or Walls. Note the perimeter of *Roman walls*, which date from the reign of Augustus and form a rectangle (754 x 572 m.). They are particularly well preserved on the west side, where the *Torre del Lebbroso* stands, now used for temporary exhibits, like the *Tour Fromage* (near the Teatro Romano); they are also well preserved on the south side, with the medieval *Torre Bramafam* (13th c.) and, near the train station, the Roman *Torre del Pailleron*.

Area Megalitica Preistorica. In the quarter of Saint Martin de Corlean, to the east of the center, near the little church of S. Martino, work is underway on an archeological park covered with megalithic tombs, lines of anthropomorphic steles, and altars from the 3rd millennium B.C. (Copper Age).

Villa Suburbana Romana. To the north of town, in the region called Consolata, an archeological area is being prepared, with remains of mosaic floors and the walls of a villa from the reign of Augustus.

Aquileia*

elev. 5 m.; pop. 3,359; Friùli-Venezia Giulia, province of Udine. Along the road to Grado, just before the last patch of plains gives way to lagoon, stands the Romanesque basilica of Aquileia. The 73-meter-tall campanile no longer towers over the solitude that was once so dear to Italy's Nobel laureate, the poet Giosue' Carducci. Aquileia is now a thriving small town set amidst prosperous farmland; it also boasts one of Italy's most interesting archeological sites. In the shade of tall cypresses, the ruins of a Roman river port evoke long-ago trade in exotic merchandise, brought from all over the Mediterranean, and precious amber, gathered on distant Baltic beaches and transported across the continent of Europe.

Historical note. The ruins of what in Roman times was Italy's fourth-largest city lie on either side of the state road 352, which runs along what was once the "cardo maximus." Founded in 181 B.C., a military base in the war against the Histri, Aquileia's distinctive square plan tells of its beginnings as a Roman camp. From camp to trading town and bazaar was a brief step, given its strategic location: to the north lay roads over the Alps, as well as the river traffic of the Danube, where amber was brought from far-off Baltic beaches; to the south lay the broad Adriatic, and the rest of the Mediterranean. Aquileia grew quickly; evidence is provided by the progressively larger series of town walls, built up to the late-3rd c. A.D. Behind these walls, Aquileia withstood the attacks of Alaric's Goths (401 and 408); it fell however to Attila's Huns in 452, never to regain its standing and wealth. It did survive as a respected bishopric, governing thirty dioceses. Aquileia was the seat of a patriarch (the term shows eastern influence) until 1451. One of Aquileia's great patriarchs, Poppo, was elected in 1019; he built new walls, enlarged the harbor, and built the "new" cathedral, the Basilica. If the 13th c. was the height of Aquileia's medieval glory, by 1420 it had fallen under Venetian rule. In the centuries that followed, it became a desolate village; in 1509 Venice ceded it to Austria; Austria gave it up in 1918.

Places of interest. **Basilica**.** *Open, Apr.-Sep., 7:30-6:30; Oct.-Mar., 7:30-12:30 and 3-5.* Among Italy's proudest Romanesque monuments, the Basilica largely looks as the patriarch Poppo built it in the 11th c.

The first religious structure to stand here dates from A.D. 313, following the Edict of Milan. In 1031, the new Basilica was completed after ten years of construction. An earthquake caused extensive damage in 1348, and restoration gave it a more Gothic appearance. Later, the Venetians added elements of Renaissance style.

The simple facade is joined by a portico, which links the church to the 9th-c. church of the Pagani and the ruins of the 5th-c. baptistery. To the left, the powerful 11th-c. bell tower stands alone. The solemn interior features 14th-c. Gothic arcades, raised on columns, and a spectacular 4th-c. **mosa-**

ic floor**, from the original church, discovered in 1909-12. Split into nine large panels, this is the largest surviving sample of early Christian mosaics in the West. In the right-hand apse, there are frescoes, also from the 4th-c. church. At the center of the stairway leading into the presbytery is an elegant Renaissance tribune*, by Bernardino da Bissone (1491). To the right of the central altar, part of a late-5th-c. mosaic, discovered in 1970, is visible. Beneath the presbytery is the *crypt*, with walls and vaults decorated with frescoes*, perhaps from the late 12th c. At the end of the left aisle is the entrance to the **crypt of the Scavi***, or excavations (*open the same hours as the Basilica*) where fragments of the 4th-c. early Christian basilica are visible, as well as fragments of 1st-c. Roman homes with mosaic floors*.

Cimitero dei Caduti. This small cemetery, behind the basilica, holds the remains of some of the first Italian soldiers to die in 1915, and the *tomb of ten Unknown Soldiers*, from battlefields of WWI.

Museo del Patriarcato. *Open, Apr.-Oct., 9:30-12:30 and 3-6; closed Mon. and Nov.-Mar.* Inaugurated in 1992, this modern museum in Viale Patriarca Popone (the Italian spelling of Poppo) casts light on the religious history of Aquileia. Of special note are the reliquary bust of St. Ermacora* (1341); altar piece with a depiction of Thomas a Becket, identified in Italian as S. Tommaso di Canterbury (12th c.); and other pieces of religious artwork.

Case Romane and Oratori Paleocristiani. The digs lie near Viale Patriarca Popone: a complex of Roman homes, some dating from the late Republic, with mosaic floors, pipes, wells, and two small early Christian oratories. Another archeological area lies to the left of the basilica, and can be entered from Piazza del Capitolo.

Museo Archeologico Nazionale*. *Open 9-2; Sun., 9-1.* It is located in the Villa Cassis, n. 1 in the Via Roma. One of Italy's leading museums of Roman antiquities, it boasts impressive collections from archeological digs in and around Aquileia. Inaugurated in 1807, it has been enlarged and renovated several times in the past two centuries. Among the items on display are: inscriptions and reliefs concerning the foundation of Aquileia; statues and busts; a Venus; a superb collection of glass, amber, and carved stones; and many remarkable mosaics.

Porto Fluviale. Discovered in the late 19th c., this river port dates from the 1st c. It can be reached from Via Gemina, but we recommend walking along the *Via degli Scavi del Porto Fluviale*, a handsome cypress-lined boulevard with altars, architectural fragments, and plaques from local excavations.

Museo Paleocristiano. *Open 9-2; Sun., 9-1.* North of the center, a vast former Benedictine convent stands on the remains of a 4th-c. *Christian basilica*, with extensive remains of 5th-c. mosaic floors*. In the ex-convent a museum has been set up, with extensive artifacts of early Christian Aquileia: mosaics, sarcophagi, and an early depiction of the Baptism of Jesus.

Roman Forum. The area of the digs is crossed by the modern state road, not far from the spectacular 1st-c. mausoleum, 17 m. tall, rebuilt in 1955. Of the late 2nd-c. Forum and Basilica, fluted columns and fragments of the mosaic pavement have been uncovered.

Sepolcreto Romano. *Open from 9 to an hour before sunset.* This necropolis, 1st/4th c., contains five family tombs.

Arezzo*

elev. 296 m.; pop. 91,626; Tuscany, provincial capital. Florence actually purchased this town twice (the second time, in 1384, for 40,000 golden scudi). From the westernmost slopes of the Alpe di Poti, Arezzo looks out over the narrow plain where the valleys of Valdarno, Casentino, and Valdichiana converge. The center of Arezzo still has a medieval appearance, which overlies its earlier incarnations (Etruscan and Roman); in this setting, Arezzo runs the Giostra del Saracino, with Aretines in medieval dress riding horses, pounding through Piazza Grande, past a menacing, whip-wielding eastern monarch, Buratto, King of the Indies.

Historical note. High on the hill, S. Francesco, the Romanesque Pieve di S. Maria, the Gothic-Romanesque Palazzo della Fraternita dei Laici, and the Gothic Duomo — all these structures recall the great centuries of Aretine history. They range from the 11th c., when Arezzo rose against the Count-Bishops, to the end of the 14th c., when the town was swallowed by the burgeoning state of Florence (1384). Between these dates stretches a glorious history of warfare with Florence and Siena, dotted with victories (Pieve al Toppo) and defeats (Campaldino; Dante Alighieri was among the opposing Florentine troops). Around the year 1200, Arezzo built new walls, which ran along what is now the Via Garibaldi; to the NE they joined the Etruscan and Roman walls. Indeed, "Arretium" had once been a major Etruscan town, and an even larger Roman city. And in the city's millennia of existence, it has produced notable citizens, from Gaius Cilnius Maecenas, the Roman patron of Horace and Vergil, up to the poet Petrarch, the artist and historian Giorgio Vasari, Francesco Redi, and a great figure of the Renaissance, Pietro Aretino, satirist and dramatist. Arezzo began its modern growth when the railway from Florence to Rome joined it to the outside world in the 1860s, but since WWII, its chaotic expansion has tumbled forth into the plain.

Getting around. Much of the area inside Arezzo's walls is closed to traffic; visitors heading for hotels may pass through. This route may be considered a walking tour.

Places of interest. **Piazza S. Francesco**. At the edge of the oldest part of town, this square was enlarged in the late 19th-c., at the expense of a wing of the Franciscan convent.

S. Francesco★★. This 13th-c. Gothic church, with an unfinished facade, was heavily restored at the turn of the 20th c.; the bell tower dates from the 16th c. The *interior* has a single aisle and a beam roof. The overall impression, amidst frescoes and austere Franciscan Gothic, is one of grandeur. In the rose window, note the stained glass by G. de Marcillat (1524); Along the right wall, Gothic and Renaissance aedicules and frescoes, some badly damaged. Note the frescoes by L. d'Arezzo, inspired by P. della Francesca; the 14th-c. wooden crucifix; and work by S. Aretino, P. Gerini, the Maestro di S. Francesco, and B. di Lorenzo; along the walls of the choir, note the **Legend of the Cross★★**, frescoes by Piero della Francesca, probably between 1453 and 1464: in their stylistic discipline and exquisite color, these are towering masterpieces of the Italian Renaissance. In the chapel to the left

of the choir, work by S. Aretino, N. di Bicci, and L. Signorelli (attributed).

Chiesa di Badia. On the elegant *Via Cavour*, the 13th-c. *Badia di S. Flora e Lucilla* was enlarged around 1550 by G. Vasari (campanile, 1650); the Neo-Gothic facade is from 1914. Inside, paintings and frescoes, by B. della Gatta (1476) and S. di Bonaventura; note ciborium by B. da Maiano. The cupola is by A. Pozzo (1703). In the nearby *former monastery*, glazed terracotta by Della Robbia; elegant 15th-c. cloister (*open, by request, contact the custodian*) attributed by G. da Maiano.

Corso Italia. Historic backbone of the medieval Arezzo (then called Borgo Maestro), it has been the main street for centuries; note old buildings and fine shops. Toward the center, on the right, is the 13th-c. church of **S. Michele**, with Neogothic facade but 14th-c. bell tower. Note 16th-c. wooden Crucifix and panel by N. di Bicci (1466).
At the corner of Via Cavour, note the 15th-c. *Palazzo Bacci* (n. 78-72), and on the right, the 13th-c. *Palazzo Altucci*. Across from the Pieve (see below), note the 13th-c. *towerhouse* (n. 24-26), the 14th-c. *Palazzo Camaiani-Albergotti* (n. 4), and the *Torre della Bigazza*, 1351.

Pieve di S. Maria★★. One of the most impressive pieces of Tuscan Romanesque, this great sandstone church was begun around 1140, as a renovation of a century-old church. Construction continued into the early 14th-c., and G. Vasari turned his hand to it in the next century. It was heavily restored in the late-19th c. The Romanesque facade★ is noteworthy, as is the central portal, with reliefs of the Months★ (1216). The bell tower★ dates from 1330.

The *interior* is vast, and features fine bas-reliefs of the Epiphany (11th c.) and a carved baptismal font by G. di Agostino. On the main altar, note the large **polyptych★★** by P. Lorenzetti (1320); also note the gilt-silver reliquary of S. Donato, the polychrome terracotta Madonna, by M. da Firenze, and the 13th-c. marble bas-relief of the Manger.

Piazza Grande★. One of Italy's most spectacular and charming squares, this is the site of the Giostra del Saracino in late August, and, monthly, a renowned antiques fair. Note the Romanesque *apse* of the Pieve S. Maria; the 16th-c. *public fountain*; the 17th-c. Palazzo del Tribunale; the elegant **Palazzo della Fraternita dei Laici★**, with a Gothic ground floor, with portal (1377) and a Renaissance upper floor, by B. Rossellino (1434) — the facade was completed in 1460 by G. and A. da Settignano with balaustrade and loggia. Lastly, note the enormous *Palazzo delle Logge*, with its shop-lined portico, designed by Vasari in 1573; on the other sides of the square, note old houses, some with walkways and towers.

Via dei Pileati. This uphill extension of Corso Italia overlooks on the left the 14th-c. *Palazzo Pretorio*; at n. 28 in Via dell'Orto is *Petrarch's reputed birthplace* (*open by request, 10-12 and 3-5; closed Sat. aft. and Sun.*), rebuilt in 1948, and devoted to studies of the great 14th-c. poet.

Passeggio del Prato. In the huge expanse of public gardens, note the *monument* to Petrarch, in the somewhat orotund style of 1928; behind it is what is left of the *Fortezza Medicea*, or Medici fortress, by G. and A. da Sangallo; fine view from the battlements.

Duomo★. Set above a flight of 16th-c. steps, this impressive Gothic structure was built between the late 13th and the early 15th c. A Neo-Gothic facade (1901-14) replaced the unfinished original; along

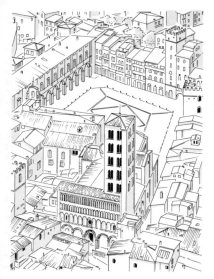

Arezzo: Pieve di S. Maria

the right side, note the Romanesque-Gothic portal (1319-37), with a group of terracotta sculptures in the lunette; the bell tower dates from 1859. The *interior*, with three broad aisles, gives an impression of great soaring height. The large stained glass windows, largely the work of G. de Marcillat (16th c.). The two marble pulpits in the nave date from the same period. In the presbytery, on the main altar, note the 14th-c. Tuscan Arca di S. Donato*, a handsome Gothic marble urn. In the left aisle, fresco* by P. della Francesca; near it, note the cenotaph * of the bishop G. Tarlati, by A. di Giovanni and A. di Ventura (1330).

Museo Diocesano. *Open, Thu.-Sat., 10-12*. With entrance at n. 13, this religious museum has art from the Duomo and other churches. Note: 12th-c. polychrome wooden Crucifix; three frescoes by S. Aretino; 15th-c. terracotta basrelief by Rossellino; panel by A. di Nerio; fresco by B. della Gatta; paintings by L. Signorelli and G. Vasari.

Palazzo del Comune. Built in 1333 as the Palazzo dei Priori, this present-day town hall has been heavily rebuilt over the years; note tower (1337), courtyard, and, inside, paintings by such local artists as P. di Spinello. If you take Via Ricasoli toward the church of S. Domenico, at n. 1 you will note the Neoclassical *Palazzo delle Statue* (1793).

S. Domenico*. Isolated in a small tree-lined square, this Gothic church has been heavily modified; note the Romanesque portal and small bell tower, with 14th-c. bells. *Inside*, badly damaged frescoes, by 14th-/15th-c. painters from Arezzo (S. Aretino, P. di Spinello, et al.) and Siena; note Gothic Dragondelli altar (1350). At middle of apse, note huge Crucifix**, youthful masterpiece by Cimabue (1265-70).

Casa Vasari*. *Open, 9-7*. At n. 55 in Via XX Settembre, a handsome piece of Mannerist domestic architecture, the home that G. Vasari built, furnished, and frescoed for himself (1540-48). Now it is the *Museo e Archivio Vasariano*, and features numerous panels and frescoes by the great Renaissance artist and critic; also paintings and other objects from his lifetime.

S. Maria in Gradi. Rebuilt in the Mannerist style (1592) by B. Ammannati, the church dates from the 11th c. Inside, note two wooden choir chancels, by S. Castellucci and B. Santini (1629-33); terracotta statue by A. della Robbia.

Museo d'Arte Medievale e Moderna*. *Open, 9-7*. Located at n. 8 in Via S. Lorentino, in the 15th-c. Renaissance *Palazzo Bruni-Ciocchi*, at the *Canto alla Croce*, a monumental crossroads lined with lovely and venerable buildings. Note the courtyard, attributed to B. Rossellino.

Arranged in about 20 halls on three floors (some feature Renaissance portals and fireplaces), the collections offer a thorough view of the art of Arezzo and Tuscany, from the 14th to the 19th c.

On the *ground floor*: sculpture, from the High Middle Ages to the early Renaissance. *Upstairs*, overlooking the Renaissance garden, are works by G. Vasari, Margaritone d'Arezzo, the Maestro della Maddalena, A. di Giovanni, Guariento, S. Aretino, S. di Spinello, B. della Gatta, L. Signorelli, the workshop of A. della Robbia. Next comes the *Salmi collection*, a gift, with works by B. di Giovanni, Empoli, A. Magnasco, L. Carracci, and A. Cecioni. On the third floor are paintings by L. Signorelli, B. Poccetti, G. Vasari, and Cigoli; also, paintings ranging from the 17th to 19th c., including work by C. Dolci, Grechetto, P. Benvenuti, and the Tuscan Macchiaioli painters: G. Fattori and T. Signorini.

Also, *upstairs*, are gold religious items, fine glass, and 15th-to 18th-c. majolica*.

SS. Annunziata. Overlooking Via Garibaldi, a long curving road around the old part of Arezzo, this Renaissance church was begun in 1490-91, possibly by B. della Gatta, and continued by A. da Sangallo the Elder (1517); the facade is unfinished, with a 14th-c. fresco by S. Aretino. *Inside*, stained glass by G. de Marcillat; painting by P. da Cortona; terracotta sculpture by M. da Firenze (ca. 1430).

Museo Archeologico Mecenate*. *Open, 9-2; closed the 1st and 3rd Mon. of each month*. Located at n. 10 in Via Margaritone, it is set in a curving former 16th-c. monastery, partly standing upon and partly overlooking the southern portion of the **Roman amphitheater** (built under Hadrian, A.D. 117-138).

With more than 20 rooms, it comprises older private collections and recent finds, from Arezzo and elsewhere in Italy.

On the *first floor*, material is arranged by geographic origin: material from archaic Arezzo, both Etruscan (gold jewels, pediment decoration) and Hellenistic (busts); and from the surrounding countryside (the Euphronios krater with volutes**), the Valdichiana (red Attic amphora* from Casalta), and the Casentino. In the Roman section, a considerable collection of the so-called **coral vases*** (this is ancient ceramic tableware, varnished red); finds from the city (mosaic floors, a marble altar, busts, furnishings from the tomb of a young girl). Also, relics of the High Middle Ages from the digs of Pionta. *Upstairs*, you will find materials from the "historical collections," especially ceramics (Attic amphora and goblet*), glass and jewels (portrait of a man, etched with gold*), coins (an Etruscan *quincussis**), Etruscan and Roman bronzes (votive figures, warriors and deities, household implements), and various collections, chief among them the Ceccatelli collection* (finds from the 7th c. B.C., mostly tomb furnishings), as well as special prehistoric and paleontological sections.

S. Maria delle Grazie*. Out of the city grid, this church stands at the southern tip of Viale Mecenate, where the ancient "Fons Tecla" once flowed; built in 1435-44, it is a solemn Gothic church, with an elegant portico*, B. da Maiano (15th c.). Inside, main altar by A. della Robbia; fresco by P. di Spinello.

Àscoli Piceno

elev. 154 m.; pop. 53,591; Marche, provincial capital. Located at the confluence of the Castellano and the Tronto, in a steep hollow, 25 km. from the Adriatic, this town is a peninsula, protected on the land side by the Colle dell'Annunziata. The city is stern, noble, and compact; a medieval cloth thrown over Roman bones, with the warm glow of the travertine of which houses, churches, towers, and bridges are built. All that is Renaissance is the work or inspiration of the architect C. dell'Amatrice; also, note the paintings of the Venetian C. Crivelli.

Historical note. Built by the ancient Piceni in an excellent tactical location, "Asculum" all the same fell to the Romans in 286 B.C., and was retaken at the cost of much life in 89 B.C., after the civil wars. The Roman city straddled the Via Salaria, which entered through the Porta Gemina, still intact, and exited across the Ponte di Cecco over the Castellano; equally important Roman relics are the Ponte di Solestà, the theater, the ruins of the Capitolium on the Colle dell'Annunziata, and the name of "rua" for many roads. The medieval town features such Romanesque monuments as the Battistero, the Palazzetto Longobardo, and the church of Ss. Vincenzo e Anastasio, all from the 12th c. Ascoli ruled itself from 1185, fought against Frederick II (who sacked the town in 1242), and competed with Fermo for access to the sea. In 1502, the town submitted to papal rule. Renaissance art and architecture prevailed in the following century, encouraged by the artist C. dell'Amatrice, who built the facade of the Duomo and the Palazzo Vescovile, rebuilt the Palazzo dei Capitani del Popolo, and probably designed the Loggia dei Mercanti. A few Baroque buildings are found, such as Palazzo Panichi and the rebuilt Palazzo del Comune and Palazzo dell'Arringo, but no further changes occurred in the town's appearance until 1860. The town has tripled in population since then, extending north and east over the rivers.

Places of interest. **Piazza Arringo***. Rectangular, vast, and monumental, this is the oldest square in Ascoli Piceno; in the shadow of the Duomo (see below), and flanked by the Palazzo Vescovile and the nearby Palazzo Comunale (which houses the Pinacoteca Civica), a complex of medieval buildings, joined by a subsequent, Baroque facade.

Pinacoteca Civica. *Open, Jun.-Sep., 9-1 and 3-7:30; Sat. 9-1, Sun. 4:30-7:30; Oct.-May, 9-1, Sun. 9-12:30.* Occupying 14 rooms, this museum's best known piece is the 13th-c. cope of Pope Nicholas IV*. In the other halls are paintings by: C. Crivelli, P. Alemanno, P. da Visso, C. dell'Amatrice, Titian, Van Dyck, Spagnoletto, Guercino, C. Maratta, Annibale Carracci, Sassoferrato, O. De Ferrari, J. Callot, Le de Morales, F. Franken, G. Reni, A. Magnasco, L. Giordano, S. Conca, G.B. Crosato, Canaletto, and F. Zuccarelli. Italian artists of the 19th and 20th c.

include: D. Morelli, F. Palizzi, A. Appiani, A. Mancini, Ximenes, Pellizza da Volpedo, and A. De Carolis.

Palazzo Vescovile. Standing alongside the Palazzo Comunale, this is an 18th-c. renovation of existing buildings. On its second floor is the **Museo Diocesano** (*open by request, contact the bishop's office*). In six halls, paintings (by C. dell'Amatrice, P. Alemanno, and L. Trasi; detached frescoes), sculptures in stone, wood, ivory, and silver, and various sacred artworks are all on display. In the 16th-c. *Palazzo Roverella*, note the frescoes by M. Fogolino (1547).

Duomo. Standing on the remains of a Roman basilica, this church preserves 15th-c. sides, with Gothic mullioned windows set between tall pilaster strips. The facade is unfinished. *Inside*, note the 15th-c. wooden stalls, the 14th-c. altar piece, and the large polyptych* by C. Crivelli (1473).

Museo Archeologico. *Open, 9:30-1:30; Sat. 3:30-5:30; closed Mon.* Set in Palazzo Panichi, in Piazza Arringo, facing the Palazzo Vescovile, this archeological museum comprises prehistoric, Italic, and Roman artifacts, statues, and mosaic floors, from Ascoli and surrounding territory.

Battistero*. *Open by request; contact the sexton of the Duomo.* Isolated, this 12th-c. octagonal baptistery stands near the left side of the Duomo; note the blind loggia and fine dome. In the Via dei Bonaparte, at n. 24, is the 16th-c. *Palazzetto Bonaparte*; note friezes.

S. Vittore. Late-12th-c. church, with pentagonal apse; inside, 14th-c. frescoes.

Piazza Matteotti. This square lies at the eastern tip of Ascoli, at the head of the rebuilt *Ponte Maggiore*. From here, to the SE, you can see the 14th-c. *Forte Malatesta* and the piers of the Roman bridge, the *Ponte di Cecco*, destroyed during WWII.

Palazzo Malaspina. At n. 224 in Corso Mazzini, which crosses Ascoli from west to east, is this stern 16th-c. palazzo; note rustication and high loggia. On the 2nd floor is the **Civica Galleria d'Arte Contemporanea** (*open, Jun.-Sep., 9-1 and 4-7; Sat. and Sun. only mornings, closed Mon.; Oct.-May, 9-1, closed Mon.*), with drawings, etchings, and prints by contemporary Italian artists.

Piazza del Popolo*. Monumental heart of the city, it is lined by low, simple, Renaissance palazzi, battlemented and porticoed; looming over the square is the Palazzo dei Capitani del Popolo, on the north side is the church of S. Francesco. A lively evening strolling ground, especially for the young, this may have been the Forum in Roman times.

Palazzo dei Capitani del Popolo*. Built, with its tower, in the 13th c., the palazzo has a statue over the portal of Pope Paul III (by S. Cioli, 1549); noteworthy courtyard. Inside, in 1982, archeologists uncovered Roman and medieval ruins (*open, by request, contact the nearby tourist office*).

S. Francesco**. Construction on this Gothic church continued from 1258 in to the 16th c. Two slender bell towers rise between its lively polygonal apses; along its right side runs the elegant five-arched *Loggia dei Mercanti** (1513). The facade features three Venetian-Gothic portals, the central one particularly rich in ornament. In the majestic and spare *interior*, the complex apse is particularly noteworthy. Note the late 15th-c. wooden Crucifix.

On the left side of the church, note the **Chiostro Maggiore**, built between 1565 and 1623; this cloister is now used as a marketplace; nearby (entrance from Via Ceci), is the 14th-c. **Chiostro Minore**.

S. Maria inter Vineas. In a small square overlooking the river Tronto is a 12th-c. church, partly rebuilt in 1954, with a massive campanile; inside, 13th-c. frescoes and a handsome Gothic-style funerary monument (1482). Nearby, adjacent to the Ponte Nuovo, is *Porta Tufilla* (1553).

Piazza Ventidio Basso. This square is enclosed by the side of the church of S. Pietro Martire (see below); also, the 11th-c. Romanesque church of **Ss. Vincenzo e Anastasio***; the facade is divided into 64 panels. Note the rich Gothic portal and low campanile; inside, the 6th-c. crypt has fragments of 14th-c. frescoes.

S. Pietro Martire. This monumental Gothic church was begun around 1280 and completed in the early-14th c. On the left side, note the portal designed by C. dell'Amatrice (1523) and the three apses. Inside, fragments of 14th-c. frescoes.

Piazzetta di S. Pietro Martire. This little square is set at the juncture of lanes that run into a notable quarter: Via delle Torri, Via dei Soderini, and Via di Solestà*. This latter street, lined by medieval towers and houses, much rebuilt in the 16th c., leads to the single-arch Roman bridge, or **Ponte di Solestà***, from the early Empire; note the gate (1230) and the medieval tower.

Via dei Soderini. This fine road still has a medieval feel to it; at n. 26 stands the tall 11th-c. *Torre Ercolani* (34 m.), the most notable of Ascoli's aristocratic towers; next to it is the 11th-c. **Palazzetto Longobardo**, now a youth hostel. Facing it, at n. 11, is another tower-house; further along, in Largo della Fortuna, is the 13th-c. church of **S. Giacomo**, in travertine, note campanile and ornate portal on left side.

Piazza Cecco d'Ascoli. At the western tip of the city is the small Roman 1st-c. **Porta Gemina**, where the ancient Via Salaria entered Ascoli. Beyond the gate is a stretch of *Roman wall*, and at the mouth of Via Angelini are the ruins of the *Roman theater*.

Piazza S. Agostino. In the western end of Corso Mazzini, this square is lined by two tall medieval towers and the 15th-c. facade of the church of **S. Agostino** (portal from 1547); inside, note the 14th-c. panel by Francescuccio di Cecco Ghissi.

Colle dell'Annunziata. This hill is partly occupied by the shaded Parco della Rimembranza, with fine views of Ascoli and the valley of the Castellano. Note the 15th-c. *former convent*, with *church* and two *cloisters*; in the refectory is a fresco by C. dell'Amatrice (1519). Just beneath the square of the church (view) are Roman ruins, commonly called the *Grotte dell'Annunziata*. Climb the hill to the *Fortezza Pia*, a fort built by Pius IV in 1560.

S. Angelo Magno. Take the quaint Via Pretoriana uphill, to this church, founded in 1292, on Roman ruins. Note bell tower and Renaissance interior, with Baroque paintings and altars.

S. Gregorio. Romanesque 13th-c. church; it incorporates fragments of a 1st-c. B.C. Roman temple (Corinthian columns on the facade; walls).

Assisi**

elev. 424 m.; pop. 24,626; Umbria, province of Perugia. The Roman city of Assisi — "Asisium" — was a large series of terraces, climbing the mountainside like a great stairway, as it was described in the words of native son Propertius. The ancient Roman poet would still recognize the landscape, if not the architecture. And Assisi still stands, wrapped in the silence and solitude of the centuries, on a ridge of Monte Subasio, overlooking the plains of the Chiascio and the Topino.

Historical note. The existing Roman foundation underlay the rectangular plan of medieval Assisi, all steep twisting lanes; some notable monuments survive. Little or nothing remains from the barbarian era, before Assisi was subjugated by the dukes of Spoleto. Around the turn of the 13th c., Assisi grew considerably, building a new set of walls and establishing some political self-rule, amid a series of wars against nearby Perugia. In those years, Francis, later saint, was born and grew up here. As a young man, he abandoned his knighthood and wealth and devoted himself to helping the poor. From 1206 until his death in 1226, St. Francis preached, meditated, built, and organized in this region. He is buried in the Basilica. St. Francis may have brought Assisi a reputation of saintliness, but war continued — first with Perugia, then the Visconti, the Montefeltro, the Fortebraccio, and Francesco Sforza, even Machiavelli's Valentino (Cesare Borgia); finally, at the turn of the 16th c., Pope Paul III Farnese ruled over the town. Assisi was described in papal reports of those years as "the remains of a town, rather than a real, complete town." Sightseeing and religious touring restored Assisi to prosperity in the 20th c.

Getting around. The first two routes that we recommend are walking routes; therefore, we suggest parking your car outside of town. In any case, traffic regulations and the steepness and narrowness of Assisi's streets should discourage the use of private vehicles. You should plan on driving or taking public transportation to visit the outlying monuments described in the third route.

The Basilica of S. Francesco and the Piazza del Comune

The basilica is the most important monument in Assisi and one of the best known artistic and religious landmarks in Italy; its counterbalance is the medieval Piazza del Comune, center of the earliest Assisi, at the far end of Via S. Francesco.

Porta S. Francesco (*A1*). This 14th c. crenelated gate is the main western entrance to Assisi; it affords a fine view* of the Convento di S. Francesco with the massive arched buttresses that make it look like a great grim fortress.

Piazza Inferiore di S. Francesco* (*A1*). Entirely

Assisi: S. Francesco

surrounded by low 15th-c. porticoes, this lower square lies in the shadow of the basilica, with its mighty bell tower* (1239). On the left, note *the Oratorio di S. Bernardino*, and the main entrance to the Sacro Convento, and, facing it, the entrance to the lower church of S. Francesco.

S. Francesco** (*A1*). The basilica, begun in 1228, two years after St. Francis's death, was consecrated in 1253. It is a monument that was designed to perpetuate Francis's message throughout Christendom.

The greatest advocate, and perhaps the mastermind behind this complex was Frate Elia, vicar general and architect of the Franciscan order, aside from a few 14th-c. additions, the church is as he built it. It comprises two churches, one atop the other. The lower church, where the saint was buried in 1230 and still rests, has a series of frescoes that are virtually unrivalled in 13th- and 14th c. Italian art.

Lower church. You enter through a late-13th-c. twin portal. The interior, built to a Greek cross, has a single aisle. Low arches divide it into five bays, with side chapels added at the end of the 13th c. In the *first bay*, 17th-c. frescoes (by C. Sermei and G. Martelli), two huge Gothic tombs, and a pulpit. On the left, chapel of St. Sebastian; beyond it, chapel of St. Catherine, with frecoes by A. de' Bartoli (1368) and stained glass. From here you can enter an attractive *little cloister** (1492-93), on the right side of the church. On the walls of the *aisle*, frescoes — partly destroyed by alterations — with scenes of the Passion (right) and stories from the life of St. Francis* (left), works by the Maestro di S. Francesco (c. 1253). Various frescoes by P. Capanna, D. Doni, the workshop of Giotto, and C. Sermei, surround the entrance to the *crypt*, with the stone urn containing the remains of the saint. In the first *chapel* on the left is an exceedingly fine series of frescoes of the Life of St. Martin**, by Simone Martini (1321-26). In the *vault* are the renowned frescoes* by the Maestro delle Vele, follower of Giotto (1315-20). In the apse, carved and intarsiaed wooden choir*

In the *right transept*, frescoes by Giotto's workshop, and a majestic **fresco**** by Cimabue (1280); a fresco* by Simone Martini. In the *left transept*, an astonishing array of frescoes** by P. Lorenzetti and his workshop (ca. 1320).

From the transepts, two stairways lead up to the *great cloister* (1476), with portico and loggia, in the shadow of the tall apsidal section of the basilica. From the terrace of the cloister, you can enter the Museo del Tesoro; a stairway leads on to the upper church.

Museo del Tesoro*. *Open 9:30-12, 2-6*. This museum contains precious reliquaries, manuscripts, and liturgical garb, as well as a fine Flemish tapestry.* Of exceptional value are: a chalice of Nicholas IV*, a 13th-c. ivory statue of the Virgin and Child*, 13th-c. Missal of St. Louis*, and altar piece of Sixtus IV* (based on drawings by Pollaiolo and F. Botticini). Among the paintings are works by S. Martini and Fra' Angelico.

Upper church. Gothic in style, with French influence, this church has a single aisle with four bays. You begin from the *transept*, entirely decorated by a vast series of frescoes by Cimabue*, begun in

Assisi 1:10000 (1 cm = 100 m)

1277, and sadly deteriorated. In the *apse*, note the wooden choir,* carved and intarsiaed by D. Indivini (1491-1501); in the vault above the main altar and on the walls, various frescoes by Cimabue. In the *aisle*, along the walls, up high, are a series of frescoes*, considered to be by Roman painters (esp. J. Torriti) and by followers of Cimabue and, perhaps, by the young Giotto. In the lower half, beneath the walkway that runs all the way around the aisle, is the renowned series of **frescoes**** by Giotto, depicting in 28 panels episodes from the life of St. Francis. Giotto began working on these frescoes in 1296. Also worthy of note are the medieval stained glass windows. Despite restorations, they constitute one of the most complete sets to be found in Italy. The oldest, in the apse, may date from before 1253.

Piazza Superiore di S. Francesco (*A1-2*). You exit the church onto the upper square, which is dominated by the simple 13th-c. facade*. Adorned with a French-style twin portal, the facade features an enormous rose window, with the symbols of the four Evangelists.

Sacro Convento (*A1*). Built with the basilica, the massive buttressing pylons were added later; inside, note the Sala Capitolare, or Chapter Hall, with fresco by P. Capanna

the enormous portico along the SW side of the convent; the monumental Refettorio, or Refectory (53 x 13 m.), with a Last Supper by F.Solimena (1717).

Via S. Francesco (A2). This long medieval road climbs straight from the basilica to the center of Assisi, and is lined by medieval houses and 17th-c. noble palazzi.

At n. 14 is the 15th-c. *Casa dei Maestri Comacini*; at n. 12, the 17th-c. Palazzo Giacobetti; and the 15th-c. former hospital, the *Oratorio dei Pellegrini*, with frescoes; at n. 3 is the 13th-c. *Portico del Monte Frumentario* (B3), and the *Oliviera fountain* (1570). Past an arch and up the Via del Seminario, you see the 12th/15th-c. *Seminario Diocesano*; the Via Portica leads past the entrance of the Museo Civico to the Piazza del Comune.

Museo Civico (B3). *Open 10-1, 2:30-5:30; closed Mon.* Located in the Romanesque *crypt of S. Nicolò* (11th c.; entrance at n. 2 in Via Portica), this is all that now survives of an old church. The museum features ancient Umbrian and Roman artifacts and art, from the local area. A corridor leads to what is thought to have been the Roman forum, with original paving.

Piazza del Comune* (B3-4). At the center of Assisi, on the site of the ancient Roman forum, this is a typical medieval square, with a 16th-c. fountain, with three stone lions. Note **Palazzo dei Priori** (1337); this heavily rebuilt complex of buildings features a handsome 16th-c. painted passageway, the *Volta Picta*. The opposite side of the square, marked by the tall crenelated *Torre del Popolo*, features the 13th-c. *Palazzo del Capitano del Popolo* (B3), victim of a 20th-c. architectural travesty. Next to it is the **Temple of Minerva**, a handsome building from the 1st c. B.C., now a Baroque church.

Pinacoteca Comunale (B3). *Open, mid-Mar./Oct., 9:30-1, 3-7; Nov./mid-Mar., 10:30-1, 3-6:30.* Located on the ground floor of the Palazzo dei Priori, this art gallery has a fine array of frescoes and paintings; note work by followers of Giotto, and Puccio Capanna, Ottaviano Nelli, Niccolò Alunno, Andrea d'Assisi, Tiberio d'Assisi, Dono Doni.

Chiesa Nuova (B4). This Baroque church (1615) stands on the remains of a medieval building (accessible), traditionally said to have been the home of St. Francis's father, Pietro Bernardone. Behind the church is the Oratorio di S. Francesco Piccolino, where the saint's mother supposedly gave birth, on a bed of hay. Inside, note fragments of 14th-c. frescoes.

The Duomo and the Roman section; S. Chiara and Borgo S. Pietro

From the Duomo, you continue into an area with clearer signs of Roman influence, until you reach the Basilica of S. Chiara, with its fine art. Borgo S. Pietro is a handsome late-medieval neighborhood.

Via S. Rufino (*B4*). Steep and twisting, it has a strong medieval appearance. From Piazza del Comune it runs up past old houses to *Piazza S. Rufino*; note 13th-c. fountain and facade of Duomo.

Duomo* (*B4*). Construction began in 1134; the Romanesque facade is majestic and austere, with three richly carved portals and three rose windows ringed by reliefs. The mighty bell tower belonged to the basilica that previously stood here; it stands on a Roman cistern (*open by request, contact the custodian; entry from the left aisle*).
Inside, note the 17th-c. stuccoes, the ancient baptismal font, and the three 16th-c. paintings by D. Doni. In the apse, noteworthy wooden choir* (1520).

Museo del Duomo (*B4*). *Open, Holy Week-4 Nov., 9:30-12 and 2:30-6; for the rest of the year, only Sat. and Sun.* You enter this museum of the cathedral along a corridor next to the right aisle, with venerable architectural fragments. The collections include illuminated codices and detached frescoes. Among the paintings, work by P. Capanna, P. di Bartolo, D. Doni, M. da Gualdo, and N. Alunno. From outside the Duomo you can also visit the ancient **crypt** (*open, Holy Week-4 Nov., 9:30-12, 2:30-6; 5 Nov.-6 Jan., 10-12 and 2:30-5:30*), with fragments of 11th-c. frescoes and a 3rd-c. Roman sarcophagus.

Via S. Maria delle Rose (*B4*). Along this road, from the Duomo, you will see the Romanesque *Palazzo dei Consoli* (1225), and, in a linden-shaded square, the ancient former church of *S. Maria delle Rose*.

Porta Perlici (*B5*). This 12th-c. gate in the medieval walls, at the end of the twisting Via Perlici, which runs from Piazza S. Rufino, has a double arch. The surrounding quarter has a Roman layout; note old houses along Via del Comune Vecchio, and the *amphitheater* (*B5*; in Via Anfiteatro, terrace offers fine view) and *theater* (*B4*; three arches in Via del Torrione), both from the late Empire.

Rocca Maggiore* (*A3-4*). *Open: 9-sunset; from 10 am in winter months; closed in bad weather.* This medieval fortress, built in 1367, stands on a peak overlooking Assisi and the valley; a road winds up from Porta Perlici. The fort is a trapezoidal wall with towers and keep with tall square tower (view* of the Valle Umbra).

Basilica di S. Chiara** (*B-C4*). Just outside the *medieval gate of S. Giorgio*, this church overlooks an immense square, with a fine view of the Valle Umbra (to the right you can see the apse and campanile of S. Maria Maggiore). Built in pure Gothic style (1257-65), it has an understated pink-and-white striped facade, with a single portal and a rose window; on the left are three large flying buttresses (1351). Alongside, overlooking the valley, is the ancient *monastery* of the Clarissan nuns (*C4; cloister: not open to tourists*).
On the stark **interior**, you will see late-13th-c. frescoes and paintings, as well as a 12th-c. Crucifix which, according to tradition, spoke to St. Francis in the church of S. Damiano.

Piazza del Vescovado (*B3*). In this square stands the church of S. Maria Maggiore (see below); from the garden, you can see ruins of the Roman walls. Near here, in the

Assisi: Duomo

since-rebuilt *Palazzo Vescovile*, St. Francis renounced his father's wealth.

S. Maria Maggiore (*B3*). Assisi's early cathedral was founded in the 10th c., and has a simple Romanesque facade and a notable semicircular apse. Inside, fragments of 14th-c. frescoes.

S. Pietro* (*B2*). This 10th-c. church was rebuilt in the 13th c., and stands on the edge of the quarter of S. Pietro. The facade has three portals and three rose windows; *inside*, note funerary monuments and fragments of frescoes, all from the 14th c. From the square, a fine view of the Assisi valley; note nearby *Porta S. Pietro*.

The places associated with St. Francis outside Assisi

Outside the town walls are a number of sites of early Franciscan history: Convento di S. Damiano, Eremo delle Carceri, Monte Subasio, the ruins of the Abbazia di S. Benedetto, and the Basilica di S. Maria degli Angeli.

S. Damiano** (*C4, off map*). Outside of *Porta Nuova* (*C4-5*), some 2.5 km south of the historic town, this simple convent was built around a country *church* where, according to tradition, in the summer of 1205, a Crucifix (now in S. Chiara) spoke to St. Francis. In 1212 St. Claire and her sisters took up residence here. Note various frescoes, by T. d'Assisi, Fra' Innocenzo da Palermo, P. A. Mezzastris, E. da S. Giorgio, and D. Doni. In the *convent* is the garden where St. Francis wrote the "Canticle of the Sun" and the dormitorium where St. Claire died.

S. Maria di Rivotorto (*C5, off map*). At 3.5 km SE on the state road to Foligno, this church was rebuilt in Neo-Gothic style in 1853; on the site where Francis and his companions first lived in 1208-11.

Eremo delle Carceri* (*B5, off map*). In a thick oak forest, at an elevation of 791 m. on the slopes of Monte Subasio, 4 km. east of *Porta dei Cappuccini* (B-C5), along a panoramic road that climbs through olive groves, is this Franciscan hermitage. The convent, built by St. Bernardino of Siena in 1426. Note the "Grotta di S. Francesco," the saint's little cell cut into living rock; stroll through the forest.

Abbazia di S. Benedetto (*B5, off map*). Further along on the same road is this 10th-c. abbey (729 m.). The original structure was largely destroyed in 1399. Continue another 11.5 km., to the peak of **Monte Subasio** (1,290 m.), with fine view* of Lake Trasimeno, Monte Amiata, and the Apennines.

S. Maria degli Angeli* (*A2, off map*). At a distance of 5 km from Assisi, in the plain (218 m.) at the foot of the city; leaving the historical center, the view of this church is notable. One of Italy's greatest sanctuaries, this basilica stands on the site where St. Francis founded his order in 1208, and later died. This monumental Renaissance building, designed by G. Alessi, was built in the 90 years from 1569 to 1679. A new, baroque facade was added in 1928. The large, solemn *interior* has three aisles, side chapels, and a deep choir. Beneath the dome is the **chapel of the Porziuncola***, a simple 10th-c. oratory. The exterior is frescoed; note the Crucifixion by P. Perugino. Inside, amidst the lamp-black stains, painting by I. da Viterbo (1393). In the presbytery, on the right, is the **Chapel of the Transito***, the cell in which St. Francis died, the evening of 3 October 1226; inside, frescoes by Spagna, a statue of the saint by A. della Robbia, and, in a case over the altar, the cord that the saint wore at his waist. On the right of the basilica is the renowned *rose garden*, with thornless rose bushes. In the refectory of the ancient *little convent* is a **Museum** (*open, Apr.-Oct., 9-12 and 2:30-6:30*) with a portrait of St. Francis by Cimabue and a Crucifix^ by Glunta Pisano.

Bari*

elev. 5 m., pop. 340,539, Puglia, provincial and regional capital. The old section of Bari is one of the two parts — perhaps one might say three parts — that make up what is now the second-largest city in continental southern Italy. Bari lies on the Adriatic Sea, midway up the coast of Puglia. If the old section lies serried and compact in a labyrinth of twisting lanes, where the entire history of Bari has had its long course, the new section developed during the 19th c. on a regular plan made up of broad straight streets. Nowadays, one might mention a third Bari, the "Bari Nuovissima", which straddled the railroad line throughout the 20th c., expanding into the industrial section and the Fiera del Levante, the site of a large trade fair.

Historical note. A quick perusal of the city map provides a graphic reading of Bari's history and a clear indication of the city's character, if you will. Built onto onto the jutting protuberance separating the Castello and the Porto Vecchio, or old port, is the Città Vecchia, or old town. The very earliest known human settlement, in the Bronze Age, lay on the very farthest tip of the little peninsula; it seems logical that the first inhabitants would settle there, as they were Illyrian adventurers who had ventured from the far shore of the Adriatic. The Città Vecchia appears as an impenetrable labyrinth of narrow lanes, enclosed courtyards, tower-houses and arches spanning the streets. And the entire history of Bari up to the end of the 18th c. took place within this cluttered and close little area. At the turn of the 19th c., Bari had a population of just 18,000; today it is the second-largest city in mainland southern Italy. Joachim Murat ruled as king of the Two Sicilies for less than 17 years, but it is safe to give him credit for undertaking the expansion of Bari (1813) with the construction of the Borgo Nuovo or Città Murattiana (a new section that bore his name, lying roughly between what is now Corso Vittorio Emanuele II and the train station).

Old town

Basilica di S. Nicola* (*B5*). This basilica, one of the archetypes of the Romanesque style of Puglia, was built to hold the body of a saint. Nicholas of Lycia, bishop of Myra in Asia Minor (the St. Nicholas whom we associate with Christmas, in Italy known as S. Nicola di Bari), died in 326 with a reputation for working miracles. In 1087, 62 seafaring men from Bari made off with the Saint's 700-year-old relics. A Benedictine abbot named Elia decided to build a new church to contain them; it was built on the site of the Corte del Catapano, the former headquarters of the Byzantine governor (Bari came under Norman rule in 1071, just five years after England did). All the features found in the Romanesque of Puglia are here: a tripartite facade (here flanked by two truncated towers) with hanging arches under the eaves, twin-light mullioned windows, three portals, and large blind arches along the sides, with little six-light loggias, an immense transept, a single wall enclosing all three apses; *inside*, note the three aisles, lined with columns and pillars, and galleries. Construction lasted from 1087 until 1197. On the main altar, note the 12th-c. ciborium*; in the apse is a remarkable marble bishop's throne* and a late-16th-c. monument to Bona Sforza, queen of Poland: the altar of St. Nicholas, made of repoussé silver (1684), can be seen in the right apse; in the left apse, note the panel* by B. Vivarini (1476); beneath the altar of the handsome crypt is the body of St. Nicholas. The treasure (*in the Museo, up in the galleries; open by advance reservations, tel. 5211205*) is exquisite; note among other things an enameled copper plaquette, possibly of 13th-c. Arab-Sicilian manufacture, depicting St. Nicholas crowning Roger II, the first Norman king of Sicily.

Facing S. Nicola is the *Portico dei Pellegrini*, rebuilt; to the right, under the 14th-c. *Arco di S. Nicola* (14th c.), is the little 11th-c. church *S. Gregorio*.

Cattedrale* (*B5*). This cathedral was built after the Norman king William I, known as "Guglielmo il Malo," practically razed Bari to the ground

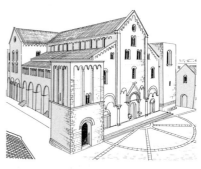

Bari: Basilica di S. Nicola

(1156). It is Romanesque, and was built on the site of the old, Byzantine cathedral. This is another notable monument of Pugliese Romanesque; note the splendid enormous window* in the apse; the large cylindrical structure along the left side, known as the "*trulla*," is an old baptistery, made into a sacristy in the 17th c. Of particular interest on the interior: the pulpit, the ciborium, and the bishop's throne, rebuilt from original fragments; also note the *crypt*, rebuilt in the 18th c. In the Archivi are priceless codices and the renowned scroll of the Exultet (prior to 1050). Beside the cathedral is the **Museo Diocesano** (*open Mon.-Thur. and Sat. 9-12:30*).

Castello* (*B4; open 9-1 and 3:30-7*). The enormous mass of the castle comprises a keep, or donjon, built on a trapezoidal plan, with two towers. Frederick II erected this version, working from the earlier Norman-Byzantine structure. It also comprises the scarps of the ramparts, and the corner towers looming over the moat (these last were added in the 16th c. to the three landward sides; the fourth side, once bathed by sea waves, still has the handsome twin-light mullioned windows of Frederick's project).

The *interior* is well worth seeing, and features a square Renaissance *courtyard*, an interesting *sculpture gallery* (Gipsoteca), with a collection of casts of the finest and loveliest monuments of the Pugliese Romanesque.

Bari 1:18000 (1 cm = 180 m) 0 200 400 m

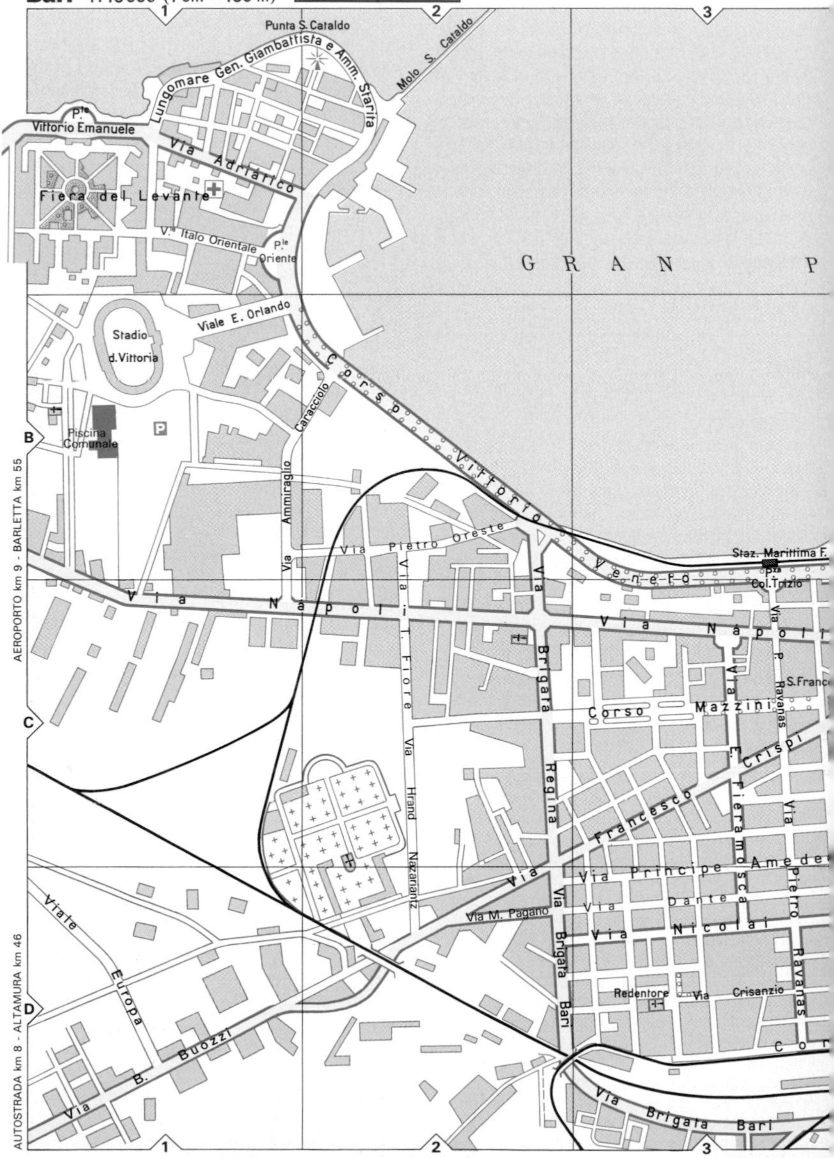

Lungomare Imperatore Augusto (*B5*). This handsome seafront promenade runs along the old walls on the east side of the Città Vecchia.

The museums

Palazzo della Provincia. This local government building stands to the SE of the Città Vecchia, on the Lungomare Nazario Sauro (*C-D5-6*); it houses the **Pinacoteca Provinciale** (*D6; open, 10-1 and 5-7; holidays 9-12; closed Mon.*), with a collection touching various aspects of the art of Puglia, including local medieval statues and paintings; work by the later school of immigrant Venetian painters (A. and B. Vivarini, Giovanni Bellini, P. Bordone, Tintoretto, and P. Veronese); work

by Pugliese and Neapolitan painters of the 17th and 18th c. (C. Giaquinto, O. Tiso); there are also Neapolitan creches, 18th-c. Pugliese ceramics, and a number of 19th-c. paintings (T. Signorini, G. Induno, and G. De Nittis).

Museo Archeologico (*D4-5*). This museum has the most complete collection of Pugliese archeological finds, and is fundamental in terms of the ancient cultures 7th/3rd c. B.C. of Dàunia (now the Tavoliere), Peucézia (now called Terra di Bari), and Messàpia (the Salento). Note the two fine-columned Attic ceramic kraters*; a hydra*, made of proto-Italic ceramics from Canosa, by the painter of Amykos; a scroll-handled krater* by the painter "delle Carnee" from Ruvo; an Apulian

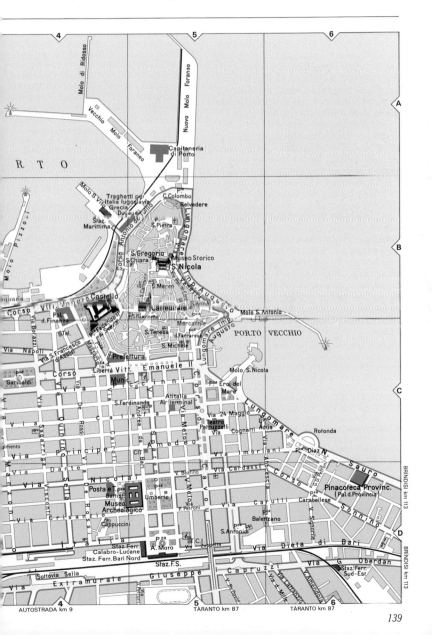

krater* with red figures, from Ceglie; tomb furnishings**, from Noicàttaro and from the Tomba Varrese**; a group of sculpted vases**; a bronze suit of armor*, part of the tomb furnishings of Conversano; a bust* and a clay group* from Egnazia.

Acquario Provinciale (*B4*). This aquarium stands at the foot of the Molo Pizzoli, a great wharf running out into the Gran Porto.

Orto Botanico (Via G. Amendola 175). This botanical garden is particularly interesting for its array of wild plants of the Puglia region.

Museo Etnografico Africa-Mozambico. This museum of African ethnography is located in the *Convento dei Cappuccini di S. Fara* (Via Gen. Bellomo 94; *open by reservation, tel. 5510037*).

Bèrgamo**

elev. 249 m.; pop. 117,886; Lombardy, provincial capital. The distinctive silhouette that can be seen from the surrounding lowlands, etched out against the mountainous background, is that of Bergamo Alta, or upper Bergamo, aloof, hushed, and ancient; this is one of the most perfect stratified assemblies of urban construction and historical memory in Lombardy, and perhaps in all of Italy. Roughly one hundred meters below, at the edge of the plain, near the mouth of the Valle Brembana and Valle Seriana, lies the thriving town of Bergamo Bassa, or lower Bergamo, the modern section, even though it has centuries of prosperous trading, banking, and manufacture behind it. Some faces you will see here: the forbidding gaze of the equestrian monument to Bartolomeo Colleoni, great condottiere, but even greater self-aggrandizer; the 16th-c. merchants who look out from portraits by G.B. Moroni; the baleful, disapproving eye that the artist Fra' Galgario casts upon the aristocrats of the 16th-c. provinces; you will also see the airy, "musical" still-lifes by E. Baschenis, you may hear melting romantic airs by Gaetano Donizetti, or the rough jokes and rapid banter of Arlecchino — Harlequin — both native sons of Bergamo.

Historical note. The dichotomy between the two cities — Bergamo Alta and Bergamo Bassa — can be seen, perhaps, as far back as the first Roman settlement, in the 2nd c. B.C. — the "civitas" stood high on the hill, while the "suburbia" lay in the surrounding plains; we do know for certain that under Longobard rule, in the 6th and 7th c., as the dukedom of Bergamo was being organized into the manorial system, the city territory was divided into two jurisdictions of two "royal courts." We have documentation of the fair in the field of Prato di S. Alessandro (now the heart of Bergamo Bassa) dating back to the 10th c.; Bergamo Alta during this same period continued to hold the reins of power, at first under a bishop, and later under Communal government (from the 12th c. on). The Visconti seized Bergamo in 1332 and, in 1428, Venice snatched the city away from them, after the Count of Carmagnola trounced the troops of Filippo Maria Visconti at Maclodio. Bartolomeo Colleoni, a Bergamasque condottiere fighting for the Venetians, staved off a new Visconti offensive a few years later, and the city remained under Venetian rule until 1796. In Bergamo Alta, an early seigneur, John of Bohemia, built the town fortress, or Rocca, to the east; on the far side of the high town, the Visconti later built the citadel: with these great works, the medieval setting of the "città alta" was complete, with its twisting streets, now so hushed

and still; further great construction came during the Renaissance, under Venetian administration. The first great project of the Venetians was the construction of the "muraine," an enclosure wall that protected both the hilltop town and the low-lying villages, or "borghi" (on the plains, the wall's one-time location is still marked by the name of Porta Nuova). The most remarkable project, however, with the farthest-reaching consequences, was the construction of bastions around Bergamo Alta (1560-1623): the two cities were split apart, with the high town held by the agrarian nobility, while the low town, more commercial, was destined to grow greatly. And in the village of Borgo Pignolo, midway between the two, were rows of the palazzi of the trading aristocracy. Bergamo remained essentially Lombard in character and in atmosphere but, like all of the "terraferma," or hinterland holdings of Venice, the town acquired a Venetian flavor and, in its turn, enriched Venetian civilization. In 1857, under Austrian rule, Bergamo was linked to Milan by railroad; the Via Ferdinandea was extended to the train station, establishing the modern-day thoroughfare of the low town (now, the Viale Giovanni XXIII and the Viale Vittorio Emanuele II). Two years later, on 8 June 1859, Garibaldi, the "libertador" of Italy, entered Bergamo, with his troops, the Cacciatori delle Alpi. Following the unification of Italy, it was decided to tear down Bergamo's "muraine," or old walls (1900); by that time, urban growth had spread far beyond the enclosure walls.

Getting around. For touring the city, we recommend two routes. You can walk the entire route, or you can use city buses and cog railways to cover short stretches of the route. Bergamo Alta is closed to motor traffic during holidays (Mar.-Sep., 2-7; Oct.-Feb., 2-5:30).

Bergamo Alta

From the modern center of town you will climb up to the heart of old Bergamo, with its famous monuments and exquisite architecture. After an excursion to the panoramic Colle S. Vigilio and a tour of the secluded and silent Borgo Canale, this route runs along a stretch of the old Venetian walls, with remarkable views.

Piazza Vittorio Veneto (*D3*). This square, with the adjoining Piazza Matteotti, Piazza Dante, and Piazza della Libertà, forms the heart of Bergamo Bassa; this orderly system of piazzas, built in the area of the long-ago demolished Fiera di S. Alessandro, is a modern piece of urban planning, done in the early-20th c. to plans by Marcello Piacentini (1914-34).

Viale Vittorio Emanuele II (*B-C2-4*). This road forms part of the long straight avenue built between 1837 and 1857 with the name of Strada Ferdinandea, linking Bergamo Bassa with Bergamo Alta, now the chief thoroughfare in the city. Midway, where the road turns beneath the walls, is the lower station of the *cog railway* (*B2*) running up to Bergamo Alta, built in 1886-87.

Porta S. Agostino (*A4*). Comprising a double curtain wall, this gate dates back to the time when the walled perimeter itself was built (16th c.). The gate takes its name from the nearby former **convent of S. Agostino**, founded at the end of the 13th c. and suppressed in 1797; the *church* of this convent have a late-Gothic sandstone facade and, inside *(closed to the public)*, fragments of frescoes, especially from the 14th and 15th c.

Via Porta Dipinta (*A-B2-3*). This street runs steep and winding among palazzi and old houses, running past the 12th-c. Romanesque church of **S.**

Michele al Pozzo Bianco (*A3*) *(open by request, tel. 247651)*, renewed in the 15th c. and again later; in the nave and aisle, note the fine frescoes (12th/14th c.): those in the chapel to the left of the presbytery are by Lorenzo Lotto (1525). Further along is the Neoclassical church of **S. Andrea** (*B3*) with a notable altar piece* by Moretto in the right chapel. Across the street is the 17th-c. *Palazzo Moroni*, with frescoed interiors and a garden on the hill.

Rocca (*A3*). *Open, Apr.-Sep., 9-12 and 3-8; Oct.-Mar., only Sat. and Sun., 10-12, 2-4 or 6. From Piazza Mercato delle Scarpe* (the upper terminus of the cog railway) a narrow lane runs up and off to the right to the 14th-c. fort, with a glacis now used as a park (Parco della Rimembranza); from atop the donjon, fine view of Bergamo, surrounding plain, and the Alpine foothills (Prealpi). On the esplanade, the building that served as barracks for the garrison now houses the *Museo del Risorgimento e della Resistenza (closed for restoration)*.

Via Gòmbito (*A-B2*). Narrow and winding, this road runs up from the Piazza Mercato delle Scarpe to the heart of Bergamo Alta. Along this distinctive road you will see a 16th-c. fountain, medieval ruins, old houses, and the 12th-c. *Torre di Gòmbito*.

Piazza Vecchia * (*A2*). With the adjoining Piazza del Duomo, this square forms the monumental center of Bergamo Alta. Built in 1440-93, it is adorned with an 18th-c. fountain. It is bounded by the late-12th-c. **Palazzo della Ragione** *, a venerable town hall with a large ground-floor loggia and three-light Gothic mullioned windows; above the 16th-c. balcony stands a lion of St. Mark's, a relic of former Venetian rule; adorning the upper hall *(open for exhibits)* are frescoes from the 14th and 15th c. from churches and palazzi of Bergamo. In particular, note the Three Philosophers, by Bramante. To the right is the 12th-c. *Torre del Comune*, with its much-rebuilt crown. Facing the Palazzo della Ragione is the *Palazzo Nuovo*, designed in 1593, but built in stages; the facade was not completed until 1927-28. This buildings houses the *Biblioteca Civica* (town library), with major collections of manuscripts and antique printed material.

Piazza del Duomo. This square contains, in picturesque asymmetry, the most noted religious monuments of Bergamo: from the left, the Duomo, S. Maria Maggiore, the Cappella Colleoni, and the Battistero, or Baptistry. The **Duomo** (*B2*), or Cathedral, with its 19th-c. facade, features paintings by A. Previtali, G.B. Tiepolo, and G.B. Moroni; behind the main altar is an inlaid 18th-c. choir.

S. Maria Maggiore ** (*B2*). *Open, weekdays, 8-12 and 3-6; holidays, 9-1 and 3-6.* This complex Romanesque construction dates from the second half of the 12th c. It has no facade; in the left transept, note the portal with the superb porch by G. da Campione (1353), with columns set on carved lions. Walk around the church toward the left to appreciate its intricate and lively architecture; you should note: another portal by G. da Campione (1367); the Renaissance structure of the Sagrestia Nuova (1491); after climbing the stairs, the apse with archwork and loggia; the campanile (14th/16th c.); the right transept with two apsidioles and portal with porch, by G. da Campione (1360); an ancient fountain, and, isolated

Bergamo: Piazza Vecchia

above the rest, the little 11th-c. church of *S. Croce*. The **interior,** with gilding and stuccoes, was renovated in the late-16th c. and in the 17th c. Along the walls, note the exquisite tapestries, made in Tuscany (16th c.) and Flanders (17th c.). In the right transept, Tree of Life, fresco by follower of Giotto (1347); in the presbytery, six bronze candelabra from 1597, note inlaid benches and chancel*, in part to designs by L. Lotto (1522-55). Across from the presbytery: Baroque confessional, carved by A. Fantoni (1704); tomb of the composer Gaetano Donizetti, by V. Vela (1855); 14th-c. monument to the Cardinal Longhi, by Ugo da Campione; tapestry of the Crucifixion (1698), and immense painting by L. Giordano.

Cappella Colleoni ** (*B2*). *Open, Feb.-Nov., 9-12 and 2-6; Nov.-Feb., 9-12 and 3-5;* winter, closed Mon. Built by Bartolomeo Colleoni, a condottiere who served the Venetian Republic, as his own funerary chapel, this is a jewel of architecture and decoration, a masterpiece by Amadeo (1476), and a crowning creation of the Lombard Rennaisance. All the features that make up the exquisite facade — pilaster strips, portal, windows, rose window, and loggias — blend in the chromatic interplay of the pink-and-white marble facing. *Inside*, amidst the 18th-c. decoration, note the Tomb of Colleoni* (in the facing wall) and the tomb of his daughter Medea*, adorned with statues and reliefs; both are by Amadeo. In the lunettes and the spandrels beneath the cupola and in the votive chapel, note frescoes* by G.B. Tiepolo (1733).

Battistero * (*A-B2*). This small octagonal baptistery, enclosed by a wrought-iron fence and crowned by a gallery with slender columns in red Verona marble, is a 19th-c. reconstruction of the original building, by G da Campione (1340). The 14th-c. statues are by Maestri Campionesi.

Museo Donizettiano (*B2*). *Open, 8:30-12 and 2-5:30; closed Sat. and holidays.* This museum is located in the

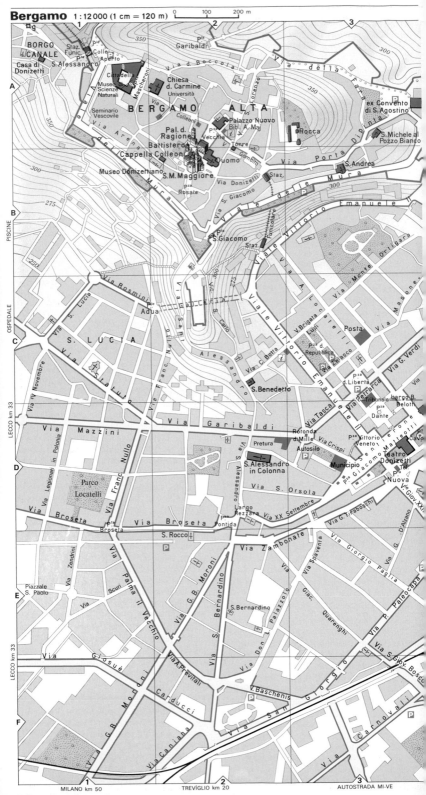

Bergamo 1:12 000 (1 cm = 120 m)

0   100   200 m

BORGO CANALE

Casa di Donizetti
S. Alessandro
Staz. Funic.
Colle Aperto
P.za Garibaldi
Via d. Boccola

Cittadella
Mascheroni
Museo di Scienze Naturali
Chiesa d. Carmine
Università

Seminario Vescovile
Via Arena
Colleoni
S. Lorenzo

BERGAMO ALTA
ex Convento di S. Agostino

Via Porta Dipinta
Palazzo Nuovo Bibl. A. Mai
Pal. d. Ragione
Battistero
Cappella Colleoni
P.za Vecchia
Torre
Gombito
Rocca
S. Michele al Pozzo Bianco

Museo Donizettiano
S.M. Maggiore
Duomo
Via Porta
Via Donizetti
Staz.
S. Andrea

P.za Rosate
Via S. Giacomo
Via delle Mura
Vittorio Emanuele

PISCINE

S. Giacomo
Staz.
Funicolare

Via Rosmini
Adua
Galleria
Viale Vittorio
S. Carlo
S. Alessandro

OSPEDALE

S. LUCIA
Via S. Lucia
Via Statuto
Via C. Botta
S. Benedetto
Viale Vittorio Emanuele

V. Brigata Lupi
Posta
Via Masone
Via Monte Ortigara
P.za d. Repubblica
Via Zelasco
P.za d. Libertà
Petrarca
Via G. Verdi

LECCO km 33

Via IV Novembre
Via Mazzini
Via Garibaldi
Via Tasca
Tribunale
Largo B. Belotti
P.za Dante
Via Nullo
Via Franc.

Rotonda d. Mille
Via Crispi
P.za Vittorio Veneto
Teatro Donizetti
Via Sentierone
Via G. Verdi
Cavour

Pretura
S. Alessandro in Colonna
Autosilo
Municipio
Via G. Giacomo Mazzini
Staz. Nuova

Parco Locatelli
Via S. Orsola
Via Papa Giov. XXII

Via Broseta
Largo Rezzara
Via XX Settembre
Fontida
Via G. Tiraboschi
Via Giorgio Paglia

P.za Broseta
S. Rocco
Via Zambonate
Via Giorgio Paglia
Via P. Paleocapa

Piazzale S. Paolo
Via Zendrini
Via Scuri
Via G.B. Moroni
Via Bernardino
S. Bernardino
Via Giac.
Via Quarenghi

LECCO km 33

Via Giosuè
Via Palma il Vecchio
Via Don J. Palazzolo
Via S. Gio. Bosco

Via G.B. Moroni
Via P. Previtali
Carducci
V. Baschenis
Via San Giorgio
Via Carnovalli
Via Caniana

MILANO km 50
TREVIGLIO km 20
AUTOSTRADA MI-VE

142

T. Morla

275

Accademia
Carrara

S.Agostino

Galleria d'Arte Moderna
e Contemporanea

Via N. Sauro

P.za G.
Oberdan

P.za

Via Giulio Cesare

Via Borgo Santa

Santa Caterina

Santuario
B. V. Addolorata

Via F. Corridoni

Via Fratelli Calvi

BORGO SANTA CATERINA

Via S. Tomaso

Via Pirentino

Via Battisti

Via della Roschia

Via Suardi

Via Codussi

Vigili
d. Fuoco

Via Fratelli

Via Pignolo

S.Alessandro
d.Croce

Parco Suardi

Palazzetto
d'Sport

Viale Muraine

Questura

Via Alessandro Noli

Via S. Giovanni

Largo
Galgario

Via S. Giovanni

Via Gagliani

S. Bernardino
in Pignolo

Via Pignolo

Parco
Caprotti

Via T. Frizzoni

T. Morla

Via Torretta

Via A. Calepio

Via Vittore Ghislandi

T. Serassi

Via Gius. Verdi

Parco
Marenzi

S.Spirito

Via Pignolo

BORGO PALAZZO

Via Carlo

Via Torquato Tasso

Via Borgo Palazzo

Via della Neve

P.za
S.Anna

S. Anna

Via Madonna della

Prefettura

Alitalia

Via M. Bianco

Via Gabriele

Via Clara Maffei

Telegrafo

Via Tord Tasaramelli

Via Angelo Mai

Via Bartolomeo

Bono

S. Anna

Via Borgo Palazzo

Via David

Via Alfredo Piatti

Via Angelo Mai

Via V. Lussana

Stazione
Autolinee

P.za F.
Lussana

Air Terminal

P.za
G. Marconi

Staz. F.S.

Via Paleocapa

Viale Giovanni XXIII

i

Via Mauro Gavazzeni

Via G. Bonomelli

Via S. Giov. Bosco

Via Zanica

Cliniche
Gavazzeni

Via Mauro Gavazzeni

Via Europa

T. Morla

Mugazzone

Circonvallazione

Palazzo della Misericordia (15th/16th c.), headquarters of the Civico Istituto Musicale, in Via Arena 9; it houses a collection of memorabilia and documents of the Bergamo-born composer Gaetano Donizetti. Not far off, in the Piazzetta Terzi, is the 16th-c. *Palazzo Terzi* (*B2*), one of the most important private homes in the historical center; the terraced courtyard has a fine view of the plain below. At n.3 in Via Donizetti is the Renaissance structure of the *Casa dell'Arciprete*, by the Bergamasque architect P.Isabello (1520); note the marble facade* with the lovely central window on the ground floor; elegant courtyard, with loggia opening out onto a vast view. This building houses the *Museo Diocesano d'Arte Sacra (open by request, tel. 211001)* with paintings, archeological finds, objects and sacred furnishings from Bergamasque churches.

Via Colleoni (*A2*). Setting off from the Piazza Vecchia along the Via Colleoni, you will find at n. 9-11 the *Casa Colleoni (open, Tue. and Fri. 9:30-11:30)*, home of the great condottiere, and headquarters of the charitable institution he founded; note 15th-c. frescoes. A bit further along is the *church of the Carmine* (*A2*), rebuilt in the 18th c., with canvases from the 16th and 17th c.

Piazza Mascheroni (*A1*). This square features the **Cittadella**, originally built in the 14th c. (note the surviving large tower), which was taken by the Venetian commanders of the occupying forces as their residence. On the second floor are the **Museo di Scienze Naturali** (*open, 9-12 and 2:30-5:30; closed Mon.*) and the **Museo Archeologico Civico** (*open, Tue.-Fri., 9-12 and 3-5:30; Sat.-Sun., 3-6; closed Mon.*), with materials ranging from prehistoric times to the Longobard period. From here, walk under an arch onto the esplanade known as the *Colle Aperto*, with the 16th-c. **Porta S. Alessandro** (*A1*), through which you can walk out to S.Vigilio and the surrounding hills.

Giardino Botanico (*A1, off map*). *Open, Apr.-Oct., 9-12; Sat.-Sun., 9-12 and 2-6; closed Tue.* You enter this botanical garden along a stairway that runs from Viale Beltrami, beyond Colle Aperto; it is especially rich in Alpine plants.

Colle S. Vigilio (*A1, off map*). A *funicular* (restored in 1991) runs up to to the top of this hill (elev. 461 m.) from the Porta S. Alessandro; from the terminus at the top, you can walk to the summit, with the **Castello** (elev. 497 m.), a simple fortress, with remains of walls and four round towers. From the esplanade, now a public park, note the fine panoramic view* of Bergamo and the surrounding plain. Not far from the Porta S. Alessandro, on the slopes of the hill, extends the distinctive **Borgo Canale**, still rural in flavor. At n. 14 in Via Borgo Canale is the *birthplace of Gaetano Donizetti* (*A1; open, Jun.-Sep., Sat.-Sun., 10-12 and 3-6*).

Viale delle Mura (*A-B1-3*) runs down from the Colle Aperto along the 16th-c. walls built by the Venetian occupiers, ending at the Porta S. Agostino. The **walls*** and the four **gates** that open into each side of the old town offer a vivid image of a 16th-c. citadel; inside the walls and gates is a series of rooms, with internal access roads, garrison halls, and gunports. You can tour them, with a guide (*tel. 213706-251233*). Along this ring of stone, which forms a sort of terrace overlooking Bergamo Bassa and the surrounding plains, is a panoramic promenade.

Bergamo Bassa

This circuit runs through ancient streets, exploring the part of Bergamo that, ever since Roman times, stood here on the plain. Setting out from the Porta S. Agostino for

a tour of the nearby Accademia Carrara, the route then reaches the modern heart of Bergamo and runs through its most elegant streets; it then ventures into the western sections of Bergamo, a place of small shops and the workshops of fine craftsmen; running up to Bergamo Alta, ending at the Porta S. Giacomo.

Pinacoteca dell'Accademia Carrara** (*A4*). *Open, 9:30-12:30 and 2:30-5:30*. This art gallery is housed in a Neoclassical palazzo (1810) which is the headquarters of the Accademia Carrara, founded at the end of the 18th c. by Giacomo Carrara. Currently the gallery, one of Italy's finest in terms of both quality and cultural depth, possesses about 1,600 paintings (especially from the Venetian and Lombard schools), as well as major collections of prints and drawings and lesser, but notable, collections of medals, bronzes, sculpture, porcelain, and miniatures. The most notable works are on permanent public display in 15 halls on the 3rd floor, arranged by date and historical consequence, from the International Gothic to Venetian painting of the late-18th c. Note celebrated masterpieces by such painters as Benedetto Bembo, Botticelli, Pisanello, Giovanni Bellini, A. Mantegna, Carpaccio, A. da Messina, V. Foppa, Bergognone, L. Lotto, Cariani, Titian, Tintoretto, El Greco, Raphael, Moroni, Dürer, Clouet, Brueghel the Elder, E. Baschenis, Fra' Galgario, G. Ceruti, Pitocchetto, P. Longhi, G.B. Piazzetta, F. Guardi, Canaletto, Bellotto, and G.B. Tiepolo. On the 2nd floor, in 7 halls that can be toured by request (enquire in the museum offices) are works from the Venetian, Lombard, and Piedmontese areas, between the 15th and 17th c., as well as Baroque works from elsewhere in Europe, and Italian paintings from the 18th to 20th c.

The Galleria d'Arte Moderna e Contemporanea (*B4*), dedicated to the art of the 20th c., will be established in the buildings overlooking the Accademia Carrara, once part of a 15th-c. convent.

Via Pignolo* (*B-C4*). This street descends steeply down from Bergamo Alta, and is lined with 16th-/18th-c. palazzi. A short distance from the corner of Via S. Tommaso, near the lovely Piazzetta del Delfino (note the 16th-c. fountain that gives this square its name) is the church of **S. Alessandro della Croce** (*B4*): inside, note the 18th-c. altar* by A. Fantoni; also note paintings by J. Bassano, L. Lotto, L. Costa, and A. Previtali. At n. 80 in Via Pignolo is the 15th-c. *Palazzo dei Tasso*; at the corner of Via S. Giovanni stands the church of *S. Bernardino in Pignolo*, founded in the 16th c. (*B4*); in the apse, note altar piece by L. Lotto (1521). At the corner of Via T. Tasso is the **church of S. Spirito** (*C4*), with rusticated facade; note bronze sculpture on the facade (1972). Inside, paintings by L. Lotto, A. Previtali, and the Bergognone.

The **Sentierone** (*D3*), in Piazza Matteotti (see route 1), is a handsome tree-lined avenue, with porticoes on one side, built by the merchants of Bergamo in 1620, and today a popular promenade and meeting spot. Note the *Teatro Donizetti*, with its late-19th-c. facade, and the church of *S. Bartolomeo* (*D4*), in the apse of which is an altar piece* by Lorenzo Lotto (1516), also known as the "Pala Martinengo"; also note choir with 16th-c. intarsia.

Via S. Alessandro (*B-C-D2*). This road runs down from Bergamo Alta, forming the central thoroughfare of one of the old "borghi" that radiate out from the old center; you reach it by following the shopping street, *Via XX*

Settembre. Just before the intersection with Via Garibaldi is the church of **S. Alessandro in Colonna** (*D2*), rebuilt in the 18th c: note paintings by L. Bassano, Romanino, L. Lotto, and the Moretto. At the corner of Via Botta is the 16th-c. church of *S. Benedetto* (*C2*), with terracotta facade and little Renaissance cloister (note frescoed lunettes). The last stretch of Via S. Alessandro is like a viaduct, running over large stone arches; this tour ends with the monumental *Porta S. Giacomo* (*B2*), the southern gate of Bergamo Alta.

Bologna*

elev. 54 m; pop. 404,322; Emilia-Romagna, regional and provincial capital. When Italy was unified and Luigi Carlo Farini became provisional dictator of the newly joined region (Emilia and Romagna), the political landscape consisted of papal legations and duchies; Parma and Modena had been capitals of states until the day before; Ferrara, which had not been an independent state for 350 years, still had the appearance of one (even Ravenna had once — briefly — been the capital of the Roman empire); the future capital of Emilia-Romagna was nothing more than the headquarters of one of the papal legations. All the same, it did boast a central location, a position that eventually made it one of the crucial centers of communications in Italy. Although it was perhaps then too early to see this clearly, it also had the raw material of its later, startling economic growth. Bologna lies along the Via Emilia, at the base of the Apennine foothills, between the rivers Reno and Sàvena, looking out over an immense arable plain. The center of Bologna, an elongated polygon stretching along the course of the Via Emilia — an ancient Roman road, once called the Via Æmilia — is medieval in layout. Its architecture dates primarily from the 17th and 18th c., brick-red in color, abounding in porticoes that are exceedingly welcome in the cold winters. This historical center was enclosed within the 14th-c. walled perimeter (the expansion beyond those walls, which now constitutes the bulk of the city, took place at the end of the last century). In the geography of Italian urban attributes, Bologna ranks as "La Dotta" and "La Grassa," literally, "the learned one" and "the fat one." The first adjective refers to the Studio, the university, more than 9 centuries old; the second refers to the rich crops, and the lavish cuisine (swine herding, it is said, dates from Celtic and Longobard times). Together, they describe, in a mysterious synthesis, the cheerfulness, cordiality, and human warmth of the people of Bologna.

Historical note. The Roman "Bononia" was founded in 189 B.C. with the settlement of 3,000 Latins, in accordance with a plan that called for colonies at regular intervals along the Via Emilia. Even so, the site had already been inhabited in prehistoric times, and was subsequently settled by Etruscans and by the Galli Boi, a tribe of Gauls. Outside of the perimeter of the Roman city, of which very little survives, Bologna expanded mainly east and west in the Middle Ages. In the preceding centuries, however, Bologna had other, intermediate rings of walls. In ancient times and the high Middle Ages, the city shrank to half its previous size, and the so-called walls of selenite (named after the variety of gypsum used in their construction) enclosed, in the SE corner of town, the remaining population. Shortly after the year 1000,

Bologna was developing one of the first Communal governments in northern Italy. The city began to expand again, occupying again the ancient section outside of the "walls of selenite"; at the end of the 11th c., the Studio was already operating. It is conventially agreed that this nucleus of Bologna's great and venerable university was founded in 1088; in 1116 the privileges conceded by the Holy Roman Emperor Henry V also marked the formal foundation of the Commune; and in the second half of the 12th c. it became necessary to build a new walled perimeter that doubled the surface area of Bologna. When these new walls — called the "Mura dei Torresotti" — were completed in 1192, Bologna was about to enter the most glorious century of its history, the 13th c. While Bologna came to dominate all of Emilia and Romagna, and after Bolognese soldiers captured the son of the Holy Roman Emperor Frederick II — Enzo, king of Sardinia — at the battle of Fossalta in 1249, construction was proceeding apace. Towers were built, streets were widened, a square was built around the two great towers of the Asinelli and Garisenda, the church of S. Francesco was built, Nicola Pisano was commissioned to create the Arca di S. Domenico, and Piazza Maggiore was expanded, with the construction of, first, the Vecchio Palazzo Comunale (literally, old town hall), on the site of the earlier Palazzo del Podestà, and then of the new town hall, known as the Palazzo di Re Enzo. These were great years for the Commune, the first government in Italy to free the serfs, with a law passed in 1256. By 1300, Bologna had a population of 50,000, and was one of the ten largest cities in Europe. In order to bring the "borghi," or quarters, that had sprung up outside the walls, into the city, a new walled perimeter was begun — the last — giving the city a six-sided plan, broader than long. These walls were barely finished in 1374, a clear indicator of the economic stagnation and political weakness that were afflicting Bologna by this time: the conflict between Guelphs and Ghibellines, in fact, led to the fall of Republican government and the establishment of seigneurial rule, first under the Pepoli; it later led to papal governments, headed by pontifical legates such as Bertrando del Poggetto and Gil Albornoz. Certainly, in the 14th c., Bologna built some new palazzi — Palazzo d'Accursio, Palazzo Pepoli in Via Castiglione, and in Piazza Maggiore the church of S. Petronio was built, the last expression of the power of the Commune, opposing that of the Cathedral — but the enormous energy of the 13th c. was gone. The city was unable to make the leap to become a regional capital, and it was increasingly hobbled by the custodianship of Rome. In the 15th c. following religious conflict of all sorts (there were even two antipopes reigning in Bologna at one point), the city fell under the rule of the house of Bentivoglio, a dynasty that collapsed at the beginning of the 16th c., along with the palazzo of the same name, under the blows of popular revolt. In 1506 the army of Pope Julius II entered Bologna, and from 1513 on, the city became a permanent part of the Papal State. From then on the city was no longer a major player on the stage of history, and until the French Revolution, the Bolognese did little more than to feast, entertain, create art, stage performances, and hold carnivals. Bologna under the pontiff, smaller though it may have been, saw considerable changes in its layout and structure during the 17th c.: the development of Strada Maggiore, the construction of the Archiginnasio with the Portico del Pavaglione and the opening of the new Piazza del Nettuno. In the centuries that followed, there were fewer significant changes: at the end of the 17th c. the rubble of the oft-destroyed Castello di Galliera, known as the Montagnola, was transformed into a public garden; in 1763, the new Teatro Comunale was built, to plans by Giovanni Bibbiena, upon another pile of historical rubble, that of Palazzo Bentivoglio. A considerable stimulus was given to higher studies during the Napoleonic era: the campus of the University was moved (1803) from the Archiginnasio to Palazzo Poggi, which formerly housed the Istituto delle

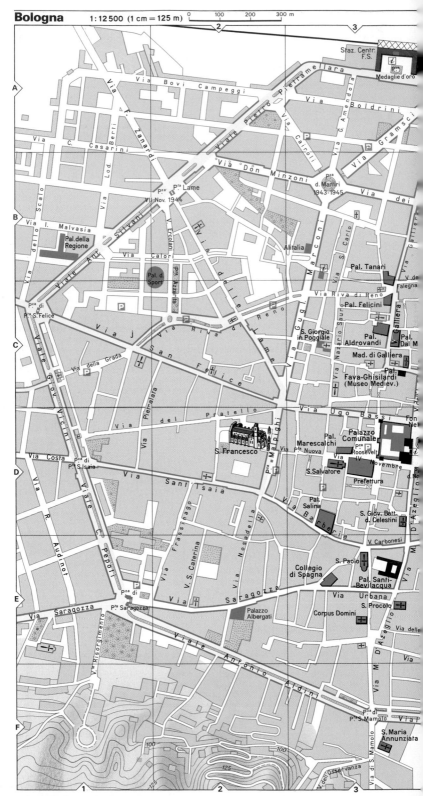

Bologna

1:12 500 (1 cm = 125 m) 0 100 200 300 m

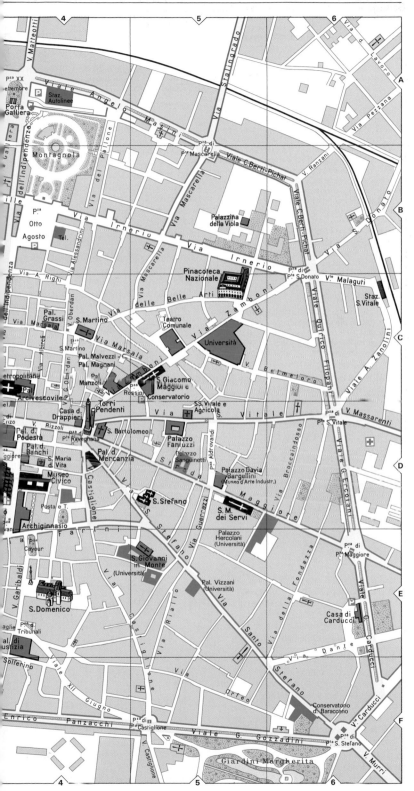

147

Scienze, or institute of sciences; this encouraged the formation in NE Bologna of a university neighborhood, which also saw the establishment of the Accademia di Belle Arti, or Academy of Fine Arts, and the Orto Botanico and Orto Agrario, botanical and agrarian gardens. It was not until the 19th c., however, after Bologna was annexed by the Kingdom of Italy, that the plan of the city again underwent modifications of considerable importance: Piazza Cavour and Via Garibaldi were opened out to the south of S. Petronio, and Via dell'Indipendenza was built to link the center with the train station; at the foot of the hill the Giardini Margherita were built. Later, toward the end of the century, Via Irnerio and Via Dante were built; in the center, Via Rizzoli was completed. In 1902 the city walls were demolished, and between WWI and WWII, Via Ugo Bassi was widened, and Via Marconi opened. In the Sixties and Seventies, when the population of Bologna nearly tripled in comparison with the early decades of the century (172,806 in 1911, 493,933 in 1973, the highest population to date), the development of the suburbs and outskirts was sufficiently great to outstrip the historic city itself in size and number of inhabitants, and the so-called "Fiera District," with office buildings and conference and trade fair facilities, was built near the ring road.

Piazza Maggiore, the Torri, the Università

Three fundamental "images" of Bologna are found along this first tour, running NE: the Piazza Maggiore, long-time heart of the town; the remarkable pair of red leaning towers; and Palazzo Poggi, nucleus of the Studio, or university, which dates from the mid-11th c., with Paris, one of the two oldest in Europe and the world.

Piazza Maggiore* (*D3-4*). This square has been the monumental center of Bologna since the early-13th c., with the church of S. Petronio, facing the Palazzo del Podestà, and the Palazzo Comunale. To the right of S. Petronio, on the southern edge of the square, is the 14th-c. *Palazzo dei Notai* (III, *B1*); to the east is the porticoed *Palazzo dei Banchi* (III, *B2*), built by Vignola (1565-68), where bankers once did business.

S. Petronio** (*D4*). Begun in 1390 but finished only in 1659, this church is a splendid example of Italian Gothic. Of the three portals, the central one ("Porta Magna") is decorated with statues** by the Siennese sculptor Jacopo della Quercia (1425-38), masterpieces of the early Renaissance. Along the right side stands the campanile, built in 1481-92.

The Gothic **interior**, with its three aisles, features remarkable artwork. Among the artists worthiest of note: T. Garelli, A. Aspertini, L. Costa, Vignola, Denijs Calvaert, Parmigianino, F. Francia, G. da Modena, and A. Torreggiani. Also note various frescoes, stained glass, marble fretwork screens, terracotta statues, inlaid choir, majolica floors, wrought-iron gates, and a vast floor sundial. One of the organs dates from 1470-75, one of the oldest in Italy. To the left of the *presbytery* is the entrance to the *Museo* (*open 10-12:30; closed Tue. and Thu.*). Among its collections are plans for the church's facade, liturgical garb, jewelry (13th/18th c.), ivory, semiprecious stones, and coral from the 15th/16th c.

Palazzo del Podestà (*D4*). *Open only for exhibitions and shows.* Built beginning in 1485, possibly to a model by A. Fieravanti, on the ancient site of

city government, this building has a ground-floor portico where two roads intersect beneath a vault; at the four corners are terracotta statues by A. Lombardi (1525), depicting the town's patron saints. Atop the palazzo is the *Torre dell'Arengo* (1212).

Palazzo Comunale* (*D3*). Also known as *Palazzo d'Accursio*, it comprises two separate buildings: the one on the left, porticoed with Gothic arches and with a tower, dates from the 13th c.; the one on the right, with terracotta mullioned windows, dates from 1428. In the middle, portal by G. Alessi (1555); on the balcony above it, a bronze statue of Pope Gregory XIII (1580). Still higher, on the left, a terracotta statue of the Virgin and Child*, by N. dell'Arca (1478). From the porticoed courtyard (1425-1508), along a great staircase attributed to Bramante (1507), you climb to the second floor, where you can tour the great *Sala d'Ercole*, or Hall of Hercules (note terracotta statue of Hercules, by A. Lombardi; also, fresco* by F. Francia); on the third floor are the *Sala Farnese* (noteworthy frescoes) and the *Salone* (marble portal and stucco frieze by Alessi). On this floor are the **Collezioni Comunali d'Arte**, with paintings of the Bolognese school, from the 13th to 19th c. Among the noteworthy artists are V. da Bologna, F. Francia, and L. Carracci. Also, miniatures, majolica, glasswork. Note the *Museo "Giorgio Morandi"* with many works by the noted Bolognese modern painter.

Piazza del Nettuno (*D3*). This square was built in 1564, set between the right wing of the Palazzo Comunale and the 13th-c. *Palazzo di Re Enzo*, restored in the early-20th c. This latter building was the "palatium novum" of city magistrates; it was named for the son of Frederick II who was taken prisoner in the battle of Fossalta (1249), and who finally died here in 1272; inside, note the Salone del Trecento, by A. di Vincenzo (1386).

Fontana del Nettuno** (*D3*). This fountain of Neptune is surely one of the finest of the 16th c.;

Bologna: Fontana del Nettuno

set on a base by T. Laureti, with statues by Giambologna: Neptune, with his trident, is calming the waves, on which putti, dolphins, and four mermaids are seen (1563-66).

Via Rizzoli (*D4*). One of the main streets of Bologna, a place to promenade and to meet in the various cafes (in the passage between Piazza del Nettuno and this street, note the few surviving fragments of ancient Roman "Bononia"). This road ends in *Piazza di Porta Ravegnana** (III, *A-B3*), with the two leaning towers and the porticoed side of the church of S. Bartolomeo (see below); at n. 1, note the *Casa dei Drappieri*, an elegant Renaissance building (1496).

Torri Pendenti (*D4*). These leaning towers are what survive of a medieval center that once bristled with towers; they are one of Bologna's hallmarks. The taller of the two (97.6 m.) is the **Torre degli Asinelli** (*open, winter, 9-5; summer, 9-6*), built around 1120, and leaning west. A staircase of 498 steps leads to the top; fine view*. The **Torre Garisenda** (*not open to the public*), probably built at the same time, is 48.16 m. tall, and leans even more sharply; on a plaque are lines by Dante describing it.

Via Zamboni (II, *C4-6*). This porticoed street is lined with magnificent 16th/18th-c. palazzi, among them: *Palazzo Manzoli* (*C4*; facade from 1760); at n. 13 a palazzo from 1560; at n. 20 *Palazzo Magnani* (*C4-5*) by D. Tibaldi (1587), with the main hall (*open by request, enquire at the Credito Romagnolo, tel. 338111*) decorated with frescoes by the Carracci (1590-92); at n. 22, the 16th-c. *Palazzo Malvezzi-Campeggi*, now part of the university. At n 30 is the 18th-c. *Teatro Comunale* (*C5*), designed by A. Bibiena, and later renovated.

S. Giacomo Maggiore* (*C5*). Founded in 1267, the facade, portal flanked by burial niches, and the apse are part of the Gothic structure (13th-/14th-c.). Along the left side runs a 15th-c. portico*, with a notable terracotta frieze. In the huge *interior*, with one aisle, the Renaissance style prevails. Artwork by I. da Imola, L. Carracci, P. Tibaldi, P. Veneziano, J. di Paolo, S. dei Crocifissi, and J. della Quercia. Note the *Bentivoglio chapel***, consecrated in 1486, with frescoes by L. Costa and a painting* by F. Francia (1494 ca.). Beneath the portico on the left side of the church, at n. 15, is the entrance to the **Oratorio di S. Cecilia** (*open by request, enquire at the sacristy of S. Giacomo*), with a remarkable series of frescoes* by F. Francia, L. Costa, and others (1506).

Conservatorio di Musica "G.B. Martini" (*C5*). Located in a former convent, this conservatory stands in Piazza Rossini, to the right of the church of S. Giacomo; among its students and professors have been Rossini, Donizetti, Martucci, and Busoni (note staircase by A. Torreggiani, 1752). One wing of the building houses the *Civico Museo Bibliografico Musicale* (*open, 9-1; closed Sun.*), one of the most important musical collections in existence.

Università (*C5*). Bologna's famous university is largely clustered around a "campus" running along Via Zamboni, though it is also scattered throughout the city and region. **Palazzo Poggi**, at n. 31 and 33 in Via Zamboni, was built in 1549, in part by P. Tibaldi, renovated in the 18th c., and made part of the Studio, or University, in 1803; it now houses museums, adminstrative offices, and uni-

versity departments. At n. 31 is the entrance to the *Accademia delle Scienze* (note 16th-c. frescoes by P. Tibaldi in the two ground-floor halls), or Academy of Science. At n. 33 you will find the main entrance, leading to: a handsome courtyard, in Roman Mannerist style; the *Aula Carducci* (*open 9-5; Sat. 9-1; closed Sun.*), a hall named for Giosuè Carducci, poet and 1906 Nobel laureate, who lectured here; the *Specola** (one of 18th-c. Europe's leading observatories); and various museums (*all the museums are open, 9-5; Sat., 9-1; closed Sun.*): *Museo di Astronomia*, devoted to astronomy; *Museo Storico dello Studio e dell'Ottavo Centenario* (*hours, tel. 259020*), concerning the eight-century-old university; *Museo delle Navi*, with a collection of 17th- and 18th-c. model ships; *Museo Ostetrico "G.A. Galli"* (*hours, tel. 259021*), on the history of obstetrics; *Museo d'Architettura Militare* (*hours, tel. 259030*), pertaining to military architecture; *Museo Indiano*, with collections of Indian history. At n. 35 in Via Zamboni is the entrance to the *Biblioteca Universitaria*, a splendid library with collections of old books, illuminated manuscripts, autograph manuscripts, and ancient papyri; the reading room has walnut bookcases; many halls are decorated with painted friezes.

Pinacoteca Nazionale** (*C5*). Open 9-2, Sun. 9-1; closed Mon. Set in the 17th-c. Palazzo di S. Ignazio, formerly the art gallery of the Accademia di Belle Arti — which joined the 18th-c. donations of Msgr. F. Zambeccari and the Marchese G. Zambeccari with the artworks taken from religious institutions following their suppression from 1794 on — this collection mirrors the artistic history of Bologna (the masterpieces by painters from other parts of Italy were executed for local churches). It documents the high points of the "scuola bolognese," including the Giotto-influenced 14th c. of Vitale da Bologna, the eclecticism of the Carracci, the Baroque of Guido Reni and Guercino. Among the earliest artists are: a follower of Giunta Pisano, the Pseudo Jacopino di Francesco, Giotto, Vitale da Bologna, Simone dei Crocifissi, L. di Dalmasio, J. di Paolo, G. da Modena. The *Renaissance section* includes: A. and B. Vivarini, F. del Cossa, L. Costa, Perugino, Cima da Conegliano, F. Francia, A. Aspertini, Raphael, Parmigianino, N. dell'Abate, L. Carracci, Agostino Carracci, Annibale Carracci. In the *Baroque section* are works by: G. Reni, F. Albani, Domenichino, Guercino, L. Pasinelli, G.M. Crespi. In the same building is the *Accademia di Belle Arti*, with several different schools teaching the visual arts from many standpoints.

Palazzina della Viola (*B5*). In Via Filippo Re, this "pleasure house" was built by A. Bentivoglio in 1497, and has frescoes by I. da Imola on the walls of the exterior loggias.

Strada Maggiore, S. Vitale, S. Stefano

The monuments you will discover in this second walk — the church of Saints Vitale and Agricola, Bologna's first martyrs, possibly located on the site of their execution; a compact group of ancient religious buildings, named for the early martyr Stefano, believed to be on the site of the Roman temple of Isis; the secluded church of S. Giovanni in Monte; the Gothic S. Maria dei Servi with Cimabue's "Maestà," to mention only the ancient churches — are all arrayed along the line of the Strada Maggiore, which, in Bologna under papal rule, was the start of the long road to the cathedral of S. Pietro, and corresponded to the Via Æmilia, to the east of Roman "Bononia."

S. Maria della Vita (*D4*).This Baroque sanctuary (1687-90), at n. 10 in Via Clavature, has a superb terracotta group* by N. dell'Arca (1463). In the adjacent *oratory*, another such group by A. Lombardi (1522).

Piazza della Mercanzia (*D4*). This was once a major intersection outside Bologna's earliest walls; it is overlooked by the Palazzo della Mercanzia, and old houses on the eastern side (n. 1 dates from the 16th c., n. 2 and 3 are Gothic).

Palazzo della Mercanzia* (*D4*). This building, with late-Gothic facade in brick and Istrian stone, was once a customs office where merchandise was unloaded; it was begun in 1384 and has been repeatedly renovated since.

Strada Maggiore (*D-E4-6*). Originally part of the ancient Roman Via Æmilia, this porticoed street runs from Piazza di Porta Ravegnana to Porta Maggiore. At the beginning, note the 17th-c. church of **S. Bartolomeo** (*D4*) with paintings by F. Albani (1632) and G. Reni (1632).

Ss. Vitale e Agricola (*D5*). At n. 44 in Via S. Vitale, this church was built in the 11th c. (original crypt), and restored more than once; inside, note the painted wax group by A. Piò, and paintings by G. Francia and Bagnacavallo. Facing the church, at n. 23, note the facade of *Palazzo Fantuzzi*, by A. da Formigine (1517-33).

Palazzo Bargellini (*D5*). This impressive 17th-c. building, at n. 44 in Strada Maggiore, houses the *Museo Civico d'Arte Industriale e Galleria Civica "Davia Bargellini"* (*open 9-2; Sun. 9-1; closed Mon.*). The collections occupy seven halls, and include fine furniture, sacred objects, ceramics, leather, miniatures, embroideries, creches, an 18th-c. Venetian marionette theater, and paintings by V. da Bologna, S. dei Crocifissi, A. Aspertini, A. Magnasco, and G. M. Crespi.

S. Maria dei Servi* (*D5*). This Gothic church, begun in 1346, enlarged in the same century, and completed in the early 16th c., features an elegant quadriporticum*; the lively apse and the campanile together form a lovely composition. Late-Gothic *interior* with Baroque furnishings. Among the noteworthy artworks seen here, a fragment of a fresco attributed to L. di Dalmasio, a 16th-c. altar by G. A. Montorsoli, a wooden inlaid choir from 1450; works by G. M. Crespi, V. da Bologna, L. di Dalmasio, V. Onofri, Cimabue, G. G. and A. Grati, A. Tiarini, I. da Imola, the Bagnacavallo, F. Albani, and A. Piò.

Piazzola di S. Stefano (*D4-5*). Aside from the buildings that make up S. Stefano (see below), in this square are the 16th-c. *Palazzo Bolognini* (n. 9-11), by Formigine, the *Case Tacconi*, with 15th-/16th-c. facades (n. 15-21), and another *Palazzo Bolognini* (n. 18), built (1451-55) by P. di Lapo Portigiani, blending classicism with local Gothic.

S. Stefano* (*D5*). A complex of medieval churches; as a whole, they are called S. Stefano, but individually there are, from the right, the 10th-c. *church of the Crocifisso*; in the center, the *church of the S. Sepolcro* (possibly dating from the 5th c., but rebuilt in the 11th and 12th c.), it contains the tomb of S. Petronio, or St. Petronius, the 5th-c. bishop of Bologna, with 13th-/14th-c. reliefs); and on the left, the *church of saints Vitale and Agricola*, Romanesque. From the church of the

S. Sepolcro you enter the 12th-c. *courtyard of the Pilato*, with an 8th-c. basin in the center. From here, you continue to the 13th-c. *church of the Trinità*, with a 14th-c. wooden Adoration of the Magi, and, to the right, on into the 11th-/12th-c. *Benedictine cloister*. From the loggia of the cloister you enter a small *Museum (open, winter, 9-12 and 3:30-5:30; summer, until 6:30)*: paintings of the Bolognese school of the 14th c. (A. de' Bartoli, S. dei Crocifissi, and L. di Dalmasio) and 17th c.; sculpture by G. di Balduccio (14th c.), and gold reliquaries.

Via S. Stefano (*D-E4-5*). Lined by 16th- to 18th-c. houses, this is a fascinating street of old Bologna. It runs from Piazza di Porta Ravegnana to Porta S. Stefano; at its start is the 30-m.-tall 12th-c. *Torre Alberici* (n. 4). This route runs only from the church of S. Stefano to the intersection with Via Guerrazzi.

S. Giovanni in Monte (*E5*). A ramp leads up to this church from Via S. Stefano. The church dates back to 1045, has been extensively renovated, and has a Venetian-style facade dating from 1474; note the terracotta eagle by N. dell'Arca (1480), above the lunette. The *interior* has a Gothic appearance. Frescoes by Giacomo Francia, on pillars. In the facade, two stained glass windows*, built to designs by F. del Cossa. Note several works by L. Costa and by Guercino, and, in the apse, inlaid choir chancel (1523). Small parish *museum (open by request, tel. 263894)* with reliquaries and paintings.

Casa di Giosuè Carducci (*E6*). At n. 5 on Piazza Carducci is the house where the Nobel-prize winning poet lived from 1890 until his death in 1907 (rooms and library are closed for restoration). The ground floor houses the *Museo del I e II Risorgimento (open 9-1; closed Mon.)*, focusing on the role of Emilia-Romagna in Italian history. To the right of the house, the intricate monument to Carducci by Leonardo Bistolfi (1924-28).

The Archiginnasio, S. Domenico

The Spanish saint, Domingo de Guzman, founder of the Dominican order, died in Bologna in 1221. His church, S. Domenico, dominates the quarter to the south of the Piazza Maggiore, through which this route runs. The saint's tomb is a masterpiece of Italian sculpture: N. Pisano began it, and in the 15th c. the great sculptor N. dell'Arca completed it; a few small statues are by the young Michelangelo.

Via Archiginnasio (*D4*). From Piazza Maggiore this street runs along the east side of S. Petronio; on the opposite side is the Portico del Pavaglione, a popular Bolognese promenade.

Museo Civico Archeologico* (*D4*). *Open 9-2; Sat. and Sun., 9-1 and 3:30-7; closed Mon.* This major archeological museum has remarkable collections, especially of prehistoric, Villanovan, and Etruscan artifacts. Many items are famous: prehistoric materials from the cave of Farneto (Hall I); tomb furnishings from the late-7th c., a bronze situla from the mid-5th c., with fine reliefs (Hall X); a Villanovan throne* from Verucchio, with scenes of ceremonies and daily life; the Zannoni stone,* with the oldest known depiction of a trip to the Underworld, Etruscan bronzes (Hall Xa). There are many Greek vases found in Etruscan tombs (Hall X): the Aureli krater* with a scene of Amazons battling, a krater with scenes of the destruction of Troy* and another with the myth of Atalanta and Hippomenes*. In the Greek section (Hall VI): the bust of Palagi*, a copy from Augustan times of the long-lost original by Phidias; 5th-c. B.C. Attic bas-relief*. Also, Roman (Halls VII, IX, and lapidary display, in the atrium and courtyard) and Egyptian antiquities (Halls III-V).

Archiginnasio (D4). This building, erected in 1563 by A. Morandi, houses the *Biblioteca Comunale*, or town library. In the porticoed courtyard, note heraldic crests of the university, which was located here until 1803; also, former church of *S. Maria dei Bulgari* (*open by request, contact custodian, weekdays, 9-1*) with frescoes by B. Cesi and D. Calvaert. Upstairs, 17th-c. *Teatro Anatomico*, damaged by bombs in 1944, and the *Sala dello Stabat Mater* (where the law was once taught).

Corte de' Galluzzi (D3). A passageway from Piazza Galvani, facing the Archiginnasio, leads to this profoundly medieval courtyard, with a tower (32 m., 1257). Another passageway leads to Via D'Azeglio and the 16th-c. church of *S. Giovanni Battista dei Celestini* (D3), with art by G. Mazza M.A. Franceschini.

S. Paolo (C1). This 17th-c. church, with sandstone and brick facade, stands in Via Carbonesi. Inside, paintings by L. Carracci (1616) and Guercino; sculpture by A. Algardi.

Collegio di Spagna (E3). Built in the 14th c. by Gattapone, for the Spanish students of the university; it was restored in 1904. A portico leads to the square courtyard, with frescoes by the young Annibale Carracci; note the Gothic church of *S. Clemente*, with polyptych* by M. Zoppo.

Corpus Domini (E3). This former convent stands in Via Tagliapietre; the church was built in the 15th c. and has a terracotta portal by S. di Bartolomeo, and, inside, fragments of 17th-c. decoration by M.A. Franceschini. Inside are paintings by L. Carracci and M.A. Franceschini and statues by G. Mazza. The Bolognese physiologist L. Galvani is buried here.

S. Procolo (E3). This church has three fine 16th-c. cloisters; across the street is the 16th-c. *Portico dei Bastardini*, part of an ancient orphanage.

Palazzo Sanuti-Bevilacqua* (E3). Built between 1474 and 1482, in sandstone, with rustication, this is said to be the finest piece of early-Renaissance architecture in Bologna. Note the elegant porticoed courtyard.

Piazza S. Domenico (E4). Oddly shaped, this square features two 17th-c. votive columns and two noted jurists — E. Foscherari, d. 1289, and R. de' Passeggeri, d. 1300; the latter is celebrated for having held his own, by letter, with Frederick II, who was threatening to raze Bologna.

S. Domenico* (E4). This church was built in 1228-38 and was renovated, attaining its current appearance, in 1728-32 (C.F. Dotti). To the left of the restored 13th-c. facade juts the Cappella Ghisilardi, designed by B. Peruzzi (1530-35). **Inside**, in the *right aisle*, note the *Cappella di S. Domenico** (1597-1605), with frescoes by G. Reni, the Arca di S. Domenico, or tomb of St. Domenick**: note the urn**, by N. Pisano, A. di Cambio, P. di Lapo, and Fra' Guglielmo (1265-67); the cyma* by N. dell'Arca (1473); statues of angel* and saints* by Michelangelo (1494). Elsewhere in the church, note work by J. Roseto (1383), Guercino (1662), Filippino Lippi (1501), B. Cesi (1595), Giunta Pisano (1250), T. Pepoli, A. Terribilia (1551), D.

Calvaert, L. Carracci, G. Reni, Albani, and F. S. Ferrucci. You can reach the **Museo**, or museum, through the sacristy at the end of the right aisle (*open by request*): note terracotta sculpture* by N. dell'Arca (1474), and paintings by L. di Dalmasio and L. Carracci; and other precious objects. From here, you can also enter the 14th-c. *Chiostro dei Morti*, or cloister of the dead; note the campanile (1336).

Piazza dei Tribunali (E4). This square is bounded by the Palazzo di Giustizia, or hall of justice, thought to have been designed by A. Palladio (1582). From the courtyard, the late-17th-c. staircase leads up to halls, with decorations by M.A. Franceschini.

S. Maria Annunziata (F3). This church is located in Via di S. Mamolo, was built in the late-15th c., and has a handsome portico; note fresco by B. Pupini (1524).

S. Francesco, the Metropolitana, the Montagnola

Near the apse of the church of S. Francesco stand the tombs of Accursio, Odofredo, Rolandino de' Romanzi, illustrious medieval jurists of the Studio, or University. The powerful French Gothic of the immense church strongly flavors the neighborhood west of Piazza Maggiore. From this first leg of the route, you cross the 19th-c. porticoed avenue of Via Indipendenza, and then you venture northward to explore a part of Bologna that mingles stern medieval architecture with opulent homes of Bologna's "senatorial" class. This tour ends with the Montagnola, the hilltop public park formed by the ruins of the Castello di Galliera, repeatedly razed and rebuilt.

Via IV Novembre (D3). Beginning from Piazza Maggiore along the left side of Palazzo Comunale, this road runs past the *Prefettura* (D3; 1603), *Palazzo Marescalchi* (n. 5; 1613), and along the side of the 17th-c. church of **S. Salvatore** (D3), with the tomb of the artist Guercino, and paintings by the Mastelletta, S. dei Crocifissi, V. da Bologna, C. Bononi, and L. da Imola. You then continue along *Via Porta Nuova*, through the 12th-c. gate of the medieval walls.

Piazza Malpighi (D2). This square features the apse with radial chapels and flying buttresses and the two bell towers of S. Francesco, the three *tombs of the Glossatori* (13th-c. scholars of jurisprudence), and the column of the Immacolata, with copper statue by G. Reni (1638).

S. Francesco** (D2). This church was built between 1236 and 1263, restored in the late-19th c., and rebuilt after WWII. The lower campanile dates from 1260; the other one, by A. di Vincenzo, from 1402. The *interior* shows clear influence of French Gothic: on the main altar, note the elegant Gothic marble altarpiece* by P. P. dalle Masegne (1392). Along the walls, note Renaissance tombs, one by F. Ferrucci (15th c.), and the tomb of Pope Alexander V, by N. Lamberti (1424) and S. di Bartolomeo (1482). The late-14th-c. *sacristy* is by A. di Vincenzo. In the convent, note the late-14th-c. *Chiostro dei Morti*, or cloister of the dead (view of the two bell towers), with tombs of the chancellors of the University, or Studio; also, the *Chiostro Grande (entrance in Piazza Malpighi; 1460-1571)*.

Via Ugo Bassi (D3). This lively road leads from Piazza Malpighi to the center of Bologna, running alongside Palazzo Comunale (fountain by T. Laureti; 1565). In the distance, you will see the two towers; on your right, the Piazza del Nettuno.

Via dell'Indipendenza (*C3-A4*). This long porticoed street was created in the late-19th c. to link the center of Bologna with the train station. The suggested route runs along it for brief stretches. Note the 16th-c. *Palazzo Scappi* (n. 3-5), with 13th-c. tower (39 m. tall); on the left, the beflowered *Casa Majani* (n. 4; 1908).

Metropolitana* (*C4*). This, Bologna's cathedral, was given its present appearance by reconstruction begun in 1605; the exceedingly tall 18th-c. facade, adorned with marble, is by A. Torreggiani; note the Romanesque campanile, with a 15th-c. pinnacle. *Inside*: note two holy-water stoups set on carved Romanesque lions, prior to the renovation; four little choir chancels, by A. Torreggiani, above the lesser arches of the nave. The presbytery was rebuilt by D. Tibaldi (1575) on the ancient crypt; in the lunette, note painting* by L. Carracci (1618-19). In the Romanesque *crypt*, note 14th-c. wooden group and 16th-c. terracotta group by A. Lombardi.

Via Altabella (*C4*). Beginning along the right side of the Cathedral (note the bell tower) this road runs past the *Torre Altabella* (12th c., on the right, 60 m. tall), and the *Palazzo Arcivescovile*, by D. Tibaldi (1575; view of the apse of the Metropolitana). If you then follow Via S. Alò, Via Albiroli, and Via Marsala, you will pass through an old and fascinating **quarter***, between the Metropolitana and S. Martino, with medieval houses and towers. In Via S. Alò note the *Torre Prendiparte* (12th c., 59 m. tall); in Via Albiroli note the medieval *tower-house of the Guidozagni* (at n. 3) and the 16th-c. *Palazzo Bocchi* (at n. 16, corner of Via Bocchi); at n. 12 in Via Marsala, *Palazzo Grassi*, with 13th-c. wooden structures.

S. Martino (*C4*). This church was built in 1227 and renovated in later centuries; note 19th-c. facade and Gothic interior, where you will see paintings from the 14th to the 19th c. Note Baroque chapel by A. Torreggiani, and frescoes and paintings by G. da Carpi, L. Dalmasio, V. da Bologna, A. Aspertini, S. dei Crocifissi, L. Costa, L. Carracci, B. Cesi, F. Francia, and P. Uccello.

Madonna di Galliera (*C3*). This church is just north of the Metropolitana, and has an interesting sandstone facade (1491); inside, painting by F. Albani.

Museo Civico Medievale* (*C3*). *Open, Mon., Wed.-Fri., 9-2; Sat.-Sun., 9-1 and 3:30-7; closed Tue.* This museum of the Middle Ages is located at n. 4 in Via Manzoni in the *Palazzo Fava-Ghisilardi**, a late-15th-c. noble home. More than 20 halls (some frescoed by the Carracci, 1584) display an odd assortment of objets d'art and applied arts, not strictly limited to the Middle Ages. Among other things: note tombs of University doctors; copper statue of Boniface VIII (1301), the pope so greatly reviled by Dante; statue by J. della Quercia; Renaissance bronzes, ivories, Murano glass, ceramics, and musical instruments; a huge collection of weapons and armor. Note the collections of naturalistic and exotic objects (Halls I and II), indications of the tastes of bygone centuries.

Via Galliera* (*B-C3*). This street is lined with venerable palazzi: among them, the 18th-c. *Palazzo Torfanini* (n. 4) and *Palazzo Aldrovandi* (*C3*; n. 8); the late-15th-c. *Palazzo Felicini* (n. 14); and the 17th-c. *Palazzo Tanari* (*B-C3*; n. 18). On the other side of the street, note *Palazzo Dal Monte* (n. 3-5, now part of the university), by Formigine (1529).

Montagnola (*A-B4*). You reach the top of this hillock, used as a public park since the late-17th c., by climbing a handsome late-19th-c. stairway, lined by statues and reliefs depicting scenes from the history of Bologna. At the foot of the hill is *Porta Galliera* (*A4*), dating from 1661.

Beyond the gates, in the hills

The church of the Madonna di S. Luca is a symbol of Bologna, marking the skyline where the plains climb gently toward the distant Apennines. Other landmarks of the hills mentioned here (Villa Aldini, the convent of Ronzano, the monastery of S. Michele in Bosco, and the church of S. Vittore) can be toured in a succession of exquisite views, beginning at the Porta di S. Mamolo and following the Via dell'Osservanza (follow markings). On Bologna's western outskirts, the Certosa, or charter house, stands on the site of an ancient necropolis. The fair, to the north, is the last stop, and attracts visitors throughout the year for its numerous events.

Museo Storico Didattico della Tappezzeria. *Open 9-1; closed Mon.* Located in the Neoclassical Villa Spada, in Via Saragozza, on the way up to the church of the Madonna di S. Luca, this unlikely museum of upholstery has a collection ranging from antique Oriental fabrics and Bolognese brocades and damasks and silk prints to rare "Fortuny" creations, and looms dating as far back as 1380. A bit further along, Via Saragozza runs under the Baroque *arch of the Meloncello* (1732), and then runs more steeply up to the sanctuary of the Madonna di S. Luca.

Madonna di S. Luca*. This is the most important sanctuary in Bologna's religious and civic history; perched atop the Colle della Guardia (291 m.), outside of *Porta Saragozza* (*E1*). You can drive up (Via di Casaglia, 10 km.), off Via Saragozza; or walk (90 minutes) following Via Saragozza, and then *Via di S. Luca*, with its 3.5-km.-long portico, built in 1674-1715. The elliptical sanctuary was built in its current form by C. F. Dotti (1723-57). Inside is a 12th-c. Byzantine icon of the Virgin; also paintings by G. Reni and Guercino. Fine view* of the city.

Villa Aldini. Take the Via dell'Osservanza from *Porta S. Mamolo* (*F3*), to this Neoclassical villa, built by a minister of Napoleon, A. Aldini. Nearby is the 15th-c. **Convento dell'Osservanza** (230 m.).

Convento di Ronzano (286 m.). *Open by request, tel. 581443.* Take Via dell'Osservanza and Via Gaibola from *Porta S. Mamolo* (*F3*), to this former convent of the order of S. Maria (Dante meets two of these monks in the Inferno, in the Malebolge: "We both were Jovial Friars, and Bolognese," or, in the Italian, "Frati godenti fummo, e bolognesi"). Inside, early-16th-c. frescoes.

Monastero di S. Michele in Bosco* (124 m.) *Open 6:30-11:30 and 3:30-8.* From *Porta Castiglione* (*F5*) along Via Castiglione and Via Putti. Now partly an orthopedic institute (fine view of Bologna), this 15th-c. *church*, rebuilt in 1517-23 by B. Rossetti, has a portal designed by B. Peruzzi (1523); inside are Renaissance sculptures and frescoes by G. da Carpi. In the *monastery*, frescoes by I. da Imola, L. Carracci, G. Reni, and other Bolognese painters.

S. Vittore (250 m.). You reach this little Romanesque church from *Porta Castiglione* (*F5*) along Via Castiglione and Via S. Vittore; built in the 11th c. and rebuilt in the 19th c., it has an elegant late-16th-c. *cloister*.

Certosa. *Open, summer, 8-6; winter, 8-5.* This ancient Carthusian monastery, or charter house, stands in Via Certosa, outside of *Porta S. Isaia*. Built in the 14th c., it was converted into a city cemetery in 1801. With many cloisters, corridors, and tunnels, and the 14th-c. church of *S. Girolamo*, it is the final resting place of Nobel laureate G. Carducci and composer O. Respighi. Note funerary monuments by L. Bartolini, V. Vela, and L. Bistolfi.

Fiera. NE of Bologna's center, this fair hosts 25 events every year; the main entrance is at n. 6 in Piazza Costituzione. Also here is the *Galleria d'Arte Moderna* (1970-75; temporary art exhibits) and the *Palazzo dei Congressi* (1975), for conferences.

Bolzano / Bozen

elev. 262 m.; pop. 98,233; Trentino-Alto Adige, capital of the autonomous region of Alto Adige. On his way south, Goethe noted the vineyards where "light-blue bunches of grapes dangle on high, ripening in the heat of the earth below," the fruit vendors in the main square, peddling peaches and pears, thriving trade, and the "bright cheerful sunshine." From the south, you are more likely to notice the Gothic appearance of the old town, at the confluence of the rivers Tàlvera and Isarco, and the sense of a mix of two worlds, Latin and Germanic, beneath the distant skyline of the Dolomites.

Historical note.   Not much is known about the ancient city, or where its center once stood. Drusus founded an outpost here in 15 B.C., as an inscription tells us, and some finds suggest Roman settlement, but not until the 12th c. is there any reliable history of Bolzano's development as a city. Amid the wars between the bishops of Trent and the counts of the Tyrol, many Gothic churches were built — notably the Duomo and the Chiesa dei Domenicani — in the area around modern-day Via dei Portici. Piazza Walther, named for its monument to the great German medieval poet, Walther von der Vogelweide, is still Bolzano's center. The town was a major trading center in the Middle Ages, with four fairs a year, each lasting two weeks. In 1635, a Mercantile Magistracy was established. The headquarters of this magistracy, until 1851, was the Baroque Palazzo Mercantile, built by the Veronese architect Perotti. Despite the existence of this and a few other Baroque buildings, the city remained largely German Gothic, until the 1500s. Meanwhile, Bolzano fell first to the counts of the Tyrol, then to the dukes of Carinthia, and from 1363, to the dukes of Austria. The Hapsburgs held the town until 1918, save for a period under Napoleon, when it was made first part of Bavaria, then part of the Kingdom of Italy. At the end of the 19th c., the elegant suburb of Gries sprang up; in the Thirties, Bolzano developed as a manufacturing center, pushing west and south.

Getting around.   Part of the historic center is closed to traffic, so we recommend following this route as a walking tour, using cars or buses only to reach the quarter of Gries, across the river Tàlvera.

Places of interest.   **Piazza Walther.** The center of Bolzano, bounded on one side by palazzi now serving as hotels, and on the other by the impressive Gothic cathedral. At the center is a monument to the great German medieval poet, Walther von der Vogelweide. Beneath the square is a parking lot.

Duomo*. *Closed Sat. aft.* This 14th-c. Gothic church has a fine apse and colorful steep-pitch roof, with 16th-c. campanile. Outside, 14th-c. portals and reliefs; inside, frescoes, and notable pulpit (1514).

Chiesa dei Domenicani. This Gothic church, once the place of worship for Italians in Bolzano, was rebuilt after heavy bomb damage in WWII; inside, note 14th-/15th-c. frescoes; an altar piece by Guercino (1655); and the **Cappella di S. Giovanni*** with remarkable frescoes of Paduan Giottesque school (note the Triumph of Death; ca. 1340). In the adjacent Gothic *cloister* (entrance through n. 19 A), frescoes by F. Pacher and paintings by local 16th-c. artist S. Müller; note also 14th-c. frescoes in *chapter hall* and *Cappella di S. Caterina* (open upon request, enquire with the parish priest, tel. 978676).

Via dei Portici*. This straight road has been the heart of Bolzano for many centuries, and is still lined with elegant shops. Note the porticoed houses, esp. n. 39 (main facade in Via Argentieri), and the Baroque *Palazzo Mercantile* (1708).

Piazza delle Erbe. This square is lined with handsome homes; this is the site of the fruit market; on one side is the 18th-c. *fountain of Nettuno*, with bronze statue by G. Mayr.

Chiesa dei Francescani. This Gothic Franciscan church has a noteworthy main altar, carved by H. Klocker (1500), and a lovely 14th-c. cloister (*closed 12-2:30*); note frescoes.

Museo Provinciale di Scienze Naturali. At the corner of Via Bottai and Via Hofer, this museum has an exhibition on the landscape and ecosystems of Alto Adige.

S. Giovanni in Villa. *Open for group tours, by request, tel. 978145.* Confined to a narrow little square is a 12th-c. church, with an immense bell tower. Inside are two series of 14th-c. frescoes.

Museo Civico*. *Open, Tue.-Sat., 9-12 and 2:30-5:30, Sun. 10-1; closed Mon.* This town museum is located in the former Casa Hurlach, at n. 14 in Via Cassa di Risparmio. It features archeological material dating from the Mesolithic (note the menhir of Lungostagno, or Renon; the mid-Bronze Age sword of Hauenstein; and a milestone from the reign of the Emperor Claudius, A.D. 46); a collection of folk costumes and domestic objects; and a gallery of local art, dating from the 13th c. on.

Ponte Tàlvera. Uphill, along the left bank of the river, runs the Lungotàlvera Bolzano, a handsome riverside promenade, which passes the *Castel Mareccio* (13th to

Bolzano: Duomo

16th c.), with four massive round towers with conical roofs, now a conference center; the promenade then joins the *Passeggiata S. Osvaldo* which runs up the slopes of Mt. Renon; fine views.

Monumento della Vittoria. Majestic triumphal arch built in 1928 by M. Piacentini; sculptures by L. Andreotti, A. Dazzi, P. Canonica, and A. Wildt. This monument has been bombed by German-speaking terrorist groups, and is entirely cordoned off.

Abbazia dei Benedettini di Gries. This *Bendictine abbey* lies amidst gardens and vineyards; popular as a spa. On the main square is the abbey with the Baroque church of *S. Agostino*, built in 1771; note frescoes and the altar piece by Tyrolian painter M. Knoller. Nearby, *Gothic parish church* (*Parrocchiale: 15th/16th c.; open, mid-Mar./end of Oct. 10:30-12 and 2:30-4, Sat., Sun. and holidays, closed*), with noteworthy altar piece by M. Pacher (1475).

Brescia*

elev. 149 m.; pop. 196,766; Lombardy, provincial capital. After Milan, Brescia is the largest city in Lombardy, both in terms of population and economic consequence. "They dig iron from its tall mountains," wrote the Mantuan chronicler Teofilo Folengo in the 16th c., once a Benedictine friar in the convent of S. Eufemia: the metal-working tradition dates back to the earliest times here. From mining it was a short step to the manufacture of weapons, in the lower Val Trompia, still a major local industry. Located between the Po Valley and the Alpine foothils, Brescia is a large and modern city, with renowned and noteworthy monuments and considerable collections of art.

Brescia 1:15 000 (1 cm = 150 m)

Historical note. Though this ancient city with a thoroughly modern appearance has been ravaged by pickaxe and steamshovel during the 20th century, shreds and tatters — but remarkable shreds and tatters — of the ancient city still survive. In the central section of the plan of Brescia, you can easily spot a roughly rectangular perimeter of avenues, where the names of gates (Porta Milano, Porta Trento, Porta Venezia) show the one-time existence of a walled perimeter; within that perimeter, the layout of the streets still adheres to a largely regular grid. In the NE corner there is a hill with castle; in the SW corner is a surprising off-kilter road (Corso Martiri della Libertà), running straight into the center, where it encounters three squares. The Castello, or castle, occupies the site of the earliest settlement, in the 6th c.B.C.; those settlers may have belonged to a Ligurian tribe. Certainly the name of the hill — Colle Cidnéo — was a learned conceit of the 16th c., a name invented to refer to a Ligurian king — "Cicno" — legendary founder of Brescia. Gallic tribesmen may have been the first to settle on the plain, below the castle. The layout of the streets hearkens back to Roman times, and to the original Roman layout. The city fell under Roman sway in the 3rd c.B.C., when the city was called "Brixia," though it was much smaller then, extending just west of what is now Piazza Paolo VI, with Piazza del Foro as its center. Expansion west and south followed; the first expansion was under Longobard rule, and included the area of what is now Piazza della Loggia (Brescia was the capital of a duchy; the "curia ducis," court of the duke, or Cordusio, was located

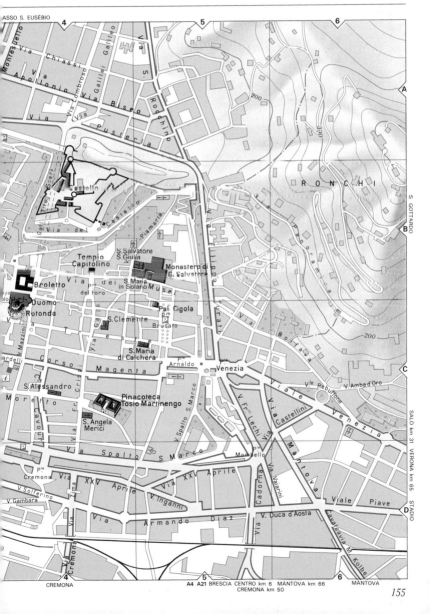

on the site of the Piazza della Loggia and Piazza della Vittoria; the important convent of S. Salvatore stood where the basilica of that name now stands); another expansion occurred when the walled perimeter was built in the 12th c. (long since demolished), extending to the west just past the church of S. Giovanni Evangelista (this was headquarters of the Communal government, first mentioned in a document dated 1120; Brescia was part of the Lombard League, which stood up against the emperor Frederick I Barbarossa; in order to be a citizen, you had to build a house of stone). The perimeter of avenues, or "viali," dates from the second set of walls, under Communal government, 1237-54; the city did not really expand beyond that perimeter until the 19th c., and with the construction of the new walls and the Broletto, Brescia seems to have exerted its last great effort for many centuries. Later, Brescia was ruled by seigneurs from outside: Ezzelino da Romano; the house of Della Scala, from Verona; the Visconti from Milan (and one local seigneury, between 1270 and 1308, under the bishop, Berardo Maggi). In 1428 Venice took Brescia from the Visconti, ruling it until 1796 (with a short French interval, 1509-1513, during the war of the League of Cambrai, with insurrection, siege, and plunder by the French nobleman and soldier Gaston de Foix, known as the "Thunderbolt of Italy"). Under Venetian rule, Brescia grew: by 1505, the population had increased from 6,000 to 65,000, the same as the population that Brescia had at the turn of the 20th c. (the plague of 1630, however, drove the population back down to 13,000). The ancient tradition of metal-working led Brescia to become a manufacturer of weapons ("Brescia has almost always been the armory of all Italy," wrote the military engineer G. Maggi in the late-16th c.). In terms of art, in the 15th c., the Brescian painter Vincenzo Foppa was the greatest artist in Lombardy, but the "Brescian school" of the 16th c., with Savoldo, Romanino, and Moretto, was equally tied to Lombardy and Veneto. The city walls were rebuilt and reinforced with bastions after 1516, along the 13th-c. perimeter; Brescia remained a citadel until Napoleonic times, when the ramparts were converted into promenades. The diagonal line of the embankment, or glacis, of Porta S. Nazaro (Piazza Repubblica) running toward the center, became the access road from the train station (1852-1854). The city walls were torn down, beginning in 1875. Industrialization followed the local tradition of "ferrarezza," or metal-working. The three squares at the heart of Brescia almost recapitulate its history. On Piazza Paolo VI, formerly Piazza del Duomo, note the monuments to religious fervor (the Rotonda, or Duomo Vecchio, and the Duomo Nuovo) and the relics of the medieval Communal government, in the Broletto; Piazza della Loggia was the center of Brescia under Venetian rule; the ambitious 20th-c. Piazza della Vittoria, which resulted in the regrettable destruction of an ancient quarter, is the center of modern Brescia.

Getting around. The route indicated runs in a ring, starting from Piazza Vittoria and ending in the nearby Piazza della Loggia, and is a walking tour.

Places of interest. Piazza della Vittoria (*C3*) is the center of modern-day Brescia, and was designed in 1932 by M. Piacentini. Among the buildings surrounding this square are the classical Palazzo delle Poste, or post office, alongside which stands the Arengario, a sort of pulpit in pink Tolmezzo stone, with reliefs by A. Maraini (episodes from the history of Brescia). Nearby is the ancient church of S. Agata (B3), rebuilt in the 15th c.; inside, 14th-c. frescoes.

Piazza della Loggia* (*B3*). Largely surrounded by Venetian-style buildings, this square is a vast and harmonious architectural complex. The dominant structure is the Loggia, facing a porticoed 16th-c. palazzo, and the Torre dell'Orologio (1540-50), or clock tower; a plaque at the foot of the tower commemorates a terrible and lethal terrorist bombing here, 28 May 1974. Bounded to the south by the Palazzo del Monte di Pietà*, two similar buildings joined by an arch: the right wing (1484-89) has Roman inscriptions and a Venetian-style loggia; the left wing was added in 1597.

Loggia* (*B3*). Now Palazzo del Comune, or city hall, this building was erected between 1492 and 1574 as a meeting hall. The ground floor (1492-1508) is partly porticoed; the upper floor (1554-74) was designed by many illustrious architects of the time, including Sansovino, Alessi, and A. Palladio, but probably chiefly by L. Beretta. A stairway climbs to the upstairs halls, partly decorated with 16th-c. paintings.

Piazza Paolo VI (*B-C4*). With two 18th-c. fountains, this square is lined by the Rotonda, or Duomo Vecchio (old cathedral), the Duomo Nuovo (new cathedral), and the Broletto.

Rotonda* (*C4*). *Open, Apr.-Sep., 8-12 and 3-6:30; closed Tue.* Brescia's premiere Romanesque monument, it sits at the square's 11th-c. level, and is circular, topped by a dome surrounded by small pilastered arches. The interior* comprises a central space covered by a hemispherical dome, ringed by an ambulatory. A presbytery and two chapels were added in the 15th c.; the left chapel holds a rich, rarely shown array of treasures; the right, paintings* by Moretto. Note mosaic floor, dating from the 1st c. B.C., and two 14th-c. sarcophagi*.

Duomo Nuovo (*B-C4*). *Open, 8-12 and 4-7:30.* Begun in 1604 and not completed until three centuries later (dome, by L. Cagnola, 1825), this cathedral's classical interior has various artworks, by Moretto, R. Scorzelli (1984), and Romanino.

Broletto* (*B4*). One of the most notable town halls in Lombardy, built between 1223 and 1298, and extensively enlarged and rebuilt in later centuries, this building is flanked by the Torre del Popolo, a tower dating from the 11th c. Note the courtyard, with a mix of medieval, Renaissance, and Baroque styles.

Castello (*B4; in summer, bus available from Piazza del Duomo*). This immense fortress, which crowns the Colle Cidnéo, dates from the time of the Communal government, though its current appearance dates from the 16th c. In the Grande Miglio is the Museo del Risorgimento (open, 9-12:30 and 2-5; closed Mon.), devoted to Italy's movement for independence and unification, covering the period from the 18th c. to Italian unity in 1870. In a number of 14th-c. rooms of the Visconti keep is the Museo delle Armi "Luigi Marzoli" (open: Oct.-May, 9-12:45 and 2-5; Jun.-Sep., 10-12:45 and 2-6; closed Mon.), with collections of weapons. Also in the castle is an observatory (Specola Cidnea; open, Mon., Wed. and Fri., from 6 pm on) and a model train layout (holidays, 3-5). The surrounding area is a park.

Via dei Musei (*B4-5*). Lined by 16th-/18th-c. aristocratic palazzi (note n. 45 and 32), this road runs along the old main street of Roman Brescia. Note the entrance to the Galleria Tito Speri (1951), a tunnel which runs under the Colle Cidnéo to the modern section to the north.

Piazza del Foro (*B4*). Covering the ancient Roman Forum only in part, this square is surrounded by the Tempio Capitolino, a number of sections of the eastern portico, the Teatro, and the Basilica. These ruins, which harmonize perfectly with the square's medieval and Renaissance architecture, are Lombardy's most important Roman complex.

Tempio Capitolino* (*B4*). *Open, 9-12:45 and 2-5; closed Mon*. This ancient temple was built in A.D. 73 under the emperor Vespasian; part of the steps, a partly rebuilt Corinthian colonnade, and the pediment, likewise reassembled, survive. Deep inside are three cellae, with a Museo Lapidario Romano, with carvings and inscriptions. On a terrace behind the temple is the archeological section of the Museo Romano* (open the same hours as the Tempio Capitolino) with fragments of reliefs and statues, as well as a 1st-c. A.D. bronze winged Victory*, six Roman busts*, and a variety of ancient objects. Adjacent are the impressive ruins of the Teatro Romano, an ancient theater partly covered by Renaissance and modern buildings.

Brescia: Tempio Capitolino

Monastero di S. Salvatore (*B5*). This monastery was founded in A.D. 753 and suppressed in 1797, when it became a barracks; it contains the churches of S. Giulia, S. Salvatore, and S. Maria in Solario (see below). This building should eventually house the Museo della Città, with documentation on all aspects of Brescia's history.

S. Salvatore* (*B5*) Open by request, tel. 59003-40679. This exquisite piece of architecture from the high Middle Ages was built in the 11th c. on the site of an 8th-c. church and Roman ruins. It has capitals from the 6th c. and a crypt, as well as 8th-c. frescoes and stuccoes; in the chapel at the base of the campanile, frescoes by Romanino.

S. Giulia (*B5*). This church was begun in 1466 and enlarged in 1599, with 16th-c. frescoes by F. Ferramola, and the Museo dell'Età Cristiana, or museum of the Christian age. S. Maria in Solario, the former oratory of the monastery, is a Romanesque structure containing 16th-c. frescoes by local artists.

Palazzo Cigola (*C5*). This 16th-c. aristocratic home was enlarged in the 18th c., and overlooks the broad, tree-lined Piazza Tebaldo Brusato. Nearby is the ancient church of S. Maria di Calchera (*C5*), with 17th-c. facade; inside, works by Romanino, Moretto, and C. Piazza.

Via A. Gallo (*B-C4*). This road begins on the site of the Roman Forum, running past Piazza Labus (*C4*), where the house at n. 3 includes ruins of the Curia, likely the municipal basilica of Roman "Brixia." From this square, a narrow lane runs to the 14th-c. church of S. Clemente (*C4*), with paintings* by Moretto and Romanino.

Pinacoteca Tosio Martinengo** (*C4*). *Open, 9-12:30 and 2-5; closed Mon.*; entrance in Via Martinengo da Barco n. 1. Two local nobles made gifts to the city of Brescia: one, an art collection; the other, the 16th-c. building that now houses one of Lombardy's largest collection of paintings. Among the artists whose work is displayed in the gallery's 22 halls are P. Veneziano, V. Civerchio, Foppa, A. Solario, Raphael, Cariani, Moretto, Romanino, Lotto, Savoldo, C. Piazza, Moroni, Tintoretto, G. Ceruti, F. Zuccarelli, and C. Ceresa.

S. Angela Merici (*C4*). This 16th-c. church, rebuilt after WWII, features paintings by F. Bassano the Younger, Tintoretto, P. da Cailina the Younger, G. C. Procaccini, Palma the Younger, and others.

Via Moretto (*C3-4*). This street is lined by numerous Baroque palazzi, notable among them Palazzo Martinengo Colleoni (n. 78) and the church of S. Alessandro (C4), with paintings by J. Bellini and V. Civerchio. Turn right in Corso Cavour to Corso Magenta, and then left along Corso Zanardelli, with porticoes, a main shopping street.

S. Maria dei Miracoli (*C3*). Built between the 15th and 16th c., this church has a luminous marble facade* (1488-1500), with bas-relief decorations; likewise, marble bas-reliefs inside.

Ss. Nazaro e Celso* (*C2-3*). This church, with an 18th-c. facade, contains fine paintings by Moretto (1541), Titian (1522), G.B. Pittoni (1740), and Romanino.

S. Francesco (*C3*). This Romanesque-Gothic church (1265) has a marble portal and rose window; inside, note 13th-/15th-c. frescoes and paintings by Moretto and Romanino. In the sacristy, note wooden intarsias by F. Morari, 1511); also, note the cloister (open, 9-11:30 and 3-5:30; closed holidays).

Torre della Pallata (*B3*). This tower was built in 1248 along the medieval walls, and raised in the 18th c. At its base, a fountain dating from 1596. Continue along Corso Mameli, one of medieval Brescia's main streets.

S. Giovanni Evangelista (*B3*). Rebuilt in the 15th c., this church was further renovated on the interior in the 17th c. Inside are notable paintings by Moretto, B. Zenale, Romanino, Francia, and Romanino.

S. Maria del Carmine (*B3*). This 15th-c. church has a stone-and-brick facade; the Baroque interior has 15th-c. frescoes (some by V. Foppa).

S. Giuseppe (*B3*). This church dates from the 16th c.; note the Museo Diocesano d'Arte Sacra (open, 10-12 and 3-5, closed holidays) with sculptures, paintings, illuminated codices, votive offerings, and sacred objects.

Bressanone / Brixen

elev. 559 m.; pop. 17,010; Trentino-Alto Adige, province of Bolzano. Two major Alpine rivers converge here, the Isarco and the Rienza; moreover, the Strada della Pusterìa, a road that runs from the eastern Tyrol, crosses the road of the Brenner pass not far off. The landscape is broad and open, dotted with cultivated hills set amidst looming mountains, green forests, and rolling meadows; in the ancient center, the city still preserves the stern flavor of its centuries of history as the capital of a large ecclesiastical principality (the power of its bishop-princes lasted eight centuries, 1027-1803). There is a Germanic flavor to the architecture, monuments, and art, stretching from Romanesque to Baroque — this is the largest center of art in Alto Adige — but beneath it all are the unique features of a cultural borderland.

Places of interest. **Via dei Portici Maggiori***. This distinctive road through the old center of town, lined with shops, is still medieval in flavor, lined with 16th-/17th-c. houses, with crenelation and overhanging windows. At n. 14, is the old *Municipio*, or Town Hall. Note, in the courtyard, painting of Solomon's Judgement; the street ends in the small and intimate Piazza della Parrocchia.

Piazza della Parrocchia. This square is dominated by the Gothic parish church of *S. Michele*; note campanile, or *Torre Bianca*. Inside, frescoes by J. Hautzinger. To the left of the church, note the Renaissance *Casa Pfaundler* (1581), a fine example of the mingling of Northern and Italian styles.

Duomo. Founded in the 10th c. and rebuilt in the 13th c., this Romanesque church was converted to Baroque in 1745-90; with its tall bell towers it dominates the tree-lined Piazza del Duomo. Inside, frescoes by P. Troger and main altar by T. Benedetti. Note tombstones of bishops, from 16th

to 19th c. On the right, renowned Romanesque-Gothic **cloister***, with notable frescoes (14th/16th c.); then you enter the *Baptistery*, with more frescoes*, and the *Treasury of the Duomo* (*open, Apr.-Oct., 10-12 and 2-5; closed Sun. and holidays*).

Palazzo dei Principi Vescovi. This palace of the bishop-princes was fortified, with a moat, and stands near Piazza del Palazzo, before the Colonna del Millennio, erected in 1909 to commemorate Bressanone's first thousand years.

This palace was built in the early 14th c. and rebuilt, from 1595 on, by the Austrians; used by the church as residence or offices until 1964. It has an elegant facade and courtyard; on the 2nd floor, note 24 terracotta statues, of members of the house of Hapsburg, by H. Reichle (1599).

Inside is the **Museo Diocesano**. *Open, mid-Mar.-31 Oct., Mon.-Sat., 10-5; closed Sun.; closed the rest of the year. Creche section, open: mid-Dec./10 Feb., every day, 10-5, except for 24 and 25 Dec.* The art collection occupies 70 halls, and ranges from medieval craftsmanship to the original furnishings of the bishops' residence, Romanesque and Gothic wooden statues, Baroque and Renaissance sculpture, and Baroque paintings by S. Kessler, J. G. D. Grasmair, F. (Sebald) Unterpergher, and P. Troger. Also, manuscripts, incunabula, fabrics, embroideries, and sacred garments. Noteworthy collection of creches.

Excursion. **The Alpine hut Città di Bressanone/Plosehütte** (2,447 m.), by cableway or by 23-km. panoramic road, through the Valle d'Eores, to *Valcrore/Kreuztal* (2,050 m.), then on foot, 1.5 hours, or by chairlift; the hut is on the south ridge of the Cima della Plose (2,504 m.), popular for winter sports (panorama*).

Càgliari

pop. 204,237; Sardinia, regional capital. Set amidst salt marshes and fish-filled ponds at the center of the broad southern gulf that extends from Cape Spartivento to Cape Carbonara, Cagliari is the main harbor and one of the "gateways" to Sardinia. The French author Auguste Bouillier, who visited it in 1864, wrote movingly of the view, with the "cupolas glittering in the setting sun," the "castle with its belt of grey walls," and the "spectral towers." Dotted with Pisan towers and a Spanish castle, Cagliari has other Spanish touches, such as its flower-lined "patios," decorated with ceramics not unlike Spain's famed "azulejos."

Historical note. Once one of three cities that thrived on the gulf in Phoenician times — "Bithia," "Nora," and "Kàralis" — only the latter survived to become present-day Cagliari. Nothing survives from those days, though graves, homes and an amphitheater bear witness to the Roman occupation, which began in 238 B.C. The Romans were succeeded by Vandals, and then Byzantines (note the central structure of the basilica of S. Saturno), and, in the 12th c., by Pisans, who built the hilltop Castello, or castle. Three gates, with three towers (S. Pancrazio, Elefante, and Leoni) shaped the growth of the quarter, and the city. Pope Boniface VIII gave the city to the kingdom of Aragon as a feudal holding, and in 1326 the Aragonese took the Castello, marking the onset of four centuries of Spanish dominion. Alongside the medieval quarters of Castello and Marina grew, to west and east, the quarters of Villanova and Stampace. Then, the Piedmontese took over in 1720, leaving little trace of their rule. The walls were torn down in 1858, opening the three main boulevards: Via Roma, Largo Carlo Felice, and Viale Regina Margherita. Since WWII, Cagliari has grown recklessly, endangering some of its finest environmental qualities and features.

Getting around. Two routes are suggested: the first starts at the Bastion of Saint Remy, southernmost tip of the Castello, and is walkable (a further excursion to the Necropolis of Tuvixeddu and the Grotta della Vipera requires driving); the other route, from Piazza Costituzione to the base of the Bastion of Saint Remy, extends to the west and east in the low section of town, or "citta' bassa," but you may want to drive to S. Saturno and Nostra Signora di Bonaria.

The Castello

"Su Casteddu" stands on a high ground, fortified in the Middle Ages by the Pisans, a symbol of Cagliari. Alongside the Cattedrale, the city museums occupy the former Arsenale Militare.

Bastione di Saint Remy (*D3*). At the southern edge of the quarter, this late 19th-c. overlook was built on the Spanish bastions.

Torre dell'Elefante (*C3*). At the end of Via Università, this tower was built by the Pisans in 1307; its name comes from a relief, set some 10 m. off the ground.

Cattedrale* (*C3*). Built in the Pisan style and later enlarged (late 13th c.), it was reshaped in Baroque style, and then restored to its original style in 1933. Note the handsome portals in the transept (above right portal, note the front of a Roman sarcophagus) and the campanile (partly rebuilt). **Inside**, note the pulpits*, originally built in 1159-62 for the Cathedral of Pisa and donated to Cagliari in 1312. Note the statue of the 14th-c. Black Madonna. In the *right transept*, Gothic chapel with a handsome triptych (attributed to G. David, or else the school of R. van der Weyden). From the presbytery, you can descend to the *sanctuary*, with its three chapels; the central chapel is decorated with 584 Baroque rose windows. In the *left transept*, note the tomb of Martin II of Aragon (1676). Adjacent to the right transept is the **Museo Capitolare** (*open, by request, tel. 663837*), featuring antiques and precious sacred decorations.

Chiesa della Purissima (*C3*). Built in 1554, with the adjacent ex-convent. Note the triptych by A. Casula (1593).

Torre di S. Pancrazio (*B3*). This tower was built in 1305 as part of the Pisan fortifications.

Cittadella dei Musei* (*B3*). This modern and panoramic complex stands on the site of the former Arsenale Militare (till 1825); note Pisan, Aragonese, Spanish, and Savoy fortifications. Included in the museum complex are the Museo Archeologico Nazionale, the Pinacoteca Nazionale, the Museo Siamese Cardu, and the Collezione delle Cere.

Museo Archeologico Nazionale*. *Open 9-7.* With materials from digs in Sardinia, it provides a lively picture of the civilizations that have occupied this island, from prehistory (6000 B.C.) to the High Middle Ages (7th and 8th c.). Ranging from the highly decorated earthenware and statuettes of mother-goddesses made of bone and rock, the

collection includes small bronzes** from the Iron Age (900-750 B.C.) to Phoenician times. Also note the jewelry, ivory, Greek vases, and Roman glass.

Pinacoteca Nazionale (*open 8:30-1:30 and 2:30-7:30*). In the collection of retables, canvases, crests, and furnishings, dating from the 15th to 18th c., note the retable "della Portiuncola," as well as art by Spanish and Sardinian painters, as well as busts by G. Sartorio and V. Vela.

Museo Siamese Cardu. This museum boasts an impressive collection of Far Eastern arms, ceramics, and objects. The original **Collezione delle Cere** (*open, Tue. and Thu., 4-7*) comprises astonishing anatomical models from 1803-1805.

Galleria Comunale d'Arte Moderna (*A3*). *Open, Tue.-Fri., 9-12:30 and 5-8; Sat.-Sun., 9-1 and 5-8; Mon. closed.* This museum has a collection of work by Italian artists of the 1960s and 1970s, and 20th-c. Sardinian art.

Anfiteatro Romano* (*B2*). Visible from the Viale Fra' Ignazio da Laconi, this 2nd-c. amphitheater is one of the finest Roman buildings in Sardinia. Note the ditch in which the wild animals were kept. Nearby, the *Villa di Tigellio* (*C2; open, by request; contact the Soprintendenza, tel. 668501*) comprises three city dwellings from the 1st c.

Necropoli di Tuvixeddu (*A1, off map*). *Open, by request; contact the Soprintendenza, tel. 668501.* In Via Falzarego, this Necropolis was first Phoenician and Punic and was later used by the Romans. Comprising roughly a hundred tombs dating from the 6th to 1st c. B.C.; note the *Tomb of the Ureo* (or Uraeus) with fine Phoenician tomb paintings, and in Via S. Avendrace, n. 81, note the *Grotta della Vipera* (*open, by request; contact the Soprintendenza, tel. 668501*), a tomb of the 1st c. A.D.

The "Città Bassa"

At the base of the Castello, the Rione Marina follows the grid of a Roman "castrum," while to the west is the Rione Stampace, to the east, the Rione Villanova. Of particular interest here are the churches.

Piazza Yenne (*C2-3*). This is the heart of Stampace, in the shadow of the Bastion of S. Croce.

S. Agostino (*D2*). This church is one of Sardinia's few pieces of Renaissance architecture. The artifacts uncovered here seem to indicate it was once occupied by baths.

S. Anna (*C2*). Set atop a high stairway, this church was bombed heavily 1943; since rebuilt.

S. Michele (*C2*) One of the finest pieces of Spanish Baroque on the island, it was built in the 17th c.

Piazza S. Giacomo (*C3*). This is the setting of the rites of Holy Week; in the adjacent *Oratorio del Crocifisso*, note the wooden statues of the Misteri della Passione (Mysteries of the Passion; G. A. Lonis, 1758), carried in Easter processions.

S. Domenico (*C4*). Rebuilt in 1954 after damage from WWII; note the handsome late Gothic *cloister*.

S. Saturno* (*D4*). Although *tourists cannot visit this church*, it is one of the most important monuments of Sardinian Christianity.

Santuario and Basilica di Bonaria (*F5*). Dedicated to the Virgin Mary, protector of sailors, this basilica is the destination of pilgrims from all over. The statue has been venerated here since the 15th c. In the sacristy, note the collection of model ships and votive offerings offered by mariners over the centuries.

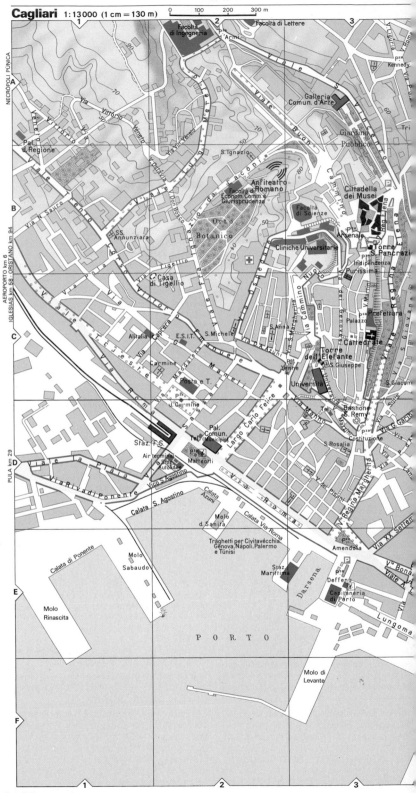

Cagliari 1:13000 (1 cm = 130 m)

0   100   200   300 m

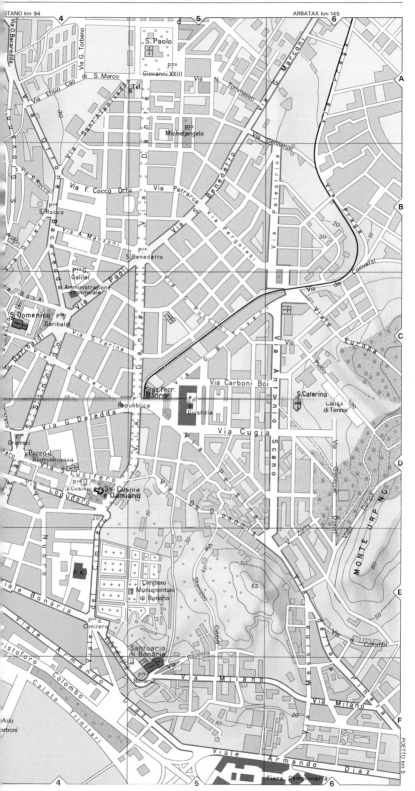

S. Paolo

Pza
Giovanni XXIII

Via G. Torbeno

Via Efisio Cao di S. Marco

Tel.

santAlenxarda

Via O. Bacaredda

Pza
Michelangelo

Via N. Tommaseo

Via Marconi

Via Genneruxi

Ollone

Via S. Rocco

Via F. Cocco Ortu

Via Petrarca

Via Benedetto

Via Pergolesi

Via Palestrina

Via Praga

Via A. Manzoni

Pza
S. Benedetto

Via Paoli

Via

Via dei Conversi

Pza G. Galilei

Amministrazione
Provinciale

S. Domenico   Pza
Garibaldi

Via S. Farina

Via Alghero

Via G. B. Tuveri

Via G. Puccini

Viale   Europa

Via   Via Antonio Scano

S. Caterina

Campi
di Tennis

Via Carboni Boi

Staz. Ferr.
Sardic

Pal.
di
Giustizia

Repubblica

Via G. Deledda

Via Cugia

Via Pietro

Via Giuseppe Dessì

Pza
Gramsci

Parco d.
Rimembranza

Via S. Lucifero

Via Da Giovanni

Via Sonnino

M O N T E   U R P I N U

Viale Europa

Via Logudoro

Pza d.
S. Cosimo   SS. Cosma
e Damiano

Viale della Pineta

Viale Bonaria

R.A.I.

Cimitero
Monumentale
di Bonaria

Via Stenisteo

Via Carboni

Via

Pza d.
Cimitero

Santuario
di Bonaria

P

Bonaria

Via Ravenna

Via Milano

Via Colombi

Viale Armando

Viale Bonaria

Cristoforo Colombo

Calata Trinitari

Via Diaz

Via   Milano

Molo
Carboni

Viale   Armando   Diaz

Fiera Campionaria

Capri (Island of)

pop. 12,399; Campania, province of Naples. The astonishing prodigies of nature, the enchantment of the landscapes, the ineffably lovely light of the sky over this massive block of limestone — only 6.5 km. in length, rising high over the deep blue sea — will always be a siren's lure to travelers.

Places of interest. You land at Marina Grande; at the far end of the beach are the ruins of the *Palazzo a Mare*, possibly inhabited by Augustus; beyond are the enormous ruins of the so-called *Bagni di Tiberio*, or Baths of Tiberius.

The world-renowned **Grotta Azzurra****, or **Blue Grotto** (*by motorboat 25 min.; by rowboat, an hour and a half; you can tour the grotto on little rowboats, 9-an hour before sunset*) takes its name from the color that sunlight acquires as it filters through the water.

Capri (elev. 142 m.), the main town on the island, is of course quite a haven for jet-setters. The **piazzetta**, a central square that lends itself admirably to effortless, enjoyable lounging, is enclosed like a courtyard, and is surrounded by an enchanting medieval quarter. Alongside the square are the Eastern-style domes of the church of *S. Stefano*.

In the **Certosa di S. Giacomo*** (*open, 9-2; Sun. 9-1*), a charter house dating from the 14th c., the little cloister dates from the 15th c. while the larger cloister dates from the 16th c. In the halls of the complex there is a *museum*.

In just 45 min. you can be at the excavations of the **Villa Iovis*** (*open, 9-an hour before sunset*), also known as the Villa of Tiberius. In 30 min., you can reach the *Arco Naturale*,* a natural arch in a landscape of savage beauty, and the *Grotta di Matromània*. In 20 min. you can reach the **Belvedere di Tragara,*** (elev. 130 m.), and from there you can descend to the beach of the *port of Tragara*, to the right of which are the immense shoals and cliffs of the *Faraglioni**; note the rare blue lizard that lives on the isolated cliff (the third one) of Scopolo.

Caserta

elev. 68 m., pop. 70,142, Campania, provincial capital. Charles of Bourbon built a royal palace here (1752) to house his newly won throne; the exterior was completed in 1774, the interior a century later — after the Bourbons had been expelled. The modern city, which developed around the "Versailles" of the Bourbon dynasty of the Two Sicilies, is in a certain sense of a by-product of the royal palace.

Places of interest. The **Palazzo Reale**** (*open, 9-1:30; Sun. 9-12:30; closed Mon.*), a royal palace built by the architect Luigi Vanvitelli, has a rectangular plan, arranged around 4 interior courtyards; the lower vestibule *, the great stairway (or *scalone d'onore**), and the upper vestibule* constitute the most remarkable architectural sections of the palazzo; the charm of the apartments is given by the Neoclassical decorations and the memories of life in the court of the Bourbon dynasty and under Joaquim Murat. You should tour: the royal apartments, the new apartment, the apartment of the King, the old apartment, an

Capri: Piazzetta

18th-c. creche with 1,200 figurines, a Pinacoteca or art gallery, and a vast hall with a Museo Vanvitelliano (with exhibits concerning the architect) and the delightful little court theater (1769).

The splendid **park**** (*open, 9-an hour before sunset; by car as well, except for on holidays*) has an array of fountains and waterfalls that extend all the way up to the hill; the **great waterfall*** with the sculptural group of **Diana and Acteon** and the **English garden** (*group tours, with the custodian*) are the most noteworthy aspects of this complex.

Surrounding areas. Three km. NW, at **San Léucio**, Ferdinand IV established a famous silk manufactory (18th c.) with the idea of creating a model city, an example of enlightened industrialization.

Castel del Monte

elev. 540 m.; Puglia, province of Bari, township of Andria (pop. 90,063). This castle can be considered the monument that is most expressive and representative of the personality of Frederick II of Swabia (1194-1250), the son of Constance of Altavilla, heiress of Sicily and Henry VI, the German emperor who preferred southern Italy - and Sicily in particular - to his northern homeland. He established his court in Sicily.

Tour. *Open Apr./Sept., 8:30-7 pm, Sun. 9-1pm; Oct./March, 8:30-2 pm, Sun. 9-1 pm.* The octogonal-plan

Castel del Monte

Castle**, built with large ashlars, is punctuated, at the corners on the exterior, by eight towers, also octogonal. Roughly halfway up the exterior wall there is a horizontal cornice, indicating the separation between the two interior floors. The entrance portal, on the east side, shows an interesting mixture of Gothic style (pointed arches, columns surmounted by lions) and echoes of classical Rome (cusped pediment). Inside, after you enter from the second hall through a pointed-arch portal of Muslim derivation, the central courtyard reiterates the octagonal plan of the building; overlooking the courtyard are three french doors on the second floor, with slender columns supporting archivolts decorated with plant motifs. There are eight trapezoidal-plan rooms surrounding the courtyard. There is a spiral staircase in one tower (the ceiling is attributed to Nicolò Pisano), which allows you to climb to the upper floor. Light comes from the exterior, through twin-light and three-light mullioned windows (panoramic view of the Murge and the Tavoliere).

Catania

elev. 10 m., pop. 333,075, Sicily, provincial capital. The second largest city in Sicily is also an illustrious birthplace of literature and music. It stands on the shores of the Ionian sea, amid the citrus groves, in the clear Mediterranean light. Mt. Etna, with its solemn silhouette, its peak brushed by clouds and snow, forms part of the cityscape and part of its destiny. The volcano made the surrounding land fertile, attracting the original founders; it is also the source of the black lava-stone of which the Roman amphitheater was built, as were the medieval cathedral and the Baroque palazzi.

Historical note. Of ancient origins (this was one of the Greek colonies of the 8th c. B.C.), Catania now has the noble, sumptuous 18th-c. Baroque appearance (at least, in the historic center) given it during the brilliant reconstruction done by the Palermitan architect Giovanni Battista Vaccarini, when the city was rebuilt following the catastrophic earthquake of 1693.

Places of interest. Piazza del Duomo* (*D3*). The 18th-c. appearance of the city strikes one immediately in the central cathedral square, with the remarkable *Fontana dell'Elefante* (G.B. Vaccarini, 1736), a fountain inspired by Bernini's Fontana della Minerva, in Rome. The elephant is an ancient one, carved of lava stone, and symbolizes Catania.

Duomo* (*D3*). The facade is also by Vaccarini; of the original 11th-c. construction, all that survives are the apses and the transept; on the immense *interior*, note the Norman structure. In the right apse is the *Cappella di S. Agata**, patron saint of Catania; from here you enter the rich *treasury (can only be viewed during religious celebrations)*.

Porta Uzeda (*D-E3*; 1696). From this gate, which opens out onto the harbor area, and from the Piazza del Duomo, runs the *Via Etnea* (*A-D3*), the main road in the reconstruction done after the earthquake. This lively city promenade runs gently up toward the base of Mt. Etna.

Piazza dell'Università (*D3*). The road is interrupted by this university square, a harmonious assembly of buildings by Vaccarini, as well as by *Piazza Stesicoro* (*C3*), to the left of which you can see the ruins of the 2nd-c. **Anfiteatro Romano,** or Roman amphitheater.

Castello Ursino* (*E3*). The vast solemn square bulk of this castle, built by Frederick II (1239-50) and rebuilt in the 16th c., houses the **Museo Civico***. This city museum comprises varied collections of archeology, ancient and modern art, ivory, terracotta, bronze, weapons, and memorabilia of local history.

The square *Piazza Mazzini* (*D-E3*) is surrounded by a peristyle of 32 marble columns, taken from a Roman basilica.

Museo Belliniano. Not far off is the Bellini Museum *(open, 9-1:30; holidays 9-12:30)* and the **Teatro Romano** (*D2-3*), or Roman theater, with an adjacent, semicircular **Odeon** *(open, 9-an hour before sunset, closed Mon.)*.

S. Francesco d'Assisi all'Immacolata. From the Piazza S. Francesco, with the Baroque facade of

Catania: Duomo

this church, begins the *Via dei Crociferi** (*D3*), slightly converging with the Via Etnea; this is another of the monumental streets designed by Vaccarini.

S. Niccolò (*D2*). Further west, the church of S. Niccolò, with an unfinished facade, is the largest one in Sicily. In it are stored 7 of the 11 "ceri," richly inlaid and painted "tapers," carried in the procession of the feast of S. Agata. Over the altars of the bare white interior, note the large canvases from the 17th/19th c. Note also the carved wooden choir chancel in the presbytery; elegant armoirs and rich ecclesiastical garb and ornaments in the Rococo sacristy. Also noteworthy is the *view** from the dome *(enquire with the sacristan)*.

Certosa di Pavìa* (Charterhouse of Pavìa)

elev. 90 m.; Lombardy, province of Pavia. Anyone who visits the Certosa, or charterhouse, is inevitably impressed by the contrast between the opulence of the house of worship and contained, balanced magnificence of the complex as a whole. From the time the cornerstone was laid, in

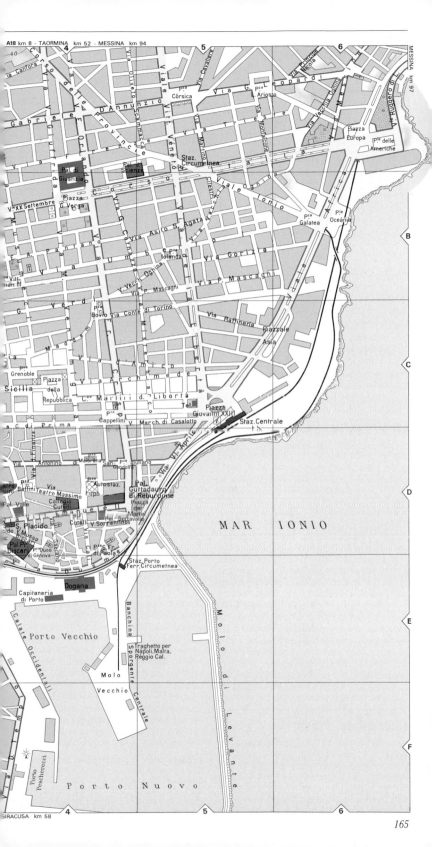

Charterhouse of Pavìa

August of 1396, construction of the imposing complex continued for over two centuries, with the contribution of the newest and most original artists of the Lombard Renaissance.

Tour. Guided tours, led by a monk *(9-11:30 and 2:30-6 pm, or 5pm in March, April, Sept., Oct;, or 4:30 pm in winter; closed on Mondays that are not holidays).* In the entrance courtyard, note the Baroque structure of the **Foresteria*** or guest quarters, by F. M. Richini (1625), which intersects with the exceedingly rich **facade**** of the church, built between the end of the 15th and the middle of the 16th c., chiefly by G. Amadeo and by C. Lombardo. The curch, which was completed in 1473, is in the transitional style between Gothic and the Renaissance. The interior has a nave and two side-aisles, and is closed at the transept by a sumptuous 17th-c. gate, and is flanked by a succession of chapels. There are exquisite **paintings*** and **frescoes*** by Perugino (15th c.), Bergognone (15th c.) and G.B. Crespi (17th c.). Also worthy of note are: two bronze *candelabra** by A. Fontana (1580); the **funerary statues of Beatrice d'Este and Ludovico il Moro***, by C. Solari (1487); a 15th-c. ivory triptych* from the Embriachi workshop; the wooden stalls of the choir* (1498); the **sepulcher of Gian Galeazzo Visconti*** by G. Romano and assistants (1487). Take a carved door, by Mantegazza, to enter the delightful *small cloister** (1462-72), with porticoes adorned with terracotta decorations. There is a magnificent view here of the right side and the transept of the curch. The large cloister is lined with the celles of the monks.

Cividale del Friùli

elev. 135 m.; pop. 11,190; Friùli-Venezia Giulia, province of Udine. Standing on the banks of the Natisone, where the river flows out of the foothills of the Julian Alps, this town has layers of history and art, dating from early Roman occupation, through the aristocratic Middle Ages, when it was the headquarters of a Patriarch, and through a peri-

od of Venetian rule; above all it is a town with a heritage of Longobard occupation. These barbarians entered Italy in A.D. 568 over the nearby Passo del Predil, ruled here for two centuries, and then vanished.

Places of interest. Piazza del Duomo. The monumental center of Cividale, on the site of the Roman Forum, this square is bounded by the Duomo, of course, the *Palazzo dei Provveditori Veneti*, designed by A. Palladio (1581-96), and the *Palazzo Comunale*, with a copy of a statue of Julius Caesar.

Duomo*. Built beginning in 1457, designed by B. delle Cisterne, it was reconstructed in the following century by P. and T. Lombardo. The simple stone facade has three portals; the middle one is by J. Veneziano (1465). Alongside, note the Baroque campanile.
Inside (designed by P. Lombardo), beneath the organ on the right is a fragment of a standard (1536) by G. da Udine; in the right chapel of the apse, Annunciation, by P. Amalteo. Note the altar piece, or Pala di Pellegrino II*, made of gilt silver (1195-1204); note frescoes by Palma the Younger.
On the right aisle is the entrance to the **Museo Cristiano** (*open 9:30-12 and 3-6, holidays from 9 am*), with remarkable 8th- and 9th-c. altars and thrones, and frescoes from the Tempietto Longobardo.

Museo Archeologico Nazionale*. *Open, 9-2; holidays, 9-1; in summer, 9-6:30.* Located in the 16th-c. Palazzo dei Provveditori Veneti, this museum has some 20 rooms with major collections ranging from Roman times to the high Middle Ages, with special focus on the Longobards and the Friùli in general. Of particular note, on the *ground floor*, is the section of epigraphs, inscriptions, reliefs, and fragments of architecture, from Roman, early-Byzantine, high-medieval, and Romanesque times; also mosaics. *Upstairs* is the Longobard section, with arms and jewelry, and the psaltery of St. Elizabeth, with 13th-c. Saxon miniatures, and a 13th-c. veil.

From the portico of the Palazzo dei Provveditori, a passage to the right leads to the *Via Monastero Maggiore*, and on to the medieval quarter of Borgo Brossana and the Tempietto Longobardo, through two gates, the *Roman arch-gate* and the *Porta Patriarcale*.

Tempietto Longobardo*. *Open, Apr.-Sep., 10-1 and 3:30-6:30; Oct.-Mar., 10-1 and 3:30-5:30.* This remarkable example of the architecture of the high Middle Ages (8th/9th c.) looms over the river Natisone, and can be reached by a short passage overlooking that river. The large square central hall is covered by a tall cross vault; the apse is split into three by columns, supporting low barrel vaults. Note detached frescoes (12th/14th c.) and the sarcophagus of Piltrude (re-used material from the 8th c.). The hall has wooden stalls and Byzantine-style frescoes (in poor condition), as well as a rich array of 8th-c. **stuccoes**** and a remarkable frieze.

S. Biagio. Across from the entrance to the Tempietto Longobardo, this little church dates from the 15th c. Returning to Piazza del Duomo you will pass the *Monastero Maggiore*, with the church of **S. Giovanni** (*open by request, contact the custodian*), with altar piece by Palma the Younger. Also, at n. 6 in Via del Monastero Maggiore is the access to the so-called **Celtic Hyogeum** (*open by request, 9-1 and 3-5; Sat. and Sun. closed*), a series of narrow tunnels cut into the rock.

Ponte del Diavolo. Built in the mid-15th c. to unite the two rocky banks of the Natisone, this bridge was demolished and rebuilt in WWI; it offers a fine view of central Cividale.

S. Francesco (*open during exhibitions*). This 14th-c. church has 14th-/16th-c. frescoes. Nearby is the *Palazzo Pontotti-Brosadola*, with a simple and handsome facade; also, the church of *S. Pietro ai Volti*, with a fine altar piece by Palma the Younger.

Como*

elev. 201 m.; pop. 88,803; Lombardy, provincial capital. The city is cupped in a small hollow, surrounded by an arc of hills, at the base of the Monte di Brunate, overlooking the southernmost tongue of its lake, the Lario, a section of Lake Como. This is the city of the Maestri Comacini, or Comacine Masters, inventors of Romanesque architecture, the town of both Plinys, Elder and Younger, who are immortalized in the statuary that adorns the façade of the Duomo, home of the silk industry, ancient but thriving as greatly as ever, and of the Italian Rationalist architecture of the early-20th c. More than for the city itself, Como is beloved and frequented for "the enchanting loveliness, the light, and the expressive mobility of the lake.» (Maurice Barrès). By noticing only the lake, however, one is deprived of the pleasure of many discoveries, of noteworthy monuments and remarkable atmospheres.

Historical note. There was a large Celtic fortification here originally, built between the 6th and 5th c. B.C., but the modern city was founded, in a certain sense, in 196 B.C., nearly 2,200 years ago: Marcus Claudius Marcellus defeated the Celts and founded a "castrum," the square Roman camp of "Comum Oppidum." Although little survives of the ancient walled perimeters, the townspeople, or Comaschi, still speak of the "città murata": they are referring to the center of Como. In the "città murata" about a third of the buildings date back before 1600, but the "borghi," or quarters outside of the walls, are also ancient. In the history of architecture the adjective "Comacini" is used with the substantive "Maestri" — the first mention of the Comacine masters is in the Edict of the Longobard king Rotari (A.D. 643). The new architecture that these builders, carpenters, masons, stonecarvers, and plasterers practiced in Como and throughout Italy developed into what we know as Romanesque; in Como the tradition takes form in the great Romanesque churches: S. Fedele, within the walls; S. Abbondio and S. Carpoforo in surrounding quarters. The town government gained strength in the early-12th c., and the defining moment of its history was its decade-long battle with Milan (1118-27); Como emerged a beaten city; the new walls and the ruins of the castle on the Colle del Baradello date from the reconstruction undertaken with the assistance of the Holy Roman Emperor Frederick I Barbarosssa. Ever since the Visconti took Como

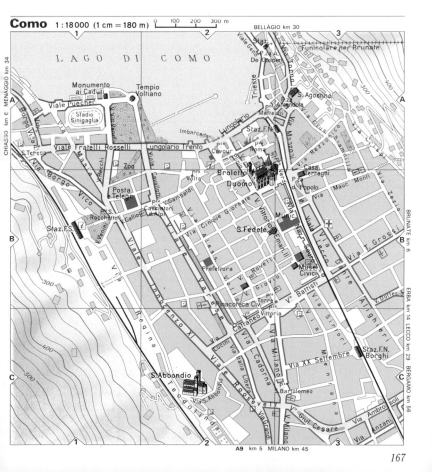

(1335), until 27 May 1859, when the city welcomed Garibaldi, who had defeated the Austrian troops on the Colle di S.Fermo, in the fight for Italian unity; Como's political history has basically been the history of Milan. The Visconti built their citadel in the NW corner of Como (between the Duomo and the lake); in 1447, when Filippo Maria Visconti died, Como proclaimed the short-lived Repubblica di S. Abbondio, and the citadel was demolished. Work resumed on the Duomo, from its beginnings in 1396: this was Como's great architectural project (the Broletto was savaged, and part of the church of S.Giacomo destroyed to make room), and work continued until the 18th c. to complete the cupola, designed by Juvarra. The Neoclassical period gave the city the appearance that Stendhal so loved, and which can still be seen in the patrician villas on the western shore of the lake and in the facades along Via Volta. From the lakefront promenade and drive of the Lungolario you can look out over the clear cold waters, standing in Piazza Cavour, which was once the port of Como (filled in with earth in 1871).

Getting around. Much of the historical center is closed to automobile traffic, especially along the thoroughfare of Via Vittorio Emanuele II; the route marked on the map can be considered a walking tour, though you may choose to take public transportation to reach the church of S. Abbondio.

Places of interest. Lungolario, a lakefront drive and promenade. (*A2*). The northern part of the city curves around the little gulf at the base of the lake. Adjoining the *Piazza Cavour*, the heart of Como, and a harbor that was filled in 1871, are the docks of the boats and hydrofoils that carry passengers across the lake.

Piazza del Duomo (*B2*). The monumental center of the city lies in this square, along which stand the Torre del Comune, the Broletto, and the Duomo.

Broletto* (*A-B2*). Once the center of Communal government, this Romanesque-Gothic town hall was built in 1215; note the marble facing, with white, grey, and pink stripes, the portico, and the mullioned windows and 15th-c. balcony. The tower, or *Torre del Comune*, was built in 1215, and rebuilt in 1927.

Duomo** (*B2*). This monument traces its origins to the architectural culture of the Comacine Masters; begun in 1396, work continued until the 17th c., when the dome was added, designed by Filippo Juvarra (1740). The Gothic-Renaissance facade is

Como: Duomo

split in three by slender pilaster strips, with portals, high windows, and a large rose windows, is enlivened with sculpture (mostly by G. and T. Rodari; 15th/16th c.). On either side of the central portal are two aedicules with statues of Pliny the Elder (who died in the eruption of Mt. Vesuvius in A.D. 79) and Pliny the Younger, his nephew. Also note the two portals, one on the right side and the other on the left (called the Porta della Rana), by Rodari; also, note the apse (1513).

The *interior* is a mix of Gothic (aisles) and Renaissance (transept) styles; note the dome, 75 m. high. Along the nave hang 16th-c. tapestries. The side altars have reliefs by Rodari and canvases by Gaudenzio Ferrari and Bernardino Luini.

Casa del Terragni (*A-B3*). Once the *Casa del Fascio*, a building used by the Fascist party, this building stands in the *Piazza del Popolo*, facing the apse of the Duomo; built by G. Terragni in 1932-36, this is one of the most notable pieces of Rationalist architecture in Italy.

S. Fedele (*B2-3*). This basilica was originally Como's cathedral, and dates from the early-12th c. The polygonal apse is crowned with a small loggia; note the portal with reliefs, in Via Vittorio Emanuele. In the little square, note two interesting 15th-c. buildings, with terracotta and wood sections, now being restored.

Musei Civici (*B3*). *Open, Apr.-Sep., 9:30-12 and 2:30-5:30; Oct.-Mar., 9-12 and 2-5; Sun., 9-12; closed Mon.* The *Museo Archeologico* is located in the Palazzo Giovio; the *Museo Storico del Risorgimento* is located in the Palazzo Olginati; and both museums, linked by a gallery, overlook the Piazza Medaglie d'Oro. They contain collections of archeological finds (from prehistoric times to Roman times) and exhibits of local history, from the Renaissance to the modern day. Now being installed are halls that will exhibit Greek, Etruscan, Phoenician-Punic, Assyro-Babylonian, and Egyptian artifacts, as well as a portrait gallery (Galleria dei Ritratti).

Pinacoteca Civica (*B2*). *Open, 11-1 and 2-6; Sun. 2-6; closed Mon.* This art gallery is housed in the 17th-c. Palazzo Volpi; it has a collection of 17th-c. Lombard canvases, frescoes and bas-reliefs from the 14th c., and work by abstract artists living in Como.

Piazza Vittoria (*B-C2-3*). Note the monument to Garibaldi, by V. Vela; on one side of this square stands the **Porta Torre**, also known as the *Torre di Porta Vittoria* (1192), a gate with two passageways and large windows on the interior, once part of the city walls, rebuilt by the emperor Barbarossa; at the corners, note the two five-sided towers. In the cellar of a nearby school are ruins of the *Torre Pretoria*, a tower dating from the Roman empire (3rd c.); in the cellars of another school in Via Carducci are ruins from the walled perimeter that dates from the Roman Republic. Yet other Roman ruins (baths and library of Pliny the Younger, 2nd c.) are found along Viale Lecco; recently, ruins of a Roman villa were uncovered at the corner of Via Tommaso Grossi and Via Zezio (*B3; private property*).

S. Abbondio* (*C2*). This basilica, built in the 11th c., is one of the masterpieces of Lombard Romanesque architecture. Note the facade, adorned with pilaster strips and cornices in relief, and the two bell towers. The interior features five aisles, divided by columns and tall piers, with a deep presbytery. In the loggia over the entrance and in the apse, there is a vast frescoed Life of Christ, by Lombard painters of the mid-14th c. To the left of the altar is a marble statue of S. Abbondio (1490) attributed to C. Solari.

On the western shore of the port is the *Giardino Pubblico*, a public park; at the water's edge is the **Tempio Voltiano** (*A1*); open, *Apr.-Sep., 10-12 and 3-6; Oct.-Mar., 2-4; closed Mon.* This classical-style building (1927) contains memorabilia and documents concerning Alessandro Volta, Como's most illustrious son, inventor of an electric battery, after whom the volt is named (1745-1827). Continue along past the *Monumento ai Caduti* (Monument to the War Dead; 1933), note a tower designed by the Futurist architect Antonio Sant'Elia. On the left is the *Stadio Sinigaglia*.

Other monuments. Villa Olmo (*off map, toward Cernobbio*). This large Neoclassical villa was built by S. Cantoni in 1782-97; it now belongs to the city of Como, and the handsome grounds are a public park. The halls are used for exhibits, conferences, and concerts (*open, 8-6, closed holidays*).

S. Agostino (*A3*). This Gothic church dates from the early-14th c., and has a Romanesque portal, decorated with reliefs. Inside, note the 15th- and 17th-c. frescoes, and canvases by Morazzone (1612). Alongside are two cloisters.

Villa Geno. Along the eastern shore of the lake runs Viale Geno (*A2*), a handsome drive or stroll leading to the *Villa Geno* (1850), on a spit of land, with a lakefront and enormous grounds, open to the public.

Museo della Seta (*C3, off map*). *Open, 9:30-12 and 2:30-5; closed Mon.* This museum in the Via Valleggio has a collection of objects and documents detailing the history of the silk industry in Como.

Museo Rivarossi. *Open by request, tel. 541541.* In the village of Sagnino (Via Pio XI, 157), this museum of model railroading has over 3,000 items from all over the world.

S. Carpoforo (*C2-3, off map*). This church stands on the SE outskirts of Como; from Via Milano you pass under the railroad tracks, with a short detour. Built in the 11th c., this basilica is one of the earliest pieces of Romanesque architecture in Como (*open by request, enquire at the adjoining religious institute, 9-12*). From here, you can continue on for about another 1.5 km., and then walk about 15 minutes, to see the ruins of the **Castello Baradello** (*open, Thu., Sat., Sun., and holidays, 10-12 and 2:30-5*) built by Barbarossa in 1158 and dismantled by the Spanish in 1527 (view of the city, the Brianza countryside, and the lakes).

Cortina d'Ampezzo*

elev. 1;211 m.; pop. 7,095; Veneto, province of Belluno. The green valley in which this town lies, in the Valle del boite in Cadore, is surrounded by a stuendous Dolomitic setting, with the peaks of the tofane Pomagagnon, Cristallo, Dorapiss, Cinque Torri, and Croda da Lago. The first Grand Hôtels were built here around 1860, just after the bell tower of the parish church was rebuilt, a classic image for the promotion of this little town (it was under Austrian rule until the end of WWI); in 1909 it was linked to Falzàrego by a new road, the Grande Strada delle Dolomiti, which had been under construction for years, for the use of the Austro-Hungarian military; the first ski competitions were held here in 1902; in 1874 a woman climbed the Cristallo, the first major Dolomitic peak scaled by a woman. The town is a legendary holiday resort, a place of elegance, renown, and luxury, where the social whirl and winter sports have long come together.

Places of interest. Corso Italia. This central thoroughfare (largely closed to traffic; pedestrians only) is lined with hotels, cafes, and elegant shops; it runs into the two central squares, Piazza Roma and Piazza Venezia, separated by the 18th-c. parish

church of the **Ss. Filippo e Giacomo,** Inside, note the wooden tabernacle by A. Brustolon (1724) and the altar piece by A. Zanchi (1679); from atop the bell tower, fine panoramic view.

Casa delle Regole. Center of the communities of Ampezzo this building is located at n. 1 in Viale Parco; in the Ladin of Ampezzo it is also called the *Ciasa de Ra Régoles*. It has a rich *Museo Geologico* (note the fossil collections of Rinaldo Zardii), a mineralogic museum and a museum of local traditions (*open, 1 Jul.-15 Sep. and 20 Dec.-end of March, 4-7; Aug. and 20 Dec.-6 Jan., also 10-12; closed Sun.*); also note the **Pinacoteca "Mario Rimoldi"** d'Arte Moderna, a ggallery with paintings by such modern artists as Massimo Campigli, Carlo Carrà, Giorgio De Chirico, Filippo De Pisis, Renato Guttuso, Giorgio Morandi, Ottone rosai, Aligi Sassu, Arturo Tosi, and others.

This now-historic Olympic ice-skating structure, on the nortthern outskirts of town, has a skating surface of 4,230 sq. m., and was built for the winter Olmpics of 1956. Facing it, on a boulder, a bronze plaque commemorates the French geologist Dolomieu who was the first, at the end of the 18th c., to describe Dolomitic rock.

Cortona*

elev. 494 m.; pop. 22,598; Tuscany, province of Arezzo. Clean air whispering through the olive trees, and a city the color of the sandstone from which it is largely carved, clustered on the steep slopes once enclosed by the vast Etruscan walls, at the edge of the plain of Valdichiana. The medieval past survives here, in the air and the buildings, for two centuries archeologists have been delving into the more distant, Etruscan past, from the Accademia Etrusca.

Getting around. Much of the historic center is close to traffic; therefore, we recommend a walking tour, though you must have a car to reach many of the monuments outside the walls.

The historic center

In the 15th c. Fra' Angelico came here to paint; a generation later, L. Signorelli, great Cortonese painter, began his career here. This Tuscan hill town is unforgettable in the melting light, when seen from high above, from the Medici fortress.

Piazza della Repubblica (*B1*). Heart of Cortona, with the 13th-c. **Palazzo Comunale**, the 12th-c. *Palazzo del Capitano del Popolo*, and the nearby *Piazza Signorelli*, with the **Palazzo Pretorio**, site of the Museo dell'Accademia Etrusca.

Museo dell'Accademia Etrusca* (*A1*). *Open, Apr.-Sep., 10-1 and 4-7; Oct.-Mar., 9-1 and 3-5; closed Mon.* Founded in 1727, with library (*open by request*), as a branch of the Etruscan Academy, this museum has remarkable collections of Etruscan artifacts. Note the great bronze lamp** with satyrs and sirens (5th/4th c. B.C.); also, Egyptian and Roman objects, a 12th-c. mosaic, medieval and modern objects of the applied arts (note the little porcelain temple by the Manifatura Ginori di Doccia; 1765), coins*, gems, medallions, seals, miniatures and costumes. Among the paintings, work by N. di Pietro Gerini, B. di Lorenzo, F

Cortona: Palazzo Comunale

Signorelli, Pinturicchio, and L. Signorelli; also, a hall of work by the Cortona-born modern painter G. Severini.

On the top floor, three rooms display finds from the Tumulo II of the digs in the so-called Etruscan "meloni" from Il Sodo (see below), including late-Archaic jewelry*.

Duomo (*A1*). Rebuilt in the 15th c., some Romanesque features survive in the facade of this cathedral; note the 16th-c. Portal of Cristofanello, under the portico.

Museo Diocesano* (*A1*). *Open, 9-1 and 3-6:30; closed Mon. and Oct.-Mar., until 5.* Set in the former *church of Gesù* (1498-1505) and adjacent buildings, facing the Duomo. In one section, artwork by P. Lorenzetti, L. Signorelli, and a 2nd-c. A.D. Roman sarcophagus*. In the *former church*, work by Sassetta, P. Lorenzetti, Fra' Angelico, B. della Gatta; in the *former sacristy*: more Lorenzetti and the celebrated Vagnucci reliquary*, by G. da Firenze (1457) and other 13th-c. paintings. Downstairs, in the *lower church*, 16th-c. frescoes, partly attributed to G. Vasari.

S. Francesco (*A-B2*). *Open by request; contact the guard, on the site.* This 13th-c. church was rebuilt in the 17th c.; inside, note the 10th-c. Byzantine ivory reliquary*.

Via Berrettini (*A2*). This steep street runs up to the 16th-c. church of *S. Cristoforo*, while Via S. Croce runs further up to S. Margherita, with fine views. Along the way is the little church of S. Nicolò.

S. Nicolò (*A2*). *Open by request; contact the guard, on the site.* This 15th-c. church stands amidst the cypresses; note the standard* painted by L. Signorelli, and fresco by same artist.

Santuario di S. Margherita (*A3*). Spectacular view from the square before this Neo-Gothic church (1856-97). Just uphill is the **Medici fortress**, 651 m. (*A3*), built in 1556 (view*); take **Via S. Margherita** (*A-B2-3*) back to town; note the mosaic *Via Crucis** by G. Severini.

Monuments outside the city walls

The clear, geometric architecture by F. di Giorgio Marini, in the church of the Madonna del Calcinaio contrasts pleasingly with the gentle views of Tuscan countryside, dotted with cypresses and olive trees.

S. Domenico (*B2*). Just outside the Porta Berarda is this late-Gothic church. Note the triptych by L. di Niccolò Gerini (1402). Take Viale Giardini Pubblici, (*B2-3*) for a walk with splendid views*.

Madonna del Calcinaio** (*B2; off map*). *Open, 3-8 (6, in winter) and by request at the parish church, tel. 603375.* Standing some 3 km. downhill from the town, near the local road from Camucìa, this elegant Renaissance church was an archetype for the sanctuaries built between the 15th and 16th c. Built in 1485-1513 to a plan by F. di Giorgio Martini, it has a luminous, Brunelleschian interior, with stained glass by G. de Marcillat (16th c.), and the main altar, from the same period, by B. Covatti.

Tanella di Pitagora (*B2; off map*). *Open by request; contact the guard, on the site.* Some 3 km. SW of town, near the Madonna del Calcinaio, is this Etruscan hypgeum, possible 4th-c. B.C., set among the cypresses.

S. Maria Nuova (*A2; off map*). Outside the walls, north of town, this mid-16th-c. church is reached by exiting the *Porta Colonia*, and was heavily rebuilt by G. Vasari.

Convento delle Celle or *Convent dei Cappuccini* (*A2; off map*). This convent stands 3.5 km. NE, out of Porta Colonia, in a handsome hillside setting, and was founded by St. Francis between 1211 and 1221.

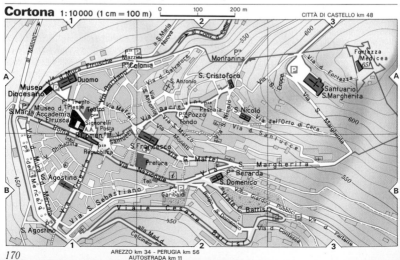

Cortona 1:10000 (1 cm = 100 m)

"**Meloni**" (*A1; off map*). *Open by request; contact the guard, on the site*. At Il Sodo, 2 km. NW of town, near the state route 71, are 4th- to 3rd-c. B.C. Etruscan hypogea, or underground burial chambers, carved or dug out of sandstone. Some of the finds here are now on display in the Museo dell'Accademia Etrusca.

Cosenza

elev. 238 m., pop. 84,614, Calabria, provincial capital. Set in a lovely hilly setting, the town has an ancient section, clinging to the Colle Pancrazio, and a modern section, set in the plain below; the two sections are linked by the Ponte Mario Martire. The Humanistic cultural tradition — which gave such renown to the Accademia, founded in the 16th c. by the great Humanist Aulo Giano Parrasio and still in existence — was recently rejuvenated with the establishment of the Università degli Studi della Calabria, at Arcavacata di Rende.

Places of interest. Piazza Campanella lies in the area where the old town meets the modern town.

Overlooking the piazza is the church of **S. Domenico**, a Baroque reconstruction of an earlier 15th-c. building, of which the entrance and a handsome rose window survive. On the *interior*, note the Madonna della Febbre, a 16th-c. statue by a Neapolitan sculptor, and the 17th-c. choir and sumptuous Cappella del Rosario.

At the center of the old town, with its intriguing medieval network of alleys and lanes, the **Duomo*** overlooks the square, with a powerful solemn Gothic facade, made of tufa, with three portals and three rose windows; a Cistercian Gothic building (12th/13th c.), it was transformed in the 18th c. and recently restored. On the *inside*, note a handsome canvas by Luca Giordano (Immaculate Conception) and the funerary monument* to Isabel of Aragon, a French creation from the late-13th c.

The **treasury** of the Duomo (including an enameled cross*, a 13th-c. creation of the Sicilian school, donated by Frederick II for the consecration of the cathedral, and ivories from the school of Cellini) has paintings dating from the 15th/18th c., goldsmithery, sacred apparel and furnishings, and parchments, is partly located in the *Bishop's Palace* (Palazzo Vescovile) and partly in the Soprintendenza ai Beni Storico-Artistici.

S. Francesco d'Assisi. This church was founded in the Gothic period, but heavily renovated during the Renaissance and in the Baroque period.

Overlooking **Piazza XV Marzo**, in the heart of the old town, are the Prefettura, or police courts building, with the extensive gardens of the *Villa Comunale*, the *Teatro Comunale* and the *Palazzo dell'Accademia Cosentina*, also the site of the **Museo Civico Archeologico** (*open, 9-1; closed holidays*).

High atop the hill stands the mighty square structure of the **Castello**, a stronghold built in various phases (Norman and Swabian era — especially the octagonal tower — and the 16th and 17th c.).

Inside the 18th-c. church of **S. Francesco di Paola** is a handsome marble sepulcher (1593), a Baroque wooden chancel, and a triptych from the early 16th-c.

Cremona*

elev. 45 m.; pop. 75,160; Lombardy, provincial capital. The river Po, flowing within the massive earth embankments, runs past the edge of Cremona,

while the Adda just a short way upstream. The surrounding countryside is well watered and fertile. A considerable portion of the city's industry and trade is driven by agriculture. The Gothic crown of the Torrazzo, visible from the surrounding fields for quite a distance, amid the low-lying Lombard plains, stands in one of the loveliest medieval squares in Italy.

Historical note. We can only speculate about Celtic and pre-Roman settlement; the Roman colony was founded in 218 B.C. The Communal government was founded in 1098; the cathedral was founded in 1107: this marked the beginning of three centuries that shaped the monumental center of Cremona, which expanded with the growing monastic settlement and projects of reclamation. The Communal government brought Cremona into the Lombard League in 1167, prior to the great battle of Legnano, but it had long been an imperial ally (the Cremonese fought alongside Barbarossa in the siege of Milan), and fought repeatedly against the Milanese (whom it defeated in 1213 at Castelleone), and again alongside the imperial troops during the reign of Frederick II. In the meantime, between 1169 and 1187, a walled perimeter had been built, which included, to the south of the ancient Roman area, the site of reclamation projects, with a set of spoke-like roads running out from the Duomo, and the Cittanova, to the north. From 1334 on, when Azzone Visconti took Cremona, the city joined its fate with that of Milan, and of the duchy of Lombardy, until the unification of Italy. Bianca Maria Visconti brought the city as part of her dowry when she married Francesco Sforza in 1441. The Renaissance brought handsome new buildings in Lombard brickwork, with terracotta decorations, and witnessed the flourishing of local paintings. Perhaps even more illustrious than the artists of Cremona, however, are its violin makers, the pride of the city's tradition and heritage; the names of the great masters, who drew exquisite music from fine wood, are well known: Andrea and Niccolò Amati (16th/17th c.), Antonio Stradivari (d. 1737), and Giuseppe Antonio Guarneri (d. 1745). In 1567 the great musician Claudio Monteverdi was born in Cremona, and in 1834 the great composer Amilcare Ponchielli was born about a dozen km. away. The walls that surrounded the city were modernized; the Castello di S. Croce was demolished, the northern bastions became a public promenade in 1787, and the rest of the walls were demolished at the turn of the 20th c., to make room for a growing town. An iron bridge over the Po, built in 1892, replaced the old bridge laid over a series of boats. The port/channel was built after WWII.

Getting around. A number of the main roads in the historic center are closed to private cars.

Places of interest. Piazza del Comune**. This is the artistic center of Cremona, and one of the loveliest medieval squares in Italy. Note the array of monuments lining the square: the Torrazzo, the Duomo, the Battistero, the Loggia dei Militi, and the Palazzo del Comune.

Torrazzo*. *Open, Apr.-Oct., 10-12 and 3-6:30; Nov.-Mar., by request, tel. 23233*. This exceedingly tall bell tower (111 m.), a symbol of Cremona, was built around 1267; the massive brick shaft has an octagonal marble top, added between 1284 and the early-14th c. A stairway (487 steps) leads to the top, with fine panoramic view*. The Renaissance *Loggia della Bertazzola* (1525; under the arcades, medieval marble carvings and 14th-c. sarcophagus, by Bonino da Campione), links the Torrazzo with the facade of the Duomo.

Duomo**. This is one of the most notable pieces of Lombard Romanesque architecture, built during

Cremona: Battistero

the 12th c. and enlarged (transept) in the 13th and 14th c. The marble facade has two orders of loggias, a handsome rose window (1274), and a 15th-c. crown, as well as a 13th-c. porch (in the front, note the strip of reliefs, depicting work in the fields*, from the school of Antelami), surmounted by an aedicule with three statues by Marco Romano (1310). Overlooking Via Boccaccino is the northern end of the late-13th-c. transept, with porch, mullioned windows, rose windows, and terracotta ornaments. As you continue to walk around the church, you will note the complex of three apses, and southern end of the transept (1342).

The **interior*** has three aisles, and is divided by lines of pillars. The rich decoration softens the somewhat stern architecture. Along the walls of the nave and the central apse note the series of frescoes depicting the lives of Mary and Jesus*, by a number of Lombard-Venetian painters (1506-73), including: B. Boccaccino, G. Romanino, and Pordenone. Note the Renaissance sculpture in the two pulpits* in front of the presbytery, with reliefs attributed, in part, to Amadeo. In the crypt, note the Arca dei Ss. Marcellino e Pietro, once attributed to B. Briosco (1506), and reassembled here in 1609.

Battistero*. This octagonal Romanesque building, crowned by a small loggia, dates from 1167.

Loggia dei Militi. Built in 1292 as a meeting hall for the captains of the city's militia. Notable portico and high mullioned windows.

Palazzo del Comune*. The headquarters of government in early Cremona, it was rebuilt in 1206-46, and has been greatly renovated since. The central pillar of the ground-floor portico bears an "*arengario*," or external pulpit, built in 1507. Upstairs, inside, note the Renaissance portal; marble fireplace (1502) in the Sala della Giunta; and in the smaller *hall of violins* (*open, 9-12 and 3-7; Sun. and holidays only morn.*), five of Cremona's finest violins — a Stradivarius, two Amatis, a Guarneri, and a Guarneri "del Gesù."

S. Agostino*. Church built in 1345, with a monumental Gothic facade; note frescoes in 3rd and 5th chapels on right.

Museo Civico "Ala Ponzone"*. *Open, 9:30-12:15 and 3-5:45; Sun. and holidays only morn.; closed Mon.* Housed in the 16th-c. *Palazzo Affaitati* (entrance at n. 4 in Via Ugolani Dati), this museum features an *art gallery, collections of fine craftwork*, the *treasure of the cathedral*, or Duomo, and other *collections*. Noteworthy **Pinacoteca**, or art gallery, with many halls containing medieval frescoes and paintings of the Cremonese school, dating from the 15th to 18th c., as well as other Italian and foreign artists, and a collection of modern Italian art.

The same building contains the **Museo Stradivariano** (entrance from n. 17 in Via Palestro; *same hours as the Museo Civico*), with collections of documents and objects linked to great musicians and instrument makers of Cremonese history. In particular, original drawings, models, and tools, made or used by Stradivarius; manuscripts by Ponchielli.

Corso Garibaldi. Lined by noteworthy buildings, especially **Palazzo Raimondi** (N. 178), built in 1496, now home to studies of ancient music and violin making. On the right, midway along the Corso, **Palazzo di Cittanova**, built in 1256 (heavily restored in the 1920s).

Other monuments. Palazzo Fodri (at n. 17 in Corso Matteotti) is an aristocratic early 16th-c. mansion.

S. Michele. This 12th-c. Romanesque church was rebuilt in the 19th c.

Palazzo dell'Arte. This modern building overlooking Piazza Marconi contains the guild of violin-makers (Istituto Professionale Liutario e del Legno) and the city *Museum of Natural History* (*open, 9:30-12:15 and 3-5:45; Sun. and holidays, only morn.; closed Mon.*).

S. Pietro al Po. Rebuilt in 1575, this church boasts artwork of the Cremonese Renaissance.

Museo della Civiltà Contadina (*off map*). *Open, 9:30-12:15 and 3-5:45; Sun. and holidays, 9:30-12:15; closed Mon.* On the Via Castelleone 51 (state road toward Milan), set in the Cascina Cambonino, this museum contains two centuries' worth of documents on the lives of Cremonese farmers, as well as many traditional farming implements.

Cuma

elev. 80, Campania, province of Naples.

Historical note. Colony of the Chalcidians of Euboea (8th c. B.C.), Cuma (orig. Cumae) has an historic importance that is not limited to the reputation of the Sybil: in its waters, the ships of Siracusa, under the tyrant, came to the city's defense against Etruscan raiders (474), who thus lost forever their dominion over the Tyrrhenian Sea. And Cumae was the cradle in Italy of reading and writing; the alphabet spread out from here. At the foot of and spreading up over a hill of lava, isolated close to the sea, the site is one of the classical birthplaces of Italian culture.

Places of interest. The **Arco Felice*** is the vault of a brick viaduct; the acropolis can be seen in the distance, stark against the sea*.

You can see the arched perimeter of the **amphitheater**, of the Campanian type, built in the early Roman Empire.

On the slopes directly above the **acropolis** (*open, 9-sunset*) note the ruins of the Greek walls, from the 5th c. B.C.

The **Antro della Sibilla Cumana**,* or Cave of the Cumaean Sibyl, is a straight gallery extending 131 m., a structure built by the Greeks in the 6th/5th c. B.C.; the room at the end of the gallery was believed to be the home — and oracular grotto — of the Sibyl.

Along the **via sacra**: the **Cripta Romana**, dating from the reign of Augustus, is a tunnel that runs through the hill, or Colle di Cuma; note the **Tempio di Apollo**, or Temple of Apollo, which still has the plaza from Greek and Samnite times, and the fragments of Augustan columns; note the **Tempio di Giove**, or Temple of Zeus, founded by Greeks, and rebuilt by Augustus, was later transformed into a 5-aisle Christian basilica (5th/6th c.).

Èrice

elev. 751 m., pop. 30,658, Sicily, province of Trapani. On the summit of Mt. Èrice, this lovely, perfectly triangular town has been a favorite stopping place for many centuries, given its perfect climate and astounding views.

Places of interest. Mura. The **walls** (well preserved, especially on the NE side) are made of megalithic blocks (5th c. B.C.) in the lower section, and are of Norman construction (12th c.) in the upper section and in the three gates.

Chiesa Matrice*. This 14th-c. church features an isolated bell tower* with mullioned windows (1312); *inside*, note the 15th- and 16th-c. chapels, and a Virgin, painted by Francesco Laurana (1469).

Museo Comunale A. Cordici *(open, 8:30 - 1:30; holidays 9 - 12).* Consists notable collections of ancient artifacts and art (prehistoric, Punic, Hellenistic, and Roman archeological finds), paintings from the 17th/19th c., local crafts work and silver, a marble Annunciation* by Antonello Gagini (1525).

To the right of the *Castello Pepoli*, at the end of a little road, stands the 12th/13th-c. *Castello di Venere* (12th/13th c.), on the round crag of the acropolis; inside, note the ruins of a temple of Venus, with a sacred well; fine view*.

Faenza

elev 35 m.; pop. 53,577; Emilia-Romagna, province of Ravenna. At the edge of the plains of Romagna, where the river Lamone crosses the Via Emilia, this city was built by the house of Manfredi (seigneurs here before the town came under the rule of the Church, 1509), and was endowed with a remarkably rich culture, in a happy conjunction with the Florentine artistic world during the Humanist age. The production of ceramics attained a spectacular level in the 15th and 16th c.; there are records of this craft as far back as 1142: the name of the town has survived in the term "faïence," indicating what the Italians call "majolica," a glaze earthenware or pottery, decorated at high heat.

Places of interest. Piazza del Popolo. Lined on both sides by porticoes and loggias, with the adjacent Piazza della Libertà this is the heart of Faenza, with the **Palazzo del Podestà**, the *Torre dell'Orologio*, and the Palazzo del Municipio; in its courtyard is the *Teatro Comunale Masini*. Overlooking Piazza della Libertà, with its monument Baroque *Fontana di Piazza*, is the Cattedrale (see below).

Cattedrale*. One of the most notable works of the early Renaissance in Romagna, this cathedral was begun in 1474 to plans by G. da Maiano; it was completed in the early-16th c. The facade is unfinished; the *interior* is clearly Tuscan in style. Note the various 15th-/16th-c. works of sculpture, including tombs of saints, with reliefs by B. da Maiano (1476). Among the paintings, note work by I. da Imola.

Corso Mazzini. One of Faenza's chief arteries, it features, at n. 21, a house built by G. Pistocchi for himself in 1788, with others at n. 47, 54, and 60. At n. 93, the 17th-c. **Palazzo Mazzolani**, with the *Museo Archeologico* and the *Galleria Comunale d'Arte Moderna*, with largely local works (A. Berti and D. Baccarini), bronze busts by A. Rodin (1908), and works by F. Carena, G. Morandi, F. De Pisis, and A. Spadini.

S. Maria Vecchia. Rebuilt in the 17th c., it preserves traces of the medieval building, especially the 9th-c. octagonal **campanile***.

Palazzo Milzetti. In Via Tonducci 15, this is a fine piece of Neoclassical architecture (G. Pistocchi; decorated by F. Giani); inside is the *Museo Nazionale dell'Età Neoclassica (open, 8-1:30, closed Sun.)*, with a research center, devoted to the Neoclassical age; also the *Museo Teatrale*, with vintage and ancient musical instruments, portraits and memorabilia of great musicians and opera singers, and a collection of modern art.

Pinacoteca Comunale*. This art gallery is located at n. 1 in Via S. Maria dell'Angelo, and features largely local artists, from the 14th to the 19th c. (G. da Rimini, Leonardo and Luca Scaletti, M. Palmezzano, G.B. Bertucci, Bagnacavallo, S. Foschi, I. da Imola, and F. Fenzoni), and of the Bolognese school, 16th to 18th c. (G. Francia, F. Albani, A. Tiarini, Domenichino, and C. Cignani). Also, note wooden statue* by Donatello; a 16th-c. Virgin and Child*; marble bust by A. Rossellino; two 15th-c. hope chests*; fine collection of still life paintings, and work by A. Lombardi and F. Guardi.

Museo Internazionale delle Ceramiche*. *Open, Apr.-Oct., 9-7; Nov.-Mar., 9:30-2; Sun., 9:30-1; closed Mon.* At n. 2 in Via Campidori, at the corner of Viale Baccarini, this museum and research center is devoted to the history and art of ceramics, in every land and era. The 38 halls include: Italian Renaissance majolica, Turkish faience, and Chinese porcelain, a wide array of Italian ceramics from the 13th to the early-20th c.; pre-Columbian and prehistoric ceramics; and a broad section devoted to contemporary international ceramics.

Chiesa della Commenda. In Borgo Durbecco (at the end of Corso Europa), this 12th-c. church has frescoes by G. da Treviso the Younger (1533), restored in 1980.

Fano

pop. 53,909; Marche, province of Pesaro and Urbino. The "Fanum Fortunae" or Temple of Fortune, which gave the town its name, is elusive in documentary sources, and has escaped all archeologists' efforts. The town is located on the Adriatic shore to the left of the mouth of the river Metauro, where the Via Flaminia reaches the sea. Of the Roman colony, all that now remains is the Arco di Augusto, or Arch of Augustus, the regular layout of the center, and the literary note of a "basilica" built here by the famous Roman architect Vitruvius; the town was shaped by the rule of the house of Malatesta, from the end of the 13th c. until 1463, when fine art and architecture were the order of the day. This is an active trading town, prospering from its fishing industry, as well as its role as a beach resort.

Places of interest. Rocca Malatestiana. This mid-15th-c. fortress has been used as a prison, and is now an art gallery. Follow a stretch of the *Augustan walls*, with cylindrical towers, then take Viale Buozzi and Viale della Rimembranza to the Arco di Augusto.

Arco di Augusto**. This arch, made of sandstone faced with travertine, was built in A.D. 2, as a monumental ornament on the Via Flaminia, in honor of Augustus, near where the great road reached the sea. Adjacent to the arch are the **loggias** of the 15th-c. church of **S. Michele***, with Renaissance portal by B. da Carona (1512).

Via Arco d'Augusto. This main street of Fano runs from the arch to the center of town, and down to the sea. Immediately on the right is the **Cathedral**, by Maestro Rainerio, with original 12th-c. facade; inside, note the Cappella Nolfi, decorated by Domenichino (1623), and paintings by L. Carracci, A. Lilli, and S. Ceccarini. Further along, past Corso Matteotti and the tree-lined Piazza Amiani, note the Gothic former church of *S. Domenico* (*open the 2nd Sun. of each month*), now a museum. Inside, frescoes by O. Nelli and others. Across the way, the monumental 18th-c. **Palazzo Montevecchio**.

Piazza XX Settembre. Set in the heart of Fano, and adorned with the 16th-c. *Fontana della Fortuna*, this square is bounded by the stern **Palazzo della Ragione*** (1299), with portico, mullioned windows, and a modern tower (inside, the 19th-c. neoclassical Teatro della Fortuna). On the right side of the building, through the Arco Borgia-Cybo (1491), you enter the courtyard of *Palazzo Malatesta*, split in two parts, one 15th-c., with portico and crenelation, the other 16th-c., by Sansovino. Here are the Museo Civico and the Pinacoteca.

Museo Civico and Pinacoteca. *Open, 8:30-12.30; Jul.-Sep. also 5-7, Sun. morn. only; closed Mon*. The *archeological section*, on the ground floor, comprises finds ranging from the Neolithic to the Roman Empire. On the mezzanine are modern paintings, by such artists as G. Induno, A. Mancini, E. Tito, F. Modesti, and G. Pierpaoli; also a collection of coins and medallions (note medallions by M. De' Pasti) and a collection of theater-related graphics (note work by G. Torelli). On the upper floor, the huge *Sala Malatestiana* with the **Pinacoteca**, with paintings by artists including B. and P. Morganti, Guercino, G. Reni, Domenichino, G.F. Guerrieri, S. Cantarini, M. Preti, A. Lilli, C. Giaquinto; in a small side room, polyptych* by M. Giambono (1420 ca.) and altarpiece by G. Santi (1487 ca.). There is also a section of local 18th-c. painters (A. Amorosi, S. Ceccarini, G. Donnini, F. Mancini, P. Tedeschi, and G.P. Zanotti) and a collection of 18th-c. ceramics.

S. Pietro ad Vallum. This 17th-c. church has a Baroque interior decorated with stuccoes, frescoes, and paintings (note dome).

Arche Malatestiane. Two *tombs** of members of the Malatesta family, the one on the right, by L.B. Alberti (1460), the other, Gothic in style, by F. di Domenico (1416-

21), both located beneath the portico of the former church of *S. Francesco*.

S. Maria Nuova. *Open, 10-12 and 4-6; closed Sun*. This church is located in Via Giovanni de Tonsis; the portico and the rich Renaissance portal, by B. da Carona, survive from the original structure. Inside, note 18th-c. stuccoes and panels by Perugino, some in collaboration with the young Raphael; also, work by G. Santi.

S. Paterniano. Dedicated to Fano's patron saint, built in the 16th c. by J. Sansovino (note Renaissance cloister).

Ferrara**

elev. 10 m.; pop. 137,336; Emilia-Romagna, provincial capital. The city lies partly concealed behind its walls and rows of trees. The river Po now flows at some distance, but its ancient bed once ran along a road in early Ferrara. The city lies on the northeast edge of Emilia-Romagna, for three centuries home to the court of the Este princes. The Este were patrons of the arts. Thus, Ferrara attracted artists and musicians who became skilled in the courtly ways of cultivating power. Aside from the masters of the "Ferrarese school," we should mention outsiders such as Piero della Francesca, Leon Battista Alberti, and Rogier van der Weyden. The poets include Boiardo, Ariosto, and Tasso. Frescobaldi, whom Bach so admired, left Ferrara at the decline of the Este. And the great Swiss historian Jacob Burckhardt called it Europe's first "modern" city, referring to the Herculean addition (the third addition in Ferrara's history), the city's architect, Biagio Rossetti, and the contrast between the Renaissance style and the narrow close-set streets of the medieval quarters.

Historical note. It was founded in the 7th c. by the Hexarchs of Ravenna; it was at one point a Byzantine "castrum," or military camp, stretching along the left bank of the river Po, which ran where Via Ripagrande now lies; the Longobards ruled here a century or so later. By the end of the eleventh century, Ferrara was fighting for its independence from the rule of Matilda, countess of Canossa, to whose family the pope had bestowed the city a century earlier. Ferrara's prosperous river trade died after 1152, when the breach of the embankment of Ficarolo, upstream of the city, shifted the Po's main course northward. The city finally won its freedom with the death of Matilda, only to be caught up in internecine strife between Guelfs and Ghibellines. A new and powerful leadership emerged with the Este family during the 13th c., and was officially recognized by Rome in 1322. The Este princes dominated Ferrara's history for centuries thereafter, bringing it prosperity and magnificence. Two Este princes, Niccolò II and Borso, worked throughout the 14th and 15th c., building the first two "additions," new walls, and the University. Late in this period, the Este court boasted such illustrious guests as Leon Battista Alberti and Piero della Francesca, along with the artists of the "Officina Ferrarese" (Cosmè Tura, Ercole de' Roberti, and Francesco del Cossa). Among their masterpieces are the frescoes of Palazzo Schifanoia. The apex of Este grandeur, however, came under Ercole I d'Este, who entrusted his architect Biagio Rossetti with the conception and construction of the third addition, in 1492. This was to be a true Renaissance city, dotted with parks and gardens. The center lies at the crossroads of Palazzo dei Diamanti, where Corso Ercole d'Este, running north-south, intersects with Corso Rossetti and Corso Porta Mare. Ferrara thus doubled in size, was girt with new walls (partly still standing), and boasted the new Palazzo dei

Diamanti and the Palazzo of Ludovico the Moor. In the 16th c., Ferrara claimed poets such as Ariosto and Tasso and painters like Dosso Dossi. Musical academies flourished here; when Ferrara's greatest composer, Girolamo Frescobaldi, moved to Rome in the early 17th c., however, the rule of the Este had already ended. Pope Clement VIII laid claim to Ferrara, and cardinals ruled here for two centuries, governing a declining city. Napoleonic rule did little to bring new vigor, nor did the return of papal rule in 1814, or the Austrian military garrison that followed. The first expansion beyond the 15th-c. walls came at the end of the 19th c. Ferrara in the 20th c. industrialized to a considerable degree, but the city is now focusing on its university and the field of applied research.

Getting around. The center is closed to private cars; these two routes are walking tours, though you may choose to use public transportation for some of the longer stretches.

The medieval city and the first expansions

A long straight roadway, comprising Viale Cavour and Corso della Giovecca, splits up the walled city. Beginning from the cathedral, studded with little loggias, this first tour captures the ancient atmosphere and hidden nooks of the southern half, the city of the early centuries, and the palazzi of Schifanoia and of Ludovico Sforza, "the Moor" (14th and 15th c.). It ends with a view of the eastern face of the city walls. Corso della Giovecca, once the Canale della Zudeca, takes you back to the city center.

Piazza Cattedrale. Overlooking this piazza in the heart of Ferrara are the Cathedral, the Town Hall, or Palazzo Comunale, and the *Clock Tower*, or *Torre dell'Orologio* (1603). At the corner of Via S. Romano stands the ancient *church of S. Romano*, rebuilt in the 15th c.

Cattedrale** (*D4*). Medieval Ferrara's chief monument, the cathedral was originally Romanesque (1135). The 13th-c. facade* is made of marble; sculptures adorn the 12th-c. portals and the 13th-c. pediment over the porch, topped by a small Gothic mullioned loggia. On the right side, concealed at its base by a 15th-c. portico lined with shops, is the marble campanile* (1441-1596); classical in design, it is attributed to Leon Battista Alberti; the late 15th-c. apse* is by Biagio Rossetti. An atrium (with 5th-c. sarcophagus) leads to the *interior*, renovated in the 18th c. and decorated in the late 19th c. On the interior of the facade, frescoes by Garofalo (1530). In the 1st altar, right, is a greatly venerated 15th-c. fresco; in the 3rd altar, right, work by Bastianino; in the right arm of the transept is a painting by Guercino (1629); on the left, bronze statues, including two 15th-c. statues by D. Paris. The main altar dates from 1728; in the choir are inlaid stalls by Bernardino Canozzi (1501-25); in the vault of the apse is a fresco of the Last Judgement*, by Bastianino (1580). In the 6th and 3rd altars, left, respectively, are paintings by F. Francia and Garofalo (1524).

Museo del Duomo* (*D4*). *Open, summer, 10-12 and 3-6; winter, until 5; closed Sun.* Climb a flight of steps from the atrium of the cathedral, on the left. This museum features artworks that once hung in the church, by such artists as Cosmè Tura and G.B. Benvenuti, known as the Ortolano; six 12th-c. marble panels* from the pulpit; two sculptures by J. della Quercia; eight 16th-c. tapestries*; 12 late 12th-c. marble panels*, with depictions of the months; 24 illuminated* missals (15th-16th c.).

Palazzo Comunale (*C4*). Built in the 13th c., this was the Este ducal residence. The facade was rebuilt in 1924. There is a small arch attributed to Leon Battista Alberti, topped by an equestrian statue of Niccolò III d'Este, and a column with a statue of Borso d'Este (the statues are modern) on either side of the *Volto del Cavallo*, which leads into the courtyard (now Piazza Municipio), which features a number of 15th-c. windows and an external vaulted stairway (1481). Inside, at the top of the main stairway (*open upon request, contact the doormen*), is the *Sala dell'Arengo*, frescoed by Achille Funi (1934-37), a Ferrarese painter, with a series devoted to the myth of Ferrara, while the *Sala del Plebiscito* features the large canvas of The Horrors of War, by G. Previati (1894), another Ferrarese painter.

Corso Porta Reno (*D4*). Beginning at Piazza della Cattedrale at the foot of the Torre dell'*Orologio*, or clock tower; on the right is the 16th-c. church of **S. Paolo**; inside are paintings by Scarsellino, Bastianino, D. Mona, and G. da Carpi.

Via delle Volte* (*D-E4*). Named after the covered arches between buildings on the Via Carlo Mayr, once the left bank of the Po, and buildings further inland; it is a nearly intact medieval street.

Via Savonarola (*D5*). Backbone of the addition by Niccolò II, this is a noble road of the early Renaissance. On the left, note the church of **S. Francesco** (*D5*), built in the 13th c., but renovated in 1494 by B. Rossetti; inside, fresco by Garofalo, paintings by I. Scarsellino, and 5th-c. sarcophagus. Further along is the main office of the University, with Renaissance portal and courtyard; it was once *Palazzo Pareschi*, and the religious reformer J. Calvin once stayed here. Opposite is the 15th-c. **Casa Romei*** (*open 9-2; closed Mon.*); around the two courtyards, note the *Sala delle Sibille* and the *Saletta dei Profeti* (note 15th-c. frescoes); also detached frescoes and sculptures.

Corpus Domini (*D5*). Convent founded in 1406; in the church, painting by G. Cignaroli. In the *Coro delle Clarisse** (*open upon request, inquire with the Clarissan nuns in Via Pergolato at n. 4; Sat. and Sun. closed*), note the Crucifixion by I. Scarsellino; also, note tombs of various members of the House of d'Este (Alfonso I, Lucrezia Borgia, Alfonso II, and Lucrezia de' Medici).

Via Scandiana (*E5-6*). First, note the church of **S. Maria in Vado** (*E5*), rebuilt from 1495 to 1518, by B. Rossetti; inside, see paintings by C. Bononi and D. Mona.

Palazzo Schifanoia** (*E5*). Best known of the Este pleasure palaces, it was begun at the end of the 14th-c., enlarged by P. Benvenuti degli Ordini (1464-69) and later by B. Rossetti. The marble portal* stands out in the brickwork facade, once frescoed. Inside, **Museo Civico** (*open, 9-7*); in the museum, the Sala dei Mesi, or Hall of Months, is decorated with a renowned series of frescoes**, by F. del Cossa, E. de' Roberti, and other Ferrarese artists of the late-15th c. (the overall plan is by C. Tura). In the other halls are collections of bronzes, ceramics, coins, jewels, and paintings. Opposite is the **Civico Lapidario** (*open 9-7*), a collection of

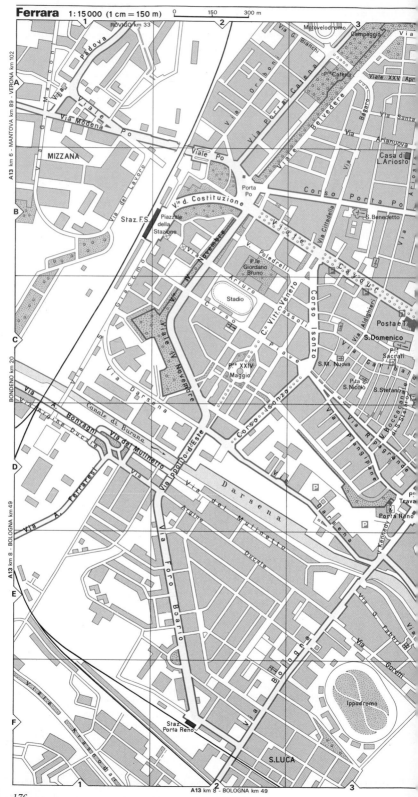

Ferrara

1:15000 (1 cm = 150 m)

0 150 300 m

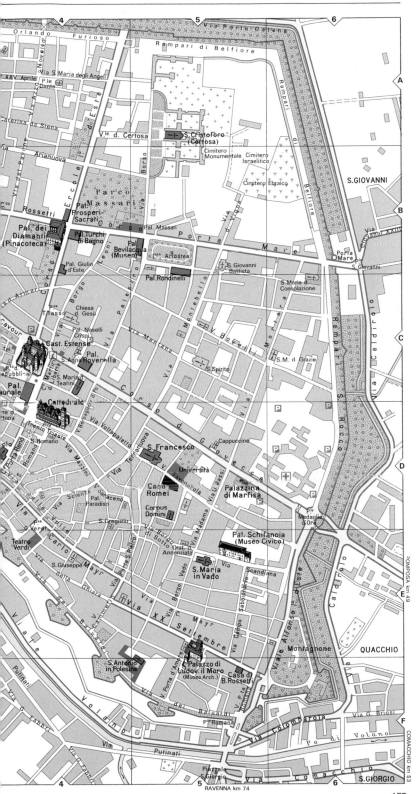

Roman marble carvings from the surrounding territory.

Palazzo di Ludovico il Moro** (*E-F5*). *Closed for restoration.* Built by B. Rossetti between 1495 and 1504, this palazzo has a fine porticoed courtyard.* It now houses the **Museo Archeologico Nazionale,*** featuring finds — especially ceramics* — from the Greco-Etruscan necropolis of Spina (over 4,000 tombs; late-6th/3rd c. B.C.), near Comacchio.

S. Antonio in Polesine (*E-F5*). This monastery once stood on an island in the Po; now in one of the loveliest settings in Old Ferrara (Vicolo Giambono n. 17). In the church, note the *Coro delle Monache**, with inlaid wooden choir stalls and three chapels with 14th-c. frescoes.

Via XX Settembre (*E-F4-5*). In this street is the Palazzo di Ludovico il Moro; straight and broad, this road was the backbone of the addition by Borso d'Este; at n. 152, decorated with terracotta, is the *home of Biagio Rossetti* (F5), which the architect built for himself in 1490.

S. Giorgio (*F5; off map*). Beyond the bridge over the Po at Volano, this 16th-c. church belongs to a complex that existed in the 7th c. The terracotta bell tower* dates from 1485; inside, paintings by local 17th-c. artist F. Naselli.

Viale Alfonso I d'Este (*E-F6*). Running along the *Montagnone*, it forms a public promenade on the city walls, and particularly on a huge heap of earth thrown up in the construction of those walls.

Corso della Giovecca* (*C-D4-6*). This popular road dates from the so-called Herculean addition, running on the course of the one-time Canale della Zudeca (named after an ancient Jewish burial ground). At n. 174 is the **Palazzina di Marfisa*** (*D5; open, winter, 9-12:30 and 2-5; summer, 9-12:30 and 3-6; 1559*), once the home of an Este gentlewoman; note grotesque paintings by C. Filippi and fine furnishings; in the garden, note the *Loggia degli Aranci*. At the far end of the Corso, at n. 476, is **Palazzo Roverella**, by B. Rossetti (1508), with an exquisite facade*, and the 17th-c. *church of the Teatini* (*C4*), with painting* by Guercino.

The "Addizione Erculea"

In 1492, work began on the new addition that more than doubled the area of Ferrara, spreading north of Viale Cavour and Corso della Giovecca. This project was the brainchild of Ercole I, the first Este duke.

Castello Estense* (*C4*). *Open 9-1 and 2-6; closed Mon.* Surrounded by a moat, the castle was built in 1385 and completed in the 16th c. Note the 15th-c. courtyard, the various frescoed halls, the Loggia degli Aranci with its hanging garden surveying the city, the corridor of the Baccanali, the chapel of Ercole II's Calvinist wife, and the dungeon, with its tragic history (Parisina, bride of Niccolò III, died a prisoner here, after falling in love with her stepson Ugo).

Corso Ercole I d'Este* (*A-C4*). This was the chief artery of the Herculean addition; at n. 16 is the majestic **Palazzo di Giulio d'Este** (late-15th c.; restored in 1932); note the **Quadrivio,*** the crossroads with Corso Rossetti and Corso Porta Mare; on the left, is the Palazzo dei Diamanti (see below), and on the right, at n. 32, the *Palazzo Turchi-Di Bagno* (1493), now part of the university; at n. 23 is the *Palazzo Prosperi-Sacrati* (1493-96), also by B. Rossetti, with a 16th-c. portal*.

Ferrara: Castello Estense

Palazzo dei Diamanti** (*B4*). The most important monument of the Herculean addition takes its name from its diamond-shaped rustication. Built largely by Biagio Rossetti (1493-1503); completed by others after 1567. Note the candelabra at the corners of the crossroads. This building houses the Pinacoteca Nazionale.

Pinacoteca Nazionale* (*open, 9-2; Sun. until 1; closed Mon.*). Occupying a number of halls of the palazzo (note the Ceremonial Hall, or *Salone d'Onore*) on the main floor, this gallery provides some idea of Ferrara's artistic heritage, especially that of the 16th c. Works by Cosmè Tura; Ercole de' Roberti; Garofalo; Dosso Dossi; Vittore Carpaccio; Gentile da Fabriano; and Andrea Mantegna. Very fine 13th-c. frescoes, by a Byzantine master, from the abbey of S. Bartolo; many 14th-c. frescoes. The palazzo houses a *gallery of modern art* and a *museum of the Risorgimento and the Resistance Movement*.

Civici Musei d'Arte Moderna (*B5*). *Open, 9-1 and 3-6:30*. Located in *two palazzi in Corso Porta Mare* (n. 7 and n. 9), the museums feature modern Ferrarese artists (among them, Filippo De Pisis); documentation concerning the "Metafisici," an artistic school that originated in Ferrara; and the works of G. Boldini. There is also a *museum of the 19th c.*, an *art gallery of the 20th c.*, and a *sculpture garden*.

Piazza Ariostea (*B5*). This broad tree-lined square was designed by Rossetti. The 17th-c. column at its center now holds a statue of Ariosto (1833), last in a succession that included a pope, the figure of Liberty, and Napoleon. At n. 10 and n. 11, *two palazzi* also designed by Rossetti.

Certosa (*A5*). Founded in the 15th c., it is now a Monumental Cemetery.

Home of Ludovico Ariosto (*B3*). *Closed for restoration*. Via Ariosto, 67. The poet purchased the late 15th-c. house and lived here. The Latin inscription reads "Small, but suited to me, beholden to no one, not miserable yet built with my own money."

Surrounding areas. At **Bondeno**, km 19.5 NW, 12th-c. *parish church*. Km 9 N, near the bridge over the Po at Ficarolo, is Stellata, with an impressive 17th-c. **Rocca**, or fortress (*open 10-12 and 3-6*).

At **San Vito**, km 26 SE, near Comacchio (you can take the Rovereto-Portomaggiore exit on the Superstrada Ferrara-Mare, the highway from Ferrara to the sea), is an 11th-c. Romanesque parish church.

At **Voghenza**, km 15 SE, is a Roman necropolis; to tour the local *antiquarium, tel. 815365.*

At **Argenta**, km 33.5 along the state road Adriatica to Ravenna, small but noteworthy *art gallery (tel. 853111)*, with works by A. Aleotti, Garofalo, F. Longhi, et al.

The **Parco-Oasi Naturalistica of the Argenta and Marmorta valleys**, km 5.5 SW. Established in 1977, the park extends over 1,600 hectares of wetlands; the local museum can be toured (*open 9:30-1 and 3-6; closed Mon.; guided tours by request, tel. 808058 and 804326*). Km. 1 from the river Reno is the small 6th-c. **Byzantine church of S. Giorgio**; worth seeing.

Fièsole*

elev. 295 m.; pop. 15,096; Tuscany, province of Firenze. The Fiesolans were Etruscans; from on high they watched the growth of the Italic village of huts that later became Florence where the river Mugnone flowed into the Arno; the Roman town of "Faesulae" was the regional capital; then Florence, the "filia", or daughter, conquered (1125) Fièsole the "mater", or mother. Set on a hill amongst other hills, this lofty balcony — with its delicate landscapes, thrilling views, archeological ruins, and art treasures — is the best known short trip from Florence. Fra Giovanni da Fiesole, better known as Beato Angelico, or Fra Angelico, was born in Vicchio di Mugello; in Fièsole he was prior in the convent of S. Domenico; the sculptor Mino da Fiesole was actually born in Papiano, a section of Montemignano in Casentino, near Poppi. For the best panoramic view of Florence, which spreads out below, you should come up here early in the morning or wait until late after noon.

Places of interest. Piazza Mino da Fiesole. This square is the heart of this small town; it was the ancient Forum, and is now bounded by the *Seminary*, the *bishop's palace* (Palazzo Vescovile), the cathedral (Duomo), and, at the far end, the handsome and large 14th c. *Palazzo Pretorio*. This is city hall, and is flanked by the ancient Oratorio di *S. Maria Primerana* (restored), with a Crucifix on panel, attributed to Bonaccorso di Cino, and fragmۍts of 14th-c. frescoes.

Duomo*. Dedicated to S. Romolo (St. Romulus), this cathedral is a Romanesque construction from the 11th c.; it was enlaarged in the 13th and 14th c. The facade was rebuilt in the 19th c., and the distinctive campanile dates from 1213, though it was rebuilt in the 1213 and 19th c. The austere basilican interior has three aisles with columns (some Roman capitals).

Area Archeologica*. *Open, Apr./mid-Sep., 9-7; mid-Sep./Mar., 9-5; closed Mon.* The entrance is from the Via Duprè; note remains of public buildings from Roman times and a small museum. The **Roman theater** dates from the early Empire; it still has its 'cavea', capable of seating 3,000, dug out of the side of the hill and divided into four sectors. The complex includes the ruins of the *hot baths*, from the 1st c. B.C., a *Roman temple* rebuilt in the 1st c. B.C., and a stretch of *Etruscan walls**, built with colossal parallelepiped blocks of stone. The **Museo Archeologico**, housed in a building made to resemble an Uonic temple, features mate-

rial from the excavations of Fièsole and surrounding territory, arranged in eight halls.

Antiquarium Costantini. *Open, the same days and hours as the archeological area.* At n. 9 in Via Portigiani, in the Palazzina Mangani, this antiquarium boasts 157 vases of Attic, Etruscan, Italic, and Greek origin; donated by Alfiero Costantini in 1985 to the township of Fièsole.

Museo Bandini. *Open, Apr.-Sep., 9:30-1 and 3-7; Oct.-Mar., 10-1 and 3-6; closed Tue.* This museum in the Via Duprè, at n. 1, has collections of Della Robbia terracotta and paintings from the 13th-/14th-c. Tuscan school, primarily, though also from the 15th c.

S. Francesco. On the top of a hill, where the ancient acropolis once stood, this church was built in the 14th c. and was rebuilt several times in ensuing centuries.

Florence / Firenze**

elev. 50 m.; pop. 403,294; Tuscany, regional and provincial capital. The inhabitants of Florence have always been justly proud of their city's remarkable qualities. Dino Compagni, a contemporary of Dante Alighieri, a merchant and a chronicler, speaks of "the fine air, the well-dressed citizens, the exceedingly handsome and well groomed women, the very impressive buildings...". And one can reasonably say that, at the time he was writing, the best was yet to come. Located on the plain that the river Arno forms between the stretta of the Incisa and that of the Gondolina, about midway between the Alpine passes and the port of Naples, all considerations that have played major roles in the city's history — a particularly remarkable history. The city lies on both banks of the river, split into unequal parts; the larger section lies on the right bank, and spreads out across the plain, touching the base of the hills of Fiesole; the other half climbs up the gentle slopes that adorn the Arno. And as for the remarkable trove of art and architecture, Alfred de Musset, lover of George Sand and the author of "Contes d'Espagne et d'Italie" (1830), noted that, after Rome, Florence "is the city with the richest array of paintings and sculpture." If we wish to sum up Italy's — and the world's — debt toward Florence, we tend to mention Dante Alighieri, the perfection of the Italian language, artists from Giotto to Michelangelo. In so doing we are correct, and, at the same time, guilty of a terrible simplification. Stendhal wrote of the subtle pleasure of being in Florence: the pleasure of watching the shifts in the Arno's colors, the age-old stones, the views from the little lanes, known as "chiassi," up at the taut lines of the dome of the cathedral, designed and built by Filippo Brunelleschi. Perhaps those who can best describe the measure, force, and elegance of Tuscan architecture, the pine trees and olive groves, the gardens and villas on the hills across the Arno, are the English, who made this part of Italy their home away from home, beginning in the 18th c.

Historical note. This was the site of an ancient Italic settlement in the 10th c. B.C.; in later, Etruscan times it was a modest offshoot of the larger, more important Fièsole. As a city, "Florentia" originated in Roman times. From the high Middle Ages, nothing survives but legendary accounts; we can say with some certainty that the importance of Florence was still minimal, since the capital of the March of Tuscia (as the marquisate of

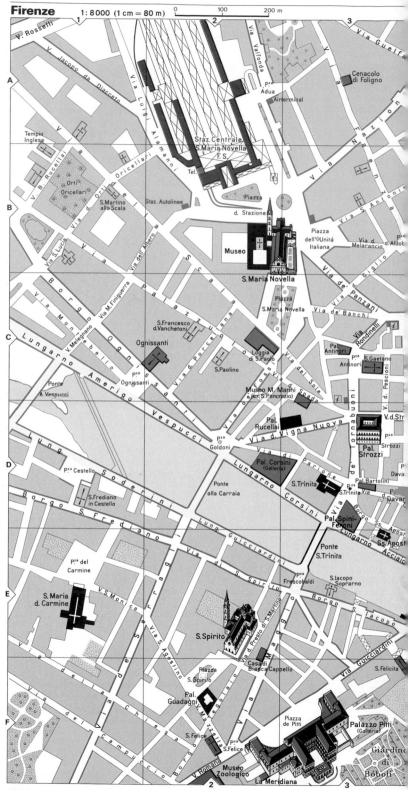

Firenze

1:8000 (1 cm = 80 m)

0   100   200 m

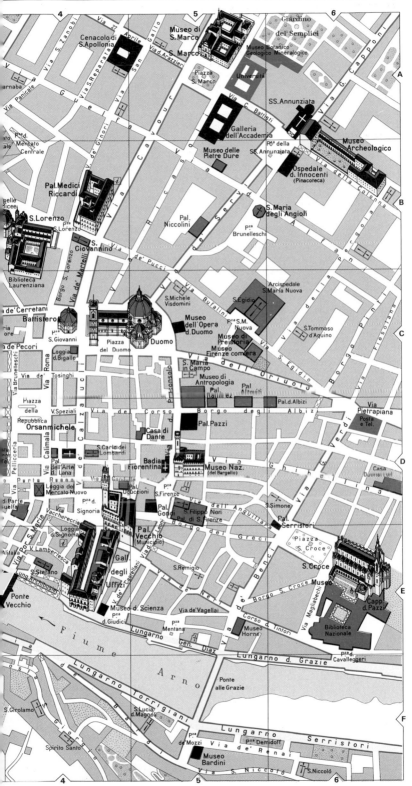

Tuscany was called in that era) was Lucca. It was not until the year 1000 that the marchese Ugo began to prefer Florence to Lucca. In the second half of the 11th c. the city, having repopulated after a long decline, was given a new walled perimeter, the first in the Middle Ages; it corresponded to the route of the Roman walls, save for the southern stretch. A bridge over the Arno, across which ran the Via Cassia, existed as early as A.D. 996; it therefore predated the 14th-c. Ponte Vecchio. It was in the 10th c., as well, that Romanesque architecture first flourished here, in the Baptistery and in the churches of S. Miniato and SS. Apostoli. After the death in 1115 of the "Great Countess" Matilda, also known as the Empress Maud, there is only an intermittent presence of a powerful central authority. The townspeople manage to establish the first autonomous government under the leadership of twelve consuls; Florence began to expand outside of its first walled perimeter. And the first city to suffer from Florence's growing ambition was Fièsole. In time, a thrusting Florence spread war over all of what is now Tuscany, in the form of coalitions of cities (Florence and Lucca against Pisa, Siena, Arezzo, and Pistoia), although the overriding conflict remained that between Florence and Pisa, a conflict that centered on the matter of access to the Tyrrhenian Sea; at the beginning of the 13th c. these wars took on the added tension of the struggle between the factions of Guelphs and Ghibellines. The Guelphs supported the papacy and the house of Anjou, the Ghibellines supported the Holy Roman Empire and the Swabians. In the meanwhile, in 1193, in the hope that entrusting power to an outsider might be a way of settling the growing conflict between aristocrats and commoners, Florence established the rule of the "Podestà." A few years earlier, in 1172, the decision had been made to build a second circle of walls, to enclose the new quarters built to house the burgeoning trade and manufacturing of Florence. The succession of Frederick II as Holy Roman Emperor then tilted the delicate Florentine political equilibrium in favor of the Ghibellines, but only briefly. The people (or "popolo") of Florence ousted the nobility, establishing their own ruling magistracy, called the Capitano del Popolo. These were the glory years of the "primo popolo," when Florence first obtained a clear chance at leadership among the cities of Tuscany. The disastrous defeat in 1260 at the battle of Montaperti was only a passing incident, and marked no permanent military setback. The decision of Florence's Guelph government to support the house of Anjou (Charles d'Anjou was "Podestà" of Florence for ten years) was a canny one. Internally, the government was increasingly controlled by merchants and craftsmen, organized into "Arti," or guilds; the Ordinamenti di Giustizia of 1293 established the hierarchic structure of Florentine government, with the leadership of the "Arti Maggiori," or leading guilds. In the same period, Florence thrashed Siena once and for all at Colle di Val d'Elsa in 1269, and in 1289 roundly defeated Arezzo at Campaldino. Pisa, instead, was defeated by an encroaching Genoa in 1284 at Meloria. These victories outside the city walls corresponded to the construction, between 1350 and 1450, of those great works of Gothic architecture that speak so clearly of Florence's wealth and power in this period: Palazzo del Podestà (known as Palazzo del Bargello), S. Maria Novella, S. Croce, S. Maria del Fiore, Palazzo Vecchio, the bell tower (by Giotto), and Orsanmichele. The decoration of the interiors was entrusted to painters such as Cimabue and Giotto, and such sculptors as Arnolfo di Cambio and Andrea Pisano. By this time, the second walled perimeter was proving insufficient, and between 1284 and 1333 a third, exceedingly extensive ring of walls was completed; this ring followed the circuit of the "viali," or outer boulevards, and it still stands in part, in Oltrarno. During the course of the 14th c., Florence consolidated its conquests and its political stability, although during the first few decades of the 14th c. it became necessary to subdue the Ghibelline uprisings led by Uguccione

della Faggiuola, Castruccio Castracani, the Holy Roman Emperor Henry VII, and the attempted takeover by the Duke of Athens. In 1343 Gualtiero di Brienne was ejected by a furious popular uprising, and Florence almost seemed to return to the golden age of the "primo popolo." Despite the massive bank failures of 1342-45, the Black Death of 1348, and the growing political strife between wealthy and poor ("popolo grasso" and "popolo minuto") which led to the revolt of the Ciompi in 1378, Florence by this time ruled over most of the rest of Tuscany. In the 15th c., the Florentine republic, based on an oligarchy of leading citizens, was transformed into a seignory, *de facto*, if not yet by law. In 1434, Cosimo de' Medici (Cosimo the Elder), who had been exiled the year previous as a citizen, returned to Florence as seigneur, or absolute ruler. As seigneur, Cosimo maintained intact the institutions of the republic, though he emptied them of meaning. His grandson Lorenzo, known as "the Magnificent," ruled Florence from 1469 to 1492, and carried on Cosimo's work. His name is often linked to that great artistic and cultural rebirth usually described as the Italian Renaissance. Great architects interpreted his spirit: F. Brunelleschi, Leon Battista Alberti, Michelozzo, Benedetto da Maiano, Giuliano da Sangallo; masterpieces were created by such painters as Masaccio, Fra' Angelico, Andrea del Castagno, Paolo Uccello, S. Botticelli, Ghirlandaio, and Benozzo Gozzoli, and sculptors including Donatello, Verrocchio, Pollaiolo, Luca della Robbia, and Ghiberti. When Lorenzo died in 1492, the splendid Medici realm was unable to withstand the brutal assault of Charles VIII of France. The exile of the Medici allowed for two episodes of restoration of the Republic (1494-1512 and 1527-30), episodes which proved however to be its swan song. In 1531, in the wake of the imperial army, Alessandro de' Medici entered the city, to become the first duke of Florence. In 1569 the duchy of Florence became the grand duchy of Tuscany, under Cosimo I de' Medici, known as Cosimo the Great, who in 1555 annexed the republic of Siena. And it was under the rule of this Medici that the "great history" of Florence can be said to have come to an end. The ancient wealth and power were never seen again. Although 16th-c. Florence was embellished with new works by Ammannati and Vasari, its true geniuses were forced to work elsewhere: Leonardo da Vinci, in Milan and France; Michelangelo in 1534 left Florence for Rome permanently. The 17th and 18th c. saw the economic and cultural decline of both city and state, as well as the end of the Medici dynasty (1737). Some small revivals of the economy, though largely agrarian in nature, marked the rule of the house of Lorraine, and especially the reign of Pietro Leopoldo, as he was known, later to become Holy Roman Emperor as Leopold II. Napoleon Bonaparte, following the hasty departure of the rulers of the house of Lorraine, placed upon the throne of Florence, in 1801, as King of Etruria, none other than Ludovico di Borbone Parma. This shortlived kingdom was annexed to the French empire in 1807, even though Elisa Baciocchi, Napoleon's sister, was made grand duchess of Tuscany. From 1815 till 1860, the house of Lorraine ruled again in Florence; with the annexation of the duchy of Lucca in 1847, they attained the outdated dream of unifying Tuscany. Following a plebiscite in 1860, Florence, with all of Tuscany, became part of the new kingdom of Italy; from 1865 to 1870, Florence was this new kingdom's second capital. It was in those years that the 14th-c. walls were razed and the outer boulevards, or "circonvallazione" (ring roads), were built, the riverfront boulevards ("lungarni") were opened up, and Viale dei Colli was linked up with Piazzale Michelangiolo. A number of downtown streets were enlarged (Via Panzani, Via Cerretani, Via Tornabuoni, and Via Martelli), and thoughtless demolition opened the perhaps excessively large Piazza Vittorio Emanuele, now Piazza della Repubblica. In the 20th c., with the renewed economic growth and increase in population, Florence expanded, incorporating new quarters. After WWII, during which Florence

Florence: Duomo

suffered extensive damage, and following the terrible flood of 1966, the city began once again to expand in all directions, but primarily NW, toward the plains and the highways. Population doubled, from the 200,000 of the turn of the century.

Getting around. Traffic jams and regulations make driving in town problematic at best; five major zones in the center of Florence are off limits to private vehicles from 7:30 until 6:30 (extending to 9 pm-12:30 am on Fri. and Sat. in the summer). Tourists with hotel reservations, or those in search of a room, are allowed to drive in; in the pedestrian zones in the more central parts of town, on the other hand, cars are forbidden entirely. You can leave your car in any of the many parking garages and areas between the main ring roads around Florence and the limited access areas. Of the seven routes suggested, the first six can be considered walking tours entirely; for the seventh — as well as the outer sections of town — you may choose to use public transportation.

The religious center

Between S. Maria del Fiore, which Arnolfo di Cambio began to build under the name of the older cathedral that stood on the same site (S. Reparata), and S. Lorenzo, the church of the Medici, in this small area you will encounter the work of some of Italy's greatest artists: Giotto, Brunelleschi, Ghiberti, Donatello, and Andrea della Robbia, Benozzo Gozzoli, and Michelangelo.

Piazza del Duomo* (*C4-5*). Along with Piazza S. Giovanni, this constitutes the heart of Florence, and features the most important religious monuments: the Battistero (Baptistery), the Basilica di S. Maria del Fiore (Cathedral, or Duomo), and the campanile of Giotto, unified by their vivid polychrome marble facings, in white, green, and pink marble, with geometric patterns. On Easter Sunday, the remarkable tradition of the "Scoppio del Carro," or "exploding carriage," should not be missed.

Battistero di S. Giovanni** (*C4*). *Open, 9-12:30 and 2:30-5:30 (5 in winter)*. At the religious heart of Florence, the Baptistery of St. John is one of the oldest and most majestic buildings in the city, mentioned by Dante as the "bel S. Giovanni." Some date it back to the 4th c., others call it an 11th-c. Romanesque structure. It has an octagonal plan, and is surrounded by a double order of pillars supporting a trabeation and, higher up,

arches; a 13th-c. attic topped by an octagonal pyramid conceals the domed roof. The most distinctive aspect is the 11th-c. white-and-green marble facing. In the three portals are the renowned bronze **doors**** arranged as a sort of giant visual Bible. The *south (entrance) portal** is the oldest, and is by A. Pisano (1330); the portal frames are by V. Ghiberti (Lorenzo's son, 1462), while the three statues over the portal are by V. Danti (1571). The *north portal** is by L. Ghiberti (1403-24), who applied a late-Gothic style, ornate and fluent, to both doors and jambs. Above the portal, statues by G.F. Rustici (1511). The *east door***, facing the Duomo, is justly famous — Michelangelo called it the **Porta del Paradiso**. This is only a copy of L. Ghiberti's masterpiece (1425-52): some of the restored original panels are now on display at the Museo dell'Opera del Duomo. Over the portal is a marble group by A. Sansovino (1502). The **interior**, to a central plan, is covered by a dome with gores and has an inlaid marble floor*; along the marble-covered walls run, lower down, an architectural composition of pillars and architraved columns, and, up high, a loggia with mullions. The cupola glitters with 13th-c. Byzantine-style mosaics*, by Venetian and Florentine artists; Cimabue possibly among them. In the apse, other mosaics by J. da Torrita (1225). Also, note the tomb of the antipope John XXIII*, attributed to Donatello and Michelozzo (1427); relief baptismal font (1371), of the Pisan school.

Loggia del Bigallo (*C4*). Set near the south door of the Battistero, at the corner of Via de' Calzaiuoli, this loggia was built in 1352-58 to offer abandoned children and orphans to public charity. It features two lovely corner arcades, and a course of mullioned windows. Inside *(closed to the public)*, in the Sala dei Capitani, a remarkable fresco from 1342 includes the earliest known depiction of the city of Florence. Note tabernacle by N. d'Antonio (1515), marble statues of angels by A. Arnoldi (1364), altar predella by R. del Ghirlandaio (1515), and Crucifix on panel, by the Maestro del Bigallo (1260).

Campanile di Giotto** (*C4*). It stands alone, to the right of the cathedral, rising 84.7 m. high; this bell tower is renowned for its slender, soaring Gothic architecture, its elegant polychrome marble facing, and its lavish plastic ornamentation. It was begun in 1334 by Giotto and A. Pisano, and completed by F. Talenti (1350-59). The base has two areas of 14th-c. bas-reliefs (copies; the originals are in the Museo dell'Opera del Duomo): by A. Pisano and L. della Robbia (first zone); A. Pisano and A. Arnoldi (second zone). Above these areas, in the niches, are statues by A. Pisano, Donatello, and N. di Bartolo (copies; the originals are in the Museo dell'Opera del Duomo). A staircase, with 414 steps, leads up to the terrace *(open, summer, 8:30-7; winter 9-4:30)*, with a fine view* of the city.

Duomo or **Basilica di S. Maria del Fiore** *(C4-5)*. This outstanding religious monument, the Cathedral of Florence, faces the Baptistery, and shows clearly the Gothic influence of broad and simple lines that was so typical of Florence.

Work began on this church in 1296 under A. di Cambio, and was halted upon his death (ca. 1310).; the project grew in size when it started back up in 1331, and was enlarged even more in 1357, under F. Talenti. In 1378, the vault of the nave was completed; in 1380 the side aisles were covered; and by 1421 the octagonal tambour was finished. Upon it, from 1420 until 1436, F. Brunelleschi built the spectacular dome. It was crowned with a lantern, built by A. del Verrocchio in 1468.

The original, half-finished **facade**, by A. di Cambio, was demolished in 1587; the current facade, less than a masterpiece, is by E. De Fabris (1871-87), who copied the motif on the sides. The bronze doors of the three portals are all less than a hundred years old. On the sides, the polychrome marble face, for all its liveliness, does nothing to diminish the sheer mass of the church; note the doors, especially the late-14th-c. *Porta dei Canonici*. Then comes the vast bulk of the *tambour*, with three huge apses and several smaller ones. Above them all stands the tall octagonal tambour (note the unfinished gallery, by B. d'Agnolo, upon which work ceased after Michelangelo's withering dismissal of it as a "cricket cage"), supporting the enormous ribbed dome by Brunelleschi. Along the *left side*, note the early-15th-c. Gothic-Renaissance *Porta della Mandorla*: in the front and the lunette, reliefs and mosaics by N. di Banco (1421), and Domenico and Davide Ghirlandaio (1491).

The **interior** has three broad aisles, divided by high pointed arches upon tall pillars, and feeding into the immense octagonal space of the tambour. The vast size and the simple purity of the composition give an impression of majestic severity. Note the three stained-glass windows by L. Ghiberti; the clock face by P. Uccello (1443); the 15th-c. tomb of Bishop A. Orso, by T. Camaino (14th c.); the bust of F. Brunelleschi, by A. Cavalcanti (1446); the tondo of Giotto, by B. da Maiano (1490); and the bust of Marsilio Ficino by A. Ferrucci (1521). From the second bay in the *right aisle*, a stairway leads down to the remains of the church of S. Reparata.

S. Reparata *(open, 10-5; closed Sun.)*. Wrongly described as the "crypt" of the church, this is what remains of the ancient cathedral of Florence, demolished in 1375, and unearthed from 1966 on. Among other things, you can see remains of houses dating back to Roman times, and the tombstone of F. Brunelleschi.

The cross vault is dominated by Brunelleschi's immense **cupola*** (91 m. tall), decorated with the fresco of the Last Judgment by G. Vasari and F. Zuccari (1579); in the oculi of the tambour, stained glass windows* done to cartoons by Donatello, Ghiberti, P. Uccello, and A. del Castagno. At the center of the octagon, a marble choir chancel, by B. Bandinelli and G. Bandini (1547-72); on the main altar, wooden Crucifix* by B. da Maiano (1497). Note, in the *Sagrestia Vecchia*, the glazed earthenware Ascension* by L. della Robbia, and numerous 15th- and 16th-c. paintings. Note the sarcophagus* with the relics of St. Zanobi, masterpiece by Ghiberti (1432-42). Next, you will see the entrance to the *Sagrestia delle Messe*, or Sagrestia dei Servi, where Lorenzo the Magnificent took refuge from the attack known as the Congiura dei Pazzi, or conspiracy of the Pazzi family; Lorenzo's brother, Giuliano de' Medici was killed in the attack (26 April 1478); note the bronze door* and the lunette (Resurrection*) by L. della Robbia (1444): on the walls and armoires, wooden intarsias* (1465). In the *left aisle*: 14th-c. stained glass, panel by D. di Michelino (1465); painted equestrian monument to "Giovanni Acuto" (John Hawkwood)**, by P. Uccello (1436); bust by B. da Maiano; and painted equestrian monument to N. da Tolentino*, A. del Castagno (1456). From the head of the aisle, you can climb up to the dome *(open, 10-5:30; 463 steps)*, of considerable interest both because of the internal structure of same, and because of the magnificent view* from the external walkway that runs around the lantern (107 m.).

Museo dell'Opera del Duomo* *(C5). Open 9-7:30 (winter, until 5:30); closed Sun.* Established in 1891, at n. 9 in Piazza del Duomo, this museum features major pieces of 14th- and 15th-c. Florentine sculpture, including many originals from the Baptistery, the Duomo, and Giotto's bell tower. In the vestibule, two terracotta lunettes by A. della Robbia; also Etruscan and Roman statuary and architectural elements. In the *Sala dell'Antica Facciata*, sculpture, mostly by A. di Cambio, from the earlier facade of the Duomo (demolished in 1587); on the right, as you enter, a 16th-c. drawing shows how that facade looked. Note some figures by N. di Banco. In two little rooms devoted to F. Brunelleschi: funeral mask of the architect; wooden model of the cupola and lantern; tools and machinery used in building the cupola. In the other halls: illuminated codices, goldsmithery, and a painting by B. Daddi (1334). On the mezzanine is a dramatic and unfinished **Pietà**, by Michelangelo (1550-53), formerly in the Duomo. On the upper floor, in the *Sala delle Cantorie*: **choir** by Donatello (1433-39), with a line of dancing putti; beneath it, Penitent Magdalene*, a wooden statue by Donatello, once in the Baptistery; **choir** by L. della Robbia (1431-38), with reliefs of boys singing and playing; 16 **statues** formerly in the niches of the Campanile, variously by A. Pisano, Donatello, and N. di Bartolo. In the adjacent *Sala delle Formelle* are displayed the relief **panels*** taken from the Campanile: those in the lower order are by A. Pisano, probably partly based on designs by Giotto, save for the last five, by L. della Robbia (1439); the panels in the upper order are by A. Pisano and A. Arnoldi. In the *Sala dell'Altare*, silver and enamel altar frontal** upon which Michelozzo, Verrocchio, and A. Pollaiolo worked, among others; note the silver Crucifix; statues by T. di Camaino, A. Pisano, and P. di Lapo; liturgical array embroidered with silk and gold to designs by A. Pollaiolo.

Via de' Martelli *(B-C4)*. This is one of the liveliest streets in Florence; note the former convent of the Jesuits and the church of *S. Giovannino degli Scolopi*, with facade by B. Ammannati (16th c.).

Palazzo Medici-Riccardi ** *(B4)*. The proud square mass of this building was the model for Florentine aristocratic mansions in the Renaissance; note the three floors of graduated rustication, the centered mullioned windows with Medici heraldic devices, and the elaborate cornice; the ground-floor windows near the corner may be by Michelangelo (1517).

Construction began in 1444, under Michelozzo, on behalf of Cosimo the Elder; the Medici kept it as their residence until the grand duchy of Cosimo I. The building then became property of the Riccardi (1659), and then the house of Lorraine, and during Florence's short stint as the capital of united Italy, it housed the Ministery of the Interior; today, it is the building of the Prefecture.

Inside, note the handsome courtyard*, which displays much of the *Riccardi Collection* of archeological material. Take the first stairway on the right to the **Cappella dei Magi*** *(open 9-12:30 and 3-5; Sun., 9-12; closed Wed.; by reservation during the height of the tourist season)*, a masterpiece of the early Florentine Renaissance, by Michelozzo. Note the frescoes of the Magi*, by B. Gozzoli (1459-60): many of the figures in the cavalcade are portraits of members of the Medici family. Back in the courtyard, a second stair climbs to the *Galleria (open, same hours as the chapel)*, a long 17th-c. Baroque loggia, in the ceiling of which L. Giordano painted the Allegory of the Medici (1682-85).

Piazza S. Lorenzo *(B4)*. Dominated by the facade of the church of S. Lorenzo, with the mighty cupola of the Cappella dei Principi; a charming market is held here, surrounded by aristocratic palazzi of the 15th and 16th c., and a marble monument to Giovanni dalle Bande Nere, by B. Bandinelli (1540).

S. Lorenzo ** *(B4)*. One of the great masterpieces of early-Renaissance Florentine religious architecture, this basilica is also bound up with the memory of the Medici family.

Built by F. Brunelleschi in 1442-46, and completed in 1461 by A. Manetti, it stands on the site of an ancient cathedral consecrated by St. Ambrose in A.D. 393, and rebuilt in Romanesque style in the 11th c. The facade has remained unfinished, though Michelangelo, among others, submitted a design for it.

The **interior**, with three aisles and columns, remains remarkably intact and perfectly composed. The mastery of Brunelleschi appears everywhere; the interior facade is by Michelangelo. In the right aisle, painting by Rosso Fiorentino* (1523); marble altar* by D. da Settignano (1460); and one of the two bronze pulpits* (a matching pulpit is in the left aisle), by Donatello (ca. 1460) and others. In the left arm of the transept, among the fine 14th-c. statues and altar pieces, note the altar piece* by Filippo

Florence: Palazzo Medici-Riccardi

Lippi and the large fresco by A. Bronzino (1565-69). From the left transept, you enter the 15th-c.

Sagrestia Vecchia **, a Renaissance jewel designed by Brunelleschi (1421-26) and decorated by Donatello (1435-43). The square plan is topped by a hemispherical cupola; against the white walls, the stone members stand out sharply, as do the medallions in colored stucco in the pendentives and lunettes and the frieze of cherubs by Donatello. Donatello also did the bronze doors* on the sides of the little chapel, and the two terracotta reliefs' above it. Although the bust* of S. Lorenzo (St. Lawrence) is attributed to Donatello, it may well be by D. da Settignano. To the left of the sacristy entrance, note the funerary monument to G. and P. de' Medici*, in porphyry and bronze, a masterpiece by Verrocchio (1472).

Biblioteca Medicea Laurenziana ** *(B-C4)*. *Tour of the halls by Michelangelo, 8-2; closed Sun.* You enter this remarkable library through the *first cloister** (entrance to the left of the facade of the basilica), in the style of F. Brunelleschi. Founded by Cosimo the Elder, the library is set in a building designed by Michelangelo (1524). The architecture of the *vestibule* and the *stairway* is daring, a forerunner of Baroque; that of the *reading room* is simple and magnificent. The ceiling, lecterns, and chairs were also designed by Michelangelo.

Cappelle Medicee ** *(B4)*. *Open, 9-2; closed Mon.* With entrance from n. 6 in Piazza di Madonna degli Aldobrandini, the Cappelle Medicee, which means "Medici Chapels," comprise the complex of the Cappella-Mausoleo dei Principi and the Sagrestia Nuova, or New Sacristy, by Michelangelo, set in the apse of the basilica of S. Lorenzo. From an immense crypt, you climb up to the Baroque **Cappella dei Principi*** (Chapel of the Princes), a splendid octagonal domed construction, lined with marble and semiprecious stones, built by M. Nigetti to plans by Giovanni de' Medici (17th c.). It holds monumental sarcophagi of the grand dukes of Tuscany (above two of them, colossal bronze statues by P. and F. Tacca). **Sagrestia**

Nuova** (or burial chapel of the Medici). This renowned prototype of Mannerist architecture was designed by Michelangelo, who began construction in 1521-24; it was completed some years later by G. Vasari and B. Ammannati. Recently restored, it has a square plan; note in particular the architectural members in "pietra serena" that stand out against the white walls, in accordance with an approach borrowed from Brunelleschi's Sagrestia Vecchia; here, they take on a daring new quality that breaks with the classicistic tradition. There are several masterpieces of sculpture by Michelangelo in this sacristy; note the Medici tombs** (1524-1533), with the figures of Dawn, Dusk, Day, and Night, and the Virgin and Child** (1521). In a small underground room to the left of the altar *(groups of no more than 12; reserve at the entrance)*, are drawings by Michelangelo, discovered in 1971.

Piazza della Signoria and the Uffizi

Art and power: this troubled link can be clearly deciphered in its Florentine version in the short walk from Orsanmichele to the Lungarno: to decorate the tabernacles on the outer walls of the granary-qua-church of Orsanmichele, the "Arti," or Guilds, summoned Donatello and Verrocchio; for the statue of David, a symbol of the Florentine Republic to be placed before Palazzo Vecchio, the job was given to Michelangelo; and when the duke Cosimo I ordered the construction of a building to house his burgeoning bureaucracy, the Uffizi, he also decided to build an area for his art collections.

Via dei Calzaiuoli *(C-D4)*. One of the main thoroughfares in Florence, it links Piazza del Duomo with Piazza della Signoria. Like much of the center, it was subjected, in 1841-44, to a "clean-up" that aroused much debate. The street is lined with elegant shops; note Orsanmichele and the Gothic church of *S. Carlo dei Lombardi (D4)*, by S. Talenti (1404).

Orsanmichele* *(D4)*. This imposing building is one of the most interesting pieces of 14th-c. architecture in Florence. Built in 1337 as a loggia/grain-exchange, it was given fine three-light mullioned windows on the ground floor, and raised two floors higher, with two-light mullioned windows. At the end of the 14th c., it was made into a church *(S. Michele in Orto)* for the guilds of Florence. On the exterior*, in the piers between the arcades, are aedicules or **tabernacles*** with statues of the patron saints of the various Guilds, executed by the leading artists of Florence in the 15th and 16th c. In the facade on Via dei Calzaiuoli, from left to right: St. John the Baptist, by L. Ghiberti; Incredulity of St. Thomas*, by A. del Verrocchio (1483); St. Luke, by Giambologna. In Via Orsanmichele: St. Peter, attributed to Brunelleschi (1413); St. Philip and the Four Crowned Saints*, by N. di Banco; St. George, by Donatello (copies; originals are in the Museo del Bargello). In Via dell'Arte della Lana: St. Matthew and St. Stephen*, by Ghiberti; St. Eligio, by N. di Banco; in Via de' Lamberti: St. Mark, by Donatello (copy; original being restored); St. James, by N. di Piero Lamberti; Madonna della Rosa, marble group by P. di Giovanni Tedesco; St. John the Evangelist, by B. da Montelupo (1515).

In the two-aisled rectangular **interior** *(entrance on Via dell'Arte della Lana)*, note the remains of late-14th-c. frescoes and stained glass. Also, note the statues by F. da Sangallo; the renowned tabernacle* by A. Orcagna, one of the loveliest creations of Florentine Gothic; and the panel painted by B. Daddi (1347).

Palazzo dell'Arte della Lana *(D4; closed to the public)*. In the Via dell'Arte della Lana, this building was, from 1308 on, the headquarters of one of the wealthiest of the Arti Maggiori, or leading guilds of the city; it consisted of a tower-house and a lower building, and on the exterior it incorporates the Gothic *tabernacle of S. Maria della Tromba* (14th c., rebuilt at the turn of the 20th c.), with a panel by J. del Casentino and a painting by N. di Pietro Gerini. In 1905 the restoration of this building was completed, and it became the headquarters of the Società Dantesca. From the interior of the palazzo you can enter the two upper halls* of Orsanmichele; in the hall on the third floor, note detached 14th-c. frescoes.

Piazza della Signoria** *(D4)*. The heart of political power and city life of Florence, ever since the Communal period, this square was opened in the 13th c. Vast and majestic, it is dominated by the structure of Palazzo Vecchio and lightened by the three spacious arches of the **Loggia della Signoria***. Built in Gothic style, between 1376 and 1382, by B. di Cione and S. Talenti, this loggia in time became a workshop for sculptors, and then an open-air art gallery.

Note from the left, n. 10, the 14th-c. *Tribunale di Mercatanzia* and, at n. 7, *Palazzo Uguccioni*, with the bronze equestrian monument to Cosimo I, by Giambologna (1594-98) and the enormous *Fountain of Neptune*, by B. Ammannati (1563-75), with Neptune surrounded by lively and elegant bronze figures of marine deities and satyrs. On the stairs of Palazzo Vecchio: the lion that symbolizes Florence, by Donatello; Judith and Holofernes, a bronze by Donatello (copy; the original is in Palazzo Vecchio); and Michelangelo's David (all three are copies, the originals of the first two are in the Museo del Bargello; the David is in the Galleria dell'Accademia), and the much-discussed group of Hercules and Cacus, by B. Bandinelli (1534). In the Loggia della Signoria: note the **Perseus***, masterpiece by B. Cellini (1554), and **Rape of the Sabines***, by Giambologna (1583); other fine sculptures by P. Fedi and Giambologna, and ancient Roman statues.

Palazzo Vecchio** *(D-E4-5). Open, 9-7; holidays, 8-1; closed Sat.* This is the most important monument of civil architecture in Florence, and certainly one of the most noteworthy medieval public palazzi in Italy.

Built, from 1299, to plans by A. di Cambio, as the *Palazzo dei Priori*, it became the *Palazzo della Signoria* in the 15th-c., and from 1540 to 1565 was the residence of the Medici. It became the "Palazzo Vecchio" when the Medici moved to Palazzo Pitti; from 1865 until 1871, when Florence was briefly the capital of Italy, it became the Parliament; since 1872, it has been city hall. It has been modified to suit its various functions over the centuries; in particular, in the 16th c., G. Vasari renovated it heavily. A few decades later, it was enlarged by G.B. del Tasso and B. Buontalenti.

The original building is a compact parallelepiped in rough ashlar, three stories tall, with two orders of elegant Gothic mullioned windows. It is crowned by tall jutting crenelation. Above that is the **tower*** (1310), 94 m. tall, with double jutting crenelations.

Inside*, the first, porticoed *courtyard*, was renovated by Michelozzo (1453), and later decorated with stuccoes and frescoes in 1565; at the center is a 16th-c. fountain, atop which is a copy of Verrocchio's Putto with Dolphin (the original is now in the Terrazzo di Giunone). Between this courtyard and the Cortile della Dogana, a monumental *staircase* designed by Vasari leads to the upper floors.

On the *second floor* is the **Salone dei Cinquecento***, an enormous hall built by A. da Sangallo (1495-96) for the meetings of the Consiglio Generale del Popolo, later transformed under Cosimo I into a reception hall (Sala delle Udienze). At the left end of the room, note the raised tribunal by B. Bandinelli; also, paintings by Vasari and others; a plaster group by Giambologna; and a **marble group*** by Michelangelo (1533-34). Adjacent rooms include: the *Studiolo di Francesco I **, lavishly decorated; the *Tesoretto (closed to the public)*, decorated by Vasari; and the *Quartiere di Leone X*, with the *hall of Leo X* (the first Medici pope), also decorated by Vasari *(closed to the public)*, now government offices.

Third floor: the Quartiere degli Elementi was decorated by G. Vasari (on the Terrazzo di Giunone, originally open to the elements, note the statue* by A. Verrocchio). A balcony overlooking the Salone dei Cinquecento takes you into the *Quartiere di Eleonora*, decorated by G. Vasari and adorned with Florentine tapestries; note the *Cappella di Eleonora**, painted by Bronzino (1545). Continue through the Cappella dei Priori, built by B. d'Agnolo (1511-14) and decorated by R. del Ghirlandaio, until you reach the *Sala dell'Udienza**, with gilded coffered ceiling by G. da Maiano and frescoes by F. Salviati (1560). Note the elegant marble portals, by B. and G. da Maiano, in the *Sala dei Gigli**, with magnificent carved and gilded ceiling and a vast fresco by D. Ghirlandaio (1485). Also, note the well restored bronzes of **Judith and Holofernes*** by Donatello. In the adjacent rooms are the Cancelleria della Repubblica Fiorentina and the Sala delle Carte Geografiche, with a huge globe (1567).

Raccolta d'Arte Contemporanea "Alberto della Ragione." *Open, 9-2; Sun., 8-1; closed Tue.* This collection of contemporary Italian art, temporarily installed in the *Palazzo della Cassa di Risparmio*, at n. 5 in Piazza della Signoria, includes works by such painters as Carrà, De Chirico, Morandi, De Pisis, Casorati, Rosai, Scipione, Mafai, Campigli, Licini, Cantatore, Sassu, Birolli, Guttuso, Morlotti, Cassinari, Severini, Maccari, Menzio, Vedova, Tosi, Guidi, and Sironi; and such sculptors as Martini, Marini, Manzù, Mirko, Fontana, and Broggini.

Piazzale degli Uffizi* (*E4*). This square extends like a majestic courtyard from Piazza della Signoria to the banks of the Arno, enclosed by the **Palazzo degli Uffizi**, a remarkable construction with portico and loggia, by G. Vasari (1560-80), who built it as the new office building for the ducal bureaucracy. Now of course the building houses the famous art gallery of the Uffizi; at the end of the square, overlooking the Arno, note the fine view* of the Ponte Vecchio and the hill of S. Miniato.

Florence: Palazzo degli Uffizi

Galleria degli Uffizi** (*E4*). *Open, 9-7; Sun., 9-2; closed Mon.* This is arguably the leading art gallery in Italy, and certainly the oldest museum in modern Europe. It possesses masterpieces of Italian painting from every period, and a select collection of work by non-Italian painters and schools. The entrance is under the portico of the Palazzo degli Uffizi, at n. 6; the collections are displayed in the halls on the fourth floor.

Built at the end of the 16th c. to house the collection of sculpture and painting of the Grand Duke Francesco I (the first architect was Buontalenti), the gallery was enlarged over time, largely due to the interest of the Medici family; it incorporated scientific and technical areas of interest as well. The collection of paintings, originally limited to what Vasari called "moderni," namely 16th-c. Florentine artists, was expanded to include Venetian and Flemish painters. In the 18th c. the Dukes of Lorraine made considerable donations, the scientific section was split, and the focus narrowed to painting and sculpture. By the late-19th c. new acquisitions of 14th- and 15th-c. paintings made the Uffizi the single most complete collection of great Italian art. As of this writing, about 2,000 works are on display, and a major renovation is planned which will make accessible to the public the other 1,800 paintings now in storage. This project was stymied, however, by the bomb blast of 27 May 1993, which endangered the safety of the halls on the third floor and in Vasari's corridors.

On the **ground floor** you can see frescoes** of illustrious men and women, by A. Castagno (ca. 1450), and a fresco by S. Botticelli (1481). The stairway, by Vasari, passes the floor of offices and takes you up to the *second floor* (**Gabinetto dei Disegni e delle Stampe**, *open only to scholars*); on the *third floor*, two vestibules lead into the gallery, with its three corridors.

First corridor. The heart of the original gallery, this hallway has ceilings decorated with grotesques; along the walls, Roman statues and busts. The first main section features Tuscan paintings in chronological order, from the 13th to the 15th c.: D. di Buoninsegna, Cimabue, Giotto, S. Martini and L. Memmi, A. and P. Lorenzetti, B.

Daddi, T. Gaddi, Giottino, L. Monaco, G. da Fabriano, Masaccio and Masolino, Fra' Angelico, P. Uccello, D. Veneziano, P. della Francesca, A. Baldovinetti, Filippo Lippi, Filippino Lippi, A. Pollaiolo, P. Pollaiolo, H. van der Goes, S. Botticelli, Leonardo da Vinci, Verrocchio, Perugino, L. Signorelli, and P. di Cosimo. The successive halls (16 to 24) are the oldest in the Uffizi. In hall 18, you can see the 1st-c. Medici Venus*, copy of an original by Praxiteles, and portraits by Bronzino. In the other halls are 15th- and 16th-c. paintings from other schools (Venetian, Lombard, Emilian, German, Flemish) and sculpture: L. Signorelli and Perugino, A. Dürer, J. Brueghel the Elder, L. Cranach the Younger, B. Vivarini, Giovanni Bellini, C. da Conegliano, Giorgione, V. Carpaccio, A. Altdorfer, H. Holbein the Younger, A. Mantegna, V. Foppa, and Correggio.

Second and third corridors. Cross the second corridor (the small hall 24 can be viewed but not entered) and continue along the third. Here, the halls are devoted to Florentine painting during the early 16th c., with works by: Michelangelo, Raphael, A. del Sarto, Pontormo, Rosso Fiorentino, and Bronzino. Then you continue to halls devoted to the schools of Venetia, Emilia and Ferrara, and Central Italy: Titian, whose work occupies an entire hall, Palma the Elder, Parmigianino, D. Dossi, Mazzolino, S. del Piombo, L. Lotto, P. Veronese, J. Bassano, El Greco, Tintoretto, and F. Barocci. Here, work by 17th- and 18th-c. artists (P. P. Rubens and A. van Dyck, Justus Sustermans) surrounds a group of fine Roman statues, copies of Greek originals; then come other halls with works by Caravaggio, F. Albani, Annibale Carracci, Rembrandt, J. Brueghel the Elder, G. M. Crespi, Canaletto, and F. Guardi. You leave the gallery through what was once the entrance, between halls 35 and 41; as you leave, you will pass 17th-c. paintings and a few notable ancient and modern sculptures.

Corridor of Vasari*. *Open by request, you must reserve in advance with the secreteriat of the Uffizi (not always possible to reserve).* You enter from the third corridor (hall 25); this corridor was built in 1565 by Vasari, to link the Uffizi to Palazzo Pitti across the Ponte Vecchio. On display are major 17th- and 18th-c. works, and part of the renowned *collection of self-portraits**, with work by painters from the 16th c. to modern times (A. del Sarto, Vasari, Bernini, Annibale Carracci, Rubens, Sustermans, Rembrandt, Van Dyck, Velazquez, Canova, Hayez, Fattori, Delacroix, Ingres, and Corot).

Museo di Storia della Scienza* (*E4*). *Open, 9:30-1, Mon., Wed. and Fri. also 2-5; closed Sun.* This Museum of the History of Science is arranged on two stories of *Palazzo Castellani*, in Piazza dei Giudici; it features a collection of scientific apparatus and instruments begun by Cosimo the Elder, on display until the mid-18th c. in the Uffizi, and the Lorraine collection of instruments and equipment for teaching and experimentation (18th c.). Of particular interest are mathematical instruments, Florentine and from elsewhere (astrolabes, mechanical calculators, measuring systems of all kinds), memorabilia of G. Galilei, optical instruments, instruments for cosmography and astronomy (an armillary sphere* built by A. Santucci delle Pomarance), clocks, magnetic and electrical instruments, pneumatic and hydrostatic apparatuses, mechanical tools, surgical tools

and instruments (Brambilla collection) and teaching models, pharmacists' equipment, and chemical instruments.

The Oltrarno

The second walled perimeter of Florence (1172) crossed over to the left bank of the Arno, when what is now called the Ponte Vecchio, or "old bridge," was the only bridge over that river. Starting in Piazza della Repubblica, you now cross the Arno over the Ponte Vecchio, stopping at the Pitti Palace, and continue on to the architectural splendor of Brunelleschi's masterpiece, the church of S. Spirito; you can also admire the newly restored frescoes by Masaccio at the church of the Carmine.

Piazza della Repubblica (*C-D4*). This late-19th-c. eclectic construction entailed the lamentable demolition of the old medieval market; on the western side, busy porticoes with popular cafes.

Palazzo Davanzati* (*D3*). This building, set in the Piazza Davanzati, is a stern aristocratic home of the 14th c., a tall narrow three-story building with centered windows and a large 16th-c. loggia. It houses the **Museo della Casa Fiorentina Antica** (*open, 9-2; closed Mon.*), which features furniture, paintings, sculpture, majolica, tapestries, fabrics, and lace from all over Europe, as well as an assortment of everyday objects from the past, a collection that offers an intriguing glimpse of domestic life and culture in Florence during the 14th/18th c. Note, in particular, the Gothic courtyard, the Sala dei Pappagalli and the Sala dei Pavoni on the second floor, and the master bedroom on the third floor.

Via Calimala (*D4*). This street runs along the **loggia of the Mercato Nuovo**, built in 1551 by G.B. del Tasso, as a marketplace for fine cloth; now Florentine crafts are sold here. On the side facing the Borsa Merci is the fountain known as the *Fontana del Porcellino* (literally, Piglet; in reality, a wild boar), a bronze copy by P. Tacca (1612; from a Hellenistic original, now in the Uffizi).

Palazzo dei Capitani di Parte Guelfa (*D4*). Behind the loggia of the Mercato Nuovo, this building dates from the early-14th c., and was enlarged in later periods by Brunelleschi and by Vasari, and restored around 1920. Inside *(undergoing restoration)*, note the magnificent hall by Brunelleschi, with a lunette in glazed terracotta by Luca della Robbia and a wooden ceiling by Vasari, who also did the elegant little exterior loggia.

Via Por S. Maria (*E4*). Completely rebuilt after WWII, this street ends with two tower-houses from the 11th and 12th c.; on the left, in a little square, is the Romanesque facade of the church of *S. Stefano al Ponte* (1233), with portal and mullioned windows in two-tone marble.

Ponte Vecchio* (*E3-4*). This is the oldest and best-known bridge in Florence, and was built in 1345 by N. di Fioravante on previous structures dating from at least 996. It was the only bridge in Florence to escape destruction, in August 1944, during the German retreat. Its span covers three arches, and it is lined by a double row of shops, once belonging to wool merchants and greengrocers, now run by jewelers; above the shops on the upstream side runs the Corridoio Vasariano, linking the Uffizi with Palazzo Pitti. From the terraces in the center, fine view of the river, Ponte S. Trìnita, and the Lungarni, or riverfront avenues.

Via de' Guicciardini (*E-F3*). Rebuilt after WWII, this road opens out into a little square dominated by the church of **S. Felicita**, heavily renovated in the 18th c.; inside, note paintings by Pontormo.

Palazzo Pitti** (*F2-3*). The most monumental of Florence's many palazzi, it was built by the Pitti, a family of merchants and bankers, around 1458, and was probably designed by F. Brunelleschi.

Simple grandeur is everywhere, in the three stories with graduated rustication, pierced by arcades; the building was enlarged by B. Ammannati and G. Parigi (1558); it attained its current appearance, with the two jutting wings, between 1764 and 1839. From 1549 on, it was the residence of the grand dukes (Medici first, then Hapsburg-Lorraine), and for a short time (1865-71) the residence of Italy's first king, Victor Emmanuel II. Today, the halls of the beautiful building, along with other structures in the adjacent Gardens of Bòboli, house several major Florentine museums: the Galleria Palatina, the Galleria d'Arte Moderna, the Museo degli Argenti, the Museo delle Carrozze, the Galleria del Costume, the Donazione Contini Bonacossi, and the Museo delle Porcellane.

From the central portal, you emerge into the majestic *courtyard** by B. Ammannati (1570): note the 17th-c. Grotto of Moscs; on the terrace above is the lovely late-16th-c. *Fontana del Carciofo*. From the courtyard, a stairway on the right leads to the Galleria Palatina and the Galleria d'Arte Moderna.

Galleria Palatina**. *Open, 9-2; closed Mon.* This collection, arranged in spectacular halls frescoed by P. da Cortona and C. Ferri, still has the appearance of a princely gallery; in particular, it boasts excellent 16th- and 17th-c. art. You enter through the Galleria delle Statue and, to the left, the Sala delle Nicchie, both featuring ancient statues. You thus reach the Sala di Venere, which takes its name from a marble **Venus**** by A. Canova. This hall has four masterpieces by Titian, and paintings by Rubens and S. Rosa. In the following halls, which are named after Greek and Roman deities, are masterpieces by Rosso Fiorentino, A. del Sarto, Titian, Tintoretto, D. Dossi, P. Veronese, P. P. Rubens, A. Van Dyck, Murillo, Giorgione, Raphael, Fra' Bartolomeo, Andrea del Sarto, Bronzino, and Perugino. In the Sala dell'Iliade, works by Raphael, R. del Ghirlandaio, A. del Sarto, and J. Sustermans. The other halls feature frescoes by P. da Cortona and paintings by Caravaggio, C. Allori, C. Dolci, Raphael, Filippo Lippi, S. Botticelli, L. Signorelli, B. Peruzzi, Pontormo, Beccafumi, Titian, P. Veronese, A. del Sarto, G. Vasari, P .P. Rubens, and S. Rosa.

Appartamenti Reali. *Open by request, for information, tel. 2388611.* These lavish rooms were home to the Medici and then the Lorraine, and reception areas for the Savoy. Recently restored to the way they looked in 1911, when they were donated to the state.

Galleria d'Arte Moderna. *Open, 9-2; closed Mon.* This gallery offers a complete view of Italian painting from Neoclassicism to the 20th c. in thirty halls; more halls will open in time, on the top floor. Notable works by: F. Hayez, G. Fattori, G. Previati, S. Lega, M. Rosso, T. Signorini, A. Puccinelli, and F. Zandomeneghi.

Museo degli Argenti*. *Open, 9-2; closed Mon.* To the left of the central courtyard, this museum of silverwork occupies the summer grand-ducal apartments and the mezzanine (take an interior staircase); it features remarkable objects made of precious metals, semi-precious stones, crystals, and ivory. An amazing array luxury items and bizarre jewelry.

Museo delle Carrozze. This museum features carriages from the courts of Lorraine and Savoy; it is on the ground floor, overlooking the roundabout to the left of the palazzo.

Giardino di Bóboli** (*F3*). *Open, 9-5:30; closed 1st and last Mon. of the month.* You enter from the Ammannati courtyard of Palazzo Pitti; this is one of the largest and most elegant of all Italian-style gardens. Extending over 45,000 sq. m. of the Bóboli hill, between Palazzo Pitti, the fortress of Belvedere, and the Porta Romana, it was designed in 1550 by N. Tribolo and others. Its current appearance developed over the centuries; it features boulevards with wide-ranging views, fountains, and statues. Among the best-known features: the great 17th-c. *amphitheater*, the 17th-c. *fountain of the Carciofo*, the *Buontalenti grotto* (1588), with its Venus by Giambologna; the *fishpond of Neptune*, with statue of same (1565); the high *garden of the Cavaliere*, with its magnificent view, and the nearby little lodge (*Casino del Cavaliere*) which houses the Museo delle Porcellane (see below), and the *Viottolone*, the long straight boulevard that runs between statues and walls of laurels, cypresses, and pine trees to the *Piazzale dell'Isolotto**, where the handsome Fountain of the Ocean stands, by Giambologna (1576).

Museo delle Porcellane*. *Open only by request (and even then, not always accessible); closed Mon.* This museum has a collection of porcelain from the Royal Manufactory of Naples, from the Ginori Manufactory of Doccia, from Sèvres and other manufactories in Paris, Chantilly, Vienna, Berlin, Meissen, and Worcester.

Palazzina della Meridiana (*F2*). This Neoclassical pavillion was begun after 1776 by G.M. Paoletti and completed in 1840 by P.Poccianti, at the SW wing of the building overlooking the Bòboli gardens. Inside, note the sumptuous Neoclassical decorations, partly retouched around 1860. Restored in 1971, it became the site of the Galleria del Costume and, temporarily, of the Donazione Contini-Bonacossi.

Donazione Contini-Bonacossi*. *Open by request, enquire at the Galleria degli Uffizi, tel. 283885.* This collection was donated to the Italian state in 1969, and is temporarily installed in a dozen-or-so rooms in the Meridiana; it includes paintings, sculpture, furniture, and objets d'art. Among the artists, let us mention: Cimabue; Sassetta; Defendente Ferrari; Giovanni Bellini; P. Veronese; Bramantino; Goya; Velàzquez; among the sculptors: G. L. Bernini and the Della Robbia family.

Galleria del Costume. *Open, 9-2, closed Mon.* This museum of fashion and costumes displays, with a two-year revolving exhibit, historical clothing, from the early-18th to the early-20th c.

S. Felice in Piazza (*F2*). This church, originally Romanesque, has a handsome Renaissance facade attributed to Michelozzo (1452-60); inside, note the Crucifix painted on wooden panel by Giotto, prior to 1307.

Museo Zoologico "La Specola" (*F2*). *Open, Mon., Thu.*

and Fri., 9-12; section of wax anatomical models, Tue. and Sat., 9-12. In the venerable old Palazzo Torrigiani, at n. 17 in Via Romana, this section of the Museo di Storia Naturale dell'Università has remarkably vast collections of zoology and wax anatomical models*, housed in 600 display cases from the 18th and 19th c. Upstairs, note the *Tribuna di Galileo*, an amphitheater (1841), with lavish marble, mosaic, and fresco decorations exalting the history of science and the scientists of Florence.

Via Maggio (*E-F2-3*). In the old days known as "Via Maggiore," this is the loveliest street in the quarter of Oltrarno; running straight and lined with 14th-/16th-c. palazzi, it has an aristocratic appearance. At n. 26, *Palazzo di Bianca Cappello* (the lover and then the wife of Francesco de' Medici), by B. Buontalenti, a fine example of a 16th-c. noble home, with facade decorated with grotesque art.

Piazza S. Spirito (*F2*). This square, with its greenery and simple fountain, is lined by 15th-c. homes; in particular, note the palazzo at n. 10, **Palazzo Guadagni***, a fine building from the Florentine Renaissance, possibly by Cronaca (1503-06). At the far end of the square, note the church of S. Spirito.

S. Spirito** (*E2*). With S. Lorenzo, this church is one of the pre-eminent creations of the architecture of the early Renaissance. Begun in 1444 by F. Brunelleschi, it was continued after 1446 on his plans by A. Antonio Manetti, and completed in 1488. The facade is stark and bare; the right side, with its simple lines, is particularly handsome. The slender campanile* on the left side is by B. d'Agnolo (1503). The *interior*, refined in its elegance and almost musical in its balanced composition, features three aisles divided by columns topped with arches, extending into the transept as well. Note the handsome niches, used as chapels. The stained glass in the facade was designed by Perugino; on the altars of the side chapels, note: copies of statues by Michelangelo; sculptures attributed to B. Rossellino and A. Sansovino; numerous panels by 15th- and 16th-c. artists, including Filippino Lippi, C. Rosselli, and A. Allori; polyptych by M. di Banco (14th c.). From the left aisle, through a vestibule* with coffered barrel vault on columns (by Cronaca, to plan by Giuliano da Sangallo), you enter the octagonal sacristy*, with two orders of pillars and ribbed cupola, also designed by Sangallo. To the left of the church is the entrance to the **Cenacolo di S. Spirito** (*open, 9-2; closed Mon.*), with an impressive fresco (Crucifixion*), by A. Orcagna, covering a whole wall, and various sculptures from the high Middle Ages to the Renaissance.

S. Maria del Carmine* (*E1*). In the Piazza di S. Maria del Carmine, this medieval church, rebuilt in 1771, is renowned for the frescoes by Masaccio and Masolino that adorn the *Cappella Brancacci*. Located at the end of the right transept, the chapel can be reached by a door to the right of the facade, by passing through the 17th-c. cloister. The frescoes were begun by Masolino and Masaccio in 1424, and finished by Filippino Lippi after 1480. The **frescoes****, recently restored, include Masaccio's masterpieces, the Expulsion from Eden, and Payment of the Tribute. The near-

by Gothic *sacristy* has various 14th- and 15th-c. paintings and frescoes by L. d'Andrea (1400).

From S. Trinita to S. Maria Novella

Via de' Tornabuoni, an understated, refined, elegant street, lay at the western extremity of both the Roman city and of the city enclosed within the first medieval circuit of walls. This route runs through the western quarters of the center of Florence, to the Dominican church of S. Maria Novella, still outside of the walls when construction began, before Dante Alighieri was born.

S. Maria Maggiore (*C3-4*). In Via de' Cerretani, one of the busiest thoroughfares in Florence, note this 13th-c. Gothic church, much renovated over the centuries. The stern interior features fragments of late-14th-c. frescoes.

Piazza degli Antinori (*C3*). This square takes its name from **Palazzo Antinori**, built (1461-69) by Giuliano da Maiano; facing it is the Baroque church of *S. Gaetano*, designed by B. Buontalenti and built during the 17th c. by M. Nigetti and Gherardo Silvani and son.

Via de' Tornabuoni* (*C-D3*). One of the most elegant streets in Florence, it is lined by exclusive shops and major palazzi of the 15th/19th c. Note the rear of Palazzo Strozzi.

Palazzo Strozzi** (*D3*). Rivalled only by Palazzo Medici-Riccardi as the finest example of Florentine Renaissance palazzo, this building was begun in 1489 by B. da Maiano, and continued by Cronaca (1497-1504); one side and part of the cornice, however, remained unfinished. It is simple yet elegant in appearance; it has graduated rustication, with two courses of centered mullioned windows, and a jutting cornice*; at the corners, note the banner lances and the wrought-iron torch-holders, also by B. da Maiano (1491-98). Inside, a porticoed courtyard and two orders of loggias, of exquisite elegance, designed and built by Cronaca. Currently, the building houses cultural institutes and major exhibitions.

Museo "Marino Marini" (*C-D3*). *Open 10-1 and 4-7 (until 6 in winter); closed Tue.* Established in 1988, this museum stands in Via della Spada, in the former church of *S. Pancrazio*. This museum features a major collection of work by the artist, from nearby Pistoia (1901-80), including paintings from the Twenties, sculpture in various materials, and canvases from the Fifties and Sixties.

Cappella Rucellai (*C-D3*). *Open only on Sat. aft. during the masses.* Adjacent to the former church of S. Pancrazio (now a museum), also in Via della Spada, this 14th-c. structure encloses the *Tempietto del S. Sepolcro*, an elegant creation of L.B. Alberti (1467), who was trying to reproduce, to scale, the Holy Sepulcher of Jerusalem.

Palazzo Rucellai* (*D3*). At n. 18 in Via della Vigna Nuova, this palazzo overlooks a piazzetta with the handsome *Loggia Rucellai* (1466). This palazzo, a masterpiece of the architecture of the early Renaissance, was built in various stages during the second half of the 15th c., by B. Rossellino to plans by L.B. Alberti; note cornices, pilaster strips, and mullioned windows. Located here are the Archivi Photografici Alinari, with the collection of a great historical photo house, and, on the ground floor, the *Museo della Fotografia Alinari* (*open, 10-7:30; closed Wed.*).

Piazza S. Trìnita (*D3*). In the center of this oddly shaped piazza is the *Colonna della Giustizia*, taken from the Baths of Caracalla in Rome. At n. 1 stands *Palazzo Bartolini-Salimbeni*; note windows with cross-bars, and the handsome courtyard by Baccio d'Agnolo (1523). At the far end, along Via de' Tornabuoni, is the creneled *Palazzo Spini-Feroni* (13th c., rebuilt more than once), with its appearance of a massive medieval fortress-palazzo.

S. Trìnita* (*D3*). One of the earliest churches in Florence, it was built in the late-11th c. and then rebuilt in the Gothic style in the 14th c., possibly by N. di Fioravante; the stone Baroque facade is by B. Buontalenti (1594). The stern *interior*, with three aisles separated by pillars with pointed arches and cross-vaults, is one of the earliest examples of Gothic art in Florence. In the 3rd chapel on the right, on the altar, Virgin on Throne and Four Saints, by N. di Bicci; on the wall, fresco and preparatory drawing, by S. Aretino. On the altar of the 4th chapel on the right, Annunciation* by L. Monaco; on the walls, frescoes, also by L. Monaco. In the sacristy, detached 14th-c. frescoes and the tomb of O. Strozzi, by P. Lamberti (1421). In the 2nd chapel to the right of the main altar (Cappella Sassetti), frescoes by D. Ghirlandaio (1483-86): on the altar, Adoration of the Shepherds*; on the walls, six Scenes from the Life of St. Francis*. In the 2nd chapel to the left of the main altar, marble tomb* of B. Federighi, bishop of Fièsole, with a handsome fascia of polychrome majolica by L. della Robbia (1454). In the 5th chapel on the left, wooden sculpture* (Magdalene), by D. da Settignano, possibly completed by B. da Maiano (c. 1455).

Borgo Ss. Apostoli (*D E3*). This distinctive street in the medieval center of Florence is lined by houses and towers from the 13th and 14th c. On the small and charming *Piazza del Limbo*, note the church of the **Ss. Apostoli***, a Romanesque building from the 11th c., renovated in the 15th/18th c., but restored to its original form in the 1930s. Note the 16th-c. central portal. Inside, note sculpture by B. da Rovezzano (tomb of O. Altoviti, 1507) and tabernacle by G. della Robbia. Other artworks, damaged by the flood of 1966, are still being restored. Nearby is the majestic *Palazzo Rosselli del Turco* (n. 19), by B. d'Agnolo (1507).

Ponte S. Trìnita* (*E3*). This majestic bridge spans the Arno with three polycentric arches; it is the masterpiece of B. Ammannati (1608), who rebuilt the five-arch bridge erected by T. Gaddi, which had collapsed in 1557. Destroyed by the retreating Germans (Aug. 1944), it was rebuilt in its original form. It offers fine views* along the riverbanks as far as the Parco delle Cascine, downstream, and of the Ponte Vecchio and the hill of S. Miniato, upstream.

Palazzo Corsini (*D2-3*). At n. 10 in Lungarno Corsini, this building dates from 1648-56, and is one of the finest examples of Florentine Baroque; note terraces decked with statues. Inside, the **Galleria Corsini** (*open by request, tel. 218994; entrance from n. 11 in Via del Parione*) is one of the most notable private collections in Italy, with spectacular rooms lined with paintings from 15th- and 16th-c. Florence (Filippino Lippi, L. Signorelli,

Pontormo, and others) and Italian and foreign artists from the 17th and 18th c.

Chiesa di Ognissanti (*C1-2*). This church, set in the Piazza di Ognissanti, was founded in 1251; it was later renovated, and has a Baroque facade (1637) by M. Nigetti, with a Della Robbia terracotta; only the slender bell tower survives from the original structure. Inside: frescoes by D. Ghirlandaio; a detached fresco by S. Botticelli; in the sacristy, a panel from the school of Giotto and a detached fresco by T. Gaddi. From the Renaissance *cloister* (17th-c. frescoes) adjacent to the church you enter (*entrance at n. 42 in Borgo Ognissanti*) the ancient refectory of the convent (*open, Mon., Tue. and Sat., 9-12*), with a fresco (The Last Supper*) by D. Ghirlandaio.

Piazza S. Maria Novella (*C2-3*). Bounded by the facade of the church of S. Maria Novella, a lovely backdrop, this square is one of Florence's most charming spots. At the center, note the two marble obelisks (1608) which marked the finish lines in the horse race of the Palio dei Cocchi; on the side opposite the church, note the handsome **Loggia di S. Paolo** (*C2*; 15th c.), with ten elegant arches on Corinthian columns; set between the arches, nine glazed terracotta medallions by Andrea della Robbia, who also did the lunette under the portico.

S. Maria Novella** (*B2-3*). One of Florence's most renowned churches, this is a masterpiece of Gothic architecture, built between 1278 and about 1350. The 14th-c. *facade**, entirely encrusted with marble, was rebuilt in 1458 to the design of L. B. Alberti; note his classical portal and the section above the central cornice, with volutes on either side. To the right of the facade, an enclosure made up of arcades with the tombs of Florence's leading families surrounds the ancient cemetery.

The **interior** is a harmonious, soaring piece of Gothic architecture, and it abounds with masterpieces of architecture, sculpture, and painting. In particular, note the work of Rossellino and D. da Settignano, L. Ghiberti, N. Pisano, B. da Maiano, Giambologna, B. d'Agnolo, G. da Sangallo, and F. Brunelleschi. Among the fine **frescoes** and paintings that adorn the interior of the church, note the work by Filippino Lippi, D. Ghirlandaio, Masaccio, N. di Cione, and A. Orcagna. In the *sacristy*, note the terracotta lavabo by G. della Robbia, the Crucifix** by Giotto, and the majestic armoire by Buontalenti.

Museo di S. Maria Novella* (*B2*). *Open, 9-2; Sun., 8-1; closed Fri.* With an entrance to the left of the church, this museum includes part of the cloisters of the old convent and a number of other rooms. The *Chiostro Verde* (or Green Cloister)

Florence: S. Maria Novella

was built after 1350 and takes its name from the frescoes in "terra verde" on the walls (Stories from Genesis*) by various early-15th-c. artists, including P. Uccello; by the latter, note in particular, the Universal Deluge* and the Drunkenness of Noah*. The *Cappellone degli Spagnoli**, once the Chapter Hall, is a spacious hall built by J. Talenti (14th c.). It is entirely frescoed by A. di Buonaiuto (1367-69), with a polyptych on the altar by B. Daddi. In the *Sala del Refettorio* (Refectory Hall), 14th-c. fresco.

Piazza della Stazione (*B2-3*). This square overlooks the handsome apse of S. Maria Novella, with its slender and elegant *campanile* (1332-33). In the distance, you can see the train station, or *Stazione Centrale di S. Maria Novella (A-B2)*, a fine example of Rationalist architecture (1932-35), built by the Gruppo Toscano, under G. Michelucci. On the side facing Piazza Adua, note the marble *Palazzina Reale (A2)*, where the king of Italy boarded his train, also by Michelucci (1934).

Ex Convento delle Monache di Foligno (*A3*). *Open by request, enquire on the spot.* At n. 40 in Via Faenza, this former nunnery features, in the refectory, a fresco of the Last Supper by assistants of Perugino and other detached frescoes by Bicci di Lorenzo, once thought to be by Raphael.

The areas around S. Marco and the SS. Annunziata

The focal points of this route lie in the Piazza S. Marco and the neighboring Piazza SS. Annunziata, both to the north of the Duomo, just outside of the second medieval walled perimeter. Around the Piazza S. Marco is the Galleria dell'Accademia and the Dominican convent where Fra' Angelico lived and painted. On one side of the Piazza SS. Annunziata, note the exquisite arches of the portico of the Spedale degli Innocenti by Brunelleschi, and the Museo Archeologico.

Via Cavour (*A-B4-5*). This road is a continuation of Via de' Martelli, known as Via Larga until the 19th c. for its broad and airy appearance; note Palazzo Medici-Riccardi and other aristocratic palazzi of the 17th and 18th c.

Cenacolo di S. Apollonia* (*A4-5*). *Open, 9-2, closed Mon.* This is the refectory of the former Benedictine nunnery of S. Apollonia (entrance from n. 1 in Via XXVII Aprile), which Andrea del Castagno decorated around 1450 with major frescoes (Last Supper**; Crucifixion; Deposition; Resurrection); also, other works by the same artist. You may wish to visit the elegant 15th-c. *Chiostro Grande**, or main cloister (entrance from n. 1 in Via S. Gallo), property of the University.

Piazza S. Marco (*A5*). Spacious and tree-lined, this square is bounded by the church of S. Marco, the adjoining convent, site of the Museo (see below), and various other buildings, including the *Università degli Studi* and the *Accademia delle Belle Arti*, with the early-Renaissance portico of the former *hospital of S. Matteo*; note the three handsome Della Robbia lunettes.

S. Marco (*A5*). This church has a Baroque facade, dates from the 14th c., but was rebuilt by Michelozzo (1437-43) and renovated in the 16th and 17th c. Inside, note various 14th-c. artworks, painting by Fra' Bartolomeo (1509), and Crucifix by Fra' Angelico (1428) on the main altar.

Museo di S. Marco** (*A5*). *Open, 9-2; closed Mon.* To the right of the church (*entrance at n. 3 in Piazza S. Marco*), this museum occupies the

handsome and well restored rooms of the Dominican convent of S. Marco, extensively rebuilt by Michelozzo (1439-44), which was a major cultural center in the 15th c. Among those who lived here were Fra' Angelico, Savonarola, and Fra' Bartolomeo. Of particular interest are the paintings by Fra' Angelico. *Chiostro di S. Antonino**: in the lunettes of the portico, a series of frescoes by Fra' Angelico. *Sala dell'Ospizio*: this hall holds a number of masterpieces by Fra' Angelico. Note the marble frame around one, by L. Ghiberti. Sala del Capitolo: note the large **Crucifixion**** by Fra' Angelico, and the Madonna, by P. Uccello. *Main Refectory*: frescoes and paintings by G.A. Sogliani, R. del Ghirlandaio, L. Lippi, and others. In the Sala di Alessio Baldovinetti paintings by the same, by B. Gozzoli, and A. Romano. In the Sala di Fra' Bartolomeo, a large altarpiece and various paintings by the same. The *Chiostro di S. Domenico (cloistered area, closed to the public)*, built by Michelozzo, can just be glimpsed through a number of windows; at the foot of the stairs is the *Sala del Cenacolo*, with a frescoed Last Supper* by D. Ghirlandaio.

The **second floor** is occupied by the cells of the monks, decorated by renowned *frescoes* by Fra' Angelico. At the end of the second corridor is the *Quartiere del Priore*, where Savonarola once lived (note the portrait by Fra' Bartolomeo). In the third corridor, note the painting by B. Gozzoli, and the *Library**, an elegant Renaissance room with three aisles, by Michelozzo.

Chiostro dello Scalzo. *Open, Mon. and Thu., 9-1.* In Via Cavour at n. 69, this small rectangular porticoed courtyard, dating from the early-16th c., has a monochrome fresco by Andrea del Sarto, working with Franciabigio (1526).

Museo di Storia Naturale. (*A5-6*). This museum of natural history is located in Via Giorgio La Pira n. 4; is run by the University, and comprises three sections. The *Museo di Mineralogia e Litologia (open, 9-1; Wed. also 3-6; closed Sun.)* has collections of minerals from all over the world; note the Brazilian topaz weighing 151 kg. (2nd-largest on earth) and a collection of beryls. The *Museo di Geologia e Paleontologia (open, 9-1, Mon. also 2-6; closed Fri. and Sun.)* is one of Italy's finest, with about 300,000 samples. The *Museo Botanico (open 9-12; closed Sat.-Sun.)* has numerous herbariums (about 4 million specimens), and the most complete tropical herbarium in Italy. Adjacent to the latter herbarium, with entrance from n. 3 in Via Micheli, is the *Orto Botanico (open, Mon., Wed. and Fri., 9-12)*, an ancient garden of simples, or medicinal herbs, founded in 1550, with about 6,000 plants.

Galleria dell'Accademia* (*A5*). *Open, 9-2; closed Mon.* At n. 60 in Via Ricasoli, this gallery is renowned for a group of sculptures by Michelangelo, but it also has a notable collection of paintings of the Florentine school (13th/16th c.). In the Galleria dei Prigioni: four enormous unfinished sculptures, known as the *Prigioni**, or Prisoners, executed around 1530 by Michelangelo for the tomb of Pope Julius II; also, an unfinished S. Matteo (St. Matthew; 1505-06), and the world-renowned **David****, carved in 1501-04, and formerly located in Piazza della Signoria. In the so-called *Sale Fiorentine*, or Florentine Halls, canvases by painters of the Florentine Renaissance: A. di Giusto; G. di Ser Giovanni, called the Scheggia;

D. di Michelino; C. Rosselli; Perugino; A. Baldovinetti; S. Botticelli; Filippino Lippi; and R. del Garbo. The large hall of the *Gipsoteca Bartolini* contains many plaster casts. In the so-called *Sale Bizantine*, or Byzantine Halls, work by Florentine painters of the 13th and 14th c.: panels and Crucifixes of the Tuscan school; P. di Bonaguida; Maestro della Maddalena; B. Daddi; T. Gaddi; G. da Milano; Maestro di S. Gaggio; and others. On the *second floor* are new halls devoted to L. Monaco and Florentine art between the 14th and 15th c.

Museo delle Pietre Dure (*B5*). This museum of semi-precious stones, with entrance in Via degli Alfani n. 78, is adjacent to the Opificio delle Pietre Dure (literally, workshop of semiprecious stones), established in 1588.

Piazza SS. Annunziata* (*B6*). This square is lined by handsome Renaissance porticoes; at the center is an equestrian statue by Ferdinando I, by Giambologna, and two elegant Baroque fountains* by P. Tacca (1629). To the right of the basilica, note the portico of the Ospedale degli Innocenti; to the left, the *loggia of the Serviti*, by A. da Sangallo the Elder and B. d'Agnolo.

Ospedale degli Innocenti* (*B6*). One of the most significant emblems of Florence's Humanist culture, this Foundling Hospital is one of the loveliest creations of the Italian Renaissance; designed by F. Brunelleschi (1419), it was completed by F. della Luna (1445). Overlooking the square is an elegant *portico** with arches on slender columns; in the spandrels of the arches, eight glazed terracotta tondos by A. della Robbia. The interior encloses a first courtyard (*Chiostro degli Uomini*); from here, two stairways lead up to the hall of the **Pinacoteca** (*open, 8:30-2, Sun. 8-1; closed Wed.*), with a small number of exquisite artworks, by great artists including: Maestro della Madonna Strauss, S. Botticelli, Luca della Robbia, Piero di Cosimo, and D. Ghirlandaio.

Basilica della SS. Annunziata* (*A6*). This renowned Florentine sanctuary contains the venerated image of the Madonna Annunziata (Annunciation to the Virgin): it was built in 1250, rebuilt in the 15th c. by Michelozzo, and subsequently renovated extensively. In front of the church is a 17th-c. portico, and from there you enter a little atrium or cloister called the *Chiostrino dei Voti* (1447). On the walls, detached and restored *frescoes** by Rosso Fiorentino (1517), Jacopo Pontormo (1516), Franciabigio, and Andrea del Sarto; also note a marble bas-relief by Michelozzo. The *interior* is notably Baroque, and features numerous artworks from the 17th and 18th c. In the 5th chapel on the right, monument to O. de' Medici, by B. Rossellino (1456). In the presbytery, enormous circular apse by Michelozzo and L.B. Alberti, surrounded by nine chapels, with paintings and statues from the 16th c. In the left transept, terracotta statue by Michelozzo. Adjoining it is the 15th-c. *Chiostro dei Morti* (Cloister of the Dead; *open by request, enquire with the sacristan*), with fresco by A. del Sarto. In the left aisle: two frescoes by A. del Castagno, in the 2nd and 3rd chapels. At the beginning of the aisle, note the *Cappella dell'Annunziata*, in the form of a little marble temple*; on the altar a 14th-c. fresco of the Annunciation.

Museo Archeologico* (*A-B6*). *Open, 9-2; Sun. 9-1; closed Mon.* In the *Palazzo della Crocetta*, in Via della Colonna n. 38, is one of the most important and fascinating archeological museums in Italy, especially noteworthy in terms of the Etruscan and Egyptian civilizations. Founded in 1824-28, it ranks second in Italy only behind the Museo Egizio of Turin.

The museum is still being reorganized following the terrible damage done by the flood of 1966, and so only a small part of the immense collection is on display; the archeological garden and the courtyard are also closed. The descriptions that follow are in part therefore indicative only.

Antiquarium Etrusco-Greco-Romano. It comprises remarkable Etruscan funerary sculpture, Roman statuary, Attic ceramics and statuary.

Museo Egizio. This Egyptian museum includes steles, sculpture, sarcophagi, mummies, wall fragments, jewelry, papyrus, ointment vases, tools, and so forth. In particular: granite group with Hathor Suckling the Pharaoh Horemhab* (14th c. B.C.), and other remarkable statues and bas-reliefs.

Museo Topografico dell'Etruria. Artifacts of the Etruscans, arranged geographically, from the 8th to the 1st c. B.C.

Via de' Servi (*B-C5*). Formerly known as "Borgo di Balla," this street ran from Piazza del Duomo toward Fiesole, and is lined by interesting palazzi. As you cross Via degli Alfani, on the left, between that street and Via del Castellaccio, note the *Rotondo di S. Maria degli Angioli* (*B5*), designed by F. Brunelleschi (1433), the core of an unfinished octagonal church. Back on Via de' Servi, n. 15 is the 16th-c. *Palazzo Niccolini*, formerly Palazzo Montalto.

Arcispedale di S. Maria Nuova (*C5-6*). Overlooking the Piazza di S. Maria Nuova, with a three-part loggia, this is the oldest hospital in Florence, founded in 1288 by Folco Portinari. Its modern-day appearance is a result of the renovation done in the late-16th c. by B. Buontalenti. At the center of the portico is the portal of the 15th c. church of *S. Egidio*; to the right of the church is the *Chiostro delle Medicherie*, a notable cloister with glazed terracotta by Giovanni della Robbia.

Museo di Preistoria (*C5*). *Open, 9:30-12:30; closed Sun.* Facing the Arcispedale, in Via S. Egidio n. 21, this museum of prehistory is housed in a former convent. It possesses various collections, concerning local and world prehistory. In the same building, but with an entrance in Via dell'Oriuolo n. 24, is the **Museo di Firenze Com'Era** (Museum of Florence As It Used to Be; *open, 9-2, Sun. 8-1; closed Thu.*), concerning the development and history of the city from the 15th c. to the modern day, with woodcuts, etchings, prints, paintings, and photographs. Note the series of twelve Views of the Medici Villas by the Flemish painter, Justus, or Giusto Utens (1599).

S. Ambrogio. This church of ancient origin (the earliest documentation is from the 10th c.), rebuilt repeatedly over the centuries, has an 18th-c. interior; on the exquisite Renaissance altars, note paintings from the 14th and 15th c. To the left of the presbytery, in the Cappella del Miracolo, marble tabernacle by M. da Fiesole (1481-83) and fresco by C. Rosselli (ca. 1486); note panel of Saints and Angels by A. Baldovinetti.

S. Maria Maddalena de' Pazzi*. At n. 58 in Borgo Pinti is this church rebuilt after 1479 to plans by Giuliano da Sangallo; note the handsome cloister. In the former Sala Capitolare (*open, 9-12 and 5-7; access from the sacristy*), Crucifixion*, fresco by Perugino.

The quarter of S. Croce

This route, which begins among the sculpture of Donatello and Michelangelo at the Bargello, leads to the Basilica di S. Croce, where Giotto painted, and where great Italians are buried, including the poet Ugo Foscolo; the route ends, across the river Arno, at the Museo Bardini.

Via del Proconsolo (*C-D5*). One of the oldest streets in Florence, it runs along the eastern edge of the first walled perimeter. At n. 12, the *Palazzo Nonfinito*, begun in 1593, perhaps to plans by B. Buontalenti, and was left unfinished (hence the name); it now houses the **Museo Nazionale di Antropologia ed Etnologia** *(open, Thu.-Sat. and 3rd Sun. of each month, 9-1)*, founded by P. Mantegazza in 1869, with anthropological and ethnological collections. To the left, in *Borgo degli Albizi**, still a clearly medieval street, note *Palazzo Ramirez de Montalvo* (n. 26), built by B. Ammannati (1568), and at n. 18, *Palazzo Altoviti* and at n. 12-14 the *Casa* and the *Palazzo degli Albizi*, rebuilt in the early-16th c.

Palazzo Pazzi* (*D5*). At n. 10 in Via del Proconsolo, this Renaissance palazzo, known as the "Palazzo della Congiura," after the great conspiracy against the Medici which was the ruin of the house of Pazzi, was built for the family by Giuliano da Maiano (1458-69). Note the splendid mullioned windows and the elegant porticoed courtyard.

Casa di Dante (*D5*). In Via Dante Alighieri *(entrance at n. 1 in Via S. Margherita)*, this building was reconstructed in 1910; it is used for exhibitions. Note the *Museo Casa di Dante (not open to the public)*, with memorabilia of the poet.

Badia Fiorentina* (*D5*). This ancient Benedictine church was enlarged in the 13th c. (the apse dates from this period) by A. di Cambio, and then further rebuilt in the 15th and 17th c. The elaborate portal, with terracotta lunette by B. Buglioni, is a 19th-c. copy of the original, which was done in 1494 by B. da Rovezzano, who also did the interior portico. Also note the 14th-c. six-sided campanile*. In the Baroque *interior*, note panel* by Filippino Lippi (1485) and various sculptures by M. da Fiesole: altar frontal with Virgin and Two Saints*; tomb of B. Giugni*; tomb of the Marchese Ugo di Toscana*. A door to the right of the presbytery leads to the *Chiostro degli Aranci*, a cloister with portico and loggia, by B. Rossellino (1432-38); in the loggia, detached frescoes and preparatory drawings, from the 15th c.

Museo Nazionale del Bargello* (*D5*). *Open, 9-2; closed Mon.* This museum is located in the rather austere *Palazzo del Podestà*, also known as the *Palazzo del Bargello**, built over the years, in several stages, from 1255 to 1345, with a tower (known as the Volognana) and handsome mullioned windows along the side. It was originally the headquarters of the Podestà and later, after 1574, of the Capitano di Giustizia, also known as the Bargello.

Opened in 1865, with a collection established with contributions from the Uffizi, the Zecca (Mint) and the Archivio di Stato (State Archives), as well as considerable private bequests, this is now one of the world's leading museums in terms of its collection of sculpture and various objects; in particular, it has an outstanding collection of Tuscan Renaissance sculpture and French medieval ivories.

Ground floor. You enter the medieval *courtyard**,

surrounded by porticoes on three sides, through the Torre Volognana; at the center of the courtyard is an octagonal well. On the walls are heraldic devices of the various Podestà; notable marble statues from the 15th-/17th-c., including six statues by Ammannati, Ocean by Giambologna, and Pescatorello (Little Fisherman) by V. Gemito (1877). *Sala del Trecento*: works originally from Orsanmichele, as well as a Virgin with Child by T. da Camaino and a group by A. di Cambio. *Sala del Cinquecento*, works by Michelangelo: the Tondo Pitti* (ca. 1504); Bacchus* (1496-97); **David-Apollo*** (1530-32); bust of **Brutus*** (1539); and other major sculpture from 16th-c. Tuscany: Bacchus* by J. Sansovino; bust of Cosimo I*, Narcissus, Apollo and Hyacinth, Ganymede*, by B. Cellini; Winged Mercury* by Giambologna.

Upstairs. In the loggia at the top of the exterior staircase, statues of animals by Giambologna; in the *Salone del Consiglio Generale**, by N. di Fioravante (1340-45), an array of works by Donatello: bust of N. da Uzzano*, in polychrome terracotta; the Marzocco (1418-20), a lion upholding the lily of Florence; Atys-Amor*, a lovely bronze depicting a winged Cupid; a marble David* (1408-09) and a bronze **David*** (ca. 1440); **S. Giorgio*** (St. George; 1416) and a bas-relief of St. George and the Princess, both from the tabernacle of Orsanmichele; Crucifixion (ca. 1450). Also, work by F. Brunelleschi and L. Ghiberti (the 2 panels of the Sacrifice of Isaac** done for the competition in 1402 for the North Door of the Battistero, or Baptistery), Michelozzo; Bertoldo; Luca della Robbia; D. da Settignano; and A. di Duccio. Next comes the *Sula Islamica* (Islamic Hall), with carpets, fabrics, and other items of Arab culture; the *Sala Carrand*, with items from the Carrand Donation of 1888 (paintings, sculpture, and, above all, objects of the applied arts, such as seals, goldwork, enamels, and glass); the *Cappella di S. Maria Maddalena* (Chapel of Mary Magdalene), frescoed by Giotto's workshop, with carved and inlaid stalls (late-15th c.); the *Sala degli Avori* (Hall of Ivory), with 265 items, ranging from the 5th to the 17th c.; the *Sala Bruzzichelli*, with 16th-c. furniture and a Virgin with Child* by J. Sansovino; and the *Sala delle Maioliche* (Hall of Majolica), with a broad array of Italian production from the 15th c.

Third floor. *Halls of the Della Robbia*: glazed terracotta by Giovanni and Andrea; *Hall of the Bronzes*: Ganymede* and Greyhound, by Benvenuto Cellini; Hercules "Exploding" Antaeus, by Antonio Pollaiolo; *Hall of Verrocchio*, with the renowned bronze David* and the marble Dama col Mazzolino* (Woman with Flowers), by Verrocchio, as well as busts and other works by A. Pollaiolo, Verrocchio, F. Laurana; opere di Antonio Rossellino, B. da Maiano, and M. da Fiesole. Last is the *Medagliere*, or collection of medals, with work by Pisanello, M. de' Pasti, Michelozzo, B. Cellini, and L. Leoni.

Palazzo di S. Firenze (*D5*). On the Piazza di S. Firenze, facing Palazzo Gondi (see below), the complex of the Filippini dedicated to S. Fiorenzo is an interesting piece of Florentine late-Baroque architecture. Now in part occupied by offices of the judiciary, it was built in 1645 as a large church, to plans by P. da Cortona; when money became scarce, only the church of *S. Filippo Neri* was built (left; inside, canvases and bas-reliefs from the 18th c.), with a facade from 1715. Next to the church, Z. Del Rosso built an *oratory* in 1772-75, repeating the facade, symmetrically, and joining it with the facade of the convent.

Palazzo Gondi* (*D5*). Overlooking Piazza S. Firenze, and built by Giuliano da Sangallo, this is an exemplary aristocratic home of 15th-c. Florence, with graduated rustication and a handsome cornice. Left unfinished, and completed in 1874 on the side facing Palazzo Vecchio, it encloses an exquisite porticoed courtyard.

Casa Buonarroti (*D6*). *Open, 9:30-1:30; closed Tue.* At n. 70 in Via Ghibellina, on the site of three houses where Michelangelo lived between 1516 and 1525, is the palazzo built by his great-grandson, the man of letters Michelangelo the Younger; note the gallery* and the studiolo*, or study — remarkable relics of 17th-c. Florence. Left by bequest to the city by Michelangelo's last descendant, Cosimo (1858), it contains the collections of art and archeology of the Buonarroti family, and, of course, work by Michelangelo: two reliefs done in his youth (Madonna della Scala*; Battle of the Centaurs*); wooden Crucifix* (attribution), model for a river god*, model for the facade of S. Lorenzo, various sketches, and a solid array of designs and drawings (attributed).

Piazza di S. Croce (*E6*). This vast and rectangular piazza was, in the 14th c. and in the Renaissance, the site of popular assemblies, jousts, and the playing field for "calcio fiorentino," a rough and ready medieval ball game that is still sometimes played in the city. Note the Basilica di S. Croce as well as the handsome palazzi, surmounted by loggias: at n. 1, **Palazzo Cocchi Serristori** (*D-E6*), from the late-15th c., attributed to Giuliano da Sangallo; at n. 20-22, *Palazzo dell'Antella*, with a jutting polychrome facade (frescoed in 1619-20) on notable corbels.

S. Croce** (*E6*). One of the most notable churches in Florence, one of the masterpieces of Florentine Gothic, renowned as the Pantheon of "illustrious Italians." It was built from 1295 on, to plans by Arnolfo di Cambio; it was completed about 1385, although the consecration only took place in 1443; the marble facade is neo-Gothic (1863), as is the campanile (1847).

The **interior**, impressive and simple, has three broad and luminous aisles, divided by large pointed arches on massive octagonal pillars, while the ceiling is open beam; along the walls are tombs, funerary monuments, and plaques commemorating illustrious personages. *Right aisle*: between the 1st and the 2nd altar, tomb of Michelangelo Buonarroti; on the facing pillar, Madonna del Latte, by Bernardo Rossellino (1478); next is the monument to Vittorio Alfieri by Antonio Canova (1810); on the 3rd pillar, magnificent marble pulpit*, by Benedetto da Maiano. Next: the tomb of Niccolò Machiavelli (1787); Annunciation*, relief by Donatello (ca. 1435) in a Renaissance aedicule in "pietra serena"; the **tomb of Leonardo Bruni****, by Rossellino (1444-45), prototype for all Florentine tombs of the Renaissance; the sepulcher of Gioachino Rossini (1900); the tomb of Ugo Foscolo (1939). In the

right arm of the transept, the immense Cappella Castellani is adorned with a series of frescoes from the 14th c., by Agnolo Gaddi and assistants: note the marble tabernacle* by Mino da Fiesole and Cross painted on wooden panel, by Niccolò Gerini. At the end of the transept, the Cappella Baroncelli, frescoed by Taddeo Gaddi with Stories of the Virgin*, a masterpiece of the artist (1338). A portal, by Michelozzo, leads into the corridor of the 14th-c. *sacristy*, decorated with frescoes by Taddeo Gaddi (Crocifissione), Niccolò Gerini, and Spinello Aretino, with glazed terracotta by Giovanni della Robbia and inlaid 15th-c. cabinets; this opens into the Cappella Rinuccini, with frescoes (Stories of the Virgin and the Magdalene*) by Giovanni da Milano and assistants (1363-66). In the nearby Cappella Medici, by Michelozzo, altar piece in glazed terracotta (Virgin, Angels, and Saints*) by Andrea della Robbia (c. 1480). *Apsidal chapels*: on the sides of the main chapel, the Cappella Peruzzi contains a series of frescoes by Giotto (Stories of John the Baptist* on the left; Stories of St. John the Evangelist* on the right), done in his later years (ca. 1320-25), whitewashed in the 18th c. and uncovered again in about 1850; also by Giotto, Stories of St. Francis** in the nearby Cappella Bardi. The *main chapel* is frescoed by Agnolo Gaddi (Legend of the Cross; 1380); the polyptych on the altar is an assembly: Virgin Mary (in the center) by Niccolò Gerini and Doctors of the Church by Giovanni del Biondo; Cross* painted by the Maestro di Figline (14th c.). In the Cappella Capponi dedicated to the Mothers of Fallen Soldiers, sculptures by Libero Andreotti (1926); in the Cappella Pulci-Berardi, frescoes by Bernardo Daddi (1330) and glazed terracotta altar piece by Giovanni della Robbia; in the Cappella Bardi di Vernio, frescoes (Stories of St. Sylvester*) by Maso di Banco (ca. 1340). At the head of the church, wrought-iron gate, from 1335 and, above the altar, the renowned wooden Crucifix* by Donatello, criticized by F. Brunelleschi for its excessive realism. *Left aisle*: monu-

Florence: Cappella Pazzi

ments to the composer and musician Luigi Cherubini, to the engraver Raffaello Morghen, and to Leon Battista Alberti; Pentecoste by Giorgio Vasari and monument to Carlo Marsuppini*, by Desiderio da Settignano, one of the most remarkable sepulchers of the 15th c.; 18th-c. tombs of Galileo and Vincenzo Viviani.

Museo dell'Opera di S. Croce* *(E6). Open, summer, 10-12:30 and 2:30-6:30; winter, 10-12:30 and 3-5; closed Wed.* Set in the building adjacent to the church, this museum houses the famous Cappella Pazzi, the entire complex was horribly damaged by the flood of 4 November 1966, when the water of the Arno rose to a level of 4.92 m. The *first cloister* remains 14th-c. in flavor; in the center are statues by H. Moore and B. Bandinelli. At the far end, note the **Cappella Pazzi****, one of the most original and harmonious creations of the early Renaissance, a masterpiece by F. Brunelleschi, who began work on it in 1429-30. Outside the chapel is a handsome portico; note the frieze, by D. da Settignano. The barrel vault ceiling of the portico opens in the center into a small cupola* decorated with with terracotta tondos and roses by L. della Robbia; note the wooden door, by G. da Maiano (1472). The **interior****, quite similar to the Old Sacristy of S. Lorenzo, is rectangular, with an apsidiole, both surmounted by cupolas. On the white walls, traced by light architectural ribbing in pietra serena, are twelve tondos by L. della Robbia. From the first cloister, you enter the 14th-c. *refectory*, with the justly renowned great **Crucifix**** by Cimabue, badly damaged by the flooding in 1966, and the gilt bronze statue of S. Ludovico* (St. Louis), by Donatello (1424), formerly in Orsanmichele; on the walls, frescoes by T. Gaddi, A. Orcagna, and D. Veneziano. You then enter a series of rooms with 14th-c. frescoes and statuary; an impressive portal, by B. da Maiano, takes you to the elegant *second cloister**, designed and built in 1453, perhaps by B. Rossellino.

Via Magliabechi *(E6).* Splitting off from *Borgo S. Croce*, this distinctive Florentine street is lined by palazzi and houses from the 15th and 16th c. (at n. 10, *Palazzo Spinelli*); it runs by the building (1911-35) of the **Biblioteca Nazionale Centrale**, the largest and richest library in Italy.

Museo della Fondazione Horne *(E5). Open, 9-1; closed Sun.* This museum, located at n. 6 in Via de' Benci, in the 15th-c. Palazzo de' Benci, believed to have been built by Cronaca, features a notable collection of paintings, sculpture, majolica, glass, and 14th-/16th-c. coins. The collection was assembled by the English scholar and collector Herbert Percy Horne, who lived in Florence around the turn of the 20th c. The collection includes works by such artists as: Masaccio, Bernardo Daddi, Pietro Lorenzetti, Giotto, Simone Martini, Beccafumi, Michelozzo, Filippino Lippi, and Antonio Rossellino.

Ponte alle Grazie *(F5).* Built in the 13th c., it was rebuilt in 1957 after being destroyed in 1944. It offers a fine view: downstream, as far as the Ponte Vecchio; straight ahead, of the hill of S. Miniato; upstream, of the 14th-c. tower-gate of S. Niccolò and the stairs that lead up to Piazzale Michelangiolo, the bridge of S. Niccolò, and the Poggio dell'Incontro.

Museo Bardini* *(F5). Open, 9-2; Sun. 8-1; closed Wed.* At n. 1 in Piazza de' Mozzi, in the Palazzo de' Mozzi, this museum comprises the enormous collection of sculpture, paintings, furniture, and ceramics donated to the city of Florence in 1922 by the collector and antiquary Stefano Bardini. Among the most notable items: Roman sculpture from the Empire; capital with Nativity and Adoration of the Magi, by a Campionese Maestro (12th c.); marble group by T. di Camaino; polychrome terracotta by B. da Maiano; group of statues in polychrome and gilt stucco by Donatello and workshop; collections of wooden chests from the 15th c.; painted terracotta relief by the workshop of J. della Quercia; St. John the Baptist by M. Giambono; statue of the Annunciation, painted terracotta from the Siennese school of the mid-15th c.; canvas by A. Pollaiolo.

The hills

These verdant hills overlook the Arno from the left bank. Up here you will find the church of S. Miniato, with its Romanesque geometry sketched out in white and green marble, and the Forte di Belvedere, a fortress that Buontalenti built for the grand duke Ferdinando I; there is an embarrassment of riches, so to speak, and you can choose which view of Florence you prefer: the view from the church, from the fort, or from the celebrated Piazzale Michelangiolo.

Viale dei Colli*. This scenic and picturesque continuation of the Viali di Circonvallazione across the Arno, is the most beautiful stroll in all Florence; it runs 6 km. over the slopes immediately south of town. The route begins in *Piazza F. Ferrucci*, where *Viale Michelangiolo* runs up to Piazzale Michelangiolo.

Piazzale Michelangiolo**. Considered the most magnificent point along the Viale dei Colli, this square offers a renowned view** of Florence; built around 1875, it balances landscape with architecture, and features a *monument to Michelangelo* (1871), a somewhat over-solemn composition on a marble pedestal.

S. Salvatore al Monte. Atop a staircase behind Piazzale Michelangiolo, surrounded by cypresses, this church was built by S. del Pollaiolo, called the Cronaca (1499), and has a simple unadorned facade. *Inside*, little survives of the Renaissance decoration. Note the Deposition in terracotta by Giovanni della Robbia.

S. Miniato al Monte*. High atop a hill, this church has a broad square with a fine view* of the city below. This is the masterpiece of Florentine Romanesque architecture, along with the Battistero di S. Giovanni, or Baptistery, and was built between 1018 and 1207. The *facade*, with geometric patterns in green and white marble, has five blind round arches, set on Corinthian pilaster strips; above that is an aedicule window surmounted by a 13th-c. mosaic. *Inside*, on the right wall, note 13th-/15th-c. frescoes; in the nave, remarkable intarsiaed marble floor*; at the end of the nave stands the Cappella del Crocifisso* (Chapel of the Crucifix), by Michelozzo (1448), with a majolica vault by Luca della Robbia and panels by A. Gaddi (1394-96) on the altar. In the presbytery, enclosed by a marble screen*, note the pulpit* that dates from 1207; inlaid wooden chancel from 1470; 11th-c. main altar with a

Crucifix by a Della Robbia. To the right of the presbytery, altar with panel by J. del Casentino (ca. 1320); to the left, panel from 1354. In the apse, girded with low handsome arches, note the enormous 13th-c. mosaic of Christ Offering Benediction, Between Mary and St. Miniato. The crypt has seven small aisles, divided by slender 11th-c. columns; in the vault, note frescoes* by T. Gaddi (1341). In the *sacristy* (entrance to the right of the presbytery), note frescoes by S. Aretino. In the left aisle, note the **Chapel of the Cardinal of Portugal***: designed by A. di Manetto (1466), it has perfect Renaissance composition; remarkable tondos* by Luca della Robbia; in the large niches: sepulcher of the Cardinal* by A. Rossellino (right), a fresco of Two Angels in Flight (far wall), and Annunciation* by A. Baldovinetti (left), above the bishop's throne, also by Rossellino.

Palazzo dei Vescovi (*closed to the public*). To the right of the church is the main building of the monastic complex, crenelated, built in the 14th c. Restored in the early-20th c., it encloses a cloister with fragments of frescoes by P. Uccello and preparatory sketches by A. del Castagno. To the left of the church you can enter the *Cimitero Monumentale* di Firenze, a monumental cemetery also known as the *Porte Sante*, built in the late-19th c.

Viale Galileo Galilei. This stretch of the Viale dei Colli after Piazzale Michelangiolo runs nearly level, with fine views of slopes dotted with olive groves, as far as *Piazzale Galileo*.

Via di S. Leonardo. This lovely country road runs between walls over which hang olive branches, and past villas, finally reaching the little romanesque church of *S. Leonardo in Arcetri* (open Sun., 8 and 11, Sat. 5 or 6), with a 13th-c. pulpit and 14th-c. Tuscan paintings. The road ends at the medieval **Porta S. Giorgio** (1224), near the Forte di Belvedere.

Forte di Belvedere*. *Open 9-20 (winter, 9-4:30); closed first and last Mon. of the month*. Also known as the *Forte di S. Giorgio*, this fortress was built by B. Buontalenti and G. de' Medici in 1590-95, linking up with the city walls and serving as both a stronghold and a suburban residence. Linked to Palazzo Vecchio via Palazzo Pitti and the Corridoio Vasariano, it consists of a platform with bastions and a star-shaped plan, dominated by the elegant 3-floor *Palazzina di Belvedere*, possibly designed by B. Ammannati; it is now used for temporary exhibitions.

Viale Machiavelli. The last stretch of the Viale dei Colli runs down from Piazzale Galileo, wending its way among villas, with fine views. It ends near **Porta Romana**, a massive lopped-off tower (1328-31) which still has its original wooden doors.

Parco delle Cascine*. This vast park covers about 118 hectares, and is a popular spot for strolling and relaxing among the Florentines; it runs over 3 km. west of the city, between the right bank of the Arno, the Canale Macinante, and the Mugnone. Opened to the public at the turn of the 19th c. (from the 16th c. on it belonged to the Medici), it has broad paths and avenues, dense woods, green clearings, and many sports facilities. At the far end of the park, in the Piazzaletto dell'Indiano, stand the *Monumento Funebre dell'Indiano*, dedicated to Rajaram Cuttraputti, Maharajah of Kolepoor, who died in Florence in 1870 and was cremated here.

The outer sections of town

Sixteenth-century knights in armor in the hall of a villa on the Colle di Montughi, a fresco by the "painter who made no mistakes" (Andrea del Sarto) in an ancient monastic refectory, codices in Hebrew: other Florentine discoveries, to the north and the east of the center, outside of the avenues of the ring road.

Museo Stibbert*. *Open, 9-1; Sun., 9-12:30; closed Thu.* At n. 26 in Via Stibbert stands one of the world's largest and richest collections of antique arms and costumes, donated to Florence by the British government in 1908, following the death of F. Stibbert (1838-1906). In this home-qua-museum, which occupies more than 60 rooms, there are a vast array of paintings and objects of the applied arts, from every era and every land: sculpture, furniture, porcelain, tapestries, embroidery, and costumes. Of special note is the collection of ancient arms and armor*, from Italy, Spain, North Africa, India, and the Far East ; note the procession of Italian and German knights* (16th-17th c.) and Ottoman horsemen (16th c.).

Museo del Cenacolo di Andrea del Sarto. *Open, 9-2; Sun. 9-1; closed Mon.* In the quarter of S. Salvi, near the Via Aretina, stands the church of **S. Michele a S. Salvi**, once a Vallombrosan monastery. Inside is the museum (entrance at n. 16 in Via S. Salvi), with early-16th-c. Florentine paintings and the funerary monument of S. Giovanni Gualberto, carved by B. da Rovezzano (1507-13); in the refectory is the famous **Cenacolo***, or Last Supper, frescoed by A. del Sarto in 1526-27, a masterpiece of 16th-c. painting.

Museo del Tempio Israelitico. *Open, Oct.-Mar., Mon. Thu., 11 1 and 3 5; Fri. and Sun. 10 1; closed Sat. (Apr-Sep., opens one hour earlier).* In Via Farini 4, near Piazza D'Azeglio, the rooms of the synagogue feature ancient codices, parchments, documents, and Jewish religious objects.

Fossanova* (Abbazia di, Abbey of)

elev. 17 m.; Lazio, province of Latina, township of Priverno (pop. 13,289). At the mouth of the valley of the Amaseno, this abbey lies between the steep slopes of the Monti Lepini. Founded by the Benedictines, it was turned over to the Cistercians (1134-35). In order to reclaim the marshland, the Cistercians dug a canal, the "Fossa Nova." The church is an acclaimed architectural masterpiece; it was a Cistercian spearhead in Italy of French Gothic architecture.

Tour. *In summer, open 8-12 and 3-6; in winter, 8-12 and 3-5:30. For groups, tour by request, tel. 93061.*

The **church*** was consecrated in 1208. The facade has a portal with Cosmatesque decoration and a great rose window; above the tall transept is the octagonal tower, with mullioned windows. The *interior* is an exquisite example of early Cistercian architecture; it has three aisles, lined with pillars. There is a transept and a rectangular choir. To the right of the church is the **abbey** complex: through the right aisle, you can enter the *cloister** with little twin columns, built between 1280 and 1300. It is Romanesque on three sides, Gothic on the fourth side, and features an aedicule with a pyramidal roof. Around the cloister stand: the *chapter hall*, dating from 1250, with two aisles lit by two large, mullioned windows; the "*calefactorium*," a hall for gatherings and meetings in the winter, around a large fireplace; a *refectory*, with a pulpit for the reading of the holy books. On the upper floor of the guest quarters is a room — since transformed into a *chapel* — in which St. Thomas Aquinas (1274) is said to have died. Separate from the monastery is the *infirmary* and other buildings.

Genoa / Genova**

elev. 25 m.; pop. 701,032; Liguria, regional capital. One of the leading ports in southern Europe, and certainly the most important port in Italy, as well as the nation's fifth-largest city. Genoa is the product of events that were played out on a larger stage than the peninsula, events, at the very least, of Mediterranean scope; one of Italy's two largest "maritime republics," as early as the Middle Ages its ships and trade were interacting and intertwining with the world of the East, extending from the Crimea to the ports of Flanders and England; the Genoan state survived and prospered for at least seven centuries. Set in the heart of the two Rivieras, at the northernmost point of the Tyrrhenian Sea, it extends, really, without a break for 30 km. from Voltri to Sant'Ilario ("Grande Genoa," as it is called), overlooking the sea, lifted high by the sharp downward plunge of the Apennine slopes. The center of Genoa, set around the narrow arch of the Porto Vecchio, or old harbor, is partly medieval, a splendid mix of Mannerism and Baroque, with a thoroughly modern, variegated, many-faceted allure. The economic life of this city is undergoing constant transformation, and it remains intensely active. Nearly half the population of Liguria is found in Genoa. It is traditionally called "La Superba," or the Proud One. The 14th-c. poet Petrarch made mention of it: "a regal city, blanketing an Alpine mount, whose men and whose walls are both full of pride, her mere appearance bespeaking her as the mistress of the sea."

Historical note. A small group of Ligurians first settled here in the 6th c. During Roman times, the settlement extended slightly downhill; in the high Middle Ages, the first walled perimeter (9th c.), erected to protect against Saracen raids, included the "castrum" or castle. In 1097 ten Genoan galleys took the port of Antiochia. The thrusting energy of Genoa, in the fields of navigation, trade, and war, had already emerged on the Mediterranean stage, and the First Crusade appeared to heighten and focus that energy. Indeed, during the same years, the "compagna communis" (the Commune, or city government), was first founded, an association of associations, as it were, or a consortium, devoted to trade, and including the bishop, nobles, and the emerging crafts and merchant classes, a sort of coalition government *ante litteram*. It was at this moment, as well, that the history of Genoa became the history of a state, a victorious sea power that ruled the Mediterranean through the 15th c., building a network of emporiums, colonies, and trading ports, a "colonial empire," covering Palestine, the islands of the Aegean, the Black Sea, Corsica, and North Africa. Various motifs intertwine through these centuries: first of all, the need to discourage Arab aggression in the upper Tyrrhenian, then the creation of a trading network, the growing control over the Rivieras, the great rivalry and conflict with Pisa (it was first triggered over rights to Corsica and it ended with the destruction of the Pisan fleet in the battle of Meloria, 1284), the seemingly endless duel with Venice (four wars in 120 years, from an early victory for Genoa in the battle of the Curzolari, 1298, when Marco Polo, by the way, was taken prisoner, all the way up to Genoan defeat in the war of Chioggia, 1378-1381). As for the first Genoa, the story of the walled perimeter pretty much sums up the development of the city itself. The walls of Barbarossa, so called because they were built (1155-63) as a defense against the incursions of that emperor, enclosed a space extending from Porta Soprana, to the east, to Porta dei Vacca to the west, and stretching up the hills to the spot now occupied by the Villetta Di Negro. Along the arc of the "ripa maris," or seafront, stand the "contrade," or quarters, of the aristocratic consortia, little plazas with porticoed houses, at first only two stories tall, and later raised, clustered around the crenelated palazzo on the cape with its well head, oven, baths, and — for the more powerful — church. What is now the historic center of Genoa, the quarter of the "carugi," or lanes, has this urban structure. In 1260 Guglielmo Boccanegra, the first "Capitano del Popolo," (leader of the popular government) had a palazzo built on the "ripa" for his city government (when he was exiled two years later, the building was converted into the customs building, and later the Casa di S. Giorgio, 1405, headquarters of Genoa's state banking system); work began in 1291 on the Palazzo del Comune, later the Palazzo Ducale. There was a light house where the Lanterna now stands, as far back as the 12th c., it served as backup to the lighthouse that stood on the breakwater that extended out from the little spit of land of the Mandraccio. The city continued to grow; and so, two "additions" were created, and then walled in: the stretch of coastline to the west, as far as what is now the Ponte dei Mille with the hills behind it (1320-27) and, to the east, the Collina di Carignano, a hill rising over the Valle del Bisagno (1345-47). This is the Genoa of Christopher Columbus's youth, a city perched on the brink of decline, a city that had failed to transform itself into a regional state, due to the competition of Venice and due to the menacing proximity of Milan and France, but above all, because of two great historical shifts: the fall of Constantinople, 1453 (Caffa, the Black Sea emporium, remained isolated, and fell to the Turks in 1475), and the decline in importance of the Mediterranean Sea, as a result of the very explorers mentioned above, who first learned to sail here. Andrea Doria, "pater patriae," built galleys on behalf of the emperor Charles V; the alliance with Spain that this statesman brought about preserved for some time the independence of the Genoan republic, while his powerful rule emphasized its oligarchic nature — with it came the Genoa ruled by bankers — as well as triggering a remarkable process of transformation of the city itself. Doria built himself a home (1529) to the west of the walls, on the hill of Fassolo, a truly splendid structure (it is the Palazzo del Principe, decorated by Gerolamo da Treviso, Perin del Vaga, the Pordenone, and Beccafumi). The nobility that ruled the state followed him in his taste for luxury: the Strada Nuova (1551; Via Garibaldi) was its neighborhood; Galeazzo Alessi (who also built the church of S. Maria Assunta in Carignano, one of the few churches built in the 16th c.) worked on the homes of the wealthy, while Rubens painted them as models for the rich of the Netherlands. At the same time, villas were built: "from Nervi all the way to Sesto and throughout the Valle di Polcévera as far as Pontedècimo, and throughout the

Valle del Bisagno, everywhere you looked were wonderful buildings, gardens and villas, to the great delight of the eye" (Agostino Giustiniani, 1537) — a chapter of Italian architecture that has never been given adequate consideration. The presence of P.P.Rubens at the beginning of the 17th c. is a clear indicator of the artistic climate; A. Van Dyck also came through town to paint the wealthy and the powerful, as well as the Via Balbi (1626); the school of Genoan painters decorated the interiors of noble homes and equally sumptuous churches (L. Cambiaso, V. Castello, the Fiasella, the Piola, the De Ferrari, the Carlone family, and the Assereto; the last great artist of Genoa, Alessandro Magnasco, worked mainly outside of Liguria). The construction of the last walled perimeter (Mura Nuove, 1626-32) cost a total of 410,000 gold "scudi," a result of the growing threat posed by the house of Savoy. The Republic, under aristocratic rule, dragged on amidst the reclusive wealth of its nobility; Louis XIV humiliated Genoa by bombarding it (1684); the history of Italy records the rebellion of Balilla (1746, War of Austrian Succession); 50 years later, the revolutionary "Armée d'Italie" arrived in Genoa; in 1805 the former Republic of Liguria became part of the Napoleonic Empire; in 1814 the duchy of Genoa was annexed to the House of Savoy, with the approval of the Congress of Vienna. Giuseppe Mazzini was a Genoan and an ardent Republican revolutionary, during the Risorgimento; from Quarto, not yet part of Genoa proper, the Ligurian-born Italian patriot Giuseppe Garibaldi sailed with his Thousand to create Italy. And once Italy had been created, Genoa became its leading port and a major industrial center. The 100,000 inhabitants of 1800 had become 200,000 by 1900. The construction of the new harbor (beginning in 1874, through the bequest of 20 million lire by Raffaele De Ferrari, duke of Galliera), the development of the modern center, uphill from the historic center (Via XX Settembre and Via Dante, which run from Piazza De Ferrari, designating the center of Genoa in the plans of the early-19th-c. urbanist C. Barabino, were built by levelling the Collina di S. Andrea), and the expansion of far-flung residential suburbs — all these were phases in the growth of the city, along with the absorption of surrounding towns.

Getting around. Of the six routes suggested here, the first three are walking tours, while the others involve travelling considerable stretches by car or public transportation. Keep in mind that in Genoa, it is particularly complicated to drive, because of restrictions on space and heavy city traffic.

The historical center, the Cathedral, and the harbor

Between the modern heart of the city and the waters of its port, this stroll will take you through many settings and quarters, differing in origin and style, offering a thorough summary of the history of Genoa, from Middle Ages to modern times.

Piazza De Ferrari (*D4*). This vast square, surrounded by impressive buildings, lies at the heart of Genoa. Overlooking the square is the *Palazzo della Borsa* (1907-12), with porticoes and a large bronze fountain (1936). Tucked away is the Neoclassical facade of the **Teatro Carlo Felice** (*D4*, 1828), damaged in WWII and recently restored. To the right is the 19th-c. building of the *Accademia Ligustica di Belle Arti*, which houses the *Pinacoteca dell'Accademia* (*open, weekdays, 9-1*), whose collections include paintings of the 16th- and 17th-c. Genoan schools.

Piazza Matteotti (*D4*). In this square stand the church of S. Ambrogio and the proud Neoclassical facade of Palazzo Ducale. The 16th-c. church of **S. Ambrogio**

Genoa: Piazza S. Matteo

(*D2-3*) is decorated inside with marble, gilt plaster, and frescoes, as well as paintings by G. Reni and P.P. Rubens. **Palazzo Ducale** (*D4*) was built in the Middle Ages (the 13th-c. section is now part of the palazzo's left wing) and expanded from the late-16th c. on; it has been recently restored and is one of Genoa's cultural centers.

Piazza S. Matteo✶✶ (*C-D4*). This square's distinct medieval flavor makes it one of the old city's loveliest places. Facing it are the black- and white-striped **houses of the Doria family**✶ (n. 15-16-17), and the 12th-c. church of **S. Matteo**✶ (*C-D4*), with its black-and-white bands and Byzantine style mosaic. Inside is the 16th-c. tomb of Andrea Doria.

Campetto (*C3*). This elongated square in the heart of old Genoa features (at n. 8) the 16th-c. *Palazzo Imperiale*, with noteworthy stucco decorations, and, nearby, the 10th-c. church of **S. Maria delle Vigne**, extensively rebuilt. Note the 12th-c. campanile, which stands atop part of a carved Roman sarcophagus.

Cattedrale✶✶ (*D3*). Dedicated to *St. Lawrence* (S. Lorenzo), and consecrated in 1118, this is the most important monument of medieval Genoa. Work continued on it for centuries after its consecration. The black- and white-striped facade, clamped between two bell towers, features three impressive 13th-c. portals with handsome sculptures.

The stern *interior* is enlivened by the two-toned marble of the nave and the 14th-c. frescoes over the central door. In the right aisle, note a British shell that hit the church in 1941, but failed to explode. In the left aisle stands the **chapel of S. Giovanni Battista**✶ (1450-65), with noteworthy marble facade and, inside, in niches, statues by M. Civitali and Andrea Sansovino; 16th-c. baldachin and 12th-c. marble Arca del Battista. To the right of the chapel is the entrance to the **Museo del Tesoro di S. Lorenzo**✶ (*open, Tue., Thu. and Sat., 9:30-11:45 and 3-5:45*), a museum which features precious objects (sacred basin supposedly used at the Last Supper, 1st-c. Roman glass); jewelry (Byzantine cross; 12th-c. Arca del Barbarossa; silver Arca di S. Giovanni✶, 1438-45; casket of the Corpus Domini✶, mid-16th c.); liturgical garb.

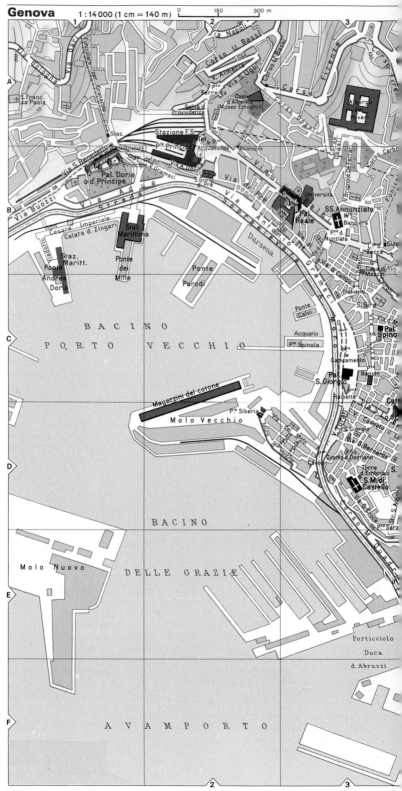

Genova

1 : 14 000 (1 cm = 140 m)   0   150   300 m

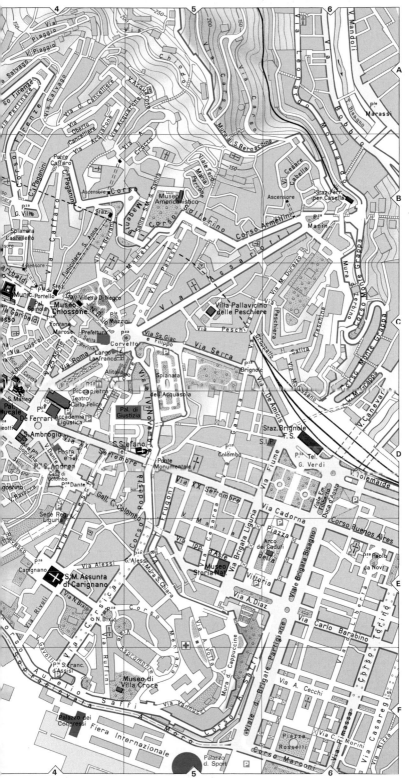

Via S. Lorenzo (*D3*). Built in the 19th c., it runs directly down to the harbor, cutting the old city in two. On either side run the alleys of Genoa, called "carugi."

Palazzo S. Giorgio* (*C3*). Ancient site of the famed Bank of S. Giorgio, this building comprises a Gothic wing (1260), with three- and four-light mullioned windows, and a Renaissance section (1570), with a frescoed facade overlooking the port. Standing alone on one side of the *Piazza Caricamento* (*C3*), the palazzo is lined by the low, busy *porticoes of Sottoripa*, once a lively market street. Between this square and the water of the Old Port runs the *elevated throughway* (1964).

Porto* (*B-F1-3*). Italy's largest harbor, Genoa is rivalled in the Mediterranean only by Marseille. It boasts 19 km of breakwaters and 28 km of wharfs. Passenger docks (for ferries and liners) are the Ponte dei Mille and Ponte Andrea Doria. For a motorboat tour of the harbor, see "Western Addition" route; the best points for a view of the harbor are the square of S. Francesco di Paola (*A1*), the Righi and the Castello de Albertis (*A2*). From an elevated vantage point, you can see the outer port, the Porticciolo (marina) of the Duca degli Abruzzi, the basin of the Grazie, the Porto Vecchio, and the basins of the Lanterna and of Sampierdarena. Far to the west, on a 140,000 sq. meter manmade island just off Cornigliano and Sestri Ponente, is *Cristoforo Colombo airport.*

Porto Vecchio* (*B-C1-3*). This old harbor is enclosed by the curve of land between the Molo Vecchio (Old Wharf) and the *tower of the Lanterna*, a venerable, 76-m.-tall lighthouse, and an emblem of Genoa (last rebuilt in 1543). Major renovations were done on this port, in the area off Piazza Caricamento, between the Molo Vecchio and Ponte Spinola, for the international expo commemorating the 500th anniversary of the discovery of America (May-Aug. 1992). Famed architect Renzo Piano renovated old harbor structures in a plan to reestablish links between the old port and the historic city center, by creating a single pedestrian zone that runs from Piazza Caricamento into the port area. The expo facilities are meant to become a permanent part of Genoa. The facilities involved renovation of the turn-of-the-century *Cotton Warehouses* (*C-D1-2*), the Molo Vecchio (to be a conference hall), the buildings of the 17th-c. *Deposito Franco* (*C3*), and the *Ponte Spinola* (*C3*), where Europe's largest *Aquarium* has been built. On the waters of the Port stands the *"Bigo,"* a structure with a maritime flavor, and a panoramic cabin that rises to an altitude of 45 m. Near the 16th-c. fortification of **Porta Siberia** (also *Porta del Molo, D2*), a new body of water changes the seaward shape of the wharf.

Via S. Luca (*C3*). One of Genoa's oldest streets, lined with 14th-/16th-c. aristocratic palazzi, it runs from Piazza Banchi, upon which both the late-16th-c. *Loggia dei Mercanti*, and the 16th-c. church of *S. Pietro in Banchi*, face. Midway down the street is the church of *S. Luca*, founded in 1188 and rebuilt in 1650.

Galleria Nazionale di Palazzo Spinola* *Open, 9-5; Sun. and Mon., 9-1.* Set in the heart of old Genoa, at n. 1, Piazza Pellicceria, this art gallery occupies an aristocratic home of the 16th/18th c., with original furnishings, and fine stucco and fresco decorations. The gallery features works by A. da Messina; J. van Cleve, A. Van Dyck, L. Giordano, G. Reni, Strozzi, Castiglione, V. Castello, Mignard, G.C. Procaccini, G.B. Gaulli, and G. Pisano.

Porta dei Vacca (*B3*). This oval-arched gate, set between two towers, was part of the walls built in 1155-60, and requires a slight detour along *Via Fossatello* (*IV, B1*) and *Via del Campo* (*VI, A1*); along the way, note the portals and reliefs

Casa di Mazzini (*B-C3*). *Open, 9-7; closed Sun. aft. and Mon.* At n. 11 in Via Lomellini stands the birthplace of a great Italian political thinker, now the site of the *Istituto Mazziniano*, with *Library* and *Archives*, and the **Museo del Risorgimento**.

S. Siro (*C3*). Genoa's first cathedral, heavily rebuilt, features 17th-c. frescoes, paintings, and reliefs; a fine example of Genoan Baroque. Next door, at the corner of Via S. Siro and Via Fossatello, stands a handsome four-story medieval *palazzo* with mullioned windows.

Via Garibaldi** (*C4*). One of Italy's most monumental streets, lined with 16th-c. buildings; hidden behind the handsome facades are lovely courtyards, porticoes, and frescoed halls. It runs from *Piazza della Meridiana* (*C3-4*), named for the sundial on a building facing it.

Palazzo Bianco (*C4*). At n. 11 in Via Garibaldi, this mid-16th-c. building has been redone in Genoan Baroque. It houses the **Galleria di Palazzo Bianco*** (*open, 9-7; closed Sun. aft. and Mon.*), one of the city's finest art collections. It has a beautifully hung collection of Genoan painters, including L. Brea, P.F. Sacchi, L. Cambiaso, Assereto, V. Castello, Fiasella, and, especially, Strozzi and Magnasco. Among the painters of other schools: F. Lippi, Pontormo, Palma the Younger, Veronese, Moretto, G. David, van der Goes, Provost, Metsys, Aertsen, Rubens, Van Dyck, Zurbaran, and Murillo.

Palazzo Rosso (*C4*). At n. 18 stands a Baroque palazzo, named for its distinctive red color; it houses the **Galleria di Palazzo Rosso*** (*open: same hours as the Palazzo Bianco*). The halls still have the feel of a princely home; the upstairs rooms are lavishly furnished and frescoed. Among the works on display are paintings by: Pisanello, Veronese, Lotto, Moretto, P. Bordone, Titian, Tintoretto, B. Licinio, Palma the Younger, Caravaggio and his followers, Genovesino, M. Preti, S. Rosa, Guercino, Reni, and various 17th-c. Genoans, including Cambiaso, Fiasella, Strozzi, Grechetto, Guidobono, and De Ferrari). Upstairs are portraits of Genoan noblemen, painted by Van Dyck during his stay, and works by Dürer, Teniers, Ribera, Murillo, and Rigaud. Various other collections are on display, including coins, antique creches, and ceramics.

Palazzo Tursi** (*C4*). This magnificent late-16th-c. building, now Genoa's town hall, stands at n. 9 in Via Garibaldi. Among the noteworthy objects here are Paganini's violin and letters by Christopher Columbus, and the document of privileges bestowed upon him by the monarchs of Spain. The rest of Via Garibaldi is lined with splendid 16th-c. *buildings*.

Piazza Fontane Marose (*C4*). One of the loveliest squares in the monumental section of Genoa; note the 15th-c. Gothic *Palazzo Spinola* (*C4*), at n. 6, with white-and-black stripes, mullioned windows, and statues of the family, set in niches.

The Hill of Castello

All that remains of the old bishop's castle is the name, but this stroll takes you to the spot where the earliest Ligurian tribes first settled. The inlet below, the Mandraccio, since filled in, was the harbor for their trade with the Greeks of Marseille and the Etruscans.

Piazza Dante (*D4*). The setting of this square is pleasantly paradoxical: two tall buildings (1940) loom over two small structures. One of them is known as the *Home of Christopher Columbus*, an 18th-c. reconstruction of the birthplace of the great navigator; the other is the 12th-c. Romanesque *cloister of S. Andrea*. Behind this, set between two battlemented towers, is the 12th-c. **city gate of S. Andrea***, or **Porta Soprana** (*climb up to the towers, Sat. and Sun., 9-12 2:30-5:30*), leading to the ancient "acropolis," or Castello.

S. Donato* (*D3*). This Romanesque church was built in the 12th and 13th c.; note the octagonal bell tower. Inside is a fine triptych* by Joos van Cleve (ca. 1515).

Museo di Architettura e Scultura Ligure (*D3-4*). *Open, with entrance from Piazza Sarzano, 9-7; closed Sun. morn. and Mon.* This museum is located in the square cloister of **S. Agostino**; the church was built in the 13th c. and later rebuilt extensively, only to be heavily damaged by bombs in 1943, and once again reconstructed. The black-and-white-striped facade, with a portal and two twin-light mullioned windows, has a three-aisle interior, with chapels that belonged to the city's various crafts guilds. The museum (*being renovated*) features architectural fragments, sculptures, detached frescoes, and other items from Genoan churches and other buildings, dating from the 6th to the 18th c. Of particular note, relics of the funerary monument to Margherita di Brabante*. Also, a Mary Magdalene by A. Canova.

The Stradone S. Agostino takes you to *Piazza Sarzano*; from the so-called *Kiosk of Janus*, a public fountain set in an elegant 17th-c. six-sided aedicule, you can see the campanile of S. Agostino, with its polychrome roof.

S. Maria di Castello* (*D3*). Originally early Christian, it was rebuilt in the 12th c. and embellished during the 15th c., when the adjacent convent was built. The facade (restored) is Romanesque. *Inside*, noteworthy 15th-c. Lombard polyptych and 8th-c. Roman sarcophagus. Around the apse and along the right side of the church are the various rooms of the **Dominican convent** (*hours, tour of the cloisters and the loggias, 9-12 and 3:30-6*); in the *Loggia dell'Annunciazione*, above one of the two 15th-c. cloisters, fresco* by Giusto d'Alemagna (1451). In one small hall is the **Museo di S. Maria di Castello** (*open by request, enquire in the sacristy*) with various artworks that once hung or stood in the church or convent.

The **Tower of the Embriaci** (*D3*), which rises high atop the Salita degli Embriaci, was built in the 12th c., with stone ashlars and parapets. When all towers in Genoa were lopped short in 1296, only this one escaped.

Ss. Cosma e Damiano (*D3*). This church is a fine piece of Genoan Romanesque architecture, built in the late 11th c.

Via di Canneto il Lungo (*D3*). One of the loveliest little streets in the neighborhood, it was once the main street of the quarter, dotted with taverns and workshops. Note the medieval construction (at nos. 23, 14, and 16) and fine Renaissance portals with reliefs (at nos. 13, 15, 21, 27, 29, 16, and 31).

The 14th-c. Addizione di Ponente (Western Addition)

This part of Genoa, running along the curve of the port, between Porta dei Vacca and Porta Pré, was enclosed by walls in the 14th c. The palazzi of the Balbi family date from the 17th c.; Andrea Doria renovated his own,

just outside the old city walls, to the west, around this time.

SS. Annunziata del Vastato* (*B3*). This, the largest and most exquisite church in Genoa, built in the 16th c., was given its current facade in 1867; it was badly damaged in WWII. The interior is a fine piece of late Genoan Mannerism, with inlaid marble, stuccoes, and frescoes. The paintings on the altar form a gallery of Genoan art of the 17th c., with works by L. Cambiaso, the Carlone, B. Strozzi, G. Assereto, G. A. Ansaldo, and D. Piola. Fine wooden statues by Maragliano. Note the "Last Supper"* by G.C. Procaccini.

Via Balbi* (*B2-3*). Like Via Garibaldi, this street is lined with monumental aristocratic homes. The Balbi family built the street in the 17th c., and built their own homes here. Note n. 1, *Palazzo Durazzo Pallavicini*, 1618; and n. 5, *Palazzo dell'Università*, 1634-50.

Palazzo Reale* (*B2-3*). At n. 10 in Via Balbi, this great building dates from the 17th c.; Carlo Fontana built the double staircase and hanging garden overlooking the port. The halls upstairs, which contain the **Galleria di Palazzo Reale** (*open, 9-1:30*), give an idea of an aristocratic home in 18th-c. Genoa, with refined furnishings (note the hall of Veronese and the Galleria degli Specchi, or Hall of Mirrors). The artwork includes: Baroque sculptures; paintings by Tintoretto, Bassano, Van Dyck, L. Giordano, J. Roos, and the Bolognese school (Reni, Guercino) and the Genoan school (Strozzi, Grechetto); tapestries and Eastern ceramics.

Piazza Acquaverde (*A-B2*). This square features the train station of *Stazione di Principe* (1854) and a monument to *Christopher Columbus* (1846-62). Toward the water is the church of **S. Giovanni di Pré** (*B2; closed for restoration*), a mix of Romanesque and Gothic, 12th to 14th c. To its left, note the *Loggia dei Cavalieri Gerosolimitani* (12th to 16th c.), or *Commenda di Pré*.

Piazza del Principe (*B1*). Overlooking the port, facing the *Stazione Marittima* and the *Ponte dei Mille* (1926-30). You can take a motorboat tour of the port, departing from the Calata degli Zingari ("*Cooperativa Battellieri*," tel. 265712).

Palazzo Doria Pamphilij** (*B1*). This is one of the most remarkable and luxurious of Genoa's 15th-c. palazzi. Renovated by Andrea Doria from

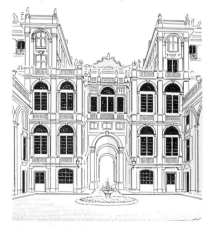

Genoa: Palazzo Reale

1529 to 1547; note the arcaded loggias, which adorn the long front facing Via S. Benedetto. Inside, frescoes and decorations by Perin del Vaga (1530); sumptuous stuccoes on the portico, Loggia degli Eroi, and the Sala dei Giganti, or Hall of Giants. In the garden (view from Via Adua), note the two 16th-c. fountains.

The Circonvallazione a Monte (Hillside Ring Road)

This route twists and turns over the hills, high above the gulf of the Porto Vecchio, along the late-19th-c. road from Piazza Acquaverde to Piazza Manin. This high section of the city — sunny and panoramic — was enclosed within city walls as early as the 17th c. These walls, the Mura Nuove, ran along the highest ridge of the astonishing natural arena above Genoa.

Circonvallazione a Monte. * This series of roads run along the spectacular slopes, in a section of modern homes.

Castello D'Albertis (*A2*). This building, erected in 1886 in neo-Romanesque style, stands at the end of Corso Ugo Bassi in a garden. It houses the *Museo di Archeologia ed Etnografia Extraeuropea* (*entrance from Corso Dogali n. 18; currently closed*), which focuses on American ethnography and pre-Columbian civilizations.

Part of the Circonvallazione a Monte, or Hillside Ring Road, Corso Firenze continues on around the huge 17th-c. *Albergo dei Poveri* (*A3*) and ends in Piazza G. Villa, beneath which lies the Spianata del **Castelletto** (*B4*), with a fine view* of city and sea. Further on, Corso Solferino, skirts the large park of the Neoclassical *Villa Grüber* (*B5*).

Museo Americanistico "Federico Lunardi" (*B5*). *Open, 9.30-12 and 3-5:30; closed Sun. morn. and Mon.* Located at Corso Solferino 29, in Villa Grüber, it features collections of pre-Columbian artifacts, especially of the classic Mayan culture (Honduras), and Central and South America. The museum also boasts a fine library, archives, and a collection of over 60,000 photographs.

Righi *. Genoans often take outings to this lovely spot, starting from Piazza Manin and climbing Via Cabella and Via Carso, or by funicular (15 minutes) from Largo della Zecca. The Righi (302 m.) offers a spectacular view* of city, gulf, valley of Bisagno with the Cemetery of Staglieno, and the quarter of Marassi, as well as the forts that dot the surrounding bluffs (the best view is from the terraces over the funicular station). An even broader view can be had from the *Peralto park*, slightly north and 60 m. higher, at the foot of the medieval *Fort Castellaccio*.

I **Forti**. The *Mura Nuove* are city walls, built in 1633, enclosing a triangle between S. Benigno and the mouth of the river Bisagno, along the shore, and running up the mountain slopes to point Sperone (489 m.). Later, forts were added (beside *fort Sperone, fort Puin*, 502 m., *Fratello Minore*, 622 m. and *Diamante*, 667 m.).

Villa Pallavicino delle Peschiere (*C5*). Possibly built by G. Alessi (1556), this is one of Genoa's finest and most intact set of villas, with a terraced garden. It is east of Via Assarotti, which runs down from Piazza Manin, terminus of the hillside ring road, to Piazza Corvetto.

Piazza Corvetto (*C4-5*). Set amongst the greenery of the Spianata dell'Acquasola and the Villetta Di Negro, this is a major traffic artery of the city; note the equestrian statue of Italian king Victor Emmanuel II (1886). West of the piazza is the entrance to the hillside *park of the Villetta Di Negro* (*C4*), with waterfalls, grottoes, and aviaries; at the entrance, a monument to Mazzini, 1882. The villa

itself was destroyed by Allied bombing in 1942, and the modern house that replaced it houses the city's **Museo "E. Chiossone"** * (*open 9-5; closed Sun. aft. and Mon.*), with its remarkable collections of Oriental art, assembled by the painter Edoardo Chiossone during the 30 years he lived in Tokyo (over 15,000 items), with later purchases as well. It offers a tour of the art and culture of the Far East, from 3,000 B.C. to the late 19th c. In the *section of large sculptures* of Japan, China, and Siam, note the Kamakura Buddha, the early Ming Buddha, and two 14th-c. Siamese busts of Buddha. The oldest painting here dates from the 11th c.; there are 17th- to 19th-c. prints, antique weapons (armor, swords, spears, daggers, and "tsubas," or saber sheaths), and masks, musical instruments, fabrics, enamels, ceramics, and lacquers. From the terrace, fine view* of city and harbor.

Spianata dell'Acquasola (*C-D5*). Public park east of Piazza Corvetto, built on the burial site for those who died of the plague of 1657; view of the Bisagno valley and eastern forts.

Via Roma (*C4*). This street runs straight down from Piazza Corvetto to Piazza De Ferrari. At the first building (n. 1), note the sumptuous 16th-c. portal, with courtyard; along the street runs the *Galleria Mazzini* (1880).

The Valle del Bisagno and the Hill of Carignano

Views of the newer section of Genoa, in a tour that includes its most luxurious street, neighborhoods built in the 1930s by covering over the last section of the Bisagno and the hill of Carignano.

Via XX Settembre (*D4-5*). This is the always crowded main avenue of modern Genoa, where the well-to-do and fashionable stroll, linking Piazza De Ferrari to Piazza della Vittoria, running beneath the 25-m.-high *Ponte Monumentale* (1895). Lined with porticoes, it runs past the church of S. Stefano, with its handsome neo-Gothic portico (1905) above which stands the church of S. Stefano.

S. Stefano * (*D5*). A mix of Romanesque and Gothic, this church was founded around 960, but the building — damaged during WWII and restored — probably dates from the 13th c. The facade has white-and-black stripes, with a Gothic portal and a rose window.

Piazza della Vittoria (*E5-6*). Set in the modern heart of eastern Genoa, this square is lined with symmetrical porticoed buildings. At the center stands the **Arco dei Caduti**, a military monument by Marcello Piacentini (1931), decorated with reliefs and statues. Nearby is the Piazza Verdi, with gardens, and the *Brignole train station* (*D6*), built in 1907; in the distance, the hills of the valley of Bisagno, topped by ancient fortifications.

Museo di Storia Naturale "G. Doria" (*E5*). *Open, 9-12 and 3-5:30, closed Mon. and Fri.* At n. 9 in Via Brigata Liguria, this museum's collections are mainly zoological in nature. A hall of paleontology, on the ground floor, features a huge skeleton of *Elephas antiquus italicus* and 11 halls of mammals; upstairs, 12 halls of birds, reptiles, fish, invertebrates, and minerals.

Circonvallazione a Mare. This seafront promenade offers a stroll along Corso Saffi (over the buildings of the *Fiera Internazionale*) and on along

Corso Quadrio (which runs beneath the medieval *walls of the Grazie*), then runs high over the rocky coast, offering fine views of the Porticciolo Duca degli Abruzzi, over the great dry docks, and the western section of Genoa (by bus, you can continue as far as Piazza Caricamento). In the gardens over the Fiera Internazionale is the **Museo di Villa Croce** (*F4, open, 9-5; closed Sun. aft. and Mon.; entrance from Via J. Ruffini, 3*), with international collections of abstract art, 1930-1980, and contemporary local artists.

Fiera Internazionale (*F4-5*). This international fair covers a huge landfill created between the Porticciolo Duca degli Abruzzi and the Foce, or mouth, of the Bisagno. Note the circular *sports hall* and the *conference center*.

S. Maria Assunta in Carignano* (*E4*). This handsome church looms over the hillside square. Built in the 16th c. by G. Alessi, it is one of Genoa's largest churches.

The Levante, or Eastern Section, from the Foce to Boccadasse

In 1874, six towns of the valley of Bisagno, to the east of the Mura Nuove, were added to Genoa, in a forerunner of the 1926 annexation of 19 towns created modern-day "Grande Genova," running from Voltri to Sant'Ilario. This route runs through the seaward section of the six towns of 1874 (Foce, San Francesco d'Albaro). Genoa absorbed an ancient network of gardens, villages, beaches, convents, and magnificent villas; many traces remain.

Passeggiata a Mare*. Comprising Corso Guglielmo Marconi and Corso Italia, this seafront promenade runs along the winding and sometimes rocky coast, looking down onto the sea; the view ranges from the promontory of Portofino to Capo Mele.

S. Giuliano d'Albaro. This small Gothic church stands amidst cypress trees on a little promontory. Founded in 1240, enlarged in the 15th c., it features fine old paintings and reliefs.

Lido d'Albaro. This popular meeting spot features bathing facilities, cafes, seaside terrace, pools, tennis courts, and "sferisterio," a sort of local pelota. At the end of Corso Italia is the charming marina of **Boccadasse***, lined with the houses of fishermen.

Via Albaro. Winding along the hill past gardens, villas, and homes. Along the way, note the **Villa Giustiniani Cambiaso*** (on the right, now Department of Engineering of the University of Genoa), a masterpiece by Alessi (1548). Further on, on the left, in Piazza Leopardi, is the 12th-c. church of **S. Maria del Prato** (*open by request, ask the nuns, at n. 4*); and nearby, the 14th-c. church of **S. Francesco d'Albaro**. The interior boasts fine frescoes.

Via Pozzo. At the beginning, on the right, note the huge 16th-c. **Villa Bombrini*** or Villa Paradiso, by Andrea Vannone, set in a garden, with two grand loggias. Via Pozzo doubles back on itself, offering fine views of Corso Buenos Aires and Via XX Settembre and the high section of Genoa.

Piazza Tommaseo. Over this square looms a *monument to Manuel Belgrano* (1927), a gift of the Italians of Argentina. Corso Buenos Aires links it directly to Piazza della Vittoria.

Cimitero di Staglieno*. You reach it by taking first Via Canevari and later Via Bobbio from Piazza Verdi through an industrial area along the banks of the Bisagno. Built from 1840 on, this hillside cemetery is famed for the lavish monuments and floral decorations; high on the hillside is the simple and austere *tomb of Giuseppe Mazzini.*

Gubbio*

elev. 522 m.; pop. 30,792; Umbria, province of Perugia. This town is grey with ancient stone, wedged into its high slope, from which it surveys plain and hills around it. Little lanes and stairways among the stern limestone houses link the main roads, running parallelel one above the other along the slope of Monte Ingino. This intact fragment of the distant past lies in NE Umbria; the waters of the river Carmignano run into the Chiascio and then into the Tiber.

Historical note. The "Tavole Eugubine," displayed in the Palazzo dei Consoli and written in an ancient Umbrian language with a mix of Etruscan and Latin letters, are relics of pre-Roman "Iguvium." A huge Roman theater at the foot of the city dates from the reign of Augustus. Little history survives from the High Middle Ages: ravaged by the Goths and recaptured by the Byzantines, Gubbio hosted Charlemagne on his return from his imperial coronation in Rome. Gubbio ruled itself from the 11th c. on, maneuvering amongst Guelphs and Ghibellines, often warring with Perugia, and attaining its height of wealth and power in the 14th c. It finally fell to the counts of Urbino (1384). Art flourished all the same, and around 1450, O. Nelli brought the style of international Gothic here; in the 16th c. Mastro Giorgio produced masterpieces in ceramics. From 1631 to 1860, Gubbio was ruled by the Papal State.

Places of interest. Piazza Quaranta Martiri. Dedicated to 40 townspeople killed in Nazi reprisals in 1944, this square opens out into the plain at the foot of town; now a park, originally a market place. Overlooked by the *church of S. Francesco* (see below), it is dominated from on high by the Palazzo dei Consoli, the long facade of the *Ospedale della Misericordia* (1326); surmounted by the *Loggia dei Tiratori* (1603), where cloth was once shaped and ironed.

S. Maria dei Laici. This small church, built in 1313, bounds the Ospedale della Misericordia. Note paintings by Gubbio-born F. Damiani and F. Barocci.

S. Francesco*. Part of a vast convent built in the mid-13th c., this church has a simple, unfinished facade, adorned with a Romanesque portal; note the twin portal and rose window on the left side, the 15th-c. campanile, and the three, original polygonal apses. In the majestic *interior*, note the 15th-c. frescoes by O. Nelli and the anonymous 14th-c. frescoes. In the convent, a notable *collection of art* (*open, by request*), with jewelry, paintings, and archeological finds.

Teatro Romano. Still used for performances, this ancient Roman amphitheater (1st c. A.D.) stands just outside *Porta degli Ortacci*, a gate in the medieval walls. The theater, one of the largest of its time, indicates Gubbio's rank under Augustus; not far off is the *Mausoleo*, a Roman tomb with barrel-vault ceiling.

S. Giovanni Battista. This 13th-c. church, with large Gothic portal and campanile, has a single-aisle interior, with diagonal arches, in a model common in Gubbio. Note panel by Perugino and 15th-c. majolica baptismal font.

Gubbio: Palazzo dei Consoli

Piazza della Signoria*. The ancient Piazza Grande, a vast manmade platform set on massive underpinnings, opens out like a terrace overlooking the rest of the town below, with a handsome view. On either side of the square are the impressive Palazzo dei Consoli and the unfinished 14th-c. **Palazzo Pretorio**, now Gubbio's Town Hall.

Palazzo dei Consoli**. *Open, Oct./mid-Mar., 10-1, 3-5; mid-Mar./Sep., 9-12:30, 3:30-6; closed Mon.* This is a noteworthy example of medieval public architecture; an elegant structure made of hewn blocks of local stone, surmounted by parapets and an elegant turret. It was built between 1332 and 1349, by A. da Orvieto, whose name appears above the main portal.

The **Museo Civico** and the **Pinacoteca Comunale** can be reached by climbing a lovely spreading staircase and passing through a Gothic portal. You will enter the *Sala Maggiore*, an enormous hall with a barrel-vault ceiling, used in public assemblies. Along the walls are numerous Roman and early medieval archeological finds. To the left is a small *chapel*, with exhibits of ancient local coins and the renowned "Tavole Eugubine*," seven slabs of bronze (3rd-/1st-c. B.C.) with inscriptions in the ancient Umbrian language, partly in Etruscan and partly in Latin characters. *Upstairs*, paintings by local artists including G. Palmerucci, O. Nelli, V. Nucci and F. Damiani, and other notable items.

Via Ducale. Climbing steeply among old buildings, this road runs past the 14th-c. *Palazzo dei Canonici*, with mullioned windows; note the enormous 16th-c. barrel preserved here. Intersecting this street, just before Palazzo Ducale, is the **Via Galeotti***, one of medieval Gubbio's most distinctive streets; note the second facade of *Palazzo Ranghiasci-Brancaleoni*.

Duomo*. Set on the highest point in the city, this cathedral was rebuilt in Gothic style on the site of the original Romanesque cathedral (of which a number of statues survive, surrounding the rose window) in the early 14th c. *Inside*, mention should be made of the 16th-c. Pietà, by D. Doni, a crèche by the school of Pinturicchio, a painting by S. Ibi (1507), the stalls of the choir, painted by B. Nucci, and the bishop's throne, carved by G. Maffei. From the portal in the fifth bay on the right, you can enter the refectory of the Palazzo dei Canonici, with a small *collection of art*.

Palazzo Ducale**. *Open, courtyard only, 9-2; holidays, 9-1*. Built, possibly by F. di Giorgio Martini, for Federico da Montefeltro, sometime after 1476. The great porticoed courtyard*, heart of the palazzo, is built in a noble Renaissance style, with a two-toned composition based on "pietra serena" and red brick. Note the exceedingly elegant windows on the top story.

Via dei Consoli*. This road is lined with late-medieval buildings; many have the "porta del morto," or "door of the dead," a narrow pointed door leading directly upstairs. In a square on the left, note the 16th-c. stone basin, called *Fontana dei Matti*; **Palazzo del Bargello** dates from 1302, and in the elegant stone front, note the window with carved casement.

S. Domenico. Located in Piazza Giordano Bruno, at the end of Via dei Consoli, and after crossing the Carmignano on the Ponte S. Martino (note view of medieval row houses along the mountain stream), this 14th-c. church has a simple, unfinished facade; inside, note paintings by local 14th-/15th-c. painters, including O. Nelli; in the apse, wooden choir (1593).

Palazzo del Capitano del Popolo. Take the handsome Via Vantaggi and Via Gabrielli, through a nearly intact medieval neighborhood, to this late-13th-c. building; upstairs, note the large Salone del Consiglio, with 16th-c. fireplace. Just outside the *Porta Metauro* is the church of *S. Croce della Foce*, with Passion Play during Holy Week (note statues of Christ and the Virgin in the main altar); inlaid gilt 16th-c. ceiling.

Via Baldassini*. Also lined by 13th-/14th-c. houses, the Palazzo dei Consoli, Piazza della Signoria — supported by four colossal arches — and the Palazzo Comunale loom over this street, with astonishing effect. Continuing along **Via Savelli della Porta**, you will see, at n. 16, *Palazzo della Porta*, with an elegant Renaissance portal.

S. Agostino. This 13th-c. church, with a brick facade dating from 1790, stands just outside *Porta Romana*, which cuts through the medieval town walls. Inside, frescoes by O. Nelli.

S. Pietro. This massive monastic complex was built before the year 1000, and rebuilt in the 13th and 16th c. The much rebuilt 13th-c. facade boasts a Romanesque portal; inside, note the monumental inlaid organ (1598), wooden 13th-c. Crucifix, and panel by R. del Colle (1510).

S. Maria della Piaggiola. This 17th-c. church, built to honor a painting by O. Nelli, can be reached by leaving Gubbio through *Porta Vittoria*.

Herculaneum (excavations of) / Ercolano** (scavi di)

elev. 18 m., Campania, province of Naples. Also located on the Gulf of Naples, though less universally renowned than the neighboring Pompeii, Herculaneum was overwhelmed by the same great eruption of Mt. Vesuvius, in A.D. 79. Unlike Pompeii, however, it was buried - not by a shower of ashes and lapilli - but by a flowing wall of mud and lava which submerged the town and then solidified, binding it in a dense blanket as hard as tufa-stone and from 12 to 25 meters in depth. Herculaneum is only a third the size of Pompeii; it is now an archeological site of equal impor-

Scavi di Ercolano 1:2000 (1 cm = 20 m)

NAPOLI km 9

TORRE DEL GRECO km 3

A3 km 1

Corso   *Ercolano*

Ingresso

Via Cortili

Decumano Massimo

Aula Superiore

Loggia

Casa del Salone I Nero

Casa del Bicentenario

Casa d. Bel Cortile

Casa dei due Atrii

Casa dii Nettuno

Casa d. Atrio Corinzio

Cardine IV

Cardine III

Palestra

Piscina

Casa del Mobilio carbonizzato

Casa d. Sacello di legno

Aula Absidata

Casa d. Telaio

Casa con giardino

Pistrinum

Terme

Casa di Galba

Casa d. Gran Portale

Casa Sannitica

Vestibolo Palestra

Decumano   Inferiore

Cardine IV

Cardine V

Pistrinum

Casa d. Tramezzo di legno

Casa d. Colonnato

Molo

Giardino

Casa d. Scheletro

Casa d. Erma di bronzo

Casa d'Alcova

Casa d. Genio

Casa del Rilievo di Telefo

Casa dell'Albergo

Casa dell'Atrio a mosaico

Casa dei Cervi

Casa d. Gemma

Casa d'Argo

Casa di Aristide

Sacelli

Area Sacra

Sepolcro di M. Nonio Balbo

Terme Suburbane

Via Mare

tance, but it has somewhat different characteristics. Herculaneum was more of a residential town; Pompeii more of a market town. The modern town has preserved, in its 18th-c. villas, the heritage of the town's first rebirth as a holiday spot.

Historical note. This renowned vacation resort for wealthy Romans and Campanians, with its charming location high over a promontory, was founded by the ancient Greeks. As punishment for its participation in the last uprising of the Italic tribes against Rome, Herculaneum was taken by storm in 89 B.C. by an army under Sulla. Damaged by the great earthquake in A.D. 62, the now-Roman Herculaneum was overwhelmed by the eruption

of A.D. 79 before reconstruction could be completed. The recent discovery of over 150 skeletons and a charred boat provides documentation that some of the people of Herculaneum headed down to the seashore in hope of getting away by water. Here, because of the tidal surge caused by the eruption, they were trapped and engulfed by the wall of lava and mud. The city thus vanished forever, and the land atop the blanket of tufa-like stone was partly settled by the present-day town of Resina; in 1969 Resina itself took the name of Ercolano (Herculaneum). All the same, folk tradition still told of the town that lay buried beneath, and in 1709 General D'Elboeuf, an Austrian prince, uncovered part of a wall of a scaena of the ancient theater, while sinking a well on land he owned there. He carried on excavations and removed statues and marble facings which finally were scattered among the museums of Europe, especially the museum of Dresden. Regular excavations were undertaken in 1738 by order of Carlo III of Bourbon, and continued until 1766 with the system of the "cunicoli," narrow tunnels dug to extract objects of interest, and then filled in again. It was not until 1828-1835 that a system of completely uncovering the excavation finally allowed scholars to form some idea of the urban layout of Herculaneum; beginning in 1927, a systematic project of excavation and restoration was pursued.

Places of interest. The **excavations****. *(open: 9-one hour prior to sunset).* The excavations cover only a minor section of the ancient city; it extends beneath the houses of the modern settlement (the excavations to the north, in fact, near the Forum, are blocked by the houses that stand above.

If the large public works that have been uncovered tend to follow a traditional layout, the types of residential structures vary widely. For example, villas of the upper classes, built on a single level with the usual succession of atrium-tablinum-triclinium, and inhabited by a single family were adjoined - particularly during the later life of the settlement - by smaller apartments that occupied a number of stories, built to take best advantage of the land available for construction and to maximize the interior space in much the same way as has been documented in Ostia. Like at Pompeii, in this archeological area as well, the ongoing efforts to restore the surviving houses and the job of consolidating the trenches surrounding the ancient city in some cases prevent the public from being able to view all of the houses and public complexes.

The most important sites are: on the Cardo IV, the *Casa dell'Atrio a Mosaico** (D2), the *Casa del Tramezzo di Legno** (C2), the *Casa Sannitica** (C2) from pre-Roman times, the *Terme*** (B-C1-2), the *Casa di Nettuno e Anfitrite** (B2); alongside it stands the best-preserved shop to survive, the *Casa del Bicentenario*** (B2); on the Cardo V, the *Palestra*** (B3) with a remarkable bronze fountain*, the *Casa dei Cervi*** (D2), one of the richest and most sumptuous houses, the *Casa del Rilievo di Telefo** (D3), the *Casa della Gemma** (D3) and the *Terme Suburbane*** (D3).

Ischia (Island of)

pop. 16,013, Campania, province of Naples. "The history of Italy comes from the sea," wrote Sabatino Moscati. Ischia (Pithecusa, as the Greeks called it) was a key site in this history. Archeologists confirm the traditional date of Greek colonization (775 B.C.), the earliest in Italy; also present were the Phoenicians.

Ischia, the main town on the island, lies at the NE extremity, and has two sections: *Ischia Porto* and *Ischia Ponte*: in the former, the inner harbor — where most of the ferries dock — is formed from an ancient volcanic crater, linked to the sea by a channel dug in 1854.

Follow Via Roma — with cafes, resaurants, and shops — and the successive Corso V. Colonna to reach the fishing village of Ischia Ponte. Take the Aragonese bridge (1438) to the little island of the castle (*Mar.- Oct.; elevator*). High atop it is the **Castello**, old but heavily renovated.

In the Piazza at **Lacco Ameno**, the sanctuary of S. Restituta comprises two churches: the smaller of the two dates from the 11th century and stands on the site of an early Christian basilica whose remains lie under the church; under the sacristy there is a **Museum** containing finds from the Bronze Age to Byzantine times, Greek kilns and ceramics laboratories (7th/2nd c.B.C.).

L'Aquila 1:12 000 (1 cm = 120 m)

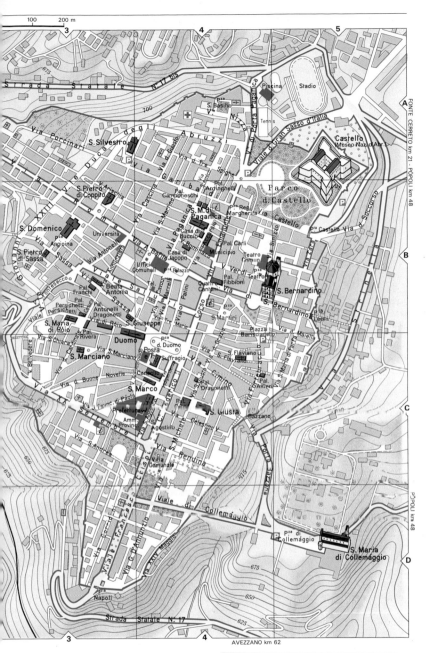

In the town of **Forìo**, the church of *S. Maria di Loreto*, built in the 14th c. but converted to the Baroque style, has a decoration of marble; the cylindrical *tower* (15th c.) formed of a system of defense against pirates; there are numerous springs yielding mineral water, and beaches, such as Spiaggia di Chiaia and Spiaggia di Citarra.

Sant'Angelo is an enchanting little fishing village, with many-colored houses arranged along stepped walkways (*cars not allowed*). Taxi boats will take to the Spiaggia dei Maronti, a pleasant beach, or to the Fumarole (hot springs).

L'Àquila*

elev. 714 m.; pop. 66,813; Abruzzo, regional capital. This ancient city, set high against the Gran Sasso d'Italia, abounds in lovely images: the corners and angles of the 16th-c. castle built by the Spanish Viceroy, Don Pedro de Toledo; the white-and-red blocks that checker the Romanesque facade of the church of S. Maria di Collemaggio, bound up with the life of the hermit, Pietro da Morrone, later pope as Celestine V, who lies in eternal rest in the classic 15th-c. church of S. Bernardino, built by Cola dell'Amatrice; lastly, the Fontana delle 99 Cannelle, or Fountain of 99 Spouts, which honored the city's original abundance (99 castles, 99 neighborhoods, 99 churches, 99 squares...). Rich in monuments, survivor of many earthquakes, L'Aquila is the greatest — if not the largest — city in the region of Abruzzo.

Historical note. At the base of the hill on which the city now stands are numerous fresh springs, which attracted the first settlement, called "Acculae." But what we now know as L'Aquila dates back only to the 13th c., after Pope Gregory IX called on the local population, in rebellion against the feudal power of the Pope's enemy, Holy Roman Emperor Frederick II, to unite their scattered castles into a single town. In 1254 the city was founded; destroyed by Frederick's successor, Manfred, it was rebuilt after 1266, with the arrival in Italy of Charles of Anjou. L'Aquila was said to boast 99 quarters, or "rioni," for each of the 99 surrounding castles. The number belongs to the realm of legend, but it was probably not unrealistically excessive. Arranged along the steeply hilly grid of the 13th-c. city, and running along the modern Corso Vittorio Emanuele, L'Aquila had been completely enclosed in walls by 1316, and just a few decades later its population of nearly 60,000 made it second only to Naples in southern mainland Italy. The city prospered (its trades included saffron, wool, silk, leather, and lace), and coined its own money until 1556, finally falling under Spanish dominion. Periodic rebellions, terrible epidemics, and ruinous earthquakes (a particularly violent one hit in 1703) laid the city low. Only in recent decades has L'Aqila again begun to swell in population; its magnificent walls have suffered from this recent growth.

Getting around. In the historical center, partly closed to cars, we recommend two routes, both starting from Piazza del Duomo. The first one returns here, after a circular walk. The second one can be walked as shown on the map, but extends outside the city walls in two different directions, for considerable distances. We recommend driving, first west, to the Fontana delle 99 Cannelle, then east, to the church of S. Maria di Collemaggio.

Piazza del Duomo and the northern quarters

This route runs through the old part of town, with fine views of the surrounding mountains. Aside from the main sights, including the church of S. Bernardino and the Museo Nazionale d'Abruzzo, the stroll is lined with lesser architectural jewels.

Piazza del Duomo (*C4*). At the heart of the city, adorned by two fountains and the site of a daily market. Overlooking it is the **Duomo** (*B-C3-4*), rebuilt after 1703, with a neoclassical facade. Inside, note the Agnifili Tomb, by S. dell'Aquila, an early Christian sarcophagus, bas-reliefs by G. de' Rettori, a painting by F. da Montereale, and a handsome view painting by V. Mascitelli.

Chiesa del Suffragio (*C4*). *Open, by request, tel. 22277.* On the south side of the square, its proudest treasure is in the apse: a 17th-c. polyptych by F. and G. C. Bedeschini. To the right, alongside the church, runs Via dei Ramieri, ending at a row of 15th-c. warehouses, called the *Cancelle*.

Corso Vittorio Emanuele (*B4*). The city's main street is a partly porticoed pedestrian mall. Midway along it is the intersection of the *Quattro Cantoni*; note the 15th-c. *Palazzo Fibbioni*, and a 14th-c. *tower*, whose bells chime 99 times, two hours after sunset, to honor the 99 castles that helped build L'Aquila.

S. Bernardino** (*B4-5*). Towering high above the city, this church was built in 1454-72, and largely rebuilt following the earthquake of 1703. The majestic facade, built by C. dell'Amatrice in 1540, is still intact. *Inside*, note: the handsome gilt carved Baroque ceiling*; the spectacular Baroque organ, built by B. Mosca; the terracotta altar-piece* by A. della Robbia; and the tombs of St. Bernardino* and Maria Pereira*, both by S. dell'Aquila.

Porta Leoni (*B5*). At the end of Via di S. Bernardino, this gate dates from the late-13th c., and is the city's oldest.

Castello* (*A-B5*). Surrounded by a large park, and offering a splendid view of the Gran Sasso d'Italia, this powerful square fort, with stout bastions, is surrounded by a deep moat. It was built by the Spanish, from 1530, until 1635, and constituted cutting-edge technology in the use of, and defense against, firearms. A monumental portal on the SE side leads into the **Museo Nazionale d'Abruzzo** (*open 9-2; Sun. 9-1*), which includes archeological, paleontological, and artistic collections. The *archeological collection* features Italic and Roman artifacts; noteworthy calendar, from the site of "Amiternum" (after A.D. 25). The *collections of art* include works by mostly local artists, ranging from the 12th to the 18th c. Among those artists are: S. dell'Aquila, N. di Buonaccorso, I. del Fiore, A. De Litio, P. Cesura, F. da Montereale, G. C. Bedeschini, L. Finson, L. Lombard, A. Mytens, C. Ruther, M. Preti, S. Conca, F. Solimena, F. De Mura. Note the processional cross* by N. da Guardiagrele (1434). Modern artists include R. Guttuso, G. Capogrossi, and D. Cantatore. Also, note the striking reconstruction of an ancestor of modern elephants, the *Archidiskodon meridionalis vestinus* (1.5 million years old), unearthed near the city in 1954.

S. Maria di Paganica (*B4*). Completed in 1308, and repeatedly ravaged by earthquakes, this church boasts a handsome carved Gothic portal (18th-c. interior). A stroll around the church includes three *palazzi* (*Ardinghelli, Camponeschi, and Carli*) and two medieval houses (*Casa di Buccio and Casa di Jacopo di Notar Nanni*).

S. Silvestro (*A3-4*). This 14th-c. church has a simple facade with a handsome portal and rose window. Inside, the central apse boasts remarkable 15th-c. frescoes. Note paintings by F. da Montereale and G. C. Bedeschini (copy; original now in the Prado, Madrid).

S. Pietro di Coppito (*B3*). Built around 1300-1350, and often restored, the carved architrave over the portal is one of the few original features of this medieval church. Inside, note the 14th-c. frescoes and the badly damaged frescoes of St. George (right and left apses).

S. Domenico (*B3*). Set in a steep, largely intact part of the medieval city, this church was rebuilt after the terrible earthquake of 1703; all that survived were the bottom of the facade, the right wall, and part of the apse.

Follow **Via Sassa** (*B3*).

The southern quarters and S. Maria di Collemaggio

This route includes two of L'Aquila's best known monuments, the Fontana delle 99 Cannelle and the church of S. Maria di Collemaggio, but also runs through areas such

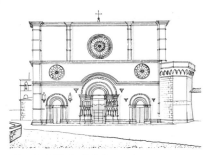

L'Àquila: S. Maria di Collemaggio

as the medieval quarter between Via Fortebraccio and Porta Bazzano, with its stepped lanes.

S. Maria di Roio (*B3*). First built in the 15th c., and rebuilt after 1703, this church is surrounded by notable *palazzi* (*Antonelli-Dragonetti, Persichetti, and Rivera*).

Fontana delle 99 Cannelle* (*B2*). A symbol of the city, this fountain has a spout and mascaron for each of the castles that reputedly helped found the city seven centuries ago. Originally built in 1272, the fountain has been heavily rebuilt over the years.

S. Marciano (*C3*). The lower section of the facade, with the elegant carved portal, is all that survives of the 14th-c. church.

S. Marco (*C4*). Built in the 14th c. and rebuilt extensively in 1750, note the original portals on the facade and right side; also note the Virgin and Child high in the facade, and another version, in wood, inside.

S. Giusta (*C4*). Begun in 1257, its solemn facade dates from 1349, with a handsome portal and Gothic rose window. Inside, note the gilt-wood main altar and inlaid Gothic choir; also, 15th-c. fresco of Virgin and Child. Around it are *Palazzo Centi* and *Palazzo Dragonetti* (*open, Tue. and Thu., 9-1 and 3-5*).

Follow **Via Fortebraccio** (*C4*).

S. Maria di Collemaggio** (*D5*). This outstanding monument of Abruzzese architecture stands just outside the Porta Bazzano, In a lovely setting. Begun in 1287, on the site of a miraculous vision of the Virgin Mary, at the behest of the hermit Pietro da Morrone, immortalized by Dante as the pope "of the great refusal," Celestine V; crowned pontiff in this church in 1294, he abdicated, making way for Dante's nemisis, Boniface VIII. The magnificent, early-14th-c. facade is adorned by white and pink blocks of stone, arranged in geometric patterns; of the three rose windows and portals, note the central one. Also, note the Porta Santa*, on the left side. The huge, three-aisled *interior* was restored in 1972-74. On the walls, 15th-c. votive frescoes, a polychrome terracotta Virgin and Child, and paintings by C. Ruther; note the tomb of S. Pietro Celestino* (1517).

Lecce*

elev. 49 m., pop. 100,491, Puglia, provincial capital. As Mannerist art and architecture gave way to Baroque, Lecce developed its own variant, virtually an original creation due to the city's isolation: the so-called "Leccese Baroque," a welter of spectacular decor, especially on the exterior

of buildings: spiral columns, outsized cornices, curving pediments, or mixtilinear, or curlicued, festoons, swag, vases full of flowers or fruit, ribbons bedecked with putti, mascarons, and caryatids. In any case, a world of spectacular architecture, making the historic center of the city entirely unique.

Places of interest. The **Piazza del Duomo*** (*D2*) is a harmonious and spectacular Baroque setting. The magnificent **Palazzo del Seminario*** (Giuseppe Cino, 1709) encloses an interior courtyard with a lovely Baroque puteale. To the left of the *Palazzo Vescovile* (1632), with a light loggia along the front, is the **Duomo***, rebuilt (1659-70) by Giuseppe Zimbalo known as Zingarello, with a spectacular facade along the side and a slender campanile* (1682); inside, note spiral columns and excellent paintings.

At **Piazza Castromediano** (*C2-3*), extending behind the partly 18th-c. *Municipio*, or town hall, note the church of the **Gesù**, dating from 1579 (lavish altars in the transept and the apse; noteworthy canvases).

S. Croce** (*C3*). Further along, note the Basilica di S. Croce (1548-1646), considered to be the most exquisite creation of Leccese Baroque; the facade was the creation of G. Riccardi (lower part), A. Zimbalo (central part) and G. Zimbalo (upper part); the pure and understated interior* is by Riccardi. To the left of the church and the **Palazzo del Governo*** is the former Celestine convent, the facade is by G. Zimbalo and G. Cino, while the enormous courtyard is by Riccardi, completed by G. Zimbalo.

To the east of the Duomo, the Baroque church of **S. Chiara** is attributed to Cino (1694). Not far off is the Roman theater (*D2*), possibly dating from the reign of Hadrian.

Another typical creation of the Pugliese Baroque is the church of **S. Matteo**, by Achille Carducci (1667-1700).

Two other interesting works of Leccese Baroque, lastly, are the **church of the Rosario** (*D1*), the last creation by G. Zimbalo, with odd inventions dotting the elaborate facade and spectacular altars on the interior, and the **church of the Carmine** (*D-E2*), rebuilt by Cino (1717).

The center of the Città Vecchia (old town) is the **Piazza S. Oronzo***, where the *Column of S. Oronzo* stands; it is considered to be one of the two columns that once marked the terminus of Via Appia (Appian Way) at Brindisi; it was erected here in 1666; the square is partly filled with the excavations of the Roman amphitheater* from the 2nd c. A.D. Overlooking the curve of the amphitheater is the *Palazzo del Seggio*, or *Palazzo del Sedile* (1592), the ancient seat of Communal government; alongside is the little former church of *S. Marco* (1543).

The **Castello** (*D3*), with a trapezoid plan and corner lancet bastions, was built at the behest of Emperor Charles V (1539-48).

The **Museo Provinciale Sigismondo Castromediano*** (*E2; open, 9-1:30 and 2:30-7:30; Sun. 9-1; closed Sat.*) is split up into three sections: the *Antiquarium*, with a notable collection of Messapic, Apulian, and Attic vases (*trozzelle*), terracottas and bronzes; the *topographic section*, with exhibits concerning towns of the ancient Salento (note

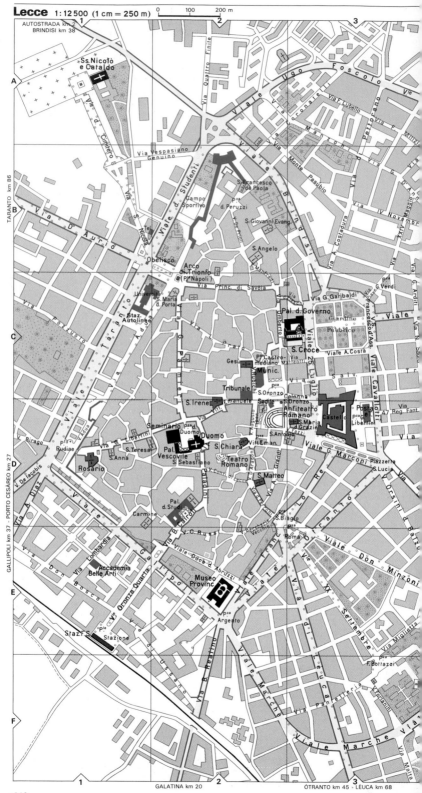

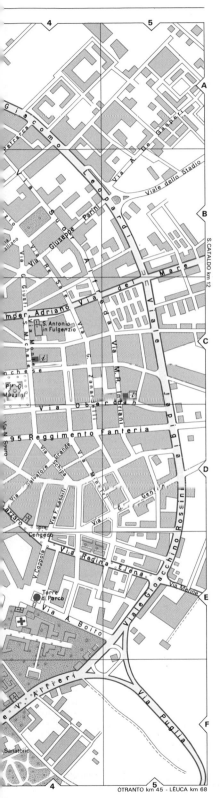

the sculptures from the local Roman theater); the *Pinacoteca*, with paintings from the Venetian, Roman, and Neapolitan schools; and work by artists and sculptors from the Salento, evangelaries in copper and enamel, 17th-18th c. ceramics from manufactories in the Abruzzi and local manufactories, Murano glass, and ivory.

The **Arco di Trionfo** (triumphal arch; *B-C2*) was built in 1548 for Charles V. Nearby, in the park of the *Palazzo Palmieri* (18th c.), a Greco-Messapic hypogaeum from the 4th c. B.C. (*not open to tourists*; plaster casts in the Museo Provinciale).

In the enclosure of the cemetery, the **church of the Ss. Nicolò e Cataldo*** (*A1*): founded by Tancred (1180), in a style that shows clear influence from the Burgundian Romanesque, with a facade rebuilt by G. Cino (1719), with an earlier portal* with fascias of floral arabesques, in a clearly Islamic style (12th c.); on the *interior*, note the three aisles, with a cupola in the middle of the nave, frescoes dating from the 15th c. to the 17th c.; 16th-c. cloister with Baroque aedicule set on spiral columns.

In Via Monte S. Michele 4 (*C4*), note the **Museo Missionario Cinese** (*open Tue., Thu. and Sat. 9-12 and 5-7*), a museum of missionary expeditions to China.

Surrounding areas. At a distance of 3 km. SW are the **excavations of Rudiae**, a Messapic town that later became Roman, and then was destroyed in the 12th c.; the birthplace of Ennius, the Latin poet. Note a number of buildings from Roman times, stretches of paved ancient road, Messapic tombs, the ruins of a small amphitheater, and remnants of city walls.

At a distance of 12.5 km. NE, facing the Rada di **San Cataldo**, is the beach of Lecce, with ruins of the *Roman port*, built by Hadrian.

At a distance of 5.7 km. south, **San Cesario di Lecce**: in the *Palazzo Ducale*, there is a notable collection of contemporary art (*8-11 and 4-7*), with work by the sculptor Aldo Calò, born here.

Also worthy of note is the **Abbey of Santa Maria di Cerrate** and the Salentine peninsula.

Lucca▲▲

elev. 19 m.; pop. 87,100; Tuscany, provincial capital. The marble sleep of the lovely and somber statue of Ilaria del Carretto, carved by J. della Quercia, in the church of S. Martino, seems a perfect symbol for this dignified and lovely city, enveloped in its proud past. Lucca is a thriving and modern town, but it jealously preserves the timeless image of the ancient city enclosed within its red walls. It stands on the left bank of the Serchio, in an exceedingly fertile alluvial plain, enclosed between the Apennine slopes of the Pizzorne and the Monte Pisano, in a landscape of olive groves and looming hills.

Historical note. The walls of Lucca, transformed two centuries ago into a pleasant tree-lined promenade, were built between 1504 and 1645, and were never used in the city's defense. Earlier walls had withstood Florentine assaults, but in time Lucca and Florence learned to live in peace and prosperity. The clearest legacy of the Roman city is the elliptical shape of the amphitheater in Piazza Mercato, oddly reflected in the shapes of the medieval houses. Tall tower-houses and narrow winding lanes are mementoes of the Middle Ages, along with large Romanesque buildings, constructed as Lucca began to

213

acquire wealth in the 12th c. The silk trade thrived here, along with banking, though the 14th c. brought huge bank failures and widespread internecine wars, followed by the rule of seigneurs. After the rule of Uguccione della Faggiuola, Castruccio Castracani, and a few others, however, Lucca regained her freedom in 1369, virtually without interruption for four centuries. Lucca never welcomed either Inquisition or Jesuits, and during the Counter Reformation, Lucca, with Venice, was the site of printshops that violated the prohibitions of the Church's Index. In 1805 Napoleon gave Lucca to his sister Elisa; in 1817, it fell to the Bourbons of Parma. Since becoming part of Tuscany in 1847, and part of Italy in 1860, Lucca has turned to trade in olive oil and fabrics.

Getting around. Much of the city within the walls is closed to traffic; tourists heading for hotels, however, are allowed through. The routes recommended are walking routes; no car is needed. You should leave your car outside the walls, or park it for a fee.

The monumental center

Piazza Napoleone, a square whose name reveals its date of foundation, was built at the same time as the tree-lined avenues along the walls; note the unrivalled monument of the church of Ss. Giovanni e Reparata and the Duomo; the narrow, attractive streets of the heart of Lucca.

Piazza Napoleone (*C2*). This vast square, lined with plane trees, is adorned by a Neoclassical monument to the duchess Maria Luisa, by L. Bartolini (1843). It is flanked by the **Palazzo della Provincia**, begun in 1578 by B. Ammannati, interior by L. Nottolini, who also built the spectacular, stucco-adorned staircase* (19th c.).

Ss. Giovanni e Reparata* (*C3*). *Open 10-1 and 2:30-5; closed Mon.* Built in the 12th c. and rebuilt in the 17th c., this church still has its original portal (1187). Recent archeological excavations (1969-90) have uncovered a series of fascinating structures.

Beneath the church, you can take an archeological tour.

Piazza S. Martino (*C3*). With the adjacent *Piazza Antelminelli*, this square forms a handsome medieval setting, dominated by the marble Duomo (see below) and bounded by low houses: left, *Palazzo Bernardi*, by B. Ammannati (1556); right, against the campanile, the typ-

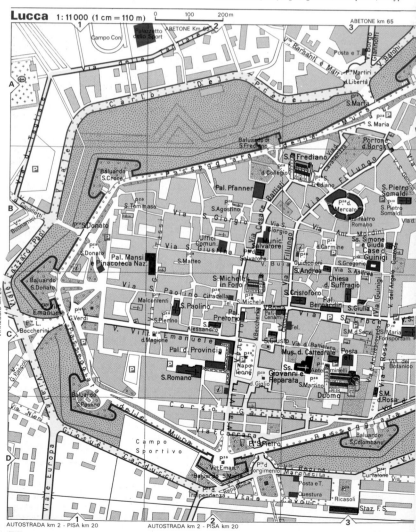

ically medieval-Lucchese *Casa dell'Opera del Duomo* (13th c.).

Duomo** (*C3*). Dedicated to St. Martin, this is Lucca's main church. It was built in Romanesque style in the 11th to 13th c., but the interior was rebuilt in the 14th/15th c. The remarkable asymmetrical marble Romanesque facade* (1204), largely by G. da Como, comprises a portico supported by three broad arches and three orders of small light loggias, with polychrome encrustations and small varied columns; on the right is a stout 13th-c. campanile, adorned with parapets. Under the portico, note the reliefs*, begun in 1233, by a Lombard Master; the reliefs of the left portal are attributed to N. Pisano; the doors of the central portal were carved by M. Civitali (1497). The sides of the cathedral date from the 14th c.; note the impressive apse*, which shows late Pisan influence. The elegant Gothic *interior*, features sculptures and paintings by artists including M. Civitali, F. Zuccari, Tintoretto, D. Ghirlandaio, P. di Noceto, D. Bertini da Gallicano, Giambologna, F. Juvarra, and

Fra' Bartolomeo. In the center of the second chapel of the *left transept*, is the justly renowned **funerary monument to Ilaria del Carretto****, masterpiece by J. della Quercia (1408), and one of the finest pieces of 15th-c. Italian sculpture.

Museo della Cattedrale (*C3*). *Open 10-1 and 2:30-5:30; closed Mon.* In Piazza Antelminelli, this museum features religious treasures from the Duomo and the church of Ss. Giovanni e Reparata, including: a 14th-c. Flemish reliquary, a painting by F. Marti, and a handsome gilt cross, called the Croce dei Pisani*. Note the paintings and sculpture from the Duomo, by J. della Quercia and Masseo Civitali.

S. Maria della Rosa (*C3*). Directly behind the *Palazzo Arcivescovile*, or Archbishop's palace, this church was originally a Pisan-Gothic oratory (1309). Renaissance portal by Matteo Civitali; inside, fragments of the 2nd-c. B.C. Roman walls. From the nearby *Baluardo S. Colombano* (*D3*), at the end of Via della Rosa, fine view of the Duomo.

Via Guinigi* (*B-C3*). Among the most attractive of Lucca's roads, this one still seems medieval. Note the **Case dei Guinigi***, a compact set of 14th-c. towers and brick houses; note the palazzo at the corner of Via S. Andrea, and the tower topped by holm-oaks (entrance from Via S. Andrea; you can climb the tower, *Mar.-Sep., 9-7:30; Oct., 10-6; Nov.-Feb., 10-4:30*).

Ss. Simone e Giuda (*B3*). This small 13th-c. church overlooks Via Guinigi; it has a simple grey stone facade, with three portals and an elegant window. In Via S. Andrea, after the entrance to the Torre Guinigi (see above), is the 13th-c. church of *S. Andrea* (*B3*); facing it is the late-14th-c. *Casa Gentili*.

Piazza del Salvatore (*B2*). In the square are a Neoclassical fountain by L. Nottolini, the medieval *Torre del Veglio*, and the 13th-c. *church of Misericordia*; note fine reliefs.

Piazza S. Michele* (*C2*). On the site of the Roman forum, this square is a pulsing center of life in Lucca; surrounded by 13th-c. buildings, its focal point is the marble church of S. Michele in Foro (see below); at the corner of Via V. Veneto is the *Palazzo Pretono*, begun in 1492, possibly by Matteo Civitali, and enlarged in 1588 by V. Civitali. Around the corner, in Via di Poggio, is the *birthplace of G. Puccini (open, Apr.-Sep., 10-6; closed Mon.)*.

S. Michele in Foro** (*C2*). This church was built between 1143 and the 14th c., and is an outstanding example of Pisan-Lucchese architecture. The tall facade is surmounted by four orders of little loggias, with a lavish decoration* of marble inlay; note the colossal Romanesque statue of the Archangel Michael; low on the right corner is a statue of the Virgin with Child, by M. Civitali (1480). The left side, with its pronounced arches and 14th-c. loggia, is particularly handsome. Note also the stout campanile, decorated with small arches; and the Pisan-influenced apse*.

The *interior* features frescoes, terracottas, paintings, and marble reliefs by such artists as G. di Simone, A. della Robbia, Filippino Lippi, A. Marti, and R. da Montelupo.

S. Paolino (*C2*). In a wide spot in the Via S. Paolino is this church, with a marble facade and handsome sides; begun in 1522 by B. da Montelupo on the site of a huge Roman building, it was completed in 1536, and is Lucca's

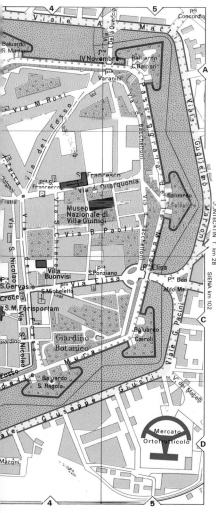

only example of a Renaissance church. *Inside*, note two holy-water fonts by N. Civitali, a painted wooden sculpture by F. Valdambrino (1414), choir chancels by N. and V. Civitali, 14th-c. painted wooden Crucifix, a 15th-c. panel of the Coronation of the Virgin, with a depiction of medieval Lucca, and a panel by A. Marti.

Palazzo Mansi* (*B-C2*). *Open 9-7; Sun., 9-2; closed Mon.* At n. 43 in Via Galli Tassi, the Pinacoteca Nazionale occupies a 17th-c. building with a handsome loggiaed courtyard. The interior is largely intact, with 18th-c furnishings. Note the *Salone della Musica*, frescoed in 1688 by G. G. Del Sole, and the *Camera degli Sposi**, with silk embroideries, stuccoes, and gilded inlaid wood; Flemish tapestries (1665).

The **Pinacoteca Nazionale** possesses paintings, from Italy and elsewhere, dating from the Renaissance to the early 18th c., arranged so as to imitate the collection of the Guardaroba Mediceo, a gift made to Lucca by Leopoldo II. Particularly noteworthy, among the *Tuscan paintings*, are works by: Beccafumi, Bronzino, V. Salimbeni, Pontormo, A. del Sarto; among the painters from other schools, mention should be made of: Veronese, J. Bassano, Ligozzi, school of Tintoretto, S. Rosa, R. da Tivoli, J. Sustermans, Barocci, Zacchia the Elder, C. Dolci, Domenichino, Borgognone, G. Reni, P. Brill, J. Miel, G. Terborch, L. Carlevarijs, and D. Calvaert.

On the **third floor**, two more sections are dedicated to 19th-c. artists from Lucca, among them: P. Batoni, B. and P. Nocchi, A. Tofanelli, and M. Ridolfi, and to *historic fabrics*, dating back to the 16th c., especially damasks, a local specialty. Note the *Tongiorgi collection* of 6th/10th-c. Coptic fabrics.

S. Romano (*C2*). This 13th-c. church has traces of its Gothic appearance (on the sides, especially) and a lively apse (1373). Inside, note the tomb* by Masseo Civitali (1490).

S. Alessandro (*C2*). This notable piece of early Lucchese Romanesque (11th c.) has a marble facade, a 13th-c. apse, and, inside, handsome Romanesque and re-used capitals (3rd/4th-c.).

S. Frediano
and the northern quarters

Via Fillungo, the medieval backbone of the historical center; note the handsome facade of the church of S. Frediano; the unique oval of Piazza del Mercato; the unrivalled treasures of Lucchese art, displayed in the Museo di Villa Guinigi.

S. Giusto (*C2*). Overlooking the Piazza S. Giusto, this late-12th-c. Romanesque church has a marble facade and a stuccoed interior.

Via del Battistero (*C3*). This handsome street runs from Piazza S. Giusto, passing by the 16th-c. *Palazzo Tegrimi Mansi*, at the corner of Via S. Donnino.

Via Fillungo* (*B-C3*). This main street of the historic center of Lucca is lined with fine shops but still has a medieval look, with old houses and towers. First, note the early-16th-c. *Palazzo Cenami* (*C2-3*), by N. Civitali, and, across from it, the 13th-c. Pisan-style church of **S. Cristoforo** (*C3*), with portal and rose window. At n. 43 is the 13th-c. *Casa Barletti Baroni*, with mullioned windows with terracotta casements; note the 13th-c. *Torre delle Ore*.

Via C. Battisti (*B2-3*). This winding street is lined with fine 17th-/18th-c. palazzi, ending with the startling presence of the large crenelated campanile* of S. Frediano (see below). At n. 33, **Palazzo Controni-Pfanner** (*B2*), 1667, with outside staircase* and 18h-c. statue-bedecked garden.

S. Frediano** (*B3*). Built in 112-47 and renovated in the 13th c., this church has a simple and noble facade, with a small loggia with architrave, surmounted by a Byzantine-style mosaic*. The lovely *interior*, with three aisles, ancient columns, and vast apse, features artwork by A. Aspertini, the Maestro del Tondo Lathrop, A. della Robbia, Matteo Civitali, F. Francia, and Masseo Civitali. Note the richly carved 12th-c. Romanesque font*, at the foot of the *right aisle*. In the *left aisle*, note the funerary slabs of L. Trenta and wife. In the *presbytery*, 12th-c. Cosmatesque mosaic floor, and the last chapel in the *left aisle* features reliefs** by J. della Quercia. Alongside the church are the relics of the 13th-c. *cemetery of S. Caterina*, in the form of a three-sided cloister.

Piazza del Mercato (*B3*). This square, just off Via Fillungo, was opened in 1830 on the site of a 2nd-c. A.D. **Roman amphitheater**, hence the elliptical shape. Parts of the original wall can be seen; the houses that had been built in the arena were demolished. Their contemporaries, the houses enclosing the piazza, were built around the shape of the arena. Via Fillungo ends with the medieval *Portone dei Borghi* (*A-B3*), a gate with two passages and round towers.

S. Pietro Somaldi (*B3*). This 12th-c. church has a Pisan facade, with grey-and-white stripes, a handsome portal, and a solid terracotta campanile. Nearby, at the intersection with Via del Fosso (see below), is a tall column, with ancient capital, crowned by a 17th-c. *statue* (*B4*); note also Neoclassical fountain by L. Nottolini.

S. Francesco (*B4*). This church was begun in 1228, rebuilt in the 14th and 17th c., and restored in the early 20th c. The white limestone facade has a portal and two aedicules, one from 1249. Inside, 15th-c. Florentine frescoes; and choir, with lectern, by L. Marti (16th c.); on left wall, funerary plaques honoring the Lucchese musicians L. Boccherini and F. Giminiani.

Museo Nazionale di Villa Guinigi* (*B4-5*). *Open 9-2; closed Mon.* This museum is set in the 15th-c. villa that once belonged to Paolo Guinigi (lord of Lucca from 1400 to 1430), a vast brickwork construction, with a ground-floor loggia and handsome mullioned windows, restored to its original appearance following WWII. Recently, it was thoroughly restored and modernized.

This museum contains almost exclusively artworks produced for the city or surrounding territories, either by local artists or outsiders working for local clients. The collections therefore give the visitor an excellent idea of Lucca's artistic history through the centuries; the collections were established mainly following the Unification of Italy, through the confiscation of ecclesiastical holdings.

Ground floor. *Archeological section*, with local finds dating from prehistoric to late Roman times, among them: furnishings from Ligurian and Etruscan tombs, Roman inscriptions, architectural fragments, mosaics, a Greco-Hellenistic relief from Vallecchia, and a huge altar uncovered (1983) in Piazza S. Michele. Halls with collections of coins and ceramics are followed by rooms of *medieval art*: fragments of architectural decorations, church furnishings, and rare examples of Longobard jew-

Lucca: Piazza del Mercato

elry and metalwork (note the shield found near the church of S. Romano), and 12th-/13th-c. sculptures and paintings. **Second floor:** Paintings and *sculpture* from the *late-13th c.* to the *17th c.*, by artists including D. Orlandi, L. Marti, P. della Quercia, V. Frediani, M. and A. Ciampanti, M. da Lucca, Matteo Civitali, F. Marti, A. Aspertini, Fra' Bartolomeo, Zacchia the Elder, A. Marti, G. Vasari, P. Guidotti, G. Reni, P. da Cortona, Lombardi, Brugieri, and Luchi. Two rooms are devoted to the work of P. Paolini and G. Scaglia, interesting 17th-c. Lucchese artists. The **gardens** contain archeological finds and medieval relics, including a 2nd-c. mosaic floor. Note the medieval lions from the city walls.

Via del Fosso (*A-C4*). One of Lucca's loveliest streets, it takes its name from the moat ('fosso'), that once lay east of the 13th-c. walls. Along Via del Fosso is the handsome *park* (*open, 9-1/30*) of the 16th-c. **Villa Buonvisi** (*C4*), with frescoes by V. Salimbeni; across from the villa is the little *church of SS. Trinità* (*B4*), built in 1589; nearby, the 13th-c. *Porta dei Ss. Gervasio e Protasio* (*C4*), handsome gate with two semicircular towers; also, against the walls, the **Giardino Botanico** (*C4-5; open, Oct.-Apr., 8-1, closed Sun. and Mon.; May-Sep., 9-12 and 3:30-6:30, closed Mon.*), established in 1820.

S. Maria Forisportam (*C3-4*). This Romanesque, Pisan-style church (13th c.) has a marble facade with fine carved portals. In the square is a granite Roman column, once used as the finish in town horse races (Palio). *Inside*, an early-Christian sarcophagus and two paintings by Guercino. In the right transept, note 17th-c. ciborium.

Via S. Croce (*C3-4*). This road runs straight, past medieval houses and aristocratic palazzi, from Porta dei Ss. Gervasio e Protasio to Via Fillungo. In the center, note the 16th-c. Palazzo Bernardini (*C3*), by N. Civitali. Behind the palazzo is the 17th-c. *church of Suffragio*, built in a plague-year burial ground (1630). To the left, the 13th-c. oratory of **S. Giulia**; inside, note 13th-c. painted Cross.

The walls*. Ancient and intact, these walls were one of the outstanding pieces of fortification in all Tuscany; they form a tree-lined ring around Lucca (4.2 km; built 1504-1645).

With 11 bastions, these walls stand about 21 m. tall, offering charming views of the city. In summer, concerts and performances are held here; the *Baluardo S. Paolino* (*D1; guided tours on weekdays: winter, 10-12:30 and 3:30-6; summer, 10-12:30 and 4-6:30*) is the site of the Centro Internazionale per lo Studio delle Cerchie Urbane.

Lucera

elev. 219 m., pop. 36,063, Puglia, province of Foggia.

Historical note. Since the Arabs in Sicily were problematic guests, the remarkable Holy Roman Emperor Frederick II moved many of them here (in several migrations, from 1224 to 1246) and since these Saracens were among his most trusted soliders, he cared for them quite well. Still some fifty years after his death the city was an Islamic enclave, until Charles II of Anjou slaughtered nearly all of the Muslims, destroyed the settlement, and renamed the town Città di Santa Maria, or town of St. Mary, a name that was soon forgotten.

Places of interest. The Gothic **Duomo*** — built at the behest of Charles II of Anjou (1302-17), possibly as a form of expiation, on the ruins of the harem of Frederick II — is one of the best preserved pieces of architecture dating from the Angevin period in Southern Italy; it is made of square-hewn, yet lively, masses of wall; among the notable artworks *inside* is a wooden 14th-c. Crucifix*.

S. Domenico. In this church, medieval but transformed into Baroque style, note the inlaid altars, a carved choir (1640), and a Neapolitan creche.

The **Museo Civico G. Fiorelli** (*open, summer, 9-2; closed Mon.; winter 9-1, Tue. and Fri. also 3-6; closed Mon.*) has a notable collection of archeological material, including a Marine Venus* from the 1st c., a bust of Proserpina*, and a Roman mosaic floor*; art gallery and bronze figurines.

S. Francesco. This church, too, was built during the reign of Charles II; inside, note frescoes from the 14th, 15th, and 17th c.

Castello* (*custodian, schedule same as the museum*). This castle occupies the terrace of the Monte Albano to the west of town; Charles I of Anjou, in the 13th c., transformed the palace of Frederick II into a castle, as French and Italian master builders set up a massive pentagonal ring of walls, with square and pentagonal towers. You can tour the ruins of Frederick's palace, and the bare interior of the vast ring of walls, with cisterns, foundations of an Angevin church, and ruins of Roman buildings.

Anfiteatro Romano. To the east of the town, this Roman amphitheater, built during the reign of Augustus, is evidence of the shift from an ancient Dàunian settlement to a Latin colony; two entrance portals have been rebuilt, and it is possible to make out the elliptical cavea, carved into the hillside.

Mantua / Mantova**

elev. 19 m.; pop. 54,228; Lombardy, provincial capital. The river Mincio flows around the city, spreading out into the three lakes, crossed by the two bridges, the Ponte dei Molini and the Ponte di S. Giorgio; thus, unless you arrive from the south, you will enter Mantua across water, not unlike Venice, with a view of the city reflected in the rippling surface. All around is the low-lying plain;

the Po is only 12 km. away. This city is marked by quiet streets, lovely colors, an overall Neoclassical patina, with the sharply distinct monuments of the Middle Ages and the Renaissance. Mantua is, of course, an ancient "capital" (of the state of the Gonzaga, which lasted nearly four centuries), one of those Italian towns in which we can see the signs of a long-ago conjunction of culture, power, wealth, high-minded patronage of the arts, splendor, and sickly decay. The lakes warded off industrial development; the city is tied to the land, in one of the most prosperous agricultural areas in Europe.

Historical note. Roman Mantua was a small "oppidum," or armed camp; it is believed that it occupied only the eastern corner of modern Mantua, the short space of the "civitas vetus" of the high Middle Ages, where the Gonzaga later built their palace. The true creation of the city may date back to another time, however. At the beginning of the Age of the Communes, great hydraulic projects were undertaken, under the supervision of Alberto Pitentino (1190), bringing the Mincio under control, directing its flow around the city, and creating lakes instead of marshes or "fens." The Rio was excavated, to link the Lago Superiore to the Lago Inferiore, and the Porto Catena was dug. Thus, the city of the "second walled perimeter" extended as far as the Rio; the Communal government built new palazzi and established markets (Broletto, Palazzo della Ragione, Piazza delle Erbe). The Commune joined the two Lombard Leagues, to fight imperial troops, and an age of prosperity and development ensued, as it had for the other cities of the Po Valley; like those cities, Mantua came under the rule of a seigneury, and formed a large territorial state. The seigneury began in 1273 with the Capitano del Popolo Pinamonte Bonaccolsi. After 55 years, there was a revolt, a famous "cacciata," or expulsion, and the Bonaccolsi were replaced by another Capitano del Popolo, Luigi Gonzaga (1328). Under the Gonzaga the state lasted until 1707, and the city of Mantua became its ambitiously crafted jewel, ornate, lovely, a renowned court during the finest centuries of Italian art, and then sadly declined into a far more provincial status. When the direct Gonzaga line died out in 1627, the succession passed to the cadet branch of the Gonzaga-Nevers. Names of dynasties and of artists punctuated the changes and progressions of taste and style. Gianfrancesco Gonzaga (1407-1444) summoned Pisanello to Mantua to paint frescoes for his court, frescoes of chivalrous grace, only recently rediscovered; around Ludovico II Gonzaga (1444-78) we find the artists of the early Renaissance: architects who studied under Brunelleschi, such as Luca Fancelli, the great Leon Battista Alberti, who designed the churches of S. Sebastiano and S. Andrea, and Andrea Mantegna, who worked for the family for most of his life. Isabella d'Este, the wife of Francesco II, played the role of high-minded patron of the arts with exquisite refinement, summoning to her court men of letters and artists, commissioning works by Leonardo da Vinci and Giovanni Bellini. In 1524 a student of Raphael arrived in Mantua — Giulio Romano, the great Mannerist artist from Rome. He was to leave his mark at court, in the city, and in the surrounding countryside (Palazzo Te lay outside the city walls, a pleasure house on an island). The height of splendor, though perhaps not of artistic excellence, came in the second half of the century; at the beginning of the 17th c. Monteverdi's "Orfeo" was first performed at court. To decide the succession of the duchy (it finally went to the house of Gonzaga-Nevers) war broke out, followed by the brutal sack and plunder by imperial troops, the plague (1630), and the beginning of the end. The ensuing decline brought Mantua under Austrian rule (1707), making it one of the strongholds of the "quadrilatero" (with Peschiera,

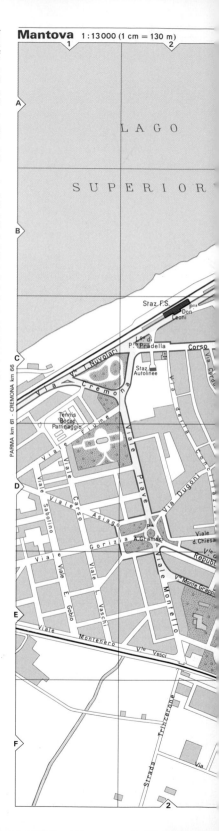

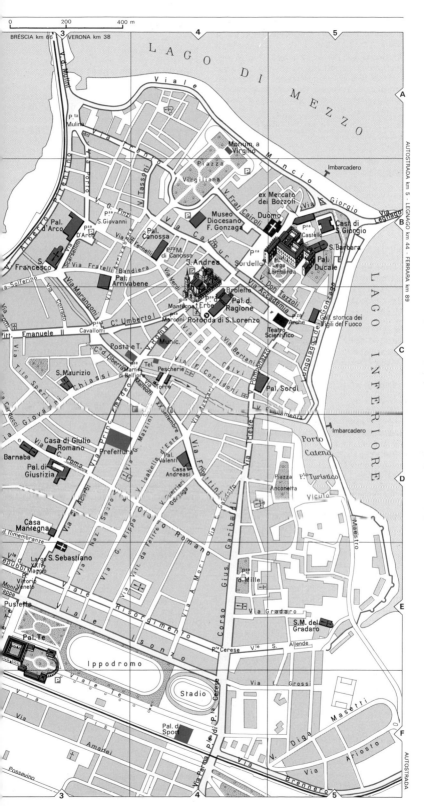

Verona, and Legnago) and a barracks town (26 barracks, at the end of the 18th c.). It became part of Italy in 1866.

Getting around. The historic center is closed to traffic (except for access to hotels) everyday from 9:30 am to midnight. Both routes recommended can be walked, though you may choose to use public transportation to return to the center from Palazzo Te, at the end of the second tour. Viale Mincio and the Lungolago dei Gonzaga, overlooking the Lago di Mezzo and Lago Inferiore, are pleasant promenades.

The ancient center and Palazzo Ducale

In the NE part of the city, the oldest section of Mantua, near the Ponte San Giorgio that divides the Lago di Mezzo from the Lago Inferiore, contains the most noted places and works. The walking tour that links them covers the masterpieces by Leon Battista Alberti, the architect of S. Andrea, and Andrea Mantegna, who painted the Camera degli Sposi in the Castello di S. Giorgio.

Piazza Mantegna (*C4*). The basilica of S. Andrea looms over this little porticoed square, at the end of Via Roma, and at the beginning of Mantua's three monumental squares (Piazza delle Erbe, Piazza Broletto, and Piazza Sordello).

S. Andrea** (*B-C4*). This Renaissance masterpiece, designed by L.B. Alberti, was begun in 1472 and completed in 1597-1600 and again in 1697-99; in 1732-65 the dome was added (F. Juvarra). The classical facade comprises a majestic arcade topped by a pediment; on the left side is a Gothic campanile (1413), with large mullioned windows. Note early-16th-c. portal, with reliefs.

The vast **interior***, grand and classical, has a single aisle and transept; note chapels, of which six are monumental, with 16th-c. frescoes and altarpieces; first *chapel* on the left commemorates A. Mantegna: tomb of the artist, with bronze bust, and paintings and decorations by school of Mantegna. In the dome, frescoes by G. Anselmi (1777-82).

Piazza delle Erbe* (*C4*). The length of the square, dating from the low Middle Ages, is a balance between the enfilade of late-Gothic and Renaissance porticos of Via Broletto, flanking S. Andrea, and a remarkable series of monumental structures. At the corner of Piazza Mantegna, just past a 15th-c. *house* with terracotta decorations, is the slightly recessed Romanesque **rotunda of S. Lorenzo*** (*open, 10:30-12:30 and 2:30-4:30*). It dates from the 11th c. but was later absorbed into the structure of the houses in the Jewish ghetto. It resurfaced in 1908 following a radical renovation; inside, ambulatory with arcades, with loggia and dome.

To the left of the rotunda, the **Torre dell'Orologio**, or clock tower, built by L. Fancelli in 1473; the astronomical-astrological clock, from that period, by B. Manfredi, was restored in 1989; adjacent is the 13th-c. **Palazzo della Ragione** (restored), with merlons and mullioned windows, and 15th-c. portico. At the end of the square is the 12th-c. **Palazzo del Podestà**, rebuilt in the 15th c. The facade on the adjacent *Piazza Broletto* has a high tower and a 13th-c. statue of Vergil. The mullioned windows and loggia over the vault

at the corner are remains of the Arengario (ca. 1300).

Museo Tazio Nuvolari (*C4*). *Open, 9-12 and 3-6; closed Mon. and Thu. morn.* At. 9 in Piazza Broletto (entrance under the loggia), this museum features trophies and memorabilia of this great Formula 1 racer.

Piazza Sordello* (*B4-5*). This rectangular plaza, unusually large for the historical center, still preserves much of its medieval appearance. Follow the short stretch of Via Broletto, through the *passageway of S. Pietro*, by G.B. Bertani; on the left, crenelated 13th-c. palazzi; on the right, the facade of Palazzo Ducale; at the far end, the Duomo.

Palazzo Ducale** (*B5*). *Guided tours, in groups (about 90 minutes), 9-1 and 2:30-4; Sun. and Mon., 9-12:30; long lines at the height of the tourist season. Sometimes, in summer, extended hours until 5 pm, with a possibility of touring the gardens and the church of S. Barbara.*

The two late-13th-c. porticoed buildings on Piazza Sordello to the right of the Duomo, along with many other buildings erected from the 13th to the 18th c., make up the Palazzo Ducale, or Ducal Palace of the Gonzaga, one of the most lavish creations of Italy under the seigneurs.

This "city within a city" extends toward the shores of the Lago Inferiore, or lower lake, enclosing palazzi, churches, inner squares, gardens, and porticoes, eloquent indications of the artistic and architectural fertility of the age of the Gonzaga. Extensive restoration is still under way, and may interfere with your tour; you should, however, be able to see paintings by D. Morone, V. Foppa, F. Bonsignori, G. Romano, G. Mazzola Bedoli, Tintoretto, Rubens, D. Fetti, G. Bazzani, and others; as well as Greek and Roman sculptures, sarcophagi, inscriptions, medieval and Renaissance sculptures (bust of F. Gonzaga*, attributed to A. Mantegna).

The most notable rooms are: the *Sala (or Hall) delle Sinopie*, with an exhibit of the preparatory drawings found on the plaster beneath the frescoes by Pisanello, discovered in 1969-72; the adjacent *Sala di Pisanello*, with the unfinished series of frescoes* painted for G.F. Gonzaga; the *Appartamento degli Arazzi*, with copies of nine tapestries made in Flanders to cartoons by Raphael; the *Appartamento Ducale*, with inlaid decorated ceilings (late-16th/early-17th c.); the 17th-c. *Appartamento dei Nani* ("Apartment of Dwarves"), actually a miniature reconstruction of the Scala Santa in Rome; the *Appartamento delle Metamorfosi*; the *Appartamento Estivale* (Summer Apartment), by G. Romano, renovated by G.B. Bertani (16th c.); the *Cortile della Cavallerizza* (16th c.); and a series of halls, frescoed and stuccoed by G. Romano and his school, by Primaticcio, and other 16th-c. artists, running from the *Galleria dei Mesi* (Hall of Months) to the majestic *Salone di Manto*; and finally the 15th-c. *Gabinetti Isabelliani*, with gilt inlaid ceilings. While touring the palace, you will also see the *Castello di S. Giorgio* (see below); in a corner tower is the **Camera degli Sposi**** (*tour limited to a few minutes, to preserve the artworks*), frescoed by A. Mantegna (1465-74) with scenes from the everyday life of the Gonzaga.

Museo del Risorgimento (*B5*). *Open by request, tel. 320280*. This museum of the Italian unification movement occupies four rooms at n. 42A in Piazza Sordello.

Mantua: Palazzo Ducale

Duomo* (*B4-5*). Built in the Middle Ages, this cathedral still has an immense Romanesque bell tower, and Gothic sections on the right side; most of the cathedral now standing dates from the 16th c. The 17th-c. facade shows the influence of Roman Mannerism and Baroque; the *interior*, by G. Romano (1545), shows classical influence, with the outer aisles and the nave featuring flat, coffered ceilings. In the right aisle, 5th-c. sarcophagus, Gothic baptismal chapel with fragments of 14th-c. frescoes; in the left aisle, note the 15th-c. *Cappella dell'Incoronata*, by L. Fancelli (1480).

Walk past the Duomo and the 15th-c. *Casa del Rigoletto*, and at the northern tip of Piazza Sordello you will see the large 19th-c. *Mercato dei Bozzoli* (*B5*), adjacent to Palazzo Ducale, which will become the site of the Museo Archeologico Nazionale di Mantova.

Castello di S. Giorgio (*B5*). This splendid urban castle, part of the complex of Palazzo Ducale, dominates the waters between Lago di Mezzo and Lago Inferiore. Built in the late-14th c. by B. da Novara, it has four crenelated towers and a broad deep moat.

Beyond the castle, along the Lungolago Gonzaga, is the outer facade of the "Rustica" by G. Romano; further along, off Piazza Arche, is the **Galleria Storica dei Vigili del Fuoco** (*C5; open, Sat. and Sun., 9:30-12:30 and 2:30-19:30*), a museum on the history of firefighting.

Teatro Scientifico* (*C5*). *Open, 9-12:30 and 3-5:30; Sun. closed.* The luminous facade of the Accademia Virgiliana, at n. 47 in Via Accademia, built by Piermarini (1771-75), can be seen on the left from Piazza Arche. The hall, a jewel of Baroque theater architecture, was built by A. Galli Bibiena (1769), and has four orders of boxes. Upstairs, *Library*, with collection of editions of Vergil's work, and collection of 18th-c. surgical instruments.

Leave Piazza Arche, turning right into Via Teatro Vecchio, along Via Scuderie Reali and Vicolo Ducale, among the secondary buildings of Palazzo Ducale, and take a passageway to the porticoed *Piazza di S. Barbara*, with the church of **S. Barbara** (*B5; open by request, enquire at the ticket window of Palazzo Ducale*), built by G.B. Bertani in 1562-72. Another passageway, to the left, leads to the porticoed **Piazza Castello**, also by Bertani, and then to the Castello di S. Giorgio; a monumental 16th-c. frescoed corridor leads to Piazza Sordello.

The "Civitas Nova" and Renaissance Mantua

Setting off from the center, you will pass through the quarters that belonged to the "city of the second walled perimeter," or the "civitas nova," the expansion that occurred at the end of the 12th c; after you cross the Rio, you will be in the later expansion of Mantua, until you reach Palazzo Te, created by the remarkable genius of Giulio Romano, at the time in broad countryside, for the pleasure house of Federico II Gonzaga.

Museo Diocesano "Francesco Gonzaga" (*B4*). *Open, 9:30-12 and 2:30-5 (Jul.-Aug., Sat. and Sun., 9:30-12 and 3-5:30), Mon. closed; Nov.-17 Mar., only Sun., 9:30-12 and 2:30-5.* At n. 55 in the huge Piazza Virgiliana, this religious museum is set in a former monastery. It features paintings by 15th-/17th-c. painters, sacred goldwork* from the Duomo and from the basilica of S. Barbara, and 15th-/16th-c. armor.

Piazza Matilde di Canossa (*B4*). Set behind the large red *Palazzo Barbetta*, built on what is now Via Cavour in 1784, this cozy little square is dominated by the impressive grotesque-work facade of **Palazzo Canossa**, built in the late-17th c., with one of the most interesting monumental staircases* of all Italian Baroque. Facing it is the little 18th-c. church of the *Madonna del Terremoto*. Follow Via Fratelli Bandiera, and at n. 17, note the 15th-c. house with carved portal and frescoes on the facade; further along, at the corner with Via Arrivabene, **Palazzo Arrivabene** (*B3*), in poor condition and much renovated, but with the original late-15th-c. porticoed courtyard.

S. Francesco (*B3*). This 14th-c. Gothic church was heavily damaged in WWII, and was restored to its original appearance; inside, 13th-/16th-c. frescoes by T. da Modena and others.

Palazzo d'Arco (*B3*). *Guided tour, Mar.-Oct, 9-12 and 3-5 (Tue., Wed. and Fri., only morn.), closed Mon.; Nov.-Feb., only Sun. and holidays, 9-12 and 2:30-4.* The long Neoclassical facade, built in 1782-84, overlooks Piazza Carlo d'Arco. Donated to the city in 1973, this building is a fine intact example of a noble residence; you can tour about 20 rooms. Note the 17th-/18th-c. furnishings, as well as paintings by F. Pourbus the Younger, F. Boselli, J. Denys, N. da Verona, and L. Lotto. Pass through the handsome courtyard to reach a 15th-c. palazzo; note the *Sala dello Zodiaco**, with frescoes by G. M. Falconetto (1520); in another wing, the collection of the 19th-c. naturalist L. d'Arco will be exhibited.

Piazza Martiri di Belfiore (*C3-4*). One of the focal points of Mantua's traffic, this square was built between 1925 and 1955, as part of the project that resulted in the filling in of the central stretch of the Rio and the demolition of the convent of S. Domenico. It extends toward Via Matteotti with an expanse of greenery that features the isolated Gothic *bell tower* of S. Domenico; behind the tower is the double portico of the **Pescherie** (*C4*), built in 1535 by Giulio Romano, across the Rio.

Palazzo Sordi (*C4-5*). Standing near the easternmost end of the distinctive *Via Corridoni*, lined by 17th- and 18th-c. buildings, this palazzo extends its vast rusticated facade at n. 23 in Via Pomponazzo. It is by the Flemish architect Frans Geffels (1680); note the courtyard and monumental staircase, with statues and stuccoes.

Palazzo Valenti (*D4*). This 17th-c. palazzo on the left side of Via Frattini (n. 7) has a handsome porticoed courtyard. Also, note, at n. 9, the 15th-c. *Casa Andreasi* and, at n. 5, a 15th-c. palazzo decorated with terracotta statues.

Via Chiassi (*C-D3*). Lined by palazzi from various eras, this street is marked by the 18th-c. Baroque facade of the church of **S. Maurizio** (*C3; undergoing restoration*), built in the early-17th c. by A.M. Viani. Just beyond, at the mouth of Via Poma, note the monumental church of *S. Barnaba* (*D3*), with an 18th-c. facade by Antonio Galli Bibiena. At n. 18 in Via Poma, note the **house of Giulio Romano** (*D3*), designed by the artist (1544), in a Neoclassical style; facing it is the **Palazzo di Giustizia** (Hall of Justice; *D3*), with its massive structure, and caryatids on the front; it was built around 1620.

Casa di Andrea Mantegna (*D3*). *Open, 9-12:30 and 3-6 (only for temporary exhibits, and by request, tel. 360506)*. At n. 47 in Via Acerbi, built in 1476, this house may have been designed and built by Mantegna himself, and has a circular courtyard. Exhibitions are held here.

S. Sebastiano* (*E3; closed to the public*). This beautiful classical church was built in 1460 to plans by L.B. Alberti; the facade was modified by restoration in 1925. Note crypt, altar in 16th-c. pergola, and Monument to the Martyrs of Belfiore.

Palazzo Te** (*E-F3*). *Open, 10-6; Mon. closed.* This spectacular suburban villa is one of the best preserved examples of 16th-c. architecture, built and decorated by G. Romano as a holiday home for Federico II Gonzaga. Made up of four low buildings around a courtyard, the building was recently restored. It is faced with imitation plaster ashlars: inside, the halls are lavishly decorated with frescoes and grotesque work, largely by G. Romano and followers: note the *Sala di Psiche**, or Hall of Psyche, with noted Manneristic frescoes, and the *Sala dei Giganti**, or Hall of Giants, praised by Vasari for its effect on the viewer. Also note the *Loggia di Davide*, linking the "cortile d'onore," or main courtyard, and the garden; the garden in turn is bounded by a monumental 17th-c. exedra and an *orchard*, used for temporary exhibits.

The building also houses the **Museo Civico di Palazzo Te** (*open, by request for the Egyptian collection and the Gonzaga section, tel. 365886*), broken up into various sections: *Donazione Mondadori*, with paintings by A. Spadini and F. Zandomeneghi; *Donazione Giorgi*, with work by this 20th-c. painter; *Sezione d'Arte Moderna* (Mantuan artists, 1850-1950); *Sezione Gonzaghesca*, with medals, coins, et al, 1328-1707; *Collezione Egizia Acerbi*, with ancient Egyptian art and artifacts.

S. Maria del Gradaro (*E5*). This 13th-c. Gothic church, with pointed portal and rose window, was used as a barracks from 1775 till 1917, and then was restored to its original appearance in 1952-66. Inside, fragments of 13th-c. Byzantine-style frescoes.

Excursions. By motorboat (*Mar.-Oct.*), on the **Lago di Mezzo**, the **Lago Inferiore**, and along the course of the river Mincio, through the **Parco del Mincio** and the locks, or Chiusa, of Governolo, as far as the Po: all the way to *Sacchetta di Sustinente*, on the Po, from the embarcadero of Ponte S. Giorgio (*B5, Motonavi Andes, tel. 668110*); as far as *San Benedetto Po* from the embarcadero of Porto Catena (*D5, Motonave Sebastiano N., tel. 668134*).

Martina Franca

elev. 431 m., pop. 46,058, Puglia, province of Taranto. The architectural setting, full of 18th-c. theatricality, with sudden surprising views through the narrow winding lanes of the dense historical center, is quite remarkable. At one end, after demolishing a Orsini fortress, the feudal lord, Duke Petracone V Caracciolo, began the construction (1669) of an enormous Ducal Palace, upon which he eventually spent 60,000 ducats. This was the beginning of a massive building campaign, which continued well into the following century.

Places of interest. Four gates are what survive of the ancient walled perimeter, which once boasted 24 towers.

The **Palazzo Ducale** (town hall) has a handsome iron balcony and 18th-c. frescoes on the interior.

The **Collegiata di S. Martino** (1774-75), with its theatrical facade, still features the Gothic bell tower of the earlier building, on the right facade; adjoining it is the *Palazzo della Corte, or Palazzo dell'Università* (1760) — *universitas*, in Southern Italy, meant the local community, as an administrative entity — with the Torre dell'Orologio (Clock Tower; 1734). Note the various picturesque little palazzi in Via Cavour. Of special note are the churches of *S. Domenico* (rococo facade, Baroque interior) and the *Carmine* (at the edge of a panoramic terrace overlooking the green Valle d'Itria), dotted with "trulli."

Massa Marittima

elev. 380 m.; pop. 9,518; Tuscany, province of Grosseto. The ancient historical center, or "città vecchia" (old town), clusters around the Duomo. This section has an intense medieval flavor and excellent artistic qualities; the "città nuova" (new town), is more orderly in design, stands higher up the hill, and was an expansion planned in 1228. At that time, this Maremma community, some 15 km. from the sea, was wealthy from its silver and copper mines, which played out in the late 14th c.; mining did not resume until 1830. Economic decline, due chiefly to malaria and ending only with the 19th-c. reclamation of the swamps, paradoxically served to preserve the remarkable townscape.

Getting around. Much of the historical center is closed to traffic; the itinerary that we suggest, is predominantly a walking tour.

Places of interest. **Piazza Garibaldi***. This monumental center of the "old town" is irregular in shape, and is closed off by the steps on which the Duomo is set at an angle. Downhill and to the left is the 13th-c. structure of the fountain known as the **Fonte dell'Abbondanza**. Opposite the Duomo, and to the right, is the stern *Palazzo Pretorio* (see below); further along is the 13th-c. *house of the Counts of Biserno* (n. 7), and the *Tower of Biserno*. Adjacent is the **Palazzo Comunale***, a huge Romanesque structure made of travertine (13th/14th c.); inside (*open by request, contact the ushers*), 16th-c. frescoes. Facing the Palazzo Comunale, the *Loggias of the Comune*, rebuilt in the 19th c.; behind it, on Via Parenti (n. 22), note the medieval *Palazzetto della Zecca*, or Mint, with handsome pointed arches on the facade.

Duomo**. Certainly one of the masterpieces of Pisan Gothic-Romanesque architecture, this cathedral was begun in the 11th c. and enlarged between 1287 and 1304. The facade is decorated with arcades and loggias; the portal is adorned with reliefs. The arcaded left side is dominated by the white-and-green covering of the nave; at the end, the massive bell tower, largely rebuilt around 1920.

The luminous *interior* features handsome capitals on the assorted columns, frescoes, a pre-Romanesque relief, and 14th-c. stained glass in the rose window. Among the fine art, note the baptismal font*, with reliefs by G. da Como (1267); the Crucifix on panel, by S. di Bonaventura (late-13th c.); another panel*, by D. di Buoninsegna; a fragmentary panel by S. di Pietro, damaged by theft; on the main altar, a polychrome wooden Crucifix* by G. Pisano; wooden inlaid 15th-c. choir stalls; and the tomb of St. Cerbone*, adorned with reliefs, a masterpiece by the Siennese artist G. di Gregorio (1324).

Palazzo Pretorio. Facing the Duomo, built around 1230; note the impressive facade. It now houses the **Musei Civici** (*open, Apr.-Sep., 10-12:30 and 3:30-7; Oct.-Mar., 9-1 and 3-5; closed Mon.*), comprising a **Museo Archeologico** and a Pinacoteca. The Archeological Museum features remarkable local finds dating back to the 8th c. B.C.

The **Pinacoteca**, or art gallery, has works by S. di Pietro, Sassetta, A. Lorenzetti, and S. Folli.

Miniera Museo. *Guided tour, Apr.-Sep., 10-12:30 and 3-7; Oct.-Jan. and Mar., 10-12 and 3-4; closed Feb. and Mon.* Beneath the "città vecchia" (*entrance in Via Corndoni*), this is a network of tunnels, used as shelters during WWII, transformed in 1980 into a museum of mining and tunnelling.

Piazza Matteotti*. This square stands in the "città nuova"; follow the steep Via Moncini, through *Porta delle Silici*. Note the dizzying arched walkway (1337) that links it with the 13th-c. *Torre del Candeliere*. All around, exceedingly old houses and no curtain walls of the huge **Siennese fort** (*open, Apr.-Sep., 11-1 and 4:30-7; mid-Jul./Aug., extended hours, from 2:30 until 7:30; closed Mon.*), built after 1335.

Museo di Storia e Arte delle Miniere. *Open, Apr.-Sep., 10-11 and 3-5; mid-Jul./Aug., 10-12 and 4-7; closed Mon.* At n. 4 in Piazza Matteotti, in the Renaissance *Palazzetto delle Armi*, this museum's four halls document the history of mining in the area. Nearby, in Piazza Beccucci, *a permanent exhibit of folk culture*; in Via Populonia, an 18th-c. oil mill (*open, Apr.-Sep., 10-12:30 and 3:30-7*).

S. Agostino. Gothic church, dating from 1299-1313, with handsome portal and polygonal apse (1348).

Matera

elev. 399 m.; pop. 55,256, Basilicata, provincial capital. From the rocky spur on which the Duomo stands, the houses run down along the steep slope as far as the steep "gravina," or gravel-lined gorge. Architectural complexes of remarkable value are intertwined in an inextricable labyrinth, crisscrossed by narrow roads and stairways, sometimes running over houses beneath. The sections in masonry, which includes the facades that closed off the caves, have loggias and balconies, mostly in 17th-c. style. These are the "Sassi di Matera."

Places of interest. S. Giovanni Battista. This church was built in the early 13th c., and has remarkable architectural details; inside, note influence of Burgundian Gothic.

S. Francesco di Assisi. In this church, rebuilt in the Baroque style in 1670, note eight panels of a polyptych* by Bartolomeo Vivarini (15th c.) on the chancel of the organ.

The **Duomo*** was built in 1268-70 in the Pugliese Romanesque style; the facade features a handsome portal and rose window; two carved portals and lavish windows along the sides; the campanile has twin-light mullioned windows.

The **Pinacoteca d'Errico** contains a notable collection of 17th- and 18th-c. paintings, chiefly of the Neapolitan school.

The scenic route, or **Strada Panoramica dei Sassi*,** allows you to enjoy a variety of views of the two valleys of Sasso Caveoso and Sasso Barisano; at a number of points it towers dizzyingly over the "gravina," or gravel-lined gorge: take the Via B. Buozzi, through the Sasso Caveoso, and you will reach the square before the little church of *S. Pietro Caveoso*; high above on the right is the crag known as the Mt. Errone. High atop it stands the church of *S. Maria de Idris*, almost wholly carved out of rock; from it, you enter another small underground church with frescoes in the 11th-c. Byzantine style.

Merano / Meran^

elev. 325 m.; pop. 32,600; Trentino-Alto Adige; province of Bolzano. The river Passirio crosses Merano, on its way to join the Adige; in the surrounding valley, hills teem with vineyards and orchards, with castles and mountains in the background. A gentle climate, fine strolls, neat parks and gardens, hotels where Hapsburg noble ladies once spent the summer and cafes where Danubian pastries and sweets tempt one to laze away the day: the cosmopolitan mountain spa preserves some of the Austro-Hungarian flavor of bygone eras. Take the waters which bubble from Monte S. Vigilio and S. Martino.

Historical note. Oddly enough, if the Gothic Duomo and the medieval houses of Via dei Portici are Merano's historical center, and the residential outskirts of Maia/Mais constitute modern Merano, in the 3rd c., the reverse was the case — the Roman "Statio Maiensis" stood among the gardens of what is now Maia Alta/Obermais. We find mention of the town again centuries later, in A.D. 857, as "Meirania." The counts of Venosta took the name from the nearby Castel Tirolo that in time spread to the entire Tyrolean region. With the decline of that house, the dukes of Carinthia took over for a while, then in 1363 the Hapsburgs moved in, building near the old center, between 1449 and 1480, the Castello Principesco (Landesfürstliche Burg), as a residence of Sigismund, archduke of Austria. Floods and landslides encroached in the 15th/16th c.; the capital was moved to Innsbruck; ravaged by the wars of the peasants, Merano declined in power and wealth. Under Napoleon, the town was made part of Bavaria. From 1814 until 1918 Austrian government gave the town new pride, making it an international spa, which remained under Italian rule after 1918. To the west and south of the old center, on the left bank of the Passìrio, are boulevards, green gardens, hotels and villas, hot baths, the Lido, a race track, tennis courts and skating rinks, as well as magnificent promenades. The new center is now in Piazza del Teatro, stretching to the Casinò Municipale (Kursaal).

Places of interest. Piazza del Teatro. This square opens next to the Ponte del Teatro overlooking the Passìrio; it is the heart of Merano, terminus of the main streets in town.

Corso Libertà. Running from the train station (Staz. F.S.) to Piazza della Rena, passing the *Casinò Municipale*, with the Kursaal (1914) and the *Pavillon des Fleurs* (1874), meeting places in town.

Duomo*. This 14th-c. cathedral, dedicated to S. Nicolò, or St. Nicholas, is Merano's main monument, with its 80-m.-plus bell tower, and buttresses. Note, along the sides, 14th-c. reliefs and frescoes. Inside, note the 15th-c. carved altar piece. Behind the cathedral is the little octagonal Gothic church of *S. Barbara*, with a fine fresco of St. Christopher.

Via dei Portici*. This is Merano's most distinctive street, lined by porticoes and shops. At n. 68, note the **Museo dell'abito e della donna attraverso il tempo** (*open 3-7; Sat. 9:30-12; closed Sun.*), with collections of historical womenswear from 1870 to 1970, including hairpins, buttons, and paper figurines. At n. 192, note the modern *Palazzo Municipale*, or town hall (1929).

Castello Principesco. *Open, 9-12 and 2-6; Sat. 10-12; closed Sun*. This princely castle stands in Via Galilei; built in 1480 by Archduke Sigismund of Austria, it boasts original furnishings and a collection of ancient musical instruments. Note the chair lift to Monte Benedetto (475 m., *in operation from Apr. to Oct.*).

Museo Civico. *Open 10-12 and 3-6; closed Sun.*; in winter also Sat. At n. 43 in Via Galilei, this museum has collections ranging from natural science and archeology to folklore and art, both medieval and modern.

Excursions. Passeggiata Lungo Passìrio*. Running along the right bank of the Passìrio, in the shadow of the poplars, this promenade runs downstream from the Ponte del Teatro to the *Lido di Merano*; upstream is the Casinò Municipale. At the *Ponte della Posta*, it changes its name to the **Passeggiata d'Inverno**, partly roofed, pushing through lush vegetation across the Ponte Romano, to the ruins of Castel S. Zeno.

Passeggiata d'Estate. Along the left bank of the Passìrio, this promenade runs from the *Ponte della Posta* (note 15th-c. Gothic church of *S. Spirito*), up the tree-shaded river to *Ponte Passìrio*. Note the marble statue of the empress Elizabeth, or "Sissi," as she is known here. You may continue to the villas, hotels, and parks of Maia Alta.

Passeggiata Tappeiner*. This promenade begins at Via Galilei, winding 4 km. over the hills to Quarazze, just below Castel Tirolo; fine views of the Conca di Merano, a valley dotted with vineyards and orchards.

Ippodromo. From Piazza del Teatro, south along Via Piave, you will reach the race track, or Ippodromo di Maia Bassa, where horse races and hurdle jumps are held.

Messina

elev. 3 m., pop. 233,378, Sicily, provincial capital. Only the name of *Zancle*, the 8th-c. B.C. Greek colony, survives; the same is true of Messana, which replaced Zancle in the 5th c. B.C.). The Roman city was described by Cicero as "civitas maxima et locupletissima," high praise indeed for a town. The modern-day city of Messina has a very up-to-date appearance, extending along the shore of the straits; the roads are broad and parallel, and buildings are relatively low, out of fear of earthquakes (though the bell tower of the cathedral stands 60 m. tall). In terms of communications, this is the gateway to Sicily, but the narrow strait that separates it from the "continent" may someday soon be spanned by a long-awaited suspension bridge.

Places of interest. Piazza Unità d'Italia. The Via Garibaldi, main thoroughfare of the city, runs in its central stretch along the waterfront, and then emerges into the *Piazza Unità d'Italia*, with the *Fontana del Nettuno** (1557), a fountain built by the Florentine sculptor and architect Montorsoli.

Piazza del Duomo. This broad square opens out against a backdrop of hills, and is adorned with the *Fontana di Orione**, another fountain built by Montorsoli (1547-50).

Duomo*. This cathedral is a painstaking reconstruction of the church that developed over the centuries from its foundation, at the behest of the Norman king, Roger II (it was consecrated in 1197). The lower section of the facade, with bands of mosaics and reliefs, is as ancient as the three Gothic portals and the two 16th-c. portals on the sides. Among the artworks found on the *interior*, note the statue of John the Baptist by Antonello Gagini (1525) and the tomb of the De Tabiatis* by the Siennese Goro di Gregorio (1333).

SS. Annunziata dei Catalani*. Don Juan of Austria, victor in the battle of Lépanto, returned from the fight with his fleet to Messina; a statue of him (by A. Calamecca, 1572) adorns the little square upon which stands *SS. Annunziata dei Catalani**, a church built in the second half of the 12th c., and shortened in the 13th c.; the facade dates from the same period. The transept, dome, and apse with blind arcades and polychrome encrustations date from the earlier building.

Museo Regionale*. The most interesting tour in the city, however, is that of the Regional Museum (along the beach, past the lighthouse; *open, summer 9-1:30 and 4-6:30, holidays only 9-1:30; winter*

Messina: Duomo

9-1:30 and 3-5:30, holidays only 9-1). The archeological section is undergoing renovation; the sections on medieval and modern art offer a priceless documentation of the city's art history, with major masterpieces. Note especially: the Madonna degli Storpi*, a sculpture by Goro di Gregorio (1333); the *polyptych of St. Gregory*** by Antonello da Messina (1473); Presentation in the Temple, Last Judgement, and Circumcision* by Girolamo Aliprandi, 1519; Scylla*, originally part of the fountain of Neptune, by Montorsoli; *Adoration of the Shepherds** and *Resurrection of Lazarus**, paintings done by Caravaggio while traveling to Messina between 1608 and 1609. One interesting curiosity are the 9 gilt slabs with the Legend of the Sacred Letter (early-19th c.), which recurs in the clock of the Duomo, as well.

Circonvallazione a Monte. Magnificent views can be enjoyed from many different points along the avenues that constitute the *"uphill ring road."*

Surrounding areas. At a distance of 10 km. is *Ganzirri*, a typical fishing village; at a distance of 14 km. is the *Punta del Faro*, also known as *Capo Peloro*.

Milan / Milano**

elev. 122 m., pop. 1,408,537; Lombardy, regional capital. Thriving, open-handed, forward-looking: the Milanese pride themselves on their city's wealth, international ties, and metropolitan sophistication. Milan is Italy's second-largest city; the population swells each day by 20 percent as commuters and travellers flock into the city; even so, the number of residents has declined in recent years. The city proper is relatively small (extending just 8 km. from the golden spire of the Duomo, or cathedral); its influence extends over the surrounding plain, which is densely populated and heavily industrialized, especially to the north. Milan is a city of executives, marketers, and financiers. It is the capital of Italy's "service industry," and boasts more than 100,000 local businesses. It stands on the brink of the brave new "post modern" world, as it quickly sheds the last remnants of its "blue-collar" past. Culturally, La Scala, the fabled opera house, is perhaps Milan's best-known landmark; La Scala is only a small part of the city's wealthy artistic heritage. Milan is vast and hard-working; were business to disappear entirely from the landscape, however, a remarkable "city of art" would still stand on the Lombard plains. On a clear, windy day, from the roof of the Duomo, or any other vantage point, one can clearly see the Alps glittering with snow to the north (and, beyond them, all of Central Europe), to the south, east, and west, the broad rolling expanse of the Po Valley, one of the wealthiest regions on earth.

Historical note. The "ring of the Navigli," or canals, the "Spanish walls" and the "bastions" — or ramparts — are still terms used everyday in Milan to give directions or to indicate neighborhoods; Milan is arranged much like a giant wagon wheel, with the Piazza del Duomo as its hub; concentric ring-roads intersect with the "spokes" that run out from the center. The Navigli, or canals, which once ringed the city, are now virtually all covered over, and only a few forlorn fragments of the Spanish walls still stand. Milan's beloved Duomo, or Cathedral, is a relative newcomer, witness to only the last six centuries of

Milan's 2,400-year history. The Piazza del Duomo took on its modern appearance in the last few decades of the 19th c., following the unification of Italy in 1861. The city has always teetered between a love of tradition and a compelling drive to demolish and rebuild; nearly every venerable monument stands out of context, surrounded by newer structures. Thus, even in the medieval center of town, the overriding style is Neoclassical, dating from the period described by Stendhal, one of Milan's illustrious "adoptive citizens."

The Insubri, a Celtic people, founded Milan around 388-386 B.C. The Romans conquered the town 150 years later, calling it "Mediolanum," or "central place," after the original Celtic name. In A.D. 286, it became the residence of the joint emperor, or "Augustus," appointed by Diocletian. Milan was roughly square in shape, with sides of 700 m. In A.D. 313, the Emperor Constantine decreed official tolerance of Christianity; the edict was published in Milan. Some six decades later, a former officer of the Empire, Ambrose, was elected bishop by the townsfolk. Honorius moved the imperial residence to Ravenna (402); when the Longobard chieftain Alboin marched into a vanquished Milan, in A.D. 569, bishop, clergy, and nobility collectively decamped to Genoa for seventy years. Milan's history during the first half of the second millennium of the Christian era strongly resembles that of Italy at large: governed by bishops, the Commune, or civic republic, Seignories, regional princes, and finally foreign occupation. The monument that best sums up the spirit of the civic republic is the innovative, Romanesque basilica of S. Ambrogio, an 11th-/12th-c. reconstruction of the ancient "basilica Martyrum." Shortly thereafter, in the mid-13th c., the Broletto Nuovo was built, marking the separation of civic government and the headquarters of the archbishop. Immediately thereafter, Milan came under a Seignory; that of the pro-Guelf Della Torre family; the pro-Ghibelline, aristocratic party, overthrew the Della Torre party in 1277, led by the archbishop Ottone Visconti; Ottone's great grandson, Matteo Visconti, was named imperial vicar in 1294.

In the 14th c., the Visconti seignory held growing sway over the towns and lands of Lombardy, Piedmont to the west, and Emilia to the south that were economically subordinate to Milan; the epiphany of Visconti rule came when Gian Galeazzo (who in 1395 had purchased the title of duke, the only one among the lords of Italy) extended his rule over much of Northern Italy and beyond the Apennines. Court sages spoke of a royal crown to come, Venice and Florence strove mightily against him, in high alarm, and then, in 1402, the Black Death conveniently swept him from the stage of history. Gian Galeazzo's younger son, Filippo Maria, was barely able to pick up the few remaining pieces of his father's empire, and was the last Visconti duke. Marriage brought the son-in-law Francesco Sforza, a mighty condottiero, whose surname meant "Stormer," into the duchy, becoming duke in 1450, following the nostalgic "Aurea Repubblica Ambrosiana," or Golden Ambrosian Republic. The peace of Lodi of 1454, opened the few happy decades of a "balance of power" among the great regional states of Italy. Work went forward on the Duomo, (which Gian Galeazzo Visconti had begun building in 1386), Antonio Filarete was introducing the concept of centrally planned buildings, as he built the vast Ospedale Maggiore, or central hospital, on land bestowed by the duke. Poetically, Filarete imagined an ideal city built to a symmetrical plan, naming it after his patron, "Sforzinda." The remarkable piece of hydraulic engineering known as the Navigli was completed (originally a system of canals outside the city walls. The network of canals was dotted with "conche," or sets of locks, allowing boats to pass from one watercourse to another at a higher or lower water level. Of the various "darsene," or wetdocks, where the water is shut in and kept at a given level to facilitate the loading and unloading of ships, the Darsena del Laghetto di Santo Stefano, now Via Laghetto, was used by the bargemen and dock workers unloading huge

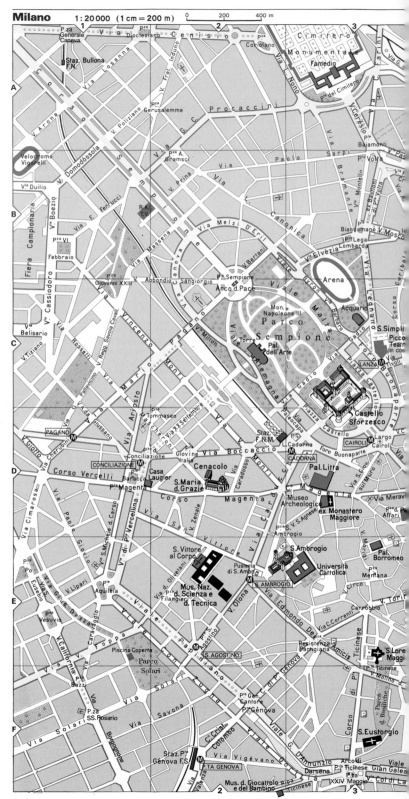

Milano

1 : 20000 (1 cm = 200 m)

227

blocks of Candoglia marble used in building the Duomo). At the turn of the 16th c., the city's population was approaching 100,000. In the words of one chronicler, "it appeared that all events heralded peace, and everyone waited only to gather great wealth, which seemed to lie at the end of every path." At the turn of the 15th c., in the Castello (Castello di Porta Giovia, as it was called then; Castello Sforzesco being the term used nowadays) Ludovico Sforza, the "Moor," and his wife Beatrice d'Este presided over what was widely called the most splendid court in Italy.

Here one could meet such luminaries as Bramante, who designed the epochal tambour of S. Maria delle Grazie, and Leonardo da Vinci, who was painting his "Last Supper" in the refectory of the convent next door to the church. The bountiful, well-irrigated, low-lying fields, manufacturing, and thriving trade with the rich lands over the Alps, all made the duchy of Milan Italy's wealthiest state. A tempting plum it was, and Louis XII of France was duly tempted; he cited a Visconti grandmother and laid claim to the duchy. Louis XII sent an army to conquer Milan in 1499; it was unsuccessful, but over the following three-and-a-half decades, as France battled Habsburg for European preeminence, Lombardy — the key to Italy — was overrun variously, changing hands until it finally fell to the Spanish (1535), who ruled it thereafter for 170 years.

The years of Spanish rule saw the construction of bastions that ringed Milan, the militant Counter-Reformation (Charles Cardinal Borromeo, was archbishop of Milan from 1560 to 1584), Mannerism and the Baroque (Alessi built Palazzo Marino, while Tibaldi started work on the church of S. Fedele dei Gesuiti). During the War of the Spanish Succession, Austrian replaced Spanish rule (1706), reigning until 1859, with only a brief interlude of the Napoleonic years. The first century of Austrian rule, especially the reign of Maria Theresa, was a time of enlightened dictatorship. The aristocratic author Cesare Beccaria, the poet Giuseppe Parini, and the architect Piermarini — who built La Scala — all helped to give Milan the refined Neoclassical style that Stendhal (1783-1842) so admired.

Between 1796 and 1814, under the rule of Napoleonic France, Milan experienced unrest, ambitious reform, heavy taxes, and grandiose plans of urban renewal — some of which were actually implemented after restoration. A second period of Austrian rule coincided with the years of Romanticism. (In Milan, Alessandro Manzoni wrote "I Promessi Sposi," while Francesco Hayez painted historic paintings and portraits of society ladies and gala evenings at the La Scala opera house). Milan grew rapidly from an agglomeration of winding medieval lanes to a modern, gas-lit city, within the ring of canals of the Navigli; between the Navigli and the outer ramparts, or Bastioni, houses and convents vied with orchards and gardens for space. As Milan grew, it gobbled up a dozen or more outlying towns and villages, attaining its current expanse in 1873. To commemorate the unification of Italy, Milan created the Piazza del Duomo and the Galleria, destroying a neighborhood to do so, and spending 43% of the city budget for twenty long years. The city grew rapidly — in 1861 the population was 196,000, roughly a tenth its current size — and construction boomed to keep pace, both within and without the Spanish walls. A similar boom followed the Allied bombings of 1943, as immigrants poured in from southern Italy, in search of work in Milan's factories. The city's architecture reflects the dizzying pace of these various decades of growth: historicistic eclecticism, "Liberty" (Giuseppe Sommaruga; the term is the Italian version of Art Nouveau), the Novecento, Rationalism, and contemporary architecture (with relatively few skyscrapers, such as the Pirelli building and the Torre Velasca). During the same decades, noteworthy schools of art developed in Milan (Divisionism, Futurism, "Novecento," "Corrente," and abstract art), right up to the work of recent generations (Transavanguardia).

Getting around. Heavy traffic and a chronic lack of parking are good reasons not to plan on using your car. There are three subway lines and plenty of public transportation; count on using these. In any case, on weekdays, from 7:30 am to 6 pm, the entire area within the Cerchia dei Navigli is closed to cars (Foro Buonaparte, Via Carducci, Via De Amicis, Via Molino delle Armi, Via S. Sofia, Via Francesco Sforza, Via Visconti di Modrone, Via S. Damiano, Via Senato, Via Fatebenefratelli, Via Pontaccio, and Via Tivoli); only vehicles with business passes, residential stickers, or tourists with written confirmation of hotel reservations can enter.

The six routes suggested can all be considered walking tours, though you may choose to make use of public transportation for the longer sections (to reach the points indicated as outlying neighborhoods and surrounding areas it is best to have your own means of transportation).

Piazza del Duomo and the "central core"

The Duomo, Corso Vittorio Emanuele, La Scala, Palazzo Marino, the Galleria, Palazzo della Ragione: famed and little-known city sights, in a stroll through memories and high society, never more than 400 m. from the golden statue of the Madonnina (literally, "Our Little Virgin Mary," high atop the Duomo's central spire).

Piazza del Duomo (*D-E4*). This vast rectangle that fronts the Duomo is the city's geographic core, the hub of the great avenues that run outward like so many spokes, in line with the 19th c. urban plan.

Working just after Italy's Unification, Giuseppe Mengoni gave this piazza much of its modern-day appearance, designing the porticoes that run its length as well as the great portal that opens into the *Galleria Vittorio Emanuele II* (1878, see below; in the center of the piazza stands an equestrian statue to this king, Italy's first), to the left of the facade of the Duomo. Opposite the Galleria, are the two loggia-structures of the *Arengario* (1939-56); beyond them lies **Piazza Diaz**, and to their left is the off-kilter space of *Piazzetta Reale*, fronting the Palazzo Reale.

Duomo** (*D4*). This monument, above all others, has come to symbolize Milan. Tradition states that the church was founded in 1386, under the rule of Gian Galeazzo Visconti, dedicated to "Maria Nascente." It magnificently dominates the eastern side of the piazza, a vast and intricately fashioned marble structure, straw-yellow in color.

The seemingly interminable process of construction began under the direction of "engineer general" Simone da Orsenigo, assisted by other "maestri lombardi"; he was succeeded by Giovannino de' Grassi, and in the first half of the 15th c. — when plan and elevation took final form — and in turn by Marco da Carona and Filippino degli Organi. Over the ensuing centuries, the supervision of construction fell to the leading "Visconti" architects, among them Giovanni and Guiniforte Solari and Giovanni Antonio Amadeo (who designed the tambour) in the second half of the 15th c., Vincenzo Seregni and Pellegrino Tibaldi in the 16th c., Lelio Buzzi and Francesco Maria Richini in the 17th c. In 1765-69 Francesco Croce completed the tambour with the main spire; atop this great spire was placed in 1774 the gilded statue of the "Madonnina." Napoleon ordered the completion of the facade (1805-13), for which one plan after another had been submitted since the 17th c., and in 1811-12 the remarkable forest of spires was finished.

As huge as the piazza itself may be, it does little to undercut the Duomo's vast size: 158 m. long,

Milan: Piazza del Duomo, and Galleria Vittorio Emanuele II

93 m. wide at the transept, with an interior area of 11,700 sq. m.; the tallest spire rises 108 m. The church boasts more than 3,400 statues, largely distributed over the 135 spires. The side view, from Piazzetta Reale, and the rear view, from Corso Vittorio Emanuele, standard fare of 19th-c. view painters, give a solid appreciation of the sheer mass of Candoglia marble, punctuated by buttresses and topped by dizzying spires. In the rear, the massive transept and polygonal apse are pierced by three enormous windows.

The *interior*, with a nave and four aisles, is crossed by a short three-aisle transept, with a deeply recessed presbytery and ambulatory. In the shadowy coolness, 52 colossal polystyle pillars line nave, transept, and apse, surmounted by huge capitals adorned by statues of saints and prophets. Most of the spectacular stained-glass **windows*** date from the 15th and 16th c., though some date from the 19th and 20th c.; especially noteworthy are the windows in the first, fifth, and sixth bays on the right and at the end of the right arm of the transept. Also, note the immense Gothic candelabrum of Trivulzio at the end of the left arm of the transept.

Overlooking the ambulatory are the 14th-c. **portals*** of the vestries; the portal on the left vestry is believed to be the earliest piece of sculpture in the Duomo, and is attributed to Giacomo da Campione (1389). The stairway facing the southern vestry leads down to the *crypt (open, 9-12 and 2:30-6)*, which contains the remains of Saint Charles Borromeo. Adjacent is the Duomo's **treasury***, featuring remarkable works of goldsmithery, the earliest dating from the 4th and 5th c.

Early Christian archeological excavations. *Open, 10-12 and 3-5; Mon. closed.* From the interior facade of the Duomo, or Cathedral, a stairway leads down to the remains of the *baptistery of S. Giovanni alle Fonti*, built around A.D. 378, to an eight-sided plan. Here St. Ambrose is said to have baptized St. Augustine.

Climb up to the roof *(by foot or elevator, from the outside of the left transept, 9-5:30; Oct-Feb., 9-4:30).* Here you will see a second, "open-air" cathedral, over which looms the elaborate tambour; from here you can enjoy a splendid view of the city*. Near the elevator is the oldest **spire** on the Duomo, built in 1397-1404.

Palazzo Reale *(E4)*. Although it was first built in the 14th c., its final, Neoclassical form is the work of Piermarini (1778); it was the residence of Spanish and Austrian governors. It was damaged by Allied bombing in 1943. It now houses the Museo del Duomo and the Civico Museo d'Arte Contemporanea (a museum of contemporary art), and various exhibition spaces.

Museo del Duomo*. *Open, 9:30-12:30 and 3-6; closed Mon.* This ground-floor museum features 600 works, largely sculpture and architecture taken from the Duomo. There are also fragments of ancient stained glass, tapestries, sketches, architectural models, and wooden carvings.

Civico Museo d'Arte Contemporanea *(E4)*. *Open, 9:30-5:30; closed last Mon. of each month.* This museum occupies the top floor of Palazzo Reale (expansion planned), and features 20th-c. Italian art , ranging from Futurism, the school of Pittura Metafisica (metaphysical painting), "Novecento," early Abstract artists, the Roman school,"Corrente," and others. There are halls devoted to the work of Boccioni, De Chirico, Sironi, Morandi, De Pisis, Fontana, and others.

Piazza Fontana *(DE15)*. This piazza takes its name from the 18th-c. fountain; it was the site of a terrorist bombing that killed 16 in 1969, marked by a commemorative plaque. The **archbishop's palace** (no. 2) dominates the square.

Corso Vittorio Emanuele II *(D4-5)*. This pedestrian zone lined by porticoes and modern architecture, movie theaters and stores, was rebuilt after the heavy bombing of 1943.

At the beginning of the Corso, on the left, overlooking Piazza del Duomo, is *La Rinascente* (rebuilt in 1950), a famous Milan department store. Worth noting along the Corso is the Art Nouveau Piazza del Liberty (n. 8), and the Neoclassical church of **S. Carlo al Corso**, built in 1839-47 (IV, *C6*).

Piazza S. Babila *(D5)*. The result of extensive urban rebuilding in the '30s and after WWII, this portico-lined piazza takes its name from the ancient church of **S. Babila**, with its 17th-c. column at the corner of Corso Monforte and Corso Venezia. The 11th-c. church was completely rebuilt between 1853 and 1906.

Corso Matteotti *(D4-5)*. Carved out as a Fascist avenue in 1926-34, this is an outstanding example of state architecture of the era. It culminates in a large disk-shaped *statue* by Arnaldo Pomodoro (1980); to the right, note

Milan: Piazza Mercanti

Piazza Belgioioso, with **Palazzo Belgioioso** (*D4*), by Piermarini (1772-81). At the corner of Via Morone is the *house* of the great 19th-c. author Alessandro Manzoni (*D4*), now the **Museo Manzoniano** (*entrance from Via Morone n. 1; open, Tue.-Fri., 9-12 and 2-4*). The brief Via Omenoni features the **Casa degli Omenoni*** (*D4*), with its mighty telamons underpinning the facade.

Piazza S. Fedele (*D4*). This pedestrian zone features a monument to Alessandro Manzoni (1883), and the church of **S. Fedele**, built to plans by P. Tibaldi (1569), but completed only in 1835. Remarkable paintings and, in the 17th-c. vestry, handsome carved cabinets.

To the left of the church, the rear facade* of **Palazzo Marino** (*D4*), built by Galeazzo Alessi (1553) in late Renaissance style, and left unaltered by the 19th-c. reconstruction. From Via Marino (n. 2), one can view the inner courtyard*, with two orders of loggias, through the former main ceremonial portal.

Piazza della Scala (*D4*). A city block was torn down in 1858 to make way for this square, designed by Luca Beltrami, who also rebuilt the facade of *Palazzo Marino*. In the center of the square stands a monument to Leonardo da Vinci (1872), overlooking La Scala.

Teatro alla Scala* (*D4*). Italy's premier opera house, possibly one of the world's finest, La Scala was built in 1776-78 by Giuseppe Piermarini, in unpretentious Neoclassical style, on the former site of the church of S. Maria della Scala, whence the name. The hall seats 3,000, has four orders of boxes, and two galleries, and is nicely finished in the Neoclassical style; partially destroyed by bombing in 1943, it was rebuilt and inaugurated with a legendary concert, directed by Arturo Toscanini.

Museo Teatrale alla Scala. *Open, 9-12 and 2-6; holidays, 9:30-12:30 and 2:30-6 (closed during afternoon performances).* Entrance through the portico to the left of the facade; major collection of operatic and theatrical memorabilia; the Raccolta Verdiana is noteworthy.

Galleria Vittorio Emanuele II* (*D4*). Traditional meeting place and watering hole of the Milanese, as well as one of the most remarkable pieces of the architecture of Milan after the Unification of Italy, the Galleria links Piazza del Duomo with Piazza della Scala. Built by G. Mengoni in 1865-78, it is crowned by a distinctive glass-and-steel roof that culminates in a central "octagon." There are four grand portals; the one facing the "Duomo," is joined with the porticoes of the piazza.

Palazzo della Ragione* (*D4*). Also called the *Broletto Nuovo*, it stands on what was once a large square, eliminated by the creation in 1867-78 of both Via and Piazza Mercanti. Built in 1233, this was the largest medieval town hall in Lombardy. The facade overlooking the piazza features a Romanesque relief* of Oldrado da Tresseno — its builder — on horseback (13th c.).

Facing the Palazzo della Ragione along Via Mercanti is *Palazzo dei Giureconsulti* (recently restored), with a portico and notable windows, almost entirely rebuilt since 1561, as have been many of the buildings along this street, dating from the 14th, 15th, and 17th c.

Brera and the "Quadrilatero della Moda"

In the northern part of town, enclosed within the Cerchia dei Navigli, this route takes you to the Pinacoteca di Brera, one of Italy's finest art galleries, through wealthy streets, studded with aristocratic mansions. The understated elegance of this neighborhood has made it a capital of Italian fashion designers.

Piazza Cordusio (*D4*). Oval in shape, with a statue to the 18th-c. poet Parini, this piazza is Milan's "business center," and features the official architectural style of the turn of the century.

Via Broletto (*D4*). This lovely old street, which continues as Via Ponte Vetero and then Via Mercato, is lined with 19th-c. office buildings, old working-class Milanese row houses, and small storefronts and businesses.

S. Maria del Carmine (*C4*). Although the slightly fanciful "Lombard-Gothic" facade dates only from 1880, the church itself was founded in the 15th c. Running off to the left from the square is the narrow Via Madonnina, intersecting with *Via S. Carpoforo* and *Via Fiori Chiari*. Long-ago a neighborhood of ill repute, these narrow lanes now teem with expensive shops and elegant nightspots; there is a fine *Mercato dell'Antiquariato*, or antiques market (3rd Sat. of each month).

Palazzo di Brera* (*C4*). This impressive building, at Via Brera no. 28, was headquarters of the Milanese Jesuits for two centuries (1572-1772); it then became home to many of the city's most important cultural institutions, including the Pinacoteca di Brera, the Biblioteca Nazionale Braidense, and the Accademia di Belle Arti.

Built in the 15th c., it was renovated by F.M. Richini (1651) and completed by Piermarini (1774). The elegant courtyard with two orders of arcades, features a heroic bronze statue of Napoleon Bonaparte I, by Antonio Canova (1811).

Pinacoteca di Brera**. *Open (hours subject to variations), 9-5:30; Sun., 9-12:30; closed Mon.* Spread out through the forty or so halls of the main floor, this is one of the leading collections of paintings in Italy; it chiefly features works of the Lombard and Venetian schools of the 15th to 18th centuries.

Founded two centuries ago as a resource for the students of the Accademia, opened in 1803, the galley grew rapidly throughout the 19th c.; the more recent acquisition of the Donazione Jesi (1976-84) gave Brera a 20th-c. dimension as well. Management problems and extensive restoration of the palazzo mean that some display rooms are closed off, and many paintings are in storage.

More than 600 works are displayed; among the artists are *15th- and 16th-c. Venetians, Lombards, and Emilians* (Jacopo Bellini, his two sons, Gentile and Giovanni Bellini, Andrea Mantegna, Carlo Crivelli, Vittore Carpaccio, Lorenzo Lotto, Titian, Paolo Veronese, Tintoretto, and Jacopo Bassano, Bernardino Luini, Correggio); *central Italian painters from the 14th and 16th c.* (Ambrogio Lorenzetti, Gentile da Fabriano, Donato Bramante, Piero della Francesca, Raphael, Luca Signorelli). Non-Italian artists include Anthony van Dyck, Rubens, and El Greco. Among the *17th-c. Italians* are Ludovico, Agostino, and Annibale Carracci, Guercino, and Caravaggio; there are *18th-c. Italians* (G.B. Tiepolo, G.B Piazzetta, Alessandro and Pietro Longhi, Francesco Guardi, Canaletto, Bernardo Bellotto); and *19th-c. Italians* (Andrea Appiani, Francesco Hayez, Silvestro Lega, Giovanni Fattori, Giovanni Pellizza). One major collection of 20th-c. work, the *Donazione Jesi*, includes paintings by Amedeo Modigliani, Umberto Boccioni, Gino Severini, Carlo Carrà, Massimo Campigli, Giorgio Morandi, Mario Sironi, Filippo De Pisis, Scipione, Picasso, and Braque; and sculpture by Medardo Rosso, Arturo Martini, and Marino Marini.

Via Brera (*C-D4*). With *Via Solferino* and *Via S. Marco*, this street runs through the heart of one of Milan's most interesting neighborhoods; here art galleries vie with fine restaurants, bars, and cafes.

Church of **S. Marco** (*C4*). Once overlooking the intersection of two canals, this church now faces out over the corner of Via S. Marco and Via Fatebenefratelli, just behind the Palazzo di Brera.

The church features the original portal, bell tower, and several statues upon the facade, dating from the 13th and 15th c.; on the interior are a number of paintings, frescoes, and other works.

Civico Museo del Risorgimento (*C4*). *Open, 9:30-5:30; closed last Mon. of each month.* This museum of Italian history is housed in the Neoclassical Palazzo Moriggia, at no. 23 in Via Borgonuovo. Along the way back to Via Manzoni, overlooking Via Verdi, is a particularly fine Baroque church, **S. Giuseppe** (*D4*), by F. M. Richini (1630).

Via Manzoni (*C-D4*). This venerable Milanese street is lined with handsome villas, many with large rear gardens.

On your left, in *Largo Croce Rossa*, is a controversial monument to the late Italian president and Resistance leader Sandro Pertini (Aldo Rossi, 1990); beyond this is the tree-lined **Via dei Giardini** (*C4*), with the remains of a 15th-c. monastic cloister, in *Piazza S. Erasmo*.
Past Via Monte Napoleone, Baroque and Neoclassical *palazzi* and churches line the road. Via Manzoni ends with the **arches of Porta Nuova**, dating from the 12th c.

Museo Poldi Pezzoli* (*D4*). *Open , 9:30-12:30 and 2:30-6; Sat. until 7:30; closed Mon. and (Apr.-Sep.) Sun. aft.* This is an outstanding example of Milanese home-qua-museum, and its 23 halls give a sterling indication of the tastes of a private collector of the 19th c., in this case, Gian Giacomo

Poldi Pezzoli. The collection includes 14th- to 19th-c. paintings and decorative arts: goldsmithery, enamels, Murano glass, Italian and European ceramics, furnishings, textiles (Persian carpet, signed and dated, 1542-43), lace and tapestries, mechanical clocks (Falck collection) and sundials (Portaluppi collection), weapons and armors. There are some masterpieces, by artists such as Piero del Pollaiolo, Botticelli, Piero della Francesca, Mantegna, Cosmè Tura, and F. Guardi; and a broad array of work by Lombard painters of the 15th and 16th c. (Bergognone, Boltraffio, Cesare da Sesto, Foppa, Luini) and 18th-c. Venetians (Tiepolo, Canaletto).

Via Monte Napoleone (*D4-5*). Almost entirely rebuilt in the Neoclassical style, lined with aristocratic palazzi, this street — with the last section of Via Manzoni, Via della Spiga, and Via S. Andrea — encloses the Quadrilatero della Moda, or "Rectangle of Fashion," featuring antique shops, jewelry stores, and designer retail outlets.

Museo Bagatti Valsecchi (*C-D5*) (*open, guided tours for groups, tel. 76006132*). This late 19th-c. home in Via S. Spirito n. 10 offers a fine view of the home of a collector. The furnishings include 16th-c. Flemish tapestries, stained glass, hope chests, and a bed decorated with bas-reliefs of Bible scenes. There are also paintings and other artworks.

Museo di Storia Contemporanea (*D5*). *Open, 9:30-5:30; closed last Tue. of each month.* Located in an 18th-c. palazzo, at no. 6 Via S. Andrea, it features documents and memorabilia of both World Wars and the period between them; upstairs is a **Museum of Milan** and a **Museum of Maritime Art**.

S. Ambrogio and the Quartiere Magenta

The centuries have left their mark in Milan, and this walk runs past the church of S. Ambrogio, a Romanesque archetype, and Santa Maria delle Grazie, where Leonardo da Vinci painted his "Last Supper," and past the Biblioteca Ambrosiana and the Pinacoteca Ambrosiana.

Piazza S. Ambrogio (*D-E2-3*). This oddly shaped square was once a broad thoroughfare — Stradone di S. Ambrogio — running alongside the basilica.

One end of the square is marked by the **Pusterla di S. Ambrogio**, built in 1939 in imitation of the medieval city gates (12th c.), and decorated by an authentic tabernacle with statues of patron saints (1360); oddly enough, this now houses a *Museo della Criminologia e delle Armi Antiche* (Museum of Criminology and Antique Weapons; *open, 10-1 and 3-7:30; Sat. and holidays until 11 pm*). Behind the basilica stand a military monument called the **Temple of Victory** (*E2-3*), an eight-sided tower (1927-30), and the **Università Cattolica del Sacro Cuore** (*E3*), a Catholic university, which features two cloisters by Bramante*.

S. Ambrogio** (*E2-3*). One of Milan's most distinctive landmarks, this basilica is a remarkable mixture of restoration and a founding monument of Lombard Romanesque.

Built in A.D. 379, as the "Basilica Martyrum," it is the final resting place of St. Ambrose, who was buried here in A.D.

Milan: S. Ambrogio

397. It was rebuilt extensively in the 9th and 10th c., and has undergone almost constant renovation since then.

Standing before the basilica is a solemn rectangular **atrium***, with porticoes (1088-99), resting upon composite columns with carved capitals. On the far side of the atrium, is the broad shed facade*, consisting of two stories of loggias: the upper loggia features five arches of declining size. On either side is a bell tower, the one on the right dating from the 9th c., the one on the left, with pilaster strips and little arches, dating from 1128-44. On the left portal, note the pre-Romanesque relief of St. Ambrose*; the central portal is adorned with minute carvings of monstrous figures and a grapevine motif (8th and 9th c.).

The *interior* is organized into a nave and three aisles, terminating in apses and separated by pillars, roofed by broad cross vaults, with galleries along the aisles, tambour, and the deep central apse. In the 3rd bay of the nave, on the left, above the sarcophagus of Stilicho (4th c.), is a **pulpit*** made of 11th-c. fragments. At the center of the presbytery, set on four porphyry columns from Roman times, is the *ciborium**, with a baldachin decorated with Lombard-Byzantine polychrome stuccoes (10th c.). Atop the **altar frontal**, or *Altare d'Oro*, is goldsmithery from the Carolingian period in gold and silver sheet (Stories of Christ and St. Ambrose) with decorations in enamel and gems, by the Maestro Volvinio (835). In the apse, note the carved Gothic wooden choir (1469-71); in the vault, note the enormous mosaic, with sections dating from the 4th and 8th c. and portions re-done in the 17th and 20th c.; in the crypt, silver urn (1897) with the bodies of St. Ambrose and two other saints. In the right aisle, fresco attributed to G. Ferrari; detached frescoes by Tiepolo; canvases and frescoes by Lanino. The 7th chapel

leads into the **Sacello di S. Vittore in Ciel d'Oro*** (4th c.): in the cupola, 5th-c. mosaics, with figures of saints. From the left aisle (1st chapel, Christ and Angels*, by Bergognone) you emerge under the *Portico della Canonica**, by Bramante (1492), rebuilt with original materials after heavy damage suffered in WWII.

Under the portico of the rectory is the entrance to the **Museo di S. Ambrogio** (*open, 10-12 and 3-5; Sat. and holidays, only aft.; closed Tue.*), which features goldwork, fabrics, tapestries, and other artwork from the basilica.

S. Vittore al Corpo (*E2*). Set back on a small rectangular piazza, this early Christian basilica was rebuilt in the late 16th c. The interior features 17th-c. paintings and a remarkable wooden choir.

To the left of the basilica is the former *monastery of S. Vittore*, now the site of the Museo della Scienza e della Tecnica (see below). Founded by Benedictines in the 11th c., the monastery was rebuilt in the 16th c. and repeatedly renovated; part of the cloisters and a few rooms survive from the original structure.

Museo Nazionale della Scienza e della Tecnica "Leonardo da Vinci"* (*E2*). *Open, 9:30-4:50; closed Mon.* Opened in 1953 as a museum documenting the development of science and industrial technology, the building extends over a vast area between Via Olona and Via S. Vittore (entry from the Piazza, at n. 21). With more than 35,000 sq. m. of exhibition area in three adjoining buildings, the museum has 28 sections. Temporary exhibits and conferences are held here; it also has a notable specialized library (about 40,000 volumes).

In the *monumental building* (once a monastery) is a great gallery devoted to Leonardo da Vinci, forming a considerable part of the museum, with extensive documentation concerning Leonardo, both as a scientist and as a technician and scholar of nature; moreover, rooms devoted to other areas of science and technology (computer science, timekeeping, acoustics, astronomy, telecommunications) and, in the sub-basement, land-based transportation, and metallurgy. On the third floor is a collection of 19th-c. paintings and sculpture, with work by Fattori, Fornara, Lega, Mancini, Michetti, and Giuseppe Pellizza. There is a *building devoted to rail transport*, with about twenty antique locomotives (steam and electric), railroad cars, signals, and other material documenting the technological development of the sector in Italy. In the *building devoted to air and sea transport*, there are sections concerning air transport (twenty antique airplanes, including a Blériot 11 from 1909) and maritime transport (the school ship "Ebe"; the bridge of the trans-Atlantic liner "Conte Biancamano"); also, a section devoted to agriculture.

In this same complex is the **Civico Museo Navale Didattico** (*open, 9:30-12.20 and 2:30-5; closed Mon.*), now being renovated.

Porta Magenta (*D1*). The city gate was demolished in 1885, but the name persists, a name that describes the elegant neighborhood stretching along Corso Magenta, Via Ariosto, Via Pagano, and the Parco Sempione. Remarkable buildings date from the turn of the century.

Cenacolo Vinciano** (*D2*). *Open, 9-1:15; Mon. closed; hours subject to variations.* On the far wall of the huge refectory of the one-time Dominican convent, to the left of the church, is Leonardo da Vinci's renowned fresco, The Last Supper** (1495-97), badly damaged by humidity, and almost destroyed by Allied bombs in the war.

S. Maria delle Grazie (D2). This church is one of the greatest monuments of the Milanese Renaissance. Built in Gothic style (1466-90), the church was given its apse in 1492, based on the design of Donato Bramante, in the shape of a huge three-apse cube, topped by a polygonal tambour with a gallery; one should note the elegant marble and terracotta decorations of the apse, and the 15th-c. marble portal in the facade.
The nave and two aisles are flanked by chapels, the bays divided by broad pointed arches set upon columns. The chapels and pillars feature remarkable artworks by such artists as Gaudenzio Ferrari and Paris Bordone.

The Renaissance **tambour** was meant to be a Sforza family mausoleum, and features a cupola set upon a drum held up by four spectacular arches. The dignified "graffito" decoration* (discovered in 1934-37 and restored in 1984-87) is attributed to Bramante; in the presbytery, an intarsiaed wooden choir (1470-1510). On the left, is the lovely little **cloister** again believed to be by Bramante. Then you enter the **Sagrestia Vecchia**, with inlaid cabinets* and early 16th-c. paintings.

Corso Magenta (D2-3). This main thoroughfare runs through the heart of the Quartiere Magenta; in the first stretch of this road only the facades survive from the 18th-c. buildings that once lined it; just past the Cerchia dei Navigli (ring of canals, many now covered over), or what is now Via Carducci, on the left (n. 24) stands the **Palazzo Litta** by F.M. Richini (1648), now offices of the State Railroads, with a rococo facade (1763) and a splendid porticoed courtyard. Facing it is the Ex **Monastero Maggiore**, once an enormous Milanese nunnery, built in the 15th c. and partly demolished in 1864-72; badly damaged in WWII; the church of S. Maurizio and the entry cloister survive, part of the Museo Archeologico.

Museo Archeologico (D3). Open, 9:30-5:30; closed last Mon. of each month. At Corso Magenta no. 15, it features remarkable **archeological and numismatic collections**. Of special interest are sculptures (Aphrodite-Aura), portraits (Maximin the Thracian*), mosaics, ceramics, oil lamps, glass, bronzes, silver; also, barbarian funerary objects. There are also remarkable *collections of Attic and other ancient pottery*. There is a large *Etruscan collection*. From the garden, one has a view of two Roman towers.

S. Maurizio* (D3). Open, Mon.-Fri., 4-6. This Renaissance church was begun in the 16th c. and completed in 1872-96. The interior features a remarkable fresco, attributed to Bernardino Luini, among others.

S. Maria alla Porta (D3). This church, built after 1652 by F.M. Richini, overlooks the Via S. Maria alla Porta, which followed the Roman "decumanus maximus." Inside, note 17th-c. canvases and sculpture. Heading back toward the mouth of Corso Magenta, you can follow the narrow Via Brisa (left) to the excavations of a large Roman building. Just behind the church is the "Quartiere degli Affari," or Financial District, the heart of which is the **Palazzo della Borsa**, by P. Mezzanotte (1931), which stands on the site of the ancient Roman theater (relics in the basement of the palazzo, *open by request, contact the Camera di Commercio, or chamber of commerce*). In

the nearby Piazza Borromeo (E3), at n. 7, is the **Palazzo Borromeo**; in the inner courtyard (open by request) note frescoes* in the International Gothic style (first half of the 15th c.).

Piazza S. Sepolcro (E3-4). This is the site of the ancient Roman Forum, though no traces survive. Overlooking the piazza is the church of **S. Sepolcro**, founded in 1030, but rebuilt in 1894-97.

Pinacoteca Ambrosiana* (E4). With its sister library, this is one of the most important cultural institutions in Milan, dating from the early 17th c. Some of the most important artwork in the collection, chiefly Lombard and Venetian, includes work by Botticelli, Bergognone, Luini, Bramantino, Leonardo, G.A. De Predis, Raphael, Tiepolo, Caravaggio, Moretto, Moroni, Titian, and J. Bassano.

The Castello Sforzesco and Porta Garibaldi

The northwestern section of the historical center of Milan clusters around the majestic structure of the Castello, its courtyards, great walls, and mighty towers redolent with the history of the Visconti and Sforza dukedom. Behind the castle lies one of the city's few stretches of greenery.

Via Dante (D3-4). One of the finest legacies of Milan under King Umberto (1890), this road provides a fitting link between Piazza Cordusio and the Castello Sforzesco; at n. 2 is the *Palazzo Carmagnola*, all that survived the wholesale demolition of the 19th c. Next to it, in Via Rovello, is the *Piccolo Teatro*, a prestigious Milanese theater founded in 1947, soon to be transferred to a new site, in Piazzale Marengo.

At the end, Via Dante opens out into **Largo Cairoli**, with a monument to Garibaldi (1895). This is the spot marking the convergence of the two tree-lined semicircles of the *Foro Buonaparte* and *Piazza Castello*, part of the unfinished Neoclassical design by Antolini (1801) for a huge circular plaza around the Castello Sforzesco.

Castello Sforzesco (C-D3). This huge fortified complex — perhaps the most significant monument from the Renaissance still standing in Milan, despite its troubled history — has housed the city museums and other major cultural institutions since the end of the 19th c.

The castle was built at the orders of Francesco Sforza (1450) on an existing 14th-c. structure. It became the home of Galeazzo Maria Sforza, duke of Milan, in 1466; the new duke summoned artists to turn the castle into a stately home; among them were V. Foppa, C. Moretto, and B. Ferrini. Ludovico the Moor, in turn, summoned Leonardo da Vinci, Bramante, Filarete, Zenale, and Butinone. After the Spanish took Milan in 1535, the Castello became one of the largest and best-served citadels in Europe by the early-17th c. It was heavily damaged by a French siege under Louis XV (1733); Napoleon Bonaparte ordered the castle demolished in 1800, though his orders were only partly carried out. It was used as a barracks by the Austrian occupying army. In 1893 Luca Beltrami undertook a fairly rough-and-tumble restoration, demolishing and rebuilding freely to recreate the "original" appearance of the Castello.

The outer ramparts were demolished at the orders of Napoleon. The Castello is now a vast square building made of brick, with long curtain walls and huge windows framed in terracotta, massive corner towers, battlements, and a moat. In the center of the facade is the so-called *Torre del Filarete*, a reproduction (1905) of the hypothetical 15th-c. tower. The arch at the foot of this tower opens out into a vast courtyard, the *Piazza d'Armi*, enclosed by three buildings (from the left): the Rocchetta, the Torre di Bona di Savoia (1477), and the Palazzo della Corte Ducale, with large terracotta Gothic windows. To the left of the entrance is the *Raccolta delle Stampe A. Bertarelli*, a collection of over 600,000 prints, ranging from the homeliest woodcuts to the most exquisite etchings. On the side of the Piazza d'Armi opposite the Torre del Filarete, you enter the *Corte Ducale* through a door surmounted by the Sforza crest, with a portico and Renaissance loggia on the left; to the right is the entrance to the Civici Musei (see below). A passageway on the left leads into the porticoed *courtyard of the Rocchetta*; note the entrance to the *Archivio Storico Civico* and to the *Biblioteca Trivulziana*, originally the private library of the Trivulzio family, purchased in 1935 by the City of Milan; rare books and incunabula. The Porta del Barco, back in the Corte Ducale, leads out into the Parco Sempione (see below); follow the moat off to the right, and you will reach the NE side of the Castello, with the *Ponticella di Ludovico the Moor*, attributed to Bramante, but largely created during the 19th-c. reconstruction.

Musei del Castello**. *Open, 9:30-5:30; closed last Tue. of each month*. These museums comprise collections of sculpture, painting, and the applied arts; they have three major sections (Civiche Raccolte) of ancient art, the applied arts, and archeology and numismatics, largely arranged by chronological order. An exception to this order can be seen in the *Sala del Gonfalone* (frescoes with heraldic devices of Spanish royalty and viceroys; gonfalon*, or banner, of Milan, painted and embroidered, 1566), the *Sala delle Asse** (frescoed vault, cartoons by Leonardo da Vinci, heavily restored; this hall contains the Belgioioso collection of Dutch and Flemish paintings of the 17th and 18th c.), the *Cappella Ducale* (15th-c. frescoes), the *Sala della Balla* (**tapestries** depicting the months*, begun in 1503, designed by Bramantino, woven in Vigevano), and the *Sala del Tesoro* (*open by request*; fresco of Argo).

Civiche Raccolte d'Arte Antica. *Collections of statuary*, largely from Milanese and Lombard monuments: note sculpture from early-Christian, Longobard, Romanesque, and Gothic periods. Sculpture and architecture from the 15th and 16th c., by A. di Duccio, A. Mantegazza, Portal of the Banco Mediceo* attributed to M. Michelozzi (in the hall of the collection of 16th-/17th-c. weapons), Bambaia, and Michelangelo (**Pietà Rondanini****). Go to the *second floor*; note the *collection of furniture**, from the 15th to the 18th c., along with tapestries, paintings, statues, and wooden bas-reliefs; note the reconstruction of a hall from the Castello di Roccabianca (Parma) with a detached series of 15th-c. frescoes*.

Next is the **art gallery**, with paintings by: A. Mantegna, B. Bembo, Giovanni Bellini, Vincenzo Foppa, Bergognone, Bramantino, C. da Sesto, Correggio, L. Lotto, Tintoretto, Fra' Galgario, Cerano, A. Magnasco, G.B. Tiepolo, and F. Guardi.

Civiche Raccolte d'Arte Applicata. This museum of the applied arts has a *ceramic section*, with porcelain and majolica, enamels, Renaissance bronze figurines, religious fabrics and clothing. *Museo degli Strumenti Musicali*, with a collection of 640 musical instruments in five sections; also note the 18th-/19th-c. costumes.

Civiche Raccolte Archeologiche e Numismatiche. This is a branch of the Museo Archeologico in Corso Magenta (see), and features a *prehistoric section*, with much material on early Lombard cultures. The Egyptian section includes everyday objects and funerary material. A new *section on Milan under Roman rule* has been added. The *medal collection* (*open by request*) includes roughly 230,000 items, from the 6th c. B.C. to modern times.

Parco Sempione (*C2-3*). Extending over an area of 47 hectares behind the Castello, this park was arranged in the English style in 1893 by E. Alemagna, with trees planted to offer a perspective on the Arco della Pace.

On your left, as you leave the Castello through the Porta del Barco, you will find the **Palazzo dell'Arte** (*C2*; 1932-33), where the Milan Triennale is held, along with other events. Note the *Torre del Parco*, formerly Torre Littoria, built in 1932 by Gio Ponti, in steel tubing, 109 m. tall. At the end of the park, in the center, stands the **Arco della Pace** (Arch of Peace; *C2*), one of the most distinctive momuments of the Neoclassical period, by L. Cagnola, begun in 1807 to honor Napoleon, and dedicated in 1838 to Francis I of Austria, and in 1859 rededicated to the independence of Italy. It directs the gaze out over the *Corso Sempione*, the first stretch of the great Napoleonic road running toward the Lago Maggiore; note the old palazzi at n. 25, 27, 33, and 36. In the park to the right of the Castello is the **Arena Civica** (*B-C3*), a Neoclassical construction from Napoleonic times, built by L. Canonica (1807). Overlooking Via Gadio (n. 2) is the **Acquario Civico** (aquarium; *open, 9:30-5:30; closed the last Tue. of each month*), with 48 tanks holding fresh-and salt-water fish, reptiles, amphibians, and invertebrates. At n. 4 in the nearby Via Quintino Sella is the *Museo Didattico del Falso nell'Antiquariato*, a private museum devoted to unmasking fake antiques (*open, Tue.-Fri., 1:30-6; Sat., 9-2; closed Sun. and Mon.*); set back between Via Tivoli and Piazzale Marengo, is the construction yard of the new *Piccolo Teatro* (Marco Zanuso; 1984).

Corso Garibaldi (*B-C3-4*). The central thoroughfare of one of the oldest and most distinctive Milanese quarters, this road runs along the ancient Roman "Way to Como," through a working-class 19th-c. neighborhood, only partly changed by the arrival of the Metropolitana. On the left (n. 17), note the reassembled facade of the *Teatro Fossati* (1858-59).

S. Simpliciano* (*C3-4*). Set back on the Piazza S. Simpliciano, to the right of Corso Garibaldi, this Romanesque basilica was founded in the 4th c. but was heavily renovated in the 19th century. Some of the outside walls date back 16 centuries, but in the facade only the central portal and some arches date back as early as the 12th c. Inside, note the large fresco* in the vault of the apse, by Bergognone (ca. 1515); also note the carved wooden 16th-c. choir.

To the right of the basilica (Piazza delle Crociate n. 6) is the former **convent of S. Simpliciano**, now occupied by the Facoltà Teologica Interregionale (*open, Mon.-Fri., 9-12:30 and 2-6, enquire with the custodian*), with a small 15th-c. cloister and a larger mid-16th-c. cloister*, possibly by V. Seregni.

S. Maria Incoronata (*B4*). Erected in the late 15th c., this church has a two-part facade that corresponds to its interior spatial organization. According to certain sources, the twin structure, with two identical aisles, was built at the behest of Francesco Sforza and his wife Bianca Maria, as a symbolic seal on the happiness of their marriage. Inside, on the right, on the walls of the chapels, note the 15th-c. funerary plaques and remains of frescoes in the apse (late-16th c.).

Cimitero Monumentale (*A3*). *Open 8:30-5:15; Sun. and Sat. and holidays, closes at 5:45; Mon. closed*. At the end of Viale Ceresio, this monumental cemetery was built in 1863-66 by C. Maciachini; at the center of the long front facade is the *Famedio*, a sort of Milanese Pantheon, where the most-prominent citizens are buried. Chapels and monuments constitute an interesting gallery of architecture and sculpture of the Lombard late-19th and 20th c. (M. Rosso, E. Butti, L. Bistolfi, A. Wildt, and F. Messina).

Porta Ticinese and Porta Romana

Along the perimeter of the Spanish bastions, there once stood ten mighty town gates (late-16th c.); in the street names of modern times, there are even a few more, each one of them the center of a specific sense of neighborhood, five of them still boasting their monumental entry. In the southern part of Milan, between Porta Ticinese and Porta Romana, there are relics of early-Christian times (S. Lorenzo), Renaissance monuments (S. Satiro, Cappella Portinari, Ca' Granda), and the surprising cityscape of the Navigli.

Piazza Missori (*E4*). A tangled welter of older and more recent architecture, this square marks the western extremity of the demolition done after WWII (the notorious "Racchetta," or Tennis Racket, of the new zoning plan of 1953).

At the mouth of the Via Albricci, at the center, note the remains of the church of *S. Giovanni in Conca*, founded in early-Christian times and rebuilt in the 11th c. To the right of the *Palazzo dell'INPS* (n. 8-10) by M. Piacentini (1929-31), is the brick facade of the 17th-c. *Collegio di S. Alessandro* (now part of the university); also note the church of **S. Alessandro**, behind Piazza Missori, begun in 1601 by L. Binago, continued by the Richini, father and son, and completed in 1710. Inside, late-17th-c. canvases and frescoes.

S. Maria presso S. Satiro (*E4*). This church, an architectural gem of the early Renaissance, was built in 1476-86, with much work by Bramante, who worked on it after 1478. The facade, set back from the Via Torino, was rebuilt in 1871. In the rear, visible from Via Mazzini, is a late-10th-c. Romanesque campanile, behind which stands the older Cappella della Pietà*, with an elegant 15th-c. exterior.

The small *interior* has a singe central nave aisle and a transept covered with broad barrel vaults; note the cupola. The asymmetrical plan resulted in the famous false painted **presbytery***, behind the main altar; this was work by the hand of Bramante. At the end of the left transept, note the *Cappella della Pietà*, a chapel that was once a separate structure (Basilica di Ansperto, 9th

c.), with a Greek-cross plan; on the altar, note the group of the Pietà, by Agostino de' Fondutis (1482-83). From the right aisle, you can enter the octagonal **Battistero*** (or sacristy), with two orders of pilaster strips and a dome, also by Bramante, decorated with a handsome frieze, also by de' Fondutis (1483).

Via Torino (*E3-4*). This major shopping thoroughfare follows the medieval road that led to the Duomo, or Cathedral. Set back at n. 3-5 in Via Spadari is the Liberty-style (Italian Art-Nouveau) facade of the **Casa Ferrario** (*E4*) by E. Pirovano (1904); a little further along, the Via Torino is dominated on the right by the tall cylindrical structure of the church of **S. Sebastiano** (*E4*; 1577-95), built to fulfill a vow made in the hopes of halting an outbreak of the plague (1576). Designed by P. Tibaldi, but heavily modified since its construction, the interior has a circular plan, and it is crowned by an 18th-c. dome. Further along, and also on the right, is the church of **S. Giorgio al Palazzo** (*E3*), founded in A.D. 750, but rebuilt in Neoclassical style by L. Cagnola (1800-21); inside, note the frescoes and panels by B. Luini (1516). At the end of Via Torino is the **Carrobbio** (*E3*), an ancient intersection of Roman origin (the name is believed to derive from the Latin for "intersection" — "quadrivium"). Set back in Via S. Sisto (n. 10), in the former church of S. Sisto, is the **Civico Museo-Studio Francesco Messina** (*E3; open, 9:30-5:30; closed last Tue. of each month*) with numerous works by this artist (bronzes, polychrome statues, paintings, drawings, sketches).

S. Lorenzo Maggiore** (*E3*). This basilica is one of the most important and the oldest monuments in Milan, of considerable weight in the history of western architecture.

Before the church lies a broad square, with a bronze copy of a statue of the emperor Constantine, in commemoration of the Edict of Milan (A.D. 313), which gave civil rights and toleration to Christians throughout the empire. Note the 16 Roman **columns*** from the empire, once part of a temple (2nd/3rd c.), transported here in the 4th c, and inserted in the great quadriporticus (later destroyed) in front of the facade.

In its basic features, this is a late-16th-c. church, which incorporates the early-Christian church, built at the end of the 4th c. as a Palatine basilica, transformed into a Romanesque church in the 12th c. The 16th-c. church still preserves the central plan of the original structure, with four

Milan: S. Lorenzo Maggiore

corner towers, and three chapels (best seen from behind).

The *interior*, with its central plan, can be likened to S. Vitale in Ravenna; the majestic circular hall, with exedrae, galleries, and an immense dome, is lined with a broad ambulatory. On the right, through an atrium with traces of 4th-c. mosaics and a Roman portal (late-1st c.), you enter the 4th-c. **Cappella di S. Aquilino****, an intact original structure, octagonal, with niches, a loggia, and dome: in two niches, more 4th-c. mosaics*; to the right of the entrance, 3rd-c. sarcophagus; on the altar, 16th-c. silver urn with the relics of S. Aquilino; a little stairway behind the altar leads down to the foundations, probably built with blocks of stone from the amphitheater. Behind the main altar of the church is the 4th-c. *Cappella di S. Ippolito*; on the left side of the church is the 6th-c. *Cappella di S. Sisto*.

Parco delle Basiliche (*E-F3*). Extending from Piazza della Vetra, behind S. Lorenzo, all the way to S. Eustorgio, this park offers a visual sweep encompassing both remarkable churches. To the right of the Basilica di S. Lorenzo stands the medieval gate of **Porta Ticinese**, built in the 12th c., rebuilt in the 14th c., and further modified in 1861-65. On the outer facade, note the tabernacle with reliefs of saints, by the school of G. di Balduccio (14th c.). Beyond the gate, *Corso di Porta Ticinese* continues out of town through the heart of the working-class Quartiere Ticinese, with much of the flavor of the original medieval "borgo."

S. Eustorgio* (*F3*). One of the most notable monuments in Milan, this basilica has a complex and stratified structure, with fragments from the 7th c. and pieces of the Romanesque structure (12th c.), set in a building that was being modified and revamped until the late-15th c. Surrounded by a broad tree-lined area, the neo-Romanesque facade dates from 1862-65; only the little loggia is intact (1597), in the left corner; at the end of the right flank, with its 15th-c. chapels, near the apse, stands the tall bell tower* (1297-1309), behind which you can see the handsome exterior of the Cappella Portinari.

Inside, in the three aisles, divided by pillars with 11th- and 12th-c. capitals, note the deep apse. In the chapels on the right, 14th- and 15th-c. funerary monuments and frescoes (in the vaults; in the 1st chapel, triptych by Bergognone; in the 4th, funerary monuments to Stefano Visconti by G. di Balduccio). In the right transept, note the *Cappella dei Magi*, with a large Roman sarcophagus which held the supposed relics of the saint until 1164. On the main altar, note the unfinished marble frontal, possibly designed by G. de' Grassi (early-15th c.) and M. da Campione. Behind the apse (where you can see the foundations of the original, 5th-c. basilica), from the pseudo-crypt you can enter the **Cappella Portinari**** (*open by request, enquire in the sacristy*) a gem of early-Renaissance Tuscan-style architecture (1466), long thought to be the work of Michelozzo. Square in plan, covered by a dome, with a sacellum in which stands the altar, this chapel has elaborate and lavish decorations, notable among them the polychrome procession of Angels* holding festoons in the tambour beneath the dome, designed by a Tuscan master, and perhaps executed by Foppa; the frescoes** high on the walls are a master-

piece by V. Foppa (1468); at the center is the marble Arca di S. Pietro Martire**, carved by G. di Balduccio (1339). The little *Museo di S. Eustorgio* (*open by request*) features 17th-c. paintings and sacred furnishings from the 17th and 18th c.; it also features underground rooms, the remains of a *Roman and early-Christian cemetery*.

Porta Ticinese (*F3*). Do not confuse this gate with the medieval gate of the same name; this one stands isolated in the center of Piazzale XXIV Maggio. One of the most notable works of Milanese Neoclassicism, it was built by L. Cagnola (1801-14) as an arch of triumph, to commemorate Napoleon's victory at Marengo. Nearby is the **Darsena** (*F2-3*), an old town port and the only basin to survive from the complex system of canals that once ringed Milan; it now marks the convergence of the *Naviglio Grande*, running from Abbiategrasso and the *Naviglio di Pavia*, which flows into the river Ticino. Overlooking the water is a distinctive quarter of old Milan, once quite working-class, now as fashionable and expensive as can be, with restaurants, bars, and nightspots. In early June, the popular *Festa dei Navigli* is held here, and, on the last Sunday of each month, the noted *Mercatone del Naviglio Grande* is held here, with merchandise ranging from fine antiques to bric-a-brac. At n. 27 in Ripa Ticinese stands the **Museo del Giocattolo e del Bambino** (*F2; open, 9:30-12:30 and 3-7:30; closed Mon. and Aug.*), a toy museum, with a rotating display of items from the 18th to the 20th c.

S. Maria presso S. Celso* (*F4*). Also known as *S. Maria dei Miracoli*, this church is a fine example of 16th-c. architecture; it was designed by Dolcebuono (1493) and completed in 1506. Before it stands a solemn quadriporticus*, a masterpiece by Cesariano from the early-16th c.; the four-order facade is by G. Alessi and M. Bassi (late-16th c.).

The *interior*, with three aisles, 16th-c. decorations, fine dome, and presbytery surrounded by ambulatory. Beneath the dome, on either side of the cross-vault, statues by S. Lorenzi and A. Fontana, who also did the statue of the Assunta (Assumption; 1586) on the altar of the Madonna (to the left of the presbytery), to which Milanese brides traditionally pay respects on their wedding day; in the presbytery, note the handsome inlaid choir (1570). On the altar of the right transept and in the ambulatory, note sculpture and paintings by P. Bordone, G. Ferrari, and the Moretto; the altar in the left transept incorporates a 4th-c. sarcophagus; in the 1st chapel on the left, note painting by Bergognone.

To the right of the church of S. Maria dei Miracoli stands the Romanesque church of **S. Celso** (*open by request, enquire in the sacristy*), built in the 10th c. but rebuilt by Canonica (1851-54); note the Lombard-Romanesque campanile and the original portal.

Corso Italia (*E-F4*). This broad thoroughfare, running out from the center, was built at the turn of the century; in part it runs along the ancient "Corso di S. Celso"; roughly halfway along this broad street is the former church of **S. Paolo Converso** (*open, 10-1 and 2:30-7:30 during exhibitions and by request, tel. 809191*), now the headquarters of an auction house. Across the street is a 17th-c. column. The church was built between 1549 and 1580; the facade is by Cerano (1613); the handsome interior is by the Cremonese architects Antonio, Giulio, and Vincenzo Campi. Further along (n. 10), is the office *building of the Touring Club Italiano* (1914-15).

Corso di Porta Romana (*E-F4-5*). Linking Piazza Missori with *Porta Romana*, this street, built in 1598, runs along the course of what was originally the Roman "decumanus maximus," and which was lined with monumental porticoes (2nd-3rd c.; you can see traces in the Missori station of the Metropolitana, line 3). In its first stretch, the Corso alternates modern buildings with ancient palazzi (at n. 6, note the 17th-c. *Palazzo Annoni*), and is dominated by the **Torre Velasca** (1958), a 26-story office and apartment building, outstanding creation of postwar Milanese architecture.

S. Nazaro Maggiore* (*E4*). This basilica was founded by St. Ambrose (A.D. 386); much of the cross-structure dates from the 4th c. It was rebuilt in the 11th c. (apse and tambour), and renovated extensively in later centuries.

Note the octagonal **Cappella Trivulzio***, built by Bramantino (1512-50), containing the family tombs in a simple room, including the Arca di G.G. Trivulzio, with the noteworthy Latin inscription: "Qui numquam quievit quiescit; tace" (He who never had rest is now sleeping; silence).

From the chapel you can descend into the basilica proper; note, in the right arm of the transept, a Last Supper by B. Lanino. To the right of the presbytery, note the 10th-c. *Basilichetta di S. Lino*; from the left arm of the transept, you can enter the 16th-c. *Cappella di S. Caterina d'Alessandria*, with fresco* by Lanino (1546).

Ca' Granda* (*E4-5. Open 8:30-7; closed Sat. and Sun.* This is the former Ospedale Maggiore, or main hospital, used for health care until 1939 (now the campus of the Università Statale); it remains one of the most noteworthy monuments of 15th-c. Milan. It was founded in 1456 by Francesco Sforza and his wife Bianca Maria, and was enlarged between the 17th and 19th c. Devastated by Allied bombing and subsequent fires in 1943, it has been radically restored.

The 15th-c. wing, on the right of the long facade, shows a style in transition from Gothic to Renaissance; built by Filarete, it consists of an arched portico below and a floor of handsome terracotta mullioned windows. The central section is a lavish imitation of the 15th-c. wing; along with the vast inner courtyard* with portico and loggia, it was built in the 17th c. by F.M. Richini, F. Mangone, and G.B. Pessina. To the right of this courtyard, note the lovely little late-17th-c. Cortiletto, a small courtyard with two orders of arcades. The notable *Quadreria dei Benefattori**, a portrait gallery, is being moved to the old stables of the abbey of Mirasole (*open by request, contact the Amministrazione degli Istituti Ospedalieri, tel. 55038278, 55038276*).

Piazza S. Stefano (*E5*). This oddly shaped space is dominated by the Baroque facade and the tall bell tower (17th c.) of the church of **S. Stefano Maggiore**, now headquarters of the *Archivio Storico Diocesano*, a religious archive; also note the 17th-c. former church of *S. Bernardino alle Ossa*, which takes its name ("Ossa," or bones) from a macabre chapel lined with human bones.

Porta Vittoria
and the "zona Venezia"

In the NE area of Milan, starting from the Verziere and continuing on beyond the walls, you will encounter relics of the Baroque age, marks of 19th-c. opulence, streets and houses decorated with "floral" motifs and the scars of a metropolis undergoing constant rebuilding.

Largo Augusto (*E5*). Standing in this small square is the Colonna del Verziere, a column erected in the 17th c. as a votive offering after the end of the plague in 1577, by Ricchino, among others.

Running into this square is the **Via Durini** (*D5*), lined by aristocratic palazzi, including, at n. 20, the *Casa Toscanini* (18th c.) and, at n. 24, the Baroque **Palazzo Durini**, also by F.M. Richini (1648). At intersection between the *Corso di Porta Vittoria* and the Cerchia dei Navigli (ring road along the course of the old canals) is the 18th-c. **Palazzo Sormani Andreani** (*E5*), now housing the *Biblioteca Centrale Comunale*. Further along is the massive looming *Palazzo di Giustizia* (Hall of Justice; *E5*) by Piacentini and Rapisardi (1932-40); set back on the Via Besana is the **Rotonda della Besana** (*E6*), a rotunda that was originally the cemetery of the Ospedale Maggiore (1713-25) and which is now used for exhibitions, with the former church enclosed by a circular portico.

S. Pietro in Gessate (*E5*). We are not sure who built this church (attributed either to P. Antonio or G. Solari), but we do know it was built from 1447-75, in a style shifting from Gothic to Renaissance. The facade was redone in 1912, and only the central portal survives. Inside, note 15th-c. Lombard frescoes and paintings. The left transept is covered with frescoes by B. Butinone and B. Zenale (1490).

S. Maria della Passione* (*D6*). This large church, second only to the Duomo, was begun to a Greek-cross plan in 1486, while the dome was completed by Cristoforo Lombardo in 1530; transformed to a Latin-cross plan at the end of the 16th c., it was given a Baroque facade in 1692-1729. On the interior, on the piers of the nave and in the enormous octagon of the dome, note paintings* by Daniele Crespi, who also created the doors of the two organs in the niches of the presbytery (the organ on the right is an Antegnati, 1558; the one on the left dates from 1610). In the right transept, Deposition, attributed to Luini; in the left transept, Last Supper by Gaudenzio Ferrari.

From the niche between the apse and the transept, you enter the **Museo della Basilica** (*open, 10-12 and 3-5; holidays only aft.; closed Sat. and Aug.*), with handsome frescoes by Bergognone, and other work by 17th-c. Lombard artists (D. Crespi, F. del Cairo, Vermiglio).

To the right of the church, in a former convent (early-16th-c. courtyard, attributed to C. Solari), is the **Conservatorio di Musica Giuseppe Verdi**, a conservatory with a remarkable *library* of musical manuscripts (18th-/19th-c.). To the left of the church (Via Bellini n. 11), note the **Casa Campanini**, one of the most remarkable examples of Milanese Liberty (a style corresponding to Italian Art-Nouveau; 1909).

Corso Monforte (*D5-6*). This chief thoroughfare of what was once the "Borgo di Monforte" features (n. 35) the **Palazzo Isimbardi**, built in the 15th c. and repeatedly renovated; it is now headquarters of the Amministrazione Provinciale, or provincial government; the vault of the Sala della Giunta (*open by request*) is decorated with a large painting by Giambattista Tiepolo.

Corso Venezia (*C-D5-6*). This major thoroughfare has a series of aristocratic palazzi and parks, giving it the dignity of a major urban boulevard; it ends with the two massive structures of the **Caselli di Porta Orientale** (*C6*), by R. Vantini (1827-28).

On the right in the first stretch of this road (n. 10), note **Casa Silvestri**, a fine example of a small Renaissance palazzo (1475), with an elegant courtyard and 14th-c. fragments; almost directly across the street (n. 11), note the portal (1652) of the **Seminario Arcivescovile**, done in 1565-77 by P.Tibaldi and V. Seregni, with a courtyard built in 1602-8 by A. Trezzi and F. Mangone. At the corner of Via S. Damiano (n. 16), note the enormous **Palazzo Serbelloni** with a Neoclassical facade (1793).

Palazzo del Senato (*C5*). This noteworthy creation of the architecture of the Counter Reformation (1608-30) has a facade by F. M. Richini and two majestic courtyards by F. Mangone. Restored after the bombing of 1943, it is now the headquarters of the Archivio di Stato, one of Italy's leading state archives.

Villa Reale* (*C5*). One of the finest creations of Milanese Neoclassicism, built in 1790 by L. Pollak for the counts of Barbiano di Belgioioso. It was the residence of Napoleon and of Eugene de Beauharnais, viceroy of Italy; the Austrian soldier Count Radetzky lived here (1857-58). Note the rear facade, overlooking the garden; inside is the Galleria d'Arte Moderna, a gallery of modern art.

Galleria d'Arte Moderna* (*C5*). *Open, 9:30-5:30; closed last Mon. of each month* (*undergoing partial restoration*). This gallery of modern art has a select collection of painting and sculpture, particularly Lombard, from the Neoclassical period (A. Canova, A. Appiani) and the Romantic era (Piccio, F. Hayez) and the late-19th c. (D. Ranzoni, T. Cremona, G. Segantini, M. Rosso). Note the *Vismara collection*, with work by A. Tosi, A. Modigliani, F. De Pisis, and G. Morandi; "*Il Quarto Stato*" by G. Pellizza, purchased with a public subscription in 1920; the *Museo Marino Marini*, with a monographic collection assembled by the sculptor himself, of his own work. The *Raccolta Grassi* is a collection comprising objets-d'art, fabrics, Oriental carpets, and especially 19th- and 20th-c. paintings of the French (Corot, Sisley, Manet, Cézanne, Gauguin, Van Gogh, Vuillard, Bonnard, Toulouse-Lautrec, Utrillo) and Italian (Lega, Ranzoni, Boldini, De Nittis, Mancini, Spadini, Pellizza, Segantini, Balla, Boccioni, Morandi) schools.

Piazza Cavour (*C5*). Set between the arches of *Porta Nuova* and the *Giardini Pubblici* (public park; see below) this square is dominated by the *Palazzo dei Giornali*, or press building, built in 1937-42 by G. Muzio, and by the tall building of the *Centro Svizzero* (1952). Set back on the right in Via Manin (n. 2) is the 18th-c. **Palazzo Dugnani**, with porticoes and loggias; inside (*open by request, during office hours*), the central hall was frescoed* by G.B. Tiepolo. The building houses the **Museo del Cinema della Cineteca Italiana** (*open, 3-6; closed Sat., Sun. and Mon.*), with documents, memorabilia, and materials on the history of film.

Via Turati (*B-C5*). At the beginning of this street, set back on the left, at n. 5 in Via Carlo Porta, is the headquarters of the Fondazione Corrente, with the *Studio-Museo di Ernesto Treccani* (*open, 4-7; closed Sat., Sun. and in the summer*). On either side of Via Turati, on a line with Largo Donegani, is the sober complex of the former *Palazzi della Montecatini* (n. 2 dates from 1936-38 and n. 1 from 1951), both by the architect Gio Ponti and associates; on the far side of Via Moscova is the eclectic residential complex called *Ca' Brütta* (1919-22). In a further stretch of Via Turati, at n. 34, is the *Museo della Permanente* (1886), where

major art exhibits are held; at the end of the street, two twin tall buildings (1960s) mark the transition to the huge, tree-lined *Piazza della Repubblica*, built in the Thirties and rebuilt after WWII.

S. Angelo (*B-C4*). Set at the beginning of Via Moscova adjoining a Franciscan convent, this church is one of the principal 16th-c. monuments in Milan, with a 17th-c. Mannerist facade. Inside, on the altars and in the sacristy, 16th- and 17th-c. canvases by A. Campi, the Fiammenghini, and by G.C. and Camillo Procaccini.

Giardini Pubblici (*C5*). Completely enclosed by a long fence, this is the oldest public park in the city; with an area of 17 hectares, it comprises a Neoclassical section (toward Corso Venezia), designed by Piermarini (1783-86), with a later English-style garden (1857-81). In these gardens, aligned along Corso Venezia, are the **Planetario** (Planetarium; 1930-55), where lectures and astronomical slide shows are held; and the Museo Civico di Storia Naturale (Natural History Museum).

Museo Civico di Storia Naturale* (*C5*). *Open 9:30-5:30; Sat. and holidays until 7:30; closed last Mon. of each month.* Founded in 1838 with the donation to the city of the collections of the naturalists Jan and De Cristoforis, this museum is housed in an immense neo-Romanesque building (1888-93). Despite heavy damage in 1943, it remains one of the leading museums of natural history in Europe, with a thriving research division (specialized library, with over 30,000 volumes; huge research collections). More than 20 halls on two floors feature minerals, fossils, and stuffed animals, as well as models, dioramas*, and explanatory panels.

Of particular interest to the history of science, note the surviving materials from the 17th-c. *naturalistic Settala museum**; also, dinosaur skeletons and eggs; the skeleton of a 19-m.-long whale; skeletons of extinct vertebrates (*Equus quagga, Alca impennis*); a single giant crystal of colorless topaz (40 kg.); and a large stuffed specimen of the *Tridacna gigantea*.

Corso Venezia (*second stretch; C5-6*). This monumental Neoclassical boulevard is lined with solemn facades overlooking the park of the Giardini Pubblici; note, at n. 40, *Palazzo Saporiti* (1812) and, at n. 51, *Palazzo Bovara* (1787); at n. 47, **Palazzo Castiglioni**, by G. Sommaruga (1900-1904), emblem of Italian Liberty (the vernacular equivalent of Art Nouveau). Other interesting examples of the Milanese early-20th-c. style can be found in the area between Corso Venezia and Viale Majno: in particular note, at Via Cappuccini n. 8, **Palazzo Berri-Meregalli** by G.U. Arata (1911-14); further along, on Via Malpighi (n. 3), note the *Casa Galimberti*, by G.B. Bossi (1903-4).

Corso Buenos Aires. (*B-C6*). This busy principal thoroughfare of the "zona Venezia," one of Milan's largest and most crowded neighborhoods, is also one of the city's main shopping streets. This is a continuation toward the outskirts of town of the Corso Venezia, along what was in the 18th c. the "Strada Regia detta di Loreto," in a densely populated late-19th-c. neighborhood, now marked by episodes of urban blight.

Grattacielo Pirelli (*A5*). Since 1978 this skyscraper has been the headquarters of the regional government of Lombardy; it is safe to call this the most prestigious creation of postwar Milanese architecture. Built in 1955-60 by Gio Ponti and associates, with the consultation of P.L. Nervi, it dominates Piazza Duca d'Aosta (standing 127

Milan: Grattacielo Pirelli

m. tall, the highest building in Milan), facing the colossal building of the **Stazione Centrale** (*A6*), massively imposing, covered with decorations, designed by U. Stacchini and built in 1912-31; from the main gallery you can enter the *Museo delle Cere* (wax museum; *open, 8-11 pm*).

Centro Direzionale (*A5*). Established by the regulatory plan drawn up after WWII, in the area between Via Fabio Filzi and Via Melchiorre Gioia, but left unfinished, this office quarter constitutes a hodge-podge of tall office buildings, mostly from the Sixites, and vacant lots; the easternmost point is the **Stazione Porta Garibaldi**, a train station built in 1963 (*A4*), with a adjacent twin *skyscrapers of the railroad corporation* (F.S.; 1990-92).

The outlying neighborhoods

The originally walled perimeter of the Spanish bastions (Bastioni Spagnoli) encloses roughly 1/16th of the town area. The other 15/16ths have been built up heavily, largely within the past century, and in some areas, within the past 20 years. In the outlying territory, note the infrastructure of the greater metropolitan area (airport, sports stadium, race track), but also fragments of outlying towns and the medieval abbeys that reclaimed the low-lying plains: the surrounding areas begin in the city.

Villa Simonetta. At n. 36 in Via Stilicone, this is a noteworthy example of a suburban aristocratic villa, built at the end of the 15th c. and rebuilt in 1547 by Domenico Giunti; restored, it is now the site of the Civica Scuola di Musica, a municipal music school.

Fiera Campionaria. This is Milan's trade fair (about 400,000 sq. m.). It has another annex in Lacchiarella, to the south of the city; it should be rebuilt and expanded before long. The main entrance is in Piazzale Giulio Cesare; not far away (Piazza Buonarroti n. 29), is the *Casa di Riposo per Musicisti*, a retirement home for musicians, with the tomb of Giuseppe Verdi (*open by request, enquire in the front office*). Further along, toward the end of Viale Monte Rosa (Via Mosè Bianchi n. 94), inside the Pontificio Istituto Missioni Estere is the small *Museo di Arte Estremo-Orientale*, with art from the Far East (*open, 9-12 and 2-6; closed Sat., Sun., Jul. and Aug.*).

S. Siro. This residential neighborhood contains the most important sports facilities in Milan, including the: Lido di Milano, the Ippodromo (horse racing track), the Trottatoio (ditto), and the Stadio G. Meazza (soccer stadium). Further north is the **Q.T.8**, another residential neighborhood, designed in 1946 for the Eighth Esposizione Triennale of Milan, and built between 1950 and 1960, covering a surface area of 878,000 sq. m.

Certosa di Garegnano. At the far NW corner of Milan, stands this former charter house, somewhat set back from Viale Certosa, in the shadow of the superhighway on-ramps. The church, all that survives, was rebuilt in the late-16th c. The interior, by V. Seregni, is lavishly decorated with frescoes* by D. Crespi (1629); in the presbytery, frescoes and paintings by S. Peterzano (1578).

Ospedale Maggiore. To the north of Milan, in the quarter of Niguarda, this hospital complex (300,000 sq. m.) replaced the obsolete structure of the Ca' Granda in the Thirties. Built by Marcovigi and Arata, it is decorated, at the end of Viale Ca' Granda, by an impressive entrance, with reliefs and statues.

Palazzina Liberty. In the gardens of Largo Marinai d'Italia, stands this handsome building by Migliorini (1908) with decorations in ceramics and floral reliefs, formerly part of a long-ago demolished central fruit-and-vegetable market; it has been restored, and is now the home of the Civica Orchestra di Fiati (City Woodwinds Orchestra).

Aeroporto di Linate. Originally named for the aviation pioneer Enrico Forlanini, this airport lies just outside the city limits, to the east of the center; the original Forlanini landing field dates from 1935-36, but it has been virtually eliminated by the various stages of rebuilding. Nearby is the large body of water (2.5 km. long) of the **Idroscalo**, built in 1928 as a landing basin for seaplanes, and now used for water sports and swimming.

Abbazia di Chiaravalle*. This abbey, to the SE of Milan, stands in farmland that is technically part of the city; it was founded in 1135 by the Cistercians, who made it a stronghold in their agricultural colonizzation of the Milanese lowlands. The *church* was built in 1172-1221 in the French Gothic style; note the bell tower. *Inside*, note the large frescoes in the nave, above the 17th-c. carved choir* and in the transepts (Fiammenghini, 17th c.), also, Virgin and Child, by Luini, in the right transept

Mòdena

elev. 34 m.; pop. 176,148; Emilia-Romagna, provincial capital. "The immense ocean of the horizon is broken, to the west, only by the towers of Modena": Stendhal described the landscape as he saw it from the hill above Bologna. The towers he described still stand: the Torre dell'Orologio, atop Palazzo Comunale, but especially the 88-m.-tall Ghirlandina, a military structure, more than a bell tower. In the ancient center of town are the Duomo (Romanesque masterpiece by Lanfranco and Wiligelmo), the curving porticoed streets of the Middle Ages and the geometric grid of streets built by the d'Este family, who held Modena for 250 years, after losing Ferrara (1598). The town is also famous for its wine (Lambrusco), food (tortellini and zampone), and tradition of fast cars (the Ferrari factory, at nearby Maranello).

Historical note. The Via Emilia still runs through the heart of town; here, in 183 B.C., between the rivers Secchia and Panaro, the Roman colony of "Mutina" was established. In the late Roman Empire, Modena almost vanished, amidst extensive flooding of the undammed rivers; time passed, and in A.D. 891 new walls were built. In 1099, work began on the new Cathedral, still standing, and in

1135, Modena began to rule herself. In 1182, Modena founded her own university, in competition with that of her arch-rival Bologna. Modena supported the imperial forces, and in the terrible defeat of Fossalta (1249), the Bolognese captured the son of Emperor Frederick II. Forty years later, Modena was subjugated by the Este family of Ferrara (1288). The following year, work began on the Castello Estense, now site of the art collections. Amid political turmoil, Modena continued to grow, trading by river and laced with canals, canals whose names still indicate streets (Corso Canal Chiaro, Via Canalino, Corso Canal Grande). In 1336, the Este finally returned to Modena, intertwining the history of the town with that of Ferrara for nearly three centuries. A new section was built, beginning in 1546, along Via Ganaceto and Corso Cavour; the canals were filled in, ducal gardens planted (now public), and beginning in 1630, the enormous square structure of Palazzo Ducale arose. Modena became the capital of the Este dukes, who had lost Ferrara to the popes; then Napoleon drove them off, and in 1814 Modena came under the rule of an Austrian Hapsburg. In 1859, Modena became part of the Kingdom of Italy, and between 1880 and 1920, the tree-lined city walls were demolished.

Places of interest. Piazza Grande. This piazza forms a monumental complex with the cathedral and its tower (see below). The 17th-c. building with porticoes, with a 13th-c. clock tower in the middle, is the *Palazzo Comunale*, or town hall; from the courtyard (*entrance in Via Scudari n. 20*), you can climb to the upper floor (*open upon request, contact Town Hall, or Municipio*), with handsome rooms, decorated with frescoes and paintings by N. dell'Abate, E. dell'Abate, and B. Schedoni, and with coffered ceilings. In the small loggia, note the wooden bucket; subject of a local feud, immortalized in the mock-heroic poem, "La Secchia Rapita," by A. Tassoni.

Cattedrale**. Modena's most important monument, and a masterpiece of Romanesque architecture, this cathedral was begun in 1099 under the direction of the Lombard master Lanfranco with the help of the sculptor Wiligelmo; it was completed in the 13th c. by Campionese masters. It features a handsome tripartite facade, with three ornate portals (note the *central portal**), a handsome loggia, and a 13th-c. Gothic rose window; of particular interest are the four bas-reliefs* by Wiligelmo (12th c.), among the earliest examples of Romanesque sculpture. Along the sides are *fine carved doors* and bas-reliefs by A. di Duccio. Adjacent to the three handsome apses is the massive bell tower, called La **Ghirlandina*** (88 m. tall), with a Gothic crown, long a symbol of Modena. The austere *interior*, powerfully designed in brick, has three aisles and cross vaults. At the end of the nave, a fine *gallery** set on slender columns, with parapet decorated with reliefs by A. da Campione (ca. 1180); above it is a 14th-c. wooden Crucifix; to the left, a 13th-c. carved ambo. Midway on the left, a pulpit by Arrigo da Campione (1322). Huge three-aisle crypt with 60 small columns (late-11th-c. capitals); on the right, a group of five polychrome statues, called the Madonna della Pappa*, by G. Mazzoni (1480). In the presbytery, a 13th-c. screen of slender columns bounds the main altar; note the inlaid choir by C. and L. Canozzi da Lendinara (1465). In the left apse, 15th-c. Tuscan bas-relief; marble statue attributed to A. di Duccio; intarsias* by C. da Lendinara (1477), and polyp-

Mòdena: Cattedrale

tych by S. Serafini (1384). In the *sacristy*, frescoes by F. B. Ferrari (1507). In the left aisle, artwork by M. da Firenze and D. Dossi. On the left side of the Cathedral, at n. 6 in Via Lanfranco, is the **Museo Lapidario** (*open by request, tel. 216078*) with Roman, Medieval, and Romanesque stonework, including eight splendid 12th-c. metopes**.

S. Vincenzo. This 17th-c. church was made the Pantheon of the Este family. *Inside*, the once-rich decorations of the nave and cupola were damaged by Allied bombing in 1944; note the numerous princely tombs.

S. Pietro*. This Renaissance church (1476-1518) has an elegant facade, and inside, fine paintings* by G. Romanino and F. Bianchi Ferrari; statues by A. Begarelli, and an inlaid choir (1543).

S. Francesco. This Gothic church, built in 1244, and since restored, has a group of terracotta sculptures by A. Begarelli (1523).

Palazzo dei Musei. This vast 18th-c. building (entrance at n. 5 in Piazzale S. Agostino), houses the many collections of the city of Modena; foremost among them, the Galleria Estense and the Biblioteca Estense (see below).

Museo Lapidario Estense. *Open Mon.-Sat., 9-7; Sun. 9-1.* Located beneath the portico, and founded in 1828, this museum of plaques and inscriptions has a Greco-Roman and a medieval-to-modern section.

Biblioteca Estense*. On the 2nd floor, this is one of the richest libraries in Italy; it has a *permanent exhibition** (*open 9-1; closed Sun.*), with illuminated codices of great note, including the 15th-c. Bible* of B. d'Este, illuminated by T. Crivelli.

Musei Civici. *Open 9-1; Tue. and Thu. also 3-6; Sun. only 10-12:30; closed Mon.* There are various sections: the **Museo Civico di Storia e Arte Medievale e Moderna** has objects of sacred art and goldsmithery, weapons, musical and scientific instruments, fabrics and embroidery, and more; 17th-/18th-c. paintings, in the **Galleria Campori**. The **Museo Civico Archeologico Etnologico**

has collections that range from prehistoric artifacts and exhibits to Roman times, as well as ethnographic material from New Guinea, Amazonia, Africa, and so on. *The Museo Civico del Risorgimento* contains weapons, uniforms, and documents of local and Italian history, from 1796 to WWI.

Galleria Estense**. *Open 9-2; Sun. 9-1; closed Mon.* Located on the top floor of the palazzo, this is one of the finest art galleries in Europe, particularly rich in works of the Emilian and Po Valley schools of the 14th to 18th c. As you enter, you will see various ancient Etruscan and Roman objects, as well as a marble bust of Francesco I d'Este* by G. L. Bernini. Among the paintings, at the start, works by early Emilian artists, including works* by T. and B. da Modena, S. dei Crocifissi, and by Tuscans, including G. di Paolo. Among the 15th-/16th-c. Ferrarese and Modenese painters are C. Tura, A. and B. degli Erri, B. Bonascia, F.B. Ferrari, G. da Carpi, D. Dossi. Bronzes by B. di Giovanni; majolicas by S. da Ravenna. Works by 16th-c. Florentines and Emilians include art by L. di Credi, Correggio, and L. Orsi. Non-Italian painters include: J. van Cleve, C. de Lyon, Velazquez, El Greco. Painters of the Venetian school include: B. Montagna, G. F. Caroto, J. and D. Tintoretto, J. Bassano, P. Veronese, and J. Palma the Younger. There are excellent medals, made for the d'Este family, by Pisanello, and G. delle Corniole. Lastly, among the 17th-c. Emilian artists are: Scarsellino, the Carracci, Guercino, G. Reni, L. Ferrari, and C. Cignani.

S. Agostino. This 17th-c. church features a terracotta group by A. Begarelli and a fresco by T. da Modena. Take the Via Emilia, Modena's main strolling street, and on the left you will see the church of **S. Giovanni Battista**, built in 1730, with a handsome polychrome terracotta group, by G. Mazzoni.

S. Maria Pomposa. This 18th-c. church was built of terracotta; next door is the house of a renowned Italian writer, L.A. Muratori, of the same period; it now houses a research center and an archive of his work.

Palazzo Ducale*. *Open upon request, tel. 225671.* In Piazza Roma is the massive and lavish ducal palace of the d'Este family; note the courtyard and facade. Construction began around 1630, incorporating a castle built in 1288. Since 1862 it has been the site of the *Italian Accademia Militare*, or war college.

Monreale*

elev. 310 m., pop. 27,217, Sicily, province of Palermo. Located in a hilly area to the SW of Palermo, Monreale owes its renown primarily to its Duomo, or cathedral, a remarkable creation of the rich Norman culture in Sicily.

Places of interest. Duomo**. The facade of this cathedral is clamped between two towers (one of which is unfinished); beneath the 18th-c. portico, note the portal, with its bronze *doors** by Bonanno Pisano (1186); along the left side, beneath the 16th-c. portico by the Gaginis, note another portal with bronze *doors** by Barisano da Trani (1179); on the exterior of the *apses*, note the interplay* of the *entwined arches* and the polychrome inlays of limestone and lava.

The interior follows a relaxed rhythm, amidst the glittering golden mosaics. In the sanctuary, the ceiling is studded with Arabic stalactites; the floor made of porphyry and granite is original; marble slabs sheath the walls, where the **mosaics**** begin. These mosaics, completed between the end of the 12th c. and the mid-13th c., depict stories of the Old and New Testament, with legends in Latin and Greek: in particular, note the *stories from Genesis**, the *Christ Pantocrator** (in the vault of the apse, the visual and symbolic center of the church), and the two panels showing William II crowned by Christ and William II offering the church to the Virgin Mary. Also, note the sarcophagi of William I and William II, the 16th-c. chapel of S. Benedetto, and the 15th-c. chapel of the Crucifix; from there, you can enter the *Tesoro (for information on the hours, tel. 540122)*, or treasury.

Fine view* from the terraces of the church *(180 steps)*.

Chiostro** *(open, holidays 9-12:30; winter 9-2:30; summer 9-12:30 and 4-7)*. This cloister, built at the same time as the church, was once part of a Benedictine monastery; it is surrounded by a portico with Gothic arches over slender twinned columns; note the fountain in an enclosure.

Monte Sant'Angelo

elev. 796 m., pop. 14,754, Puglia, province of Foggia. It is believed that the sanctuary dates from the late-6th c., when the Longobards were organizing — politically and religiously — their dukedom of Benevento.

Places of interest. Santuario di S. Michele.* Standing nearly at the end of the little oblong town, this sanctuary fronts a little square, at the foot of the octagonal *campanile* (1274); two arcades lead into the atrium, with a stairway leading down to the courtyard of the church, which has a Romanesque portal with bronze doors* (made in Constantinople, 1076). The *interior* has a single aisle and Gothic arches. In the Grotta dell'Arcangelo, or Grotto of the Archangel, note the statue of St. Michael, by A. Sansovino (16th c.), as well as a 12th-c. bishop's throne*, and a niche that collects the water dripping from the rock, believed to be miraculous. A number of digs beneath the floor of this grotto have unearthed crypts dating back before A.D. 493, with frescoes from the time of the emperor Otho.

A stairway in front of the bell tower of the sanctuary leads to the ruined church of S. Pietro and the so-called **Tomba di Rotari***, probably a baptistery rebuilt around 1109 *(contact the custodian)*. Alongside is the Romanesque church of **S. Maria Maggiore** (1170), with a carved portal (1198) and fragments of Byzantine-style frescoes (13th/16th c.) on the interior walls.

The **Museo Tancredi di Arti e Tradizioni Garganiche** *(open, 9-12 and 3-6)*, installed in a former Franciscan convent, contains ancient objects and pieces of folk art, along with costumes and documents of local folkways.

The **Castello**, a castle built on a Norman plan, was enlarged by the Aragonese (1494).

The *Rione Junno*, overlooking the cliff, with row houses

— many dating from the 17th c. — occupies the SW area of town.

Excursion. At a distance of 9.2 km.SW,note the ancient abbey church of **S. Maria di Pulsano**, rebuilt in the 12th c.

Montepulciano*

elev.605 m.; pop. 13,856; Tuscany,province of Siena. A statue of Pulcinella strikes the hours on the town bells, and the chimes echo through noble streets atop the ridge,in the town center,and in steep narrow lanes, below arches and vaults. Set high on a hilltop,Montepulciano overlooks the valley of the Orcia and the Valdichiana. Among the architects who built this town are Michelozzo,A.da Sangallo the Elder, B. Peruzzi, and Vignola. The great scholar and poet Politian was born here, as Agnolo Ambrogini; he took his pen name from his birthplace (in medieval Latin,"Mons Politianus").

Getting around. The area within the town walls is off limits to private cars: in summer (Jun.-Sep.) round the clock; the rest of the year from 7 am until 8 pm; tourists can drive to their hotels, after receiving a permit at the Ufficio Turistico Comunale in Piazza Don Minzoni (near Porta al Prato).The route shown inside the walls is a walking tour; you may wish to drive to S. Biagio and S. Maria delle Grazie.

The city within the walls

Via di Gracciano,Via di Voltaia,Via dell'Opio,to each add "nel Corso";Via Ricci,Via del Poggiolo,Piazza Grande: all these names are rich in history, in an urban setting that has maintained, virtually intact,its Renaissance flavor.

Porta al Prato. Spreading out before it is the 19th-c. *garden of Poggiofanti*; this gate is the main entrance to the historical center of Montepulciano, and was originally part of the 13th-c. walls. It was rebuilt in the early-16th c. by A. da Sangallo the Elder; note the two immense trapezoidal buttresses.

Via di Gracciano nel Corso*. Backbone of the "Borgo di Gracciano," this is the first leg of the Corso,which has been the central traffic artery of Montepulciano since the 16th c.; note the many aristocratic palazzi from that time.

On your right,at n.91,note **Palazzo Avignonesi**, by the architect Vignola; across the road is a 19th-c. copy of the *Column of Marzocco* (the original is in the courtyard of the Museo Civico). Note the Florentine lion, which replaced the Siennese she-wolf in 1511. At n. 82 is the *Palazzo Tarugi*, also by Vignola, then **Palazzo Cocconi** (n. 68-72), believed to be by A. da Sangallo the Elder. At n. 73,*Palazzo Bucelli* (in poor condition); note, embedded in the base, Etruscan and Latin urns and inscriptions. Next is the church of S.Agostino (see below) and, facing it, the brick **Torre di Pulcinella** (1524), with a metal-and-wood figure of Pulcinella, or Punch, which strikes the hours. Further on,at n. 12,note *Palazzo Venturi*'s fine windows; after the *Arco della Cavina*, the road enters *Piazza delle Erbe* near the three arches of the late-16th-c.**Loggia del Grano** (also by Vignola).

S. Agostino. This 15th-c. church, with a late-Gothic/Renaissance facade* by Michelozzo,has a noteworthy portal with festoons and terracotta reliefs, also by Michelozzo; note rose window.

Inside, panel by G. di Paolo; painted wooden Crucifix attributed to Donatello. Note original choir chancel, by a follower of Pomarancio, the Crucifix attributed to A. Pollaiolo, and Crucifixion by L. di Credi.

Via di Voltaia nel Corso. This second leg of the Corso runs through the southern part of the center, amid 16th-c. palazzi: on the left, at n. 21, is **Palazzo Cervini***, believed to be by A. da Sangallo the Younger; next to it is *Palazzo Bruschi* (n. 31), site of the popular 19th-c. *Caffè Poliziano*.

At n.55,*Palazzo Gagnoni-Grugni*, by Vignola; note the 17th-c. *Collegio dei Gesuiti*, and the Baroque **church of Gesù** (1689-1733), with unfinished brick facade: the elegant, slightly elliptical interior is by A. Pozzo, while the false vault was added by S. Cipriani.

Via dell'Opio nel Corso. Last leg of the Corso, this road continues as *Via del Poliziano* toward the church of S. Maria dei Servi. At the intersection of Via delle Farine and Via del Teatro, at n. 1 in the Via del Poliziano is the **birthplace of Politian**, Renaissance scholar and poet. Via del Teatro, running up to Piazza Grande and the center, is dominated by the 18th-c. **Teatro Poliziano** (*open by request, contact the Ufficio Turistico*), with four rows of boxes, renovated in 1881.

Piazza Grande*. Monumental, hilltop center of town, sloping slightly; this square was given its modern-day appearance in the 15th c. by Michelozzo. One side is filled by the facade of the Duomo, on another side the Palazzo Comunale dominates (see below). Facing the Duomo is **Palazzo de' Nobili-Tarugi** (n.3), attributed to A. da Sangallo the Elder; to its left, behind the late-Renaissance well (**Pozzo de' Grifi e de' Leoni**, 1520), is the originally Gothic Palazzo del *Capitano del Popolo*. Also, at n. 13, note the Renaissance **Palazzo Contucci**, begun in 1519 by Antonio da Sangallo the Elder, and completed by B. Peruzzi.

Palazzo Comunale*. *Open during the working hours of the town government; you can climb up to the tower, 8-1; closed Sun*. Built in several stages between the end of the 14th c. and the middle of the 15th c., this building's stone facade was by Michelozzo (1424), while its overall structure is reminiscent of the Palazzo della Signoria in Florence. Crowned by corbels and Guelph (or swallowtail) crenelations, the facade overlooking the square — with a high rusticated base and a single stark portal — is in turn topped by a crenelated tower, offering a fine view* of the city, the Valdichiana, and the valley of the Orcia. Note the 14th-c. courtyard, with cistern and loggias, recently restored.

Duomo*. This enormous late-Renaissance church, by I.Scalza (1586-1630), has an unfinished facade and an unfinished 15th-c. bell tower, surviving from the previous parish church. The vast *interior* features a funerary statue* by Michelozzo (15th c.). Note two 15th-c. Siennese wooden statues, and, on the main altar, the large triptych* by T. di Bartolo (1401), as well as a painting by S. di Pietro; an early-14th-c. baptismal font; and a bas-relief by B. da Maiano.

Museo Civico. *Open, Easter-Sep., 9:30-1 and 3-6, closed Mon.and Tue.; the rest of the year,by request; contact the Biblioteca Civica (across the street), Mon.-Sat., 9:30-1*. Largely the creation of 19th-c.

bequests, this museum is housed in the Gothic *Palazzo Neri-Orselli*, at n. 10 in Via Ricci. Among the artists are Margaritone d'Arezzo, the Maestro di Badia a Isola, B. di Lorenzo, J. Sustermans, J. di Mino del Pellicciaio, G. di Benvenuto, L. di Tommè, Sodoma, A. Puccinelli, Spagnoletto, P. Bordone, and A. della Robbia.

Via del Poggiolo. Lined, like Via Ricci, by lordly medieval and Renaissance homes, this road begins at *Piazza S. Francesco*, with a fine view* of the valley and S. Biagio; the church of *S. Francesco (closed to the public)* has a handsome Gothic portal. Downhill is the church of **S. Lucia**, with a mix of early Baroque and Mannerist styles in the facade by F. del Turco (1633); inside, painting by L. Signorelli. Then you return to Piazza delle Erbe.

Churches and sanctuaries outside the walls

From the masterpiece of S. Biagio to the modest church of S. Agnese, four buildings offer evidence of the historic and economic standing of Montepulciano between the 14th and 17th c.

S. Biagio * *. Set in a lovely location SW of the historic center, on a natural terrace overlooking the surrounding hills, this church is a masterpiece by A. da Sangallo the Elder (1518-45), a solemn and harmonious travertine building with a Greek-cross plan, topped by a high cupola, and flanked by two bell towers. *Inside*, note the majestic cupola again, with rose windows, and, on the main altar, a 14th-c. fresco of Virgin and Child and St. Francis. Overhead, a stained glass window by M. da Cortona (1568).

S. Maria dei Servi. Built in the 14th c., this church has a simple Gothic facade, with a solemn splayed portal; inside, note the Virgin with Child*, attributed to D. di Buoninsegna.

S. Agnese. On Piazza Don Minzoni, north of town, is an early-14th-c. church, rebuilt extensively. Inside, stained glass rose window by M. da Cortona and fresco by S. Martini.

S. Maria delle Grazie. Roughly 1 km. north of town, along Viale Calamandrei, this late-16th-c. church is by I. Scalza. Inside, note gilt stuccoes by

Montepulciano: S. Biagio

A. da Cremona (1605), fine polychrome glazed terracotta by A. della Robbia, and rare Renaissance organ.

Naples / Napoli**

elev. 10 m., pop. 1,066,663, Campania, provincial and regional capital. This city, the third-largest in Italy and the largest in the "Mezzogiorno," or Southern Italy, was for many centuries the capital of the largest Italian state, prior to the 19th-c. Risorgimento and unification. It served as a center of attraction in much the same way that Paris did for France or Madrid did for Spain, and that Rome has - only recently - for the Italian peninsula. (Indeed the roots of modern Naples' urbanistic and demographic problems sink deep into those long-ago times). In one of the loveliest natural settings in all of Europe, celebrated throughout history for the variety of panoramic views, the mild weather, the luminous sea, and the gentle breezes, Naples is endowed with a superb heritage of monuments and artistic collections, at the center of an archeological zone that extends from Cumae to Pompeii, and is an attraction that draws visitors from all over the world. "Grand, luminous, and noble city," as one of its most illustrious sons, Giambattista Vico, once called it; Vico, the great historical philosopher, was an example of Naples' cultural and philosophical rigor that has always been the other face of the unassuming Neapolitan humanism, immortalized by such actors as Salvatore Di Giacomo and Eduardo De Filippo.

Historical note. The origins of the earliest Greek settlement ("Palaeopolis," or "Parthenope") are linked to the expansionistic policies of Cumae, whose colonists settled on the slopes of Monte Echia. "Neapolis" (meaning, the new city) remained a Greek town, even when it was downgraded from a Roman ally (326 B.C.) to a "municipium" (90 B.C.); a Greek city, or nearly. In any case, the Romans of the ancient Republic and those of the newer Empire, captivated by the allure of ancient Greek culture, chose this as a place of study and leisure. In the villa of Lucullus, whose name has become a byword for rich living and fine cuisine, and whose home stood on the present-day site of the Castel dell'Ovo, Virgil composed his "Georgics"; an odd twist of fate brought the last emperor of Rome - Romulus Augustulus - to die in the same spot, in A.D. 476. Twenty years earlier, during the reign of Valentinian III, a new walled perimeter was built to enclose Naples within the bounds of the ancient city until the 10th c., when the ring of walls was enlarged to the SW to include the sites of the churches of Gesù Nuovo, S. Chiara, S. Maria la Nova, and S. Pietro Martire. Naples, in the meanwhile, after a short Gothic interlude, had become again, and definitively, Greek in A.D. 553 - or Byzantine; from that time on an influx of Byzantines restored the never entirely vanished Graeco-Latin bilingual tradition. The population had dropped to 20,000, but in the course of a few centuries, it redoubled. In continual conflict with the bordering Longobard duchy of Benevento, the small Neapolitan state - which included Cuma, Pozzuoli, Nola, and Sorrento - gradually became increasingly independent, until independence was complete in A.D. 763 with duke Stefano II; this latter ruler assured hereditary ducal rule for his own descendants, while still maintaining nominal loyalty to Byzantium. The centuries that followed may well have been the most glorious years in the history of Naples: Neapolitan fleets, along with those of Amalfi and Gaeta, faced off against the naval power of the Saracens, winning many great victories (among them, the famous triumph of Ostia, immortalized by Raphael in the Stanze Vaticane). Trade prospered too, as Naples exported the cloth it manufactured to the Arabs, between one battle and the next, in exchange for fine carpets. Still, in 1139, after prolonged resistance, even Naples was forced to yield before the steadily encroaching Normans under King Roger. With the end of the duchy, the political importance of Naples declined; it became part of a vast kingdom with its capital at Palermo. Its commercial might remained, however, and was even augmented by a period of relative peace and by the decline of Amalfi. The city of Naples continued to develop, both inland, where the Castel Capuano was erected, and along the seashore, where an existing fortress was enlarged into the Castel dell'Ovo. The Normans in time were replaced by the Swabians; these new rulers encountered tacit but implacable Neapolitan hostility; the populace often sought the support of the pope against the Swabians. When Corradin was beheaded in 1268, the Swabians were replaced by the house of Anjou, who moved the capital from Palermo to Naples. Naples thus became the leading city in a kingdom that was called the Kingdom of Sicily by diplomats, but was commonly described as the Kingdom of Naples by one and all. The Angevins endowed their new capital with a new set of monuments. King Charles I erected the Castel Nuovo to serve as his palace, and the city spread to the area surrounding the new palace. The walled perimeter spread south from Castel Capuano to the area of the marketplace and west as far as Port'Alba. The port, which was brought within the ring of walls for the first time, was further protected by the great Molo Angioino. During this period, some of the loveliest churches in Naples were erected (S. Lorenzo Maggiore, S. Chiara, S. Domenico Maggiore, S. Pietro a Maiella, and S. Maria Donnaregina). The third Angevin king, Roberto, built the Castel S. Elmo. The capital grew even greater with the advent of the first king of the house of Aragon, in 1442, Alfonso the Magnanimous. He ruled until 1501. To the east stood tall and handsome walls; in part they can still be seen alongside the Via Rosaroll, and they included the entire Castel Capuano. To the west these walls extended as far as the present-day Via Toledo, and along the Via S. Brigida, the citadel of the Castel Nuovo. In the 14th c., Angevin Naples had attracted such painters as Pietro Cavallini from Rome, Simone Martini from Siena, Giotto from Florence, and such scholars and men of letters as St. Thomas Aquinas, Petrarch, and Boccaccio. The Renaissance court of Alfonso the Magnanimous witnessed the flowering of poetry brought by such names as Panormita, Pontano, and Sannazaro. This splendid season was quickly ended by the wars between France and Spain over the southern kingdom; finally in 1503 the general Consalvo de Cordoba reduced Naples from its standing as the capital of a state to the humble rank of administrative center of a Spanish province. The authoritarian, repressive, and centralizing rule of the viceroys brought the immigration of barons into Naples, along with their clients and workers from the provinces, as well as Spanish nobles, officials, and soldiers. Here the foundations of the architectural and demographic problems of Naples were first laid; these problems were further aggravated by the remarkable birthrate of the city. The viceroy Pedro de Toledo attempted, during his twenty-year reign, to solve this problem by undertaking one of the largest efforts at urban renewal in the history of Naples: the entire area between the Aragonian walls and the slopes of the Vómero as far as the present-day Corso Vittorio Emanuele, filled up with houses and tall buildings. The Via Toledo was built, running north to south, and for three centuries this was the main street of Naples and one of the best-known avenues in all of Europe. In a few decades, the population, which in Angevin times had been about 60,000, and by the turn of the 16th c. had risen above 100,000, at this point swelled to about 200,000. In the 17th c., despite rebellions which were put down with bloody violence (Masaniello led a famous revolt in 1647) and despite outbreaks of disease

and plague (one famous outbreak in 1656 reduced the population - then well over 360,000 - by 200,000), the viceroys continued to finance monumental works, such as the new Palazzo Reale and the Palazzo degli Studi (now the site of the Museo Archeologico Nazionale), as well as a great many Baroque churches. The events of the European wars led an Austrian army to occupy Naples in 1707 without firing a shot. For 27 years Naples was the capital of a province, once Spanish and newly Austrian. In 1734 the great European powers assigned Naples to Charles of Bourbon, and once again the city became the capital of a kingdom. Naples was embellished with the Teatro S. Carlo, the Palazzo Reale di Capodimonte, the Albergo dei Poveri, and the Foro Carolino (the present-day Piazza Dante). The walls and many of the town gates were demolished, the outlying suburbs were joined with the city, and the Naples of early Bourbon rule came to resemble the Naples of the present day: the site of a royal court and seat of many foreign ambassadors, the city began to acquire a much higher tone, as is documented by the many accounts offered by foreign travellers making the Grand Tour. Under Napoleon, in 1799, the city was the capital of the short-lived Parthenopean Republic; after a very brief return of the Bourbon dynasty, it was again capital of the kingdom, ruled first by Napoleon's brother Joseph and later by his brother-in-law, Joaquin Murat (1806-1815). The decade under French rule produced a number of new features: among them were the road that runs from the Palazzo degli Studi up to Capodimonte, the Via di Posillipo, known then as Corso Napoleone, the Orto Botanico or botanical gardens, and the Osservatorio Astronomico, an observatory. During the second period of Bourbon rule (1815-1860) the Foro Ferdinandeo (now Piazza del Plebiscito) was opened, while along the Riviera di Chiaia the Villa Reale was built (now Villa Comunale), and Corso Maria Teresa (now Corso Vittorio Emanuele) was laid out. Gregorovius described that last-named avenue as one of the loveliest streets on earth. Between the end of the period of Bourbon rule and the earliest years of Italian unity (the population of Naples was already 450,000) Via del Duomo and Corso Garibaldi were built, cutting through the city from north to south, to provide air and a healthier setting in place of the dark and narrow alleys; but it was not until after the outbreak of cholera in 1884 that it was decided to demolish the lower area of the old city, with the creation of the Via Depretis, Via Sanfelice, and the broad avenue of Corso Umberto I, the most notable phases in the urban renovation that lasted for many many years, with the massive destruction caused during WWII. Between the two wars the city expanded into the new quarter known as the Rione Vasto near the central station, into the Rione Vómero and the Rione Regina Elena to the west, the Rione Arenella and the Rione Materdei to the north, the Rione Luzzatti to the east, the Rione Speme on the slopes of Posillipo, and Rione Fuorigrotta in the area of the Phlegraean Fields; the galleries that ran under the hills of Posillipo and Pizzo Falcone, and the funiculars made communications among the various quarters much easier. Urban renewal proceeded apace (Quartiere Cari-tà), and along Via Diaz the new public buildings of the two decades of Fascism were erected. The chaotic reconstruction of the postwar period focused around the port, giving rise to the new Via Marina, and then developed an ultimately unsuccessful traffic center between Via Toledo, Via Medina, and Piazza del Plebiscito. In the meanwhile, the city continued to grow, on the hills of Posillipo, in the Vómero-Arenella area, while economic trends and residential development pushed north (Secondigliano) and NE (Barra, Ponticelli). It was not until 1972 that the new urban zoning plan was approved, to replace the plan of 1939; there were no detailed plans for implementation however, leading to further delay and abuse. The exceedingly recent classification of the historical center of Naples as a "world cultural heritage" status seems an official signal of a change in direction in the treatment of the "ancient heart" of the capital of Southern Italy.

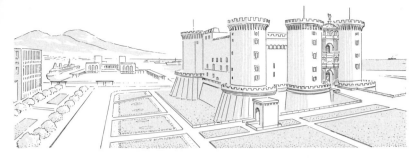

Naples: Castel Nuovo

Getting around. Traffic jams and regulations make driving in town problematic at best; part of the center of Naples is off limits to private vehicles. Of the five routes suggested, only the third and part of the first can be considered walking tours entirely; for the others, you may choose to use a taxi because public transport (the railway and the four cable railways for tha Vòmero are an exception) is inadequate and unreliable.

From the harbor to the main museums

Besides maintaining their key role as the centers of political and administative power in the city, the Municipio (town hall), Castel Nuovo e Palzzo Reale bear interesting testimony to the history of Italy's southern capital. Via Toledo takes us back to the beginnings of Spanish rule; proceeding under another name, it then leads on to the Museo Archeologico Nazionale, commissioned by King Ferdinand IV to house the Farnese Collection and the archeological finds of the Herculaneum and Pompeii digs. The great Farnese collection of art also led to the foundation of the city's second-largest museum, the Capodimonte Gallery, recently renovated and opened to the public.

Harbor *(E4)*. Naples' harbor is one of the most important in the Mediterranean; the Stazione Marittima (E5) is located on the *Molo Angioino*; to the north is the Rococo building of the *Immacolatella* (D.A.Vaccaro, 18th c.); to the south is the Calata Beverello.

Piazza del Municipio *(D4)*. At the far end of this lush green square, note the 19th-c. *Palazzo del Municipio*, which incorporates the 16th-c. church of **S. Giacomo degli Spagnoli** built at the behest of the viceroy Pedro da Toledo; inside, behind the main altar note the *sepulcher** by G. da Nola (1539).

The Castel Nuovo** *(E4; open 9-19, closed Sun.)* or Maschio Angioino (because it was built under Angevin rule, or "Angioino"; 1279-82) was entirely rebuilt at the behest of Alphonse I of Aragon (15th c.); it now has the massive 15th-c. appearance given it by Catalonian and Tuscan architects, with a trapezoidal plan and round towers; its entrance, flanked by two towers, is the lovely *triumphal arch**, a celebrated 15th-c. creation by a number of sculptors, including F.Laurana; note in particular the relief of the triumph of Alphonse. Access to the courtyard, rebuilt in the 18th c., lies beyond the portal; on the far side, opposite the entrance, a 15th-c. outside staircase leads to the *Sala dei Baroni*, whezre local council sessions are held. *Inside*. The **Museo Civico** includes the **Palatine**

Chapel (14th c.), the only surviving feature of the Angevin palace, with a Madonna by F. Laurana (1474). Sculptures belonging to the 14th and 15th c., and paintings from the 15th-18th c. are collected in the two floors of the west wing of the castle; many notable works by 19th c. Neapolitan artists.

Piazza del Plebiscito *(E4)* In this harmonious and monumental square, the elliptical curves of the colonnades join the pronaos of the sober Neoclassical church of **S. Francesco di Paola** - built at the behest of King Ferdinand I, to celebrate the return of the Bourbons (1815) - with its large cupola (P.Bianchi, 1817-46); of the two equestrian statues of Charles III and Ferdinand I, the former is by Canova.

Palazzo Reale* *(E4; open 9-1:30; Thur. and Sat. also 4-7:30; closed Mon.)*. It faces the church of S. Francesco di Paola, enclosing the NE side of the Piazza del Plebiscito. It was built by D. Fontana (1600-1602), restored and enlarged in 1743-48, and then subjected to further renovations and restorations; this was the palace of the Bourbons from 1734 to 1860. You can tour the Cortile del Fontana (the Fontana Courtyard, named after the architect); the Scalone d'Onore (ceremonial stairway). In the atrium at the base, note the bronze door* by the Parisian Guglielmo Monaco (1468) with reliefs, originally in the Castel Nuovo. The **Appartamento Storico**, or Historical Apartment, now a museum, has halls and rooms furnished with genuine 18th- and 19th-c. furniture and frescoes of the Neapolitan school (17th and 18th c.); it houses the Teatro di Corte (Court Theater, F.Fuga, 1768). The *Appartamento delle Feste* is occupied by the **Biblioteca Nazionale Vittorio Emanuele III**, a library where numerous manuscripts, including those of T.Tasso and G.Leopardi, and the burnt papyri* discovered the Villa dei papiri at Herculaneum, are preserved.

Teatro S. Carlo *(E4)*. This celebrated "temple of the opera," dates from 1737 but was rebuilt in the Neoclassical style during the 19th c. Directly opposite begins the *Galleria Umberto*, from the end of the 19th c., a chief meeting spot for Neapolitans.

Via Toledo *(E-C4)*. From Piazza Trieste e Trento (E4), extending up to the Museo Archeologico Nazionale, runs the Via Toledo, the lively main thoroughfare of old Naples, the most popular strolling promenade. Note along this route the church of S. Nicola alla Carità (17th c.), the baroque *Palazzo Carafa di Maddaloni*, the church of *Spirito Santo (C4)* , rebuilt in the 18th c.

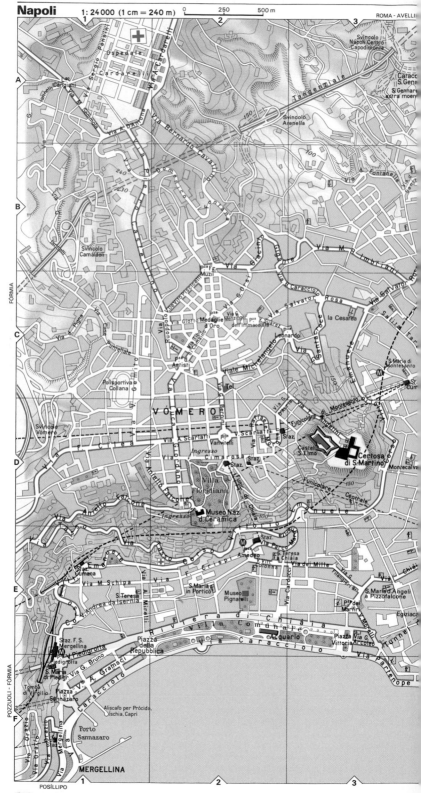

Napoli

1:24000 (1 cm = 240 m)

0   250   500 m

VÓMERO

MERGELLINA

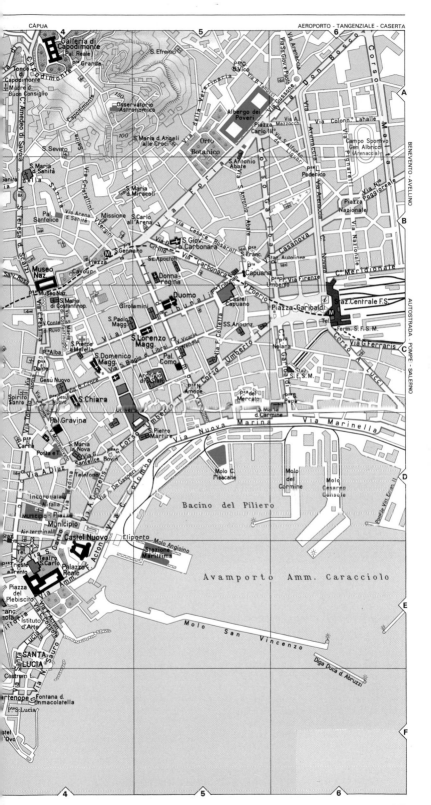

Museo Archeologico Nazionale** *(C4; open summer 9-7, Sun.9-1; winter 9-2, Sun.9-1; undergoing partial restoration).* Installed in a building that was once a cavalry barracks and later the headquarters of the University, the Museo Archeologico is one of the world's leading archeological museums; Roman replicas of Greek sculpture, unearthed in the cities buried by the eruption of Mt. Vesuvius, were one of the great sources of knowledge of Greek art, prior to the discovery of the few, rare originals; mosaics and paintings and minor collections complete the wonderful array of objects from Greco-Roman classical antiquity. The number of works is enormous, and they are arranged in over a hundred halls.

Among the **marble sculptures***, to mention only the most important: the Tyrannicides*, a funerary stele* from the 5th c. B.C.; an Athena* clearly derived from the work of Phidias; Eurydice and Hermes**, an Augustan-period copy of an original from the school of Phidias; the Aphrodite of the gardens*; an excellent copy of the renowned Doriforo** , or Offering bearer, by Polyclitus; a Diomedes from Cumae*; the Palestrita*; the Venus Callipige* from a Hellenistic original, a bronze statuette of Herakles; the colossal Farnese Hercules*; torsos of Ares* and Aphrodite*; a Psyche* from Capua; a Venus from Capua*; the renowned Farnese Bull**, the largest surviving group of marble statuary from antiquity; the Diana Ephesina*; a Seated Matron,* believed to depict Agrippina; a bust of Caracalla*; a bronze horse's head, possibly dating from the 3rd c. B.C., once attributed to Donatello; the Augustus of Fondi*; a bust of Homer*; a statuette of a Dancing Faun,* from Pompeii, the renowned sculptures of the Sleeping Satyr*, the Drunken Silene*, and Hermes Resting*, and a portrait said to be of Seneca*; and, last but not least, the Farnese Atlas*, a Hellenistic sculpture.

Among the **paintings and mosaics***, aside from the world-renowned Battle of Isso**, a mosaic based upon an Alexandrian painting, of unique historical and artistic worth, you should also note the other major mosaics* from Pompeii, such as the Strolling Musicians*, Plato and His Disciples in the Gardens of Academe*, a bust of a woman* and a Cat Biting a Quail*; a collection of paintings*, including murals from Pompeii, Herculaneum, and Stabia: among the most notable items are a group of women performing a funerary dance* from Ruvo, women playing astragalomacy* (divination by means of small bones or dice) in the Neo-Attic style, and Pasquius Proculus with his wife.

A special section contains artworks and other objects unearthed in the 18th c. at Herculaneum in the **Villa dei Papiri***.

Also note the collection of **valuables**, among which you should note two gladiatorial helmets*, a vase in dark-blue glass*, a table of 115 pieces from the Casa del Menandro (House of Menander) in Pompeii, and the Tazza Farnese** a cup in sardonyx, from the Alexandrian school. The exquisite collection of Campanian, Apulian, Lucanian, Etruscan, and Attic vases* can only be seen in part.

Naples: Palazzo Reale di Capodimonte

The **Sale del Tempio di Iside** have been arranged to gather together frescoes and archeological finds discovered in Pompeii in 1764-66.

Palazzo Reale di Capodimonte *(A4).* On the site of what used to be a small village, King Charles of Bourbon decided to open the famous porcelain manufactory in 1739. A building to contain the art collections which came to him via his mother, Elisabetta Farnese, was also established there. The manufactory was operative for just 20 years, while the palazzo, commissioned in 1734, has housed the Museo and the Gallerie di Capodimonte since 1957.

Museo di Capodimonte and Gallerie di Capodimonte** *(A4; open 9-2).* The Galleria Nazionale (art gallery) is one of the most versatile and significant collections of paintings in Italy. Among the masterpieces to be seen here: St. Louis of Toulouse Crowns His Brother Robert of Anjou King of Naples** by Simone Martini; the Crucifixion** by Masaccio; the Transfiguration** by Giovanni Bellini; the Zingarella,** or Gypsy Girl, by Correggio; Pope Paul III with His Nephews Ottavio and Alessandro Farnese** by Titian; the Parable of the Blind Men* by Pieter Bruegel; the Flagellation** and the Seven Acts of Mercy** by Caravaggio. Also worthy of note are the: Galleria dell'Ottocento, or Gallery of the 19th c., with numerous major works by Neapolitan painters; the Appartamento Storico e Museo - or Historic Apartment and Museum - with a collection of porcelain and majolica, the vast Collezione De Ciccio*, the David* by Pollaiolo, and the Salottino di Porcellana** (1757-59), a masterpiece of porcelain produced by the manufactory of Capodimonte, from the palace of Portici.

In the handsome **park** stands the Fabbrica di Porcellane di Capodimonte (porcelain manufactory; active from 1743 until 1759).

Old Naples

This route covers the heart of the city and the straight street called "Spaccanapoli" (so named because it splits the city center; "spaccare" means to split). Some of the city's most important monuments are located in this area. Apart from renowned churches like S. Chiara and S. Domenico Maggiore, veritable treasure troves of artworks, the area features some more typical characteristics of the city: jewelry shops, the Christmas creche workshops in Via San Gregorio Armeno, and the picturesque neighbourhood of Forcella.

Church of the Incoronata *(D4).* Along the Via Medina you will see: the church of the Incoronata, which has, in its two Gothic aisles, frescoes from the 14th and 15th c.

S. Maria la Nova *(D4)*. Along Via Monteoliveto, this 15th-c. church has two Renaissance cloisters; farther on, the **Palazzo Gravina*** *(D4)* is built in the Tuscan Renaissance style.

Church of S. Anna dei Lombardi *(D4)*. The

nearby church of S. Anna dei Lombardi* can be considered a museum of Renaissance sculpture. Among other things: note the marble altar piece by Benedetto da Maiano (1489); the Pietà in terracotta by G. Mazzoni (1492); a Manger and Saints* by Antonio Rossellino (1475); the Monument to Maria of Aragon* by Antonio Rossellino and Benedetto da Maiano; frescoes by Vasari and inlaid stalls* in the Old Sacristy.

Spaccanapoli (Via B. Croce and Via S. Biagio dei Librai) runs along an ancient "decumanus." Following this route, you will pass a number of renowned churches and old palazzi; note Palazzo Filomarino, where the philosopher Benedetto Croce lived and died.

Church of Gesù Nuovo *(C4)*. It is a fine example of Neapolitan Baroque, especially in the interior, with its rich decoration of colored marble.

S. Chiara* *(C4)*. It was rebuilt in the original style (1310-28), with a clear Provençal Gothic inspiration; it is one of the foremost monuments of medieval Naples; inside, note the Tomb of Marie de Valois* by Tino da Camaino and assistants (1333-38) and fragments of the funerary monument of Robert I Anjou by Giovanni and Pacio Bertini from Florence (1343-45); the inscription "Cernite Robertum regem virtute robertum", which comments on the arts of the Trivium and Quadrivium, or pillars of Medieval Scholasticism, who are shown watching over the funerary statue of the dead king, is said to have been dictated by the poet Petrarch. Adjacent are the Convent of the Minorites, with a handsome portal* leading into the choir, and the **Cloister of the Clarisse*** *(open, winter 8:30-12:30 and 4-an hour before sunset; summer 8:30-12:30 and 4-6:30; closed Sun. afternoon)*, a spacious rectangle containing a splendid garden, laid out in 1742, at its center; the outside wall of the garden, the seats and the pillars are covered with marvelous colored majolica*.

Church of S. Domenico Maggiore* *(C4)*. In

the convent adjacent to the church, Thomas Aquinas once taught and both Pontano and Giordano Bruno once studied; inside the church, frescoes attributed to Cavallini (circa 1308) and, in the Cappellone del Crocifisso, a Crucifix* on panel, from the 13th c., which supposedly spoke to St. Thomas, and a Deposition, attributed to Colantonio.

Cappella Sansevero *(C4; entrance in Via De Sanctis 19)*. With 18th-c. decoration of colored marble, it is celebrated for the virtuoso statues of Disinganno (Disillusionment, by Queirolo), Pudicizia (Modesty, by A. Corradini) and Christ Veiled* (G. Sammartino, 1735).

S. Angelo a Nilo *(C4)*. Known also as the "Cappella Brancaccio," it is a church set on a little square with an ancient statue of the god of the River Nile, and contains the sepulcher of Rinaldo Cardinal Brancaccio*, by Donatello, Michelozzo, and Pagno di Lapo Portigiani (1426-28).

No less interesting is the **Via Tribunali**, another of the

ancient "decumani." S. Paolo Maggiore (C5) dei Teatini (1583-1603) is a church set high atop a stairway in the Piazzetta S. Gaetano, the site of the ancient Greco-Roman Forum; the interior is richly decorated with marble inlay and frescoes *(tours in the morning, enquire with the priests)*.

S. Lorenzo Maggiore** *(C5)*. One of the most important Medieval Neapolitan churches. The first church was built in the 6th c. on top of Roman structures which have only recently been brought to light during excavations; this same church was then rebuilt at the express wish of Charles I and Charles II in 1270-75. Of the Baroque renovation, only the facade (1742) remains. The **interior** of this church has a Provençal Gothic inspiration; note the Gothic sepulcher of Catherine of Austria* by Tino di Camaino and assistants; from the 18th-c. cloister you can enter an area of Greek, Roman, and medieval archeological excavations *(open 9-1; closed Sun.)*.

Girolamini *(C5)*. The interior of the church of the Girolamini (16th/18th c.) is an interesting composite example of Baroque decoration, though it is badly damaged; adjacent to the main cloister is a small **Pinacoteca** (picture gallery; *open 9-1; closed Sun. holidays)*.

Pio Monte della Misericordia *(C5)*. Such were the confraternity tasks (corporal works of mercy) that, when the building was undergoing construction (1658), the architect was asked to carve out a space for a portico in the lower part of the facade where the needy could be welcomed. In the 17th-c. **church**, note sculpture by Andrea Falcone and paintings by B. Caracciolo, L. Giordano, and others; the *Pinacoteca*, or art gallery, includes paintings from the Neapolitan school of the Pio Monte della Misericordia.

Via del Duomo follows an ancient "cardo" of the Greco-Roman city. The Renaissance **Palazzo Como*** *(C5; 1460-90)*, also called "Cuomo", possibly designed by Giuliano da Maiano, is the site of the Museo **Civico Filangieri** *(open, 9-2; closed Mon.)*, with an estimable collection of Neapolitan paintings, Italian and Spanish arms and armor (16th/18th c.), European and Oriental ceramics and porcelain, and embroideries from the 16th c.

S. Giorgio Maggiore *(C5)*, rebuilt in the 17th c. by C. Fanzago, still preserves, at the entrance, the apse of the early-Christian church, dating from the 4th/5th c.

The Duomo** *(C5)* still maintains the soaring 13th-c. Gothic interior, with pointed arches and piers, against which 110 ancient columns have been placed. The third chapel in the right aisle is the 17th-c. **Cappella di S. Gennaro***, with a bronze gate by Fanzago, and frescoes by Domenichino and Lanfranco, a silver altar frontal dating from 1695, a statue of the Saint, little flagons of miracle-working blood, and the saint's cranium, in a 14th-c. French reliquary. The Assumption of the Virgin* by Perugino and assistants, is in the second chapel in the right transept; frescoes dating from the late 13th c. to the 16th c., a mosaic floor from the 13th c., a Siennese polyptych from the 14th c. and the two tombs of the Minutolo family in the Cappella Minutolo** *(if closed, enquire in the sacristy)*; a large 14th-c. fresco with a Jesse Tree in the second chapel in the left transept. From the left aisle, you can descend to the church of **S. Restituta** , the first Christian basilica in Naples (4th c.); in the 5th-c. **baptistery,** fragments of original mosaics*; in the sixth chapel in the left aisle, Virgin and Saints, in mosaic, by Lello da Orvieto (1322).

S. Maria Donnaregina *(B5)*. There are two churches named S. Maria Donnaregina*: one is Baroque (1649), and has an interior frescoed and decorated with polychrome marble; the other is an important medieval Franciscan Gothic monument, and contains the sepulcher of Mary, Queen of Hungary* by Tino di Camaino and Gagliardo Primario (1326) and, in the nuns' choir, frescoes* from the first half of the 14th c., by F. Rusuti and others.

Castel Capuano *(C5)*. At the end of Via dei Tribunali, it is also known as the Vicaria (C5); built by the Normans and enlarged the Swabians, it was the royal palace until the 15th c.

Porta Capuana * *(B5)*, built in 1484 to a plan by Giuliano da Maiano, is one of the great masterpieces of the Renaissance.

S. Giovanni a Carbonara * *(B5)*, which stands high atop an 18th-c. staircase, is a church that was founded in 1343, rebuilt at the beginning of the 15th c., and then modified and enlarged; note in particular the sculptures, such as the Monumento Miroballo* (16th c.), the monument to King Ladislaus* (1428) and the sepulcher of Ser Gianni Caracciolo*, one of the lovers of Queen Jane II, stabbed to death at her orders.

The Vomero

This quarter may be considered a city within the city; it is hard to beleive that the hill slopes were once dotted with farmhouses, patrician residences and villas.

Piazza Vanvitelli *(D2)*. The very center of a quarter which developed at the end of the 19th c. Once characterized by handsome Art Nouveau architecture, its appearance is that of an anonymous middle-class quarter, spoilt by real estate speculation.

The Floridiana * *(D2)*. King Ferdinand I gave to his morganatic wife, Lucia Partanna, Duchess of Floridia, the villa (1817-19) now known as the Floridiana. The magnificent park is famous for its abundance of splendid camelias; the Neoclassical mansion houses the **Museo Nazionale della Ceramica Duca di Martina** * *(open, 9-2; closed Mon.)*, an exquisite collection of porcelain and majolica from the main manufactories of Europe and the East.

Castel S. Elmo *(D3; open 9-2; closed Mon.)*. A massive star-shaped fortress, rebuilt in the 16th c. It later became a prison (in 1799 revolutionaries were jailed here, as were many patriots of the Risorgimento). Splendid view** over the city and gulf from the terraces.

Certosa di S. Martino ** *(D3; open 9-2; closed Mon.)*. G.A. Dosio, C. Fanzago, and other architects made the Certosa di S. Martino, a charterhouse on a ridge of the Vomero hill, into the most complete and exquisite work of 17th-c. Neapolitan Baroque.

Naples: Certosa di S. Martino

The church **, glittering with marble inlays, is itself a gallery of 17th-c. Neapolitan painting. You then pass through the interesting area of the convent; from the square in front of the Certosa, splendid panoramic view*.

Located inside the Certosa is the **Museo Nazionale di S. Martino** ** *(open, 9-2; closed Mon.)* the museum includes: a Naval Section, Historical Souvenirs and Memorabilia of the Kingdom of Naples, the Neapolitan Topographical Section, the Section of Feasts and Costumes, the Section of Creches, with the large Cuciniello Creche* and, across the handsome main cloister*, is the lavish Pinacoteca, or Art Gallery, the Sculpture Section, and the Section of Applied Arts and memorabilia of the Certosa.

The Riviera

The legendary view of Naples was celebrated by painters in the 18th c., only to be followed by photographs and postcards in the 19th c. In touring this part of the Gulf of Naples - perhaps by car along the Posillipo hill - one can understand why people used to say " See Naples and die."

S. Lucia *(E-F4)*. Take Via N. Sauro, the first stretch of the magnificent beachfront promenade, or Lungomare**, as far as Mergellina, and you will arrive at the Porto di S. Lucia with its quay that leads to the Borgo Marinaro (fishing village); at the end of Via N. Sauro, note the *Fontana dell'Immacolatella (F4)*, a Baroque fountain.

The Castel dell'Ovo *(F47.* It was built in the 12th c. (though its current appearance dates from 1691), on the site of a villa that once belonged to Lucullus, a great general and bon-vivant of Ancient Rome.

Riviera di Chiaia *(E2-3)*. This elegant road used to be the site of the old Neapolitan promenade, famous for its views and 17th-19th-c. houses, important examples of which, especially in the opening stretch, still remain.

Villa Pignatelli *(E2; open 9-2; closed Mon.)*. Surrounded by a beautiful garden, it houses the **Museo Principe Diego Aragona Pignatelli Cortes** which still preserves the flavor of the original patrician residence; note the large araucarias in the garden, as well as the *Museo delle Carrozze* (Museum of Carriages).

Villa Comunale *(E 2-3)*. The gardens of the Villa Comunale separate the Riviera di Chiaia from the beach-front promenade, or Lungomare of Via Caracciolo, and enclose the **Acquario*** (Aquarium; *E2; open, summer, 9-6, holidays 10-6; winter 9-5; closed Mon.)*.

Piedigrotta *(E-F1)*. The Piedigrotta quarter (so called because it is on this side of tunnel - "grotta"- underneath the hill of Posillipo dug in the 1st c. B.C.) features the church of S. Maria di Piedigrotta *(F1)*, originally built in the 13th c., with a Siennese wooden Madonna from the 14th c.

Parco Virgiliano *(F1)*. Here you can visit the Tomb of Giacomo Leopardi and the so-called Tomb of Vergil, which was actually a Roman dovecote.

Mergellina *(F1)*. Continuing along Via Caracciolo, you will reach one of the most enchanting sites in Naples: the inlet of Mergellina. In **S. Maria del Parto** is the tomb of the Neapolitan Humanist poet Jacopo Sannazaro and the famous "Diavolo di Mergellina," a panel from the 16th c. showing St. Michael besting the Devil.

Posillipo*. A crossroads along the panoramic Via di Posillipo* is the starting point for promenades and walks through the enchanting "region" of Posillipo*, which takes its name from the Greek words for "assuaging pain or grief." The Via di Posillipo will take you to: Capo di Posillipo, with a group of houses by the sea, and a little marina; to the little fishing village of **Marechiaro**, high over the sea, where a plaque on a house atop a cliff indicates the "fenesta ca lucive" from the song by Salvatore Di Giacomo; lastly, on the Pozzuoli shore of the gulf, on the **island of Nìsida**, note the ancient volcanic crater, joined to the mainland by a breakwater/bridge.

The remarkable vistas and views in this area are all of particular note, but perhaps the finest panorama** of Naples is the one from the Belvedere of the **Eremo dei Camàldoli** (Hermitage of the Camaldolites, elev. 458 m., the highest point in the Campi Flegrei, or Phlegrean Fields, to the NW of the river; exit from A1).

Noto*

elev. 152 m., pop. 21,803, Sicily, province of Siracusa. Set in a landscape of quarries and marshes, but also surrounded by citrus groves, almond orchards, and vineyards, Noto is a remarkable town, rebuilt in a lavish Baroque style following the ravages of the earthquake of 1693.

Places of interest. Corso Vittorio Emanuele*. The main street of Noto, which widens into three squares, from which monumental staircases ascend.

Piazza Immacolata. If you enter town from the Porta Nazionale, the first of these three squares is the Piazza Immacolata, with a stairway up to the *church of the Immacolata* (or of S. Francesco) and the *convent of the SS. Salvatore.*

Museo Civico. In the last-mentioned convent is the town museum *(tel. 836462)*, which comprises an archeological section, with prehistoric and Greek finds, as well as a modern section.

Piazza del Municipio. In this square stands the elegant *Palazzo Ducezio** (V. Sinatra, 18th c.) and the staircase that climbs up to the **Duomo**, with a spectacular 18th-c. facade; the interior is closed to the public because of the collapse of the dome in March 1996.

Piazza XXIV Maggio. Continuing along the Corso, you will see this square, after the *church of the Collegio*; note the church of *S. Domenico.*

Crocifisso. In the high part of Noto, this Baroque church contains a Virgin with Child* by F. Laurana (1471).

Noto Antica. Passing through this section of town, you can continue on to the Val di Noto and the Monti Iblei.

Surrounding areas. At a distance of 20 km. are the beach resorts of Marzamemi and Portopalo.

Orvieto*

elev. 325 m.; pop. 21,419; Umbria, province of Terni. The bluff of yellowish tufa on which Orvieto is built rises like a shoal, at the head of the green valley of the Paglia. An island in time, just as it may long ago have been an island in a gulf along the Tyrrhenian coast, Orvieto soars above the surrounding countryside. L. Maitani was summoned from Siena in 1290 when the walls of the Cathedral seemed about to collapse; he repaired them and began to design the remarkable facade, which was later completed by A. Pisano and A. Orcagna. The golden Gothic triptych of the facade should be seen from a distance, glittering in the sunset — words hardly suffice to describe it.

Historical note. With the Latin name of "Urbs Vetus," or 'old city,' Orvieto is barely mentioned in the high Middle Ages, in the writings of Paulus Diaconus and Saint Gregory the Great. Whatever the ancient name of Orvieto, it certainly was a flourishing Etruscan town between the 7th and 3rd c. B.C. In the 11th and 12th c. the city developed a Communal government and was recognized in 1157 by the pope. Orvieto tried to expand its rule over surrounding territory, but the civil factions of Guelphs and Ghibellines produced strife here, as they did in much of 13th-c. Italy. Romanesque architecture thrived: note the churches of S. Andrea and S. Giovenale, the various towers, and the spectacular Palazzo del Popolo. A little later, the Gothic style pervaded Orvieto, in the churches of S. Francesco and S. Domenico, the Palazzo Papale, and above all, the Duomo, a masterpiece of Italian Gothic. Even then, Orvieto — which of course never required walls — occupied virtually all of the surface of the tufa plateau. Civil discord was quashed in 1354 by the Cardinal Albornoz who recognized Orvieto's government but built the fortress of the Rocca and reiterated the dedication of the town to the purposes of the Church. As the quarrels raged between popes and anti-popes, between Rome and Avignon, Orvieto was tossed among outside rulers, but in 1448 it came under the rule of Pope Nicholas V, and its medieval history subsided into order. The remarkable well, or Pozzo di S. Patrizio, was built, as were various 16th-c. palazzi; all modern expansion of the city has taken place at the foot of the plateau.

Getting around. We suggest leaving your car in one of the parking areas outside of town, and taking a bus into Orvieto. The cable car restored to service in 1990 links the train station with Piazza Cahen.

Places of interest. Piazza Cahen. Across from the Rocca (see below); it can be reached from the train station by *cable car*, built in 1880 and recently restored to service. Near the square is the ancient *Porta Postierla*.

Rocca. This fortress was built at the orders of the Cardinal Albornoz (1364), destroyed by the townspeople in 1390, and rebuilt in 1450. Used as a fort until the 18th c., it is now a park (fine view of the Paglia valley). Note tufa ruins of the Etruscan **Temple of Belvedere**, late-5th c. B.C.

Pozzo di S. Patrizio*. *Open: Oct.-Mar., 10-6; Apr.-Sep., 9-7.* This well, a unique and daring piece of architecture, was built, along with other cisterns and wells, at the order of Pope Clement VII after the Sack of Rome, in order to ensure that Orvieto would have an adequate water supply during a siege. Begun by A. da Sangallo the Younger in 1528, it was completed in 1537. It comprises a cylindrical chamber (diameter 13 m.) that drops to a depth of 62 m.; around it run two broad staircases, stacked in a double spiral, illuminated by 72 great window along their length. In this way, men and mules could efficiently descend and climb with loads of water.

Corso Cavour. This main street winds its way through the center of Orvieto, lined with 16th-c. palazzi and medieval houses. At the beginning, a small lane on the right leads to the 13th-c. church of *S. Maria dei Servi*, entirely rebuilt in Neoclassical style. On the left is the Romanesque church of **S. Stefano**, and on the left, the medieval church of *S. Angelo*, one of Orvieto's oldest, entirely rebuilt in 1828. A little further on, facing the *Teatro Mancinelli* (1864), is the 16th-c. facade of *Palazzo Petrucci*, begun, but not finished, by M. Sanmicheli.

Torre Civica. This medieval tower stands 42 m. tall, and is topped by a bell, cast in 1316 for Palazzo del Popolo, with the 24 symbols of the Arts. At the base lies Via del Duomo. Next to it is **Palazzo dei Sette**, built around 1300, partly rebuilt in the 16th c., and now used as a cultural center.

Piazza del Duomo. This cozy square with its odd shape and proportions emphasizes the massive Duomo. The northern end of the square is bounded by *low medieval houses*; at the corner with Via del Duomo stands a *clock tower* (1349) with a bronze figure that strikes the hours; originally designed to ensure steady work on the Duomo. Across the little square is Palazzo Faina, with the Museo Civico; to the right of the Duomo is Palazzo Soliano, site of the Museo dell'Opera del Duomo and the Museo "Emilio Greco" (see below).

Duomo**. Begun in 1290 and carried on (1310-30) by L. Maitani, who worked especially on the facade and the terminal section, this is certainly one of the finest creations of Italian Gothic architecture. The *facade*, which was completed in the 16th c., is shaped like an immense triptych, glowing and glittering with polychrome marble, statuary, and mosaics (it was redone in the 17th and 18th c.). The central portal and the rose window* — by A. Orcagna — are particularly noteworthy. Also note the statues of prophets and apostles. The four pillars that frame the portals are lined with **reliefs**** based on the Bible, by L. Maitani and helpers (early 14th c.); the same artists made the bronze symbols of the Evangelists above the pillars and the group in the lunette over the central portal.

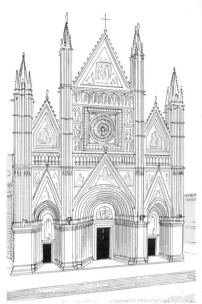

Orvieto: Duomo

In the majestic **interior**, the three *aisles* are still Romanesque, while transept and presbytery are Gothic in style. Note the baptismal and holy-water fonts, wrought-iron, and reliefs by R. and F. da Montelupo. At the end of the right arm of the *transept* is the early-15th-c. *Cappella Nuova*, renowned for the **frescoes**** by Luca Signorelli. Originally begun by Fra' Angelico (1477), with the help of B. Gozzoli, G. d'Antonio Fiorentino, and G. da Poli, the frescoes — outstanding masterpieces of Italian art history — were completed by L. Signorelli (1477-1504) with the theme of the Last Judgment. In the vault, the prophets shown with Christ the Judge are by Fra' Angelico and helpers, 1447; in the lunette, on the left, in the scene of the Antichrist preaching, the two figures in black are portraits of Signorelli and Fra' Angelico; also note the figures of poets from Homer to Dante. The raised *presbytery* is decorated with 2,500 sq. m. of frescoes by U. di Prete Ilario (1370-80); they are unusual in both size and subject (Glory of Mary). Note the majestic inlaid wooden choir* by G. Ammannati (1331-40). On the right wall of the left arm of the transept, note the panel*, 1320, by L. Memmi. On the altar, a marble Gothic tabernacle (1358) contains a famed reliquary** containing a blood-stained cloth, supposedly from a host that bled to confound a Bohemian priest, doubtful concerning the dogma of Transubstantiation (the Mass of Bolsena, 1263). The reliquary, by the Siennese U. di Vieri (1338), is a masterpiece of Italian goldsmithery. Nearby is a fresco* by G. da Fabriano (1425).

Palazzo Faina. This 19th-c. palazzo across from the Duomo houses the *Raccolta Archeologica Civica* and the *Museo "Claudio Faina"*, comprising the city's collection and the archeological collections of Count Claudio Faina, a gift to Orvieto. Among the more notable items: 6th-/4th-c. B.C. Attic vases*, and a 4th-c. B.C. Etruscan sarcophagus* with traces of polychrome paint.

Palazzo Soliano*. This immense austere building made of tufa, with a large exterior staircase and trifores, or three-light mullioned windows, was built at the orders of Pope Boniface VIII (1297-1304); the upper section was left unfinished, and was completed in the 16th c. The Guelph-style crenelations date from the late-19th-c. The ground floor houses the Museo Emilio Greco (see below) and, upstairs, the **Museo Civico e dell'Opera del Duomo***, with its collections of sculpture, painting, liturgical objects, jewelry, largely from the Cathedral and other churches of the diocese. Among the artists whose work is featured in this museum: C. di Marcovaldo, S. Martini, L. Signorelli, A. Pisano, L. Maitani; reliquary of S. Savino* by U. di Vieri and V. di Lando.

Museo "Emilio Greco". *Open, Oct.-Mar., 10:30-1 and 2-6; Apr.-Sep., 10:30-1 and 3-7; closed Mon.* Opened in 1991, on the ground floor of Palazzo Soliano, this museum features sculpture and art, donated by the artist himself (1947-present). Nearby, the Manneristic *Palazzo Buzi* (1580), by I. Scalza.

Museo Archeologico Nazionale. *Open, 9-1:30 and 2-6, in summer 3-7; Sun. 9-1.* To the right of the Duomo, this archeological museum is located in the 12th-c. **Palazzo Papale**, restored in 1958. The museum comprises state collections and the collections of the Opera del Duomo, which document the process of its construction. Note the Etruscan funereal furnishings, and frescoes from the necropolis of Settecamini, with life-size figures; also, intact Etruscan suit of armor.

The "Grotte." *Guided tours available by request; contact the APT.* The bluff of Orvieto is made largely of tufa, and over the centuries countless chambers have been carved into the soft stone; they are referred to as the "Grotte," or caves. They constitute a sort of underground city, now being studied systematically for the first time. An intricate network of passages and galleries links the many cavities, dating from different eras, and built for different purposes. The Etruscans built the narrow oval tunnels, storerooms for crops, and a number of very deep wells, along with more than 100 cisterns for water. In the Middle Ages, the "butti" were dug, and used to toss rubbish; the cisterns with grey plaster, the furnaces, and the ruins of Orvieto's first aqueduct also date from the Middle Ages. Many rooms date from the Renaissance, as well. The tours are limited to the safest and most accessible areas.

S. Francesco. Founded in 1240 at the highest point in Orvieto, the walls and facade are original (note rose windows and portal). Inside, note the 14th-c. wooden Crucifix.

S. Lorenzo de Arari. This little 13th-c. church has a lovely interior, with 14th-c. frescoes; the main altar features an Etruscan altar, and a 12th-c. ciborium. Nearby is the *Porta Romana* (1822), built on the site of the ancient *Porta Pertusa* (ruins); from the park area, with the medieval *Palazzo Medici*, fine view of the valley of the river Povero, spanned by the medieval aqueduct. If you skirt the western edge of the bluff, you will reach the octagonal church of *S. Giovanni*; inside, 14th-c. fresco, and, in adjacent convent, fine Renaissance cloister.

S. Giovenale. This church was founded in 1004; note the simple Romanesque facade and fortified bell tower. The interior, with tufa columns, was modified in the 13th c.; note fragments of 13th-c. frescoes, and carved altar piece from 1170. Nearby, handsome medieval homes and the 13th-c. former church of *S. Agostino*, with Baroque interior. The Museo della Ceramica will be installed here.

Via Malabranca. This handsome road runs along a slope on the surface of the bluff, through a well preserved medieval neighborhood. At n. 14-18, notable old houses; at n. 22, the Renaissance *Palazzo Simoncelli* (by B. Rossellino); at n. 15, the 16th-c. *Palazzo Caravajal*. Turn onto **Via della Cava**, running downhill between rows of medieval houses to Porta Maggiore. Next to the church of *Madonna della Cava*, note the *well*, a deep cylinder drilled into the tufa, used from 1428 to 1546.

Piazza della Repubblica. Center of Orvieto ever since the Middle Ages, this square is dominated by the long facade of the 16th-c. *Palazzo Comunale*, by I. Scalza; on the same square is the simple facade of the 11th-c. church of **S. Andrea***, with a 12-sided tower. The portico on the left side was built during restorations (1926-30). The interior has fragments of 14th-c. frescoes; beneath the church, Villanovan and Etruscan remains, and 6th-c. mosaic floors.

Palazzo del Popolo**. Begun around 1250, inspired by the "broletti" of Lombardy, with a huge meeting hall over an open loggia, this building was enlarged at the end of the 13th c., with the addition of the residence of the Capitano del Popolo — equivalent to mayor — and a bell tower. As the politics of Orvieto changed, this building fell into neglect, and was used variously as a prison, workshop, warehouse, and silo. Restored in recent years (1987-90), it has recently been used for conferences and meetings; digs have uncovered Etruscan temples, a medieval aqueduct, and a large cistern. In the upper hall, note 14th-c. frescoes. On the square, note the little church of *S. Rocco*, built by M. Sanmicheli around 1525; also, the 16th-c. *Palazzo Simoncelli*.

S. Domenico. This church, built in 1264, was drastically amputated in 1934; only the transept survived. Inside, note the monument to Cardinal Braye*, by A. di Cambio (1285); beneath apse, note chapel by M. Sanmicheli.

Excursion. **Etruscan necropolis of the Crocifisso del Tufo** *(open, 8:30-sunset),* 1.5 km on state road 71. Dating from the 6th-c. B.C., this necropolis is quite orderly, with tombs lined up along two parallel roads.

Òstia Antica*

elev. 2; Lazio, province and township of Rome. The Tiber runs past the medieval borgo, or village, near the Castello — Renaissance in style, military in purpose — built by B. Pontelli, at the behest of Giuliano Cardinal della Rovere (later Pope Julius II). Nearby are the silent tombs, baths, temples, theaters, and forum of the port of ancient Rome, a set of ruins as startling as those of Pompeii and Herculaneum.

Historical note. In 1575 flooding shifted the course of the Tiber, which once ran past the Castello, moving it northward; for centuries, however, the deposits brought by the river had been pushing the seashore out, some 4 m. per year. It is now 6 km. away. Archeologists tell us that Ostia was founded in the early 4th c. B.C., a small camp some 400 m. from the ancient beach. By the 1st c. B.C., Ostia was given a new set of walls some 2.5 km in circumference. The Empire saw an even larger, thriving port city. Claudius built a new harbor, Trajan enlarged it, establishing a second city "Portus," that would in time supplant Ostia. The capital of the Empire moved from Rome to Constantinople; the Goths ravaged Ostia, and of a once mighty city of 100,000, nothing remained but haunted ruins. Two industries now flourish here, however: an incessant series of archeological digs, and a steady flow of fascinated sightseers.

Places of interest. Castello di Giulio II*. *Open 9-1; closed Sun.* Standing in the heart of the 15th-c. Rocca, or fortress, it was built in 1483-86, by B. Pontelli. Triangular in plan, with two mighty circular towers and a pentagonale keep. In the adjacent Palazzo Episcopale, a series of frescoes* by B. Peruzzi (1508-1513) were found in 1977-79.

Via Ostiense. The ancient road from Rome to the port is the modern entrance to the **archeological site of Ostia Antica** (*open, winter 9-5; summer 9-6 or 7*).

Terme di Nettuno. These baths, built by Hadrian and adorned with handsome mosaics, stand near the *barracks of the "Vigiles"*, or police, dating from the same period.

Teatro**. The first structure here was built under Agrippa (1st c. B.C.), but a later, brick structure dates from A.D. 196; from the step-seats, excellent view* of the digs. Behind the proscenium extends the *Piazzale delle Corporazioni**, designed during Augustan times as a sort of lobby for intermissions: the double portico, rebuilt under Hadrian, contains the mosaics donated by various guilds. To the west is the *Mithreum of the Seven Heavens*, one of 17 sanctuaries consecrated to Mithras in the 2nd and 3rd c., and *four little temples* dedicated to the female deities that protected commerce in the early 1st c. B.C.

Via della Casa di Diana. Running among multi-story apartment buildings; note, at the end of the road, a 3rd-c. *"thermopolium"* (cafeteria) with counter, sinks, and a fresco advertising food and beverages.

Museo Ostiense*. *Open 9:30-2.* In the 11 halls of the 15th-c. *Casone del Sale*, this museum features the finest materials found in 40 years of digs. Of particular note, sarcophagi, Greek statuary, busts of emperors (esp. Trajan), paintings, and mosaics.

Foro. Ostia's political center, this Forum was given the appearance we see today under Hadrian's rule. Overlooking it are: the *Capitolium*, Ostia's main temple (staircase and high podium survive); the houses of the Triclinii, with the *baths of the Forum*, opened under Antoninus Pius and used till the 5th c.; the *temple of Rome and Augustus* (a statue of Roma and part of the pediment, with a Winged Victory, survive); the *"Judiciary Basilica,"* built by Domitian or Trajan; to its right is a *round 3rd-c. temple*, for the emperor cult.

Via della Foce. Starting from the "Bivio del Castrum," this road runs past the *"Horrea Epagathiana,"* a 2nd-c. warehouse, near the Late-Empire *Domus of Amor and Psyche*; nearby stand many popular apartment *houses* and baths (Caseggiato di Serapide, *Casette Tipo, Caseggiato degli Aurighi, Terme della Trinacria*, and *Terme dei Sette Sapienti*). The road ends at the *Palazzo Imperiale*.

Insula delle Muse. One of the richest residential complexes to survive from the middle Empire, it lies in a part of Ostia that was rebuilt under Hadrian. Note the *Case a Giardino*, with 8 apartments sharing a "yard"; the *Porta Marina (C2)*, where the main street hit the ancient coastline; and the oldest **Synagogue*** in the West (1st c.).

Schola del Traiano. This was the headquarters of the guild of shipbuilders; it takes its name from a statue of Trajan found here.

Cardine Massimo. Running roughly north to south, this "cardo maximus" was the main street of Ostia; nearby is the *Campo della Magna Mater*, dedicated to one of the oldest cults in the Roman world.

Domus della Fortuna Annonaria. Aristocratic home of the Late Empire; nearby is a Roman laundry, with original *dyeing vats*.

Padua / Padova*

elev. 12 m.; pop. 215,025; Veneto, provincial capital. Padua has an irregular urban layout, in which the thread of history is tangled and difficult to read, amongst the long low porticoes of the old town, the weeping willows that line the banks of the Bacchiglione and the area of Prato della Valle, and amongst the thriving modern sections devoted to business and manufacturing. The city has a seven-century-plus tradition of university studies. Among its art treasures are Giotto's frescoes in the Scrovegni Chapel, Donatello's work, at the "Santo," and work by the young Titian, at the Scuola del Santo, masterpieces of Italian art history.

Historical note. Near the University, or Bo', you can still see the Tomb of Antenor, a Trojan hero who, according to tradition, founded Padua in 1184 B.C. Certainly, Padua was founded later, not before the 8th or 7th c. B.C. The Paduan historian, Titus Livius, known as Livy, attests Padua's existence in 302 B.C. Livy also tells us that the river Brenta once ran through Padua, and that the Brenta naturally changed its course, so that the Paduans were forced to divert the nearby river Bacchiglione into the old bed of the Brenta. The part of Padua enclosed by the two branches of the river, between the Specola, or Observatory, and the Porte Contarine, corresponds to the Roman city. In the 12th c., the first city walls were built along this watercourse; in this same period, Padua began to assert itself as a major political force in northern Italy. Following the wars against Frederick I Barbarossa, in the second half of the 12th c., Padua subjugated Vicenza, Bassano, and Feltre. In these years, the Palazzo della Ragione was built (1218-19), the University was founded by students and masters who left Bologna (1222); in these same years, amidst the turmoil of factional infighting, a Franciscan monk from Portugal preached counsels of peace — he was to become St. Anthony of Padua, and the people of the city began to build a vast and sumptuous basilica to his memory, immediately after his death (1231). Ezzelino da Romano took advantage of the continual factional fighting to rule Padua for several decades, but the Communal government survived to enjoy free rule; during that time Giotto was summoned to fresco the Scrovegni Chapel and the University had Dante Alighieri as an honored guest. It was in this same period that Padua built its porticoes, so rare among cities of Veneto; this development may possibly have been due to the influence of the University, a direct scion of the University of Bologna, city of porticoes par excellence. Over the next century or so, the Da Carrara family ruled the city, beginning in 1318, yielding to the Visconti (1389), who in turn ceded Padua to Venice (1405). During this period, Padua was home for a while to the poet Petrarch. Although Padua had lost its political independence, it preserved, in the 15th c., a certain artistic supremacy over Venice, with the work of Donatello and Mantegna. A new, larger ring of walls was built. In the 19th c., when the walls were partly demolished, the city finally began to spread south (Bassanello) and north (Borgomagno). In that century, the historic center was gutted, to make way for the Corso del Popolo; the same happened in the 20th c. for the Corso Milano, when many of Padua's canals were filled in and paved over (Riviera is the name that now marks each of these former waterways).

Getting around. For your tour of Padua, we recommend two routes; you may walk the entire distance, or take public transportation for part of the way.

The old historic center

The Piazza delle Erbe, P. della Frutta, and P. dei Signori, the romantic oxbow curve of the Bacchiglione, the Bo', or University, the Neoclassical Caffè Pedrocchi, Giotto's Scrovegni Chapel, the Eremitani, S. Sofia and its "Byzantine" apse, the historic center and the modern heart of Padua, all lie within a short distance from the great keel-roof of the Palazzo della Ragione, the "Salone," an ancient courthouse.

Piazza delle Erbe (*C3*). A lively fruit and vegetable market is held here; it is lined by the Palazzo della Ragione, the Palazzo Comunale, and old buildings with porticoes.

Palazzo Comunale, now *Palazzo del Municipio*, or town hall (C3). This building dates from the 13th c. (note the tower on the right side), and was rebuilt by A. Moroni in the mid-16th c. and enlarged in 1904.

Palazzo della Ragione* (*C2-3*). Also known as the "Salone," this majestic building was founded in 1218-19 and enlarged in 1306-1309; it was badly damaged by a fire in 1420, which destroyed fine frescoes by Giotto.

The *interior* (open, Apr.-Oct. , 9-6; Nov.-Mar., 9-12:30 and 3-6, closed Mon.) comprises a single huge room, 27 m. wide, 78 m. long, and 27 m. tall; the walls are decorated with frescoes, redone in 1430. Note the wooden reproduction of Donatello's equestrian statue of the Gattamelata (see below for original).

Duomo (*C2*). Founded in the High Middle Ages, rebuilt in the 9th c. and again by 1124, today this cathedral bears the marks of the renovation begun in 1551, to plans by Michelangelo. The facade is unfinished, and the interior is starkly majestic. On the transept walls are 14th-c. funerary monuments. In the Sacristy, 14th-c. panels and paintings by P. Bordone, J. da Montagnana, G. Tiepolo, and others. On the right of the Duomo is the Baptistery (see below); behind it, in Via Dietro Duomo 15, is the *Museo Diocesano* (open 9-12:30, Sat. 9-12; closed Thu., Sun. and Jul.-Aug.), with paintings, sculptures, and sacred objects.

Battistero* (*C2*). This 13th-c. Romanesque baptistery, with a square plan and a broad round cupola, has an interior covered with *frescoes**, the masterpiece of G. de' Menabuoi (1374-76; also note his polyptych on the altar); note the 13th-c. baptismal font. The square is flanked by the *Palazzo del Monte di Pietà*, the 14th-c. Palazzo Vescovile, and various medieval houses.

Piazza dei Signori (*C2*). Note in particular the elegant marble **Loggia del Consiglio*** (1496-1553); also, the *Palazzo del Capitanio* (1605), with a **triumphal arch**, by G.M. Falconetto (1532), which holds the first clock in Italy, built in 1344, but rebuilt in 1437.

Past the arch is the *Corte Capitaniato*, with 16th-c. buildings, and the **Liviano**, designed by G. Ponti (1939), and now part of the University. In the atrium, frescoes by M. Campigli and a statue of Livy by A. Martini (1942). A spectacular *stairway** leads up to the vast 16th-c. *Sala dei Giganti* (open upon request, contact the department), decorated with huge figures of kings and heroes (in a corner, 14th-c. portrait of Petrarch). Adjacent to the Department of Archeology is the *Museo di Scienze Archeologiche e d'Arte* (open as above), with ancient and Renaissance artifacts and artworks (Donatello, B. Ammannati).

Piazza Insurrezione (*C2-3*). At the heart of modern Padua, this square is near the 18th-c. church of **S. Lucia**, with noteworthy paintings (D. Campagnola, Sassoferrato, Padovanino) and, up high, monochromatic canvases by G. Ceruti and G. B. Tiepolo. Adjacent is the **Scuola di S. Rocco** (*C2-3; open, Tue.-Fri., 3:30-6:30; Sat. also 10-12:30; Sun. only 10-12:30*), built in the 15th/16th c., and frescoed by D. Campagnola, G. del Santo, and others. At the mouth of Via Marsilio da Padua is the so-called *Casa di Ezzelino**, a handsome 13th-c. dwelling.

I Carmini (*B2-3*). This Romanesque church was completed in 1494, and almost immediately rebuilt to plans by L. da Bologna. Note the Renaissance sacristy*. Adjacent is the **Scuola del Carmine*** (*open upon request, contact sexton*), built in the 14th c. and frescoed by D. and G. Campagnola, G. del Santo, and others.

Cappella degli Scrovegni** (*B3*). Open 9-6; closed Mon. in winter. This funerary chapel stands in the public gardens of the Arena, which take their name from the scattered ruins of the 1st-c. A.D. *Roman amphitheater*. The little church, also known as *Madonna dell'Arena* or *S. Maria dell'Annunciata*, was built at the behest of Enrico Scrovegni, and consecrated in 1305.

Inside are the renowned **frescoes by Giotto****, executed before 1305 by the great master and his helpers, a towering masterpiece of Italian painting. Above the entrance, the Last Judgement; on the side walls, on the base, depictions of the 7 *Virtues** (right) and the 7 *Capital Sins** (left); above, in 38 panels, are Stories of Mary and Christ, showing Giotto's finest qualities: monumental composition, concise and expressive depiction, solid plasticism, emotional drama. In the presbytery, above the altar, statues by G. Pisano*; behind the altar, tomb of E. Scrovegni (d. 1336).

Museo Civico (*B3*). Open 9-6; closed Mon. Set in the old Convento degli Eremitani (note remains of frescoes from various eras), to the left of the church. The Museum comprises: an *archeological section*, with pre-Roman and Roman, Egyptian, Etruscan, and early-Christian materials; the *Museo Bottacin*, with 19th-c. artwork and a valuable coin collection; the *Quadreria Emo Capodilista*, featuring more than 500 paintings by Venetian and Flemish artists, including Titian, Giorgione, and Giovanni Bellini; the *Pinacoteca*, with paintings by artists of the Venetian schools, from the 14th to the 18th c., including Giotto, Guariento, B. Boccaccino, A. Vivarini, J. Bellini, P. Bordone, P. Veronese, J. and L. Bassano, J. Tintoretto, G. Romanino, G.B. Tiepolo, F. Guardi, M. and S. Ricci, and others; the *Raccolta dei Bronzetti e delle Placchette*, with creations by artists working in bronze, from the 14th to the 17th c. (A. Briosco, B. Ammannati, Sansovino, T. Aspetti); the *Raccolta di Ceramiche e Vetri* and the *Raccolta di Incisioni e Stampe*, with collections of, respectively, ceramics and glass, and prints and engravings.

Museo di Geologia e Paleontologia and Museo di Mineralogia. *Open upon request, tel. 656010*. This museum belongs to the University; set in the 16th-c. Palazzo Cavalli, in Via Giotto 36, it has collections of geology, paleontology, and mineralogy.

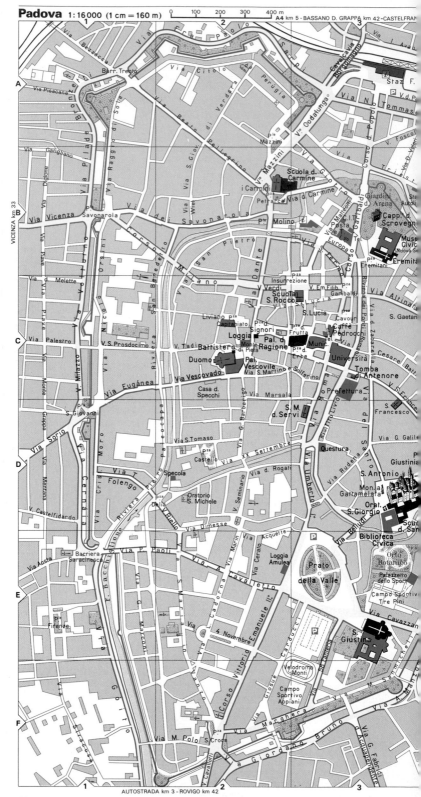

Padova

1:16000 (1 cm = 160 m)

0   100   200   300   400 m

A4 km 5 - BASSANO D. GRAPPA km 42 - CASTELFRAN

AUTOSTRADA km 3 - ROVIGO km 42

Eremitani* or *Church dei Ss. Filippo e Giacomo* (*B3*). This Romanesque-Gothic church was built between 1276 and 1306; partially destroyed by bombing in 1944 (especially the apse), it was faithfully rebuilt. The lower section of the facade, in stone, has a large portal and other arcading that continues along the right side; note the Renaissance portal on that side with carvings of the Months, by the Florentine N. Baroncelli (ca. 1442).

Inside (*open, Mon.-Sat., 8:15-12 and 3:30-5:30 or 6:30; Sun. from 9*), along the walls of the single aisle, with wooden ceiling, tombs and statues from the 14th to 16th c.: tombs of J. da Carrara* (left) and U. da Carrara (right); two 15th-c. altar-fronts; enormous tomb of M. M. Benavides, by B. Ammannati (1546). Note the *Cappella Ovetari**, once famed for the frescoes by A. Mantegna, A. da Forlì, B. da Ferrara, and others, destroyed by bombs. What has survived are several religious paintings and a terracotta altar piece by N. Pizzolo. In the presbytery and other chapels in the apse, 14th-c. frescoes and funerary monuments.

S. Sofia* (*C4*). This Romanesque church is the oldest in Padua and may have been founded in Carolingian times; it was rebuilt in the 11th c. and remodeled in the 14th c. Note the facade, the apse*, and the remarkable ambulatory.

Piazza Cavour (*C3*). A lively center of the city; in a nearby square, note the **Caffè Pedrocchi** (*C3*), a Neoclassical coffee shop dating from 1831, famous watering spot of the city's students and intelligentsia.

Via VIII Febbraio. This street is flanked by the University on the left and the Palazzo del Municipio, or town hall, on the right. The **University** (C3), commonly called *the Bo'*, is one of Europe's oldest (1222). Galileo taught here, as did G.B. Morgagni; it is considered the cradle of modern medicine. Note the handsome *old courtyard**, studded with coats of arms, and the stairs to the upper floors (*guided tours by request, in summer*). Note the *anatomical theater**, the first of its kind (1594), the *Sala dei Quaranta* (where Galileo taught), and the *Aula Magna* (coats of arms).

The Cittadella Antoniana

This route runs through the southern section of central Padua, and begins at the square of the Tomb of Antenor, near the University, where the previous tour ended. High point of this tour is the Basilica del Santo, but of considerable interest are the Oratorio di S. Giorgio and the Scuola del Santo. Along the route, other notable stops are the Orto Botanico (Europe's oldest botanical garden), the Prato della Valle, and the church of S. Giustina; you return to the center along Via Umberto and Via Roma.

Via S. Francesco. (*C-D 3-4*) On the Piazzale Antenore, which this road crosses, is the so-called **Tomb of Antenor** (*C3*), built in 1283, with an urn long said to contain the remains of Antenor, mythical founder of Padua, but actually holding the remains of a warrior of the 2nd/4th c. A.D. Along the road, note, at n. 9, the *Palazzo Romanin Jacur*, a Neogothic reconstruction, and the church of **S. Francesco** (*C-D3*), with notable frescoes.

Piazza del Santo (*D3*). Heart of the Cittadella Antoniana, this square, featuring the monument to Gattamelata, is surrounded by the Basilica del Santo, the Oratorio di S. Giorgio, the Scuola di S. Antonio, and a series of porticoed houses.

Monumento a Erasmo da Narni** (*D3*). Built to commemorate this great condottiere of the Venetian Republic, known as the **Gattamelata**

Padua: S. Antonio

(1370-1443). This statue is one of Donatello's masterpieces (1453).

S. Antonio** (*D3*). *Open 7-7.* This basilica, known locally simply as **the "Santo"**, is one of Italy's most renowned sanctuaries. It was built in a mixed Romanesque and Gothic style between 1232 and about 1350, to house the tomb of St. Anthony of Padua (born in Lisbon in 1195, died in Padua, at L'Arcella, in 1231). The simple facade boasts handsome portals, arches, and rose windows. The eight *cupolas* of the roof show a mixture of Byzantine, Venetian, and French Romanesque (Perigord) influences, while the little towers and the two octagonal bell towers give the church an eastern flavor. *Inside*, the three soaring aisles with huge pillars lead to a deep presbytery surrounded by a lavishly adorned ambulatory. In the right aisle is the tomb of a great soldier, Gattamelata (15th c.). In the *right transept*, the 14th-c. **Cappella di S. Felice***, is adorned with lovely frescoes* by Altichiero (1374-78). In the *presbytery*, the main altar is adorned with exceedingly fine **bronzes by Donatello**** (1443-50) and assistants. To the left of the altar, an astonishing bronze candelabrum* by A. Briosco (1515). Along the walls, 12 bronze bas-reliefs by B. Bellano and A. Briosco. Around the *presbytery*, with the *ambulatory*, with chapels opening out like rays; the 5th chapel, the Cappella delle Reliquie, by F. Parodi (as are the statues; 1689) contains an impressive treasury*: note the reliquaries (one supposedly holds St. Anthony's tongue, 13th c.), incense boats, and wooden caskets that held the saint's remains. Further along are two other chapels; the Cappella del Beato Luca Belludi (1382) is decorated with frescoes* by G. de' Menabuoi.

In the *left transept* is the **Cappella dell'Arca del Santo***, begun in 1500 (stucco ceiling by G. M. Falconetto, 1533): on the walls, reliefs by T. and A. Lombardo and J. Sansovino; other remarkable monuments in this section by T. Aspetti, P. Lombardo, and M. Sanmicheli. From the right aisle, you can enter the **cloisters** (13th/15th c.). The first cloister, called the *Chiostro del Capitolo* or della Magnolia (1240), leads into the Consiglio della Presidenza dell'Arca (*open, Tue. and Thu., 10-12*), where you can admire a very handsome fresco by A. Mantegna. In the nearby *Chiostro del Noviziato*, with well-curb dating from 1492, monument to C. Musso by A. Briosco; from the Chiostro del Generale (1434), you can climb up to the *Biblioteca Antoniana*, a library with 85,000 volumes and many incunabula.

S. Giorgio* *(D3). Open, Apr.-Sep., 9-12:30 and 2:30-6:30; Feb.-Mar. and Oct.-Nov. until 4:30; Jan. and Dec. mornings only.* This 14th-c. oratory stands to the right of the basilica; on the interior, note the **frescoes*** by Altichiero and assistants (1379-84), one of the most interesting pieces of 14th-c. Italian painting.

Scuola del Santo*. *Open the same hours as the Oratorio di S. Giorgio.* Built beginning in 1427, and raised in 1504, this building has its upper halls adorned with a series of frescoes* by Venetian artists, including several by Titian; the finest set of early-16th-c. paintings in Padua.

Palazzo Giustiniani *(D4).* This building, in Via Cesarotti, n. 21, was a theatrical center for 16th- and 17th-c. Padua.

Orto Botanico *(E3). Open, Mon.-Sat., 9-1; in summer also 3-6; Sun. (summer only) 10-1.* Founded in 1545, this botanical garden is the oldest in Europe, and one of the finest in Italy.

Prato della Valle *(E3).* This is one of Europe's largest squares (1775). Note the tree-covered islet in the center, the *Isola Memmia*, adorned with 78 statues and surrounded by a canal.

S. Giustina* *(E3).* This enormous brick 16th-c. church, with a bare facade and eight cupolas, has a late-16th-c. bell tower, set on the base of the medieval one.
The *interior* is huge and solemn. From the right transept, you can reach the *Sacello di S. Prosdocimo**, part of the 6th-c. basilica, with original iconostasis. Note the *old choir* (open, enquire in the front office of the monastery)* dating from 1462, with fine inlaid stalls. In the apse, carved and inlaid walnut *choir** (1566) and large altar piece by P. Veronese (1575). Note, in the left transept, the Arca di S. Luca, or Tomb of St. Luke, with alabaster reliefs (1316). In the 2nd chapel on the left, painting by S. Ricci. To the right of the church, note the Benedictine *monastery*, now partly used as a barracks.

Via Umberto I *(D3).* Along its left side, note the porticoes and old buildings; esp., at n. 8, *Casa Olzignani*, a Renaissance-Gothic mix (15th c.), rebuilt between 1900 and 1922.

Via Roma *(C-D3).* One of Padua's liveliest streets, lined by porticoes, and by the church of **S. Maria dei Servi** *(D3)*, Gothi-Romanesque (1372-92); note the frescoes (note Pietà*, by J. da Montagnana).

Paestum**

elev. 18 m., pop. 180, Campania, province of Salerno

Historical note. This was a colony of Sybaris (late-7th c. B.C.) and was called Poseidonia, from the name of the god of the sea; the town's prosperity, in fact, came from maritime trade; the Lucanians conquered it (circa 400 B.C.), and it then became a Roman colony (273 B.C.) with the name of Paestum.

Places of interest. As you pass through the walls of the **Porta Aurea**, the **zone of monuments**

Paestum: Poseidonion

and excavations is on the right *(open, 9-two hours before sunset).*

There are three Greek temples: the **Basilica***, from the mid-6th c. B.C., is the oldest of the temples of Paestum; the **Poseidonion****, or temple of Neptune (450 B.C.), is considered by some to be the most beautiful Doric temple in the Greek world; set apart from the others is the smaller **Tempio di Cerere***, or Temple of Ceres, dating from the end of the 6th c. B.C., and probably dedicated to the goddess Athena.

The Roman **Forum** occupies the site of the Greek *agora*; there is still a building that may have been the *Curia*, ruins of *baths*, the **Italic temple** (273 B.C., modified in 80 B.C.), perhaps the *Comitium*, and the *amphitheater*.

The route of the **Via Sacra**, a street used for religious processions, skirts a residential section; the *documanus maximus* runs past what may have been the *Gymnasium* and a sacred enclosure, with an *underground votive chapel** in the center (2nd half of the 6th c.).

A natural complement to this tour is a visit to the **Museum****, of particular importance for the archaic **metopes**** of the "*thesauros*" and the **metopes**** of the main temple (late 6th c. B.C.), which all come from the sanctuary of Hera at the mouth of the river Sele; a seated statue of Zeus** (mid-6th c. B.C.); the painted slabs from the Tomba del Tuffatore*, or Tomb of the Diver, an exceedingly rare example of Greek painting.

Palermo**

elev. 14 m., pop. 695,742, Sicily, provincial and regional capital. Set on the north coast of Sicily, with the stern Monte Pellegrino as the constant point of reference throughout the landscape, dotted with the citrus groves of the Conca d'Oro, the city of Palermo preserves the memories, monuments, and atmosphere of Arab and Norman times as one of its two urban faces; the more remarkable and original of the two. The other face is that of the Baroque architecture that dates from the 17th/18th c., from the time of the Spanish viceroy and the Bourbon monarchs. The city can be considered as being split in two by the axis of Via Cavour and Via Volturno; to the north, near the port, is the modern section, with rectangular blocks and broad roads; to the south is the intricate and chaotic structure of the old section, once enclosed by medieval and Spanish walls. Two Spanish viceroys, the Duke of

Toledo (1565-66) and Maqueda, who governed Sicily from 1598 to 1601, built two straight avenues: the first is Corso Vittorio Emanuele, running from the Marina to the Palazzo dei Normanni; the second avenue runs perpendicular to the first and parallel to the sea: Via Maqueda. These two avenues divide Palermo roughly into four quarters, of about the same size, and they meet in the little Piazza Vigliana, or Quattro Canti, once the city center.

Historical note. Not much survives of Phoenician, Roman and Byzantine Palermo. Its economic and political power began with the Arabs, who held this town from 831 until 1072, making it the capital of Arabian Sicily. The Arabs were succeded by the Normans, and Palermo enjoyed great prosperity and a level of artistic and cultural achievement never again equalled. This period created magnificent buildings, in which Arab, Latin and Byzantine features mingle and merge, engendering a remarkable character and allure: the Cappella Palatina and the Martorana, with their splendid Byzantine mosaics; the churches of S. Giovanni degli Eremiti, S. Cataldo, the pavillions of La Zisa and La Cuba, with a distinctive Muslim appearance; the exceedingly grand cathedral, whose interior was subsequently greatly altered. Palermo declined under Anjou rule; the Anjou were expelled from the city by the famous Revolt of the Vespers in 1282; under the rule of the House of Aragon Palermo recovered somewhat. The artistic tradition of the Normans can be clearly seen in the great Palazzo Chiaramonte and Palazzo Sclàfani, both from the 14th c. In the 15th c., the style and shapes of Catalonian Gothic came to dominate, providing inspiration for M. Carnelivari, who designed Palazzo Abatellis and Palazzo Ajutamicristo and the lovely church of S. Maria della Catena. Under Spanish rule, in the 17th and 18th c., the city took on the festive Baroque appearance that it still preserves, in part. It was then that the churches of S. Giuseppe dei Teatini, S. Caterina, and Gesù were built; they are decorated inside with spectacular marble inlays. Later, in the 18th c., the various oratories (S. Cita, Rosario, S. Lorenzo) acquired their spirited joyful arrays of stuccoes, by a great master of the style, Giacomo Serpotta.

Getting around. The first three routes suggested for a visit to the center of Palermo can be undertaken on foot or public transport. All three strart from Quattro Canti, an important piazza where Corso Vittorio Emanuele and Via Maqueda converge. To reach the monuments and resorts which lie in the ouskirts of the town, described in the other three routes, a car is useful.

The western section
of the old town

Starting from Quattro Canti, running along the western stretch of Corso Vittorio Emanuele, the first route takes in the oldest part of the city. This area is called Càssaro (from the Arabic "el Kasr", for castrum or castle) and lay at the hearth of the city even in Medieval times, when the construction of the Norman Palace and the Cathedral made it the center of political and religious power.

S. Giuseppe dei Teatini *(E4)*. Immediately adjacent to the Quattro Canti stands this lavish Baroque church, with its remarkable, marble-studded interior, bedecked with stuccoes and frescoes.

Via Maqueda *(D4-F5)*. Built in 1600 by the viceroy Maqueda, it runs from Porta Vicari *(F5)* also called Porta S. Antonino, to Piazza Verdi *(D4)*. Note the 17th-c. *Church of S. Nicola da Tolentino* and the Palazzo S. Croce (18th c.).

Chiesa del Gesù* *(E4)*. This church of Jesus, as the Italian has it, or Chiesa della Casa Professa, was built in 1564 and later enlarged; the dome dates back to the mid-17th c.; the church has an interior covered with wood inlays and marble carvings. It is a sterling example of Sicilian Baroque.

Palazzo Sclàfani *(E3)*. A Gothic palazzo, a fine instance of Gothic civil architecture. Note the facade with its high interwined archwork, surrounding twin-light mullioned windows.

Cattedrale** (E3). This majestic Cathedral stands at the end of a verdant square; it is a monument of great interest. You should pay close attention to details of its construction, as it is the result of a complex series of rebuildings, ranging from the first structure (1185) to renovation and addition of the dome by Fuga (1781-1804). On the left side of the facade (14th/15th c.), note the **Loggia dell'Incoronazione** (12th c.; rebuilt in the 16th c.) from which the monarchs of Sicily used to greet the populace, following their coronation. On the right side, note the portico, in flamboyant Catalonian Gothic style; the *apsidal section**, set between two little towers, comprises three apses with intertwined arcades and polychrome encrustations; it preserves the style of the original Norman building.

Inside. In the Neoclassical interior, note: in the right aisle the renowned **imperial and royal tombs*** of Henry VI, Frederick II, Constance, and Roger II; in the chapel to the right of the presbitery, a silver urn (1631) containing the relics of Santa Rosalia, the patron saint of Palermo; and, in the left aisle, a Madonna* by F. Laurana (1469). Exquisite precious objects are preserved in the **Tesoro**, or "treasure," along with the golden tiara of Constance of Aragon, wife of Frederick II; in the sacristy, note the Madonna by Antonello Gagini (1503), the leading member of a family of Palermitan sculptors (originally from Bissone, in the Canton Ticino, birthplace of Antonello's father, Domenico). The *crypt* dates from the 12th c.

In the **Palazzo Arcivescovile**, or archbishop's palace, note the *Museo Diocesano*, with a notable array of sacred art from the 12th c.

Piazza della Vittoria *(E-F3)*. Immense green space in front of the norman Palace; its present appearance dates back to the 16th c. when an enormous open area was created for public events. Its current name commemorates the success of a local revolt against the Bourbon garrison in 1820. It is almost entirely taken up by the palmtree-lined park of *Villa Bonanno.*

Palazzo dei Normanni* *(F3)*. On the other side of Villa Bonanno stands a vast and majestic building, the Palace of the Normans, one of Sicily's most significant monuments. Originally built by the Arabs, later a sumptuous royal palace under Norman rule, and then the court of Frederick II. During this period, this building lay at the heart of great cultural changes, mingling the ancient classical heritage with Arab and Byzantine traditions (here, the "Scuola Siciliana" gave birth to Italian poetry).

Cappella Palatina* *(entrance from Piazza Indipendenza, F3; open 9-12 and 3-5. Sun. 9-10 and 12-1.; closed Sat.)*. Upstairs is the Palatine chapel,

Palermo: Cattedrale

one of the finest creations of the entire Norman monarchy (Roger II, 1132-40). This three-aisle structure is divided by rows of Gothic arches set on ancient columns; note the mosaic floors and exquisite marble lining the lower half of the walls. There is an exceptional wooden ceiling, modeled with stalactite and honeycomb shapes, in distinctly Arab style (ca. 1143), over the nave. Near the sanctuary, note the mosaic ambo* on columns, and a 13th-c. Paschal candelabrum*; above the marble lower panels, the walls are adorned with splendid 12th-c. **Byzantine mosaics**** on a gold background, with Bible stories and stories of Saints Peter and Paul; there are Latin phrases stretching the length of the aisles, as well as scenes from the Gospels, with phrases in Greek, in the sanctuary. Note the Christus Pantocrator, or all-powerful Christ, surrounded by Archangels, Prophets, and Evangelists in the dome. **Appartamenti Reali.** In these, the royal apartments, you should particularly note the Sala di Ercole (or Sala del Parlamento), where the Assembly of Sicily now convenes. Also, note the Sala di Re Ruggero, or King Roger, with mosaics* of hunting scenes (ca. 1170).

S. Giovanni degli Eremiti* *(F3; open 9-1; Sun. 9-12:30. Mon. and Thur. also 3-5).* This Norman church stands in a lovely garden, and is one of the most enchanting sites in Palermo. In the garden, full of exotic plants, note the exquisite 13th-c. cloister*, with lovely little twin columns.

The southeastern section of the old town

Starting once again from Quattro Canti, it is possible to explore the SE sector of the city, bounded by the eastern stretch of Corso Vittorio Emanuele and the southern stretch of Via Maqueda. Following on from Palazzo Abatellis, which houses the important Galleria Regionale (art gallery), the route takes in the ancient Kalsa quarter, a fortified stronghold built by Muslims in 937.

Piazza Pretoria *(E4).* Adjacent to the Quattro Canti, it is almost entirely occupied by the fanciful **Fontana Pretoria***, a great fountain built by the Florentine Mannerists, F. Camilliani and M. Naccherino (1555-75).

S. Cataldo* *(E4).* This church, with blind arcades on the exterior walls, Arabic crenelation and three little cupolas, a bare and lovely interior, is a perfect example of pure Norman style (ca. 1160).

Martorana**. This church, also known as S. Maria dell'Ammiraglio (named after an admiral, George of Antioch, who had the church built), is another jewel of the Norman period. It dates from 1143, but it was partly rebuilt in the 16th and 17th c.; note the addition of a Baroque facade along the side. The **bell tower**** is truly original, 4 stories tall, with mullioned windows, corner columns, and polychrome intarsia.

Inside**, the original Greek-cross plan, with the later addition of a series of bays, features two mosaics: Roger II being crowned by Jesus and George of Antioch at the feet of the Virgin Mary, on the pediment of what was once a portico. Also note the splendid 12th-c. **Byzantine mosaics**** in the sanctuary; there is Christ Pantocrator (ruler of the universe), along with the Archangels, the Prophets, and the Evangelists, in the dome. Note a Birth of Jesus and a Death of the Virgin Mary. Mosaic screens enclose the apses.

Palazzo Ajutamicristo *(E5).* Elegant palazzo built by M. Carnelivari in 1590-95, late Catalonian Gothic in style; note the portal.

Oratorio di S. Lorenzo* *(E5; undergoing restoration).* The stucco decoration - with symbolic statues, stories from the lives of Ss. Lorenzo and Francesco (Saints Lawrence and Francis), and rejoicing cherubs - that adorns this oratory is considered to be Giacomo Serpotta's masterpiece, in terms of expressivity and maturity.

Palermo: S. Cataldo and Martorana

S. Francesco d'Assisi* *(E5)*. This Gothic church, one of the most important in Palermo, was built between 1255 and 1277, altered and enlarged several times; badly damaged during the bombardments of 1943. It features a series of Gothic and Renaissance chapels, flanking the smallest of the three aisles.

Palazzo Chiaramonte* (D6). Set on the vast Piazza Marina, with the palm trees and rare plants of the Giardino Garibaldi at the square's center, is the Palazzo Chiaramonte, also known as the Steri (from Latin "hosterium," in the sense of fortified palace). This stern and compact structure, with Gothic twin- and triple-light mullioned windows, and tufa-and-pumice intarsias, is a noble example of a medieval Sicilian palazzo; it was the headquarters of the ecclesiastical courts.

Museo Internazionale delle Marionette *(D6; Via Butera 1; open 9-1 and 4-7; closed Sun.)*. This international museum of marionettes includes in its collections: "pupi siciliani," puppets from the Neapolitan theater, and puppets and marionettes from many nations, as well as Asian shadow-theater puppets.

Palazzo Abatellis* *(E6)*. In this palazzo, note the strong architecture, a blend of Catalonian Gothic and Renaissance style (1495).

Galleria Regionale della Sicilia* *(open, 9-1:30; Sun. 9-12:30; Tue.-Fri. aft. as well)*. Housed in Palazzo Abatellis, it is a major art collection. In particular, note the marvelous **Annunciation**** by Antonello da Messina. Other fine masterpieces are three saints*, also by Antonello, the lovely **bust of Eleanor of Aragon**** by Francesco Laurana, a famous fresco of the **Triumph of Death**** from the mid-15th c., originally in Palazzo Sclafani, the Madonna del Latte* by Giovanni di Nicola, the **Malvagna triptych**** by the Flemish painter Mabuse, and the exquisite Malaga vase*, a piece of Hispanic-Moorish ceramics.

Foro Italico *(D-E6)*. Opened in the 16th c., this beachfront promenade stretches from Monte Pellegrino to Monte Catafano with a superb view of the Gulf of Palermo. Nearby, the *Piazza della Kalsa*, whose name comes from the Arabic "el Khalisa," originally given to the surrounding quarter, a fortified stronghold. At the end of the piazza, note the church of **S. Teresa** *(E6)*, one of the most important examples of Palermo Baroque architecture.

The northeastern section of the old town

The route leaves again from Quattro Canti, and takes in the area to the north of Corso Vittorio Emanuele, running along Via Maqueda towards Piazza Verdi, and the lively Via Roma towards Piazza Olivella. The Museo Archeologico Regionale, one of the most importatnt in Italy, is the highlight of the route.

Corso Vittorio Emanuele. It runs from the Marina to the Palazzo dei Normanni. From the Quattro Canti, following an eastern route, along this road or near it, you will find many interesting monuments.

S. Matteo *(E4)*. A Baroque church built in 1633-47; inside, note the marble and four fine statues by Giacomo Serpotta.

S. Antonio Abate *(D5)* Isolated on an embankment, near the crossroads of Corso Vittorio Emanuele and Via Roma, it was built in the 12th c. and rearranged in the 14th c.; the facade is from the 19th c. Along the left side, you can walk down to Palermo's oldest market, the much loved Bocceria Vecchia, known as the **Vucciria**.

S. Maria di Porto Salvo *(D5)*,. Built in Renaissance style in 1526 and renovated in 1581, when the opening of Corso Vittorio Emanuele resulted in the destruction of the apsidal section, later replaced by a portal.

S. Maria della Catena* *(D5-6)*. The name comes from the chain, or "catena" used to close off the harbor. In front of the church there is a flight of steps and a portico. The church dates from the late 15th c., hovering in style between Catalonian Gothic and the Renaissance.

Oratorio del Rosario di S. Domenico* *(D4-5; ring for the custodian, Via Bambinai 16)*. The interior of this oratory is a masterpiece of grace and elegance, especially the stucco decorations** by G. Serpotta; canvases by L. Giordano and the Monreale painter, P. Novelli, considered the greatest Sicilian artist of the 17th c.; and a canvas on the altar by A. van Dyck.

Oratorio di S. Cita* *(D4; ring for the custodian)*. The entrance is beside the church of S. Cita, known also as S. Zita. There are other excellent stuccoes* by Serpotta in this oratory*.

S. Giorgio dei Genovesi *(C-D5)*. This fine church dates from the late-16th c. and was built for the colony of Genoese people in Palermo.

Museo Regionale Archeologico** *(D4; open, 9-1:30; Tue. Wed. and Fri. also 3-6:30)*. This major archeological museum occupies the 17th-c. building of a former convent. The entrance is through the lower cloister, with a fountain at its center; some of the archeological finds discovered beneath the sea are housed here, including a vast and comprehensive collection of stone, lead and iron anchors*. In the hall dedicated to *classical sculptures*, particularly noteworthy among the enormous collections are the **sculptures from Selinunte**** especially the 3 metopes** from temple C (mid-6th c. B.C.), two half metopes* from temple F (5th c. B.C.), and 4 renowned metopes** from temple E (460-450 B.C.). At the center of the great hall is the so called **Efebo di Selinunte*** (Selinunte Ephebe), a 5th c; BC bronze Greek statue. Other sections include prehistoric finds, Greek ceramics, Roman mosaics and frescoes.

The new city and Monte Pellegrino

This route takes in the modern areas of the city - whose development began in 1778 and continued into the 19th c. with the opening of Viale della Libertà - and areas lying outside the city too; the routes covers a visit to the Parco della Favorita and a suggested trip up the panoramic Monte Pellegrino, where the celebrated Sanctuary of S. Rosalia stands.

Piazza Giuseppe Verdi *(D4)*. Following the extensive demolition work carried out at the end of the 19th c., this spacious tree-lined piazza is situated on the border of the new city and the old city. The imposing structure of the **Teatro Massimo** *(D3-4)*, built between 1875 and 1897, one of the temples of Italian opera music and one of the largest theaters in Europe (7,730 sq. m. surface area), dominates the piazza.

Piazza Castelnuovo *(C3)*. Together with the adjoining Piazza Ruggero Settimo, it forms a vast open space set off with monuments and palm trees. To the right, the vast bulk of the **Teatro Politeama** stands out. built between 1867 and 1874 in classical style, the theater houses the Civica Galleria d'Arte Moderna.

Civica Galleria d'Arte Moderna E. Restivo *(C3; entrance from Via Turati; open, 9-1; Wed. also 3-6 closed Mon.)*. This modern art gallery has an interesting collection comprising work by 19th-c. artists and contemporary artists.

Viale della Libertà *(A2-C3)*. From the square in front of the art gallery, leads this broad and elegant boulevard, lined with villas and parks.

Parco della Favorita* This magnificent park lies at the base of Monte Pellegrino, and was built in 1799 at the orders of the Bourbon king of the Two Sicilies, Ferdinand, when he was forced to take refuge in Sicily, after being rudely chased from Naples by a French army.

Museo Etnografico Pitrè *(open 9-1. Wed. also 3:30-5:30; closed Fri.)*. Alongside the Palazzina Cinese, an early 19th-c. Chinese-style mansion built by a Bourbon king, is the Museo Etnografico Pitrè, one of the leading museums in the field of Sicilian traditions, costumes, and folkways. It comprises 31 halls.

Santuario di S. Rosalia*. Set high on the craggy limestone massif of Monte Pellegrino (606 m.), this sanctuary of the patron saint of Palermo (15 km. north) is made up of a convent and a cave-chapel (with a small natural spring said to flow with holy water that works miracles). In this cavern, the saint lived in penitence until her death (1166); a road leads further on to a broad square, with a colossal statue of S. Rosalia and a splendid view of sea and coastline.

In the outskirts to the south and west

Villa Giulia* *(E6)* . Known also as Villa Flora, it is a lovely 18th-c. park with one side overlooking the sea. Adjacent is the **Orto Botanico** *(open 9-5; summer 9-6; Sat. and Sun. 9-1)*, a botanical garden, one of Europe's finest, founded in 1789; it has plants from all over the earth.

S.Giovanni dei Lebbrosi. In Corso dei Mille, in the southernmost section of Palermo, note this church, which dates from 1070.

S. Spirito* (in the enclosure of the cemetery of S. Orsola). This squared-off church dates from the 12th c. In the plaza before the church, the anti-Anjou revolt of Palermo against its French garrison, known as the "Vespri Siciliani," or Sicilian Vespers, was triggered on 31 March 1282. Inside is a 15th-c. painted wooden cross.

S. Maria di Gesù*. This 15th-c. church stands on the lower slopes of Monte Grifone in the southernmost section of Palermo.

Zisa**. *(D1; open 9-1:30, Sun. 9-12:30. Tue. and Fri also 3-5.)*. This building which stands in the west-

ern part of Palermo was erected in the 12th c. by the Norman kings of Sicily, William I and William II and is a masterpiece of Muslim architecture. Its name derives from the Arabic word for splendid, "aziz"; it follows the Muslim architectural tradition of the pleasure house.

Cuba* *(F1; Corso Calatafimi 100; in the courtyard of the Caserma Tuköry, a barracks; ask the sentinel)*. This buildings was one of the pavillions in the park built by William II (1180); its appearance is exquisitely Islamic; there is even an inscription in Arabic in the frieze.

Surrounding areas. At a distance of 11 km. NW (from A2), note the elegant beach resort of **Mondello**, next to a venerable old fishing village, north of Monte Pellegrino; near Punta Priola are a number of interesting caverns, inhabited in prehistoric times (note the paleolithic graffiti in the Grotta Addàura).

At a distance of 15 km. to the east is **Bagherìa** (80 m.): Palermo's nobility built villas here from the 17th to the 19th c., in the countryside dotted with vineyards and citrus orchards; architecturally, the finest one is the Villa Valguarnera (1721), but the most famous is without a doubt the Villa Palagonìa, renowned for its statues of dwarfs, beggars, Moors, Turks, musicians, chickadees, all sorts of cripples and freaks; these statues line the high ground of the enclosure. The architect of the two villas was the Dominican monk, Tommaso Maria Napoli.

Solunto*. Standing at an elevation of 217 m., this town on a ridge of Monte Catalfano (18 km. east of Palermo) has a spectacular view of the sea. The Phoenicians founded an early trading town here, but the ruins *(open, 9-an hour before sunset; closed Mon)* date from the city in the Hellenistic-Roman period (4th c. B.C.-2nd c. A.D.): running off the from the main road at right angles, are smaller roads, sometimes with steps, that follow the slope of the mountain; note the ruins of houses, the so-called Gymnasium (actually a home with a peristyle and atrium), a theater, and a "bouleuterion," or ancient Greek council chamber; the artifacts found in the digs are on display in an antiquarium.

Terrasini. This seaside village, about 15 km. west of Carini, boasts a notable Museo di Storia Naturale *(open, 9-12:30; closed Mon.)*, with exhibits of natural history, and the Museo del Carretto Siciliano (Palazzo D'Aumale, on the beachfront; *open, 9-12:30; closed Mon.*), a museum devoted to the history of the remarkable painted Sicilian cart.

Palestrina

m 450; ab. 15 802; Lazio, provincia di Roma. When a sightseer goes to the museum in Palazzo Barberini, to see the mosaic depicting the flooding of the Nile, that sightseer will climb the same stairs up which people once climbed to consult the oracle. Medieval in appearance, this site is actually a mix of Middle Ages with the relics of the Temple of Fortuna Primigenia, a venerated ancient Roman sanctuary. Set on the southern slope of the Monte Ginestro, a ridge of the Monti Prenestini overlooking the Roman countryside, this complex stands on an ancient road running between the valleys of the Sacco and the Tiber.

Historical notes. «Civitas Praenestina,» was the medieval name, hence Penestrina, and finally Palestrina; the medieval village gradually grew up on the site of the ancient, enormous, and long-abandoned sanctuary of Fortuna Primigenia, whose oracle had made the Roman city of «Praeneste» renowned throughout the Empire. From remains of the cyclopic walls, inscriptions, and funerary furnishings, we know that «Praeneste» existed in the 7th c.B.C.When the emperor Theodosius abolished all pagan worship, it spelled the end for the temple of Fortuna Primigenia and for the city.The medieval village formed on the temple's ruins; ruled by the powerful Colonna family, it suffered much destruction in periodic wars with the popes, until, in 1630, Francesco Colonna sold it to Carlo Barberini, brother of Pope Urban VIII. In 1525 the great composer Giovanni Pierluigi da Palestrina was born here. It was damaged by bombing in WWII, but the devastation was a blessing in disguise, allowing many of the structures of the ancient sanctuary to come to light, revealing one of the greatest monumental complexes in pre-Christian Italy.

Places of interest. Piazza Regina Margherita. This central square probably occupies the site of the Forum in early «Praeneste.» Overlooking it is a monumental, multistory building, in which you can see remains of ancient walls and four Corinthian semicolumns; note the 2nd-c. B.C. inscription. From the square, through the door to the left of the Seminary, you enter the Sacred Area, a huge basilican space dug out of the side of the hill. On the right is the hall with apse, identified as the hall of the oracle; once the great mosaic of the Nile stood here; it is now in the Museo Archeologico. On the opposite side of the Sacred Area is the so-called *Antro delle Sorti*, or Cave of Destinies, a natural cavern that has been enlarged and built up, adorned with a mosaic floor depicting the bottom of the sea (1st c. B.C.), of which only fragments survive.

Duomo. This cathedral was built on the site of a Roman building made of tufa (possibly the «lunonarium»), of which some relics survive. Only the facade and the bell tower remain of the original Romanesque structure. In the left aisle is a copy of Michelangelo's Palestrina Pietà (the original is in Florence, at the Galleria dell'Accademia).

Palestrina: Palazzo Barberini

Santuario*. *Open 9-one hour before sunset; June-August still 7:30 p.m.; closed Mon.* You enter this monumental complex, dedicated to the goddess «Fortuna Primigenia», dating from the mid-2nd-c. B.C., and built on manmade terracing, from Piazza della Cortina. Three terraces rise, one above the other, the terrace of the Emicicli, the terrace of the Fornici, and the terrace of the Cortina. Overlooking the last terrace is the spare **Palazzo Barberini**, built in 1640 and now the site of the Museo Archeologico; at the base of the building is a handsome staircase between architraved columns (15th c.).

Museo Archeologico Prenestino*. *Open, Winter 9-4; Summer 9-7:30.* Arranged in the 17th-c. Palazzo Barberini, this museum comprises collections of artifacts found in the sanctuary and the territory. In particular, one should note a 4th-c. relief (Triumph of Constantine); a large 2nd-c. B.C. statue,* perhaps of Fortune, badly damaged; bronze mirrors* and toiletries, including cylindrical recipients; a renowned **mosaic*** of the flooding of the Nile, probably dating from 80 B.C.

S. Rosalia. This church, next to Palazzo Barberini, was built in 1656-60. In the rich Baroque interior, with four tombs by Barberini, a Pietà by Michelangelo, known as the Palestrina Pietà, once stood. It is now in Florence.

Via degli Arcioni. This street takes its name from the deep arches in the huge retaining wall that holds up the terracing of the hill where the sanctuary was built. Recent excavations here have unearthed remains from the 1st c. B.C. The 17th-c. Porta del Sole leads into town.

Villa Imperiale. Not far from the cemetery stand the ruins of a 2nd-c. building, now called "Hadrian's Villa."

Parma**

elev. 52 m.; pop. 168 905; Emilia-Romagna, provincial capital. The cities along the Via Emilia are united by their similar plains setting, with nearby hill country, vigorous Po Valley architecture, cuisine with simple rich flavors, and courtly manners; each of these cities has a distinctive personality born of its history. Parma shows many aspects of its personality in the medieval monuments upon which Antelami worked, and in the delightful artwork created by Correggio. The city is also a treasure trove of opera and "bel canto," Stendhalian in the refinement of its culture, and then, primarily, ducal, if we may use the term (referring to the three centuries, before Italian Unity, of Farnese and Bourbon rule, with the interlude of the ruler that the people of Parma still like to call, with affectionate pretension, "la nostra Maria Luigia," known to us as Marie Louise). Parma still maintains the atmosphere and quality of life of a lesser European capital.

Historical note. The city is divided practically in two by the river Parma, which runs through it from south to north, but most of Parma's political and artistic history has been concentrated on the right bank of that stream; and the center of Parma is still there, on the right bank. It expanded concentrically from there between the 11th and 14th c., around the plan of the old Roman colony, founded in 183 B.C. The religious center of Parma developed to the north of the Roman walls: the Duomo, or Cathedral, which existed as early as 1046, was destroyed by fire in 1055, was rebuilt and then damaged by earthquake in 1117, and then was finally rebuilt shortly there-after, this time to a rectangular plan, rather than a square one, in the Romanesque style that we now know. The Battistero, or Baptistery, on which Benedetto Antelami worked, was begun in 1196. These spectacular years of artistic creativity were years of terrible conflict in polit-ical terms. Once the conflict between the Guelphs and Ghibellines had come to a halt, Parma enjoyed a peri-od of peace in the second half of the 13th c., during which the Communal government gained in strength. The early decades of the 14th c., on the other hand, wit-nessed worsening conflict between the powerful fami-lies of the Correggeschi and the Rossi; as neither faction managed to prevail, the city fell under foreign rule. The house of Della Scala was followed by the Visconti in 1346. The Visconti held Parma for a century, until 1447; from 1449 until 1500 the city was under Milanese rule, under the Sforza. The last major expansion of the walled perimeter to the south and east took place under the Visconti, extending to the Porta Nuova and Porta S. Michele and, to the south, the Monastero delle Cappuccine. In the first 20 years of the 16th c., Parma repeatedly fell into the hands of the French and the popes, until 1521, when it definitively became part of the Papal State, with Francesco Gucciardini as governor. In 1545 Pope Paul III Farnese gave Parma and Piacenza in fief to his son Pier Luigi; this was the origin of the duchy — which survived until 1860 — that had Parma as its capital (Piacenza was capital for a short period, until 1556). The architectural and cultural Renaissance brought about by the house of Farnese resulted in the construction of the Palazzo della Pilotta with the adja-cent Teatro Farnese, inaugurated in 1628 to the notes of music by Monteverdi; Palazzo Ducale with its grounds; the new Palazzo del Comune; and the great privileges and bequests given to the Università. In 1731 the house of Farnese died out, in a time of economic stagnation, and the Treaty of Aix-la-Chapelle in 1748 recognized the existence of the duchy (to which Guastalla was added, where a branch of the Gonzaga family had just died out), and awarded it to the Spanish prince Phillip of Bourbon, born to a Farnese mother. Parma experi-enced, under him and under his son Ferdinand, both guided by the minister Du Tillot, a new period of eco-nomic and cultural activity. The Bourbon penchant for collecting lies at the origin of the Galleria Nazionale, the Biblioteca Palatina, and the Museo Archeologico Nazionale. The Università grew considerably, and Bodoni established the ducal printing house. Following the tur-moil of the Napoleonic period, the duchy did not fall back into the hands of the Bourbons, but was given as a lifelong holding to the second wife of Napoleon, and daughter of Francis I of Austria, Marie Louise (or Maria Luigia, as she is known here), who continued the works of generosity begun by her predecessors. She went down in popular myth as "l'amata sovrana," or "the beloved sov-ereign." During her reign, a new ducal theater was built, which we now know as the Teatro Regio, a symbol of Parma's musical life and one of Italy's most renowned opera houses. In 1847, after the death of Marie Louise, Parma once again fell under the rule of the Bourbon dynasty, who reigned here until 1860, when a plebiscite determined that it would be joined to the kingdom of Sardinia, and then to the kingdom of Italy (Regno d'Italia). Between the end of the 19th c. and the early 20th c., Parma's walls were demolished; at that time, there had been few buildings outside Parma's walls, and much farmland within those walls. At the turn of the 20th c., work began on the riverfront boulevards — the Lungoparma — and on the ring roads, or Viali di Circonvallazione, completed in 1932. Today, Parma, chiefly due to the enormous development of the food indus-try, has expanded greatly in all directions, but especial-ly to the north and along the Via Emilia: the 50,000 inhab-itants of the early 20th c. have now become more than 150,000.

Parma: Duomo and Battistero

Places of interest. Piazza del Duomo* (*C4*). Intimate and silent, this square truly preserves its medieval character; surrounded by the Duomo, the Battistero, and the Palazzo del Vescovado.

Duomo** (*C4*). This cathedral is certainly one of the masterpieces of the 12th-c. Romanesque architecture of the Po Valley. Its austere facade is enlivened by three orders of loggias; the central portal extends into a porch surmounted by an aedicule, by G. da Bissone (1281). Note the high terracotta Gothic *bell tower* (1294).

The *interior* features pillars with handsome cap-itals. The walls of the high nave are frescoed (G. M. Bedoli, 16th c.); note the copper statue of the Archangel Raphael (1294). There are 15th-c. fres-coes in various chapels, and an inlaid Baroque pulpit (1613). In the cupola, note the majestic **fresco**, by Correggio (1526-30). On the right wall of the right transept, note the **relief** by B. Antelami (1178). In the *apse*, note the 12th-c. episcopal throne*, with excellent high reliefs by Antelami; inlaid choir by C. da Lendinara (1473). In the huge *crypt*, note the fragments of polychrome mosaics (especially the early Christian depiction of fish).

Battistero** (*C4*). Open 9-12 and 3-7, or 5 in winter. This lively Romanesque-Gothic Baptistery (1196-1270), with an octagonal plan, is combed with lovely architraved loggias. In the lower sec-tion, the reliefs* on the three portals and the decorative fillets and the statues* in the niches, by B. Antelami, are one of the masterpieces of Italian Romanesque sculpture.

The octagonal interior, with niches, two orders of small loggias, and a high ribbed cupola, contains high-reliefs of the **Months***, the **seasons*** (note Winter and Spring), and the **signs of the Zodiac***; the frescoes with a Byzantine flavor, in the lunettes and cupola, are largely from the late 13th c.; in the center of the Baptistery, a double baptismal font (13th c.).

Storica Spezieria di S. Giovanni Evangelista (*C4*). Open 9-2; holidays 9-1; closed Mon. At n. 1 in Borgo Pipa, behind the Benedictine monastery of S. Giovanni, is the old pharmacy of the Benedictines, founded in 1201. In operation until 1766, it was restored and reopened to the pub-lic in 1959. In the three rooms, adorned with 16th-c. frescoes, furniture, and shelves, note the 192 ceramic pharmacy jars, from the 15th to 17th c.

Also, note the giant mortars; in a fourth room, note the alembics, retorts, and ancient instruments.

S. Giovanni Evangelista* (*C4*). This Renaissance church (1510), has a facade and bell tower from the early 17th c. *Inside*, set in exceedingly elegant architecture, are renowned series of **frescoes**** by Correggio and Parmigianino. Vaults and candelabra were decorated by M. Anselmi (1520-21) under the guidance of Correggio; painted lacunar ceiling and frieze are by F.M. Rondani, working on drawings by Correggio (1522-23). In the *apse*, note the inlaid and carved choir* by M.A. Zucchi (1512-13); and paintings by G. M. Bedoli (ca. 1556). In the transepts, note four terracotta statues by A. Begarelli. Also worthy of note are the sacristy with inlaid early-16th-c. armoires, and three 16th-c. cloisters of the monastery (*open by request, ask porters*). In the Sala Capitolare (enter from 2nd cloister), there are two detached frescoes* by Correggio.

S. Sepolcro (*C5*). This 13th-c. church was renovated in the 15th c. (note carved candelabra, 1501, on the unfinished facade); various paintings and statues inside, worthy of note. In particular, however, in the 1st chapel on right, note the late-15th-c. fresco* and the Apulian oil amphorae, unearthed below the church, evidence of human occupation of this site in Republican Roman times.

Piazza Garibaldi (*C3*). Called Piazza Grande in the 19th c., this square lies in the center of Parma; note monument to Garibaldi, *Palazzo del Governatore* with its *Torre* (1673), or tower, and the porticoed Palazzo del Comune (1673). Also, to right, the former *Palazzo del Podestà* (13th c.).

Pinacoteca "Giuseppe Stuard" (*C-D3*). *Closed for restoration*. In Via Cavestro at n. 14 is the leading private collection of Parma (1834), owned by the church. The collection comprises over 270 paintings; note work from early Tuscan naive painters (P. di Giovanni Fei, B. Daddi, and G. di Francesco) and 17th-/18th-c. painters (B. Schedoni, Guercino, S. Ricci, and F. Fontebasso).

Università (*C3*). Set in a stern, majestic 16th-c. building, once a Jesuit college, the University offers interesting **Raccolte di Storia Naturale** (*open, 3-5, closed Mon., Fri. and Sun.; entrance from Via Università n. 12*), or natural history collections, in such fields as paleontology, mineralogy, and zoology, as well as the Museo Zoologico Eritreo "Bottego," or Eritrean zoo and the Raccolta "Piola," with ethnographic and zoological collections from the former Belgian Congo (present-day Zaire).

Strada Garibaldi (*B-C3-4*). This road runs past the Neoclassical **Teatro Regio** (1829), one of Italy's most renowned opera houses (hall with four orders of boxes). Almost directly across the road is the church of the Madonna della Steccata (see below). From Piazza Garibaldi the Strada Mazzini leads to the *Ponte di Mezzo*, a bridge over the river Parma; take the underpass along the right bank to see the remains of the *Roman bridge* of the Via Emilia, from the reign of Augustus, and used until the course of the river shifted in the 12th. c.

Madonna della Steccata* (*C3*). This church, designed by B. and G. F. Zaccagni (1521-25), is a Renaissance structure, with large semicircular apses, and cupolas adorned with loggias. The majestic *interior* is decorated with frescoes by artists of the 16th-c. Parmesan school, among them B. Gatti, M. Anselmi, G. Mazzola-Bedoli, and Parmigianino. Also, note the funerary monument by L. Bartolini and, in the sacristy, inlaid wooden

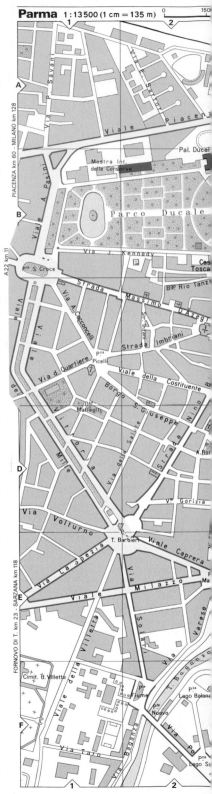

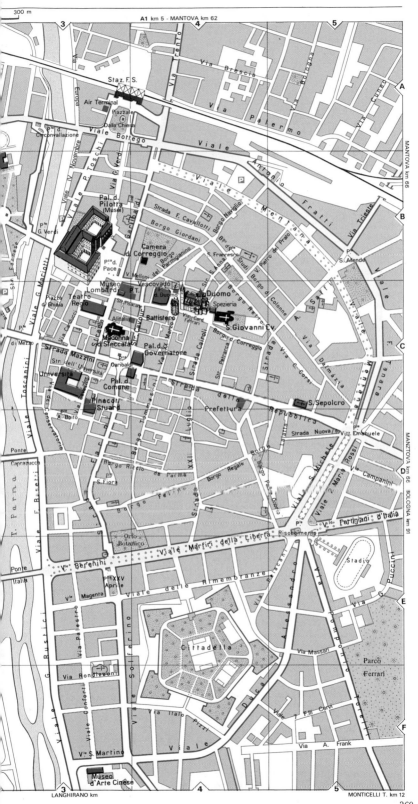

Staz. F.S.
Air Terminal
Piazzale
Dalla Chiesa
P.za d.
Circonvallazione
P.le G. Verdi

Viale Bottego

Viale Mentana

Via Trieste

Strada F. Cavallotti
Borgo Giordani
Pal. d. Pilotta (Musei)
Camera
d. Correggio
P.za d.
Pace
V. Melloni
Museo
Lombardi P.T.
Vescovado
d. Duomo
Duomo
Spezieria
Battistero
S. Giovanni Ev.
Teatro
Regio
Alitalia
Madonna
d. Steccata
Pal. d.
Governatore
Università
Garibaldi
Pal. d.
Comune
Pinacot.
Stuard
A. Boito
S. Sepolcro
Prefettura
Repubblica
Strada Nuova
Vitt. Emanuele
Borgo Riccio de Parma
S. Fiora
Via Campanini
P.le Partigiani d'Italia
Orto
Botanico
Viale Martiri della Libertà
Risorgimento
V.le Berenini
Stadio
P.za XXV
Aprile
V.le Magenta
Viale delle Rimembranze
Parco
Ferrari
Cittadella
Via Massari
Via Rondizzoni
Via Italo Pizzi
Via A. Frank
V.le S. Martino
Museo
d'Arte Cinese

armoires. Beneath the church are the tombs of the Farnese, dukes of Parma.

Piazza della Pace (*B3*). In this square, note the *Monumento al Partigiano* (1955), or monument to the WWII resistance fighter, and a *monument to G. Verdi* (1913). At the far side of the square, Palazzo della Pilotta (see below). Overlooking the square, in Strada Garibaldi at n. 15, in the Neoclassical *Palazzetto di Riserva* (note stuccoes by E. Petitot), is the **Museo "Glauco Lombardi"** (*C3; open 9:30-12:30 and 3-5, or 4-6 (Apr.-Sep.); holidays 9:30-1; closed Mon.*). This museum has a collection of memorabilia and documents from the entire period of Bourbon rule (18th/19th c.), and especially from the reign of Marie Louise, duchess of Parma (1816-1831), as well as the Napoleonic era. Note paintings, largely by 18th-c. French artists.

Camera del Correggio**, or *of S. Paolo* (*B4*). *Open 9-1; closed Mon.* A major center of Parmesan culture, adjacent to the former Benedictine nunnery of S. Paolo, it can be reached from the Strada Macedonio Melloni. Originally part of the private apartment of the abbess, it was renovated and decorated from 1514 on, at the behest of Giovanna da Piacenza. Correggio worked here in 1519, in his first major project, achieving one of the masterpieces of the full Italian Renaissance. The hall is covered with an umbrella vault, divided into 16 gores, set on lunettes: Correggio painted a pergola with putti set in tondos, and in the lunettes*, he painted classical monochrome figures. In an adjacent room, frescoes by A. Araldi (1514).

Palazzo della Pilotta (*B3*). Impressive building erected by the Farnese in 1583-1622, unfinished. Its name comes from the game of "pelota," played in a courtyard. It houses the Museo Archeologico Nazionale, the Galleria Nazionale — one of Italy's finest galleries — and the Biblioteca Palatina.

Museo Archeologico Nazionale*. *Open 9-2; Sun. and holidays 9-1; closed Mon.* Founded by Phillip I of Bourbon in 1760, in conjunction with the dig at Veleia, this is one of Italy's earliest archeological collections, stocked largely with local finds. Note: sculpture from the great Farnese and Gonzaga collections; an Egyptian collection; Greek, Italiot, and Etruscan ceramics; Greek and Roman coins; a fine 1st-c. B.C. bust of the head of a youth; and other notable material. Moreover, there are local collections of prehistoric material, and Celtic artifacts as well. All sorts of Roman material (amphorae, bronzes, marble, mosaics) come last.

Galleria Nazionale**. *Open 9-2; holidays 9-1; closed Mon.* Of special importance in terms of Parmesan painting from the 15th to the 18th c.; this gallery boasts a number of masterpieces by Correggio, among others. As a surprising and theatrical atrium to the Galleria you will pass through the magnificent **Teatro Farnese*** (1617-18), one of the most attractive theaters on earth, rebuilt in the 1950s, following the damage from Allied bombing in 1944. The collections are arranged in sections, by school and chronological order. In the medieval section you will find capitals and sculptural fragments, including three capitals by B. Antelami. Early painting of the 14th and 15th c. includes works by A. Gaddi, P. Veneziano, Fra' Angelico, and B. Daddi. Then come

frescoes and paintings by A. and B. degli Erri, F. Francia, and Leonardo da Vinci. In the section of 17th-c. Emilian painters are F. Mazzola, D. and B. Dossi, and Garofalo; among the 16th-c. Italian paintings are several Virgins with Christ Child (by M. Anselmi, G. Gandini del Grano) and canvases by S. del Piombo and G. Romano. The section featuring the Parmesan school of the 16th and 17th c. includes works by G. M. Bedoli, G.B. Tinti, and L. Spada; there are also works from the Flemish school (J. Sons, D. Calvaert), the Venetian (D. Tintoretto, Palma the Younger, El Greco), the Emilian (the Carracci) and the Lombard (G. C. Procaccini). The 17th-c. section features works by painters of various schools: Bolognese (C. Aretusi, Guercino), Genoan (Genovesino, G. A. De Ferrari), Spanish (Murillo, Giobbe*), Flemish (A. Van Dyck), and Lombard (C. F. Nuvolone). From 18th-c. Venice, works by G.B. Tiepolo, G.B. Piazzetta, Canaletto, and S. Ricci. The 19th-c. section (*it can also be toured separately from the rest of the gallery*) is noteworthy chiefly for some of the most important works by Correggio and Parmigianino.

In the same building is housed the *Biblioteca Palatina*, a library endowed with almost 700,000 volumes, 6,620 manuscripts, 70,100 manuscripts, 3,041 incunabula, and 50,479 prints, engravings, and illuminated codices from the 9th/10th c.; part of the library is the *Museo Bodoniano*, with a collection of editions by the great court printer.

Palazzo Ducale (*B2*). *Open by request, enquire at the Corpo di Guardia dei Carabinieri, 8:30-12:30.* This ducal palace is set in a lovely park, created in 1561 on 20 hectares of land along the left bank of the river Parma. The palace was designed by Vignola, and enlarged by Petitot in 1767. Note halls frescoed by Agostino Carracci, A. Tiarini, G. Mirola and 18th-c. stuccoes.

Casa di Toscanini (*B2*). *Open, 10-1; closed Sun. and holidays.* At n. 13 in Borgo Tanzi is the birthplace of Maestro A. Toscanini; memorabilia.

The outlying quarters

Cittadella (*E-F4*). This citadel was built by P. L. Farnese in the 16th c., to a pentagonal plan, with five bastions and a moat; handsome marble portal. Inside is a park.

Museo di Arte Cinese (*F3*). *Open 3-6; closed Mon., Tue. and Jun.-Sep.* This museum of Chinese art is located in the *Istituto Saveriano per le Missioni Estere*, in Viale S. Martino n. 8; it has a collection of bronzes and porcelains, dating back to the 3rd millennium B.C.

Surrounding areas. The **Certosa di Parma** (*open, Mon.-Fri., 9-12 and 3-5; Sat. and Sun. 9-12*), or Charterhouse of Parma, 4 km. NE. Founded by Carthusian monks in 1285, this building figured in the novel by Stendhal; it is now a school for prison guards. Note, in church, frescoes by S. Galeotti and F. Bibiena.

The **Castello di Torrechiara*** (*open 9-1; closed Mon.*), 17.5 km south, on the left bank of the Parma is one of the largest castles in the area. Built by P.M. Rossi (1448-60), it has three concentric sets of walls, with corner towers. Inside, note frescoes by C. Baglione and B. Bembo* (1463).

Pavìa*

elev. 77 m.; pop. 80,073; Lombardy, provincial capital. Lying along the Ticino's left bank, just upstream from the river's confluence with the Po, Pavia is surrounding by verdant riverine landscapes. "Centium turrium," a 14th-c. chronicler wrote, calling it the town of "100 towers." Ancient, brick-red towers, silent streets, snug little squares, and warm Lombard terracotta — this is the historic center, where 18th- and 19th-c. opulence is facade to an underlying structure that dates back to the Middle Ages. Two famed Romanesque churches are benchmarks of Italian art. Pavia's venerable university with its 16th-c. "collegi," are noteworthy presences here.

Historical note. The 48 "insulae," or blocks of Pavia in Roman times stretch from Corso Carlo Alberto south to Corso Garibaldi; the checkerboard layout can still be seen, with "cardo" and "decumanus," echoed by the center's chief roads (Strada Nuova, Corso Cavour and Corso Mazzini). Pavia was capital of the Kingdom of Italy in the High Middle Ages. During the time of the communes (11th c. on), the thriving city had 40,000 inhabitants, one of the largest in northern Italy. Walls built then (13th.c.) enclosed the modern center (bounded by the Ticino-Viale della Libertà-N.Sauro-Gorizia-della Resistenza). At the same time, early medieval churches were rebuilt in brilliant Romanesque Pavian brickwork and masonry: first and foremost, S. Michele; also, S. Pietro in Ciel d'Oro and twin basilicas where the Duomo now stands. The tradition of study here dates back to A.D. 825; the University to 1361, when it was founded by a Visconti and by the emperor Charles IV. To help the school grow, the Visconti forbade their subjects to study elsewhere. A burst of activity after Milan subjugated Pavia in 1359 resulted in the Castello Visconteo, the Piazza Grande (or Piazza della Vittoria), and the Strada Nuova, running to the bridge over the Ticino, built and covered during the 13th c. Construction began on the university campus in 1485. Artists working in Pavia included Michelino da Besozzo, Pisanello, Foppa, Bramante, Leonardo da Vinci, and Solari. The construction of the Duomo crowned an age of great artistic achievement. Bramante and Leonardo both worked on the design of the tambour that rose at the axis of the Greek cross plan, though it was not completed till centuries later.
In a famed 1525 battle here, the Holy Roman Emperor's troops captured France's King Francis I. Spanish occupation was followed by Savoy rule (1743). Pavia declined to a military border town, with a venerable university, that was enlarged under the rule of Austrian monarchs Maria Teresa and Joseph II. Great poets and scientists, such as A. Volta, L. Spallanzani, Vincenzo Monti, and Ugo Foscolo lectured here. During the 19th and 20th c., the city prospered and became industrialized (the first synthetic silk mill in Italy opened here in 1905).

Getting around. A section of the historical center is closed to cars. The route shown is wholly a walking tour; you'll probably want to take public transportation back from Borgo Ticino.

Places of interest. S. Pietro in Ciel d'Oro**. This splendid Romanesque church was consecrated in 1132. The facade echoes the architecture of S. Michele, in a smaller version; the portal is adorned with fine carvings. Above the main altar is the Gothic marble Arca di S. Agostino* (tomb of St. Augustine, whose bones were moved to Pavia in the 8th c.), executed by Lombard sculptors (1362). Behind the altar is a sarcophagus with the bones of Boethius, a late Roman philosopher executed by the Longobard king Theodoric as a traitor in A.D. 524.

Castello Visconteo**. Great square brick building, with corner towers, and two orders of Gothic mullioned windows and crenelations. Built by Galeazzo II Visconti in 1360; its north side was badly damaged during the Battle of Pavia in 1525. The moat is temporarily the site of the stone remains of the Torre Civica which collapsed in 1989. Note the

huge *courtyard**, surrounded by a portico on three sides, with terracotta decorations. Many halls of the castle are part of the yet unfinished **Museo Civico** (*open, 9-1:30; Sun., 9-1; closed Mon.*). You can see collections of *medieval archeology*, *sculpture*, mosaics, and the frescoes of S. Agata al Monte (15th c.); the **Pinacoteca Malaspina*** features work by Foppa, Boltraffio, Bergognone, Butinone, Giambono, Giovanni Bellini, and Correggio. There is a Renaissance model of the Duomo.

Strada Nuova. Pavia's main street runs north-south, from the Castello to the Ticino. Along it are the **Teatro Fraschini** (undergoing restoration), designed by Antonio Galli Bibiena and built in 1771; and the **University**, founded in 1485. Giuseppe Piermarini designed the Neoclassical building that now stands here; inside are five handsome courtyards. Two of those lead to the adjacent former *hospital of S. Matteo* (now part of the university). In the nearby *piazza* stand three *Romanesque towers* and a medieval *crypt*.

Chiesa del Carmine. Built in 1390, it has a monumental facade. Inside, works of art dating from the 15th / 16th c.

Piazza della Vittoria or *Piazza Grande*. In the heart of Pavia, edged with porticoes and and 14th- and 15th-c. houses. On one side is the ancient Town Hall, or **Broletto** (12th c.), with two orders of loggias (1563).

Piazza del Duomo. Adorned with statuary, the huge *Torre Civica* stood here, till its collapse in 1989. Damage can still be seen on nearby houses.

Duomo*. Major monument of the Lombard Renaissance. Bramante, Leonardo da Vinci, and Francesco di Giorgio worked on this church (1490), but work continued on it almost to the end of the 16th c. Facade and cupola are from the late-19th c. The *interior* is built to a Greek cross plan. Note the high, vast central cupola. Work by Bramante adorns the vaults of the crypt.

S. Michele**. Founded by the Longobards, this basilica was rebuilt in the mid-12th c. It is Pavia's chief monument and a masterpiece of Romanesque architecture. Kings and emperors — Frederick Barbarossa, for one — were crowned

Pavia: S. Michele

here. Note the sandstone facade*, with loggia and pilaster strips. Carvings and reliefs (12th c.) adorn walls and the three portals.

Inside, note late-10th-c. Crucifix, carved main altar (1383), and late-15th-c. fresco.

S. Teodoro. This Romanesque church dates from the 12th c. Inside, three aisles and raised transept; note the 13th- and 14th c. frescoes; also, view of Pavia (1522), with its many medieval towers.

Ponte Coperto sul Ticino. Destroyed by Allied bombing in 1944, this is a partly faithful reconstruction of the bridge built in 1354. Across the bridge lies the *Borgo Ticino*, with the 12th-c. Romanesque church of **S. Maria in Betlem**.

Perugia**

elev. 493 m.; pop. 144,732; Umbria, regional capital. Set amidst the green valley of the Tiber and not far from Lake Trasimeno, Perugia is perched on a jagged hill, carpeting the ridges and slopes. N. and G. Pisano worked on the great fountain, or Fontana Maggiore, seven centuries ago; A. di Duccio planned and carved the facade of the church of S. Bernardino, the artist Perugino (from nearby Città della Pieve) frescoed the Sala dell'Udienza, and the local Renaissance architect G. Alessi constructed his first buildings here. The image is even older and more complex: Etruscan walls and arches, stern stone towers, the carved marble of palazzi and churches, the Guelph lion and the proud city griffon on the walls of Palazzo dei Priori. At sunset, you can see the lovely heart of Umbria, from a garden where the Rocca Paolina once stood, a fortress built by Pope Paul III, and designed by A. da Sangallo the Younger. It was destroyed by the angry citizenry. Perugia is a perfect example of the Italian art of shaping mere cities into astonishing atmospheres.

Historical note. Perugia is an accretion of the original Etruscan and Roman settlements, with three extensions that crept over outlying ridges. The oldest inhabited section is of course on the hilltop, and is enclosed by the Etruscan walls that link Porta Marzia, Porta S. Ercolano, Porta Sole, the Arco Etrusco and the Arco della Mandorla. Here, from the 4th to the 1st c. B.C., was one of the capitals of Etruscan Italy, alternately allied with and fighting against the burgeoning power of Rome. During the great civil wars following the assassination of Julius Caesar, Perugia supported Mark Antony, and when Octavian triumphed, becoming the Emperor Augustus, Perugia paid the price, suffering siege and sack in 40 B.C. Byzantines ruled here, and Goths took the town in A.D. 54, followed by Longobards. Perugia ruled herself after the year 1000, though many popes resided here, and five conclaves were held here, away from the poisonous intrigues of Rome. Beginning in 1321, new and larger walls were built, and around the Palazzo dei Priori, streets were extended, while the Duomo and the churches of S. Francesco, S. Domenico, and S. Agostino rose. The 14th c. was a time of war, and Perugia held her own, until the popes cast their eyes on her. In time, Perugia had one seigneur after another, the best known being Braccio Fortebraccio da Montone, who began building Renaissance Perugia. Construction went on under the Baglioni: particularly Palazzo dei Capitani del Popolo and the Oratorio di S. Bernardino. Pope Paul III finally decided to bring Perugia into the papal fold, and on the ruins of the houses of the Baglioni, he built the powerful Rocca Paolina (1540). The fortress was destroyed as Italy began to acquire its inde-

Perugia 1 : 12 000 (1 cm = 120 m)

RACCORDO AUTOSTRADALE A1 - AS

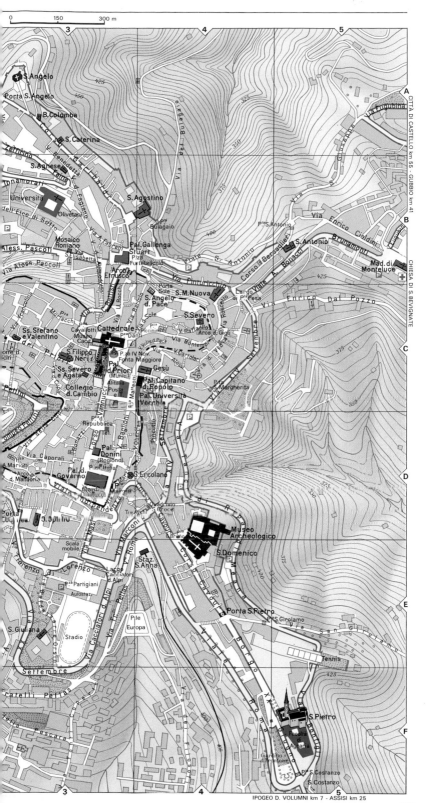

0   150   300 m

CITTÀ DI CASTELLO km 55 - GUBBIO km 41

CHIESA DI S. BEVIGNATE

S. Angelo
Porta S. Angelo
B. Colomba
S. Caterina
Tetticino
S. Agnese
Innamorati
Università
dell'Elce di Sotto
Olivetani
Mosaico
Romano
S. Isabella
Alessi. Pascoli
Via Aless. Pascoli
Arco
Etrusco
S. Agostino
Bulagaio
Pal. Gallenga
Stuart
Fortebraccio
P.za S. Antonio
Via Enrico Cialdini
Mad. di
Monteluce
S. Antonio
Brunamonti
Via Enrico Dal Pozzo
Porta
Sole
S. Angelo
d. Pace
S. M. Nuova
Largo di
P. za Febbea
S. Severo
Ss. Stefano
e Valentino
Cattedrale
Museo
Capit.
Dante
S. Filippo
Neri
Ss. Severo
e Agata
Pal.
Priori
Piazza IV Nov.
Fonte Maggiore
Gesù
Collegio
d. Cambio
Pal. Capitano
d. Popolo
Pal. Università
Vecchia
P. za
S. Margherita
Repubblica
Pal.
Donini
(Regione)
Via Caporali
Pal. d.
Governo
S. Ercolano
Porta
Oubbrea
S. Giuliano
Scala
mobile
Museo
Archeologico
S. Domenico
Staz.
S. Anna
S. Lorenzo
P. za
Partigiani
Autostaz.
Pile
Europa
S. Giuliana
Stadio
Settembre
Fratelli Pellas
Porta S. Pietro
P.za S. Girolamo
Via San Girolamo
Tennis
S. Pietro
Facoltà
di
Agraria
Giardino
d. Frontone
P.za S. Costanzo
S. Costanzo

IPOGEO D. VOLUMNI km 7 - ASSISI km 25

Perugia: Piazza IV Novembre, Palazzo dei Priori, and Fontana Maggiore

pendence and unity, from 1848 to 1860. Perugia has expanded onto the plains at the foot of the hill during the 20th c.

Getting around. We suggest three routes: the first winds entirely through the older, monumental heart of Perugia, within the Etruscan walls; the other two run through the northern and southern quarters, within the 14th-c. walls. Because of Perugia's steep narrow streets and traffic regulations, prohibiting cars in much of the center, we do not recommend that you drive. Elevators and escalators will take you from parking lots outside of the center up to the high part of town. Buses will take you to the more distant monuments.

The city within the Etruscan walls

This route runs almost completely through the high part of town, within the Etruscan walls. From Piazza IV Novembre it follows Corso Vannucci to Piazza Italia. It runs down to Piazza Matteotti, and then follows Via dei Priori through a lovely medieval section of town, ending at the convent of S. Francesco al Prato.

Piazza IV Novembre* (*C3*). This square has been the heart of Perugia since Etruscan times; the center of religious and political power and of artistic achievement: note the Fontana Maggiore, Palazzo dei Priori, the Cathedral, and the Loggia di Braccio Fortebraccio.

Fontana Maggiore** (*C3*). Emblematic of the medieval "Commune" and symbol of Perugia, this fountain was built in 1275-78 to plans by G. and N. Pisano, as the outlet of the aqueduct from Monte Pacciano. It comprises two concentric marble basins, adorned with sculptures, and bronze cup with a group of three Nymphs, or Theological Virtues, depending on the eye of the beholder. Note the lovely reliefs depicting the Months of the Year** and the 24 statuettes of the upper basin.

Loggia di Braccio Fortebraccio (*C3*). This loggia was built in the 15th c., under the rule of B. Fortebraccio. Note the fragment of Roman wall. Also, note the *Palazzo Arcivescovile*, with the **Museo di Storia Naturale** (*open, Wed. and Fri., 9-1; Thu. and Sat., 9-1 and 3-6; Sun., 10-1*) with collections of natural history.

Via Maestà delle Volte* (*C3*). Leading down from Piazza IV Novembre to Piazza Felice Cavallotti, this road passes before 13th-c. houses and beneath dark passages; this is one of the most

evocative settings of medieval Perugia. Note the white-and-red striped Gothic arch, all that remains of the 14th-c. Oratory of the *Maestà delle Volte*.

Cattedrale* (*C3*). Begun as a Gothic church in 1345 on the site of a Roman building, work on this cathedral went forward by fits and starts (1437-1587) but was never finished. The unfinished left side, partly covered in pink and white marble, overlooks the square. Overlooking the steps on this side is a statue of Pope Julius III, by V. Danti (1555); to the right of the 16th-c. portal (G. Alessi), is a pulpit from which Bernardino da Siena once preached. *Inside* you will find a wide array of styles and decorative approaches. In the chapel of S. Bernardino is a Deposition by F. Barocci. Across from it is chapel which holds the revered relic of the Virgin's supposed wedding ring (1498) which can be seen only on 30 July. In the apse, note the carved and inlaid choir*, by G. da Maiano and D. del Tasso (1486-91).

Museo Capitolare (*C3*). Adjacent to the Cathedral, this museum features paintings and frescoes by Umbrian and Siennese artists of the 14th to 16th c., including B. Caporali, L. Signorelli, and M. di Guido da Siena.

Palazzo dei Priori** (*C3*). Built in several stages (1293-1443) in a rigid Gothic style, this is one of the largest and most impressive "palazzi pubblici" of the period, a combination of courthouse and town hall. It is now Perugia's Town Hall. The oldest section comprises the three mullioned windows on the left, overlooking the piazza, and the first ten mullioned windows overlooking Corso Vannucci. Note the handsome portal (ca. 1326) on the Corso, and the staircase and large Gothic portal, surmounted by bronze statues of the Guelph lion and the Perugian griffin (1281). Through this portal is the large **Sala dei Notari*** (*open, 9-1 and 3-7; closed Mon.*).

Galleria Nazionale dell'Umbria** (*C3*). *Open, 9-1:30, 3-7; Sun., 9-1*. On the fourth floor of Palazzo dei Priori, this gallery has one of the most important collections of 13th- to 18th-c. art of Central Italy, especially for Umbria, Tuscany, and the Marche.

Founded in 1863, it was given to the Italian State in 1918 as the Regia Pinacoteca Vannucci; it comprises the art given up by religious institutions following the Unification of Italy, and the works owned by Perugia's Accademia di Belle Arti. It has been located in the Palazzo dei Priori since 1879. Since 1918, the collection has grown constantly, through gifts and purchases; the museum owns over 1,500 artworks. For years, restoration and modernization have been underway. With time, more and more halls will be opened to the public.

Among the artists whose work is on display (in chronological order), the most important are: M. da Perugia, M. da Siena, D. di Boninsegna, F. da Rimini, O. Nelli, L. Salimbeni, L. di Velletri, B. Gozzoli, and G. Boccati. Thoroughly represented here is Perugian painting of the late-15th c., including: B. Bonfigli, N. Alunno, F. di Lorenzo, Fra' Angelico, F. di Giorgio Martini, P. della Francesca, and Pinturicchio. There are many paintings by Perugino and by his followers of the 15th/16th c., among them G. di Paolo, B. di Giovanni, D. Alfani. Then come works by painters of the Mannerist period, especially those of Central Italy. Among them are: V. Danti, G.B. Naldini, and M. Venusti.

Up the spiral staircase, you can see works by artists of the 17th to 19th c., including: P. da Cortona, O. Gentileschi, V. de Boulogne, S. Conca, P. Subleyras, C. Giaquinto, and F. Trevisani. The last hall has many works by J. B. Wicar (a compete series of sketches** for his painting of Pope Pius VII, now near Rome, in Castel Gandolfo).

Collegio della Mercanzia* (*C3*). *Open, Mar.-Oct., 9-12:30 and 3-6; Nov.-Feb., 8-2; Sun. 9-12:30, closed Mon.* On the ground floor of Palazzo dei Priori, with entrance to the right of the main portal, was the headquarters of the powerful guild of the merchants. Inside, the richly inlaid wood of the *Sala dell'Udienza* is particularly impressive.

Collegio del Cambio** (*C3*). *Open, Mar.-Oct., 9-12:30 and 2:30-5:30; Nov.-Feb., 8-2; Sun., 9-12:30; closed Mon.* Headquarters of the powerful guild of the moneychangers, this building was built in 1452-57 at the far end of the Palazzo dei Priori. From the vestibule (*Sala dei Legisti*) with its baroque wooden benches, you enter the *Sala dell'Udienza**, one of the great bequests of Renaissance culture. The magnificent wooden tribunal was carved and inlaid by D. del Tasso (1493); the walls and ceiling are frescoed, by **Perugino**** and workshop (possibly Raphael among them). In the adjacent *Chapel of S. Giovanni Battista*, note the frescoes by G. di Paolo (1513-28), and the altar piece by M. di Ser Austerio (1512), student of Perugino.

Corso Vannucci (*C-D3*). Perugia's most elegant street, and the main drag since Etruscan times; note the *Palazzetto dei Notari* (1438-46), and, at the other end, the 18th-c. *Palazzo Donini* (*D3*).

Piazza Italia (*D3*). This 19th-c. square was laid out after the destruction of the 16th-c. papal fortress, the Rocca Paolina (1860); the far end is occupied by the porticoed *Palazzo del Governo* (*D3;* 1872), behind which are the *Giardini Carducci* (*D3*), gardens with a spectacular view** of the heart of Umbria.

Piazza Matteotti (*C3*). Built in the late-13th-c. on artificial terracing, it faces the long facade of the *Università Vecchia*, or Old University (1490-1514), and the elegant **Palazzo del Capitano del Popolo*** (*C4*) (1472-81), with fine portals, windows, and balcony. The arch at n. 18 leads to a covered market (1932) and a panoramic terrace. Note the 14th-c. porticoed *Via Volte della Pace*.

Chiesa del Gesù (*C4*). At the north end of Piazza Matteotti is this 16th-c. church, with splendid Baroque altar, frescoes, and paintings by S. Amadei; see the *three oratories* below the church, with frescoes.

Via dei Priori (*C3*). This road passes under the Palazzo Comunale, through the *Arco dei Priori*, and descends through a quarter with a strong medieval flavor. On the left is the little 14th-c. church of *Ss. Severo e Agata*, with fine frescoes; facing it is the odd, twisting *Via Ritorta;* further along, on the right, is the Baroque church of **S. Filippo Neri** (*C3;* 17th c.), with altar piece by P. da Cortona (1662); then, the church of *Ss. Stefano e Valentino*, built in the 12th c. Last, on the left, the high **tower of the Sciri*** (13th c.); then the road ends at the medieval *Porta Trasimena*. Note the 16th-c. church of the **Madonna della Luce*** (*C2*).

S. Bernardino** (*C2*). This church is a gem of Renaissance architecture and sculpture; it was built in honor of a saint who often preached in Perugia. The harmonious facade is by A. di Duccio (1457-61); note statues and reliefs. Inside, the main altar is a 4th-c. Roman sarcophagus.

S. Francesco al Prato (*C2*). This immense Gothic church was built in the mid-13th c., and rebuilt often thereafter. Next door is the *Accademia di Belle Arti*, or Academy of Fine Arts, founded in the 16th c.; the *Museum* (*open, 10-1; closed Sun.*) has a large collection of statues, paintings from the 19th and 20th c., drawings, and prints.

The northern quarters

This route covers the expansion of Perugia northward, beyond the Etruscan walls. From Piazza Danti, you follow Corso Garibaldi, to Porta S. Angelo; then, from Piazza Fortebraccio, you continue to the church of S. Maria Nuova and Corso Bersaglieri, heart of the medieval Borgo di S. Antonio. You then return to the center along the Colle del Sole, enjoying a fine view from the Piazza Rossi Scotti.

Piazza Danti (*C3*). Stretching along the right side of the Cathedral, this was Perugia's marketplace in the Middle Ages. At n. 18 is the entrance to the **Pozzo Etrusco** (*open, Apr.-Sep., 10:30-6; Oct.-Mar., 10-12.30 and 2:30-4:30*), or Etruscan Well, a 3rd-c. B.C. structure of notable size: 37 m. deep, 5.6 m. across. *Via Cesare Battisti* (*B-C3*), a terrace road built in 1901, runs past a long stretch of Etruscan walls (fine view to the north), and drops down to Piazza Fortebraccio. Next to the Arco Etrusco (see below) is the 17th-c. church of *S. Fortunato*.

Arco Etrusco* (*B3*). This Etruscan Arch was built in the 3rd c. B.C., and was the main gate of the Etruscan walls. Note the later Doric frieze, with the Roman inscriptions "Augusta Perusia" and "Colonia Vibia." The loggia and fountain on the left side are from the 16th c.

Piazza Fortebraccio (*B3-4*). This square is dominated by the Baroque *Palazzo Gallenga Stuart* (1748-58), now the Università Italiana per Stranieri. In the nearby *Via S. Elisabetta*, note the large 2nd-c. Roman *mosaic* (*B3; open, 8-8; Sat. 8-1; closed Sun.*).

Corso Garibaldi (*A-B3*). This narrow street climbs through a medieval neighborhood, lined with small, old buildings. On the right, the church of **S. Agostino** (*B4*) has several fine works of art: 14th- and 16th-c. frescoes, wooden choir by B. d'Agnolo (1502), and altar piece by G. di Paolo. Along the Corso, at n. 179, is the **monastery of S. Caterina** (*A3*), built in 1574, perhaps by G. Alessi; at n. 191, the *monastery of the Beata Colomba* — note painting by G. Spagna; nearby, the *monastery of S. Agnese* (*B3*), with fresco* by Perugino.

S. Angelo* (*A3*). This remarkable early Christian church (5th or 6th c.), with a central plan, has a 14th-c. Gothic portal. Inside, an ambulacrum, marked by 16 columns with Roman capitals, runs around a central space. On the walls, detached frescoes; in the baptistery, frescoes by an Umbrian painter of the 15th c.

Porta S. Angelo (*A3*). Largest of Perugia's medieval gates, with parapets and loopholes, it marks the end of the long Corso Garibaldi; beyond it, in Via Monte Ripido, is the 13th-c. church of *S. Matteo degli Armeni* (*A2*).

Via Pinturicchio (*B-C4*). Return to Piazza Fortebraccio and follow this road to the 13th-c. church of **S. Maria Nuova** (*C4*). The portal on the Via Pinturicchio and the bell tower are from the 16th c., possibly by G. Alessi. *Inside*, banner painted by B. Bonfigli (1471); wooden choir* (1456); and 15th-c. frescoes by L. Vasari. Then take the 13th-c. *Arco dei Tei* to Corso Bersaglieri (*B4-5*) which leads through the Borgo di Porta S. Antonio, last fragment of medieval Perugia, running past the church of S. Antonio, to the 14th-c. *Porta di S. Antonio* (*B5*).

S. Maria di Monteluce (*B5*). Founded in the 13th c., rebuilt in 1451, this church has a handsome twin portal and a marble face in red-and-white panels. Inside, note frescoes, including one by F. di Lorenzo. The adjacent monastery is now a hospital.

S. Severo (*C4*). In the small and isolated Piazza Raffaello, this ancient church, traditionally said to have once been a temple to the Sun, now has an 18th-c. appearance. The adjacent **oratory of S. Severo** (*open, Apr.-Sep., 10:30-6; Oct.-Mar., 10-12:30, 2:30-4:30; closed Mon.*) has a fine fresco* by Raphael (1505-08), completed in the lower half by Perugino (1521).

Le Prome (*C4*). The highest *square* in Perugia, once the acropolis, set high atop a retaining wall with great arches (1374). Excellent view. Note the little church of *S. Angelo della Pace* (*C4;* 1545) and the 17th-c. *Palazzo Conestabile della Staffa*, now a library.

The southern quarters

From Porta Marzia, in the eastern bastion of the long-destroyed Rocca Paolina, the route follows Corso Cavour, through the historic Borgo di Porta S. Pietro. The quarter first extended to the Porta S. Pietro, enclosed by 13th-c. walls; and a few centuries later extended to Porta di S. Costanzo, just past the church of S. Pietro. One then returns, after various excursions, up the stairs of Paradiso, through the Arco della Mandorla.

Porta Marzia (*D3*). Set alongside the Via Porta Marzia, this Etruscan gate probably dates from the 2nd c. B.C.; it is now part of the *Rocca Paolina*, a fortress built by A. da Sangallo the Younger in 1540, and destroyed in 1860. The gate is one of the entrances to the subterranean **Via Bagliona** (*open till sunset*), which runs through the eerie remains of the medieval quarter upon which the fortress was erected.

S. Ercolano (*D3-4*). Set against the ancient walls, this Gothic church (1297-1326) has a Roman sarcophagus as its main altar. To the right of the church, a stairway leads up to the Etruscan *arch of S. Ercolano* (*D3-4*), rebuilt in Gothic times.

S. Domenico* (*E4*). This impressive church was built during the 14th c., perhaps to plans by G. Pisano. Construction continued until 1482; note the truncated campanile. The *interior* shows clear marks of the 17th-c. renovation by C. Maderno. Note the altar-frontal* by A. di Duccio (1459); also,

note the funerary monument to Pope Benedict XI* (early 14th c.), by a follower of A. di Cambio.

Museo Archeologico Nazionale dell'Umbria* (*D-E4*). *Open, summer, 9-1 and 3-7:30; winter 9-1 and 2:30-6; closed Sun. aft. and Mon.* Largely housed in an ancient Dominican convent, this museum comprises a Roman-Etruscan section and a prehistoric section. The collections originated with a gift in 1790, and include a wide array of artifacts uncovered in Umbria and other parts of Italy. Apart from major finds from the Bronze and Iron ages, there is a substantial collection of documents concerning the history of Perugia under the Etruscans. Note the "Cippo di Perugia" (3rd/2nd c. B.C.), the lengthy Etruscan text of a property agreement.

Porta S. Pietro* (*E4*). This gate has two faces: the interior is a simple 14th-c. construction; the exterior is an elegant monumental arch, built in the Renaissance by A. di Duccio and P. di Stefano (1475-80), but left unfinished.

Borgo XX Giugno (*E-F4-5*). This 15th-c. quarter is dominated by the church and monastery of S. Pietro; the street was widened in the 19th c.

S. Pietro** (*F5*). This basilica, located in a 10th-c. convent complex, preserves parts of the original structure and, beneath it, a small early Christian temple. Over it towers an elegant polygonal campanile; before it is a handsome 17th-c. cloister. *Inside*, the three aisles with ancient columns are splendidly decorated; the original basilica structure has been maintained. In the *nave*, wooden 16th-c. ceiling and a series of large paintings by Aliense (1592). On the walls and altars of the *aisles* are paintings by E. da San Giorgio, Sassoferrato, Guercino, Perugino, G. Reni, and others; in the 15th-c. *sacristy* are four small paintings* by Perugino. In the *presbytery*, two carved chairs (1556) and a remarkable inlaid wooden choir*, considered to be among the finest in Italy (1525-26).

The former *Benedictine monastery* is now part of the university, and has two cloisters: the *Chiostro Maggiore*, and the *Chiostro delle Stelle*, by G. Alessi (1571).

Giardino del Frontone (*F4-5*). Once an Etruscan necropolis, this area was laid out as a garden in the 18th c. The handsome tree-lined avenues end in a small amphitheater, and a fine view of Assisi and Monte Subasio.

Porta S. Costanzo (*F5*). This 16th-c. gate marks the end of the Borgo XX Giugno. Just beyond it is the church of *S. Costanzo*, dating from the 11th c. but rebuilt in the 19th c.

S. Giuliana (*E3*). This church, built in 1253, has fragments of 13th- and 14th-c. frescoes; in the adjacent former convent, 14th-c. cloister.

Porta Eburnea (*D3*). This unadorned town gate dates from 1576; a stairway leads from the church of *S. Spirito* (1579-1689), not far from a Franciscan convent. Nearby is the ancient church of *S. Prospero* (*D2*), first built in the 7th c., with 13th-c. frescoes.

Arco della Mandorla (*D3*). This pointed arch, at the top of the *stairs of Paradiso* (*D3*), is a medieval version of an ancient Etruscan gate. The narrow but charming *Via Caporali* (*D3*) takes you back to the center of Perugia.

Surrounding areas. The **Ipogeo dei Volumni***, or Hypogeum, lies 7 km. SE, if you take Viale Roma and head down toward the Tiber (Tevere). The underground chamber (*open 9:30-12:30 and 3-5; Jul.-Aug. 9:30-12:30 and 4:30-6:30; closed Sun. afternoon*) is located near a level railroad crossing near a viaduct. This is an artistocratic Etruscan tomb complex, from the late-2nd c. B.C.. Take a steep stairway down, and from the underground atrium, you will see a number of cells. The furthest one contains seven cinerary urns*.

Piazza Armerina

elev. 697 m., pop. 22,549, Sicily, province of Enna

Places of interest. The source of this place's great fame is the extraordinary archeological complex of the **Villa Romana del Casale**** (5.5 km. SW; *open, 9-sunset*), a huge Roman country villa (late 3rd/early 4th c.). It is an intriguing hypothesis, though not at all certain, that this villa belonged to a wealthy importer of wild African animals for the Roman games; the celebrated, brilliant **mosaic floors****, some of the largest and most impressive ones surviving from antiquity, are believed to be the work of African master craftsmen, based on certain similarities with mosaic floors found in Roman-occupied North Africa.

Numerous elaborate buildings, built in the late-Roman architectural style, are arrayed around the *large peristyle** (in a square vestibule, the imperial family with handmaidens* in the mosaic floor; on the north side, halls with mosaics of Eroti pescatori* and the hunt for small game*): the baths, with the three classical sections of the *frigidarium*, the *tepidarium*, and the *calidaria*; the Corridoio della Caccia Grossa, or corridor of the hunt for big game*, with a long mosaic depicting hunting scenes*, the capture of wild beasts* and predatory animals attacking prey in the wild* a composition that tells a story clearly related to the trade in animals for gladiatorial games in the amphitheaters of ancient Rome; the Sala delle 10 Ragazze, or hall of the 10 girls*, which takes its name from the floor mosaic of 10 young girls** intently engaging in athletic pursuits, covered in skimpy two-piece outfits that appear surprisingly modern to us.

On either side of the *basilica* are numerous rooms, many with splendid mosaic floors, including one of Arione on the dolphin with an entourage of naiads and sea monsters*.

An *elliptical peristyle* lies before the hall of the *triclinium**, with mosaics of the Labors of Hercules*, the Glorification of Hercules*, the Defeated Giants* and Lycurgus and Ambrosia*.

Pienza**

elev. 491 m.; pop. 2,330; Tuscany, province of Siena. This silent hilltop town with a spectacular view was built by a Renaissance architect, for a Humanist pope: the ideal city of Renaissance philosophy.

Historical note. The ancient village of Corsignano belonged to the abbey of Monte Amiata as early as the 9th c.; it then fell to Siena, and finally to the Piccolomini family. In 1405 Enea Silvio Piccolomini was born here; in 1458 he became Pope Pius II. He renamed his native town after his papal name — Pienza — and hired a great Renaissance architect, B. Rossellino, to rebuild it. The new, very rigorous little city was built in three years, and the pope then ordered a number of cardinals to build houses there in the same style.

Places of interest. Piazza Pio II**. Set on the highest point of the hill, this masterpiece by Rossellino resulted from the remodelling of the town, between 1459 and 1462. The deaths of architect and pope, both in 1464, prevented completion of the project.

Rossellino demolished freely, reshaping the square and the buildings to trapezoidal plans, in agreement with the concepts of perspective set forth in "De re aedificatoria" by L. B. Alberti and other Renaissance texts, that called for reason, proportion, and symmetry in all architecture.

The "rear wall" of this ideal "drawing room in the open air" — and the herringbone brickwork lined with travertine on the ground only emphasizes this — is the facade of the Cathedral; on the right is Palazzo Piccolomini (see below), with a handsome well curb* before it, also designed by Rossellino (1462). Opposite is the stern **Palazzo Vescovile** (once Palazzo Borgia). Opposite the cathedral is the **Palazzo Pubblico** (1463; restored), and to the left of it is Palazzo Ammannati, and next to it, a 15th-c. house.

Cattedrale**. This cathedral, with its octagonal campanile, was inspired by the German "Hallenkirchen" which Pius II much admired; among the art in the church, all specially commissioned by Pius II, are works by G. di Paolo, M. di Giovanni, Vecchietta, and S. di Pietro. Beneath the apse is the crypt (open by request, contact the Museo della Cattedrale), with a baptismal font* designed by Rossellino.

Palazzo Piccolomini**. *Guided tours for groups, 10-12:30 and 4-7 (Jun.-Sep), or 3-6 (Apr. and May), or 3-5 (Oct.-Mar.); closed Mon.* Larger than the cathedral beside it, its handsome perspective arrangement is cunningly arrayed, and is clearly inspired by Palazzo Rucellai in Florence (likewise built by Rossellino to plans by L. B. Alberti). The fine inner courtyard leads to a hanging garden*, beneath the great three-story loggia* facing south. The rooms on the second floor are decorated in 15th-c. style, with fine antiques and priceless art; excellent view* of garden and the Orcia valley.

Museo della Cattedrale*. *Open, 10-1 and 4-6 (Jun.-Aug.), or 3-5 (Mar., Apr., Sep., Oct.), or 2:30-4:30 (Nov.-Feb.); closed Tue.* This museum of the cathedral should be moved into a larger setting in

Pienza: Piazza Pio II

Palazzo Vescovile. Note the cope**, said to have belonged to Pius II, and other lavish fabrics and liturgical items. Also, note panel* by B. di Fredi; triptych* recently attributed to the Maestro dell'Osservanza.

Corso Rossellino. Main street of Pienza, lined with buildings and aristocratic homes designed by Rossellino. Toward Porta al Murello, beyond Palazzo Piccolomini and Palazzo Ammannati, the 13th-c. church of S. Francesco is the only medieval building left in the town.
In the opposite direction, toward *Porta al Ciglio*, see the 15th-c. **Palazzo Jouffroy** (n. 30) and Palazzo Gonzaga (n. 38); an arch leads into Via del Castello which takes you back to Piazza Pio II, with fine views*.

Pisa**

elev. 4 m.; pop. 98,928; Tuscany, provincial capital. The columns of the Battistero, or Baptistery, were brought across the sea from Elba and Sardinia; the Camposanto, or Cemetery, encloses earth brought by galleon from Golgotha, in the Holy Land (1203). Even before the architect Buscheto began designing the Duomo, in the 11th c., he had been influenced by the Islamic architecture of the Levant, as well as by architecture from Armenia. The breezes from across the sea are a fundamental component of this city — straddling the river Arno — which certainly holds a place of high honor in Italian art.

Historical note. Although its first origins are distant and uncertain, the Romans certainly made Pisa a city, recognizing in its excellent harbor a base for pushing north and west across the Mediterranean. In those times, Pisa stood on the sea, where the Arno meets the Serchio, in the northern area of the modern town, between the Duomo, Porta a Lucca, and S. Zeno. The center soon shifted south, and the section of Pisa just described came to be known as "città vecchia," or 'old town'. The first walls were built in the 10th c., when Pisa was already a mighty sea power; in the 11th c. her ships, with those of Genoa, chased Arabs from Sardinia, and hunted them as far as Bône, in what is now Algeria, and in 1063 the Pisan fleet helped the Normans take Palermo. The Duomo was completed at the end of that century, and a larger ring of walls was built, the last walls the city built. The 12th c. was the golden age of the Pisan Maritime Republic. After supporting the First Crusade and founding colonies in the Near East, the Pisans held their own crusade against the Saracens in the Balearic Islands (1113-14); they stormed and sacked Amalfi, eliminating it as a seafaring power (1135-37); they controlled the entire Tyrrhenian coast, from Portovenere to Civitavecchia, as well as Sardinia (1162-5), received in fief from the emperor Frederick Barbarossa. These were also the years of artistic splendor: alongside the Duomo, or Cathedral, work began on the Battistero and the renowned Torre Pendente, or leaning tower, although the tower in question did not yet lean. Power and wealth bred new and revived old rivalries — with Lucca, over Apennine passes; with Genoa, over Eastern trade, and over Corsica and Sardinia; with Florence, over access to the sea. Still, Pisa defeated Genoa at Giglio (1241) and Acre (1258), and Florence at Montaperti (1260; Dante Alighieri fought in this battle). With the decline of imperial power, however, Pisa's might ebbed. Lucca and Florence grew bold, and in 1284 the Pisan fleet was destroyed by Genoa. In the 14th c., Pisa declined and more or less fell. Art and culture survived: the University thrived; the Camposanto was completed; and in the Duomo G. Pisano carved the famous pulpit; on the Lungarno S. Maria della Spina was built. Internal strife tore Pisa, however, and it was ruled, in succession, by Uguccione della Faggiuola, the Della Gherardesca family, the Gambacorta family (with Florentine patrons), the Visconti (1399), and, finally, by Florence (1406). Florence languished in the late 15th c. As silting drove the seacoast west, Pisa lost its harbor, while malaria raged in the countryside; the population fell to about 8,000. As the Medici duchy became a grand-duchy, times improved; vast reclamations were undertaken, a canal linked Pisa to the new port of Livorno, the University built the first botanical garden in Europe. And in 1562 Cosimo I instituted the Order of the Knights of St.Stephen to fight piracy, in a last revival of maritime valor. Twelve galleys of the Order fought the Turks at Lepanto (1571). But that spark died out, and Livorno supplanted Pisa both in trade and war. Under the Medici grand-duchy, Pisa built the Fortezza Nuova, the Ponte di Mezzo, the buildings in Piazza dei Cavalieri (G. Vasari), the Logge di Banchi, and many buildings on the Lungarni. After becoming part of Italy, Pisa expanded north and south. Manufacturing and one of Italy's finest universities now bring Pisa prosperity.

Getting around. Due to traffic and parking problems, both the routes recommended, shown on the map, are in pedestrian zones; public transportation may be useful for the longer stretches, as well as for returning to your starting point.

The Medici center and the Campo dei Miracoli

From the Ponte di Mezzo, the sight of the imposing ranks of venerable palazzi overlooking the Arno foreshadows — after you make your way through the 16th-c. Medici center of Pisa — the spectacular geometric perspective of the Campo dei Miracoli, a must for any visitor.

Ponte di Mezzo (*C4*). This oldest bridge in Pisa was rebuilt after WWII. It crosses the Arno in a single span, opening north onto Piazza Garibaldi. Note the bronze monument (1892).

Borgo Stretto (*C4*). One of the main streets of the old quarter, lined with handsome porticoes.

Note, in a 17th-c. tabernacle, at the head of the right portico, the copy of a wooden sculpture by N. Pisano (original is at the Museo di S. Matteo). A bit further on, note the church of S. Michele (see below).

S. Michele in Borgo* (*C4-5*). Built in the 11th c., modified in the 14th c., this church has a strong Pisan-style facade (14th c.); note portals and loggias. Inside, note 13th-c. fresco and 14th-c. marble Crucifix.

Piazza dei Cavalieri* (*B4*). Once the center of Pisa, under the Republic, this square was renovated under the Medici, to accommodate the 16th-c. headquarters of the Ordine dei Cavalieri di S. Stefano (Order of the Knights of St.Stephen). Many of the buildings on the square are by G.Vasari, but one of them stands out: Vasari's **Palazzo dei Cavalieri*** (1562): massive curving facade, double stairway, statue and fountain by P.Francavilla (1596); on the right, the church of S. Stefano dei Cavalieri (see below). Note Vasari's **Palazzo dell'Orologio**; this building is said to stand on the site of the captivity of Count Ugolino della Gherardesca, whose horrible death is recounted by Dante (Inf. XXXIII, 1-90).

S. Stefano dei Cavalieri* (*B4*). Church and bell tower are by G.Vasari (1569); the marble facade dates from 1606. Inside: on the walls, three fragments of a 17th-c. processional ship; canvases and ceiling by Cigoli, Allori, Empoli, and Ligozzi. Note painting by Bronzino (1564).

Pisa: Duomo, Battistero, and Campanile

S. Sisto (*B4*). This 11th-c. Romanesque church has an unassuming facade and sides decorated with hanging arches and ancient Pisan ceramic bowls, as decoration (copies; originals in the Museo di S. Matteo). Inside, note late-13th-c. panel.

Via S. Maria (*B-C3*). Perhaps the most distinctive of Pisa's streets, lined with 17th-/18th-c. buildings; some of these buildings belong to the university. Toward the Arno, at n. 26, the Domus Galilaeana (*C3; currently closed to the public*), with a major library of works by and about Galileo Galilei. Note, at the corner of Via Volta, a 13th-c. towerhouse; also, the church of S. Giorgio dei Tedeschi (*B3*), and the 15th-c. Ospizio dei Trovatelli*.

Orto Botanico (*B3*). Open 8-1, 2-5:30; closed Sat. aft. and Sun.; entrance from Via Ghini n. 5. This botanical garden was moved here from its previous site on the Arno in 1595 by Ferdinando I. It covers over 2 sq. km., with greenhouses as well as open plantings.

Piazza del Duomo** (*A3*). Also known as the Campo dei Miracoli, or Field of Miracles, this square holds the finest masterpieces of Pisan Romanesque art, and is one of the best known and most popular monuments in Italy. On the broad meadow, against the backdrop of crenelated medieval walls, stand the Duomo, Battistero, Campanile, and Camposanto (Cathedral, Baptistery, Bell Tower, and Cemetery). Built in different periods, they are wonderfully homogeneous in color and style.

Campanile** (*A3*). Also known as the Leaning Tower, it is the emblem of Pisa and one of the most famous towers on earth, both for its elegant white marble and for its decidedly odd tilt. Work began in 1173, was halted as the ground began to sink, and was begun again in 1275, to be finished after 1350. Cylindrical, it has the same decorative motif as the apse of the Cathedral. Inside is a 294-step winding staircase, leading to the 54-m.-tall top of the tower. From here, Galileo is said to have performed his experiments concerning the pull of gravity on falling objects.

Duomo** (*A3*). Open, 7:45-1 and 3-7; Mar. and Oct., closes at 5:30 and, Nov.-Feb., at 5 (holidays, at 6). This impressive white building, with its elegant decoration, was built between 1064 and the 12th c. by Buscheto and Rainaldo, and is the crowning creation of Pisan Romanesque architecture. The facade is spectacularly adorned with four orders of small loggias, and decorated with marble statues and inlay. Followers of Giambologna made the bronze doors of the three portals. To the left of the apse is the Portal of S. Ranieri, with handsome bronze doors* by B. Pisano (1180).

The **interior**, solemn and beautifully lit, sheathed in black and white marble, has five aisles divided by close-set columns, an elliptical dome, and a deep apse. In the central aisle, note the handsome bronze holy-water fonts by F. Palma (1621); at the end of the aisle, marble **pulpit**** by Giovanni Pisano (1302-11), a complex masterpiece of Italian Gothic sculpture. Almost directly across from it is the "lamp of Galileo," made of bronze, and designed by B. Lorenzi (1587); its swinging motion was long believed to have inspired Galileo's discoveries concerning the pendulum (it is now known, however, that these discoveries were made six years before the lamp was installed). Right aisle: note the paintings by A. del Sarto and G. A. Sogliani. Right transept: 14th-c. mosaic, partly hidden by the chapel of S. Ranieri; also note the tomb of the Holy Roman Emperor Henry VII* by T. di Camaino. Cross vault of the transept: remarkable 13th-c. Cosmatesque mosaic floor. Presbytery: two bronze angels by Giambologna (1602); 15th-c. inlaid stalls*; and paintings by A. del Sarto and Sogliani. On the altar, bronze Crucifix by Giambologna. In the vault of the apse, note the large 13th-c. mosaic of the Savior between Mary and St. John, the Evangelist* (the head of the latter is by Cimabue); below, paintings by Beccafumi, Sodoma, and Sogliani.

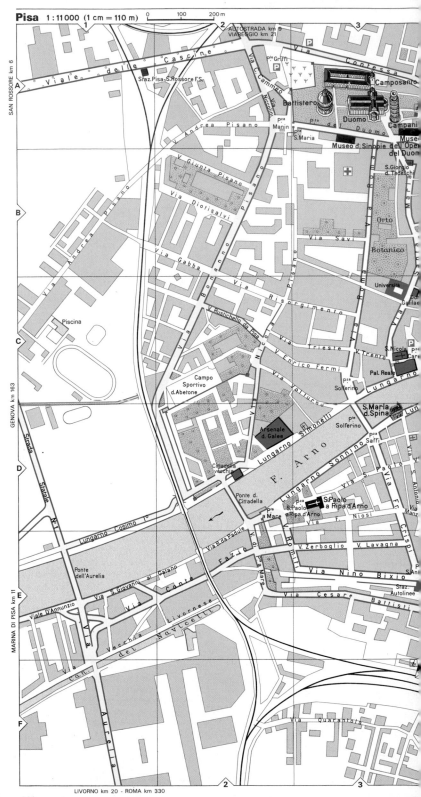

Pisa 1:11000 (1 cm = 110 m)

0   100   200 m

SAN ROSSORE km 6

ALTOSTRADA km 9
VIABEGGIO km 21

Viale delle Cascine

Via G. Cammeo

Sraz.Pisa-S.Rossore F.S.

A

Via Niccolini

P.za Grifi

Battistero

Camposanto

Duomo

Campanile

V. Andrea Pisano

P.za Manin

P.za del Duomo

Museo

S.Maria

Museo d. Sinopie dell'Opera
del Duomo

V. Giunta Pisano

S.Giorgio
d. Tedeschi

Via Diotisalvi

Bonanno Pisano

B

Via Andrea Pisano

Via Gabba

Orto

Via Savi

Botanico

Via Risorgimento

Università

Galilei

V. Rustichello da Pisa

Piscina

Via Trieste

V.Trento

S.Nicola

C

Via Enrico Fermi

GENOVA km 163

Pal. Reale

P.za
Solferino

Campo
Sportivo
d. Abetone

Via Valturno

Lungarno

S.Maria
d.Spina

Lungarno Simonelli

P.za
Solferino

Arsenale
d. Galee

F. Arno

P.za
Saffi

Strada

D

Cittadella
vecchia

Lungarno

Lungarno Sonnino

Via Paolo

Via Fr.

Via Antonio

Ponte d.
Cittadella

Via B. da Padule

S.Paolo
a Ripa d'Arno

S.Paolo
a Ripa d'Arno

Via Manz

Strada

Via Garibaldi

a Mace

Via Romiti

Via F. Niosi

Via Crispi

Lungarno Cosimo

V. Zerboglio

V. Lavagna

S.An

Ponte
dell'Aurelia

MARINA DI PISA km 11

E

Fazio

V. d. Padule

Via Nino Bixio

Sraz.
Autolinee

Viale D'Annunzio

Via S.Giovanni al Gatano

Via Conte

Via del Navicelli

Via Cesare

Battisti

Via Vecchia del Navicelli

Via Con.

F

Via Quarantola

Aurelia

2

3

LIVORNO km 20 - ROMA km 330

280

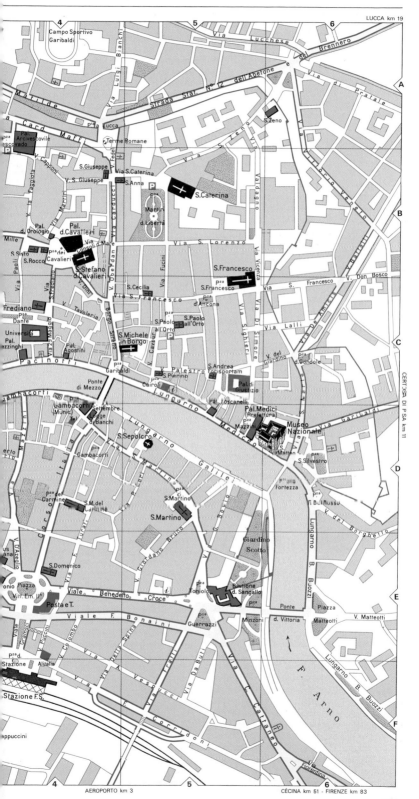

Battistero** (*A3*). *Open mid-Apr./Sep., 8 am-8 pm; first half of Apr., 8-7:30; Mar. and Oct., 9-6; Nov.-Feb., 9-5.* This majestic round Romanesque building, made of white marble, girded by arches and loggias with elegant Gothic crowning ornamentation, was begun in 1152 by Diotisalvi, continued in the next century by N. and G. Pisano, and completed around 1350, with a pyramidal eight-sided dome* by C. di Nese. The Baptistery has four exceedingly fine portals*: particular note should be given to the one facing the Cathedral.
Inside, note the octagonal baptismal font* by G. da Como (1246); on its left, supported by carved stone lions bearing columns on their backs, is the *pulpit*** by N. Pisano (1260). Before the altar, 13th-c. Cosmatesque marble floor. Along the walls, large statues* by N. and G. Pisano and school, formerly set on the exterior of the Baptistery.

Camposanto** (*A3*). *Open mid-Apr./Sep., 8-8; first half of Apr., 8-7:30; Mar. and Oct., 9-6; Nov.-Feb., 9-5.* This perfect rectangular structure, with blind arcades, was begun in 1277 by G. di Simone; an inner gallery surrounds the meadow of the ancient cemetery. Of the two simple portals, the right one is surmounted by an elegant Gothic tabernacle, (school of N. Pisano, 1350).

Ravaged in July 1944 by a fire, sparked by combat, its current appearance is the result of painstaking restoration.

Intended for the burial of noble and illustrious citizens of Pisa, from the 15th c. on many funerary monuments were moved here (most are now restored to their original locations), along with a collections of mostly Roman sarcophagi*. The walls were decorated with frescoes, largely destroyed by time or the terrible fire; many of the few that survive are protected in a room, which can be reached from the north arm.
West arm: several remarkable Roman sarcophagi; a large marble Etruscan vase; the family tomb of the Conti della Gherardesca (1315-20), by a follower of G. Pisano; on the wall, chains from the old port of Pisa.
North arm: Greek and Roman funerary objects. In the Ammannati Chapel, monument to L. Ammannati (died in 1359), from the school of G. Pisano. To the left of the chapel, the hall of frescoes*: by the so-called Maestro del Trionfo della Morte (1360-80; some identify this Master as Bonamico Buffalmacco), Trionfo della Morte, or Triumph of Death**, Last Judgement, Inferno, and a Slaughter of Anchorites*; Landscape by Taddeo Gaddi. In a huge hall next to the chapel, a series of large prints show the frescoes as they originally were. Also, note the 2nd-c. B.C. Greek marble vase*. In the Aulla Chapel, note the 2nd-c. A.D. "sarcophagus of Countess Beatrice"* (it and the Greek vase, above, served as inspiration for N. Pisano's pulpit in the Baptistery); sarcophagus of the Sponsali*.
East arm. Completely stripped of its original frescoes; note the tomb of G. Buoncompagni by B. Ammannati (1574); tomb of O. Massotti, with a female figure by G. Dupré; and the renowned statue of the "Inconsolable Woman," by L. Bartolini (1842).
South arm: tablets concerning the original Roman

colony of Pisa, mosaics, two headless 2nd-c. statues, and Roman and medieval sarcophagi.

Museo delle Sinopie* (*A3*). *Open 9-1 and 3-7; Mar. and Oct., closes at 6 and, Nov.-Feb., at 5.* This museum in Piazza del Duomo has collections of preparatory drawings (usually ochre in color), of the frescoes that once decorated the Camposanto. It is the largest and most interesting collection of drawings by great 14th-c. artists. Note the work* by the Maestro del Trionfo della Morte, and the large Crucifixion*, for the first fresco done in the Camposanto (1320-30), by F. Traini; also, note work by T. Gaddi, P. di Puccio, S. Aretino, B. Gozzoli, and A. Bonaiuti.

Museo dell'Opera del Duomo* (*A3-4*). *Open mid-Apr./Sep., 8-8; Oct., 9-6; Nov.-Feb., 9-5; Mar., 9-1 and 3-6; first half of Apr., 8-7:30.* This large museum comprises collections of art from the monuments of the Campo dei Miracoli, and stands at the far eastern side of Piazza del Duomo. On the ground floor and in the cloister is the core of the collections: 11th-/14th-c. statuary. Note Islamic bronze {??}griffon; 12th-c. Burgundian wooden Christ; masterpieces by Nicola and G. Pisano, T. di Camaino, Nino Pisano, Andrea Guardi, and Matteo Civitali. Moreover, in the Duomo's Tesoro, or Treasury: ivory carvings by G. Pisano, and fine religious metalwork. Upstairs, a vast array, from illuminated codices to Egyptian and Etruscan artifacts.

Piazza dell'Arcivescovado (*A-B4*). The 15th-c. Palazzo Arcivescovile stands here; continuing along Via Maffi, with fine view of the Duomo's apse and bell tower, and along the Largo del Parlascio, you will see ruins of 2nd-c. A.D. Roman baths; on the left is the Porta a Lucca (A4; 1544), from outside the gate, fine view of the medieval walls* (1155).

S. Caterina* (*B5*). Built in the late-13th c., this church has a Pisan-style marble facade and a large rose window; the terracotta campanile is decorated with ceramic bowls. Inside, note the marble statues* by N. Pisano (1360); in the sacristy, paintings by Fra' Bartolomeo (1511) and F. Traini (ca. 1350).

S. Zeno (*A5-6*). Standing at the end of Via S. Zeno, alongside the 13th-c. Porta di S. Zeno, outside of which is a fine view of the medieval walls*, this church was founded before the year 1000, rebuilt in the 13th c., deconsecrated in 1809, and used as a warehouse until 1972. The interior is usually closed.

S. Francesco* (*B-C5*). Construction of this convent church, which first began in 1211, was undertaken again by G. di Simone in 1265-70 and completed in the 14th c.; the facade dates from 1603. Inside, Baroque altars and large canvases by Empoli, Passignano, and S. di Tito. Note frescoes by T. Gaddi (1342) and marble altar piece by T. Pisano (14th c.). At the corner of the left transept, note structures supporting the campanile. In the sacristy, note frescoes by T. di Bartolo (1397).

S. Cecilia (*C5*). In Via S. Francesco, this small Romanesque church (1103) is made of stone and brick; not far off is the church of S. Paolo all'Orto, built in the 12th c. but later renovated.

S. Pierino (*C5*). This Romanesque church was built between 1072 and 1119; inside, fragments of frescoes, and a 13th-c. mosaic floor. Behind main altar, 13th-c. Crucifix.

Piazza Cairoli (*C5*). This cozy little square has a column with a 16th-c. statue of Abundance; note the Via delle Belle Torri, one of Pisa's loveliest streets, despite damage done in WWII. Along it are 12th-/13th-c. tower-houses.

S. Andrea Forisportam (*C5*). This simple 12th-c. Pisan-style church, is decorated with hanging arches and terracotta bowls (copies). Handsome, original Romanesque interior.

Museo Nazionale di S. Matteo ** (*D5-6*). *Open 9-7; Sun., 9-1:30; closed Mon.* Overlooking the Lungarno Mediceo, since 1949 this museum has occupied part of the convent of the Benedictine nuns of S. Matteo, a building adjacent to the 11th-c. bell tower, with a 13th-c. porticoed courtyard.

Among the museum's vast collections, we should make special note of the collections of Pisan sculpture, Tuscan paintings of the 12th/15th c., and Pisan and Islamic medieval ceramics. A separate section in the former Palazzo Reale will house the works from private gifts and from the collections of the houses of Medici, Lorraine, and Savoy.

Ground floor. Remarkable collection of medieval ceramics: series of ceramic basins*, some of 11th-c. Islamic origin, others from 13th-c. Pisa, used as ornaments on the exterior walls of Pisan churches; also, ceramic archeological finds from all over Pisa. Armor from the Gioco del Ponte, an example of rough sport begun in Pisa by the Medici in the 16th c.; also, one of the most important European collections of antique metal arms and armor (about 900 pieces).

Second floor. Sculpture from the 12th/14th c., eloquent examples of Pisan art: fragments of Romanesque buildings and statues. Among the artists: follower of G. Pisano, T. di Camaino, N. Pisano, F.Traino; A. and N. Pisano, F. di Valdambrino; A. di Giovanni. Rock-crystal cross, late-13th-c. Venetian school. Sculpture from the 15th c., including work by: Donatello**, a follower of Michelozzo*, workshop of Verrocchio*, Della Robbia. Painting from 12th/13th c., by Berlinghiero, E. di Tedice, Giunta Pisano, Maestro di S. Martino, 14th c., work by D. Orlandi, S. Martini, G. di Nicola, L. di Tommè, B. Daddi, Maestro di S. Torpè, L. Memmi, C. di Pietro, B. da Modena, S. Aretino, M. di Bartolomeo, T. di Bartolo; and 15th c., work by G. da Fabriano, Masaccio, Fra' Angelico, G. da Milano, A. Veneziano, D. Ghirlandaio, B. Gozzoli, P. Schiavo, N. di Bicci, and L. di Bicci.

Lungarno Mediceo (*C-D5-6*). This riverfront quay runs from the Ponte alla Fortezza to Piazza Garibaldi: at the corner of Piazza Mazzini is the 13th-c. Palazzo dei Medici (D5), greatly modified during a restoration in the early-20th c. Further along is the 16th-c. Palazzo Toscanelli.

S. Maria della Spina
and the quarters on the left bank

The miracle of the little church of S. Maria della Spina, seemingly floating upon the waters of the Arno, the simple facade of the church of S. Paolo, and the lively left bank, a quarter which sprang up in the 19th c.

Lungarno Pacinotti (*C3-4*). Stretching from Piazza Garibaldi to Ponte Solferino, this quay offers handsome views of the opposite bank. At n. 26, Palazzo Agostini (*C4*), and at n. 43, Palazzo Upezzinghi, designed by C. Pugliani (1594).

S. Frediano (*C4*). Not far from the university campus is this 11th-c. Pisan Romanesque church. Inside, note 12th-c. Crucifix and painting by A. Lomi (1604).

Palazzo Reale (*C3*). The huge building at n. 56 on Lungarno Pacinotti was begun in 1559 by Cosimo I de' Medici, and later enlarged; across the Arno, note the marble church of S. Maria della Spina (see below). It will eventually house part of the collections of the Museo Nazionale di S. Matteo, especially items from the collections of the houses of Medici, Lorraine, and Savoy, becoming a museum of court life and art.

It now exhibits the **Raccolta Ceci** (*open by appointment, 9-2, tel. 926511; closed Sun.*): among the artists, note F. Francia, A. Boscoli, B. Strozzi, Magnasco, P. Brueghel, F. Francken, Jan Bruegel the Elder. Other collections are being installed.

S. Nicola (*C3*). Behind Palazzo Reale, part of this church's lower facade and the remarkable bell tower* date from the 13th c. Inside, note painting by F. Traino and statues by G. and Nino Pisano.

S. Maria della Spina ** (*D3*). This exquisite piece of Romanesque-Gothic architecture and art, originally a small church on the banks of the Arno, it was was enlarged in 1323; it takes its name from a thorn ("spina") believed to be from the true crown of thorns (now in S. Chiara). Disassembled and moved to higher ground to save it from the flooding of the river (1871), the church is girt by arcades enclosing mullioned windows and portals. Note statues* on facade and spires by T. Pisano.

Lungarno Sonnino (*D2-3*). Across from this riverbank boulevard you can see the huge brick sheds, once boat yards (Arsenale delle Gallee, D2) of the Cavalieri di S. Stefano. At the end of Lungarno Simonelli, at the Ponte della Cittadella, is the Cittadella Vecchia (D2), the ruins of a Florentine fortress (1405).

S. Paolo a Ripa d'Arno * (*D3*). This handsome Pisan Romanesque church of the 11th c. has the same decorative pattern as the Duomo. Inside (much restored after damage sustained in WWII), note the handsome columns supporting pointed Arab-style arches. Also, painting by T. Vanni (1397). Behind the apse is the separate, octagonal **Cappella di S. Agata***, built in the 12th c.

S. Antonio (*E4*). Only the lower order of the facade survives from the original 14th-c. church. To the left, in Via Mazzini n. 71, is the Domus Mazziniana (*E4; open 8-1:30; Sat., 8-12; closed July and holidays*), commemorating G. Mazzini, Italian revolutionary.

Corso Italia (*D-E4*). This lively pedestrian street links the train station to the historic center of Pisa. Along the way are two churches: S. Domenico (*E4*), built in the 14th c., and badly damaged in WWII; and the 14th-c. S. Maria del Carmine (*D4*), with inside paintings by Allori, A. Lomi, and B. Lomi Gentileschi. When the Corso reaches the Arno, on the left, note the vast Loggia di Banchi, built in 1603-05 by C. Pugliani, for wool and silk traders. At the mouth of the Ponte di Mezzo, fine view of the north banks of the Arno.

Lungarno Galilei (*D4-5*). Between Ponte di Mezzo and Ponte alla Fortezza, this boulevard offers handsome views of the Lungarno Mediceo. Note the octagonal church of S. Sepolcro* (D5), by Diotisalvi (1153). Inside, note the tomb stones of Pisan aristocrats, and painting by the school of B. Gozzoli.

Via S. Martino (*D4-5*). Main street of the old quarter of Chinzica, once inhabited Arab and Turkish traders. In a square, note the church of S. Martino (D5), built in 1332. Inside, frescoes and paintings by G. di Nicola, A. Veneziano, A. Lomi, and E. di Tedice.

Bastione Sangallo (*E5*). This bastion and the nearby walls are all that survive of the 15th-c. Cittadella Nuova, built by the Florentines, destroyed by the Pisans, rebuilt by G. da Sangallo. Note fine park: Giardino Scotto.

Surrounding areas. The **Parco Naturale di Migliarino, S. Rossore, Massaciùccoli** (for information, call the Consorzio per il Parco, tel. 525500), established in 1979; this park extends over 21,000 hectares along the coast between Viareggio and Livorno; it comprises the lake of Massaciùccoli, much maquis, beaches, forests, pine groves, and marshes.

Pistoia*

elev. 67 m.; pop. 87,830; Tuscany, provincial capital. Set within the diamond shape of the 14th-c. walls, the juxtaposition of light-and-dark striped marble, so typical of the medieval architecture of Pisa, Tuscany, and Liguria, here becomes more minute and subtle, setting a forest green against the pure white. Thus, the architecture here is perfectly matched with the surrounding landscape, and the stone blends with the plain of the river Ombrone and the nearby spurs of the Apennines. This harmony may seem surprising from a city that spawned so much art yet so much violence: the medieval chronicler, Giovanni Villani, recalls "lo mal seme venuto di Pistoia di parte bianca e nera," or "the bad seed that came from Pistoia, engendering black and white factions," the source of the raging factions that drove Dante Alighieri, a member of the "white" faction, into lifelong exile; another poet, Cino da Pistoia, was of the "black" faction, and was also exiled. This "stilnovista" wrote that he liked to "veder colpi di spada altrui nel volto, e navi andare a fondo," literally, "to see others smitten in the face by blows of a sword, and ships sent to the bottom of the sea."

Historical note. The walls, which still stand, were first built by Pistoia itself in the early 14th c., and later fortified by the Medici. Within them we can still see the plan of the Roman city of "Pistoria"; the Longobard city too, in the 8th c., lay within this area. For centuries all life at Pistoia remained within their bounds.

Pistoia's true glory, however, began in the 11th c., and culminated with the 13th c., when Pistoian bankers lent money to French princes and kings. Within the walls, the Pistoians were building their great Romanesque Cathedral and other churches, and by the end of the 13th c., they began work on the Palazzo del Comune. Pistoia's growth was soon thwarted, however, by Lucca in one direction, and Florence in the other. In 1306, the Pistoians surrendered to the joint forces of the two rival cities, who sacked the town. Political decline ensued, and the great banking houses dwindled and died. In 1329, the Pistoians made peace a second time with a belligerent Florence, falling under its sway; in 1401, Pistoia was tucked into the Medici duchy. Centuries of silence and poverty followed, broken only in the late 18th c., with a reforming Jansenist bishop, Scipione de' Ricci. After 1850, the city grew timidly beyond its 14th-c. walls. More recently, the city has thrived, growing in all directions.

Places of interest. Piazza del Duomo*. The historical and artistic center of Pistoia, bounded by medieval buildings, this square holds, of course, the Duomo, with its tall bell tower, the Palazzo Vescovile, and the Battistero, with the Palazzo del Pretorio and Palazzo del Comune facing each other. At the corner of Via Tomba stands the medieval Torre di Catilina, whose name marks the fact that Catiline, a Roman conspirator denounced by Cicero, fled here and was defeated (62 B.C.), and then buried near Pistoia's walls.

Duomo**. This Romanesque cathedral, in the Pisan style, was built in the 12th and 13th c., and has a stone facade with three orders of loggias, with a marble portico (late 14th c.). The lunette over the central portal has an enameled terracotta bas-relief*, by A. della Robbia (1505), who also did the decorations of the barrel vaults. Note the enormous campanile.

The *interior* is majestic, and you should note numerous works of art. Among them: in the right aisle, early-14th-c. funerary monument of C. da Pistoia; Crucifix on panel by C. di Marcovaldo (1275); monumental silver **altar frontal of S. Jacopo****, begun in 1287 and finished in the mid-15th c. At the end of the aisle is the entrance to the sacristy, mentioned by Dante in the 24th Canto of "Inferno." Note the Cappella di S. Atto, with painting by M. Preti; also, fine bronze candelabrum by M. di Bartolomeo (1440). In the chapel to the left of the presbytery, canvas* by L. di Credi (1485), and stele commemorating the bishop D. de' Medici by A. Rossellino. At the foot of the left aisle, monument to N. Cardinal Forteguerri (1419-73): the statues of Faith and Hope are by A. Verrocchio; those of Christ and angels are by Verrocchio's students, among them L. di Credi. Note baptismal font by A. Ferrucci da Fiesole, designed by B. da Maiano.

Battistero**. *Open, Oct.-Mar., 9:30-12:30 and 3:30-6:30; Apr.-Sep., 9:30-12:30 and 4-7; Sun., 9:30-12:30; closed Mon.* A handsome piece of Gothic architecture, octagonal in shape, this baptistery was begun in 1338 by C. di Nese, to plans by A. Pisano, and completed in 1359. With white-and-green marble facing, it is surmounted by a blind gallery, and has three fine portals, with reliefs and statues. Inside, 14th-c. full baptismal font, restored in 1960.

Palazzo dei Vescovi. *Guided tours, Tue., Thu. and Fri., 10, 11:30, 3:30.* This 14th-c. building with loggia and mullioned windows is a major piece of Pistoian civil architecture of the Middle Ages, renovated in later centuries. It houses the Museo Capitolare, with exquisite artwork and sacred objects from the Treasure of the Duomo, as well

Pistoia: Piazza del Duomo

as frescoes and paintings. Also, note sculpture by M. Marini and paintings by G. Boldini; in the cellars, archeological finds.

Palazzo del Podestà. This stern building dates from 1367, and was enlarged in the mid-19th c. Note mullioned windows and porticoed courtyard, studded with family crests in marble and terracotta; to the left of the entrance is a stone "judge's bench," restored in 1507, where the accused were tried.

Palazzo del Comune*. This stern and majestic town hall, built with local Tuscan stone called "pietra serena," was begun in 1294, enlarged in 1334-85. To the left of the large central window, crowned by a Medici crest, with papal keys honoring Leo X (1513), is an odd head carved of black marble, probably depicting Musetto, the king of Majorca, defeated by the Pistoian G. de' Ghisilieri (1113-14). This palazzo now houses the Museo Civico (see below); in the courtyard, sculpture by M. Marini.

Museo Civico. *Open, 9-1 and 3-7; closed Sun. aft. and Mon.* Pistoia's town museum is set on the two upper floors of the Palazzo del Comune, where the handsome public halls have frescoes and carved ceilings; note especially, in the main hall, the wooden ceiling, the long 16th-c. bench, and the city crest, in marble, by the workshop of A. Verrocchio. In the museum proper, 13th- and 14th-c. paintings are on display. Note the rare panel with scenes from the life of St. Francis (1260-70), and a polyptych from 1310; wooden sculpture by F. di Valdambrino. From the 15th and 16th c., note the altar pieces from local churches, by L. di Credi, G. Gerini, R. del Ghirlandaio, Fra' Paolino da Pistoia, G.B. Volponi, and B. del Signoraccio. A section features canvases from the 17th and 18th c., by such artists as G. Gimignani, F. Vanni, M. Rosselli, P. Batoni, L. Cigoli, and others. Also note the Collezione Puccini, with works ranging from 17th-c. Florence to 19th-c. furniture. A hall is also devoted to contemporary local painters.

Madonna dell'Umiltà*. This basilica, a major piece of Renaissance architecture, was built by V. Vitoni (1494-1522), and may have been designed by G. da Sangallo; it has an octagonal plan and is surmounted by a vast dome, by G. Vasari. On the main altar, fresco by P. Tacca; chapels decorated by B. Ammannati.

S. Francesco. Begun in 1294 and completed in the 15th c., this large church was heavily renovated over the centuries, especially in Baroque times; the white-and-green striped marble facade dates from 1717. Inside, note fragments of frescoes from the 14th and 15th c.: work by P. Capanna, and others of the school of Giotto or of local schools; in the sacristy, frescoes in the manner of N. di Pietro Gerini, as well as fine work in the 14th-c. Chapter Hall.

S. Andrea**. This 12th-c. church has a Romanesque facade in the Pisan style; over the architrave of the central portal, note reliefs by Gruamonte and Adeodato (1166). Inside is one of the masterpieces of 12th-/13th-c. Italian sculpture: the **pulpit**** (1298-1301) by G. Pisano, who also carved the wooden Crucifix* in a 15th-c. tabernacle, midway up the right aisle. Also note frescoes by G. da Pistoia, and 14th-c. baptismal font.

Ospedale del Ceppo*. Founded in the 13th or 14th c., this hospital is named for a log in which charity was collected. Note the Florentine-style portico (1514), with medallions and a frieze* in polychrome terracotta, by G. della Robbia and S. Buglioni (1525-26).

S. Bartolomeo in Pantano. Literally, "St. Bartholomew in the Swamp," this Romanesque church was built in 1159; portal by Gruamonte (1167). Inside, note the pulpit* by G. da Como (1250), and fragments of 14th-c. frescoes.

Palazzo Rospigliosi. *Open, 10-1; Tue., Thu. and Fri., also 4-7; closed Mon.* This palazzo is a combination of several buildings from different eras, the oldest of which is adjacent to the cathedral. The entrance is from Ripa del Sale, up a double staircase. Upstairs is a lavish apartment, named after Clement IX, a Pistoian pope believed to have lived here. Note the 17th-c. furniture and paintings. Also, note the Museo Diocesano, with sacred objects and artwork from local churches.

S. Pietro Maggiore. All that survives of the 13th-c. church is the right side and the lower order of the facade.

Fortezza di S. Barbara. This square fortress, in a park, stands on the site of a medieval fort; it was built in the 16th c. by G.B. Bellucci and B. Buontalenti.

S. Paolo. This church in the Pisan style (1291-1302), has a handsome facade and portal with carved lunette; note Gothic tombs. Inside, a 14th-c. wooden Crucifix.

S. Domenico. Built in the late-13th c. and enlarged in 1380, this church holds a funerary monument to Filippo Lazzari, by B. and A. Rossellino (1462-68).

S. Antonio del Tau. Named after the "tau," or Greek "T," worn by its monks on their habits, this church was built in 1340 by Fra' Giovanni Guidotti; it has not been used for worship for two centuries. Inside, note the 14th- and 15th-c. frescoes**.
In the former convent, restored in 1987, is the **Fondazione Marino Marini** *(open, 9-1 and 3-7; closed Sun. aft. and Mon.)*, with collections of the work of the Pistoian artist, including etchings, lithographs, and sculpture.

S. Giovanni Fuorcivitas**. Begun in the 12th c. and completed in the 14th c., this is one of Pistoia's largest churches. Note the facing with bands of travertine and greenish marble; in the portal, architrave by Gruamonte (1162). Inside, note: marble pulpit* by Fra' Guglielmo da Pisa (1270); holy-water font* with reliefs by G. Pisano. In the presbytery, polyptych* by T. Gaddi (1353-55), fragments of frescoes from the early 14th c., and terracotta group* by the Della Robbia school.

Via Roma. At the beginning of this street, note the imitation-Renaissance Palazzo della Cassa di Risparmio (1905); nearby, on the opposite side of the street, is the Palazzo del Capitano del Popolo (late-13th c.), at the corner of Via della Stracceria, lined with medieval homes and workshops.

Pompeii** (excavation of) / Pompei** (scavi di)

Campania, province of Naples, city of Pompei; pop. 25,177. Set on the last low buttress to the SW of Mt. Vesuvius not far from the gulf of Naples, Pompeii is known throughout the world for its tragic destruction and for its miraculous discovery. This is a unique memento of the topography of a city of the ancient world; here life came to a sudden halt on 24 August A.D. 79.

Historical note. The site occupied by Pompeii was endowed perfectly by nature for trade and commerce. This city was exceedingly wealthy during Samnite times, when the area between the Via della Fortuna and the Via Stabiana was built up (this is where most of the public buildings were located), while the area to the north, between the Herculaneum gate and the gate of Nola remained largely residential. After taking part in the war of the Italic towns against Rome, in 80 B.C., Pompeii was forced to open its gates to Sulla, accepting a colony of veteran legionaries. Pompeii rapidly became a Roman town, in language, customs, and architecture. During this period, the theaters and the amphitheater were built; and many Samnite houses were rebuilt or at least redecorated. In A.D. 62 Pompeii was damaged by an earthquake that was a prelude to the catastrophe of A.D. 79, the terrifying eruption — vividly described in two letters from Pliny the Younger to Tacitus — that was announced by a giant black cloud. Scorching lapilli and a shower of ash rained down, covering people and buildings under a blanket that stood 4 to 5 meters deep. In the 19th c. casts were made of the bodies that came to light. The corpses, which had the appearance of a person sleeping, much more than that of a dead person, had been preserved by pumice and ashes; pumice tended to cover the dead body, preserving the skeleton without flesh, while the ashes solidified upon the corpse, creating a sort of cast. All that was required was to inject plaster into these "moulds" in order to obtain a vivid image of the last seconds of life of those who were unable to get away over the water. Animals included. Over the centuries, an additional 2 m. of earth and plants were added, and even the folk memory of where the city had once stood was eventually lost. The first accidental discoveries took place on the deserted hill, or Collina della Civita at the end of the 16th c. during the reclamation of the Valle del Sarno; but it was not until 1748, under the rule of Carlo III of Bourbon, that the first subterranean explorations began, like those in Herculaneum. With the discovery in 1763 of an inscription, the site was identified as that of Pompeii. Excavations proceeded apace in 1806-1815 under Joseph Bonaparte and Joaquin Murat, and again under the restored Bourbon dynasty (1815-1859). As of this writing, 60 percent of the ancient city has been uncovered; ancient Pompeii covered roughly 66 hectares, and it is believed that the town had a population of 20,000 or 30,000.

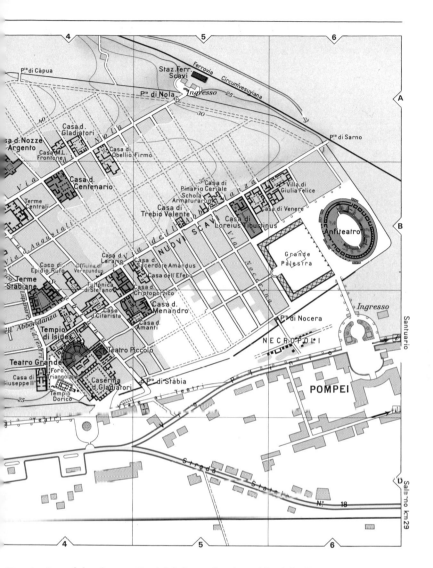

The urban layout. In few other excavations in Italy does one have as clear an idea as one has in Pompeii of just how the ancient Romans organized a city. The town that was destroyed by Mt. Vesuvius was, in fact, much like Ostia, a particularly complete example of a market town, with a clear distinction between quarters serving a public function and residential areas. That is because the eruption basically put a seal upon the Roman settlement, arresting its development sharply and definitively on 24 August A.D. 79. On that date, Pompeii was still almost entirely encircled by walls, in which no fewer than eight gates opened out to allow communications with the chief settlements of the surrounding area (the names of the gates often indicated the places toward which the roads led). The walls were punctuated at regular intervals by towers. Only to the south — overlooking the sea — did the walled perimeter serve, during the Empire, to support the panoramic terraces of the homes of particularly wealthy citizens. The urban layout within the walls was structured in accordance with a traditional ancient city plan. There were two main arteries running east-west ("decumani"); they were intersected at right angles by the "cardines," running north-south. The diagonal Via

Consolare and the winding Vicolo del Lupanare, as they are now called in Italian, were characterized by an irregular layout. Both of the largest routes were paved with large paving stones and were lined with sidewalks, while the "decumani" in particular were outfitted, at the most important intersections, with raised walkways allowing pedestrians to cross the street easily. The leading arteries of the town can be clearly recognized by the deep ruts left by the passage of chariots and carts (Via dell'Abbondanza and Via Consolare were in some areas actually carved with "tracks" by the heavy wheels). There were public fountains at crossroads. Smaller roads, in turn, split up the urban grid into "insulae," literally islands, blocks that were grouped into quarters (the so-called "regiones"). These blocks were often occupied by one or more residential buildings, but it was not uncommon for several "insulae" to be joined and used for the construction of a large public facility (amphitheater, theater, baths). Another outcome of this geometric organization were the addresses ("regio VI, insula V," or "regio V, insula XIV") which a visitor can see on nearly every corner. They serve to tell you what part of Pompeii you are in, while the "street address" of the structures overlooking the street identify a progression of shops, vestibules of homes, and manufactories, the same block after block.

The Pompeian house. Arrayed around a square courtyard (atrium), where the "impluvium" for the collection of rain water was located, the archaic Pompeian house had, directly facing the entrance, the "tablinum" (dining room and living room) and, on either side, the bedrooms ("cubicula") and the storerooms ("cellae"). This simple style of home was enlarged by adding, in the back, a Hellenistic peristyle, which surrounded the garden ("viridarium") with its colonnade; around the peristyle stood the "triclinium" (dining hall, moved here from the "tablinum") and other rooms for domestic use and for entertaining ({oeci}, exedrae); the rooms on the facade were used as shops; the upstairs area was used by tenants or slaves. The interior walls were decorated with the well-known Pompeian murals, in tempera or by encaustic process (pigments mixed with wax and applied while hot); these murals are generally divided into four styles (usually numbered): the first style, employing encrustation (Samnite era), imitating a marble facing in stucco; the second style, architectural (1st c. B.C.), in which false perspectives framed figured compositions; the third style, which imitated the Egyptian manner (Imperial age, until A.D. 62), in which the architectural elements serve as ornamentation; the fourth style, highly ornamental (A.D. 62-79), in which the figurative depictions are enclosed by complicated and capricious architectural assemblies. The archaic city, which occupied a small area around the Forum and had an elliptical plan, grew according to a more comprehensive and rationalized scheme, as is the case with modern cities.

The Pompeian styles. One of the fundamental points of reference for the study of the development of Roman art is the heritage that has survived in Pompeii. The Pompeian frescoes have been split up by scholars into four successive chronological periods. The "first style" (2nd c.-turn of the 1st c. B.C.) was actually Greek in origin and is characterized by imitation of architectural elements (socles, columns), in colored stucco or jutting features; these features typified the buildings and tended to be brightly colored. The "second style" (1st c. B.C.) caught on in the wake of Roman colonization; at first this style echoed the interplay of light and shadow in the reliefs of the previous style, and then tended toward more developed and fanciful elevations and solutions, making use of jutting panels ("pinakes"), with plant motifs, masks, and human figures. The "third style" (end 1st c. B.C.-first half of the 1st c. A.D.) developed as a direct reaction to the previous style; in this style, spaces were no longer constructed through perspectival illusion, but rather on a rigid horizontal and vertical gridwork. The scenes depicted usually appeared at the center of the panel, accompanied by Egyptian motifs, enclosed by candelabra featuring plant motifs and small heads, while the landscapes developed into veritable miniatures, with a few spare strokes. The "fourth style" (mid-1st c. to A.D. 79) at first carried on the refined design that characterized the latest phase of the previous style — with a sharp prevalence of panels embellished with textile-based decorative techniques, interrupted by narrow views and airy architectural structures — with a greater emphasis on colors (particularly prevalent was golden yellow and shades that allowed sharp contrasts). Following the earthquake of A.D. 62, there was a progressive stiffening of shapes and the stereotypical repetition of decorative motifs, though the taste for illusionistic solutions returned, with architectural backdrops reminiscent of set design. There has been much debate, ever since the first discoveries, concerning the pictorial techniques used by the ancients. We have more reliable information on the colors, or paints, once again thanks to Pliny the Elder, who listed a great many colors in his "Naturalis Historia." Even then, distinctions were made between natural and artificial colors, between dark and light shades, and there were different prices, as well. Usually, bright colors were the most

expensive (and the owner of the house would provide the painters with them directly), though they were also the colors that lasted longest, provided they were applied carefully and on walls that were not exposed to atmospheric agents (Vitruvius, for instance, recommends against using cinnabar red on surfaces exposed to the sun, as it tends to darken with light). As we observe walls with fragments of frescoes nowadays, we should keep in mind that dark colors, which certainly prevail over bright colors, are in many cases the result of the eruption and the centuries, much more than of inexpert painters or poor-quality paints, although most Pompeiians did indeed use mid-to-low price paints. Almost wholly shrouded in mystery are the painters themselves. Only one signed his work - a certain Lucius - while all the other frescoes are anonymous.

The **excavations**** (*open, 9-an hour before sunset*) have uncovered roughly 60 percent of the city's area, a mix of Oscan, Etruscan, and Greek cultures, later occupied by Samnites (end 5th c. B.C.) and by Romans only after 80 B.C.; it was damaged by an earthquake in A.D. 62, before it was buried by the ash and lava of the eruption (A.D. 79).

The entire city seems to leap alive from the shattered ruins; the paved streets are marked by the ruts left by passing chariots, wagons, and carts; there are sidewalks and large stones at the intersections, marking pedestrian crossings; amongst the residential homes, painted and carved signs indicate the many hotels (*hospitia*), shops (*tabernae*), taverns (*cauponae*), and the bars (*thermopolia*), with pouring-tables on the street; painted slogans or scratched-in graffiti support this or that candidate for elected public office, or announce upcoming gladiatorial matches; huge phallic symbols were used to ward off the evil eye.

The **Antiquarium** (*C3*) features materials from excavations and the dramatic **casts*** of victims of the disaster.

Of particular note: the rectangular plaza of the *Forum*** (*C3*) with the podium of the Temple of Jove, the building of Eumachia, headquarters of the guild of the "fullones" (cleaners, dyers, and manufacturers of cloth) and the *basilica**, the site of the administration of justice and business; the Hellenistic *great theater*** (*C4*; 200-150 B.C.), which was later enlarged, on the hillside slope; the elegant *small theater*** (*C4*); the *amphitheater** (*B6*) dating from 80 B.C., the earliest sur-

Pompeii: Forum

viving amphitheater known; and the *Terme Stabiane*,** or Baths of Stabia (*B-C4*).

Among the best-known residential houses are: the *Casa del Menandro** (House of Menander; *C5*), richly decorated with frescoes; the *Casa di Loreius Tiburtinus** (*B5*) with a triclinium decorated with scenes from the *Iliad* and the Labors of Hercules; the *Praedia di Giulia Felice** (*B6*), in which, alongside the house of the proprietress (Julia Felix), are a public bath and a rental block with shops; the exemplary *Casa dei Vettii*** (House of the Vettii; *B3*) in which the great *triclinium** is decorated with lovely ancient paintings; the *Casa degli Amorini Dorati** (House of the Gilded Cherubs; *B3*); the *Casa del Fauno** (House of the Faun; *B3*); the *Casa del Poeta Tragico* (House of the Tragic Poet; *B3*) offers a fine example of a middle-class dwelling.

Outside of the enclosure around the excavations is the **Villa dei Misteri*** (*A1*): the huge painting, from the 1st c. B.C., on the walls of one hall, depicting the Initiation of the Brides to the Dionysian Mysteries** is a remarkable and exquisite piece of ancient art.

Portofino*

pop. 646; Liguria, province of Genoa. This town lies on the southernmost extremity of the Monte di Portofino. Around a little seaside square and along the natural port is a fringe of Ligurian houses, tall, narrow, and brightly colored. In the water, during the high season, luxury yachts flying every imaginable flag and elegant parties are the rule here. Inland, among the pines and holm-oakks, are the villas that were exclusive and elegant at the turn of the 20th c.

Places of interest. The **port**. As you stroll through the main square and then along the waterfront, you will enjoy remarkable scenes and landscapes of all sorts. The natural setting becomes even more spectular if you go to a corner of the square, and take the Salita S. Giorgio up to the *church of S. Giorgio*, which grandly surveys two bodies of water (on one side the open sea, on the other the bay); the church was rebuilt after WWII. From the church courtyard you can enter the **Castello di S. Giorgio** (*open, 10-4; in summer until 6 pm; closed Tue.*), a 19th-c. adaptation of an existing building; beneath the church, a little lane runs out among the Mediterranean pine trees of the promontory, leading to the lighthouse at the *tip of the Cape*; from ere you will enjoy a majestic view of the Golfo del Tigullio and the coast as far south as Sestri Levante.

Pozzuoli

elev. 28 m., pop. 77,586, Campania, province of Naples. The phenomenon of bradyseism here can be detected through the holes dug by rock-boring sea mollusks in the columns of the so-called Serapaeum, indicating that as the land rises and falls, the complex is alternately submerged and lifted out of the water.

Places of interest. The **Serapaeum***, partly underwater, was the *macellum* or public market of the Roman town of Puteoli under the empire; the sixteen Corinthian columns, with the mollusk-burrowed holes mentioned above, supported a dome.

The **Duomo**, which was built around a Roman temple of the earliest Republic, was rebuilt in the 17th c., but a fire (1964) uncovered its original structure; excavations then showed that the podium incorporates the ruins of a temple made of tufa during the Republican era, identified as the "Capitolium" of the earliest Roman colony (194 B.C.).

In the **Anfiteatro Flavio***, or Flavian amphitheater (*open, 9-until times that can range from 2:45 to 6, depending on the season*), built in the 2nd half of the 1st c. A.D., *naumachiae* (staged sea battles) were held, along with fights and hunts of wild beasts; a tour of the intriguing **cellars*** includes the shafts up which the cages of the wild beasts were hoisted into the arena.

The traditional name of Temple of Neptune is used to indicate a structure that actually comprises the impressive remains of a bath structure; the nearby Temple of Diana is actually the ruins of a nymphaeum.

The waters of a number of hyperthermal springs are used in the baths, or **Terme Puteolane** (*for information tel. 081-5261303*) and in the **Terme La Salute**.

Ravello*

elev. 350 m., pop. 2,458 , Campania, province of Salerno. The center of town is the Piazza Vescovado.

Places of interest. High atop a stairway is the **Duomo***, founded in 1086, built in the 12th c., and heavily renovated in the 18th c.; note the bronze door* (1179) and the 13th-c. campanile. *Inside*: pulpit* decorated with mosaics and reliefs by Niccolò di Bartolomeo da Foggia (1272) and ambo* from circa 1130.

Partly surrounding the **Piazza Vescovado** is the park of **Villa Rufolo*** (*open, 9:30-1 and 2-5; summer 9.30-1 and 3-7*). In the complex of Moorish Sicilian style buildings (13th c.) note in particular the courtyard,* not unlike a small cloister; in a building adjacent to the Villa, note the Antiquarium; also note the *garden** with exotic plants.

After you pass the church of *S. Francesco*, with its romantic Gothic cloister, you continue on to the **Villa Cimbrone***: the courtyard features superb ancient fragments; at the end of the garden, note the famous **Belvedere Cimbrone****.

Ravenna**

elev. 4 m.; pop. 135,435; Emilia-Romagna, provincial capital. The unexcelled allure of this city springs from a chance twist of ancient history. In A.D. 402, the emperor Honorius shifted the capital of the Western Roman Empire from Milan to this village on the Adriatic coast, with a strategic lagoon defending it inland. For the ensuing century-and-a-half, Ravenna was, variously, the heart of a moribund empire; the court of a Gothic king educated in Constantinople named Theodoric,; and the center of Byzantine Italy (lavishly adorned with earnings made in the wars against the Goths). Classical influence, Christian faith, and plentiful funds made this a spectacular proving ground for the growing Byzantine artistic canon. And the centuries of quiet papal rule that followed left Ravenna magically intact. In the 15 centuries since Ravenna's foundation, the Adriatic has receded to a distance of 12 km, but maritime trade still thrives here.

Historical note. The emperor Augustus was the first to glimpse Ravenna's potential as a port. This modest Roman colony stood on a littoral strip, protected by the Adriatic on one side, and by a vast lagoon to the landward. It became the second naval base of the Roman empire; and, in A.D. 402, capital of the empire (Milan was threatened by the Goths). Despite the empire's decline, Ravenna began to accumulate its astonishing trove of monuments. In 476, Odoacre deposed the last Roman emperor; his successor, Theodoric, ruled here from 493 to 526. More monuments were built: Theodoric's mausoleum, the basilica of S. Apollinare Nuovo, the church of S. Spirito, and the Arian baptistery. Byzantium declared war on the Goths, and in 540 the Byzantine general Belisarius took Ravenna. Three decades of peace followed, during which time such monuments as the churches of S. Vitale and S. Apollinare in Classe were built. With the Longobard invasion of 568, Ravenna was reduced to the capital of the Hexarchate (the Byzantine military district that held out for two centuries). The river Po shifted its course northward, further isolating the city. In 751 Ravenna fell to the Longobards. Its glory had ended. In the centuries that followed, Ravenna was ruled by archbishops and an assortment of local nobility. The Da Polenta family, who ruled from 1302 to 1441, gained some small immortality by offering hospitality to Dante Alighieri, who died and was buried here. Venice held sway here from 1441 to 1509; new monuments were built for the first time in many centuries. Modern-day Piazza del Popolo became the center of Ravenna. In front of the Palazzo del Comune, two columns were built, reminiscent of St. Mark's Square in Venice. The "Palazzetto Veneziano" was built, and handsome, Venetian-style houses were constructed in what is now Via Cairoli. After 1509, the Papal State held sway here; no noteworthy monuments date from this period, nor from the 19th c. The industrial boom of the 1950s and 1960s led to environmental problems, but also to the restoration and preservation of Ravenna's historical center. The extraction of water and methane has exacerbated the centuries-long sinking of Ravenna's monuments.

Getting around. We recommend two routes; each begins from a centrally located piazza. The first route is a walking tour; the second route, at least partly walkable, may require public transportation for the second half, which is on the outskirts of town.

S. Vitale, the Duomo, the Baptisteries

The baptistery of the Arians; the complex of S. Vitale with its remarkable windows and light and the tomb of Galla Placidia (sister of emperors, wife of a Visigoth king, and in time herself empress), the Duomo with the baptistery of the Orthodox; and the ivory throne of Maximian in the Museo Arcivescovile — these are the three highlights of the route through the western part of Ravenna, beginning from the Piazza del Popolo.

Piazza del Popolo. Heart of Ravenna, with two Venetian columns (1483), the 15th-c. **Palazzo Comunale**, and the porticoed *Palazzetto Veneziano* (1462; note the 6th-c. capitals, with the signet of Theodoric).

Battistero degli Ariani. *Open 8:30-12 and 2:30-sunset.* Octagonal building, probably early 6th c.; dome with

Ravenna: S. Vitale

mosaics. Adjacent is the late-5th-c. church of **Spirito Santo**, renovated in the 16th c. Byzantine capitals; 6th-c. ambo; ancient sarcophagus.

Via S. Vitale. At n. 28, 13th-c. house with mullioned windows. At the end of the street, on the right, the basilica of *S. Vitale* and the tomb of Galla Placidia.

S. Vitale**. *Open, winter, 9-4:30; summer, 9-7.* Construction began in A.D. 526; consecrated in 547-48 by the bishop Maximian, this basilica is one of the greatest early Christian monuments. Built to an octagonal plan, with a narthex at one face, even its brick exterior reveals a Roman conception of space reworked in Byzantine style. The **interior*** has a strikingly original structure; it is lavishly adorned with marble and mosaic; stunning effects using natural light. The dome is exceedingly light, made with rings of hollow terracotta pipes; painted in 1780. On one side extends the *presbytery*, its walls adorned with remarkable **mosaics*** that date from mid-6th c., still classical in style. Two panels in the lower section of the apse (the emperor Justinian* and the empress Theodora*, with respective entourages) are more properly Byzantine in their stylization. At the center of the presbytery, note the 6th-c. altar, with a translucent slab of alabaster*.

Mausoleo di Galla Placidia**. *Open, winter, 9-4:30; summer, 9-7.* Chapel, built to a Greek cross plan, built in the mid-5th c. The interior boasts remarkable **mosaics****, prior to 450, perhaps the earliest in Ravenna. Three ancient sarcophagi in apse and each transept.

Museo Nazionale*. *Open, 8:30-1:30; closed Mon.* An eclectic array of collections, built around a nucleus dating from the early 18th c. Noteworthy collection of Roman and early Christian artwork; arranged around three cloisters of a Benedictine monastery, the museum also has collections of ancient fabrics, ivories, icons, paintings, and various other artwork.

Piazza Kennedy, formerly Piazza del Mercato. Note Palazzo Rasponi delle Teste (early 18th c.), and facing it, *Palazzo Rasponi Murat* (15th c.).

Duomo. The Basilica Ursiana, built here in the early-5th c. and demolished in 1733, was replaced by this Baroque structure; on the left side stands the round, 10th-c. *campanile*; inside, at the end of the central nave, the ambo* of the archbishop Agnellus (late-6th. c.).

Battistero Neoniano. *Open, winter, 9:30-4:30; summer, 9-7*. Also called Baptistery of the Orthodox, eight-sided, brick, it was probably built during the first half of the 5th c. The mosaics date from just after 450. Inside, two orders of arcades support the **mosaic-lined dome**, divided in three areas: Baptism of Jesus in the Jordan, the river personified as an old man; the Apostles; and symbolic depictions of altars and thrones.

Museo Arcivescovile*. *Open, winter, 9:30-4:30; summer, 9-7*. Behind the Duomo, in the Arcivescovado, or archbishopric, this museum preserves collections of materials from the ancient cathedral and other churches, including a headless porphyry statue*, early 6th-c. mosaics*, and the celebrated 6th-c. ivory throne of Maximian.

S. Apollinare Nuovo
and the Mausoleo di Teodorico

The handsome marble statue of Guidarello, man of arms (Pinacoteca), the tomb of Dante Alighieri, who lived his last years in exile here, and the so-called Palace of Theodoric, king of the Goths, all mark this tour through the eastern portion of Ravenna. Although the barbarian king never lived in the palace that bears his name, he did build the church of S. Apollinare Nuovo, a curious mixture of barbarian style and classical ambitions.

Piazza S. Francesco. This is the heart of the "zone of Dante." Lord Byron once lived in Casa Oriani, which overlooks the piazza; it now contains the Biblioteca di Storia Contemporanea, a library of contemporary history.

S. Francesco. Fifth-c. basilica, rebuilt in the 10th c., damaged in WWII. The main altar consists of the Urn of Liberius, adorned with reliefs; the crypt, now flooded, dates from the 9th and 10th c.

Tomba di Dante. *Open 9-12 and 2-5*. For the last five years of his life, Dante Alighieri was a guest in Ravenna of Guido Novello da Polenta; he died during the night of 13 September 1321, and was buried here. The modern-day tomb was built in 1780; the relief by Pietro Lombardo, depicting Dante reading, dates from 1483. Adjacent is the *Museo Dantesco (open 9-12)*.

S. Agata Maggiore. In Via Mazzini, 5th/6th-c. church; restored in the late 15th c. Round campanile; inside, columns with Roman, Byzantine, and Renaissance capitals.

S. Maria in Porto. Late-16th-c. church with noteworthy paintings (esp. by Palma the Younger) and Greek Madonna*, a late Byzantine marble relief. Adjacent is a *former monastery*, with a noteworthy early 16th-c. **loggia**, a handsome Renaissance cloister*, and the **Pinacoteca Comunale**, or town art gallery* (*open, Tue.-Sat., 9-1; Tue. and Fri. also 2:30-5:30; Sun. 10-2; closed Mon.*). The collections include artworks by L. Monaco; Guercino; C. Bravo; N. Rondinelli; and the famed sepulchral statue of Guidarello Guidarelli*, a soldier of Ravenna, by T. Lombardo (1525).

Palazzo di Teodorico. Long said to be the sumptuous royal residence depicted in a mosaic still preserved in S. Apollinare Nuovo, this is actually a late-7th.-c. building, perhaps a barracks or a secretariat.

S. Apollinare Nuovo**. *Open, winter, 9:30-4:30; summer, 9:30-7*. Built by Theodoric in 493-96, for the Arian sect, the church has received various additions: the cylindrical campanile* in the 9th or 10th c., the small portico in the 16th c., the gilt coffered ceiling in the 17th c. The walls of the nave are lined with **mosaics****, in three zones: the two upper zones date from the reign of Theodoric, and show the style of late classicism; the lower zone dates from slightly later, and is exquisitely Byzantine in composition and style.

**S. Giovanni Evangelista*. Fifth-c. basilica, restored and rebuilt after heavy damage was sustained during the war. In front is a Gothic portal* adorned with bas reliefs; to the right of the facade is a sturdy square 10th-c. bell tower. Inside are ancient columns, fragments of floor mosaics (displayed on the walls), and, in the chapel to the left, fragments of 14th-c. frescoes.

Rocca di Brancaleone. This square fort, with its four circular towers, built by Venice in the late 15th c., once commanded the city. It is now a playground, and is used for outdoor concerts and performances.

**Mausoleo di Teodorico*. *Open, winter, 8:30-1:30; summer, 8:30-7*. Standing alone against a backdrop of cypresses, about 2 km. NE of the center. The king of the Goths ordered it built around A.D. 520. An odd structure, with a mixture of barbarian and classic styles, its dome is a single enormous block of limestone (1 m. thick; 11 m. across; it was probably damaged during construction). In the upper chamber, the porphyry sarcophagus must once have contained the king's body.

Surrounding areas. The **Basilica di S. Apollinare in Classe****, 5 km. south, on the state road Adriatica. From the intersection for Lido di Dante, entrance to the *archeological site of Classe* (open, winter, 9-4; summer, 9-7), with relics of the late-Roman and Byzantine port facilities. Just past this, on the left of the state road, is **S. Apollinare in Classe**, a basilica consecrated in 549, and an outstanding monument of Ravenna's Byzantine artistic heritage. The round *campanile*, with its progression of one-, two-, and three-light mullioned windows, was built sometime after the 9th c. Inside (*open, winter, 8-12 and 2-5; summer, until 6:30*), the aisles are separated by columns made of Greek marble, topped by Byzantine capitals; in particular, note the mosaics* (6th/7th c. and later).

Reggio di Calabria

elev. 31 m., pop. 178,524, Calabria, provincial capital.

Historical note. The Chalcidians of Euboea found their "promised land" in the Ionian "gulf" that the coastlines of Sicily and the Italian peninsula form, before squeezing into the strait: in just a few years, toward the end of the 8th c. B.C., they founded Naxos and Zancle (Messina) on the Sicilian shore, and Rhegion on the opposite shore.

Places of interest. The **Museo Nazionale****
(*B2; open 9-7; closed 1st and 3rd Mon. of the month*) is the first and most interesting stop in any tour of the city. The immense archeological collections, with material unearthed at sites in

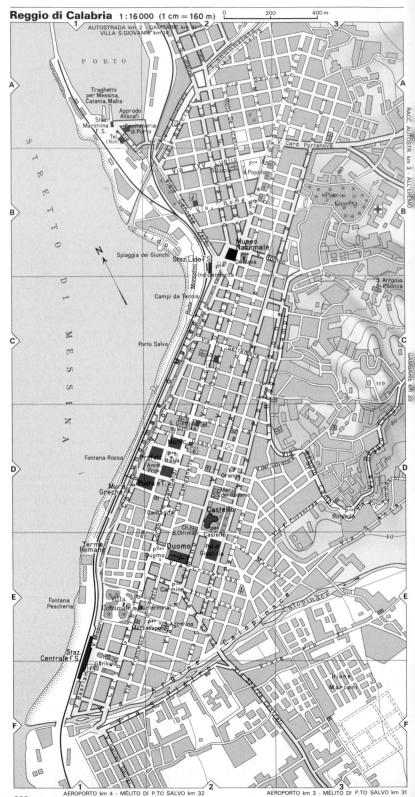

Reggio di Calabria

1:16 000 (1 cm = 160 m)

0   200   400 m

PORTO

Traghetto
per Messina,
Catania, Malta

Approdo
Aliscafi

Staz.
Marittima
F.S.
Tel.
(Noti.)

Capitaneria
di Porto

P.za
d.Popolo

Via XXV Luglio

S.Luca

Via Roma

RACC. AUTOSTR. km 3 - ALL'EREMO

S T R E T T O

Parco
Caserta

N

Spiaggia dei Giunchi

Staz.Lido F.S.

Via Romeo

Museo
Nazionale

De Nava

S. Antonio
di Padova

Via Indipendenza

D I

Campi da Tennis

Porto Salvo

Via Settembre

119

M E S S I N A

S. Giorgio al Corso
S. Giorgio d.Vittoria

Munic.

GAMBARIE km 35

V.Sbarre

Fontana Rossa

Prefett.

Italia

Amm.
Prov.

Orange

P.za
Italia

Mura
Greche

Posta e T.

Maria
SS.del Rosario

V.del Salvatore

Camagna

Castello

P.za
Rotonda

Ch.Ca
d.Ottimati

Castello

Via F.Cuzzocrea

Via S.Anna

Terme
Romane

Duomo

Pal.di
Giustizia

P.za
Duomo

Via Marsala

Fontana
Pescheria

P.za
Carmine

Via XXI Agosto

Villa
Comunale

Autterminal

Viale Calopinace

P.za
Mercadante

S.Agostino

Rione
Marconi

Staz.
Centrale F.S.

Garibaldi

292
AEROPORTO km 4 - MÉLITO DI P.TO SALVO km 32
AEROPORTO km 3 - MÉLITO DI P.TO SALVO km 31

Calabria and Basilicata, are fundamental for those who wish to understand the ancient culture of this section of Magna Graecia; a further attraction is constituted by the world-renowned **Bronzes of Riace****, two large statues of warriors, Greek originals from the mid-5th c. B.C., attributed to Phidias or his school. Of considerable interest are the artifacts found in ancient Locri with the *pinakes** (terracotta tablets) depicting in relief the myth of Persephone, a terracotta group with an Ephebus on Horseback (5th c. B.C.) and the marble group of the Dioscuri (early-5th c. B.C.). In the section of medieval and modern art, note two small panels by Antonello da Messina, with St. Jerome* and Abraham and the Angels* (1457) and the Return of the Prodigal Son* by Mattia Preti.

There is a magnificent **promenade** with a panoramic view of the strait of Messina, the Monti Peloritani, and Mt. Etna, on the **Lungomare*** (*C-D1-2*); at its southern extremity, you can see a stretch of **Greek walls** (*D1*), dating from the 4th c. B.C., and ruins of the *Terme Romane* (Roman Baths; *E1*).

The **Duomo** (*E2*) was rebuilt following the earthquake.

Of the **Castello** (*D2*), built during Aragonese rule (15th c.), only two circular towers and a stretch of the curtain walls still survives.

Rìmini

pop. 128,119; Emilia-Romagna, provincial capital. Long sunny days on the beach, warm nights on the dance floor: Rimini is the heart of Romagna's Riviera, the spectacular playground of Europe. This was just a fishing village when the first adventuresome bathers ventured into the waves, in hats and ample suits. The 18th- and 19th-c. breakwaters changed the shape of the beach, increasing the eastern shores with fine iridescent sand, and eroding the western ones. And overlooking the eastern beach is the luxurious Grand Hotel, so dear to Fellini. Rimini itself dates back to the 3rd c. B.C.; 17 centuries later, the local ruler, Sigismondo Malatesta (1429-1468), had P.della Francesca paint his portrait, and asked Leon Battista Alberti to transform a little local church into the Tempio Malatestiano, a major masterpiece of the early Renaissance.

Places of interest. Piazza Cavour. Historically the heart of Rimini, this square has a statue of Pope Paul V (1613) and a 16th-c. fountain. On the NW side are the 16th-c. *Palazzo Comunale* and the 13th-c. *Palazzo dell'Arengo* (note loggia and mullioned windows; upstairs, note the large detached frescoes), and, at the end, the 14th-c. Gothic *Palazzo del Podestà*. Also note the 19th-c. *Teatro Amintore Galli.*

Castel Sismondo, in the huge Piazza Malatesta, surviving relics of the castle, completed in 1446, designed by Sigismondo Malatesta with the advice of F.Brunelleschi. Inside is the **Museo delle Culture Extraeuropee** (*open 8-1, closed Sun.*), with African, Australian, and Precolumbian ethnographic collections.

S. Agostino. This Romanesque-Gothic church dates from 1247, and has a fine tall campanile*; inside, 14th-c. frescoes, paintings by G. da Rimini,

Rìmini: Tempio Malatestiano

frescoes by the Maestro dell'Arengo, and a large 14th-c. Crucifix*.

Piazza Tre Martiri. This square lies on the ancient Roman Forum, where Julius Caesar exhorted his troops in 49 B.C. after crossing the Rubicon. Also note *Torre dell'Orologio*, or the clock tower (1547), and the 17th-c. octagonal church of *S. Antonio.*

Arco d'Augusto*. Oldest of the surviving Roman arches, with medieval crenelations, it was built in 27 B.C. in honor of Augustus, who rebuilt the Via Flaminia, which joined the Via Emilia at Rimini.

Anfiteatro Romano. This Roman amphitheater dates from Hadrian's reign, and could originally seat 10,000. Discovered in 1844 and unearthed in 1926-35, it now comprises little more than parts of the arena and cavea and the exterior portico.

Tempio Malatestiano**. This church symbolizes Rimini, and is considered one of the masterpieces of the early Renaissance. A 13th-c. chapel stood here, and was almost entirely rebuilt by L. B. Alberti (1447-1460), at the behest of Sigismondo Malatesta. Heavily damaged in WWII, the church was restored in the Fifties. The majestic façade (unfinished) takes its style from Roman triumphal arches; along the side, solemn arches hold the tombs of famous men and women.

The Gothic *interior* was renovated by the Veronese architect M. de' Pasti. The handsome decoration is by A. di Duccio. Note the tomb of S. Malatesta, to the right of the entrance. Note also detached fresco** by P. della Francesca (1451), the tomb of Isotta degli Atti*, perhaps by M. de' Pasti, and Crucifix on panel**, painted by Giotto around 1312. Also note bas-reliefs* and tomb* by A. di Duccio (1454).

Museo della Città. *Open 8-1; Fri. and Sun. also 4-6; closed Mon.* Set in a huge ex-convent, still being restored (entrance at n. 1 in Via Tonini), this Museum has Roman epigraphs, a Pinacoteca, or art gallery, and archeological and naturalistic sections. In the **Lapidario Romano**, of particular note: colossal Augustan milestone* from the "Via Aemilia," two altars* to Iuppiter Delichenus, mosaic floors. The **Pinacoteca** features works by 14th-c. Riminese artists; among them: G. da Rimini, Giovanni Bellini, D. Ghirlandaio, and G. Cagnacci.

Ponte di Tiberio*, or Tiberius's Bridge, originally spanned the river Marecchia (since shifted northward). Begun by Augustus and completed under Tiberius (A.D.

14-21), it has five arches. Nearby is the 16th-c. church of **S. Giuliano**, with paintings by P.Veronese and Bittino da Faenza (1409).

Surrounding areas. The **riviera of Rimini**, made up of a series of tree-lined boulevards, with hotels, pensioni, and seaside resort villages. To the NW, 4.5 km., is **Viserba**, with the villages of *Viserbella* and *Torre Pedrera*. To the SE, 7 km., is Miramare, after Rivazzurra. In Miramare is the Istituto Talassoterapico (salt-water and sand cures).

Rome / Roma**

elev. 20 m.; pop. 2,775,250; Lazio, regional capital, provincial capital, and capital of the Italian Republic. "If," Stendhal once wrote, "as you run from one monument to the next in your Roman mornings, you should have the courage to become bored through lack of social interchange, no matter how indifferent you might be to the little conceits of the drawing room, in the end you will feel the joy of the arts..." This many-faceted city envelops and penetrates with its endless array of images, with its kaleidoscopic stimuli: the "walls and the arches," as one writer summed it up, the umbrella pines of Villa Borghese, the creations of Raphael and Michelangelo, Bernini and Borromini, the Spanish Steps at the Trinità dei Monti, seen through the eyes of Goethe or Keats, the old travertine from which you can hear echoing the biting wit and violent jibes of the "romanesque" poetry of Belli, where you can imagine the fanciful irony created by the late, great Federico Fellini, and the rushing, "blonde" Tiber. This city is incomparable, and part of its allure may lie in its history, which saw chapters of great splendor followed by chapters of melancholy decadence. Rome, however, has always been reborn; hence its nickname of "The Eternal City." It has heaped treasures and memories, and it boasts the allure of a cityscape that still survives the assault of its suburbs.

Historical note. It all began here around the middle of the 8th c. B.C. — according to legend, on 21 April 754 B.C. — on the Palatine Hill, where settlements date back as far as the Bronze Age. This early Rome gradually spread out to cover, one by one, the other six hills — the Esquiline, Caelian, Viminal, Quirinale, Capitoline, and Aventine — and it was enclosed within the Servian walls (by the semi-legendary king, Servius Tullius). These walls of Rome were thoroughly rebuilt after the invasion of the Gauls in 378 B.C.; in comparison with the Aurelian walls of the 3rd c., they left out the Pincio, to the north, as well as the modern section of town to the east, bordered by the Rione Castro Pretorio, the Tiburtine, and the Lateran; excluded to the south was the entire area of the Baths of Caracalla, and to the west, Testaccio, Trastevere, and Campo Marzio. In the five centuries of the Roman Republic (509-31 B.C.), while Rome was becoming mistress of the entire Mediterranean basin, the city grew until, in the 1st c. B.C., it had attained a population of 400,000. For the first time, public works began to acquire a certain grandeur, as we can see from the Tabularium on the Campidoglio or the theater of Marcellus. With Augustus (27 B.C.- A.D. 14) began the final development of the Imperial Forums, or Fori Imperiali, while Nero made the Palatine the site of a vast imperial palace. Rome attained its definitive appearance, however, only with the Flavian emperors (A.D. 69-96), who built the Colosseum and the Arch of Titus. In the 2nd c. Rome reached its greatest urban and demographic expansion, with a population of more than a million; by the beginning of the century, Trajan had built the largest of the Imperial Forums, known as Trajan's Forum. The 3rd c. began with the construction of the Baths of Caracalla, but the threat of barbarian invasions led the emperor Aurelian to build a new walled perimeter around Rome, between 271 and 275. The city continued to develop within those walls until 1870; they still enclose the historical center. Only a few major works (the Baths of Diocletian, the Basilica of Maxentius, the Arch of Constantine) were erected thereafter in Rome, until, with the transfer to Byzantium of the imperial court (A.D. 330), Rome lost the title of capital of the empire. Despite the restorations undertaken by Honorius at the turn of the 5th c., the Aurelian walls failed to protect Rome from the Goths in 410, nor from the Vandals in 455 and 472. In Christian and Byzantine Rome, afflicted with political turmoil and declining population (at the end of the Western Empire, there were only 100,000 people in the city), the neglected ancient monuments stood in the shadow of new churches, the latter often being built with architectural fragments and valuable materials taken from the former. The formal prohibition of transforming temples into churches moved the center of town from the Forums and the Palatine to the Lateran, residence of the bishop of Rome. The first major city works of the Middle Ages were defensive in nature, and followed the sack by the Saracens (A.D. 846) of the basilicas of S. Pietro and S. Paolo (St. Peter and St. Paul). Pope Leo IV fortified part of the city, on the right bank of the Tiber, building new walls and linking them with the mausoleum of Hadrian, which was in turn transformed into a fortress (Castel S. Angelo): this was the birth of the "Leonine city." Though by this point the pope was the true lord of Rome, the 9th-11th c. were centuries of turmoil and bloody conflict among the local nobility, and between that nobility and the Holy Roman Emperors of Germany. In 1084, the Normans sacked the town; destruction was especially severe around the Caelian; population shifted away from areas furthest from the river, and into the oxbow curve of the Tiber. The so-called Consular Commune formed in the mid-12th c., and from then to the end of the 13th c., many towers and palace-fortresses were built by the nobility, often incorporating ancient buildings. Rome in those years had shrunk to one-fourth of its ancient expanse; the population hovered between 17,000 and 50,000, and was clustered along the curving bank of the Tiber, between the bridges of Ponte S. Angelo and Ponte Rotto (the ancient Aemilian bridge). During the 13th and 14th c., the autocratic power of the pope and his family grew, outweighing that of the Commune and the nobility; at the head of the nobility were the house of Orsini (pro-pope) and the house of Colonna (pro-emperor); the former controlled the strongholds along the Tiber, the latter controlled the area between the Mausoleum of Augustus and the Lateran. The celebration of the first Jubilee (1300) occurred in a thriving Rome, on its way to new glory, a Rome that attracted such great artists as Giotto, Pietro Cavallini, and Jacopo Torriti. The long "Avignonese captivity," also known as the "Babylonian captivity," the plague of 1341, the earthquake of 1349, and the failure of the attempt by Cola di Rienzo to establish a supreme government that would encourage trade while keeping the local barons at bay, returned Rome to long decades of poverty and misery.

The return of the papal court from Avignon marked the beginning of a time of recovery. The popes held temporal power as the princes of Rome and in 1417, Pope Martin V Colonna was the first Roman pope in 40 years not opposed by an Avignonese antipope; his reign also marks the dawn of the Renaissance. His projects of reconstruction were carried on primarily by the first Humanist pope, Nicholas V, who commissioned work from L.B. Alberti and the architect B. Rossellino, who designed the new Basilica of S. Pietro (St. Peter's). Sixtus IV (1471-1484) undertook the first real program of urban reconstruction, beginning with the Ponte Sisto. Julius II (1503-

Rome: Piazza S. Pietro

1513) brought the great architect Bramante to Rome, finally beginning work on the long-delayed Basilica di S. Pietro (St. Peter's); he also built the Via Giulia, Rome's first great straight avenue; he commissioned Michelangelo to paint the ceiling of the Cappella Sistina (Sistine Chapel), and Raphael to paint the ceilings and walls of the new papal apartments. The Medici popes Leo X and Clement VII brought a Florentine conception of city-planning to Rome, and built the Tridente, comprising the central Via del Corso and the lateral Via di Ripetta and Via del Babuino. The Sack of Rome in 1527 brought work to a halt only temporarily. Pope Paul III Farnese commissioned Michelangelo to transform the Piazza del Campidoglio, with the placement of the great and ancient equestrian statue of Marcus Aurelius in the center of the piazza. Michelangelo also produced a new design for St. Peter's and built the Via dei Condotti, leading up to the church of Trinità dei Monti. The Protestant Reformation pushed the popes to reorganize their dominion and to work even harder (and spend even more lavishly) to make their capital a luxurious and magnificent city. In the second half of the 16th c., during the Counter Reformation, Pius IV built the arrow-straight Strada Pia (now the Via del Quirinale and Via XX Settembre), Gregory XIII built the straight roads of Via Gregoriana and Via Merulana and built the Convents of the Agostiniani, the Teatini, the Filippini, and the Jesuits, whose churches dominated the cityscape of late-16th-c. Rome.

The great renewal came with Pope Sixtus V, however, who in just five years (1585-90) gave Rome the appearance that we know today. The plan called for a series of roads radiating out from the great Basilica of S. Maria Maggiore (Sixtus's favorite church) to the churches of S. Giovanni in Laterano (St. John Lateran), S. Lorenzo Fuori le Mura, and Trinità dei Monti. As early as 1586 the Strada Felice was being built — corresponding to the modern-day Via Depretis, Via Quattro Fontane, and Via Sistina — followed by the boulevards that became modern-day Via Panisperna and Via S. Giovanni in Laterano. Sixtus V was also a great erector of obelisks, installing them in Piazza S. Pietro (St. Peter's Square), Piazza S. Giovanni in Laterano (St. John Lateran), Piazza del Popolo, and Piazza dell'Esquilino. The Rome of Sixtus V was given its crowning Baroque touches by Pope Alexander VII (1655-67) with the work of G. L. Bernini on the colonnade of Piazza S. Pietro (St. Peter's Square) and on the fountains of Piazza Navona. Between the late-17th c. and the early-18th c., Rome attained the height of its formal and theatrical

splendor: the Spanish Steps of the church of the Trinità dei Monti and the Trevi Fountain are the most spectacular expressions of that period. At the end of the 18th c., the waning political influence of the papacy and the growing economic crisis of the Papal State led to a slowing of construction. French occupation and annexation led to new political ideas, which found expression in Neoclassical architecture and art. A series of truly ambitious reconstruction projects were intended to make Rome the second capital of Napoleon Bonaparte's new empire, but in the five short years available (1809-1814) the French project was completed only in the Pincio and the rebuilding of Piazza del Popolo and Piazza della Colonna Traiana (Trajan's Column). With the return of Pius VII (1815), Rome turned in upon itself, and for the rest of the 19th c., declined in artistic and cultural importance.

After 1870, when Rome was newly established as the capital of the kingdom of Italy, it began to grow rapidly, by 1900 it had 400,000 inhabitants, twice the population of 30 years before. Among the new boulevards built were the Via Nazionale, Via Cavour, and Corso Vittorio Emanuele II; also newly built were the quarters of the Esquilino (Esquiline Hill), the Celio (Caelian Hill), the Testaccio, and Prati. Among the results of the Exposition of 1911 were the urbanization of the quarter of Vittoria and the reconstruction of Valle Giulia; by the end of WWII, the quarters of Flaminio, Salario, Nomentano, Ostiense, and Monteverde Vecchio had all been built. Major archeological digs were undertaken in central Rome, and some buildings and sections were destroyed that we can only regret; other major and laudable projects were undertaken and completed, among them the Città Universitaria (central university campus, the Foro Mussolini (now Foro Italico), Cinecittà (the film studios), and the satellite city of EUR, designed to house the Universal Exposition of 1942 (WWII of course prevented that). During the Fifties, EUR was completed, becoming a major business and office center. Rome's population, which had reached one million in the Thirties, was 1.5 million by the end of WWII. Since then it has nearly doubled, and only in the past few years has there been a decline. This led to chaotic expansion and construction, with the usual real-estate speculation and illegal development. In 1990 a new law was passed for Rome, the capital city: Rome's future depends on the planned projects in the fields of archeology, the environment, traffic control, university expansion, and convention centers.

Città Giudiziaria

Uff. Giudiziari

Piazzale Clodio

Via Golametto

Via dei Cavalieri di Vittorio Veneto

Via Clodia

Via Dardanelli

Via Sabotino

Via Monte Santo

Via Oslàvia

Via Monte Zebio

Cristo Re

Via G. Mazz

Piazza G. Mazzini

Viale G. Mazzini

Circonvallazione

P.za d. Prati d. Strozzi

Via della Giuliana

Via Angelica

Viale Giuseppe Mazzini

Corte d. Conti

Posta T. e Tel.

Via L. Sette

Via Rodi

Via Andrea Doria

Piazza Giovine Italia

Via Lante

Via G.

Via Bazzoni

Via S. Pellico

Viale delle Milizie

Via Broffério

Via G. Ferrari

Via Legnano

Via Damiata

Via Lepanto

LEPANTO M

Largo Trionfale

Via Barletta

Cesare

Viale Giulio

Via P. Duilio

S. Gioacchi

P.za dei Quiriti

Via P. Magn

Via Andrea Doria

Via Candia

Via Leone

OTTAVIANO M

Viale Ottaviano

Germanico

Via Fabio Massimo

Via Paolo Emilio

Via Ennio

Via Rienzo

P.za dell'Unità

Via Cola

Regolo

Prat

Ingresso Vaticano Viale Vaticano ai Musei

Piazza d. Risorgimento

Via S. Porcari

Via Crescenzi

Via Terenzio

Via Ovidio

Via Virgilio

I.C.I.

CITTÀ

Musei Vaticani

Via di P.za Angelica

P.za A. Capponi

V. Vitelleschi

Castel S. Angelo (Museo)

DEL

VATICANO

S. Pietro in Vaticano

P.za d. Città Leonina

Via di Porta Angelica

Via di Corridori

Borgo S. Angelo

P.za S. Maria in Traspontina

Pal. Torlonia

P.za Pia

Piazza S. Pietro

Piazza S. Pietro

Via d. Conciliazione

Ponte S. Angelo

Lung. Vaticano

Staz.

Sagrestia

Aula delle Udienze Pontificie

Largo di P.ta Cavalleggeri

Borgo Santo Spirito

S. Spirito in Sassia

Ospedale di S. Spirito in Sassia

S. Spirito

Ponte Vitt. Eman.

Ponte S. Angelo

Lung. d. Altoviti

Via d. Penitenzieri

Galleria P.

Villa Barberini

V. Aurelia

P.za

Gregorio VII

P.za Cavalleggeri

Via A. De Gasperi

Via delle Mura Aurelie

Via del Crocifisso

P.za Amedeo

P.te Amedeo

Via Acciaioli

Lungot. G.

S. Giov. d. Fiorentini

Sacchetti

Lungotevere

P.za S.M. alle Fornaci

V. Innocenzo III

Staz. S. Pietro F.S.

Via delle Fornaci

Monte del Gallo

Gianicolense

Pal. Salviati

Museo di Criminologia

S. Onofrio al Gianicolo (Museo)

Oratorio Gonfalo

Gianicolense

Quercia d. Tasso

P.le G. Mazzini

0   100   200 m

1   2   3

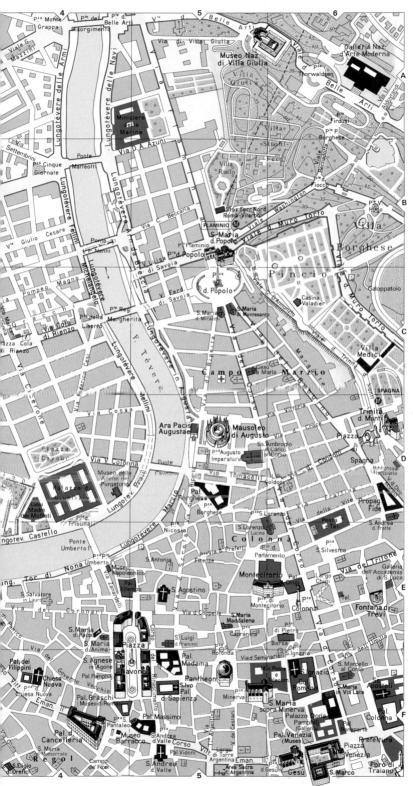

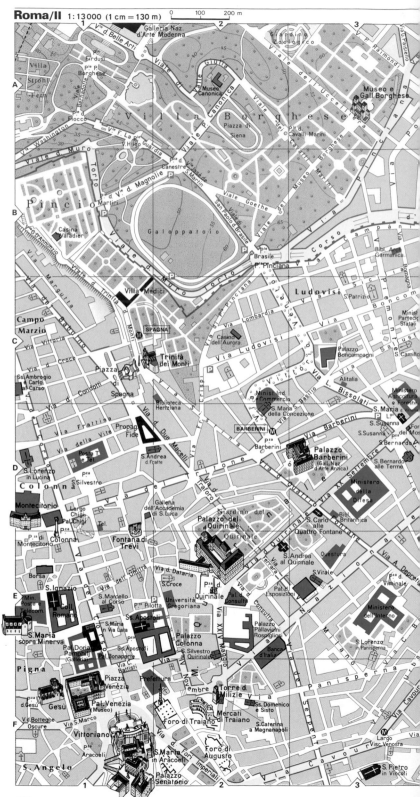

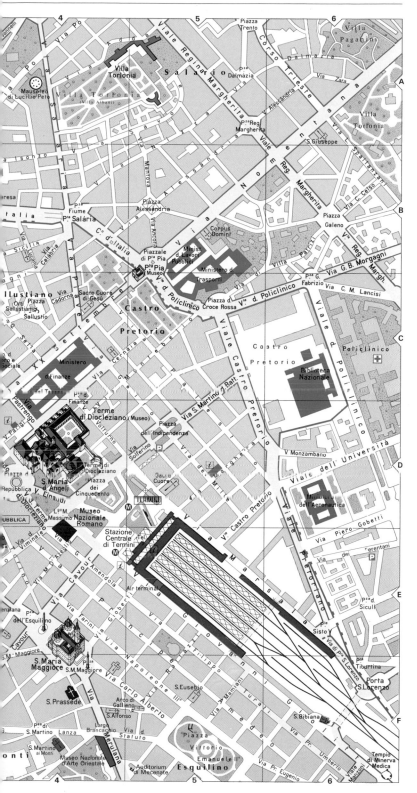

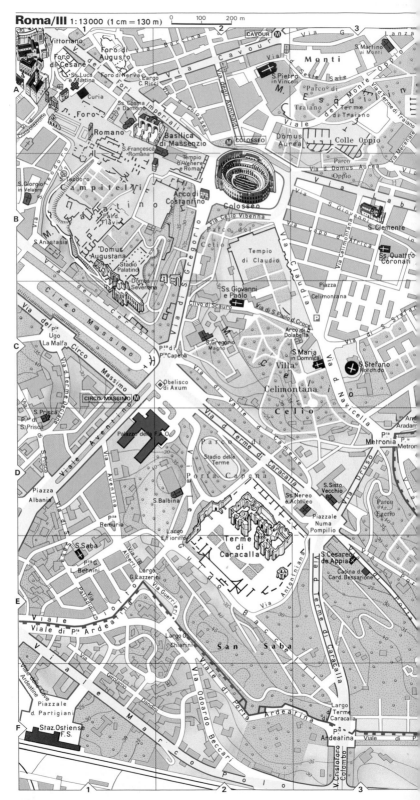

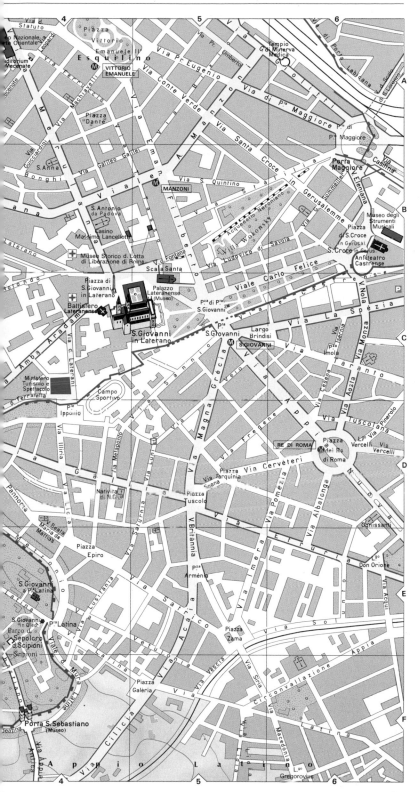

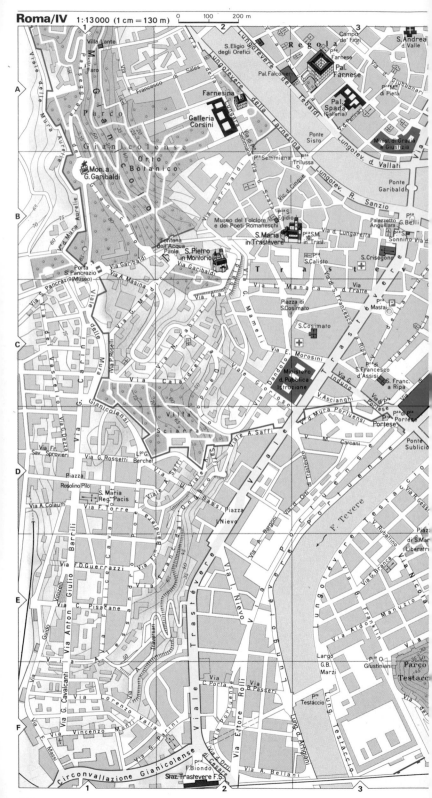

0   100   200 m

Villa Lante
Villa Vante

S. Eligio
degli Orefici
Lungotevere della Farnesina

Campo
de' Fiori

S. Andrea
d. Valle

R e g o l a

P.za
Farnese

Pal.Falconieri

Pal. Farnese

Pal.
Spada
(Galleria)

p.za
Giubbonari
di Pietà

Faro
Francesco

Sales

Farnesina

Galleria
Corsini

Ponte
Sisto

Minist. di Grazia
e Giustizia

P a r c o

G i a n i c o l e n s e

Orto
Botanico

P.za Settimiana Trilussa

P.za
Trilussa

Lungotev. d. Vallati

Ponte
Garibaldi

Mon. a
G. Garibaldi

Via di
Settimania

Vic. d. Cinque

Lungotev. R. Sanzio

G
i
a
n
i
c
o
l
o

Museo del Folclore
e dei Poeti Romaneschi

S.
Egidio

P.za
Anguillara

G. Belli

Fontana
dell'Acqua
Paola

S. Maria
in Trastevere

P.za S M
in Trast.

Via d. Lungaretta

Sonnino

Porta
S.Pancrazio
(Museo)

S. Pietro
in Montorio

Via Garibaldi

S.Calisto

S. Crisogono

T r a s

t

e

Via
d. Fratte

P.za
Mastai

Piazza di
S.Cosimato

Via L. Manara

Via d. Fratte

S.Cosimato

Via E. Morosini

Via
Induno

S. Francesco
d'Assisi

V i l l a
S c i a r r a

Ministero
d. Pubblica
Istruzione

S. Franc.
a Ripa

V. Ascianghi

Via d. Mura Portuensi

P.za
Porta
Portese

Porta
Portese

Viale A. Saffi

V. M. Garcani

Ponte
Sublicio

Via Fr.
Sprovieri

Via G. Rossetti

L.go G.
Berchet

F. Tevere

Piazza
Rosolino Pilo

S. Maria
Reg. Pacis

Via F. Torre

Via I. Nievo

Piazza
I. Nievo

Piaz
di S.Mar
Liberati

Via A. Colauti

Via
Onorato
Bassi Orti

Via F.D.Guerrazzi

Via G.
Branca

Via C. Pisacane

Largo
G.B.
Marzi

P.za O.
Giustiniani

Parco
Testacc

Via
C. Porta

Via
B. Passeri

P.za
Testaccio

Via G. Cavalcanti

Via Vincenzo Monti

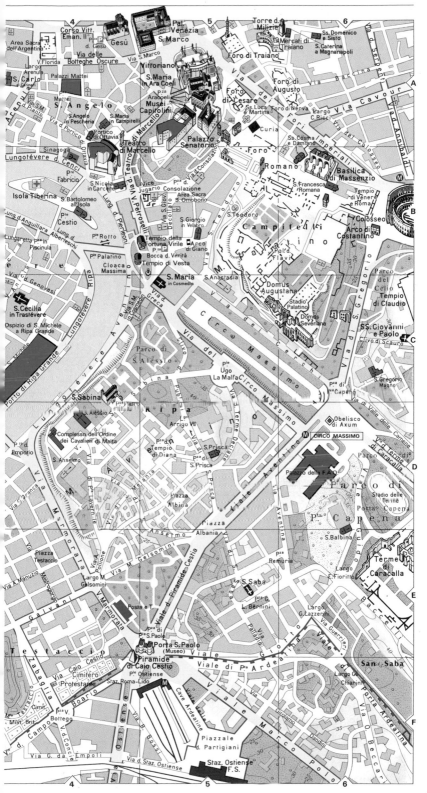

Getting around. Rome should be toured on foot, if for no other reason than to enjoy the allure of a city with a history dating back more than 25 centuries. This applies in particular to the historical center, enclosed within the bounds of the walls built by Aurelian, where it is particularly difficult to park — at times, impossible. Moreover, some areas of this central section are off limits to traffic, or require special permits. Public transportation is inevitably crowded, but it offers a good way of getting around; especially useful are the two metro lines (subway), which were recently extended. Far more problematic are buses and trolleys, which are often caught in traffic jams. Therefore the 13 routes shown here are printed, each with a small detail map, showing the suggested route and the chief sights that each route features.

1 The Campidoglio, the Fori Imperiali, and the Colosseum

A first sample of the splendor of classical times can be had along this route, which runs from the high-flown oratory of the monument to Victor Emmanuel II, on Piazza Venezia, all the way to the magic of Michelangelo's Piazza del Campidoglio, and then on to much-criticized Via dei Fori Imperiali, alongside the expanse of ruins of the Imperial Forum, and within sight of the impressive mass of the Colosseum.

Piazza Venezia* (II, *F1*). Geometric center of Rome and the focal point of intense flows of traffic, it lies between Palazzo di Venezia and the Vittoriano (see below).

Palazzo di Venezia** (II, *F1*). This building, begun in 1455, was the first major civil construction of the Roman Renaissance, based on the ideas of L. B. Alberti. From 1564 to 1797 it was the residence of the Venetian ambassador. In following years it was home to the ambassadors of France and then Austria, then a museum (see Museo del Palazzo di Venezia, below) and, in this century, the headquarters of the Fascist Gran Consiglio. Note the 15th-c. portal and the fine porticoed courtyard.

Museo del Palazzo di Venezia*. *Open: 9-2; Sun. 9-1; closed Mon.* An extremely varied grab-bag of the applied arts, this museum was established in 1922 in the former Cybo and Barbo Apartments, and has just been renovated. Note the church furnishings of the late Middle Ages, the Christ Pantokrator* (central-southern Italy, 13th c.), the Sterbini collection of 14th-c. paintings, the Orsini cross (1334), the 14th-c. triptych* from Alba Fucens, the extensive collections of ceramics, majolica, and porcelain, the 113 bronzes of the Auriti collection and the terracotta figures of the Gorga collection, and silver from all over Europe.

Basilica di S. Marco** (II, *F1*). This church of St. Mark's is the palatine chapel of the Palazzo di Venezia, and overlooks the Piazza S. Marco. Little survives of the original 4th-c. structure, though the bell tower dates from 1154 and a handsome mosaic in the apse dates from the 9th c. Note, in the largely Baroque *interior*, the 15th-c. carved ceiling; in the sacristy, reliefs by M. da Fiesole and G. Dalmata, and a St. Mark Evangelist by M. da Forlì. Excavation of the 9th-c. crypt is now underway.

Palazzetto Venezia** (II, *F1*). Built by Pope Paul II in 1464 as a porticoed open garden, it was moved to its present site in 1911-13, to make way for the Vittoriano (see below). In a corner of the facing piazza is a colossal female bust, from classical times, known to the people as Madama Lucrezia; like several other statues throughout Rome, this was used as a sort of bulletin board for satires and invectives against sovereigns and prelates.

Vittoriano** (II, *F1*). This monument to United Italy's first king, Victor Emmanuel II, was begun in 1885 by G. Sacconi and substantially completed in 1911. A notable feature of the Roman skyline, this vast white marble structure is topped by enormous bronze chariots (1927), and before them a grand stairway leads up to the *Altar of the Fatherland*. In the central niche stands a statue of Rome, by A. Zanelli. Beneath the statue is the tomb of Italy's Unknown Soldier; on either side, stairways lead up to a bronze equestrian statue of Victor Emmanuel II, by E. Chiaradia and E. Gallori; on the statue's base are depictions of the chief cities of Italy. Higher still is a portico (fine view*), with statues of the Regions of Italy.

Museo Centrale del Risorgimento. *Closed to tourists.* Located in the Vittoriano, it is connected with an historical institute (Istituto per la Storia del Risorgimento Italiano). Tourists can visit the *Sacrario delle Bandiere delle Forze Armate* (*open: 9:30-1:30; closed Mon.*), with exhibits of military history.

Campidoglio* (II, *F1*; IV, *A5*). Of the seven hills of ancient Rome, this, the Capitoline Hill, was the acropolis and the religious center (in 509 B.C. the temple of Capitoline Jove was inaugurated here, the most important sanctuary of Latinity, dedicated to the triad of Jove, Juno, and Minerva). Ever since, it has always been the heart of Rome's government. It consists of the "Capitolium" prop-

er, to the right, and the "arx," on which stands the church of Aracoeli. Between them is a saddle, with the Piazza del Campidoglio. Climbing up the west slope of the hill is the stairway of S. Maria d'Aracoeli and the monumental graded ramp*, designed by Michelangelo and modified by G. della Porta; at the top is a balustrade, decorated with late-Empire statues of the Dioscuri, the so-called trophies of Marius (1st c.), statues of Constantine and his son Constans I (4th c.), and two milestone columns from the Via Appia Antica.

Piazza del Campidoglio** (IV, A5). Michelangelo designed the monumental architecture of this square, surrounded by three buildings (in the middle, Palazzo Senatorio; on the right, Palazzo dei Conservatori; on the left, Palazzo Nuovo), the elegant base that once held an ancient equestrian statue of Marcus Aurelius (a copy now stands here, while the original has stood since 1981 on the ground floor of the Museo Capitolino), and the pavement, actually installed in 1940.

Rome: Piazza del Campidoglio

Palazzo Senatorio* (IV, A5). Rome's city hall, it stands on the Tabularium (see below), and was designed by G. della Porta and G. Rainaldi (1605), based on a plan by Michelangelo. Note the bell tower (1582), with the statue of Minerva-Goddess Roma; also, inside, statue of J. Caesar* (1st c. B.C.).

Tabularium. *Closed for restoration.* This Roman archives, built in 78 B.C., survives only in fragments; from here, you have a remarkable view of the Roman Forum*.

Palazzo dei Conservatori** (IV, A5). This building, on the SW side of the Piazza del Campidoglio, was designed and built by Michelangelo, with the help of G. della Porta (1568). The porticoed façade is crowned by a statue-lined balustrade; in the courtyard, note the fragments of a colossal statue of Constantine and trophies from a temple to Hadrian; Michelangelo also designed the facing **Palazzo Nuovo**, built by G. and C. Rainaldi (1655). These two buildings hold the collections of the Musei Capitolini.

Musei Capitolini**. *Open: 9-8; closed Mon. The Braccio Nuovo and the Museo Nuovo are closed for reinstallation.* These museums comprise the Appartamento dei Conservatori, the Museo del Palazzo dei Conservatori, the Braccio Nuovo, the Museo Nuovo, and the Pinacoteca Capitolina — all of which are located in the Palazzo dei Conservatori — and the Museo Capitolino, which is located in the Palazzo Nuovo. They originated from a donation made in 1471 by Pope Sixtus IV to the City of Rome, consisting of the bronzes formerly preserved in the Lateran. To this donation was added, in 1733, the Albani collection; under Benedict XIV, works from Hadrian's Villa at Tivoli were added, along with the "Forma Urbis Romae," dating from the reign of Severus. After Italy was unified, all materials from excavations carried out there came into these collections.

The Appartamento dei Conservatori — which is reached along a stairway lined with honorary reliefs of Marcus Aurelius and Hadrian and a late-13th-c. statue of Charles of Anjou — comprises a series of richly decorated halls, with notable 16th-c. frescoes and friezes telling the history of Rome; these rooms are used as an official reception area by the city government. Among the works assembled here, ranging from the 5th c. B.C. to the 18th c., let us point out in particular: the statues of Urban VIII* by G. L. Bernini (1635-39) and of Innocent X* by A. Algardi (1645-50) in the Sala degli Orazi e Curiazi; the Spinario* (boy removing a thorn from his foot), and a bronze statue from the 1st c. B.C., believed to be a portrait of Junius Brutus*, in the Sala dei Trionfi; the renowned Capitoline Lupa, or She-Wolf*, a bronze from the beginning of the 5th c. B.C. (Romulus and Remus were added in the 15th c. by Pollaiolo), in the Sala della Lupa; the Views of Rome* by G. Vanvitelli in the passage leading to the Museo del Palazzo dei Conservatori.

*The Museo del Palazzo dei Conservatori** has several remarkable collections: statuary found on the Esquiline Hill, in the Orti Lamiani (note Esquiline Venus* from the early Empire, and a bust of Commodus, depicted as Hercules) and in the Orti Mecenaziani (Marsias Hanging; and a Fighting Hercules); Greek original statuary (torso of an Amazon, from about 510 B.C.; a late-6th-c. B.C. funerary stele with a girl holding a dove; a lion's head from the early-5th c.); Egyptian art; early Christian epigraphs and sarcophagi; and the Castellani collection of vases, among them Greek (7th/6th c. B.C.; the krater of Aristonothos** depicting the Myth of Ulysses and Polyphemus), Etruscan, Corinthian, and Attic examples. Note the Capitoline Tensa*, a cart used to carry images of deities in procession (4th c. B.C.), and various bronzes, among them a colossal head of Constantine.

The *Braccio Nuovo* and the *Museo Nuovo*, opened to house the sculpture unearthed since 1870, are being reorganized to contain the sculptural groups scattered throughout the Musei Capitolini, so as to create proper documentation of the decorative phases of Rome's greatest monuments. It is planned for installation in the former Ostiense Terminal, near Porta S. Paolo (see route 11). These collections include 5th-c. B.C. Greek pediment sculpture, a horse's head from the school of Lysippus, and garden sculpture from Imperial Rome.

The *Pinacoteca Capitolina** is an art gallery with paintings from various schools, dating from the 14th to the 18th c. It was inaugurated by Benedict XIV in 1748. Among the *Emilian* and *Ferrarese painters of the 16th c.*, let us mention F. Francia, Garofalo, Ortolano, and D. Dossi. Among those from the *15th-/16th-c. Venetian school* are G. G. Savoldo, Palma the Elder, Titian, L. Lotto, and D. Tintoretto. From the rest of *17th-c. Europe* come works by A. Van Dyck, P. P. Rubens, and D. Velázquez. Among the *Umbrian, Tuscan, and Emilian painters of the 14th and 15th c.*, we should list the works of M. d'Alba, C. dell'Amatrice, and N. di Bicci. *Italian 17th-c. painting* is exemplified by Caravaggio, Guercino, Domenichino, G. Reni, P. da Cortona, and G. Lanfranco. The Galleria Cini boasts a remarkable collection of fine 18th-c. porcelain*.

The Museo Capitolino, which occupies the entire Palazzo Nuovo, has collections largely made up of ancient Roman copies of Greek statuary; it is arranged according to Neoclassical criteria. In the courtyard is the **equestrian statue of Marcus Aurelius**, brought here from the Piazza del Campidoglio, following its time-consuming

restoration (1981-90); this is an exceedingly rare example of ancient bronze statuary; only a case of mistaken identity saved it from being melted down in the Middle Ages — it was believed to depict the first Christian emperor, Constantine. It became a model for equestrian statuary in the Renaissance. The section devoted to *Eastern cults and monuments in Rome* (statues, reliefs, busts, and inscriptions dedicated to Mithras, Isis, and Serapis) and to sarcophagi in general (see the 2nd-c. sarcophagus of Amendola*) is followed by a thorough array of Hellenistic statuary and copies of originals. Among them are: the Capitoline Venus*, a Roman copy from a Hellenistic original influenced by the Cnidian Venus (3rd c. B.C.); Wounded Amazon*, copy of the masterpiece by Cresilas (5th c. B.C.); Dying Galatian*, Roman copy of a 3rd-c. B.C. original from the school of Pergamon; Amor and Psyche*, from a Hellenistic original (3rd/2nd c. B.C.); and Resting Satyr*, from an original by Praxiteles. Among the *mosaics* is a splendid depiction* of four doves drinking from a vase, from Hadrian's Villa. Among the *portraits*, we may mention 65 busts of emperors and 79 busts of philosophers (note Homer, Cicero, and Lysias), providing a vast sampling of Roman tastes from the 1st to the 3rd c. Among the *bronzes* is a tablet with the "lex de imperio Vespasiani," with which the Roman Senate conferred power on Vespasian.

Antiquarium Comunale. *Not yet properly installed.* This institution was created in 1890 to house the applied and decorative arts unearthed during the urban renovation involved in making Rome Italy's new capital. The collections, largely in storage (a small portion can be viewed in the Casino di Cesare Salvi al Celiu, see route 10), include tomb furnishings from Rome's earliest necropolises (9th/7th c. B.C.), architectural decorations, and votive objects, vases with Etruscan inscriptions, a marble plan of Rome (age of Severus), and the sarcophagus of Crepereia Thryphaena*, with a jointed ivory doll.

S. Maria in Aracoeli** (IV, *A5*). This church was built on the site of a temple to Juno, and takes its name from a supposed apparition of the Virgin Mary to the Emperor Augustus. Construction went on intermittently from the 13th to the 17th c., though it was first consecrated in 1291. The simple brick facade dates from the 13th c. It has a basilican *interior*, and offers a rich sampling of Roman art from the 13th to 18th c. Note the rich carved ceiling (1575), and the 13th-c. Cosmatesque floors. Among the notable works of art are funerary monuments, by A. Bregno and by Donatello; frescoes by Pinturicchio (1486); a tomb, by A. di Cambio; two pulpits by L. and J. di Cosma (about 1200); frescoes by P. Cavallini, by N. Martinelli, and by B. Gozzoli (ca. 1454-58). The Cappella di S. Elena, in the left transept (1605), has a Cosmatesque altar depicting the Emperor Augustus kneeling before the apparition of the Virgin Mary.

Via dei Fori Imperiali (IV, *A-B5-6*). This broad avenue, linking Piazza Venezia to the Colosseum, was built in 1931-33, and involved the destruction of dense and ancient neighborhoods.

Fori Imperiali. These were the Forums built outside the Roman Forum, first by J. Caesar, and by various later emperors.

Foro di Cesare (IV, *A5*). *Open by request, contact the X Ripartizione del Comune.* This Forum was dedicated in 46 B.C., during J. Caesar's lifetime, but was completed by Augustus. It was partly excavated in 1932.

Ss. Cosma e Damiano (IV, *B6*). The facade dates from 1947, but the basilica is much older; note the ancient mosaics* in the triumphal arch and apse.

S. Francesca Romana (IV, *B6*). Built in the 9th c., it boasts a shrine by G. L. Bernini (1649), 12th-c. mosaics*, and a 5th-c. icon*.

Colosseo** (III, *A-B2*; IV, *B6*). *Open, 9-two hours before sunset; Wed. and holidays 9-1.* The Colosseum's real name — *Flavian Amphitheater* — indicates that Flavian emperors built it, as a venue for public spectacles and combat between gladiators and wild beasts. Vespasian began work on it, but Titus inaugurated it in A.D. 80, with games said to have lasted for 100 days. (It is mere legend that Christian martyrs ever died here). Badly damaged by earthquakes, the Colosseum was turned into a fort during the Middle Ages, and a quarry during the Renaissance. Pope Benedict XIV put an end to the destruction of the monument in the 18th c., but efforts at restoration began only in the 19th c. (the most recent large-scale effort began in 1992).

This enormous monument has an elliptical plan. Its NE side is virtually intact, and stands 48.5 m. tall; note the three orders of arcades and the attic above, with windows and square openings from which the "velarium" — a huge cloth that shaded the spectators — was hung. Four entrances led into the arena, which held about 50,000 spectators and measured 80 x 54 m. The podium was reserved for the leading figures of the Empire; beneath the arena were galleries containing the animals and the structures for the spectacles, winched up into place.

Tempio di Venere e Roma (IV, *B6*). Built by Hadrian, from A.D. 121 on was completed by Antoninus Pius.

Arco di Costantino** (IV, *B6*). To commemorate Constantine's victory over Maxentius Rome's Senate and People ordered the construction of this arch in A.D. 315, re-using statues, friezes, and medallions from monuments dating from the reigns of Trajan, Hadrian, and Marcus Aurelius (those created for this arch stand above and on either side of the archway). It has been restored several times, most recently in 1981-87. Recent studies suggest the arch may be far older than was thought, by as much as three centuries.

Domus Aurea (III, *A-B2-3*). *Closed for restoration.* Enclosed by the park of the Colle Oppio (one of the summits of the Esquiline) is the great palace that Nero ordered built following the great fire of Rome in A.D. 64 (the structures that comprised the great imperial home occupied all of what is now the Piazza del Colosseo, where there was an artificial lake); it was later overshadowed by the Baths of Trajan, designed by Apollodorus of Damascus, archetype of all later bath buildings (part of it was the nearby cistern, known as the "Cisterna delle Sette Sale"). The ruins of the imperial palace include a series of huge rooms, partly decorated with stuccoes and paintings, in a style that came to be known as "grotesque."

Foro di Nerva (IV, *A6*). *Open by request, contact the X Ripartizione del Comune.* Begun by Domitian in the narrow space between the nearby *Forum of Peace* (on one exedra of this forum stands the Torre dei Conti; see route 9) and the Forum of Augustus (Foro di Augusto, see below). It was completed in A.D. 97 by Nerva. Note the surviving columns of the portico, topped by a frieze, and the core of the podium of the temple of Minerva.

Foro di Augusto* (IV, *A6*). *Open by request, tel. 69941020; entrance at n. 1 in Piazza del Grillo.* Decreed in 42 B.C. and inaugurated in 2 B.C., this forum mirrors the plan of the nearby Forum of Caesar. At the end is a rusticated enclosure wall, with the ruins of the temple of Mars Ultor (note three surviving trabeated columns). To the left of this is a portico and an exedra, upon which stood in the 15th c. the **House of the Knights of Rhodes*** *(open same hours as above).* Dating from Augustan times is the splendid porticoed atrium. The house is now the side of the *Antiquarium del Foro di Augusto (closed for restoration),* with materials found in the excavations of 1924-32.

Mercati di Traiano* (IV, *A5-6*). *Open, Oct.-Mar., Tue.-Sat., 9-1:30, Sun. 9-1; Apr.-Sep., Tue., Thu. and Sat., 9-6, Fri. and Sun. 9-1:30; closed Mon.; entrance at n. 94 of Via IV Novembre.* The architect Apollodorus of Damascus planned this immense complex, known as Trajan's Market, adjacent to Trajan's Forum (see below); in the Middle Ages, other structures were added (for the Torre delle Milizie, see route 8). The front of the structure curves in a huge exedra; behind it runs the Via Biberatica, lined by shops, and to the left of this there is a huge roofed two-story hall filled with shops (through which you enter from the Via IV Novembre); this was probably a trading room. Recently, an exhibit of architectural decorations from the Forums of Trajan and Augustus was put on display.

Foro di Traiano* (IV, *A5*). *Open same hours as the Mercati di Traiano.* Largest of the Fori Imperiali, it was also built by Apollodorus of Damascus (A.D. 107). You can still see the "Basilica Ulpia" — columns at the center of the excavated area — and **Trajan's column****, commemorating his victory over the Dacians (A.D. 101-103 and 107-108), nearly 40 m. tall, with a spiral frieze depicting episodes from the Dacian Wars. A spiral staircase inside the column leads to the top, where a statue of St. Peter replaced the statue of Trajan, in 1587.

2 The Archeological Area of the Foro Romano and the Palatine Hill

This is the archeological route par excellence, running through the sites that gave birth to the Eternal City. An unbroken succession of basilicas, arches, temples, and imperial residences, enclosed by verdant vegetation, with views straight out of a postcard; there is a great deal of restoration work being carried on here, as well as new digging, with surprising finds from time to time.

Foro Romano** (IV, *A-B5-6*). *Open 9-two hours before sunset; Tue. and holidays 9-1. You enter from Largo Romolo e Remo.* This is the Roman Forum, for centuries the heart of public life in ancient Rome; it was originally a marshy valley set between the Capitoline, Palatine, Viminal, and

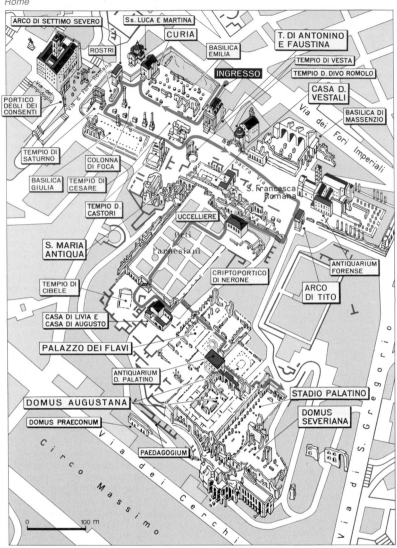

Quirinal hills, and occupied by one of the oldest burial grounds in the city. Its history as a great forum began when construction of Rome's great sewer, the Cloaca Maxima, permitted drainage of the marsh; by the late-7th c. B.C., it reached its standing as Rome's religious, political, commercial, and juridical center. Its final appearance was attained under Caesar and Augustus; earthquakes and barbarians reduced its splendor, and in the High Middle Ages its buildings were used, first as churches and fortresses, and later as quarries, and even as pasture land (Campo Vaccino). Archeological excavation has almost never ceased since the 19th c.

Basilica Emilia. Set at the bottom of the ramp leading into the archeological area, this basilica was founded in 179 B.C. and rebuilt a century later; it was destroyed by a fire when the Goths under Alaric sacked Rome. Trade was conducted here, and justice was administered; the basilica consisted of a large hall divided by rows of columns, with a two-story porch overlooking the Forum. The ruins now visible date from the restoration done by Augustus.

Curia*. According to tradition, Tullius Hostilius founded this building to house the Senate, although the brick building you now see was rebuilt under Diocletian following a fire in A.D. 283.

Inside, the rectangular hall still preserves the low ledges on which the senators sat. Also seen here are the so-called Plutei di Traiano*, temporarily housed here; they once decorated the tribune of the Rostri.

Tomba di Romolo. Standing before the Curia, beneath a modern shelter, is a square slab of black marble ("Lapis Niger"), a monument that the ancient Romans believed covered the tomb of Romulus, founder of the city; it is now thought to have been a sanctuary of the god Vulcan. A stele with a religious inscription dating from the 6th

c. B.C. was found here, believed to be the earliest document in the Latin language. Behind the Curia — and outside of the archeological area — are the churches of *Ss. Luca e Martina*, a domed building by P. da Cortona (1635-64), and S. Giuseppe dei Falegnami; beneath the latter is the entrance to the **Carcere Mamertino** (*open 9-12, 2:30-5*), the state prison in ancient Rome (2nd c. B.C.). It is said — with no historical foundation — that St. Peter was confined in the lower cell, and that he miraculously created a spring of fresh water, with which he baptized his jailers.

Arco di Settimio Severo**. This arch dedicated to Septimius Severus was built in A.D. 203 to honor the emperor and his sons for their victories over the Parthians, and Arabs; on the attic, the name Geta was cancelled after he was murdered by his brother, Caracalla.

Rostri. The high platform to the left of the arch of Septimius Severus was used as a speaking podium; under Caesar it replaced the one that had been decorated in 338 B.C. with the beaks ("rostra") removed from the ships captured at Anzio.

Tempio di Saturno**. This temple to Saturn is one of the oldest in the Forum (dedicated in 497 B.C.); the podium (42 B.C.) and eight Ionic columns still stand. Behind this temple, you will find the *Tempio della Concordia* (367 B.C.), the *Tempio di Vespasiano** (Temple of Vespasian), built by Domitian in A.D. 81 (three Corinthian columns), and the *Portico degli Dei Consenti*, the last monument in Rome devoted to the pagan cult.

Piazza del Foro. Extending before the Rostri, this almost rectangular piazza is paved with travertine; note the *Colonna di Foca*, the last monument erected in the Forum (A.D. 608), and dedicated to a ruler of the Eastern Empire.

Basilica Giulia**. Separated from the Piazza del Foro by the *Via Sacra*, which ran east and west across the Forum (the paving remains; note the seven bases of honorary columns from the reign of Diocletian), this basilica was built by J. Caesar, completed by Augustus, and rebuilt by Diocletian. On the floor of this huge rectangular buildings, there are still several gaming boards, etched into the marble. Along the east side of the complex runs the "*Vicus Tuscus*," a road lined with Etruscan shops, which linked the Roman Forum to the Foro Boario and the earliest port of Rome.

Tempio dei Castori**. Dedicated in 484 B.C. to the Dioscuri (Castor and Pollux), this temple was rebuilt more than once. Note the tall podium, with three elegant trabeated Corinthian columns, from the reign of Tiberius.

S. Maria Antiqua*. This church was built in the 6th c., in part of the Palazzi Imperiali, behind the temple. It is the oldest Christian church in the Forum; abandoned in the 9th c., after terrible earthquakes, it was unearthed in 1900. Before it is the *Oratorio dei Quaranta Martiri*, with 8th-c. frescoes. A remarkable array of paintings* from the high Middle Ages (6th/8th c.) can be seen inside.

Tempio di Cesare. Octavian dedicated this temple to Caesar in A.D. 29, on the site where his grandfather's body had been cremated, marked by the hemicycle with an altar in the center.

Edicola di Giuturna. Near this small building, restored in 1954, a 2nd-c. B.C. basin marks the site of a legendary freshwater spring.

Tempio di Vesta*. Circular in plan, this temple is as it was when rebuilt, under Septimius Severus. In the *house of the Vestals*, behind it, lived the Vestal Virgins, who guarded the sacred fire of Vesta, believed to have been burning since it was first lit by Numa Pompilius, a legendary Sabine king of Rome of the 7th c. B.C. The complex clustered around a huge courtyard, surrounded by a two-story portico. Along the sides of the courtyard were the living quarters of the virgins. Bases and statues commemorated the priestesses that lived here between A.D. 291 and 364.

Regia. This was said to have been the home of Numa Pompilius, second of Rome's seven kings, as well as the home of the chief priest and a sacrarium dedicated to Mars, where sacrifices were also made to other deities.

Tempio di Antonino e Faustina*. This temple was at first dedicated to Faustina alone; after the death of Antoninus Pius (A.D. 161), it was also dedicated to the emperor; in the 7th c., it was transformed into the church of S. Lorenzo in Miranda. Note the Corinthian columns of the pronaos.

To the right of the temple, a patch of green marks the *ancient necropolis* (10th-8th c. B.C.), discovered in 1902 (some material is now in the Antiquarium Forense).

Tempio del Divo Romolo. This temple is said to have been dedicated to Romulus, son of Maxentius, though theories abound as to its real identity. It was certainly undertaken by Maxentius (the portal, flanked by two porphyry columns, frames the original bronze door*; note the lock, one of the oldest in existence) and completed by Constantine. In the 6th c., it was incorporated in the Basilica dei Ss. Cosma e Damiano. Across the Via Sacra, walls and fortifications have been identified, dating from 730 to 540 B.C.

Basilica di Massenzio**. Among the most impressive buildings of ancient Rome, we should list this basilica begun by Maxentius (308) and finished by Constantine. The original front overlooked the Colosseum, and a niche held a statue of its builder, the emperor Maxentius; Constantine built a new facade, overlooking the Via Sacra, in which another niche held a statue of Constantine, which now stands in the courtyard of the Palazzo dei Conservatori.

Antiquarium Forense. Occupying what was once the monastery of S. Francesca Romana (see route 1), this museum contains the tomb furnishings of the archaic necropolis of the Palatine Hill, as well as ancient imported Greek pottery, architectural terracotta decorations, portraits of emperors and reliefs from various basilicas, and detached frescoes from the churches of S. Adriano and S. Maria Antiqua.

Arco di Tito**. This arch, dedicated to Titus, was built at the highest point along the Via Sacra to honor the victories of Vespasian and Titus over the Hebrews in A.D. 71. It was restored by G. Valadier in 1821. In the archway, note the reliefs* showing booty brought back from Jerusalem and Victory crowning Titus.

Palatino** (IV, B-C5-6). It is on this, the Palatine

Hill, high over the oxbow curve of the Tiber, overlooking the valley of the Forum and the first port of Rome, that the city's earliest memories are set. The earliest remains of huts date from the early Iron Age, precisely where tradition has it that Romulus's house was located; this home of the founder of Rome (754 B.C.) was continually restored until Imperial times. During the Republic, the Palatine was the residence of wealthy citizens, and from Augustus on, it was the official residence of the emperor (hence the term, "palace"). In the Middle Ages it declined, as did the Forum; a period of renewed splendor came in the 16th c., when the Farnese built a splendid villa here; that villa was dismantled by relentless archeologists, from the late 19th c. onward.

Uccelliere. These aviaries are all that survive of the Orti Farnesiani, a 16th-c. complex of gardens, by Vignola. Note the fine view of the Forum. The garden behind it, from 1625 the earliest botanical garden in the world, extends over the "Domus Tiberiana," of which nothing can be seen from the surface.

Tempio di Cibele. Built in 204 B.C., this temple was rebuilt under Augustus. Nearby is a remarkable find from the earliest settlement of Rome: three *huts** from the early Iron Age, identified by holes left by the roof poles and drainage ditches.

Casa di Livia*. An inscription found on a water conduit has led scholars to identify this as the home of Livia, wife of Augustus. A typical mansion of the late Republic, this house is famous for the frescoes found in the rooms overlooking the square atrium. Recently unearthed to the south of this Casa di Livia is the **Casa di Augusto***, or home of Augustus, later incorporated into the Palazzo dei Flavi.

Palazzo dei Flavi*. Just before the opening of the *cryptoporticus of Nero* (a gallery that linked the various sections of the Palazzi Imperiali, or Imperial Palaces), you climb up to the emperor's reception area (the "Domus Flavia"), with three halls for religious and political functions, a huge peristyle and triclinium, with two adjacent nymphaeums with fountains, and part of the original marble floor. Beneath this palace, archeologists have found the *Aula Isiaca*, consecrated by Caligula to the cult of Isis; the *House of the Griffins* (late-2nd c. B.C.), decorated with late-Pompeiian-style paintings; and the *"Domus Transitoria"*, residence of Nero prior to the great fire of A.D. 64.

Antiquarium del Palatino. This gallery contains statues unearthed on the Palatine Hill after 1870 (head of Athena Promachos, late-6th c. B.C.; head of Meleager, Flavian copy from an original by Scopas), along with stuccoes and frescoes from various periods.

"Domus Augustana."* Beginning with Domitian, and up until Byzantine times, the Roman emperors lived here; the home was arranged on two or three stories to accommodate the steep slope of the hill toward the Circus Maximus, which it overlooked.

Stadio Palatino*. Domitian ordered the construction of this immense building, surrounded by a portico which features, at the center of the eastern side, the enormous niche of the imperial loggia. The oval enclosure of the race track was probably added by Theodoric.

"Domus Severiana."* Equipped with its own heating system (there are traces near the curve of the Stadium), this building originated as an extension of the "Domus Augustana," at the behest of Septimius Severus. From the terrace, you can enjoy a magnificent view* of the valley of the Circus Maximus below, and the Aventine Hill beyond it.

3 The Corso, Via dei Condotti, and Piazza di Spagna

This is a section of the historical center of Rome, where the sea of automobiles has been replaced by a flood of tourists, flowing along through the posh art galleries, churches built during the Counter Reformation, exclusive shops, and past the buildings of Italy's national government, and then resting by the soothing sounds of some of the loveliest fountains in Rome.

Via del Corso* (I, C-F5-6). At one end of this road is the Vittoriano (see route 1) and at the other, about 1.5 km. away, is the Flaminian obelisk in Piazza del Popolo (see route 5). Running along the ancient Via Flaminia, with street numbers running in opposite directions on either side of the street, the Corso is Rome's traditional street for festivities and processions of illustrious visitors. In the 18th c. it became a magnet for cafes, bookstores, and newspaper offices. It is now partly a pedestrian mall, thronged especially on Saturdays with young people shopping for clothes.

Palazzo Doria Pamphilj* (I, F6). Chief among the aristocratic buildings overlooking the Corso, and one of the very few that are still inhabited by the family that built it, this building's facade* was the work of G. Valvassori (1731-34). The building itself was erected in the 15th c. Valvassori closed off the courtyard to install the private art gallery (see below). Across the Corso, in a small square further along, is the Baroque facade (C. Fontana) of the church of *S. Marcello al Corso*, rebuilt in 1519 by J. Sansovino, A. da Sangallo the Younger, and A. Lippi on the site of a late-4th-c. church.

Galleria Doria Pamphilj**. *Open, Tue., Fri., Sat. and Sun., 10-1. Entrance is at n. 1A in Piazza del Collegio Romano.* This gallery began in 1651 with the collection of Pope Innocent X Pamphilj; marriages and purchases enlarged the collections (especially the dowry brought by Olimpia Aldobrandini), resulting in one of Rome's most notable private collections. The gallery maintains its original layout, with four arms and over 400 paintings, covering the period from the 16th to the 18th c. Among the more noteworthy artists featured here, let us mention: Correggio, Tintoretto, Raphael, L. Lotto, P. Bordone, Titian, Caravaggio, A. Algardi, Guercino, M. Preti, F. Duquesnoy, L. Carracci, G. di Paolo, A. Solario, J. Bassano, Parmigianino, D. Beccafumi, J. van Schorel, J. Brueghel the Elder, P. Brueghel the Elder, D. Velázquez, and G. L. Bernini. The *private apartment**, with sumptuous furnishings that give a good idea of how Roman nobility once lived, contains artworks by F. Lippi, S. del Piombo, L. Lotto, A. Algardi, F. Salviati, and J. Brueghel the

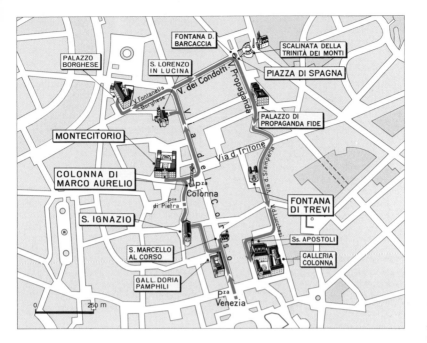

Elder, as well as splendid tapestries from Tournai (mid-15th-c.).

S. Ignazio** (I, F6). Enclosed in the structure of the *Collegio Romano*, this church was built for the Jesuits, beginning in 1582, at the behest of Ignatius of Loyola. It was completed in 1685, though the cupola was added later. The travertine facade and the broad nave, adorned with gilt, frescoes, and marble, are reminiscent of those of the church of the Gesù. Note the renowned fresco of the vault, by A. Pozzo; the remarkable perspective is best seen from the disk of yellow marble in the center of the nave. Many other paintings and frescoes are by Pozzo, and by A. Algardi. Facing the church are the so-called *Burro* (I, E6), architectural oddities by F. Raguzzini (1728).

Palazzo della Borsa (I, E6). This Roman branch of the stock exchange is located in a building that includes the Temple of Hadrian, dedicated by the emperor to his son Antoninus Pius in A.D. 145. Note the 11 tall fluted columns, overlooking Piazza di Pietra.

Piazza Colonna (I, E6). This is the only monumental square along the Via del Corso, with the column of Marcus Aurelius (see below). Surrounding it are: to the north, *Palazzo Chigi** (now head of the executive branch of the Italian government), begun in 1580-86; to the east is the *Galleria Colonna* (early 20th c.); to the west, is the 19th-c. *Palazzo Wedekind*, with a portico incorporating 11 columns unearthed at Veio.

Colonna di Marco Aurelio** (I, E6). The continual frieze that winds along the 28 cylinders of marble that make up this Column to Marcus Aurelius narrate his victories over the German tribes on the Danube. Built in A.D. 180-193, the column is 29.6 m. tall, and is now topped by a bronze statue of St. Paul (1588-89).

Palazzo di Montecitorio* (I, E5-6). This palazzo

overlooks the Piazza di Montecitorio, and the *obelisk of Psamtik II* (early-6th c. B.C.), which Augustus had shipped here from Heliopolis as part of a giant sundial. Pope Pius VI moved it here in 1792. The building was begun in 1653 by G.L. Bernini, who designed the slightly convex facade, and was completed by C. Fontana. Since 1871 it has been the *Chamber of Deputies of the Italian parliament (open during the sessions of the Chamber of Deputies)*.

S. Lorenzo in Lucina (I, D-E6). This church was founded in the 4th c., and was heavily modified over the centuries; it was largely restored to its original form in the 19th and 20th c. Note the 12th-c. bell tower and portico. Inside, the grate on which St. Lawrence supposedly was martyred; bust of G. Fonseca by G.L. Bernini; on the main altar, Cruxifix* by G. Reni.

Palazzo Borghese* (I, D5). This building, which may have been designed by the Vignola, and which was completed by F. Ponzio in 1605-1614, belonged to another famous Roman family. Piazza Borghese is the site of a lively market of used books and old prints.

Via dei Condotti (I, D6). Built in the 16th c., this boutique- and gallery-lined street runs off from Via del Corso, with a view of the Spanish Steps (Scalinata della Trinità dei Monti, see below) and the church of the same name (see route 5) in the distance. It runs over the water conduits of the ancient Aqua Virgo (hence the name) and has notable 17th-/18th-c. palazzi. At n. 86, note the venerable *Caffè Greco*, a centuries-old meeting place for writers and artists.

Piazza di Spagna* (I, D6). This is one of the most charming and theatrical settings of Baroque Rome, and a destination for sightseers from around the world ever since the 16th c. Inns and taverns made way in the 19th c. for photographers and antiques dealers, who still hold sway in the

Rome: Scalinata della Trinità dei Monti

nearby Via Babuino and Via Margutta. At the center of the square is the original **fountain of the Barcaccia** (1629), designed by P. and G. L. Bernini for Pope Urban VIII (note the image of the sun and the bees, symbol of Urban's family, the Barberini), set low in the street because of insufficient water pressure.

Scalinata della Trinità dei Monti** (I, *D6*). F. De Sanctis built this scenic stairway in 1723-26 to bridge the steep incline between the square and the Pincio; in springtime, the stairway, covered with blooming azaleas, frames the church of Trinità dei Monti (see route 5), and is used for fashion presentations. In the building to the right of the stairway is the *Keats-Shelley Memorial Foundation (open, winter, 9-1 and 2:30-5:30; summer, 9-1 and 3-6; closed Sat. and Sun.)*, and on the other side is *Babington's*, the oldest tearoom in Rome.

Palazzo di Propaganda Fide* (I, *D6*; II, *D1-2*). Built on the SE side of Piazza di Spagna, with a simple terracotta facade by G. L. Bernini (1644), it has a more elaborate facade on Via di Propaganda by F. Borromini. Note the column of the Immaculate Conception (Colonna dell'Immacolata Concezione); on 8 December a procession led by the pope terminates here.

S. Andrea delle Fratte (II, *D1-2*). F. Borromini built the bell tower and the drum of the cupola of this church, working on it from 1653 until his death; work was completed by M. De Rossi. Inside, note two angels carved by G.L. Bernini.

Galleria dell'Accademia di S. Luca (II, *D1*). *Open, Mon., Wed., Fri. and last Sun. of each month, 10-1; closed Jul. and Aug.* Set in the 16th-c. *Palazzo Carpegna* (elliptical ramp and interior loggia by F. Borromini), it features works from the 17th-/19th c., by artists from the academy, as well as by others. Among the artists whose work is found here, note: Baciccia, Raphael, J. Bassano, G. P. Pannini, J. Asselijn, A. Van Dyck, and P.P. Rubens.

Fontana di Trevi** (II, *D-E1*). The 18th-c. Trevi fountain is a remarkably successful and theatrical fusion of architecture and sculpture. N. Salvi conceived it as a whirl of reefs, statues, and sprays of water (note, in the central niche, Ocean riding a chariot drawn by seahorses, by P. Bracci);

according to popular belief, tossing a coin in the fountain assures that you will return to Rome.

Basilica dei Ss. Apostoli* (II, *E1*). Note the late-15th-c. portico; although this church was built in the 4th c., it was almost entirely rebuilt in 1702-1708 by C. and F. Fontana. Among the sculptures arranged under the portico, note the 2nd-c. relief with an imperial eagle, and the funerary stele by A. Canova (1807). The rich Baroque interior features a fresco by Baciccia. There are also 15th-c. frescoes* (*open by request, enquire in the sacristy*). To the left of the apse is a monument to Pope Clement XIV, Canova's first project in Rome (1789).

Galleria Colonna* (II, *E1-2*). *Open, Sat., 9-1; closed Aug. Entrance at n. 17 in Via della Pilotta.* This major patrician collection, begun by Girolamo Colonna in 1654-65, is housed in the 18th-c. *Palazzo Colonna.* We should mention works by Bronzino, J. Tintoretto, and Annibale Carracci, as well as works from the 17th c. (F. Albani, Guercino, O. Borgianni) and a series of landscapes by G. Dughet and J. F. van Bloemen. Note the nearby *Museo delle Cere* (wax museum), at the corner of Via IV Novembre (*open, summer, 9-9; winter, 9-8*).

4   The "Quartiere del Rinascimento"

This route runs through the section of Rome that lies around the great oxbow curve in the Tiber; even in the dark centuries of the Middle Ages, this section was inhabited, and beginning in the Renaissance, a few of the most powerful Roman families chose to build their homes here (Palazzo Massimo, Palazzo Farnese, Palazzo Spada). The churches in this section are often linked to the "nations" that they represented (S. Giovanni dei Fiorentini, S. Maria dell'Anima, S. Luigi dei Francesi).

Il Gesù** (I, *F6*). This is the principal church of the Jesuits in Rome (built at the behest of Ignatius of Loyola, founder of the order, who is buried here) and the model for the churches of the Counter-Reformation; it was begun in 1568 to a plan by Vignola, and completed by G. della Porta, who designed the facade in travertine (1571-77). The late-Baroque *interior*, with a single aisle, glitters with marble, bronze, gold, and frescoes. Note the frescoed vault, by Baciccia, and the chapel of St. Ignatius, by A. Pozzo (1696-1700). Adjacent to the church are the *rooms* where St. Ignatius once lived (*open 4-6; Sun. 10-12; entrance at n. 45 in Piazza del Gesù*).

Corso Vittorio Emanuele II (I, *F3-6*). This extension of Via Nazionale toward St. Peter's (S. Pietro), was built from 1883 through the neighborhood known as the "Quartiere del Rinascimento," destroying a dense section of Rome dating from the Middle Ages.

Area Sacra dell'Argentina* (I, *F5*). *Open by request.* The ruins of temples that jut from the center of this chaotic Largo, or square, constitute the most extensive complex from Republican times still visible in Rome; it was unearthed in 1926-29. The circular structure is known as Temple B, possibly dedicated in 101 B.C.; to the right of it is Temple A, built in the mid-3rd c. B.C.; to the left is Temple C, the oldest in the complex, possibly dedicated to the Italic deity Feronia; beyond it is Temple D, from the beginning of the 2nd c. B.C., largely covered by the modern road surface.

S. Andrea della Valle* (I, *F5*). This church too — built from 1591 to 1650, and largely shaped by C. Maderno — follows the model of the Gesù; less, however, in the cupola* (second-tallest in Rome, after St. Peter's) or the facade (C. Rainaldi and C. Fontana, 1656-65), than in the interior, with a complex and impressive body of paintings by G. Lanfranco, Domenichino, and M. Preti.

Palazzo Massimo "alle Colonne"* (I, *F5*). The Massimo family still lives here, and documentation dates the family back to the 10th c., though they claim to trace their roots back to Quintus Fabius Maximus Verrucosus, "Cunctator," who harassed Hannibal's army without risking a pitched battle. The family entrusted B. Peruzzi with rebuilding the entire block after the Sack of Rome in 1527; the Florentine architect built a convex facade with a six-column portico. Note the frescoes on the facade of the adjacent *Palazzo Massimo "Istoriato."*

Farnesina ai Baullari (I, *F4*). Originally called the *Palazzetto Leroy*, after a Breton prelate who began it in 1522-23, the Farnese name was a misnomer caused by the use of the French lilies (also symbol of the Farnese family). Wrongly said to be by Michelangelo, the Renaissance facade overlooks Via de' Baullari and Vicolo dell'Aquila. This is the site of the Museo Barracco.

Museo Barracco*. *Open 9-1:30; Tue. and Thu. also 5-8; Sun. 9-1; closed Mon.* This major collection of sculpture was the product of the efforts in the late 19th c. of the Baron G. Barracco, who emphasized his interest in ancient originals. Note in particular the sphinx of Queen Hatshepsut (1504-1450 B.C.), the head of an *ephebe** (late-6th-c. B.C. original), head of the Kassel Apollo (copy of original by Phydias), mosaic from the Villa of Livia at Prima Porta, and others.

Palazzo della Cancelleria** (I, *F4*). This masterpiece of Renaissance architecture was built between 1485 and 1511-3. Once thought to be the work of Bramante, it is now thought that he worked only on the three-order courtyard*.

Campo de' Fiori (I, *F4*; IV, *A3*). This ancient market maintains the popular flavor of past centuries; one tradition that, happily, has been abandoned here is that of executions (the monument to Giordano Bruno commemorates the Neapolitan philosopher and scientist, burnt at the stake here in 1600).

Palazzo Farnese** (IV, *A3*). Set in the Piazza Farnese, this building's facade (note the magnificent cornice* adorned with the Farnese lilies) overlooks two fountains built with material from the Baths of Caracalla. Construction began in 1517, under the direction of A. da Sangallo the Younger; work continued under Michelangelo (cornice and balcony), and Vignola, and G. della Porta (facade overlooking the Tiber). *The interior is not open to the public*; atrium* and courtyard* are noteworthy; as is the 2nd-floor gallery, frescoed by Annibale and Agostino Carracci, with the help of Domenichino and G. Lanfranco. This building now houses the French Embassy.

Palazzo Spada* (IV, *A3*). Italian government offices occupy part of this 16th-c. building; note the stucco and statuary of facade and courtyard. On the ground floor, note the 9-m. gallery* which F. Borromini succeeded in making appear quite large through tricks of perspective. Inside is also the **Galleria Spada*** (*open 9-2; Sun. 9-1; closed Mon.*), with paintings hung in rows according to the decorative tastes of the 17th c., with the flavor of an aristocratic collection. Canvases are by 16th/17th-c. artists, including: F. Muratori, Baciccia, Guercino, F. Trevisani, M. Cerquozzi, L. Baugin, and O. Borgianni.

Via Giulia* (I, *E-F3-4*; IV, *A2-3*). Now a pedestrian street, with the numbers running in opposite directions on either side, the Via Giulia was designed by Bramante in the early-16th c. for Pope Julius II, as a location for the offices of the main

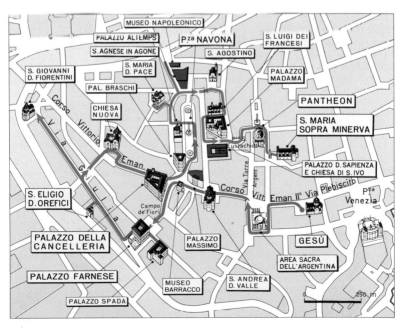

institutions of the papal state. Note the palazzi (*Palazzo Falconieri*, n. 1, overlooking the Lungotevere with a loggia by F. Borromini; *Palazzo Sacchetti*, n. 66, 16th c.) and churches: **S. Eligio degli Orefici** (I, *F4*; IV, *A2*; *open by request, enquire at n. 9 in Via di S. Eligio*), designed by Raphael, and *S. Giovanni dei Fiorentini* (I, *E3*), begun under Leo X in 1519 by J. Sansovino, completed in 1602-1620 by C. Maderno (18th-c. facade, however), who, with F. Borromini, was buried here.

Museo di Criminologia *(Open: Tue., 9-1 and 2:30-6:30; Wed., 9-1; Thu., 2:30-6:30; Fri. and Sat., 9-1; closed Sun., Mon. and Aug.; entrance at n. 29 in Via del Gonfalone)* This museum of criminology is located in the Prigioni, a former prison. The nearby **Oratorio del Gonfalone*** (I, *F3*; *open by request, enquire at n. 1B in the parallel Vicolo della Scimmia*) features a notable Mannerist fresco (1572-75).

Chiesa Nuova* (I, *F4*). This church is properly known as *S. Maria in Vallicella*, and was rebuilt at the behest of St. Philip Neri (1575). Consecrated in 1599; both facade and Baroque interior are reminiscent of the Gesù. Inside, artwork by P. da Cortona, P.P. Rubens (1606-1608), O. Longhi, and F. Barocci. To the left of the church is the **Palazzo dei Filippini*** (1621-66), largely by F. Borromini.

Palazzo Braschi (I, *F4*). This is the last building of a Roman family that produced a number of popes; Pius VI commissioned C. Morelli to plan and build it in 1791; note the magnificent interior staircase, with ancient columns. The rear facade features the famed Pasquino, best-known of Rome's "talking statues"; this damaged Roman statue was used by the people of Rome as a sort of bulletin board for satires and tracts against the authorities. Inside is the **Museo di Roma*** (*closed for restoration*), dedicated to the history of Rome (note the watercolors by E. Roesler Franz), and the *Gipsoteca Tenerani (closed for restoration)*, with copies of sculptures by Tenerani.

Piazza Navona** (I, *E-F4-5*). This remarkable Baroque square takes its size and shape from the Stadium of Domitian, upon which it stands. Ruins of the stadium are found in some of the houses on the north side of the square; they can be seen from the Piazza di Tor Sanguigna. Also, note the crypt under S. Agnese in Agone (see below). This square was a traditional site of festivities and processions, especially during Carnival. At its center is the **Fontana dei Fiumi**** by G. L. Bernini (1651): a circular basin holds a reef supporting an obelisk from the reign of Domitian, as a lion and horse drink thirstily; allegorical statues of the rivers Nile, Ganges, Danube, and Rio de la Plata express, with their gestures, Bernini's contempt for his rival, F. Borromini, who built the nearby church of S. Agnese in Agone.

S. Agnese in Agone* (I, *F4*). This church stands on the site where St. Agnes was said to have been pilloried nude, only to be miraculously covered by her hair; G. and C. Rainaldi began the rebuilding of the church in 1652, and it was completed by F. Borromini who gave it a concave facade, set between two bell towers. Beneath it are the ruins of the Stadium of Domitian.

S. Maria dell'Anima (I, *E4*). This church was built in the early-16th c. atop a chapel in a hospice for German, Dutch, and Flemish pilgrims. The *interior (entrance at n. 20 in Piazza di S. Maria della Pace)* is modelled on German churches; in the presbytery, note painting by G. Romano (1522); to the right, monument to Pope Adrian VI, architecture by B. Peruzzi.

S. Maria della Pace* (I, *E4*). Probably, B. Pontelli undertook the reconstruction of this church around 1480, but P. da Cortona designed the facade**, during the restoration done in 1656. The facade is a theatrical backdrop, closing off the intimate little Piazzetta di S. Maria della Pace. In the arch of the 1st chapel on the right are the Sybils** painted by Raphael in 1514; on the altar of the facing chapel is a fresco by B. Peruzzi. Various chapels and altars were designed by A. da Sangallo the Younger, and C. Maderno. The small adjacent *cloister** (open 10-12 and 4-6; Sun. 9-11; entrance at n. 5 of the Arco della Pace)*, surrounded by a portico surmounted by a loggia, was Bramante's first project in Rome (1500-1504). The nearby *Via dei Coronari* is now a street of antiques dealers.

Palazzo Altemps (I, *E4*). This building (erected in 1471 on medieval foundations) has been under reconstruction since 1984, and is meant to house — in the context of the new Museo Nazionale Romano (see route 8) — the famous and remarkable **Ludovisi collection** of ancient art, assembled by Cardinal Ludovico in the 17th c. to decorate his own villa.

Museo Napoleonico (I, *E4*). *Open, Mon.-Sat., 9-1:30; Sun. 9-1; closed Mon.* Located in Palazzo Primoli, this museum documents — through paintings, statues, miniatures, prints, and manuscripts — the story of the Bonaparte family, related by marriage with the house of Primoli. Beyond the Ponte Umberto I is the massive *Palazzo di Giustizia* (III, *D4*; 1888-1910), or hall of justice, known by the pejorative nickname of "Palazzaccio" for its pompous architecture.

S. Agostino* (I, *E5*). A high stairway leads up to the white facade of this church, enlarged and renovated twice, once in 1479-83 and again in 1756-61 by L. Vanvitelli. Note statues by J. and A. Sansovino, the main altar by G. L. Bernini (1627), a fresco** by Raphael (1512), and an altarpiece** by Caravaggio (1605).

S. Luigi dei Francesi (I, *E5*). This is the church of the French in Rome; begun in 1518 and completed by D. Fontana in 1589. Inside, note paintings by Domenichino, and three masterpieces* by Caravaggio (1597-1602).

Palazzo Madama* (I, *F5*). The "Madama" for whom this building is named was Margaret of Austria, a Medici widow. Built in 1503, and enlarged in the 17th c., this is the Italian Senate building. Its lavish facade overlooks *Corso del Rinascimento* (I, *E-F5*), which was built in 1936-38. In the *Palazzo della Sapienza* (I, *F5*) next door, the university of Rome — known as "La Sapienza" — was located until 1935. Founded by Pope Boniface VIII in 1303, it is now in the Città Universitaria (see route 9). In the courtyard is a masterpiece by F. Borromini, the church of **S. Ivo*** (1642-50), with a remarkable spiral cupola*.

Pantheon** (I, *F5*). This is one of the most impressive monuments of antiquity, as well as a fascinating example of Roman construction techniques.

Built by Marcus Vipsanius Agrippa in 27 B.C., its was completely rebuilt by Hadrian, in A.D. 118-125, though the original inscription remained on the pediment. It became a Christian church in A.D. 608, with the name of S. Maria ad Martyres, and a fortress in the Middle Ages. The bronze coating of the portico was removed in 1625, and used to cast the baldachin of St. Peter's and the cannons of Castel S. Angelo. (Hence the famous Pasquinade, lampooning Pope Urban VIII Barberini, "quod non fecerunt barbari, fecerunt barberini," or "What the barbarians did not do, the Barberini did."). The gates of the pronaos, erected to prevent the marketplace from overflowing into the church, were removed after the Unification of Italy, when the Pantheon became the burial place and shrine of the kings of Italy.

The *pronaos* comprises 16 monolithic Corinthian columns, which support the triangular pediment. The brick *rotunda* stands 43.3 m. tall, and is covered by a cupola of the same diameter. The *interior** is illuminated by only one light source, the 9-m.-diameter oculus; the floor is largely original. Note the lacunar ceiling. Note also frescoes by M. da Forlì and Lorenzetto (commissioned by Raphael for his own tomb); buried here are kings Victor Emmanuel II and Humbert I and queen Margherita.

S. Maria sopra Minerva** (I, *F5-6*). This church overlooks the square of the same name, with a marble elephant, designed by G. L. Bernini, supporting a 6th-c. B.C. Egyptian obelisk, the so-called "Pulcin della Minerva," or "chickadee of the Minerva." The church was built on the ruins of a temple wrongly thought to be dedicated to Minerva Calchydica. The church dates from 1280, was handsomely rebuilt by G. da Sangallo and C. Maderno, and then blighted architecturally in the 19th c. On the simple facade are lines marking (right corner) the level of the floods of the Tiber, from 1422 to 1870. *Inside* are handsome tombs and monuments, by such great artists as A. Romano, M. da Fiesole, Verrocchio, G. da Maiano, G. di Cosma, Michelangelo, A. da Sangallo the Younger, and G. L. Bernini. Note the frescoes* by Filippino Lippi (1488-93). Buried here is Fra' Angelico (1455), with monument by I. da Pisa.

5 From Piazza Barberini to Piazza del Popolo through the Pincio

Among the views that Rome offers, the ones you can enjoy along this route are some of the best known and most photographed. Flashes also pop regularly inside the church of S. Maria del Popolo, an incredible concentration of masterpieces, near the green cupola of the mausoleum of Augustus, and in the glassed-in pavillion of the Ara Pacis Augustae.

Via del Tritone (II, *D1-2*). This street is lined by palazzi from the late-19th c., and runs from Via del Corso to Piazza Barberini, linking the historical center of Rome with the sections around Via Veneto and the train station.

Piazza Barberini (II, *D2*). This square received its name in 1625, when it was surrounded by aristocratic villas with vast grounds. G.L. Bernini

built the *Fontana del Tritone**, the fountain that decorates the center of the square, in 1642-43, for Pope Urban VIII, a Barberini. Also by Bernini, at the corner of Via Veneto (see route 7), is the *Fontana delle Api* (1644), with its motif of bees.

Palazzo Barberini** (II, *D2-3*). Construction began in 1625, under the supervision of C. Maderno, who merged the lines of an urban patrician mansion with the broad green spaces of a villa. Following him, G. L. Bernini added the glassed-in loggia atop the portico and the stairway with a square well, leading up to the Galleria Nazionale d'Arte Antica (see below), while F. Borromini designed the spiral staircase* on the right of the facade.

Galleria Nazionale d'Arte Antica**. *Open 9-2; Sun. 9-1; closed Mon.* This collection of artwork from the 12th to the 18th c. was moved from its original site, in Palazzo Corsini, in 1949, and installed in Palazzo Barberini. Some of the paintings are still in storage; officers' clubs of the Italian army should soon be moved, to make room for them. Among the masterpieces now on display, let us mentions works by such artists as: B. Berlinghieri, the Maestro di Palazzo Venezia, F. Lippi, P. di Cosimo, F. di Giorgio Martini, A. Romano, Perugino, L. da Viterbo, A. del Sarto, D. Beccafumi, Raphael, G. Romano, Bronzino, Tintoretto, Titian, El Greco, Caravaggio, M. Preti, G. Reni, Guercino, H. Holbein, Q. Metsys, G. L. Bernini, G. Bonito, and M. Benefial. Note the great *fresco by P. da Cortona***, and the *Appartamento Barberini*, with lavish Rococo furnishings and remarkable collections of the applied arts.

Via Sistina (II, *C-D2*). This street extends the first stretch of the Strada Felice, which Sixtus V (born Felice Peretti) built between the Trinità dei Monti and S. Maria Maggiore. At n. 24 in Via Crispi, the *Galleria Comunale d'Arte Moderna*, the museum of modern art of the city of Rome (*open, Tue.-Sat., 10-5:30; Sun. 9-12:30; closed Mon.*), was recently installed with works by Italian artists of the 19th and 20th c.

Chiesa della Trinità dei Monti* (II, *C1*). It was begun in 1502 at the order of Louis XII of France, and consecrated in 1585. The interior has some

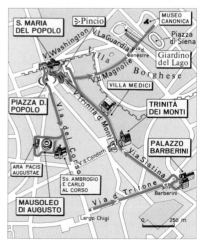

traces of late-Gothic style; note frescoes by D. da Volterra and P. del Vaga. In front of the church is the *Sallustian obelisk*, placed here in the late-18th c. (the hieroglyphics are a Roman imitation of genuine Egyptian hieroglyphics). Note the fine view*.

Villa Medici* (II, *C1*). Built by N. di Baccio Bigio and A. Lippi in 1564-75, this villa was purchased by the Medici and later taken over by the French in 1804, and used as the headquarters of a foundation established in 1666 by Lous XIV to allow French artists to study on Rome. Note the bas-reliefs and statues on the facade overlooking the *gardens (open, Apr.-Jun., Sun., 10-12).*

Pincio (II, *B1*). Along the with the reconstruction of the Piazza del Popolo (see below) G. Valadier organized, at the turn of the 19th c., on the summit of the hill of the Pincio, the park of the same name, with the Neoclassical lodge, or *Casina Valadier.* From the terrace, panoramic view** of Rome, from Monte Mario to the Vatican and the Janiculum.

Villa Borghese* (II, *A-B1-3*). This park, originally the garden of the 17th-c. estate of Cardinal Scipione Borghese (see route 7), is lined with busts of the famous. An early renovation of the estate came in the 18th c., when *Piazza di Siena** was opened (II, *A-B2*; the horse track is still used) and the *Giardino del Lago* (II, *A1-2*) was laid out; from 1800-1830, many of the Neoclassical structures were built, along with the "medieval" fortress, the Fortezzuola, which now houses the *Museo Canonica* (II, *A2; open 9-1:30; Tue. and Thu. also 3-7:30; Sun. 9-1; closed Mon.*), dedicated to the sculptor of that name.

S. Maria del Popolo** (I, *B5*). It was the people of Rome who collected the money to build the first church on this site, between the 11th and 12th c. (hence the name); it was rebuilt in 1475-77, probably by A. Bregno. G. L. Bernini later modified both facade and **interior**, adapting Baroque style to the original structure. Note chapels by A. Bregno, C. Fontana, Raphael, Bernini, and A. Sansovino; among the artwork, an early-13th-c. Byzantine panel*, remarkable stained glass, and frescoes by Pinturicchio; the choir was remodelled by Bramante between 1500 and 1509. The chapel to the left of the *presbytery* contains two masterpieces by Caravaggio (1601-1602). In the *sacristy*, note the marble altar** by A. Bregno and the 14th-c. Siennese Madonna.

Porta del Popolo* (I, *B5*). Replacing the Porta Flaminia in the Aurelian Walls, this gate was, for over a thousand years, the main entrance into Rome for those who arrived from the north. The outer facade was built in 1561-62 by N. di Baccio Bigio, while the inner facade was added by G.L. Bernini in 1655, on the occasion of the arrival of Queen Kristina of Sweden.

Piazza del Popolo* (I, *C5*). Rebuilt at the turn of the 19th c. by G. Valadier, who gave it the two hemicycles, statues, and fountains, this square is focused on the **Flaminian obelisk** (about 1200 B.C., placed here in 1589); also note the twin

churches of *S. Maria dei Miracoli*, built in 1675-81 by C. Rainaldi and C. Fontana, and *S. Maria di Montesanto* (1662-79), upon which G. L. Bernini also worked.

Mausoleo di Augusto** (I, *D5*). *Open by request, contact the X Ripartizione del Comune.* Built in 27 B.C., during Augustus's lifetime, as a mausoleum for the first Roman emperor and his heirs, it fell into neglect in the Middle Ages, and was used as a quarry for marble and stone, and later as a theater. It was rediscovered in 1936-38; only the lower section is part of the ancient structure.

Ara Pacis Augustae** (I, *D5*). *Open 9-1; closed Mon.* To celebrate the peace earned through his victories in Spain and Gaul, Augustus decided to build this Altar of Peace, and inaugurated it in 9 B.C. The reliefs (some originals and some moulded copies) are important doucments of late-1st-c. B.C. Roman art.

Ss. Ambrogio e Carlo al Corso (I, *D5-6*). This is the church of the Lombards in Rome, and was designed in 1610 by O. and M. Longhi the Younger, and completed by P. da Cortona in 1668-69. Inside, note the unusual ambulatory.

6 The Basilica di S. Pietro, or St. Peter's, and the Musei Vaticani

The Vatican once ruled Rome, and it remains a true city within the city, a treasure trove of remarkable sights. Devout pilgrims, the faithful, and the simply curious all consider it the eighth wonder of the world: they arrive in crowds from every corner of the world to pray before the altar of St. Peter's (S. Pietro) and to tour the remarkable Museums, where the most popular attractions are the masterpieces of Michelangelo and Raphael.

Ponte S. Angelo* (I, *E3*). The 'core' of the structure of this bridge dates back to the reign of the emperor Hadrian, when it was known as the "pons Aelius." Still, its modern appearance was the creation of G. L. Bernini, who placed ten statues of angels* on the balustrade. For centuries, this was the main bridge connecting St. Peter's with the center of Rome; note the splendid views of Castel S. Angelo and the dome of St. Peter's (see below).

Castel S. Angelo** (I, *D-E3-4*). This fortress provides an exceptional example of successive stratification and a wide array of utilizations over history (it is now the site of the Museo Nazionale di Castel S. Angelo, see below). It was first built as a mausoleum for Hadrian and his heirs, around A.D. 123. The "Hadrianeum" was transformed into a fortified bridgehead across the Tiber, and it became a papal fortress, linked to the Vatican by the little bridge known as the "passetto." Here pontiffs took refuge in cases of extreme danger (popular uprisings, invasions, etc.). Much of the structure is ancient and original; note the copy of the statue of the angel (after which the castle is named) sheathing its sword.

Museo Nazionale di Castel S. Angelo*. *Open 9-5.* Of note, both for the collections of ceramics, arms, and paintings, and for the history of the building, originally the mausoleum of the Emperor Hadrian. The *ambulatory* around the Roman walls features the surviving decorations from Hadrian's

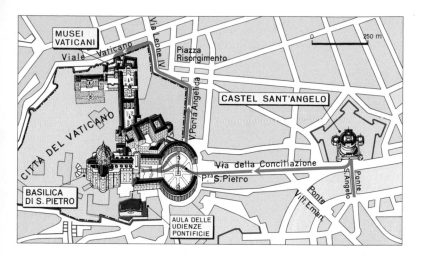

time. The *spiral ramp** leading to the room of imperial urns dates from the same period. Note the five architectural models of the castle, over time. The *Sale di Clemente VIII* feature frescoes by P. del Vaga, as well as Renaissance sculptures; while the *Sale di Clemente VII* were decorated by N. di Liberatore, L. Signorelli, and C. Crivelli. Note stuccoes and frescoes by G. da Udine and G. Siciolante (1543; *Loggia di Paolo III*, attr. to A. da Sangallo the Younger). The rooms that overlook the *"giretto" of Pius IV* (view*) were papal court residences, and later prison cells; the *Loggia di Giulio II*, overlooking Ponte S. Angelo (view*), is attributed to G. da Sangallo. The *Appartamento di Paolo III** (1542-49), former residence of the pope, is a fine example of Roman Mannerism. The *chamber of the Adrianeo*, or Hadrianeum, features a frieze with mythological scenes and ancient Roman monuments. The *Cagliostra*, with art by L. Luzi, was once a prison cell for Cagliostro, famous 18th-c. Italian adventurer and impostor. The *Sala delle Colonne* has 13th/18th-c sculpture. The *Appartamento del Vicecastellano* features paintings of the castle itself. From the *terrace*, at the foot of the statue of the angel (1752), excellent view**.

Museo delle Anime del Purgatorio (I, *D4*). *Open 7-11 and 5-7; closed Sun.*. Located in the church of the Sacro Cuore del Suffragio, this Museum of the Souls of Purgatory is devoted to the manifestations of the dead, around the turn of the 20th c.

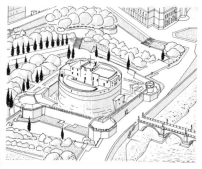

Rome: Castel S. Angelo

Via della Conciliazione (I, *E2-3*). The first plan for this boulevard — designed as a monumental accessway to St. Peter's — dates from 1936 (M. Piacentini and A. Spaccarelli); it was completed in 1950. It resulted in the destruction of a lovely Renaissance and medieval neighborhood (you can sense from the nearby Borgo Pio and Borgo Vittorio what it looked like). Also note the church of *S. Maria in Traspontina* (I, *D-E3*; begun in 1566, completed in 1668); note the dome, built lower than planned so as not to interfere with cannon fire from Castel S. Angelo Also note *Palazzo Torlonia* (I, *E2*; 1500-1520).

Città del Vaticano (I, *C-E1-2*). The Vatican City is located on the Colle Vaticano in the western part of Rome; it is an independent state, established formally in 1929. The pope comprises all three branches of government (legislative, executive, and judiciary). The state has its own currency and stamps, a daily newspaper ("L'Osservatore Romano"), and its own police force (including the Swiss Guards). The election of a new pope is usually held in the Sistine Chapel, by cardinals who are "locked in" (hence the term "conclave"). The election is announced by a puff of white smoke; deadlocks are announced by puffs of black smoke.

Enclosed within the Vatican walls, but with enclaves in Rome proper (in fact, the four basilicas, the Palazzo del Laterano, the Palazzo della Cancelleria, and the Palazzo di Propaganda Fide, as well as the Pope's summer residence at Castel Gandolfo, all enjoy the privilege of extraterritoriality), the Vatican City, which covers 0.44 sq. km., dates from the 9th c. You can visit the famed Musei Vaticani, but you can also tour the *Vatican City* itself (*open by request, enquire in the Ufficio Informazioni Pellegrini e Turisti, tel. 69884341*) as well as the Vatican Gardens.

Piazza S. Pietro** (I, *D-E2*). In 1656-67, G. L. Bernini designed a four-fold colonnade, in two great hemicycles, surmounted by 140 statues, so as to embrace the square (St. Peter's Square) standing before the basilica, creating a solemn vestibule (when seen from the circular stone set between the obelisk and the fountains, the colonnade appears to have only a single row of columns). At the center stands the **Vatican obelisk** (25.5 m. tall); it was brought from Alexandria under Caligula and set in the Circus where St. Peter met his martyrdom; it was then moved here by

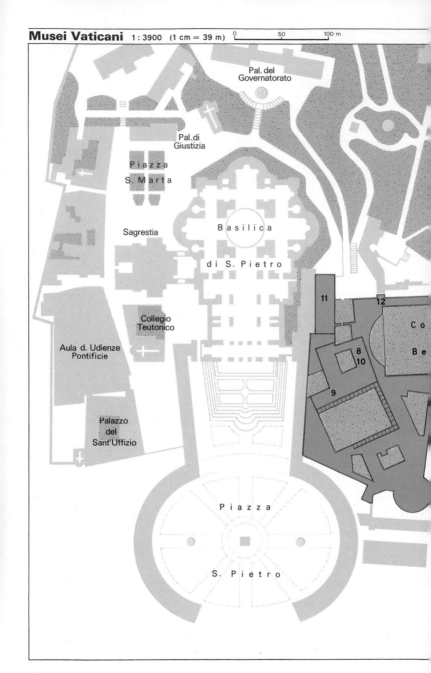

Pal. del
Governatorato

Pal. di
Giustizia

P i a z z a
S. M a r t a

Sagrestia

B a s i l i c a

d i S. P i e t r o

11   12

Collegio
Teutonico   8
10

Aula d. Udienze   9
Pontificie

Palazzo
del
Sant'Uffizio

P i a z z a

S. P i e t r o

D. Fontana. (An anecdote tells of how, as the obelisk was being raised, it seemed the ropes were about to give; one Ligurian sailor had the presence of mind to cry out, "Water on the ropes!" The obelisk was thus saved; a grateful pope gave the sailor a monopoly on all palm leaves sold in Rome for a certain time thereafter). The fountains are by C. Maderno (right; 1613) and C. Fontana (left; 1677).

Basilica di S. Pietro** (I, *E1*). St. Peter's Cathedral is the heart of the Catholic religion,

throughout the world, and is certainly the largest and most impressive church in Christendom (it covers a total surface area of 22,067 sq. m.), is 218 m. in length, and stands, from the ground to the cross atop the dome, 136 m. tall). It is said to stand on the tomb of St. Peter.

In 1452 Pope Nicholas V decided to rebuild the original basilica, founded by the emperor Constantine around A.D. 320. Work did not begin until 1506, under Pope Julius II, with designs by Bramante, and later, by Raphael, B. Peruzzi, and Antonio da Sangallo the Younger. The shape of the floor plans wavered between a Greek and Latin

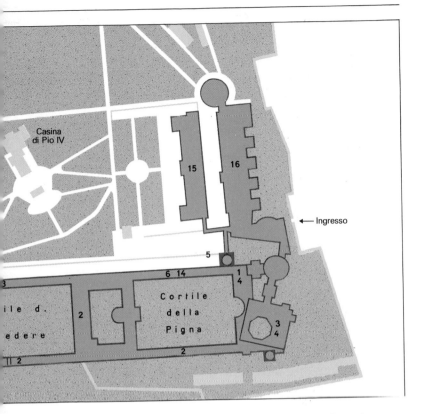

Casina di Pio IV

15

16

← Ingresso

5

3

6 14

1 4

ile d.

edere

2

Cortile della Pigna

2

3 4

II 2

2

cross. Michelangelo, put in charge in 1546, envisioned a Greek cross topped by a cupola, set in the center of a square; this plan was followed by plans by Vignola, P. Ligorio, G. della Porta, and D. Fontana. At the orders of Pope Paul V, C. Maderno returned to the Latin cross plan, extending the nave of the church with three additional chapels on each aisle; he also built the facade. On 18 November 1626, Pope Urban VIII consecrated the church.

Facade. The three-level stairway leads up to the facade, with eight great columns, topped by a trabeation and balustrade; atop this are statues of Christ, John the Baptist, and the Apostles (except St. Peter), and two clocks. The *central balcony* over the portico is where the pope gives Rome his benediction. The **cupola****, designed by Michelangelo, was built by G. della Porta and D. Fontana. Five arches lead into the *portico*; five bronze doors lead into the church.

Interior. The best idea of this vast interior can be had from the papal altar. *Nave.* Along the floor, markers show the sizes of other churches. Note the statue of St. Peter, by A. di Cambio (13th c.). The luminous **cupola**** stands upon four pillars (in the niches, 17th-c. statues of saints). Beneath the cupola is the papal altar, covered by the great **baldachin*** (1633) cast by Bernini with bronze pried from the Pantheon; the bees, symbols of the Barberini family, on the columns, are reminders of Pope Urban VIII. In the Confessione, 99 perpetual lamps mark the "tomb of St. Peter." *Right aisle.* In the first chapel, note

the **Pietà****, the masterpiece of a young Michelangelo (1498-99). Note the wooden Crucifix by P. Cavallini, the wrought-iron gates by F. Borromini, and the gilded ciborium by Bernini (1674). *Right transept.* Monument to Clement XIII*, by A. Canova (1784-92) *Apse.* Remarkable bronze statue of the throne of St. Peter, by Bernini (1656-65), with a gilt stucco "Gloria." In the niches on either side, monuments to Urban VIII* by Bernini (right; 1627-47) and Paul III* by G. della Porta (left; 1551-75). *Left aisle.* The tomb of Pius VII by B. Thorvaldsen (1823) is the only work by a Protestant artist in St. Peter's. Tomb of Innocent VIII* by Pollaiolo (1498). Note the monument to the Stuarts, by A. Canova. The *baptistery* features a porphyry basin that may have been taken from the tomb of Hadrian.

Museo Storico Artistico-Tesoro di S. Pietro. *Open: winter, 9-5:30; summer, 9-6:30; entrance from the corridor of the sacristy.* This museum is all that remains of the papal treasury, plundered repeatedly but still rich in masterpieces. Note the column upon which Christ purportedly rested in the temple of Jerusalem; a Byzantine dalmatic*, long (and wrongly) said to belong to Charlemagne; a 6th-c. cross*; a ciborium by Donatello, the monument to Pope Sixtus IV* by Pollaiolo; and candelabra by B. Cellini; the sarcophagus of Junius Bassus* (4th c.).

Sacre Grotte Vaticane. *Open: winter, 7-5; summer, 7-6; entrance from the cupola, near the pillar of S. Longino.* These grottoes lie beneath the nave, and contain the tombs of popes (note the tomb of Boniface VIII*, in part by Arnolfo di Cambio); there are also chapels, mosaics, and reliefs. You may also tour the *Necropoli Precostantiniana** *(open by request, contact the Ufficio Scavi della Fabbrica di S. Pietro, tel. 69885318)*, a pagan cemetery with later Christian tombs.

Climb up to the **Cupola di S. Pietro**, or the Dome of St. Peter's*. *Open: winter, 8-5; summer, 8-6; entrance from the right side of the basilica.* An elevator will take you up to the terrace (view* of the main dome and the two side domes, added by Vignola for decorative effect); two stairways lead up to the circular corridor (view of the mosaics inside the cupola) and to the lantern, where a spiral staircase leads to the outer gallery: panoramic view**.

Palazzi Vaticani (I, *D1*). Since 1378 this has been the residence of the popes, who previously lived in the Lateran. These buildings were erected under Nicholas V, and continued under Sixtus IV (Sistine Chapel), Julius II (Cortile del Belvedere), Leo X (Logge di S. Damaso), Paul III (Cappella Paolina and Sala Regia), Sixtus V (buildings on Piazza S. Pietro), and Urban VIII (Scala Regia). As the art collections grew, sections were made into museums (Palazzetto di Innocenzo VIII), and various additions and renovations were made.

Musei Vaticani** (I, *D1*). *Open 8:45-1; closed Sun., except for the last Sun. of each month, 9-1. Entrance from the Viale Vaticano.* The transfer of the Museo Storico Vaticano into the Palazzo Lateranense in 1987 was the most recent of the various transitions that have affected the collections assembled by different popes since the Renaissance. The opening of the Museo Pio-Clementino was the first instance of a museum housed in the Palazzi Vaticani: Gregory XVI founded the Museo Gregoriano Egizio and the Museo Gregoriano Etrusco; Leo XIII opened the Borgia Apartments to the public, while Pius XI, John XXIII, and Paul VI helped to set up the picture gallery and collections once displayed in the Palazzo Laterano.

Museo Gregoriano Egizio*. This Egyptian museum was opened in 1839 by Gregory XVI; it has been newly arranged, and features steles and statues, dating from Ancient Egypt to the 6th c. A.D. The collections included mummies, sarcophagi, jewelry, vases, and reliefs (including Assyrian reliefs, with possible traces of the great fire that destroyed Nineveh).

Cortile della Pigna. The great statue of a pine cone that gives its name to this courtyard stands on a stairway beneath the great niche designed by Bramante, along with the larger courtyard (1587-88).

Museo Chiaramonti. The museum still follows the arrangement by A. Canova, who laid out the collections of ancient statuary and inscriptions for Pope Pius VII. The *Museo Chiaramonti* proper comprises numerous Roman copies of Greek works, and a few originals. The *Galleria Lapidaria* (open by request, tel. 69883041) includes the collection begun by Clement XIV. The *Braccio Nuovo* is a neoclassical gallery; among the noteworthy works are a **statue of Augustus***, a Wounded Amazon (5th c. B.C.); the Nile*; and others.

Museo Pio-Clementino*. The Greek and Roman sculptures in this museum came from the collections of Clement XIV, with additions made by Pius VI. Among them are outstanding masterpieces

of ancient art: the sarcophagus of Lucius Cornelius Scipio Barbatus, consul in 298 B.C.; the **Apoxyomenos***, sole surviving copy of a renowned bronze by Lysippus (340-320 a.C.); the **Belvedere Apollo***, from a 4th-c. B.C. Greek original; the renowned **Laocoön****, copy attributed to the sculptors Agesander, Athenodorus, and Polydorus of Rhodes, found in the Domus Aurea in 1506 — this statue served as an inspiration to Michelangelo and the Mannerists; a **Hermes**, the Meleager*, a Roman copy of a 4th-c. B.C. Greek statue; a remarkable Apollo Saurochthonos*, based on a bronze original by Praxiteles; the Barberini candelabra* (2nd c.); the **Cnidian Venus***, a Roman copy of a renowned statue by Praxiteles (4th c. B.C.); the **torso of the Belvedere****; the Jove of Otrìcoli*; the 4th-c. sarcophagi of St. Helena** (mother of Constantine) and Constantina** (daughter of that emperor). By A. Canova are the statues of Perseus* (1800) and of two wrestlers. Behind the Apoxyomenos is the *stairway by Bramante*, built around the turn of the 16th c.

Museo Gregoriano Etrusco*. Founded by Pope Gregory XVI in 1837, this museum of Etruscology is one of the earliest. The halls are arranged as they were in the 19th c., are in some cases still decorated with 16th-c. art. Tomb furnishings and ceramics document the earliest Etruscan and Latin Iron Age (9th/8th c. B.C.). From the Regolini-Galassi tomb** in Cervèteri come splendid jewelry and bronzes (mid-7th-c. B.C.); from the same period dates the Calabresi urn. The Mars of Todi* (late-5th-c. B.C.) was donated to a public figure of Celtic descent, as the inscription in Umbrian language along the edge of the armor indicates. Note also 6th-c. B.C. Attic vases, the B. Guglielmi collection (7th/5th c. B.C.), the G. Guglielmi collection of Greek and Etruscan ceramics, and the Falcioni collection. Also from Vulci come remarkable items of ancient jewelry as well as an ancient Roman doll, with moving limbs, and remarkable glasswork*.

Galleria degli Arazzi. Following the *Sala della Biga* (this room, lined with Carrara marble, is named after the biga, or ancient two-wheeled chariot,* reassembled in the late-18th c.) and the *Galleria dei Candelabri* (named for the candle holders under each arch), which feature materials from classical antiquity, this room contains tapestries* woven in the 16th c. at Brussels by P.van Aelst, based on cartoons by students of Raphael. The following 120-m.-long *Galleria delle Carte Geografiche* is decorated with wall paintings of maps, by A. Danti in 1580-83; note the accuracy, as well as the central location of Rome in each map.

Stanze di Raffaello**. *The great flow of tourists makes it necessary to see the rooms in reverse order.* Pope Julius II, in 1508, decided to decorate several of the rooms in the apartments of Nicholas V. At the suggestion of Bramante, he contacted Perugino, Sodoma, B. Peruzzi, and L. Lotto, but finally settled on Raphael, who worked there until 1517. The *Sala di Costantino* was then completed in 1525 by G. Romano and by G. F. Penni. Among the three rooms, or "stanze," particular note should be given, in the *Stanza di Eliodoro**, to the **Mass of Bolsena****, depicting a miracle of 1263, and the **Liberation of St. Peter,****

renowned for its light effects, with reference to the imprisonment of Pope Leo X during the battle of Ravenna; in the *Stanza della Segnatura***, note the **Disputation of the Sacrament****, and, on the facing wall, the **School of Athens**** with Plato and Aristotle and the great minds of Antiquity, as well as **Parnassus***. In the *Stanza dell'Incendio*, note the Fire of Borgo*, executed by G. Romano and G. F. Penni, to cartoons by Raphael.

Loggia di Raffaello*. *Open by request, tel. 69883041.* This is part of the Loggias of S. Damaso, commissioned by Julius II in 1512, first by Bramante, and then continued by Raphael; they were finished under Leo X in 1518. Designed by Raphael but completed by his pupils, the frescoes depict scenes from the Old and New Testaments. The stuccoes and grotesques are by G. da Udine.

Cappella di Niccolò V*. You enter this chapel from the Sala di Costantino through the Sala dei Chiaroscuri; it is entirely decorated with frescoes** by Fra' di Beato Angelico (1448 and 1450).

Appartamento Borgia*. These rooms take their name from Pope Alexander VI Borgia, who lived here and had it painted by Pinturicchio and students (1492-95). Of the six rooms — occupied by part of the Collezione d'Arte Religiosa Moderna (see below) — three are in the Torre Borgia, three are in the Palazzo di Niccolò V. In particular, note the Sala dei Santi**, masterpiece by Pinturicchio, and the Sala dei Misteri della Fede*, with students (in one lunette, note the portrait of Alexander VI).

Collezione d'Arte Religiosa Moderna *. This collection of modern religious art was inaugurated in 1973 by Pope Paul VI; it occupies 55 halls and offers a thorough repertory of all major world schools.

Cappella Sistina**. The Sistine Chapel is the official private chapel of the pope. Here, the conclaves in which the popes are elected are held. It may fairly be called the most famous room in the Musei Vaticani, because of the remarkable frescoes that adorn it. It was built in 1475-81 under Sixtus IV; it was during that initial phase of construction that the marble screen* dividing the rectangular chapel into two areas was built, as was as the railing around the choir; both are by M. da Fiesole, G. Dalmata, and A. Bregno. The frescoes were executed in three different periods: those on the side walls and facing the altar were done in 1481-83, those in the ceiling and in the lunettes above the windows date from 1508-1512, and those on the far wall are from 1536-41. *Side walls and facing the altar.* This decorative complex was executed by the leading Tuscan artists of the late-15th c., for Pope Sixtus IV, and includes Stories from the Life of Moses (note work by S. Botticelli and L. Signorelli) and Stories from the Life of Jesus (again, work by Botticelli, as well as work by D. Ghirlandaio and Perugino); between the windows, portraits of popes, by Ghirlandaio, Botticelli, C. Rosselli, and Fra' Diamante. *Ceiling.* It is decorated with the **frescoes**** (restored 1981-90) that Michelangelo began for Julius II on 10 May 1508 and completed on 31 October 1512, creating, upon a surface of some 800 sq. m. a mixture of architectural, plastic, and pictorial elements that — at that time — was unprecedented. The work is organized on three levels: in the central zone, Stories from Genesis (note the Creation of Adam**) and Stories from the Old Testament; between the panel, note the pairs of "ignudi," ** or nude figures, supporting medallions; beneath them, monumental figures of Prophets and Sibyls; in the lunettes over the windows and in the gores of the ceiling, Ancestors of Christ. *Wall over the altar.* Here, Michelangelo frescoed for Pope Paul III the **Last Judgement**** (1536-41), the painter's interpretation of the apocalyptic "Dies Irae," or Day of Wrath. The restoration carried out in 1990-93 to recreate the ancient splendor of color eliminated the work done by D. da Volterra, who — at the order of Pope Pius IV — had covered the nudity of many figures, earning the scornful nickname of "braghettone," or "britches."

Biblioteca Apostolica Vaticana. This library is located just beyond the *Sala delle Nozze Aldobrandine*, named after a splendid fresco (Nozze di Alessandro Magno e Rossane, or Wedding of Alexander the Great and Roxanne), possibly from the age of Augustus, and unearthed in 1605; and the little *Museo Sacro*, established by Pope Benedict XIV in 1756. The library was founded by Sixtus IV in 1475, and moved to its present location by Sixtus V; note the Salone Sistino*, decorated with fine frescoes. Later, the *Museo Profano* was founded, to hold the Etruscan, Roman, and medieval collections assembled by popes Clement XIII and Pius VI.

Pinacoteca Vaticana**. It was also Pope Pius VI who founded this remarkable collection, housed in the palazzo that Pius XI built in 1932; the collection includes the paintings from the Palazzi Pontifici, following the Treaty of Tolentino (the finest works found their way to France, and only 77 were recovered, through the efforts of A. Canova). Among the masterpieces of Italian art here, note works by Margaritone d'Arezzo, B. Daddi, Giotto and helpers, P. Lorenzetti, S. Martini, G. di Paolo, Saccotta, G. da Fabriano, Fra' Angelico, Fl Lippi, M. da Forlì, E. de' Roberti, C. Crivelli, Perugino, Raphael, Leonardo da Vinci, Giovanni Bellini, Titian, P. Bordone, Domenichino, Caravaggio, G. Reni, G. M. Crespi, and F. Mancini. Also, examples of Byzantine, Slavic, Greek, and Russian sacred art.

Museo Gregoriano Profano*. This museum was first housed in the Palazzo Lateranense, where Pope Gregory XVI displayed, in 1844, Greek and Roman materials, found mainly in digs conducted in the Papal State; in the late-19th c., a collection of pagan epigraphs was added. The section of original Greek statuary includes the stele of Palestrita* (an Attic relief from the mid-5th c. B.C.), numerous fragments of sculptures* from the Parthenon in Athens, and a head of Athena similar to works from Magna Grecia (mid-5th c. B.C.). In the section of Roman copies and versions of Greek originals, note the statue of Marsyas*, a statue of Sophocles, and a relief showing Menander and the Commedia. The section of 1st- and early-2nd-c. Roman sculpture includes a relief with personifications of the Etruscan cities of Tarquinia, Vulci, and Vetulonia, and the Altar of Vicomagistri* (about A.D. 30-40). The section of sarcophagi includes items from the 2nd to the 4th c. In the section of 2nd- and 3rd-c.

Roman sculpture, a torso of a statue, possibly depicting Trajan or Hadrian, stands out.

Museo Pio Cristiano. This museum, too, founded by Pius IX in 1854, was originally located in the Palazzo Lateranense, and was transferred here by John XXIII. Remarkable architectural and sculptural exhibits, along with mosaics (note an inscription, on the stele of Abercius, dating from the reign of Marcus Aurelius, the earliest Christian reference to Mass).

Museo Missionario-Etnologico. This museum offers a description of religious, social, and economic life in countries outside Europe, and exhibits of Christian art in the missionary context.

Museo Storico Vaticano. This is a separate section of the same museum, located in the Palazzo Lateranense (see route 9); it illustrates the history of the Papal State through carriages, litters, and antique automobiles.

7 The "Quartiere delle Regioni", the museums of Villa Borghese, the Foro Italico

This route runs through a part of Rome that should really, by this point, be considered part of the center, even though it does lie outside the walls; it offers a very pleasant stroll through a world of art. It ranges from ancient, pre-Christian times (Museo Etrusco di Villa Giulia), to the collections of the 17th c. (Museo Borghese and Galleria Borghese), and on to the most recent trends in contemporary art (collections of the Galleria Nazionale d'Arte Moderna). And the Foro Italico offers an interesting view of the architecture that developed under Fascism.

Via Veneto (II, *B-D2-3*). This is, by definition, the street of luxury hotels in Rome, as well as of cafes and the sites of the famous "Dolce Vita."

At the beginning of the climb up this sloping street, a double-staircase marks the church of *S. Maria della Concezione* (II, *D2*), also known as the *Church of the Capuchins* (Chiesa dei Cappuccini), built in 1626-30; you will find paintings by G. Reni, G. delle Notti, and Caravaggio here. Beneath the church is the *cemetery of the Capuchins* (Cimitero dei Cappuccini), comprising five chapels lined with skeletons and bones. In the second curve of Via Veneto stands *Palazzo Boncompagni* (II, *C3*; 1886-90), also known as *Palazzo Margherita*, and now the site of the U.S. embassy.

Casino dell'Aurora (II, *C2*). *Open by request, enquire at n. 44 in Via Ludovisi.* This is all that survives of the 17th-c. Villa Ludovisi, devoured by the growing city in the late-19th c. Note frescoes by Guercino in the Sala dell'Aurora, by A. Circignani in the Sala del Camino and, perhaps, by Caravaggio in a room on the ground floor. This villa once held the famous collezione Ludovisi collection of ancient marble statues, now in the Museo Nazionale Romano.

Porta Pinciana (II, *B2*). This simple arch of travertine, flanked by two cylindrical towers, was built by the Byzantine general Belisarius during a siege by the Goths; it runs through the Aurelian Walls (see route 10). Beyond this gate is an entrance to Villa Borghese (see route 5).

Museo e Galleria Borghese** (II, *A3*). *Open: Museo, 9-2; Sun. 9-1; closed Mon.* Set in the Casino Borghese that was built at the orders of the Cardinal Scipione in 1608-1617 (arch. F. Ponzio), this has been described as the "queen of all private collections on earth"; it is divided into a remarkable collection of materials from classical times, and a gallery of paintings, along with major pieces of Baroque and neoclassical sculpture.

The *Museo Borghese* was founded in 1608, when works from old St. Peter's were added to the collection of the Cardinal. What we see today is only part of a once far vaster collection; a great deal was given by Camillo Borghese to France under Napoleon, and now constitutes the core of the Louvre's classical collection. Among the works from Roman times, still arranged according to 19th-c. tastes, one should note: a mosaic with scenes of hunting in the Circus and gladiatorial fights (310-320), the Athena Parthenos copied from the original, by Phidias, and others. Also, note the masterpieces by Antonio Canova (Statue of Pauline Borghese**, sister of Napoleon) and G. L. Bernini (David with Sling*, in which the face is a self-portrait of the sculptor; Apollo and Daphne**, 1624).

The *Galleria Borghese* too originated from a collection belonging to Cardinal Scipione, to which were added other collections, chief among them that of Olimpia Aldobrandini. Among the paintings (moved in 1994, because of construction and renovation, to the former Hospice of S. Michele a Ripa Grande: see route 12) note those by: S. Botticelli, Fra' Bartolomeo, Raphael, Pinturicchio, A. del Sarto, L. Cranach the Elder, Bronzino, G. G. Savoldo, L. Lotto, Palma the Elder, Domenichino, P. da Cortona, Caravaggio, G. L. Bernini, P. P. Rubens, A. Sacchi, J. Bassano, Ortolano, F. Francia, Correggio, D. Dossi, Titian, Giovanni Bellini, A. da Messina, V. Carpaccio, and P. Veronese.

Giardino Zoologico (II, *A2-3*). *Open: winter, 9-1 and 2:30-5:30; summer, 9-1 and 2:30-6:30.* This zoo was founded in 1911 in the park of Villa Borghese; inside is the *Museo Civico di Zoologia (open the same hours as the Giardino Zoologico).*

Galleria Nazionale d'Arte Moderna* (I, *A6*). *Open 9-2; Sun. 9-1; closed Mon.; undergoing partial restoration.* This national gallery of modern art is housed in the *Palazzo delle Belle Arti* built in Valle Giulia by C. Bazzani for the Esposizione Internazionale of 1911.

Originally (1883) intended for Italian artists only, the gallery opened its doors to non-Italian artists in 1909; at the same time, the collection was installed in this Palazzo, which was later enlarged. This is one of the largest collections of Italian painting, sculpture, and graphics of the 19th and 20th c.

The *left wing* of the building is devoted to the 19th c., featuring works by such Neoclassicists and Romantics as A. Appiani, F. Podesti, A. Canova, and Fr. Hayez; among the Tuscan Macchiaioli, we should cite G. Fattori, S. Lega, and T. Signorini, while among the Neapolitans, are D. Morelli, M. Cammarano, and V. Gemito; Social Realism is represented by T. Patini and V. Vela, Divisionism by G. Previati and G. Pellizza; note the sculpture M. Rosso and Roman landscapists (G. De Nittis, G. Boldini; among the non-Italians, note works by G. Courbet, E. Degas, C. Monet, V. Van Gogh, and A. Rodin. In the *right wing*, the 20th c. begins with symbolist works by G. Klimt and G. De Chirico, continuing with U. Boccioni, G. Balla, G. Severini, G. Braque, C. Carrà, A. Modigliani, G. Morandi, and P. Mondrian; between the wars, work was created by such artists as M. Marini, G. Manzù, M. Sironi, A. Savinio, M. Campigli, M. Mafai, F. Pirandello, P. Fazzini, F. De Pisis, M. Maccari, M. Reggiani, and C. Badiali; from

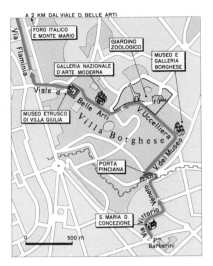

A 2 KM DAL VIALE D. BELLE ARTI

FORO ITALICO E MONTE MARIO
GIARDINO ZOOLOGICO
MUSEO E GALLERIA BORGHESE
GALLERIA NAZIONALE D'ARTE MODERNA
Viale d. Belle Arti
MUSEO ETRUSCO DI VILLA GIULIA
Villa Borghese
V. Uccelliera
V. del Museo
PORTA PINCIANA
V. Veneto
S. MARIA D. CONCEZIONE
V. Vittorio
0   500 m
P.za Barberini

the 1950s and '60s, work by Italians such as L. Fontana, A. Burri, E. Morlotti, E. Vedova, and A. Giacometti, and such non-Italians as D. Spoerri, J. Pollock, H. Moore, and H. Hartung.

Villa Giulia* (I, A5-6). Built for Julius III by B. Ammannati, G. Vasari, and Vignola nel 1551-55, this villa presents a series of three courtyards, with a loggia* by Ammannati (note the signature on the right pillar) and a nymphaeum, with fountain.

Museo Etrusco di Villa Giulia**. *Open, Tue. and Thu.-Sat., 9-2, Wed., 9-7; Sun., 9-1; closed Mon.* The material of this remarkable Etruscan museum is arranged by place of discovery, including Latium, Umbria, and southern Etruria. The museum was founded in 1889; the Etruscan and Faliscan civilizations are documented, both through locally produced items and items imported, especially from Greece. From the digs done at "Pyrgi" come three gold laminae** with Etruscan and Punic inscriptions. Dating from 1916 and 1939 the finds, at Vejo, of clay statues (Goddess with Child*; Herakles) from the temple of Portonaccio, masterpieces of Etruscan sculpture of the 6th c. B.C, while from the tombs of Cervèteri come the famous sarcophagus of the Married Couple (Sposi)* (ca. 530 B.C.) and Greek vases of the 7th/6th c. B.C. From the area around Vejo comes the Chigi oenochoe* (640-625 B.C.), and from Castro come bronze chariot handles* (530-520 B.C.). The Castellani collection, acquired in 1919, contains a vast and complete array of Greek and Etrusco-Italic ceramics from the 8th to the 1st c. B.C., as well as glasswork and goldwork; the Pesciotti collection comprises bronze cineraria, bucchero pottery*, and amphorae. Note the decorations* from the Etrusco-Italic temple of "Falerii Veteres" (now Civita Castellana), dating from the 6th to 1st c. B.C. From Palestrina come the furnishings** of the Barberini and Bernardini tombs, including ivory, gold, silver, and bronze objects of Syrian and Cypriot production (mid-7th-c. B.C.). Lastly, the Ficoroni cist* dates from the end of the 4th c. B.C..

Via Flaminia (I, A-D5). This road runs along the route of the old Via Flaminia, inaugurated in 223-219 B.C. by the censor Caius Flaminius; it ran to "Ariminum" (modern-day Rimini). At the center of the green strip that separates it from the parallel Viale Tiziano is the church of **S. Andrea**, built by the Vignola. The *Stadio Flaminio* (1957-59) and the *Palazzetto dello Sport* (1956-58) are sports facilities built for the 1960 Olympics, held in Rome. The Via Flaminia crosses the Tiber on the *Ponte Milvio*, or Milvian Bridge, built in wood in the 3rd c. B.C. and rebuilt in tufa stone in 109 B.C.; it was rebuilt by G. Valadier, however (1805).

Villa "ad Gallinas Albas". Not open for sightseeing. When this villa belonged to Livia, the wife of Augustus, it was in the open countryside. It is now on the edge of the Roman suburb, or Borgata di Prima Porta, along the Via Flaminia. The villa, where the famous statue of Augustus of Prima Porta was found in 1863-64 (now in the Musei Vaticani), featured remarkable frescoes and a bath facility.

Foro Italico. Set at the foot of Monte Mario, this is an athletic complex built at the behest of Mussolini, to celebrate the fusion of sports and Fascist ideology; work began in 1928, but it was not finished until after WWII. An obelisk that was originally built in honor of Mussolini, and named after him, marks the entrance; behind it is the Viale del Foro Italico, a broad avenue decorated by mosaic pavement and punctuated by blocks commemorating important dates in the history of the Italian Empire and Republic, leading to the *Stadio dei Marmi* (1932), with its low tiers decorated with statues of athletes, and to the *Stadio Olimpico*, built in 1950-53 and roofed over in 1990.

On the slopes of Monte Mario you will also find *Villa Madama** (*not open to the public*), designed by Raphael in 1518, and once the home of Madama Margherita di Parma (hence the name), and the Osservatorio Astronomico e Meteorologico, with the adjoining *Museo Astronomico e Copernicano (open, Wed and Sat 9:30-1)*. There is also a military museum adjacent to the *Istituto Storico e di Cultura dell'Arma del Genio (open by appointment, tel. 3725446)*, founded in 1906 at the behest of Victor Emmanuel III.

8 The Quirinale, Porta Pia, and the Museo Nazionale Romano

This route runs through the NE section of Rome, within the walled perimeter, past a nerve center of the Italian government (Palazzo del Quirinale) and two churches central to the famed rivalry between two great architects, Bernini and Borromini (churches of S. Andrea and S. Carlino); the route then leads to a trove of Roman antiquities, namely the baths of Diocletian and the limitless collections of the Museo Nazionale Romano. A short detour out through the gate of Porta Pia, where an Italian army of unification once stormed the walls of Rome (1870); here you will see the ancient complex of S. Agnese Fuori le Mura, which contains the famous Mausoleo di S. Costanza.

Largo Magnanapoli (II, F2). Overlooking this square, on the right, is the church of *S. Caterina a Magnanapoli* (1628-41), in the shadow of the 13th-c. **Torre delle Milizie**, the largest surviving baronial tower in Rome, built on the site of the Mercati di Traiano (Trajan's Market, see route 1). To the left, atop a stairway, is the Baroque church of *Ss. Domenico e Sisto*, begun in 1569 and completed around 1650.

Palazzo Pallavicini Rospigliosi (II, E2). Begun by F. Ponzio in 1605 and completed by C. Maderno in 1616, this palazzo now belongs to the Pallavicini family. The *Casino Pallavicini (open, the 1st of each month, 10-12 and 3-5)* was frescoed by G. Reni in 1614, with his famous Aurora* (Dawn). The *Galleria Pallavicini (not open to the public)* is one of the leading galleries in Rome, and

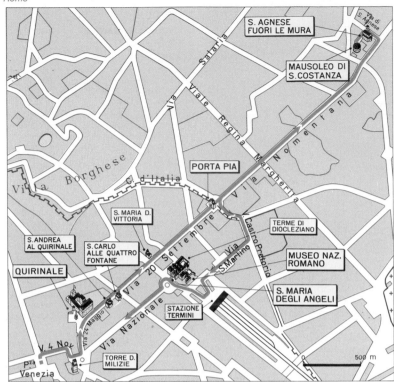

contains work by P.Brill, P.da Cortona, L.Lotto, L.Giordano, Giampietrino, P.P. Rubens, Tintoretto, and D. Velázquez.

Piazza del Quirinale* (II, *E2*). Overlooking one of the finest views of Rome, this square was given its current appearance in the 18th c., when the **fountain of Montecavallo**, in the center of the square, was built, with the ancient Roman replica of a 5th-c. B.C. statue of the Dioscuri* (Roman replica of a Greek original, 5th c. B.C.); also note the obelisk, from the mausoleum of Augustus. The *Palazzo della Consulta* (F.Fuga, 1732-34), now houses Italy's highest court, the Corte Costituzionale.

Palazzo del Quirinale* (II, *D-E2*). This building complex has always belonged to the powerful in Rome: it was a summer residence of the popes, then the Savoy royal family, and, since 1946, the president of Italy. Begun in 1573, a remarkable series of architects worked on it: M. Longhi the Elder, O. Mascherino, D. Fontana, F. Ponzio, C. Maderno, and G. L. Bernini. The *interior (open, Sun., 9-12)* is noteworthy, especially the great stairway, by Ponzio, and the Cappella Paolina, built by Maderno to rival in size the Sistine Chapel. Fine art abounds; the gardens still maintain their 16th-c. design.

S. Andrea al Quirinale* (II, *E2*). Overlooking Via del Quirinale with a curving pronaos, this church is one of the masterpieces of G.L. Bernini (1658). Inside, note the lavish Baroque style.

S. Carlo alle Quattro Fontane* (II, *D3*). F. Borromini worked all his life on this church, especially on the facade, which he left unfinished at his death in 1667; he built the interior to the size of a pier of the cupola of St. Peter's. Note the odd adjacent little cloister*, with an octagonal plan (1635-36). The *intersection of the Quattro Fontane* is the crossroads of two main papal roads.

S. Maria della Vittoria* (II, *D3*). Built by C. Maderno (1608-1620), the interior of this church is a sumptuous example of Baroque decoration. Among artwork by Domenichino, of particular note, in the left transept, is the famous marble statue of St. Theresa in ecstasy** by G. L. Bernini (1646). Across the road is the *Fontana del Mosè* (D. Fontana, 1587), and nearby is the late-16th-c. church of *S. Bernardo alle Terme*.

Museo Numismatico della Zecca Italiana (II, *C-D4*). *Open by appointment, tel. 85083699.* This numismatic museum of the Italian mint is located in the building of the Ministry of the Treasury, and features medals from as far back as the 15th c., as well as a collection of coins from the Kingdom of Italy, the Italian Republic, and the various sovereign states of the Italian peninsula.

Orti Sallustiani (II, *C4*). *Open by request, contact the Soprintendenza Archeologica di Roma.* These gardens stand at the center of Piazza Sallustio, sunk 14 m. down, a result of the gradual rise of the level of the surrounding ground. The ruins that you can still see are those of a circular hall, once part of a larger building, originally owned by Julius Caesar, later owned by Tiberius, and thereafter part of the imperial estates. It was heavily damaged by the Goths under Alaric.

Porta Pia** (II, *B-C5*). Built in 1561-64, at the end of the Strada Pia, to a design by Michelangelo, this is the only Roman gate to face inward toward the city (the outer facade was added in 1853-

69). Its prominent place in Italian history dates from 1870 when the Aurelian walls were "breached" on 20 September, and Papal Rome fell to the army of the Risorgimento; there is a commemorative column, topped by a statue of Victory. In the courtyard is the *Museo Storico dei Bersaglieri (open, Tue., Thu. and Sat., 9-1)* dedicated to the sharpshooters of the Italian army.

Via Nomentana (II, *A-B5-6*). This broad tree-lined boulevard follows the route of an ancient Roman road that ran toward "Nomentum," modern-day Mentana. An Ionic porch on the right marks the entrance to the grounds of the 19th-c. *Villa Torlonia* (II, *A6*), once the private residence of Benito Mussolini. The grounds were made a public park in 1978, and feature a number of interesting buildings erected in the last two centuries.

S. Agnese Fuori le Mura*. From the Via Nomentana you can see the 15th-c. campanile of this church, first built in the 4th c. From the courtyard of n. 349, a staircase takes you inside: note the handsome columns, the wooden ceiling, and the statue of the saint by N. Cordier. The 7th-c. mosaic in the apse is a particularly fine piece of Byzantine art. You can also tour the *catacombs of S. Agnese (open 9-12 and 4-6; closed Sun. morn. and Tue. aft.)*, which are well preserved.

Mausoleo di S. Costanza**. After touring the complex of S. Agnese, you may turn to this major early Christian monument, built in the early-4th c. as a mausoleum for the daughters of Constantine, Constance and Helena. It was soon turned into a baptistery and, later (13th c.), a church. The round ambulatory is adorned with exceedingly fine 4th-c. mosaics**.

Piazza dei Cinquecento (II, *D4*). This square, named in honor of those who died in the battle of Dògali, was rebuilt in 1950 after the completion of the *Stazione Centrale di Termini*, which was begun in 1937 in view of the Universal Exposition, planned for 1942 and rendered impossible by WWII. To the left of the entrance to the station are notable ruins of the so-called *Servian walls*, supposedly built by Servius Tullius, one of the legendary seven kings of Rome.

Museo Nazionale Romano** (II, *D-E4*). *Only the ground floor is open, 9-1:30; Sun. 9-1; closed Mon.* This museum is under renovation, and its collections — drawn from digs done after 1870 and from the former Museo Kircheriano — will be shown in three different locations. The Baths of Diocletian will house the Epigraphic Department (see below), Palazzo Altemps will display the historical collections (including the renowned Ludovisi collection, see route 4), and the **Palazzo dell'ex-Collegio Massimo**, will house the main core of the collections.

In the century-old Palazzo dell'ex-Collegio Massimo, the five sections open to the public illustrate five aspects of Roman artistic culture between the 1st c. B.C. and the late Empire. A series of portraits (note the **statue of Augustus from the Via Labicana**) are used to show the shifts in style from the late Republic to the Augustan age. Also in the collections you will find notable ancient bronzes and the Ludovisi throne** (5th c. B.C.). Among the *statuary* are copies of Greek works used to decorate imperi-

al residences and public buildings, as well as official busts and portraits. Also noteworthy are the so-called ships of Nemi*, bronze decorations from floating platforms once anchored before the villa of Caligula. Two villas, one **"ad Gallinas Albas,"**** the other at Castel di Guido along the Via Aurelia, are the sources of many of the most fascinating paintings and mosaics, along with the **frescoes** and stuccoes **from the Villa della Farnesina***, an Augustan complex overlooking the Tiber. The *numismatic section* analyzes coins in economic terms, ranging from trade routes to depressions and slumps; the *jewelry section* features some items found with the mummy of Grottarossa.

Terme di Diocleziano** (II, *D4*). The Baths of Diocletian offer an important example of structures put to continual use; built as a public facility between A.D. 298 and 306, they were then used as a church in the 16th c., and finally, in 1889, they were adopted as the site of the Museo Nazionale Romano. The renovation underway since 1983 calls for the Baths to hold the *Epigraphic Department (inauguration planned for 1997)*, with 10,000 inscriptions; this section will illustrate the political, social, and religious development of Rome from the 1st c. B.C. to the late empire.

S. Maria degli Angeli** (II, *D4*). You enter from *Piazza della Repubblica*. This church was built by Michelangelo, who adapted the ancient "tepidarium" and adjacent rooms. In the mid-18th c., L. Vanvitelli shifted the church's orientation considerably, restructuring the main interior nave to accommodate the altar pieces* taken from St. Peter's, which still adorn the walls (note the ones by P. Batoni and P. Subleyras). In the right arm, note the funerary monuments to V. E. Orlando, Admiral P. Thaon di Revel (both by P. Canonica), and Marshall A. Diaz, all Italian leaders in WWI.

Sala della Minerva (II, *D4*). *Open 10-1 and 3-6.* This is another room of the enormous complex of the baths of Diocletian; it was converted into a planetarium in 1928, and in 1991 the statues that once adorned the baths of ancient Rome were placed on display here.

Via Nazionale (II, *D-E2-4*). When this street was built, in the 19th c., it was meant to be the monumental entrance to Rome, along with Piazza dell'Esedra, for those who arrived in the new

Rome: Mausoleo di S. Costanza

capital of Italy by train; it is now a major artery linking the Stazione Termini with Piazza Venezia. Midway along it, a stairway runs down to the church of *S. Vitale* (II, *E3*), consecrated in A.D. 412, and rebuilt more than once. Note the nearby *Palazzo delle Esposizioni* (P. Piacentini, 1877-83). *Palazzo della Banca d'Italia* (II, *E-F2*) is a noteworthy work of late-19th-c. Roman eclecticism.

9 Between the Viminal Hill, the Esquiline Hill, and the Lateran

You can tour one early-Christian basilica after another here; though often restored and even rebuilt, the churches that you will see along this route in SE section of Rome (within the walls) are often of exceedingly ancient origin. Surrounding them is a section of Rome built in the late-19th c., to accommodate the civil servants of Italy's new capital, on ground previously occupied by villas and verdant countryside.

Via Cavour (II, *E-F2-4*). This avenue was built in the late-19th c. to ease traffic between the Forums and the Stazione Termini over the hills of Quirinal and Esquiline; the *Torre dei Conti* was built in the early 13th c. (II, *F2*).

S. Pietro in Vincoli* (II, *F3*). First built in the 5th c., and still standing amidst an exceedingly ancient residential neighborhood, this church was restored in the late-15th c., and again in the early-18th c. by F. Fontana. It was named for the chains ("vincula") of St. Peter, subject of a miracle involving St. Leo I the Great, in the 5th c. In the transept is the mausoleum of Pope Julius II*, only partly completed by Michelangelo; of the statues that he planned and partly executed, only the famous **Moses**** is still here (1514-16?; the Prisoners are now in Paris and Florence), though he worked on the statues of Lia and Rachel. In the confession, or shrine, note two bronze doors, attributed to Caradosso, behind which are the supposed chains of the saint; also, in the 2nd altar on the left, note the 7th-c. mosaic.

S. Martino ai Monti (II, *F4*). The *towers of the Capocci and the Graziani* which stands the Piazza di S. Martino ai Monti are medieval, while the basilica of S. Martino ai Monti dates from the 5th c., although it was rebuilt to some extent after 1636. Surviving from the original structure are a set of columns and a hall (*open by request, contact the sacristan*) that dates back to the 3rd c.; note the Roman and medieval architectural fragments, bits of 9th-c. frescoes, and a 6th-c. mosaic.

S. Prassede* (II, *F4*). This basilica was founded in A.D. 489, and features two of the finest pieces of Byzantine art in Rome. In the 9th-c. *Cappella di S. Zenone***, note the portal, floor, and mosaics; the triumphal arch bears fine 9th-c. mosaics*, as does the apse (less certain).

S. Maria Maggiore** (II, *E-F4*). This is one of the four patriarchal basilicas, and the most important Roman church dedicated to the Virgin Mary.

Legend has it that the church was first built on the site of a miraculous snowfall in August of A.D. 356. Various renovations were done throughout the centuries, and in the 18th c. F. Fuga gave the church a new facade; note the 14th-c. bell tower. In the loggia over the portico are late-13th-c. mosaics by F. Rusuti.

The **interior*** still appears much as the ancient basilica must have. The *nave* still has part of the 12th-c. floor and a magnificent 16th-c. wooden ceiling; tradition has it that the gold used to gild it was the first to arrive from the New World. Above the trabeation are 5th-c. mosaic panels*, extensively restored in 1593; in the triumphal arch, exquisite mosaics* from the same century. Before the papal altar, with baldachin by Fuga, is the confession, with relics, supposedly of the crib of Bethlehem. The huge *apse* is covered with an equally vast mosaic* by J. Torriti (1295). Note the paintings, frescoes, and sculptures by P. Cavallini, G. Guerra and C. Nebbia, A. di Cambio, G. di Cosma, the Cavalier d'Arpino, and G. Reni. Various chapels were designed by D. Fontana, F. Ponzio, and Michelangelo.

Piazza dell'Esquilino (II, *E4*). This is the terminus of the long avenue of the Strada Felice (see route 5); in 1587, Sixtus V erected here one of the obelisks that were originally located at the entrance of the mausoleum of Augustus. The nearby church of *S. Pudenziana* dates from the 4th c., as you can see from the mosaic* in the apse.

Via Merulana (II, *F4*; III, *A-B4*). Pope Gregory XIII built this road, in part along an ancient route, linking the basilicas of S. Maria Maggiore and S. Giovanni in Laterano (St. John Lateran); it was completed by Sixtus V. At the beginning of this chaotic thoroughfare (one of the main arteries in the late-19th-c. quarter of the Esquiline), slightly to one side, is the *Arco di Gallieno* (II, *F5*), originally the Porta Esquilina in the Servian walls, but rebuilt in Augustan times, and dedicated to the emperor Gallienus in A.D. 262.

Museo Nazionale d'Arte Orientale (II, *F4*). *Open 9-2; Sun. 9-1; closed Mon.* Located in *Palazzo Brancaccio* (1886-1912), this museum of eastern art was established in 1957, and comprises collections of materials from digs conducted by the Istituto per il Medio e l'Estremo Oriente (IsMEO), in Iran, Pakistan, and Afghanistan. The museum is divided into sections that document the history and culture of the enormous territory stretching from Iran to Japan. The Iranian section ranges from the 4th millennium B.C. to the 8th c. A.D.; note the finds from Afghanistan (Ghazni, 11th/12th c.). There is much material from ancient Gandhara, scrolls and statues from Southeast Asia, and Chinese bronzes (14th c. B.C.-1st c. A.D.), and Japanese and Korean bronzes and pottery.

Piazza di S. Giovanni in Laterano (III, *B-C4-5*). The *Obelisco Lateranense***, or Lateran obelisk, which stands in the center of this square, is the tallest (31 m.) and oldest (it stood before the temple of Amon in Thebes as early as 1500 B.C., and it was erected in the Circus Maximus in A.D. 357) obelisk still standing in Rome; it was placed here as the crowning touch to the renovation of this area in the late-16th c. by Sixtus V.

Palazzo Lateranense (III, *C4-5*). Built by D. Fontana in 1586-89, this building was later used as a hospital and to house the museums that were subsequently moved into the Vatican; it enjoys the privilege of extraterritoriality, and is not subject to Italian law. It now houses the *Museo Storico Vaticano (open, 1st Sun. of each month, 8:45-1)*, comprising the Papal Apartment (note frescoes by Mannerist painters) and the Historical Museum proper. It was damaged by a terrorist bombing in June 1993.

Battistero Lateranense* (III, *C4*). The emperor

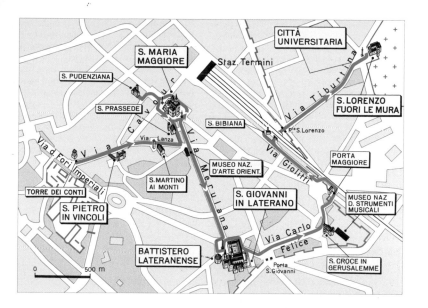

Constantine had this baptistery built, on the site of a 1st-c. villa and 2nd-c. baths, in the Cappella di S Rufina note the 5th-c. mosaics; in the C. di S.Venanzio note the 7th-c.mosaic decorations of the apse and triumphal arch; and in the C. di S. Giovanni Evangelista note the late-12th-c. bronze doors.

S. Giovanni in Laterano** (III, *C4-5*). This, the Cathedral of Rome, better known as St. John Lateran, was built between 313 and 318 by order of Constantine; it was renovated repeatedly, especially by D. Fontana, and by F. Borromini. The facade, surmounted by 15 statues, is by A. Galilei (1732-35); in the portico, the central doorway has bronze doors* taken from the Roman Curia. The **interior*** has five aisles and a vast transept; stretching over the nave is a 16th-c. wooden ceiling.* Statues of apostles date from the 18th c. An ogival tabernacle dates from 1367, decorated with frescoes from the same period, later retouched by A. Romano and F. di Lorenzo; it houses the relics of the supposed heads of Saints Peter and Paul. Note sculptures, frescoes, and mosaics by A. Bregno, I. da Pisa, Giotto, A. di Cambio, J. Torriti, J. da Camerino, and the Cavalier d'Arpino. From the transept, you can enter the *museum* of the basilica. The adjacent *cloister*** is by the Vassalletto (1215-32); along the walls are fragments of architecture and sculpture for the ancient basilica, and Roman and early Christian archeological finds.

Scala Santa (III, *C5*). Sixtus V asked D. Fontana to build this structure, which covers what is said to have been a set of steps that Jesus climbed prior to his trial. Even now, the faithful climb it on their knees, to peer through grates at the Sancta Sanctorum*, a chapel decorated with 13th-c. mosaics and frescoes. At n. 145 in nearby Via Tasso, note the *Museo Storico della Lotta di Liberazione di Roma (open, Tue., Thu. and Fri., 4-7; Sat. and Sun., 9:30-12:30; closed Aug.)*, or Museum of the Liberation of Rome. This was the headquarters of the SS; in Via Aleardi, note the *Casino Massimo Lancellotti (open, Tue., Thu. and Sun., 9-12 and 2-4)* with frescoes by the Nazareni, German painters of the early 19th c.

S. Croce in Gerusalemme* (III, *B6*). The earliest documentation of a place of Christian worship here dates from the early 4th c., when Helena, mother of Constantine, consecrated a room in her own home to Christian worship; the church, however, was rebuilt in the form of a basilica in 1144-45 and, again, in 1743 by Pope Benedict XIV. The church is now largely 18th c. in style, though the floors are Cosmatesque; the apse has a fresco attributed to A. Romano (1492 ca.); the tomb of Cardinal F. Quiñones* is by J. Sansovino (1536). In the Cappella di S. Elena, at the foot of the right aisle, is a mosaic* in the vault, by M. da Forlì or B. Peruzzi (1510 ca.).

Museo degli Strumenti Musicali (III, *B6*). Open 9-1:30; closed Sun. This museum of musical instruments has collections dating from antiquity to the 20th c., largely from the collection of Evan Gorga; note the famous Barberini harp* and a pianoforte* built by Bartolomeo Cristofori in 1722.

Porta Maggiore* (III, *B6*). This gate is the beginning of the Via Prenestina and the Via Labicana; it made use of arches of aqueducts built by Caligula in A.D. 38, and completed by Claudius in A.D. 52. On Piazzale Labicano, near the central archway, is the *tomb of Eurisax* (1st c. B.C.), a baker, as one can see from the frieze showing the production and sale of bread. Nearby, next to the earthen bank of the railroad, is the entrance to the **Basilica di Porta Maggiore** *(open by request)*, a 1st-c. subterranean sanctuary, decorated with very fine stuccoes*, discovered in 1917.

Tempio di Minerva Medica (III, *A6*). Scholars still debate the function of this ten-sided hall, built in the 4th c.; it is named for a statue of the goddess Minerva, with a serpent, found here. Further along is the church of *S.Bibiana* (II,*F6*), founded in early-Christian times and rebuilt in 1624-26 by G.L. Bernini (note his statue of the saint* on the main altar).

S. Lorenzo Fuori le Mura**. This basilica is one of the four patriarchal churches, and is the result of a fusion of two churches. Built around 330, it was ordered to be built by Constantine as a shrine for the burial of the relics of Christian martyrs.

Bombed and damaged on 19 July 1943, it was restored; in particular, note the portico*, which supports a trabeation adorned with frieze, and the Romanesque campanile.

Inside, you can readily perceive the sections of the two different churches. The ambos and paschal candelabra in the nave are by the Cosmati (13th c.). The presbytery is older: la trabeation* dates from the 4th c., the mosaic on the triumphal arch, from the 6th c., and the ciborium, from 1148. The adjacent Romanesque *cloister* dates from the late-12th c.

Città Universitaria (II, *C-D6*). This giant campus, designed by M. Piacentini, was built in the 1930s, and enlarged in the 1960s.

10 The "Passeggiata Archeologica" and the churches of the Celio, or Caelian Hill

Little known to the majority of tourists, who venture no further than the immense Baths of Caracalla, this southern section of Rome is full of astonishing sights. The first surprise is the vast expanse of greenery, a relic of the grounds of the numerous villas that were found here until 1870, when the new capital of Italy began to grow rapidly; you will also note a seemingly endless succession of churches, largely of ancient origin, made more appealing by the bucolic setting.

Via di S. Gregorio (III, *B-C2*). Running past the Palatine, where the ruins of *Nero's aqueduct*** can be seen; also note the *obelisk of Axum*, brought from Ethiopia in 1937, and the *offices of the FAO.*

S. Gregorio Magno (III, *C2*). Largely Baroque, this church features a miraculous fresco, which supposedly once spoke to the saint; in the nearby *oratory of S. Andrea*, frescoes by G. Reni, Domenichino, Pomarancio, and G. Lanfranco.

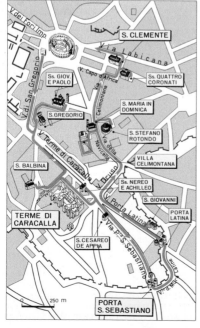

Ss. Giovanni e Paolo* (III, *C2*). In the late-4th c., the first nucleus of this church was built on the site of the house of the two martyrs; later destroyed by the Goths under Alaric and by Norman invaders, it was rebuilt by Pope Paschal II in the late-12th c.; from that period date the Romanesque abse, the buttresses along the side, and the architraved portico on the face, with adjacent campanile* — note embedded ceramic basins. The rest of the church is later in style. Underneath the church (*open by request, contact the Soprintendenza Archeologica di Roma*) are rooms dating from classical antiquity, used in the 2nd c. by one of the earliest Christian communities in Rome (the nymphaeum features a 3rd-c. fresco).

Terme di Caracalla** (III, *D-E2*). *Open 9-4; Sat.-Sun., until 1.* The impressive ruins of the Baths of Caracalla, inaugurated by that emperor in A.D. 217, and which continued to operate until the 6th c., are the most notable monument in the Passeggiata Archeologica, or Archeological Promenade, established between 1887 and 1914 to protect the Roman ruins thus far excavated; this praiseworthy project was perverted, under Fascism, to transform the walkways into arteries for automobile traffic toward the EUR section. The baths, which occupied a total area of 330 sq. m., presented the traditional succession of frigidarium-tepidarium-calidarium, and had not only gymnasiums, but also libraries.

S. Balbina (III, *D2*). This church, first consecrated in A.D. 595, was restored in 1927-30; inside, note the Crucifixion, possibly by M. da Fiesole and G. Dalmata.

Ss. Nereo e Achilleo (III, *D3*). Founded by Pope Leo III on the site of a 4th-c. church; note the mosaics in the triumphal arch. Other sections of the church, including the main altar and the bishop's throne, date from the 12th c.

Via di Porta S. Sebastiano* (III, *E-F3-4*). This street, lined by low walls, runs through one of the last green areas to survive the burst of construction of the past 120 years; unfortunately it has a became a fast-traffic artery linking the Colosseum with the Via Appia Antica. The church of *S. Cesareo de Appia** (III, *E3; closed for restoration*) features a late-16th-c. ceiling and a 2nd-c. mosaic. Near the end of the road is the entrance to the **tomb of the Scipioni** (*closed for restoration*), a powerful Roman family buried here from the beginning of the 3rd c. to 139 B.C.

Porta S. Sebastiano** (III, *F4*). Before this gate stands the *Arch of Drusus* (211-216) which supported the aqueduct that conveyed water to the Baths of Caracalla; it is surely one of the most monumental gates in the walls of Aurelian (built against the barbarian onslaughts; 3rd c.A.D., rebuilt in the 5th c. by Honorius, and restored in the 6th c. by the Byzantine eunuch general Belisarius). It takes its name from the basilica, toward which the Roman Appian Way, or Via Appia, led. Inside the gate is the *Museo delle Mura di Roma (open 9:30-2; Tue., Thu. and Sat. also 4-7; Sun. 9-1, closed Mon.)*, which illustrates the history of the Roman walls. This museum is the beginning of the walking tour of the **walls of Aurelian**, which are particularly well preserved between this gate and the Nuova Porta Ardeatina, 400 m. to the west; 6 m. tall, with a square tower every 100 feet, they were built on existing walls, they have been repeatedly restored and reinforced, especially after the Sack of Rome in 1527.

Porta Latina (III, *E4*). This gate has Roman features; note the travertine arch, the moulding of the cornice, and the merlons. Just inside is the *Oratorio di S. Giovanni in Oleo*, rebuilt in the early 16th c. and restored by F. Borromini.

S. Maria in Domnica* (III, *C3*). Set atop the Celio, or Caelian Hill, with a portico by A. Sansovino, this church was first rebuilt in the 9th c. and again in the 16th c. by Pope Leo X. Inside, beneath the wooden lacunar ceiling (1566) is a frieze with heraldic devices by G. Romano; on the triumphal arch and in the apse, mosaics* from the reign of Pope Paschal I (early-9th c.). To the left of the church is the entrance to the *Villa Celimontana* (III, *C-D2-3*), a public park. On the right, note the 13th-c. portale*, by J. and C.; beyond which is the *Arch of Dolabella* (III, *C3*), possibly a gate in the Servian Walls. Across the Via della Navicella, a wall conceals the 5th-c. church of **S. Stefano Rotondo*** (*entrance at n. 7 of the Via S. Stefano Rotondo*), the oldest church with a round plan in Rome; note the original colonnade in the outer wall.

Ss. Quattro Coronati* (III, *B3*). In one version, this church is dedicated to four soldiers who became martyrs because they refused to worship a statue of Aesculapius; in another, it was four Dalmatian sculptors who refused to carve such a statue. In any case, it was built before the end of the 6th c., rebuilt in 1111, and given its cloister and oratory in the late 13th c. Note the frescoes, in the church and in the *oratory of S. Silvestro** (*you can request the key from the Ruota delle Monache*), as well as the star-and-cross decoration, with five majolicas, unique in Rome. Also, note the rare 13th-c. liturgical calendar.

S. Clemente** (III, *B3*). The first church was built here in the 3rd c. atop a house built in the 2nd

Rome: S. Clemente

c.; burnt by Norman invaders in 1084, it was replaced with the church that now stands, by Pope Paschal II. Renovations were done in 1713-19. The lovely interior of the *upper basilica*, with Roman columns and Cosmatesque floor, looks much as it did in the 12th c. (despite the 18th-c. frescoes in the nave); the schola cantorum*, the ciborium, and the bishop's throne are all from the 12th c. The apse is decorated with a magnificent 12th-c. mosaic**; the fresco beneath it is from the 14th c. The Cappella di S. Caterina, in the left aisle, is adorned with frescoes** done between 1428 and 1431 by M. da Panicale, and perhaps by Masaccio. The *lower basilica (open 9-12:30 and 3:30-6; Sun. 10-12 and 3:30-6; entrance from the sacristy)* preserves, in the fresco in the nave, one of the earliest examples of vernacular Italian. Beneath the basilica are ancient Roman ruins, as well as a 3rd-c. *mithreum* and a 6th-c. Christian baptistery.

11 The Foro Boario, the Aventine Hill, and S. Paolo Fuori le Mura, or St. Paul without the Walls

From the noisy confusion of ancient marketplaces to the silence of early-Christian churches, this route runs through the heart of ancient Rome, tucked away in the oxbow curve of the Tiber, near the Isola Tiberina, and Rome's earliest river port; it then runs up into the quiet of the Aventine Hill, a haven of silence just a short walk from the center, where little villas surrounded by greenery stand beside churches founded in ancient times. A pleasant side trip is the Basilica di S. Paolo Fuori le Mura, or St. Paul without the Walls, inside the 19th c. exterior, it conceals masterpieces from the 13th c.

Via del Teatro di Marcello (IV, *A-B4-5*). Another avenue built under Fascism (1926-41), as part of the route linking Rome and the Lido di Ostia, wiping away a section of the city dating from the Middle Ages.

S. Maria in Campitelli (IV, *A4*). C. Rainaldi built this remarkable example of late Roman Baroque in 1662-67; the main altar contains the image (said to work miracles) of S. Maria in Portico Campitelli, dating from the 11th c. The nearby block (between Via de' Funari, Via Caetani, Via delle Botteghe Oscure, and Via Paganica) once belonged to the family of the Mattei. Worth noting are: at n. 32 in Via Caetani, *Palazzo Mattei di Giove*, begun by C. Maderno in 1598 ; *Palazzo Mattei di Paganica*, built in 1541, perhaps by Nanni di Baccio Bigio, on the ruins of the theater of Balbus (13 B.C.). At the center of Piazza Mattei is the *Fontana delle Tartarughe** (Fountain of Turtles), designed by G. della Porta (1581-84; the turtles were added in 1658, probably by G.L. Bernini).

Teatro di Marcello** (IV, *A-B4*). Begun by Julius Caesar and dedicated in 13 or 11 B.C. by Augustus to his nephew Marcellus, this theater had been abandoned by the 5th c.; it was reused in 1523-27 by B. Peruzzi for the construction of the *Palazzo Orsini*.

Portico di Ottavia (IV, *A4*). The five Corinthian columns with trabeation once formed part of a building erected in 146 B.C. and rebuilt by Augustus in 27-23 B.C. for his sister Octavia; it was again rebuilt by Septimius Severus and Caracalla (A.D. 203). The propylaeum was, from the Middle Ages to the 19th c., the site of a lively market, dealing especially in fish (hence the name of the church of *S. Angelo in Pescheria*). On the left side of Via del Portico d'Ottavia are unremarkable buildings where the Jewish ghetto once stood (from 1555 to 1848); in the

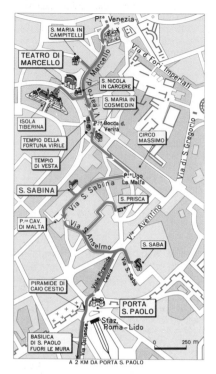

according to legend, by Tarquinius Priscus, to drain the Valle del Foro.

S. Maria in Cosmedin* (IV, *C5*). Built in the 6th c., it was given to the Greek community, who so embellished it that it was called "Kosmidion," or lovely (hence, Cosmedin). The bell tower* to the right of the portico dates from the 12th c. In it is the famous Bocca della Verità**, or Mouth of Truth, a sewer cover, carved with a mascaron, which popular tradition said would bite the hand of a liar. *Inside* is an 8th-c mosaic floor, a Gothic baldachin by D. di Cosma il Giovane (1294), and 8th-c. frescoes; the fragment of mosaic* in the sacristy came from the original St. Peter's.

Circo Massimo (IV, *C-D5-6*). This, the Circus Maximus, clearly visible from Piazzale Ugo La Malfa, was begun, according to tradition, by Tarquinius Priscus, one of the seven kings of Rome, in the valley between the Palatine and the Aventine hills, and it remained in use until A.D. 549. It seated 300,000, and is now a park. From the square, view* of the ruins of the Palazzi Imperiali on the Palatine; also a fine view of the nearby *Parco Savello* (IV, *C4-5*).

S. Sabina** (IV, *C-D4*). The restoration in the first half of the 20th c. restored this basilica's original appearance; this may be the most complete example of a 5th-c. Christian church; cloister and bell tower date from the 13th c. In the atrium, the portal preserves the original 5th-c. carved wooden doors**. The *interior* features a fragment of mosaic over the doorway, with inscription* in golden letters commemorating the foundation of the church; the frieze with red and green panels over the arcades dating from the 5th c.; and the schola cantorum, or chancel, made of reassembled ancient fragments (5th/9th c.).

Complesso dell'Ordine dei Cavalieri di Malta (IV, *D4*). *Open by request, contact the Ordine di Malta, at n. 68 in Via Condotti.* This headquarters of the Order of the Knights of Malta is enclosed within a massive wall (if you peek through the keyhole, you can see the dome of St. Peter's), and was given its present appearance in the 18th c. by G.B. Piranesi, who rebuilt the church of S. Maria del Priorato, as well as the villa and the grounds.

S. Prisca (IV, *D5*). An archeological complex, worth a tour, lies under the church, which is dedicated to a 1st-c. martyr. The complex in question is a *Mithraeum (open by request, contact the Soprintendenza Archeologica di Roma)* with partial ruins of a 1st-c. home, a nymphaeum built during the reign of Trajan, and a number of rooms dedicated to the ancient Persian god Mithras, decorated with frescoes depicting initiatory rites into the cult.

S. Saba* (IV, *E5*). Legend has it that this church was built on the site of the house of the mother of Pope Gregory I the Great; certainly an old monastery stood here, at one point Cistercian. Note the portal by J. di Lorenzo di Cosma, dated 1205; the floor inside is also Cosmatesque, and there are handsome late-13th-c. frescoes.

Porta S. Paolo** (IV, *E4-5*). This was the ancient "Porta Ostiensis" in the Aurelian walls (the inner front, with two passages, dates from the 3rd c.; the outer front, set between two semicylindrical crenelated towers, dates from the reign of Honorius), and it marked the beginning of the Via Ostiensis, which led to the seaport of ancient Rome. The adjacent **Piramide di Caio Cestio***

Sinagoga Nuova, or New Synagogue, there is an historical exhibit (*Mostra della Comunità Ebraica di Roma; open 9:30-2 and 3-5; Sun. 9:30-12:30; closed Fri. aft. and Sat.*). Further along in the same road is the *Casa dei Manili**; on the facade is the date of construction (2221 after the foundation of Rome, i.e., A.D. 1468).

S. Nicola in Carcere (IV, *B4*). The facade, by G. della Porta, re-uses two columns from an ancient temple of Juno (197 B.C.); the right side features two others from the Temple of Hope (built after the First Punic War); the left side, columns from the Temple of Janus (260 B.C.). This medieval church makes much use of ancient material. Across the street, note the *Area Sacra di S. Omobono* (open by request)*, dating from the 6th c. B.C.

Isola Tiberina* (IV, *B4*). Linked to the Tiber's left bank by the 2,000-year-old *Ponte Fabricio**, and to the right bank by the *Ponte Cestio* (the central arch is ancient, the rest was rebuilt in the 19th c.), this ship-shaped island was sacred to Aesculapius. Pope Otto III built the church of *S. Bartolomeo all'Isola*, rebuilt in the late-16th c. From the island's southern tip, you can see the remains of Rome's first stone bridge (181-179 B.C.).

Piazza della Bocca della Verità (IV, *B-C4-5*). This square stands on the site of the Foro Boario (the livestock market in classical times), and is lined by two temples from the Republic: the square-plan *Tempio della Fortuna Virile** (IV, *B5; open by request*), and the round-plan *Tempio di Vesta** (IV, *B4-5; open by request*), the oldest surviving marble temple. The *Casa dei Crescenzi** dates from 1040-65, and includes classical decorative motifs. Dating from Roman times are the monuments in the nearby Via del Velabro: the 4th-c. *Arco di Giano** (IV, *B5*), or Arch of Janus; the *Arco degli Argentari*, to the left of the medieval church of *S. Giorgio in Velabro* (the Romanesque portico and campanile were almost entirely destroyed by a terrorist bombing in July 1993, and have almost been rebuilt), was dedicated by the moneychangers in A.D. 204 to Septimius Severus and his family. The *Cloaca Maxima (open by request)* was built,

(IV, *E-F4*), a pyramide standing 36 m. tall, was built in just 330 days in the late-1st c. B.C.

Ex-terminal Ostiense (III, *F1*). This modern structure, behind the *train station of Roma Ostiense* that was inaugurated in 1938 on the occasion of a visit to Rome by Hitler, was built for the World Cup games of 1990. It will be used to house the collections of the Braccio Nuovo and the Museo Nuovo of the Musei Capitolini (see route 1).

S. Paolo Fuori le Mura*. Largest of the patriarchal basilicas, after St. Peter's, it was built in the time of Constantine on the grave of St. Paul, and consecrated in 324; it was enlarged and embellished over the centuries, until it was entirely razed by a fire on 15-16 July 1823. It was rebuilt to the plan and size of the original, and consecrated in 1854. On the Via Ostiense stands the campanile, known as the "faro," or "lighthouse," for its unusual shape. The *interior**, 131.7 m. long, 65 m. wide, and 29.7 m. tall, glitters with marble, mostly from the 19th c. To the right of the main entrance are the bronze doors* of the ancient basilica (1070). The frieze over the arcades features medallions with portraits of the popes from St. Peter to John Paul II. The triumphal arch bears 5th-c. mosaics. Over the main altar, note the Gothic ciborium** by A. di Cambio (1285), with bas-reliefs and statues; on the right, paschal candelabrum* by N. di Angelo and P. Vassalletto (12th c.). In the apse, mosaic* from the time of Honorius III. The adjacent *cloister**, completed by 1214, is in part by the Vassalletto. Note *paintings* by Bramantino and Cigoli.

12 Trastevere

This was a section of Rome originally frequented by merchants and pilgrims, who arrived in town near the Isola Tiberina, and received care and assistance in the many hospitals and hospices in the area. Trastevere still has a quintessentially Roman atmosphere; the Viale di Trastevere runs through a maze of narrow lanes, and small squares where you can often find open-air restaurants. There are also numerous churches and art collections, as well as breathtaking views, such as the one you can enjoy from the top of the Janiculum.

S. Carlo ai Catinari (IV, *A4*). Barnabite monks had this church built by R. Rosati, who designed and erected it (1612-20; note the cupola), and G.B. Soria, who did the facade (1636-38). The frescoes on the interior of the facade are by M. and G. Preti, those in the spandrels of the cupola are by Domenichino; the Cappella di S. Cecilia* features decorations by A. Gherardi (1692-1700); the panel on the main altar is by P. da Cortona.

S. Crisogono (IV, *B3*). Standing just behind the 13th-c. *Palazzetto Anguillara*, with tower, on Piazza Sonnino, is the church of S. Crisogono, first built as a basilica in the 5th c., and rebuilt in its present form in 1123-29, then restored in 1620-26. Inside, note the 17th-c. stucco decorations and the wooden coffered ceiling, the 13th-c. Cosmatesque floor, and mosaic from the school of P. Cavallini in the vault of the apse. In the nearby church of *S. Agata* note the image of the Madonna de' Noantri, patron saint of the "rione," or neighborhood.

S. Cecilia in Trastevere* (IV, *C4*). This 9th-c. church was built on the site of the house of the saint's husband; she was martyred under the reign of Marcus Aurelius. Much of the interior and the facade were rebuilt in the 18th c., though the mosaic frieze in the portico and the campanile

date from the 12th c. In the vestibule, funerary monuments, by P. Taccone (right; late-14th c.) and M. da Fiesole (left; ca. 1473). At the foot of the right aisle, a corridor, with frescoes by P. Brill, leads to the calidarium (note the ancient steam pipes), where the saint was steamed to death over three days. In the presbytery, the Gothic ciborium* by A. di Cambio (1293); beneath the main altar, statue of S. Cecilia* by S. Maderno (1600), who depicted the body as it was found in its tomb, in 1599; over the apse is a great mosaic* dating from ca. 820. The *nun's choir (open, Tue. and Thu., 10-11:30)* is decorated with a Last Judgment* by P. Cavallini (ca. 1289-93, and rediscovered in 1900; the finest piece of pre-Giotto painting in Rome).

Ospizio di S. Michele a Ripa Grande (IV, *C-D3-4*). Originally a school for boys in the 17th c., and later the chief center for education and charity in Rome, it was turned over to the state in 1969, and made the headquarters for the Ministero per i Beni Culturali and for the Istituto Centrale per il Restauro e la Documentazione; you will also find that the collection of paintings from Galleria Borghese has been temporarily placed here (see route 7).

S. Francesco a Ripa (IV, *C3*). The original church was founded in the 10th c., but was completely rebuilt in 1681-85 by M. De Rossi; when St. Francis came to Rome he stayed in the adjacent convent. In the left transept, note the statue of the Blessed Ludovica Albertoni* by G.L. Bernini (1671-75).

S. Maria in Trastevere** (IV, *B2-3*). In the heart of Trastevere, this church dates from the 4th c. but was rebuilt in its modern form in 1138-48. The facade preserves a 13th-c. mosaic; before it is a portico, to the side a Romanesque bell tower. You enter under three doorways with re-used cornices from the imperial period. *Inside*, three aisles with large ancient trabeated columns run beneath a rich wooden coffered ceiling designed by Domenichino (1617). The mosaics** near the windows are by P. Cavallini (1291). In the chapel to the left of the apse, note the 6th-c. encaustic painting**

Museo del Folclore e dei Poeti Romaneschi (IV, *B2*). *Open 9-1; Tue. and Thu. also 5-7:30; Sat. and Sun., 9-1; closed Mon.* This museum of Roman folklore and poetry documents the Roman popular traditions, from

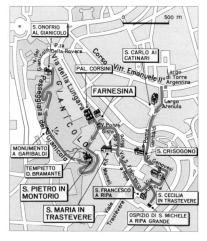

the 18th c. onward; note the watercolors by E. Roesler Franz and the reconstructions of rooms.

Piazza Trilussa (IV, B2-3). This square stands on the riverfront boulevard, or Lungotevere, at the *Ponte Sisto* (IV, A-B3), a bridge rebuilt under Pope Sixtus IV in 1473-75 (the only bridge built over the Tiber from classical times until 1870) on the site of an older span; it is adorned with the 17th-c. *Fontana dell'Acqua Paola* and a monument to the Roman poet Trilussa.

Via della Lungara (IV, A-B2). This marks the beginning of a boulevard built by Julius II, to plans by Bramante, along with the parallel Via Giulia (see route 4), and the *Porta Settimiana* (IV, B2), a reconstruction of a passage through the Aurelian walls built by Alexander VI. At the end of the first road off to the left from Via della Lungara is the *Orto Botanico*, or botanical garden (*open by request*).

Palazzo Corsini (IV, A2). This building takes its name from the last family to own it; the Corsini purchased it in 1736. In the 17th c., queen Kristina of Sweden lived here, and it was founded by the Accademia dell'Arcadia. F. Fuga designed the facade overlooking Via della Lungara. The "cultural" tradition of the palazzo continues even now, as it houses both the *Accademia dei Lincei*, founded in 1603, and the Galleria Corsini.

Galleria Corsini*. *Open, Tue.-Sat., 9-2; Sun. 9-1; closed Mon.* The recent restoration of this, the only private Roman collection still intact, to its original locale has given it new splendor; it was begun in the mid-18th c. by the Cardinal Neri Corsini. Among the 16th/17th-c. artists, Italian and not, whose work is featured here, we should mention: G. da Milano, F. Francia, Fra' Angelico, Fra' Bartolomeo , J. Bassano, P.P. Rubens, A. Van Dyck, Murillo, J. van Cleve, A. Algardi, G.B. Foggini, Caravaggio, O. Gentileschi, Maestro del Giudizio di Salomone, N. Tournier, P. Wouwerman, G. Dughet, A. Brueghel, C. Berentz, C. Maratta, N. Poussin, G.B. Piazzetta, G. Reni, G. Lanfranco, D. Creti, M. de Caro, Spagnoletto, D. Gargiulo, and L. Giordano. The Corsini goblet and throne are Roman works dating from the 1st c. B.C.

Farnesina** (IV, A2). *Open 9-1; closed Sun.* This villa, a masterpiece of Renaissance architecture, was built by B. Peruzzi (1506-1520) for the Siennese banker A. Chigi. In 1580 it became property of the Farnese family; it lost its gardens and the loggia (attributed to Raphael) when the Lungotevere, or boulevards running along the Tiber, were built. Inside, where the Gabinetto Nazionale delle Stampe is located, you can tour: the Loggia of Psyche, frescoed** to cartoons by Raphael, 1517; the Sala del Fregio, with mythological scenes, painted partly by Peruzzi; the Sala di **Galatea**, with frescoes** by Raphael (1513-14), S. del Piombo, Peruzzi, and D. Beccafumi; the Salone delle Prospettive, painted by Peruzzi (1518-19); and the bedroom, with fresco by Sodoma (1517).

S. Pietro in Montorio** (IV, B2). This church was heavily rebuilt in the late 15th-c.; its name comes from the ancient name of the Janiculum ("Mons Aureus"). Inside is a Flagellation* by S. del Piombo, and a chapel designed by G.L. Bernini. In the cloister, to the right of the church, is a little **temple by Bramante****, 1508-1512, sup-posedly on the site of St. Peter's crucifixion. Fine view* from the square in front of the church.

Passeggiata di Gianicolo* (IV, A-B1). Beginning from the **fountain of the Acqua Paola** (IV, B2), built by F. Ponzio and G. Fontana for Paul V (1608-1612), this offers one of the loveliest strolls in Rome, overlooking the city. The finest view can be had from the *equestrian monument to G. Garibaldi* (IV, B1; 1895), though another fine panorama can be enjoyed from the *Faro* (IV, A1; III, F2), a lighthouse, given to Rome by the Italians of Argentina.

S. Onofrio al Gianicolo (I, F2). This church was begun in 1439 and completed in the 16th c. (the frescoes in the portico are by Domenichino, those in the apse are by B. Peruzzi, or perhaps by J. Ripanda). In the nearby convent the great poet Torquato Tasso lived, and died here in 1595.

Villa Doria Pamphilj. This is the largest public park in Rome, once a hunting preserve and pleasure park in the 18th c. (note the *Casino d'Allegrezze*). The avenues are named after major events in the history of the Roman Republic.

13 The Via Appia Antica and the EUR

In the southern section of Rome, you will find two major tourist attractions. The first of the two is certainly the best known, and comprises a succession of ancient tombs from the dawn of Christianity, and Roman ruins, lining the ancient Appian Way; many are, sadly, in a state of neglect. The second attraction is unique: the EUR. Here you will see buildings that hearken back to classical style, erected to glorify Roman Fascism of the 1920s-40s.

Via Appia Antica**. The "queen of the roads" of ancient Rome was opened in 312 B.C. by the censor Appius Claudius Caecus; the Appian Way followed an older route toward the Alban Hills, and eventually extended all the way to Brindisi, becoming the main route to the East; it fell into disrepair in the Middle Ages, and was replaced in the 16th c. by the Via Appia Nuova. It was rediscovered in the late-18th c. Not until 1988 did the Region of Lazio establish an archeological park along the road. This park is noteworthy both for the ancient artifacts displayed and for the lovely natural setting, as yet undeveloped.

Domine Quo Vadis? Here, it is said, Jesus appeared to St. Peter as he fled Rome; when the apostle asked Christ, "Domine quo vadis?" (Lord, where are you going?), Christ supposedly replied, "Eo Romam iterum crucifigi," (I am going to Rome, to be crucified once again). Peter then returned to the city, where he was martyred. The church was given its modern appearance in the 16th c.

Catacombe di S. Callisto*. *Open: winter, 8:30-12 and 2:30-5; summer, 8:30-12 and 2:30-5:30; closed Wed.* This was the official cemetery of the popes in the 3rd c.; discovered in 1849. Note the Crypt of the Popes, the tomb of St. Cecilia, with 9th-c. frescoes, and the Cubicles of the Sacraments, adorned with early-3rd-c. paintings.

S. Sebastiano*. This basilica, founded in the 4th c. near the cemetery where the apostles Peter and Paul were briefly interred and where St. Sebastian was buried, was rebuilt in the 17th c. by F. Ponzio and G. Vasanzio. In the first chapel on the right is a stone with a footprint imbedded in it, sup-

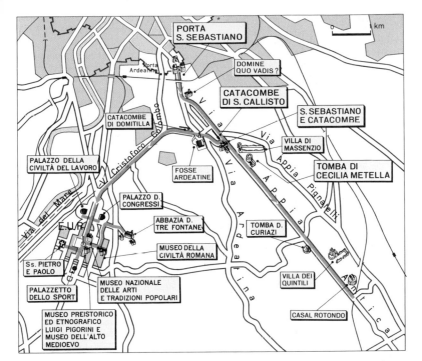

posedly left by Jesus in the story known for the famous phrase, "Domine quo vadis?"; also, note statue of St. Sebastian by A. Giorgetti (1671-72). Beneath the church are the ancient **catacombs of S. Sebastiano** *(open: winter, 8:30-12 and 2:30-5; summer, 8:30-12 and 2:30-5:30; closed Thu.)*, unfortunately in poor shape. Note a bust of the saint by G.L. Bernini and a chapel dedicated to Pope Honorius III, with 13th-c. frescoes.

Villa di Massenzio. *Open: winter, 9-1; summer, 9-1 and 3:30-7:30; closed Mon.* The villa of Maxentius (3rd/4th c.) comprises the Circus of Maxentius (it seated 10,000), and the mausoleum of Romulus, built by Maxentius for his son; still to be excavated is the imperial palace, set between the circus and the tomb.

Tomba di Cecilia Metella*. *Open: winter, 9-3:30; summer, 9-sunset; closed Mon.* As an inscription on a plaque notes, a monument in this road commemorates the daughter of Metellus Creticus — and wife of Crassus — and was erected around 50 B.C. Set on a square base is a cylindrical structure, crowned by a frieze with relief carvings; the crenelation dates from the Middle Ages, when this tomb was used as the donjon of a fortified castle.

Tomba dei Curiazi. Set in the heart of the ancient section of the Via Appia, and amidst the lovely landscape of the Roman Campagna, dotted with ruins and umbrella pines; this small hillock, supposedly the Tomb of the Curiatii, actually covers ruins from the late Roman Republic. According to tradition, this is where the combat was fought between the three Horatii brothers, champions of Rome, and the three Curiatii brothers, champions of Alba Longa, to determine which city should rule the other. Note the nearby tombs of the Horatii, also from the late Republic.

Villa dei Quintili. *Open by request, contact the Soprintendenza Archeologica di Roma.* This villa, originally the property of the family of the Quintili, and later

of the emperor Commodus, was so large that the area is still known as "Old Rome." From the Via Appia you can see the majestic arches of the aqueduct that supplied water to the villa. Note the *Casal Rotondo*, a cylindrical tomb.

Fosse Ardeatine. *Open: winter, 8:30-5; summer 8:30-6.* The atrocious massacre that made these Ardeatine Caves sadly famous occurred on 24 March 1944, when, as a reprisal for a partisan attack in Via Rasella, the Germans slaughtered 335 civilians in these pozzolana quarries. The adjacent *museum (open same hours as above)* contains documents on the Nazi occupation of Rome, following Italy's attempted separate peace.

Catacombe di Domitilla. *Open 8:30-12 and 2:30-5; closed Tue.* These catacombs developed between the 3rd and 5th c., and extend underground through nearly 15 km. of tunnels. The church of *Ss. Nereo e Achilleo* above them was built in the late 4th c. to house the relics of martyrs who were killed under Diocletian; one of the little columns of the ciborium bears a rare depiction of the Beheading of a Martyr.

Via Cristoforo Colombo (III, *F3*). This was originally part of the Via Imperiale which linked Piazza Venezia to the Lido di Roma; its name changes as soon as it exits the Aurelian walls. The stretch that runs to the EUR passes through a built-up zone developed after WWII. On the left, near the Fiera di Roma, is the *Museo dell'Energia Elettrica (open 9-1 and 4-8).* The road then runs through the pine forest of Castel Fusano as far as Lido di Ostia.

EUR. The planned Universal Exposition of 1942 offered Italy's Fascist regime an excuse to build a new quarter to the south of Rome, planned in monumental style, in the wake of the victorious war in Ethiopia, by M. Piacentini. Work was halted in 1943. Following WWII, the project was altered, making it more of a business center, but the original architectural design was maintained; the sports facilities were built for the Rome Olympics of 1960.

Palazzo della Civiltà del Lavoro*. The "Square Colosseum," as this building is also called, was based on the Flavian amphitheater, and was built (1938-43) with a distinctive array of 216 arches on its four faces. Facing it is the *Palazzo dei Congressi* (VII, *B2-3*) designed by A. Libera and built from 1938 to 1954.

Museo Nazionale delle Arti e Tradizioni Popolari. *Open 9-2; Sun., 9-1.* Set in a building erected from 1939 to 1942, surrounding *Piazza Marconi*, this museum is devoted to Italian customs and traditions, from the earliest times until the 20th c. Note the 750 costumes and 3,000 pieces of jewelry in the collection.

Museo Nazionale Preistorico-Etnografico "Luigi Pigorini"*. *Open 9-7; Sun. 9-1; the ethnographic collections are being reinstalled.* This is one of the leading European museums in the field of ethnography, and since 1962 those collections have been housed in the Palazzo delle Scienze (1939-43); they originated in the 17th c. from the "scientific research" of Athanasius Kircher, who wished to "document the lives of modern-day savages in order to understand those of prehistoric savages." The collection grew greatly through the tireless efforts in the late-19th c. and early-20th c. of Luigi Pigorini.

The *prehistoric section* contains material from Lazio (Latium), the region of Rome, dating from the late Paleolithic (remains of pre-Neanderthal man, ca. 200,000 years ago) to the early Bronze Age (tombs of a warrior and a woman with skull fractures, perhaps a human sacrifice), and much material concerning the transition from the late Bronze Age to the early Iron Age (10th c. B.C.); also material on the Villanovian culture of Etruria.

Ss. Pietro e Paolo. This "neighborhood church" has a distinctive cupola; built in white marble, it was designed in 1938 and consecrated in 1955.

Palazzo dello Sport. Perched high atop a hill, overlooking a manmade lake around which Via Cristoforo Colombo runs, splitting into two, is what may fairly be called the finest athletic facility built for the 1960 Olympics, held in Rome. Designed by M. Piacentini and P.L. Nervi (1958-60), this sports arena holds 16,000 spectators. The modern building on the eastern shore of the lake houses the *Museo delle Poste e delle Telecomunicazioni* (*open 9-1; closed Sun.*), a museum devoted to the history of the mail and telecommunications, with collections ranging from the earliest known letter slot (1633) to the automatic electronic calculator "ELEA 9003," designed by E. Fermi.

Museo dell'Alto Medioevo. *Open 9-2; Sun. 9-1; closed Mon.* This museum of the high Middle Ages has collections that include tomb furnishings, goldwork, reliefs, and Coptic fabrics.

Museo della Civiltà Romana*. *Open 9-1; Tue. and Thu. also 3-6; closed Mon.; undergoing partial reinstallation.* This museum occupies a building in the Fascist style, constructed in 1939-52 for the chairman of Fiat. The materials displayed here, all casts and models designed to illustrate Roman civilization and its spread through the ancient world, come from two major exhibitions: the "Mostra Archeologica" held at the Baths of Diocletian in 1911 and the "Mostra Augustea della Romanità" of 1937; they were placed in this museum in 1955. Of special note are the **model of Rome** in the time of Constantine, in 1:250 scale,

and the casts of Trajan's Column (Colonna Traiana), made at the behest of Napoleon III in 1860.

Abbazia delle Tre Fontane. According to legend, the three fountains mentioned in the name of this abbey originated when the head of St. Paul, who was decapitated here, bounced three times; archeologists tell us only that there was a Christian cemetery here in the 3rd c., a church in the 4th c., and a new church and abbey built in 1140 by the followers of St. Benedict. The complex comprises the church of *Ss. Vincenzo e Anastasio**, founded by Honorius I in 625 and completed by Honorius III in 1221, the church of *S. Maria Scala Coeli*, built by G. della Porta (1581-84) and, at the end of the avenue, the church of *S. Paolo*, rebuilt in 1599-1601 by G. della Porta, and containing the three fountains in question (the mosaic floor comes from Ostia).

Sabbioneta*

elev. 18 m.; pop. 4,490; Lombardy, province of Mantova. It is said that the duke Vespasiano Gonzaga, a valiant soldier wounded time and time again in battle, carried vitruvius's renowned architectural treatise with him at all times, even during hard campaigning. When the 16th-c. duke drew up the plans for his little capital city, he imagined it as perfectly finished in every detail, within the star-shaped perimeter of the walls. Sabbioneta — honored as a 'small latter-day Athens' for the enlightened and very learned court that was held there — is an exemplary model of an 'ideal city', conceived and built to suit its prince, in perfect accordance with the canons of Renaissance urban planning.

Hours. *Guided tours for groups through the main buildings; starting from the "Pro Loco" (Piazza Castello); Apr-Sep., 9-12 and 2:30-6, holidays until 7; Jul. closed Mon.; Oct.-Mar., 9-12 and 22:30-5, holidays until 5:30, closed Mon.; for reservations, tel: 52039.*

Piazza Ducale* (also *Piazza Garibaldi*). This is the center of Sabbioneta; partly bounded by ssmall portico-fronted palazzetti, this square preserves its ancient appearance. Note the Palazzo Ducale and the **Parrocchiale** (1581); on the interior, the 18th-c. Cappella del Sacro Cuore; by Antonio Bibiena.

Palazzo Ducale*. This ducal palace was built in 1568 and has a ground-level portico; a "piano nobile" (or main floor) with marble windows, and a turret in the center of the facde. On the interior are halls with carved wooden ceilings and frescoes by Bernardino Campi, Alberto Cavalli; and others. In particular, note the four wooden equestrian statues of the Gonzagas, and the Galleria degli Antenati, with busts in stucco of the dynasty.

Behind the palazzo is the **church of the Incoronata** (1588), with octagonal plan; with the mausoleum of Vespasiano Gonzaga by G.B. Della Porta (1592); note the bronze statue* of the duke, by Leone Leoni (1588).

Museo d'Arte Sacra. *Open, Apr.-Nov., 9:30-12:30 and 2:30-6:30; closed Mon., Fri. aft. and Sun.-Aug.; in the other months, by request, tel. 52035.* Not far away, the parrocchiale, or parish church, in Via Pesenti 6, contains the treasure of the Gonzaga dynasty: ancient silver, fabric, and clothing, manuscripts, charters, and a portable organ from the 16th c.

Teatro Olimpico*. Masterpiece by Vincenzo Scamozzi, who built it in 1588. The interior has a rectangular plan, with tiered steps and loggia. On the walls, excellent frescoes of the Venetian school.

Piazza Castello. This is the ancient 'piazza d'armi' (or parade ground), with a roman column in the center. It is surrounded on one side by the long buildings of the *Galleria degli Antichi* (1584), joined by an overpass with the Palazzo del Giardino.

Palazzo del Giardino*. Built between 1577 and 1588 as a pleasure palace for the prince, this holiday home is filled with halls and antechambers, decorated with frescoes, stuccoes, and grotesques by the Campi brothers and the school of Giulio Romano; from here you pass into the *Galleria degli Antichi**, 97 m. long, with a wooden ceiling and walls decorated with frescoes.

Salerno

elev. 4 m., pop. 147,010, Campania, provincial capital. The old town lies on a slope, with all its Norman landmarks and monuments, overlooking the sea.

Places of interest. Narrow, twisting, rich in atmosphere, the **Via dei Mercanti** is the central thoroughfare of the old town. Follow it and you will reach: the church of the **Crocifisso** (10th/11th c.), with ancient columns and frescoes in the apse (15th c.) and crypt (13th c.); as well as the Baroque church of **S. Giorgio** (in a side street): this church has frescoes by Solimena (1675); note the *Arco di Arechi*, remains of a princely palazzo (8th c.). *S.Pietro a Corte* is an ancient palatine church; the little bell tower dates from Longobard times, while the frescoes inside date from the 11th c.

The **Duomo**** is a remarkable monument, with a long and complex architectural history; it was built (1076-85) at the behest of Robert Guiscard, when Salerno was the capital of the Norman realm. It stands at the top of a stairway with, alongside, a campanile* (12th c.), surmounted by intertwined arches; with ancient columns; raised Islamic arches; the intarsiaed mullioned loggia of the great atrium — all indicate the composite culture of the Norman era. The Romanesque portal has celebrated bronze doors* from Constantinople (1099). In the three-aisle *interior*, note the exquisite works of art: the two mosaic-encrusted ambos** (13th c., on the right; 12th c., on the left) adjacent to the iconostasis* (1175); mosaics in the right apse, where Pope Gregory VII is buried, in the vault of the left apse, and on the marble screen of the main altar ; the monument to queen Margherita di Durazzo* (15th c.) and a Baroque *crypt* with supposed relics of the Evangelist Matthew.

The **Museo del Duomo** (*open, 9-12; 4-7*) contains, among other items, an illuminated Exultet* from the 13th c. and an ivory frontal** from the 12th c.

High overhead stands the impressive **Castello di Arechi** (elev. 263 m.), a castle built by successive waves of Byzantines, Longobards, and Normans; fine view, and an exquisite collection of ceramics, ranging from the 8th to the 19th c. (*open, 9-1*).

Salerno: Duomo

At a distance of 11 km., **Pontecagnano** has a local **Museum** (*open, 9-7*) featuring the materials found in Iron Age necropolises (9th c. B.C.).

S. Clemente a Casàuria* (Abbazia di, or Abbey of)

elev. 194 m.; Abruzzo, province of Pescara, township of Castiglione a Casàuria (pop. 902). This Benedictine abbey lies in the valley of the river Pescara, not far from the Rome-Pescara highway. It was founded by Louis II, emperor of the West and king of Italy, in A.D. 871; in so doing, the emperor was fulfilling a vow he had taken while imprisoned in the duchy of Benevento. In the following year, he had the relics of the pope and martyr St. Clement brought there, through the concession of Pope Adrian II. The abbey suffered devastation and looting but was rebuilt in the 12th c., and remained a powerful institution until the 14th c. The remarkable architecture of the church can be glimpsed at the end of a short drive; only the ground floor

S. Clemente a Casàuria: interior

of the monastery survives. The name Casàuria comes from "Casa Aurea" or "Casa Urii," Latin names that hearken back to a temple of Jove Urios, bringer of winds.

Places of interest. Abbey church**. The modern building dates substantially from the 12th-c. reconstruction. The facade, with a handsome portico*, has a lovely central portal with bronze doors* (1192). In the nave, note the pulpit* set on four columns, with lavish decorative friezes and rosettes in the classical style. Note the 12th-c. candelabra for the Paschal candles; in the apse an early-Christian sarcophagus serves as an altar, beneath a 15th-c. ciborium*. In the *crypt* part of the 11th-c. apse survives, set within its 12th-c. successor. In the surrounding park, note Roman and medieval architectural fragments.

San Gimignano*

elev. 324 m.; pop. 6,956; Tuscany, province of Siena. In the 13th c. there were nine "hospitatores," or hotels, for the merchants who flocked here; the pride of the newly rich families were 72 tall towers (by law, none could overtop the Rognosa, the tower of the town government). Saffron, too, was processed here, and sold throughout Europe. Nowadays, of the original 72, 15 towers survive; a sudden economic decline preserved this skyline, so typical of a medieval hill town.

Getting around. The area inside the walls is closed to private traffic; with prior authorization, tourists may drive to their hotels. Large parking areas are located near the walls, but at the height of the season, these may be full. The routes shown are walking tours.

Places of interest. Porta S. Giovanni. This 13th-c. gate has a distinctive Siennese flathead arch, and is part of the **medieval walls*** that surround the center (rebuilt in 1262). To the right is the little privately owned Museo di Arti e Mestieri, a museum of crafts and trades.

Via S. Giovanni. This road runs slightly uphill past many 12th-/13th-c. buildings: at n. 69, the remains of the Pisan Romanesque facade of **S. Francesco**; then tower-houses and, on left, at n. 40, the elegant **Palazzo Pratellesi**, now the town library, which boasts a collection of over 10,000 manuscripts. Becoming more medieval still, on the left is the tall Torre Cugnanesi, and just beyond, the **Arco dei Becci**, through which you enter Piazza della Cisterna; on right, the Torre dei Becci.

Via Quercecchio. Along this road, note the Oratorio di S. Francesco, now a small Museo Ornitologico (*open, Apr.-Sep., 9:30-12:30 and 3-5:30; Oct.-Mar., 9:30-12:30, 2:30-5:30 and closed Mon.*), or museum of ornithology. A series of stairways leads up to the Rocca di Montestaffoli, a fortress built in 1353 and dismantled in 1558. Note pentagonal plan and surviving walls; from sole surviving tower, fine view** of the town's central group of towers.

Piazza della Cisterna**. Triangular in shape, this plaza is linked to Piazza del Duomo by an open passageway, forming a harmonious set of spaces that have been the center of San Gimignano since the 13th c. The cistern, at the center of the huge space paved with herringbone brickwork, dates from 1237 and was enlarged in 1346. To the right of the Arco dei Becci, entering the square, are Casa

San Gimignano: Piazza della Cisterna

Razzi, Casa Salvestrini (now a hotel), and the 13th-c. Palazzo Tortoli-Treccani (n. 22). Across the square, Palazzo dei Cortesi (n. 5), with the tall Tower "del Diavolo"; also note the twin Ardinghelli towers, built in the 13th c. and diverging slightly.

Piazza del Duomo*. Linked to Piazza della Cisterna, and paved with the same herringbone brickwork, this square is lined with medieval houses and towers. Overlooking it is the Collegiata, to the left of which is the facade of Palazzo del Popolo (see below). Across the square is the ancient **Palazzo del Podestà*** (1239), with handsome loggia, and massive tower called the Torre Rognosa (51 m. tall); nearby, at the mouth of Via S. Matteo, is the Chigi tower (1280) and the twin Salvucci towers.

Collegiata**. *Open, Apr.-Sep., 9:30-12:30 and 3-6; Oct.-Mar., 9:30-12:30 and 2:30-5:30*. This 12th-c. Romanesque building, with a simple 13th-c. facade, has been renovated and restored many times. Inside, note paintings and sculpture by great artists such as G. and B. da Maiano, T. di Bartolo, B. Gozzoli, J. della Quercia, B. da Siena and G. da Asciano, B. di Fredi, D. Ghirlandaio, and A. da Colle. In particular, note the chapel of St. Fina* (open, 9:30-12:30 and 3-5:30). From the left aisle, you enter the 14th-c. cloister of S. Giovanni.

Museo d'Arte Sacra. *Open, Apr.-Sep., 9:30-7:30; Oct.-Mar., 9:30-12:30 and 2:30-5:30, closed Mon. only in winter.* Enter the minute Piazza Pecori, on the left of the Collegiata, passing under an arch topped by a 14th-c. statue of the town's patron saint and namesake; on the right is the little Chiostrino di S. Giovanni. Catty-corner is the 12th-c. Palazzo della Propositura; note mullioned windows. On the left, at n. 1, is the entrance: five halls comprise the ancient "Dormitorio dei Cappellani," or dormitorium. Note 16th-c. Egyptian floral-pattern carpet*, marble bust by B. da Maiano (1493); 15th-c. frontal of the "golden doves," * panel by B. di Fredi, painted wooden Crucifix* by G. da Maiano. Adjacent is the Museo Etrusco, with collections from Roman and Etruscan excavations.

Palazzo del Popolo*. Built in 1288 and enlarged in 1323, this building has lost its crenelation but preserves its mayoral crests and three orders of windows; note on left two large arcades* and, on right, the *Torre Grossa** (54 m. tall; 1311). Fine view from top*. (Open during the same hours as the

Museo Civico). In courtyard, note cistern (1361); fresco by Sodoma (1507). An exterior stairway leads up to the Museo Civico.

Museo Civico*. *Open, Apr.-Sep., 9:30-7:30; Oct.-Mar., 9:30-1:30 and 2:30-4:30, closed Mon. only in winter.* On the second floor of Palazzo del Popolo is the enormous Sala di Dante, adorned by the Maestà*, a fresco by L. Memmi (1317); an inlaid door leads to the Sala delle Adunanze Segrete ("Hall of Secret Assemblies"; note the chairs, from 1475) and another adjacent room, with pharmacist's vases from Faenza (16th/17th c.), Florence, and Siena. Third floor: Camera del Podestà, frescoed by M. di Filippuccio, and three halls used as a gallery, with paintings of the Tuscan school (13th/15th c.): C. di Marcovaldo, B. Gozzoli, Filippino Lippi, Pinturicchio, N. di Ser Sozzo, T. di Bartolo, and M. di Filippuccio.

Via del Castello. Lined by 14th-c. buildings, this road runs off the Piazza della Cisterna, and ends at the 13th-c. church of S. Lorenzo in Ponte (closed to the public); note the 15th-c. marble portal of the former convent of S. Domenico, now a prison. A plaque notes that the monk, reformer, and martyr G. Savonarola stayed here.

Via S. Matteo*. Northernmost stretch of the Via Francigena that ran through San Gimignano, it is lined by medieval houses and palazzi. First, note the twin towers, the Torri Salvucci, Palazzo Pettini and Torre Pettini (n.2); pass through the Arco della Cancelleria, once a city gate. Note the 13th-c. Palazzo della Cancelleria and the Romanesque church of **S. Bartolo**. At n. 12-14, is a late-13th-c. tower-house, the **Casa Pesciolini**, and at n.52, the slightly rusticated 15th-c. Casa Francardelli. At n. 60-62, Palazzo Tinacci, and, facing it, at n.97, Palazzo Bonaccorsi. Last comes Porta S. Matteo (A1; 1262).

Piazza S. Agostino. Irregular in shape, it is dominated by the church of S. Agostino; on one side is the little 11th-c. church of S. Pietro (closed to the public), with a simple facade adorned with rose window.

S. Agostino*. This imposing Romanesque-Gothic church, built in 1280-98, has a stark brick facade, and four Gothic windows on the right side. Inside, note artwork by S. Mainardi (1500), B. da Maiano (1494), P. F. Fiorentino, B. di Fredi, P. del Pollaiolo (1483), frescoes by B. Gozzoli and G. d'Andrea (1465), L. Memmi (1320). From the left transept, you can enter the cloister of the adjacent convent.

Spedale di S. Fina. Built in the 13th c. and still used as a hospital, this building overlooks Via Folgore da S. Gimignano: inside, frescoes by S. Mainardi and busts of saints by P. Torrigiani. Ahead, on the left, is the 13th-c. church of S. Jacopo (closed to the public), and from there, you can turn right to follow the city walls, reaching Porta alle Fonti, and from there climb down to the Fonti, which are springs covered with Gothic arches (12th/14th c., restored in 1852).

San Marino

elev. 739 m.; pop. 4,207; capital of the Republic of San Marino. Two stonecarvers fleeing persecution as Christians took refuge on Elba, and became saints. One was St. Leo, the other was St. Marinus, or "Marino," after whom San Marino is named. Monte Titano, a jagged limestone ridge with a handsome silhouette, visible from the beaches, stands between the valleys of Marecchia and the Conca, between Romagna and Montefeltro; on it stands the medieval village that constitutes the capital, overlooking the countryside of the rest of the republic at its base (61,131 sq. km.; pop. 22,966). For anyone who is vacationing on the Riviera di Romagna, the thrill of this venture out of Italian territory is exciting and enjoyable. A must.

Places of interest. S. Francesco (B2). Adjacent to the *Porta di S. Francesco* (1451), the main entrance to the town, is this church, which dates from 1361, but was greatly transformed in the 17th and 18th c. The facade, the apse, and the adjoining portico still have traces of the original 14th-c. structure. The adjoining **Museo di S. Francesco** *(open, May-Sep., 8-8; Dec.-Feb., 9-12:30 and 2:30-5; Mar.-Apr. and Oct-Nov., until 6)* contains a small gallery of paintings, with an Adoration of the Magi, a fresco by Antonio Alberti.

Piazzetta del Titano (B2). This teeming square was originally the site of one of the town gates of the second walled perimeter. Overlooking it is the *Palazzo Pergami Belluzzi*, which is slated to become the new site of the **Museo di Stato**.

The collection of the museum, which is to be reordered and organized, is, as of writing, in storage. The collection comprises two main parts: historical and archeological, on the one hand, and art. In the first section are excavated materials and tools from the Neolithic, Bronze, and Iron ages, along with pottery and other objects. Much of the artwork was donated in the 19th c., and there are canvases by Michele Giambono and Bernardo Strozzi, as well as paintings from the Tuscan school of the 15th c. and the Bolognese school of the 17th c.

Via Carducci (B1-2). This road runs from the lively Piazzetta del Titano to the 15th-c. *Porta della Rupe*; lining its length are aristocratic buildings from the 16th and 17th c. (numbers 145, 146, 151, and 152). Among them, note *Palazzo Valloni*, at n. 141, once the site of the Museo di Stato, or state museum.

Piazza della Libertà (B2). This square is the heart of town with a fine panoramic view, and the **Palazzo del Governo**, or *Palazzo Pubblico*, built in the late-19th c. in 14th-c. style, with a spectacular interior. Slightly uphill is the Neoclassical Basilica of *S. Marino*, built in 1836, on the site of the ancient pieve, or parish church. In the surrounding area, note the *Museo delle Cere*, or Wax Museum *(open, summer, 8-8; winter, 8:30-12:30 and 2:30-5)*, with effigies of local celebrities and great opera singers.

Rocche*. *Open, Jun.-Sep., 8-8; Dec.-Feb., 9-12:30 and 2:30-5; Mar.-Apr. and Oct.-Nov. until 6.* Set on the three knobs of the ridge of Monte Titano, almost sheer above the plains, stand three fortresses, called either the Rocche or the *Penne*. The first of the three, known as either the **Rocca** or *Guaita* (A2), at an elevation of 738 m., may date from the 11th c., but was rebuilt in the 15th c. and again later. It now houses temporary exhibitions. The second one, known as the **Cesta** (B2), at an elevation of 749 m., dates from the 13th c. but was rebuilt; it now houses the **Museo delle Armi Antiche**, or museum of ancient weapons, with cutting arms and firearms from all over. The third, called the **Montale** (off map), was built in the 13th

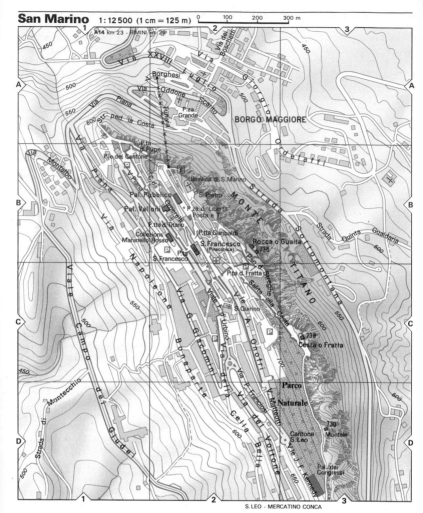

1 : 12 500 (1 cm = 125 m)

BORGO MAGGIORE

MONTE TITANO

S. LEO - MERCATINO CONCA

c., and was almost entirely rebuilt in 1935. Immense panoramic view* of the Romagna plains below, the sea, and the distant Apennines.

Collezione Maranello Rosso (*B2*). *Open, 10-1 and 2-6, closed Tuesday; Nov.-Feb. only on Sun. and holidays.* Located by the ancient town walls, in Via Tonnini at n. 10, is a display of 27 legendary Ferraris, dating from as early as 1951 to recent times.

Borgo Maggiore. In this little village at the base of the mountain — an obligatory route for all those entering S. Marino — is the very modern church of the *Beata Vergine della Consolazione* (1966); note, in the Via Boschetti, the **Museo delle Auto d'Epoca** (*open, Apr.-Sep., 9-12 and 2-8; Oct.-March, 10-12:30 and 2-7*), with over 160 vintage automobiles dating from as early as 1908, manufactured in Italy and elsewhere.

Sàssari

elev. 225 m.; pop. 122,339; Sardinia, provincial capital. Sardinia's second-largest city lies along the slopes of a limestone tableland stretching down to the Gulf of Asinara, only about 10 km away. Sassari in the north rivals Cagliari in the south, and prides itself on its culture and its music. In 1899 the king

of Italy, Umberto I, came here on an official visit; proud horsemen in traditional costume paraded before the king, originating the tradition — still very much alive — of the "Cavalcata Sarda."

Historical note. Originally a haven for those in flight from Saracens, Pisans, and Genoans, Sassari fell under the rule of the latter through the end of the 13th c. As the city grew, it built walls (early 14th c.; still visible in Corso Trinità) which entirely contained the city until the early 18th c. After four centuries of Spanish rule, Sassari became Piedmontese in the 18th c. Beginning in the mid-19th c., Sassari destroyed its walls, its Pisan towers, and its Aragonese castle, building a new, more modern city alongside the old one, with straight roads and broad squares, on the Piedmontese model. This development continued in this century, pushing up the Hill of the Cappuccini and toward the plain of Baddi Mannu. Though life, perhaps, improved, much of Sassari's historic heritage was thus lost.

Places of interest. Piazza Castello. The fortress that gave this square its name was razed in the late-19th c.

Museo Nazionale "Sanna"*. *Open 9-1:45; Sun., 9:30-1.* Since 1932 this museum has occupied the palazzo built by the Sanna family for their own collections and for the archeological material of the University. The *archeological section* begins with the prehistoric period. A major section is devoted to the Sardinian civilization of the "Nuraghe," with the so-called "tombs of the giants" and remarkable 10th-c. B.C. bronzes. The Phoenician period features pottery, bronzes, and statuettes; the Punic a series of funerary stelae, as well as scarabs and amulets; the Roman, glass, gold, mosaics, and a bronze tablet. Coins date from Roman and Carthaginian times. The *art gallery* features a 14th-c. triptych of the Pisan school, as well as work by the Cavaro, B. Vivarini, Mabuse, and G. Marghinotti. Local folklore and customs are also documented.

Corso Vittorio Emanuele II. This avenue runs through the old part of town, with buildings in the 15th-c. Catalan Gothic style (note *Casa Farris*, n. 23, and the *Casa di Re Enzo*, n. 42) standing alongside 19th-c. buildings. The church of *S. Antonio* features an 18th-c. retable, by B. Augusto.

Mura Medievali. Fragments of the city walls, built by Pisans and Genoans in the 13th and 14th c., and demolished in the 19th c., still stand along Corso Trinità. Near the church of the Trinità, you can see the *Fonte Rosello*, built in 1605-1606.

Duomo*. In the heart of the medieval section, the Cathedral was rebuilt in the late-15th c., on the site of a 12th-c. parish church. The *interior*, like the exterior, is Gothic in style; note the 14th-c. Siennese tempera on the main altar and the wooden choir. The adjacent *Museo del Tesoro del Duomo* features a late-15th-c. processional standard* and a silver statue of St. Gavin, said — inaccurately — to have been made in Mexico. Nearby, the *Palazzo Ducale* (1775-1805) is a breath of Piedmontese style.

S. Maria di Betlem. All that remains of the original 12th-c. church is the lower half of the facade; the upper half, with rose window, dates from 1465. *Inside*, note the early-15th-c. wooden statues, and the *cloister* with the 16th-c. Fontana del Brigliadore.

S. Pietro in Silki. Although a church of this name stood here in the 12th c., the oldest portion still standing is the base of the bell tower (13th c.). Inside, note the Sardinian version of Catalan Gothic in the 1st chapel on the left; the 4th houses a venerated 14th-c. simulacrum.

Segesta*

elev. 318, Sicily, province of Trapani.

Historical note. This was once a city of the Elimi, a western Sicilian people that blended Greek customs with Phoenician and Carthaginian influences. The city vanished in the high Middle Ages, but the magnificent temple remains, standing on a rise.

Places of interest. Vast against the green landscape, the **temple**** (*open, 9-sunset*) has a peristyle of 36 un-fluted Doric columns, supporting a trabeation with flat metopes and two pediments. This construction dates from the 5th c. B.C., comprising the single circuit of columns still standing, enclosing the open-air altar of an indigenous cult; Segesta was a rival of Selinunte, and may have had a seaside market town and harbor near what is now Castellammare del Golfo.

On your way up to the Monte Bàrbaro (415 m.),

note along the road the ruins of the ancient city (a tower, a fortified gate, ruins of a ring of walls). Then you will reach the **theater***, dating from Hellenistic times (3rd/2nd c. B.C.); the view* extends all the way to the distant Monte Érice.

Selinunte*

elev. 32, Sicily, province of Trapani.

Historical note. Westernmost of the ancient Greek colonies in Sicily, this town was settled in 628 B.C. by the colonists of Megara Hyblaea, rose to its peak of glory in the 5th c. B.C., and was destroyed by Carthage in 409 B.C. It is notable for its temples.

Places of interest. You can begin your tour of the **archeological park** (*open, 9-an hour before sunset*, with an antiquarium under preparation in the Cascina Ancona) with the **eastern temples***.

This is a group of three temples (indicated with alphabetical letters, since we no longer know to which deities each was sacred). A single column emerges from the mass of ruins of *temple G*, one of the largest of Greek antiquity, Doric, with an eight-column peripteros, and a three-aisle cella; it seems to have been begun in 550 B.C., and left unfinished, possibly because of the Punic invasion in 409 B.C.

Majestically standing out from the landscape, on the other hand, is **temple E****, all of whose columns have been raised, with part of the trabeation and of the walls of the cella. This magnificent Doric construction dates from the first two decades of the 5th c. B.C., and has a six-column peripteros; 4 handsome metopes of its sculptural decoration are now in the Museo Archeologico in Palermo.

The smaller temple F has a six-column peripteros (560-540 B.C.)

Acropolis*. Walking for a stretch along the *walls* made of enormous square blocks of stone, you climb up to the broad, high acropolis*; it was crossed by two intersecting roads, and there are ruins of a number of temples: base of *temple O*; base and drums of fluted columns of *temple A*; twelve raised columns and part of the trabeation of *temple C*, the oldest one in the acropolis (mid-6th c. B.C.; three remarkable metopes from this temple are now in Palermo); ruins of Punic houses (4th/3rd c. B.C.), and the base of a small archaic temple, possibly the source of 6 other small metopes, now in Palermo.

Selinunte: Temple E

At the northern tip of the acropolis is the main gate, defended on the outside by magnificent *fortifications**.

Siena**

elev. 322 m.; pop. 56,956; Tuscany, provincial capital. Certainly the most distinct and homogeneous of all Tuscany's cities, Siena lies in a hilly landscape similar to that seen in the famous 14th-c. fresco in Palazzo Pubblico, "Assedio del Castello di Montemassi da parte di Guidoriccio da Fogliano"; located in the heart of the Tuscan highland, on the rises that separate the valley of the river Arbia, tributary of the Ombrone, from the valley of the river Elsa, tributary of the Arno. Compact and clearly 14th-c. in style, Siena is a city of a single era, with a single past, a city that never ventured down from the three hills along which its steep hillside slope, safely girded by the perimeter of its walls. From Duccio di Buoninsegna to Sassetta, the Siennese artistic tradition has always been separate from, and in some sense counterposed to the art of Florence. It is said that the finest Italian spoken is the version found here.

Historical note. Within Siena's walled perimeter, you can clearly see three hills, which lay at the origin of the three "terzieri" (instead of quarters) into which the town is divided: the "terziere di Città" corresponds to the original core of the city. The earliest historical documents known date from Longobard times, when Siena was the headquarters of a "gastaldo," an officer of the royal court. During the barbarian invasions, Siena's strategic hilltop position made it an easily defended site; its population grew accordingly. Little is known of the long dark centuries before this. Ancient "Sena," apparently founded by the Senoni tribe of Gauls, was called "Sena Etruriae" to distinguish it from another city, "Sena Gallica" (modern Senigallia); it became an Etruscan town. It later became a Roman military colony, and was called "Sena Julia." With the Frankish conquest, the Longobard "gastaldi" were replaced by Carolingian counts who were in turn faced with the encroachments of increasingly powerful bishops; under the patronage of those bishops, Communal government developed, taking power largely for itself. "Consoli," or consuls, were named for the first time in 1147, and under their rule Siena began to extend its dominion outside the city walls, which by now enclosed all three hills in a single fortified perimeter. Siena's expansion toward Poggibonsi and the Val d'Elsa may have had imperial approval, but it necessarily led to conflict with the Guelph city of Florence. An endless series of wars, prompted by trade issues, thus broke out, as Siena became one of the main Ghibelline strongholds in Tuscany. The government of Siena had meanwhile shifted from rule by the "Consoli" to rule by a "Podestà," but real power remained firmly under the control of the rich merchant families of town, who traded throughout Europe, and who were threatened by competing towns, especially Florence. Fighting continued from 1141 until 1235, when a heavy military defeat led to political reform; the power of the Podestà was now moderated, with the establishment of the Consiglio dei Ventiquattro (Council of 24), with equal representation of nobles and commoners. The Italian activities of the Swabian emperors bolstered the ambitions of Ghibelline Siena; in 1260 Siena defeated Florence at Montaperti, regaining Montepulciano and Montalcino. The attack of Charles of Anjou, however, proved fatal: the defeat at Colle marked the end of Ghibelline Siena's ascendancy.

A papal excommunication had already hurt the merchants and bankers of the city, making it difficult for them to obtain repayments of their loans and bills; this led to a shift of allegiance for many merchants, from Ghibelline to Guelph. As a result, a Guelph government was formed in 1270. This government remained in power until 1355. It was the best government Siena had ever had. Peace was made with Florence, and Siena was able to tend to the prosperity of its possessions; there were years of triumphant Gothic architecture and art. Siena became what we see today. Between the turn of the 14th c. and about 1350, the Siennese built Palazzo Pubblico, with the Torre del Mangia, the Palazzo del Capitano del Popolo, and Palazzo Tolomei, the first privately owned palazzo; work continued on the Duomo, only to be broken off in 1339 to begin work on the colossally ambitious Duomo Nuovo, or New Cathedral, a church so large that the existing Duomo was meant to serve merely as its transept; among the projects actually completed were the Cappella di Piazza, the Battistero, or Baptistery, and the churches of S. Domenico and S. Francesco, later renovated. In this same period, Siennese Gothic art began its stunning development: in 1308 Duccio di Buoninsegna was commissioned to paint a major altar piece for the Duomo; in 1315 Simone Martini frescoed his "Maestà" in Palazzo Pubblico; a decade later, the fresco of the "Assedio del Castello di Montemassi" (Siege of the Castle of Montemassi) was painted; between 1338 and 1340 Ambrogio Lorenzetti depicted in his frescoes the concept of good government. In Siena, Gothic became synonymous with art, and Gothic buildings were erected throughout the first half of the 15th c. (Loggia della Mercanzia, Palazzo Buonsignori). It was not until the years between 1460 and 1480 that the Florentine Renaissance, with Palazzo Piccolomini and Palazzo Spannocchi, began to appear in Siena. This new influence, however, went beyond art: Siena was politically subjugated by Florence and by Angevin politics; war with Pisa, the famine of 1326, and the Black Death of 1348 had all provoked discontent and uprisings. In 1399 Siena offered itself to the duke of Milan, Gian Galeazzo Visconti; when he died, however, civil unrest broke out again, in spite of the sermons on peace preached by St. Catherine (S. Caterina) and St. Bernardino. In 1487 power was seized by Pandolfo Petrucci, who governed Siena until his death (1512). His successors were unable to cement their power, and Siena fell into an imperial wardship. An insurrection took place, the emperor's Spanish garrison was driven out, and war followed, with a terrible siege. In 1555 a broken, starving Siena surrendered to an imperial army led by Cosimo I de' Medici. A small band of diehards retreated to Montalcino and kept the banner of the Siennese republic flying until 1559. The peace of Cateau-Cambrésis put an end to Republic freedom in Siena, and a new overlord took over, in the person of Cosimo I. The unification of Tuscany brought little if any benefit to Siena over the next two centuries: during that entire period, the grand duchy of Tuscany maintained a customs barrier between the former state of Siena and the state of Florence, with serious economic repercussions for Siena. It was not until a Hapsburg-Lorraine ruler took over, Pietro Leopoldo, in the late-18th c., that agriculture and trade began to revive. Construction and expansion practically ceased, and the only notable monument from that period is the Baroque church of S. Maria di Provenzano. In 1779 the ancient fortress of Lizza was transformed into a public park, and was enlarged further after Italy was unified. And it was not until the 20th c. that Siena expanded beyond its walls: the fortress of S. Barbara was converted into a public park, and new quarters were built, among them, S. Prospero. Nowadays, Siena is home to a number of prestigious cultural institutions, such as the Università (one of Italy's oldest universities), and the Accademia Musicale Chigiana.

The Palio. This remarkable, centuries-old horse race takes place in the heart of Siena, twice a year. Held in the Piazza del Campo, the race is run to commemorate

Siena: Piazza del Campo

the holidays of the Madonna di Provenzano (2 July) and the Assumption (16 August). This is the deepest-rooted, and, in a sense, the most authentic of Italy's folk events. Competing, by turn, are ten of the city's seventeen historic "contrade," or neighborhoods. The names of these "contrade" are: Aquila, Bruco, Chiocciola, Civetta, Drago, Giraffa, Istrice, Leocorno, Lupa, Nicchio, Oca, Onda, Pantera, Selva, Tartuca, Torre, Valdimontone (literally, Eagle, Caterpillar, Snail, Owl, Dragon, Giraffe, Porcupine, Unicorn, She-Wolf, Shell, Goose, Wave, Panther, Forest, Tortoise, Tower, and Valley of the Ram). Each has a banner with an image corresponding to its name. Before the race, as the excitement builds among the townspeople (understandable excitement; the horses are raced bareback, ridden by jockeys who will do nearly anything to eliminate their rivals), a spectacular historical procession takes place, in costume, in which each "contrada" marches, with banners, followed by the Carro del Trionfo, or Carroccio, literally the Carriage of Triumph, with the "palio," a splendid silk drape awarded to the winning "contrada."

Getting around. Almost all of the area inside Siena's walls is closed to traffic; tourists heading for hotels can enter if they have written reservations or special permits for loading and unloading luggage, but they cannot park, even in the evening and at night. There is plenty of parking outside town, served by shuttle buses; in the summer, and on holidays, it is tough to find parking near the gates of town and on the ring roads.

The Campo and the "terzo" di S. Martino

Siena branches out into three hilltop ridges, or "terzi," each of which is then split up into "contrade." From the Campo, in the shadow of Palazzo Pubblico, the "terzo" of S. Martino extends east to Porta Romana.

Piazza del Campo** (*D3*). This outstanding testimony to the city's medieval harmony of layout and composition, the Piazza — called the **Campo** by the Siennese — with its remarkable shell shape, has always lain at the heart of life in the city. First paved with elaborate brickwork in 1347, the square is dominated by the facade of Palazzo Pubblico and the elegant silhouette of the Torre del Mangia, which marks the perspectival vanishing point; along the other sides of the square extends a line of ancient palazzi, some

of them crenelated and turreted, broken by narrow lanes and "chiassi" that lead toward the broader streets behind.

The square was first cleared and built in 1169. As early as 1297, a decree of the Republic, one of the first zoning regulations known to history, established standards for buildings facing the Campo. These palazzi were continually improved and beautified over the centuries; some were then radically rebuilt in the 18th c., and then restored to their original Gothic style in the 19th c.

Fonte Gaia, a rectangular basin in the center of the Campo, was created in 1419 by J. della Quercia; the originals of the exquisite marble panels are now in the Museo Civico. Note, to the right of the fountain, the curving facade of **Palazzo Sansedoni**, and to the left, the crenelated **Palazzo d'Elci.**

Palazzo Pubblico** (*D3*). Symbolic of the independence and wealth of Siena's oligarchic ruling class, this town hall is certainly one of the finest achievements of Gothic civil architecture in Tuscany. As if to underscore the shift from a fortress to a residential palazzo, the popular government "of the Nine" ordered the central, taller wing of this building erected between 1284 and 1305; the two side wings were completed in 1310, with another story added in 1680. The stone lower section of the facade, once lightened by great doors, balanced the brick upper section, still punctuated by two orders of elegant, three-light, mullioned windows. It is crowned by parapets and the vast disk of the "monogram of Bernardino" (1425). As work continued on the exterior, the greatest painters of Siennese art were summoned to decorate the interior, in celebration of the wisdom and taste of the leaders of the Republic. The artworks they created now form the collections of the Museo Civico (see below); a number of halls, used by the city government, are generally closed to the public. From atop the left wing rises the soaring profile of the **Torre del Mangia*** (102 m. tall), built in 1325-48. The sober brick shaft is crowned by a stone corbel structure, probably designed by L. Memmi; it in turn works as the base for a stone structure which

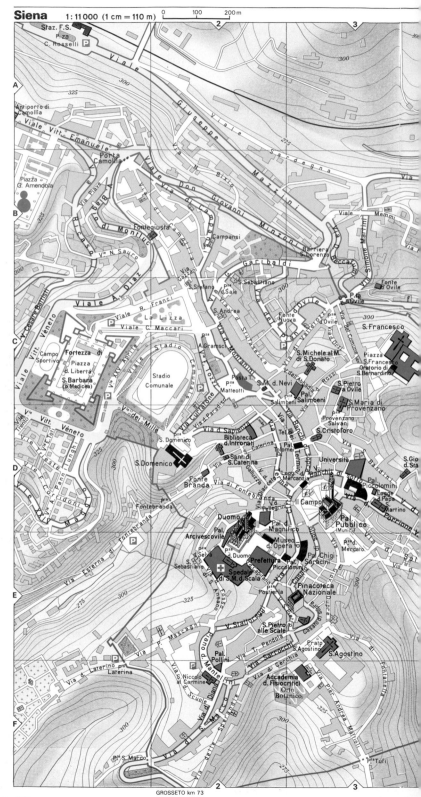

0   100   200 m

Staz. F.S.
P.za
C. Rosselli
Viale
Antiporto di
Camollia
Viale Vitt. Emanuele
Porta Camollia
Piazza
G. Amendola
Viale di Camp.
Viale Giuseppe Mazzini
Viale Sardegna
Via
Viale N. Bixio
Via Garibaldi
Fontegiusta
Via N. Sauro
Campansi
Viale di Montluc
Barriera
S. Lorenzo
Garibaldi
Viale A. Diaz
Via Gazzani
S. Stefano
P.za d. Sale
S. Sebastiano
Fonte d'Ovile
Viale R. Franci
La Lizza
Viale C. Maccari
S. Andrea
Fonte Nuova
P.za d'Ovile
S. Francesco
Viale Vitt. Veneto
Fortezza di
Campo Sportivo
Piazza d. Libertà
S. Barbara (o Medicea)
Stadio Comunale
P.za A.Gramsci
Posta T.
S.M. d. Nevi
S. Michele al M. di S.Donato
Piazza S.Francesco
Oratorio di S.Bernardino
Viale Vitt. Veneto
Viale XXV Aprile
Via Tozzi
Via di Abbadia
S. Pietro a Ovile
S. Maria di Provenzano
Via dei Mille
Via Curtatone
P.za Matteotti
P.za Salimbeni
Pal. Salimbeni
Provenzano Salvani
S. Cristoforo
Università
S. Gio d. Sta
Via d. Sapienza
Biblioteca d. Intronati
Sant. di S. Caterina
Tel. e Tel.
Pal. Tolomei
Loggia d. Mercanzia
Banchi di Sotto
Pal. Piccolomini
Loggia d. Papa
S. Domenico
S. Domenico
Fonte Branda
Via di Fontebranda
Il Campo
Pal. Pubblico (Municipio)
Porrione
Fontebranda
Duomo
Pal. Arcivescovile
Pal. Magnifico
Museo d. Opera
Pal. Chigi Saracini
P.za d. Mercato
Via Esterna di Fontebranda
S. Selva
S. Sebastiano
d. Duomo
Prefettura
Pal. Piccolomini
Spedale di S.M.d.Scala
Pinacoteca Nazionale
Postierla
V. Stalloreggi
S. Pietro alle Scale
Via P. Mascagni
Pal. Pollini
V. Sarrocchi
Prato d'Agostino
S. Agostino
Laterina
Via d. Laterina
S. Niccolò al Carmine
Pal. Mandoli
Accademia d. Fisiocritici
Orto Botanico
P. S. Marco
P. Tufi

GROSSETO km 73

342

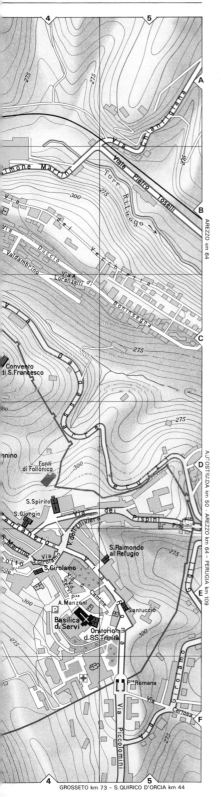

AREZZO cm 64

AUTOSTRADA km 50 – AREZZO km 64 – PERUGIA km 109

serves as the belfry. At the base of the tower, the **Piazza chapel** is a marble loggia joined to the facade of Palazzo Pubblico; built from 1352 to 1376 to fulfill a vow taken during the Black Death of 1348, its upper section was completed in 1461-68. The sadly deteriorated fresco over the altar was by Sodoma (1537-39).

The portal to the right of the Piazza Chapel leads to the porticoed *courtyard of the Podestà* (1325). At the far side, on the right, is the *Teatro dei Rinnovati (open by request, enquire at the Museo Civico)*, once the hall of the Gran Consiglio della Repubblica, rebuilt as a theater in 1560, and once again rebuilt, after two fires, by A. G. Bibiena in 1753. On the left, entrance to the 503-step stairway to the top of the Torre del Mangia *(you can climb the tower, maximum, 30 persons at a time: mid-Jun/mid-Sep., 10-7; mid-Nov./mid-Mar., 10-1:30; in the other months, 10-5 or 10-6)* with its fabulous view* of Siena. Further to the right, the entrance to the *Magazzini del Sale*, partly subterranean rooms with brick vaults, used for temporary exhibits, and to the Museo Civico.

Museo Civico** *Open, mid-Mar./mid-Nov., 9:30-7:45; Sun. and mid-Nov./mid-Mar., 9:30-1:45.* This museum comprises an impressive gallery of paintings as well as the monumental halls of Palazzo Pubblico. From the courtyard of the Podestà, you climb first of all to the 19th-c. *Hall of the Risorgimento* (late-19th-c. frescoes by Tuscan artists, including C. Maccari). A steep staircase leads up to the loggia (see below), followed by the *Sala (or Hall) di Balìa*, with 15th-c. frescoes; the *Sala dei Cardinali*, with sculptures by a student of J. della Quercia and detached frescoes; the *Sala del Concistoro*, featuring a carved portal* by B. Rossellino (1446) and frescoes by D. Beccafumi in the vault. The little *forechapel*, with frescoes by T. di Bartolo (1414), contains ancient gold jewelry, including the mid-15th-c. gold rose of Pope Pius II; the *chapel**, with wrought-iron gate (1437) and inlaid wood choir** (1415-28) by D. di Niccolò, features fine frescoes by T. di Bartolo (1407) and, an altar piece* by Sodoma. In the *Sala del Mappamondo*, a great hall where the Council of the Republic met, on the far wall, the renowned fresco of the **"Maestà"**** by Simone Martini (1315), recently restored. Facing it is "Siege of the Castle of Montemassi by Guidoriccio da Fogliano"** (1328-29), a fresco long attributed to Simone Martini, now debated. The hall contains other fine artworks, by S. di Pietro, Sodoma, and Duccio di Buoninsegna. In the *Sala della Pace*, or Hall of Peace, you can see the remarkable **"Allegory of Good and Bad Government,"**** a set of frescoes painted for the Government of the Nine, by Ambrogio Lorenzetti in 1338-40. Next comes the *Sala dei Pilastri*, with Siennese paintings from the 13th to the 15th c., including works by: G. da Siena, A. Lorenzetti, N. di Bartolomeo, and M. di Giovanni. The *gallery* features Italian and especially Siennese paintings from the 16th to the 18th c., notable among them works by J. Roos and B. di David. Upstairs, the *Loggia dei Nove*, overlooking the Piazza del Mercato and the Siennese countryside, displays the fragments of the Fonte Gaia* by J. della Quercia, reassembled in 1904 *(undergoing restoration, to be moved)*.

Università degli Studi (*D3*). At the corner of Via S. Vigilio, overlooking Via Banchi di Sotto (n. 55-57), this *former convent* was founded in the 11th c. and repeatedly renovated until the neo-Renaissance version of 1891. Now the office of the Rector of the University of Siena, this building has, since 1816, been the headquarters of the ancient Siennese Studio, which dates back to the 13th c. Note the Gothic *funerary monument* in the courtyard. If you follow *Via S. Vigilio*, a covered entrance (on the left, after Via Angiolieri) leads into the Courtyard of the **Castellare degli Ugurgieri**, a medieval fortress-home. On Via Bandini note the Renaissance palazzi of the *Bandini Piccolomini* family (n. 25-29).

Palazzo Piccolomini* (*D3*). This impressive piece of architecture from the later Florentine Renaissance was built from 1469 on by P.P. del Porrina, probably to a plan by B. Rossellino, and enlarged in the 17th c. The light rustication of the facade overlooking Via Banchi di Sotto (n. 52) is crowned by a broad cornice: note the two large marble crests over the main doorway, with the heraldic device of the Piccolomini family. This building contains the *State Archives*, with vast collections of historic documents, and, especially, the records of the Siennese Republic. Four halls on the third floor contain the **Museo dell'Archivio di Stato*** (*open, 9-1; Sun. closed*), *featuring the collection of the Biccherne***, 103 painted wooden tablets which served as covers for books of public records, commissioned from 1258 and 1659, and painted by such great artists as Ambrogio and Piero Lorenzetti, G. di Paolo, Vecchietta, S. di Pietro, F. di Giorgio Martini, and D. Beccafumi. The Archives also contain documents concerning episodes or persons mentioned in Dante's Divine Comedy, the last will and testament of Boccaccio, and writings of St. Catherine of Siena.

Logge del Papa (*D3*). This elegant Renaissance loggia with three arcades marks the eastern end of Via Banchi di Sopra; it was built by A. Federighi (1462) at the behest of Pope Pius II Piccolomini.

S. Martino (*D3*). Nearby is one of Siena's oldest churches, which gave its name to the "terzo" (or quarter) of S. Martino. Built in 1537, with a solemn facade from 1613, the church has nothing of the original, much-older structure; inside, note the Baroque ciborium by G. Mazzuoli (1649) and marble altars, with paintings by G. Reni and D. Beccafumi.

Salicotto (*E3-4*). Linked to Via del Porrione and Via S. Martino by many steep cross-lines, this old quarter of Siena was largely "sanitized" in the 1930s; where it comes closest to Via S. Martino, the buildings on the right of Vicolo delle Scotte, once part of the Ghetto, include the classical Sephardic *Synagogue*, by G. del Rosso (1756).

S. Girolamo (*E4*). *Open by request, enquire at the nearby convent.* This convent church was founded in 1354 by the Jesuits; inside is a painting by S. di Pietro.

Basilica dei Servi* (*E4*). This immense church was begun in the 13th c., and was not completed and consecrated until 1533, with the 15th-c. facade still unfinished. Alongside it stands a 14th-c. campanile (completely restored in 1926). From the broad stairway before it, you have a fine view* of the walled city, the Torre del Mangia, and the Loggia dei Nove of Palazzo Pubblico, as well as the Cathedral, with its tall Romanesque bell tower and the distinctive silhouette of the unfinished "great facade."
The luminous *interior*, with three aisles and slen-

der marble columns, preserves the original Renaissance plan, though it is sadly marred by 19th-c. "restorations." Of special interest, among the many artworks by the Siennese school, between the 13th and 16th c., are those by: C. di Marcovaldo, M. di Giovanni, N. di Segna, S. di Bonaventura, P. Lorenzetti, B. Fungai, T. di Bartolo, and G. di Paolo.

Oratorio della SS. Trinità (*E4-5*). *Open by request, enquire in the Contrada di Valdimontone, tel. 222590.* Just behind the Basilica dei Servi, overlooking Via Valdimontone, this oratory was built around 1380 and was renovated at the end of the 16th c.; inside, stuccoes and frescoes by V. Salimbeni, A. Casolani, and L. and C. Rustici.

Via Roma (*E4-5*). This twisting road links Via di Pantaneto with Porta Romana. Set back at the end of Via del Refugio is the church of *S. Raimondo al Refugio (open by request, enquire in the nearby collegiate church)*, with work by some of the leading Siennese painters of the late-16th c., including F. Vanni, S. Folli, and R. Manetti. Further along is the little church of the **Santuccio**, founded in the 14th c. and rebuilt in the 16th c. Note 17th-c. frescoes by V. Salimbeni. In the sacristy is the *Museo della Società di Esecutori di Pie Disposizioni (entrance at n. 71; open by request, tel. 220400, 9-12; Sun. closed)*, with work by 14th-/16th-c. Siennese painters.

Porta Romana* (*F5*). Built after 1328, this is the largest of the gates in the 14th-c. walls.

S. Maria degli Angeli in Valli. *Open by request, enquire in the parish church of S. Mamiliano in Valli, Via Piccolomini n. 153.* This 15th-c. church, standing outside the walled perimeter of Siena (on the left, as you descend Via Piccolomini), was once the convent church of a monastery destroyed in the 18th c.: note the elegant Renaissance marble portal; inside, on the main altar, note Virgin with Child, by R. del Garbo (1502).

S. Spirito (*D4*). Overlooking the oddly shaped Piazza S. Spirito, with its handsome 16th-c. *Fountain* of the "Pispini," this solemn brick Renaissance church features a portal believed to be by B. Peruzzi (1519). Inside, paintings by Sodoma and D. Beccafumi, and a terracotta creche by A. della Robbia.

Via di Pantaneto (*D-E3-4*). Lined by 16th- and 17th-c. buildings, this road runs out to the *Porta di S. Maurizio*; to the left of the gate, note the 14th-c. *Fonte di S. Maurizio*.

S. Giorgio (*D4*). This church dates from the Middle Ages and overlooks Via di Pantaneto with a vast Roman Baroque facade, by G.P. Cremona (1730-38); inside, painting by F. Vanni.

S. Giovannino della Staffa (*D3*). *Open by request, enquire in the Contrada del Leocorno, tel. 289021.* Set back on Piazzetta Grassi along Via di Follonica, this 13th-c. church was rebuilt in 1563 by G.B. Pelori. Inside, note paintings by R. Vanni, R. and D. Manetti, B. Mei, and F. di Vannuccio.

The Duomo, the Pinacoteca Nazionale, and the "terzo" di Città

Its skyline marked by the 13th-c. dome of the Cathedral and by its white- and black-striped bell tower, the "terzo di Città" is the oldest part of Siena. With the paintings of the Pinacoteca, the pulpit by Nicola Pisano in the Cathedral, and the "Maestà" by Duccio in the Museo dell'Opera, this route becomes a short course in some of the finest art that Italian history has to offer.

Loggia della Mercanzia* (*D3*). This elegant Gothic-Renaissance structure (1417-44) is made of three broad arcades, with statues in niches and 16th-c. frescoes and stuccoes beneath its vaults; note the two 15th-c. marble benches, with carved reliefs.

The loggia stands near the *Croce del Travaglio*, Siena's central crossroads, where Via Banchi di Sotto and Via Banchi di Sopra, once part of the medieval Via Francigena, meet Via di Città, which leads to the Spedale and the Duomo.

Via di Città* (*D-E2-3*). The refined main avenue of the section of ancient Siena where the Longobard Gastaldo once lived, is still distinctly medieval in flavor; it climbs in a gentle curve, lined with elegant stores and 14th- and 15th-c. aristocratic palazzi. Just past *Chiasso del Bargello*, with a charming view of Palazzo Pubblico, the 14th-c. *Palazzo Patrizi* (n. 75-77) is the headquarters of the Accademia degli Intronati, a celebrated Siennese cultural institution founded in the 16th c. Further on is the vast curving facade of the 13th-c. *Palazzo Marescotti*, now called **Palazzo Chigi-Saracini*** (n. 89); note the handsome courtyard. This is the headquarters of the respected *Accademia Musicale Chigiana*, which holds fine concerts here, and has one of Italy's finest private art collections (*the collection can be toured by scholars, call the Monte dei Paschi, tel. 296832*), featuring archeological artifacts, sculptures, furniture, ceramics, and Tuscan paintings from the 14th to the 17th c., including works by Sodoma, Sassetta, and Beccafumi. Practically facing it is **Palazzo Piccolomini*** (n. 126), now an office building for the Banca d'Italia; it was almost certainly built by B. Rossellino (1495). Also note the 14th-c. *Palazzo Marsili* (n. 132), heavily restored in the 19th c.

Piazza Postierla (*E2*). Dominated by the medieval *tower-house of the Forteguerri*, this square has a 15th-c. *column* and is lined by the 16th-c. *Palazzo Chigi Piccolomini alla Postierla*, designed by Riccio (in Via del Capitano, n. 1), also, the 13th-c. *Palazzo del Capitano del Popolo* (n. 15), heavily renovated in 1854, restored to early Gothic.

Piazza del Duomo* (*E2*). Dominated by the black-and-white marble mass of the Duomo, high atop its stepped platform, the asymmetrical piazza features some of Siena's oldest and most important buildings.

To the left of the cathedral is the **Palazzo Arcivescovile**, built in 1718-24 in 14th-c. Gothic style; facing it is the long facade of the *Spedale di S. Maria della Scala* (see below) and, to the right of the cathedral, the 16th-c. **Palazzo del Governatore dei Medici**, now the seat of police business and provincial government. Further along is *Piazza Jacopo della Quercia*, originally planned as the site of the three aisles of the gargantuan but unbuilt Duomo Nuovo; relics of this project can seen in the colonnade and in the surrounding buildings, as well as in the "facciatone," the unfinished facade of this giant "new cathedral."

Duomo** (*D-E2*). The pride of Siena, intended to be the "the greatest monument in Christendom," this is one of the most successful creations of Italian Romanesque-Gothic.

An earlier cathedral was built here around the 9th c.; a larger one was built in its place and consecrated in 1179, but beginning in 1215-20 the building was rebuilt and enlarged; only the crypt remained intact. All scholars now agree that the architect was Nicola Pisano. Work

Siena: Duomo

began on the facade in 1284. In 1339 work began on the ambitious — even overweening — project to make the Cathedral merely a transept of another, immense cathedral, the Duomo Nuovo; the Siennese gave up this folly in 1357. Between 1377 and 1382 facade and apse were completed.

The majestic *facade*, largely the Romanesque-Gothic creation of G. Pisano, stands out for its exquisite decorations and many sculptures, largely by Pisano and his school. Many of the originals are now in the Museo dell'Opera Metropolitana. Note, on the right side of the Cathedral, the large Gothic windows and the Porta del Perdono: in the lunette, bas-relief by Donatello; the original is in the Museo dell'Opera. The tall Romanesque *bell tower** was built in the late 13th c. White- and black-striped, it has a progression of mullioned windows, ranging from one-light to six-light, at top.

The **interior**, built to a Latin-cross plan, has three huge aisles; the grandiose proportions are underscored by the black-and-white stripes of the walls, and by the **marble floor**** with marble decorations, in color and with etched depictions. This immense artwork, with its 56 panels depicting sacred and profane scenes, unique in art history, is covered for protection, and can only be seen during solemn occasions. Among the artists who worked on it, from 1373 to 1547, were G. di Stefano, N. di Bartolomeo, A. Federighi, Pinturicchio, Beccafumi, and F. di Giorgio Martini. Worn down by the shoes of the faithful, part of the floor was completely redone in the 19th c., by A. Maccari. Noteworthy counter-facade, with *central portal* and columns attributed to G. di Stefano. Above it, over the arcades, along the nave and the presbytery runs a 15th-/16th-c. cornice with terracotta busts of the popes.

The **transept**, with its double aisle, has hexagonal cross vaults and a great dome, with a twelve-sided base. Six large gilded statues of saints (G. di Stefano, 1488) stand beneath a blind gallery, adorned with depictions of patriarchs and prophets. At the opening of the *right transept* is the circular Baroque *Chapel of the Vow*, attributed to G.L. Bernini (1662), who also did the two marble statues. Inside the chapel, 13th-c. Madonna del

Voto, and a masterpiece by M. Preti (1670). In the middle of the *presbytery*, note the main altar by B. Peruzzi (1532), topped by a bronze ciborium* by Vecchietta, which replaced Duccio's "Maestà" in the early-16th c.; on the nearby pillars, the various angels are by G. di Stefano (1489), F. di Giorgio Martini (1490) and Beccafumi (1548-51). In the *apse*, note the 14th-c. wooden choir,* partly inlaid by Fra' Giovanni da Verona (1503), assembled here in the 19th c. but originally from Monte Oliveto Maggiore; on high, note exquisite circular stained glass* of 1288 (one of the earliest made in Italy) to cartoons by D. di Buoninsegna. To the left of the presbytery, note the fine holy-water stoup* by G. di Turino (1434) at the entrance to the *sacristy (open by request)*, with frescoes by B. di Bindo (1412). From here, you can reach the Chapter Hall, with portraits of Siennese popes and bishops, and two paintings by S. di Pietro.

In the *left transept*, note the octagonal marble **pulpit**** by N. Pisano (1266-68), a masterpiece of Italian Gothic sculpture (also by his son Giovanni, and others, including A. di Cambio); the stairs are by B. Neroni, the Riccio (1543).

At the beginning of the left transept is an elegant portal by Marrina, through which you enter the Renaissance *Cappella di S. Giovanni Battista** (1492), with paintings by Pinturicchio (1504-06), partly redone by Rustichino (1615-16); throughout, sculpture by Donatello (1457), A. Federighi (ca. 1460), G. di Stefano, N. di Bartolomeo (1487), T. di Camaino (1317), and F. Vanni (1596).

At the end of the left aisle is the entrance to the **Libreria Piccolomini**** *(open, mid-Mar./Sep, 9-7:30; Oct., 9-6:30; Nov./mid-Mar., 10-1 and 2:30-5)*, a Renaissance library built beginning in 1492 by the future pope Pius III, to hold the books of his uncle, Pope Pius II. The marble facade was decorated in classical style by Marrina (1497), and bears a fresco by Pinturicchio; note the polychrome wooden group of sculptures by A. di Betto (1421). The walls of the library are frescoed** by Pinturicchio (1502-1509): in the middle is the group of the Three Graces*, a 3rd-c. Roman copy from a Hellenistic original; on display are exquisite illuminated 15th-c. choir books*. Next to the entrance, in the aisle of the cathedral, note the huge Piccolomini altar*, begun by A. Bregno in 1481: four of the statues of saints are by Michelangelo (1503-04), while the Virgin with Child (center, top) is attributed to J. della Quercia.

Spedale di S. Maria della Scala *(E2)*. This huge medieval hospital complex was built to serve pilgrims and the poor, between the 9th and 11th c.; the facade was renovated repeatedly through the 13th/15th c., and features large mullioned windows. Of particular note, inside *(open by request, 8:30-1, tel. 299410)* is the vast *infirmary*, or "Pellegrinaio," with a series of frescoes* depicting the hospital's history and everyday operation, by D. di Bartolo, P. della Quercia, and Vecchietta (1440-44). Part of the facade is the flank of the 13th-c. church of **SS. Annunziata**, rebuilt in 1466; inside, note the Crucifix (ca. 1330) and impressive 15th-c. organ; also, statue* by Vecchietta (1476) and fresco by S. Conca (1732). As Siena's new polyclinic is completed, the Spedale is being retired as a working hospital; there are plans to convert it into a museum.

Museo Archeologico Nazionale *(E2)*. *Open, 9-1:30; Sun., until 12:30; closed first and last Mon. of each month*. With a separate entrance at the beginning of the Via del Capitano, this Museum was recently (1993) renovated and reinstalled in two huge halls in the Spedale di S. Maria della Scala. Its collections comprise materials (vases, urns, kraters, coins, and jewelry) from prehistoric, Etruscan, and Roman periods, largely drawn from the 19th-c. private collections that constitute the museum's historical core; these are found in the "*antiquarium*." In the so-called *topographic section* are archeological finds, mostly tomb furnishings, found in Siena and its territory (Murlo, Chianti, and the Upper Val d'Elsa).

Museo dell'Opera Metropolitana* *(E2)*. *Open, mid-Mar./Sep., 9-7:30; Oct., 9-6:30; Nov./mid-Mar., 10-1 and 2:30-5*. Housed in a building in Piazza Jacopo della Quercia, built as early as the 15th c. in what had been intended as the right aisle of the planned Duomo Nuovo, or New Cathedral, this museum comprises works of art from the decoration and furnishing of the Cathedral. On the *second floor*, the *Sala di Duccio* features, on the facing wall, the front of the **"Maestà"**** by Duccio di Buoninsegna (1308-11), masterpiece of Siennese art, commissioned for the main altar of the Cathedral; on the other side of the room, the back of the altar piece. On the right wall, a notable triptych** by P. Lorenzetti (1342), and a Madonna* done by Duccio in his youth* (ca. 1283). In the three other rooms on this floor, wooden statues, golden reliquaries, ivory crosiers, and illuminated choir books outdo one another in splendor. Note the small wooden Crucifix* by G. Pisano; also, three wooden busts of saints*, by F. di Valdambrino (1409).

Third floor. In the middle of the first hall, an early 13th-c. "Madonna dagli occhi grossi"* (named for her outsized eyes); four saints by A. Lorenzetti; and various works by such artists as G. di Paolo, S. di Pietro, a follower of Sassetta, G. di Cecco. In the other rooms: M. di Giovanni, D. Beccafumi, Pomarancio; also altar pieces, liturgical garb, and other objects. From the last room, you can climb up to the top of the unfinished facade of the Duomo Nuovo, known in Siena as the "facciatone," or "great facade" (fine view*).

Ground floor. At the center, a relief by J. della Quercia**, and a bas-relief tondo** by Donatello; along the walls, ten statues** by G. Pisano (1284-96), once on the facade of the Cathedral, masterpieces of Gothic sculpture. You leave through the deconsecrated 17th-c. church of *S. Niccolò in Sasso*.

S. Giovanni Battista* *(D2)*. This is Siena's *baptistery*, and is located beneath the apse of the Duomo, on Piazza S. Giovanni. You take a 15th-c. staircase down to it, through the **portal*** by G. di Agostino, meant as part of the right side of the giant Duomo Nuovo (1345); midway down is the *Crypt of Statues*, used for exhibitions.

The church, built amid the arches that support the extended apse of the Duomo over Valle Piatta, has a Gothic facade, with three large splayed portals. Inside, amid frescoes by many mid-15th-c. artists, including Vecchietta, note the great hexagonal **baptismal font**** (1416-34), a masterpiece of the early Tuscan Renaissance, believed to have been built under the overall direction of J. della Quercia. J. della Quercia also did the marble ciborium with statue of John the Baptist and bas-reliefs; the bronze angels are by Donatello and G. di Turino, who also did the bas-reliefs, along with G. di Neroccio, J. della Quercia, T. di Sano, and L. Ghiberti.

Palazzo del Magnifico (*D2*). Overlooking Piazza S. Giovanni and Via dei Pellegrini, to the left of the baptistery, this palazzo was named for P. Petrucci, seignor of Siena between 1487 and 1512. It was built in 1504-09, by G. Cozzarelli, the facade is in poor condition. Facing the church of S. Giovanni Battista, in the facade of n. 12/13, a bust marks the birthplace of the architect F. di Giorgio Martini.

Pinacoteca Nazionale** (*E3*). *Open, 8:30-2 (Sun., 8-1); Jul.-Sep., Tue.-Sat., extended hours, until 7.* On the left in Via S. Pietro, this art gallery is located in the early-15th-c. *Palazzo Buonsignori* (n. 29), and the adjacent Gothic *Palazzo Brigidi*, both of which have been restored in the Romantic style of the 19th c.

This gallery dates from the 18th c., when a great scholar named G. Ciaccheri began to collect the work of Siennese "primitive" artists, and it has been in the present location since 1930, filling some thirty rooms; this is certainly one of the most important collections for an understanding of Siennese painting as it developed from the late-12th c. to the early 17th c.

From the elegant courtyard of Palazzo Buonsignori, a stairway (right) leads to the **3rd floor**. *Siennese painters* featured include, from *the 13th c.. G. da Siena, Maestro del S. Pietro, Maestro del S. Giovanni;* from *the 14th c.*: D. di Buoninsegna, N. di Segna, U. di Nerio, B. di Fredi , L. di Tommè, S. Martini, L. Memmi, A. Lorenzetti, P. Lorenzetti, P. di Giovanni Fei, B. Bulgarini, D. di Bartolo, M. da Besozzo, L. Monaco, S. Aretino, and T. di Bartolo; from *the 15th c.*: G. di Paolo, Sassetta, Maestro dell'Osservanza, M. di Giovanni, N. di Bartolomeo, F. di Giorgio Martini, P. di Domenico, G. di Benvenuto, S. di Pietro, and Vecchietta. You descend to the **2nd floor**, where there are other works by *Siennese painters of the 15th c.*: G. da Cremona, P. degli Orioli, G. Genga, Pinturicchio, and B. Fungai; and of the *16th c.*: D. Beccafumi, Sodoma, and Brescianino. On the **4th floor** is the *Collezione Spannocchi*, featuring works by northern Italian and central European artists of the 15th and 16th c., among them: A. Dürer, L. Lotto, Sofonisba Anguissola, Q. Massys, P. Bordone, and Palma the Younger.

S. Pietro alle Scale (*E3*). Founded in the 13th c. and rebuilt in the 18th c., this church has fragments of frescoes by L. da Verona and segments of a polyptych by A. Lorenzetti; on the main altar, note canvas by R. Manetti.

S. Agostino (*E3*). *Open by request, enquire in the parish church of S. Pietro in Castelvecchio, Via S. Pietro.* Built in the 13th c. and renovated in 1747-55 by L. Vanvitelli, this church overlooks the *Prato S. Agostino*; before it extends a 19th-c. portico by A. Fantastici. The luminous, neoclassical interior holds works by Perugino, A. Lorenzetti, F. di Giorgio Martini, L. Signorelli, R. Manetti, and Sodoma. Also note a marble altar by F. del Turco (1608), majolica floors, and a 15th-c. wooden Virgin.

Accademia dei Fisiocritici (*F3*). *Hours of the museum, 9-1 and 3-6; closed Thu. aft., Sat. and Sun.* This respected academy for the study of science was founded in 1691 by P.M. Gabrielli, and still does extensive research, Located at n. 5 in Prato S. Agostino, across from the church, the academy has many collections of the life sciences, with part of the **museum** installed in the cloister, and on the ground and 2nd floor; outside is a *botanical garden (open by request, enquire in the Accademia).*

S. Niccolò al Carmine (*F2*). This church overlooks the vast semicircular expanse of Piano dei Mantellini, and can be reached from Prato S. Agostino along the distinctive *Via T. Pendola*, with its venerable old homes, and then down along Via di S. Quirico, past the 16th-c. *Palazzo Pollini* (n. 39-41). The church was founded in the 14th c. and renovated often in the 15th/16th c.; note the campanile attributed to B. Peruzzi (1517). Inside, note paintings by Beccafumi, Sodoma, A. Casolani (1604), and G. del Pacchia; note main altar, by T. Redi. To the right of the church (n. 40), note the Neoclassical facade of *Palazzo Incontri*, designed by S. Belli (1799-1804).

Via Stalloreggi (*E2*). This road twists and turns past craftsmen's workshops with a medieval flavor, extending Via di Città along the hill of Castelvecchio; at the far end, near Piano dei Mantellini, is the *Arco delle Due Porte*, an old city gate incorporated in the surrounding buildings; on the inner side, 14th-c. fresco by B. di David. Returning toward Piazza Postierla, on the right, *Via di Castelvecchio* runs through a series of houses and lanes that make up a medieval quarter; at the intersection of Via Stalloreggi and Via di S. Quirico, note the *tabernacle*, with a Pietà by Sodoma.

The "terzo" di Camollìa and S. Domenico

In the northern part of town, heavily modified in the 19th and 20th c., you can still find the memories of two great, eloquent Siennese saints: St. Bernardino would preach in the oratory near S. Francesco; the son of a washerman, Caterina Benincasa, or St. Catherine of Siena, lived near the Fonte Branda, in a house that had been turned into a sanctuary as early as the 15th c.

Via Banchi di Sopra (*D3*). The backbone of the "terzo," or quarter of Camollìa, this road climbs with a slight curve from the Croce del Travaglio, breaking off at the *Piazza Tolomei*, with its column, topped by the she-wolf of Siena (1610). On the left, the 13th-c. **Palazzo Tolomei*** (n. 11); on the right side of the palazzo, in Vicolo della Torre, a plaque bears the verses from Dante's Divine Comedy concerning Pia dei Tolomei, believed to have lived in this house.

S. Cristoforo (*D3*). Facing Palazzo Tolomei, still in the "terzo" of S. Martino, this Romanesque church has a neo-Classical brick facade; inside, canvas by G. del Pacchia (1508); outside, a handsome little 12th-c. cloister (rebuilt in 1921) with view of the intact original apse.

S. Maria di Provenzano (*C-D 3*). This majestic basilica, with a fine view of the surrounding walls and hillsides, was built immediately after the Medici conquest, in 1595-1604; inside, marble floor (1685) and immense main altar by F. del Turco (1617-31), with the 15th-c. terracotta image of the Madonna di Provenzano.

S. Pietro a Ovile (*C3*). *Open by request, enquire in the church of S. Maria di Provenzano.* Cattycorner to the

Basilica di Provenzano, this former church overlooks Via del Giglio and is now used as a university lecture hall: note paintings by G. di Pietro; and G. di Paolo (ca. 1440).

S. Francesco (*C3*). This huge 14th-c. Franciscan basilica, flanked by the Oratory of S. Bernardino (see below) stands on a large square overlooking a panoramic landscape stretching to the hills of Chianti, in the distance. It was completed in 1482, partly destroyed by fire in 1655, and restored to the original Gothic form by G. Partini in 1885-92; the neo-Gothic facade dates from 1894-1913. Inside, note the fragments of frescoes that once adorned Porta Romana, by Sassetta and S. di Pietro (1447-50), and other 14th-c. frescoes by P. Lorenzetti, A. Lorenzetti, and L. Vanni. Also note the portal, by F. di Giorgio Martini.

Convento di S. Francesco (*C3*). To the right of the church (n. 7), this former convent is now largely used by the university: it encloses a large Renaissance cloister, with a handsome Gothic portal by D. di Agostino, leading to the great 15th-c. *crypt*, now a university library.

Oratorio di S. Bernardino* (*C3*). *Open, Apr.-Oct., 10-1 and 2-5; Nov.-Mar., by request, enquire in the Museo dell'Opera Metropolitana.* Built in the 15th c. on the site where St. Bernardino da Siena once preached, this two-level oratory has a fine Renaissance portal (1574). In the *lower oratory*, note 17th-c. frescoes, and painting by S. di Pietro, as well as two 16th-c. terracotta statues. A vestibule with exquisite relief** by G. di Agostino (ca. 1336), precedes the *upper oratory**; note 15th-c. inlays and stuccoes as well as frescoes* and panels by Sodoma, G. del Pacchia, and Beccafumi (1518-37).

Porta Ovile (*C3*). Built in the 13th c., this gate was incorporated in the 14th-c. walls; from S. Francesco take the steep *Via del Comune*. In the small aedicule, note the fresco by S. di Pietro. Then, outside the walls, note the 13th-c. *Fonte d'Ovile* (fountain). Climb back up *Via di Vallerozzi* toward the center, and you will pass on the right the **Oratorio di S. Rocco** (*C3; open by request, enquire at the Contrada della Lupa, tel. 270777*), with paintings by R. Vanni and V. Salimbeni and frescoes by Rutilio Manetti, B. Mei, and S. Salimbeni. Behind the Oratorio, in *Via del Pian d'Ovile*, note the **Fonte Nuova d'Ovile** (*C2-3*), a fountain built in 1295-1303, a fine medieval blend of monumental form and practical function. As you walk from Via di Vallerozzi to Via dell'Abbadia, note the church of **S. Michele al Monte di S. Donato** (*C3*), built in 1147, and extensively renovated since; inside, wooden group by Vecchietta. Facing the church is the enormous *Rocca dei Salimbeni*, a 13th-c. fortress rebuilt in Gothic style in 1883-87 (see below).

Piazza Salimbeni (*C2-3*). "Invented" at the end of the 19th c. by the architect G. Partini as part of a greater Siennese "Gothic revival," at its center is a *monument to S. Bandini* (1880); on the left is the mid-16th-c. *Palazzo Tantucci*, by Riccio.

On the right side is the neo-Renaissance facade, by G. Partini (1877-82), of *Palazzo Spannocchi*, an imitation of the original, by G. da Maiano (1473), in Via Banchi di Sopra. At the far end stands **Palazzo Salimbeni**, once part of a fortress; the 14th-c. Gothic facade is largely the fruit of 19th-c. restorations by Partini (1871-79). The entire complex serves as the offices of *Monte dei Paschi*, an important Siennese bank dating from the Middle Ages; noted historical archive and fine art collections (*open by request, for scholars, enquire at the Monte dei Paschi, tel. 296832*).

S. Maria delle Nevi (*C2*). *Open by request, enquire at the Soprintendenza.* This small oratory was built in 1471 by F. di Giorgio Martini; the sober Renaissance facade overlooks Via dei Montanini; inside, altar piece by M. di Giovanni (1477).

Biblioteca Comunale degli Intronati (*D2*). *Open, Mon.-Fri., 9-7; Sat., 9-2; closed Sun.* At n. 5 in Via della Sapienza, in the building where Siena's Studio, or university, was founded, is a major city institution, based on an 18th-c. donation; it now has more than half-a-million volumes, including codices illuminated by 12th-/15th-c. Siennese artists (L. Vanni, Sassetta, S. di Pietro) and a major collection of drawings and prints. A bit further along, the steep *Costa di S. Antonio* offers a fine view of the Duomo and its quarter; continue down, along the Vicolo del Tiratoio to the Santuario della Casa di S. Caterina (see below) and the Fonte Branda; then return to the center along the **Via della Galluzza**, renowned for the succession of medieval arches through which it passes.

Santuario della Casa di S. Caterina (*D2*). *Open, 9-12:30 and 3:30-6.* You reach the complex of buildings that has grown up around the birthplace of Caterina Benincasa, Siennese mystic and saint (St. Catherine of Siena, 1347-80), patron saint of Italy (with St. Francis), along the *Portico dei Comuni d'Italia* (1941); note the 15th-c. well. An atrium with loggia, attributed to B. Peruzzi, leads to the right to the *church of the Crocifisso*, with a 13th-c. Crucifix, before which the saint supposedly received her stigmata; facing it is the *Oratorio Superiore*, with gilt lacunar ceiling and majolica floors (16th c.), adorned with 16th-/17th-c. paintings by A. Casolani, A. Salimbeni, F. Vanni, R. Manetti, and B. Fungai. Continue down to the *Oratorio della Camera*, with frescoes by A. Franchi (1896); at the altar, 16th-c. masterpiece by G. di Benvenuto; adjacent is the cell of the saint; still further down is the *Oratorio di S. Caterina in Fontebranda* (1465-74), still in use; inside are frescoes by Sodoma, G. del Pacchia, and others; on the altar, wooden statue* of the saint by N. di Bartolomeo (1475). Beneath the Oratorio is the

Siena: S. Domenico and Fonte Branda

"miraculous cellar," where the saint produced a bounty of wine.

Fonte Branda (*D2*). At the end of Via S. Caterina, this is the best-known of Siena's fountains, standing in the shadow of S. Domenico. Mentioned by Boccaccio, and documented as early as 1081, it was rebuilt in 1246, entirely in brick; the merlons and cornice of small arches is modern. Nearby is the panoramic *Vicolo di Camporegio*, with steps, leading up to S. Domenico.

S. Domenico* (*D2*). The nucleus of the huge brick Gothic basilica, now standing, was built between 1226 and 1262-65.

Enlarged around 1350, the church had a difficult existence: badly damaged by fire (1443 and 1531), war (1548-52), and earthquake (1798), it was extensively restored and modified in 1941-62.

Devoid of *facade*, the basilica has a 15th-c. campanile, lopped short in 1793, and still has much of its Cistercian apse. *Inside*, note the high mullioned windows; the huge transept has six apsidal chapels (from the apsidal terrace, fine view* of central Siena, the Duomo, and the Fonte Branda, below). On the right as you enter, is the *Cappella delle Volte*, with a fresco of St. Catherine, by A. Vanni, believed to be the only accurate portrait of her. Along the right wall of the church, 14th-c. wooden Crucifix and marble portal to the **Cappella di S. Caterina**, with frescoes* by Sodoma and paintings by F. Vanni; the marble tabernacle (G. di Stefano; 1466) contains a reliquary with the saint's head. In the sacristy, standard by Sodoma; at the end of the aisle, painting by F. di Giorgio Martini and fresco by P. Lorenzetti.

On the modern main *altar*, note the elegant marble ciborium* and the candle-holding angels* by B. da Maiano (1475). Note paintings by M. di Giovanni, B. di Giovanni, F. di Vannuccio, Sodoma, R. Manetti, S. di Pietro, and B. Salimbeni.

Fortezza di S. Barbara (*C1*). This huge square fort with corner bastions was built at the orders of Cosimo I de' Medici, and designed by B. Lanci (1561). Now a public park, it offers a fine view of hills and city. Inside is the *Enoteca Italiana* (*open, 3-12 midnight*), a wine cellar, with tastings and sale of local varieties. Nearby is the *garden of La Lizza* (*C1-2*), established as a park in 1779 and enlarged at the turn of the 20th c.

Chiesa di Fontegiusta (*B2*). Set back on the left of Via di Camollìa, near the customs office of the *Porta di Pescaia* (closed in 1368), this church was built in 1482-84 with a brick facade (1489). Inside, note the marble main altar*, by Marrina (1517), with late-14th-c. fresco and, on the far wall, painting by F. Vanni (1590).

Porta Camollìa (*B1*). This 17th-c. reconstruction of a 14th-c. gate still bears an inscription honoring Ferdinando I de' Medici, a symbol of Siennese hospitality: "Cor magis tibi Sena pandit" (Siena opens its heart to you, wider than this gate). Outside the gate, along Viale Cavour, is the tall crenelated *Antiporto di Camollìa* (*A1*; 1270); at the end of the road, near where it meets the Via Cassia, is the medieval Palazzo dei Diavoli, restored in 1859.

Syracuse / Siracusa**

elev. 17 m., pop. 127,148, Sicily, provincial capital. Until Roman times, this was the most powerful and magnificent city in all of Sicily. Today, it is an impressive and intriguing sight, with a mixture of late-Baroque architecture — vivid yet damaged

by the passage of time, from the reconstruction of the city following the terrible earthquake of 1693 — and ancient classical architecture. It stands in an exquisite landscape of sea, rocks, Mediterranean vegetation, under a clear blue sky. Recent expansion of the city has largely followed the road leading to Catania.

Historical note. Siracusa was founded, according to tradition, in 734 B.C. by Greek settlers from Corinth; it had soon attained such wealth that in turn Siracusa founded a number of colonies in Sicily. Internal dissension caused it to fall under the rule of the tyrant Gelon in 485 B.C.; Siracusa enjoyed remarkable prosperity under him and under his successor, Hiero. In 466 B.C., Siracusa returned to democratic government, extended its influence over nearly all of Sicily, and the city finally entered into harsh conflict with Athens, trouncing the city soundly (414 B.C.). Over the course of the centuries, the city had grown considerably and become quite lovely; of all its monuments, however, only the ruins of the temple of Apollo have survived, along with the spectacular remains of the temple of Athena, incorporated into the Duomo. With the elimination of the Athenian menace, Siracusa was threatened by the even more dangerous threat of Carthage. The city managed to withstand the new threat under the rule of Dionysius (406-367 B.C.), who built the Castello Eurialo, one of the most perfect works of fortification of the ancient world; later, in 343 with the generous assistance of Timoleon, who sailed from Corinth to the rescue of Siracusa with a thousand soldiers; and finally under Agathocles (316-289 B.C.). The government of the two tyrants may have brought Siracusa to its greatest peak of glory. The growing threat of Carthage remained on the horizon, however, and it was only under the rule of Hiero II (265-215 B.C.) that the city enjoyed a period of relative peace. Hiero II was responsible for the almost total reconstruction of the theater and the great sacrificial altar that stood before the theater. Finally, caught up in the great war between Carthage and Rome, Siracusa was laid waste in 212 B.C.; under the Romans, it became the capital of Sicily, but this was the start of a slow decline. It still built a few monuments, such as the complex of the Ginnàsio and the amphitheater; enormous catacombs speak to the presence of a large Christian community.

Places of interest. **Isola di Ortigia** (*D-F5*). This island was the site of the earliest Greek settlement; it is now an enchanting labyrinth of narrow lanes. In the midddle of the island is the *Piazza Archimede* (*E5*), with the modern fountain of Artemis.

Piazza del Duomo (*E5*) is a handsome Baroque architectural complex.

Duomo**. This cathedral features an 18th-c. Baroque facade by A. Palma (1728-54; note the chiaroscuro), but it was built with the inclusion of the intact outer colonnade of a Doric temple of Athena (5th c. B.C.; the capitals and shafts of the columns can be seen protruding from the side wall in Via Minerva); the nave of the church was once the cella of the temple; among the furnishings of the church, note the baptismal font, made of a Hellenistic krater, supported by little bronze 13th-c. lions. Also note the painting of St. Zosimo*, attributed to Antonello da Messina (it has been removed as a precautionary measure), as well as 16th-c. paintings* by Antonello Gagini.

Fonte Aretusa* (*F5*). This spring bubbles forth into a basin overlooking the sea; note the papyrus plants growing in abundance; it has a romantic renown linked to the myth of the nymph

Syracuse: Piazza del Duomo

Arethusa who threw herself into the sea to elude the pursuit of Alphaeus; according to the myth, she reappeared as a spring, while Alphaeus transformed himself into an underwater river to follow her, till they finally merged their waters; the fresh-water spring of the "*Occhio della Zillica*," feeding into the harbor, is said to be Alphaeus.

Palazzo Bellomo (*E5*). A 13th-c. building, renovated heavily in the 15th c., with Catalonian mullioned windows, the Palazzo Bellomo (*E5*), houses the **Galleria Regionale*** (*tel. 65343*); the interior boasts fine architecture, a collection of *statues*, and a good *art gallery*, with an Annunciation** by Antonello da Messina (1474) and a Burial of St. Lucy* by Caravaggio, as well as an enormous 18th-c. model of the city.

Castello Maniace* (*F5; not open for tours*). The far tip of the island is occupied by this castle, built by Frederick II in 1239; it is square, with round corner towers, a Gothic portal*, and, overlooking the sea, a great three-light mullioned window*.

Via Vittorio Veneto (*D-E5*). This neighborhood, built in the Middle Ages, extends along the eastern side of the island. The road was once the **Mastrarua**, the main street of Spanish Syracuse. Along it are narrow lanes, notable churches, and Baroque palazzi.

Acradina. Of all the sections of the Greek city, this one probably has the least to offer a tourist.

Foro Siracusano (*C-D3*). A shaft and several bases of columns are all that rest of the ancient agora in this great modern square.

Ginnasio Romano (*C3*; 1st c. A.D.). Of the *quadriporticus* that surrounded the old Roman gymnasium, only the perimeter is still visible.

Parco Archeologico della Neapoli** (*A1-2; B1-2; open, 9-4*). The heart of any archeological tour of Syracuse is the archeological park of the Neapolis (Greek for "new town").

Ara di Ierone II (*B1*). The base cut into the rock indicates the altar of Hieron II, which was built for public sacrifices (3rd c. B.C.); during the Roman Empire, an immense porticoed plaza stood before it, with a large pool in the middle.

Anfiteatro Romano* (*B2*). This Roman amphitheater is largely carved from the living

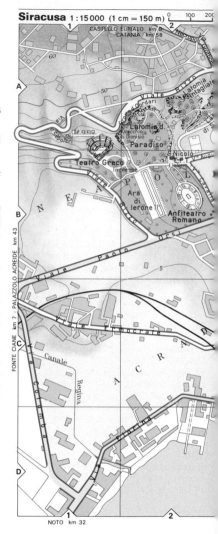

rock; built in the 3rd c. A.D., it was only slightly smaller than the Arena of Verona.

Chiesetta di S. Nicolò (*B2*). Facing the entrance of the amphitheater is this small 11th-c. church, with original apse and small side portal.

Teatro Greco** (*A-B1*). This marvelous Greek theater, cut almost entirely out of living rock, appears as it was following the renovation in 230 B.C., during the reign of Hieron II; still, the theater existed as early as the 5th c. B.C., when tragedies by Aeschylus were performed here, and it was further adapted in Roman times. The semicircular cavea is still intact; it was enormous (with a capacity of 15,000 spectators), and it still has 46 of the original 61 tiers of seats; it encloses the orchestra, behind which was the platform of the scena, little of which remains intact (Charles V used it as a quarry for materials with which to fortify Ortigia); *fine view** of the city from the terrace at the top of the tiers of seats.

Latomia del Paradiso** (*A2*). In the enormous former quarry of the Latomia del Paradiso, literally Prison of Paradise, now partly a garden, is the Orecchio di Dionisio, or Ear of Dionysius, and the Grotta dei Cordari. The name of the **Orecchio di Dionisio***, an artificial excavation that tapers almost to a Gothic arch at the top, was given by the painter Caravaggio (1608), who believed the legend that Dionysius, the ruthless "tyrant" of 4th-c. B.C. Siracusa, used this as a prison because of its remarkable acoustic properties of amplification; the tyrant could thus hear every word the unwary prisoners uttered.

Grotta dei Cordari*. For centuries, and until just a few decades ago, rope and cable makers practiced their profession in the Grotta dei Cordari, a long cave supported by narrow pillars, with odd lighting effects and walls decked with moss and maidenhair ferns.

In the quarter of Tiche

Piazza della Vittoria (*B3*). In this square, archeologists have uncovered a stretch of paved road, running east-west, the backbone of the city layout in Hellenistic and Roman times.

S. Lucia al Sepolcro (*B4*). This church, rebuilt in the 17th c., with a great tree-lined square before it, was built on the site indicated by tradition as that of the martyrdom of St. Lucy, a virgin of 3rd-/4th-c. Syracuse; among the remarkable artworks once here, especially, the Burial of St. Lucy* by Caravaggio, *most are now in Palazzo Bellomo*.

Villa Landolina (*A-B4*). Further inland is the garden of the Villa Landolina, which houses the Museo Regionale (*open, 9-1 and 3-6:30; closed Mon. and holidays*). This is one of the leading archeological museums in all of Italy. In particular, one should note the *finds from the cache of Adrano** (8th c. B.C.); the sculptures of the *Kouros*** and the *Kourotrophos**, archaic Greek statuary from Megara Hyblaea; a marble cornice* with waterspouts in the shape of lions' heads and an acroterial statue of a *Winged Victory**, from the temple of Athena in Syracuse, and an archaic limestone head* from the area around the springs, or Fonti del Ciane.

S. Giovanni* (*A3*). From the ruins of this little church, razed by the earthquake of 1693, you can descend to the *crypt of S. Marciano* (the first bishop of Syracuse); note the Greek-cross plan, the fragments of frescoes from various periods on the walls, and the **catacomb of S. Giovanni***, a 4th-/5th c. underground necropolis, with thousands of burial niches in the main gallery, as well as rotundas and crypts.

Piazza dei Cappuccini (*A5*). A handsome view of the sea and the city can be had from this square; adjacent is the enormous L**atomia dei Cappuccini***, a former prison according to its name, with oddly shaped piers, giant bridges, and remarkable settings in the lush vegetation.

Surrounding areas. At a distance of 8 km. to the west, note the **Castello Eurialo**** (*open, summer, 9-7; winter 9-5; from A1*), the finest and most intact military structure to survive from Greek times, built (402-397 B.C.) by Dionysius the Elder atop the Epipolis to provide security against the Carthaginians; it was partly rebuilt in Byzantine times. The site is as interesting in terms of archeology as of landscape; among the materials on display in the *antiquarium* located in the little home of the custodian, note two colossal dripstones shaped like lion's heads*. At a distance of 30 km. is the *Necropolis of Pantàlica*, the largest cliffside necropolis in Sicily, with over 5,000 cavern tombs on a limestone terrace.

Sorrento

elev. 50 m., pop. 16,911, Campania, province of Naples.

Places of interest. The center of the little town is the **Piazza Tasso** (named for the poet Torquato Tasso, who was born here in 1544); a terrace overlooks the gorge that runs down to the Marina Piccola. The *Basilica di S. Antonino*, a transformed 14th-c. oratory, has an 11th-c. portal on the side. An odd and whimsical bell tower, set on an arch atop four ancient columns, stands before the **Duomo**, rebuilt in the 15th c.; *inside*, note — among other things — the choir, a fine piece of intarsia of the Sorrento school. Note the ruins of a *Roman arch* in the 16th-c. walls on the side uphill of the town.

Near the entrance to the **Villa Comunale**, note the handsome public park, dotted with palm trees overlooking the sea, and the church of *S. Francesco*, with a little *cloister* of Arab-style intertwined arches (14th c.).

Surrounding areas. At the **Punta del Capo*** note the ruins, called the **Bagni della Regina Giovanna** (Baths of Queen Jane; 1st c. A.D.), of the **Villa di Pollio Felice**.

Spoleto*

elev. 396 m.; pop. 37,763; Umbria, province of Perugia. "When you draw near Spoleto," wrote Montesquieu, who was on his way from Rome, "the landscape changes entirely: fertile, well-tended, populous lands; lush hills and mountains; and many olive groves." This is in fact the landscape of the Valle Umbra. Rocky, compact, and austere, grey in the intense green, the Rocca, or fortress, surveys the medieval town below. This is the setting of the "Festival dei Due Mondi," or "Festival of the Two Worlds." Everywhere, the art, history, and culture of many centuries intertwine: a handsome 19th-c. theater alongside a creation of Alexander Calder.

Historical note. Nearly every period of history has left a major mark in Spoleto. The large polygonal stones of the walls date from the pre-Roman Umbrian settlement; the square blocks are from the Roman "colonia," while those shaped like parallelepipeds date from the age of Sulla. Dating from Augustus's reign are the Ponte Sanguinario, the Arco di Druso, and the ruins of a Roman house. From a few centuries later are a temple, the theater, and the amphitheater. Though the early-Christian churches of S. Salvatore and S. Pietro still stand, nothing survives from the high Middle Ages, when Spoleto was the powerful capital of a flourishing duchy, Longobard and later Frankish and Carolingian. The duchy reached its height in A.D. 889, when Guido II was crowned king of Italy and, two years later, Holy Roman Emperor. The duchy declined politically, as Romanesque flourished: note the churches of S. Eufemia, S. Gregorio Maggiore, and S. Giovanni e Paolo. In 1155 Frederick I Barbarossa destroyed the defiant city, with its ancient cathedral; the modern Duomo was built on the site, and consecrated in 1198. By 1231, the "duca-tus spoletinus" had been incorporated into the papal state. Loss of independence did not mean loss of artistic excellence: the Gothic church of S. Domenico, the Rocca, between the 14th and 15th c., the Renassiance frescoes of Filippo Lippi and the Baroque church of S. Filippo. In the late-18th c. G. Valadier worked here, on the Duomo and outside of town (Villa Pianciani). In the late-19th c., the Teatro Nuovo and the Teatro Caio Melisso were built, and later made famous by the Spoleto "Festival dei Due Mondi."

Getting around. For the tour of the historical center, we recommend a walking tour; a second route runs toward the monuments outside the walls, and we recommend driving or taking public transportation.

The historic center

This route runs past Spoleto's chief monuments, with the most notable Roman ruins, S. Eufemia, the Duomo, the Rocca, and Palazzo Comunale. From the dense medieval center of Spoleto, this route runs all the way to the Ponte Sanguinario, near Porta Garibaldi, at the northern end of the old city.

Piazza della Libertà. Set in the center of Spoleto, this square is bounded to the south by the Neoclassical Palazzo Ancaiani. Look down on the ruins of the **Teatro Romano**, from the early empire (partly rebuilt in 1954), in the shadow of the medieval church and monastery of S. Agata (now the Museo Archeologico).

Via Brignone. This road runs up from Piazza della Libertà to the monuments in the center of Spoleto. On the right, Palazzo Mauri; not far off, the Arco di Monterone, one of the mighty gates in the Roman walls, possibly from the 3rd c. B.C.

Arco di Druso*. This travertine arch was built in the 1st c. B.C. as a monumental entrance to the Roman forum; it stands next to the 11th-c. church of S. Ansano. Next to the arch and in part beneath the church are the ruins of a Roman temple, with pronaos with six marble columns.

S. Ansano. Completely rebuilt in the late-18th c., this church has a fragment of a fresco by Spagna. In the 11th-c. crypt*, with 8th-c. columns, note fragments of Byzantine-style frescoes.

Piazza del Mercato. This square lies at the end of Via Arco di Druso; note 17th-c. Palazzo Leti. It occupies a small part of the vast Roman Forum. Note the lovely Fonte di Piazza (1746-48), built in the Roman style of fountains.

Palazzo Comunale. Completely rebuilt in the late-18th c., this town hall preserves only the massive 13th-c. tower and some fragments of the 15th-c. frescoes in the great Salone delle Udienze. Upstairs is the **Pinacoteca Comunale** (*open, 10-1 and 3-6; closed Mon.*), with two detached frescoes by Spagna, originally in the Rocca. Among the painters whose work is in this gallery, let us mention the Maestro di Cesi, A. de Saliba, N. Alunno, Maestro di S. Alò, Guercino, S. Conca, and S. Parrocel. The western wing of Palazzo Comunale, added in 1913, stands on the ruins of a wealthy Roman house (entrance from Via Visiale; open 10-1, 3-6; closed Mon.), believed to have belonged to the mother of the emperor Vespasian.

Piazza Campello. Take the short Via del Municiplo to this square, and note the glimpses between old buildings on your right. This park-like square overlooks all Orvieto, and is bounded by Palazzo Campello (1597-1600), the

13th-c. former church of *Ss. Simone e Giuda*, with the 17th-c. Fontana del Mascherone. Towering overhead is the **Rocca**, a fortress built in 1359-70 by Gattapone for Cardinal Albornoz.

Via dei Duchi. With its old shops, with stone counters, set within the arches of the church of S. Donato, this road takes its name from an enormous Roman building, partly buried, which was believed to be the palace of Theodoric, the Longobard king. At the corner of Via Fontesecca, note the Casa dei Maestri Comacini, home of master builders of the Romanesque period.

Palazzo Arcivescovile. Last rebuilt in the 17th c., this bishop's palace overlooks the 16th-c. facade of *Palazzo Martorelli-Orsini.* Upstairs is the Raccolta Diocesana, a collection of religious art and objects: note paintings by D. Beccafumi and F. Ragusa. On the palazzo grounds are ruins of a major 1st-c. B.C. Roman building, and the little church of S. Eufemia.

S. Eufemia*. Located in the courtyard of Palazzo Arcivescovile, this ancient church was rebuilt in the early-12th c. and again rebuilt often in the centuries that followed. Note the 13th-c. frontal and the fresco in the apse.

Piazza del Duomo. This spectacular square is bounded by the elegant facade of the Duomo; on the right is the 16th-c. *Palazzo Rancani.* On the far side of the square stands the **Palazzo della Signoria**, a complex of buildings, supported by massive piers. At one end is the Casa dell'Opera del Duomo (1419); at the far end, near the Duomo, is the octagonal church of *S. Maria della Manna* (1528). In the middle is the little *Teatro Caio Melisso* (1877-80); note the 3rd-c. A.D. sarcophagus, now a fountain.

Duomo**. Built in Romanesque style in the 12th c. atop the older church of S. Maria in Vescovado, this cathedral has a majestic facade and a mighty campanile. Note the intricate rose window, with four smaller rose windows and symbols of the four Evangelists; also, enormous Byzantine-style mosaic (1207). Fine Romanesque portal (prior to 1198). The **interior** was radically transformed in the early-17th c., but the 12th-c. mosaic floor in the

Spoleto: Duomo

nave is largely original. Note the bronze bust of Pope Urban VIII, by G. L. Bernini (1640) and fresco* by Pinturicchio. In the right transept, canvas by Annibale Carracci and tomb of the painter Filippo Lippi (who died in Spoleto in 1469), designed by his son Filippino. To the right of the presbytery, note chapel of the SS. Icona, with a 12th-c. Byzantine panel, donated to Spoleto by the emperor Frederick I Barbarossa. In the apse, **frescoes**** by Filippo Lippi (with Fra' Diamante and M. d'Amelia; 1467-69); main and lateral altars by G. Valadier (1792). Also, note Crucifix by A. Sozio (1187), painted on parchment and applied to a shaped panel.

S. Filippo Neri. In Piazza Mentana, this church was built around 1650; note painting by S. Conca.

Ss. Giovanni e Paolo. *Open by request, contact the custodian of the Galleria d'Arte Moderna e Contemporanea.* This small Romanesque church, consecrated in 1178, stands near Via Filittèria. Inside, note the 12th-c. frescoes, and a depiction of the murder of St. Thomas à Becket in the Cathedral of Canterbury.

Galleria d'Arte Moderna e Contemporanea. *Open, 10-1 and 3-6; closed Mon.* Located in the *Palazzo Rosari-Spada*, at the end of a downhill lane running off Corso Mazzini, this gallery of modern art came into existence when the town of Spoleto acquired the award-winning artworks of the "Premio Nazionale Spoleto" (1953-66); more art was donated over time; among the artists are C. Accardi, A. Burri, M. Ceroli, G. Capogrossi, P. Consagra, and P. Pascali. A hall is devoted to L. Leonardi, a Spoleto-based painter and sculptor. Also, the original version of the Teodolapio, a large bronze by A. Calder, which has stood in front of the train station since 1962.

Monastero di S. Agata. Built upon the houses of the Corvi family (1395) and later modified, this Benedictine monastery has the stern appearance of a fortified residence; inside, handsome 16th-c. cloister with terracotta pillars. The church stands on buttresses sunk in the Roman theater; inside, fragments of 13th-c. frescoes. In the former monastery, the **Raccolta Archeologica Statale** (*open, 10-1 and 3-6; closed Mon.*) with artifacts, mostly Roman, found during digs in the Spoleto area.

S. Domenico. Built in the late-13th c., with white-and-red bands, this church boasts notable 14th- and 15th-c. frescoes. Also, inside, 14th-c. panel, 15th-c. fresco, altar piece with gold background (Maestro di Fossa, early-14th c.), and carved 14th-c. Crucifix. Nearby, the Teatro Nuovo (1854-64) is the headquarters of the Foundation of the "Festival dei Due Mondi."

Via Cecili. Bounded by a well-preserved stretch of tall **city walls** (6th and 3rd c. B.C.), with Roman and medieval strata, this road runs from Piazza Torre dell'Olio; on the left, the medieval Porta Fuga, commemorates the defeat of the besieging Carthaginians; alongside the medieval Palazzo Vigili stands the tall Torre dell'Olio; this 12th-c. tower was long believed, wrongly of course, to have been crucial in the defeat of Hannibal's troops, 14 centuries before it was built. In any case, its name (Tower of Oil) indicates that boiling oil must have been poured from it onto some troops, though probably not Carthaginians.

S. Nicolò. This former church was built in the early-14th c., and is now used for conferences and cultural events. Beneath it, the little 14th-c. church *S. Maria della Misericordia* still has traces of old frescoes.

S. Gregorio Maggiore*. This 12th-c. church has much of the original Romanesque building, and stands beside a huge 12th-c. bell tower; note the 16th-c. portico, with baptistery on the left (note 14th-c. frescoes). Inside, note 12th-/15th-c. frescoes.

Piazza Garibaldi. Next to Porta Garibaldi, a city gate last rebuilt in the 15th c., this square is also strategically close to the Roman bridge of Ponte Sanguinario. The three-arch bridge was built during the reign of Augustus, and was left behind when the course of the river shifted (access by a partly hidden stairway). Nearby are ruins of an enormous 2nd-c. A.D. Roman amphitheater, visible in the courtyard of the military Caserma Minervio, in Via Anfiteatro.

The monuments outside the walls

This tour involves religious buildings of remarkable architectural and artistic quality, including the churches of S. Pietro and S. Salvatore, built outside Spoleto's walls; also, the ancient church of S. Paolo inter Vineas, SW of the center, and the spectacular Ponte delle Torri.

S. Paolo inter Vineas. Built in early-Christian times, this church was refounded in the 10th c. as a Benedictine convent and was rebuilt in 1234. Inside, note 13th-c. frescoes*.

S. Pietro** (*D2*). Built upon Roman ruins, enlarged in the 13th c., and later enlarged, this church stands on the lowest slopes of Monteluco. Note in particular the 12th-c. facade* of finely carved stone, and in particular the carved branch motifs around the central portal; also note emblems and the bas reliefs depicting scenes from the New Testament. *Inside*, note the 15th-c. baptismal font and holy-water font.

Ponte delle Torri*. This majestic bridge stands 76 m. tall and stretches 230 m. in length; its ten arches now support foot traffic but once brought water to the Rocca. It spans the Tessino, linking Colle S. Elia with Monteluco; it was first built in the 12th c. and was then restructured by Gattapone in the 14th c. You can reach it from the road for Monteluco (left at the first hairpin turns), or walk up from Piazza Campello.

S. Ponziano. Believed to have been built on the grave of a martyr, this 12th-c. Romanesque church stands just beyond the Tessino, next to the state road Flaminia. Note the cornices and hanging arches, simple portal, and rose window with symbols of the Evangelists. Note the peculiar crypt and fine reused columns.

S. Salvatore**. This early-Christian basilica (4th/5th c.) stands on the slopes of the Colle Luciano, just over 1 km. from Piazza della Vittoria. Rebuilt over the centuries, the front and apse are original; the facade has three marble portals. Inside, note the fragments of 14th-c. frescoes, and in a niche in the center of the apse, a 9th-c. painted gem-encrusted cross.

Taormina*

elev. 204 m., pop. 10,255, Sicily, province of Messina.

Places of interest. At the entrance into town from *Porta Messina*, in the *Piazza Vittorio Emanuele*, which lies on the former site of the Forum, stands the 15th-c. **Palazzo Corvaia***, with a crenelated facade, mullioned windows with slender columns, and a Catalonian Gothic portal on the side facing the little church of S. Caterina.

Behind the church, note the **Odeon**, a building from Imperial times, with five wedge-shaped arrays of steps; the front of the scaena was constituted by the side of a Hellenistic temple; you can still see some of the steps of that temple's base.

From the piazza you can stroll to the **Greek theater**** (*open, summer, 9-7; winter 9-4*), which dates from the Hellenistic period (3rd c. B.C.), and was entirely rebuilt in Roman times (perhaps the 2nd c. A.D.): the cavea was built in a natural hollow on the side of a hill; of the scaena, which had a facade of columns and niches, major ruins survive (something quite rare for an ancient theater), and slender cypresses peek out from among them. The *view*** from cavea and from the terraces above the scaena is as it was described by Goethe.

Pleasant cafes and elegant shops line **Corso Umberto**, which runs from one end of the city to the other.

Downhill from the first section of this thoroughfare, the **Naumachia** features a monumental facade in brick, with niches, while the terracing of the hillside dates from Imperial times; this is one of the most significant Roman ruins in Sicily.

Interrupting Corso Umberto is the panoramic terrace of the Piazza IX Aprile, with the Gothic former church of *S. Agostino* (1448).

Through the gate and under the *Torre dell'Orologio*, or clock tower, you enter the medieval quarter; portals and mullioned windows, in Romanesque and Gothic style, embellish the houses.

Further along lies the square, with a 17th-c. fountain, and the **Duomo***, surmounted by crenelation; originally built in the 13th c., this cathedral has a long history of construction; the two side portals are, one from the 15th c., the other Gothic from the 16th c.; on the inside are 15th- and 16th-c. polyptychs of the school of Messina (Visitation, by A. Giuffrè; Virgin and Saints, by Antonello De Saliba).

The "corso" ends at the *Porta Catania* . On the left note the vast mullioned windows of the **Palazzo Duca di Santo Stefano*** (14th/15th c.).

Surrounding areas. Above the city (*by trail, 30 min. from the Circonvallazione, or follow the road for Castelmola*) stands the medieval structure of the **Castello di Taormina** (398 m.), with a magnificent panoramic view* of the ancient acropolis.

At a distance of 5 km., note the picturesque little town of **Castelmola**, built high atop a crag (529 m.); the setting is archaic yet refined, and there is another celebrated *view** from the terrace of the Caffè S. Giorgio.

Tàranto

elev. 15 m., pop. 222,070, Puglia, provincial capital. An islet set between two peninsulas almost completely separates the Mar Grande (inlet of the Gulf of Taranto, bounded by the Chéradi islands and by harbor breakwaters) from the inner Mar Piccolo. The city mostly occupies the islet (the Città Vecchia, or old town) and the peninsula to the SE.

Historical note. Archita of Taranto is a name of some renown in the history of science: he delved into the fields of mathematics, astronomy, music, and cosmogony, as well as ethics and politics. Between 367 and 361 B.C. he ruled the city of Taranto, and for the town, an ancient Spartan colony said to have been founded in 706 B.C., this may have been its finest moment: it was the most important city in all Magna Graecia (the ancient colonial cities and settlements of Greece in southern Italy) and it had introduced the Apulian tribes of the inland cities to Greek culture. There was a pact with Rome of mutual non-interference, so that Roman ships were, under no conditions, to sail past the Lacinian promontory (now Capo Colonna). But the Roman ships did indeed venture past the promontory, and war broke out (280 B.C.). It did the Tarentines little good to appeal to Pyrrhus, the greatest general of his age; with 25,000 troops and the first elephants used in battle in Italy, he beat the Romans, but so suffered in beating them that he achieved what was henceforth known as a Pyrrhic, victory. Finally, the Romans took Taranto (then known as Tarentum). Among the slaves taken to Rome was a boy called Livius Andronicus: the father of Roman dramatic and epic poetry. Although it had been subjugated, Taranto remained a Greek city until the time of the Roman Empire. Thus, the museum of Taranto is an absolute must for anyone who wishes to understand the history of Magna Graecia.

Places of interest. Museo Archeologico Nazionale** (*open, 9-2; holidays 9-1*). The main collection of material found in the national museum here comes from the town of Taranto: Greek statuary, either imported or Tarantine, tomb furnishings from the necropolis, a wide array of ceramics, exquisite women's jewelry and adornments from the Hellenistic period, and terracotta figures, all providing a lively picture of the art and civilization of Magna Graecia. Among the more noteworthy items in the succession of halls: two kore*; a bust of Artemis or Aphrodite** from the school of Praxiteles; the funerary stele* of a warrior, showing him offering a pomegranate to the chthonian serpent; a bearded head* from the school of Lysippus; two statues of Dionysus* from the school of Praxiteles; portraits* of ordinary Romans; Roman mosaic floors*; reliefs* from the necropolis; an architectural sarcophagus**; a Corinthian aryballos* or oil jar; Laconian goblets**; a red-figured Attic lekythos*, a taller variety of oil jar, depicting Athena waking Theseus; vases* with theatrical portrayals; sheet-gold diadems*; a set of jewels from Mòttola (a ring*, a spiral bracelet*); funerary furnishings** from the tomb of the Ori in Canosa, with a silver jewel box** and a golden diadem**, precious stones and enamels; gilt terracottas*; Tarantine figured terracottas with genre subjects (statuettes* from Hellenistic tombs) or theatrical subjects (figures of actors and masks**). The *topographical section* contains, among other things, vases* from the Varrese hypogaeum in Canosa and two proto-Italic scroll-work kraters** from Ceglie del Campo. In the *prehistoric section*, note the paleolithic Venuses* from Parabita, neolithic finds from the caves of: Scaloria* in Manfredonia, S. Angelo* in Ostuni, S. Angelo* in Taranto-Statte, Erba* in Avetrana, Badisco** in Otranto; stone sculptures* from a cave-tomb in Arnesano; and documents concerning the Mycenaean presence* in Puglia in the 16th/15th c. B.C.

In Via Roma 3, in the Istituto Talassografico, is the *Museo Oceanografico* (Museum of Oceanography; *weekdays open, 9-12*).

In the lovely park of **Villa Peripato**, with palm trees and pine trees, opening out over the Mar Piccolo, is the **Museo del Sottosuolo**, a museum of speleology, or the study of caves.

Along the Mar Grande is a handsome promenade among palm trees and pine trees and oleanders, the **Lungomare Vittorio Emanuele III**.

Beyond the swing bridge over the Canale Navigabile,

note the **Castello**, a castle built in 1480, headquarters of the Comando della Marina, or Navy Command Post (Taranto is a major naval base), with a small Museo della Marina.

The **Via del Duomo** runs across the islet of the Città Vecchia, almost exactly as it was during the Middle Ages, with, on either side, a labyrinth of alleys and lanes. At the beginning of the road, note three columns, surviving from a *Greek temple* dating from the 6th c. B.C. Further along (in Via Paisiello, *plaque*) note the birthplace of the composer Giovanni Paisiello.

The **Duomo** dates from the 10th/11th c.; it was later modified and renovated. Note the Baroque facade (1713).

S. Domenico Maggiore. In this church, set high atop a long staircase, note the Baroque altars in the Leccese style; facade and presbytery both belong to the original construction of the early 14th c.

Tarquinia*

elev. 133 m.; pop. 14,020; Lazio, province of Viterbo. The great Etruscan city of "Tarxuna" stood on a strategic highland, now the plain of Civita; its port later became the Roman colony of Gravisca. The city now appears predominantly medieval, dense with towers and buildings dotted with dark volcanic tufa. It is set on a hill not far from the original settlement; close by is a renowned Etruscan necropolis, unrivalled for its tomb paintings.

Places of interest. **Palazzo Vitelleschi** * *.This palazzo, built by the lords of Corneto in 1436-39, now houses the Museo Nazionale Tarquiniense (see below). A mix of Gothic and Renaissance styles, the palazzo boasts a handsome loggia and an elegant inner *courtyard** adorned with sarcophagi and carved slabs. Little of the original interior decoration has survived.

Museo Nazionale Tarquiniense * *. *Open: winter, 9-2, Sun. 9-1; summer, 9-7; closed Mon.* This museum, founded in 1916, comprises the Collection Bruschi-Falgari and various materials belonging to the town of Tarquinia; it was subsequently enriched with material from the excavations of the necropolis and the ancient settlement on the plain of Civita. Most of the material dates from the 6th to the 3rd c. B.C. The collections include funerary slabs and sarcophagi, both Etruscan and Roman (note the Magnate, the Obeso, and the Sacerdote), the so-called **Cavalli Alati** (Winged Horses, a relief from the temple known as the Ara della Regina); Villanovian tomb furnishings and early ceramics; the **vase of Bochoris***, from the tomb of an Egyptian pharaoh, proof of trade between Etruria and the eastern Mediterranean as early as the 7th c. B.C.; Greek vases* of Corinthian and Attic production; and bronze mirrors. Yet to be displayed are frescoes* removed from the tombs of the Olimpiadi, the Letto Funebre, and the Triclinio.

Palazzo Comunale. Originally Romanesque, rebuilt in Baroque style, this buildings stands in the hilltop Piazza Matteotti.

S. Francesco. Consecrated in the 12th c., this church is a mix of Gothic and Romanesque.

Palazzo dei Priori. Set near the 13th-c. former church of *S. Pancrazio*, it comprises four 12th-c. towers, in the heart of the intricate **medieval quarter** — note the church of **S. Martino*** and the 17th-c. *Duomo*.

S. Maria di Castello*. *Open, by request; enquire in the house to the left of the church.* Set in the oldest part of Tarquinia, called *Castello*, high overlooking the valley of the river Marta, still enclosed by medieval walls with towers. Note the central portal. *Inside*, note the lovely capitals on the pillars, the mosaic floors**, the octagonal baptismal font**, the pergamon by G. di Guittone (1209), and the ciborium. On the southern slopes of Castello, is the Romanesque church of *S. Maria di Valverde (closed for restoration)*.

Excursion. To the **Etruscan necropolis of Monterozzi*** (*open: mid-Jun./mid-Sep., 9-7; rest of the year, 9-2; Sun., 9-1; closed Mon.; to safeguard the tombs, only six of them can be toured*), in the countryside to the east of town. The expanse of underground tombs, some marked by mounds, dates from the 7th c. B.C. to Roman times, and are decorated with wall paintings. Among the most interesting tombs are the *Tori*, with a depiction of Achilles's ambush of Troilus, and the *Auguri**, with scenes of combat (both late-6th c. B.C.), the *Barone** (6th/5th c. B.C.) with ritual scenes (note flutist and horsemen), the *Caccia* and the *Pesca* (about 530 B.C.), *Cardarelli* (about 500 B.C.) with scenes of dancing, the *Giocolieri* (about 530-520 B.C.), the *Leonesse* (about 530 B.C.) with dancers, the *Leopardi* (5th c. B.C.) with musicians, the *Orco*, with Greek-style deities (4th/3rd c. B.C.).

Tìvoli

elev. 235 m.; pop. 52,372; Lazio, province of Rome. Overlooking the Roman countryside from a ridge of the Monti Tiburtini, Tivoli stands among centuries-old olive groves; the river Aniene runs around it in an oxbow curve, tossing itself off rocky heights in astonishingly romantic waterfalls. In Roman times this was a famed vacation spot, with fine climate and natural features (among those who spent their summers here were Sallust, Catullus, Horace, and Maecenas); after the 16th c., aristocratic villas gilded the lily, with fountains, grottoes, overlooks, terraces, statues, and brooding rows of cypress trees. Hadrian's Villa lies beneath it.

Places of interest. **Villa d'Este***. *Open from 9 until an hour before sunset.* Built by P. Ligorio in the 16th c. for Cardinal Ippolito II d'Este, this building was originally a Benedictine convent; Ligorio also designed the park and many fountains. The fairly rigorous palazzo features halls frescoed by such 16th-c. Roman painters as L. Agresti, F. Zuccari, and G. Muziano. From the superb loggia you enjoy a fine view of the **garden***, which drops away in symmetrical terraces, clad in rich vegetation and enlivened by numerous fountains and sprays. From the stairway, you climb down past the *Fontana del Bicchierone*, perhaps by Bernini (on left, the stuccoed *Grotta di Diana*), to the entrancing *Viale delle 100 Fontane*, with fountains and statues. Everywhere are fountains, representing the *fontana di Tivoli*, miniature versions of *Rome, dragons*, and even *organs*. The central avenue ends at the *Rotonda dei Cipressi*, with its centuries-old cypresses.

S. Maria Maggiore. Founded in the 13th c. and rebuilt in the 16th c., this church has late-Gothic portal and rose window; inside, artworks by B. da Montelupo, J. Torriti, and B. da Siena.

S. Pietro alla Carità. Founded in the 5th c., this church boasts handsome columns, possibly taken from Hadrian's Villa, and a Romanesque facade and bell tower. The quarter in which it is set is dotted with late medieval houses.

S. Silvestro. Set in the small oblong *Piazza del Colonnato*, named for its portico of Roman columns, this Romanesque church has an apse decorated with 13th-c. frescoes. Not far off, facing the 16th-c. church of *S. Nicola*, is a group of two-story medieval houses.

Duomo. With a portico dating from 1650 and a medieval Romanesque bell tower, this church possesses some fine artwork, including a large 13th-c. group of wooden statues of the Deposition* and an exquisite 12th-c. triptych (*covered, visible only on solemn occasions*).

Next to the Duomo is an 18th-c. washing tank and the **mensa ponderaria** (*open, by request; contact the Assessorato alla Cultura, 9-1; closed Sun.*), an ancient Roman public scale, with weights and marble slabs with measures of capacity. Along the steps of the *Via del Duomo*, lined by medieval houses, you will reach the *Palazzo Comunale*, rebuilt at the end of the 19th c.

Tempio di Vesta*. On the site of the ancient acropolis, on a rocky ridge overlooking the valley with its waterfalls, is a small round well-preserved 2nd-c. temple, dedicated either to Vesta or to Hercules. Near it is the **temple of Tiburnus**, founder of Tivoli.

Villa Gregoriana*. *Open: Oct.-Mar., 9:30-4:30; Apr. and Sep., 9:30-6; May-Aug., 10-7:30; access from Lungo S.Angelo.* This immense park is built around the **waterfall**** of the river Aniene (vertical drop of 160 meters). First you descend to the *overlook* of the Grande Cascata, where the water plunges from a manmade channel, inaugurated in 1835 by Pope Gregory XVI. Next you tour the *Grotta delle Sibille*, and two other *waterfalls* — the *Cascatelle Piccole* and the *Cascata Bernini* — before you reach the astonishing and deafening *main overlook** of the Grande Cascata. Then you continue on to two more grottoes: the *Grotta della Sirena*, where the water rushes straight down, and the *Grotta di Nettuno*, heavily encrusted with mineral residues.

Rocca Pia. This powerful fortress, built by Pius II (1461), dominates Viale Trieste. Near it are the ruins of a great imperial *amphitheater* (2d c. A.D.). Further east is the 15th-c. church of **S. Giovanni**; with frescoes attributed to A. Romano (1475).

Todi*

elev. 400 m.; pop. 16,722; Umbria, province of Perugia. If you head south along the Tiber from Perugia, high on a bluff over the valley appears a patch of medieval Umbria, ancient bell towers and colorful roofs amid the green and yellow.

Historical note. In Todi, the strongest influence is still the 13th c., when the last and largest circle of walls was built, along with many of the buildings on the central square, and the enormous church of S. Fortunato. In ancient times, Todi belonged to the Umbrians, and marked the boundary with the Etruscans (the name "Tuder" means border), and eventually became an Etruscan town. The Roman period has left some noteworthy relics, among them the great niches of the Mercato

Vecchio. Of the monuments produced in later centuries, when Todi was under papal rule, the most notable is the 16th-c. church of S. Maria della Consolazione, just outside the city walls.

Places of interest. Piazza del Popolo*. This square stands atop the hill, at the center of town. Overlooking it are the Gothic **Palazzo dei Priori**, on the south, and the Palazzo dei Popolo and the Palazzo del Capitano, to the west. To the north is the Cathedral, or Duomo. Near the Duomo is Palazzo Cesi, attributed by some to A. da Sangallo the Younger.

Palazzo del Popolo* or P. del Podestà. Stern Gothic architecture, from 1214-28, marks this building, linked by an exterior stairway to the **Palazzo del Capitano del Popolo**, from 1290. On the fourth floor are the Pinacoteca, the Museo Etrusco-Romano and the Library.

The Pinacoteca (closed for renovations) has 14th-c. frescoes and paintings. The Museo Etrusco-Romano (closed for renovations) features artifacts from the area.

Duomo*. This cathedral was begun in the 12th c., and renovated in the 13th and 14th c. Note the Gothic portals and rose window in the facade. Inside, note the fresco by F. da Faenza (16th c.), fresco by Spagna (1525), and altar pieces. A ramp to the left of Duomo leads, through a portal by Vignola, to the Palazzo Vescovile, built in 1593.

S. Fortunato*. This church was begun in 1292. Set dramatically atop a stairway, with two little Romanesque lions before it. In the 15th-c. facade, note the Gothic central portal*. In particular, note the Virgin and Angels* by M. da Panicale (1432); also, fragments of paintings by the school of Giotto. In the apse, a fine carved wooden choir (1590). In the 16th-c. crypt Jacopone da Todi (1230-1306), a religious poet, is buried.

Piazzale IV Novembre. On the right of S. Fortunato; note the ruins of the 14th-c. fort, and the view*.

Piazza del Mercato Vecchio. This square is lined by the ruins of a huge Roman building from the 1st-c. B.C. Also note the medieval fountain.

S. Maria in Camuccia. Small 13th-c. Romanesque church, in a setting of medieval buildings.

Todi: Duomo

S. Maria della Consolazione*. Standing in isolation, outside the medieval walls, in a lovely hilly setting, this church is one of the masterpieces of the Umbrian Renaissance. Begun in 1508, among its architects were Bramante, B. Peruzzi, Vignola, and M. Sanmicheli.

Mura Medievali, or Medieval Walls. Built in the 13th c.; a well preserved section, with square towers, can be seen along the outer ring road that runs from the Tempio della Consolazione to Porta Romana.

Convento di Montesanto. This convent was built in the early-13th c. in a site holy to the Etruscans, and came, with later additions, to resemble a fortress. Marvelous view from the entrance square.

Torcello*

Veneto, province and township of Venice. The stern cathedral; the nearly millennium-old campanile that rears up over this little village, marking it from afar; the few scattered buildings and ruins, clustered around a grassy clearing, commemorating the main square of a long-vanished town. Torcello was the heir to the Roman townn of Altino; and had a population of 20,000, a bishop; a port, salt marshes; this, when the site of Rialtine Venice was still swept by wind and waves. Now Torcello is an island of gardens, where outt-of-season fruit and vegetables are cultivated, or where artichokes are grown; surrounded by silent waters and other islands, it lies in the NE section of the lagoon 10 kilometers from Piazza S. Marco.

Places of interest. S. Maria Assunta**. Dating from the 7th c., but rebuilt in the 11th c., along with its campanile, the cathedral of the first major lagoon settlement stands by the remains of the baptistery and by a narthex which was enlarged in the 14th and 15th c. The *interior* has three aisles with columnnns topped with classical and Byzantine capitals; the floor is decorated with marble inlay and mosaics, from the 11th c. In the counter-facade, note the reemarkable Giudizio Universale, or Last Judgement*, a large 12th-/13th-c. mosaic; in the nave, iconostasis with marble plutei (or dwarf walls between pillars) with bas-reliefs (10h c.) and 15th-c. paintings in the architrave. To the left of the altar, note the original inscription commemorating the foundation of the church (A.D. 639), believed to be the earliest document of Venetian history.

S. Fosca*. This Romanesque construction with a central plan (11th c.) is surrounded on the outside by a pen-

tagonal portico and with apses with two orders of arcades; the interior has a Greek-cross plan.

Museo di Torcello. *Open, 10:30-12:30 and 2-4; closed Mon.* This museum is housed in the 14th-c. *Palazzo dell'Archivio* and *Palazzo del Consiglio*: it features archeological material from Altino and the lagoon (reliefs, bronzes, ceramics) and various objects from the 11th to 16th c. (sculpture, paintings), including the remmains of the ancient silver altarpiece of the cathedral (13th c.).

Trani

elev. 7 m., pop. 51,812, Puglia, province of Bari. From the Piazza del Duomo the view is unforgettable. The sea crashes with foaming spray at the foot of this pink cathedral, with its towering campanile; the church juts so into the water that it seems as if it is about to set sail.

Places of interest. Cattedrale**. Begun in the 12th c. and completed midway through the 13th c., this cathedral is one of the most complete and refined examples of Pugliese Romanesque. The central portal features exquisite bronze doors* by Barisano da Trani (1180 ca.). The campanile was rebuilt after WWII with original materials. *Inside*, beneath the transept, is the *crypt of S. Nicola**, dense with slender columns; from here you can enter the church of *S. Maria*, a 3-aisled crypt, which extends the length of the church, underground. Still lower is the *Hypogaeum of S. Leucio*, pre-Romanesque.

Nearby is the **Museo Diocesano** (*open, weekdays 8:30-1 and 12:30-5:30*) with medieval paintings and architectural and sculptural fragments.

The **Castello**, a castle built by Frederick II (1233-49), was rebuilt in the 15th c. and in the 16th c., and later damaged; it has been restored.

Ognissanti. This church formed part of the Ospedale dei Templari, or Hospital of the Knights Templar, in the 12th c.

In the historical center, with its virtually intact medieval structure, are the synagogue and various interesting churches, including *S. Giacomo; S. Andrea* (Byzantine style, with a Greek-cross plan); and *S. Francesco*, consecrated in 1184.

The **Museo delle Carrozze** (Carriage Museum; *reserve by phone, tel. 46032*) is located in the 18th-c. Palazzo Antonacci.

Trent / Trento*

elev. 194 m.; pop. 101,430; Trentino-Alto Adige, capital of the region. The town stands at the convergence of the valleys that run through Trentino (Giudicarie, Anaunia, Avisio, Valsugana); it has always been the focal point of its region, and is surrounded by mountains drained by the Adige, a river linking the Po Valley to the Alps and all that lies beyond. Trent is a town of stern medieval and Renaissance architecture, where mountains greet the gaze on every hand.

Historical note. In the Stone Age, primitive peoples lived on the Doss Trento, which towers over 100 m. above the banks of the Adige. This was a fortress in Roman times, though the town of "Tridentum" stood on the other bank of the Adige, near the historical center. Abandoned in the high Middle Ages for the Doss (early-Christian ruins), Trent was slowly repopulated, with a surge in the

Torcello: S. Fosca

13th c., when the Adige ran along the modern locations of the Via Torre Vanga and Via Torre Verde. Back then, Trent had been detached, along with the entire Marca Veronese, from the Kingdom of Italy, and incorporated into Bavaria by the emperor Otto I in 952. That marked the beginning of Trent's German identity. Shortly after the year 1000 the German Holy Roman Emperors had given the bishops of Trent temporal power, in a bid to keep the strategic mountain passes open. And the prince-bishops immediately found themselves caught up in the rivalry between the pro-pope Guelphs and the pro-emperor Ghibellines. In 1273 the bishops of Trent were stripped of their power by the counts of the Tyrol, incorporating the town in fact. Trent then fell to Rudoph of Hapsburg, with a popular uprising in 1407, supported by Venice, that ended in a bloody Tridentine defeat, and, a century later, a treaty with Maximilian I. From 1516 to 1539 Trent was ruled by a bishop, Bernardo Cardinal di Cles, who gave the city its Renaissance appearance, and built the Castello del Buonconsiglio and the church of S. Maria Maggiore. He also laid the groundwork for the Council of Trent, which met from 1545 and 1563, largely in the Duomo and S. Maria Maggiore, and which started the Counter Reformation. The following century, under the bishops of the Madruzzo family, was Trent's golden age; successive ages are largely occupied with military history, with a siege in 1703, French occupation in 1796 and 1801, a brief annexation to Bavaria (1806-1809) and to Napoleon's Kingdom of Italy (1810-1813). The Austro-Hungarian Empire ruled until 1918; a time of growing prosperity. The course of the Adige was shifted, and the city grew, northward and southward.

Getting around. Part of the historic center of Trent is closed to traffic; especially Via Manci, Via Belenzani, and Piazza del Duomo. The route we recommend is a walking tour, except for the visit to the Museo d'Arte Moderna e Contemporanea in Palazzo delle Albere, which can be reached by car or by public transport.

Places of interest. Piazza della Fiera. This square is lined by about 100 m. of *crenelated walls*, built in 1230; to the west, at the end of Via Mazzini, is the *Torrione*, ruins of a 16th-c. round tower, recently taken over as living quarters. Ample underground parking.

Museo Tridentino di Scienze Naturali. *Open 9-12 and 3-5:30; closed Mon.* Housed in the 16th-c. *Palazzo Sardagna*, in Via Calepina at n. 14, with halls frescoed by Fogolino, this museum of natural science has collections of geology, prehistory, zoology, and botany. Note the prehistoric art from the Tridentine region.

Piazza del Duomo*. Monumental center of Trent, adorned by the 18th-c. *Fontana del Nettuno*, this square is surrounded by noble residences and buildings. On the south is the long side of the Duomo; to the east is the 13th-c. *Palazzo Pretorio*, with mullioned windows, site of the Museo Diocesano (see below, note excavation of Roman ruins), and the *Torre Civica*; to the NE, the two 16th-c. *Cazuffi houses*, with facades frescoes by Fogolino; note the small *Fontana dell'Aquila*.

Duomo**. This cathedral, a stern mixture of Romanesque and Gothic (12th/13th c.), with a powerful 16th-c. bell tower, is flanked by charming little loggias, with large rose windows in facade and transept, lavish portals, and a handsome apse (adjacent to which is the so-called Castelletto, a battlemented 13th-c. building, with mullioned windows). *Inside*, three high aisles, with polystyle piers and cross vaults. Note the flying staircases cutting diagonally across the walls at the foot of each side aisle. Along the walls, various 16th-c. funerary mon-

Trent: Duomo

uments. Note the Altar of S. Anna with altar piece by Fogolino; nearby, the *Cappella del Crocifisso* contains an historic wooden Crucifix (16th c.) by the German sculptor S. Frey, here, the decrees of the Council of Trent were promulgated. At the head of the left aisle, 13th-c. stone statue of the Madonna degli Annegati (named after the fact that those drowned in the river Adige were brought before the statue to be identified, when it still stood in a niche outside the church).

Beneath the church, remains of the 6th-c. *early-Christian basilica* (*open, Mon.-Sat., 10-12 and 3-6*), unearthed in 1977, with mosaic walls and fragments of sculpture.

Palazzo Pretorio (*closed for archeological excavation*). It lines the east side of Piazza del Duomo and houses the Museo Diocesano (see below). Next to it is the 13th-c. *Torre Civica* (41 m. tall).

Museo Diocesano*. This religious museum features the most precious treasures of the Cathedral: seven Flemish *tapestries**, carried out in Brussels by P. van Aelst at the turn of the 16th c.; carved altars and statues, panels and paintings, all from the 14th to 18th c.

Via Belenzani*. This broad, elegant road is one of the loveliest in Trent; it is lined by Renaissance Venetian-style palazzi, some with frescoed facades. In particular, note at n. 20, the 16th-c. *Palazzo Geremia*; at n. 32, the *Casa Alberti Colico*, with frescoes by Fogolino. Across the street, *Palazzo Thun*, now town hall. At the end of the street is the church of *S. Francesco Saverio*, the finest Baroque church in Trent.

Via Manci. This street is lined by remarkable palazzi, among them n. 63, the Baroque *Palazzo Galasso*, 1602; n. 57, the 16th-c. *Palazzo Pedrotti*, headquarters of the Società degli Alpinisti Tridentini (SAT, an association of mountaineers), with *Alpine museum* (*open, only Sat., 10-12 and 3-5*); and just beyond, the 16th-c. *Palazzo Salvadori*, once a synagogue. At the end of the road, the early-16th-c. *Palazzo del Monte* — note the frescoes of the Labors of Hercules, executed around 1540.

Castello del Buonconsiglio**. Ancient residence of the bishop-princes, this castle stands within an enclosure wall studded with low keeps.

The castle comprises several wings: to the north, topped by the round *Torre Grande*, the battlemented 13th-c. *Castelvecchio*, modified in 1475, with a lovely central courtyard with stacked loggias; note frescoes by Fogolino and others. In the center, the so-called *Giunta Albertiana*, a wing built to join north and south wings in the 17th c.; to the south, the *Magno Palazzo*, Renaissance in style, with a broad loggia overlooking the Cortile dei Leoni, Note splendid frescoes by G. Romanino (1531-32).

Inside, the **Museo del Castello del Buonconsiglio*** (*open, Oct.-Mar., 9-12 and 2-5; Apr.-Sep. until 5:30; closed Mon.*), the Trent section of the larger *Museo Provinciale d'Arte*, with sections also in Castel Beseno, Castel Stenico, and Castel Thun, features ancient, medieval, and modern art. From the entrance, you cross the garden, and on the right you can see the cells of Italian heroes D. Chiesa, C. Battisti, and F. Filzi, executed here in 1916. The Museum, with artifacts, coins, codices, sacred objects, and paintings, occupies many rooms in the Magno Palazzo and the Castelvecchio; note carved wooden ceilings and frescoes by D. Dossi, Romanino, and Fogolino. Note the frescoes of the *12 Months** (*March* has been lost) by 15th-c. anonymous artists (*to safeguard the art, only 20 persons are allowed in, with guide*).

In one restored building in the complex, you will find the **Museo Civico del Risorgimento e della Lotta per la Libertà** (*open: same hours as the Museo del Castello*), with memorabilia and documentation of WWI and the Italian Resistance movement of WWII.

Piazza Raffaello Sanzio. Note the yellow-and-green tiled *Torre Verde*, dating from the 13th c., with fragments of the ring of walls of which it formed part.

Piazza Dante. Set between the modern *Palazzo della Regione* (A. Libera, 1954-62) to the east, the train station to the NW, and the Palazzo della Provincia to the north, this square boasts a large public garden with a famed *monument to Dante*, by C. Zocchi (1896), a symbol of Italian resistance under Austrian domination. To the west, note the 12th-c. Romanesque church of *S. Lorenzo*, rebuilt in 1955 after heavy damage from bombing in WWII.

S. Apollinare. Across the river Adige, this 14th-c. Romanesque-Gothic church has a portal and rose window in red Veronese porphyry.

Palazzo delle Albere . *Open 9-12 and 2:30-6; closed Mon.* This square "suburban" villa with corner towers and moat was built around 1535 by the bishop-prince C. Madruzzo. It is the site of the Tridentine section of the **Museo d'Arte Moderna e Contemporanea di Trento e Rovereto**, with documentation of fundamental phases of Italian art, from Romanticism and Divisionism, and the period of Ca' Pesaro to the Novecento, from Spatialism to the Informal. Among the Trent-born artists, note E. Prati, U. Moggioli, L. Bonazza, T. Garbari, and F. Depero.

Torre Vanga. Square and crenelated, this tower was built in the 13th c. to protect a bridge over the river Adige.

S. Maria Maggiore. Renaissance church (1520-1524), with noteworthy portal and campanile, the site of many of the meetings of the Council of Trent; inside, artwork by P. Ricchi (1664) and G.B. Moroni (1551); marble chancel choir by V. and G. G. Grandi (1534).

Continuing along Via Rosmini, near n. 18, in a garden-courtyard, note the mosaic floor of a 2nd-c. A.D. *Roman villa*.

Treviso*

elev. 15 m.; pop. 83,222; Veneto, provincial capital. Narrow porticoed streets, lovely vignettes, and astonishing monuments rearing high, a welter of medieval lanes set within the old walls, Gothic and Renaissance paintings — Treviso, set at the confluence of the river Botteniga (once called the Cagnan) with the Sile, is also "entwined with the restless filigree of water, studded everywhere with emerald patches of trees and gardens" (G. Comisso). Small and mid-sized businesses drive the economy, though its many gardens and orchards make Trevisan cuisine, to say it again with Comisso, "human and complete, based on a thorough understanding of the health and tastes of living creatures."

Historical note. Etchings of the 16th/18th c. show us a fortified Treviso, the work of a newly alert Venice immediately following the great defeat of Agnadello (1509). The walls of this stronghold can still be seen in part, with the only three gates: Porta Altinia, P. Santi Quaranta, and P. S. Tomaso. Within the haven of those walls stood, for many centuries, medieval Treviso; bombardments of WWI and bombing in WWII destroyed that town only partially, happily enough. Treviso was born in the Middle Ages. Even though under Augustus an ancient settlement was elevated to Roman outpost, with the name of "Tarvisium," the city — off the main roads but with a river port — grew especially during the high Middle Ages. It prospered under Goth and Longobard rule, and became a capital in Carolingian times. The center grew in an "island" between the two branches of the river Cagnan, where the Romans had lived, building on the site of a pagan temple: the Duomo, Battistero, and Episcopio, or bishop's palace. Treviso fought against the emperor in league with the Po Valley towns, and from 1207, ruled itself. In 1210, Treviso built the Palazzo dei Trecento, or 300, named after the 300 members of the city council. It was a major center for troubadors, such as Sordello, attracted by the city's love of poetry and song. Even when self-rule gave way to seigneurs, Treviso kept its reputation as a prosperous town of book-lovers and connoisseurs of poetry. Venice took Treviso in 1339, lost her in 1381, and took her back in 1388. The town slumbered for centuries in an agrarian backwater; and under Austrian rule (1813-1866) the railroad link to Venice shifted the center of the town south, to the station; from here to Porta S. Tomaso, along the walls, at the turn of the 20th c., was built a promenade that still sets Treviso apart.

Places of interest. S. Nicolò**. This Gothic church dates from the 13th c., and is made entirely of brickwork, with tall windows and apses. The *interior* has three aisles, transept, and five chapels. Note the colossal round pillars. Among the artists whose work adorns the church, we should mention: T. da Modena; L. Bregno; A. da Treviso; M. Pensaben and G. Savoldo; and Andrea da Murano. Note the remarkable organ, built by A. Palma, with doors painted by G. Lauro. In the chapel to the right of the *presbytery*, 14th-c. frescoes (also note frescoes in sacristy); on the altar is a canvas by Anonymous Venetian. Also, note the *monument to the Senator Agostino Onigo***, by the sculptor Giovanni Buora and the painter Lorenzo Lotto.

Seminario Vescovile. Adjacent to the church, in a former convent, is the *Sala del Capitolo dei Domenicani* (*open, 8-1 and 3-5; summer until 7*), decorated with noteworthy frescoes by T. da Modena (1352), and two small museums: the *Museo Etnografico "Dino Grossa"* (*both are open, Sun. 9-12 and by request, tel. 412010*) features tribal objects from Amazonia; the *Museo Zoologico "Giuseppe Scarpa"* features Italian vertebrates and exotic reptiles.

Museo Civico "Luigi Bailo" *. Open 9-12 and 2-5; Sun. 9-12; closed Mon.* Located at n. 22 in Borgo Cavour, this museum houses the archeological and art collections of the town of Treviso. In the *archeological section* are objects from the Copper, Bronze, and Iron ages (axes, buckles, swords*), Roman artifacts (urns, plaques, sculptures, portraits, bronzes) as well as sculptures from early-Christian times and the High Middle Ages. In the *gallery* are paintings and statues: in particular, Venetian and local artists: G. da Treviso the Elder, G. da Treviso the Younger, P.M. Pennacchi, and L. Pozzoserrato. Special note should be given to the works by G. da Fabriano, Giovanni Bellini, C. da Conegliano, L. Lotto, Titian, Pordenone, P.Bordone, J. Bassano, R. Carriera, F. Guardi , P. and A. Longhi. Also, works by 19th-c. painters (F. Hayez, I. Caffi) and a sculpture by A. Canova.

In the *Galleria Comunale d'Arte Moderna* (*located here temporarily*) are works by the Trevisan sculptor Alberto Martini: note the bust of Lilian Gish.

Museo della Casa Trevigiana. *Being renovated; part of the collection can be seen only during temporary exhibitions, or by request, tel. 658442.* Located in the *Casa da Noal*, at n. 38 in Via Canova, this late-Gothic building houses a collection of medieval and Renaissance marble sculptures, terracotta, wooden statues, ancient weapons, and musical instruments. Next door, at n. 40, is the Renaissance *Casa Robegan*; in the nearby Via Riccati, which leads to Piazza del Duomo: at n. 52-56 note the mid-15th-c. house, and, across the street, a series of 15th-and 16th-c. houses, frescoed.

Duomo **. Originally built in the Middle Ages (Romanesque sections on the left side, column-bearing lions on either side of the pronaos), the apse of this cathedral was rebuilt in the 15th/16th c., and the rest was rebuilt in the 18th c.; before it stands a Neoclassical six-pillar pronaos, built in 1836. The three-aisle *interior*, with seven cupolas, includes artworks by noteworthy painters and sculptors. Among them are: A. Vittoria, A. Lombardo, P.Bordone, G. da Treviso the Elder, Titian, G. A. Pordenone, P. and T. Lombardo, and L. Bregno. Note the 11th-c. *crypt*, with a forest of little columns and re-used capitals (possibly 8th c.).

Battistero. To the left of the Duomo, this Romanesque baptistery (11th c.) has a 14th-c. bas-relief on the pediment, Roman friezes on either side of the portal, and, inside, fragments of 12th-c. frescoes in the apses. Note the large 11th-c. bell tower.

Museo Diocesano di Arte Sacra. *Open, Mon.-Thu., 9-12; Sat. 9-12 and 3-6; closed Fri. and Sun.* Entrance to this museum of sacred art is at n. 9 in Via Canoniche. Note the various marble reliefs*, the fresco by T. da Modena, the tapestries and other objects from the Treasury of the Cathedral.

Calmaggiore. This lovely and busy main street of the old town is lined by 15th- and 16th-c. porticoes and homes.

Piazza dei Signori*. Set in the middle of Treviso, its medieval flavor is due to the complex of Communal buildings (many of them rebuilt) on three sides. To the east, **Palazzo dei Trecento***, from about 1210 (wholly rebuilt, 1946-52), then *Palazzo del Podestà* with the *Torre Civica*, and, on the west side, the ancient *Palazzo Pretorio*.

Loggia dei Cavalieri. Romanesque arcaded structure

Treviso: Piazza dei Signori

(1276-77), once a meeting place for Treviso's nobility.

Piazza del Monte di Pietà. Behind Piazza dei Signori is the ancient *Palazzo del Monte di Pietà*, with the **Cappella dei Rettori*** (*open upon request, tel. 654320*), a small 16th-c. room, richly decorated with paintings and decorated leather walls (17th c.).

S. Lucia and S. Vito. In Piazza S. Vito, these two medieval churches have been joined into one. Of the two, **S. Lucia**, with frescoes by T. da Modena, is the more interesting, though both are worth a visit.

Pescheria. This islet on the river Botteniga is the site of the fish market; note the welter of canals and little lanes that converge here.

S. Francesco*. This Gothic church, built in 1230, was rebuilt in 1928; note the frescoes by T. da Modena; note the tombs of Francesca, daughter of Petrarch (d. 1384); and Pietro, son of Dante Alighieri (d. 1364).

Porta S. Tomaso. The most monumental of the three gates in Treviso's Venetian-built walls, it dates from 1518 (G. Bergamasco); note the lion of St. Mark's, emblem of Venice.

S. Caterina dei Servi di Maria. *Open 3-6; Jun.-Sep. also 10-12; closed Sun.* This 14th-c. church was devastated by Allied bombing in 1944, restored, and made into an art gallery. Note the paintings, by T. da Modena, and others.

S. Maria Maggiore. This Gothic church was built in 1473, and has a handsomde 15th-c. *cloister*.

Villa Manfrin. As you head toward Conegliano, note this huge estate, dating from 1783, with vast gardens open to the public.

Surrounding areas. The Parco Naturale Regionale del Fiume Sile is a natural park running the length of the river Sile (about 95 km.); flora and fauna are one attraction; noble villas and industrial archeology are two more (boat trips are available on the lower course of the Sile; *for information, tel. 8186663*).

Trieste*

elev. 2 m.; pop. 229,216; Friùli-Venezia Giulia, regional capital. If you first see Trieste from the Adriatic waves, or from a train, or if you arrive by car, dropping down along the road that descends from the Karstic highlands, it appears set as on a stage, between the lighthouse to the north and the modern harbor to the south. In the words of Italian poet Umberto Saba, "young city, with its masculine adolescence, formless and unrestrained, growing between the sea and the harsh hills behind." Some consider the finest architecture and urban settings of Trieste to be found in the courtly order of the "Borgo Teresiano" (named after the empress Maria Theresa; her father, the emperor Charles VI, laid the foundations for the growth of modern Trieste, by establishing the free port here). Unquestionably, the 19th-c. buildings that line the shore speak eloquently of the city's past as the great maritime outlet of the Austro-Hungarian Empire (the name Trieste comes from an ancient word meaning "market"). The cultural tradition here is intensely Italian, yet cosmopolitan and open to Europe. The view of the Gulf of Trieste and the Adriatic beyond is alluring; these is a sense of the sea, in the light of summer and even winter, when the impetuous "bora" wind brings good weather.

Historical note. Trieste became what it is today in the 18th and 19th c.; before, it was a tiny village. A Roman colony named "Tergeste" in the late-1st c., it was triangular in plan, with the seashore as the base, and the hill of S. Giusto as the tip. The medieval walls ran down from the Castello to the sea like two long arms, enclosing the same triangle.

What survives from Roman times are the ruins of the basilica of the Forum, on the hill, the Roman theater, and the so-called arch of Riccardo, probably a gate in the walls. From medieval times, only the cathedral of S. Giusto is worthy of any note. Trieste, which was for many years under Byzantine rule, and was only briefly ruled by Goths and Longobards, became part of the Carolingian empire around 788. In 948 the king of Italy, Lothar II, gave the bishop John and his successors temporal power over Trieste. This date marks the beginning of Trieste's growth as an independent town. In 1236 another bishop named John, in financial straits, sold his rights to govern the city; pressed by the patriarch of Aquileia and the counts of Gorizia and Venice, Trieste surrendered itself in 1382 to the duke of Austria Leopold II. Trieste thus survived, leading a modest existence within the realm of the Hapsburgs, in relative independence. The structure of the city remained that of the medieval town it had once been, right up until the 17th c., when it had a population of just 3,000. Everything changed in the 18th c. The Hapsburgs, following their victories over the Turks, penetrated into the Balkans and Charles VI, following the War of Spanish Succession, ruled as the King of Naples for 20 years. Having proclaimed, in defiance of Venice, freedom of navigation in the Adriatic Sea, the emperor gave Trieste in 1719 the status of free port. That was only the beginning. The empress, queen, and archduchess Maria Theresa did even more to encourage maritime trade, promoting the creation of a large market, attracting merchants and bankers, small businessmen and craftsmen, laborers and porters. At the end of the century, Trieste had a population of 30,000. On the area that was once occupied by ancient salt flats — which offered a meager income, enough to allow the city's waning aristocracy to eke out its existence — rose a new city, on a checkerboard layout. The "borgo teresiano," or

"quarter of Theresa," followed, on an area reclaimed from the sea at the foot of the Colle di S. Vito, by the "borgo giuseppino," or "quarter of Joseph." Following the crisis of three occupations by Napoleonic troops, development continued in a frenzy. During this period the most renowned Neoclassical edifices were built: Palazzo Carciotti, Palazzo della Borsa, the church of S. Antonio Nuovo, the Teatro (now Teatro Verdi); and between 1831 and 1838 the most important companies were established: Assicurazioni Generali, Lloyd Austriaco (now Lloyd Triestino), the Arsenale del Lloyd, and the Riunione Adriatica di Sicurtà. By 1819 Trieste had established Italy's first steamship line. The last decades of the 19th c. and the early years of the 20th c. witnessed further development of Trieste, which grew from a population of 176,000 in 1900 to a population of 247,000 in 1913, the fourth largest city in the Austro-Hungarian empire. The city continued to grow to the east of what is now Via Carducci, in the "borgo franceschino" and in the so-called "rioni industriali" which gobbled up farm villages in the surrounding area. The city began to grow once again, expanding into the outskirts and developing residential districts, when it was annexed by Italy (1918), after the political shifts in its hinterland drastically reduced its importance as a port, pushing Trieste toward greater industrialization. In the period following WWII as well, Trieste hovered in a limbo as a potential Free Territory for almost ten years, and then became part of Italy again only in 1954; in these years, the industrial zone of Zaule was created, along with the satellite town of Borgo San Sergio; low-cost housing was also built for tens of thousands of refugees from Istria. Despite this massive immigration, Trieste, after a long period of demographic stagnation, is declining sharply in population, and is now the 15th largest city in Italy (in 1921 it was the 7th largest). Trieste's current economic situation — which lost nearly all of its regional and provincial territory after 1945, and which has a national boundary only a few kilometers from its city center — is not an easy one, nor does a promising future appear from the bloody reports of war and death from the neighboring lands that were once Yugoslavia.

Getting around. The three routes recommended here can be considered walking tours, though you may wish to take public trasportation for some of the longer stretches, or to return to your point of departure. It should in any case be kept in mind that traffic regulations discourage the use of private cars in the historic center, and that cars are less than practical in other parts of town, where space is limited.

Piazza dell'Unità d'Italia and the "città vecchia," or "old city"

On the Colle di S. Giusto the walls ran down from the Castello to the sea like two long arms, enclosing the "città vecchia," or "old city." Trieste lived within this narrow space until the 18th c. From the modern heart of Trieste, the sunny "stage" of Piazza dell'Unità d'Italia, the route runs up to the Colle, or hill, discovering both the view and the past.

Piazza dell'Unità d'Italia (*C2-3*). The heart of old Trieste, built on landfill of the ancient Roman port, this square was opened to the sea in the 19th c., to become a sort of stage, with an eclectic backdrop in the **Palazzo Comunale** (1875), by G. Bruni.

Two monumental *flagpoles* (1933) mark the edge of the square overlooking the Bacino di S. Giusto; before the Palazzo Comunale, on the right, is a Baroque *column* with *statue of Charles VI*, who made Trieste a free port, and the reassembled *Fountain of the Four Continents* (1751). Along the left side of the square is the *Palazzo del Governo* (1904-5), a bulky revue of Italian architectural styles, by E. Artmann, and the 19th-c. *Casa Stratti*, with the historical mirror-lined *Caffè degli Specchi*. On the right side, the immense **Palazzo del Lloyd Triestino**, by H. Ferstel (1880-83), with two allegorical fountains; alongside, a building styled after the French Renaissance (1875), now a hotel, and the elegant **Palazzo Pitteri** (1785), a blend of Baroque and Neoclassical.

S. Maria Maggiore (*C3*). Behind Palazzo Comunale, this church on the slopes of the hill of S. Giusto overlooks an area that was ravaged in the 1930s by urban renewal. Built in 1627-82 and enlarged by A. Pozzo, it has a handsome Baroque facade; to the right of the main altar, note the venerated painting by Sassoferrato. To the right, downhill, the little 11th-c. basilica of **S. Silvestro** (*open, Thu.-Sat., 10-12*), restored in the 1920s; the simple facade has a handsome Gothic rose window, while inside, you can see fragments of ancient frescoes.

Arco di Riccardo (*C3*). Behind S. Maria Maggiore, at the beginning of Via del Trionfo, this arch is one of the gates of ancient Roman Trieste, built by Octavian in 33 B.C. Recently restored, the arch has a single passageway, and is decorated with pilaster strips. Continue downhill along Via del Trionfo, past the notable early-19th-c. Neoclassical facade of **Casa Pancera**, by M. Pertsch (1818). Climb up Via S. Michele and, on the right (n. 13), and you will see Trieste's *Anglican church* (1830-31), now an art gallery. Set back on Via Madonna del Mare, at the heart of one of the old town's most distinctive and neglected quarters, is the Istituto Magistrale Carducci (n. 11), built atop the remains of an early-Christian **basilica**, with 5th-c. mosaic floors (*open by request, contact the Soprintendenza, Wed., 10-12*).

Museo di Storia e Arte (*C3*). *Open, 9-1; closed Mon.* This is the main collection of Trieste's museums of art and history, with eight rooms of a collection that is largely archeological, located at n. 15 in Via della Cattedrale; the road offers fine views of the old town. In the museum, note the prehistoric artifacts (from the Paleolithic to the Iron Age, especially from the necropolis* of S. Lucia di Tolmino; 8th/5th c. B.C.). Also, fine collections* of Greek and Italic vases and terracottas, silverwork, bronzes, glass, ceramics, ivory, amber, and classical sculptures and reliefs.

The museum also contains collections (*open by request, for scholars only*) of Greek, Roman, and medieval coins (mints of Aquileia, Trieste, and Venice) and a collection of prints and designs, featuring 274 drawings* by G.B. Tiepolo (Sartorio collection). Next to the museum is the **Orto Lapidario** (*open same hours as the museum*), or lapidary garden, with inscriptions and architectural fragments from ancient to modern Trieste, Aquileia, and Istria; opened in 1843. A small classical building, commemorating the great German archeologist J.J. Winckelmann (murdered in a Triestine tavern in 1768), will house a collection of Roman sculpture.

Piazza della Cattedrale (*C3*). This large tree-lined square, atop the hill of S. Giusto, is bounded by the bastions of the Castello. The Cattedrale di S. Giusto, with the little 14th-c. Gothic church of *S. Michele al Carnale* next to it, stands atop the stairway that concludes Via della Cattedrale.

On the left, facing the campanile of S. Giusto, is a *column* (1560), originally topped by an imperial eagle, which

Trieste: S. Giusto

was removed under Napoleon, and replaced by symbols of Trieste; to the left of the stairway, overlooking the gulf is an *altar* (1929) commemorating the end of WWI. At the base of the Castello extends the *Roman "platea,"* or plaza, with ruins of the 2nd-c. A.D. *basilica* and the so-called *Capitoline temple* (1st c.A.D.); note the *Monumento ai Caduti*, a somber monument by A. Selva (1934) (fine view* of city and port).

S. Giusto** (*C3*). This is Trieste's greatest monument and symbol, built in the 14th c. by joining two 5th-c. Romanesque basilicas: S. Giusto (right) and Assunta (left). The simple *facade* features a large 14th-c. Gothic rose window; the central portal contains fragments of a Roman stele. The 14th-c. campanile, with its fortified appearance, stands on the ruins of a Roman temple; note the Byzantine-Romanesque statue of S. Giusto.

The *interior* has five asymmetrical aisles; the nave, straddling the two ancient buildings, has a 16th-c. painted vault, rebuilt in 1905; the central apse is also modern (1843) with a mosaic by G. Cadorin (1932), based on fragments of an original. In the right apse, blind arch with 13th-c. frescoes and a notable mosaic; note also fragments of the 5th-c. mosaic floor. In the right apse, note 12th-c. Venetian mosaics*; in the left aisle, panel by B. Carpaccio (1540). Also, note the Baptistery, with 9th-c. baptismal basin.

Castello (*C3*). *Open, 8-sunset.* The castle that now stands was built between 1470 and 1630, on the site of an older Venetian fortress, which in turn stands on what was probably once a prehistoric fortification. Restored and refitted in the 1930s, converted to a museum and open-air theater (Cortile delle Milizie), its bastions offer fine views of Trieste and its gulf. In the square 15th-c. tower, and in the building next to it, is the **Civico Museo del Castello** (*open, 9-1, closed Mon.*), a museum in a furnished setting: Chapel (17th-c. wooden statue of Christ, statue of John the Baptist, 15th-c. Friulan art, and paintings of sacred subjects); Venetian room, from the home of noted Triestine historian G. Caprin (16th-c. chests, 17th-c. Flemish tapestries); the Appartamento del

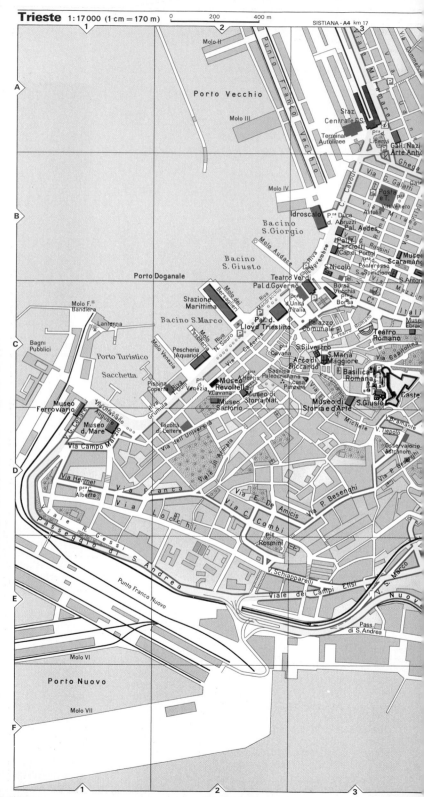

Trieste

1:17 000 (1 cm = 170 m)

0   200   400 m

SISTIANA - A4 km 17

Porto Vecchio

Molo II

Molo III

Molo IV

Punto Franco Vecchio

Staz.
Centrale F.S.

Terminal
Autolinee

P.za
Libertà

Gall. Nazi.
Arte Antic

Via G. Galatti

Posta
e T.

Cavour

Via N. Venezia

Via Milano

Alfalia

Ghed

Idroscalo

P.za Duca
d. Abruzzi

Bacino
S.Giorgio

Molo Audace

Bacino
S.Giusto

Riva 3 Novembre

Pal. Aedes

Pal. Carciotti
(Cap.di Porto)

Via S. Rossini

P.za
Pontorosso

Museo
Scaramang

Porto Doganale

Teatro Verdi

S.Nicolò

S.Spiridione

S.Anton

Stazione
Marittima

Molo Bersaglieri

Molo
Pescheria

Molo
Venezia

Pal. del
Municipio

Pal. d.Governo

Pal. d.
Lloyd Triestino

P.za
d.Unità
d'Italia

Borsa
Vecchia

P.za d.
Borsa

Mazzini

Italia

Muse
Ebraic

Molo F.lli
Bandiera

Lanterna

Bagni
Pubblici

Porto Turistico

Sacchetta

Bacino S.Marco

Pescheria
(Aquario)

Piscina
Coperta

Palazzo
Comunale

P.za
Cavana

Teatro
Romano

S.Silvestro

S. Maria
Maggiore

Via Capitolina

Museo
Revoltella

Arco di
Riccardo

Basilica
Paleocristiana

Casa
Panzera

Basilica
Romana

Castel

Museo di
Storia Nat.

Museo
Sartorio

Museo di
Storia d'Arte

S.Giusto

Via S. Michele

Museo
Ferroviario

Via G. Cesare

Museo
d. Mare

Via Campo Marzio

Vecchia Via Augusto

Riva Grumula

Facoltà
di Lettere

Via dell'Università

V.Cavana

Bramante

V. Tiepolo

Osservatorio
Astronom

Via P. Besenghi

Via Hermet

P.za C.
Alberto

Via
Franca

Via
Lorchi

Viale XX Settembre

Via R. De Amicis

Via C. Combi

ple
Rosmini

Via P. Besenghi

Viale R.Gessi

Passeggio di S. Andrea

V. Schiapparelli

Viale dei Campi Elisi

V. S. Marco

N u o v o

Punto Franco Nuovo

Pass.
di S.Andrea

Molo VI

Porto Nuovo

Molo VII

364

Capitano, or residence of the castle's commander. In the two huge rooms of the watch, a collection* of antique weapons (in particular, 17th-c. inlaid ivory powder flask). In the Cortile delle Milizie, note the newly restructured "bottega del vino," or wine shop; the so-called "flowering bastion" holds temporary exhibits.

The "borgo teresiano" and the modern city

Along this route, running north of the hill, or Colle di S. Giusto, you will see the 19th-c. center of business, trade, and international commerce, as well as the relaxed, Neoclassical atmosphere of the urban expansion brought about by Maria Theresa.

Piazza della Borsa (*C3*). This broad, triangular plaza, in front of the Borsa, or stock exchange, is linked by Via Capo di Piazza to Piazza dell'Unità d'Italia, and is one of the centers of life in Trieste.

At the center of the plaza is a *column* with a bronze *statue* of emperor Leopold I (1673); on the left, coming from Piazza dell'Unità d'Italia, the *Tergesteo* (1842), once a critical link in international commerce at Trieste. Also, note the **Palazzo della Borsa Vecchia**, by A. Molari (1806-9) and facing it, *Casa Bartoli* (n. 7B), an Art Nouveau home by M. Fabiani (1905); on the left at the corner of Corso Italia (n. 9), *Palazzo Romano* (1760-70), renovated in 1919, a significant example of Triestine Baroque.

Teatro Comunale G. Verdi (*C3; undergoing restoration*). Behind the Tergesteo, this Neoclassical theater (1801) had among its architects G.A. Selva, M. Pertsch, and G. Piermarini; the *Museo Teatrale* is located at Via Imbriani n. 5.

S. Nicolò 'dei Greci' (*B3*). Overlooking the Riva III Novembre, on the left side of Piazza N. Tommaseo, near a famous cafe, this Greek Orthodox church was built in 1784-87, and has a sober Neoclassical facade with twin bell towers, by M. Pertsch (1819-21).

Canal Grande (*B3*). Dredged in 1750-56, this canal offered safe anchorage and a more convenient way to unload ships directly into warehouses in the new "borgo teresiano," reclaimed with landfill from the surrounding salt marshes. At the canal's mouth, on the right, note **Palazzo Carciotti** by M. Pertsch (1802-5), and the old *Hôtel de la Ville* (1839, rebuilt more than once), now offices of a bank. On the opposite bank, at the head of Via Rossini, is **Palazzo Aedes**, by A. Berlam (1926-28). At the end of the Canal Grande is the spectacular Neoclassical facade of the church of **S. Antonio Nuovo**, by P. Nobile (1827-42).

Piazza Ponterosso (*B3*). The oldest square in the "borgo teresiano," it takes its name from a wooden drawbridge that once linked the two banks of the Canal Grande, replaced in 1840. Adorning the square, which is surrounded by buildings in the eclectic "official" style, stands an 18th-c. fountain, surmounted by the popular figure of "Giovannin." Dominating the space between Piazza Ponterosso and the neighboring Piazza S. Antonio Nuovo is the glittering mass of the church of **Ss. Trinità and S. Spiridione Taumaturgo**, built by the Serbian Orthodox community, to plans by Carlo Maciachini (1869); inside, note the lavish 19th-c. iconostasis and the remarkable silver accessories and furnishings. At n. 1 in Via F. Filzi, across the Canal Grande, is the **Museo Scaramangà di Altomonte** (*open, Tue.-Fri., 10-12*), a small but important collection concerning the history and art of Trieste, with rotating shows. As you approach

Corso Italia, this section of the "borgo teresiano" blends the sort of eclectic architecture seen in the office buildings on Piazza della Repubblica, with interesting examples of a transition from Liberty (Italian Art Nouveau) to Rationalism, as in the former *Casa Smolars*, by R. Depaoli (1906-07), at the corner of Piazza della Repubblica and Via Dante (n. 6), *Casa Fontana* (Via Mazzini 5, at the corner of Via Roma), and the bank offices at n. 9 in Via Roma.

Corso Italia (*C3-4*). This busy avenue linking Piazza della Borsa to the eastern quarters of Trieste, is the site of the traditional "liston" (or stroll).

Along it are large buildings by major architects of Fascism, such as the *building of the Assicurazioni Generali* (n. 1-3) and the *offices of the Banco di Napoli* (n. 5), both by M. Piacentini (1935-39), or the *"skyscraper"* by U. Nordio (1936) in Largo Riborgo, as well as surviving bits of the old Austro-Hungarian "Corso." Among them, note the Neoclassical *Casa Steiner* (n. 4), by M. Pertsch (1824); *Casa Hierschel* (n. 9), by A. Buttazzoni (1833), the neo-Tuscan *Casa Ananian* (n. 12), by G. Polli (1905), and the building at the corner of Piazza Goldoni (n. 22), with Art Nouveau pediment, by R. Depaoli (1908).

Teatro Romano* (*C3*). This Roman theater, on the slopes of the hill of S. Giusto, was partly unearthed in 1938; it seated 6,000 and dates from the early-2nd c. A.D. Behind it, in Via di Donota, is a small **Antiquarium** (*open, Thu., 10-12*) with artifacts from the digs, from a 1st-c. A.D. home and a slightly later cemetery, used until the 6th c.

Museo della Comunità Ebraica (*C3*). *Open, Sun., 5-8; Tue., 4-6; Thu., 10-1*. Located at Via del Monte n. 7, parallel to Corso Italia, where a Polish Ashkenazi synagogue stood in the 1920s; it was founded in 1993 to house collections of Jewish art and culture of Trieste, especially religious furnishings.

Civico Museo "M. Morpurgo de Nilma" (*C4*). *Open, 10-1; closed Mon.* Set back from Corso Italia, at n. 5 in Via Imbriani, this eclectic palazzo by G. Berlam (1875), built for a family of Triestine bankers and merchants, now houses several sections of the Civici Musei. On the *2nd floor* is the *Museo Teatrale "C. Schmidl"*, featuring old instruments, theater memorabilia, portraits, and posters; on the *3rd floor* is the former home of Mario Morpurgo de Nilma, furnished in the late-19th-c. middle-class Triestine style: paintings by Delacroix and Daubigny, sculpture (wooden polychrome statues by Veit Stoss; 15th/16th c.); prints, Bohemian crystal, ceramics. In this building are the collections of the *Civico Museo di Storia Patria* (*open by request, only for scholars*); the *Stavropulos collection* was being installed in the Civico Museo Sartorio in 1993.

Via Carducci (*B-C4*). This major boulevard was built in 1850, upon a covered-over drainage canal. Follow it from Piazza Goldoni, until you reach Viale XX Settembre and Via Battisti on the right. Via Battisti leads to the 19th-c. *Giardino Pubblico*; the tree-lined Viale XX Settembre, a popular promenade, is lined with cafes, theaters, and movie houses: at n. 35, the **Teatro Eden** (*B4*), is a fine piece of Liberty, or Italian Art Nouveau, by G. Sommaruga (1906); while at n. 45 is the *Politeama Rossetti* (*B5*; 1878), a landmark in the history of Italian theater and of the city of Trieste. Continue along until you reach the western extremity of the "Boschetto," the city's **botanical gardens** (*B5; entrance from Via Marchesetti n. 2; closed for renovation*). Take a left from Via Battisti into Via Donizetti and, at n. 4, at the corner of Piazza Giotti, you will see the monumental **Synagogue** (*B4*), by R. and A. Berlam (1906-12).

Piazza Oberdan (*B4*). Built as an impressive entrance to Trieste in the 1920s-30s, it stands on the site where, in 1882 the Italian patriot G. Oberdan was hanged by the Austrians.

In the piazza is the terminus of the exceedingly popular *"Opicina tram"* (cable tramway built in 1902); it is marked on the right by three monumental buildings set on large arcades, by U. Nordio (1929-39). At n. 4 in Via XXIV Maggio, the *Casa del Combattente*, a military monument, includes, on the ground floor, the **Sacrario Oberdan** *(open, 9-1; closed Mon.)*, commemorating an Italian national hero, hanged by the Austrians, with the cell in which he spent his last night, and monument to Oberdan by A. Selva. On the 2nd floor, the **Civico Museo del Risorgimento** *(same hours as the sacrarium)*, with memorabilia and documentation of the history of Trieste and of the Irredentists.

Piazza della Libertà *(A3)*. Monumental square built at the end of the 19th c., surrounded by stern buildings; among them note *Palazzo Economo* (n. 7), see below; it is dominated by the huge neo-Renaissance facade of the *Stazione Centrale* (1878), or main train station. Nearby, note the bus station, built in 1986-89 from old *grain silos* (1890).

Galleria Nazionale d'Arte Antica *(A3)*. *Open, 9-1; Sun. closed.* Located on the 3rd floor of Palazzo Economo, at n. 7 in Piazza della Libertà, this museum basically comprises the Collezione Mentasti of 15th-/19th-c. Italian paintings. The seven rooms of the Galleria contain drawings by Canaletto (10 sketches); detached frescoes by Romanino; paintings by L. Cranach il Vecchio, G. Assereto, G. A., and F. Guardi, F. Solimena, Fra' Galgario, G.M. Crespi, G. Tominz; and a "salone piemontese," 18th-c. room with mirrors and boiseries, from Palazzo S. Tommaso in Turin.

As you climb up into the early-20th-c. quarter above the station, first Via Udine, and then the *Salita di Gretta*, lead to the panoramic *Via del Friùli*, and on to the **Faro della Vittoria** *(A3, off map; Apr.-Set, 9:30-11:30 and 3:30-6:30; Oct.-Mar, holidays only, 10-3)*, a monumental lighthouse by A. Berlam (1927), commemorating those who died at sea; fine view* of the Gulf of Trieste. Overlooking *Via Commerciale (A4)* are several notable Art Nouveau *houses* (n. 21, 23, 25).

The harbor and the Rive

Facing east, Le Rive (the banks, or shore) are Trieste's majestic face, overlooking the water of the port, and gleaming in the light of the gulf. Extending into the waves are the great jetties, from which great ocean liners once set sail. Along the "passeggiata," or sea-front promenade, lie the aquarium and five museums.

Molo Audace *(B2)*. This jetty, the panoramic "promenade on the sea" of Trieste, is named after a torpedo boat that landed Italian soldiers here on 3 November 1918; the jetty divides the Bacino di S. Giusto from the Bacino di S. Giorgio.

From the head of the Molo Audace, there is a fine view* of Trieste's waterfront. To the right of the jetty, the Bacino di S. Giorgio was used between the wars for seaplanes (first civilian flight in 1926); note the old terminal, or *Idroscalo*, by R. Pollack (1930), now abandoned. Nearby is the **Porto Vecchio** *(A-B 2-3)*, which extends north to Bàrcola, with a breakwater (1868-90). Over Bàrcola, on the Colle di Gretta, stands the *Faro della Vittoria*, a lighthouse; in the distance, the *Castello di Miramare*. To the left of the Molo Audace, the Bacino di S. Giusto, with **customs offices** *(B-C 2)*; further along the marina.

Le Rive *(A-C 2-3)*. These broad sea-side avenues lined by handsome Neoclassical buildings are joined with the great piers between the *Porto Vecchio* and the *Lanterna (C1)*, at the tip of the Molo Fratelli Bandiera.

Molo dei Bersaglieri. This jetty, with its monument to N. Sauro, holds the 1930s **Stazione Marittima** *(C2)*, by U. Nordio, now a conference center. Further along the sadly deteriorating Art Nouveau **Pescheria** *(C2)*, or aquarium, by G. Polli (1913), with the adjacent **Civico Acquario Marino** *(open, Apr.-Sep., 9-6:30; Oct.-Mar, 9-1; closed Mon.)*, with 40 tanks of Adriatic fish and marine invertebrates, and some tropical fish, as well as freshwater fish, amphibians, and reptiles, from Friùli-Venezia Giulia.

Museo Revoltella* *(C2)*. *Open to groups (rules subject to change), 9, 10:30, 12, 3, 4:30, 6; closed Tue. and Sun. aft.* The entrance is at n. 27 in Via Diaz; this neo-Renaissance building, by F. Hitzig (1852-58), was donated, with 19th-c. furnishings, to the city of Trieste in 1866-69 by a businessman and patron of the arts, P. Revoltella. Enlarged from the 1960s on by C. Scarpa ("Scarpa wing," completed in 1992), it has become the **Galleria d'Arte Moderna** Triestina, with a major collection of 19th-/20th-c. sculpture and painting, from Italy and Mitteleuropa (some 40 rooms). Of note: statues by A. Canova and J.A. Houdon; paintings by G. Tominz, F. Hayez, D. Induno, F. De Nittis, L. Nono, L. Balestrieri, G. Previati, I. Zuloaga, F. Casorati, A. Nathan; decorative panels by V. Timmel; and contemporary artwork by G. Manzù, L. Minguzzi, R. Guttuso, L. Fontana, and Afro. From the terrace in the Scarpa wing, fine view* of Trieste.

Civico Museo di Storia Naturale *(C2)*. *Open, 9-1; closed Mon.* This museum of natural history occupies some 20 rooms on the 2nd and 4th floor of the *Palazzo della Biblioteca Civica*, or Library, at n. 4 in Piazza Hortis. Founded in 1846, it features collections of paleontology, marine zoology, comparative anatomy, botany, and entomology, as well as collections of amphibians, reptiles, and birds. It also has a set of late-19th-c. herbaria and a specialized library, with nearly 10,000 volumes.

Civico Museo Sartorio *(C2)*. *Open, 9-1; closed Mon. (being reinstalled, tours only of the first floor).* This fine example of a late-19th-c. home is set in an 18th-c. city villa, rebuilt in Neoclassical style in 1820-38 by N. Pertsch, at n. 1 in Largo Papa Giovanni XXIII. *Ground floor:* collection of antique European ceramics* and temporary exhibitions. *Second floor:* rooms furnished in neo-Gothic and Biedermeier style, 17th-/19th-c. paintings (note work by Tiepolo and followers). On the third floor are rotating exhibitions of Triestine collections, especially from the 18th c. Recently installed is the *Stavropulos Collection* * of Italian, German, and Hungarian painting and sculpture (paintings by A. Martini, P. Brill, G. Tominz, and Mihály Munkácsy; sculpture by Veit Stoss, P. Breuer, and V. Mukina).

Civico Museo del Mare* *(D1)*. *Open, 9-1; closed Mon.* Located in a modern building at n. 5 in Via di Campo Marzio, this museum of the sea was founded at the turn of the century. It now occupies about 30 rooms on three floors, providing a general history of shipbuilding up to the 19th c. and a section on the history of fishing, with special attention to the systems, equipment, and boats of the Adriatic; note models of how various types of nets are deployed.

Museo Ferroviario *(C-D1)*. *Open, 9-1; Mon. closed.* Located in the handsome, Art Nouveau former station Campo Marzio, by R. Seelig (1907; closed in 1960), this railroad museum was founded in 1984. It features documents, models, and memorabilia; outside, about 15 locomotives, mostly steam engines, stand on rails, alongside early-20th-c. cars from the Italian, Austrian, Hungarian, and German railways.

Other monuments. Risiera di S. Sabba *(F4, off map).* *Open, 9-1; closed Mon.* In the industrial section south of Trieste, in Ratto Pileria n. 1 (take the Valmaura exit from the ring road), stands a former rice-husking plant, now a national monument, notorious for its use, under Nazi occupation, first, as a marshalling yard for Jews bound for concentration camps, and later, as a death camp. Note the *Museo della Resistenza*, with documents and photographs concerning the Italian resistance movement.

Foiba di Basovizza *(A6, off map).* As you leave town, on the right of state road n. 14 toward Basovizza, a plaque commemorates the karstic sinkhole, now a national monument, where hundreds, possibly thousands, of victims of military and political reprisals were tossed between 1943 and 1945, during the occupation, first by the Nazis, and later by Tito.

Troia

elev. 439 m., pop. 7,875, Puglia, province of Foggia.

Places of interest. Cattedrale**. This cathedral is the monument for which this little town, arrayed along a ridge of a hill overlooking the Tavoliere, is widely known. Founded in 1093 on the structure of an existing Byzantine building, it is considered a masterpiece of the Romanesque architecture of the Capitanata, with Byzantine influence and subtle Muslim traces. The rose window* in the facade is framed by a large arcade, and is closed off with fretwork screens. The bronze door* is by Oderisio da Benevento (1119). In the three-aisle *interior*, decorated with tiny reliefs (1169), the first two pillars of the presbytery incorporate Byzantine porphyry columns.

The *treasury* (including 3 celebrated illuminated scrolls of the Exultet, from the 12th and 13th c., silver, Arab ivory caskets, and enamels) is scheduled to be moved to the Museo Diocesano, partly arranged in the Benedictine nunnery across from the cathedral *(for the treasury and the museum, enquire in the treasury).*

S. Giovanni. This church is Baroque; also note the proto-Romanesque church of *S. Basilio* (11th c.).

Of particular interest is the facade of the *Palazzo Tricarico* (17th c.), with diamond-point ashlars.

The **Museo Civico**, in the *Palazzo Vasto (enquire at the headquarters of the local police)*, is a museum with an archeological section and a modern section.

Turin / Torino*

elev. 239 m., pop. 991,870; Piedmont, regional capital. The city lies along the left bank of the river Po; founded in ancient times at the confluence of the Dora Riparia with the Po, Turin now extends along the course of the Po from the confluence with the Stura di Lanzo, downstream, to that of the Sangone, upstream. On the opposite bank rises the Collina, or hills, which loom over the city and make up a very pleasant part of the lives of the Turinese. In the distance, one can make out the silhouette of the Alps. Turin is a major city, the fourth-largest in Italy; it is thoroughly up-to-date, busy, and courteous. At the heart of the city, both architecturally and historically, is the ancient capital of the dynasty of the Savoia, or Savoy;

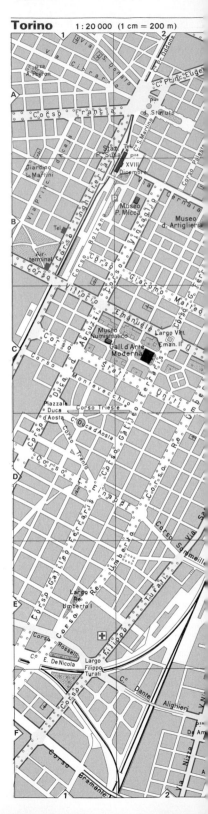

Torino   1 : 20 000   (1 cm = 200 m)

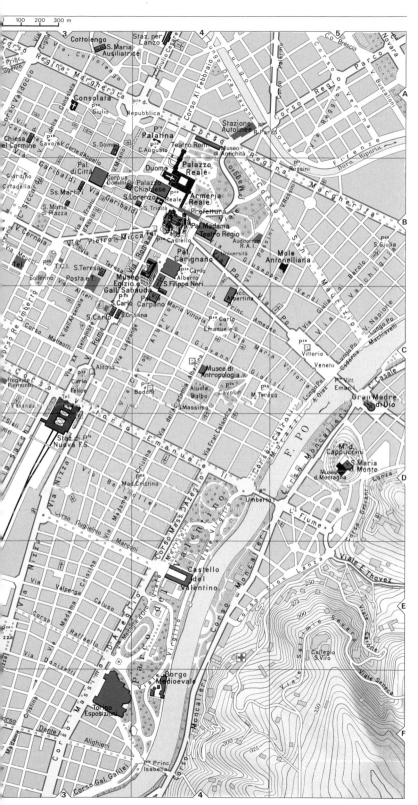

dramatic, Baroque, and abounding in fine buildings, this central area has extended its restrained regularity to outlying neighborhoods of varied and dignified nineteenth-century construction, with ample piazzas, broad straight boulevards, and long lines of shade trees. Turin is known best as an industrial metropolis, and as Italy's car-manufacturing capital; socially, it has a reputation of formal "drawing-room" entertaining, in the neighborhoods of Piazza San Carlo, Via Roma, and surrounding areas. The city, however, also boasts a surprisingly rich artistic and cultural life, and a wealth of monuments.

Historical note. It is customary to attribute Turin's checkerboard layout to the grid of the Roman colony, but that is only a partial explanation: this is a city that grew in carefully planned expansions, becoming a regional, then ducal, and finally royal capital. The location was first chosed by the Ligurian tribe of the Taurini; the Roman colony, which must have existed under Caesar, was refounded by Augustus around 29 B.C.; the "Julia Augusta Taurinorum" occupied the rectangular area, less than 800 m. long, with 72 "insulae," or blocks, between what is now Palazzo Madama and Via della Consolata, between Porta Palatina, Porta Romana, and Via S. Teresa. The medieval history of Turin is intricate and relatively marginal: the Savoy enter into the city's history when the town was already a thousand years old: in 1046 Adelaide, daughter of Olderico Manfredi II, marchese di Turin and its march, married Oddone di Savoia, son of Umberto Biancamano. The house of Savoy only established permanent possession of the city in 1280, under Tommaso III. The city remained within the Roman perimeter (until the 17th c.); in the 13th c. Guglielmo di Monferrato built a fortress-home against the Porta Decumana, the first structure of what would one day be Palazzo Madama; in 1404 the university was founded, at the behest of Ludovico di Savoia, approved by Benedict XIII, the pope in Avignon, and by the emperor Sigismund; Meo del Caprina designed and decorated (1491-98) for the bishop Domenico della Rovere the Duomo, or cathedral, almost the only Renaissance monument in Turin. The house of Savoy had possessions on both sides of the Alps, in parts of what are now Switzerland and France, as well as Italy, and they rarely lived on the Italian side of the Alps; the capital of the Savoy duchy was Chambery, and the Italian possessions seemed of marginal interest. In the European wars of the early-16th c., the duchy came close to catastrophe. Emanuele Filiberto led the Spanish army in a decisive battle against the French in northern France; he regained the duchy through the Peace of Cateau-Cambrésis, 1559, with a solemn entry into Turin, finally freed of French occupation, on 7 February 1563. Thus began the history of Turin as a capital city, more than two centuries of transformations that turned it into the city we know today. Emanuele Filiberto immediately gave the city a mighty fortified stronghold, the Cittadella, a five-pointed star at the SE corner of the Roman rectangular camp (1564-1568; only the keep survives, at the corner of Via Cernaia and Corso Galileo Ferraris). There were three major enlargements of the city, one under Carlo Emanuele I, a second beginning in 1673 (Amedeo di Castellamonte), and a third after 1714 (under Vittorio Amedeo II, with Filippo Juvarra as architect). Then, beginning in 1736, under Carlo Emanuele II, the Via Dora Grossa (now Via Garibaldi, originally the Roman "decumanus") was rebuilt, in Gothic times, it had been a porticoed market street. Among the epochal constructions were the church of S. Maria del Monte on the Monte dei Cappuccini (Vittozzi, late-16th c.); the Castello del Valentino, on the banks of the Po, was transformed by Carlo and Amedeo di Castellamonte (1630-1660); and the Basilica di Superga, by Juvarra (1716), supposedly to fulfill a vow made by Vittorio Amedeo II during the siege of 1706. The city now

had its appearance of a Baroque capital, but as De Brosses observed, "there was none of the usual unpleasantness of seeing huts next to palaces." In effect, the original aspect of the Turinese Baroque palazzo (four, six, or eight to an "isola," or block) was a sort of social integration: the owner lived on the main floor, or "piano nobile," middle class families above them, and the poor on the upper floors. In the Napoleonic era, all of the city's fortifications were dismantled; Turin became a haven for those working to unite Italy. As the beacon of a united nation, Turin began to grow and modernize. In 1853 the city had a population of 160,000; tree-lined boulevards were built (there were a total of 130), and called "Corsi." On 14 March 1861 in a wooden pavilion in the courtyard of Palazzo Carignano, the Italian parliament voted unanimously to make Victor Emmanuel II king of Italy. Turin was the first capital of a united Italy (1861-65); there were two days of riots when it was learned that Florence was to become capital in its place. Then came a period of industrialization, with Turin's new status as the peak of the "industrial triangle," (with Genoa and Milan); now Turin was the "capital of the automobile." A remarkable piece of engineering, the Mole Antonelliana began to lift its spire above the surrounding town (it was begun as a Jewish synagogue in 1863, it was completed by the city in 1897); in 1899 FIAT was founded, although automobiles were already being built in Turin; in 1923 the factory of the Lingotto began operations; on the roof was a test track, where models such as the Balilla and the Topolino made their first runs. In the census of 1939 Turin had a population of 700,000; the modern population is about a million, a result of massive immigration from the south of Italy and the incorporation of surrounding villages into the city.

Getting around. Turin has no large pedestrian zone (save for a stretch of Via Garibaldi), but its famed porticoes, distinctive features of the historical center, offer a long and pleasant covered walkway, extending for a good 18 kilometers.

Palazzo Madama and "Turin the Capital"

The oldest buildings along this square-shaped route through the heart of the city date primarily from the 17th c. Some of the most illustrious sites in this capital city — first of a Savoy duchy, and later of a Savoy kingdom — are found here, many of them by the hands of the "court architects" G. Guarini and F. Juvarra; this was also a Roman colony, many centuries ago, and traces of that period can be seen in the regular checkerboard pattern of streets, as well as in other details. The Roman walled perimeter, within the bounds of which Turin remained until the 17th c., also enclosed the medieval city.

Piazza Castello (*B4*). This immense square is surrounded by regular porticoed palazzi (the 90-m.-tall skyscraper that stands on the western side dates from 1934), and was designed in 1584 by A. Vittozzi. This is the heart of Turin.

Isolated at the center of the square stands the Palazzo Madama. A 19th-c. wrought-iron gate separates it from the Piazza Reale, beyond which you can see the dome of the Cappella della S. Sindone and the bell tower of the Duomo; opposite Palazzo Madama rises the dome of the church of S. Lorenzo. On the eastern side of square is the 18th-c. facade of the **Teatro Regio**; the rest of this theater was recently rebuilt, reopening in 1973 (adjoining it is a small Museo Teatrale, or museum of the theater, open when performances are being stage); further off is the Mole Antonelliana (see). On the western side of this square, opposite Palazzo Madama, are the offices of the regional government of Piedmont.

Palazzo Madama** (*B4*). This great palazzo in the center of the square sums up in its long process of construction the history of Turin itself. It incorporates the remains of an ancient Roman gate (front towers), which was transformed in the Middle Ages into a castle; this castle, enlarged in the 15th c. by the house of Savoy, with corner towers and mullioned windows, became the home of Madama Reale (hence its current name) Maria Cristina, the widow of Vittorio Amedeo I and the regent of Carlo Emanuele II, in the 17th c.; in 1721 F. Juvarra designed and built the monumental Baroque facade. The palazzo now holds the **Museo Civico di Arte Antica*** (*closed for renovation*), featuring artwork, largely from Piedmont, including sculpture (by T. di Camaino*); wooden carvings; paintings (by A. da Messina, Pontormo, M. Spanzotti, M. d'Alba, D. Ferrari, and G. Jaquerio); illuminated books (the Très Belles Heures of the Duke de Berry**, illuminated by the brothers van Eyck and their school); furniture*, tapestries, glass, ceramics, ivory, and embroideries.

S. Lorenzo* (*B4*). This small church, of great architectual interest, is one of the loveliest in Turin. Devoid of facade — it has the elevation of a palazzo instead — it was built between 1668 and 1680; it is one of the major works by G. Guarini. Note the complex structure of the central-plan interior, decorated with polychrome marble, stuccoes, and gilding; especially, note the cupola.

Armeria Reale* (*B4*). *Open, Tue. e Thu., 2:30-7:30; Wed., Fri. e Sat., 9-2; closed Sun. e Mon.*). Beneath the portico to the right of the fence around Palazzo Reale, alt n. 191, is the entrance to one of the most notable collections of arms and armor in all of Europe. Of special note: the weapons of Emanuele Filiberto (1561); arms and armor for parade, from Milanese, French, and Flemish manufactories (16th c.); firearms from the finest German smiths (17th c.); firearms from Brescia and the other leading European armsmakers; weapons from different places in Asia, and other remarkable specimens

Palazzo Reale* (*B4*). *Open, 9-2; closed Mon.* Built in 1660, this enormous royal palace with its stern facade was, until 1865, the residence of the house of Savoy. The interior features spectacular examples of furnishing and decoration from the 17th and 19th c.; note especially the painted and carved coffered ceilings and the parquetry in the wooden floors; interesting collection of large vases from the Far East. The *Scala delle Forbici*, a stairway that runs from the entry hall to the upstairs apartments, is a remarkable creation of F. Juvarra, who also designed the decorations in the remarkable little *Chinese room*. Behind the palace (accessible from the courtyard) extend the **royal gardens** (*open in the summer, 9-5*), created in the French style in the late-17th c.

Museo Nazionale del Cinema (*B4*). Set in the 17th-c. *Palazzo Chiablese*, to the left of the Piazza Reale, this museum of film was inaugurated in 1958; exhibits illustrate the technical, artistic, and industrial development of film and photography; the first halls are devoted to "precinema," i.e., to old forms of entertainment, based on viewing static or moving images.

Duomo* (*B4*). This cathedral was built in 1491-98, and has a Renaissance facade, the only one in Turin, made of white marble, with three portals in the Tuscan style; standing alone on the left of cathedral is the mighty *bell tower*, built in Romanesque style around 1470, and built still taller in 1720. The interior contains three colomned naves, simple and austere; on the wall, near the entrance, note the mausoleum of Giovanna d'Orlier de la Balme, around 1493. To the side of the presbytery, you can climb up to the **Cappella della S. Sindone*** (*open, 7:30-12 e 3-6; closed aft. of holidays and Mon.*), a remarkable chapel designed by G. Guarini (1668-94), entirely faced with black marble, and with a conical cupola comprising six stacked orders of arches. On the walls, note four monuments to members of the house of Savoy; above the sumptuous altar is a silver urn containing the *S. Sindone*, the shroud that is believed to have been used to wrap the body of Jesus after it was taken down from the Cross; it supposedly bears the miraculous impressions of His face and hands. This precious relic, which became a possession of the house of Savoy in 1430 and was first placed here in 1694, is displayed to the public only on rare occasions; in the left aisle of the Duomo you can see a life-sized photograph.

Piazza Cesare Augusto (*A4*). In this square there are a number of items of archeological interest: remains of walls, a stretch of Roman road (between the two statues of Caesar and Augustus), and the **Porta Palatina***, 1st c. A.D., with four vaults topped by two orders of windows and flanked by two polygonal towers, forming part of the city walls. To the left of the Duomo, beyond a fence that runs along the NW wing of the Palazzo Reale, are the remains of the **Roman theater** (1st-3rd c.).

Museo di Antichità (*A4*). *Open, 9-1 e 3-7; closed Sun. e Mon.; 1st and 3rd Sun. of each month, 9-1.* At n. 105 of Corso Regina Margherita is the entrance to this museum of antiquities. It occupies what were once the greenhouses of Palazzo Reale, and contains archeological material, ranging from prehistoric times to late Latinity and barbarian times. Of particular importance: Cypriot and Greek ceramics; the Etruscan collection; silver from the treasure of Marengo, with a portrait of Lucius Verus; collection of Roman glass.

S. Domenico (*A3*). This Gothic 14th-c. church, restored in 1906-08, has a portal. In the chapel at the end of the left aisle, note the heavily restored 14th-c. frescoes.

Corso Regina Margherita. On the right side of this avenue, in the Via Cottolengo, is the **Cottolengo** (*A3*), or Piccola Casa della Provvidenza, a hospital founded by S. Giuseppe Cottolengo in 1828, a celebrated institution of Christian charity, and the headquarters of the *Opere Salesiane*, founded by S. Giovanni Bosco (1846); note the adjoining church of **Maria SS. Ausiliatrice** (1868).

Santuario della Consolata* (*A3*). Formed by the union of two churches, this sanctuary was built in 1678 by G. Guarini, who transformed the existing church of S. Andrea into a vestibule of the new sanctuary. To the right of the Neoclassical facade (1860) is the 11th-c. Romanesque bell tower, part of the original structure. The *interior* is built to a hexagonal plan, and is surrounded by elliptical chapels and decorated with lavish marble and gilt stucco; in the chapel to the left of the presbytery, note the kneeling statues of the queens Maria Teresa and Maria Adelaide, by V. Vela (1861). As you continue along the Via della Consolata you will see, at the corner of the Piazza Savoia, the *Palazzo Martini di Cigala* (1716), attributed to Juvarra, with a handsome atrium opening out onto the courtyard.

Church of the Carmine (*A3*). Designed by Filippo Juvarra, with an austere 19th-c. facade, this church has a luminous interior, with a barrel vault ceiling. Not far off, at n. 1 in Via della Consolata, stands the 18th-c. *Palazzo Saluzzo di Paesana*, with a loggia-lined courtyard, once one of the most luxurious homes in Turin.

Via Garibaldi (*B3-4*). This street is off-limits to automobiles, and is lined with 18th-c. houses and palazzi; it is clearly a shopping street. Continuing along this street toward Piazza Castello you will see, on the right, the church of the **Ss. Martiri** (*B3*), built to plans by P. Tibaldi after 1577, with decorations inside of marble, stucco, and bronze. Next to the church is the **Cappella dei Banchieri e Mercanti** (chapel of bankers and merchants; *open holidays, 10-11; Sat., 2:30-6*), a fine example of Baroque architecture of the late-17th c., with a number of canvases by A. dal Pozzo. Further along, on the left, is the *Palazzo di Città*, dating from 1659-63, whose main facade overlooks the Piazza di Città, with a monument to the Conte Verde (1853).

Corpus Domini (*B3*). A short detour to the left, along the narrow Via Porta Palatina, leads to the church of Corpus Domini, built to plans by A. Vittozzi (1609-71) on the site of a miracle that supposedly occurred 150 years previous (the miracle involved a mule and a stolen monstrance, or ostensory).

SS. Trinità (*B4*). Continuing further along the Via Garibaldi, just before you reach Piazza Castello, note (on the left) the Neoclassical facade of the church of the SS. Trinità, designed by Ascanio Vittozzi (1606), with an interior built to a circular plan and dome, lavishly faced with marble by Filippo Juvarra (1718).

The 19th-c. Corsi and the "modern" heart of Turin

This late-16th-c. citadel and the fortifications with which Turin defended itself against a French siege in 1706 were demolished under Napoleon. In the spaces thus freed up (this route runs along them in part), these 19th-c. avenues and the broad tree-lined boulevards, laid out before the invention of the automobile, interpreted in a new architectural language the old and aristocratic image of Turin. This route ends along Via Roma, the best-known road in Turin: central thoroughfare of a Baroque addition, renovated in questionable style in the early-20th c., it remains, with the Baroque square that lies across its middle, the "drawing room" of Turin.

Via Pietro Micca (*B3-4*). Lined by buildings in the eclectic architectural style, it runs from the western corner of Piazza Castello and is one of the most elegant streets in Turin, with porticoes along the right side; it was built with a diagonal line of demolition in 1894 through an old neighborhood.

S. Maria di Piazza (*B3*). Set back along a cross street of Via Pietro Micca, this small church was rebuilt in 1751 to plans by Antonio Vittone, but the facade dates

from 1830. The interior is interesting; note the cupola and the theatrical altar.

Cittadella (*B2*). At the beginning of the long porticoed Corso Galileo Ferraris, in a garden, stands the keep of the Cittadella, all that remains of the enormous fortress built by Emanuele Filiberto of Savoy in 1564-68. It houses the **Museo Storico Nazionale dell'Artiglieria** (*open, Tue. e Thu., 9-1:45; Sat. e Sun., 9-11:45*) which features a collection of firearms and memorabilia of the Piedmontese corps of artillery and engineers.

Museo Pietro Micca (*B2*). *Open 9-2; closed Mon.* Not far off, to the west, at n. 7 in Via Guicciardini, in an area once occupied by a fortress, stands a museum with models, maps, and memorabilia of the Cittadella di Torino (Citadel of Turin) during the time of the French siege, in 1706. A custodian will take you into the underground chambers beneath the building (they once extended 14 km. under the city); a certain Pietro Micca was executed here. Follow the porticoes of *Corso Vinzaglio* and you will reach the broad and tree-lined **Corso Vittorio Emanuele II**, a central thoroughfare in the modern section of Turin; once you reach *Largo Vittorio Emanuele II* (*C2*), in which looms a monument dating from 1899, you will take a right into Corso Galileo Ferraris, and soon you will reach the Galleria d'Arte Moderna.

Galleria d'Arte Moderna* (*C2*). *Closed for renovation.* At n. 31 in Via Magenta, this is one of the leading collections of modern art in Italy; it occupies a modern building with 19th-c. art on the second floor: the works are predominantly by Piedmontese painters (M. d'Azeglio, Fontanesi, Avondo, Delleani, Grosso, Quadrone, Reycend, and G. Pellizza), although the Lombards (Hayez, Cremona, Induno), Tuscans (Fattori, Lega, Signorini), Venetians, and painters from other parts of Italy are well represented too. The third floor is devoted to the Futurists, early-20th-c. painters (Spadini, Modigliani, De Chirico, Carrà, Tosi, Casorati, Morandi, Scipione, Rosai, and De Pisis) and painters of later generations (Mafai, Menzio, Paulucci, Spazzapan, Birolli, Guttuso, Cassinari, Morlotti, and Santomaso) all the way up to the modern avant-gardes. Among the sculptors, we should mention: Canova, Marocchetti, Vela, Gemito, Medardo Rosso, Andreotti, Martini, Marini, Manzù, Fazzini, and Mastroianni. European art is present with works by Courbet, Renoir, Léger, Utrillo, Pascin, Klee, Ernst, and Chagall, as well as the contemporary artists Tobey, Hartung, Le Moal, Manessier, Gischia, Tal Coat, and Tamayo.

Civiche Raccolte di Numismatica, Etnografia e Arti Orientali (*C1*). *Open, 1:30-6:30; Sun., 9-12:30; closed Mon.* Not far from the Galleria d'Arte Moderna, at n. 8 in Via Bricherasio is this collection of Greek, Roman, Byzantine, and Italian coins, from the Middle Ages to modern times, along with plates, seals, and medals; there are also collections of materials from Africa, the Americas, and Oceania, archeological finds from Gandhâra, in India, and items of Chinese art.

Stazione di Porta Nuova (*C-D3*). Return to Largo Vittorio Emanuele II and then take the Corso Vittorio Emanuele II to the train station of Porta Nuova (1860-68), with a broad portico on the facade.

Piazza S. Carlo (*C3*). This square is joined to Piazza Carlo Felice, on one side, and Piazza Castello, on the other, by *Via Roma*, Turin's main thoroughfare, lined with porticoes and elegant shops. This square was given its current appear-

Turin: Piazza S. Carlo

ance — with symmetrical porticoed palazzi along the main sides — during the 17th c. The southern end features the two churches of *S. Cristina* (Baroque, by F. Juvarra) and *S. Carlo*, whose 19th-c. facade reproduces many of the architectural motifs found in S. Cristina; at the center of the square is an equestrian monument to Emanuele Filiberto, by C. Marocchetti (1838).

S. Teresa (*B3*). This Baroque church (1642-74) may have been built to plans by A. Costaguta; the facade dates from 1764. Inside, note the rich marble decoration and the spectacular altar of S. Giuseppe* by Juvarra (1735). Alongside the church, at n. 5 in Via S. Teresa, is the *Museo della Marionetta* (*open, 9-12; Sun., 3-6; closed Mon.*), with puppets, marionettes, backdrops, and costumes created by the Lupi brothers for the traditional theater of "Gianduia."

The Galleria Sabauda, the Museo Egizio, and the Baroque addition

When the city was still enclosed within its fortified walled perimeter, expansions took place through well-planned projects, beginning with the shift outward of bastions and ramparts. The quarter to the SE of Piazza Castello, explored by this route, was added from 1673 on, and still shows the stern style of the Piedmontese Baroque, lit up by the brilliant flashes of architectural genius of Guarino Guarini. Marks of cultural continuity can be seen in the two most prestigious collections of art in Turin, the Galleria Sabauda and the Museo Egizio.

Palazzo Carignano (*B4*). Overlooking Piazza Carignano, with a statue of the Turin-born Italian philosopher and politician Vincenzo Gioberti (1859); among the stern buildings that surround it is the *Teatro Carignano*, where, in 1775, Vittorio Alfieri's first tragedy, "Cleopatra," was performed. Built by G. Guarini (1679-85), the palazzo belonged to the Carignano branch of the house of Savoy; Carlo Alberto (1798) and Vittorio Emanuele II (1829; later king of Italy, known as Victor Emmanuel II) were born here; the kingdom of Italy was proclaimed in the courtyard, on 14 March 1861; Italy's first parliament met here, until the capital was moved to Florence (1865). A new wing that closes off the courtyard and the monumental facade overlooking Piazza Carlo Alberto were built in the 19th c. The palazzo contains the **Museo Nazionale del Risorgimento Italiano** (*open, 9-6:30; holidays, 9-12:30; closed Mon.*), with a major collection of documents, memorabilia, and other material concerning the period of the

struggle for Italian unification, with manuscripts by Garibaldi, Cavour, Mazzini, and Vittorio Emanuele II; a section is devoted to the Italian Resistance movement in WWII.

Palazzo dell'Accademia delle Scienze (*B4*). This imposing brick Baroque building, by Guarino Guarini (1678), houses two of the most important collections in Turin: the Museo Egizio and the Galleria Sabauda.

Galleria Sabauda★★ *Open 9-2; closed Mon.* Set on the third and fourth floors of the Palazzo dell'Accademia delle Scienze, this is a first-rank collection of paintings, boasting among other things remarkable paintings of the Flemish and Dutch schools. There are works by Piedmontese painters of the 15th and 16th c.: M. d'Alba, Spanzotti, G. and D. Ferrari, Sodoma, and Giovenone. There is a notable group of works by Tuscan painters: B. Daddi, Fra' Angelico, Pollaiolo, L. di Credi, and Bronzino. Among the Venetians we should mention: Mantegna, B. Montagna, Veronese, Tintoretto, Bassano, Schiavone, and Savoldo. There are many works by 17th- and 18th-c. Italian painters: Carracci, Reni, Guercino, B. Strozzi, O. Gentileschi, G.B. Tiepolo, Magnasco, Bellotto, Piazzetta, Ricci, and Guardi. Particularly noteworthy is a group of Flemish and Dutch paintings, by: J. van Eyck, R. van der Weyden, Memling, Petrus Christus, van Dyck, G. Dou, Rembrandt, J. van Ruisdael, P. Potter, and others. The collection of the princes of Savoy includes portraits by François Clouet and van Dyck. Also worthy of note is the *Gualino collection*, comprising a major group of paintings by early Italian masters, including a painter working prior to Giotto, Botticelli, E. de' Roberti, and P. Veronese, as well as Chinese sculpture and medieval furniture.

Museo Egizio★★ (*B4*). *Open, 9-2; closed Mon.* Located in the Palazzo dell'Accademia delle Scienze, this is one of the most notable collections of Egyptian antiquities in all of Europe. On the ground floor is the statuary section, with remarkable material: 10 seated statues and 11 standing statues of the lion-headed goddess, Sachmis; the pharaohs Thutmose I (1505-1493 B.C.), Thutmose III (1490-1436 B.C.), Amenhotep II (1438-1412 B.C.), Haremhab (1333-1306 B.C.), and Ramses II* (1290-1224 B.C.). Of special note is the reassembled "speos"* (little cliff temple) of El-Lesiya, with bas-reliefs dating from 1450 B.C., a gift (1966) from Egypt to Italy. On the second floor are collections of various material: sarcophagi, mummies, canopic vases, statuettes, weapons, tools, papyrus (Book of the Dead), and paintings, which document various aspects of Egyptian civilization (everyday life, culture, religion, the funerary cult, etc.). Especially noteworthy is a small room with material from the tomb of a married couple, Kha and Merit (1430-1375 B.C.), uncovered intact.

S. Filippo Neri (*B-C4*). Begun in 1675, this church was completed in 1772 by F. Juvarra. Before it is a classical pronaos (1835); note the vast interior, with stuccoed relief, marble, and paintings. Alongside the church is the *Oratorio di S. Filippo* (*C4*), also designed by Juvarra; facing it is the *Palazzo Carpano*, built in 1686 to a design by Michelangelo Garove, student of Guarini. Note the spiral columns.

Piazza Carlo Emanuele II (*C4*). Built at the end of the 17th c., this square has, at its center, a *monument to Cavour* (1873). Not far off are the *Museo di Antropologia e di Etnografia* (museum of anthropology and ethnography, at n. 17 in Via Accademia Albertina), and the *Museo di Scienze Naturali*, at n. 36 in Via Giolitti (museum of life sciences; *both are closed for renovation*).

Piazza Cavour (*C4*). The square, with little hillocked flowerbeds, dotted with trees and 19th-c. homes, is adjacent to the so-called *Aiuola Balbo*, a large garden created in 1835 on the site of ancient fortifications. From Piazza Cavour, continuing further along the Via Giolitti, you will soon reach the *Piazza Maria Teresa*, a placid tree-lined square in a residential neighborhood, which still shows the style of early-19th-c. Turin.

Piazza Vittorio Veneto (*C5*). This large rectangular square, surrounded on three sides by porticoes, was designed and built between 1825 and 1830 in the area in which the 17th-c. Porta di Po once stood. Overlooking the river Po, it has as a backdrop the large church of the Gran Madre di Dio (see below) and the Collina, or hills, behind it.

Via Po (*B-C4-5*). This broad thoroughfare is lined with uniform rows of buildings with porticoes; built in 1675, it links the enormous Piazza Vittorio Veneto with Piazza Castello. In a cross street on the right, Via Montebello, stands the **Mole Antonelliana*** (*B5*), a remarkable construction by A. Antonelli, now an emblem of the city (begun in 1863, and completed toward the end of the century, it was originally built entirely in masonry and stone, and stands 165.15 m. tall; the spire, torn down by a hurricane on 23 May 1953, has since been rebuilt). Originally built as a synagogue, it is now used for temporary exhibitions; it has a huge single hall some 85 m. tall; the original structure has been reinforced by a skeleton in reinforced cement. Take an elevator up (*9-7; closed Mon.*) to a broad terrace above the cupola for a remarkable view of Turin and the surrounding area.

Galleria dell'Accademia Albertina (*C4*). *Open on request to scholars and small groups, tel. 8397008.* Set in the Palazzo dell'Accademia Albertina di Belle Arti, at n. 6 in the Via dell'Accademia Albertina, this museum contains paintings and drawings by G. and D. Ferrari, Spanzotti, Filippo Lippi, and other 17th-c. artists from Italy (O. Gentileschi; Cavarozzi) and elsewhere in Europe (P. Brill; S. Vouet). On the Via Po, just before Piazza Castello, on the right you will see the stern facade of the **University** (*B4*), built in 1713 to plans by M. Garove,

with porticoed courtyard and a loggia decorated with statues and busts of illustrious historical figures.

The banks of the River Po

The river Po, and the Collina, or surrounding hills, which rise verdant over the opposite bank, are some of the most distinctive features of Turin, deeply rooted in the mindset and customs of its population. All the same, the city discovered the delights of the banks of the Po fairly late; aside from the Castello del Valentino, a princely outlying villa, Turin did not turn to the riverbanks until the 19th c. It then made the riverbanks into a public park, as well as a showcase: the medieval "Borgo," Torino Esposizioni, and the buildings of the Centennial Celebrations of the Unification of Italy (1961) are three approaches to the concept of "showing the city's best face," in three different times and three different cultural contexts.

Gran Madre di Dio (*C5*). From Piazza Vittorio Veneto (see above) the *Ponte Vittorio Emanuele I* (1810-15), the oldest masonry bridge in Turin, leads up to this large church, built to commemorate the return of the house of Savoy in 1814, following the Napoleonic period. Built between 1818 and 1831 by F. Bonsignore in Neoclassical style (modelled after the Pantheon), the church houses, in the crypt, the *Ossuary of the Caduti della Guerra* 1915-18 (the Italian dead of WWI). To the side of the bridge are the Neoclassical 19th-c. **Murazzi** (*C-D5; embarcadero for boat rides on the river*).

Monte dei Cappuccini (*D5*). This isolated wooded hill served as a fortified position protecting the city. On the hilltop (284 m.) stands the church of *S. Maria del Monte*; this church, with a luminous interior richly decorated with marble, was built by A. Vittozzi (1583-96), who also designed the adjoining convent. Alongside it is the **Museo Nazionale della Montagna Duca degli Abruzzi*** (*open, 8:30-7:15; Sat., Sun. e Mon., 9-12:30 e 2:45-7:15*), with a vast array of documentary material concerning mountains and mountain climbing: history and techniques of climbing, geology, landscapes, culture and peo-

Turin: Gran Madre di Dio

ples of the mountains, and expeditions outside of Europe. From the square in front of the building, remarkable view* of the city and the Alps, from Monviso to Monte Rosa.

Parco del Valentino* (*D-F4; May-Sep., 9-11; Oct.-Apr., 9-7*). Public park, on the left bank of the Po, built in 1830. On the grounds, lined with boulevards and paths, is the large **Castello del Valentino** (*E4*), built in 1630-60 by C. di Castellamonte on the model of French castles of the 16th and 17th c., with a broad rectangular courtyard opening out to the city, and a majestic terracotta facade overlooking the river Po; to the left of the castle is the entrance to the *University's Orto Botanico* (*open, 8:30-1; closed Sat. e Sun.*) one of the leading botanical gardens in Italy, and one of the first (1729). Further along, near the banks of the Po, stand the **medieval village** and **castle** (*F4; open, 9:30-16; Sun., 10:30-16; closed Mon.*), a remarkable array of faithful reproductions of medieval houses and castles from the Valle d'Aosta, built for the International Exposition of 1884. The *Palazzo Torino Esposizioni* (*F4*; 1948), at the southern edge of the park, on Corso D'Azeglio, is a complex of pavillions, some designed by Pierluigi Nervi and Riccardo Morandi.

Museo dell'Automobile "Carlo Biscaretti di Ruffia"*. *Open, 10-6:30, closed Mon.* At n. 40 in Corso Unità d'Italia, this car museum offers a remarkable array of material on the history and development of the automobile in Italy, and the broad outlines of world production. Among the many cars on exhibit, note the "Itala" that won the race from Peking to Paris in 1907, the earliest steam-driven cars, the first Fiat (1899), the cars that raced in the first Giro d'Italia (1901), racers, and limousines; there is also a section devoted to the early years of the Touring Club Italiano.

Not far from the museum, in a park area overlooking both Po and Collina, stand various buildings, including the *Palazzo del Lavoro*, by Pier Luigi Nervi, now the headquarters of the Organizzazione Internazionale del Lavoro and other professional institutions, and the *Palazzo delle Mostre*, an exhibition hall with a remarkable "sail" roof; both buildings were erected to commemorate the Centennial of Italian Unity, for the Expo "Italia 61."

Corso Agnelli. This road is lined by the *FIAT Mirafiori* factories, built in 1938 and later enlarged; to one side of the complex is the auto test track. In Via Nizza stands the old **FIAT Lingotto factory**, built after WWI, and now used for art exhibits. Note the multi-story construction; cars can drive on any story and from one story to another, through the helical ramps, culminating in the remarkable test track on the roof of the factory.

Surrounding areas. Basilica di Superga*, elev. 670 m., 10 km east of Turin. This remarkable hillside church was built at the behest of Vittorio Amedeo II (Victor Amadeus II) to fulfill a vow taken during the French seige of 1706; it was built by F. Juvarra (1731), in "regal" classical style. The *crypt* (*open, summer 8:30-12:30 e 2:30-6:30; winter 8:30-12:30 e 2:30-5:30*) contains the tombs of the Savoy kings up to Carlo Alberto as well as numerous princes of the house; behind the basil-

ica is a plaque that commemorates the tragic plane crash that occurred here in 1949, killing the entire "Torino" soccer team.

Villa Reale di Stupinigi* (*open, weekdays, 9:30-5; holidays, 10-1 e 2-5; closed Mon.*), 10.5 km. to the SW of town; the celebrated Rococo architecture by F. Juvarra was built in 1730 as a hunting lodge for Vittorio Amedeo II (Victor Amadeus II). It is surrounded by vast grounds, and it now houses the interesting *Museo di Storia, Arte e Ammobiliamento*, with furniture and decorations from the 17th and 18th c., from the royal residences of Piedmont.

Udine*

elev. 112 m.; pop. 99,157; Friùli-Venezia Giulia, provincial capital. From the high hill of the Castello, you can see quite a bit of the "Patria del Friùli," the great plain stretching to the Alps. When a patriarch moved here in the 13th c. from Cividale, Udine became capital of Friùli, a great marketplace, a cultural center, and crossroads of the Alps. At the foot of the hill, beneath the Castello, is a piazza in which Venetian, Gothic, and Renaissance architecture all blend and mingle. The young artist Tiepolo, at the time just 30, came to paint Bible stories in the palace of the bishop.

Historical note. In all likelihood, the castle was built as an outpost during the raids of the Huns; it is documented as early as 983 as the castle of "Udene." In the 13th c., Udine became the residence of the patriarch, the capital of Friùli (the Pieve di S. Maria in Castello dates from this period, almost alone). During the 14th c., Udine was torn by factions, and in 1420 Udine – and all of Friùli – became possessions of the Venetian Republic, largely left to administer themselves amid new artistic and economic growth. The 15th and 16th c. witnessed the construction of Piazza della Libertà, the Palazzo del Comune, the Porticato di S. Giovanni, and even the modern structure of the Castello. In the 18th c. Tiepolo decorated the Duomo, the Palazzo Arcivescovile, and the Oratorio della Purità. Venice fell, Napoleon fell, and even the Austrians were firmly ejected – in 1866, Udine and Friùli became part of united Italy. Only after WWI did the city grow beyond the walls, and it continues to expand even now.

Getting around. Part of the historic center of Udine is closed to traffic from 10 to 6, and the entire area within the ring roads is heavily regulated. The routes we recommend map are walking tours, though you may choose to take public transportation to the Galleria di Arte Moderna.

Piazza della Libertà, the Castello, and the Duomo

The "Venetian" piazza and the monuments of "Patriarchal" and Venetian rule stand at the foot of the hill of the Castello, historical cradle of Udine, set high enough to enjoy quite a panoramic view.

Piazza della Libertà**. Elegant focal point of all Udine, it stands at the base of the Castello hill, surrounded by an harmonious complex of Venetian-style buildings.

Once Piazza Nuova, then Piazza Contarena, its modern appearance has changed little from how it looked in the 16th c. In particular, you should note the *Loggia del Lionello* and the *portico of S. Giovanni* (see below), to the left of which an arch leads into the Castello.

Loggia del Lionello*. This is the *Palazzo del*

Ùdine: Piazza della Libertà

Comune, or town hall, built in 1448-56 by B. delle Cisterne to plans by the Udinese goldsmith N. Lionello, in elegant Venetian Gothic style. Faced with alternating bands of white and pink stone, it is dominated by the large ground-floor loggia, with balustrade. Note the statue of the Virgin, by B. Bon (1448).

Porticato di S. Giovanni*. This spectacular piece of Renaissance architecture, by B. da Morcote (1533), comprises a long portico on slender columns, topped by the elegant *Torre dell'Orologio* (1527), or clock tower, with the Venetian lion of St. Mark's and two Moors, who strike the hours. At the center, a broad arch leads to the *Cappella di S. Giovanni*, now Pantheon dei Caduti, dedicated to the soldiers killed in war.

Note the *statues of Peace, Justice, Hercules, and Cacus*; on the right, a 15th-c. column with the *lion of St. Mark's*, and a handsome *fountain*, by G. da Carrara (1542).

Castello. This sober 16th-c. castle, built from 1517 on by G. Fontana and G. da Udine upon the site of the earlier castle of the patriarchs of Aquileia.

It was badly damaged by an earthquake in 1976; it has gradually been reopening during the Nineties. Take *Salita al Castello* (1563) from Piazza della Libertà, and pass through the *Bollani arch*, by Palladio (1556), and stroll through the lovely *Lippomano portico* (1487). Note the observatory ("*specola*," with its spectacular view*).

Civici Musei and Gallerie di Storia e Arte*. *Open, 9:30-12:30 and 3-6; closed Sun. aft. and Mon.* These museums and galleries have been located in the Castello since 1906; the complex comprises four main sections: the Galleria d'Arte Antica on the main floor; the Museo Archeologico and the Raccolte Numismatiche, on the ground floor and mezzanine of the right wing; the Gabinetto dei Disegni e delle Stampe on the fourth floor of that wing, along with the Biblioteca d'Arte, Storia ed Etnografia with over 20,000 volumes, and the Fototeca, or photographic archives. On the main floor, the *Salone del Parlamento** features frescoes by P. Amalteo, G.B. Grassi, and G.B. Tiepolo.

The **Galleria d'Arte Antica**, organized chronologically, has a collection comprising paintings from the late Middle Ages to the 19th c., including Friulian and Italian artists. Of particular note, works by G.B. Tiepolo, early Friulan artists, and the school of "Tolmezzo" (14/15th c.), and Renaissance and 18th-c. artists, such as: D. da Tolmezzo; V. Carpaccio; A. Bellunello; P. da San Daniele; P. Amalteo; G.A. da Pordenone; Palma the Younger; Caravaggio; A. Carneo; S. Bombelli; B. Strozzi; L. Carlevarijs; M. and S. Ricci; N. Grassi. Also, works by 19th-c. artists, including: O. Politi, B. Bison, and F. Giuseppini.

The **Museo Archeologico** has collections – including glass, arms and armor, and ceramics – that range from the Mesolithic to the Iron Age, through ancient Roman times, and on up through the Middle Ages to the Renaissance.

Moreover: solid **numismatic collections** (note the *Colloredo Mels collection**), with about 50,000 items, including Roman, Byzantine, barbarian, and medieval coins; *Toppo collection** of amber, semiprecious stones, glass, and Roman perfume jars and jewelry from Aquileia; *Torrelazzi collection** of Roman and 18th/19th-c. gems. **Gabinetto dei Disegni e delle Stampe** exhibits a rotating selection of the rich array of prints and drawings (some 10,000 items) in the museum, including work by A. Dürer, G.B. Tiepolo, G.A. Pordenone, and F. Chiarottini.

S. Maria di Castello*. *Open upon request, in the Museo del Castello*. Documented from the 6th c. A.D., this church was enlarged in the 12th c. and modified frequently; damaged by earthquake in 1976 and restored, it boasts an elegant facade and massive bell tower, by G. Negro. Note the fragments of 13th-c. frescoes* in arches and apses.

The church is joined to the Castello by the *Grimani arch* (1522); next to it is the entrance to the *Gothic Casa della Confraternita di S. Maria al Castello*; the **Casa della Contadinanza**, built after 1511, damaged in the earthquake in 1976, and is being restored.

S. Maria delle Grazie. Overlooking the great tree-lined oval of Piazza 1° Maggio, this 18th-c. basilica by G. Massari was given a Neoclassical pronaos by V. Presani (1838-51). Inside, behind the main altar, Virgin with Child by L. Monteverde (1522).

Palazzo Arcivescovile. This imposing 16th-c. palazzo overlooks Piazza Patriarcato; on the second floor, **gallery*** with early fresco by G.B. Tiepolo (1726-28), and rooms frescoed by Tiepolo and G. da Udine; note *library* by D. Delfino (1709).

The building will house the **Museo Diocesano d'Arte Sacra**, featuring objects of sacred art from early-Christian times to the 19th c., from Udine and Aquileia. Note the 15th-c. wooden altars of the "School of Tolmezzo." To the right, at n. 3, the 17th-c. **Palazzo Antonini Belgrado** (open upon request) has frescoes by G. Quaglio (1698).

Duomo*. Despite extensive remodelling over the centuries, this cathedral preserves its impressive 14th-c. Gothic form, especially in the handsome sharply splayed central portal (with carved lunette), and in the German-school 14th-c. portal* on the left side (near the campanile); on the right side, Renaissance portal by C. da Carona. The unfinished campanile was built in the 15th c. atop the octagonal base of the 14th-c. Baptistery.
Inside, note paintings by G.B. Tiepolo; organ doors painted by P. Amalteo; and a carved wooden pulpit (1737). The entrance to the theatrical Baroque complex of the presbytery and the cross vault, with spectacular stucco decorations, is flanked by two organs with decorations by Pordenone, F. Floreani, and G.B. Grassi; note the statues and marble carvings on the main altar (1717) and the two colossal *tombs of the Manin*, by M. Calderoni and F. Picchi (18th c.).

To the left of the presbytery is the entrance to the **Museo del Duomo** (*closed for restoration*), which includes the 14th-c. *chapel of S. Nicolò* with frescoes* by V. da Bologna (1348-49) and panels by his pupil the Maestro dei Padiglioni; also in the museum is the ancient *Baptistery*, beneath the campanile, with handsome architecture and monuments.

Oratorio della Purità. *Open upon request, in the sacristy of the Cathedral, or Duomo.* Directly across from the right side of the Duomo, this 18th-c. oratory, by L. Andreoli, has paintings and frescoes by G.B. Tiepolo and G.D. Tiepolo.

Madonna del Carmine. On the outskirts toward the railroad station, in the Via Aquileia, this 16th-c. church has a fine 14th-c. funerary monument, by F. De Sanctis.

S. Francesco. *Open only for temporary exhibitions.* Of the original Romanesque convent church (12th c.), heavily damaged in the fighting in 1945, all that survives is the left side, and the apse and campanile overlooking the modern Piazza Venerio. Inside, where concerts and exhibitions are held, note the fragments of 14th-/15th-c. frescoes of the School of Rimini.

Museo Friulano di Storia Naturale. *Open, Oct.-Apr., 9-12 and 3-6; May-Sep., 9-12 and 4-7; Sun. aft. and Mon. closed.* Located in the 18th-c. Palazzo Giacomelli, at n. 1 in Via Grazzano, this museum of natural science has a broad array of exhibits documenting various aspects of Friùli-Venezia Giulia.

Piazza Matteotti and the Galleria di Arte Moderna

The different aspects of Udine and the life of its streets can be seen in the western section, amid venerable churches (the 18th-c. Baroque Cappella Manin), palazzi of the 1500s, and museums – if last, not least, the Galleria di Arte Moderna, abounding in masterpieces of the Italian Novecento.

Via Rialto. Among the most attractive streets of the historical center, this was the main street in medieval "Villa Udin," as the town was called. Cars prohibited.

Behind the *Loggia del Lionello*, it begins with the monumental *municipal office building*, by R. D'Aronco (1911-30). Beneath the portico, but on the parallel *Via Cavour* side, is the historic *Caffè Contarena* (1925).

Piazza Matteotti. "Piazza S. Giacomo" to the Udinese, this may be the town's oldest square, documented back in 1248 with the name of "Forum Novum." Its modern layout – square, surrounded by houses with low porticoes – was the brainchild of T. Lippomano (1486); note the *fountain*, by G. da Udine (1542).

S. Giacomo. Built in the late-14th c., this church has a lively Lombardesque facade, by B. da Morcote; note paintings inside.

Museo Friulano delle Arti e Tradizioni Popolari. *Closed for restoration.* Set in the 17th-c. Palazzo Gorgo-Maniago, at n. 3 in Via Viola, this museum of Friuli's crafts and traditions features popular costumes*, furnishings, and everyday utensils and tools, from the 17th c. to today.

Monumento alla Resistenza. At the center of Piazzale XXVI Luglio, this huge monument to Italy's Resistance movement in WWII was designed by G. Valle and F. Marconi (1959-69); sculpture by D. Basaldella. On the north side of the square is the *Tempio-Ossario dei Caduti d'Italia*, a funerary shrine to Italy's dead in WWI, built in 1931; it holds the remains of 20,000 soldiers.

Via Zanon. Lined by one of the few surviving stretches of Udine's distinctive non-porticoed "rogge," or irrigation ditches this street has several handsome palazzi, mostly from the 18th c. At the corner of Via dei Torriani is the 13th-c. *Torre di S. Maria*, surviving relic of the old walls. Behind it, beyond the sober front of *Palazzo Torriani* (n. 4), is the 18th-c. **Cappella Manin** (*B1; open upon request*), a jewel of Baroque architecture.

Via Mercatovecchio. One of the most popular strolling streets in Udine, this was also the town's first marketplace, a distinction that dates from 1223. Broad and slightly curving, this handsome street is lined with porticoes; note the building of the **Monte di Pietà** (1690). Beneath the portico, in the middle, is a *chapel* with fine wrought-iron and frescoes* by G. Quaglio (1694).

Palazzo Antonini. Now a bank, at n. 3 in Via Gemona, this palazzo was built, beginning in 1570, to a plan by A. Palladio. Unfinished though it may be, its facade is quite distinguished and original. Practically facing it, on the right of Via Antonini, is the 17th-c. *Palazzo Antonini-Cernazai*, now part of the university.

Galleria d'Arte Moderna*. *Open, 9:30-12:30 and 3-6; Sun. aft. and Mon. closed.* This separate section of the *Musei Civici* is set in the *Palamostre* (1968) in Piazzale Paolo Diacono (n. 22) and occupies two stories in a succession of "open space" areas.

The museum's collections include works by Italian and especially Friulian and Venetian artists; it offers a broad and thorough array of 20th c. schools of art. Of special note, the Astaldi collection (about 200 works) with masterpieces by Italian artists from the 1920s to the 1960s.

On the *upper floor*, along with a section on modern and contemporary architecture (original drawings by R. D'Aronco), there are exhibits of works by artists from Friùli-Venezia Giulia, including Pellis, Crali, Pittino, Music, Pizzinato, Zigaina, and Alviani, as well as artworks by A. Martini, M. Mafai, C. Cagli, and F. Casorati, and a collection of 1970s American art (W. De Kooning).

The *ground floor* is primarily taken up with the *Astaldi collection*** which includes, in particular, works by G. Severini, G. De Chirico, Savinio, M. Sironi, G. Morandi, M. Campigli, O. Rosai, F. Pirandello, and C. Carrà; in a separate space are works by the Udinese artists Dino, Mirko, and A. Basaldella.

Urbino**

elev. 485 m.; pop. 15,114; Marche, province of Pesaro e Urbino. Montaigne wrote that "It is said that the duke's palace has as many rooms as there are days in the year." The writer visited the city and palace when the last duke was still alive; he expressed disappointment. The result of peevishness? Or an indication that there are fashions in everything? The location, a hilly spur on the reliefs dividing the valleys of Metauro and Foglia, midway between the Adriatic and the ridge of the Apennines, was inhabited in prehistoric times. Today, Urbino, with its "astonishing palace" (Vasari), "so expensive and daunting to build," as Raphael's father once wrote, is a university town rich in memories of an illustrious court (among the artists and architects who worked here, let us mention L. Laurana, F. di Giorgio Martini, P. della Francesca, and perhaps S. Botticelli); it seems that every detail of this town was carved, painted, or planned by a superior mind. Raphael and Bramante both came from here (the latter from Fermignano, 5 km. south).

Historical note. This town still lies within the walls built in 1507, on two hills separated by the hollow of Piazza della Repubblica; one hill lies SE, with the Duomo and Palazzo Ducale; one lies NW, with Piazza Roma. Time seems to have stopped in the Renaissance here; most of Urbino's buildings date from the 15th and 16th c. The Baroque barely grazed this town, and little if anything seems to have survived from earlier times. No monuments survive from the major Roman municipium of "Urbinum Metaurense," only inscriptions. The age of the Goths, the sack by the Byzantine general Belisarius, Longobard rule, the Carolingians, and the Church — none left a trace. Little survives of Romanesque Urbino, though the Gothic age survives in the churches of S. Agostino, S. Domenico, S. Francesco, all renovated since. The counts of Montefeltro became the dukes of Urbino in 1443; the second duke was Federico II, the most famous member of the dynasty, renowned for the portrait by P. della Francesca, now in the Uffizi. A skillful condottiere, Federico served popes, Florence, and Naples, and tripled his realm as he did; he was more illustrious in peace than war, as his court attracted the great minds of the Humanist Renaissance, among them L. B. Alberti, Pisanello, P. della Francesca, M. da Forlì, P. Uccello, D. da Settignano, D. Rosselli, and others still. From Flanders and Spain came painters and weavers of tapestries; for 14 years, 30/40 scribes worked to make Federico's library the richest in Europe. The architect L. Laurana rebuilt the Palazzo Ducale, one of the masterpieces of Renaissance architecture. This was Urbino's golden age. Federico's son married a Gonzaga and held high the splendor of a court immortalized by B. Castiglione ("The Courtier"). As if a spell had been cast, Raphael was born in Urbino in 1483, and Bramante, in 1444, not far away. The Della Rovere family took over in 1508, and Urbino flourished one last time; in 1626 it was ceded to the pope. Stripped of its treasures, Urbino declined sharply, and the Napoleonic occupation did the rest. After Italian unification, the university began to restore the city to health and prosperity.

Getting around. The area contained within the walls is off limits to private cars; the route we recommend, shown on the map, is a walking tour.

Places of interest. Piazza del Mercatale. This enormous plaza, at the foot of the town walls, is now a parking lot. With the 17th-c. sandstone Porta Valbona, this is the main entrance to Urbino; note, inside the semicircular 15th-c. bastion, the spiral ramp of steps, designed by F. di Giorgio Martini (restored in 1976); it leads directly into the center, to the porticoes of Corso Garibaldi.

Corso Garibaldi. Flanked by a long portico and overshadowed with the three tall apses of the Duomo and the west side of Palazzo Ducale — with two slender towers and three stacked loggias — this road runs past the brick Teatro Sanzio (C2; 1853), on the left. By Ghinelli, this fine opera house stands on the semicircular 15th-c. bastion overlooking Piazza del Mercatale.

Piazza della Repubblica. At the center of Urbino, set between the two hills, this square is the hub of all roads. On the north side, note the stern Collegio Raffaello (1705).

Duomo. Designed by F. di Giorgio Martini and built at the orders and expense of Federico da Montefeltro, this cathedral was almost entirely rebuilt in Neoclassical style by G. Valadier, following the earthquake of 1789; the facade is by C. Morigia (1802). Inside, note paintings by C. Maratta, C. Cignani, and C. Unterpergher.

In the left aisle, painting by F. Barocci. From the right aisle, you can enter the **Museo "Albani"** (open, 10-12 and 3-5), featuring paintings of the 14th/16th c. (Barocci, A. da Bologna), an English 13th-c. bronze lectern*, a Paschal candelabrum* by F. di Giorgio Martini; illuminated parchments and music. In the crypt (open by request, contact the sexton), note the marble Pietà* by G. Bandini.

Urbino: Palazzo Ducale

Piazza Rinascimento. Bounded on one side by the mullioned windows in the long facade of Palazzo Ducale, this square boasts an Egyptian obelisk, brought here from Rome in 1737; opposite is the Gothic former church of **S. Domenico**, now a gallery, with elegant portal (1451; in lunette copy of terracotta by L. della Robbia, original in Palazzo Ducale). Note the Palazzo dell'Università, once the residence of the Montefeltro family (heraldic device on portal).

Palazzo Ducale. The most important monument in Urbino, it constituted the model for the unfortified princely residence of the Renaissance. The palazzo houses both the Galleria Nazionale delle Marche and the Museo Archeologico Urbinate (see below).

This was the creation of the Dalmatian architect L. Laurana, who was summoned in 1465 by Duke Federico da Montefeltro to enlarge the original structure, the part with elegant twin-light mullioned windows, overlooking Piazza Rinascimento (ca. 1444). Laurana concentrated the building around the handsome courtyard*, and gave it the famed facade overlooking the valley to the west, with small stacked balconies, flanked by slender towers*. The two wings facing Piazza Duca Federico were completed by F. di Giorgio Martini, while the elegant decoration of portals and windows was done by A. Barocci.

Galleria Nazionale delle Marche. *Open, Oct.-Jun., 9-2; Sun. and fest 9-1; Jul.-Sep. until 7; closed Mon.* Housed in the Palazzo Ducale since its foundation in 1912, this is the region's leading museum. On the ground floor, adjacent to the Museo Archeologico, are displayed 71 panels depicting the machinery of war and peace built by A. Barocci in the late 15th c., to plans by F. di Giorgio Martini. The monumental stairway, known as the Scalone d'Onore* leads up to the loggias, where handsome inlaid doors lead into the various rooms of the Galleria Nazionale.

Apartment of Jole. In the older, eastern wing of the palazzo, this suite comprises seven rooms, foremost among them the Sala della Jole. Note the carved fireplace, by M. di Giovanni da Fiesole; also worthy of note is the artwork by L. della Robbia, A. di Duccio, and F. di Giorgio Martini. In the other rooms, there are badly damaged frescoes attributed to G. Boccati; bedroom* of Federico da Montefeltro, a rare example of 15th-c. furnishings, with painted decorations by G. da Camerino; and paintings by G. Boccati and G. di Giovanni. *Apartment of the Melaranci.* In these three rooms you will find an array of 14th-c. artworks, as well as frescoes* by the Maestro di Campodonico; a polyptych* by G. Baronzio (1345); a Crucifix by the Maestro di Verucchio; a triptych by the Maestro dell'Incoronazione di Urbino; a Virgin with Child by A. Nuzi. *Apartment of the Ospiti*, or Guests. You will see 15th-c. wooden sculptures, ceiling stuccoes by F. Brandani, a trove of 103 15th-c. gold coins, and works by C. and V. Crivelli, A. Vivarini, and Giovanni Bellini.

Apartment of Duke Federico. This apartment includes the most exquisite rooms in the palazzo: the Sala delle Udienze, a receiving hall with handsome stone decorations, as well as the **Flagellation** ** and the **Madonna of Senigallia**, paintings by P. della Francesca; the little Chapel of Guidobaldo, with stuccoes by F. Brandani; the Study* of Duke Federico, with, below, inlays by B. Pontelli, executed to drawings by Botticelli, F. di Giorgio Martini, and Bramante, and, above, 14 panels ** by Justus van Gand and P. Berruguete, with Portraits of Illustrious Men (there were originally 28 portraits, but 14 are now in Paris, in the Louvre); the Guardaroba del Duca, with a 15th-c. decorative strip depicting cupids hunting boar; the Cappellina del Perdono* (spiral staircase), with marble decorations; and the Tempietto delle Muse (originally decorated with paintings of the Muses, now in the Galleria Corsini in Florence, by G. Santi and T. Viti); the Camera da Letto del Duca, with carved fireplace, attributed to D. Rosselli and F. di Simone Ferrucci, portrait of Federico da Montefeltro and his son Guidobaldo*, by P. Berruguete, and a Virgin with Child, school of Verrocchio. The duke's apartment is completed by the spectacular Sala degli Angeli, overlooking the hanging garden, with its immense fireplace with a frieze of putti*, by D. Rosselli, fine inlaid doors* with design attributed to S. Botticelli, and the artworks: Communion of the Apostles* by Justus van Gand, Miracle of the Profaned Host* by Paolo Uccello, View of an Ideal City*, attributed to L. Laurana; a bas-relief by T. Fiamberti and a 15th-c. carved inlaid chest with a view of a city. The Sala delle Veglie (where Baldesar Castiglione set his book, the "Libro del Cortegiano," or "The Courtier") connects the apartments of duke and duchess; here you can see works by L. Signorelli and G. Santi. *Apartment of the Duchess*. Here are a number of rooms, decorated later than the rooms toured so far, with 16th-c. works. In the vestibule, see the stained glass by T. Viti, and a fine Florentine bas-relief. In the Salotto della Duchessa (note the stucco ceiling* by F. di Simone Ferrucci), works by: Raphael, Bramantino, and T. Viti; in the bedroom, various 16th-c. artists, as well as Titian, Raffaellino del Colle, and V. Pagani, and notable Flemish tapestries. In the wardrobe and adjacent room, works by Tibaldi, Zuccari, and Brandani (ceiling). In the immense Throne Room (35 m. by 15), seven handsome tapestries based on cartoons by Raphael.

Appartamento Roveresco. The third floor, completed during the reign of Guidobaldo II della Rovere, to the design of B. Genga, is devoted to the paintings of F. Barocci, early-17th-c. artists, and ceramics. In particular, note the work of Barocci and his pupils (Vitali, Marini); and works by O. Gentileschi, G.F. Guerrieri, A. Lilli, Mastelletta, S. Cantarini, and C. Ridolfi. In the last rooms, 15th-c. terraces that were enclosed in the 16th c., you can see, variously, work by F. Barocci, A. De Carolis, and ceramics from Faenza, Deruta, Siena, and other local centers. Last comes the long Galleria del Pasquino (note the 15th-c. battlements, built into the enclosure walls) with the furnishings for the wedding of F. U. della Rovere and Claudia de' Medici (1621), the work of C. Ridolfi and G. Cialdieri.

Cellars. These huge, recently restored rooms can be reached from the courtyard down a ramp. First you see the stables, then, on the left, the kitchens, baths, and storerooms, and on the right the laundry rooms, ice room, and other facilities.

Museo Archeologico Urbinate. *Open the same hours as the Galleria Nazionale.* This archeological museum is accessible directly from the courtyard of Palazzo Ducale: it has a collection of funerary epigraphs. Note the Lastra del Marmorarius Eutropus* (early 4th c.A.D.) and a relief of Ulysses and the Sirens (1st c. A.D.).

Oratorio di S. Giuseppe. *Open, Mon.-Sat., 10-12 and 3-5 (Jul.-Oct. until 6); Sun., 10-12:30.* In Via Barocci, this church has a fine old crèche* by F. Brandani (1522); fine paintings.

S. Giovanni Battista* (*open the same hours as the Oratorio di S. Giuseppe*). This oratory, just beyond the oratory of S. Giuseppe, dates from the late-14th c. (the facade is modern). The single-aisle interior with a handsome wooden ceiling, is decorated with a series of frescoes* by the brothers I. and L. Salimbeni (1416). From the stairs on the left of the building, a fine view of the Palazzo Ducale and its towers.

Via Raffaello. This distinctive road runs steeply up from Piazza della Repubblica to Piazzale Roma; fine views. It begins at the 14th-c. church of S. Francesco; inside, note 16th-c. reliefs in the Cappella del Sacramento; canvas by F. Barocci. Uphill, on the left, the Casa di Raffaello, birth place of Raphael (open, 9-1 and 3-7; winter and holidays, 9-1), with copies of work by the great artist, and a few paintings (by Raphael's father, G. Santi, G. Romano, and T. Viti); note fresco, done by Raphael when young.

Piazzale Roma. Atop one of Urbino's hills, this square offers a vast view* of the surrounding mountains. Note the monument to Raphael (1897). From here, along the Viale Buozzi, you have a fine view of the 16th-c. walls, with the Fortezza Albornoz.

Colle dei Cappuccini. At about 1 km. from Piazza del Mercatale, this hill is the campus of the university, built in 1966 to a plan by G. De Carlo.

Venice / Venezia**

elev. 2 m.; pop. 308,717; Veneto, regional capital. This town has exhausted every adjective, and outstripped all astonishment. In the earliest times, the pilgrims who came here to take ship for the Holy Land noted this city "set in the middle of the sea, built neither on mountain slope nor in bounteous plain, but only upon wooden poles, something that, for those who have never seen

Venice, may seem unbelievable," and where "you go by boat, from house to house, through every street" (Dietrich von Schachten). The mainland is only 4 km. away, and the sea is just 2 km. away; the city has more than 100 islands, as many canals, over 400 bridges, and just one "piazza" (every other square, circle, and triangle is either a "campo" or a "campiello"). Venice is at once unreal and exceedingly real — many have pointed this out. It seems to emerge from the void at the meeting ground of two infinities, the water and the sky, the ground here being so understated and hidden that it hardly counts. This city-republic's long and glorious political history extends over a millennium (tradition lists 120 Doges of Venice); a good portion of its history cannot be described as a chapter of Italy's history, but rather as part of something much larger; for more than a century, Venice was the capital of the entire Mediterranean Sea, and hence, the center of world trade. In its golden and sensuous autumn, Venice knew that it was still the European capital of theater, of celebration, of the joy of living, the desire of every educated mind. "Those days are long gone, but the beauty is still here" (Lord Byron): Venice survived the end of the Venetian Republic, trailing a great series of unsolved problems. The city now represents for all humanity (a humanity that loves Venice with so suffocating a love that it may yet prove fatal) the unattainable dream of a place where time stands still, the alluring Fata Morgana of a completely different way of life.

Historical note. Of course, in reality Venice did not spring out of a void, nor was it miraculously born of the sea, as the city's chroniclers long maintained, anxious to nullify any historical claims that either the Papacy or the Holy Roman Empire might choose to enforce. The Venetians, these "strange animals who neither plow, nor sow, nor harvest" (Cassiodorus, 6th-c. Roman historian), amazed even the earliest visitors, who were ready and willing to believe the local mythology. Recent archeological research, on the other hand, has clearly shown that there was a continuous settlement of the lagoon area that dates back to Roman times. And it is widely accepted that the Longobard invasion of the 6th c. forced various tribes of "Venetia," which formed part of the Augustan X Regio, to seek refuge among the islets of the lagoon. The center of these new settlements was first known as "Civitas Nova," and later Heraclea, in the long-vanished lagoon of Oderzo, later Malamocco, and finally, at the beginning of the 9th c., the island of Rialto, called the "Civitas Rivoalti." These lands were invariably dependent upon Byzantium, and neither Longobards nor Franks ever managed to set foot upon them; they were governed first by maritime tribunes, and later by a single officer, the duke, or Doge, at first named by the Byzantine rules, but as early as the 8th c., elected by the people's assembly. It was the anomalous environmental setting in which Venice rose that saved the city from those harsh wars that tattered and bloodied the cities of the mainland throughout the Middle Ages. In the 8th c., Venice was already substantially the city that we know, with its "calli," "campi," churches, palazzi, and "fonteghi." And yet it is a radically different city because, having no other territory into which it could expand, Venice was forced to do all its new building on the same area, rebuilding and raising its buildings, covering over the shoals and sandbanks of the lagoon, extending the walkways (bridges and "fondamenta") as canals and "rii" became narrower. In the 14th c., the population of Venice was already more than 130,000, roughly the same as the population at the end of the Republic, at the turn

of the 19th c. During those five centuries, Venice took to the seas, acting at first in the name of the Eastern Roman Empire, or Byzantium, to which it formally belonged, but in reality looking only to its own self-interest, ignoring everything that was happening on the mainland behind it. The first goal was to establish free rein over the Adriatic Sea. The major steps involved treaties with the Istrian cities, an expedition into Dalmatia in the year 1000 against the pirates that operated from there, and a campaign — at the behest of Byzantium — against the Normans, who were trying to control both shores of the channel of Otranto further south. The Venetians thus attained their first objective. Venice had unimpaired access to the routes of the Levant, and thus became a competitor of Pisa and Genoa. While the conflict with Pisa over the trading ports of Syria was soon dampened by the instability of those outposts, constantly under attack by the Saracens, the parallel conflict with Genoa over the possession of the trading ports of the Aegean Sea in time led to a fight to the death. The astute and cynical Venetian masterpiece of politics and military strategy — the conquest of Constantinople in 1204 by Crusaders transported by Venetian ships — allowed the Venetian Republic to take control of "la quarta parte e mezzo dell'impero," i.e., "a quarter and an eighth of the Empire."

Early in the 13th c., then, Venetian power in the Levant had reached its peak. The profits that came from the Venetian trade fleet were so enormous that they allowed the construction of the astonishing city of marble and stone that we see today, already the wonder of the 13th and 14th c. So mighty a sea power could hardly help but come into conflict with Genoa, on the Tyrrhenian coast, working to cultivate the same trade routes with the Levant. Just as Venice had played the card of the Crusaders in 1204, Genoa in 1261 played the card of the Greek rulers of Byzantium, lending its great fleet to the restoration of the Paleologus dynasty of emperors in Constantinople, in exchange for immense commercial concessions. For over a century the two maritime republics fought sea battles, neither one ever quite eliminating their rival; then Genoa tried to deliver a final blow by taking the war to Chioggia, in the Venetian lagoon. It brought Genoa a defeat from which the city never quite recovered. For Venice, the Peace of Turin of 1381 that ended the "War of Chioggia" reconfirmed its almost total control of trade with the Levant, which was, as Fernand Braudel later wrote, tantamount to dominion over all international trade of that time. For nearly a century, from that fateful 1381 until 1498, the year in which Vasco da Gama made his triumphant return to Lisbon, after his circumnavigation of Africa, Venice held the status that in later centuries fell to Antwerp, London, and New York. Everything passed through her hands: gold from Africa, silver from Central Europe, and the pepper, spices, cotton, and silk carried from the Far East by caravan and then loaded onto ships in the ports of Egypt and Syria. Despite the Turkish threat, increasingly menacing following the fall of Constantinople in 1453, this was the Golden Age of the Venetian Republic. On the Piazza di Rialto, near the little church of S. Giacometto, merchants and bankers held their "borsa," or exchange, while manufactories produced woolen cloth and silk fabrics and exquisite glass objects, exported around the world. In the Arsenale, anywhere from 2,000 to 3,000 master craftsmen stood ready to produce a hundred galleys in just two months' work. In order to safeguard its back, Venice expanded during the 15th c. from its stronghold of Treviso, in the hinterland, taking control of Padua, Vicenza, Verona, Belluno, Feltre, Udine, Brescia, Bergamo, Ravenna, and later, Cremona and Ferrara. The 16th c., on the other hand, marked the end of this centuries-long triumph: on the mainland, by the leagues that the states of Europe and Italy formed against Venice (Venice's defeat at Agnadello in 1509 marked an end to all further expansion on land); at sea, by the exhausting wars Venice fought against the Turks, wars that — despite the

Venice: Piazza S. Marco

great victory at Lepanto in 1571 — were to end with the loss of Cyprus and most of the trading ports in the Aegean and in the Peloponnesus; in the field of trade, because the great currents of sea traffic were slowly but inexorably shifting westward, out of the Mediterranean Sea and into the great Oceans; likewise because of the development of mighty nation-states. Fully aware that its prosperity was coming to an end, Venice spent part of its enormous wealth in the 16th c. on a thorough revamping of its urban image. In the 16th c., the aristocracy of Venice accentuated the ongoing competition to build palazzi on the Grand Canal, a competition that was to continue throughout the following centuries, culminating in the great monumental waterway that it is today. In the 17th c., Venice still had the strength to take positions against the pope, the Hapsburgs, and Spain, in the controversy over the interdiction, in the wars of Uscocchi and Gradisca, and in the so-called conspiracy of Bedmar, from the name of the Spanish ambassador who was behind it. In later years, the remaining energy of the Venetian Republic ebbed away in further wars against the Turks, finally culminating in 1669 in the loss of the island of Candia (Crete), inadequately counterbalanced by Venetian conquests in Dalmatia and the temporary reconquest of the Peloponnesus (Morea). After the peace of Passarowitz (1718), which obliged Venice to cede Morea, out of all its far-flung maritime holdings ("da mar"), all that remained were the Ionian isles. Venice's long and glorious history was coming to an end. The decline in manufacturing, trade, and military might, almost seemed to prompt Venice to attempt to establish itself as a new European capital of festivities and theater, and of a tourism *ante litteram*. And after so many carnival celebrations, in 1797 a Corsican general named Bonaparte put an end to this aristocratic Republic that had outlived itself. For Venice, no longer capital, this was to be the beginning of a new, more modest life. For many years it was occupied by Austria, save for a brief rebellion in 1848-49, until it was unified with Italy in 1866. These various political events left marks in the city itself.

After the Unification of Italy, between 1868 and 1871, a new road was built, running parallel to the Grand Canal, linking Rialto with the train station; it was called the Strada Nuova. Beginning in 1880 construction began on the new port, known as the Marittima. Between 1880 and 1882 the Calle Larga XXII Marzo was built, and, slightly further out along the Grand Canal, along the Riva degli Schiavoni and at Lido, the major hotels were built. Beginning in 1922, the pavilions of the Biennale were built; between 1930 and 1933, the automobile bridge was built, followed by the construction of the great parking garage in Piazzale Roma; and during the same years,

the opening of the Rio Nuovo provided an alternative to the Grand Canal. With the creation of the great industrial zone on the mainland, Mestre and Marghera were joined with Venice in 1926, constituting a single municipality. The great decline in population in the historical center in the last 40 years has brought the population of Venice proper from 184,000 in 1950 to the current low level of fewer than 90,000 (140,000 with all of the islands and the littoral strip), as against more than 200,000 on the mainland. This has only worsened the city's problems, which include the ravages of high water ("acqua alta"), the immense challenge of restoring the architectural heritage, and the great dangers to the city posed by the invasions of tourists that pour constantly through Venice.

Getting around. In Piazzale Roma, the terminus of automobile access to Venice, there certainly are paid parking areas, but, particularly on weekends and at the height of the tourist season, there is considerable danger of long lines, traffic jams, and endless delays; it is therefore advisable to leave your car at the Tronchetto parking area, with connections to the historical center by "vaporetto" or by private water taxis. As an alternative, you may choose to park your car in Mestre or Marghera and continue by bus or train to Venice, across the Ponte della Libertà. More than any other city, perhaps, on earth, Venice is a city for walking, and you should plan to walk extensively, through "calli" and "campielli," over bridges, discovering the always astonishing charm of lesser-known quarters and areas that have escaped the crush of mass tourism. The handiest way to move from place to place in Venice and to reach the various areas of town is by the "vaporetti" run by the public transportation system — ACTV. They provide an extensive and reliable network of connections and destinations. A useful and not particularly expensive way to get across the Grand Canal, from bank to bank, is the "traghetto in gondola," or "ferry gondola"; the "gondola di rappresentanza," or luxury gondola, while one of the symbols of this lagoon city, is used only for sightseeing, and can be found in specific "gondola stands," so to speak, scattered throughout Venice, at rates established by the city government.

The Grand Canal

The great aristocratic families of Venice competed in building lovely palazzi on the Grand Canal, "the loveliest thoroughfare, I believe, in the whole world" (Philippe de Commynes); but in long-ago times, the ground floor areas were stocked with merchandise, the mezzanines were used for keeping count of everything that was loaded into or unloaded from the galleys that docked directly at the front doors, and the Ponte di Rialto, a

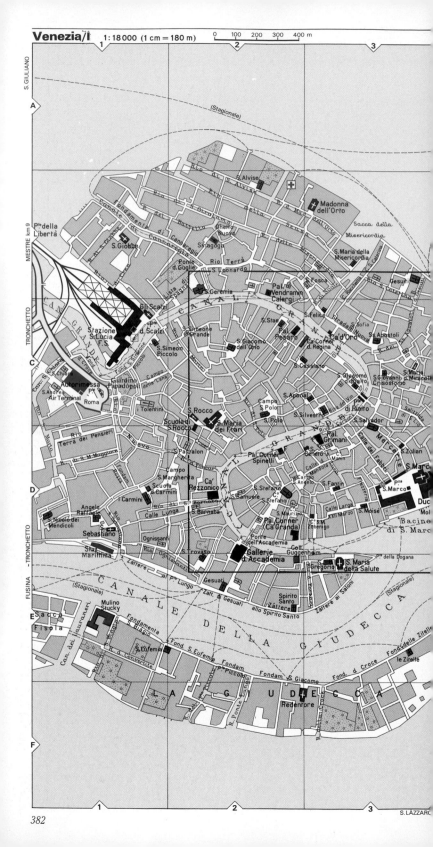

Murano

S.Michele
in isola

Cimitero

Isola
di S.Michele

Ss.Giovanni
e Paolo

S.Francesco
d.Vigna

M.Formosa

S.Lorenzo

Sc. di S.Giorgio
d.Schiavoni

Darsena
Grande

S.Zaccaria

S.M.
d.Pietà

Torri d. Arsenale

S.Giovanni
in B'agora

Riva degli Schiavoni

Museo
Navale

Pal.d.Sport

S.Biagio

S.Pietro
di Castello

Isola
di S.Pietra

C A N A L E

Via Garibaldi

Riva dei Martiri

S.Anna

Secco Marina

D I

S. M A R C O

Bacino

S.Giorgio
Maggiore

Isola
di S.Giorgio
Maggiore

Teatro
Verde

d. Grazia

Esposizione
Internazionale
d'Arte Moderna
Giardini
Pubblici

Campo
Indipendenza

V.le 24 Maggio

Isola
di S.Elena

Campo
Sportivo

S.Elena

V. Vittorio Veneto

S.ERASMO

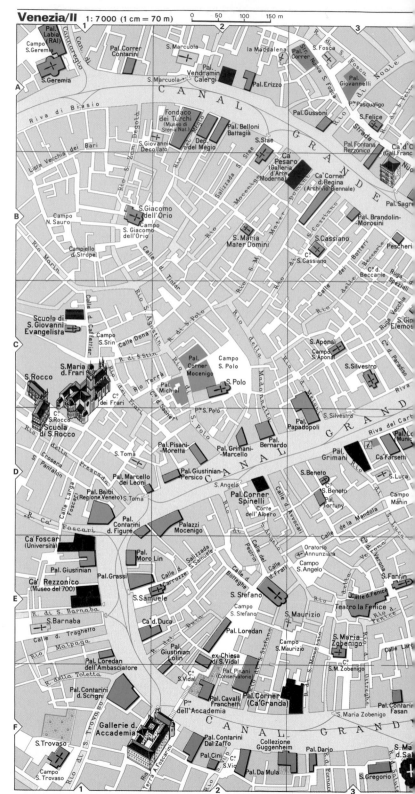

Venezia/II 1:7000 (1 cm = 70 m)

0   50   100   150 m

A
Pal. Labia (RAI)
Campo S.Geremia
S.Geremia
Pal.Correr Contarini
S.Marcuola
Pal. Vendramin Calergi
S.Marcuola
la Maddalena
Pal. Correr
S. Fosca
S. Maria Nuova S.Fosca
Pal. Erizzo
C A N A L
Pal. Giovannelli
P.za Pasqualigo

Riva di Biasio
Pal.Gussoni
S.Felice
Strada
Fondaco dei Turchi (Museo di Storia Nat.)
Pal. Belloni Battagià
Pal. Fontana Rezzonico
Ca'd'O (Gall.Franc
Lista Vecchia dei Bari
S. Giovanni Decollato
Dep. del Megio
S.Stae
G R A N D E
Ca' Pesaro (Galleria d'Arte Moderna)
Ca' Corner d. Regina (Archivio Biennale)
Pal. Sagre

B
Campo N. Sauro
S.Giacomo dell'Orio
Campo S. Giacomo dell'Orio
Pal. Brandolin-Morosini
S.Maria Mater Domini
S.Cassiano
Pescheri
Campiello d.Strope
Rio Marin
C°. S.Cassiano
Ruga d. Spezial

C
Scuola di S. Giovanni Evangelista
Campo S.Stin
Pal. Corner Mocenigo
Campo S. Polo
S.Aponal
Campo S.Aponal
S.Silvestro
S. Gio. Elemos

C
S.Rocco
S.Maria d. Frari
C°. dei Frari
Pal. Michiel
S.Polo
P.za S. Polo
C°. S.Rocco
Scuola di S. Rocco
S.Silvestro
Pal. Papadopoli
Riva del Carb
Pal. Lc Munic

D
S.Toma
Pal. Pisani-Moretta
Pal. Bernardo
Pal. Grimani-Marcello
Pal. Grimani
Ca'Farsetti
S. Pantalon
Pal. Marcello dei Leoni
Pal. Giustinian-Persico
S.Angelo
S. Beneto
S.Luca
Pal. Balbi (Regione Veneto)
S.Toma
Pal. Corner Spinelli
C°. S.Beneto
Pal. Fortuny
Campo Manin
Pal. Contarini d. Figure
Palazzi Mocenigo
Corte dell'Albero

E
Ca'Foscari (Università)
Pal. Moro Lin
Oratorio Annunziata
Campo S.Angelo
S.Fanfin
Pal. Giustinian
Pal.Grassi
Calle Carrozze
Calle Boteghe
Teatro la Fenice
Ca'Rezzonico (Museo del '700)
S.Samuele
S. Stefano
Campo S. Stefano
S.Maurizio
S.Barnaba
Ca'd. Duca
Pal. Loredan
Campo S.Maurizio
S.Maria Zobenigo
Pal. Loredan dell'Ambasciatore
Pal. Giustinian Lolin
ex-Chiesa di S.Vidal
C°. S.M. Zobenigo
Calle Larg
Pal. Contarini d. Scrigni
C°. S.Vidal
Pal. Pisani (Conservatorio)
Pal. Corner (Ca'Granda)
Pal. Contarin Fasan
S. Maria Zobenigo

F
Gallerie d. Accademia
Pal. Cavalli Franchetti
P.za dell'Accademia
S.Trovaso
Pal. Contarini Dal Zaffo
Collezione Guggenheim
Pal. Dario
S. Ma d. Sa
Campo S.Trovaso
Pal. Cini
C°. S.Vid
Pal. Da Mula
S.Gregorio

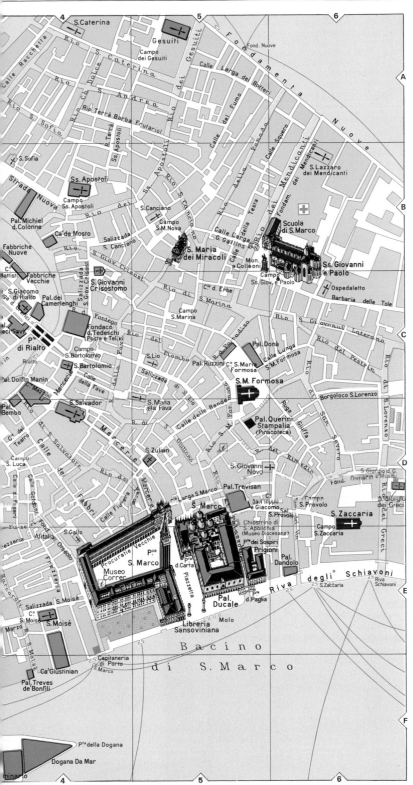

wooden bridge back then, could be drawn up to let ships pass through. The wealth of Venice derived from trading in goods, and its beauty certainly sank its roots in that activity. This route runs the length of the Grand Canal, from Piazzale Roma to the Bacino di S. Marco, or Basin of St. Mark's, with descriptions of the most notable buildings along that body of water. Many of these *palazzi* will be featured in subsequent routes, with more detailed descriptions, of the interior as well, when the buildings house museums or collections of art.

Grand Canal**. This is Venice's main interior waterway, and it runs through the city from NW to SE, linking the various quarters. The canal is 3,800 m. in length, and ranges from 30 to 70 m. in breadth; it winds in a broad, backward S; ever since the 14th c., work has been going on to straighten and reinforce the banks of the Grand Canal, giving it its present-day appearance. It orig-

inally served as part of the harbor of Venice, and was used to transport merchandise to the market of Rialto; from the 16th c. on, it became the place where the Venetian nobility built its lavish homes and *palazzi*. It is lined with unbroken successions of sumptuous residences (the distinctive mooring poles that stand before each *palazzo* are often emblazoned with painted heraldic devices) which range in age from the 13th c. (the Byzantine "case-fondaco," or homes-qua-warehouses of the 13th and 14th c.) to the 18th c.; the stunning array of facades along the Grand Canal expresses the full array of styles, from Gothic to Renaissance and Baroque, but translated into the distinctive architectural language of Venice, with airy fretwork, mullioned windows with pointed arches, and impressive loggias.

Left bank	Right bank
	Pontile S. Chiara, this bridge leads to **Piazzale Roma** (I, *C1*), where the Ponte della Libertà (1933) connects Venice to Mestre, on the mainland.
The *Venice-S. Lucia railroad station* (I, *C1*), built in the late-19th c. on the site of the convent of S. Lucia, and rebuilt in 1954.	*Giardino Papadopoli* (I, *C1*), this garden occupies the area where the convent of S. Croce once stood.
Pontile degli Scalzi. (The term Pontile refers to a smaller and more rudimentary bridge than, say, the Ponte di Rialto; it is used throughout this listing).	
Gli Scalzi* (I, *B1*), Baroque church built by B. Longhena for a community of Carmelites, who moved here from Rome around 1650.	*S. Simeon Piccolo* (I, *B1*), Neoclassical church (1738), with a green cupola.

Ponte degli Scalzi (I, *B1*), built in stone in 1934; this is one of the three bridges that cross the Grand Canal.

Canale di Cannaregio (I, *B1-2*), the second-largest canal in Venice, after the Grand Canal, crossed by the handsome *Ponte delle Guglie*. On the left, *S. Geremia* (II, *A1*), 18th-c. church with broad facade (1871) and Romanesque bell tower in terracotta. Adjacent to it is the 17th-c. **Palazzo Labia** (II, *A1*), regional headquarters of RAI television; the spectacular Salone delle Feste is frescoed by G.B. Tiepolo (1745-56).	
Palazzo Correr Contarini (II, *A1*), sumptuous 17th-c. building, called "Ca' dei Cuori" after the hearts featured in the family crest.	**Fondaco dei Turchi** (II, *A2*), Venetian-Byzantine in style, but heavily restored in 1858-69; it houses the *Museo di Storia Naturale*.
Pontile di S. Marcuola.	*Depositi del Megio* (D. del Miglio; II, *A2*), ancient granary of the Venetian Republic, a stern crenelated terracotta building, dating from the 15th c.
Palazzo Vendramin Calergi* (II, *A2*), an elegant Renaissance building, designed by M. Codussi and completed by the Lombardo brothers (1509). R. Wagner died here, 13 February 1883; it is the winter location of the Casinò Municipale.	*Palazzo Belloni Battagia* (II, *A2*), 17th-c. architecture by B. Longhena, with an ample loggia on the "piano nobile," or main floor.
Palazzo Erizzo alla Maddalena (II, *A2*), 15th-c. Gothic, subsequently heavily renovated.	Pontile S. Stae.
	S. Stae (S. Eustachio; II, *A-B2*), 17th-c. church with a lively Baroque facade, by D. Rossi (1709).
Palazzo Gussoni (II, *A3*), elegant 16th-c. building, attributed to Sanmicheli; its facade was once decorated with frescoes by Tintoretto.	**Ca' Pesaro*** (II, *B2-3*), a spectacular example of Venetian Baroque, begun by B. Longhena (1628) and completed by A. Gaspari (1710); it houses the *Galleria d'Arte Moderna and the Museo d'Arte Orientale*.

Left bank	Right bank
	Ca' Corner della Regina (II, *B3*), this impressive classical work, by D. Rossi (1724), has two stories of loggias; it is the headquarters of the *Archivio Storico della Biennale di Venezia*.
Palazzo Fontana-Rezzonico (II, *A-B3*), built in the 16th/17th c., in the late style of Sansovino.	
Ca' d'Oro** (II, *B3*), sumptuous 15th-c. Gothic architecture, rebuilt in the 19th c.; it houses the *Galleria G. Franchetti*.	*Palazzo Brandolin-Morosini* (II, *B3*), 15th-c. Gothic building, on a Byzantine plan, with two elegant loggias; rebuilt in the 14th c.
Pontile Ca' d'Oro.	
Palazzo Sagredo (II, *B3*), Byzantine in origin, rebuilt in Gothic style.	
	Pescheria (II, *B3*), this neo-Gothic porticoed building was built in 1907, as the center of Venice's fish market.
Palazzo Michiel dalle Colonne (II, *B4*), renovated in the late-17th c., with a ground-floor portico and elegant loggias.	
Ca' da Mosto (II, *B4*), typical 13th-c. "casa-fondaco," or "house/warehouse," heavily renovated, with two stories added; in the lower section, it still has Byzantine features. From the 16th to 18th c., this was the famous Albergo Leon Bianco.	*Fabbriche Nuove* (II, *B4*), building designed by Sansovino (1554-56), with long ground-floor portico; it houses the Tribunale (Law Courts).
	Fabbriche Vecchie (II, *B-C4*), extensive porticoed building, part of the complex of structures built by Scarpagnino (1522); it is now used as a fruit and vegetable market.
	Palazzo dei Camerlenghi (II, *C4*), elegant Renaissance building, possibly by G. Bergamasco (1528), with two floor of arched loggias.
Fondaco dei Tedeschi (II, *C4*), rebuilt in 1505-1508 by Scarpagnino to a plan by G. Tedesco, with ground-floor portico; its facade was once decorated with frescoes by Giorgione and Titian.	

Ponte di Rialto* (II, *C4*). This is the best-known bridge in Venice, rebuilt in 1591 by A. da Ponte. It is 48 m. long and 22 m. wide, and has a single arch, with a chord of 28 m. and a height of 7.5 m. Above it are a series of arcades.

Left bank	Right bank
	Palazzo dei Dieci Savi (II, *C4*), porticoed Renaissance building, constructed by Scarpagnino in 1521.
Pontile di Rialto.	Riva del Vin.
Palazzo Dolfin Manin (II, *C-D4*), Renaissance building by J. Sansovino (1536-75), with ground-floor portico; now holds offices of the Banca d'Italia.	
Palazzo Bembo (II, *C-D4*), late-Gothic building, built upon Venetian-Byzantine structures, which can be faintly detected in the structure.	
Palazzo Loredan and Ca' Farsetti (II, *D3*; Municipio), Venetian-Byzantine buildings from the 12th/13th c., with one floor of unbroken loggias.	Pontile S. Silvestro.
Palazzo Grimani* (II, *D3*), impressive three-story Renaissance building, with broad arcades set on pilasters and columns; masterpiece of M. Sanmicheli (1556-75), it now houses offices of the judiciary.	
	Palazzo Papadopoli (II, *C-D3*), sumptuous mid-16th c. home, with two orders of spacious loggias.
	Palazzo Bernardo (II, *D2*), 15th-c. Gothic, richly adorned.
Palazzo Corner Spinelli* (II, *D2*), a fine piece of early Renaissance architecture, with two stories of large twin-light mullioned windows, designed by M. Codussi (late-15th c.).	*Palazzo Grimani-Marcello* (II, *D2*), elegant Lombardesque style (early-16th c.), with three-arch loggias on the upper floors.

Left bank

Pontile S. Angelo.

Palazzi Mocenigo (II, *D1-2*), a complex of four buildings of the 16th-18th c. Residents have included Giordano Bruno (1592) and Lord Byron (1818).

Palazzo Contarini delle Figure (II, *D-E1*), Renaissance building, from the first half of the 16th c.; its name comes from the caryatids over the portal.

Palazzo Moro-Lin (II, *E1*), 17th c., known as the "house of the 13 windows."

Palazzo Grassi (II, *E1*), Baroque, with imposing classical style, by G. Massari (18th c.): headquarters of the Fondazione Grassi, it is used for major events and art exhibitions. On the stairway, note the lively frescoes by M. Morlaiter (18th c.).

S. Samuele (II, *E1-2*), church originally built in the 11th c., with a charming little Venetian-Romanesque bell tower (12th c.); temporary exhibitions are held here.

Ca' del Duca (II, *E1-2*), dates from the 19th c., but includes sections from the 15th c.: it houses collections of 18th-c. Venetian porcelain and Oriental art *(closed for restoration and reorganization).*

Palazzo Giustinian Lolin (II, *E-F2*), Baroque building, by B. Longhena (1630 ca.), with two stories of tall loggias.

Right bank

Palazzo Pisani-Moretta (II, *D2*), Gothic (first half of the 15th c.), with two handsome loggias with interlaced arches.

Palazzo Giustinian-Persico (II, *D2*), Renaissance architecture (16th c.).

Palazzo Marcello dei Leoni (II, *D1*), named after the two Romanesque lions on either side of the door.

Pontile S. Tomà.

Palazzo Balbi (II, *D1*), called "in volta di Canal," this large classical building was constructed to a design by A. Vittoria in 1590; it holds the offices of the Region of Veneto.

Ca' Foscari* (II, *E1*), begun in 1452, with two lovely eight-arched loggias, this was certainly one of the most sumptuous homes of Gothic Venice; it is now part of the university.

Palazzi Giustinian (II, *E1*), elegant Gothic buildings from the late-15th c., with long facades punctuated by mullioned windows. In one of these buildings, R. Wagner composed "Tristan and Iseult."

Ca' Rezzonico* (II, *E1*), a spectacular Baroque building begun by B. Longhena (1649) and completed by G. Massari (ca. 1750); it houses the *Museo del Settecento Veneziano.*

Pontile di Ca' Rezzonico.

Palazzo Loredan dell'Ambasciatore (II, *E1*), late-Gothic, from the 15th c.; in two niches on the facade, two Lombardesque putti bearing shields.

Palazzo Contarini degli Scrigni (II, *F1*), comprising two sections: one is late-Gothic, the other was designed by V. Scamozzi (1609).

Gallerie dell'Accademia (II, *F1-2*), housed in the former convent of *S. Maria della Carità.*

Pontile dell'Accademia.

Ponte dell'Accademia (II, *F2*), wooden, built in 1934 to replace a 19th-c. iron bridge.

Palazzo Cavalli Franchetti (II, *F2*), dates from the 15th c., enlarged and renovated at the end of the 19th c.

Palazzo Cornèr della Ca' Granda* (II, *F2-3*), magnificent building by J. Sansovino (1533-36 ca.), with a three-order classical facade; it is now the headquarters of the Prefecture.

Pontile S. Maria Zobenigo.

Palazzo Contarini Dal Zaffo (II, *F2*), a fine example of early-Renaissance Venetian architecture, possibly by G. Buora.

Palazzo Cini (II, *F2*), the Renaissance facade is reflected in the little Rio S. Vio; this building houses the *Collezione V. Cini (open in the summer months, and for temporary exhibits)*, with 13th-/14th-c. Tuscan paintings.

Palazzo Da Mula (II, *F2*), late-Gothic, from the end of the 15th c., with three orders of four-light loggias.

Palazzo Venier dei Leoni (II, *F2-3*), designed in 1749, it houses the *Peggy Guggenheim Collection of Contemporary Art.*

Palazzo Dario (II, *F3*), Renaissance building, attributed to P. Lombardo (1487), with a facade marked by triple four-light loggias.

Former Abbey of S. Gregorio (II, *F3*), founded in 1160, extensively rebuilt, with a 14th-c. Gothic portal.

Left bank

Palazzo Contarini Fasan (II, *F3*), a fine example of flamboyant Gothic style (1475); it is commonly called the "House of Desdemona."

Palazzo Treves de' Bonfili (I, *F4*), dates from the 17th c., with a classical facade; the interior is exemplary in terms of Neoclassical furnishings and decorations (turn of the 19th c.).

Ca' Giustinian (II, *E-F4*), late-Gothic (1474), with three orders of windows and loggias; this is the headquarters of the administration of the Venice Biennale.

Pontile S. Marco.

Right bank

Pontile della Salute.

S. Maria della Salute* (II, *F3*), Baroque masterpiece by B. Longhena.

Punta della Salute, or *Punta della Dogana* (II, *F4*), this handsome landmark frames the entrance to the Bacino di S. Marco, with the long low building of the *Dogana da Mar,* which existed in the 15th c. as a customs dock, repeatedly rebuilt since.

The area around St. Mark's

This was the heart of the Venetian state: from high atop the campanile the government was summoned to council; the Doge would walk majestically around the square in procession; St. Mark's was the Doge's chapel; in the Doge's Palace, government councils would convene, the Doge had his apartments, and judgement was passed by the Venetian Inquisition. Often those judged unfavorably would be executed at one of the columns in the Piazzetta; beneath the portico, crews were recruited while galleys lay at dock on the Molo, or wharf. This elite architectural image was meant to reflect the power of the Venetian Republic and the culture of the aristocracy that ran it. The route recommended here is limited to St. Mark's Square (Piazza S. Marco) and the smaller Piazzetta S. Marco.

Piazza S. Marco** (II, *E15*). This magnificent space, St. Mark's Square, has long been both a symbol and the drawing room of the Venetian community. Rectangular in shape, surrounded by porticoes, with cafes and stores, the square culminates in St. Mark's Cathedral, with its slender, solitary bell tower. Bounding it on the north are the **Procuratie Vecchie**, a long 12th-c. building, with two orders of loggias, rebuilt in the 16th c., in part by J. Sansovino. This building was once the headquarters of the highest magistrates of the Venetian Republic; to the east is the **Torre dell'Orologio** (1496-99, M. Codussi), topped by bronze statues of two Moors, which strike the hour on a great bell. Facing this building, on the south side of the square, stretch the **Procuratie Nuove**, built from 1582 (V. Scamozzi) to 1640 (B. Longhena), and continuing the motif of the adjacent Libreria Sansoviniana. Under the porticoes are various fine cafes; chief among them, the 18th-c. *Caffè Florian.* The narrow west end of the square is closed off by the *Ala Napoleonica* (1810); inside, note the monumental staircase.

Basilica di S. Marco** (II, *E5*). At the heart of the religious and public life of Venice, this church was the place where the Doge was consecrated, and one of the prime symbols of Venice and its history. Founded in the 9th c. to house the body of the Evangelist St. Mark, patron saint of Venice (the body was stolen from Alexandria in Egypt in A.D. 828), the building clearly shows, in its complex and articulated structure, the different phases of construction, with early Romanesque Byzantine sections juxtaposed with Gothic and 16th-c. architecture. Rebuilt in many different areas and at many different times, this church acquired the distinctive outline of a Byzantine church, with a large central dome and hemispheric cupolas, topped by smaller onion domes.

The *facade* comprises two stories and five arcades, with a cuspidate Gothic crown (14th and 15th c.), with aedicules and statues. The lower order, with its five portals with bronze doors, presents a complex interweaving of arches, columns, and marble decorations; in particular, you should note the 13th-c. reliefs in the central arch (Months, Virtues, Prophets), and those in the intrados of the largest arch (the Trades and Vocations; 15th c.). The mosaics in the facade, except for those in the vault of the first arch, were redone in the 17th and 18th c. On the upper terrace, copies of the four horses brought in 1204 from Constantinople (originals are in the Museo di S. Marco).

On the *northern side* is a portal decorated with a 13th-c. relief, Byzantine bas-reliefs from the 12th c., and the tomb of Daniele Manin (1868). On the *southern side*, is one of the two side entrances, before which stand two pillars adorned with reliefs, brought here from the town of Acre after 1256; some call these Syrian art of the 5th c., others believe them to be Byzantine-Islamic work of the 12th c. At the corner with the Porta della Carta (see Palazzo Ducale), note the porphyry group of the Tetrarchs (or Four Kings), possibly a Syrian creation of the 4th c.; near the corner of the square is the "pietra del bando," or the "stone of proclamations," a fragment of a Syrian column from which the decrees of the Republic were once read aloud; it was shattered by the collapse of the bell tower in 1902.

In the *atrium,* or narthex, before the entrance to the church proper, the marble mosaic floor dates from the 11th and 12th c. The walls have a facing of marble and columns; vaults and little cupolas glitter with Venetian-Byzantine mosaics* (Stories from the Old Testament) of the 12th and 13th c. Three portals, with bronze doors from the 11th c., open into the church. In the arcade of the central door, you can look up into the 16th-c. mosaic vault of the Arcone del Paradiso.

The **interior**** *(open, summer, 9:45-5, Sun. 2-5;*

winter, 10-4, Sun. 2-4) is a typical Byzantine structure, built to a Greek cross, with three aisles in each arm, divided by colonnades above which are galleries; massive arches support the five mosaic-lined cupolas. The floor, which has dips and humps due to the settling of the building on the dense forest of wooden poles that constitute the foundation, is in mosaic, with geometric patterns (12th c.; partly redone).

The **mosaics****, with their golden background, decorating the upper walls and the cupolas, are one of the Basilica's greatest adornments and riches. Created by Byzantine and Venetian craftsmen in the 12th to 14th c., they were partly redone during the 16th and 17th c., to cartoons by Titian, Tintoretto, P.Veronese and others. Among the earliest mosaics, easily recognized by the stylized forms and the hieratic poses of the figures, note those that run along the walls of the side aisles (Christ, Mary, Prophets, and Apostles), those in the cupolas, and especially the scene of the Ascension in the main cupola.

The *Battistero*, or Baptistery *(undergoing restoration)*, built in the 14th c. by closing off part of the atrium, is located in the right aisle of the base of the Greek cross. It contains the tombs of various doges and a baptismal font by J.Sansovino (1545); in the little cupolas of the ceiling, note the 14th-c. mosaics.Adjoining is the *Cappella Zen*, a chapel decorated with 13th-c. mosaic, with a 16th-c. bronze altar and the great sepulcher of the Cardinal G.B. Zen (1501), by P. Savin.

The **presbytery** *(open, entrance fee, 10-4; Sun. 1:45-4)* is set above the crypt and enclosed by a marble screen (iconostasis), surmounted by statues of the Dalle Masegne (1394).The main altar, which contained the body of St.Mark (S.Marco), is supported by four columns* made of alabaster, carved with reliefs, and with 12th-c. capitals, surmounted by a ciborium decorated with six statues from the 13th c. Behind the main altar is the renowned **Pala d'Oro****, a notable piece of Byzantine and Venetian goldwork (10th-14th c.), studded with enamels and gems. In the niche to the left of the apse, note the bronze door* of the sacristy, the last creation of J.Sansovino (1546-69). In the left transept is the *Cappella della Madonna Nicopeia*, with a 12th-c. image of the Virgin, taken from Constantinople, and considered the protectress of the city.

You can enter the **Tesoro di S. Marco** *(open, entrance fee, with cumulative ticket, same hours as the presbytery)* from the end of the right transept. This collection, certainly one of the richest arrays of sacred art in all Italy, contains liturgical objects of Byzantine goldsmithery, much of it plundered from Constantinople (1204). Installed in three halls, this collection comprises vases, goblets, chalices, reliquaries, Gospels, and altar frontals, largely from the 12th and 13th c.

Museo di S. Marco. *Open 10-4.* This museum is located on the same level as the Gallerie; you can reach them from the atrium of the Basilica. The museum's collection includes illuminated choir books, fragments of mosaics from the Basilica, a polyptych by P.Veneziano (1345) and 15th-c. paintings, 16th-c. tapestries, and ancient Persian carpets. In one hall are the **four horses*** in gilded bronze, a Greek creation from the 4th or 3rd c. B.C., or possibly Roman art from the 4th c., transported to Venice from the hippodrome of Constantinople in

1204 as plunder for the Doge Dandolo during the Fourth Crusade.

Piazzetta dei Leoni (II,*D5*).To the left of the Basilica, this little square takes its name from two lions made of red Verona marble (1722). At the end of the piazza, note the Neoclassical *Palazzo Patriarcale* (1837-70).

Campanile di S. Marco (II,*E5*). *Climb up it, 10-4.* This bell tower of St. Mark's cathedral stands alone, rising 96.8 m. over Venice. Built in the 12th c., probably atop a watch tower, and rebuilt in the 16th c., it was entirely rebuilt once again in 1912, following the sudden early-morning collapse of the old tower (happily, no one was hurt and damage to surrounding buildings was limited) on 14 July 1902. From the top of the tower, panoramic view* of Venice and of the lagoon.At the base, note the marble **loggia***, an elegant piece of architecture by J. Sansovino (1537-49), who also did the bronze statues.

Museo Civico Correr* (II,*E4*). *Open 10-4; closed Tue.* Set in the Ala Napoleonica and in the Procuratie Nuove, this museum has exhibits of all sorts, concerning life and art in the Serenissima from the 14th to the 18th c. Note A. Canova's Dedalus and Icarus. Major art gallery **(Pinacoteca*)**, with Venetian paintings from the 14th to the 16th c., as well as Ferrarese, Flemish, and German. The gallery possesses masterpieces by J. Bellini, and by his two sons Gentile and Giovanni; A. Vivarini, V. Carpaccio, C. Tura, A. da Messina, L. Lotto; as well as by German (L. Cranach) and Flemish painters (Van der Goes, D. Bouts). In the same building is the **Museo del Risorgimento e dell'800 Veneziano** *(entrance from the Museo Correr, same hours)*, with documents and memorabilia of Venetian history, from the late-18th c. until it became part of Italy (1866).

Piazzetta S. Marco* (II,*E5*). Set between Palazzo Ducale and the Libreria Sansoviniana, overlooking the Molo di S. Marco, with the island of S. Giorgio in the distance.At the bank are two 12th-c. *columns*, once the site of executions.

Palazzo Ducale** (II,*E5*). Residence of the Doge and headquarters of the highest magistracies of the Republic, this building is the symbol of the power and glory that was Venice. Founded as a castle in the 9th c., it attained its current size in the 14th and 15th c., a masterpiece of Venetian Gothic architecture. Above the ground-floor portico (note the capitals of the columns and the corner reliefs) runs a very elegant loggia. Two magnificent balconies (15th/16th c.) interrupt the series of large Gothic windows that stretch along the facades overlooking both wharf and square. The Gothic *Porta della Carta*, by G. and B. Bon (mid-15th c.), adjacent to the wall of St. Mark's basilica, leads into a very handsome **courtyard****, with two bronze 16th-c. well heads in the center. The courtyard is a mix of Gothic (W and S sides) and Renaissance (E side) styles.Near the entrance is the Baroque facade of the clock (1615) and the *Foscari Arch*, a Gothic monument (1470) by A. Rizzo. Facing this is the *Scala dei Giganti**, designed by Rizzo, with statues of Mars and Neptune by J.Sansovino (1554); here, a newly elected Doge swore to uphold the laws of Venice.

Interior. *Open 9-4; only by guided tour, for some halls, and for the Prigioni, or Prison.* Along a stairway beneath the SE side of the portico, you climb up to the Gothic loggia gotica; from here, the *Scala d'Oro** (1558; note gilt stuccos by A. Vittoria in the ceiling) to the main floor on the second story, where you cross the great *Sala delle Mappe* (note the maps on the walls) to the rooms that were once the *residence of the Doge*. Here, amidst spectacular Renaissance ceilings and fireplaces, paintings and frescoes by Giovanni Bellini, Titian, and V. Carpaccio. Cross back through the Sala delle Mappe, and then you enter the *Sala degli Scudieri* (two paintings by D. Tintoretto). You then climb to the main floor on the third story, where you can tour the council rooms of the highest magistracies of the Serenissima. The tour begins from the *square atrium*: in the 16th-c. wooden ceiling, note canvases by J. Tintoretto; on the walls are paintings by Veronese and F. Bassano. *Sala delle Quattro Porte*, named for the four monumental doorways, decorated with statues and columns: ceilings frescoed by Tintoretto; on the wall is a famed painting* by Titian (1556). In the *Anticollegio*, fine paintings adorn walls (Tintoretto, P. Veronese, J. Bassano) and ceiling. *Sala del Collegio*: on the walls are canvases by Tintoretto and Veronese; the carved ceiling boasts panels by Veronese. *Sala del Senato*: at the center of the spectacular ceiling is a painting by J. and D. Tintoretto; on the walls, canvases by Palma the Younger. *Sala del Consiglio dei Dieci*: in the carved gilt ceiling, panels* by P. Veronese. *Sala della Bussola*: near the door, a little slot, from which secret accusations were handed in through the "mouth of the lion" outside. *Sala dei Tre Capi del Consiglio dei Dieci*: in the ceiling, panels* by Veronese and Zelotti; on the walls, paintings by H. Bosch. *Sala d'Armi del Consiglio dei Dieci*: armor, weapons, and trophics of war. You then descend to the *passage of the Maggior Consiglio*, with canvases by Tintoretto and Palma the Younger, and from there, you enter the *Sala della Quarantia Civil Vecchia* and the *Sala dell'Armamento*, where you can see what survives of the great fresco of Heaven, by Guariento (1365-67), irreparably damaged by a terrible fire in 1577; in the next loggia are statues of Adam and Eve* by A. Rizzo (1464). *Sala del Maggior Consiglio* (53 x 24 m.): like the subsequent Sala dello Scrutinio, the decorations of this room date from after the fire in 1577. The walls feature paintings by Tintoretto (in particular, note the painting of Heaven*, 7.45 x 24.65 m. in size, done on several canvases by J. and D. Tintoretto, with the help of Palma the Younger, and others), L. Bassano, Aliense, Palma the Younger, and others; also note the frieze with 76 portraits of Doges (the portrait of Marin Faliero, beheaded in 1355 for conspiracy, is covered with black paint), by J. and D. Tintoretto; at the center of the spectacular ceiling, Apotheosis of Venice* by Veronese; in the ovals on either side, canvases by Palma the Younger and Tintoretto. *Sala della Quarantia Civil Nuova* and *Sala dello Scrutinio*: on walls and ceilings of these two rooms, paintings by Tintoretto, Aliense, Palma the Younger, A. Vicentino, and others. After you descend to the Loggia, you can see some of the Prigioni Vecchie

(Old Prison), known as the *Pozzi* (Wells), dank, dark, narrow cells. After crossing the **Ponte dei Sospiri** (Bridge of Sighs), comprising two corridors, one above the other, you can tour the *Prigioni Nuove* (New Prison), from the late-16th c.

Libreria Sansoviniana** (II, *E5*). This masterpiece of 16th-c. Venetian architecture by J. Sansovino was completed, after the architect's death (1570), by V. Scamozzi. This luminous classical building is the old site of the Biblioteca Marciana, but can now be toured only during temporary exhibitions; a monumental stairway climbs to the vestibule, with ceiling* frescoed by Titian, and to the great hall, with paintings by Veronese, Tintoretto, and Schiavone.

Museo Archeologico. *Open 9-2, weekdays and holidays; entrance at n. 17 in the portico of the Libreria.* This archeological museum occupies a number of rooms in the Procuratie Nuove, with a major collection of Greek and Roman sculpture, including a series of Greek statues of goddesses* from the 5th and 4th c. B.C. (Demeter; Hera; Athena); three wounded Gauls (3rd c. B.C.); the Hellenistic Grimani altar*; busts of Trajan and Vitellius; the Hellenistic Zulian cameo*. Also, marble fragments, epigraphs, and Roman coins.

Palazzo della Zecca (II, *E5*). Extending from the Libreria Sansoviniana, on the Molo, is a stern palazzo built by J. Sansovino (1537-66) and used as a mint. It now holds the *Biblioteca Nazionale Marciana*, based on a bequest by the Cardinal Bessarione (1468). Among the most important works in this library is the Grimani breviary, from the late 15th c., with exquisite miniatures.

Ponte della Paglia (II, *E5*). This bridge is called, literally, the Bridge of Straw, because this was the docking point where that material was unloaded for conveyance to the prison and stables of Palazzo Ducale (Doge's Palace); the bridge spans the Rio di Palazzo. From atop the bridge you can see the east side (Renaissance) of Palazzo Ducale with the 17th-c. Ponte dei Sospiri (Bridge of Sighs; see above), through which prisoners were led from their cells to face the State Inquisitors. Beyond the bridge is the Riva degli Schiavoni, with the vaporetto stops of the Linee Interlagunari (cross lagoon lines).

The Accademia, Ca' Rezzonico, and the Zattere, as far as S. Maria della Salute

Venetian art, perhaps the finest in the world, is scattered everywhere: you will find it in churches, palazzi, and of course in art galleries. It is found in the other routes, as well, but this route, extending in a ring to the west of St. Mark's Square, on the far side of the Grand Canal, covers perhaps the most celebrated treasures of Venetian art: the Accademia, with masterpieces by Bellini, Giorgione, Carpaccio, Tiziano, Tintoretto, an unrivalled collection; Ca' Rezzonico, with its 18th-c. paintings and frescoes; S. Sebastiano, where P. Veronese painted. The art of the Venetian masters should certainly be counted as one of the foremost charms of this city; nor can you really sense the meaning, style, and substance of that art anywhere else on earth. After running the length of the Fondamenta delle Zattere, this route ends at the church of S. Maria della Salute.

Campo S. Moisè (II, *E4*). The regular shape of the Campo is bounded by the facade of the church of **S. Moisè** (1668), a refined example of the spectacular Venetian Baroque (inside, note fine sculpture and paintings, including a later work by Tintoretto). Another fine example of exuberant Baroque decoration can be seen in the facade of the church of **S. Maria del Giglio** (or *Zobenigo*; II, *E3*; 1683), located a little further along, in Campo S. Maria Zobenigo. Rebuilt after 1750, it contains notable paintings: in particular, works by P. P. Rubens, Palma the Younger, S. Ricci, and J. Tintoretto.

Campo S. Fantin (II, *E3*). This charming and venerable square is bounded by elegant, white facades; the well-heads date from the 15th c. The famed **Teatro La Fenice** stands here; almost entirely destroyed by a severe fire on January 29, 1996, it is now being restored; facing it is the Renaissance church of **S. Fantin**, begun by Scarpagnino (1507-49), and completed by J. Sansovino (1564), whose work can be seen in the apse and in the marble chancel inside. On the left is the former *Scuola di S. Fantin* (late-16th c.), which since 1812 has been the headquarters of a literary and scientific academy founded by Napoleon Bonaparte.

Campo S. Stefano, or *Campo Morosini* (II, *E2*). At the center of this square is a statue of N. Tommaseo (1882); the square lies at the intersection of major Venetian thoroughfares. It is lined by notable buildings, including, at n. 2945, *Palazzo Loredan*, a long building dating from 1536, now housing the Istituto Veneto di Scienze, Lettere ed Arti, founded in 1810. Overlooking the square is the church of S. Stefano.

S. Stefano* (II, *E2*). Church built in the 14th c. with Gothic portal (1442). Vast interior, with fine Renaissance monuments and Gothic choir (1488). In the sacristy, paintings by P. Veneziano, B. Vivarini, Palma the Elder, and Tintoretto. From left aisle, you reach the 16th-c. cloister.

Palazzo Fortuny (II, *D3*) This 15th-c. palazzo, once known as Palazzo Pesaro degli Orfei, dominates the Campo S. Beneto with its Gothic facade. Inside is the **Museo Fortuny** *(open 9-7; closed Mon.)*, with a collection of work by the Spanish painter and decorator Mariano Fortuny y Madrazo (1861-1949), in halls that he himself decorated and furnished. On the upper floors are the *Centro di Documentazione Fotografica* (a photographic institute) and the *Donazione Virgilio Guidi (open 10-12 and 3-7)*, with 80 paintings by the Roman artist who lived in Venice for many years. Nearby is the 17th-c. church of *S. Beneto*; note the altarpiece by B. Strozzi and a painting by G.D. Tiepolo.

Palazzo Pisani (II, *E-F2*). This majestic 16th-/18th-c. palazzo, headquarters of the Conservatorio di Musica "Benedetto Marcello," stands in the Campiello Pisani. To the right of Campo S. Stefano is the 18th-c. church of *S. Vidal*, deconsecrated, and now used for art exhibitions; note the handsome altarpiece* by V. Carpaccio (1514) and canvas by G.B. Piazzetta (1730).

Ponte dell'Accademia (II, *F2*). This bridge was built in 1934 to replace a 19th-c. iron bridge. It offers a fine view of the Grand Canal: in one direction as far as the mouth of the Bacino di S. Marco, with the church of S. Maria della Salute; on the other, as far as the curve in the canal known as the "Volta del Canal."

Gallerie dell'Accademia** (II, *F1-2*). *Open 9-7; weekdays and holidays; ticket window closes at 6*. This is the greatest collection of work by painters of Venice and Venetia, from the 14th to the 18th c. Originally a collection of work by the students of the Accademia, the galleries were enriched by Napoleon's suppression of religious institutes, and then by private bequests.
Beginning with a hall devoted to artists working from the *late-14th c. to the mid-15th c.* (P. and L. Veneziano, J. del Fiore), you then pass through a series of halls with *works of the 15th c.*, by artists such as: Giovanni Bellini, V. Carpaccio, C. da

Conegliano, M. Basaiti, B. Montagna, and G. Buonconsiglio, as well as C. Tura, A. Mantegna, and P. della Francesca. The Gallerie also feature masterpieces of *15th-c. Venetian art*, by such masters as: Giorgione, L. Lotto, P. Veronese, Titian, Tintoretto, Tiepolo, Palma the Elder, and J. Bassano. *Artists of the 17th and 18th c.* include: Ricci, Guardi, Canaletto, Solimena, Strozzi, Piazzetta, P. and A. Longhi, and Zuccarelli. In Sala XX are eight *huge canvases* painted in the late-15th c. by Gentile Bellini, V. Carpaccio, G. Mansueti, and L. Bastiani, while the Sala XXI, features the *Ciclo di S. Orsola*, by V. Carpaccio (1490-96). The tour ends with paintings by A. Vivarini, G. d'Alemagna, and Titian.

Collezione Peggy Guggenheim (II, *F2-3*). *Open 11-6; closed Tue*. This major collection of European and American avant-garde art is installed in the 18th-c. *Palazzo Venier dei Leoni*, on the Grand Canal; this was the Venetian home of the American collector and patron of the arts, Peggy Guggenheim. The works are arrayed according to school; note works by P. Mondrian, P. Klee, G. Balla, G. Severini, M. Ernst, J. Miró, G. De Chirico, and P. Picasso. Among the works from the period after WWII note the ten paintings by J. Pollock, done between 1942 and 1947.

Ca' Rezzonico* (II, *E1*). Impressive Baroque residence, built on the Grand Canal from 1649 (B. Longhena) to 1750 (G. Massari). It houses the **Museo del Settecento Veneziano*** *(open 9-4; closed Fri.)*, which displays, in luxurious rooms (note frescoed ceilings by G.B. Tiepolo), documentation on 18th-c. Venetian life and culture. The art gallery includes works by: G.B. Piazzetta, F. Zuccarelli, G. Zais, P. Longhi, Rosalba Carriera, Canaletto, Guardi. Note frescoes* by G.A. Guardi and G.D. Tiepolo.

Campo S. Margherita (I, *D2*). This distinctive center of local nieghborhood life serves as a marketplace, and is lined by old homes. At the northern corner, you can see the lopped-off bell tower of the former church of *S. Margherita* (17th c.), partly enclosed by the surrounding houses; in the center of the "campo," two wellheads that date back to 1529.

Scuola Grande dei Carmini (I, *D1*). *Open 9-12 and 3-6; closed Sun*. This 17th-c. building, once the headquarters of a very powerful confraternity, is believed to be by Baldassarre Longhena. The halls are decorated with stuccoes, wooden frontals, and paintings from the 17th and 18th c.; in the upstairs hall, note the exquisite ceiling, with nine canvases* by G.B. Tiepolo (1739-44), masterpiece of the artist's late period; also note the painting of Judith and Holofernes, by G.B. Piazzetta.

I Carmini (I, *D1*). Convent church from the 14th c., with a Renaissance facade with a curving crown (early 16th c.) and a 14th-c. portal on the left side. Inside, note the three aisles lined with monolithic columns, and the lavish 17th-c. decorations in the nave. Among the many paintings and sculptures, note work by C. da Conegliano (ca. 1509), F. di Giorgio Martini (ca. 1474), and L. Lotto (1529). Alongside the church is the entrance to a one-time *monastery*, with a handsome 16th-c. cloister.

S. Sebastiano* (I, *D1*). This elegant Renaissance church is noteworthy primarily for the paintings and frescoes** done here by P. Veronese (1555-65). Veronese was buried here in 1588. Also note statues and monuments by T. Lombardo and Sansovino; in the vestibule, a Titian.

Angelo Raffaele (I, *D1*). Said to have been founded in the 7th c., and certainly rebuilt in 1639, this church has a largely 17th-c. interior. In particular, note the paintings by G.A. Guardi, which adorn the parapet of the organ. Not far off is the church of **S. Nicolò dei Mendicoli**, one of the oldest in Venice, rebuilt between the 12th and 16th c., with porch; the campanile is Romanesque. Inside, note ancient columns and rich array of canvases, statues, and ornaments of all sorts, as well as fine gilt and carved wooden frames (late-16th c.).

Zattere (I, *E1-3*). This pleasant promenade extends along the broad Canale della Giudecca, which runs between Venice proper and the large island of Giudecca. The exceedingly long "fondamenta," or quay (nearly 2 km.) is split up into four stretches, named after an outstanding building or landmark: Zattere al Ponte Lungo, Zattere ai Gesuati, Zattere allo Spirito Santo, Zattere ai Saloni. As you walk along the first stretch, you pass the 16th-c. church of **S. Trovaso** (II, *F1*), with two virtually identical facades (inside: note the 18th-c. organ by G. Callido; 15th-c. painting by M.Giambono; Renaissance relief with Angels and Symbols of the Passion, in the chapel in the right transept). In the presbytery, the chapel to its left, and the Cappella del Sacramento, note canvases by J. and D.Tintoretto, including a remarkable Last Supper*. Continue along toward the Punta della Dogana and you will find the 18th-c. church of the **Gesuati** (I, *E2*); the elegant interior features artwork by Tiepolo, Piazzetta, and Tintoretto; also note statues and reliefs by G.M. Morlaiter (18th c.) on the walls.The church of the *Spirito Santo*, which gives its name to the next stretch of the Zattere, has a simple Renaissance facade (1506).

Punta della Dogana (II, *F4*). This "customs point" extends from the mouth of the Grand Canal to the Canale della Giudecca, extending out into the Bacino di S.Marco, facing the island of S.Giorgio. Note the long low building of the **Dogana da Mar** (Maritime Customs; 1677), built as early as the 15th c. to process merchandise arriving by sea; the spectacular point, designed as a ship's prow with loggia, has a corner tower with a group of 17th-c. bronzes, depicting two Atlases supporting the terrestrial orb, with a revolving figure of Fortune (by B. Falcone).

S. Maria della Salute (II, *F3*). This masterpiece of Baroque architecture was built by B. Longhena (1631-87); the Venetian Senate voted for the construction in gratitude for surviving an outbreak of plague.This majestic marble structure, with an octagonal plan, is studded with statues and topped by a great dome; one of the outstanding features of the Venetian skyline.

The majestic *interior* culminates in the high cupola and the main altar. To the left is the *great sacristy*: on the altar and in the ceiling, paintings by Titian; to the right of the altar, large canvas by Tintoretto.

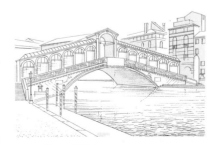

Venice: Ponte di Rialto

Campo della Salute (II, *F3-4*). One of the few "campi," or squares, that overlook the Grand Canal, this one offers a spectacular view of the basin of St. Mark's (Bacino di S. Marco). To the left of the church of the Salute, set high on its stepped base, is the *Seminario Patriarcale* (III, *F4*), a stern building designed and built by B. Longhena (1671), organized around a cloister and a monumental staircase. Adjoining it is the remarkable **Pinacoteca Manfrediniana** *(open by request, enquire at the Seminario, tel. 5225558)*, with noteworthy works by 15th-/18th-c. artists, among them: Giorgione, C. da Conegliano, Filippino Lippi, and Beccafumi. Among the sculpture, note two Renaissance reliefs by T. Lombardo and a terracotta bust by A. Canova.

The Mercerie, Rialto, the Frari, and the Scuola di S. Rocco

The nobles of Venice would return from the meetings of the state council along the Mercerie, where even now fine goods are offered invitingly for sale along the most popular promenade in the city; after the work of government, the aristocrats would head back to their ledgers, accounts, and correspondence, across the Grand Canal, in Rialto, which back then was the commercial and financial heart of Venice, and is nowadays the main food market. This route runs over the Grand Canal over the Ponte di Rialto, and on through the two Sestieri of S. Polo and S. Croce, wrapping around the first curve in the canal, to the church of the Frari (Franciscan friars) and the Scuola di S. Rocco, both remarkable treasures of exquisite painting. You will then return to the Ponte di Rialto, via Campo S. Polo and Campo S. Aponal.

Mercerie* (II, *D4-5*). Broken up into several sections, with constantly changing names, running from St. Mark's Square to Rialto, this is one of Venice's liveliest streets, dotted with shops (hence the name). At the end of the first segment (Merceria dell'Orologio) is the church of **S. Zulian** (II, *D5*), rebuilt by J.Sansovino (1553-55); inside are paintings by P.Veronese and Palma the Younger.

S. Salvador (II, *D4*). Nearly at the end of the Merceria is the 16th-c. church of S.Salvador, with its white Baroque facade (1663), overlooking Campo S. Salvador. Inside, in a setting of stern elegance, is an abundance of fine art: note the monument to the Procuratore Andrea Dolfin by G. del Moro, and the monument to the Doge Francesco Venier* by Sansovino (1561); also work by Titian (1560 and 1566), and P. Bordone. To the right of the church is the former *convent of S. Salvador*, built in the 16th c., which features two cloisters.

Campo S. Bartolomio (II, *C4*). In the past, a lively marketplace, this is now one of the busiest and most exciting meeting spots in Venice, at the convergence of routes from Piazza S. Marco, from Rialto, and from the train station. At the center of the square is a monument to Carlo Goldoni (1883); also note the 18th-c. church of *S. Bartolomio*, long the place of worship of the German comunity that lived in the nearby Fondaco.

Ponte di Rialto* (II, *C4*). Until the 19th c., this renowned bridge was the only solid link between the two banks of the Grand Canal. It is lined by double arcades, packed with shops; the sides bear 16th-c. reliefs. Handsome view of the Grand Canal. On the right bank, to the right, the *Palazzo dei Camerlenghi*; to the left, *Palazzo dei Dieci Savi*.

Campo S. Giacomo di Rialto (II, *C4*). Formerly the center of Venice's financial activity, this square spreads out to the right of the *Ruga degli Orefici*. Bounded by the porticoes of the *Fabbriche Vecchie*, it features the 16th-c. statue of the "Gobbo di Rialto," a hunchback, supporting the stairway; decrees and condemnations were once proclaimed here. Note the facade, with 15th-c. portico, of the church of **S. Giacomo di Rialto** (S. Giacometto), said to be the oldest church in Venice, but actually built in the 12th c. and rebuilt in 1601. Inside, note the handsome medieval columns, and artworks by Marco Vecellio, V. Scamozzi, and G. Campagna (1604).

S. Cassiano (II, *B3*). This 17th-c. church turns its right side to the Campo S. Cassiano, a busy thoroughfare. Founded in early times, but repeatedly rebuilt, this church still has a 13th-c. terracotta bell tower; inside, in the presbytery, three canvases by Tintoretto, including a Crucifixion* (1568).

Ca' Corner della Regina (II, *B3*). This classical-style building, by D. Rossi (1724), with a double loggia, belonged to the family of Caterina, queen of Cyprus, who was born here in 1454. It now contains the *Archivio Storico della Biennale di Venezia* (archives of the Venice Biennale; *open, weekdays, 9-1*), an international center for the study of contemporary art.

Ca' Pesaro* (II, *B2-3*). One of the largest palazzi on the Grand Canal, it features a broad courtyard with a large well, by J. Sansovino, and a majestic entrance hall. On the 2nd and 3rd floors is the **Galleria d'Arte Moderna**, with work from the Venice Biennale. It boasts work by great names of the 20th c.: Morandi, Boccioni, Savinio, Carrà, Sironi, Rosai, Miró, De Pisis, Chagal, Kandinsky, Klimt (painting); Moore, Messina, Martini, Arp, Pomodoro, Calder (sculpture). Also, major artists of the 19th c., including: G. Pellizza, Hayez, Fattori, De Nittis, Corot, Bonnard. On the 4th floor is the **Museo d'Arte Orientale*** *(open 9-2; holidays, 9-1; closed Mon.)*, with one of the largest collections of Japanese art from the Edo period (1614-1868), as well as Chinese (porcelain and jade) and Indonesian art (fabrics, shadow puppets).

Campo S. Maria Mater Domini (II, *B2*). Regular in shape, this square has a 14th-c. well head in the center and, all around, late-Byzantine and Gothic buildings. It takes its name from the adjoining Renaissance church of **S. Maria Mater Domini** (1502-40), with a facade attributed to J. Sansovino and a harmonious interior built to a Greek cross. Inside, paintings by V. Catena (1520) and a very young Tintoretto.

S. Giacomo dell'Orio (II, *B1*). In one of the few tree-lined squares of central Venice, this church, one of Venice's oldest, still preserves its 12th-c. structure in the apsidal area; note the 13th-c. terracotta campanile. Inside, note the 14th-c. wooden ceiling, and many exquisite works of art: a 13th-c. holy water font and a Lombardesque pulpit; wooden 14th-c. Crucifix by P. Veneziano; Virgin and Saints* by L. Lotto (1546); and paintings by P. Veronese (1572 and 1577) and Palma the Younger (1575).

Fondaco dei Turchi (II, *A2*). This exemplary 13th-c. "casa-fondaco," or "warehouse/home," was used from 1621 until 1838 as a warehouse and hotel for Turkish traders. Transformed by restoration in the 19th c., it now houses the **Museo Civico di Storia Naturale** *(open 9-1:30; holidays 9-1; closed Mon.)*, with collections of fossils, mammals, minerals, and marine fauna, herbaria, and entomological and ethnographic collections.

Scuola Grande di S. Giovanni Evangelista* (II, *C1*). From an elegant Renaissance courtyard, by P. Lombardo (1481), you enter to find, facing each other, the Gothic church of *S. Giovanni Evangelista*, and the Scuola Grande, whose blends of style testify to the long period of construction (14th/18th c.). Inside, note the spectacular staircase* (M. Codussi, 1498), a hint of things to come,

both in the huge Gothic hall on the ground floor and in the lavish 18th-c. room upstairs. Note paintings by J. Guarana, G.D. Tiepolo, D. Tintoretto, P. Longhi, Palma the Younger, and others.

S. Maria Gloriosa dei Frari* (II, *C-D1*). Marked by the massive 14th-c. campanile (second-tallest in Venice, after St. Mark's), this church was built by the Franciscans from 1340 to 1443. Gothic in style, it has a stern facade, marble portals, along the flanks as well, and a handsome apse. The portal on the facade has statues by B. Bon, P. Lamberti, and A. Vittoria.

The **interior** is vast and majestic and features monuments and fine art. In the center of the *nave*, note the Gothic-Renaissance choir* of the monks, with marble screen and carved inlaid wooden stalls. *Right aisle*: note monument to Titian and statue by A. Vittoria. *Right transept*: monuments by P. Lombardo and L. Bregno. *Sacristy*: triptych** by Giovanni Bellini (1488), in the original frame; certainly one of his masterpieces. The *apsidal chapels on the right* houses various Gothic tombs, with a polyptych by B. Vivarini (1482), and a wooden sculpture by Donatello (ca. 1450). *Presbytery*: altar piece** by Titian; monument to the Doge F. Foscari*, by A. and P. Bregno; funerary urn of the Doge Niccolò Tron*, by A. Rizzo, a masterpiece of the Venetian Renaissance. *Apsidal chapels on the left*: paintings and statues by B. Licinio, A. Vivarini, M. Basaiti, B. Vivarini, and J. Sansovino. *Left aisle*: altar piece** by Titian; note the colossal "funerary machine," conceived by B. Longhena for Doge Giovanni Pesaro (1669); and pyramidal monument to A. Canova, designed by himself.

Scuola Grande di S. Rocco* (II, *D1*). *Open: 28 Mar.-2 Nov., 9-5:30; 3 Nov.-27 Mar., 10-1, Sat., Sun. until 4; 26 Dec.-6 Jan. and week of Carnevale, 10-4*. This building was erected between 1516 and 1560, at first to plans by Bartolomeo Bon, and later under the supervision of Sante Lombardo and Scarpagnino; in the facade, elements of the early Renaissance (ground floor) mix with bellwethers of the Baroque (upper floor). *Inside*, the vast halls are decorated with the full series of large **canvases** by Jacopo Tintoretto, done between 1564 and 1587, at the peak of his creative prowess. The tour begins on the upper floor, which you reach by climbing the immense stairway* by Scarpagnino (1544-46); on the wall, The Plague of 1630, masterpiece by Antonio Zanchi (1666). In the *Sala dell'Albergo*, decorated by Tintoretto, monumental Crucifixion* (1565) and dramatic scenes of the Passion; in the splendid ceiling, S. Rocco in Glory, the first canvases done here by the master. On easels: Christ Carrying the Cross*, attributed variously to Giorgione and Titian; Ecce Homo, youthful work by Titian. In the ceiling of the impressive *Sala Maggiore*, decorated between 1576 and 1581, 21 canvases with stories from the Old Testament; on the walls, 12 stories from the New Testament; on the altar, Glory of S. Rocco, also by Tintoretto. On either side of the altar, on easels: Annunciation, by Titian; Visitation and Self-Portrait, by Tintoretto; Abraham Visited by Angels and Hagar Succoured by Angels, by G.B. Tiepolo. In the *hall* on the ground floor, note the eight large canvases that Tintoretto painted in 1583-87; note in particular, Annunciation, Flight into Egypt, St. Mary Magdalene and S. Maria Egiziaca; on the altar, S. Rocco, statue by Girolamo Campagna (1587).

S. Rocco* (II, C1). This church, rebuilt in the 18th c., features paintings* by Tintoretto; also, by S. Ricci and G.A. Pordenone.

Campo S. Polo (II, C2). This is one of the largest and most distinctive "campi," or squares, in Venice. It was once used as a setting for popular festivals. It is lined by palazzi (14th-/18th-c.), as well as the apse of the ancient church of **S. Polo**, Byzantine in origin, but repeatedly modified, and largely rebuilt at the turn of the 19th c. On the side, note the large 15th-c. Gothic portal and a 14th-c. campanile; inside, note the wooden keel ceiling, and paintings by J. Tintoretto, G.B. Tiepolo, and Palma the Younger; the organ was built by G. Callido, 1763.

Campo S. Aponal (II, C3). This small but lively square features the former church of **S. Aponal** (S. Apollinare), rebuilt in the Gothic style in the 15th c., with a brick facade and a handsome Romanesque-Gothic campanile with mullioned windows.

S. Silvestro (II, C3). This ancient church was rebuilt around 1850, with a Neoclassical facade from the early-20th c.; it features a few notable paintings by J. Tintoretto and Carl Loth. Between the two altars is the entrance to the *Ex Scuola dei Mercanti di Vino* (16th c.); note canvases by G. Diziani.

S. Giovanni Elemosinario (II, C3-4). This ancient church breaks up the dense line of buildings along *Ruga Vecchia S. Giovanni*, the main thoroughfare linking Rialto and S. Polo. Destroyed by fire in the early-16th c., and rebuilt by Scarpagnino in 1538, it still has the late-14th-c. bell tower. The interior is simple and elegant, built to a Greek cross: on the main altar, painting by Titian (1533); also, paintings by G.A. Pordenone (1530).

Ss. Giovanni e Paolo, S. Maria dei Miracoli, and Ca' d'Oro

The great churches of the two medieval orders of preaching monks seem to preside spiritually over Venice, from their adjacent sites: the Frari, to the west, and Ss. Giovanni e Paolo (S. Zanipolo) of the Dominicans, to the north of the square. In this route "behind" St. Mark's, and through part of the *Sestiere di Castello*, the church of Ss. Giovanni e Paolo and its "campo," with the renowned monument to Colleoni by Verrocchio, comes midway, after Pinacoteca Querini Stampalia, a valuable introduction to life in Venice in bygone eras, and before the delicate Lombard-style church of S. Maria dei Miracoli and final luminous view of the Grand Canal, at the Ca' d'Oro.

Campo S. Maria Formosa (II, C5). You reach this Campo from the church of S. Zulian (see preceding route) by following the Calle delle Bande. One of the liveliest and most interesting "campi," or squares, in Venice, and once used as an open-air theater, it is lined with noteworthy palazzi: at n. 5866, *Palazzo Ruzzini* (1580); at n. 6121 and n. 6125-26, three *Palazzi Donà*, the first of them dating from the late-16th c., the other two, Gothic, from the 15th c.; at n. 5246, *Palazzo Vitturi*, a rare example of Venetian-Byzantine architecture (13th c.); at n. 5250, *Palazzo Malipiero*, dating from the 16th c. but renovated in the 19th c.

S. Maria Formosa* (II, C-D5). This church was first built in the 7th c., and rebuilt in 1492 by M. Codussi; the facades are from the 16th c. and the bell tower, from the 17th c. Inside, artworks by B. Vivarini, Palma the Elder, and L. Bassano.

Palazzo Querini Stampalia* (II, D5). Built around 1528, this building overlooks a handsome little "campiello," along the Rio di S. Maria Formosa. Headquarters since 1869 of the *Fondazione Querini Stampalia*, it houses a major library, and, on the 3rd floor, an impressive *Pinacoteca (open 10-12:30, closed Mon.)*. In the 20 halls, decorated with 18th-c. stuccoes and furnishings, are works by Venetian painters from the 14th to the 18th c., including: D. and C. Veneziano, Giovanni Bellini, L. di Credi, V. Catena, Palma the Elder, L. Giordano, P. Vecchia, G.B. Tiepolo, P. Longhi, F. Zugno, and G. Bella.

Campo dei Ss. Giovanni e Paolo* (II, B-C5). After St. Mark's Square, this is the most monumental in Venice; distinctly marked by the facades of the church of Ss. Giovanni e Paolo (in terracotta) and the adjacent Scuola di S. Marco; at its center is a 16th-c. well head. The fulcrum of the "campo" is the **statue of Bartolomeo Colleoni*** (II, B-C5), a masterpiece of Renaissance statuary, by A. Verrocchio (1481-88).

Ss. Giovanni e Paolo, or S. Zanipolo** (II, B-C6). This grand Gothic church was built by the Dominicans from 1246 to 1430, and it was established from about 1450 on as the site of the solemn funerals of the Doges. In the impressive terracotta facade, which was left unfinished, note the marble portal by Bartolomeo Bon (1461); pay special attention to the right side and the polygonal apses*.

The **interior**, with its solemn soaring Gothic structure, is similar to that of the church of the Frari, and like the Frari it contains monuments to doges, commanders, and other illustrious personages of the ancient Venetian Republic, from the 14th to the 17th c. *Counterfacade*: three monuments to the Mocenigo, among them the monument of the Doge Pietro Mocenigo* by Pietro Lombardo (1481). *Right aisle*: 1st altar, Virgin and Saints, attributed to Francesco Bissolo; on the next wall, monument to Marcantonio Bragadin (the defender of Famagosta), attributed to Vincenzo Scamozzi; 2nd altar, polyptych by a young Giovanni Bellini (ca. 1465). At the end of the aisle is the *Cappella di S. Domenico* (1716), in the carved and gilded ceiling of which is the Glory of St. Domenick* by G.B. Piazzetta (1727). *Right transept*: altarpiece by Lorenzo Lotto (1542); large Gothic window with painted glass (15th c.). On the walls of the *presbytery*, with its luminous polygonal apse, note the tombs of the Doges: on the left, monument of the Doge Andrea Vendramin* by Pietro and Tullio Lombardo (15th c.); on the same wall, the Gothic monument of the Doge Marco Corner*, with statues of the Virgin and Saints by Giovanni Pisano. At the end of the left transept, under the monument of the Doge A. Venier (15th c.), is the entrance to the 16th-c. *Cappella del Rosario**, devastated by fire in 1867; in the rebuilt ceiling, canvases* by Paolo Veronese; in the presbytery, statues and two bronze candelabra by Alessandro Vittoria. *Left aisle*: beneath the 18th-c. organ by Gaetano Callido, triptych by Bartolomeo Vivarini; among other things, note the monument of the Doge Tomaso Mocenigo, executed by Tuscan artists in 1423, and the monument of the Doge Nicolò Marcello, by Pietro Lombardo (completed after 1474).

Scuola Grande di S. Marco* (II, *B5-6*). This building is now a hospital; its long elegant marble facade was built in the early Venetian Renaissance by P. and T. Lombardo and G. Buora (1487-90); the curved coping is by M. Codussi (1495); the lunette over the portal is by B. Bon. Inside, note the handsome blue-and-gold coffer ceiling, and paintings by Palma the Younger, Tintoretto, and G. Mansueti. Also, note the former *Dominican convent of Ss. Giovanni e Paolo*, rebuilt by B. Longhena in 1660-75.

S. Maria dei Miracoli** (II, *B5*). This small, isolated church in the narrow Campo dei Miracoli is one of the most exquisite creations of the early Venetian Renaissance. Built by Pietro Lombardo, with the help of his sons Antonio and Tullio (1489), this church has a facing of polychrome marble which enlivens the elegant architecture of the sides and the front; it is crowned with a semicircular pediment. The interior is equally elegant, with marble facing, a lacunar vault, with busts of saints, painted by P.M. Pennacchi (1528); note the fine sculptural decorations by T. Lombardo. The hanging choir over the entrance is adorned with a Virgin and Child by Palma the Younger.

S. Giovanni Crisostomo (II, *B-C4*). This Renaissance church was built by Mauro Codussi (1497-1504). Inside, note paintings by Giovanni Bellini (1513) and S. del Piombo, and a marble altarpiece by Tullio Lombardo.

Ss. Apostoli. (II, *B4*). Renovated in 1575, possibly to a design by A. Vittoria, this church features the Renaissance Cappella Corner, attributed to M. Codussi (1499), with sculpture believed to be by T. Lombardo (16th c.) and a painting by G.B. Tiepolo (1748) on the altar.

Strada Nuova (II, *A-B3-4*). This broad thoroughfare was built in 1871 to link Rialto with the train station; it laid waste a great deal of old Venetian architecture. Its southern side is lined by the secondary facades of the palazzi overlooking the Grand Canal; in the *Calle della Ca' d'Oro* stands the entrance to the Ca' d'Oro (see below). At the end of the street, at Campo S. Felice, you will see the left side of the church of *S. Felice* (II, *A3*; 1531-46), with clean and elegant Renaissance lines.

Ca' d'Oro** (II, *B3*). Built in the Gothic style, by B. Bon and M. Raverti (1422-40), this palazzo takes its name from the gold that once adorned the facade overlooking the Grand Canal; this facade still presents polychrome marble, a lower portico and two upper loggias with lovely balconies and remarkable crenelation. Inside is a fine courtyard, with well head by B. Bon (1427).

With the adjacent *Palazzo Giusti*, it houses the **Galleria Giorgio Franchetti*** *(open weekdays and holidays 9-2)*, created from the private collection of the Turinese musician Giorgio Franchetti, who donated it to the Italian state in 1916, along with the Ca' d'Oro. The remarkable collection includes European and Italian paintings, marbles, bronzes, and Venetian ceramics. In the halls near the broad Porteghi overlooking the Grand Canal, are works by: (2nd floor) A. Vivarini, A. Mantegna, V. Carpaccio, G. da Rimini, B. Diana, M. Giambono, G. Ferrari, L. Signorelli, C. Braccesco, A. di Bartolo, and J. del Sellaio. Among the sculptures: Apollo (1498), by P.J. Alari; bronzes and marbles by T. Lombardo, V. Gambello, and G.M. Mosca; and medals by Pisanello, Gentile Bellini, and S. Savelli.

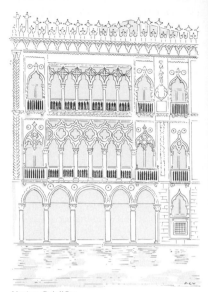

Venice: Ca' d'Oro

A 15th-c. carved staircase leads up to the 3rd floor, were 16th-c. Flemish tapestries and busts by A. Vittoria are displayed; among the paintings are works by: Titian, Tintoretto, F. Guardi, H. Van Eyck, and other Flemish and Dutch artists.

Cannaregio: from the Scalzi to the Gesuiti and the Island of S. Michele

The route suggested here remains in the Sestiere di Cannaregio, in NW Venice, bounded by the Grand Canal and the lagoon. From the church of the Scalzi, near the train station of S. Lucia, the route runs past major churches, along lively city thoroughfares, and through evocative little squares; you will walk along the broad canal of Cannaregio for a stretch, and then, after you tour the church of S. Giobbe, you will head east and enter the Ghetto, one of the most picturesque sections of Venice, with its tall distinctive tower-houses and exquisite old synagogues. This route ends in the NW section of the Sestiere, in secluded areas of remarkable beauty.

Gli Scalzi* (I, *C1*). Built by B. Longhena beginning in 1654, this building's lavish interior is reminiscent of the Roman Baroque. Note frescoes by G.B. Tiepolo.

S. Giobbe* (I, *B1*). This church, built from 1450 in Gothic style, and completed by P. and T. Lombardo in Renaissance style, boasts a finely carved portal, a marble altar piece by A. Rossellino (15th c.), and, in the sacristy, a 16th-c. ceiling. Cross over the 17th-c. *Ponte dei Tre Archi* (I, *B1*) to reach the Fondamenta di Cannaregio.

Ghetto Nuovo (I, *B2*). This, the New Ghetto, was built in one of the three sectors that make up the Venetian Ghetto, where the Jews were forced to live, from 1516 until 1797; this is a small block, or island, surrounded by a ring of water and tall buildings. Note the **Museo d'Arte Ebraica** *(open 10-4; closed Sat.)*, which features collections of objects, sacred furnishings, tapestries, codices, and other interesting examples of Jewish art in Venice in the 17th/19th c. In the dense architectural structure of the Ghetto, small cupolas mark the presence of synagogues, also known as Scuole (or Schools) for the variety of functions they served. The most spectacular is the *Scuola Levantina* (I, B2) in the Ghetto Vecchio (or Old Ghetto), founded in 1538 and renovated in the 17th c., possibly by B. Longhena.

S. Alvise (I, B2). This church, built in the 14th c., overlooks a solitary square; inside are paintings by G.B. Tiepolo. In the nave, note an early "barco" (hanging choir chancel, for nuns)', supported by columns.

Madonna dell'Orto* (I, B3). This 15th-c. church with a terracotta facade overlooks a lovely little Campo; note the portal and bell tower, with cupola by B. Bon. Inside, paintings by J. Tintoretto, who was buried here in 1594. Also, painting by C. da Conegliano (ca. 1493).

S. Maria della Misericordia (I, B3). Founded, with the adjoining abbey, in the 10th c., this church was rebuilt in the 13th c., and modified repeatedly in the following centuries. At an angle with the Baroque facade (1651-59) is the 15th-c. elevation of the *Scuola Vecchia di S. Maria della Misericordia*, built in 1310 and enlarged several times thereafter. The two angels on the architrave of the portal are all that survives of a relief by Bartolomeo Bon, now in the Victoria and Albert Museum, London. Not far off is the *Scuola Nuova di S. Maria della Misericordia*, designed by J. Sansovino, and built between 1534 and 1583.

I Gesuiti (II, A5). The original church of the Crociferi was rebuilt between 1715 and 1730 for the Jesuits, with a Baroque facade, based on Roman church architecture. The interior is spectacular, and is decorated with marble inlay and white and gold stucco. Note paintings by Titian (1558) and by a young J. Tintoretto. A major series of paintings, done by Palma the Younger between 1583 and 1591, is found in the nearby *Oratorio dei Crociferi*, founded in the 13th c. and rebuilt at the end of the 16th c. From this church, you can easily reach the *Fondamenta Nuove*, with a notable view of the broad expanse of water and the first islands of the northern lagoon (S. Michele and Murano).

Isola di S. Michele (I, A-B4-5; *vaporetto from the Fondamenta Nuove*). This remarkable Venetian island cemetery is filled with white crosses and rare monuments; the church of *S. Michele in Isola* (I, A4), with its elegant Renaissance facade, is by Mauro Codussi (1469-78).

S. Zaccaria, the Arsenale, and the Rive. The Islands of S. Giorgio and Giudecca

The "Rive," or shores, from the Zecca east, are the "facade of Venice," a city that shows its best face to those who arrive from the sea; the square in front of the church of S. Giorgio Maggiore on the island of S. Giorgio offers a remarkable view of that facade. This route will take you there, after a walk through the Sestiere di Castello, with tours of the church of S. Zaccaria and the canvases by Carpaccio in the Scuola di S. Giorgio degli Schiavoni, as well as an examination of the Venetian maritime tradition (the entrance to the Arsenale, the Museo Navale). S. Giorgio is a brilliant, luminous church, designed by Palladio; the tour concludes with the church of the Redentore on the island of Giudecca, another Venetian masterpiece by the same great architect.

Palazzo Trevisan (II, D5). The Renaissance facade, attributed to Bartolomeo Bon (early-16th c.), can be seen particularly well from the nearby *Ponte della Canonica*. On the right, view of the Rio di Palazzo, with the rear facade of the Palazzo Ducale (Doge's Palace) and the Ponte dei Sospiri (Bridge of Sighs). At the end of the Fondamenta, entrance to the former Benedictine convent of S. Apollonia (12th/13th c.), now housing the **Museo Diocesano d'Arte Sacra** *(open 10:30-12:30)*. In the restored Romanesque cloister is the *Lapidario Marciano*, with a collection of Roman and Byzantine fragments, largely from the Basilica di S. Marco (St. Mark's); upstairs are paintings, liturgical garb, and sacred accessories from Venetian churches no longer open for worship.

Campo S. Zaccaria (II, D-E6). You enter through a portal, in the flamboyant Gothic style, surmounted by a relief dating from around 1430, possibly by a Tuscan artist. This "campo" is small and charming; it is dominated by the facade of the church of S. Zaccaria, to the right of which is a distinctive terracotta campanile (13th c.), while to the left stand the arcades (occupied by shops) of the 16th-c. cloister of the ancient monastery. The "campo" is bounded to the north by late-15th-c. arches, which once surrounded the monastery's cemetery; a 16th-c. portal (n. 4693) marks the entrance to the onetime *Benedictine nunnery*, once the wealthiest and most prestigious in Venice (now a barracks of the Carabinieri).

S. Zaccaria* (II, D-E6). Built in Gothic style in the 15th c., completed by M. Codussi (1480-1515), who built the multi-order facade, a fine creation of the Venetian Renaissance. The church boasts paintings and frescoes by Giovanni Bellini, Tintoretto, G.B. Tiepolo, A. del Castagno and F. da Faenza, A. Vivarini, and G. d'Alemagna. Note the inlaid choir (1455-64).

S. Giorgio dei Greci (II, D6). This 16th-c. church (1561) of the Greek Orthodox community was the most important foreign church in Renaissance Venice; the interior of the rectangular hall is solemn and majestic, lavishly decorated (stalls, marble icon stalls with late-Byzantine paintings, with gold background). On the left, near the Istituto Ellenico (Greek Institute), is the *Museo dei Dipinti Sacri Bizantini (open 9-1 and 2-5; closed Sun.)*, with a collection of about 80 Byzantine icons.

Scuola di S. Giorgio degli Schiavoni* (I, D4). *Open 10-12:30, 3:30-6; Sun. 11-12:30; closed Mon.* This church was built in the early-16th c. It is particularly renowned for the **paintings by V. Carpaccio****, in the ground floor hall (1501-11); they are considered masterpieces.

S. Francesco della Vigna (I, C4). This large 16th-c. church, designed by Jacopo Sansovino, has a classical-style facade, by A. Palladio (1564-70). The vast interior abounds in fine artworks: note work by Fra' Antonio da Negroponte (1450) and sculptures by Pietro Lombardo and students (1495-1510); in the presbytery, funerary monuments to the doge Andrea Gritti and others, possibly by Sansovino; also, note paintings by Giovanni Bellini (1507) and Paolo Veronese (1551).

Campo Bandiera e Moro (I, D4). At the edge of the more popular walking routes, this square is bounded to the north by the Gothic facade of the *Palazzo Gritti* (late-14th c.); note the five-light mullioned window, adorned with polychrome marble. In this square stands the Gothic church of **S. Giovanni in Bràgora**, rebuilt in 1475, with a distinctive brick facade. Inside are notable paintings, by C. da Conegliano (1502), A. Vivarini, and F. Bissolo. In the presbytery, with vault decorated with stuccoes by A. Vittoria (1596): note paintings by C. da Conegliano (1494) and P. Bordone. In the left aisle, note two paintings by A. Vivarini (1490-93).

Arsenale (I, *C-D5*). *Not open to the public*; part of this area however can be seen by taking the n. 5 vaporetto line through the inner canal. A tall, crenelated walled perimeter, surrounded by canals, marks off the impressive complex of boatyards that dates back to the 12th or early-13th c., and was enlarged repeatedly over the centuries. This is where the fleets of Venice were built, fleets that constituted the foundation of centuries of wealth and power for the ancient maritime republic. The entrance on the land side is marked by a *portal** (1460), believed to date from the early Venetian Renaissance; it is surmounted by a great lion (symbol of St. Mark), attributed to Bartolomeo Bon. In 1692-94 a terrace was built in front of the portal, adorned with Baroque allegorical statues; on either side of this terrace are two stone lions, originally from Greece (the one on the left was located in the harbor of the Piraeus). To the right are two other, smaller lions, one of which comes from the island of Delos. The area of the Arsenale contains buildings of considerable architectural and historical interest, among them: the *building of the Bucintoro* (in the Arsenale Vecchio), where the Doge's vessel was docked; the *Gaggiandre* (Darsena Arsenale Nuovissimo), two enormous wet docks built in 1568-73, supposedly to plans by J. Sansovino; the *Corderie della Tana* (south side of the Arsenale), 300 m. in length, where hemp was stored and the great cables were made for the ships (now a site for temporary exhibitions). The *Officina Remi* (or Oar Workshop) now houses a detached section of the Museo Storico Navale (see below).

Isola di S. Pietro (I, *D6*). Just behind the Arsenale, this island is a secluded and lovely enclave at the easternmost tip of Venice; from the 8th to the early-19th c. this was the center of religious power in the city. Note the church of *S. Pietro di Castello*, which was, until 1807, the cathedral of Venice. Founded over a thousand years ago (9th c.), rebuilt and renovated repeatedly in the 16th and 17th c., this church has a monumental facade from 1594-96 and an isolated campanile, by M. Codussi (1482-90).

Museo Storico Navale

Museo Storico Navale (I, *D5*). *Open 9-1; closed Sun.* In Campo S. Biagio, at the end of the Riva degli Schiavoni, this museum can be seen, set in an austere, late-16th-c. building, that was formerly a granary of the Venetian Republic. This museum offers documentation of the history of the Venetian navy (16th/18th c.) and the Italian Marina Militare (navy) from 1860 to modern times, with memorabilia, models, etchings, and other material. Of particular interest: a model of the Bucintoro, a splendid galley that was once used by the Doge in the ceremony of the wedding between Venice and the Sea; a large model of a 16th-c. Venetian galleass; models of frigates and sailing ships of the 18th c. A separate section of the Museo Navale, with actual historical vessels, is set up in the Officina Remi in the Arsenale.

Giardini Pubblici (I, *E-F5-6*). This great park was built in the Napoleonic era, and modified around 1850 to suit the Romantic tastes of the time. In it are the various pavillions of the *Biennale d'Arte* (Venice Biennale), a major international fair of painting, sculpture, graphics, and decorative arts, established in 1895. The pavillions of the individual nations reflect the architectural trends of more than half-a-century (1907-64), and some are quite excellent.

Riva degli Schiavoni* (II, *E6*; I, *D-E4*). This broad walkway along the Bacino di S. Marco takes its name from the sailors of Schiavonia (or Slavonia, the Dalmatian coast), who moored here. Following the Riva toward St. Mark's, you will see the 18th-c. church of **S. Maria della Visitazione** (I, D4), particularly silent inside (built in part as a concert hall); note the ceiling, frescoed by G.B. Tiepolo. Further on is an equestrian monument to Victor Emmanuel (E. Ferrari, 1887). After the *Ponte del Vin* (II, *E6*), the Riva tends to be crowded with sightseers; note the Gothic *Palazzo Dandolo*, now the *Hotel Danieli*, and the massive *Prigioni Nuove* (1589-1614).

S. Giorgio Maggiore* (I, *E4*). *Vaporetto from Riva degli Schiavoni, lines 5 and 8*. This church stands on the island of the same name; it was designed and partly built by A. Palladio (1565-83, completed in 1611). Majestic interior, with paintings by S. Ricci, G. Campagna, Tintoretto, and V. Carpaccio (1516). From the 18th-c. campanile *(you can climb up, 9-12:30 and 2-5)*, fine view* of Venice and the Lagoon.

Monastero di S. Giorgio Maggiore (I, *E4*). *Open by request, for groups only, tel. 5289900*. Headquarters of the Fondazione "Giorgio Cini," this is a complex of rooms arranged around two *cloisters**; some of the finest architects from ca. 1500 to ca. 1700 worked on it, among them: A. Palladio, G. and A. Buora, and B. Longhena. On the ground floor, on the far wall of the *Refettorio* (Refectory), by A. Palladio, is the Wedding of the Virgin, by J. Tintoretto; a monumental double staircase by B. Longhena (1643-44) climbs up to the 2nd floor, where the *Biblioteca Longheniana*, furnished with carved 17th-c. bookshelves, contains over 100,000 volumes of art history. In the large grounds, you can see the *Teatro Verde* (I, *E4*; 1951) in which open-air performances are staged.

La Giudecca (I, *E-F1-4*). *Vaporettos from Riva degli Schiavoni or from the Zattere ai Gesuati, lines 5 and 8*. Narrow and elongated, set between the Canale della Giudecca and the south lagoon, this strip of land may take its name from the settlement of Jews ("Giudei") here during the Middle Ages. Because of its location, secluded but still on the Bacino di S. Marco, from the 16th c. on it became a favored site for pleasure gardens and villas, where the homes of the nobles alternated with gardens, orchards, and monasteries. In the 19th c., with the decline of the Venetian aristocracy and the suppression of convents, the island slowly became the domain of barracks, prisons, factories, and large working class quarters. A long stroll on the "fondamenta," or quay, which has different names in the various stretches, runs around the whole island, offering excellent views of the Canale della Giudecca. From the *Zitelle* (I, *E3*), a large complex comprising a church and a hospice for poor young women, built in 1579-86 (perhaps designed by A. Palladio), you will reach the church of the Redentore (see below). To the west, past the 11th-c. church of *S. Eufemia* (I, *E1-2*), with sumptuous 18th-c. decorations inside, you will continue along the *Fondamenta di S. Biagio* (I, *E1*), the westernmost stretch of the island, marked by industrial buildings. At the end of the Fondamenta, across a metal bridge, stands the impressive neo-Gothic structure of the *Mulino Stucky* (1896), now abandoned.

Redentore* (I, *F2-3*). This votive temple was built by the Venetian Senate during a terrible pestilence; set on the island of Giudecca, it was conceived as the final destination for the solemn procession of the Redentore (3rd Sun. in Jul.), which crossed the canal on a bridge of boats. Considered one of A. Palladio's masterpieces, it was begun in 1577, and completed by A. da Ponte in 1592, after Palladio's death. Classical and majestic, it has a single nave and a fine cupola. On the altars and in the sacristy, paintings by F. Bassano, Palma the Younger, J. Tintoretto, G. Campagna, A. Vivarini, F. Bissolo, and P. Veronese.

Verona**

elev. 59 m.; pop. 252,689; Veneto, provincial capital. The river Adige lingers lovingly as it passes through this city on the last foothills of the Monti Lessini, overlooking the boundless plains spreading out before it. Here the timeless past meets the city's everyday life, as well: the Veronese still attend the ancient Roman Arena; they pray in the Romanesque church of S. Zeno before Andrea Mantegna's altar piece; they stroll over the red Scaliger bridge, sawtoothed with parapets; and they shop in the ancient Piazza delle Erbe. A city of farmers, manufacturers, and merchants, it has always been the crossroads for Italy's trade with Germany and Europe to the north. "There is no world without Verona walls," says Romeo upon being banished, with Juliet in his heart; the same phrase can describe the enviable completeness of the universe that is Verona.

Historical note. When Theodoric, the great 6th-c. king of the Goths, built a castle atop the hill of S. Pietro (a 19th-c. Austrian castle now stands on that site), the left bank of the Adige had been set aside solely for worship and sport (the Romans had built a temple and a theater, still visible). Verona's founders, however, had first settled here, where the hill overlooks the narrowest turn in the serpentine oxbow curve of the river. By the first century B.C., when Verona became a Roman city, the city occupied the entire peninsula described by the river's right bank; its southern face was bounded by a wall in which two gates opened (they still exist; Porta dei Borsari and Porta dei Leoni). Piazza delle Erbe was the Forum. Three centuries later, the emperor Gallienus built new walls far enough south to include the great 1st-c. amphitheater. Two bridges spanned the river (one, the Ponte della Pietra) still stands. It was only in the 12th c. that Verona's Communal government expanded the city, building walls that can still be seen in Via del Pallone, and digging a moat — the Adigetto — from the Castelvecchio to the bridge of Aleardi. Later, the Della Scala family came to rule Verona, and Cangrande I attempted to form a vast northern Italian state, only to be thwarted by an alliance among the alarmed leaders of Venice, Florence, and Milan. Some indication of the breadth of his ambitions can be had from the vast new walls he built, which stood until the turn of the 20th c. Cangrande's successors were less warlike, and were content to embellish Verona with marble bridges, the Arche Scaligere, and the fountain of Madonna Verona, or to build the spectacular Castelvecchio and the Scaliger bridge. None of this saved them from Visconti domination in 1387, or from Venetian rule shortly thereafter, in 1405. The Venetians brought great art but economic decline; Verona suffered more atrophy after the great plague of 1630. The treaty of Lunéville in 1801 established the boundary between French and Austrian empires along the Adige. The city was made part of the Republic of Italy; while the left bank became Austrian, and took the name of Veronetta. From 1815 on, Verona fell under Austrian rule, until Italy's unification 50 years later. Since WWII, the city has expanded sharply thrusting east, west, and south.

Getting around. The historic center of Verona is partly a pedestrian zone (Via Mazzini, Via Cappello, and

Verona: Piazza delle Erbe

Piazza Bra') and partly reserved to limited traffic according to certain schedules (in the triangle comprising the church of S. Lorenzo-church of S. Anastasia-Duomo). Tourists are in any case always allowed to drive to their hotels. The first route suggested is really a walking tour, since the monuments are all relatively close; the second route, on the other hand, is far longer, and may require the use of public transportation.

Roman Verona and Veronetta

The Roman city of Verona lay within the oxbow curve of the river Adige, around modern-day Piazza delle Erbe, then the Forum: this is Verona's ancient nucleus, though the prevailing flavor is medieval, with influence of the Della Scala rule and Venetian domination. On the left bank of the river, between Ponte Nuovo and S. Giorgio in Braida, you are in Veronetta.

Piazza delle Erbe* (*C5*). On the site of the Roman Forum, this rectangular square is lined with venerable houses and towers. At its center, amidst the stands of the daily market, you can see the *Market column* (1401); the *Berlina* or *Capitello* (16th c.), where town leaders took office; and the *fountain of Madonna Verona** (1368). On the SW side of the square is the 14th-c. *Casa dei Mercanti*, with mullioned windows and parapets; on the far end is the *Gardello tower* (1370); on the NE side are the 15th-c. *Mazzanti houses*, the Palazzo del Comune with the tall Lamberti tower (see below) and the *Costa arch* (1470; named for the whale rib, or "costa," that hangs from it), leading to Piazza dei Signori.

Piazza dei Signori* (*C5*). Once the administrative heart of Verona, it stands as a courtyard enclosed by monumental buildings linked by arcades. At its center stands a 19th-c. *monument to Dante*.

Palazzo del Comune or *Palazzo della Ragione*. Dating from the late-11th c., this town hall was heavily reworked in the 16th c.; the *courtyard**, or Mercato Vecchio, is Romanesque, with a round-arched portico and mullioned windows; note the 15th-c. exterior staircase made of red marble. Part of this building is the 84-m.-tall *Lamberti tower* (open, elevator available, 8-6:30; in winter until 2; closed Mon.), built between 1172 and 1450 ca.; excellent view from the top.

Palazzo del Capitanio, formerly *Tribunal*, is a 14th-c. building, renovated in the 19th c. Note portal by M. Sanmicheli.

Palazzo della Prefettura. Once the Della Scala residence (both Dante and Giotto were guests here), it was built in the 14th c. and restored in 1929-30. Again, portal by Sanmicheli (1533).

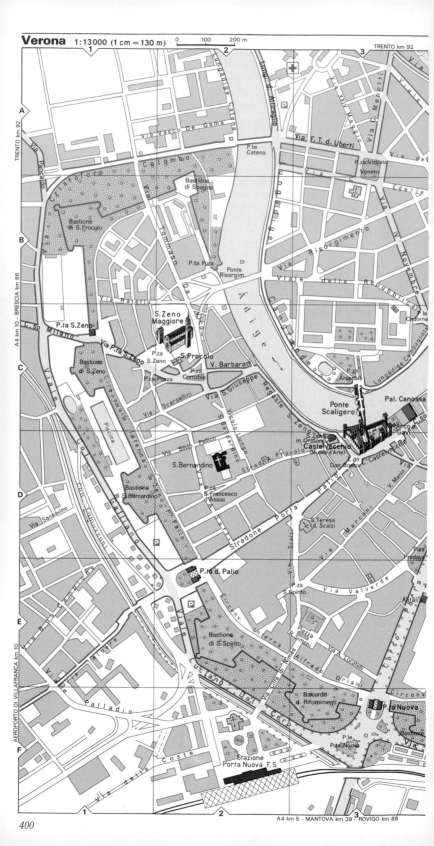

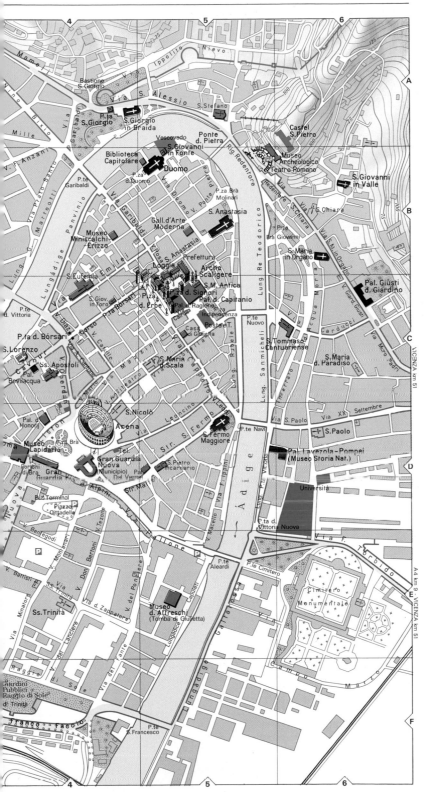

Loggia del Consiglio*. Built in the late-15th c. for the city council, this is a splendid piece of Veronese Renaissance architecture, with purity of line and artistic composition. Note the elegant portico and twin mullioned windows set between small pillars; lively color and handsome sculptures enliven the facade. On its left is the *Domus Nova*, a 17th-c. reconstruction of the Della Scala home of the Podestà, or mayor.

Arche Scaligere* (*B-C5*). To the right of the Palazzo del Governo, you enter the Piazzaletto delle Arche, one of the loveliest spots in Verona. Here is the little Romanesque church of *S. Maria Antica* (12th c.), with its handsome interior, and the Arche Scaligere, monumental tombs of the lords of Verona. Enclosed by a 14th-c. iron gate with the heraldic "ladder" ("Scala"), the aedicules are crowned by Gothic baldachins, and adorned with 14th-c. statues. Above the portal of the church — one of the earliest pieces of Veronese Romanesque — is the **sarcophagus of Cangrande I**, who died in 1329, and a copy of an equestrian statue of this condottiere.

S. Tommaso Cantuariense (*C6*). Across the *Ponte Nuovo*, this 15th-c. church has an unfinished terracotta facade with a marble portal. Nearby, in Via Muro Padri, the late-15th-c. church of **Ss. Nazaro e Celso** (*C6; off map*) features a Gothic facade and, inside, works by Venetian Renaissance painters. Note the *chapel of S. Biagio**.

Palazzo Giusti del Giardino (*C6*). Late 16th c., this mansion has a lovely garden (*open, 8-8; in winter, until sunset*), with cypress-lined avenues, a maze, and a terrace with view.

S. Maria in Organo* (*B6*). This fine piece of architecture dates from 1481; its facade is a mix of Gothic and Renaissance styles. The interior features handsome frescoes and altarpieces. The magnificent *choir** and sacristy (*open by request, contact the sacristan*) boast excellent intarsias (end 15th/early 16th c.). Note the crypt, with fragments of the 7th-c. church and of the Roman walls.

S. Giovanni in Valle* (*B6*). Founded in the High Middle Ages, and rebuilt in Romanesque style in the late 12th c., this church boasts fine apses, cloister, and campanile. Inside, 14th-c. frescoes. In the crypt, the *Arca dei Ss. Simone e Giuda**, carved in the 4th c.

Area Archeologica del Teatro Romano* (*B5-6*). *Open 8-1:30; closed Mon*. This remarkable complex, set on the hill of S. Pietro, comprises chiefly the ancient Roman *theater* (built early 1st c.A.D.). Above it stands the little church of *Ss. Siro e Libera* (rebuilt in the 14th c.). The theater is used for drama and dance in the summer.

Museo Archeologico. *Open, same hours as the Teatro*. Set in a 15th-c. convent, the entrance is located atop the steps of the theater (elevator; handsome view); it especially features relics of Roman Verona. From the 15th-c. cloister, you enter the *church*; note frescoes and fine triptych altarpiece. From terraces, excellent views of Verona.*

S. Stefano (*A5*). Founded in the 5th c., partly rebuilt in the 12th c., this church preserves some of its original structure. Note the handsome facade and octagonal terracotta tambour, as well as the 10th-c. crypt.

S. Giorgio in Braida* (*A4-5*). With its massive dome, by Sanmicheli, this church overlooks the river Adige's oxbow curve. Built between 1477 and 1536, its white marble facade dates from the 17th c. The interior, solemn and harmonious, with a single aisle, is decked with paintings by Jacopo Tintoretto, Paolo Veronese, Moretto da Brescia, Girolamo dai Libri, and G.F. Caroto. Before the church is the early-16th-c. **Porta S. Giorgio**.

Ponte della Pietra (*A-B5*). Roman in origin, this bridge was destroyed in WWII and rebuilt with original materials in 1957-59. Excellent view of the banks of the Adige.

S. Anastasia* (*B5*). This Gothic church is made entirely of terracotta, and was built by the Dominicans between 1290 and 1481, when the bell tower was finished. The unfinished facade has a splendid 14th-c. *portal**.

The majestic *interior* boasts fine works of art. In particular, note the holy water fonts, with the odd "hunchbacked" statues supporting them (16th c.); the Fregoso altar (1st on the right) by Sanmicheli (1565); frescoes by Liberale da Verona; a handsome Renaissance altar (1502), with a painting by Girolamo dai Libri; a major fresco by Altichiero (1370 ca.); two Gothic tombs and terracotta reliefs by Michele da Firenze (1435); a large fresco of the Last Judgement, by the 14th-c. Maestro del Giudizio Universale; and a tomb by Nanni di Bartolo (1429). From the left transept (note painting by F.Morone) a door leads to the Giusti chapel (*inquire if it is closed*), which contains a fresco of St. George and the Dragon* by Pisanello.

To the left of the church, note the Gothic *arch* and *church*.

Via Duomo. At the beginning of this street, on the left, in Via A. Forti n. 1, is the 18th-c. *Palazzo Forti-Emilei* (in the courtyard, note the Romanesque wing), which houses temporary exhibits, the *Museo del Risorgimento*, and (entrance from Vicolo Vòlto Due Mori), the **Galleria Comunale d'Arte Moderna e Contemporanea** (*open 8-6:30; closed Mon.*). In the halls of this museum, various works by 19th- and 20th-c. artists, including paintings by F.Hayez, G. Fattori, M. Bianchi, F. De Pisis, and U. Boccioni and sculptures by M. Rosso, G. Manzù, and G. Duprè.

Duomo* (*B5*). Dominating the Piazza del Duomo, this 12th-c. Romanesque cathedral was renovated in the Gothic style (15th c.) and has Renaissance additions. On the front, note the monumental two-story *porch**, adorned with reliefs by Maestro Nicolò (1139); another porch from the same period stands on the right side; the 16th-c. campanile, Romanesque at the base, was designed by Sanmicheli, and was left unfinished. The 12th-c. *apse**, in tufa stone, is one of the most exquisite creations of Veronese Romanesque architecture; it is studded with pilaster strips and a very fine frieze in the cornice. The Gothic *interior* has broad arches set on tall pillars. In the chapels and the presbytery, enclosed by a semicircular columned *choir* by Sanmicheli (1534), are various paintings and statues from the 14th/16th c.

On the left of the Duomo is a Romanesque *cloister* with twinned columns (ca. 1140), with fragments of mosaic floors from the early-Christian basilica; you can enter the little church of *S. Elena* (Romanesque, on early-Christian foundations and structures) and the ancient baptistery of *S. Gio-*

vanni in Fonte (13th-c. octagonal baptismal font*), both from the 12th c. Behind the Duomo, the *Palazzo del Vescovado* has a Renaissance facade decorated with Venetian merlons (1502) and a portal adorned with statues.

Biblioteca Capitolare (*B5*). *Open 9:30-12:30; Tue. and Fri. also 4-6; closed Thu., Sun. and Jul.* Housed in the *Palazzo del Canonicato* (rebuilt in 1948), to the left of the Duomo, this is one of the leading ecclesiastic libraries in Europe. Among its most precious manuscripts, note the 4th-c. Vergil, the 6th-c. Codex of Justinian, various illuminated books, and the Canonical Archives, with 11,000 parchments. Also located in this building is the *Museo Pinacoteca Canonicale*, with paintings and sculpture from the 14th to 19th c.

Museo Miniscalchi-Erizzo (*B4*). *Open 10-12:30 and 3:30-7; closed Mon. and Tue., Jan. and Feb.* In the newly restored 15th-c. Palazzo Miniscalchi-Erizzo, in Via S. Mammaso 2/A, this museum has 16 halls with collections of archeological material, bronzes, scultures, majolicas, weapons, armors, drawings, and paintings by Venetian masters of the 16th to 18th c.

Corso di Porta Bórsari. This typical road of old Verona runs along the course of the Roman "decumanus maximus." Note the little Romanesque church of *S. Giovanni in Foro* (C4).

Porta dei Bórsari* (*C4*). This was the main entrance to Verona in Roman times. It was built in the middle of the 1st c.

S. Eufemia (*C4*). This long narrow Gothic church was completed in the 14th c.; note the handsome portal from 1476. Transformed in 1739, it has frescoes from the 14th c. and Venetian paintings from the 14th to 16th c.

The "Addizione Scaligera"

The ambitious southward expansion marked by the walls built under Cangrande I della Scala was sufficient for Verona's growth through the 19th c.: the Arena, Castelvecchio and the Scaliger bridge, and S. Zeno Maggiore (with Andrea Mantegna's noteworthy altarpiece) are the three high points of the area contained between the southern and western ramparts.

Piazza Bra' (*D4*). Once a country field ("braida"), this garden-like square is now the center of Verona, a meeting place for the Veronese. To the NE is the Arena (see below); to the SE is the Neoclassical **Gran Guardia Nuova**, or *Palazzo Municipale* (town hall; 1838); to the south is the Baroque building of the *Gran Guardia* (begun in 1610, completed in 1836, housing temporary exhibitions) and the two arcades and the pentagonal tower of the *Portoni della Bra'*, built ca. 1480. Nearby is the complex of the *Accademia Filarmonica* (with Library-Museum, for scholars only) and the **Museo Lapidario Maffeiano** (*open 8-1:30; closed Mon.*), founded in the 18th c. by Scipione Maffei, containing plaques and marble from Greek, Etruscan, and Roman times (mithriac relief* from the 2nd c.), as well as from early Christian and medieval periods. To the NW, various palazzi (at n. 16, the *Palazzo degli Honorij*, later Palazzo *Guastaverza*, by Michele Sanmicheli, 1554) with porticoes, along which runs the "Listón," an elegant and lively stone-slab promenade.

Arena** (*D4*). *Open (entrance from the fifth arcade), 8-6:30; closed Mon.; during the opera season, until 1:30.* One of the largest surviving Roman amphitheaters (after the Colosseum and the amphitheater of Capua), the Arena was built in the 1st c. Built of blocks of limestone from the Valpolicella, all that survives of the outer ring are four arcades of three orders, while the second ring maintains intact 72 arcades of two orders.

In the oval-shaped interior (44.43 x 73.58 m.), a tribune (cavea) with 44 tiers (restored), with a capacity of 22,000, surrounds the stage, or "platea." Operas are performed here in the months of July and August.

Via Mazzini (*C4-5*). This road links Piazza Bra and Piazza delle Erbe; it is a pedestrian mall, lined with elegant shops and clubs.

Casa di Giulietta (*C5*). *Open 8-6:30, closed Mo*n. In Via Cappello, at n. 21-23, is what is believed to be the *house of Juliet Capulet* (Casa di Giulietta, a 13th-c. Gothic building, with the renowned balcony, rebuilt). Continuing along Via Leoni, note the remains of the Roman gate, or **Porta dei Leoni*** , from the 1st c B.C..

S. Fermo Maggiore* (*D5*). This church comprises two buildings, superimposed; the lower building dates from the 11th/12th c., while the upper one is Gothic, and dates from the 13th/14th c.; it has a handsome facade with a large, deeply splayed Romanesque portal (on the left, Arca di Fracastoro, tomb of a physician to the house of Della Scala in the 14th c.) and a twin portal (1363) with a porch on the left side. Note the complex of apses (the smaller *apses* are Romanesque, the largest one is Gothic).

The *interior* of the **upper church**, with a single aisle and a keel roof (1314), abounds in 14th- and 15th-c. frescoes and 15th- and 16th-c sculpture; in the lunette of the portal, Crucifixion attributed to Turone; on the right, near the ambo, Angels with Scrolls*, fragment of a detached fresco by S. da Verona; midway up the left side is the Baroque Cappella della Madonna, with 16th-c. paintings, and altar piece by G.F. Caroto (1528). At the 1st altar on the left, altar piece by Battista dal Moro; in the corner, the *Monument to Brenzoni*, by the Florentine N. di Bartolo (1430), framed by the renowned fresco of the Annunciation* by Pisanello. From the right transept, you can enter the remains of the ancient Romanesque *cloister* (*open by request, contact the sacristan*) and then descend to the **lower church**, with three aisles (the nave is divided midway by slender pillars), and fragments of frescoes from the 11th/13th c.; behind the main altar, 14th-c. wooden Crucifix.

Palazzo Lavezola Pompei* (*D6*). Standing on the left bank of the river Adige, beyond the Ponte delle Navi, at n. 9 in Lungadige Porta Vittoria, is this mid-16th-c. palazzo, one of the finest creations of Sanmicheli; nowadays it is the site of the **Museo Civico di Storia Naturale*** (*open 8-7; closed Fri.*), one of Italy's finest museums of natural history, with an especially notable collection of fossil fauna and flora*, from Bolca. The Museum also includes a specialized library, a photographic archive, and research laboratories.

Stradone S. Fermo (*D5*). This road is lined with notable houses and palazzi, from the 16th to 19th c., partly rebuilt; in particular, at n. 13 is the *Palazzo Della Torre*, from the school of Sanmicheli (16th c.), with a fine courtyard and garden. At the end of the street is the church of *S. Pietro Incarnario*, built on Roman foundations, with its 14th-c. bell tower and, inside, detached 12th-c. fresco (Crucifixion). After the dogleg, the name changes to Stradone Maffei, and here you will find *Palazzo Dal Verme*, where the great dramatist, scholar, and soldier Scipione Maffei was born and died. At the end of the road is a stretch of crenelated *walls*, built by the Della Scala family.

Museo degli Affreschi (*E5*). *Open 8-6:30; closed Mon.* Take a left off Via del Pontiere, and, in a complex formed by the cloister and church of *S. Francesco al Corso*, this museum contains the most important series of Veronese frescoes, detached from their original sites since the 19th c. In particular, note the 16th-c. frescoes, including the lovely allegorical scenes by D. Brusasorci. From the cloister, a stairway leads down to the so-called *Tomba di Giulietta* (Tomb of Juliet), where the star-crossed lover of Romeo was supposedly buried.

Corso di Porta Nuova. Designed by Sanmicheli, this broad thoroughfare runs from the Portoni della Bra' in the center to the train station. At the end of the Corso stands the massive, isolated **Porta Nuova** (*F3*), built by Sanmicheli (1546) as well.

Viale L. Dal Cero. This road runs just outside the *Baluardo dei Riformati* and the *Bastione di S. Spirito*, fortifications constructed by the Austrians in place of earlier walls built by the Della Scala, which still circle the city, extending over a circumference of about 10 km. On the left is the *train station of Porta Nuova* (*F2*); to the right, in Via Città di Nimes, entrance to the zoo (*Giardino Zoologico; E2, open 8:30-5*), with European and exotic animals.

Porta del Palio* (*E2*). So-called because the horse race of the Palio once ran along it (mentioned by Dante Alighieri), this is the loveliest of the gates designed by Sanmicheli for Verona's walled perimeter.

S. Bernardino* (*D2*). Built in the mid-15th-c., in a transitional style between Gothic and Renaissance, this church features a large cloister before the facade. The two-aisle interior contains many fine 15th/16th-c. Veronese paintings and frescoes. Domenico Morone painted the organ doors (1481); and the library, now called the **Sala Morone*** (1503, *open by request, contact the custodian*).

S. Zeno Maggiore** (*C1-2*). *Open 8:30-12:30 and 3-6:30*. This masterpiece of Italian Romanesque architecture is, with the Arena, one of Verona's two most celebrated monuments. It stands in a broad, quiet square, set between a 13th-c. tower of the ancient abbey (on the left) and a solitary bell tower (11th c.). Built in the 9th c. upon the tomb of Verona's first bishop, who died in 380, it was so badly damaged in an earthquake in 1117 that it was entirely rebuilt in the 12th and 13th c. The elegant tufa facade, adorned in the center with the wheel of fortune, a great 13th-c. rose window, has a *portal** with reliefs by Maestro Nicolò (1138), and an exquisite *door* with 24 12th-c. bronze **panels***, depicting Bible stories and lives of the saints.

The *interior* is simple and majestic, and features a Crucifix by Lorenzo Veneziano (1360 ca.); at the head of the right aisle, an octagonal 12th-c. baptistery. Noteworthy frescoes and statues of the 13th c. On the main altar, a **triptych**** by Andrea Mantegna (1459). Noteworthy wooden Gothic choir. From the left aisle, you can step out to the handsome Romanesque *cloister*.

Regaste S. Zeno (*C2-3*). Running along the river Adige, this road is lined by a large wall, and offers a fine view of both river and castle. At the end of the road is the little 13th-c. Romanesque church of *S. Zeno in Oratorio*, with its Gothic facade. Inside, note the stone on which, according to legend, the saint used to sit while fishing in the river Adige.

Castelvecchio** (*C-D3*). The principal monument of civil architecture of medieval Verona, it was built by Cangrande II della Scala as a residence and fortress in 1354-57; the keep was added in 1375. This massive terracotta structure, with towers and battlements, comprises two centers divided by the battlemented bridge: the eastern, rectangular building surrounds a great courtyard; the western one was the palace, and has a double set of walls, two courtyards, and drawbridges. This castle houses the Civico Museo d'Arte.

Civico Museo d'Arte*. *Open 8-6:30; closed Mon.; entrance from the main courtyard*. This museum houses fine collections of art, chiefly of the Veneto school, 14th to 18th c. Extensive work by Veronese artists, including the early painters Turone, Altichiero, Stefano da Verona, Pisanello; the 15th-c. artists Francesco Morone, Liberale, Paolo Cavazzola, G. F. Caroto; and the 16th-c. artists Paolo Veronese and Paolo Farinati. Among the other Veneto artists, let us mention: A. Mantegna, J. Bellini, Giovanni Bellini, C. Crivelli, B. Montagna, A. Vivarini, B. Strozzi, J. Tintoretto, G.B. Tiepolo, and F. Guardi. Various Flemish artists. Note the many ancient artifacts, including fragments of early Christian glass, 7th-c. gold work, the Tesoretto di Isola Rizza, with 4th-c. silver; cloth and silk from the Arca, or tomb, of Cangrande I; miniatures. Arms from Longobard times to the 17th c. Excellent 14th-c. Veronese statuary, including the **equestrian statue of Cangrande I***, from the Arche Scaligere.

Ponte Scaligero* (*C3*). This bridge links the Castelvecchio with the other bank of the river Adige; it is a massive structure, with three arches on pillars with towers, entirely made of brick. It was rebuilt after destruction in WWII.

Corso Cavour* (*C3-4*). This is one of the loveliest streets in Verona; it runs from the Piazzetta di Castelvecchio, where the reassembled 1st-c. **Arco dei Gavi** stands, a rare example of a four-pier Roman arch, all the way to the Porta dei Bórsari. It is lined with aristocratic palazzi: at n. 44, *Palazzo Canossa*, by Sanmicheli (1537); at n. 19, the spectacular **Palazzo Bevilacqua*** (*C4*), a masterpiece, also by Sanmicheli (ca. 1534). Facing this palazzo is the Gothic entrance arcade of the 12th-c. Romanesque church of **S. Lorenzo**; note two round towers and remarkable interior. A little further along, on the right, note the small bell tower and the side of the Romanesque church of the *Ss. Apostoli*; from the sacristy, you can enter the partly subterranean little 8th-c. church of *Ss. Tosca e Teuteria*.

Vicenza*

elev. 39 m.; pop. 107,076; Veneto, provincial capital. This town stands in the gentle green Venetian plain, now an industrialized area, at the foot of the Monti Bèrici; other mountains loom on the horizon. This town is linked with the name of Andrea Palladio. The 16th-c. Paduan architect was certainly thinking of his Vicentine clients when he rejoiced at having "found gentlemen of so noble and generous a spirit and such excellent discrimination, that they believed in my reasoning and abandoned that old-fangled manner of building without a line of decoration or a single thing of beauty...". This "new" beauty – Neoclassical and Palladian – pervades the city, harmonizing with the fragments of Venetian Gothic, and with another face of Vicenza, with bridges, canals, haunting vignettes, and sudden views of hills and alpine foothills.

Vicenza: Basilica

Historical note. All of Vicenza's history can be recounted in the growth of the urban grid. "Vicetia" (from "vicus," Latin for village), became Roman with Padua, in 49 B.C. The Roman municipium was small, but its layout can still be seen. Modern Vicenza traces its origin back to the 12th c., when the Commune joined the league against the emperor Frederick I, Barbarossa, Vicenza finally became a Venetian holding in 1404. But those two centuries marked the layout of the town. As Vicenza stagnated and even shrank in later years, the city's outline remained fixed. Later, under Venice, the city expanded south, to Porta Lupia and P. Monte, and NW, to Porta Pusterla. Within its walls, Vicenza remained stable: its population was 30,000 at the end of the 16th c. and the same at the turn of the 20th c. Still, from 1450 to 1600, Vicenza so changed its architecture that the city was never the same. The great culmination was the work of A. Palladio. The Basilica, Palazzo Chiericati, the Teatro Olimpico, and the Rotonda are all prototypes of a Neoclassical architecture that developed, with Scamozzi, until 1800. After WWII, the suburbs grew so rapidly that Vicenza soon doubled in area.

Getting around. Much of the historic center is closed to traffic; visitors going to hotels are allowed through, however. The route recommended can be covered entirely on foot.

Places of interest. Piazza dei Signori*. This is the monumental center of Vicenza; here you will find: on the south side, the Basilica, alongside which stands the slender 82-m.-tall *Torre di Piazza* (12th c.); at the far end, the two *columns of the Piazza*, one topped by the Lion of St. Mark's (1520), the other by a statue of the Savior (1640); on the NE side, are the **Loggia dei Capitaniato***, also known as *Loggia Bernarda*, an unfinished work by A. Palladio (1571) and the long facade of the 16th-c. Palazzo del *Monte di Pietà*, with the Baroque facade of the church of *S. Vincenzo* in the center (1614; inside, marble Deposition* by O. Marinali).

Basilica**. *Open, Tue.-Sat., 9:30-12 and 2:30-5; Sun. 10-12; closed Mon.* The most important monument in Vicenza, one of the outstanding buildings of the Venetian Renaissance, built between 1549 and 1617. One of the masterpieces of A. Palladio, who enclosed the existing 15th-c. Gothic *Palazzo della Ragione* in a sumptuous marble sheath, featuring classical portico and loggia. The term 'Basilica,' first used by Palladio himself, here means a building in which justice was administered. On the right side, a stairway leads up to the loggia, and from here you enter the Gothic hall, which occupies the entire upper floor of the building. Nearby, in the Piazza delle Erbe, stands the medieval *Torre del Girone*, or *Torre del Tormento*.

S. Maria in Foro. This 15th-c. church overlooks the nearby Piazza delle Biade; inside, altar piece by B. Montagna.

Casa Pigafetta. Located at n. 9 in Via Pigafetta, this house was built in a flamboyant Venetian Gothic style in the 15th c. It was the birthplace of A. Pigafetta, who sailed with Magellan on the first circumnavigation of the earth (1519-22), and wrote a detailed account of the journey.

S. Nicola da Tolentino. *Open upon request (ring bell on the left side).* This 16th-c. church is decorated with stuccoes that frame numerous paintings by F. Maffei, G. Carpioni, A. Zanchi, and others. From the nearby *bridge of S. Michele* (1623), you have a fine view of the center of Vicenza; in the Contrà Piancoli, note buildings at n. 4, 6, and 8.

Piazza del Duomo. This square has the cathedral of Vicenza, or Duomo, and, at n. 11, the *Palazzo Vescovile*, or bishop's palace, rebuilt in Neoclassical style in 1819 and partly rebuilt after being damaged in WWII; in the courtyard, note the splendid **Loggia Zeno***, a Renaissance creation by B. da Milano and T. da Lugano. On the south side of the square, next to Palazzetto Roma (now offices of the APT), you can enter the **Roman cryptoporticus** *(open, Sat., 10-11:30)*, part of a 1st-c. A.D. Roman house.

Duomo*. Built as it stands today (restored following WWII) from the 13th to 16th c., this cathedral has a Gothic facade (1467), with polychrome marble, attributed to D. da Venezia, and an elegante Renaissance apse (1482-1508), with an 11th-c. Romanesque bell tower, on Roman foundations, across the street.

The Gothic interior, with a single vast aisle and cross vaults, features paintings by F. Maffei, L. Veneziano, and B. Montagna. In the vaults, below, Roman ruins.

Piazza Castello. This square features *Palazzo Piovini* (1656-58), now a warehouse, and the unfinished *Palazzo Porto*, built by V. Scamozzi to plans by Palladio (late-16th c.). At the end of Corso Palladio, see below, stands a mighty *tower*, the only relic of the medieval castle of the Della Scala family. Outside the *Porta Castello* are the *Salvi public gardens*; note the *Loggetta Valmarana*, a small loggia in Palladian style (1592), set alongside a stream of running water.

Ss. Felice e Fortunato*. This basilica looms large in the religious history of Vicenza; Romanesque in style, following the restoration of the early-20th c., it was built in the late-10th c. Note the mosaic floors, from the 4th and 5th c., remaining from an earlier building on the same site. Note the distinctive little 12th-c. bell tower with 14th-c. additions.

Corso Andrea Palladio* (*1st part*). This main street runs through Vicenza, east-west, amidst a series of monumental homes and churches, dating from the 14th to the 18th c. At n. 13, the enormous *Palazzo Thiene*, later *Bonin-Longare*, attributed to Palladio and completed by Vincenzo Scamozzi; at n. 45, the Renaissance *Palazzo Capra-Clementi* (late-15th-c.); at n. 47, the Venetian Gothic *Palazzo Thiene*, with handsome five-light mullioned window; at n. 67, the elegant Venetian Gothic *Palazzo Braschi-Brunello*, with a portico.

Corso Fogazzaro. One of Vicenza's liveliest streets, it is lined by fine Baroque and Renaissance homes; on the right, at n. 16, the solemn *Palazzo Valmarana-Braga* (1566) by Palladio; further along, the *Palazzo Repeta*, by F. Muttoni (1711).

S. Lorenzo*. Impressive Franciscan church, in brickwork and Gothic style (13th c.). In the facade, note the statue-studded *portal** (1344). Inside, amidst round pillars, various funerary monuments from the 14th/16th c.; note the altar reliefs by the Pojana and a fresco by B. Montagna. The cloister (1492) features a round-arch portico.

Chiesa del Carmine. In Corso Fogazzaro, this neo-Gothic construction preserves portals and other elements from the long-demolished 14th-c. church of S. Bartolomeo (14th-15th c.). *Inside*, paintings by P. Veronese, J. Bassano, and B. Montagna.

Galleria d'Arte Municipale. *Open, Tue. and Sat., 10-12:30 and 4-7; Sun., 10-12.* Set in a 16th-c. former church, in a nook in Corso Palladio, this town art gallery features paintings by local artists such as G.B. and A. Maganza, S. Prunato, and G.A. Fumiani.

Palazzo Trissino-Baston*. Now city hall, at n. 98 in Corso Palladio, it has a tall portico with Ionic columns. A masterpiece by V. Scamozzi (1592), it has a handsome courtyard and, on the third floor (*open upon request, contact porter*), is the Sala della Giunta, or Council Hall, adorned with a frieze by G. Carpioni, and the Sala degli Stucchi, with 17th-c. decorations.

Contrà Porti*. This road runs past a number of splendid palazzi: at n. 6-10, the 15th-c. Venetian Gothic *Palazzo Cavalloni-Thiene*; at n. 11, the vast **Palazzo Barbaran-Porto**, by Palladio (1571), soon to become the Museo Palladiano. At n. 12, the Renaissance *Palazzo Thiene* (office of the Banca Popolare), designed by Palladio, with facade by L. da Bologna (1489). At n. 14, the Gothic *Palazzo Trissino-Sperotti* (1450-60), with an elegant balcony; at n. 17, the Venetian Gothic *Palazzo Porto-Breganze* (1481), with a handsome Renaissance portal and a porticoed courtyard; at n. 16, the Renaissance *Palazzo Porto-Fontana*; at n. 19, the magnificent Venetian Gothic *Palazzo Porto-Colleoni* (late 14th c.); at n. 21, the unfinished *Palazzo Iseppo da Porto*, later *Palazzo Festa*, by Palladio (1552).

S. Marco, 18th-c. church with a lavish facade; inside, painting by S. Ricci.

Contrà Zanella. This street is lined with notable buildings: at n. 2, *Palazzo Sesso-Zen*, a rare piece of Vicentine Gothic; at n. 1, on the Piazzetta S. Stefano, the crenelated Renaissance *Palazzo Negri De Salvi*; to the left, the Baroque church of *S. Stefano* (note painting* by Palma the Elder); further along, the Palladian rear facade of Palazzo Thiene (see above).

Corso Palladio* (*2nd part*). At n. 147, **Palazzo Dal Toso-Franceschini-Da Schio***, known as *Ca' d'Oro*, a gem of Venetian Gothic architecture of the 14th/15th c. After you pass, on the left, the garden of the 13th-c. church of S. Corona, see below, at n. 165-67, you will see the *Casa Cogollo*, inaccurately but frequently called *Casa di Palladio*, with a late-Renaissance facade (1559-62), possibly by G.A. Fasolo.

S. Corona*. *Open, Oct.-May, 9:30-12:30 and 3-6; Jun.-Sep., 8:30-12:30 and 3-6:30; closed Mon. morning.* This Dominican church, built beginning in 1261, has an enormous marble central portal and an elegant campanile. The *interior* has three Gothic aisles, with a deep, raised Renaissance presbytery (1489), built by L. da Bologna. On various altars throughout the church are paintings by P. Veronese (1573), Giovanni Bellini, L. Bassano, and B. Montagna. Also, note the main altar (1669); the 15th-c. inlaid wooden choir, and the handsome 14th-c. reliquary, which supposedly contains a Thorn from the Crown of Christ, *displayed only on Good Friday*.

In the adjacent cloisters are a *Museo Naturalistico*, with exhibits of natural history, and the **Museo Archeologico** (*open the same hours as the church*), with collections ranging from the Stone Age to the High Middle Ages.

Piazza Matteotti. This broad green space is flanked by Palazzo Chiericati, site of the Museo Civico (see below), and, to the left, in a garden scattered with carved marble, the Teatro Olimpico (see below); behind the theater rises a crenelated medieval tower.

Museo Civico*. *Open 9-12:30 and 2:30-5:30; closed Sun. aft. and Mon.* Located in the **Palazzo Chiericati***, which was built by Palladio (1551), this museum opened in 1855, and has a *section of medieval art*, a fine **Pinacoteca***, or Gallery, rich in work from the Venetian school from the 16th to 18th c. Note the ceilings of three halls on the ground floor, with frescoes by D. Brusasorci, G.B. Zelotti, and E. Forbicini. In the first section, work by P. Veneziano, B. da Vicenza, G. Buonconsiglio, and others. The Pinacoteca features work by 15th- and 16th-c. artists such as C. da Conegliano, B. Montagna, P. Veronese, J. Tintoretto, J. Bassano, and 17th- and 18th-c. artists such as G. Carpioni, F. Maffei, S. and M. Ricci, P. della Vecchia, G. Zais, G.B. Tiepolo; there are also noteworthy still-lifes and landscapes from the 17th and 18th c. Also: B. Boccaccino, F. del Cairo, L. Giordano, and especially the Flemish artists H. Memling and Van Dyck; note the Virgin and Child*, a terracotta by J. Sansovino. The museum also has a precious collection of drawings by A. Palladio.

Teatro Olimpico**. *Open, mid-Mar./mid-Oct., 9:30-12:20 and 3-5:30; holidays, 9:30-12:20; mid-Oct./mid-Mar., 9:30-12:20 and 2-4:30; closed Sun. aft.* The last creation of Palladio (1580), completed by his son Silla in 1582-83. The largest of the halls adjacent to the Teatro is the Odeo, or Odeon, a meeting hall for the Accademia degli Olimpici, built by V. Scamozzi in 1608, with frescoes by F. Maffei. Then comes the *Antiodeo*; from here, along stairways that lead to the upper loggias, you enter the Teatro. This theater, built of wood and stucco, imitates the form of classical theaters of antiquity; its cavea comprises thirteen semi-elliptical steps, and a lush scaena, on two orders, adorned with 95 statues, and architectural perspectives of the seven roads of the ancient city of Thebes, designed by V. Scamozzi.

S. Maria in Aracoeli. One of Vicenza's few Baroque monuments, designed by G. Guarini and built by C. Borella (17th c.), it has an elliptical plan.

S. Pietro. This Gothic church has a late-16th-c. facade and fine paintings inside. The nearby hospice (note monument to founder, in atrium, on right, by A. Canova) includes a 15th-c. *cloister**.

Surrounding areas. Villa Valmarana*, known as *Villa ai Nani* and **La Rotonda***, about 3 km. SW. The **Villa Valmarana*** (*open, mid-Mar./Apr., Tue.-Sat., 2:30-5:30; May-Oct., Tue. and Fri., 3-6, Wed., Thu., Sat. and Sun., 10-6; closed Mon.*), was built in 1665-70, with later work in 1736 by F. Muttoni, is decorated with renowned frescoes** by G.B. Tiepolo and his son G. D. (1757). The famed **Villa La Rotonda***, to which you can easily walk from Villa Valmarana (*open, Tue.-Sun., 10-12 and 3-6; interior only Wed.; closed Mon.*), is Palladio's best known creation (1550), the upper section was completed by V. Scamozzi (1606). Note frescoes in cupola by L. Dorigny.

Villa Adriana (Hadrian's Villa)*

elev. 76; Lazio, province of Rome, comune di Tivoli. This was the largest of the ancient Roman imperial villas; Hadrian oversaw the project for over 20 years, lavishing his thorough knowledge of late-Hellenistic culture on it, building theaters and libraries as well as tributes to places he had seen in his extensive travel through the eastern provinces. Work ended only four years before Hadrian's death. This vast field of ruins, devastated, plundered, forgotten, and then rediscovered (1450), mingles the allure of history and archeology with a lovely landscape, near the river Aniene, at the base of the Monti Tiburtini.

Tour. *Open: 9-an hour before sunset.* Follow the route shown on the map to tour the renowned archeological area. Other tours are available (by subject) and are indicated at the *Museo Didattico*.

Pecile. This huge rectangular quadriporticus (232 x 97 m.) was used as a gymnasium; it also contained a garden and had a large pool in the center. The western side stands atop a tall buttressing, containing the so-called *Cento Camerelle*, numerous small rooms, distributed over four stories; used either as warehouses or slave quarters.

Teatro Marittimo. You enter from the NE corner of the Pecile through a large rectangular hall, the *Sala dei Filosofi* (it is believed that the seven niches in the apse contained statues of the Greek Seven Wise Men). The Teatro Marittimo takes its name from its shape (theater-like) and the marine-motif decorations; it comprises two concentric parts: an Ionic-columned portico and a little round islet, separated by a ring-shaped canal, spanned with movable bridges; on the island itself was a miniature Roman "domus," with rooms arrayed around a peristyle. This was the emperor's personal retreat. South of the Teatro Marittimo are the ruins of a *bath house*; note the "heliocaminus," a round pool used for sunbathing, and a "frigidarium," or pool of cold water, surround on three sides by porticoes.

A *building with three exedrae*, possibly a banqueting hall, opens at the SE corner of the Pecile; at the center is a rectangular hall, with basin and surrounded by four courtyards. You then continue through a long *nymphaeum*; note peristyles and polychrome marble floors.

Terme*. This huge bath house is divided into **Grandi Terme** and **Piccole Terme**, or Large and Small Baths. The smaller baths may have been for women, and were surrounded by courtyards with exedrae and gardens; they comprised a large oblong room, an octagonal hall surrounded by smaller roooms, and a "frigidarium," or cold bath, with two curving basins.

In the larger baths, for men, you may note the "frigidarium," with large open-air rectangular pool and a semicircular basin; the adjacent hall has fine stuccoes in the vault. Grouped around a circular hall in the same complex are various rooms, one of them the "calidarium," with a pool and three furnaces to heat it.

Canopo. Set in a little manmade valley, girt by a wall to the east and by a two-story row of rooms to the west, this is an architectural tribute to the Egyptian town of Canopus, noted for its huge *temple of Serapis*. Along the edge of the long pool (119 x 18 m.) are column fragments and casts of statues: note four caryatids and two Sileni. At the northern extremity, two sculptural groups, the Tiber and the Nile. Note the *Serapeo*, or Serapeum, possibly used as a banqueting hall.

Antiquarium. Located just to the right of the Canopo, this small museum contains statues, portraits, and mosaics; note the originals of the caryatids in the Canopo.

Pretorio. Just behind the Grandi Terme is this three-story building, once believed to be barracks for Pretorian Guards, but actually warehouses. Note the series of rooms, still with plaster, possibly dwellings of the staff. From here, if you climb up to the olive grove to the east of the Piccole Terme you will note a large *quadriporticus* with a large fish-basin; below it is an *underground portico*, reserved for the emperor's summertime strolls (on the plaster, note signatures of 17th-c. visitors).

Palazzo Imperiale. The ruins of the imperial palace, believed to be the emperor's winter residence due to the discovery of a sophisticated heating system, covers a total area of 50,000 sq. m., comprising three complexes of residential and official rooms, distributed around three peristyles. To the SE is the *Piazza d'Oro*, or Golden Square, named for the lavish artifacts found here. On the central line of the square is the monumental semicircular *Ninfeo di Palazzo*, or Palace Nymphaeum, which may have been used as a summertime triclinium, or dining area. Adjacent to it is the *Hall of the Doric Pillars*, with a courtyard and fluted pillars.

Cortile delle Biblioteche. This Courtyard of the Libraries, which architecturally links the older parts of the villa with the later expansions, takes its name from two multi-story buildings, known respectively as the *Greek Library* and the *Latin Library*, with tower-shaped triclinia. On the southern side of the courtyard, under the terrace of Palazzo Imperiale, is a *cryptoporticus* from the time of the Republic, with four galleries cut out of the tufa. On the NE side is a huge room in which we find ten guest rooms (*hospitalia*), with black-and-white mosaic floors; in each room, we see three rectangular sleeping niches.

Terrazza di Tempe. At the SE corner of this terrace is the tree-shaded *Padiglione di Tempe*, a lofty three-story belvedere, overlooking the *Valle di Tempe*, a valley named after the Vale of Tempe, in Thessaly, sacred to Apollo.

Teatro Greco. This Greek Theater – near the *Ninfeo*, the little *Tempietto di Venere*, and the 18th-c. lodge called the *Casino Fede* – still possesses a few features of the original theater.

Viterbo*

elev. 326 m.; pop. 58,380; Lazio, provincial capital. This town has two particularly noteworthy features: an abundance of handsome, cheerful fountains, and an intense, exquisite medieval atmosphere. Set on a rolling plain on the slopes of the Cimini mountains, along the Via Cassia, this was the historical capital of Upper Lazio, the ancient Tuscia of the Romans. It still has battlemented, turreted city walls, with seven gates. The Palazzo dei Papi is a reminder of the looming papal presence in Viterbo's history. One memorable conclave resulted in the election of Gregory X, but only after 33 months of attempts. The Capitano del Popolo Raniero Gatti, on the advice of St. Bonaventure, locked the quarrelsome cardinals in the Palazzo, tore the roof off the council hall, and stopped sending in food....

Historical note. The eight rows of great stone blocks on the Ponte del Duomo and a few fragments of city walls are all that remain of what was probably once a Etruscan town. The name Viterbo is often derived from the Latin "vetus urbs," or "old city." Certainly, the city's triangular plan is medieval, based on the original village at the confluence of two rivers, where Piazza S. Lorenzo now stands, the site of the ancient castle. The nearby medieval quarter of S. Pellegrino, with 13th-c. architecture and atmosphere, reminds the visitor that the 1200s were Viterbo's most flourishing century. After long wars with Otto IV and then Frederick II, and even the city of Rome, Viterbo became the capital of the papacy in 1257, when Pope Alexander IV fled here from the Eternal City. Many popes reigned here, until the people finally rebelled, and were excommunicated en masse. After two centuries, the papal state conquered Viterbo with an army. After surviving practically intact for centuries, 20 years of Fascist rule, the Allied bombings of 1944, and the frenzied construction of the past 50 years have done more damage than the previous seven centuries.

Places of interest. Piazza del Plebiscito. The political heart of the city since the mid-13th-c., as the medieval *Palazzo del Podestà* indicates, along with the facing 18th-c. *Palazzo della Prefettura*, both adorned by columns with the lion symbolizing Viterbo. The *Palazzo dei Priori*, now city hall, was built in the 15th c. under Pope Sixtus IV, and later renovated. The 15th-c. facade conceals a courtyard with a fine view of the river valley below. Also overlooking the square is the church of *S. Angelo in Spatha*, Romanesque but rebuilt; note the copy of the Sarcophagus of the Bella Galiana (the original is in the Museo Civico); also note, inside, the fragment of 14th-c. triptych. In Via Ascenzi, note the handsome 14th-c. portal* of the Gothic church of *S. Maria della Salute*.

Via S. Lorenzo. Linking the political heart of Viterbo with the religious heart, the street runs through a dense medieval quarter. Note the 15th-c. *Palazzo Chigi* and the medieval *tower of Borgognone*. Just beyond is the Piazza del Gesù, with the 11th-c. Romanesque *church* of the same name; note the 17th-c. fountain.

S. Maria Nuova*. This Romanesque church, one

of Viterbo's oldest (1080), features – at the left corner of the facade – the pulpit from which St. Thomas of Aquinas once preached. The *interior** is basilican; note the 15th-c. ceiling with tempera panels. Also worthy of note are a 13th-c. Crucifix; from the same period, a triptych* on leather; and artwork by Balletta, M. Giovannetti, and Pastura. On the left side of the church, you can enter the adjacent Longobard *cloister* (*open 10-1 and 4-7:30*).

Loggia di S. Tommaso. Part of the 13th-c. Palazzo di S. Tommaso, it houses the Museo delle Confraternite (*open, by request; contact the Ente per il Turismo, tel. 345229*), devoted to the ancient brotherhoods of the area.

Palazzo Farnese. Beyond the Ponte del Duomo, a bridge that includes a number of Etruscan blocks (visible, descending, on right), you can recognize the palazzo by the twin-light mullioned windows on its right side. These 14th-c. features were reused in building this 16th-c. Renaissance residence.

Cattedrale*. This Cathedral was built in the 12th c. The campanile* was built a century later, and shows Tuscan influence. The facade was completed in 1570. *Inside*, note the columns on the capitals and the Cosmatesque floors. Note the late-15th-c. baptismal font by F. da Ancona, 14th-c. fragments of frescoes, and the late-13th-c. Madonna della Carbonara*.

Palazzo dei Papi**. Built in 1255-67 as a papal residence, this is Viterbo's best known monument and the most important example of Viterbese Gothic architecture. Some exceedingly lively conclaves took place here. A staircase leads up to the battlemented facade; to the right runs the elegant loggia** (view*); the fountain dates from the 15th c. Note the *Museo d'Arte Sacra*, with 17th-c. paintings and sculptures in wood and stone.

Via S. Pellegrino*. This is the main street of the *medieval quarter***, dotted with towers, mullioned windows, and elevated walkways. In the handsome little Piazza S. Pellegrino* note the **Palazzo degli Alessandri**, a 13th-c. home with balcony, and nearby two medieval towers. At n. 60, note the *Museo della Macchina di S. Rosa* (*open, Sat. and Sun., 10-12 and 4-7*), devoted to a local saint.

Viterbo: The Medieval Quarter

Fontana Grande. Beyond the 15th-c. *Case dei Gatti** is the most famous fountain in Viterbo, functioning since 1279.

S. Sisto*. Built in the 9th c. on the site of a pagan temple, enlarged in the 12th and 13th c., and rebuilt after heavy bombing in WWII, the church boasts an ancient apse, and two bell towers, one based on the transept, the other rising from the city walls. Note the unusual columns near the triumphal arch and, in the apse, the main altar, built of 4th- and 5th-c. material.

Casa Poscia. Another typical example of an early-14th-c. Viterbese home; note the "profferlo," distinctive exterior staircase supported by a hanging arch.

S. Maria della Verità. Built in the 12th c. just outside the *city walls*, this church was badly damaged in WWII; inside, note the Mazzatosta Chapel, with frescoes* by L. da Viterbo (1469).

Museo Civico*. *Open, Oct.-Apr., 10-6; May-Sep., 10-7; closed Mon.* It is located in a former convent; note the Gothic cloister*. Among the *archeological finds* displayed here are sarcophagi; in particular, the Roman one, known as the Sarcophagus of the Bella Galiana*, with scenes of hunting. Among the *painters*, we should mention S. del Piombo, Pastura, and G. F. Romanelli. Noteworthy collection of pharmacy vases.

S. Giovanni in Zoccoli. This 11th-c. church, rebuilt after the war, features a rose window surrounded by the symbols of the four evangelists. Inside, a polyptych by Balletta.

S. Rosa. This church, with the 13th-c. saint's nearby home (*open, Thu. and Sun., 9:30-12 and 4-5:30*), forms the saint's sanctuary; inside, another polyptych by Balletta.

S. Marco. Founded by Cistercian monks and consecrated by Innocent III in 1198, this church features an apse frescoed by G. F. d'Avanzarano.

Rocca Albornoz. Cardinal Albornoz began work on this fortress in the mid-14th c. Numerous popes carried on construction, at one point summoning Bramante (he designed the courtyard). Restored in the 1960s, the Rocca now houses the Museo Archeologico Nazionale.

Museo Archeologico Nazionale*. *Open 9-6: closed Mon.* The section that can now be viewed in the Rocca Albornoz provides documentation of the archaic Etruscan architecture of Viterbo and surrounding areas, through material excavated at San Giovenale (1956-65) and Acquarossa (1966-78). Providing, respectively, materials ranging from the Stone Age to the Middle Ages, and the structure of an entire Etruscan city of the 7th c. B.C., the finds offer such fascinating details as painted tiles from pitch roofs, an entire portico, and primitive siding as well as terracotta fixtures.

S. Francesco. The reconstruction done after WWII maintained the church's Gothic style (13th c.). Inside, note the tomb of Pope Adrian V* (d. 1276), believed to be the first monument by A. di Cambio.

Volterra*

elev. 531 m.; pop. 12,879; Tuscany, province of Pisa. "At the summit of a high hill," recalls Stendhal, Volterra surveys the surrounding heights between the valleys of the Era and the Cècina. The landscape mingles lush greenery with hard white lines of ridges and erosion. This city is stern and medieval in its skyline. All around are workshops where craftsman shape the alabaster taken from the ground here; chalky dust is everywhere. The Museo Guarnacci features fine alabaster work done by the Etruscans, long ago.

Historical note. Etruscan civilization reached this town, originally called "Velathri," relatively late: around the end of the 7th c. B.C., probably from Populonia along the course of the river Cècina. The town flourished immediately, prospering on trade in metals (it controlled Elba and Corsica) and lumber, grain, and alabaster. The Etruscan walls ran 7 km. and enclose 102 hectares; that is three times the length and area of the medieval walls, which encompass the modern town. Roman "Volaterrae" declined when the Pisa-Tortona road across the Apennines cut it out of the mainstream of commerce (109 B.C.). For more than a thousand years, Volterra slumbered quietly. The 13th and 14th c. saw a prosperous town, fighting against local lords and the towns of San Gimignano, Pisa, Siena, and Florence; it was Florence that finally subjugated Volterra, and Lorenzo the Magnificent built the Fortress of the Rocca Nuova as an emblem of that subjugation.

Getting around. The area inside the town walls is closed to traffic from 10 to 1 and from 5 to 8 (from 10 to 8 on holidays); visitors heading for hotels are allowed in to drop off or pick up luggage. The route is a walking tour; you may wish to drive to the Balze (see below).

Places of interest. **Piazza dei Priori***. This square has been the site of markets since A.D. 851. One of Italy's loveliest medieval squares, it is lined with handsome buildings, some of which are original.

Palazzo dei Priori*. Built in 1208-54, this massive crenelated building is punctuated by three orders of mullioned windows, and a handsome tower. Still serving as the town hall, you can go to the second floor (open, 9-1; only weekdays) and visit the Sala del Consiglio (note frescoes and painting) and the Sala della Giunta, with inlaid 15th-c. desk. Note the terracotta heraldic devices everywhere.

Duomo*. Behind Palazzo dei Priori, overlooking Piazza S. Giovanni, this Romanesque cathedral dates from the 12th c.; the facade is simple and understated, while the interior is rich and lavishly covered with marble. Among the artists who worked on the cathedral, note R. Cioli, M. da Fiesole, F. di Valdambrino, M. Albertinelli, and B. Gozzoli. Also, note the handsome pulpit* on four columns, assembled in the 16th c. with 13th-c. sculptures; the 13th-c. gild and silver-plated polychrome wooden group; and the handsome Gothic wooden choir (1404). Facing the Duomo is the **Battistero**, or **Baptistery** (closed for restoration), a fine octagonal 13th-c. building with a Romanesque portal, and green-and-white striped front; inside, baptismal font* by A. Sansovino (1502).

Museo Diocesano di Arte Sacra. *Open, 9-1.* Entrance at n. 1 in Via Roma, from the portico behind the bell tower of the Duomo. This museum has collections of sculpture, architectural fragments, metalwork, and paintings of religious nature. Note works by A. della Robbia, A. Pollaiolo, Giambologna, and R. Fiorentino.

Quadrivio dei Buomparenti*. This fascinating crossroads in the historical center features the very tall *Casa-Torre Buomparenti**, a 13th-c. tower-house, connected by a catwalk to the Torre Buonaguidi.

Via Ricciarelli. This road is lined with medieval and Renaissance churches and houses.

Pinacoteca* and **Museo Civico**. *Open, Apr.-Oct., 9:30-1 and 3-6:30; Nov.-Mar., 9:30-1:30.* At n. 1 in Via dei Sarti, the art gallery and town museums are located in the Palazzo Solaini, attributed to A. da Sangallo the Elder. The fifteen halls feature Florentine, Siennese, and Volterran artists, from the 14th to the 17th c.; among them are T. di Bartolo, B. di Giovanni, F. di Valdambrino, D. Ghirlandaio, L. Signorelli, Rosso Fiorentino, P. de Witte, B. Franceschini, D. da Volterra; also medals and coins.

Palazzo Incontri-Viti. Open by request, contact the owners. This 16th-c. palazzo, with entrance at n. 41 in Via dei Sarti, has a facade attributed to B. Ammannati. The interior is worth touring; note the Volterran alabasters*.

S. Michele Arcangelo. Overlooking the "piazzetta" of the same name, this church has a handsome Romanesque facade and, inside, a Della Robbia terracotta and a painting by the Pomarancio. Note the 13th-c. Toscano tower-house.

Teatro Romano. *Open, Mar.- Oct., 11-4; closed in bad weather.* This Roman theater, built under Augustus, can be clearly seen from Via Lungo le Mura del Mandorlo, at the outer end of Via Guarnacci.

Fortezza. Not open to the public. Still used as a prison, this is one of the most formidable fortresses built during the Italian Renaissance. From Piazza XX settembre, you can enter the public gardens; note the interesting Parco Archeologico Enrico Fiumi (*open, Mar.-Oct., 11-4; closed in bad weather*).

Museo Etrusco Guarnacci*. *Open, Apr.-Oct., 9:30-1 and 3-6:30; Nov.-Mar., 9-2.* Entrance at n. 15 in Via Don Minzoni; the museum features noteworthy collections** of Etruscan cinerary urns made of tufa, alabaster, and terracotta, sculpture*, and a collection* of more than 3,000 Etruscan, Greek, and Roman coins.

Via Matteotti*. Handsome road through the most truly medieval section of Volterra. It is lined with 13th-c. tower/houses; at the end, on the left (n. 25), the stern Palazzo Maffei, 1527.

Porta all'Arco*. This gate is the center of the alabaster workshops; the gate itself is a mix of Roman and Etruscan features; note the three heads of Etruscan deities.

Viale dei Ponti. Beginning in Piazza Martiri della Libertà this road offers a fine stroll with excellent views* of the Cècina valley.

Surrounding areas. At the Balze*, 2 km. NW, leaving through Porta S. Francesco. The Balze are a vast and spectacular sink of gullies and ravines. Remains of Etruscan walls can be seen, though many other buildings have been swallowed up by the slow progressive collapse of the soil. Note the 11th-c. Abbey (being restored and reinforced).

Italy: Instructions for Use

Arriving in Italy

Citizens of Australia, Canada, New Zealand, and the United States can enter Italy with a valid passport, and stay for a period of not more than 90 days; citizens of Great Britain and Ireland, as members of the European Union, can travel either with valid passport or with valid identification card.

Helpful addresses

Foreign Embassies in Italy
(use initial zero only when phoning within Italy)

Australia:
Via Alessandria 215 - Rome, tel. (06) 852721

Canada:
Via G.B. de Rossi 27 - Rome, tel. (06) 445981

New Zealand:
Via Zara 28 - Rome, tel. (06) 4404035-4402928

United States of America:
Via Vittorio Veneto 119/A, Palazzo Margherita, Rome, tel. (06) 46741

Great Britain:
Via XX Settembre 80 - Rome, tel. (06) 4825441

Ireland:
Largo Nazareno 3 - Rome, tel. (06) 6782541

Foreign Consulates in Italy

Australia:
Via Borgogna 2
Milan, tel. (02) 76013330 - 76013852

Canada:
Via Vittor Pisani 19 - Milan, tel. (02) 6758001

New Zealand:
Via F. Sforza 48 - Milan, tel. (02) 58314443

United States of America:
Lungarno A. Vespucci 38 - Florence,
tel. (055) 2398276
Via Principe Amedeo 2/10 - Milan,
tel. (02) 290351
Piazza Repubblica 2 - Naples,
tel. (081) 5838111
Via Re Federico 18/bis - Palermo,
(consular agency), tel. (091) 6110020

Great Britain:
Via S. Paolo 7 - Milano, tel. (02) 723001
Via F. Crispi 122 - Napoli, tel. (081) 663511

Italian Embassies and Consulates around the World

Australia:
12 Grey Street - Deakin
Canberra, tel. (06) 273-3333

Consulates at: Adelaide, Brisbane, Melbourne, Perth, Sydney.

Canada:
275 Slater Street, 21st floor
Ottawa (Ontario), tel. (613) 2322401

Consulates at: Montréal, Toronto, Vancouver.

New Zealand:
34 Grant Road
Wellington, tel. (4) 4735339 - 4736667

United States of America:
1601 Fuller Street, N.W.
Washington D.C., tel. (202) 328-5500
Consulates at: Boston, Chicago, Philadelphia, Houston, Los Angeles, Miami, New York, New Orleans, San Francisco.

Great Britain:
14, Three Kings Yard
London W.1, tel. (0171) 3122200

Consulates at: Edinburgh, Manchester.

Ireland:
63/65, Northumberland Road
Dublin 4, tel. (01) 6601744

ENIT

In order to have general information and documentation concerning the best known places in Italy, you can contact the offices of the Ente Nazionale Italiano per il Turismo (ENIT), run by the Italian government; they are open Mon.-Fri., from 9 to 5.

Canada:
Office National Italien du Tourisme/Italian Government - Travel Office
Montreal, Quebec H3B 3M9
1 Place Ville Marie, Suite 1914
tel. (514) 866-7667/866-7669
fax 392-1429

United States of America:
Italian Government Tourist Board
630 Fifth Avenue
New York, NY 10111
tel. 212-245-4961
fax 212-586-9249
Italian Government Travel Office
Chicago 1, Illinois 60611-401, North Michigan Avenue, Suite 3030
tel. (312) 644-0996, fax 644-3019
Italian Government Travel Office
Los Angeles, CA 90025
12400, Wilshire Blvd. Suite 550
tel. (310) 820-0098/820-1898, fax 820-6357

Great Britain:
Italian State Tourist Board
London W1R 6AY, 1 Princes Street
tel. (0171) 408-1254, fax 493-6695

The climate: when to visit Italy

O Sole Mio, the famous Neapolitan song, in praise of the fine southern sun, is the most stereotypical image of Italy's good weather.
The truth is that it rains almost as much in Rome as it does in London, and that the winter climate of Turin is virtually identical to that of Copenhagen. In any event, the Italian climate really is one of the finest on earth, with dry hot summers and mild winters. Roughly speaking, there are three distinct types of climate to found in the Italian peninsula: continental, in the north; moderate in the lake region; Mediterranean along the coasts.

August is the least advisable month in which to travel in Italy. It is not so much a matter of heat; rather, this is when the vast majority of Italians take their vacations. The major cities, especially in the north, are desolate and virtually empty; in the week straddling the 15th of August, Ferragosto or Feast of Our Lady of the Assumption, you may even have difficulty finding a restaurant open. If the cities are empty, vacation spots are teeming with crowds; equally jammed are highways, trains, and airplanes. And all tourist-related services cost more during this month.

For the art capitals the best period to come is in the fall and the spring, ideal times in which to enjoy the Italian landscape at its finest, with the color of flowers in spring and the colors of trees and grapevines in the fall.

From December to March the happiest visitors to Italy are those skiing on the slopes of the Alps and the Apennines.

The hot dry Italian summer is perfect along the coastline, where fresh breezes often cool the air, save for the area around Venice, which is humid and muggy. On mountain paths, in the Alps and Apennines, conditions are ideal for hiking. Because of the heat, however, you should plan to avoid both the northern plains and the hills of central Italy.

Customs requirements

For travellers from countries that do not form part of the European Community the following limitations are set: on tobacco (200 cigarettes, 50 cigars, 250 gr. of tobacco), alcohol (2 liters of table wine and 1 liter of liquors with more than 44 proof), perfumes (50 ml. of perfume and 0.25 liters of *eau de toilette*), coffee (500 gr. of coffee and 250 gr. of concentrate or extract) and tea (100 gr. of tea and 40 gr. of concentrate or extract).

For travellers from countries which belong to the European Community, from 1 July 1993, all fiscal and customs border inspections have been suspended, with the exception of a few specific objects (works of art, antiques, weapons, ammunition, and so on); for those, you must have proper authorization and documentation.

Money and banks

The monetary unit is the lira (the symbol is either £ or else Lit.), plural: lire. Banknotes in circulation range from 1,000, 2,000, 5,000, and 10,000, up to 50,000 and 100,000 lire; the coins have denominations of 50, 100, 200, and 500 lire.

Banks are open from Monday to Friday, generally from 8:30 to 1:30 and from 3 to 4. Many money-changing windows operate separately from banks, in air terminals, the main railroad stations and terminals, and in heavily touristed areas.

All of the major credit cards — American Express, Diner's Club, Visa, and Master Card — are accepted in hotels, car rentals, and department stores. A number of restaurants and stores in smaller cities will not accept them.

Travelling in Italy

By train. The extensive Italian railroad system is run by the agency Ferrovia dello Stato (FS).

Outside of Italy, services are available to travellers in the agencies of the Compagnia Italiana Turismo (CIT), at the following addresses:

Australia
Melbourne, 450 Little Collins Street, 2nd floor - Suite 250 - Sydney, 123 Clarence Street

Canada
Montreal, 2055 Peel Street - Suite 102 P.Q.
Toronto, 111 Avenue Road Concourse Level

Great Britain
Londra, Wasteels Travel, Victoria Station

United States
New York, 594 Broadway - Suite 307
Los Angeles, 6033 West Century Blvd. - Suite 1090

The trains are classified by speed; they include:
* *Pendolino (ETR 450)*. This is the bullet train between Rome and Milan; it takes just 4 hours, with stops at the stations of Bologna and Florence; 5 trains a day, one of them non-stop;
* *EC-Eurocity* and *EN-Euronight*, with 1st-class sleeping cars; reservations are required;
* *IC-Intercity*, with seat reservations required, reservations free of charge;
* E-Long-distance express, or "*Espresso*";
* *D-Diretto* (Direct) and *IR-Interregionale* (Interregional) which stop in most stations;
* *R-Regionale* (Regional), of local interest, and which stop in all stations.

A number of trains, especially long-distance trains, are equipped with: restaurant car or self-service car, snack bar or "minibar," public pay telephones, sleeping car, bunk sleeping cars (4/6 beds per car), or *sleeperettes* (with reclining seats).

First- and second-class tickets are sold both at ticket windows in railroad stations and in travel agencies, at no extra charge; they must be used within 2 months of date issued.

Attention: travellers are obliged by law to validate their tickets (this is done by punching it in a special time-clock available in all stations) before starting the trip, in both directions; if you fail to do so, a fairly stiff fine can and may be levied.

In the CIT agencies outside Italy, listed above, you can buy train tickets at discount prices. The major packages include:
* *Biglietti Turistici di Libera Circolazione (BTLC)*, meaning Tourist Tickets for Free Circulation, with validity of 8/15/21/30 days; with these you can travel anywhere on the Italian railroad system; they are for individuals, for use only by purchaser, and available only to travellers residing outside of Italy;
* *Biglietti Chilometrici*, or Kilometric Tickets, are for use only by purchaser/s, and can be made out for as many as 5 people; they allow the bearer/s to travel for a maximum of 3,000 km., within 2 months of date issued.

Detailed information on train schedules can be found on *Televideo Rai*, on page 477.

By airplane. National transportation is offered by the national airline, *Alitalia*, which flies from Rome to a number of Italian cities: Bari, Bologna, Cagliari, Catania, Florence, Genoa, Milan/Linate and Milan/Malpensa, Palermo, Pisa, Reggio di Calabria, Turin, Trieste, Venice, Verona.

For reservations on national or domestic flights: Rome, tel.(06) 65641; Milan, tel. (02) 26851;

For information: Rome, tel.(06) 65643, Milan, tel. (02) 26853.

From outside of the metropolitan areas of Rome or Milan, dial: for reservations on national or domestic flights: tel. 1478/65641; for information: tel. 1478/65643.

The Italian airline, *Meridiana*, offers flights between Rome and: Arbatax, Catania, Milan Malpensa, Olbia, Palermo, Venice, and Verona. The reservations lines can be reached by calling: Alghero, tel. (0789) 69300, Milan, tel. (02) 864771, Rome tel.(06) 478041.

Air One is a new Italian airline, which has a heron as its symbol (in Italian, "airone" means heron). It offers 26 flights a day between Rome Fiumicino and Milan Linate. For information and reservations, tel. (06) 478766.

Detailed information on plane schedules can be found on *Televideo Rai, on page 432.*

By motorcoach. The motorcoach lines, Eurolines Italia (reservations office: Florence, Via Mercadante 2/B, tel. (055) 357110) offers connections between all of the main Italian cities, and a number of cities outside of Italy, in such countries as Belgium, Czech Republic, France, Great Britain, Holland, Poland, Spain, and Hungary.
Other major Italian motorcoach lines include:

- *Autostradale Viaggi* in Piazza Castello 1, Milan, tel. (02) 72001304, which operates primarily in Lombardy and in northern and central Italy;
- *Autolinee Lazzi*, Via Mercadante 2, Florence, tel. (055) 363041, with lines chiefly connecting Tuscany and central Italy;
- *SITA*, Viale dei Cadorna 105, Florence, tel. (055) 47821, operating an extensive national network, though not in Sicily or Sardinia.

By car. Italy possesses a good road and highway network, which covers the entire country. The road markings and signs are in line with international norms; you drive on the right and you pass on the left; safety belts are mandatory on front seats. Main and secondary roads are marked by signs with a dark-blue background and white letters; highways have signs with a green background.
On the highways (with the exception of a few, such as for example the A3 Salerno-Reggio di Calabria) you must pay a toll; in order to facilitate the payment, and in order to avoid getting caught in long lines at the toll barrier, motorists can purchase a prepaid card, *Viacard*, which is valid in the entire highway system.
Speed limits are as follows: 50 km/h in residential centers, 90 km/h on secondary roads, 110 km/h on primary roads, 130 km/h on highways.

Roadside assistance. This is a national service offered by *ACI (Automobile Club Italiano)*, with an operations network with over 900 centers, working 24 hours a day. On the highways, note the special yellow SOS calling poles, placed every 2 km.
Dial 116 for assistance, from any telepone; road-

side assistance is free for all cars with foreign plates; non-Italian tourists who fly to Italy and rent a car at the airports of Rome Fiumicino, Milan Malpensa, and Milan Linate can enjoy the same free service.

Automobile rentals. This is the handiest solution for travellers who fly to Italy and wish to travel freely. In the arrivals hall of most airports there are offices of the major multinational rental corporations (*Hertz, Avis, Maggiore, Europcar, etc.*). Hotels in the larger towns and cities often have direct ties with leading local rental firms. Credit cards are required, and most rental firms demand a deposit.
In order to rent a vehicle you must in any case be 21, and in some cases, 23; you must have had your license for over a year. Experience shows that, in case you do have an accident or are caught breaking a traffic regulation, it is quite useful to have an international driver's license, issued by the automobil associations of your country of origin; the international driver's license is useful because it can be immediately understood by Italian police officers.

Emergencies. For emergency phone calls, police, or an ambulance, dial 113.

By ship. The main Italian islands are linked to the mainland by regular ferry service, carrying both cars and passengers. During the summer, there is also frequent hydrofoil service. Schedules and frequency vary according to the season.

Major islands. The *Tirrenia* line (Rione Sirignano 2, Naples, tel. 081/7201111) offers regular service to Sicily (between Genoa and Naples and Palermo; between Cagliari and Trapani) and Sardinia (between Genoa and Arbatax, Cagliari, Olbia, and Porto Torres; between La Spezia and Olbia; between Civitavecchia and Arbatax, Cagliari, Golfo Aranci, and Olbia; between Naples, Palermo, and Trapani and Cagliari).

Smaller islands. Capri and Ischia are served regularly by ferryboats and hydrofoils run by the *Alilauro* line (Via Caracciolo 11, Naples, tel. 081/7614250) leaving from Naples and Sorrento and by the *Caremar* company (Molo Beverello, Naples, tel. 081/5515384), leaving from Pozzuoli and Naples.
The *Navarma* line (Piazzale Premuda, Piombino, tel. 0565/276077) links Piombino and Portoferraio, on the Isle of Elba.
Note the services of the *Siremar* line (Via Principe di Belmonte 1/c, Palermo, tel. 091/582688) with boats from the Sicilian ports of: Milazzo for the Isole Eolie; Palermo for Ustica; Trapani for the Isole Egadi and Pantelleria; Porto Empedocle for Linosa and Lampedusa.

Lakes. The *Navigazione Laghi* line (Via Ariosto 2, Milan, tel, 02/4812086) transports vehicles and passengers between the main towns on Lake Maggiore, Lake Garda, and Lake Como.

In town. *Taxi.* Taxis can be recognized by the luminous sign, while the actual color of the car may vary from city to city (yellow, white, green). Be wary of unoffical taxi drivers who may approach travellers on line in train stations and in airports; their cars have no official lighted taxi sign, and there is no fare meter, making it impossible for you to monitor the fare. In official taxis, the fare meter should display a running tab; it is proper for there to be extra charges for suitcases, dogs, night service, or holiday service.

Buses, electric trolley-buses, and trolleys run in most cities; in Venice, there is the "vaporetto." Tickets, or discount booklets, can be purchased in cafes, bars, tobacco shops, and from automatic vending machines and at newsstands (for information, contact local tourist offices).

Hotels

The hotels are classified, the number of "stars," ranging from one star (*) to five-star deluxe (*****L) when the hotel is located in a building of special historical or architectural note. Standards, comfort, and service may vary — rating aside — from area to area. Often, especially far away from the big cities, hotels with (**) or (***), family-run, can be surprisingly affordable, in terms of the quality/price ratio.

In order to find European standards, you should choose hotels that belong to the major chains in Italy: Jolly Hotels, Best Western, Starhotels, Monrif Hotels, Forte, Agip Hotels, etc., all notable for the fine accommodations and the careful, efficient service; the less exclusive hotel chains, such as Mercure, Novotel, Sofitel, Ibis, Family Hotels, Notturno Italiano, etc. offer comfortable lodgings and handy, reliable service.

Requirements. Hotels are required to inform the police of all guests, and they therefore always require that the guest provide identification, and fill out a personal information sheet.

Prices. A chart of prices must be displayed in every hotel room. There are differences, sometimes quite considerable, between prices in high season and off season. In general, the high season in major cities coincides with important fairs and other business events; in the art capitals it ranges from Easter to October; in coastal areas, from July to August; in the mountains, from Christmas to Easter for the ski season, and the month of August in the summer. Everywhere in Italy, Christmas-time (20 December to 6 January) and the week of Easter are considered the high season.

Reservations. It is always advisable to make reservations, but it becomes mandatory during the high season. Local offices of tourism have a list of hotels, can provide information concerning vacancies, and in some cases can offer to make reservations for you. When you reserve, or when you check in, it is always wise to ask about the rates that apply in the period in question.

Rates. These may be based on 1) a single or double hotel room (for 2 persons) with or without a continental breakfast; for children, if another bed is required, there will likely be a supplementary charge; 2) the "mezza pensione," or half board, including continental breakfast and a full meal (in general, dinner); 3) "pensione completa," or full board, including continental breakfast, lunch, and dinner. In many resorts and towns, in the high season you must have either half or full board.

Other accommodations

Houses and apartments. It is quite common to be able to rent apartments and houses in resort towns and areas, even for short stays (minimum, one week). You can enquire with local tourist agencies and offices.

Agritourism. It is becoming increasingly common to find fine accommodations in the countryside, often in homes that have a certain atmosphere; a vast array of possible opportunities is listed in the *Guida dell'Ospitalità Rurale* published in Italian by *Agriturist* (Corso Vittorio Emanuele 101, Rome, tel. 06/6852342).

Youth hostels. In Italy there are 54 youth hostels; in order to use them, you must be a member of the AIG (Associazione Alberghi per la Gioventù, Via Cavour 44, Rome, tel. 06/4871152). There is no age limit, but when the rooms are limited, young people below the age of 25 have priority of access. Other possibilities of cheap accommodations for young people are offered by student unions and religious institutions; enquire with the local offices of tourism.

Camping. Italy has over 2,200 campsites and tourist villages, generally open from Easter to September. Information is available from ENIT, Federcampeggio (Via V. Emanuele 11, 50041 Calenzano, Florence), and local offices of tourism. The publication *Campeggi e Villaggi Turistici in Italia* published by TCI in Italian, contains a complete list of reliable structures. You are allowed to camp outside of official campsites, especially in central and southern Italy, if you have the permission of the owner, or authorization from town hall (Municipio), if you wish to camp on public lands.

Restaurants

Unlike for hotels, there is no single official classification of restaurants in Italy. The fame of Italian cuisine as one of the finest on earth is fairly deserved, but not always borne out in every single meal. Restaurants range from refined temples to food, with fine cooking and excellent service, to more modest "osterias" or "trattorias," home-style and unassuming, while in pizzerias the range is vast, as is the price range. In order to avoid surprises, we strongly recommend you read the menu that is displayed outside the restaurant; in any case, once you are seated, you should ask for a written menu listing prices: it is a risky business to trust to the spoken presentation of the restaurateur. Most restaurants offer a "house wine" at a reasonable price. If you order a finer bottle, check the price on the wine list. Despite the constant rises in price, dining out in Italy is still reasonably cheap, especially if you consider the average price of wine outside of Italy. To figure out the final price of a meal, count on adding between 2,000 and 4,000 lire each for bread and tablecloth ("pane e coperto") and about 15 percent for service. It is a good idea to leave a small tip.

Lastly, the "tourist menus" ("menù turistico") and "sample menus" ("menù degustazione") are two formulas that can save you from the horrible surprise of an astronomical check. The difference between the two types of menu is considerable, however. The former is convenient, often cheap, and is usually made up of less original dishes. The latter, on the other hand, is a new innovation offered by some of the more creative restaurateurs in Italy; it consists of a selection from their daily or season specialties.

Food and wines

A traditional Italian meal consists of an *antipasto*, or appetizer (salami or vegetables), a primo (rice or pasta), a *secondo* (meat or fish) often accompanied by a *contorno*, or side dish (salad, pototoes, or beans) and, to finish up, cheese, fruit, sweets, and black espresso coffee. That is why, in the worldwide division between those who eat to live and those who live to eat, the Italians will always be solidly in the second category, at least by stereotype.

All of this applies now only as a general rule. First of all, because the traditional meal is now a rarity, and is found only on special occasions, but also because the struggle to lose weight, especially in the north, has undermined the love of good food. It remains true that in Italy, the culinary art has a deep and solid cultural tradition. And for some time now it has been chic to eat Italian all over the world; Italian food is almost as fashionable as Italian clothing.

In the field of cuisine and the culinary arts, the saying that there is a different Italy in every region holds particularly true; those differences can be quite substantial, at least as great as the differences in climate. In an imaginary voyage from north to south, here is a tour of the specialties you should sample. There are many more, of course, but the ones mentioned here are the most representative of the region, and often the easiest to sample in restaurants. Not in all restaurants, but certainly in those that are proud to maintain a time-honored local tradition.

Valle d'Aosta: chamois or venison, generally haunch or filet, marinated in red wine with herbs, sauted in the pan, sprinkled with grappa; the local coffee — "caffè valdostano" — is quite memorable; it is consumed, taking turns, from a wooden goblet with a number of spouts; aside from the piping hot coffee, it contains lemon rinds and a generous dollop of grappa. **Piedmont**: *bagna cauda*, or "hot bath", is a sauce made of oil, garlic, and anchovies, which must boil continually and never cool off; into it you dip Jerusalem artichoke, green, yellow, and red peppers, or celery stalks; or there is "fonduta", a sort of fondue, served piping hot and covered with a cheese-based melted "crema di formaggio" (Fontina Valdostana). **Liguria**: aside from the fish specialties, found also in other coastal regions (baked, grilled, or in broth), we can recommend the savory vegetable pies; the best known is the "Pasqualina", and it has a filling of boiled minced beets, mixed with curdled milk, parmesan cheese and other ingredients; at the end, hard-boiled eggs are added, left whole. **Lombardy**: "risotto alla milanese", cooked in meat broth, colored with saffron, and mixed with butter and parmesan cheese. **Veneto**: calf's liver "alla veneziana", thinly sliced and cooked in oil, butter, and abundant chopped onion. **Emilia Romagna**: "lasagne alla bolognese", egg pasta half-

boiled and laid in a baking pan and layered with ragù, bechamel, and grated parmesan cheese; "tortellini" is the most famous stuffed pasta in Italy, and it contains meat and cheese, and is served dry or in broth; when dry, with tomato sauce, meat sauce, or cream. **Tuscany**: "trippa alla fiorentina," or Florentine-style tripe, is the main feature of many trattorias; it is boiled, cut into thin slices, and sauted with oil and herbs, and finally cooked with tomatoes and basil. **Umbria**: "porchetta" is a famous and elaborate regional dish; preparation has been simplified in recent years, but the original recipe called for a hog weighing roughly 40 kilograms (90 pounds), gutted and cleaned, and stuffed with minced innards mixed with wild fennel, pepper, garlic, and salt; then run through with a large spit and turned slowly in a wood-burning oven. **Lazio**: "gnocchi alla romana," little round shapes made of semolina flour cooked in milk, set in a baking pan with butter and cheese, baked, and served "au gratin." An ideal meat dish that can accompany them is "saltimbocca," slices of veal pounded thoroughly, stuffed with "prosciutto," or ham, and a leaf of sage, cooked in butter and white wine. **Abruzzo**: among all the culinary souvenirs Italy can offer, the "confetti" of Sulmona are certainly among the best known and most sought after. **Campania**: this is the unquestioned homeland of pizza and spaghetti; what more can we add. We can only recommend that you venture beyond spaghetti with tomato sauce, and try "spaghetti con le vongole veraci," or spaghetti with clam sauce; absolutely the white clam sauce, not the red. **Puglia**: the "orecchiette," literally "little ears," are a pasta made with a hand-worked semolina flour, shaped into a little shell or ear shape; they are served with a rich and flavorful meat sauce (ragù), or else with vegetables (turnip greens) and minced anchovies. **Sicily**: a variety of vegetables is the secret to an excellent antipasto: the "caponata." Cook spinach, cauliflower, endives, and celery, separately at first, and then saute them in olive oil, sprinkled with vinegar, and filled out with olives, anchovies, and capers. In the Italian region that lies closest to Africa, the most popular dish just had to be couscous, an Arab food, made of granular semolina flour, served along with various type of fish, shellfish, and "frutti di mare."

Wines. Culinary civilization would not be complete without a fine wine, judiciously selected, accompanying the right dishes. This is a rule that holds true everywhere, but especially here, in Italy, where wine is good and generally affordable. Keep an eye out, however: fraud is common, and you should generally choose wines that have labels marked DOC ("denominazione d'origine controllata," meaning "officially certified vintage and variety") or DOCG ("denominazione d'origine controllata e garantita," meaning "officially certified and guaranteed vintage and variety") which indicate quality wines. Every region has its own wines. The best known among the red wines (rossi) are the Piedmontese varieties (Barolo, Barbera, Barbaresco, and Grignolino); the Venetian Valpolicella and Bardolino; the Emilian Lambrusco; and the famous Tuscan Chianti. Among the white wines (bianchi): Spumante from

Asti in Piedmont; Soave in Veneto; Albano in Emilia; Orvieto in Umbria, Verdicchio in the Marche, Frascati or Vino dei Castelli in Lazio; Greco di Tufo in Campania, and Malvasia in Sicily; from this last wine a strong liquorous dessert wine is made: Marsala.

And at the end of a hearty meal, irrigated with fine wines, the logical ending is to have a cup of coffee. The other popular and famous Italian beverage, the "cappuccino," is really best enjoyed for breakfast in the morning or at an afternoon coffee break; not after a big meal.

Post office & telephones

Post offices are generally open from 8:30 to 1:30; but the main post offices in the larger cities are open to the public in the afternoon as well.

Stamps are sold in the post offices but also in tobacconists, and can often be purchased at the reception desk in hotels.

Public telephones. You can make national or international phone calls from public telephones; some take a phone debit card, sold at tobacconists and at newsstands, while others take phone tokens or 100, 200, or 500 lire coins.

International dialing prefixes:

calling from Italy		calling to Italy	
Australia	0061	Australia	00139
Canada	001	Canada	01139
New Zealand	0064	New Zealand	0039
United States	001	United States	01139
Great Britain	0044	Great Britain	0039
Ireland	00353	Ireland	0039

Electricity

Electric current is either 200 or 220 volts, 50 cycles. The sockets are different in shape from American sockets; you will need an adapter, which can be purchased at any electrical equipment or hardware store.

National holidays

1 January (Capodanno, or New Year's Day), 6 January (Epifania, Easter Monday, 25 April (Festa della Liberazione, or Liberation Day, WWII), 1 May (Festa del Lavoro, or Labor Day), 15 August (Assunzione, or Assumption of the Virgin), 1 November (Ognissanti, or All Saint's Day), 8 December (Immacolata Concezione, or Immaculate Conception), 25 and 26 December (Natale and Santo Stefano, or Christmas and St. Stephen's Day).

Local holidays and festivals throughout the year

Arezzo: Giostra del Saracino, or Joust of the Saracen, a competition in medieval costume, 1st Sunday in September.
Ascoli Piceno: Torneo della Quintana, a historic tournament, 1st Sunday in August.
Assisi: Calendimaggio, Festa della Primavera, or Kalends of May, Feast of Spring, 1st week in May.
Asti: Palio or horserace, procession in historic costume , 3rd Sunday in September.
Bari: Sagra di San Nicola, a marine procession in historical costumes, 1st Saturday and Sunday in May.

Cagliari: Sagra di Sant'Efisio, a religious procession in traditional garb, 1 May.
Florence: Scoppio del Carro, or Explosion of the Cart, a fireworks display and folk event on the cathedral square.
Gubbio: Palio dei Balestrieri, tournament in historical costume, last Sunday in May.
Perugia: Umbria Jazz, a two-part jazz festival: the better-known of the two is in the summer, but the winter version is gaining popularity.
Rome: Festa dell'Epifania, Epiphany, in Piazza Navona, during the month of December, market stalls selling manger figurines.
Festa de Noaltri, meaning Our Own Party, parades, with dancing and folk songs, from 16 to 24 July.
Sassari: Cavalcata Sarda, or Sardinian Cavalcade, an equestrian parade in medieval costumes, 3rd Sunday in May.
Siena: Palio delle Contrade and Palio dell'Assunta, two all-Siena horseraces, no holds barred, respectively on 2 July and 16 August.
Spoleto: Festival dei Due Mondi, or Festival of Two Worlds: with productions of opera, theater, music, and dance, from June to July.
Venice: Carnevale, or Carnival, February, theatrical and musical performances in the lanes and theaters of Venice. You must wear a costume.
Il Redentore, Feast of the Savior, with nocturnal procession of bunting-covered boats and spectacular fireworks show, 3rd weekend in July.
Historical gondola regata along the Grand Canal, 1s Sunday in September.
Mostra del Cinema, or Film Festival, at Lido, in September.
Viareggio: Carnevale, or Carnival, procession of allegorical floats and masked parades, February.

We could devote a chapter just to the numerous processions of Holy Week, before Easter, popular and spectacular, in the south especially. The most famous processions are those of the Addolorata and of the Misteri (Mysteries) in Taranto, and on Good Friday in Trapani. Of course, the most popular event in this period is the solemn benediction of the Pope, on Easter Morning, in Piazza San Pietro (St. Peter's Square).

For more information you can contact ENIT, Via Marghera 2, 00185 Rome, tel. (06) 49711, fax 4463379.

Shopping: where and when

Fashion. If Italy means fashion, fashion means Milan: the mental association is inevitable and it is completely accurate. The most famous designers all have their show-rooms in the heart of the capital of Lombardy, concentrated among Via Montenapoleone, Via della Spiga, and Via Durini. Here it is easy to satisfy your dream of dressing like a movie star, though it is certainly expensive to attain such a dream. They are all here: Armani, Versace, Prada, Gianfranco Ferré, Nicola Trussardi, Mila Schön, Laura Biagiotti, Krizia and Moschino. Even Valentino and Fendi, who have chosen Rome as their base of operations, have their most luxurious stores in these Milanese streets.
So you cannot overlook Milan, the center and starting point of the world of fashion, but an ideal

shopping trip for fine Italian clothing extends throughout Italy. And the right item or perfect outfit can be found in the more elegant shops on the main streets of any number of Italian cities, even cities far from the main areas of production indicated below.

In the Veneto, in particular in Treviso, you can dress with taste and flair, without hurting your bank account too badly, in the youthful style of Benetton and Stefanel. Then come back to Lombardy, to Como and along the shores of Lake Como, for fine silks. In Piedmont (Biella) and in Tuscany (Prato) you can buy first-rate woolen fabrics. A stopover in Florence to buy purses and belts, especially those by Gucci. For shoes, go back to Lombardy, especially to Vigevano (in the provinice of Pavia). Last comes the Veneto (Vicenza, in particular), the perfect place to find the crowning touch — jewelry. And then of course there is the great tradition of Tuscan goldsmithery, in Arezzo and in Florence, and the other remarkable tradition of coral-working, at Torre del Greco, in the province of Naples.

Culinary specialties. A less costly sort of souvenir or gift is wine or culinary specialties, perfect, original gifts for all occasions. For the wine, the only problem is selection, but there is an equally vast array of options involved in choosing food *Made in Italy*: from the marzipan of Sicily to the "gianduiotti," luscious milk chocolates from Turin; cheeses, pasta, including the classic "maccheroni" from the south (don't miss the delightful handmade noodles "alla chitarra," named for their resemblance to guitar strings) and the more elaborate forms of meat and vegetable ravioli from Emilia Romagna.

Glass. At first glance glass might seem to pose problems of logistics, but it is actually a practical purchase: glass dealers are great experts in the art of packing glass for shipment, even in particularly complicated cases. Venice and the island of Murano are the two best places to buy glass; you will most often be tempted to buy vases or pieces of fine design, but there are excellent sets of glasses or even the smaller chandeliers.

Lace and embroideries. Remaining in the same area, on the other little Venetian island of Burano, you can buy lace, a great tradition of Italian craftsmanship; sadly, it has become prohibitively expensive, and is increasingly undercut by competition from Taiwan. Often, Italian lace is sold alongside Taiwanese lace, but the difference is obvious, and not only in the prices. Another region in which this tradition lives on gloriously is Umbria, where the most exquisite embroideries, used in religious fabrics as well, use the famous "Punto Assisi."

Antiques. Another excellent resource consists of antiques of all sorts — from knick-knacks to books, from porcelain to paintings — in the twofold option: real antiques, or excellent "recreations." The important thing is not to be confused between the two. Easier said than done; you should definitely get a certificate of authenticity, though often that is not enough, as the "recreations" can be really well done. You should develop a relationship of trust with the antiques dealer; ideally you should get a name from friends or trusted acquaintances. (Customs regulations concerning the export of antiques may also become an insurmountable obstacle to a purchase; another good reason to have a trusted reliable dealer).

Hours. Stores are generally open from Monday to Saturday, from 8:30 or 9 until 12:30 or 1 and from 3:30 or 4 until 7:30 or 8 in the evening. Usually, stores close Sunday and one other halfday during the week; a day that varies from one region to another. In the large cities, especially in the north, it is becoming more common for stores to stay open all day (9-7), especially department stores and supermarkets.

Useful things to know

The official hours of museums, art galleries, churches, and offices vary throughout Italy, from region to region. In general, in the north, the hours are much like the rest of Europe: you will often find that places stay open all day, or close only for an hour for lunch. In the south, the lunch-time break tends to be longer, especially in the warmer months, as is the case in other Mediterranean countries.

Hours of museums and monuments: this guide lists the hours in each instance.

Visiting churches: it is rare to find a religious building open from 1 pm until 3 or 4 pm; being open in the afternoon is limited to the more important cathedrals and basilicas, and not always. It is fairly common to find smaller churches entirely closed, especially if they contain valuable artworks and if the sacristan is not around to keep an eye out. Usually, if you enquire at the busiest café or shop in the area, you will soon find someone who has a key. In any case, before you enter churches, it is always wise to make sure that you have 100-, 200-, or 500-lire coins: many of the chapels, with frescoes or fine paintings, have coin-operated timed lighting, and without the right change, you cannot enjoy the art. You should not try to tour churches during religious services; in any case, dress appropriately — no short shorts or skimpy outfits.

Entertainment

Casinos: there are four casinos in Italy, all in the north — Venice, Campione (on Lake Lugano), San Remo (Imperia), and St. Vincent (Aosta). In order to get in, you must be 18 years of age, and you must show your passport of identification.

Theater and concerts. Fine performances can be found in all the main cities. To purchase tickets, you should either go directly to the theater, or else to the office of tourism, where you can find out where tickets are on advance sale (often in the largest music stores, especially for pop and rock concerts). For the most popular performers and performances, you had better be ready for an ordeal: getting a ticket to the opera at La Scala in Milan, for instance, can be quite a challenge.

Movies. In Rome, Milan, and other large cities, there are movie houses that show movies in the original language ("versione originale," or "V.O."); they are listed in the local newspaper; in all other cases, movies are dubbed into Italian.

Sports

Soccer. This game is a national obsession, the subject of endless discussions in cafes throughout Italy, every Monday morning (games are on Sunday afternoons). Tickets can be purchased at the stadium or in the surrounding areas, sold by "bagarini," or scalpers. There are amateur teams everywhere, and so you can try playing yourself. For information: Federazione Italiana Gioco Calcio, Via G. Allegri 4, 00198 Rome, tel. 06/84911.

Bicycling. The *Giro d'Italia* is a famous international bicycle race, in which the leading champions compete; it is held every year, and it is as popular as soccer. The mountain bike is a fad that has been spreading for a few years now; there are associations that organize outings and rentals. For information, you can contact the tourist offices in the larger cities.

Golf. This game has caught on more slowly in Italy than in other European countries, but there are now quite a few courses, especially in the NW and in the more expensive resort areas; many golf clubs welcome guests and rent equipment. For information: Federazione Italiana Golf, Viale Tiziano 74, 00196 Rome, tel. 06/3231825.

Mountain sports. In the summer, there is an excellent network of trails and mountain huts, especially in the Alps; it is run by the Club Alpino Italiano (CAI), which can also connect you with organizations that provide guides for the more challenging hikes and for climbing. For information: local tourist offices, or else CAI, Via Silvio Pellico 6, Milan, tel. 02/86463516. There are lovely hikes, often less daunting than the Alps, in the Apennines; note the Parco Nazionale d'Abruzzo. For information: Ufficio di Zona del Parco, Via Consultore 1, Pescasseroli, tel. 0863/91955.

In winter in the Alps, especially in the Valle d'Aosta and in the Dolomites, all sorts of skiing take places: downhill, cross-country, and by helicopter. The most expensive and chic resorts are Cortina, Courmayeur, and Cervinia where you can also iceskate, or, if you are feeling daring, go bobsledding.

Water sports. Sailing and windsurfing are popular all along the Italian coasts; the most famous spots are in Liguria, Sardinia, and along the coasts of Tuscany and Lazio. There are excellent schools for both pursuits on both Lake Como and Lake Garda. For information: Federazione Italiana Vela, Via Brigata Bisagno 2/17, Genova, tel; 010/565723. The best Italian sailing school is the Centro Velico Caprera, which offers only live-in courses in the Arcipelago della Maddalena, between Sardinia and Corsica. For information: CVC, Corso Italia 10, 20122 Milan, tel. 02/86452191.

Tennis. The finest hotels have tennis courts, which are in some cases open to those not staying at the hotel; many private tennis clubs accept guest players, and so playing a game of tennis is not a difficult thing to do. For information contact the local office of tourism.

Horseback riding. Horseback tours of the countryside are an absolute must in many centers of agritourism, especially in Tuscany, Umbria, and Lazio; in the larger cities there are also riding stables. For information: you can contact offices of tourism, but you can also contact the Associazione Nazionale per il Turismo Equestre, Via A. Borelli 5, 00161 Roma, tel. 06/4441179.

Information for Travellers
Hotels, Restaurants, and Services for Tourists

The places indicated in this section correspond either to towns described on their own, in the guidebook proper, or to towns mentioned in the routes or elsewhere, provided that they are equipped with hotels of some note. For every town, we indicate the province (abbreviation), the postal code ⊠ and the telephone prefix code ☎. As of 18th December 1998 the code must also be dialled for local calls. For those calling Italy from abroad, the local code (including the 0) must be dialled after the international code for Italy, followed by the subscriber's number. The information has been carefully checked before going to print. We would, however, advise readers to confirm certain data which is susceptible to change, before departure. All observations and suggestions are gratefully accepted.

Public offices of interest to travellers and sightseers. For the most important towns, we list addresses and telephone numbers for offices providing information and assistance to travellers and tourists (APT, Pro Loco, and so on, according to various regional organizations, often changing over time), with the symbol ⬛; for the train station, with the symbol ⬛; for the closest toll booth station, within 20 km., with the symbol ⬛, followed by the official number of the highway; for the airport, with the symbol ✈; for passenger shipping, with the symbol ⬛

Hotels. The list contains a selection of Hotels, arranged by categories according to the official classification established by the Italian Tourism Law (from ⬛⬛⬛ to ✶). For every hotel listed, we provide the postal code and the telephone prefix code, when those are different from the codes provided in the main heading of the place; we also provide the address, the telephone number, the fax number where available, the total number of rooms (with bathrooms, baths, or showers ⬛), the periods in which the hotel is open (if it is seasonal), the months or periods of closing, and, with special graphic symbols, we indicate whether or not the hotel has air conditioning ⬛, a garden or grounds ⬛, a pool ⬛, a private parking garage ⬛, or special parking arrangements ⬛, a parking lot ⬛, and – lastly – whether it is easily accessible to handicapped customers ⬛.

Restaurants. The list offered here includes restaurants chosen by TCI and arranged in five different categories (from ⬛ to ⬛). This is not an official classification, only an indicative ranking, meant to serve as a "scout," through a complex array of criteria, indicating the levels of quality, comfort, setting, and price, in declining order, from the top luxury restaurant to the most unpretentious and affordable restaurants. For each restaurant, we provide the name, the address, the telephone number, and fax number where available; we also indicate the capacity for seating (where two numbers are given, that indicates min./max. capacity when the usual dining hall is somehow expanded, perhaps by gardens or terraces), the days and periods of the year when the restaurant is closed. Also, special graphic symbols indicate: whether it is necessary to reserve ⬛, whether there is private parking ⬛, a garden ⬛, or air conditioning ⬛. The symbol ⬛ specifies the type of cooking (either classical Italian, regional, or distinctly local, international, or simply fine cuisine) as well as indications of any culinary specialties.

Facilities for winter sports. For the main resorts for winter sports, we provide a brief description of the facilities, following the symbol ⬛.

References to maps. Public offices and items of interest to sightseers, hotels, and restaurants in the towns for which maps are provided are followed by a letter and number which should refer you to its location on the map itself (when there is more than one map, the references are identified by a Roman numeral for the map). The phrase *not shown on map* means, of course, that the hotel or restaurant is off the map.

Aeolian Islands / Isole Eolie (ME)   ☎ 090

🅹 *AA*, at Lipari, Corso Vittorio Emanuele 239, tel. 9880095, fax 9811190; *Information Office*, Corso Vittorio Emanuele 202, tel. 9880095.

⚓ Transportation to Messina and Milazzo.

at Lipari   ✉ 98055

Hotels and restaurants

**** **Villa Meligunis** Via Marte 7, tel. 9812426, fax 9880149; closed November-February; 37 rms. ▥; 🕮🕯.

*** **Carasco** township of Porto delle Genti, tel. 9811605, fax 9811828; seasonal; 89 rms. ▥; 🕮 ℗.

*** **Giardino sul Mare** Via Maddalena 65, tel. 9811004, fax 9880150; 40 rms. ▥; 🖭; 🕮 🗛.

👖👖 **Filippino** Piazza Municipio, tel. 9811002 ⊠; fax 9812878; ⑂ Aeolian (seafood); 200 capacity; closed Monday in the off season, for a certain period of time between November and December; 🖭.

👖 **E Pulera** Via Diana, tel. 9811158 ⊠; ⑂ Aeolian; 80 capacity; seasonal; ❀.

at Panarea   ✉ 98055

Hotels

*** **Cincotta** (no restaurant), Contrada S. Pietro, ⊠ 98050, tel. 983014, fax 983211; seasonal; 29 rms. ▥; 🖭🕮🗛🕯.

*** **La Piazza** (no restaurant), Via S. Pietro, tel. 983176, fax 983003; seasonal; 25 rms. ▥; 🕮🗛 🕯.

at Malfa, on the Isola Salina   ✉ 98050

Hotels

*** **Signum** Via Scalo 15, tel. 9844222, fax 9844102; 16 rms. ▥; 🕮.

at Santa Marina Salina, on the Isola Salina   ✉ 98050

Restaurants

👖 **Portobello** Via Bianchi 1, tel. 9843125; ⑂ Aeolian (seafood); 25/100 capacity; closed Wednesday in winter, November.

at Strómboli   ✉ 98050

Hotels

*** **La Sirenetta** township of Ficogrande, Via Marina 33, tel. 986025, fax 986124; seasonal; 43 rms. ▥; 🕮 🗛.

at Vulcano   ✉ 98050

Hotels

*** **Eolian** at Porto Ponente, tel. 9852151, fax 9852153; seasonal; 88 rms. ▥; 🕮 ℗ 🕯

Agrigento   ✉ 92100 ☎ 0922

🅹 *AAPT*, Viale della Vittoria 255, tel. 401354, fax 25185 (*B3*); *AA*, Via Battisti 15, tel. 20454 (*A2*).

🚉 *Stazione F.S. (State railway station)*, Piazza Marconi 3, tel. 25669.

Hotels and restaurants

**** **Kaos** Villaggio Pirandello, tel. 598622, fax 598770; 105 rms. ▥; 🕯🕮 🗛 ℗; (*C1*).

**** **Villa Athena** Via dei Templi 33, tel. 596288, fax 402180; 40 rms. ▥; 🖭🕮 🗛 ℗; (*B-C2*).

👖 **Black Horse** Via Celauro 8, tel. 23223; ⑂ Sicilian (seafood); 55 capacity; closed Sunday; (*A2*).

at Villaggio Mosè, km. 8

Hotels

**** **Jolly dei Templi** Parco Angeli, tel. 606144, fax 606685; 146 rms. ▥; 🖭🕮 🗛 ℗ 🕯.

*** **Tre Torri** Contrada Fegotto, tel. 606733, fax 607839; 118 rms. ▥; 🖭 🗛 ℗.

Alberobello (BA)   ✉ 70011 ☎ 080

🚉 *Stazione F.S. (State railroad station)*, Via Margherita, tel. 9323308.

Hotels and restaurants

**** **Dei Trulli** Via Cadore 32, tel. 9323555, fax 9323560; 28 rms. ▥; 🖭🕮 🗛 ℗.

*** **Astoria** Viale Bari 11, tel. 9323320, fax 721290; 47 rms. ▥; 🕮🖩 ℗ 🕯.

👖👖 **Il Poeta Contadino** Via Indipendenza 21, tel. 721917 ⊠; ⑂ Pugliese fine cuisine; 70 capacity; closed Sunday evening and Monday except in summer, for a certain period of time in January and between June and July; 🖭 ℗.

👖 **Chiusa di Chietri** state road (S.S.) 172 at km. 29.800, tel. 9325481; ⑂ Pugliese and classical; 600 capacity; closed Tuesday, November; 🖭 ❀ ℗; also hotel.

👖 **Trullo d'Oro** Via Cavallotti 27, tel. 721820; ⑂ Pugliese and classical; 100/150 capacity; closed Monday, Epiphany (6 January)/beginning-February; 🖭 ❀.

Alghero (SS)   ✉ 07041 ☎ 079

🅹 *AA*, Piazza Portaterra 9, tel. 979054, fax 974881; *EPT, Information Office*, Aeroporto Fertilia, tel. 935124 (seasonal).

🚉 *Stazione Ferrovie della Sardegna*, Via don Minzoni, tel. 950785.

✈ *Airport* at Fertilia (10 km. to the NE), tel. 935033. *Alitalia*, airport, tel. 935033.

Hotels and restaurants

**** **Calabona** township of Calabona, tel. 975728, fax 981046; seasonal; 110 rms. ▥; 🖭🕮 🗛 ℗ 🕯.

**** **Villa Las Tronas** Lungomare Valencia 1, tel. 981818, fax 981044; 29 rms. ▥; 🖭🕮 🗛 ℗.

*** **Continental** (no restaurant), Via F.lli Kennedy 66, tel. 975250, fax 981046; seasonal; 32 rms. ▥; 🕮🗛 ℗.

*** **Florida**, Via Lido 15, tel. 950500, fax 985424; 78 rms. ▥; 🖭🕮 🗛 ℗.

👖👖 **La Lepanto** Via Carlo Alberto 135, tel. 979116; ⑂ Sardinian; 160 capacity; closed Monday in winter; 🖭.

👖 **Al Tuguri** Via Maiorca 113, tel. 976772 ⊠; ⑂ Sardinian (seafood); 35 capacity; closed Sunday, mid-December/mid-January; 🖭.

at Fertilia, km. 6   ✉ 07040

Hotels

*** **Bellavista** Lungomare Rovigno 13, tel. 930166, fax 930124; 46 rms. ▥; 🖭.

Amalfi (SA)   ✉ 84011 ☎ 089

🅹 *AA*, Corso Roma 19/21, tel. 871107.

♰ *Vietri* (A3) km. 20.

Hotels and restaurants

**** **Il Saraceno** Via Augustariccio 25, tel. 831148, fax 831595; seasonal; 56 rms. ▥; 🖭🕮 🗛 ℗.

**** **Miramalfi** Via Quasimodo 3, tel. 871588, fax 871287; 48 rms. ▥; 🗛 ℗.

*** **Aurora** (no restaurant), Piazzale dei Protontini 7, tel. 871209, fax 872980; seasonal; 29 rms. ▥; 🕮 🖭.

★★★ **Dei Cavalieri** Via M. Comite 26, tel. 831333, fax 831354; 60 rms. 🅿️🅿️🅿️🅿️🅿️

★★★ **La Bussola** Lungomare dei Cavalieri 16, tel. 871533, fax 871369; 63 rms. 🅿️🅿️🅿️

🍴 **Gemma** Via Fra' Gerardo Sasso 10, tel. 871345 🅿️; 🍴 Classical (seafood); 40/60 capacity; closed Wednesday except in summer, mid-January/mid-February; 🅿️.

🍴 **La Caravella** Via M. Camera 12, tel. 871029 🅿️; 🍴 Amalfi (seafood); 40/50 capacity; closed Tuesday, and for a certain period of time in November; 🅿️.

🍴 **Smeraldino** Piazzale dei Protontini 1, tel. 871070; 🍴 Amalfi (seafood); 120/200 capacity; closed Wednesday, and for a certain period of time between January and February; 🅿️.

Anagni (FR) ✉ 03012 ☎ 0775

📋 *Pro Loco*, Piazza Innocenzo III, tel. 727852.

🚉 *Stazione F.S. (State railroad station)*, Anagni Scalo km. 9, tel. 767077.

🚶 *Anagni-Fiuggi T.* (A1) km. 7.

Hotel and restaurants

★★★ **Villa La Floridiana**, Via Casilina at km. 63.700, tel. 769960, fax 769961; closed for a certain period of time between August and September; 9 rms. 🅿️🅿️🅿️🅿️.

🍴 **Della Fontana** at Osteria della Fontana, Via Casilina 23, tel. 768577; 🍴 Ciociaria and classical (seafood); 200 capacity; closed evening of Sunday and of Monday, and for a certain period of time in August.

Ancona ✉ 60100 ☎ 071

📋 *APT*, Via Thaon de Revel 4, tel. 33249 *(D6)*; *Information Office*, Stazione Centrale, seasonal, tel. 41703 *(E1)*.

🚉 *Stazione F.S. (State railroad station)*, Piazza Rosselli, tel. 43933.

🚶 *Ancona Nord*, km. 15, *Ancona Sud*, km. 13 (A14).

✈ *Aeroporto Raffaello Sanzio*, Falconara Marittima, township of Castelferretti (18 km. NW), tel. 56257. *Alitalia, Passenger agency*, Piazza Roma 21, tel. 2075892 (C3).

⚓ *Stazione Marittima (Marine Terminal)*: information c/o Capitaneria di Porto, Banchina Sauro, tel. 2074697; oppure *IAT*, seasonal, tel. 201183.

Hotels and restaurants

★★★ **G.H. Palace** (no restaurant), Lungomare Vanvitelli 24, ✉ 60121, tel. 201813, fax 2074832; closed Christmas-Epiphany (6 January); 41 rms. 🅿️🅿️🅿️.

★★★ **Jolly Miramare** Rupi di Via XXIX Settembre 14, ✉ 60122, tel. 201171, fax 206823; 89 rms. 🅿️🅿️🅿️🅿️.

★★★ **City** (no restaurant), Via Matteotti 112/114, ✉ 60121, tel. 2070949, fax 2070949; 39 rms. 🅿️🅿️🅿️.

★★★ **Fortuna** (no restaurant) Piazza Rosselli 15, ✉ 60126, tel. 42663, fax 42662; 57 rms. 🅿️🅿️🅿️.

🍴 **Passetto** Piazza IV Novembre 1, ✉ 60124, tel. 33214; 🍴 Marche and classical; 60/80 capacity; closed Monday and Sunday evening, and for a certain period of time in August; 🅿️🅿️.

🍴 **Moretta** Piazza Plebiscito 52, ✉ 60121, tel. 202317 🅿️; 🍴 Marche (seafood); 80/100 capacity; closed Sunday, and for a certain period of time in January; 🅿️🅿️.

at Portonovo, km. 12 ✉ 60020

Hotels

★★★ **Emilia** Via Poggio 149, tel. 801145, fax 801330; closed January-February; 30 rms. 🅿️🅿️🅿️🅿️🅿️.

Aosta/Aoste ✉ 11100 ☎ 0165

📋 *Ufficio Regionale Informazioni Turistiche*: Palazzo del Municipio, Piazza E. Chanoux 8, tel. 236627, fax 34657; *APT*, Piazza E. Chanoux 3, tel. 33352, fax 40532.

🚉 *Stazione F.S. (State railroad station)*, Piazza Manzetti 1, tel. 262057.

🚶 *Aosta* (A5) km. 5.

Hotels and restaurants

★★★ **Europe** Piazza Narbonne 8, tel. 236363, fax 40566; 71 rms. 🅿️🅿️🅿️🅿️.

★★★ **Valle d'Aosta** (no restaurant), Corso Ivrea 146, tel. 41845, fax 236660; closed for a certain period of time in December; 105 rms. 🅿️🅿️🅿️🅿️.

★★★ **Ambassador** Via Duca degli Abruzzi 2, tel. 42230, fax 236851; 41 rms. 🅿️🅿️🅿️.

★★ **Mignon** (no restaurant), Viale Gran S. Bernardo 7, tel. 40980, fax 43227; 26 rms. 🅿️🅿️🅿️.

🍴 **Le Foyer** Corso Ivrea 146, tel. 32136, fax 239474 🅿️; 🍴 fine cuisine; 50 capacity; closed Tuesday, and for a certain period of time in January and July; 🅿️.

🍴 **Vecchia Aosta** Piazza Porte Pretoriane 4, tel. 361186 🅿️; 🍴 Val d'Aostan and French; 90 capacity; closed Wednesday, and for a certain period of time in June and October; 🌸.

🍴 **Vecchio Ristoro** Via Tourneuve 4, tel. 33238 🅿️; 🍴 Val d'Aostan and classical; 34 capacity; closed Sunday and at midday on Monday, period of closing may vary.

Aquilèia (UD) ✉ 33051 ☎ 0431

📋 *APT*, seasonal, Piazza Capitolo, tel. 919491.

🚶 *Palmanova* (A4) km. 14.

Hotels and restaurants

★★★ **Patriarchi** Via Giulia Augusta 12, tel. 919595, fax 919596; 23 rms. 🅿️🅿️🅿️.

🍴 **Colombara** at La Colombara, Via S. Zilli 42, tel. 91513 🅿️; 🍴 Friulian (seafood); 140 capacity; closed Monday; 🅿️.

Arezzo ✉ 52100 ☎ 0575

📋 *APT*, Piazza Risorgimento 116, tel. 23952, fax 28042 *(B-C1)*; *Information Office*, Piazza della Repubblica 28, tel. 377678.

🚉 *Stazione F.S. (State railroad station)*, Piazza della Repubblica 1, tel. 22663; *Stazione La Ferroviaria Italiana*, Via Concini, tel. 355872.

🚶 *Arezzo* (A1) km. 11.

Hotels and restaurants

★★★ **Etrusco** Via Fleming 39, tel. 984067, fax 382131; 80 rms. 🅿️🅿️🅿️🅿️.

★★★ **Europa** (no restaurant), Via Spinello 43, tel. 357701, fax 357703; 46 rms. 🅿️🅿️🅿️.

★★★ **Milano** Via Madonna del Prato 83, tel. 26836, fax 21925; 27 rms. 🅿️🅿️🅿️.

★★★ **Minerva** Via Fiorentina 4, tel. 370390, fax 302415; 132 rms. 🅿️🅿️🅿️🅿️.

🍴 **Buca di San Francesco** Via S. Francesco 1, tel. 23271; 🍴 Arezzo; 60 capacity; closed Monday evening and Tuesday.

🍴 **Cantuccio** Via Madonna del Prato 76, tel. 26830; 🍴 Arezzo and classical; 60 capacity; closed Wednesday, and for a certain period of time in August.

Arona (NO)   ✉ 28041 ☎ 0322

- *i* IAT, Piazzale Duca d'Aosta, tel. 243601.
- *Stazione F.S. (State railroad station)*, Piazzale Duca d'Aosta, tel. 242044.
- ⵜ *Arona (A26) km. 7.*

- ★★★ **Atlantic** Corso della Repubblica 124, tel. 46521, fax 48358; 79 rms. 🕮; 💷 &;
- ★★★ **Florida** (no restaurant), Piazza del Popolo 32, tel. 46212, fax 46213; closed November-December; 25 🕮.
- ★★★ **Giardino** Corso della Repubblica 1, tel. 45994, fax 249401; 56 rms. 🕮; ♨ &.
- ▯▮▯ **Taverna del Pittore** Piazza del Popolo 39, tel. 243366, fax 48016 ✕; 〗Ⅱ fine cuisine; 48 capacity; closed Monday, November and Christmas.
- ▮▮ **Vecchia Arona** Lungolago Marconi 17, tel. 242469 ✕; 〗Ⅱ fine cuisine; 35 capacity; closed Friday, and for a certain period of time in June and in November; 💷.

Ascoli Piceno   ✉ 63100 ☎ 0736

- *i* APT, Corso Mazzini 229, tel. 257267 (B2-3); Information Office, Piazza del Popolo 1, tel. 253045, fax 252391).
- *Stazione F.S. (State railroad station)*, tel. 341004.
- ⵜ *access at km. 2* (Highway intersection Ascoli P.-Porto d'Ascoli/A14).

Hotels and restaurants

- ★★★ **Gioli** (no restaurant), Viale De Gasperi 14, tel. 255550, fax 255550; 56 rms. 🕮; 💷.
- ★★★ **Marche** Viale Kennedy 34, tel. 45475, fax 342812; 32 rms. 🕮; &.
- ★★★ **Pennile** (no restaurant), Via Spalvieri, tel. 41645, fax 342755; 28 rms. 🕮; ♨ 💷.
- ▮▮ **Gallo d'Oro** Corso Vittorio Emanuele 13, tel. 253520 ✕; 〗Ⅱ Marche fine cuisine; 150 capacity; closed Sunday, Christmas-New Year's Day, and for a certain period of time in August; 💷.
- ▮▮ **Tornasacco** Piazza del Popolo 36, tel. 254151 ✕; 〗Ⅱ Marche; 56 capacity; closed Friday, and for a certain period of time in July and at Christmas; 💷.

at Colle San Marco, km. 12

Hotels

- ★★★ **Roxy Miravalle** tel. 351100, fax 351100; mid-May/September; 52 rms. 🕮; ♨ ♨ 💷 &.

Asolo (TV)   ✉ 31011 ☎ 0423

- *i* IAT, Via Santa Caterina 258, tel. 529046.

Restaurants

- ▮▮ **Hosteria Ca' Derton** Piazza D'Annunzio 11, tel. 529648 ✕; 〗Ⅱ Venetian; 45 capacity; closed Monday, and for a certain period of time between July and August; 💷.
- ▮▮ **Tavernetta** Via Schiavonesca 45, tel. 952273; 〗Ⅱ Venetian regional and classical; 45 capacity; closed Tuesday, and for a certain period of time in July; 💷.

Assisi (PG)   ✉ 06081 ☎ 075

- *i* APT, Piazza del Comune 27, tel. 812534, fax 813727 (B3-4).
- *Stazione F.S. (State railroad station)*, Santa Maria degli Angeli, km. 4, tel. 8040272.
- ⵜ *Perugia* (Highway intersection Perugia-Bettolle / A1) km. 18.

Hotels and restaurants

- ★★★ **Subasio** Via Frate Elia 2, tel. 812206, fax 816691; 61 rms. 🕮; 💷; (A1).
- ★★★ **Dei Priori** Corso Mazzini 15, tel. 812237, fax 816804; March/November, and Christmas-Epiphany (6 January); 34 rms. 🕮; 💷 &; (B4).
- ★★★ **Umbra** Via degli Archi 6, tel. 812240, fax 813653; closed mid-January/mid-March; 25 rms. 🕮; ♨ &; (B3).
- ★★★ **Windsor Savoia** Viale Marconi 1, ✉ 06082, tel. 812210, fax 813659; 34 rms. 🕮; ♨ &; (B1-2).
- ▮▮ **Frantoio** Vicolo Illuminati, tel. 812977, fax 812841; 〗Ⅱ Umbrian (truffles); 300 capacity; 💷; also hotel; (A-B2).
- ▮▮ **Medio Evo** Via Arco dei Priori 4/B, tel. 813068 ✕; 〗Ⅱ Umbrian and classical; 80/120 capacity; closed Wednesday and evening of Sunday, and for a certain period of time January and July; 💷; (B3).
- ▮▮ **Taverna dell'Arco-da Bino** Via S. Gregorio 8, tel. 812383 ✕; 〗Ⅱ Umbrian; 90 capacity; closed Tuesday, Epiphany (6 January)/mid-February, and for a certain period in July; (B3).

Bari   ✉ 70100 ☎ 080

- *i* EPT, Piazza Moro 33/a, tel. 5242361 (D5); Information Office, tel. 5242244.
  AA, Corso Vittorio Emanuele II 68, tel. 5219951 (C5).
  TCI, Via Melo 259/261, tel. 5242448 (D5).
- *Stazione F.S. (State railroad station)*, Piazza Moro, tel. 5216801; *Ferrovia Bari-Nord*, Piazza Moro 50/b, tel. 5213577; *Ferrovie Appulo Lucane*, Corso Italia 6, tel. 5725111; *Ferrovie Sud-Est*, Via Oberdan, tel. 5530274.
- ⵜ *Bari Nord (A14 and A16) km. 8; Bari Sud (A14) km. 9.*
- ✈ *Aeroporto Civile (Town Airport)* Bari-Palese km. 10, tel. 5382370.
  Alitalia, Via Calefati 37/41, tel. 5244440 (C5).
- ⚓ *Stazione Marittima (Marine Terminal)*, Molo San Vito, tel. 5235205.

Hotels and restaurants

- ★★★ **G.H. Ambasciatori** Via Omodeo 51, ✉ 70125, tel. 5010077, fax 5021678; 177 rms. 🕮; 💷 ♨ ♨ 💷 💷 &; (not shown on map).
- ★★★ **Jolly** Via G. Petroni 15, ✉ 70124, tel. 5564366, fax 5565219; 164 rms. 🕮; 💷 💷 &; (D5).
- ★★★ **Palace Hotel** Via Lombardi 13, ✉ 70122, tel. 5216551, fax 5211499; 200 rms. 🕮; 💷 💷 💷; (C4).
- ★★★ **Victor** (no restaurant), Via Nicolai 69/71, ✉ 70122, tel. 5216600, fax 5216600; 77 rms. 🕮; 💷 💷; (D4).
- ★★★ **Boston** (no restaurant), Via Piccinni 155, ✉ 70122, tel. 5216633, fax 5246802; 70 rms. 🕮; 💷 💷; (C4).
- ★★★ **Windsor** (no restaurant), Via Parallela Amoruso 62/7, ✉ 70124, tel. 5610011, fax 5510011; 79 rms. 🕮; 💷 💷; (not shown on map).
- ▮▮ **Ai 2 Ghiottoni** Via Putignani 11, ✉ 70121, tel. 5232240; 〗Ⅱ Pugliese and classical; 180 capacity; closed Sunday, and for a certain period of time in August; 💷; (C5).
- ▮▮ **Nuova Vecchia Bari** Via Dante 47, ✉ 70121, tel. 5216496 ✕; 〗Ⅱ Bari; 100 capacity; closed Friday and evening of Sunday, and for a certain period of time in August; (C5).
- ▮▮ **Piccinni** Via Piccinni 28, ✉ 70122, tel. 5211227 ✕; 〗Ⅱ Pugliese and classical; 60 capacity; closed Sunday, and for a certain period of time in August; 💷 ❀; (C5).

Bellagio (CO) ☒ 22021 ☎ 031

ℹ️ *IAT*, Piazza della Chiesa 14, tel. 950204, fax 951551 (*A-B1*).

🚂 *Stazione F.S. (State railroad station)*, Lecco km. 22, tel. 0341/361317.

Hotels and restaurants

✯✯✯ **G.H. Villa Serbelloni** Via Roma 1, tel. 950216, fax 951529; seasonal; 85 rms. 🕮; 🏤 ♨ ⛵ 🍽️ 🅿️ ♿.

✯✯✯ **Belvedere** Via Valassina 31, tel. 950410, fax 950102; seasonal; 58 rms. 🕮; ♨ ⛵ 🍽️ 🅿️.

✯✯✯ **Florence** Piazza Mazzini 46, tel. 950342, fax 951722; seasonal; 33 rms. (31 🕮); ♿.

✯✯ **Fioroni** Viale D. Vitali 2, tel. 950392, fax 951970; 14 rms. 🕮; 🅿️.

🍴 **Silvio** Via Carcano 12, tel. 950322; 🍽️ Lake Como; 200 capacity; closed Epiphany (6 January)/February; ♣ 🅿️; also hotel.

Bergamo ☒ 24100 ☎ 035

ℹ️ *APT*, Viale V. Emanuele 20, tel. 210204-213185, fax 230184 (*C2-3*); *IAT*, Viale Papa Giovanni XXIII 106, tel. 242226, fax 242994 (*E4*) and Vicolo Aquila Nera 2, tel. 232730 (seasonal, *A2*).

🚂 *Stazione F.S. (State railroad station)*, Piazza Marconi 7, tel. 247624.

🏩 *Bergamo* (*A4*) km. 3.

✈️ *Airport* at Orio al Serio, km. 3.5, tel. 326323.
Alitalia, Via Casalino 5, tel. 224425 (*D4*).

Hotels and restaurants

✯✯✯ **Cappello d'Oro** Viale Giovanni XXIII 12, ☒ 24121, tel. 232503, fax 242946; 120 rms. 🕮; 🏤 🍽️ 🅿️ ♿; (*D3*).

✯✯✯ **Starhotel Cristallo Palace** Via B. Ambiveri 35, ☒ 24126, tel. 311211, fax 312031; 90 rms. 🕮; 🏤 ⛵ 🍽️; (*not shown on map*).

✯✯✯ **Arli** (no restaurant), Largo Porta Nuova 12, ☒ 24122, tel. 222014, fax 239732; 56 rms. 🕮; 🍽️ 🅿️ ♿; (*D3*).

✯✯✯ **Piemontese** (no restaurant), Piazza G. Marconi 11, ☒ 24122, tel. 242629, fax 230400; 57 rms. 🕮; 🏤 🍽️; (*E4*).

🍴🍴🍴 **Vittorio** Viale Giovanni XXIII 21, ☒ 24121, tel. 218060 ☒; 🍽️ Bergamasque and classical; 130 capacity; closed Wednesday, and for a certain period of time in August; 🏤 🅿️; (*D4*).

🍴🍴 **Lio Pellegrini** Via S. Tomaso 47, ☒ 24121, tel. 247813 ☒; 🍽️ Tuscan and fine cuisine; 50 capacity; closed Monday and at midday on Tuesday, and for a certain period of time in January and in August; ♣; (*B4*).

🍴 **öl Giopì e la Margì** Via Borgo Palazzo 27, ☒ 24125, tel. 242366 ☒; 🍽️ Bergamasque; 80 capacity; closed Sunday evening and Monday, and for a certain period of time in January and August; 🏤; (*C5*).

in Bergamo Alta

Hotels and restaurants

✯✯ **Agnello d'Oro** Via Gombito 22, ☒ 24129, tel. 249883, fax 235612; 20 rms. 🕮; (*A2*).

🍴 **Trattoria del Teatro** Piazza Mascheroni 3, ☒ 24129, tel. 238862; 🍽️ Bergamasque; 80 capacity; closed Monday, and for a certain period of time in July; 🏤; (*A1*).

Bologna ☒ 40100 ☎ 051

ℹ️ *APT*, Piazza Maggiore 6, tel. 239660 (*D3*); Stazione F.S., tel. 246541 (*A3*); airport, tel. 6472036.

🚂 *Stazione F.S. (State railroad station)*, Piazza Medaglie d'Oro 4, tel. 246490.

🏩 *Bologna Borgo Panigale* (*A1*) km. 8; *Bologna Arcoveggio* (*A13*) km. 5; *Bologna San Lazzaro* (*A14*) km. 8.

✈️ *Aeroporto G. Marconi*, Borgo Panigale, Via Triumvirato 84 (6 km. toward the NW), tel. 311578.
Alitalia, Via Marconi 34, tel. 6300111 (*B3*).

Hotels

✯✯✯ **Al Cappello Rosso** (no restaurant), Via de' Fusari 9, ☒ 40123, tel. 261891, fax 227179; 33 rms. 🕮; (*D3*).

✯✯✯ **Corona d'Oro 1890** (no restaurant), Via G. Oberdan 12, ☒ 40126, tel. 236456, fax 262679; closed for a certain period of time in August; 35 rms. 🕮; 🏤 🍽️ ♿; (*C-D4*).

✯✯✯ **Holiday Inn Bologna Tower** Viale Lenin 43, ☒ 40138, tel. 6010909, fax 6010700; 150 rms. 🕮; 🏤 🍽️ 🅿️ ♿; (*not shown on map*).

✯✯✯ **Internazionale** (no restaurant), Via dell'Indipendenza 60, ☒ 40121, tel. 245544, fax 249544; 120 rms. 🕮; 🏤 🍽️ ♿; (*B4*).

✯✯✯ **Royal Hotel Carlton** Via Montebello 8, ☒ 40121, tel. 249361, fax 249724; 251 rms. 🕮; 🏤 ♨ 🍽️; (*B3*).

✯✯✯ **Starhotel Milano Excelsior** Via Pietramellara 51, ☒ 40121, tel. 246178, fax 249448; 70 rms. 🕮; 🏤 🍽️; (*A3*).

✯✯✯ **Astoria** (no restaurant), Via F.lli Rosselli 14, ☒ 40121, tel. 521410, fax 524739; 38 rms. 🕮; 🏤 🍽️ 🅿️ ♿; (*A-B2*).

✯✯✯ **City Hotel** (no restaurant), Via Magenta 10, ☒ 40128, tel. 372676, fax 372032; 60 rms. 🕮; 🏤 ♨ 🍽️ 🅿️; (*not shown on map*).

✯✯✯ **Dei Commercianti** (no restaurant), Via de' Pignattari 11, ☒ 40124, tel. 233052, fax 224733; 35 rms. 🕮; 🏤 🍽️ ♿; (*D3-4*).

✯✯✯ **La Pioppa** Via M. Emilio Lepido 217, tel. 400234, fax 402079; 42 rms. 🕮; 🏤 ♨ 🍽️ 🅿️; (*not shown on map*).

✯✯✯ **Orologio** (no restaurant), Via IV Novembre 10, ☒ 40123, tel. 231253, fax 260552; 31 rms. 🕮; 🏤 🍽️; (*D3*).

✯✯✯ **Re Enzo** (no restaurant), Via Santa Croce 26, ☒ 40122, tel. 523322, fax 554035; 51 rms. 🕮; 🏤 ♿; (*C1*).

✯✯✯ **San Felice** (no restaurant), Via Riva Reno 2, ☒ 40122, tel. 557457, fax 558258; closed mid-July/at the end of August; 36 rms. 🕮; 🍽️; (*C1*).

✯✯✯ **Touring** (no restaurant), Via de' Mattuiani 1/2, ☒ 40124, tel. 584305, fax 334763; 31 rms. (29 🕮); 🏤 🍽️; (*E4*).

Restaurants

🍴🍴🍴 **Pappagallo** Piazza Mercanzia 3, ☒ 40125, tel. 232807, fax 232907 ☒; 🍽️ Emilian and classical; 80 capacity; closed Sunday in summer at evening on Saturday; 🏤; (*D4*).

🍴🍴🍴 **Antica Trattoria del Cacciatore** Via Caduti di Casteldebole 25, ☒ 40132, tel. 564203, fax 567128; 🍽️ Emilian and classical; 300 capacity; closed Monday and evening of Sunday, New Year's-Epiphany (6 January), and for a certain period of time in August; 🏤 ♣ 🅿️; (*not shown on map*).

🍴🍴🍴 **Bitone** Via Emilia Levante 111, ☒ 40139, tel. 546110 ☒; 🍽️ Emilian; 90 capacity; closed Monday and Tuesday, August; 🏤; (*E6, not shown on map*).

🍴🍴🍴 **Rodrigo** Via della Zecca 2/H, ☒ 40121, tel. 220445, fax 220445 ☒; 🍽️ Bolognan and classical; 65 capacity; closed Sunday, and for a certain period of time in August; 🏤; (*D3*).

🍴🍴🍴 **Rosteria Luciano** Via Sauro 19, ☒ 40121, tel. 231249, fax 260948 ☒; 🍽️ Bolognan; 45/60 capacity; closed Wednesday, mid-July/mid-August; 🏤; (*C3*).

¶¶ Carlo Via Marchesana 6, ⊠ 40124, tel. 233227 ⊠; ⅗⅟ Bolognan and classical; 40/120 capacity; closed Tuesday and evening of Sunday, and for a certain period of time in January and in August; ✦; (D4).

¶¶ Diana Via dell'Indipendenza 24, ⊠ 40121, tel. 231302 ⊠; ⅗⅟ Emilian; 100/150 capacity; closed Monday, and for a certain period of time in January and August; ▣ ✦; (C3-4).

¶¶ Duttòur Balanzon Via Fossalta 3, ⊠ 40125, tel. 232098; ⅗⅟ Bolognan and classical; 180 capacity; closed Tuesday; ▣; (D4).

¶¶ Nuovi Notai Via de' Pignattari 1, ⊠ 40124, tel. 228694 ⊠; ⅗⅟ Emilian; 65/80 capacity; closed Sunday; (D3-4).

¶¶ Trattoria Leonida Vicolo Alemagna 2, ⊠ 40125, tel. 239742 ⊠; ⅗⅟ Emilian; 55/75 capacity; closed Sunday (except for a certain period of time of fiera), and a certain period of August; ▣ ✦; (D4).

at San Làzzaro di Sàvena, km. 6   ⊠ 40068

Hotels

★★★ Le Siepi a Idice, Via Emilia 514, tel. 6256200, fax 6256243; closed for a certain period of August and December; 39 rms. ▨; ♯ P &.

Bolzano/Bozen   ⊠ 39100 ☎ 0471

▣ *APT*, Piazza Walther 8, tel. 970660, fax 980300, *Ufficio Provinciale per il Turismo*, Piazza Parrocchia 11, tel. 993808.

🚆 *Stazione F.S. (State railroad station)*, tel. 974292.

✟ *Bolzano Sud or Bolzano Nord (A22) km. 5.*

Hotels and restaurants

★★★ Alpi Via Alto Adige 35, tel. 970535, fax 971929; 110 rms. ▨; ▣ ▣.

★★★ Parkhotel Laurin Via Laurin 4, tel. 311000, fax 311148; 96 rms. ▨; ▣ ♯ ≋ ▣.

★★★ Scala-Stiegl Via Brennero 11, tel. 976222, fax 981141; 65 rms. ▨; ♯ ≋ ▣ P.

★★★ Città-Stadt Piazza Walther 21, tel. 975221, fax 976688; 92 rms. (82 ▨); ▣ P &.

★★ Lewald Via Maso della Pieve 17, tel. 250330, fax 251916; closed for a certain period of time in February and in July; 14 rms. ▨; ♯ ≋ ▣ P.

¶⅟¶ Belle Epoque Via Laurin 4, tel. 311000, fax 311148 ⊠; ⅗⅟ classical; ▣ ✦; of the Park Hotel Laurin.

¶¶ Da Abramo Piazza Gries 16, tel. 280141, fax 288214 ⊠; ⅗⅟ classical; 70/100 capacity; closed Sunday, and for a certain period of time in August; ✦.

¶ Posta Vicolo Parrocchia 6, tel. 974043; ⅗⅟ classical; 100/130 capacity; closed Tuesday.

Bordighera (IM)   ⊠ 18012 ☎ 0184

▣ *IAT*, Via Roberto I (Palazzo del Parco), tel. 262322.

🚆 *Stazione F.S. (State railroad station)*, tel. 262209.

✟ *Bordighera (A10) km. 4.*

Hotels and restaurants

★★★ G.H. Cap Ampelio Via Virgilio 5, tel. 264333, fax 264244; closed November/Christmas; 100 rms. ▨; ▣♯≋ ▣ P.

★★★ G.H. del Mare Via Portico della Punta 34, tel. 262201, fax 262394; closed mid-October/mid-December; 107 rms. ▨; ▣ ♯ ≋ P &.

★★★ Astoria Via T. Tasso 2, tel. 262906, fax 2621612; closed November; 24 rms. ▨; ♯ P.

★★★ Bel Sit Via dei Colli 120, tel. 264114, fax 264134; 25 rms. ▨; ▣ ♯ ≋ P.

★★★ Villa Elisa Via Romana 70, tel. 261313, fax 261942; closed November/mid-December; 35 rms. ▨; ♯≋ ▣ P.

¶⅟¶ Via Romana Via Romana 57, tel. 266681 ⊠; ⅗⅟ Mediterranean (seafood); 40 capacity; closed Wednesday and midday, and a certain period of time of February and October; ▣.

¶¶ Carletto Via Vittorio Emanuele 339, tel. 261725 ⊠; ⅗⅟ Ligurian; 35 capacity; closed Wednesday, and for a certain period of time in July, and between November and December; ▣.

Brescia   ⊠ 25100 ☎ 030

▣ *APT*, Corso Zanardelli 38, tel. 45052, fax 293284 (C4); *IAT*, Corso Zanardelli 34, tel. 43418 (C4).

🚆 *Stazione F.S. (State railroad station)*, Viale Stazione, tel. 37961.

✟ *Brescia Ovest (A4) km. 6; Brescia Centro (A21) km. 6.*

Hotels and restaurants

★★★ Vittoria Via X Giornate 20, ⊠ 25121, tel. 280061, fax 280065; 66 rms. ▨; ▣ ▣ P &; (B-C3).

★★★ Ambasciatori Via S. Crocefissa di Rosa 92, ⊠ 25128, tel. 399114, fax 381883; 64 rms. ▨; ▣ ▣ ▣ P &; (not shown on map).

★★★ Alabarda (no restaurant), Via Labirinto 6, ⊠ 25125, tel. 3541377, fax 3541300; 38 rms. ▨; ♯ P &; (not shown on map).

★★★ Industria Via Orzinuovi 58, ⊠ 25125, tel. 3531431, fax 347904; 70 rms. ▨; ▣ ▣ ▣ P &; (not shown on map).

¶⅟¶ La Sosta Via S. Martino della Battaglia 20, ⊠ 25121, tel. 295603, fax 292589 ⊠; ⅗⅟ Brescian and classical; 100/200 capacity; closed evening on Monday and Sunday and New Year's /Epiphany (6 January), and for a certain period of time in August; ▣ ✦; (C4).

¶¶ Olimpo - Il Torricino Via Fura 131, tel. 347565 ⊠; ⅗⅟ classical; 100/250 capacity; closed Monday, and for a certain period of time in August; ✦ P.

Bressanone/Brixen (BZ) ⊠ 39042 ☎ 0472

▣ *Associazione Turistica*, Viale Stazione 9, tel. 836401, fax 836067.

🚆 *Stazione F.S. (State railroad station)*, tel. 83368.

✟ *Bressanone (A22) km. 6.*

⅟ a number of chairlifts, skilifts, and crosscountry skiing.

Hotels and restaurants

★★★ Elefante Via Rio Bianco 4, tel. 832750, fax 836579; open March/mid-November and Christmas/Epiphany (6 January); 44 rms. ▨; ▣ ♯≋ ▣ P.

★★★ Grüner Baum Via Stufles 11, tel. 832732, fax 832607; closed for a certain period of time between November and December; 80 rms. ▨; ♯ ≋ P &.

★★★ Bel Riposo (no restaurant) Via Dei Vigneti 1, tel. and fax 836548; 15 rms. ▨; ♯ P.

★★★ Jarolim Piazzale Stazione 1, tel. 836230, fax 833155; 35 rms. ▨; ♯ ≋ P.

¶¶ Fink Via Portici Minori 4, tel. 834883; ⅗⅟ Alto-Adige; 60 capacity; closed Tuesday evening and Wednesday, July; ▣.

¶¶ Oste Scuro-Finsterwirt Vicolo del Duomo 3, tel. 835343 ⊠; ⅗⅟ Alto-Adige; 50/80 capacity; closed Sunday evening and Monday, and for a certain period of time between January and February and June.

Breuil-Cervinia (AO)   ⊠ 11021 ☎ 0166

▣ *APT*, Via Carrel 29, tel. 949136, fax 949731.

✟ *Saint-Vincent-Châtillon (A5) km. 28.*

⅟ numerous cableways, chairlifts and skilifts.

Hotels and restaurants

★☆★ **G.H. Cristallo** Via Piolet 6, tel. 943411, fax 948377; seasonal; 100 rms. 🐾; ♨♨ 📺 📇.

★☆★ **Hermitage** Strada Cristallo, tel. 948998, fax 949032; seasonal; 36 rms. 🐾; ♨ 📺 📇.

★★★ **Astoria** Piazzale Funivie, tel. 949062, fax 949062; seasonal; 30 rms. 🐾; 📺.

★★★ **Excelsior-Planet** Piazzale Planet 1, tel. 949426, fax 948827; seasonal; 46 rms. 🐾; ♨ 📺 📇.

★★★ **Les Neiges d'Antan** at Cret Perrères, tel. 948775, fax 948852; 28 rms; 🐾; ♨ ♿ 📇; also restaurant.

🍴 **Cime Bianche** Località La Vieille, tel. 949046 ✉; 🍽 Val d'Aostan; 70 capacity; closed Monday, mid-May/mid-July; 📇; also hotel.

Burano (VE)　　　　✉ 30012 ☎ 041

🚢 Transportation from Venice.

Restaurants

🍴 **Gatto Nero-da Ruggero** Fondamenta della Giudecca 88, tel. 730120; 🍽 Venetian (seafood); 80/150 capacity; closed Monday, and for a certain period of time in January and between November and December.

🍴 **Da Romano** Piazza B. Galuppi 221, tel. 730030, fax 735217; 🍽 Venetian (risotto); 200 capacity; closed Tuesday, mid-December/mid-January.

Busseto (PR)　　　　✉ 43011 ☎ 0524

ℹ c/o Municipio, Piazza Verdi 10, tel. 92487.

🕇 Cortemaggiore (A21 Dir.) km. 13.

Hotels

★★★ **I Due Foscari** Piazza Rossi 15, tel. 92337, fax 930039; 20 rms. 🐾; 📧 ♨ 📇.

Cagliari　　　　✉ 09100 ☎ 070

ℹ *EPT*, Piazza Deffenu 9, tel. 654811, fax 663207 (*E3*); *Information Office*, Aeroporto Elmas, tel. 240200. *AA*, Via Mameli 97, tel. 664195, fax 658200 (*C2*); *Information Office*, Piazza Matteotti, tel. 669255 (*D2*). *ESIT*, Via Mamoli 97, tel. 60231, fax 664636 (*C2*).

🚆 *Stazione F.S. (State railroad station)*, Piazza Matteotti, tel. 656293; *Stazione Ferrovie della Sardegna*, Piazza Repubblica, tel. 491304.

✈ *Aeroporto Elmas* (7 km. to the NW), tel. 240119. *Alitalia*, Passenger agency, Via Caprera 14, tel. 60107 (*C2-3*).

🚢 Transportation with car ferry from Civitavecchia, Naples, Palermo, Trapani and seasonally from Genoa.

Hotels

★☆★ **Mediterraneo** Lungomare Colombo 46, ✉ 09125, tel. 301271, fax 301274; 140 rms. 🐾; 📧 ♨📇 ♿; (*F4*).

★☆★ **Panorama** Viale Diaz 231, ✉ 09126, tel. 307691, fax 305413; 97 rms. 🐾; 📧 ♨♨ 📺 ♿; (*F6*).

★☆★ **Regina Margherita** (no restaurant), Viale Regina Margherita 44, ✉ 09124, tel. 670342, fax 668325; 99 rms. 🐾; 📧 ♨♨ 📇 ♿; (*D3*).

★★★ **Al Solemar** (no restaurant), Viale Diaz 146, ✉ 09126, tel. 340201, fax 340201; 42 rms. 🐾; 📧 📇; (*F5-6*).

★★★ **Forte Agip** Circonvallazione Nuova 626, ✉ 09134, tel. 521373, fax 502222; 129 rms. 🐾; 📧 📇 ♿; (*A5, not shown on map*).

★★★ **Italia** (no restaurant), Via Sardegna 31, ✉ 09124, tel. 660410, fax 650240; 113 rms. 🐾; 📧; (*D2*).

Restaurants

🍴 **Dal Corsaro** Viale Regina Margherita 28, ✉ 09124, tel. 664318, fax 653439 ✉; 🍽 Sardinian (seafood); 80 capacity; closed Sunday, August and Christmas-Epiphany (6 January); 📧; (*D3*).

🍴 **Flora** Via Sassari 45, tel. 664735 ✉; 🍽 Sardinian; 70/110 capacity; closed Sunday, and for a certain period of time in August; 📧 ❀; (*C2*).

🍴 **St. Remy** Via Torino 16, ✉ 09124, tel. 657377 ✉; 🍽 Sardinian and classical (seafood); 35/60 capacity; closed Saturday at midday, and Sunday, September; 📧; (*D3*).

Camogli (GE)　　　✉ 16032 ☎ 0185

ℹ *IAT*, Via XX Settembre 33, tel. 771066.

🚆 *Stazione F.S. (State railroad station)*, tel. 771137.

🕇 *Recco* (A12) km. 5.

Hotels and restaurants

★☆★ **Cenobio dei Dogi** Via Cuneo 34, tel. 7241, fax 772796; 107 rms. 🐾; 📧 ♨♨ 📇 ♿.

★★ **La Camogliese** Via Garibaldi 55, tel. 771402, fax 774024; closed November; 16 rms. 🐾.

🍴 **Vento Ariel** Calata Porto 1, tel. 771080 ✉; 🍽 Ligurian; 25/30 capacity; closed Wednesday, and for a certain period of time in January.

Capri (Island of) (NA)　　✉ 80073 ☎ 081

ℹ at Capri: *AA*, Piazzetta Cerio 11, tel. 8375308; Via Padre Cimmino, tel. 8370424; Via Marina Grande (Information) tel. 8370634; Piazza Umberto I, tel. 83/0686; ad Anacapri: *AA*, Via G. Orlandi 19/a, tel. 8371524.

✈ *Airport* at Naples-Capodichino, tel. 7096259-7896245.

🚢 Transportation with car ferry (if cars are allowed on the island) from Naples; only for passengers from Sorrento and Positano.

at Capri　　　　　　　✉ 80073

Hotels

★☆★ **G.H. Quisisana** Via Camerelle 2, tel. 8370788, fax 8376080; seasonal; 150 rms. 🐾; 📧 ♨♨ ♨.

★☆★ **La Palma** Via Vittorio Emanuele 39, tel. 8370133, fax 8376966; 72 rms. 🐾; 📧 ♨♨ 📺.

★☆★ **La Pazziella** (no restaurant), Via P. Reginaldo Giuliani 4, tel. 8370044, fax 8370085; 20 rms. 🐾; 📧 ♨♨.

★☆★ **Punta Tragara** Via Tragara 57, tel. 8370844, fax 8377790; seasonal; 47 rms. 🐾; 📧 ♨♨.

★☆★ **Syrene** Via Camerelle 51, tel. 8370102, fax 8370957; seasonal; 34 rms. 🐾; 📧 ♨♨.

★★★ **Gatto Bianco** (no restaurant), Via Vittorio Emanuele 32, tel. 8370446, fax 8378060; seasonal and Christmas/New Year's Day; 37 rms. 🐾; ♨ 📧.

★★ **Florida** (no restaurant), Via Fuorlovado 34, tel. 8370710, fax 8370042; closed January-February; 19 rms. 🐾; ♨♨ 📺 📇.

Restaurants

🍴 **Canzone del Mare** at Marina Piccola, Via Marina Piccola 93, tel. 8370104, fax 8370541; 🍽 Campanian; 150 capacity; Easter/ October at midday.

🍴 **Capannina** Via delle Botteghe 12 bis, tel. 8370732, fax 8376990 ✉; 🍽 Campanian (seafood); 100/120 capacity; seasonal; and end-December/Epiphany (6 January); 📧.

🍴 **Gemma** Via Madre Serafina 6, tel. 8377113 ✉; 🍽 Campanian (seafood); 150 capacity; closed beginning January/beginning February.

¶ **Grottelle** township of Arco Naturale 5, tel. 8375719 ⊠; ⑭ Campanian (seafood); 30/80 capacity; seasonal; closed Thursday.

¶ **Paolino** at Marina Grande, Via Palazzo a Mare 11, ⊠ 80070, tel. 8375611 ⊠; ⑭ Campanian (grilled fish and meat); 200 capacity; seasonal at evening; closed Tuesday in the off season; ✿.

at Anacapri   ⊠ 80071

Hotels and restaurants

★★★ **Europa Palace** Via Capodimonte 2/B, tel. 8373800, fax 8373191; seasonal; 90 rms. ▥; ⊠ ♨ ⚐ 📷 🅿.

★★ **Bianca Maria** (no restaurant), Via Orlandi 54, tel. 8371000, fax 8372060; seasonal; 24 rms. ▥ ♨.

¶ **Cucciolo** at Damecuta, Via La Fabbrica 52, tel. 8371917; ⑭ Campanian; 80 capacity; seasonal; closed Tuesday in the off season; ✿ 🅿.

Caserta   ⊠ 81100 ☎ 0823

🆔 *EPT*, Palazzo Reale, tel. 326300 (*C-D2*); *Information Office*, Piazza Dante, tel. 321137.

🚆 *Stazione F.S. (State railroad station)*, Piazza Ferrovia, tel. 327170.

⋔ *Caserta Nord* km. 3 (A1, A30/A3, A30/A16) and *Caserta Sud* km. 7 (A1).

Hotels and restaurants

★★★ **Europa** Via Roma 19, tel. 325400, fax 32540; 60 rms. ▥; ⊠ 📷 🅿 ♨.

★★★ **Jolly** Viale Vittorio Veneto 9, tel. 325222, fax 354522; 107 rms. ▥; ⊠ 📷 ♨.

¶ **Ciacco** Via Majelli 37, tel. 327505 ⊠; ⑭ Campanian and classical (seafood); 70 capacity; closed Sunday except in summer; 🅿.

at San Léucio, km. 4   ⊠ 81020

Restaurants

¶ **Antica Locanda** Piazza della Seta, tel. 305444 ⊠; ⑭ Campanian; 40/60 capacity; closed evening of Sunday and Monday, and for a certain period of time in August; ✿.

Castelfranco Veneto (TV)   ⊠ 31033 ☎ 0423

🆔 *Pro Loco*, Via Francesco Maria Preti 39, tel. 495000.

🚆 *Stazione F.S. (State railroad station)*, Via Melchiorri, tel. 491991.

Hotels and restaurants

★★★ **Alla Torre** (no restaurant), Piazzetta Trento e Trieste 7, tel. 498707, fax 498737; 39 rms. ▥; ⊠ 📷.

★★★ **Al Moretto** (no restaurant), Via S. Pio X 10, tel. 721313, fax 721066; 36 rms. ▥; ⊠ ♨ 🅿 ♨.

★★★ **Roma** (no restaurant), Via F. Filzi 39, tel. 721616, fax 721515; 68 rms. ▥; ⊠ 🅿 ♨.

¶ **Alle Mura** Via Preti 69, tel. 498098 ⊠; ⑭ classical (seafood); 80 capacity; closed Thursday, mid-January/mid-February; ✿.

¶ **Al Teatro** Via Garibaldi 17, tel. 721425 ⊠; ⑭ Venetian (seafood); 35 capacity; closed Monday, mid-July/August.

Catania   ⊠ 95100 ☎ 095

🆔 *AAPT*, Largo Paisiello 5, tel. 312124, fax 316407 (*C2-3*); *Uffici Information*: Staz. Centrale F.S., tel. 531802 (*C5*); Airport, tel. 341900. *AA*, Corso Italia 302, tel. 373084, fax 373072.

🚆 *Stazioni F.S. (State railroad stations)*: Centrale, Piazza Giovanni XXIII, tel. 531625; Acquicella, Via Adamo, tel. 340227. *Ferrovia Circumetnea*, Via Porto, tel. 531402.

⋔ *Catania Nord* (A18) km. 8; *Catania Sud* (A19) km. 5.

✈ *Aeroporto Civile*, Catania-Fontanarossa km. 5, tel. 578296.
Alitalia, Corso Sicilia 111, tel. 252333 (*C4*).

⚓ *Capitaneria di Porto*, Via Dusmet, tel. 531667.

Hotels and restaurants

★★★★ **Excelsior** Piazza Verga 39, ⊠ 95129, tel. 537071, fax 537015; 163 rms. ▥; ⊠ 📷 ♨; (*B4*).

★★★ **Jolly Trinacria** Piazza Trento 13, ⊠ 95129, tel. 316933, fax 316832; 159 rms. ▥; ⊠ 🅿; (*B3*).

★★★ **Forte Agip** (no restaurant), Via Messina 628, ⊠ 95126, tel. 7122300, fax 7121856; 56 rms. ▥; 🅿; (*A6, not shown on map*).

¶¶¶ **Costa Azzurra** Via De Cristofaro 2, ⊠ 95126, tel. 497889, fax 494920; ⑭ Sicilian and classical (seafood); 180/250 capacity; closed Monday; 🅿; (*A6, not shown on map*).

¶¶¶ **Siciliana** Viale Marco Polo 52/A, ⊠ 95126, tel. 376400, fax 7221300 ⊠; ⑭ Sicilian; 100 capacity; closed Monday and evening of Sunday and holidays, and for a certain period of time in August; ✿; (*A3, not shown on map*).

¶ **Poggio Ducale - Da Nino** of the Hotel Poggio Ducale Via Paolo Gaifami 5, ⊠ 95126, tel. 330016; ⑭ Sicilian (seafood); 160 capacity; closed Sunday evening and Monday at midday, and for a certain period of time in August; 📷 🅿.

Certosa di Pavia (PV)   ⊠ 27012 ☎ 0382

🆔 *APT* at Pavia, tel. 22156; *IAT*, seasonal in loco.

🚆 *Railroad station (Stazione F.S.)*

⋔ *Pavia* (Highway intersection Pavia-Bereguardo/A7) km. 10.

Restaurants

¶¶¶ **Vecchio Mulino** Via al Monumento 5, tel. 925894, fax 933300 ⊠; ⑭ Lombard; 45/120 capacity; closed Sunday evening and Monday, and for a certain period of time in January and in August; ✿ 🅿.

¶ **Chalet della Certosa** Piazzale Monumento 1, tel. 925615; ⑭ Lombard and classical; 100/150 capacity; closed Monday, except holidays, period of closing may vary; 📷 ✿ 🅿.

Chioggia (VE)   ⊠ 30015 ☎ 041

🆔 *APT*, Sottomarina, Lungomare Adriatico 101, tel. 401068, fax 5540855.

🚆 *Stazione F.S. (State railroad station)*, tel. 400462.

⚓ Transportation to Pellestrina.

Restaurants

¶¶¶ **El Gato** Campo S. Andrea 653, tel. 401806, fax 405224 ⊠; ⑭ Venetian (seafood); 70/100 capacity; closed Monday and at midday of Tuesday, January/mid-February; 📷.

¶ **Mano Amica** Piazzetta Vigo, tel. 401721; ⑭ Venetian (seafood); 80/160 capacity; closed Monday, January; 📷.

at Sottomarina, km. 1   ⊠ 30019

Hotels

★★★ **Bristol** Lungomare Adriatico 46, tel. 5540389, fax 5541813; closed January; 65 rms. ▥; ⊠ ♨ ⚐ ♨ 🅿.

★★★ **Al Gambero d'Oro** Viale Venezia 1, tel. 5500424, fax 403054; closed mid-January/mid-February and mid-November/Christmas; 20 rms. ▥; ⊠ ♨ 📷 🅿.

★★★ **Park Hotel** Lungomare Adriatico, tel. 4965032, fax 490111; 41 rms. ▥; ♨ 🅿.

Cividale del Friuli (UD) ✉ 33043 ☎ 0432

🛈 *Azienda Regionale per La Promozione Turistica,* Largo Boiani 4, tel. 731398.

🚋 *Stazione Ferrovia Udine-Cividale,* tel. 731032.

Hotels and restaurants

★★★ **Roma** (no restaurant), Piazza Picco, tel. 731871, fax 701033; 50 rms. 🏧 ♨ 🅿.

🍴 **Alla Frasca** Via de Rubeis 8/A, tel. 731270; 🍽 Friulan and classical (mushrooms); 40/60 capacity; closed Monday, for a certain period of time in January; ❀.

Como ✉ 22100 ☎ 031

🛈 *APT,* Piazza Cavour 17, tel. 262091, fax 261152 (*A2*); *IAT,* Piazza Cavour 16, tel. 269712 (*A2*); and Stazione F.S., tel. 267214 (*B2*).

🚋 *Stazione F.S. (State railroad station),* Piazzale San Gottardo 1, tel. 261494. *Stazione Ferrovie Nord Milano,* Como Lago, Largo Leopardi 3, tel. 304800.

🛣 *Como Sud* (A9) km. 5; *Como Nord* (N2, Svizzera) km. 5.

Hotels and restaurants

★★★ **Como** Via Mentana 28, tel. 266173, fax 266020; 76 rms. 🏧; 🔲 ♨ 🔲 🅿 ⚒; (*C3*).

★★★ **Le Due Corti** Piazza Vittoria 15, tel. 328111, fax 328800; 60 rms.; 🔲♨🔲 🅿 ⚒.

★★★ **Villa Flori** road to Cernobbio 12, tel. 573105, fax 570379; closed December/January; 45 rms. 🏧; 🔲♨🔲 🅿 ⚒; (*A1, not shown on map*).

★★★ **Continental** Viale Innocenzo XI 15, tel. 260485, fax 273343; 68 rms. 🏧; 🔲 🅿 ⚒; (*B2*).

★★★ **Park Hotel** (no restaurant), Viale F.lli Rosselli 20, tel. 572615, fax 574302; seasonal; 41 rms. 🏧 🅿 ⚒; (*A1*).

🍴 **Imbarcadero** Piazza Cavour 20, tel. 270166, fax 300808 ⊠; 🍽 classical; 170 capacity; closed Christmas/Epiphany (6 January); 🔲; (*A2*).

🍴 **Sant'Anna 1907** Via Turati 1/3, tel. 505266, fax 520531 ⊠; 🍽 Lombard fine cuisine; 40/70 capacity; closed Friday and at midday on Saturday, and for a certain period of time between July and August; 🔲; (*C2, not shown on map*).

Cortina d'Ampezzo (BL) ✉ 32043 ☎ 0436

🛈 *APT,* Piazzetta San Francesco 8, tel. 3231, fax 3235; *Information Office,* Piazza Roma 1, tel. 2711.

🛣 *Vittorio Ven. Nord* (A27) km. 65.

🎿 ample availability of cableways, chairlifts, skilifts, and crosscountry skiing.

Hotels

★★★ **Miramonti Majestic G.H.** Via Peziè 103, tel. 4201, fax 867019; seasonal; 105 rms. 🏧; ♨♨🔲 🅿 ⚒.

★★★ **Ancora** Corso Italia 62, tel. 3261, fax 3265; seasonal; 64 rms. 🏧; 🔲 🅿 ⚒.

★★★ **De la Poste** Piazza Roma 14, tel. 4271, fax 868435; seasonal; 80 rms. 🏧; 🔲 🅿 ⚒.

★★★ **Europa** Corso Italia 207, tel. 3221, fax 868204; closed mid-October/mid-December; 50 rms. 🏧; 🔲 🅿 ⚒.

★★★ **Capannina** Via dello Stadio 11, tel. 2950, fax 868317; seasonal; 30 rms. 🏧; ♨🔲 🅿.

★★★ **Columbia** (no restaurant), Via Ronco 75, tel. 3607, fax 3607; seasonal; 19 rms. 🏧; ♨🔲 🅿.

★★★ **Pontechiesa** Via Marangoni 3, tel. 2523, fax 867343; seasonal; 31 rms. 🏧; ♨🔲 🅿.

★★★ **Villa Resy** Via Riva 49, tel. 3303, fax 866065; 14 rms. 🏧; 🅿.

Restaurants

🍴🍴 **El Toulà** Via Ronco 123, tel. 3339, fax 2738 ⊠; 🍽 Ampezzan; 70 capacity; seasonal; closed Monday; 🅿.

🍴🍴 **Tivoli** Via Lacedel 34, tel. 866400, fax 3413 ⊠; 🍽 fine cuisine; 50/70 capacity; seasonal; closed Monday in the off season; 🅿.

🍴 **Beppe Sello** Via Ronco 68, tel. 3236, fax 3237 ⊠; 🍽 Ampezzan and classical; 100 capacity; seasonal; closed Tuesday; 🅿; also hotel.

🍴 **El Zoco** Via Cademai 18, tel. 860041 ⊠; 🍽 Venetian (mushrooms); 40 capacity; seasonal; closed Monday; 🅿.

🍴 **Leone & Anna** township of Alverà 112, tel. 2768 ⊠; 🍽 Sardinian; 35 capacity; seasonal; closed Tuesday; 🅿.

at Pocol, km. 6

Hotels

★★★ **Sport Hotel Tofana** tel. 3281, fax 868074; seasonal; 83 rms. (73 🏧); ♨🔲 🅿.

★★ **Pocol** tel. 2602, fax 2707; seasonal; 23 rms. 🏧; ♨🅿.

Cortona (AR) ✉ 52044 ☎ 0575

🛈 *Via Nazionale 42, tel. 630352 (*B2*).

🛣 *Cortona* (Highway intersection Perugia-Bettolle/A1) km. 10.

Hotels and restaurants

★★★ **Il Falconiere** at San Martino a Bocena, tel. 612679, fax 612927; 12 rms. 🏧; 🔲♨♨ 🅿 ⚒.

🍴🍴 **Il Falconiere** at San Martino a Bocena, tel. 612679, fax 612927 ⊠; 🍽 Tuscan and fine cuisine; 20/50 capacity; closed Wednesday in winter, period of closing may vary; 🔲 ❀ 🅿.

🍴 **Tonino** Piazza Garibaldi 1, tel. 630500 ⊠; 🍽 Tuscan and Umbrian; 200 capacity; closed Monday evening and Tuesday; 🔲; (*B2*).

at Pòrtole, km. 9

Hotels

★★★ **Portole** Via Umbro Cortonese 39, tel. 691008, fax 691035; seasonal; 20 rms. 🏧; ♨ 🅿.

Cosenza ✉ 87100 ☎ 0984

🛈 *APT,* Corso Mazzini 92, tel. 27821, fax 27304; *IAT,* Via Rossi 70, tel. 390595.

🚋 *Stazione F.S. (State railroad station),* Piazza Matteotti, tel. 482333; *Ferrovie Calabro Lucane,* Via Medaglie d'Oro, tel. 413124.

🛣 *Cosenza* (A3) km. 2.

Hotels and restaurants

★★★ **Centrale** Via del Tigrai 3, tel. 73681, fax 75750; 50 rms. 🏧; 🔲 🅿 ⚒.

🍴 **Giocondo** Via Piave 53, tel. 29810 ⊠; 🍽 Calabrian; 80 capacity; closed Sunday, August; 🔲.

🍴 **Luna Rossa** Via Sicilia 94, tel. 32470; 🍽 Calabrian; 180 capacity; closed Tuesday, and for a certain period of time in August; 🔲 🅿.

at Castiglione Cosentino Scalo, km. 6 ✉ 87040

Hotels

★★★ **President** Via A. Volta 47/49, tel. 839101, fax 837522; 65 rms. 🏧; 🔲 🔲 ⚒.

Courmayeur (AO) ✉ 11013 ☎ 0165

🛈 *APT,* Piazzale Monte Bianco, tel. 842060, fax 842072.

🛣 *Morgex* (A5) km. 12.

🎿 ample facilities, crosscountry skiing.

Hotels and restaurants

★★★ **Pavillon** Strada Regionale 62, tel. 846120, fax 846122; seasonal; 50 rms. 🏧; ♨♨🔲 🅿 ⚒.

★★★ Royal e Golf Via Roma 87, tel. 846787, fax 842093; seasonal; 92 rms. 🐾; ♨ ♨ 🖥 🅿 ♿; also restaurant.

★★★ Cristallo Via Roma 142, tel. 846666, fax 846327; seasonal; 27 rms. 🐾; 🖥 🅿 ♿.

★★★ Mont Blanc-Perrier state road (S.S.) 26 n. 18, tel. 846555, fax 846633; seasonal; 40 rms. 🐾; ♨ 🖥 🅿.

★★ Svizzero (no restaurant), state road (S.S.) 26 n. 14, tel. 842035, fax 846464; seasonal; 27 rms. 🐾; ♨ 🖥 🅿.

🍴 Cadran Solaire Via Roma 122, tel. 844609 ⌧; 🍴 Val d'Aostan and classical; 70 capacity; closed May and October.

🍴 Pierre Alexis 1877 Via Marconi 54, tel. 843517 ⌧; 🍴 Val d'Aostan; 80 capacity; closed Monday and at midday on Tuesday (in the winter), October/beginning of December; 🅿.

at Entrèves, km. 3

Hotels and restaurants

★★★ La Brenva Strada La Palud 14, tel. 869780, fax 869726; closed May and October; 12 rms. 🐾; ♨ 🅿.

★★★ Pilier d'Angle tel. 869760, fax 869770; seasonal; 19 rms. 🐾; ♨ 🖥 🅿.

🍴 La Maison de Filippo tel. 869797 ⌧; 🍴 Val d'Aostan; 160 capacity; closed Tuesday, June and November/mid-December; 🅿.

Cremona   ⌧ 26100 ☎ 0372

ⓘ *APT* and *IAT*, Piazza del Comune 5, tel. 23233, fax 21722.

🚂 *Stazione F.S. (State railroad station)*, Via Dante 68, tel. 22237.

🕇 *Castelvetro P.* (A1) km. 8; *Cremona* (A21) km. 5.

Hotels and restaurants

★★★ Continental Piazza della Libertà 26, tel. 434141, fax 434141; 57 rms. 🐾; 🖥 🅿.

★★★ Ibis Cremona Via Mantova, tel. 452222, fax 452700; closed for a certain period of time in August; 100 rms. 🐾; 🖥 🅿 ♿.

★★★ Este Viale Po 131, tel. 32220, fax 458188; 24 rms. 🐾; ♨ 🅿.

🍴 Cigno Vicolo del Cigno 7, tel. 21361 ⌧; 🍴 Cremona; 60 capacity; closed Sunday, and for a certain period of time between July and August; 🖾.

Desenzano del Garda (BS)   ⌧ 25015 ☎ 030

ⓘ *IAT*, Via Portovecchio, tel. 9141510, fax 9144209.

🚂 *Stazione F.S. (State railroad station)*, Viale della Stazione, tel. 9141247.

🕇 *Desenzano* (A4) km. 3.

Hotels and restaurants

★★★ Park Hotel Lungolago C. Battisti 17, tel. 9143494, fax 9142280; 65 rms. 🐾; 🖥 ♨ 🖥 ♿.

★★★ Residence Oliveto Lungolago C. Battisti, tel. 9911919, fax 9911224; closed mid-December/mid-January; 63 rms. 🐾; 🖥 ♨ ♨ 🅿 ♿.

★★★ City (no restaurant), Via Sauro 29, tel. 9911704, fax 9912837; closed mid-December/mid-January; 39 rms. 🐾; 🖥 🅿.

★★★ Piccola Vela Via Dal Molin 36, tel. 9914666, fax 9914666; 43 rms. 🐾; 🖥 ♨ ♨ 🅿.

★★★ Piroscafo Via Porto Vecchio 11, tel. 9141128, fax 9912586; closed mid-Jan/mid-Feb; 32 rms. 🐾; 🖾.

🍴🍴 Cavallino Via Gherla 30 corner of Muracchette, tel. 9120217, fax 9912751 ⌧; 🍴 Lake Garda; 30/50 capacity; closed Monday and at midday on Tuesday, January; 🌺.

🍴🍴 Esplanade Via Lario 10, tel. 9143361, fax 9143361 ⌧; 🍴 fine cuisine; 40 capacity; closed Wednesday; 🌺 🅿.

Elba (Island of) (LI)   ☎ 0565

ⓘ *APT*, Portoferraio, Calata Italia 26, tel. 914671, fax 916350.

⛴ Transportation with car ferry from Piombino.

at Capoliveri   ⌧ 57031

Hotels

★★★ Antares at Lido di Capoliveri, tel. 940131, fax 940084; seasonal; 47 rms. 🐾; ♨ 🅿 ♿.

★★★ Le Acacie at Naregno km. 5, tel. 966111, fax 967062; open mid-May/September; 39 rms. 🐾; ♨ ♨ 🅿 ♿.

★★ Dino at Pareti, tel. 939103, fax 968172; seasonal; 30 rms. 🐾; ♨ 🅿 ♿.

at Marciana   ⌧ 57030

Hotels and restaurants

★★★ Del Golfo at Pròcchio, tel. 907565, fax 907898; seasonal; 102 rms. 🐾; 🖥 ♨ ♨ 🅿 ♿.

★★★ Bel Tramonto at Patresi, tel. 908027, fax 908280; seasonal; 20 rms. 🐾; ♨ 🅿.

★★★ Valle Verde at Pròcchio-Spartàia, tel. 907545, fax 907965; seasonal; 42 rms. 🐾; ♨ 🅿.

🍴 Lo Zodiaco at Pròcchio, Via del Mare 19, tel. 907630 ⌧; 🍴 Leghorn; 30/90 capacity; seasonal; closed Monday; 🌺.

at Marciana Marina   ⌧ 57033

Hotels

★★★ La Conchiglia Via XX Settembre 43, tel. 99016, fax 99488; seasonal; 42 rms. 🐾; ♨ ♨.

★★★ Marinella Viale Margherita 38, tel. 99018, fax 996895; seasonal; 57 rms. 🐾; ♨ ♨ 🅿.

at Marina di Campo   ⌧ 57034

Hotels and restaurants

★★★ Riva del Sole Viale degli Eroi 11, tel. 976316, fax 976778; seasonal; 57 rms. 🐾; 🖥 🅿 ♿.

★★★ Dei Coralli Via degli Etruschi 81, tel. 976336, fax 977748; open Easter/mid-October; 62 rms. 🐾; 🖥 ♨ ♨ 🅿.

🍴 Bologna Via Firenze 27, tel. 976105; 🍴 Leghorn and classical; 120/300 capacity; seasonal; closed Tuesday in the off season; 🌺.

at Porto Azzurro   ⌧ 57036

Hotels

★★★ Belmare Banchina IV Novembre 21, tel. 95012, fax 958245; closed mid-November/mid-December; 27 rms. 🐾.

at Portoferràio   ⌧ 57037

Hotels and restaurants

★★★ Hermitage at La Biòdola, tel. 936911, fax 969984; seasonal; 127 rms. 🐾; 🖥 ♨ ♨ 🅿.

★★★ Villa Ottone at Ottone, tel. 933042, fax 933257; seasonal; 80 rms. 🐾; 🖥 ♨ ♨ 🅿.

★★★ Il Caminetto at San Martino, tel. 915700, fax 915271; seasonal; 17 rms. 🐾; ♨ ♨ 🅿.

★★★ Paradiso at Viticcio, tel. 939034, fax 939041; seasonal; 46 rms. 🐾; ♨ ♨ 🅿.

🍴 Ferrigna Piazza della Repubblica 22, tel. 914129; 🍴 Livornese; 80 capacity; open March/mid-November; closed Tuesday.

at Rio Marina   ⌧ 57038

Hotels

★★★ Marelba at Cavo, Via Pietri, ⌧ 57030, tel. 949920, fax 949776; seasonal; 52 rms. 🐾; ♨ 🅿.

★★★ Rio Via Palestro 31, tel. 924225, fax 924162; seasonal; 35 rms. 🐾.

Erice (TP) ✉ 91016 ☎ 0923

- *i* *AA*, Viale Conte Pepoli 11, tel. 869388, fax 869544; *Information Office*, Piazzale Funivia, tel. 565055.

- ✚ *Trapani* (A29 Dir.) km. 9.

Hotels and restaurants

- ★★★ **Moderno** Via Vittorio Emanuele 63, tel. 869300, fax 869139; 40 rms. ▧; ▣.
- ★★ **Edelweiss** Cortile Padre Vincenzo 3, tel. 869420, fax 869252; 15 rms. ▧; ▣.
- ¶ **Cortile di Venere** Via Sales 31, tel. 869362; ⅋ Trapani; 90/150 capacity; closed Wednesday, period of closing may vary.

Faenza (RA) ✉ 48018 ☎ 0546

- *i* *IAT*, Piazza del Popolo 1, tel. 25231.

- ▦ *Stazione F.S. (State railroad station)*, Piazza Battisti 7, tel. 28482.

- ✚ *Faenza* (A14) km. 5.

Restaurants

- ¶ **Turandot** Corso Mazzini 195/13, tel. 24750 ▨; ⅋ fine cuisine; 30/50 capacity; closed Wednesday, August; ▣.

Fano (PS) ✉ 61032 ☎ 0721

- *i* *APT*, Viale Battisti 10, tel. 803534, fax 824292; *Information Offices*, seasonal, Torrette, Via Boscomarina 10, tel. 884779; Marotta, Viale Cristoforo Colombo 31, tel. 96591.

- ▦ *Stazione F.S. (State railroad station)*, tel. 803627.

- ✚ *Fano* (Highway intersection Fossombrone-Fano/A14) km. 2.

Hotels and restaurants

- ★★★ **G.H. Elisabeth** Viale Carducci 12, tel. 804241, fax 804242; closed Christmas; 37 rms. ▧; ▣ ♨ ▣.
- ★★★ **Angela** Viale Adriatico 13, tel. 801239, fax 803102; 28 rms. ▧; ▣ ♨ ▣ ⅋.
- ★★★ **Corallo** Via L. da Vinci 3, tel. 804200, fax 803637; closed Christmas Epiphany (6 January); 27 rms. ▧; ▣ ▣.
- ¶ **Ristorantino-da Giulio** Viale Adriatico 100, tel. 805680 ▨; ⅋ Marche; 50/80 capacity; closed Tuesday, period of closing may vary.

Ferrara ✉ 44100 ☎ 0532

- *i* *APT*, Corso Giovecca 21, tel. 209370, fax 212266 (*C4*); Piazzale Kennedy 2, tel. 765728, fax 760225 (*D3*)

- ▦ *Stazione F.S. (State railroad station)*, tel. 770340.

- ✚ *Ferrara Nord* (A13/A4) km. 6; *Ferrara* (Highway intersection Porto Garibaldi-Ferrara/A 13) km. 6.

Hotels and restaurants

- ★★★ **Duchessa Isabella** Via Palestro 70, tel. 202121, fax 202638; closed August; 28 rms. ▧; ▣ ♨ ▣ ⅋; (*B-C5*).
- ★★★ **Astra** Viale Cavour 55, tel. 206088, fax 247002; 66 rms. ▧; ▣ ▣ ⅋; (*C3*).
- ★★ **Jolly de la Ville** Piazzale Stazione 11, tel. 772635, fax 772645; 85 rms. ▧; ▣ ⅋; (*B2*).
- ★★★ **Ripagrande** Via Ripagrande 21, tel. 765250, fax 764377; 40 rms. ▧; ▣ ▣ ▣; (*D3*).
- ¶ **Centrale** Via Boccaleone 8, tel. 206735 ▨; ⅋ Ferrarese; 100 capacity; closed Sunday and evening of Wednesday (except in exhibition period); ♣; (*D4*).

Provvidenza Corso Ercole I d'Este 92, tel. 205187

- ¶ **Provvidenza** Corso Ercole I d'Este 92, tel. 205187 ▨; ⅋ Ferrarese and classical (fish and mushrooms); 80/110 capacity; closed Monday, and for a certain period of time in August; ▣ ♣ ▣; (*A4*).
- ¶ **Quel Fantastico Giovedì** Via Castelnuovo 9, tel. 760570 ▨; ⅋ fine cuisine; 40 capacity; closed Wednesday, and for a certain period of time in January and between July and August; ▣; (*E4*).
- ¶ **Il Bagattino** Via Correggiari 6, tel. 206387 ▨; ⅋ Ferrarese; 80 capacity; closed Monday, and for a certain period of time in August; ▣; (*D4*).

Fiesole (FI) ✉ 50014 ☎ 055

- *i* *IAT*, Piazza Mino 36, tel. 598702.

- ✚ *Firenze Nord* (A11) km. 12.

Hotels and restaurants

- ★★★ **Villa Aurora** Piazza Mino 39, tel. 59100, fax 59587; 27 rms. ▧; ▣ ♨ ▣.
- ★★★ **Villa San Michele** Via Doccia 4, tel. 59451, fax 598734; seasonal; 41 rms. ▧; ▣ ♨ ▣.
- ★★★ **Villa Bonelli** Via F. Poeti 1, tel. 59513, fax 598942; 20 rms. ▧; ♨ ▣.
- ¶ **Cave di Maiano** at Maiano, Via delle Cave 16, tel. 59133 ▨; ⅋ Tuscan; 120 capacity; closed Monday at midday, and for a certain period of time in August; ♣ ▣.

Florence ✉ 50100 ☎ 055

- *i* *APT*, Via Manzoni 16, tel. 23320, fax 2346286 (*D6, not shown on map*), *APT-Provincia-Comune*, Via Cavour 1r, tel. 290832 (*E4*); *Uffici Informazioni del Comune (City Information Offices)*, Chiasso Baroncelli 17/19r, tel. 2302124 (*E4*); Stazione S.M.N. (outdoor shelter), tel. 212245 (*B2*).

- ▦ *Ferrovie dello Stato*, information for travellers for all the stations in town: Stazione Santa Maria Novella, tel. 288785.

- ✚ *Firenze Nord* (A11) km. 10; *Firenze Sud* (A1) km. 8; *Firenze Certosa* (Highway intersection Siena-Florence/A1) km. 7.

- ✈ *Aeroporto Vespucci*, Via del Termine 11 (4 km. to the NW), tel. 373408; *Air terminal for the Airport Galilei* di Pisa. Stazione S.M.N., tel. 216073 (*B2*). *Alitalia*, Lungarno Acciaiuoli 10/12r, tel. 27888 (*E4*).

Hotels

- ★★★★ **G.H. Villa Medici** Via il Prato 42, ✉ 50123, tel. 2381331, fax 2381336; 103 rms. ▧; ▣ ♨ ♨ ▣; (*B1*).
- ★★★ **Excelsior** Piazza Ognissanti 3, ✉ 50123, tel. 264201, fax 210278; 168 rms. ▧; ▣ ▣ ▣ ⅋; (*C-D1-2*).
- ★★★ **G.H. Villa Cora** Viale Machiavelli 18, ✉ 50125, tel. 2298451, fax 229086; 48 rms. ▧; ▣ ♨ ♨ ▣ ⅋; (*not shown on map*).
- ★★★ **Regency** Piazza D'Azeglio 3, ✉ 50121, tel. 245247, fax 2346735; 35 rms. ▧; ▣ ♨ ▣; (*not shown on map*).
- ★★★ **Bernini Palace** Piazza S. Firenze 29, ✉ 50122, tel. 288621, fax 268272; 86 rms. ▧; ▣ ▣ ⅋; (*D-E5*).
- ★★★ **Brunelleschi** Piazza S. Elisabetta 3, ✉ 50122, tel. 562068, fax 219653; 96 rms. ▧; ▣; (*C-D4*).
- ★★★ **Croce di Malta** Via della Scala 7, ✉ 50123, tel. 218351, fax 287121; 98 rms. ▧; ▣ ♨ ♨ ▣ ⅋; (*C2*).
- ★★★ **Executive** (no restaurant), Via Curtatone 5, ✉ 50123, tel. 217451, fax 268346; 38 rms. ▧; ▣ ▣; (*B-C1*).
- ★★★ **Jolly Carlton** Piazza Vittorio Veneto 4/A, ✉ 50123, tel. 2770, fax 294794; 167 rms. ▧; ▣ ♨; (*not shown on map*).

*** **Lungarno** (no restaurant), Borgo S. Jacopo 14, ☒ 50125, tel. 264211, fax 268437; 66 rms. 🗽; 🅿 🗎; (E3).

*** **Montebello Splendid** Via Montebello 60, ☒ 50123, tel. 2398051, fax 211867; 54 rms. 🗽; 🅿 ♨ 🗎; (not shown on map).

*** **Park Palace** Piazzale Galileo 5, ☒ 50125, tel. 222431, fax 220517; 26 rms. 🗽; 🅿 ♨ ♒ 🅿.

*** **Rivoli** (no restaurant), Via della Scala 33, ☒ 50123, tel. 282853, fax 294041; 65 rms. 🗽; 🅿 ♨ ♒ 🗎; (B-C2).

*** **Savoy** Piazza della Repubblica 7, ☒ 50123, tel. 283313, fax 284840; 101 rms. 🗽; 🅿 🗎 & ; (C-D4).

*** **Starhotel Michelangelo** Viale F.lli Rosselli 2, ☒ 50123, tel. 2784, fax 2382232; 137 rms. 🗽; 🅿 🗎 & ; (not shown on map).

*** **Alba** (no restaurant), Via della Scala 22, ☒ 50123, tel. 282610, fax 288358; 24 rms. 🗽; 🅿 🗎; (B2).

*** **Albion** Via il Prato 22/r, ☒ 50123, tel. 214171, fax 283391; 21 rms. 🗽; 🅿 🗎; (not shown on map).

*** **Capitol** Viale Amendola 34, ☒ 50121, tel. 2343201, fax 2345925; 92 rms. 🗽; 🅿 🗎; (not shown on map).

*** **David** (no restaurant), Viale Michelangiolo 1, ☒ 50125, tel. 6811695, fax 680602; 26 rms. 🗽; 🅿 🅿; (not shown on map).

*** **Il Guelfo Bianco** (no restaurant), Via Cavour 29, ☒ 50129, tel. 288330, fax 295203; 29 rms. 🗽; 🅿 🗎 & ; (B4-5).

*** **Loggiato dei Serviti** (no restaurant), Piazza SS. Annunziata 3, ☒ 50122, tel. 289592, fax 289595; 29 rms. 🗽; 🅿 🗎; (A-B5-6).

*** **Pagnini** (no restaurant), Via Montebello 40, ☒ 50123, tel. 2381468, fax 216685; 19 rms. 🗽; 🅿; (C1).

*** **Palazzo Benci** (no restaurant), Piazza Madonna Aldobrandini 3, ☒ 50123, tel. 213848, fax 288308; 35 rms. 🗽; 🅿 ♨ (B3).

*** **Villa Liberty** (no restaurant), Viale Michelangiolo 40, ☒ 50125, tel. 6810581, fax 6812595; 16 rms. 🗽; ♨ 🅿; (not shown on map).

** **Casci** (no restaurant), Via Cavour 13, ☒ 50129, tel. 211686, fax 2396461; closed for a certain period of time in January; 25 rms. 🗽; 🗎; (B4).

** **Desirée** (no restaurant), Via Fiume 20, ☒ 50123, tel. 2382382, fax 2382382; closed for a certain period of time in August; 20 rms. 🗽; 🗎; (A-B3).

** **Liana** (no restaurant), Via Alfieri 18, ☒ 50121, tel. 245303, fax 2344596; 18 rms. 🗽; ♨ 🅿 & ; (not shown on map).

Restaurants

🍴🍴🍴 **Enoteca Pinchiorri** Via Ghibellina 87, ☒ 50122, tel. 242777, fax 244983 ☒; 🍴 fine cuisine; 80 capacity; closed Sunday and at midday on Monday and Wednesday, Christmas and August; ❀ ; (D6).

🍴🍴 **Alle Murate** Via Ghibellina 52/r, ☒ 50122, tel. 240618, 🍴 fine cuisine; 65 capacity; open only evening; closed Monday, August; 🅿; (D5-6).

🍴🍴 **Cibreo** Via dei Macci 118, ☒ 50122, tel. 2341100 ☒; 🍴 Tuscan and classical; 70 capacity; closed Sunday and Monday, New Year's-Epiphany (6 January) and August; ❀; (not shown on map).

🍴🍴 **Harry's Bar** Lungarno Vespucci 22/r, ☒ 50123, tel. 2396700 ☒; 🍴 Tuscan and classical; 55/65 capacity; closed Sunday, Christmas-Epiphany (6 January); 🅿; (D2).

🍴🍴 **Oliviero** Via delle Terme 51/r, ☒ 50123, tel. 287643, fax 2302407 ☒; 🍴 Tuscan fine cuisine; 80 capacity; closed Sunday, August; (D3).

🍴🍴 **Paoli** Via dei Tavolini 12/r, ☒ 50122, tel. 216215 ☒; 🍴 Tuscan; 80 capacity; closed Tuesday, and for a certain period of time in August; (D4).

🍴 **Acquerello** Via Ghibellina 156/r, ☒ 50122, tel. 2340554 ☒; 🍴 Tuscan; 65 capacity; closed Thursday; 🅿; (D5-6).

🍴 **Al Lume di Candela** Via delle Terme 23/r, ☒ 50123, tel. 294566, fax 283815 ☒; 🍴 Tuscan and classical; 35/50 capacity; closed Sunday, and at midday on Monday; 🅿; (D3).

🍴 **Buca Lapi** Via del Trebbio 1/r, ☒ 50123, tel. 213768 ☒; 🍴 Tuscan; 80/130 capacity; closed Sunday, at midday of Monday, August; (C3).

🍴 **Buca Mario** Piazza Ottaviani 16/r, ☒ 50123, tel. 214179 ☒; 🍴 Tuscan; 100 capacity; closed Wednesday, and midday on Thursday, August; 🅿; (C2).

🍴 **Fonticine** Via Nazionale 79/r, ☒ 50123, tel. 282106 ☒; 🍴 Tuscan and Emilian; 100 capacity; closed Sunday and Monday, end July/August; (A3).

🍴 **I' Toscano** Via Guelfa 70/r, ☒ 50129, tel. 215475 ☒; 🍴 Tuscan; 60/80 capacity; closed Tuesday, August; (A4).

🍴 **Sagrestia** Via Guicciardini 27/r, ☒ 50125, tel. 210003; 🍴 classical; 100 capacity; closed Monday; 🅿; (F3).

🍴 **Taverna del Bronzino** Via delle Ruote 25-27/r, ☒ 50129, tel. 495220 ☒; 🍴 classical; 75 capacity; closed Sunday, August; 🅿; (not shown on map).

Forte dei Marmi (LU)   ☒ 55042 ☎ 0584

ℹ️ *IAT*, Viale Achille Franceschi 8, tel. 80091, fax 83214.

🎿 *Versilia* (A12) km. 4.

Hotels and restaurants

**** **Augustus** Viale Morin 169, tel. 787200, fax 787102; seasonal; 68 rms. 🗽; 🅿 ♨ ♒ 🅿.

*** **Byron** Viale Morin 46, tel. 787052, fax 787152; 30 rms. 🗽; 🅿 ♨ ♒ 🅿.

*** **Raffaelli Park** Via Mazzini 37, tel. 787294, fax 787418; 28 rms. 🗽; 🅿 ♨ ♒ 🅿.

*** **Ritz Forte dei Marmi** Via F. Gioia 2, tel. 787531, fax 787522; 32 rms. 🗽; ♨ ♒ 🅿.

*** **Adam's Villa Maria** Via Lungomare 110, tel. 752424, fax 752112; seasonal; 37 rms. 🗽; ♒ 🅿.

*** **Franceschi** Via XX Settembre 19, tel. 787114, fax 787471; 55 rms. 🗽; 🅿 ♨ 🅿 & .

*** **Le Pleiadi** Via M. Civitali 51, tel. 881188, fax 881653; seasonal; 30 rms. 🗽; ♨ 🅿.

🍴🍴🍴 **Magnolia** Viale Morin 46, tel. 787052, fax 787152; 🍴 Tuscan and classical (seafood); 90 capacity; closed November; 🅿 🅿; of the Albergo Byron.

🍴 **Maitò** Via Arenile 28, tel. 80940 ☒; 🍴 classical; 80/100 capacity; open only evening in summer; closed Monday in winter, period of closing may vary; ❀ 🅿.

Frascati (RM)   ☒ 00044 ☎ 06

ℹ️ *AA*, Piazza Marconi 1, tel. 9420331, fax 9425498.

🎿 *Monte Porzio Catone* (A1 Dir.) km. 4.

Hotels and restaurants

** **Eden Tuscolano** Via Tuscolana 15, tel. 9408589, fax 9408591; 32 rms. (26 🗽); ♨ 🅿 & .

** **Giadrina** (no restaurant), Via A. Diaz 15, tel. 9419415, fax 9420440; 23 rms. 🗽; & .

🍴 **Cacciani** Via A. Diaz 13, tel. 9420378 ☒; 🍴 Roman and classical; 140 capacity; closed Monday (from November to March and evenings, on holidays), for a certain period of time in August; 🅿.

Gardone Riviera (BS)   ☒ 25083 ☎ 0365

ℹ️ *IAT*, Via della Repubblica 37, tel. 20347.

Hotels and restaurants

★✦★ **G.H. Gardone** Corso Zanardelli 74, tel. 20261, fax 22695; seasonal; 180 rms. 🕮; 🖭 ⚶ ♨ 🖩 🅿 ♣.

★✦★ **Spiaggia d'Oro** at Barbarano di Salò, Via Spiaggia d'Oro 15, ⊠ 25087, tel. 290034, fax 290092; seasonal; 39 rms. 🕮; 🖭 ⚶ ♣.

★★★ **Bellevue** Corso Zanardelli 40, tel. 290080, fax 290088; seasonal; 33 rms. 🕮; ⚶ ♨ 🖩 🅿.

★★★ **Monte Baldo** Corso Zanardelli 110, tel. 20951, fax 20952; seasonal; 45 rms. (40 🕮); ⚶ ♨ 🅿.

🍴🍴🍴 **Villa Fiordaliso** Corso Zanardelli 132, tel. 20158, fax 290011 ⊠; 🕪 Lombard-Venetian regional; 60/150 capacity; seasonal and December; closed Monday and at midday of Tuesday; ❦ 🅿; also hotel.

at Fasano del Garda, km. 3　　　　　⊠ 25080

Hotels and restaurants

★✦★ **G.H. Fasano** Corso Zanardelli 160, tel. 290220, fax 290221; seasonal; 87 rms. 🕮; ⚶ ♨ 🖩 🅿 ♣.

🍴🍴 **Lidò 84** Corso Zanardelli 168, tel. 20019 ⊠; 🕪 Lake Garda (seafood); 160 capacity; seasonal; closed Tuesday; ❦ 🅿.

Genoa　　　　　⊠ 16100 ☎ 010

🄸 *APT*, Via Roma 11/4, tel. 541541, fax 581408 *(C4)*; *IAT*, staz. Principe, tel. 2462633 *(B2)*; Aeroporto C. Colombo, tel. 2415247.

🚆 *Stazioni F.S. (State railroad stations)*, Porta Principe e Brignole; travellers information, tel. 284081.

⛟ *Genova Ovest* (A10, A6, A26, A7) km. 4; *Genova Est* (A12) km. 6.

✈ *International Airport* C. Colombo at Sestri Ponente (km. 7 to the west), tel. 2415410. *Alitalia*, Via XII Ottobre 188/r, tel. 54938 *(C4-5)*.

⛴ *Stazione Marittima (Marine Terminal)*: information c/o Consorzio Autonomo del Porto di Genova, P.te del Mille, tel. 2411.
Passenger shipping lines: ferry boat, for passengers with or without cars, to Sicily, Sardinia, Corsica, and Tunisia.

Hotels

★✦★ **Bristol Palace** (no restaurant), Via XX Settembre 35, ⊠ 16121, tel. 592541, fax 561756; 133 rms. 🕮; 🖭 🖩 ♣; *(D4)*.

★✦★ **City** (no restaurant), Via S. Sebastiano 6, ⊠ 16123, tel. 55451, fax 586301; 64 rms. 🕮 🖩; *(C4)*.

★✦★ **Jolly Hotel Plaza** Via M. Piaggio 11, ⊠ 16122, tel. 8393641, fax 8391850; 147 rms. 🕮; 🖭 🖩 ♣; *(C4-5)*.

★✦★ **Sheraton Genova** Via Pionieri e Aviatori d'Italia, ⊠ 16154, tel. 65491, fax 6549004; 284 rms. 🕮; 🖭 🅿 ♣; *(not shown on map)*.

★✦★ **Starhotel President** Corte Lambruschini 4, ⊠ 16129, tel. 5727, fax 5531820; 193 rms. 🕮; 🖭 🖩 ♣; *(D6)*.

★★★ **Agnello d'Oro** (no restaurant), Via delle Monachette 6, ⊠ 16126, tel. 2462084, fax 2462327; 35 rms. 🕮; 🅿; *(B2)*.

★★★ **Alexander** (no restaurant), Via Bersaglieri d'Italia 19/r, ⊠ 16126, tel. 261371, fax 265257; 35 rms. 🕮; 🖭 🖩; *(B2)*.

★★★ **Europa** (no restaurant), Vico delle Monachette 8, ⊠ 16126, tel. 256955, fax 261047; 38 rms. 🕮; 🖭 🅿; *(B2)*.

★★★ **Galles** (no restaurant), Via Bersaglieri d'Italia 13, ⊠ 16126, tel. 2462820, fax 2462822; 20 rms. 🕮; 🖩 ♣; *(B2)*.

★★★ **Viale Sauli** (no restaurant), Viale Sauli 5, ⊠ 16121, tel. 561397, fax 590092; 56 rms. 🕮; 🖭 🖩; *(D5)*.

Restaurants

🍴🍴🍴 **Antica Osteria del Bai** at Quarto dei Mille, Via Quarto 12, ⊠ 16148, tel. 387478, fax 392684; 🕪

Ligurian and classical; 60/80 capacity; closed Monday, and for a certain period of time in January and in August; 🖭; *(not shown on map)*.

🍴🍴🍴 **Gran Gotto** Viale Brigata Bisagno 69/R, ⊠ 16121, tel. 564344 ⊠; 🕪 Ligurian fine cuisine; 60 capacity; closed Saturday at midday and Sunday, and for a certain period of time in August; 🖭; *(E-6)*.

🍴🍴🍴 **La Bitta nella Pergola** Via Casaregis 52, ⊠ 16129, tel. 588543; 🕪 Ligurian fine cuisine; 40/60 capacity; closed Sunday evening, Monday, New Year's/Epiphany (6 January), and for a certain period of time in August; 🖭 ❦ 🅿; *(F6)*.

🍴🍴🍴 **Saint Cyr** Piazza Marsala 4, ⊠ 16122, tel. 886897 ⊠; 🕪 Ligurian and classical; 40 capacity; closed Sunday and at midday on Saturday, Christmas and a certain period of time in August; 🖭 🅿; *(C5)*.

🍴🍴🍴 **Zeffirino** Via XX Settembre 20, ⊠ 16121, tel. 591990, fax 586464 ⊠; 🕪 Ligurian and classical; 180 capacity; *(D5)*.

🍴🍴 **Baldin** Piazza Tazzoli 20/r Sestri Ponente, ⊠ 16154, tel. 6531400; 🕪 Ligurian (fish, mushrooms); 70 capacity; closed Sunday and Monday evening, a certain period of time in January and August; 🖭; *(not shown on map)*.

🍴🍴 **Bruxaboschi** at San Desiderio, Via Mignone 8, ⊠ 16133, tel. 3450302; 🕪 Ligurian (mushrooms); 150 capacity; closed Sunday evening and Monday, Christmas-Epiphany (6 January), and August; ❦ 🅿; *(not shown on map)*.

🍴🍴 **Genio** Salita S. Leonardo 61/r, ⊠ 16128, tel. 588463 ⊠; 🕪 Genoese; 55 capacity; closed Sunday, August; *(D4)*.

🍴 **Enoteca con Cucina Sola** Via C. Barabino 120/r, ⊠ 16129, tel. 594513; 🕪 Ligurian; 40 capacity; closed Sunday, and for a certain period of time in August.

Gubbio (PG)　　　　　⊠ 06024 ☎ 075

🄸 *APT*, Piazza Oderisi, tel. 9220693, fax 9273409; *Associazione Maggio Eugubino*, Corso Garibaldi 50, tel. 9273912.

🚆 *Stazione F.S. (State railroad station)*, Fossato di Vico km. 21, tel. 075/919230.

Hotels and restaurants

★★★ **Park Hotel ai Cappuccini** Via Tifernate, tel. 9234, fax 9220323; 95 rms. 🕮; 🖭 ⚶ ♨ 🖩 🅿 ♣.

★★★ **Bosone Palace** (no restaurant), Via XX Settembre 22, tel. 9220688, fax 9220552; 30 rms. 🕮; ♣.

★★ **Oderisi-Balestrieri** (no restaurant), Via Mazzatinti 2-12, tel. 9220662, fax 9220663; closed February; 40 rms. 🕮; 🖭.

🍴🍴🍴 **Taverna del Lupo** Via Ansidei 21, tel. 9274368, fax 9271269 ⊠; 🕪 Umbrian (mushrooms and truffles); 150 capacity; closed Monday; 🖭.

🍴🍴🍴 **Villa Montegranelli** township of Monteluiano, tel. 9220185, fax 9273372 ⊠; 🕪 Umbrian and Apulian (mushrooms and truffles, fish); 130/400 capacity; ❦ 🅿; also hotel.

🍴🍴 **Federico da Montefeltro** Via della Repubblica 35, tel. 9273949; 🕪 Umbrian (mushrooms and truffles); 250/300 capacity; closed Thursday (except August and September), February; ❦.

Hercolaneum (NA)　　　　　⊠ 80056 ☎ 081

⛟ *Ercolano* (A3) km. 1.

Hotels

★✦★ **Punta Quattroventi** Via Marittima 59, tel. 7773041, fax 7773757; 37 rms. 🕮; 🖭 ⚶ ♨ 🅿.

Ischia (Island of) (NA)   ☎ 081

🅙   at Ischia: *AA*, Via Colonna 126, tel. 983066; *Information Office*, Via Jasolino, tel. 991146.

✈   *Airport* at Naples-Capodichino, tel. 7896259-7896245.

⛴   Transportation with car ferry from Naples and Pozzuoli.

at Ischia   ✉ 80077

Hotels and restaurants

★★★ **G.H. Punta Molino Terme** Lungomare C. Colombo 23, tel. 991544, fax 991562; seasonal; 82 rms. 🕭; 🅿 ♨ ♨ P.

★★★ **Continental Terme** Via M. Mazzella 74, tel. 991588, fax 982929; seasonal; 244 rms. 🕭; 🅿 ♨ ♨ P.

★★★ **G.H. Excelsior** Via E. Gianturco 19, tel. 991522, fax 984100; seasonal; 74 rms. 🕭; 🅿 ♨ 🅿 🔳.

★★★ **Jolly delle Terme** Via De Luca 42, tel. 991744, fax 993156; seasonal; 208 rms. 🕭; 🅿 ♨ ♨ P ♿.

★★★ **Bristol Hotel Terme** Via Marone 10, tel. 992181, fax 993201; seasonal, 61 rms. 🕭; ♨ 🅿 🔳.

🍴🍴🍴 **Damiano** Nuova Circonvallazione, tel. 983032 ⌧; ⅋⅋ Ischian and classical; 50 capacity; seasonal; closed at midday from April to September.

🍴🍴🍴 **Gennaro** Via Porto 66, tel. 992917, fax 983636 ⌧; ⅋⅋ Ischian and classical; 60 capacity; seasonal; closed Tuesday in the off season.

🍴 **Giardini Eden** Via Nuova Cartaromana 68, tel. 985015; ⅋⅋ Neapolitan; 130 capacity; seasonal; ❋ P; also hotel.

at Barano d'Ischia   ✉ 80070

Hotels

★★★ **Parco Smeraldo Terme** at Lido dei Maronti, Via Maronti 21, tel. 990127, fax 905022; seasonal; 72 rms. 🕭; 🅿 ♨ ♨ P.

★★★ **San Giorgio Terme** at Lido dei Maronti, Via Maronti 42, tel. 990098; seasonal; 80 rms. 🕭; ♨ ♨ 🔳.

at Casamìcciola Terme   ✉ 80074

Hotels

★★★ **Elma Park Hotel Terme** Corso Vittorio Emanuele 57, tel. 994122, fax 994253; 73 rms. 🕭; 🅿 ♨ ♨ P ♿.

★★★ **Manzi** Piazza Bagni 1, tel. 994722, fax 980241; seasonal; 62 rms. 🕭; 🅿 ♨ ♨.

★★★ **L'Approdo** Via Eddomade 29, tel. 994077, fax 980185; seasonal; 33 rms. 🕭; 🅿 ♨ ♨ P.

at Forio   ✉ 80075

Hotels

★★★ **Parco Maria** at Cuotto, Via Provinciale Panza 212, tel. 909040, fax 909100; seasonal; 98 rms. 🕭; ♨ ♨ P.

★★★ **La Bagattella** at San Francesco km. 3 Via T. Cigliano 8, tel. 986072, fax 989637; seasonal; 53 rms. 🕭; 🅿 ♨ ♨ P.

at Lacco Ameno   ✉ 80076

Hotels

★★★★ **Regina Isabella e Royal Sporting** Piazza S. Restituta, tel. 994322, fax 900190; closed mid-January/early April; 134 rms. 🕭; 🅿 ♨ ♨ 🔳 P ♿.

★★★ **La Reginella** Piazza S. Restituta, tel. 994300, fax 980481; seasonal; 83 rms. 🕭; 🅿 ♨ ♨ P.

★★★ **Parco Hotel Terme Michelangelo** Via Provinciale Fango 77, tel. 995134, fax 995553; seasonal; 71 rms. 🕭; ♨ ♨ P.

★★★ **San Montano** Via Montevico, tel. 994033, fax 980242; seasonal; 67 rms. 🕭; ♨ 🅿 ♨ P.

★★★ **Don Pepe** Via Campo 25, tel. 994397, fax 996696; seasonal; 70 rms. 🕭; 🅿 ♨ ♨ P.

★★★ **Villa Angelica** Via IV Novembre 28, tel. 994524, fax 980184; closed mid-November/Christmas and mid-January/mid-February; 20 rms. 🕭; ♨ ♨ 🔳.

at Sant'Angelo   ✉ 80070

Hotels and restaurants

★★★ **Park Hotel Miramare** Via C. Maddalena 29, tel. 999219, fax 999325; seasonal; 54 rms. 🕭; ♨ ♨.

★★★ **San Michele Terme** Via S. Angelo 60, tel. 999276, fax 999149; seasonal; 52 rms. 🕭; ♨ ♨.

🍴 **Pescatore** Piazza O. Troia 5, tel. 999206 ⌧; ⅋⅋ Campanian (seafood); 70 capacity; closed Tuesday in the off season, February; 🅿.

L'Aquila   ✉ 67100 ☎ 0862

🅙   *EPT*, Piazza S. Maria di Paganica 5, tel. 410808, fax 65442 (*B4*); *AA*, Via XX Settembre 10, tel. 27486 (*C3*); *Information Office*, Corso Vittorio Emanuele 49, tel. 410859 (*B4*).

🚆   *Stazione F.S. (State railroad station)*, tel. 419290.

🛣   *L'Aquila Ovest* km. 3 o *L'Aquila Est* km. 5 (A24).

Hotels and restaurants

★★★ **G.H. del Parco** Corso Federico II 74, tel. 413248, fax 65938; 36 rms. 🕭; 🔳 P ♿; (*C4*).

★★★ **Duca degli Abruzzi** Viale Giovanni XXIII 10, tel. 28341, fax 61588; 120 rms. 🕭; 🅿 🔳 P ♿; (*B3*).

★★★ **Duomo** (no restaurant), Via Dragonetti 9, tel. 410893, fax 413058; 30 rms. 🕭; 🔳; (*C4*).

★★★ **Le Cannelle** Via Tancredi da Pentima 2/A, tel. 411194, fax 412453; 140 rms. 🕭; ♨ ♨ 🔳 P; (*B2*).

🍴🍴🍴 **Tre Marie** Via Tre Marie 3, tel. 413191 ⌧; ⅋⅋ Abruzzese; 80 capacity; closed Sunday evening and Monday, Christmas-Epiphany (6 January); (*B4*).

🍴 **Grotta di Aligi** Viale Rendina 2, tel. 65260; ⅋⅋ of Abruzzo and classical; 120/270 capacity; closed Monday; 🅿 ❋; del G.H. del Parco; (*C4*).

Lecce   ✉ 73100 ☎ 0832

🅙   *EPT*, Via Monte S. Michele 20, tel. 314117 (*C4*); *Information Office*, Piazza S. Oronzo Sedile, tel. 304443 (*C-D2*). *AA*, Via Zanardelli 66, tel. 316461.

🚆   *Stazione F.S. (State railroad station)*, Viale Quarta, tel. 301016. *Ferrovie Sud Est*, Viale Quarta 38, tel. 241931.

Hotels and restaurants

★★★ **President** Via Salandra 6, tel. 311881, fax 372283; 154 rms. 🕭; 🅿 🔳 ♿; (*C5*).

★★★ **Delle Palme** Via Leuca 90, tel. 347171, fax 347171; 96 rms. 🕭; 🅿 P ♿; (*F3*).

🍴 **Barbablu** Via Umberto I 7, tel. 241183 ⌧; ⅋⅋ of Salento (seafood, herbs); 40/60 capacity; closed Sunday evening and Monday; (*C2-3*).

🍴 **Villa della Monica** Via Ss. Giacomo e Filippo 40, tel. 458432; ⅋⅋ of Salento and classical; 500 capacity; closed Tuesday, and for a certain period of time in January; 🅿 ❋ P; (*B-C4*).

Lérici (SP)   ✉ 19032 ☎ 0187

🅙   *IAT*, Via Gerini 40, tel. 967346.

🛣   *Sarzana* (A12) km. 6.

Hotels and restaurants

★★★ **Europa** Via Carpanini 1, tel. 967800, fax 965957; 35 rms. 🕭; 🅿 P.

★★★ **Shelley & delle Palme** Lungomare Biaggini 5, tel. 968204, fax 964271; 49 rms. 🕭; 🔳.

🍴 **Calata** Via Mazzini 4, tel. 967143 ⌧; ⅋⅋ classical (seafood); 50/70 capacity; closed Tuesday, and for a certain period of time in January and between November and December; 🌸.

at Fiascherino, km. 4   ✉ 19030

Hotels

★★★ **Cristallo** (no restaurant) tel. 567291, fax 564269; seasonal; 35 rms. ▦; 🅑 ⚏ 🅟.

★★★ **Il Nido** tel. 967286, fax 964225; seasonal and Christmas, New Year's; 36 rms. ▦; ⚏ 🔲 🅟.

at Tellaro, km. 4,5   ✉ 19030

Restaurants

🍴🍴🍴 **Miranda** Via Fiascherino 92, tel. 968130, fax 964032 ☒; 🍽 fine cuisine (seafood); 35 capacity; closed Monday, mid-January/February; 🅟; also hotel.

Lèvanto (SP)   ✉ 19015 ☎ 0187

▦ *Stazione F.S. (State railroad station)*, tel. 808457.

🏕 *Carrodano* (A12) km. 12.

Hotels and restaurants

★★★ **Nazionale** Via Jacopo da Levanto 20, tel. 808102, fax 800901; closed beginning November/beginning December, and Epiphany (6 January)/mid-March; 32 rms. ▦; ⚏ 🅟.

🍴🍴 **Hostaria da Franco** Via privata Olivi 8, tel. 808647 ☒; 🍽 Ligurian and Umbrian; 70 capacity; closed Monday except in summer, November; 🌸.

Lido di Ostia (RM)   ✉ 00121 ☎ 06

ℹ️ *Pro Loco*, Piazzale Stazione Lido Centro 34, tel. 562/892.

▦ *Stazione Ferrovie Cotral*, travellers information, Rome, tel. 57532323.

Hotels and restaurants

★★★ **Airport** Viale dei Romagnoli 165, tel. 5692341, fax 5695993; 260 rms. ▦; 🅑 🔲 ⚏.

★★★ **Satellite** Via delle Antille 49, tel. 5693841, fax 5695993; 256 rms. ▦; 🅑 ⚏ 🔲 ⚏.

★★★ **Ping Pong** Lungomare Toscanelli 84, tel. 5601733, fax 5621236; 28 rms. ▦; ⚏.

▲▲▲ **Sironetta** Lungomare Toscanelli 46, tel. 5626700, fax 5622310; 56 rms. ▦; ⚏ 🅟.

🍴 **Ferrantelli** Via Claudio 5/7, tel. 56304269 ☒; 🍽 classical (seafood); 100 capacity; closed Monday and Sunday evening in winter; period of closing may vary; 🅑.

🍴 **Sbarco di Enea** at Ostia Antica, Via dei Romagnoli 675, ✉ 00119, tel. 5650253; 🍽 classical (seafood); 230 capacity; closed Monday, February; 🌸.

Lucca   ✉ 55100 ☎ 0583

ℹ️ *APT*, Piazza Guidiccioni 2, tel. 491205, fax 490766 (*B3*); *Information Office*, Vecchia Porta San Donato, Piazzale Verdi, tel. 419689 (*C1*).

▦ *Stazione F.S. (State railroad station)*, Piazza Ricasoli, tel. 47013

🏕 *Capannori* (A11) km. 5; *Lucca* (A11/A12) km. 2.

Hotels and restaurants

★★★ **G.H. Guinigi** Via Romana 1247, tel. 4991, fax 499800; 158 rms. ▦; 🅑 🅟 ⚏; (*C5, not shown on map*).

★★★ **La Luna** (no restaurant) Via Fillungo corner of Corte Compagni 12, tel. 493634, fax 490021; closed for a certain period of time in January; 30 rms. ▦; 🔲 🅟; (*B3*).

★★★ **Piccolo Hotel Puccini** (no restaurant) Via di Poggio 9, tel. 55421, fax 53487; 14 rms. ▦; 🅟; (*C2*).

★★★ **Rex** (no restaurant), Piazza Ricasoli 19, tel. 955443, fax 954348; 25 rms. ▦; 🅑 ⚏; (*D3*).

★★ **Stipino** (no restaurant), Via Romana 95, tel. 495077, fax 490309; 21 rms. (19 ▦); 🅑 ⚏ 🅟; (*B5, not shown on map*).

🍴🍴🍴 **Antico Caffè delle Mura** Piazza Vittorio Emanuele 2, tel. 47962 ☒; 🍽 Lucchesia; 100/300 capacity; closed Tuesday, and for a certain period of time in January; 🌸; (*D2*).

🍴🍴 **Del Teatro** Piazza Napoleone 25, tel. 493740 ☒; 🍽 Tuscan and classical (seafood); 70/110 capacity; closed Thursday; 🌸; (*C2*).

at Massa Pisana, km. 4   ✉ 55050

Hotels and restaurants

★★★★ **Locanda L'Elisa** state road (S.S.) for Pisa, tel. 379737, fax 379019; 10 rms. ▦; 🅑 ⚏ 🔲 ⚏.

🍴🍴🍴 **Gazebo** state road (S.S.) for Pisa, tel. 379737 ☒; 🍽 Tuscan and classical; closed Sunday; 🌸 🅟.

at Ponte a Moriano, km. 9   ✉ 55029

Restaurants

🍴🍴🍴 **Mora** Via Sesto di Moriano 1748, tel. 406402, fax 406135 ☒; 🍽 Lucchesia and Garfagnana; 40/60 capacity; closed Wednesday, and for a certain period of time in January; 🌸.

at San Macàrio in Piano, km. 6   ✉ 55056

Restaurants

🍴🍴🍴 **Solferino** road to Villa Pardini 2, tel. 59118, fax 329161 ☒; 🍽 Tuscan (seafood, mushrooms); 80 capacity; closed Wednesday and at midday on Thursday, and for a certain period of time in January; 🌸 🅟.

at San Michele in Escheto, km. 4   ✉ 55050

Hotels

★★★★ **Villa San Michele** (no restaurant), Via della Chiesa 462, tel. 370276, fax 370277; closed Epiphany (6 January)/February; 22 rms. ▦; 🅑 ⚏ 🅟 ⚏.

Madonna di Campiglio (TN)   ✉ 38084 ☎ 0465

ℹ️ *APT*, Via Pradalago 4, tel. 42000, fax 40404.

▦ *Stazione F.S. (State railroad station)*, at Trento km. 74, tel. 0461/234545.

🎿 numerous chairlifts and skilifts, crosscountry skiing.

Hotels and restaurants

★★★★ **Cristallo** Via Dolomiti di Brenta 53, tel. 441132, fax 440687; seasonal; 43 rms. ▦; 🔲 🅟 ⚏.

★★★★ **Savoia Palace** Via Dolomiti di Brenta, tel. 441004, fax 440549; seasonal; 55 rms. ▦; 🔲 🅟.

★★★ **Alpina** Via Sfulmini 5, tel. 441075, fax 443464; seasonal; 27 rms. ▦; ⚏ 🅟 ⚏.

★★★ **Bonapace** Via Spinale 18, tel. 441019, fax 440570; seasonal; 50 rms. ▦; ⚏ 🔲 🅟.

★★★ **Chalet dei Pini** (no restaurant), Via Campanile Basso 24, tel. 441489, fax 441489; seasonal; 10 rms. ▦; ⚏ 🔲 🅟.

★★★ **Oberosler** Via Monte Spinale 27, tel. 441136, fax 443220; seasonal; 39 rms. ▦; ⚏ 🔲 🅟 ⚏.

★★ **Hermitage** Via Castelletto 65, tel. 441558, fax 441618; seasonal; 41 rms. ▦; ⚏ 🔲 🅟.

🍴 **Artini** Via Cima Tosa 47, tel. 440122; 🍽 classical (mushrooms); 160 capacity; seasonal; 🅑.

🍴 **Crozzon** Via Dolomiti di Brenta 96, tel. 442217 ☒; 🍽 of Trento and classical; 90 capacity; seasonal; 🌸; also hotel.

433

at Campo Carlo Magno, km. 3

Hotels

⁎ **Golf Hotel** Via Cima Tosa 3, tel. 441003, fax 440294; seasonal; 124 rms. ℡; ♨ ℙ ♿.

Mantua
✉ 46100 ☎ 0376

ℹ *APT*, Piazza Mantegna 6, tel. 328253, fax 363292 (*C4*).

🚊 *Stazione F.S. (State railroad station)*, Piazza don Leoni, tel. 363888.

✈ *Mantova Nord* (A22) km. 5.

Hotels and restaurants

⁎ **San Lorenzo** (no restaurant), Piazza Concordia 14, tel. 220500, fax 327194; 32 rms. ℡; 🏧 🖳; (*C4*).

*** **Bianchi Stazione** (no restaurant), Piazza Don Leoni 24, tel. 326465, fax 321504; 53 (52 ℡) rms.; 🏧 ♨ 🖳 ℙ ♿.

*** **Mantegna** (no restaurant), Via Filzi 10, tel. 328019, fax 368564; closed Christmas-Epiphany (6 January); 39 rms. ℡; 🏧 🖳 ℙ; (*C4*).

¶¶ **Aquila Nigra** Vicolo Bonacolsi 4, tel. 327180, fax 226490 ✕; ⅋ Mantuan; 65 capacity; closed Sunday evening, except April/May and September/October and Monday, and for a certain period of time in August; 🏧; (*B4*).

¶ **Cigno-Trattoria dei Martini** Piazza d'Arco 1, tel. 327101 ✕; ⅋ Mantuan and classical; 80 capacity; closed Monday and Tuesday, and for a certain period of time in January and in August; 🏧 ❀; (*B3*).

¶ **Ochina Bianca** Via Finzi 2, tel. 323700 ✕; ⅋ Mantuan; 80 capacity; closed Monday and at midday on Tuesday, and for a certain period of time in January and between July and in August; 🏧 ❀; (*B3-4*).

Marina di Ravenna (RA)
✉ 48023 ☎ 0544

ℹ *IAT*, seasonal, Viale delle Nazioni 159, tel. 530117; Marina Romea, seasonal, tel. 446035; Punta Marina, seasonal, tel. 437312; Lido Adriano, seasonal, tel. 495353.

✈ *Ravenna* (A14 Dir.) km. 19.

Hotels and restaurants

⁎ **Park Hotel Ravenna** Viale delle Nazioni 181, tel. 531743, fax 530430; seasonal; 144 rms. ℡; 🏧 ♨ ♨ ℙ ♿.

*** **Bermuda** Viale della Pace 363, tel. 530560, fax 531643; closed mid-December/mid-January; 20 rms. ℡; 🏧 ♨ ℙ.

¶¶ **Gloria** Viale delle Nazioni 420, tel. 530274, fax 503377 ✕; ⅋ of Romagna (seafood); 65/160 capacity; closed Wednesday, August; ❀ ℙ.

at Marina Romèa, km. 3 beyond the harbor channel

Hotels

*** **Columbia** Viale Italia 70, tel. 446038, fax 447202; 44 rms. ℡; ♨ ℙ.

Martina Franca (TA)
✉ 74015 ☎ 080

ℹ *AA*, Piazza Roma 37, tel. 705702.

🚊 *Stazione Ferrovie Sud Est*, tel. 8808151.

Hotels and restaurants

*** **Dell'Erba** Viale dei Cedri 1, tel. 4301055, fax 4301639; 49 rms. ℡; 🏧 ♨ ♨ ℙ ♿.

¶ **La Rotonda** Villa Comunale Garibaldi, tel. 4807052; ⅋ Tarantina and Barese; 100/250 capacity; closed Tuesday, and for a certain period of time in January; ❀.

Massa Marittima (GR)
✉ 58024 ☎ 0566

ℹ Via Parenti 22, tel. 940242.

Hotels and restaurants

*** **Il Sole** (no restaurant), Via della Libertà 43, tel. 901971, fax 901959; 51 rms. ℡; 🖳 ♿.

** **Duca del Mare** Piazza Alighieri 1, tel. 902284, fax 901905; closed mid-November/mid-December; 19 rms. ℡; 🖳 ♿.

¶¶ **Bracali** at Ghirlanda, ✉ 58020, tel. 902318; ⅋ Tuscan and classical; 30 capacity; closed Tuesday, period of closing may vary; 🏧 ❀ ℙ.

Matera
✉ 75100 ☎ 0835

ℹ *APT*, Via De Viti De Marco 9, tel. 331983, fax 333452; *Information Office*, tel. 333541.

🚊 *Ferrovie Appulo Lucane*, Stazione Villa Longo, tel. 388192; Stazione Centrale, Piazza Matteotti, tel. 332861.

Hotels and restaurants

*** **De Nicola** Via Nazionale 158, tel. 385111, fax 385113; 119 rms. ℡; ♨ 🏧 🖳 ♿.

*** **Il Piccolo Albergo** (no restaurant), Via De Sariis 11, tel. 330201, fax 333122; closed for a certain period of time in August; 11 ℡.

¶ **Casino del Diavolo** Via La Martella 48, tel. 261986; ⅋ Lucanian; 160 capacity; closed Monday; 🏧 ❀ ℙ.

at Venùsio, km. 7

Restaurants

¶¶ **Venusio** Via Lussemburgo 2, tel. 259081, fax 259082 ✕; ⅋ Lucanian and Apulian (seafood); 60/80 capacity; 🏧 ❀ ℙ.

Merano / Meran (BZ)
✉ 39012 ☎ 0473

ℹ *APT*, Corso Libertà 45, tel. 235223, fax 235524.

🚊 *Stazione F.S. (State railroad station)*, tel. 447500.

⛷ some facilities at Merano 2000.

Hotels and restaurants

⁎ **Kurhotel Schloss Rundegg** Via Scena 2, tel. 234100, fax 237200; closed Epiphany (6 January)/mid-February; 30 rms. ℡; ♨ ♨ 🖳 ℙ.

⁎ **Palace** Via Cavour 2/4, tel. 211300, fax 234181; 124 rms. ℡; ♨ ♨ ℙ ♿.

*** **Villa Tivoli** Via Verdi 72, tel. 446282, fax 446849; seasonal; 25 rms. ℡; ♨ 🖳 ℙ.

*** **Europa Splendid** Corso Libertà 178, tel. 232376, fax 230221; 54 rms. ℡; 🖳.

*** **Isabella** Via Piave 58, tel. 234700, fax 211360; seasonal; 25 rms. ℡; ♨ 🖳 ℙ ♿.

*** **Mendelhof** Via Winkel 45, tel. 236130, fax 236481; seasonal; 36 rms. ℡; ♨ ♨ ℙ.

¶ **Flora** Via Portici 75, tel. 231484 ✕; ⅋ fine cuisine; 26 capacity; open April/mid-November; closed Sunday and at midday on Monday; 🏧.

¶ **Sissi** Via Plankenstein 5, tel. 231062 ✕; ⅋ fine cuisine; 24 capacity; closed Monday, period of closing may vary; 🏧.

at Fragsburg, km. 7

Hotels

⁎ **Castel Fragsburg** Via Fragsburg 3, tel. 244071, fax 244493; seasonal; 18 rms. ℡; ♨ ♨ ℙ ♿.

Messina
✉ 98100 ☎ 090

ℹ *AAPT*, Via Calabria is. 301 bis, tel. 674236, fax 601005; *AA*, Piazza Cairoli 45, tel. 2935292, fax 694780.

🚊 *Stazioni F.S. (State railroad stations)*: Centrale, Piazza Stazione, tel. 675234; Marittima, Via Calabria, tel. 675234.

ⵈ *Messina Boccetta* (A20) km. 3; *Messina Centro* (A18) km. 4.

✈ at Reggio di Calabria-Ravagnese, tel. 0965/642232. *Alitalia*, Via del Vespro 52/56, tel. 679940.

⚓ *Capitaneria di Porto*, Via Vittorio Emanuele, tel. 41896.

Hotels and restaurants

*** Jolly dello Stretto Via Garibaldi 126, ✉ 98126, tel. 363860, fax 5902526; 96 rms. ▯; 🅿 ⅋.

*** Royal Palace Hotel Via Cannizzaro 224, ✉ 98122, tel. 6503, fax 2921075; 106 rms. ▯; 🅿 ⅋.

¶¶ **Pranpron** Via Ugo Bassi 157, ✉ 98123, tel. 2938584; ✗ Messinese (seafood); 100 capacity; closed Sunday evening and Wednesday, September; 🅿.

¶¶ **Savoya** Via XXVII Luglio 36/38, ✉ 98123, tel. 2934865 ☒; ✗ Sicilian (seafood); 100 capacity; closed Monday, and a certain period of time in August; 🅿.

Mestre (VE)   ✉ 30170 ☎ 041

ⓘ Nuova Rotatoria Autostrada, Marghera, tel. 937764.

🚂 *Stazione F.S. (State railroad station)*, Piazzale Favretti, tel. 715555.

ⵈ *Mestre M.* (A4) km. 2.

Hotels and restaurants

*** Bologna & Stazione Via Piave 214, ✉ 30171, tel. 931000, fax 931095; 129 rms. ▯; 🅿 🔲.

*** Michelangelo Via Forte Marghera 69, ✉ 30173, tel. 986600, fax 986052; 51 rms. ▯; 🅿⅋🔲🅿 ⅋.

*** President (no restaurant), Via Forte Marghera 99/A, ✉ 30173, tel. 985655, fax 985655; 51 rms. ▯; 🅿 🔲🅿.

¶¶¶ **Dall'Amelia** Via Miranese 113, ✉ 30171, tel. 913955, fax 5441111; ✗ Venetian regional and fine cuisine (seafood); 150/250 capacity; closed Wednesday; 🅿 ❀; also hotel.

¶¶ **Valeriano** Via Col di Lana 18, ✉ 30171, tel. 926474 ☒; ✗ Venetian and classical (seafood); 60 capacity; closed Sunday evening and Monday, and for a certain period of time in August; 🅿.

Milan   ✉ 20100 ☎ 02

ⓘ *APT* and *IAT*, main headquarters, Palazzo del Turismo, Via Marconi 1 corner of Piazza Duomo, tel. 809662, fax 72022999 (*D-E4*); Stazione Centrale (Galleria di Testa; i.e., main atrium), tel. 6690532-6690432 (*A6*).
Information Office of the Comune di Milano, Galleria Vittorio Emanuele II corner of Piazza della Scala, tel. 878363 (*D4*).
TCI, Corso Italia 10, tel. 85261 (*E4*).

🚂 *Ferrovie dello Stato*, travellers information for all destinations in Milan: Stazione Centrale, Piazza Duca d'Aosta, tel. 675001.

🚂 *Stazione Ferrovie Nord Milano*, Piazzale Cadorna 14, tel. 85111.

✈ *Airports: Internazionale Forlanini* at Linate (km. 7 east of the center), tel. 28106306. *Intercontinentale della Malpensa*, near Gallarate (km. 45 NW), passenger information for both airports (SEA), tel. 26800613.
Alitalia (Passenger agencies): Via Albricci 5, tel. 62817 (*E4*) and Corso Como 15, tel. 62811 (*A4*); for information and reservations tel. 26853.

ⵈ *access from Viale Certosa and from Piazzale Kennedy* (A4, A8, A9), *from Corso Lodi* (A1), *from Via La Spezia* (A7); a ring road links the various highways without having to drive through the city.

Hotels

***L Four Seasons Via Gesù 8, ✉ 20121, tel. 77088, fax 77085000; 98 rms. ▯; 🅿 ⚶ 🔲 ⅋; (*D4*).

***L Palace Piazza della Repubblica 20, ✉ 20124, tel. 63361, fax 654485; 216 rms. ▯; 🅿 🔲 ⅋; (*B5*).

***L Principe di Savoia Piazza della Repubblica 17, ✉ 20124, tel. 62301, fax 6595838; 299 rms. ▯; 🅿 ⅋; (*B5*).

*** Carlton Via Senato 5, ✉ 20121, tel. 76015535, fax 783300; closed August; 63 rms. ▯; 🅿 🔲 ⅋; (*C-D5*).

*** G.H. et de Milan Via Manzoni 29, ✉ 20121, tel. 723141, fax 86460861; 95 rms. ▯; 🅿 🔲; (*D4*).

*** Antares Hotel Rubens (no restaurant), Via Rubens 21, ✉ 20148, tel. 40302, fax 48193114; 87 rms. ▯; 🅿 🔲 🅿; (*not shown on map*).

*** Bristol (no restaurant), Via Scarlatti 32, ✉ 20124, tel. 6694141, fax 6702942; closed for a certain period of time in August; 68 rms. ▯; 🅿 🔲; (*A-B6*).

*** Brunelleschi Via Baracchini 12, ✉ 20123, tel. 8843, fax 804924; 128 rms. ▯; 🅿 🔲⅋; (*E4*).

*** Carlyle Brera Hotel (no restaurant), Corso Garibaldi 84, ✉ 20121, tel. 29003888, fax 29003993; 96 rms. ▯; 🅿 🔲 ⅋; (*C3*).

*** Century Tower Hotel Via F. Filzi 25/B, ✉ 20124, tel. 67504, fax 66980602; 148 rms. ▯; 🅿⚶🔲 ⅋; (*A5*).

*** De La Ville Via Hoepli 6, ✉ 20121, tel. 867651, fax 866609; closed August; 109 rms. ▯; 🅿 🔲; (*D4*).

*** D'Este (no restaurant), Viale Bligny 23, ✉ 20136, tel. 58321001, fax 58321136; 79 rms. ▯; 🅿 🔲; (*F4*).

*** Excelsior Gallia Piazza Duca d'Aosta 9, ✉ 20124, tel. 67851, fax 66713239; 237 rms. ▯; 🅿 🔲 🅿; (*A5*).

*** Hermitage Via Messina 10, ✉ 20154, tel. 33107700, fax 33107399; 131 rms. ▯; 🅿 ⚶ 🔲; (*A2-3*).

*** Hilton Via Galvani 12, ✉ 20124, tel. 69831, fax 66710810; 320 rms. ▯; 🅿 🔲 🅿; (*A5*).

*** Jolly President Largo Augusto 10, ✉ 20122, tel. 77461, fax 783449; 220 rms. ▯; 🅿 🔲; (*D-E5*).

*** Jolly Touring Via Tarchetti 2, ✉ 20121, tel. 6335, fax 6592209; 301 rms. ▯; 🅿 🔲 🅿 ⅋; (*B5*).

*** Lloyd (no restaurant), Corso di Porta Romana 48, ✉ 20122, tel. 58303332, fax 58303365; 57 rms. ▯; 🅿 🔲; (*F6*).

*** Mentana (no restaurant), Via Morigi 2 corner of Piazza Mentana, ✉ 20123, tel. 86454255, fax 865382; 33 rms. ▯; 🅿 🔲; (*D3*).

*** Michelangelo Via Scarlatti 33 corner of Piazza L. di Savoia , ✉ 20124, tel. 6755, fax 6694232; closed for a certain period of time in August; 300 rms. ▯; 🅿 🅿; (*A6*).

*** Regency (no restaurant), Via Arimondi 12, ✉ 20155, tel. 39216021, fax 39217734; closed for a certain period of time in August, and Christmas holidays; 59 rms. ▯; 🅿 🔲; (*not shown on map*).

*** Starhotel Ritz Via Spallanzani 40, ✉ 20129, tel. 2055, fax 29518679; 195 rms. ▯; 🅿 🔲 ⅋; (*B6*).

*** Starhotel Rosa Via Pattari 5, ✉ 20122, tel. 8831, fax 8057964; 185 rms. ▯; 🅿 🔲 ⅋; (*D4*).

*** Starhotel Splendido Viale Andrea Doria 4, ✉ 20124, tel. 6789, fax 66713369; 165 rms. ▯; 🅿 🔲 ⅋; (*A6*).

*** Albert (no restaurant), Via Tonale 2, ✉ 20125, tel. 66985446, fax 66985624; closed for a certain period of time in August; 62 rms. ▯; 🅿 🔲 ⅋; (*not shown on map*).

*** Canada (no restaurant), Via S. Sofia 16, ✉ 20122, tel. 58304844, fax 58300282; 35 rms. ▯; 🅿 🔲 ⅋; (*F4*).

*** City (no restaurant), Corso Buenos Aires 42/5, ✉ 20124, tel. 29523382, fax 2046957; closed for a certain period of time in August and Christmas-New Year's; 55 rms. ▯; 🅿 🔲; (*B6*).

★★★ **Imperial** (no restaurant), Corso di Porta Romana 68, ✉ 20122, tel. 58318200, fax 58318027; 36 rms. ▨; 🅿️; (F5).

★★★ **Mennini** (no restaurant), Via Napo Torriani 14, ✉ 20124, tel. 6690951, fax 6693437; closed for a certain period of time in August; 65 rms. ▨; ▨; (A6).

🍽 **Savini** Galleria Vittorio Emanuele II, ✉ 20121, tel. 72003433, fax 86461060 ✉; 🍴 Lombard, Piedmontese and Venetian; 200/420 capacity; closed Saturday at midday, Sunday, August and Christmas-New Year's; ▨ ✿; (D4).

🍽 **Aimo e Nadia** Via Montecuccoli 6, ✉ 20147, tel. 416886, fax 48302005 ✉; 🍴 classical and fine cuisine; 40 capacity; closed Saturday at midday and Sunday, August and New Year's-Epiphany (6 January); ▨; (not shown on map).

🍽 **Biffi Scala and Toulà** Piazza della Scala, ✉ 20121, tel. 866651, fax 866653 ✉; 🍴 classical; 140 capacity; closed Saturday at midday and Sunday, and for a certain period of time in August; ▨; (D4).

🍽 **Boeucc** Piazza Belgioioso 2, ✉ 20121, tel. 76020224, fax 796173 ✉; 🍴 Lombard and classical; 140/160 capacity; closed Saturday and at midday on Sunday, August, Christmas and New Year's; ▨; (D4).

🍽 **Hong Kong** Via Schiapparelli 5, ✉ 20125, tel. 67071790 ✉; 🍴 Chinese; 30/80 capacity; closed Monday; ▨; (not shown on map).

🍽 **L'Ulmet** Via Olmetto 21, ✉ 20123, tel. 86452718, fax 72002486 ✉; 🍴 fine cuisine; 60 capacity; closed Sunday and at midday on Monday, August and Christmas-Epiphany (6 January); ▨; (E3-4).

🍽 **Sadler** Via Conchetta corner Via Troilo 14, ✉ 20143, tel. 58104451, fax 58112343 ✉; 🍴 fine cuisine; 55 capacity; open only evening; closed Sunday, and for a certain period of time in January and August; ▨; (not shown on map).

🍽 **Sambuco** Via Messina 10, ✉ 20154, tel. 33610333, fax 33611850 ✉; 🍴 classical (seafood); 90 capacity; closed Saturday at midday and Sunday, and for a certain period of time in August and Christmas-New Year's; ▨ 🅿️; (A2-3).

🍽 **Suntory** Via Verdi 6, ✉ 20121, tel. 8693022, fax 72023282 ✉; 🍴 Japanese; 150 capacity; closed Sunday, and for a certain period of time in August; ▨; (D4).

🍽 **Alfredo-Gran San Bernardo** Via Borgese 14, ✉ 20154, tel. 3319000, fax 29006859 ✉; 🍴 Lombard; 60 capacity; closed Sunday (in June-July also Saturday), August; ▨; (not shown on map).

🍽 **Bice** Via Borgospesso 12, ✉ 20121, tel. 76002572 ✉; 🍴 Tuscan and classical; 95 capacity; closed Monday and at midday on Tuesday, Easter, August and Christmas-Epiphany (6 January); ▨; (C5).

🍽 **Bistrot di Gualtiero Marchesi** Via S. Raffaele 2, ✉ 20121, tel. 877120, fax 877035 ✉; 🍴 Lombard; 90/120 capacity; closed Sunday and at midday on Monday, and for a certain period of time in August; ▨; (D5).

🍽 **Le Cinque Terre** Via Appiani 9, ✉ 20121, tel. 6575177, fax 653034 ✉; 🍴 Ligurian (seafood); 50/60 capacity; closed Saturday at midday and Sunday, and for a certain period of time in August; ▨; (B4).

🍽 **Porto** Piazza Cantore, ✉ 20123, tel. 89407425, fax 8321481 ✉; 🍴 classical (seafood); 90 capacity; closed Sunday and at midday on Monday, August; ▨; (F2).

🍽 **Torre di Pisa** Via Fiori Chiari 21, ✉ 20121, tel. 874877 ✉; 🍴 Tuscan; 100 capacity; closed Saturday at midday and Sunday, and for a cer-

tain period of time in August and Christmas-New Year's; ▨; (C3).

🍽 **Valtellina** Via Taverna 34, ✉ 20134, tel. 7561139, fax 7560436 ✉; 🍴 Valtelline (pizzoccheri, mushrooms); 40/60 capacity; closed Monday, New Year's-Epiphany (6 January) and for a certain period of time in August; ✿ 🅿️; (not shown on map).

🍽 **Al Girarrosto-da Cesarina** Corso Venezia 31, ✉ 20121, tel. 76000481 ✉; 🍴 Tuscan and classical (seafood); 90 capacity; closed Saturday and at midday on Sunday, August and Christmas-Epiphany (6 January); ▨; (C-D5).

🍽 **Al Mercante** Piazza Mercanti 17, ✉ 20123, tel. 8052198; 🍴 classical; 160 capacity; closed Sunday, and for a certain period of time in August and in January; ▨ ✿; (D4).

🍽 **Bandiere** Via Palermo 15, ✉ 20121, tel. 86461646 ✉; 🍴 Venetian, of Trento, Friulian; 60 capacity; closed Saturday at midday and Sunday, and for a certain period of time in August and Christmas-New Year's; ▨; (C3-4).

🍽 **Berti** Via Algarotti 20, ✉ 20124, tel. 6694627, fax 6884158 ✉; 🍴 Lombard; 100/200 capacity; closed Sunday, and for a certain period of time in August and Christmas-Epiphany (6 January); ✿; (not shown on map).

🍽 **Cavallini** Via M. Macchi 2, ✉ 20124, tel. 6693771; 🍴 classical; 150 capacity; closed Saturday and Sunday, August and Christmas-Epiphany (6 January); ▨ ✿; (B6).

🍽 **Grand Hotel Pub** Via A. Sforza 75, ✉ 20141, tel. 89511586 ✉; 🍴 Po Valley; 80 capacity; closed Monday, and for a certain period of time in August; ✿; (not shown on map).

🍽 **Il Verdi** Piazza Mirabello 5, ✉ 20121, tel. 6590797; 🍴 classical; 60 capacity; closed Sunday, a certain period of time in August, and Christmas-New Year's; ▨; (C4).

🍽 **Masuelli San Marco** Viale Umbria 80, ✉ 20135, tel. 55184138 ✉; 🍴 Lombard and Piedmontese; 45 capacity; closed Sunday and at midday on Monday, mid-August/mid-September and Christmas-Epiphany (6 January); ▨; (not shown on map).

🍴 **Osteria Via Prè** Via Casale 4, ✉ 20144, tel. 8373869 ✉; 🍴 Ligurian; 60/80 capacity; closed Monday, and for a certain period of time in August; ▨; (F2).

Modena ✉ 41100 ☎ 059

ℹ️ APT, Via Scudari 30, tel. 222482, fax 214591.

🚉 Stazione F.S. (State railroad station), Piazza Dante, tel. 218226; Stazione ATCM, Piazza Manzoni, tel. 308011.

✈️ Modena Nord (A1) km. 5; Modena-Campogalliano (A22) km. 8.

★★★ **Canalgrande** Corso Canal Grande 6, tel. 217160, fax 221674; 78 rms. ▨; ▨ 🏊 🖥️.

★★★ **Central Park Hotel** (no restaurant), Viale Vittorio Veneto 10, tel. 225858, fax 225141; closed Christmas-Epiphany (6 January), and August; 48 rms. ▨; ▨ 🏊 🅿️.

★★★ **Real Fini** (no restaurant), Via Emilia Est 441, tel. 238091, fax 364804; closed for a certain period of time in August, and Christmas-Epiphany (6 January); 92 rms. ▨; ▨ ▨ 🅿️ ♿.

★★★ **Eden** (no restaurant), Via Emilia Ovest 666, tel. 335660, fax 820108; 84 rms. ▨; ▨ 🏊 🖥️ 🅿️ ♿.

★★★ **Europa** (no restaurant), Corso Vittorio Emanuele II 52, tel. 217721, fax 222288; 120 rms. ▨; 🖥️.

Restaurants

Fini Rua Frati Minori 54, tel. 223314, fax 220247 ⊠; 〗ୋ Modenese and classical; 120 capacity; closed Monday and Tuesday, Christmas-New Year's, and for a certain period of time between July and August; ⊠ Ⓟ.

Borso d'Este Piazza Roma 5, tel. 214114 ⊠; 〗ୋ Emilian; 40 capacity; closed Saturday at midday and Sunday, August; ⊠.

Le Temps Perdu Via Sadoleto 3, tel. 220353 ⊠; 〗ୋ classical (seafood); 35 capacity; open only evening; closed Monday, and for a certain period of time in August; ⚘ Ⓟ.

Oreste Piazza Roma 31, tel. 243324; 〗ୋ Emilian and classical; 80 capacity; closed Sunday evening and Wednesday, and for a certain period of time in July; ⊠.

Zelmira Largo S. Giacomo 17, tel. 222351 ⊠; 〗ୋ Modenese; 40/80 capacity; closed Thursday, and for a certain period of time between January and February; ⊠ ⚘.

Monreale (PA) ⊠ 90046 ☎ 091

AAPT, Piazza Duomo, tel. 6564570.

Palermo (A19) km. 11.

Restaurants

La Botte state road (S.S.) 186, Contrada Lenzitti 20, tel. 414051 ⊠; 〗ୋ Sicilian and classical; 75/90 capacity; closed from Monday to Thursday, July and August; ⚘ Ⓟ.

Taverna del Pavone Vicolo Pensato 18, tel. 6406209 ⊠; 〗ୋ Sicilian; 35/50 capacity; closed Monday for a certain period of time between September and October.

Montepulciano (SI) ⊠ 53045 ☎ 0578

Chiusi-Chianciano T. (A1) km. 20.

Hotels and restaurants

Granducato (no restaurant), Via delle Lettere 62, tel. 758610, fax 758597; 54 rms. ▥; ▣ Ⓟ ♿.

Il Marzocco Piazza Savonarola 18, tel. 757262, fax 757530; closed for a certain period of time between November and December; 16 rms. (15 ▥); ▣ Ⓟ.

La Grotta township of San Biagio, tel. 757607 ⊠; 〗ୋ Tuscan; 50 capacity; closed Wednesday, Epiphany (6 January)/end February; ⚘.

Monterosso al Mare (SP) ⊠ 19016 ☎ 0187

IAT seasonal, Via Fegina (sotto la stazione) tel. 817506.

Stazione F.S. (State railroad station), Via Fegina, tel. 817458.

Hotels and restaurants

Porto Roca Via Corone 1, tel. 817502, fax 81788; seasonal; 43 rms. ▥; ♨ ⊠.

La Colonnina (no restaurant), Via Zuecca 6, tel. 817439, fax 817788; closed November; 20 rms. ▥; ♨.

Gigante Via IV Novembre 9, tel. 817401; 〗ୋ Ligurian; 180 capacity; closed Tuesday; ⚘.

Monte Sant'Angelo (FG) ⊠ 71037 ☎ 0884

Stazione F.S. (State railroad station), Manfredonia km. 16, tel. 0884/581015.

Hotels and restaurants

Rotary Road to Pulsano, tel. 562146, fax 562146; 24 rms. ▥; Ⓟ ♿.

Al Grottino Corso Vittorio Emanuele 179, tel. 561132; 〗ୋ Apulian; 70/120 capacity; closed Monday; ⊠.

Murano (VE) ⊠ 30121 ☎ 041

Transportation from Venice

Restaurants

Ai Frati Fondamenta Venier 4, tel. 736694; 〗ୋ Venetian (seafood); 150 capacity; closed Thursday, February.

Naples ⊠ 80100 ☎ 081

EPT, Piazza dei Martiri 58, tel. 405311, fax 401961 (*E3*); Information Office, Stazione Centrale, tel. 268779 (*B-C6*). AA, Information Office, Piazza del Gesù Nuovo 78, tel. 5523328 (*C4*).

Railroad stations: Napoli Centrale (Naples Main Station), Piazza Garibaldi; Mergellina, Piazza Piedigrotta; Campi Flegrei, Piazzale Tecchio. For all of them, tel. 5543188.
Ferrovia Circumvesuviana, Corso Garibaldi 387, tel. 7792444.
Ferrovia Cumana, Piazza Montesanto, tel. 5513328.

access from Via G. Ferraris or from the ring road (A1, A3, A16).

Airport Naples-Capodichino km. 7, tel. 7896259-7896245.
Alitalia, Via Medina 41, tel. 5425333 (*D-E4*).

Stazione Marittima (Marine Terminal), Molo Beverello, tel. 5523968; *Aliscafi Mergellina*, Via Caracciolo 10, tel. 7612348.

Hotels

Britannique Corso Vittorio Emanuele 133, ⊠ 80121, tel. 7614145, fax 660457; 88 rms. ▥; ▦ ♨ ▣ Ⓟ; (*E2*).

Excelsior Via Partenope 48, ⊠ 80121, tel. 7640111, fax 7649743; 102 rms. ▥; ▣ ⊠; (*F4*).

G.H. Oriente Via A. Diaz 44, ⊠ 80134, tel. 5512133, fax 5514915; 132 rms. ▥; ▣ ⊠; (*D4*).

G.H. Vesuvio Via Partenope 45, ⊠ 80121, tel. 7640044, fax 5800380; 167 rms. ▥; ▣ ⊠ ♿; (*F4*).

Jolly Ambassador's Via Medina 70, ⊠ 80133, tel. 416000, fax 5518010; 250 rms. ▥; ▣ ⊠; (*D2*).

Miramare (no restaurant), Via N. Sauro 24, ⊠ 80132, tel. 7647589, fax 7640775; 31 rms. ▥; ▣ ⊠; (*E4*).

Paradiso Via Catullo 11, ⊠ 80122, tel. 7614161, fax 7613449; 74 rms. ▥; ▣ ⊠; (*F1*).

Palace Piazza Garibaldi 9, ⊠ 80142, tel. 267044, fax 264306; 102 rms. ▥; (*B-C5-6*).

Rex (no restaurant), Via Palepoli 12, ⊠ 80132, tel. 7649389, fax 7649227; 40 rms. (37 ▥); ▣ ⊠; (*F4*).

Splendid Via A. Manzoni 96, ⊠ 80123, tel. 7145630, fax 7146431; 44 rms. ▥; ▣ ♨ Ⓟ ♿; (*not shown on map*).

Restaurants

Cantinella Via Cuma 42, ⊠ 80132, tel. 7648684, fax 7648769 ⊠; 〗ୋ Campanian and classical; 80 capacity; closed Sunday, and for a certain period of time in August; ▣ Ⓟ; (*E4*).

Sacrestia Via Orazio 116, ⊠ 80122, tel. 664186, fax 7611051; 〗ୋ Campanian and classical; 130 capacity; closed Monday, and for a certain period of time in August; ⊠ ⚘ Ⓟ; (*F1*).

A' Fenestella Calata Ponticello a Marechiaro 25, ⊠ 80123, tel. 7690020, fax 5750686; 〗ୋ

437

Neapolitan (seafood); 180 capacity; closed Wednesday, open in August only evening; at lunch and Sunday at dinner; Sunday in VII and VIII, a certain period of time in August; 🅿; (*not shown on map*).

🍴🍴🍴 **Ciro a Santa Brigida** Via S. Brigida 71/73, ⊠ 80132, tel. 5524072 ⊡; ☽ Neapolitan and classical; 150 capacity; closed Sunday, a certain period of time in August; ▧; (*D-E4*).

🍴🍴🍴 **Giuseppone a Mare** Via F. Russo 13, ⊠ 80123, tel. 5756002, fax 7640195 ⊡; ☽ Campanian and classical; 180 capacity; closed Monday, and for a certain period of time in August and Christmas-New Year's; 🅿 ▧; (*not shown on map*).

🍴🍴🍴 **San Carlo** Via Cesario Console 18/19, ⊠ 80132, tel. 7649757, fax 2451166 ⊡; ☽ Campanian and classical (seafood); 60/70 capacity; closed Sunday, and for a certain period of time in August; ▧ 🅿; (*E4*).

🍴🍴 **Bersagliera** Borgo Marinaro 10/11, ⊠ 80132, tel. 7646016; ☽ Neapolitan (seafood); 150/250 capacity; closed Tuesday, period of closing may vary; (*F4*).

🍴🍴 **Cavour** Piazza Garibaldi 34, ⊠ 80142, tel. 283122; ☽ Neapolitan; 250 capacity; also hotel; ▧ 🅿; (*B-C5-6*).

🍴🍴 **Don Salvatore** Via Mergellina 5, ⊠ 80122, tel. 681817, fax 661241 ⊡; ☽ Campanian (seafood); 100 capacity; closed Wednesday; ▧ 🅿; (*F1*).

🍴🍴 **Poeta** Piazza S. Di Giacomo 133, ⊠ 80123, tel. 5756936 ⊡; ☽ Campanian (seafood); 80/130 capacity; closed Monday, and for a certain period of time in August; ▧ ❀ 🅿; (*not shown on map*).

🍴🍴 **Salvatore alla Riviera** Riviera Chiaia 91, ⊠ 80122, tel. 680490; ☽ Campanian (seafood); 180 capacity; closed Tuesday, and for a certain period of time in July; ▧; (*D5*).

🍴🍴 **Sbrescia Antonio** Rampe S. Antonio a Posillipo 109, ⊠ 80122, tel. 669140 ⊡; ☽ Neapolitan and classical (seafood); 120/140 capacity; closed Monday; ▧ 🅿.

🍴 **Cinquantatré** Piazza Dante 53, ⊠ 80135, tel. 5499372 ⊡; ☽ Campanian; 160 capacity; ▧; (*C4*).

at Agnano Terme, km. 11 ⊠ 80125

Hotels

★★★★ **San Germano** Via Beccadelli 41, tel. 5705422, fax 5701546; 105 rms. ⫼; ▧ ≋ ▤ 🅿.

Noto (SR) ⊠ 96017 ☎ 0931

ℹ *AAPT*, Piazzale XVI Maggio, tel. 836744 (*B2*).

🚉 *Stazione F.S. (State railroad station)*, tel. 838733.

at Lido di Noto, km. 8

Hotels

★★★ **Helios** township of Pizzuta, tel. 812366, fax 812378; 141 rms. ⫼; ▧ ♣ ≋ 🅿.

Nùoro ⊠ 08100 ☎ 0784

ℹ *EPT*, Piazza Italia 19, tel. 30083, fax 33432.

🚉 *Stazione Ferrovie della Sardegna*, Via Lamarmora 10, tel. 30115.

Hotels and restaurants

★★★ **Grazia Deledda** Via Lamarmora 175, tel. 31257, fax 31258; 72 rms. ⫼; ▧ ▤ ♿.

★★★ **Grillo** Via Mons. Melas 14, tel. 38678, fax 32005; 46 rms. ⫼; ▤.

★★★ **Paradiso** Via Aosta 44, tel. 35585, fax 232782; 42 rms. ⫼; ▤ 🅿 ♿.

🍴🍴 **Canne al Vento** Viale Repubblica 66, tel. 201762; ☽ "Barbaricina"; 130/150 capacity; closed Sunday, and for a certain period of time in August and December; ▧.

🍴 **Giovanni** Via IV Novembre 9, tel. 30562; ☽ "Barbaricina" and classical; 40/60 capacity; closed Sunday.

Olbia (SS) ⊠ 07026 ☎ 0789

ℹ *AA*, Via Catello Piro 1, tel. 21453, fax 22221.

🚉 *Stazione F.S. (State railroad station)*, tel. 22477.

✈ *Aeroporto Costa Smeralda* (4 km. to the SE).

Meridiana, Airport, tel. 52634; to reserve flights, tel. 69300.

⛴ Transportation with car ferry from Genoa, Civitavecchia e Livorno.

Hotels and restaurants

★★★★ **Mediterraneo** Via Montello 3, tel. 24173, fax 24162; 74 rms. ⫼; ▧ 🅿.

★★★ **Centrale** (no restaurant), Corso Umberto I 85, tel. 23017, fax 26464; 23 rms. ⫼; ▧.

🍴🍴🍴 **Gallura** Corso Umberto 145, tel. 24648, fax 24629 ⊡; ☽ classical; 80 capacity; closed Monday, and for a certain period of time between December and January; ▧; also hotel.

🍴🍴 **Leone e Anna** Via Barcellona 90, tel. 26333 ⊡; ☽ Sardinian (seafood); 30/70 capacity; closed Wednesday in the off season, January/mid-February; ▧ ❀ 🅿.

at Lido di Pittulongu, km. 7

Hotels

★★★★ **Stefania** Strada Panoramica, tel. 39027, fax 39186; period of closing may vary; 28 rms. ⫼; ▧ ≋ 🅿 ▤.

Orbetello (GR) ⊠ 58015 ☎ 0564

🚉 *Stazione F.S. (State railroad station)*, Orbetello Scalo km. 4, tel. 862105.

Restaurants

🍴 **Pergola** Via Roma 14, tel. 867585 ⊡; ☽ Maremman; 70/90 capacity; closed Thursday, and for a certain period of time in December.

on the Via Aurelia

Hotels and restaurants

★★★ **Corallo** (no restaurant), ad Albinia, Via Paolieri 27, ⊠ 58010, tel. 870065, fax 870571; 26 rms. ⫼; ♣.

★★★ **Vecchia Maremma** at Quattrostrade, Via Aurelia at km. 146, ⊠ 58016, tel. 862147, fax 862347; 50 rms. ⫼; ▧ ♣ ≋ 🅿 ♿.

🍴🍴 **Ruota** at Orbetello Scalo, ⊠ 58016, tel. 862137; ☽ of Maremma; 100/150 capacity; closed Thursday in the off season; also hotel; ❀ 🅿.

Orvieto (TR) ⊠ 05018 ☎ 0763

ℹ *APT*, Piazza del Duomo 24, tel. 41772, fax 44433. Orvieto Scalo, Via Costanzi 75, tel. 301507, fax 301487.

🚉 *Stazione F.S. (State railroad station)*, Orvieto Scalo km. 5, tel. 300434.

⛙ *Orvieto* (A1) km. 6.

Hotels and restaurants

★★★★ **Maitani** (no restaurant), Via Maitani 5, tel. 342011, fax 342011; closed for a certain period of time in January; 40 rms. ⫼; ▧ ▤.

★★★ **Valentino** (no restaurant), Via Angelo da Orvieto 32, tel. 342464, fax 342464; closed for a certain period of time between January and February; 17 rms. ⫼; ▤ ♿.

🍴🍴🍴 **Giglio d'Oro** Piazza Duomo 8, tel. 341903; ☽ Umbrian fine cuisine and classical; 50 capacity; closed Wednesday; ▧.

¶ **Grotte del Funaro** Via Ripa di Serancia 41, tel. 343276 ⊠; ⅀ Umbrian (pasta dishes); 110/150 capacity; closed Monday, except July and August; 🅟.

¶ **Sette Consoli** Piazza S. Angelo 1/A, tel. 343911 ⊠; ⅀ Umbrian; 35 capacity; closed Wednesday, period of closing may vary; ❀.

¶ **Trattoria Etrusca** Via Maitani 10, tel. 344016; ⅀ Umbrian; 90 capacity; closed Monday, and for a certain period of time between January and February; 🅟.

at Orvieto Scalo, km. 5   ⊠ 05019

Hotels

★★★ **Villa Ciconia** township of Ciconia, state road (S.S.) 71 to Arezzo, tel. 92982, fax 90677; closed for a certain period of time in January or February; 10 rms. 🏨; ♨ 🅟.

★★★ **Gialletti** (no restaurant), Via Costanzi 71, tel. 90381, fax 92264; 51 rms. 🏨; 🅿🅗🅟 ♿.

Padua   ⊠ 35100 ☎ 049

ℹ *APT*, Riviera dei Mugnai 8, tel. 8750655, fax 650794 (*B3*); *Information Office*, Stazione F.S., tel. 8752077 (*A3*); *TCI*, Via Verdi 7, tel. 8754227 (*C2*).

TCI, Ufficio di Padova, Via Verdi 7, tel. 8754227.

🚂 *Stazione F.S. (State railway station)*, tel. 8751800.

🛣 *Padova Est* (A4) km. 5; *beginning of highway* (A13) km. 4.

Hotels

★★★ **Biri** Via Grassi 2, ⊠ 35129, tel. 776566, fax 776566; 99 rms. 🏨; 🅿🅗🅟 ♿; (*C6*).

★★★ **Milano** Via P. Bronzetti 62, ⊠ 35138, tel. 8712555, fax 8713923; 80 rms. 🏨; 🅿🅿 ♿; (*B1*).

★★★ **Plaza** Corso Milano 40, ⊠ 35139, tel. 656822, fax 661117; 142 rms. 🏨; 🅿🅗 ♿; (*B-C2*).

★★★ **Europa** Largo Europa 9, ⊠ 35137, tel. 661200, fax 661508; 64 rms. 🏨; 🅿🅢; (*B3*).

★★★ **Leon Bianco** (no restaurant), Piazzetta Pedrocchi 12, ⊠ 35122, tel. 8750814, fax 8756184; 22 rms. 🏨; 🅿🅢; (*C3*).

★★ **Al Cason** Via Paolo Sarpi 40, ⊠ 35138, tel. 662636, fax 8754217; 48 rms. 🏨; 🅿🅢; (*A2-3*).

Restaurants

¶ **Antico Brolo** Corso Milano 22, ⊠ 35139, tel. 664555 ⊠; ⅀ Venetian regional and Emilian; 55 capacity; closed Monday and at midday on Sunday, and for a certain period of time in August; 🅟; (*B-C2*).

¶ **Belle Parti** Via Belle Parti 11, ⊠ 35139, tel. 8751822 ⊠; ⅀ Venetian regional and classical (seafood); 45/90 capacity; closed Sunday, and for a certain period of time in August; 🅟; (*C2*).

¶ **Trattoria Bertolini** Via Altichiero 162, tel. 600357 ⊠; ⅀ Venetian; 120/150 capacity; closed Friday evening and Saturday, and for a certain period of time in August; 🅿 ❀ 🅟.

at Ponte di Brenta, km. 5   ⊠ 35020

Hotels

★★★ **Le Padovanelle** Via Chilesotti 2, tel. 625622, fax 625320; 40 rms. 🏨; 🅿♨♿🅟.

Paestum (SA)   · ⊠ 84063 ☎ 0828

ℹ *AA*, Via Magna Grecia 152, tel. 722322; *Information Office*, Via Nazionale, tel. 811016.

🚂 *Stazione F.S. (State railway station)*, km. 1, tel. 722171.

Hotels and restaurants

★★★ **Le Palme** at Laura, Via Sterpinia 33, tel. 851025, fax 851507; seasonal; 50 rms. 🏨; 🅿♨♿🅗🅟 ♿.

★★★ **Cristallo** at Laura, Via P. della Madonna 39, tel. 851077, fax 851468; 36 rms. 🏨; ♨🅟.

★★★ **Esplanade** Via Sterpina, tel. 851043, fax 851600; 28 rms. 🏨; 🅿♨♿🅟 ♿.

★★★ **Park Hotel** coast road for Agropoli, tel. 811134, fax 722310; 28 rms. 🏨; ♨🅗🅟.

¶ **La Pergola** at Capaccio Scalo, Via Nazionale 1, tel. 723377 ⊠; ⅀ local (seafood, mushrooms); 35 capacity; closed Monday (except in summer), period of closing may vary.

¶ **Nettuno** Via Principe di Piemonte 2, tel. 811028; ⅀ Campanian and classical (seafood); 160/250 capacity; closed Monday, Christmas; ❀ 🅟.

Palermo   ⊠ 90100 ☎ 091

ℹ *AAPT*, Piazza Castelnuovo 34/35, tel. 583847, fax 582788 (*C3*); *Information Office*, Piazza Cavalieri del Santo Sepolcro, tel. 6161361 (*E4*); *AA*, Salita Belmonte, tel. 540122, fax 6375400 (*A4*).

🚂 *Stazioni F.S. (State railroad stations)*: Centrale, Piazza G. Cesare, tel. 6161806; Notarbartolo, Via Notarbartolo, tel. 343409.

🛣 *Palermo* (A19 and A20) km. 4; *Palermo* (A29 and A29 Dir.) km. 12.

✈ *Aeroporto Civile (Town Airport)* Palermo-Punta Raisi km. 31, tel. 591414.
Alitalia, Via Mazzini 59, tel. 6019333 (*B3*).

⚓ *Capitaneria di Porto*, Via Crispi 153, tel. 582944.

Hotels and restaurants

★★★ **Villa Igiea Grand Hotel** Salita Belmonte 43, ⊠ 90142, tel. 543744, fax 547654; 117 rms. 🏨; 🅿♨♿🅟 ♿; (*not shown on map*).

★★★ **Forte Agip** Viale Regione Siciliana 2620, ⊠ 90145, tel. 552033, fax 408198; 105 rms. 🏨; 🅟; (*not shown on map*).

★★★ **Jolly del Foro Italico** Foro Italico 22, ⊠ 90133, tel. 6165090, fax 6161441; 235 rms. 🏨; 🅿♨♿ 🅟; (*E6*).

★★★ **Europa** Via Agrigento 3, ⊠ 90141, tel. 6256323, fax 6256323; 73 rms. 🏨; 🅿; (*B3*).

¶¶¶ **Charleston** Piazzale Ungheria 00, ⊠ 90141, tel. 321366, fax 321347; ⅀ Sicilian and classical (seafood); 120/200 capacity; seasonal; closed Sunday; 🅟; (*C-D3*).

¶¶¶ **L'Approdo, Ristorante Renato** Via Messina Marine 242, ⊠ 90123, tel. 6302881 ⊠; ⅀ Sicilian fine cuisine; 60 capacity; closed Sunday, and for a certain period of time in August; 🅟; (*not shown on map*).

¶¶¶ **Il Ristorantino** Piazzale De Gasperi 19, ⊠ 90146, tel. 512861, fax 6702999 ⊠; ⅀ Sicilian; 60/80 capacity; closed Monday, August; 🅿 ❀; (*not shown on map*).

¶¶¶ **Scuderia** Viale del Fante 9, ⊠ 90146, tel. 520323, fax 520467 ⊠; ⅀ Sicilian and classical (seafood); 180/280 capacity; closed Sunday evening, for a certain period of time in August; 🅿 ❀ 🅟; (*not shown on map*).

¶ **Stella** Via Aragona 6, tel. 6161136 ⊠; ⅀ Sicilian; 80 capacity; closed Sunday (Wednesday in winter), and for a certain period of time in August; (*E5*).

at Mondello, km. 10   ⊠ 90151

Hotels and restaurants

★★★ **Mondello Palace** Viale Principe di Scalea 2, tel. 450001, fax 450657; 83 rms. 🏨; 🅿♨♿🅗🅟 ♿.

★★★ **Splendid Hotel la Torre** Via Piano Gallo 11, ⊠ 90151, tel. 450222, fax 450033; 179 rms. ▩; ▤ ⚿ ⛾ ⛳.

℣℣℣ **Charleston-le Terrazze** Viale Regina Elena, tel. 450171; ♪ Sicilian and classical (seafood); 400 capacity; seasonal.

Palestrina (RM) ⊠ 00036 ☎ 06

ℹ *Pro Loco*, Piazza S. Maria degli Angeli, tel. 9573176.

⋔ *Valmontone* (A1) km. 12.

Hotels

★★ **Stella** Piazzale della Liberazione 3, tel. 9538172, fax 9573360; 28 rms. (24 ▩); ⛳.

Parma ⊠ 43100 ☎ 0521

ℹ *APT*, Piazza Duomo 5, tel. 234735 (*C4*).

🚉 *Stazione F.S. (State railroad station)*, Piazzale Dalla Chiesa 11, tel. 771118.

⋔ *Parma* (A1) km. 5; *Parma Ovest* (A15) km. 11.

✈ *Airport*, Via dell'Aeroporto 44/a, tel. 982626 (km. 3 to the NW).
Alitalia, Via Mazza 2, tel. 230063 (*C3-4*).

Hotels

★★★ **Palace Hotel Maria Luigia** Viale Mentana 140, tel. 281032, fax 231126; 101 rms. ▩; ▤ ▣; (*B4*).

★★★ **Park Hotel Stendhal** Via Bodoni 3, tel. 208057, fax 285655; 60 rms. ▩; ▤ ▣; (*B4*).

★★★ **Daniel** Via Gramsci 16, tel. 995147, fax 292606; closed for a certain period of time in August and Christmas; 32 rms. ▩; ▤ ℙ; (*B1, not shown on map*).

★★★ **Farnese International Hotel** Via Reggio 51/A, tel. 994247, fax 992317; 76 rms. ▩; ▤ ⚿ ▣ ℙ ⛳; (*A3, not shown on map*).

★★★ **Savoy** (no restaurant), Via XX Settembre 3/A, tel. 281101, fax 281103; closed Christmas-New Year's and August; 27 rms. ▩; (*B4*).

Restaurants

℣℣℣ **Angiol d'Or** Vicolo Scutellari 1, tel. 282632, fax 282747 ⊠; ♪ Parmesan fine cuisine; 50/70 capacity; closed Sunday, Christmas-New Year's; ▤ ❦; (*C4*).

℣℣℣ **Charly** at San Lazzaro Parmense, Via E. Lepido 89, ⊠ 43026, tel. 493974 ⊠; ♪ Emilian and classical; 60 capacity; closed Sunday evening and Monday; ❦ ℙ.

℣℣℣ **Parizzi** Via Repubblica 71, tel. 285952, fax 285027 ⊠; ♪ Parmesan and fine cuisine; 80/90 capacity; closed Monday and, in summer, also Sunday evening; ▤ ℙ; (*C-D5*).

℣℣ **Parma Rotta** Via Langhirano 158, tel. 966738, fax 968167; ♪ Parmesan (pasta dishes); 120 capacity; closed Monday and, in summer, Sunday; ❦ ℙ; (*not shown on map*).

Pavia ⊠ 27100 ☎ 0382

ℹ *APT*, Via Fabio Filzi 2, tel. 22156, fax 32221.

🚉 *Stazione F.S. (State railroad station)*, Piazzale Stazione, tel. 23000.

⋔ *access at km. 2* (Highway intersection Pavia Bereguardo/A7).

Hotels and restaurants

★★★ **Ariston** Via A. Scopoli 10/D, tel. 34334, fax 25667; closed Christmas-Epiphany (6 January); 60 rms. ▩; ▤ ⛳.

★★★ **Excelsior** (no restaurant), Piazza Stazione 25, tel. 28596, fax 26030; 20 rms. ▩; ▣ ⛳.

★★★ **Rosengarten** (no restaurant), Piazzale Policlinico 21/23, tel. 526312, fax 525186; 61 rms. (59 ▩); ▤ ▣ ℙ.

℣℣℣ **Locanda Vecchia Pavia** Via Cardinal Riboldi 2, tel. 304132, fax 304132 ⊠; ♪ Lombard and classical; 60 capacity; closed Monday and at midday on Wednesday, and for a certain period of time in January and in August; ▤.

℣℣ **Osteria della Madonna-da Peo** Via dei Liguri 28, tel. 302833 ⊠; ♪ classical; 40/70 capacity; closed Sunday, and for a certain period of time in August; ▤.

Perugia ⊠ 06100 ☎ 075

ℹ *APT*, Via Mazzini 21, tel. 5725341, fax 5736828 (*C3*); *Information Office*, Piazza IV Novembre 3, tel. 5736458 (*C3*).

🚉 *Stazione F.S. (State railroad station)*, Piazza Vittorio Veneto, tel. 5007467, *Stazione Ferrovia Centrale Umbra*, Via Sant'Anna, tel. 5729121.

⋔ *access at km. 4* (Highway intersection Perugia-Bettolle/A1).

✈ *Aeroporto Regionale Umbro*, Sant'Egidio (km. 15 to the west), tel. 6929447.
Alitalia, Via Fani 14, tel. 5731226 (*C3*).

Hotels

★★★★ **Brufani** Piazza Italia 12, ⊠ 06121, tel. 5732541, fax 5720210; 24 rms. ▩; ▤ ▣ ℙ ⛳; (*D3*).

★★★★ **Giò Arte e Vini** Via R. D'Andreotto 19, ⊠ 06124, tel. 5731100, fax 5731100; 130 rms. ▩; ▤ ⚿ ⛳; (*C1*).

★★★★ **Grifone** Via Pellico 1, ⊠ 06126, tel. 5837616, fax 5837619; 50 rms. ▩; ▤ ▣ ℙ ⛳; (*not shown on map*).

★★★★ **La Rosetta** Piazza Italia 19, ⊠ 06121, tel. 5720841, fax 5720841; 95 rms. ▩; ❦ ▣; (*D3*).

★★★★ **Perugia Plaza Hotel** Via Palermo 88, ⊠ 06129, tel. 34643, fax 30863; 108 rms. ▩; ▤ ⚿ ⚿ ▣ ⛳; (*not shown on map*).

★★ **Ideal** (no restaurant), Via Tuderte 1/G, ⊠ 06126, tel. 30869, fax 30869; 19 rms. ▩; ❦ ▣ ℙ; (*not shown on map*).

Restaurants

℣℣ **Aladino** Via delle Prome 11, ⊠ 06122, tel. 5720938 ⊠; ♪ Sardinian fine cuisine; 55/65 capacity; open only evening; closed Monday, for a certain period of time in August; ▤; (*B-C4*).

℣℣ **Da Giancarlo** Via dei Priori 36, ⊠ 06123, tel. 5724314 ⊠; ♪ Umbrian; 60 capacity; closed Friday, and for a certain period of time between August and September; (*C3*).

℣℣ **Del Sole** Via Oberdan 28, ⊠ 06121, tel. 5735031; ♪ Umbrian; 180 capacity; closed Monday, Christmas-Epiphany (6 January); (*D4*).

℣℣ **Enoteca Giò** of Hotel Giò Arte e Vini, Via D'Andreotto 19, ⊠ 06124, tel. 5731100; ♪ Umbrian; 250 capacity; closed Sunday evening and Monday at midday; ▤ ℙ.

at Bosco, km. 10 ⊠ 06080

Hotels

★★★★ **Relais San Clemente** tel. 5915100, fax 5915001; 64 rms. ▩; ▤ ⚿ ⚿ ℙ ⛳.

at Ponte San Giovanni, km. 8 ⊠ 06087

Hotels

★★★ **Tevere** Via Manzoni 421/E, tel. 394341, fax 396641; 50 rms. ▩; ▤ ⚿ ▣ ℙ ⛳.

Pescara ⊠ 65100 ☎ 085

ℹ *EPT*, Via Fabrizi 171, tel. 4212939, fax 298246; *Information Office*, Piazza I Maggio, tel. 4224546.

🚉 *Stazione F.S. (State railroad station)*, tel. 378172.

⋔ *Pescara-Chieti* (A14) km. 10; *Pescara-Villanova* (A25) km. 11.

✈ *Aeroporto Pasquale Liberi* (4 km. to the SW); for information, *SAGA*, tel. 4311962.
Alitalia, general agency *Cagidemetrio*, Via Ravenna 3, tel. 4213022.

⚓ *Capitaneria di Porto*, Piazza della Marina 1, tel. 694140.

Hotels and restaurants

★ **Carlton** Viale della Riviera 35, ☒ 65123, tel. 373125, fax 4213922; 71 rms. ▥; ▤ ℙ.

★ **Plaza** Piazza Sacro Cuore 55, ☒ 65122, tel. 4214625, fax 4213267; 68 rms. ▥; ▤ ▦.

★ **Singleton** (no restaurant), Piazza Duca d'Aosta 4, ☒ 65121, tel. 374241, fax 28233; 77 rms. ▥; ▦.

★★★ **Alba** (no restaurant), Via M. Forti 14, ☒ 65122, tel. 389145, fax 292163; 50 rms. ▥; ▦ ⛿.

★★★ **Ambra** (no restaurant), Via M. Forti 38 corner of Quarto dei Mille, ☒ 65122, tel. 378247; 61 rms. ▥; ▦.

★★★ **Salus** Lungomare Matteotti 13, ☒ 65121, tel. 374196, fax 374103; closed Christmas-New Year's; 23 rms. ▥; ▤ ⛲ ℙ.

†¶† **Guerino** Viale della Riviera 4, ☒ 65123, tel. 4212065, fax 4212065; ⅔ of Pescara; 90 capacity; closed Thursday, Christmas-Epiphany (6 January).

†¶ **Abruzzo in Tavola** Via delle Riviera 173, ☒ 65123, tel. 4710304; ⅔ of Abruzzo; 50/60 capacity; closed Friday, in July or August.

†¶ **Cantina di Jozz** Via delle Caserme 61, ☒ 65127, tel. 690383; ⅔ of Abruzzo; 120 capacity; closed Sunday evening and Monday, Christmas-Epiphany (6 January), and for a certain period of time between June and July; ▤.

Piazza Armerina (EN)   ☒ 94015 ☎ 0935

ℹ *AA*, Via Cavour 1, tel. 680201, fax 684565.

Hotels and restaurants

★★★ **Park Hotel Paradiso** Contrada Ramaldo, tel. 680841, fax 684908; 35 rms. ▥; ▤ ℙ ⛿.

† **Da Battiato** Contrada Paratore Casale 11, tel. 685453, fax 685453; ⅔ Sicilian (grilled roasts); 200/350 capacity; ❀ ℙ; of the Albergo Mosaici.

Pienza (SI)   ☒ 53026 ☎ 0578

ℹ *Pro Loco*, Via Casenuove 22, tel. 748072; *Ufficio Turistico Comunale*, seasonal, Piazza Pio II 59, tel. 748502.

✚ *Chiusi-Chianciano Terme* (A1) km. 32.

Hotels and restaurants

★★★ **Relais il Chiostro di Pienza** Corso Rosellino 26, tel. 748400, fax 748440; 28 rms. ▥; ⛲ ⛲ ℙ ▦.

† **Buca delle Fate** Corso Rossellino 38/A, tel. 748272 ☒; ⅔ Tuscan; 120 capacity; closed Monday, and for a certain period of time in June.

Piombino (LI)   ☒ 57025 ☎ 0565

ℹ *IAT* seasonal, Via Cellini 102, tel. 49121.

🚃 *Stazione F.S. (State railroad station)*, Piazza Niccolini, tel. 225263.

⚓ Transportation with car ferry to the isle of Elba.

Hotels and restaurants

*★★ **Centrale** Piazza Verdi 2, tel. 220188, fax 220220; 41 rms. ▥; ▤ ▦ ⛿.

★★★ **Esperia** Lungomare Marconi 27, tel. 42284, fax 42284; 14 rms. ▥; ℙ.

†¶ **Centrale** Piazza Edison 2, tel. 221825; ⅔ Tuscan (seafood); 50/150 capacity; closed Saturday and Sunday, Christmas-Epiphany (6 January), and for a certain period of time in August; ▤.

Pisa   ☒ 56100 ☎ 050

ℹ *APT*, Viale Benedetto Croce 24/26, tel. 40096, fax 40903 (*E5*); *Information offices*, Piazza Duomo, tel. 560464 (*A3-4*); Piazza Stazione, tel. 42291 (*F3-4*).

🚃 *Stazioni F.S. (State railroad stations)*, Centrale and San Rossore, tel. 41385.

✚ *Pisa Nord* (A11) km. 9; *Pisa Centro* (A12) km. 7.

✈ *Aeroporto G. Galilei*, Via Aeroporto San Giusto (km. 2 to the south), tel. 500707.
Alitalia, Ufficio Prenotazioni (Reservations office), Via Puccini 21, tel. 501570 (*E-F4*); *Passenger agency*, Via Corridoni, tel. 48027 (*E-F4*).

Hotels and restaurants

★ **G.H. Duomo** Via S. Maria 94, ☒ 56126, tel. 561894, fax 560418; 94 rms. ▥; ▤ ▦ ⛿; (*B3*).

★ **Jolly Hotel Cavalieri** Piazza Stazione 2, ☒ 56125, tel. 43290, fax 502242; 100 rms. ▥; ▤ ▦ ⛿; (*E-F4*).

★★★ **Roma** (no restaurant), Via Bonanno Pisano 111, ☒ 56126, tel. 554488, fax 550164; 27 rms. ▥; ▤ ⛲ ℙ; (*A B2*).

★★★ **Verdi** (no restaurant), Piazza Repubblica 5, ☒ 56127, tel. 598947, fax 598944; 32 rms. ▥; ▤ ⛿.

†¶† **Ristoro dei Vecchi Macelli** Via Volturno 49, ☒ 56126, tel. 20424 ☒; ⅔ Tuscan; 45 capacity; closed Wednesday and at midday on Sunday, and for a certain period of time in August; ▤; (*C2*).

†¶ **Artilafo** Via Volturno 38, tel. 27010 ☒; ⅔ Tuscan fine cuisine; 25/65 capacity; open only evening; closed Wednesday, August; ❀; (*C2-3*).

†¶ **Osteria del Porton Rosso** Vicolo del Porton Rosso 11, ☒ 56126, tel. 580566 ☒; ⅔ Tuscan (seafood); 35 capacity; closed Sunday, and for a certain period of time between July and August; ▤; (*C4*).

Pistoia   ☒ 51100 ☎ 0573

ℹ *IAT*, Piazza Duomo 4, tel. 21622, fax 34327.

🚃 *Stazione F.S. (State railroad station)*, Piazza Dante Alighieri, tel. 20789.

✚ *Pistoia* (A11) km. 3.

Hotels and restaurants

★★★ **Leon Bianco** (no restaurant), Via Panciatichi 2, tel. 26070, fax 26675; 27 rms. ▥; ▦.

★★★ **Milano** (no restaurant), Viale Pacinotti 10/12, tel. 975700, fax 32657; 55 rms. ▥; ℙ.

★★★ **Patria** (no restaurant), Via Crispi 6/8, tel. 25187, fax 368168; 28 rms. (23 ▥).

†¶ **Casa degli Amici** Via Bonellina 111, tel. 380305; ⅔ Tuscan; 100/200 capacity; closed Monday evening and Tuesday, August; ❀ ℙ.

at Castagno di Pitèccio, km. 12

Restaurants

†¶† **Castagno di Pier Angelo** Via del Castagno 46/B, tel. 42214 ☒; ⅔ Tuscan (seafood, mushrooms); 50/150 capacity; open midday only with reservation; closed Monday in January, in August and in November; ❀ ℙ.

Pompei (NA)   ☒ 80045 ☎ 081

ℹ *AA*, Via Sacra 1, tel. 8507255; *Information Office*, Piazza Porta Marina Inferiore 11, tel. 8610913, fax 8632401; Via Colle S. Bartolomeo, tel. 8503232.

🚃 *Stazione F.S. (State railroad station)*, tel. 8506176.

✚ *Scafati-Pompei* (A3) km. 1.

Hotels and restaurants

★★★ **Bristol** Piazza Vittorio Veneto 1/3, tel. 8503005, fax 8631625; 50 rms. ▥; ▦.

★★★ **Forum** (no restaurant), Via Roma 99, tel. 8501170, fax 8506132; closed Christmas; 19 rms. 🏠; 📶 🏊 📺 👶.

★★★ **Giovanna** (no restaurant), Via Acquasalsa 18, tel. 8506161, fax 8507323; 24 rms. 🏠; 📶 🏊 🅿.

🍴🍴 **Il Principe** Piazza B. Longo 8, tel. 8505566, fax 8633342 ✉; 🍴 Campanian and classical, fine cuisine; 40/150 capacity; closed Sunday evening and Monday (except April/June and September/October), Christmas; 📶.

🍴 **Zi' Caterina** Via Roma 20, tel. 8507447; 🍴 Neapolitan; 370 capacity; closed Tuesday; 📶 🅿.

Porto Cervo (SS)   ✉ 07020 ☎ 0789

📋 at Arzachena (see).

✈ *Airport* at Olbia km. 34, tel. 0789/69300.

Hotels and restaurants

★☆★ **Balocco** (no restaurant), tel. 91555, fax 91510; seasonal; 35 rms. 🏠; 📶 🏊 🏊 🅿.

🍴🍴 **Pescatore** tel. 92296 ✉; 🍴 Sardinian; 100/220 capacity; open only evening, May/October.

at Cala di Volpe, km. 8

Hotels and restaurants

🟰🟰🟰 **Cala di Volpe** tel. 976111, fax 976617; seasonal; 123 rms. 🏠; 📶 🏊 🏊 🅿.

★★★ **Valdiola** tel. 96215, fax 96652; 33 rms. 🏠; 📶 🏊 🏊 🅿 👶.

🍴🍴🍴 **Pevero Golf Club** township of Pevero, tel. 96124, fax 96572 ✉; 🍴 classical (seafood); 60/120 capacity; seasonal.

at Liscia di Vacca, km. 2

Hotels

🟰🟰🟰 **Pitrizza** tel. 930111, fax 930611; seasonal; 51 rms. 🏠; 📶 🏊 🏊 📺 🅿.

at Romazzino, km. 9

🟰🟰🟰 **Romazzino** tel. 97711, fax 96258; seasonal; 91 rms. 🏠; 📶 🏊 🏊 🅿 👶.

Portofino (GE)   ✉ 16034 ☎ 0185

📋 *IAT*, Via Roma 35-37, tel. 269024.

🏕 *Rapallo* (A12) km. 10.

Hotels and restaurants

★☆★ **Nazionale** (no restaurant), Via Roma 8, tel. 269575, fax 269578; seasonal; 12 🏠.

★☆★ **Piccolo Hotel** Via Duca degli Abruzzi 31, tel. 269015, fax 269621; closed for a certain period of time between November and December; 23 rms. 🏠; 🏊 📺 🅿 👶.

★☆★ **Splendido** Viale Baratta 13, tel. 269551, fax 269614; closed January/mid-March; 69 rms. 🏠; 📶 🏊 🏊 📺 🅿.

★★ **Eden** (no restaurant), Vico Dritto 18, tel. 269091, fax 269047; 12 rms. 🏠; 🏊.

🍴🍴🍴 **Pitosforo** Molo Umberto I 9, tel. 269020 ✉; 🍴 Ligurian and classical; 120 capacity; open only evening; closed Monday and Tuesday, November/December; 📶.

🍴🍴🍴 **Puny** Piazza Martiri dell'Olivetta 5, tel. 269037 ✉; 🍴 Ligurian and classical; 40/70 capacity; closed Thursday, mid-December/mid-February.

🍴 **Da ü Batti** Vico Nuovo 17, tel. 269379 ✉; 🍴 Ligurian; 25/70 capacity; closed Monday, mid-November/mid-January.

🍴 **Delfino** Piazza Martiri dell'Olivetta 40, tel. 269081; 🍴 classical; 80/200 capacity; closed Monday in the off season, mid-January/mid-February.

Portovènere (SP)   ✉ 19025 ☎ 0187

📋 *IAT*, Piazza Bastreri 1 (at the entrance to town), tel. 900691.

🏕 *La Spezia* (A15) km. 16.

Hotels and restaurants

★☆★ **Royal Sporting** Via dell'Ulivo 345, tel. 790326, fax 77707; seasonal; 62 rms. 🏠; 📶 🏊 🏊 📺 👶.

★★★ **Paradiso** Via Garibaldi 34, tel. 790612, fax 792582; 22 rms. 🏠; 📶 👶.

🍴🍴🍴 **Taverna del Corsaro** Calata Doria 102, tel. 790622, fax 790622 ✉; 🍴 Ligurian (seafood); 70 capacity; closed Monday evening and Tuesday evening of the season, a certain period of time between November and December.

at Le Grazie, km. 3   ✉ 19022

Hotels and restaurants

★★★ **Della Baia** Via Lungomare 111, tel. 790797, fax 790034; 38 rms. 🏠; 🏊 🅿.

🍴 **Gambero** Viale Libertà 143, tel. 790325 ✉; 🍴 Ligurian (seafood); 120 capacity; closed Monday, November.

Positano (SA)   ✉ 84017 ☎ 089

📋 *AA*, Via Saraceno, tel. 875067-875760.

⚓ Transportation to Capri.

Hotels and restaurants

🟰🟰🟰 **Le Agavi** Via G. Marconi 127, tel. 875733, fax 875965; seasonal; 70 rms. 🏠; 📶 🏊 🏊 🅿.

★☆★ **Le Sirenuse** Via C. Colombo 30, tel. 875066, fax 811798; 60 rms. 🏠; 📶 🏊 🅿.

★☆★ **Buca di Bacco** Via Rampa Teglia 4, tel. 875699, fax 875731; seasonal; 53 rms. 🏠; 🏊.

★★★ **Casa Albertina** Via della Tavolozza 3, tel. 875143, fax 811540; 21 rms. 🏠; 📺.

★★★ **Pupetto** Via Fornillo 37, tel. 875087, fax 811517; seasonal; 30 rms. 🏠; 🏊 🅿.

★★★ **Savoia** (no restaurant), Via C. Colombo 73, tel. 875003, fax 811844; seasonal; 44 🏠.

🍴 **Cambusa** Piazza A. Vespucci 4, tel. 875432 ✉; 🍴 Campanian (seafood); 70/120 capacity; 📶.

🍴 **Chez Black** Via del Brigantino 19/21, tel. 875036 ✉; 🍴 Campanian (seafood); 60/120 capacity; closed for a certain period of time between January and February; 📶.

Pozzuoli (NA)   ✉ 80078 ☎ 081

📋 *AA*, Via Campi Flegrei 3, tel. 5261481; Via Matteotti 1, tel. 5266639.

🚉 *Stazione F.S. (State railroad station)*, Via Oriani 2, tel. 5262304.

⚓ Transportation to Procida and, car ferry, to Ischia.

Hotels and restaurants

★★★ **Santa Marta** at Arco Felice, Via Licola Patria 28, ✉ 80072, tel. 8042404, fax 8042406; 34 rms. 🏠; 🅿 👶.

★★ **Mini Hotel** (no restaurant), state road (S.S.) Domiziana at km. 61.700, tel. 5263223, fax 5263223; 23 rms. 🏠; 📶 🏊 🅿.

🍴 **Ninfea** Via Italia 1, tel. 8661326, fax 8665308; 🍴 Campanian; 900 capacity; closed Tuesday in the off season; 📶 🌿 🅿.

Rapallo (GE)   ✉ 16035 ☎ 0185

📋 *IAT*, Via Diaz 9, tel. 54573, fax 63051.

🚉 *Stazione F.S. (State railroad station)*, tel. 231000.

🏕 *Rapallo* (A12) km. 2.

Hotels and restaurants

****** **Astoria** (no restaurant), Via Gramsci 4, tel. 273533, fax 62793; closed December/mid-January; 20 rms. ▥; ▨ ℙ.

****** **Eurotel** Via Aurelia Occidentale 22, tel. 60981, fax 50635; 63 rms. ▥; ▨ ♨ ♨ ▣ ℙ.

*** **Giulio Cesare** Corso Colombo 52, tel. 50685, fax 60896; closed Nov/mid-Dec; 33 rms. ▥; ▣ ⅍.

*** **Minerva** Corso Colombo 7, tel. 230388, fax 67078; closed for a certain period of time in December; 37 rms. ▥; ♨ ℙ ⅍.

*** **Riviera** Piazza IV Novembre 2, tel. 50248, fax 65668; closed Nov/mid-Dec; 20 rms. ▥; ▨ ♨ ℙ.

¶¶ **Roccabruna** Via Sotto la Croce 6, township of Savagna, tel. 261400 ▨; Ж fine cuisine; 25 capacity; closed Monday, and for a certain period of time in November; ❀ ℙ.

Ravello (SA)   ▨ 84010 ☎ 089

ℹ *AA*, Piazza Duomo 1, tel. 857977.

Hotels and restaurants

****** **Palumbo** Via Toro 16, tel. 857244, fax 858133; 21 rms. ▥; ▨ ♨ ▣ ℙ.

****** **Rufolo** Via S. Francesco 1, tel. 857133, fax 857935; closed February; 30 rms. ▥; ▨ ♨ ♨ ▣ ℙ ⅍.

*** **Graal** Via della Repubblica 8, tel. 857222, fax 857551; 33 rms. ▥; ▨ ♨ ♨ ▣ ⅍.

¶¶¶ **Confalone** of the Albergo Palumbo.

¶¶ **Salvatore** Via Boccaccio 2, tel. 857227; Ж of Amalfi; 180 capacity; closed Monday from November to March; ❀.

Ravenna   ▨ 48100 ☎ 0544

ℹ *APT*, Via Salara 8/12, tel. 35404; *Information Office*, seasonal, Via delle Industrie 14, tel. 451539.

▨ *Stazione F.S. (State railroad station)*, Piazza Farini, tel. 36450.

╫ *Ravenna* (Intersection A14 Dir.) km. 6.

Hotels and restaurants

****** **Jolly Hotel Mameli** Piazza Mameli 1, tel. 35762, fax 216055; 83 rms. ▥; ▨ ▣.

*** **Argentario** (no restaurant), Via di Roma 45, tel. 35555, fax 35147; 28 rms. ▥.

*** **Diana** (no restaurant), Via Rossi 47, tel. 39164, fax 30001; 33 rms. ▥; ▨ ♨ ▣ ⅍.

¶¶¶ **Tre Spade** Via Faentina 136, tel. 500522, fax 500820 ▨; Ж Romagna and classical (fish, mushrooms); 60/100 capacity; closed Sunday evening and Monday, and for a certain period of time in August; ▨ ❀ ℙ.

¶¶ **Chilò** Via Maggiore 62, tel. 36206 ▨; Ж Romagna (pasta dishes); 80/110 capacity; closed Thursday; ❀.

Reggio di Calabria   ▨ 89100 ☎ 0965

ℹ *APT*, Via Roma 3, tel. 21171, fax 890947 (*B2*); *IAT*, Corso Garibaldi 327, tel. 892012 (*D2*); Stazione Centrale F.S., tel. 27120 (*E-F1*).

▨ *Stazione Centrale F.S.*, Piazza Garibaldi, tel. 898123.

╫ Access from Via Cardinale Portanova or from Via S. Caterina (A3).

✈ *Aeroporto Civile dello Stretto*, Ravagnese km. 4, tel. 642232.
Alitalia, Corso Garibaldi 521/523, tel. 331444 (*E1*).

⚓ *Stazione Marittima (Marine Terminal)*, Via Florio, tel. 895524.

Hotels and restaurants

****** **G.H. Excelsior** Via Vittorio Veneto 66, ▨ 89121, tel. 812211, fax 893084; 84 rms. ▥; ▨ ▣ ⅍; (*B2*).

¶¶ **Baylik** Vico Leone 3, ▨ 89121, tel. 48624; Ж Calabrian; 80/110 capacity; closed Thursday, period of closing may vary; ▨; (*not shown on map*).

Rimini   ▨ 47037 ☎ 0541

ℹ *APT*, Piazzale Federico Fellini 3, tel. 51101, fax 26566; Via Dante, tel. 51331; *Information offices*, Miramare, tel. 372112; Viserba, tel. 738115.

▨ *Stazione F.S. (State railroad station)*, Piazzale Battisti, tel. 53512.

╫ *Rimini Sud* (A14) km. 4.

✈ *Aeroporto Civile Miramare*, at Miramare (km. 7 to the south), tel. 373132.
Alitalia, airport, tel. 370017.

Hotels

****** **Club House** Viale Vespucci 52, tel. 391460, fax 391442; 28 rms. ▥; ▨ ♨ ♨ ℙ.

****** **Milton** Viale C. Colombo 2, tel. 54600, fax 54698; seasonal; 75 rms. ▥; ▨ ♨ ♨ ℙ.

****** **Park Hotel** Viale Regina Elena 6, tel. 391640, fax 390634; 65 rms. ▥; ▨ ♨ ♨ ℙ.

*** **Acasamia** Viale Parisano 34, tel. 391370, fax 391816; 40 rms. ▥; ▨ ♨ ▣ ℙ.

*** **Lotus** Via Rovani 3, tel. 381680, fax 392506; open mid-May/September; 46 rms. ▥; ♨ ♨ ℙ ⅍.

*** **Nancy** Viale Leopardi 11, tel. 381731, fax 387374; open Easter/mid-September; 32 rms. ▥; ℙ.

*** **Napoleon** (no restaurant), Piazzale Battisti 22, tel. 27501, fax 50010; 64 rms. ▥; ▨ ▣ ℙ.

*** **Villa Lalla** Viale Vittorio Veneto 22, tel. 55155, fax 23570; 40 rms. ▥; ▨ ♨ ℙ.

** **Donau** Viale Alfieri 12, tel. 381302, fax 381302; open May/September; 19 rms. ▥.

Restaurants

¶¶¶ **Rivadonda** Via Farini 13, tel. 27657, fax 21348 ▨; Ж local regional; 45/90 capacity; closed Monday, and for a certain period of time in January; ▨ ❀.

¶¶ **Oberdan-il Corsaro** Via Destra del Porto, tel. 27802; Ж local regional (seafood); 75 capacity; seasonal; closed Wednesday, except in August. ℙ

at Marebello, km. 5

Hotels

*** **Carlton** Viale Regina Margherita 6, tel. 372361, fax 374540; 67 rms. ▥; ▨ ♨ℙ.

at Miramare, km. 7   ▨ 47045

Hotels

****** **Ascot** Viale Principe di Piemonte 38, tel. 371561, fax 372012; closed November/January; 63 rms. ▥; ▨ ♨ ℙ ⅍.

*** **Due Mari** Viale Principe di Piemonte 53, tel. 370660, fax 375610; 60 rms. ▥; ▨ ℙ.

*** **Giglio** Viale Principe di Piemonte 18, tel. 372073, fax 377490; Easter/September; 40 rms. ▥; ▨ ♨ ℙ.

at Rivazzurra, km. 6

Hotels

*** **De France** Viale Regina Margherita 48, tel. 371551, fax 710001; seasonal; 65 rms. ▥; ▨ ♨ ℙ.

Riva del Garda (TN)   ▨ 38066 ☎ 0464

ℹ *APT*, Giardini di Porta Orientale 8, tel. 554444, fax 520308.

╫ *Rovereto Sud-Lago di Garda Nord* (A22) km. 19.

*** G.H. Riva Piazza Garibaldi 10, tel. 521800, fax 552293; closed for a certain period of time in December and in February; 77 rms. ▥; ⌂.

*** International Hotel Liberty Viale Carducci 3/5, tel. 553581, fax 551144; 84 rms. ▥; ⚒ ⚎ ℗ ⌂.

*** Astoria Viale Trento 9, tel. 552658, fax 521222; seasonal; 94 rms. ▥; ⚒ ⚎ ℗.

*** Luise Viale Rovereto 9, tel. 552796, fax 554250; closed November; 58 rms. ▥; ⚒ ⚎ ℗.

†¶† Vecchia Riva Via Bastione 3, tel. 555061, fax 555550 ⊠; ⅀ Tridentine and fine cuisine (seafood); 30/50 capacity; closed Tuesday in the off season, period of closing may vary; ▣ ❀.

†¶ Al Volt Via Fiume 73, tel. 552570; ⅀ Tridentine; 70 capacity; closed Monday, mid-February/mid-March.

Rome ⊠ 00100 ☎ 06

ⓘ *EPT*, Via Parigi 11, tel. 488991, fax 4819316 (II, *D4*); *Information Offices*: Via Parigi 5, tel. 48899228 (II, *D4*); Stazione Termini, tel. 4871270 (IV, *E4-5*); Aeroporto Leonardo da Vinci, Fiumicino, tel. 65954471.

TCI, Via del Babbuino 20, tel. 3203886.

▦ *Ferrovie dello Stato*, travellers information for all the stations in the city: Stazione Termini, tel. 4775; *Ferrovie del Gargano*, Stazione Tiburtina: for information, San Severo, tel. 0882/321414, reservations and tickets c/o Agenzia Piccarozzi, Via G. Mazzoni 12, tel. 4404495; *Ferrovie Cotral*: Rome-Civita Castellana, Roma-Nord, Rome-Lido and Rome-Greater Lazio, travellers information, tel. 57532323.

╫ *access from Via della Magliana* (A12); *from the Via Salaria and A1 Dir.* (A1); *from the Circonvallazione Tiburtina* (A24 and A25); *from the Via Casilina and Tuscolana, then A1 Dir.* (A1). The Grande Raccordo Anulare is a ring road that links the various parts of town and the highways, without having to drive through town.

✈ *Airports: Aeroporto Intercontinentale Leonardo Da Vinci*, Fiumicino (26 km. to the SW), tel. 65951; *G.B. Pastine*, Ciampino (15 km. to the SE), Via Appia Nuova, tel. 794941.
Alitalia, information, tel. 65643; *Passenger agencies*: Via Bissolati 13 (II, *C3*), Via A. Marchetti 111 (*not shown on map*), information, tel. 65621.

Hotels

┋┋┋ Aldrovandi Palace Via U. Aldrovandi 15, ⊠ 00197, tel. 3223993, fax 3221435; 137 rms. ▥; ▣ ⚒ ▤ ℗; (*not shown on map*).

┋┋┋ Bernini Bristol Piazza Barberini 23, ⊠ 00187, tel. 4883051, fax 4824266; 125 rms. ▥; ▣ ▤ ⌂; (II, *D2*).

┋┋┋ Cavalieri Hilton Via Cadlolo 101, ⊠ 00136, tel. 35091, fax 35092241; 376 rms. ▥; ▣ ⚒ ⚎ ▤ ℗ ⌂; (*not shown on map*).

┋┋┋ Excelsior Via Vittorio Veneto 125, ⊠ 00187, tel. 4708, fax 4826205; 327 rms. ▥; ▣ ▤ ℗; (II, *C3*).

┋┋┋ Hassler Piazza Trinità dei Monti 6, ⊠ 00187, tel. 699340, fax 6789991; 100 rms. ▥; ▣ ⚒ ▤ ⌂; (II, *C1-2*).

┋┋┋ Le Grand Hotel Via Vittorio Emanuele Orlando 3, ⊠ 00185, tel. 4709, fax 4747307; 170 rms. ▥; ▣ ▤; (II, *D3-4*).

┋┋┋ Lord Byron Via G. de Notaris 5, ⊠ 00197, tel. 3224541, fax 3220405; 37 rms. ▥; ▣ ⚒ ▤; (*not shown on map*).

*** Artdeco Via Palestro 19, ⊠ 00185, tel. 4457588, fax 4441483; 49 rms. ▥; ▣ ▤; (II, *C5*).

*** Atlante Garden (no restaurant), Via Crescenzio 78/A, ⊠ 00193, tel. 6872361, fax 6872315; 60 rms. ▥; ▣ ▤ ℗ ⌂; (I, *D2*).

*** Atlante Star Via Vitelleschi 34, ⊠ 00193, tel. 6873233, fax 6872300; 61 rms. ▥; ▣ ⚒ ▤ ℗ ⌂; (I, *D3*).

*** D'Inghilterra Via Bocca di Leone 14, ⊠ 00187, tel. 69981, fax 69922243; 105 rms. ▥; ▣ ▤; (I, *D6*).

*** Farnese (no restaurant), Via A. Farnese 30, ⊠ 00192, tel. 3212553, fax 3215129; 22 rms. ▥; ▣ ▤; (I, *B4*).

*** Jolly Leonardo da Vinci Via dei Gracchi 324, ⊠ 00192, tel. 32499, fax 3610138; 256 rms. ▥; ▣ ▤ ⌂; (I, *C4*).

*** Jolly Midas Via Aurelia 800, ⊠ 00165, tel. 66396, fax 66418457; 347 rms. ▥; ▣ ⚒ ⚎ ℗; (*not shown on map*).

*** Jolly Vittorio Veneto Corso d'Italia 1, ⊠ 00198, tel. 8495, fax 8841104; 203 rms. ▥; ▣ ▤ ⌂; (II, *B3*).

*** Massimo D'Azeglio Via Cavour 18, ⊠ 00184, tel. 4870270, fax 4827386; 202 rms. ▥; ▣ ▤; (II, *E4*).

*** Mediterraneo Via Cavour 15, ⊠ 00184, tel. 4884051, fax 4744105; 262 rms. ▥; ▣ ▤; (II, *E4*).

*** Mondial (no restaurant), Via Torino 127, ⊠ 00184, tel. 472861, fax 4824822; 84 rms. ▥; ▣ ▤ ℗; (II, *D-E4*).

*** Napoleon Piazza Vittorio Emanuele 105, ⊠ 00185, tel. 4467264, fax 4467282; 80 rms. ▥; ▣ ▤; (III, *A4*).

*** President Via Emanuele Filiberto 173, ⊠ 00185, tel. 770121, fax 7008740; 180 rms. ▥; ▣ ▤ ⌂; (III, *B5*).

*** Rivoli Via Taramelli 7, ⊠ 00197, tel. 3224042, fax 3227373; 54 rms. ▥; ▣ ℗; (*not shown on map*).

*** Arcangelo (no restaurant), Via Boezio 15, ⊠ 00192, tel. 6874143, fax 6893050; 33 rms. ▥; ▣ ℗; (I, *D3*).

*** Canada (no restaurant), Via Vicenza 58, ⊠ 00185, tel. 4457770, fax 4450749; 70 rms. ▥; ▣ ▤; (II, *D5*).

*** Corot (no restaurant), Via Marghera 15/17, ⊠ 00185, tel. 44700900, fax 44700905; 20 rms. ▥; ▣ ▤; (II, *D5*).

*** Domus Aventina (no restaurant), Via di S. Prisca 11/B, ⊠ 00153, tel. 5746135, fax 57300044; 26 rms. ▥; ▣ ▤; (IV, *D5*).

*** Helios (no restaurant), Via Sacco Pastore 13, ⊠ 00141, tel. 8603982, fax 8604355; 50 rms. ▥; ▣ ▤; (*not shown on map*).

*** Miami (no restaurant), Via Nazionale 230, ⊠ 00185, tel. 4817180, fax 484562; 34 rms. ▥; ▣ ▤ ⌂; (II, *E3*).

*** Mozart (no restaurant), Via dei Greci 23/B, ⊠ 00187, tel. 36001915, fax 36001735; 34 rms. ▥; ▣ ▤; (I, *C5-6*).

*** Piccadilly (no restaurant), Via 0Magna Grecia 122, ⊠ 00183, tel. 70474858, fax 70476686; 55 rms. ▥; ▣ ▤ ℗; (III, *D5*).

*** Villa del Parco (no restaurant), Via Nomentana 110, ⊠ 00161, tel. 44237773, fax 44237572; 23 rms. ▥; ▣ ⚒ ▤ ℗ ⌂; (*not shown on map*).

*** Villa Florence (no restaurant), Via Nomentana 28, ⊠ 00161, tel. 4403036, fax 4402709; 33 rms. ▥; ▣ ⚒ ▤ ℗; (II, *B5*).

Restaurants

†¶† Relais le Jardin Via G. de Notaris 5, ⊠ 00197, tel. 3220404, fax 3220405 ⊠; ⅀ classical; 60 capacity; closed Sunday, and for a certain period of time in August; ▣ ℗; of the Albergo Lord Byron; (*not shown on map*).

†¶† Alberto Ciarla Piazza S. Cosimato 40, ⊠ 00153, tel. 5818668, fax 5884377 ⊠; ⅀ of Lazio (seafood); 70/100 capacity; closed Sunday; ▣; (IV, *C2*).

Rosetta Via della Rosetta 8, ⊠ 00187, tel. 6861002, fax 6872852 ⊡; "marinara"; 50 capacity; closed Saturday at midday and Sunday, and for a certain period of time in August; ▣; (I, *E5*).

Sans Souci Via Sicilia 20, ⊠ 00187, tel. 4821814, fax 4821771 ⊡; fine cuisine; 80/100 capacity; open only evening; closed Monday, and for a certain period of time in August; ▣; (II, *C2-3*).

Terrazza Via Ludovisi 49, ⊠ 00187, tel. 478121, fax 4821584 ⊡; Mediterranean; 65 capacity; ▣; (II, *C2*).

Agata e Romeo Via Carlo Alberto 45, ⊠ 00185, tel. 4466115, fax 4465842 ⊡; Lazio and of Sannio; 35/42 capacity; closed Sunday, period of closing may vary; ▣; (II, *F4-5*).

Convivio Via dell'Orso 45, ⊠ 00186, tel. 6869432 ⊡; fine cuisine; 30 capacity; closed Saturday at midday and Sunday, period of closing may vary; ▣; (I, *E4-5*).

Sabatini Piazza di S. Maria in Trastevere 13, ⊠ 00153, tel. 5812026, fax 5898386 ⊡; Roman and "marinara"; 85/285 capacity; closed Wednesday, Christmas and for a certain period of time in August; ▣; (IV, *B3*).

San Luigi Via Mocenigo 10, ⊠ 00192, tel. 39720704, fax 39722421 ⊡; fine cuisine; 50/60 capacity; closed Sunday, and for a certain period of time in August; ❀ ▣; (I, *C1*).

Ceppo Via Panama 2, ⊠ 00198, tel. 8419696 ⊡; Marche and classical; 110 capacity; closed Monday, and for a certain period of time in August; ▣; (*not shown on map*).

Cesarina Via Piemonte 109, ⊠ 00187, tel. 4880828; Romagna; 160 capacity; closed Sunday; ▣; (II, *B3*).

Charly's Saucière Via di S. Giovanni in Laterano 270, ⊠ 00184, tel. 70495666; French-Swiss; 36/48 capacity; closed Sunday, and for a certain period of time in August; ▣; (III, *B-C4*).

Checco er Carettiere Via Benedetta 10, ⊠ 00153, tel. 5800985 ⊡; Roman and "marinara"; 60/120 capacity; closed Sunday evening and Monday, and for a certain period of time in August; ▣ ❀; (IV, *B2-3*).

Girarrosto Toscano Via Campania 29, ⊠ 00187, tel. 4821899 ⊡; Tuscan; 80/115 capacity; closed Wednesday; ▣; (II, *B-C2-3*).

Ortica Via Flaminia Vecchia 673, ⊠ 00191, tel. 3338709; Neapolitan; 70 capacity; closed Sunday, and for a certain period of time in August; (*not shown on map*).

Pavone Via Palestro 19/b, ⊠ 00185, tel. 4465433, fax 4441483 ⊡; of Lazio and classical; 33/80 capacity; closed Saturday at midday in summer and Sunday; ▣; (II, *C5*).

Peppone Via Emilia 60, ⊠ 00187, tel. 483976 ⊡; Roman and classical; 100 capacity; closed Sunday, holidays and before holidays in August; ▣; (II, *C2*).

Scoglio di Frisio Via Merulana 256, ⊠ 00185, tel. 4872765; Neapolitan; 200 capacity; closed at midday on Saturday and Sunday; ▣; (II, *F4*).

Taberna de' Gracchi Via dei Gracchi 268, ⊠ 00192, tel. 3213126; classical (grilled meat and fish); 180 capacity; closed Sunday, and at midday on Monday, Christmas, Easter and 15th August; ▣; (I, *C3*).

Agustarello a Testaccio Via G. Branca 98, ⊠ 00153, tel. 5746585 ⊡; Roman; 40 capacity; closed Sunday and holidays, for a certain period of time in August; ❀; (IV, *E3*).

Felice Via Mastro Giorgio 29, ⊠ 00153, tel. 5746800 ⊡; Roman; 60 capacity; closed Sunday, and for a certain period of time in August; (IV, *E4*).

Il Dito e la Luna Via dei Sabelli 51, ⊠ 00185, tel. 4940726 ⊡; Sicilian; 70/90 capacity; (II, *F6, not shown on map*).

Tram Tram Via dei Reti 44/46, ⊠ 00185, tel. 490416 ⊡; Roman and Apulian (seafood); 50 capacity; (II, *F6, not shown on map*).

EUR

Hotels and restaurants

★★★★ **Aris Garden** Via Aristofane 101, ⊠ 00125, tel. 52362443, fax 52352968; 106 rms.; ▣ ♣ ≋ Ⓟ ♿.

★★★★ **Shangri Là Corsetti** Viale Algeria 141, ⊠ 00144, tel. 5916441, fax 5413813; 52 rms.; ▣ ≋ Ⓟ.

★★★★ **Sheraton Roma** Viale del Pattinaggio, ⊠ 00144, tel. 5453, fax 5940689; 643 rms.; ▣ ♣ ≋ Ⓟ ♿.

Vecchia America-Corsetti Piazza Marconi 32, ⊠ 00144, tel. 5911458; Lazio and classical (seafood); 200 capacity; ▣ ❀.

Sabbioneta (MN) ⊠ 46018 ☎ 0375

Pro Loco, Via V. Gonzaga 15, tel. 52039, fax 52039.

Restaurants

Parco Cappuccini Via Santuario 30, tel. 52005; Mantuan and classical; 80/250 capacity; closed Monday and evening of Wednesday, and for a certain period of time in January; ❀ Ⓟ.

Saint-Vincent (AO) ⊠ 11027 ☎ 0166

APT, Via Roma 48, tel. 512239, fax 513149.

Stazione F.S. (State railroad station), km. 2, tel. 61200.

Saint-Vincent-Châtillon (A5) km. 3.

Hotels and restaurants

★★★★ **G.H. Billia** Viale Piemonte 72, tel. 5231, fax 523799; 246 rms.; ▣ ♣ ≋ Ⓟ ♿.

★★★ **Elena** Piazza Zerbion 2, tel. 512140, fax 537459; closed mid-November/mid-December; from May to October restaurant I Due Nani; 48 rms.; ▣ Ⓟ.

★★ **Leon d'Oro** Via E. Chanoux 26, tel. 512202, fax 537345; 50 rms.; ♣ ▣.

Batezar Via G. Marconi 1, tel. 513164, fax 512378 ⊡; Val d'Aostan and Piedmontese; 30 capacity; open only evening holiday and before holidays also at midday; closed Wednesday, and for a certain period of time in November and between June and July.

Le Grenier Piazza Zerbion 1, tel. 512224 ⊡; Val d'Aostan and classical; 60 capacity; closed Tuesday and at midday on Wednesday, for a certain period of time in July and in January; Ⓟ.

Sala Comacina (CO) ⊠ 22010 ☎ 0344

Restaurants

Taverna Blu Via Puricelli 4, tel. 555107 ⊡; Lake Como; 60 capacity; closed Tuesday, and for a certain period of time in March and September; ❀ Ⓟ.

on the Isola Comacina

Restaurants

Locanda dell'Isola tel. 55083, fax 57022; Lake Como; 150 capacity; seasonal; closed Tuesday in the off season; ❀.

Salerno ⊠ 84100 ☎ 089

🛈 *EPT*, Via Velia 15, tel. 224322, fax 251844; *Information Office*, Piazza Ferrovia, tel. 231432. *AA*, Via Roma 258, tel. 224744; Via Torrione, tel. 790469.

🚉 *Stazione F.S. (State railroad station)*, Piazza Vittorio Veneto, tel. 252200.

🛉 *Salerno Centro or Salerno Fratte* (A3, A30, Highway intersection Avellino-Salerno/A3).

⚓ *Stazione Marittima (Marine Terminal)*, Molo Manfredi.

Hotels and restaurants

*** **Jolly delle Palme** Lungomare Trieste 1, ⊠ 84121, tel. 225222, fax 237571; 104 rms. 🕮; 🖭 📠 🅿.

*** **Fiorenza** (no restaurant), Via Trento 145, ⊠ 84131, tel. 338800, fax 338800; 30 rms. 🕮; 🖭 📠 🅿.

*** **Plaza** (no restaurant), Piazza Vittorio Veneto 42, ⊠ 84123, tel. 224477, fax 237311; 42 rms. 🕮; 📠 🅿.

🍴 **Al Cenacolo** Piazza Alfano I 4, ⊠ 84125, tel. 238818 ⊠; 🍽 Campanian (seafood); 30/50 capacity; closed Sunday evening and Monday, and for a certain period of time in August and in December.

Salò (BS) ⊠ 25087 ☎ 0365

🛈 *IAT*, Lungolago Zanardelli 39, tel. 21423.

🚉 *Stazione F.S. (State railroad station)*, Desenzano del Garda km. 20, tel. 030/9141247.

Hotels and restaurants

*** **Laurin** Viale Landi 9, tel. 22022, fax 22382; closed mid-December/mid-January; 37 rms. 🕮; 🏥 🚞 🅿.

*** **Benaco** Lungolago Zanardelli 44, tel. 20308, fax 20724; 20 rms. 🕮; 🅿 📠.

** **Panoramica** Via del Panorama 28, tel. 41435, fax 521210; 20 rms. 🕮; 🏥 🚞 🅿.

🍴🍴🍴 **Laurin** of the Albergo Laurin.

🍴 **Lepanto** Lungolago Zanardelli 67, tel. 20428 ⊠; 🍽 classical (lake and sea fish, mushrooms); 45/95 capacity; closed Thursday, mid-January/February; ❀; also hotel.

San Gimignano (SI) ⊠ 53037 ☎ 0577

🛈 *Pro Loco*, Piazza Duomo 1, tel. 940008.

🛉 *Poggibonsi* (Highway intersection Siena-Florenze/A 1) km. 13.

Hotels and restaurants

*** **Villa San Paolo** (no restaurant), road for Certaldo, km. 4, tel. 955100, fax 955113; closed Epiphany (6 January)/mid-February; 18 rms. 🕮; 🖭 🏥 🚞 🅿 🕭.

*** **Da Graziano** Via Matteotti 39/A, tel. 940101, fax 940101; closed Epiphany (6 January)/mid-February; 11 rms. 🕮; 🅿.

*** **La Cisterna** Piazza della Cisterna 24, tel. 940328, fax 942080; closed Epiphany (6 January)/mid-March; 49 rms. 🕮; 🖭 🕭.

*** **Leon Bianco** (no restaurant), Piazza della Cisterna 13, tel. 941294, fax 942123; closed Epiphany (6 January)/mid-February and for a certain period of time between November and December; 24 rms. 🕮; 📠 🅿.

🍴 **La Griglia** Via S. Matteo 34/36, tel. 940005; 🍽 Tuscan and classical; 90/200 capacity; closed Thursday, mid-December/mid-February; 🖭.

🍴 **Le Terrazze** Piazza della Cisterna 24, tel. 940328 ⊠; 🍽 Tuscan; 100 capacity; seasonal; closed Tuesday and at midday on Wednesday; 🖭; of the Albergo La Cisterna.

San Marino ⊠ 47031 ☎ 0549
(Repubblica of)

🛈 *Ufficio di Stato per il Turismo*, Palazzo dei Congressi, tel. 882998 (*B2*).

🛉 *Rimini Sud* (A14) km. 23.

Hotels and restaurants

*** **G.H. San Marino** Viale Onofri 31, tel. 992400, fax 992951; closed mid-December/mid-Feb; 63 rms. 🕮; 🖭 📠 🕭; (*C2*).

*** **Panoramic** Via Voltone 91, tel. 992359, fax 990356; closed mid-January/mid-February and for a certain period of time in November; 30 rms. 🕮; 🏥 📠 🅿; (*D3, not shown on map*).

*** **Quercia Antica** Via Capannaccia 7, tel. 991257, fax 990044; 26 rms. 🕮; 🖭 🏥 📠 🅿; (*C2*).

*** **Rossi** at Domagnano, Via XXV Marzo 13, tel. 902263, fax 906642; period of closing may vary; 34 rms. 🕮; 📠 🅿.

🍴 **La Fratta** Salita alla Rocca 14, tel. 991594; 🍽 classical (truffles and mushrooms); 200/350 capacity; closed Wednesday in winter, for a certain period of time between November and December, and January and February; ❀; (*B2*).

🍴 **Righi-la Taverna** Piazza Libertà 10, tel. 991196 ⊠; 🍽 fine cuisine; 80 capacity; closed Wednesday in winter, for a certain period of time between November and December; 🖭; (*B2*).

🍴 **Buca San Francesco** Piazzetta Feretrano 3, tel. 991462; 🍽 Romagna; 60/70 capacity; closed Friday in winter, mid-November/mid-December; (*B2*).

San Remo (IM) ⊠ 18038 ☎ 0184

🛈 *APT*, Largo Nuvoloni, tel. 571571, fax 507649.

🚉 *Stazione F.S. (State railroad station)*, Piazzale Battisti, tel. 531890.

🛉 *San Remo* (A10) km. 8.

Hotels

***ᴸ **Royal Hotel** Corso Imperatrice 80, tel. 5391, fax 661445; seasonal; 142 rms. 🕮; 🖭 🏥 🚞 📠 🅿 🕭.

*** **Eveline Portosole** Corso Cavallotti 111, tel. 503430, fax 503431; 25 rms. 🕮; 🖭 📠 🏥.

*** **Nazionale** Corso Matteotti 3, tel. 577577, fax 541535; 78 rms. 🕮; 🖭 📠 🕭.

*** **Principe** Via F.lli Asquasciati 96, tel. 531919, fax 532811; closed mid-October/Christmas; 50 rms. 🕮; 🏥 🚞 📠 🅿 🕭.

*** **Lolli** *Palace* Corso Imperatrice 70, tel. 531496, fax 541574; 48 rms. 🕮; 🖭 📠 🅿.

*** **Paradiso** Via Roccasterone 12, tel. 571211, fax 578176; 41 rms. 🕮; 🏥 📠 🅿.

*** **Villa Maria** Corso Nuvoloni 30, tel. 531422, fax 531425; 38 rms. 🕮; 🏥 🅿.

** **Corso** Corso Cavallotti 194, tel. 509911, fax 509231; closed November; 18 🕮; 🖭 🅿.

Restaurants

🍴🍴 **Paolo e Barbara** Via Roma 47, tel. 531653 ⊠; 🍽 Ligurian; 30 capacity; closed Wednesday (at midday on Thursday), for a certain period of time in December, January and July; 🖭.

🍴 **La Pignese** Piazza Sardi 7, tel. 501929 ⊠; 🍽 Ligurian; 100 capacity; closed Monday for a certain period of time in June; 🖭.

Sansepolcro (AR) ⊠ 52037 ☎ 0575

🛈 *IAT*, Piazza della Repubblica 2, tel. 740536.

🚉 *Stazione Ferrovia Centrale Umbra*, Piazza Battisti 1, tel. 742094.

Hotels and restaurants

***ᴸ **La Balestra** Via dei Montefeltro 29, tel. 735151, fax 740282; 54 rms. 🕮; 🏥 📠 🅿.

★★★ **Fiorentino** Via Pacioli 60, tel. 740350, fax 740370; 26 rms. (23 🛏); 🅱.

🍴🍴🍴 **Oroscopo di Paola e Marco** at Pieve Vecchia, Via Togliatti 66/68, tel. 734875 ☒; 〰 Tuscan; 30 capacity; open only evening; closed Sunday, period of closing may vary; also hotel.

🍴 **La Balestra** Via dei Montefeltro 29, tel. 735151; 〰 Tuscan; 300 capacity; closed Sunday evening and Monday, and for a certain period of time between July and August; ✿ 🅿.

Santa Margherita Ligure (GE)   ☒ 16038 ☎ 0185

ℹ️ *APT*, Via XXV Aprile 4, tel. 287485, fax 290222.

🚆 *Stazione F.S. (State railroad station)*, Piazza Nobili, tel. 286630.

🛤 *Rapallo* (A12) km. 5.

Hotels and restaurants

★★★ **Imperiale Palace Hotel** Via Pagana 19, tel. 288991, fax 284223; seasonal; 102 rms. 🛏; 🅱 ♿ ⚓ 🅿 ⚕.

★★★ **Continental** Via Pagana 8, tel. 286512, fax 284463; 76 rms. 🛏; 🅱 ♿ ⚓ 🅿 ⚕.

★★★ **G.H. Miramare** promenade Milite Ignoto 30, tel. 287013, fax 284651; 84 rms. 🛏; 🅱 ♿ ⚓ 🅱 🅿 ⚕.

★★★ **Regina Elena** promenade Milite Ignoto 44, tel. 287003, fax 284473; 105 rms. 🛏; 🅱 ♿ ⚓ 🅿 ⚕.

★★★ **Nuovo Hotel Garden** Via Zara 13, tel. 285398, fax 290439; 31 rms. 🛏; ♿ 🅿 ⚕.

★★★ **Tigullio et de Milan** Corso Rainusso 3, tel. 287455, fax 281860; closed mid-November/mid-December; 42 rms. 🛏; ♿ 🅿 ⚕.

🍴 **Il Frantoio** Via Giunchetto 23 A, tel. 286667 ☒; 〰 Ligurian; 80 capacity; closed Tuesday and for a certain period of time between January and February.

🍴 **Paranza** Via Ruffini 46, tel. 283686 ☒; 〰 Ligurian; 80 capacity; closed Thursday, and for a certain period of time in November.

🍴 **Trattoria Cesarina** Via Mameli 2/C, tel. 286059 ☒; 〰 Ligurian (fish, mushrooms); 50 capacity; closed Tuesday, Epiphany (6 January)/February.

Santa Teresa Gallura (SS)   ☒ 07028 ☎ 0789

ℹ️ *AA*, Piazza Vittorio Emanuele I, tel. 754127, fax 754185.

🚆 *Stazione Ferrovie della Sardegna*, at Palau km. 25, tel. 0789/709570.

Hotels and restaurants

★★★ **G.H. Corallaro** township of Rena Bianca, tel. 755475, fax 755431; 81 rms. 🛏; 🅱 ♿ ⚓ 🅿 ⚕.

★★★ **Belvedere** Piazza della Libertà 2, tel. 754160, fax 754937; seasonal; 22 🛏.

★★★ **Miramare** Piazza della Libertà 6, tel. 754103, fax 754672; seasonal; 14 🛏.

🍴🍴🍴 **Bacchus** Via Firenze 5, tel. 754556 ☒; 〰 Sardinian (seafood); 60/100 capacity; closed Monday in the off season, for a certain period of time between December and January; 🅱 ✿; also hotel.

Sassari   ☒ 07100 ☎ 079

ℹ️ *EPT*, Viale Caprera 36, tel. 299546, fax 299415; *AA*, Viale Umberto I 72, tel. 233534, fax 237585.

🚆 *Stazione F.S. (State railroad station)*, Corso Vico 10, tel. 260362; *Stazione Ferrovie della Sardegna*, Viale Sicilia, tel. 241301.

Hotels and restaurants

★★★ **Grazia Deledda** Viale Dante 47, tel. 271235, fax 280884; 127 rms. 🛏; 🅱 🅱 🅿 ⚕.

★★★ **Frank Hotel** Via A. Diaz 20, tel. 276456, fax 276456; 103 rms. 🛏; 🅱 🅱 🅿 ⚕.

★★★ **Leonardo da Vinci** (no restaurant), Via Roma 79, tel. 280744, fax 280744; 118 rms. 🛏; 🅱.

🍴 **Florian** Via Capitano Bellieni 27, tel. 236251 ☒; 〰 classical (seafood, mushrooms); 50 capacity; closed Sunday, for a certain period of time in August; 🅱.

Selinunte (TP)   ☒ 91020 ☎ 0924

ℹ️ *AAPT*, Via G. Caboto.

🚆 *Stazione F.S. (State railroad station)*, km. 1.

at Marinella, km. 1

Hotels

★★★ **Paradise Beach Hotel** Contrada Belice di Mare, tel. 46333, fax 46477; seasonal; 250 rms. 🛏; ♿ ⚓ 🅿.

Siena   ☒ 53100 ☎ 0577

ℹ️ *APT*, Via di Città 43, tel. 42209, fax 281041 (*D3*); *Information Office*, Piazza il Campo 56, tel. 280551 (*D3*).

🚆 *Stazione F.S. (State railroad station)*, Piazzale Rosselli, tel. 280115.

🛤 *Siena* (Highway intersection Siena-Florence/A1) km. 4.

Hotels

★★★ **Executive** Via Orlandi 32, tel. 333173, fax 333178; 73 rms. 🛏; 🅱 ♿ 🅱 🅿 ⚕; (*not shown on map*).

★★★ **Jolly Excelsior** Piazza La Lizza, tel. 288448, fax 41272; 126 rms. 🛏; 🅱 ⚕; (*C2*).

★★★ **Villa Scacciapensieri** Via di Scacciapensieri 10, tel. 41441, fax 270854; closed January/mid-March; 30 rms. 🛏; 🅱 ♿ 🅿 ⚕; (*not shown on map*).

★★★ **Antica Torre** (no restaurant), Via Fieravecchia 7, tel. 222255, fax 222255; 8 rms. 🛏; (*D-E4*).

★★★ **Castagneto Hotel** (no restaurant), Via dei Cappuccini 39, tel. 45103, fax 283266; 11 rms. 🛏; open mid-March/mid-December and Christmas; ♿ 🅿.

★★★ **Duomo** (no restaurant), Via Stalloreggi 38, tel. 289088, fax 43043; 23 rms. 🛏; 🅱; (*E2*).

★★★ **Santa Caterina** (no restaurant), Via Piccolomini 7, tel. 221105, fax 271087; closed Epiphany (6 January)/February; 19 rms. 🛏; 🅱 ♿ 🅿; (*F5*).

Restaurants

🍴 **Al Mangia** Piazza del Campo 42, tel. 281121; 〰 Tuscan; 40/150 capacity; closed Monday in the off season; (*D3*).

🍴 **Antica Trattoria Botteganova** Via Chiantigiana 29, tel. 284230 ☒; 〰 Tuscan and fine cuisine; 50 capacity; closed Monday, period of closing may vary; 🅱 🅿; (*A-B5*).

🍴 **Guido** Vicolo Pier Pettinaio 7, tel. 280042; 〰 Tuscan; 85/110 capacity; (*D3*).

🍴 **Medio Evo** Via dei Rossi 40, tel. 280315; 〰 Tuscan; 150/200 capacity; closed Thursday, and for a certain period of time in July; (*C3*).

Syracuse   ☒ 96100 ☎ 0931

ℹ️ *AAPT*, Via S. Sebastiano 43 and 47, tel. 67710, fax 67803 (*A3*); *AA*, Via Maestranza 33, tel. 464255 (*E5*).

🚆 *Stazione F.S. (State railroad station)*, Piazzale Stazione, tel. 67964.

⚓ *Capitaneria di Porto*, Largo IV Novembre, tel. 66713.

★★★ Forte Agip Viale Teracati 30, tel. 463232, fax 67115; 87 rms. ▨; ▨ Ⓟ ♿; (A3).

★★★ Jolly Corso Gelone 43/45, tel. 461111, fax 461126; 100 rms. ▨; ▨ Ⓟ ♿; (C3).

★★★ Panorama (no restaurant), Via Necropoli Grotticelle 33, tel. 412188, fax 412188; 55 rms. ▨; Ⓟ; (not shown on map).

♟♟ Jonico-'a Rutta 'e Ciauli Riviera Dionisio il Grande 194, tel. 65540 ▨; ◗▯ Sicilian (seafood); 80/160 capacity; closed Tuesday, Christmas, Easter Monday, 15th August; ❀; (A-B5).

♟ Minosse Via Mirabella 6, tel. 66366; ◗▯ Sicilian (fish and mushrooms); 140 capacity; closed Monday, and for a certain period of time in July; ▨; (D5).

Sirmione (BS) ✉ 25019 ☎ 030

ⓘ IAT, Viale Marconi 2, tel. 916114, fax 916222.

♜ Sirmione-San Martino della Battaglia (A4) km. 9.

Hotels and restaurants

★★★ Broglia Via Piana 36, tel. 916172, fax 916586; seasonal; 34 rms. ▨; ♨ ⚒ ▣ Ⓟ.

★★★ Ideal Via Catullo 31, tel. 9904245, fax 9904245; seasonal; 33 rms. ▨; ♨ Ⓟ.

★★★ Golf & Suisse (no restaurant), Via Condominio 2, tel. 9904590, fax 916304; seasonal; 30 rms. ▨; ♨ ⚒ ▣ Ⓟ.

♟♟ La Rucola Via Strentelle 3, tel. 916326 ▨; ◗▯ classical; 25/35 capacity; closed Thursday, January/mid-February; ▨.

at Lugana, km. 4 ✉ 25010

Hotels

★★★ Derby Via Verona 122, tel. 919482, fax 9906631; closed mid-December/January; 14 rms. ▨; ▨ ⚒ Ⓟ.

Sorrento (NA) ✉ 80067 ☎ 081

ⓘ AA, Via L. De Maio 35, tel. 8074033.

♜ Castellammare di Stabia Città (Highway intersection Castellammare di S.-Pompei/A3) km. 20.

⛴ Transportation to Capri.

Hotels

★★★ Bristol Via del Capo 22, tel. 8784522, fax 8071910; 142 rms. ▨; ▨ ⚒ Ⓟ.

★★★ Carlton International Via Correale 15, tel. 8072669, fax 8071073; seasonal; 76 rms. ▨; ♨ ⚒ ▣ Ⓟ.

★★★ Central Corso Italia 254, tel. 8073330, fax 8781372; 60 rms. ▨; ▨ ⚒ ▣ Ⓟ.

★★★ G.A. Excelsior Vittoria Piazza T. Tasso 34, tel. 8071044, fax 8771206; 106 rms. ▨; ♨ ⚒ Ⓟ.

★★★ G.H. Ambasciatori Via Califano 18, tel. 8782025, fax 8071021; 103 rms. ▨; ♨ ⚒ Ⓟ ♿.

★★★ G.H. Royal Via Correale 42, tel. 8073434, fax 8772905; seasonal; 96 rms. ▨; ♨ ⚒ Ⓟ ♿.

★★★ Imperial Tramontano Via Vittorio Veneto 1, tel. 8782588, fax 8072344; closed for a certain period of time between January and February; 115 rms. ▨; ♨ ⚒ ▣ Ⓟ.

★★★ La Solara Via del Capo 118, tel. 5338000, fax 8071501; 38 rms. ▨; ▨ ♨ ⚒ Ⓟ.

★★★ President Via Colle Parise 4, tel. 8782262, fax 8785411; seasonal; 102 rms. ▨; ♨ ⚒ Ⓟ.

★★★ Rivage Via Capo 11, tel. 8781873, fax 8071253; 48 rms. ▨; closed for a certain period of time between January and February; ▨ Ⓟ ♿.

★★ La Minervetta Via del Capo 25, tel. 8073069, fax 8773033; 12 rms. ▨; Ⓟ.

★★ La Tonnarella Via del Capo 31, tel. 8781153, fax 8782169; 21 rms. ▨; ▨ ♨ Ⓟ.

Restaurants

♟♟♟ Caruso Via Sant'Antonino 12, tel. 8073156, fax 8072899 ▨; ◗▯ Campanian and classical (seafood); 90 capacity; closed Monday; ▨.

♟♟♟ Favorita-o' Parrucchiano Corso Italia 71/73, tel. 8781321, fax 8772905; ◗▯ Campanian, fine cuisine; 250/300 capacity; closed Wednesday from mid-November to mid-March; ❀ Ⓟ.

♟♟ Mulino Via Fuorimura 7, tel. 8781216; ◗▯ Neapolitan and classical; 300/600 capacity; closed Tuesday; ❀.

Spoleto (PG) ✉ 06049 ☎ 0743

ⓘ APT, Piazza della Libertà 7, tel. 220311, fax 46241.

♨ Stazione F.S. (State railroad station), Piazzale Polvani, tel. 48516.

Hotels and restaurants

★★★ Dei Duchi Viale G. Matteotti 4, tel. 44541, fax 44543; 49 rms. ▨; ▨ ♨ Ⓟ ♿.

★★★ Gattapone (no restaurant), Via del Ponte 6, tel. 223447, fax 223448; 15 rms. ▨; ▨ ♨.

★★★ Charleston (no restaurant), Piazza Collicola 10, tel. 220052, fax 222010; 18 rms. ▨; ▣.

★★★ Clarici (no restaurant), Piazza della Vittoria 32, tel. 223311, fax 222010; 24 rms. ▨; ▨ Ⓟ.

♟♟♟ Apollinare Via S. Agata 14, tel. 223256, fax 221885 ▨; ◗▯ Umbrian fine cuisine; 55/95 capacity; closed Tuesday; ▨; also hotel.

♟♟♟ Tartufo Piazza Garibaldi 24, tel. 40236 ▨; ◗▯ Umbrian (mushrooms and truffles); 70/80 capacity; closed Sunday evening and Monday, period of closing may vary; ▨.

♟♟ Pentagramma Via Martani 4, tel. 223141 ▨; ◗▯ Umbrian fine cuisine (pasta dishes); 80 capacity; closed Monday, and for a certain period of time between July and August.

Stresa (VB) ✉ 28838 ☎ 0323

ⓘ APT and IAT, Via Principe Tomaso 70/72, tel. 30150-30416, fax 32561.

♨ Stazione F.S. (State railroad station), Via G. Carducci 1, tel. 30472.

♜ Stresa (A26) km. 6.

⛴ Transportation to the Isole Borromee.

Hotels and restaurants

★★★ G.H. des Iles Borromées Corso Umberto I 67, tel. 938938, fax 32405; 173 rms. ▨; ▨ ♨ ⚒ Ⓟ ♿.

★★★ G.H. Bristol Corso Umberto I 73, tel. 32601, fax 33622; seasonal; 250 rms. ▨; ▨ ♨ ⚒ Ⓟ ♿.

★★★ La Palma Corso Umberto I 33, tel. 933906, fax 933930; seasonal; 124 rms. ▨; ▨ ♨ ⚒ ▣ Ⓟ ♿.

★★★ Du Parc Via Gignous 1, tel. 30335, fax 33596; seasonal; 21 rms. ▨; ♨ Ⓟ.

★★★ Flora Via Sempione Nord 26, tel. 30524, fax 33372; seasonal; 23 rms. ▨; ♨ Ⓟ.

★★★ Primavera (no restaurant), Via Cavour 39, tel. 31286, fax 33458; seasonal; 31 rms. ▨; ▣ ♿.

♟♟♟ Emiliano Corso Italia 50, tel. 31396, fax 33474 ▨; ◗▯ classical; 50 capacity; closed Tuesday and at midday of Wednesday, for a certain period of time between December and January.

♟♟ Piemontese Via Mazzini 25, tel. 30235 ▨; ◗▯ Piedmontese and classical; 60 capacity; closed Monday, for a certain period of time between December and January.

at the Mottarone, km. 20, or by cableway

✉ 28836

Restaurants

🍴 **Eden** tel. 924873; 🍴 Piedmontese (mushrooms); 150/300 capacity; closed Tuesday in the off season, and for a certain period of time in November; ⚜ Ⓟ; also hotel.

Taormina (ME) ✉ 98039 ☎ 0942

📋 *AA*, Piazza S. Caterina, tel. 23243, fax 24941.

🚉 *Stazione F.S. (State railroad station)*, km. 5, tel. 51511.

🛉 *Taormina* (A18) km. 4.

Hotels and restaurants

★★★ **San Domenico Palace** Piazza S. Domenico 5, tel. 23701, fax 625506; 111 rms. 📶; ♨♨☕ 🔲 Ⓟ ♿.

★★★ **Excelsior Palace** Via Toselli 6, tel. 23975, fax 23978; 88 rms. 📶; 🔲 ♨☕ Ⓟ ♿.

★★★ **Villa Diodoro** Via Bagnoli Croce 75, tel. 23312, fax 23391; 102 rms. 📶; ♨☕ Ⓟ 🔲.

★★★ **Continental** Via Dionisio Primo 2/A, tel. 23805, fax 23806; 43 rms. 📶; 🔲 ♨ Ⓟ.

★★★ **Vello d'Oro** Via Fazzello 2, tel. 23788, fax 626117; open February/November; 58 rms. 📶; Ⓟ.

★★★ **Villa Belvedere** (no restaurant), Via Bagnoli Croce 79, tel. 23791, fax 625830; seasonal and Christmas-Epiphany (6 January); 48 rms. 📶; ♨☕ Ⓟ.

🍴🍴🍴 **La Giara** Vico Floresta 1, tel. 23360, fax 23233 ✉; 🍴 fine cuisine (seafood); 100 capacity; closed at midday and Monday from October to March, for a certain period of time between January and February; 🔲.

🍴 **Al Duomo** Vico Ebrei 11, tel. 625656 ✉; 🍴 Sicilian; 45/80 capacity; closed Wednesday in the off season; 🔲.

🍴 **Griglia** Corso Umberto 54, tel. 23980 ✉; 🍴 Messina (seafood); 80 capacity; closed Tuesday; 🔲.

at Capo Taormina, km. 3 ✉ 98030

Hotels

★★★ **G.A. Capotaormina** Via Nazionale 105, tel. 24000, fax 625467; seasonal; 203 rms. 📶; 🔲 ♨ ☕ 🔲 Ⓟ ♿.

Taranto ✉ 74100 ☎ 099

📋 *EPT*, Corso Umberto I 121, tel. 4532397, *Information Office*, Corso Umberto I 113, tel. 4532392.

🚉 *Stazione F.S. (State railroad station)*, Piazza Libertà, tel. 4711801; *Ferrovie Sud Est*, Via Galeso, tel. 4704463.

🛉 *access at km. 20* (A14).

Hotels and restaurants

★★★ **G.H. Delfino** Viale Virgilio 66, tel. 7323232, fax 7304654; 200 rms. 📶; 🔲♨ ☕ Ⓟ ♿.

★★★ **Park Hotel Mar Grande** Viale Virgilio 90, tel. 7351713, fax 7369494; 93 rms. 📶; 🔲 ♨☕ Ⓟ.

🍴🍴🍴 **Monsieur Mimmo** Viale Virgilio 101, tel. 372691; 🍴 Taranto and classical; 140 capacity; closed Tuesday in the off season; 🔲 Ⓟ.

🍴 **Il Caffè** Via D'Aquino 8, tel. 4525097; 🍴 "marinara"; 105 capacity; closed Tuesday, period of closing may vary.

Tarquìnia (VT) ✉ 01016 ☎ 0766

📋 *AA*, Piazza Cavour 1, tel. 856384, fax 840479 (*B2*).

🚉 *Stazione F.S. (State railroad station)*, km. 3, tel. 856084.

🛉 *beginning of highway section Civitavecchia-Roma* (A12) km. 11.

Restaurants

🍴 **Bersagliere** Via B. Croce 2, tel. 856047; 🍴 Lazio (seafood); 150/250 capacity; closed Monday and Sunday evening, Christmas-Epiphany (6 January), and for a certain period of time in July; 🔲 ⚜ Ⓟ.

at Tarquinia Lido, km. 7 ✉ 01010

Hotels

★★★ **G.H. Helios** Via Porto Clementino, tel. 864618, fax 864295; 95 rms. 📶; 🔲 ♨ ☕ Ⓟ.

★★★ **La Torraccia** (no restaurant), Viale Mediterraneo 45, tel. 864375, fax 864296; closed Christmas-Epiphany (6 January); 18 rms. 📶; 🔲 ♨.

Tivoli (RM) ✉ 00019 ☎ 0774

📋 *AA*, Largo Garibaldi, tel. 21249, fax 331294.

🚉 *Stazione F.S. (State railroad station)*, Viale Mazzini, tel. 20268.

🛉 *Castel Madama* (A24) km. 6.

Restaurants

🍴 **Cinque Statue** Largo S. Angelo 1, tel. 335366 ✉; 🍴 classical; 90/150 capacity; closed Friday and Sunday evening, and for a certain period of time between August and September.

at Bagni di Tivoli, km. 9 ✉ 00011

Hotels

★★★ **G.H. Duca d'Este** Via Tiburtina Valeria 330, tel. 3883, fax 388101; 184 rms. 📶; 🔲 ♨ 🔲 Ⓟ.

Todi (PG) ✉ 06059 ☎ 075

📋 *APT*, Piazza Umberto I 6, tel. 8943395.

🚉 *Stazione Ferrovia Centrale Umbra*, Ponte Rio km. 3. tel. 8942092.

Hotels and restaurants

★★★ **Villa Luisa** Via Cortesi 147, tel. 8948571, fax 8948472; 40 rms. 📶; 🔲 ♨ ☕ Ⓟ ♿.

🍴 **Umbria** Via S. Bonaventura 13, tel. 8942737 ✉; 🍴 Umbrian (truffles); 70/150 capacity; closed Tuesday; 🔲.

Torcello (VE) ✉ 30012 ☎ 041

🚢 *Transportation from Venice*.

Restaurants

🍴🍴🍴 **Locanda Cipriani** Piazza S. Fosca 29, tel. 730150, fax 735433; 🍴 classical (seafood); 250 capacity; closed Tuesday, Epiphany (6 January)/mid-February; 🔲 ⚜.

🍴 **Ostaria al Ponte del Diavolo** Via Borgognoni 10/11, tel. 730401, fax 730250 ✉; 🍴 Venetian (seafood); 150 capacity; closed Wednesday, mid-December/mid-February; 🔲 ⚜.

Torre del Greco (NA) ✉ 80059 ☎ 081

🚉 *Stazione F.S. (State railroad station)*, Via S. Maria La Bruna, tel. 8833252.

🛉 *Torre del Greco* (A3) km. 1.

Hotels

★★★ **Sakura** Via E. De Nicola 26, tel. 8493144, fax 8491122; 65 rms. 📶; 🔲 ♨ ☕ 🔲 Ⓟ ♿.

★★★ **Marad** Via S. Sebastiano 24, tel. 8492168, fax 8828716; 79 rms. 📶; 🔲 ♨ ☕ 🔲 Ⓟ.

Trani (BA) ✉ 70059 ☎ 0883

📋 *AA*, Corso Cavour 140, tel. 588825; *Information Office*, Piazza Repubblica, tel. 43295.

🚃 Stazione F.S. (State railroad station), Piazza XX Settembre, tel. 588801.

🕇 Trani (A14) km. 8.

Hotels and restaurants

☆ **Royal** Via De Robertis 29, tel. 588777, fax 582224; 45 rms. 🅼; 🅱🅴🅿 ♿.

🍽 **Torrente Antico** Via Fusco 3, tel. 47911 ☒; ⅀ "marinara"; 35 capacity; closed Sunday evening and Monday, and for a certain period of time in January and in July; 🅱.

🍽 **Il Patriarca** Lungomare Colombo 72, tel. 45904 ☒; ⅀ of Bari and classical; 150 capacity; closed Tuesday, period of closing may vary; 🅱 🅿.

Trent   ☒ 38100 ☎ 0461

ℹ APT, Via Alfieri 4, tel. 983880, fax 984508.

🚃 Stazione F.S. (State railroad station), Piazza Dante, tel. 234545; Stazione Ferrovia Trento-Malè, Via Secondo da Trento, tel. 822725.

🕇 Trento Centro (A22) km. 2.

Hotels and restaurants

☆ **Buonconsiglio** (no restaurant), Via Romagnosi 16/18, tel. 272888, fax 272889; 45 rms. 🅼; 🅱🅴 ♿.

*** **America** Via Torre Verde 50, tel. 983010, fax 230603; 50 rms. 🅼; 🅱🅴🅿 ♿.

*** **Everest** Corso Alpini 14, tel. 825300, fax 824527; 123 rms. 🅼; 🅱🅿 ♿.

🍽 **Chiesa** Parco S. Marco, tel. 238766, fax 986169 ☒; ⅀ Tridentine; 100 capacity; closed Sunday and at midday on Monday, August; ❀.

🍽 **Osteria a le due Spade** Via Don Rizzi 11, tel. 234343 ☒; ⅀ Tridentine fine cuisine; 40 capacity; closed Sunday and at midday on Monday; 🅱.

at Cognola, km. 3   ☒ 38050

Restaurants

🍽 **Villa Madruzzo** Ponte Alto 26, tel. 986220; ⅀ Tridentine and classical (mushrooms); 80/120 capacity; closed Sunday; of the Albergo.

Treviso   ☒ 31100 ☎ 0422

ℹ APT, Via Toniolo 41, tel. 547632, fax 541397.

🚃 Stazione F.S. (State railroad station), Piazzale Duca d'Aosta, tel. 541352.

🕇 Treviso Nord (A27) km. 8; Treviso Sud (A27) km. 7.

✈ Airport, Via Noalese 63/e (km. 4 to the SW), tel. 20393.
Alitalia, Via Collalto 3, tel. 410103.

Hotels

☆ **Ca' del Galletto** (no restaurant), Via S. Bona Vecchia 30, tel. 432550, fax 432510; 60 rms. 🅼; 🅱🅿 ♿.

☆ **Carlton** Largo Porta Altinia 15, tel. 411661, fax 411620; 93 rms. 🅼; 🅱🚭 🅿.

*** **Al Foghèr** Viale della Repubblica 10, tel. 432950, fax 430391; 55 rms. 🅼; 🅱 🅿.

*** **Scala** Viale Felissent 1, tel. 307600, fax 305048; 20 rms. 🅼; 🅱 🅿.

** **Campeol** (no restaurant), Piazza Ancillotto 11, tel. 56601, fax 540871; 14 rms. 🅼.

Restaurants

🍽 **Alfredo** Via Collalto 26, tel. 540275 ☒; ⅀ classical (seafood); 60 capacity; closed Sunday evening and Monday, August; 🅱.

🍽 **Al Bersagliere** Via Barberia 21, tel. 579902 ☒; ⅀ Trevisan (seafood); 50/70 capacity; closed Sunday and at midday on Saturday, and for a certain period of time in August; 🅱.

🍽 **Antica Torre** Via Inferiore 55, tel. 53694 ☒; ⅀ Trevisan (seafood); 38/55 capacity; closed Sunday, and for a certain period of time in August; 🅱.

🍽 **Beccherie** Piazza Ancillotto 10, tel. 540871 ☒; ⅀ local; 100 capacity; closed Sunday evening and Monday, and for a certain period of time in July; 🅱.

🍽 **L'Incontro** Largo di Porta Altinia 13, tel. 547717 ☒; ⅀ Venetian regional and classical; 60/75 capacity; closed Wednesday and at midday on Thursday, and for a certain period of time in August; 🅱.

Trieste   ☒ 34100 ☎ 040

ℹ Azienda Regionale per la Promozione Turistica (Regional Chamber of Tourism), Via Rossini 6, tel. 363952, fax 365496 (B3); APT, Via San Nicolò 20, tel. 369881, fax 369981 (C3); Information Office, stazione F.S., tel. 420182 (A3).

🚃 Stazioni F.S. (State railroad stations), Centrale, Piazza Libertà 8, tel. 418207; Villa Opicina, tel. 211682.

🕇 Trieste Miramare-Sistiana (A4/A23) km. 19.

✈ Airport, Ronchi dei Legionari (km. 34 to the NW), tel. 0481/773224-773225.
Alitalia, Via Milano 15, tel. 631484.

⚓ Stazione Marittima (Marine Terminal), Molo Bersaglieri, tel. 6732261.

Hotels and restaurants

☆ **Jolly** Corso Cavour 7, ☒ 34132, tel. 7600055, fax 362699; 174 rms. 🅼; 🅱🅴 ♿; (B3).

☆ **Starhotel Savoia Excelsior** Riva del Mandracchio 4, ☒ 34124, tel. 77941, fax 638260; 155 rms. 🅼; 🅱; (C2).

*** **Novo Hotel Impero** (no restaurant), Via S. Anastasio 1, ☒ 34132, tel. 364242, fax 365023; 50 rms. 🅼; 🅱; (A3).

*** **San Giusto** (no restaurant), Via C. Belli 3, ☒ 34137, tel. 762661, fax 7606585; 62 rms. 🅼; 🅱🅿; (D4).

🍽 **Antica Trattoria Suban** Via Comici 2, ☒ 34128, tel. 54368, fax 579020 ☒; ⅀ of Trieste; 80 capacity; closed Monday at midday and Tuesday, and for a certain period of time in January and in August; ❀; (B6, not shown on map).

🍽 **Ai Fiori** Piazza Hortis 7, ☒ 34124, tel. 300633 ☒; ⅀ of Trieste (seafood); 40/50 capacity; closed Sunday and Monday, Christmas-New Year's, and for a certain period of time in July; 🅱; (C2).

at Villa Opicina, km. 7   ☒ 34016

Restaurants

🍽 **Daneu** Via Nazionale 194, tel. 211241; ⅀ of Trieste; 150/200 capacity; closed Monday; ❀ 🅿; also hotel.

Turin   ☒ 10100 ☎ 011

ℹ APT and IAT, Via Roma 226 (Piazzetta CLN), tel. 535181, fax 530070 (C3); Information Office, Stazione Porta Nuova, tel. 531327 (C-D3).
TCI Ufficio di Torino, Piazza Solferino 3 bis, tel. 5627070 (B3).

🚃 Stazioni F.S. (State railroad stations), Porta Nuova and Porta Susa: travellers information, tel. 5613333.

🕇 access from Corso G. Cesare (A4 and A5); from Corso Trieste (A6 and A21); from the ring road that links all the highways (A32 and Highway intersection Turin-Pinerolo).

✈ *International Airport* at Caselle (km. 15), tel. 5676361.
Alitalia, Via Lagrange 35, tel. 57698 (*C3*).

★★★ **G.H. Sitea** Via Carlo Alberto 35, ✉ 10123, tel. 5170171, fax 548090; 117 rms. ▥; 🅿 ♨ ♿; (*C4*).
★★★ **Jolly Hotel Ambasciatori** Corso Vittorio Emanuele II 104, ✉ 10121, tel. 5752, fax 544978; 199 rms. ▥; 🅿 ♿; (*C1*).
★★★ **Jolly Hotel Ligure** Piazza Carlo Felice 85, ✉ 10123, tel. 55641, fax 535438; 169 rms. ▥; 🅿 🅿 ♿; (*C3*).
★★★ **Jolly Hotel Principi di Piemonte** Via Gobetti 15, ✉ 10123, tel. 5629693, fax 5620270; 107 rms. ▥; 🅿 🅿; (*C3*).
★★★ **Starhotel Majestic** Corso Vittorio Emanuele II 54, ✉ 10123, tel. 539153, fax 534963; 152 rms. ▥; 🅿 🅿; (*C3*).
★★★ **Turin Palace Hotel** Via Sacchi 8, ✉ 10128, tel. 5625511, fax 5612187; 123 rms. ▥; 🅿 🅿 ♿; (*C3*).
★★★ **Villa Sassi** Strada Traforo del Pino 47, ✉ 10132, tel. 8980556, fax 8980095; closed August; 17 rms. ▥; 🅿 ♨🅿 ♿; (*not shown on map*).
★★★ **Boston** (no restaurant), Via Massena 70, ✉ 10128, tel. 500359, fax 599358; 61 rms. ▥; 🅿 ♨ 🅿; (*D2*).
★★★ **Crimea** (no restaurant), Via Mentana 3, ✉ 10133, tel. 6604700, fax 6604912; 49 rms. ▥; 🅿; (*D5*).
★★★ **Genio** (no restaurant), Corso Vittorio Emanuele II 47, ✉ 10125, tel. 6505771, fax 6508264; 90 rms. ▥; 🅿 🅿; (*C-D3*).
★★★ **Genova e Stazione** (no restaurant), Via Sacchi 14/B, ✉ 10128, tel. 5629400, fax 5629896; closed August; 57 rms. ▥; 🅿 🅿 ♿; (*D3*).
★★★ **Giotto** (no restaurant), Via Giotto 27, ✉ 10126, tel. 6637172, fax 6637173; 50 rms. ▥; 🅿 🅿 🅿; (*F3*).
★★★ **Gran Mogol** (no restaurant), Via Guarini 2, ✉ 10123, tel. 5612120, fax 5623160; closed August; 45 rms. ▥; 🅿 🅿; (*C3*).
★★★ **Piemontese** (no restaurant), Via Berthollet 21, ✉ 10125, tel. 6698101, fax 6690571; 35 rms. ▥; 🅿 🅿; (*D3*).
★★★ **Plaza** (no restaurant), Via Potitti 18, ✉ 10126, tel. 6632424, fax 678351; 65 rms. ▥; 🅿 🅿 ♿; (*F2*).

♦♦♦ **Carignano** Via Carlo Alberto 35, ✉ 10123, tel. 5170171, fax 548090 ⊠; ♦♦ Piedmontese and classical; 60/80 capacity; closed Saturday evening and Sunday, August; 🅿; del G.H. Sitea; (*C4*).
♦♦♦ **Del Cambio** Piazza Carignano 2, ✉ 10123, tel. 546690, fax 535282; ♦♦ Piedmontese and classical; 60/150 capacity; closed Sunday, New Year's-Epiphany (6 January) and August; 🅿; (*B4*).
♦♦♦ **Neuv Caval 'd Brôns** Piazza S. Carlo 151, ✉ 10123, tel. 5627483, fax 543610 ⊠; ♦♦ Piedmontese and classical; 20/65 capacity; closed Sunday, and for a certain period of time in August; 🅿; (*B-C4*).
♦♦♦ **Vecchia Lanterna** Corso Re Umberto 21, ✉ 10128, tel. 537047, fax 530391 ⊠; ♦♦ classical (seafood); 35/60 capacity; closed Saturday at midday and Sunday, and for a certain period of time in August; 🅿; (*C3*).
♦♦♦ **Villa Sassi-El Toulà** Strada Traforo del Pino 47, ✉ 10132, tel. 8980556, fax 8980095 ⊠; ♦♦ classical; 50 capacity; closed Sunday, August; ❀ 🅿; of the Albergo Villa Sassi; (*not shown on map*).
♦♦♦ **Villa Somis** Strada Val Pattonera 138, ✉ 10133, tel. 6614266, fax 6613086 ⊠; ♦♦ fine cuisine; 150 capacity; closed Monday from October to May, also at midday week-days, and for a certain period of time in August; ❀ 🅿; (*not shown on map*).

♦♦ **Balbo** Via A. Doria 11, ✉ 10123, tel. 8395775, fax 8151042 ⊠; ♦♦ Piedmontese and fine cuisine (seafood); 60/80 capacity; closed Monday, and for a certain period of time between July and August; 🅿; (*C4*).
♦♦ **Tiffany** Piazza Solferino 16, ✉ 10121, tel. 535948 ⊠; ♦♦ classical (seafood); 80 capacity; closed Saturday at midday and Sunday, and for a certain period of time in August; 🅿; (*B3*).
♦♦ **Al Bue Rosso** Corso Casale 10, ✉ 10131, tel. 8191393; ♦♦ classical; 60 capacity; closed Monday and at midday on Saturday, for a certain period of time in August; 🅿; (*C5*).
♦♦ **Mina** Via Ellero 36 bis, ✉ 10126, tel. 6963608 ⊠; ♦♦ Piedmontese; 140/240 capacity; closed Monday (also Sunday evening from mid-June to mid-September), August; 🅿; (*not shown on map*).
♦♦ **Porta Rossa** Via Passalacqua 3/B, ✉ 10122, tel. 530816 ⊠; ♦♦ classical; 40/50 capacity; closed Saturday at midday and Sunday, August; 🅿.
♦♦ **San Giorgio** Viale E. Millo 6, ✉ 10126, tel. 6692131 ⊠; ♦♦ Piedmontese and classical; 300 capacity; closed Tuesday and at midday on Wednesday, August, and for a certain period of time in January; (*F4*).
♦ **Ij Brandè** Via Massena 5, ✉ 10128, tel. 537279 ⊠; ♦♦ Piedmontese; 50/60 capacity; closed Sunday and at midday on Monday, August; 🅿; (*C3*).

Udine   ✉ 33100 ☎ 0432

🛈 *Azienda Regionale per la Promozione Turistica (Regional Chamber of Tourism)*, Piazza I Maggio 7, tel. 295972, fax 504743.

TCI, Uffico di Udine, Via P. Sarpi 14, tel. 512101.

🚃 *Stazione F.S. (State railroad station)*, Viale Europa Unita 90/6, tel. 503656.

🛣 *Udine Nord* (A23) km. 8; *Udine Sud* (A23/A4) km. 6.

✈ *Airport*, Ronchi dei Legionari (km. 43 to the SE), tel. 0481/773224-773225.
Alitalia, general agency, Via Carducci 26, tel. 294601.

★★★ **Ambassador Palace** Via Carducci 46, tel. 503777, fax 503711; 87 rms. ▥; 🅿 🅿.
★★★ **Astoria Hotel Italia** Piazza XX Settembre 24, tel. 505091, fax 509070; 75 rms. ▥; 🅿 🅿.
★★★ **Friuli** Viale Ledra 24, tel. 234351, fax 234606; closed Christmas-Epiphany (6 January); 100 rms. ▥; 🅿 🅿 ♿.
★★★ **La' di Moret** Viale Tricesimo 276, tel. 545096, fax 545096; 60 rms. ▥; ♨ ♨ 🅿 ♿.
♦♦ **La' di Moret** Viale Tricesimo 276, tel. 545096 ⊠; ♦♦ Friulian (seafood); 100/300 capacity; closed Sunday evening and Monday evening; of the Albergo; 🅿 ❀ 🅿.
♦♦ **Vitello d'Oro** Via Valvason 4, tel. 508982, fax 508982 ⊠; ♦♦ Friulian and classical; 100 capacity; closed Wednesday, and for a certain period of time in July; 🅿 ❀ 🅿.

Urbino (PS)   ✉ 61029 ☎ 0722

🛈 *APT*, Piazza Rinascimento 1, tel. 2613, fax 2441.

🛣 *Fossombrone Ovest* (Highway intersection Fossombrone-Fano/A14) km. 18.

★★★ **Bonconte** Via delle Mura 28, tel. 2463, fax 4782; 25 rms. ▥; ♨ 🅿 ♿.
★★★ **Mamiani** Via Bernini 6, tel. 322309, fax 327742; closed for a certain period of time in January; 72 rms. ▥; 🅿 ♿ 🅿.

★★★ **Raffaello** (no restaurant), Via S. Margherita 40, tel. 4896, fax 328540; closed for a certain period of time in December and in July; 14 rms. 🖫.

🍴 **Il Cortegiano** Via Puccinotti 13, tel. 320307; 🍴 Marche (truffles); 100 capacity; closed Monday, mid-December/mid-January; 🎫 ❀.

Venice 　　　　　🖂 30100 ☎ 041

ℹ️ *APT*, San Marco 71/c, tel. 5226356, fax 5298730 (II, *E4*); Stazione F.S., tel. 719078 (I, *C1*); Lido, Gran Viale S. Maria Elisabetta 6/a, tel. 5265721, fax 5298720.

🚉 *Stazione F.S. (State railroad station)*, Fondamenta Santa Lucia, tel. 715555.

🚏 *Mestre Est* (A27) km. 14; *Mestre M.* (A4/A13) km. 10.

✈ *Aeroporto Marco Polo*, Tessera (km. 13 to the north), tel. 2609260.
Alitalia, San Marco, Bacino Orseolo 1166, tel. 5216222 (II, *E4*).

🛳 *Stazione Marittima (Marine Terminal)*, tel. 5334725; San Basilio, tel. 5334745.

★★★ᴸ **Danieli** Castello 4196, Riva degli Schiavoni, 🖂 30122, tel. 5226480, fax 5200208; 231 rms. 🖫; 🎫 🔲; (I, *E6*).

★★★ᴸ **Gritti Palace ITT Sheraton** S. Marco 2467, Campo S. Maria del Giglio, 🖂 30124, tel. 794611, fax 5200942; 93 rms. 🖫; 🎫; (II, *F3*).

★★★ **Amadeus** Cannaregio 227, Lista di Spagna, 🖂 30121, tel. 715300, fax 5240841; 63 rms. 🖫; 🎫 🏃 🔲; (I, *B2*).

★★★ **Cavalletto & Doge Orseolo** S. Marco 1107, Calle del Cavalletto, 🖂 30124, tel. 5200955, fax 5238184; 96 rms. 🖫; 🎫 🔲; (II, *E4*).

★★★ **Gabrielli Sandwirth** Castello 4110, Riva degli Schiavoni, 🖂 30122, tel. 5231580, fax 5209455; closed December/mid-February; 100 rms. 🖫; 🎫 🏃 🔲; (I, *D4*).

★★★ **Luna Hotel Baglioni** S. Marco 1243, Calle Larga de l'Ascension, 🖂 30124, tel. 5289840, fax 5287160; 118 rms. 🖫; 🎫 🔲 🔥; (II, *E4*).

★★★ **Starhotel Splendid Suisse** S. Marco Mercerie 760, 🖂 30124, tel. 5200755, fax 5286498; 166 rms. 🖫; 🎫 🔥; (II, *D4*).

★★★ **Abbazia** (no restaurant), Cannaregio, Calle Priuli 68, 🖂 30121, tel. 717333, fax 717949; 39 rms. 🖫; 🎫 🏃; (I, *B1*).

★★★ **Ala** (no restaurant), S. Marco 2494, Campo S. Maria del Giglio, 🖂 30124, tel. 5208333, fax 5206390; 85 rms. 🖫; 🎫; (II, *F3*).

★★★ **American** (no restaurant), Dorsoduro 628, Fondam. Bragadin (S. Vio), 🖂 30123, tel. 5204733, fax 5204048; 29 rms. 🖫; 🎫 🔲; (I, *E2*).

★★★ **Ateneo** (no restaurant), S. Marco 1876, Calle Minelli, 🖂 30124, tel. 5200777, fax 5228550; 20 rms. 🖫; 🎫; (II, *E3*).

★★★ **Bisanzio** (no restaurant), Castello 3651, Calle della Pietà, 🖂 30122, tel. 5203100, fax 5204114; 42 rms. 🖫; 🔲; (I, *D4*).

★★★ **Casanova** (no restaurant), S. Marco 1284, Frezzeria, 🖂 30124, tel. 5206855, fax 5206413; 50 rms. 🖫; 🎫 🔲; (II, *E4*).

★★★ **Giorgione** (no restaurant), Cannaregio 4587, Campo SS. Apostoli, 🖂 30131, tel. 5225810, fax 5239092; 70 rms. 🖫; 🎫 🏃 🔥; (I, *B4*).

★★★ **La Fenice et Des Artistes** (no restaurant), S. Marco 1936, Campiello della Fenice, 🖂 30124, tel. 5232333, fax 5203721; 69 rms. (67 🖫); 🎫 🏃 (II, *E3*).

★★★ **Olimpia** (no restaurant), S. Croce 395, Fondamenta delle Burchielle, 🖂 30135, tel. 711041, fax 5246777; 35 rms. 🖫; 🎫 🏃; (I, *C1*).

★★★ **Pausania** (no restaurant), Dorsoduro 2824, Fondamenta Gherardini, 🖂 30123, tel. 5222083, fax 5222989; 26 rms. 🖫; 🎫; (I, *D1*).

★★★ **Spagna** (no restaurant), Cannaregio 184, Lista di Spagna, 🖂 30121, tel. 715011, fax 715318; 19 rms. 🖫; 🎫 🔲; (I, *B2*).

★★ **Agli Alboretti** Accademia 884, rio terrà A. Foscarini, 🖂 30123, tel. 5230058, fax 5210158; 20 rms. 🖫; 🏃 🔲; (II, *F2*).

🍴🍴🍴 **Antico Martini** S. Marco 1983, Campo S. Fantin, 🖂 30124, tel. 5224121, fax 5289857 🖂; 🍴 classical (seafood); 40/85 capacity; closed Tuesday and at midday on Wednesday; 🎫; (II, *E3*).

🍴🍴🍴 **Harry's Bar** S. Marco 1323, Calle Vallaresso, 🖂 30124, tel. 5285777, fax 5208822; 🍴 Venetian and classical; 80/100 capacity; 🎫; (II, *E-F4*).

🍴🍴 **Antico Pignolo** San Marco 451, Calle dei Specchieri, 🖂 30124, tel. 5228123 🖂; 🍴 Venetian and classical (seafood); 300 capacity; closed Tuesday in the off season; 🎫 ❀; (II, *D5*).

🍴🍴 **Covo** Castello 3968, Campiello della Pescaria, 🖂 30122, tel. 5223812 🖂; 🍴 Venetian (seafood, game); 50 capacity; closed Wednesday and Thursday; 🎫; (I, *C-D4*).

🍴🍴 **Osteria da Fiore** S. Polo 2202, Calle del Scaleter, 🖂 30125, tel. 721308, fax 721343 🖂; 🍴 Venetian regional (seafood); 45/55 capacity; closed Sunday and Monday, Christmas/mid-January and August; 🎫; (II, *C2*).

🍴 **Ai Gondolieri** Dorsoduro 366, S. Vio, 🖂 30123, tel. 5286396 🖂; 🍴 Venetian regional; 40 capacity; closed Tuesday, period of closing may vary; 🎫; (II, *F3*).

🍴 **Ai Mercanti** S. Marco 4346/A, Calle dei Fuseri, 🖂 30124, tel. 5238269 🖂; 🍴 Venetian regional (seafood); 50/60 capacity; closed Sunday and Monday at midday; 🎫; (II, *D4*).

🍴 **A la Vecia Cavana** Cannaregio 4624, rio terrà SS. Apostoli, 🖂 30131, tel. 5287106 🖂; 🍴 Venetian (seafood); 70/120 capacity; closed Thursday, period of closing may vary; 🎫; (II, *B4*).

🍴 **Al Conte Pescaor** S. Marco 544, piscina S. Zulian, 🖂 30124, tel. 5221483; 🍴 Venetian (seafood); 100/120 capacity; closed Sunday, and for a certain period of time between January and February; 🎫; (II, *D5*).

🍴 **Antica Besseta** S. Croce 1395, salizzada de Ca' Zusto, 🖂 30121, tel. 721687 🖂; 🍴 Venetian (seafood); 46/70 capacity; closed Tuesday and at midday on Wednesday; (II, *B1*).

🍴 **Antica Carbonera** S. Marco 4648, Calle Bembo, 🖂 30124, tel. 5225479; 🍴 Venetian; 80/100 capacity; closed Tuesday and Sunday in the high season, Epiphany (6 January)/mid-February and July; 🎫; (II, *D4*).

🍴 **Corte Sconta** Castello 3886, Calle del Pestrin, 🖂 30122, tel. 5227024, fax 5227513 🖂; 🍴 Venetian (seafood); 50/70 capacity; closed Sunday and Monday, and for a certain period of time between January and February, and mid-July/mid-August; ❀; (I, *C4*).

🍴 **Giardinetto-da Severino** Castello 4928, Ruga Giuffa, 🖂 30122, tel. 5285332; 🍴 Venetian (seafood); 100/300 capacity; closed Thursday, January; ❀; (II, *D6*).

🍴 **Graspo de Ua** S. Marco 5094, Calle dei Bombaseri, 🖂 30124, tel. 5200150, fax 5233917 🖂; 🍴 Venetian regional (fish and shellfish); 110 capacity; closed Monday and Tuesday, and for a certain period of time in January and in August; 🎫; (II, *C4*).

🍴 **Bruno** Castello 5731, Calle Paradiso, 🖂 30122, tel. 5221480; 🍴 Venetian regional (seafood); 60/110 capacity; closed Tuesday, and for a certain period of time in July; 🎫; (II, *C5*).

¶ **Osteria Alle Testiere** Castello 5801, Calle del Mondo Novo, ✉ 30122, tel. 5227220 ✉; ⅹ Venetian; 25 capacity; closed Sunday, and for a certain period of time in March and August; ⓑ; (II, C5).

Lido di Venezia

Hotels and restaurants

✭✭✭ **Excelsior** Lungomare Marconi 41, ✉ 30126, tel. 5260201, fax 5267276; seasonal; 193 rms. ⌂; ⓑ ⚎ ⚎ ▣ Ⓟ ⚹.

✭✭✭ **Biasutti (Adria-Urania-Villa Nora)** Via E. Dandolo 27/29, ✉ 30126, tel. 5260120, fax 5261259; closed December/January; 68 rms. ⌂; ⓑ ⚎Ⓟ.

✭✭✭ **Belvedere** Piazzale S.M. Elisabetta 4, ✉ 30126, tel. 5260115, fax 5261486; 30 rms. ⌂; ⓑ Ⓟ.

✭✭✭ **Biasutti (Villa Ada)** Via Dandolo 24, ✉ 30126, tel. 5260120, fax 5261259; closed December/January; 17 rms. ⌂; ⓑ ⚎ Ⓟ.

✭✭✭ **Villa Pannonia** Via Doge Michiel 48, ✉ 30126, tel. 5260162, fax 5265277; closed for a certain period of time in December; 32 rms. (30 ⌂); ⚎ Ⓟ.

¶ **Al Vecio Cantier** Via della Droma 76-Alberoni, ✉ 30011, tel. 5268130 ✉; ⅹ Venetian (seafood); 70 capacity; closed Monday and at midday on Tuesday, January and November/mid-December; ⚹.

Verona ✉ 37100 ☎ 045

ℹ *APT,* Via Leoncino 61, tel. 592828, fax 8003638 (D4); Piazza delle Erbe 42, tel. 8030086 (estivo, C5).

🚉 *Stazione F.S. (State railroad station),* Piazzale XXV Aprile, tel. 590688.

🛣 *Verona Sud* (A4/A22) km. 5.

✈ *Aeroporto Valerio Catullo di Verona Villafranca,* Caselle (km. 12 to the SW), tel. 8095666. *Alitalia,* Corso di Porta Nuova 61, tel. 8035700 (E3).

Hotels

✭✭✭ **Due Torri Baglioni** Piazza S. Anastasia 4, ✉ 37121, tel. 595044, fax 8004130; 91 rms. ⌂; ⓑ Ⓟ ⚹; (B5).

✭✭✭ **Firenze** (no restaurant), Corso Porta Nuova 88, ✉ 37122, tel. 8011510, fax 8030374; 52 rms. ⌂; ⓑ ▣ ⚹; (E3).

✭✭✭ **San Luca** (no restaurant), Via Volto S. Luca 8, ✉ 37122, tel. 591333, fax 8002143; closed Christmas-Epiphany (6 January); 41 rms. ⌂; ⓑ ▣ ⚹; (D3-4).

✭✭✭ **Giulietta e Romeo** (no restaurant), Via Tre Marchetti 3, ✉ 37121, tel. 8003554, fax 8010862; 30 rms. ⌂; ⓑ ▣ ⚹; (C4).

✭✭✭ **Italia** (no restaurant), Via Mameli 58/64, ✉ 37126, tel. 918088, fax 8348028; 58 rms. (30 ⌂); ⓑ ▣; (A4).

✭✭✭ **Piccolo Hotel** (no restaurant), Via Camuzzoni 3/B, ✉ 37138, tel. 569400, fax 577620; 42 rms. ⌂; ⓑ ▣; (E1-2).

✭✭ **Torcolo** (no restaurant), Vicolo Listone 3, ✉ 37121, tel. 8007512, fax 8004058; closed for a certain period of time in January; 19 rms. ⌂; ⓑ; (D4).

Restaurants

¶¶ **Arche** Via Arche Scaligere 6, ✉ 37121, tel. 8007415, fax 8007415 ✉; ⅹ Venetian (seafood); 60 capacity; closed Sunday and at midday on Monday, January; ⓑ; (B-C5).

¶¶ **Nuovo Marconi** Via Fogge 4, ✉ 37121, tel. 591910, fax 595295 ✉; ⅹ classical (seafood); 90 capacity; closed Sunday, and for a certain period of time between June and July; ⓑ; ⚹; (B-C5).

¶¶ **Tre Corone** Piazza Brà 16, ✉ 37121, tel. 8002462, fax 8011810 ✉; ⅹ Venetian regional and classical; closed Thursday, January; ⓑ; (D4).

¶ **Antica Trattoria-da l'Amelia** Lungadige Rubele 32, ✉ 37121, tel. 8005526; ⅹ classical; 50/75 capacity; closed Sunday and at midday on Monday, for a certain period of time in January and in August; ⚹; (C5).

Viareggio (LU) ✉ 55049 ☎ 0584

ℹ *APT,* Viale Carducci 10, tel. 962233, fax 47336.

🚉 *Stazione F.S. (State railroad station),* Piazza Dante, tel. 44350.

🛣 *Viareggio-Camaiore* (A12) km. 4.

Hotels

✭✭✭ **Astor Hotel** Viale Carducci 54, tel. 50301, fax 55181; 68 rms. ⌂; ⓑ ⚎ ▣ Ⓟ ⚹.

✭✭✭ **Excelsior** Viale Carducci 88, tel. 50726, fax 50729; seasonal; 83 rms. ⌂; ⓑ ▣ Ⓟ ⚹.

✭✭✭ **Palace Hotel** Via Gioia 2, tel. 46134, fax 47351; 68 rms. ⌂; ⓑ ▣.

✭✭✭ **Garden** Via Foscolo 70, tel. 44025, fax 45445; 40 rms. ⌂; ⓑ ▣ ⚹.

✭✭✭ **Liberty** (no restaurant), Lungomare Manin 18, tel. 46247, fax 46249; seasonal; 49 ⌂.

✭✭✭ **Miramare** Viale Carducci 27, tel. 48441, fax 963637; 26 ⌂; ⓑ.

Restaurants

¶¶ **Montecatini** Viale Manin 8, tel. 962129 ✉; ⅹ Tuscan and classical (seafood); 40/80 capacity; closed Monday; ⚹.

¶ **Mirage** Via Zanandelli 12/14, tel. 48446; ⅹ Tuscan and classical (seafood); 120/150 capacity; closed Tuesday (except in July and in August), January; ⓑ; also hotel.

¶ **Tito del Molo** Lungomolo C. del Greco 3, tel. 962016, fax 962016; ⅹ Tuscan and classical (seafood); 100/250 capacity; ⚹.

Vicenza ✉ 36100 ☎ 0444

ℹ *APT,* Piazza Matteotti 12, tel. 320854, fax 325001.

🚉 *Stazione F.S. (State railroad station),* tel. 325046.

🛣 *Vicenza Ovest* (A4) km. 5; *Vicenza Nord* (A31) km. 7.

Hotels and restaurants

✭✭✭ **Alfa** Via dell'Oreficeria 50, tel. 565455, fax 566027; 90 rms. ⌂; ⓑ ⚎ Ⓟ ⚹.

✭✭✭ **Campo Marzio** Viale Roma 21, tel. 5ʹ5700, fax 320495; 35 rms. ⌂; ⓑ ▣ Ⓟ ⚹.

✭✭✭ **Jolly Hotel Europa** state road (S.S.) Padana to the Verona, tel. 564111, fax 564382; 127 rms. ⌂; ⓑ ▣ ⚹.

✭✭✭ **Quality Inn Viest** (no restaurant), Strada Pelosa 241, tel. 582677, fax 582434; 61 rms. ⌂; ⓑ ⚎ ▣ Ⓟ ⚹.

✭✭✭ **Continental** Viale G.G. Trissino 89, tel. 505476, fax 513319; 55 rms. ⌂; ▣ Ⓟ ⚹.

¶¶ **Nuova Cinzia e Valerio** Piazzetta Porta Padova 65/67, tel. 505213, fax 512796 ✉; ⅹ Venetian regional (seafood); 30/50 capacity; closed Sunday evening and Monday, August; ⓑ.

¶ **Antico Ristorante Agli Schioppi** Contrà del Castello 26/28, tel. 543701; ⅹ Venetian regional; 50/80 capacity; closed Saturday evening and Sunday, and mid-July/mid-August; ⓑ.

¶ **Da Remo** Via Caimpenta 14, tel. 911007 ✉; ⅹ Vicenza; 30/80 capacity; closed Sunday evening and Monday, Christmas-Epiphany (6 January) and for a certain period of time between July and August; ⚹ Ⓟ.

Vieste (FG)　　　　　🖂 71019 ☎ 0884

📝 *AA*, Piazza Kennedy, tel. 707130-708806.

⛴ Seasonal transportation from Manfredonia and for the main sites of the Gargano.

Hotels and restaurants

★★★ **Pizzomunno Vieste Palace** Spiaggia di Pizzomunno (beachfront), tel. 708741, fax 707325; seasonal (annual for meeting); 183 rms. 🏨; 🅱 ⚴ ⚎ 🇪 🅿.

★★★ **Scialara** at Scialara, Lungomare Mattei 30, tel. 706684, fax 706114; seasonal; 38 rms. 🏨; 🅱⚴ 🇪 🅿.

🍴 **San Michele** Viale XXIV Maggio 72/74, tel. 708143 ☒; 🍽 Apulian; 40/70 capacity; closed Monday, January/February; 🅱.

Villa Adriana　　　🖂 00010 ☎ 0774
(Hadrian's Villa) (RM)

📝 c/o Villa Adriana, tel. 530203.

Restaurants

🍴🍴 **Adriano** Via Villa Adriana 222, tel. 382235 ☒; 🍽 Roman; 60 capacity; ❀ 🅿; also hotel.

Viterbo　　　　　　🖂 01100 ☎ 0761

📝 *EPT*, Piazza dei Caduti 16, tel. 304795, fax 326206; *Information Offices*: seasonal, Piazza della Morte, tel. 345229; service station Tevere Ovest, tel. 948391; *AA*, Piazza Verdi 4/A (Palazzo Santoro), tel. 226666, fax 346029.

🚃 *Stazioni F.S. (State railroad stations)*, Porta Fiorentina and Porta Romana; travellers information, Porta Fiorentina, tel. 340955; *Stazione Ferrovie Cotral*, Viale Trieste, tel. 342902.

🚏 *Attigliano* (A1) km. 25.

Hotels and restaurants

★★★ **Mini Palace Hotel** (no restaurant), Via S. Maria della Grotticella 2/B, tel. 309744, fax 344715; 38 rms. 🏨; 🅱 🇪 🅿 ♿.

★★★ **Balletti Palace Hotel** (no restaurant), Via F. Molini 8, tel. 344777, fax 344777; 105 rms. 🏨; ⚴ 🅿 ♿.

🍴 **Grottino** Via della Cava 7, tel. 308188 ☒; 🍽 Lazio and classical; 30 capacity; closed Tuesday, and for a certain period of time in December; 🅱.

🍴 **Richiastro** Via della Marrocca 16/18, tel. 228009 ☒; 🍽 Lazio; 60 capacity; open from Thursday to Sunday at midday; closed July/August; ❀.

at San Martino al Cimino, km. 7　　🖂 01030

Hotels

★★★ **Balletti Park Hotel** Via Umbria 2/A, tel. 3771, fax 379496; 40 rms. 🏨; 🅱 ⚴ ⚎ 🅿 ♿.

Volterra (PI)　　　　🖂 54048 ☎ 0588

📝 *Pro Loco*, Via Turazza 2, tel. 86150.

🚃 *Stazione F.S. (State railroad station)*, km. 9, tel. 44116.

Hotels and restaurants

★★★ **San Lino** Via S. Lino 26, tel. 85250, fax 80620; 43 rms. 🏨; ⚎ 🅱 ♿.

★★★ **Sole** (no restaurant), Via dei Cappuccini 10, tel. 84000, fax 84000; 10 rms. 🏨; 🅿.

🍴 **Etruria** Piazza dei Priori 6/8, tel. 86064; 🍽 Tuscan; 90/150 capacity; closed Thursday, for a certain period of time in January and February, and in November; ❀ 🅱.

🍴 **Trattoria del Sacco Fiorentino** Piazza XX Settembre 18, tel. 88537 ☒; 🍽 Tuscan; 50 capacity; closed Friday, and for a certain period in June and in winter; 🅱.

Index of Places

The numbers in Roman type refer to the "Excursions" chapters or "Italy A to Z", while those in Italics refer to the "Information for Travellers" chapters.

Index of Maps and Plans

HB BETTOJA HOTELS

For information and booking
call the Booking Center
Tel. +39/06/4814798-4883288
Fax +39/06/4824976
Toll-free number 1678-860004
E-Mail: hb@bettojahotels.it
internet: http://www.bettojahotels.it

In Rome

Four four-star hotels with varied tariffs and one three-star hotel, facing or adjoining each other in the city center, near the Termini railway station, the Air Terminal and the Subway, offer their traditional and professional services for meetings, congresses, business trips and other incentives. The large number of rooms and conference halls, as well as two restaurants and the roof garden bar at Hotel Mediterraneo satisfy the most varied requirements.

MEDITERRANEO **
Via Cavour 15 - 00184 Rome
Tel. +39 06 4884051 - Fax +39 06 4744105

MASSIMO D'AZEGLIO **
Via Cavour 18 - 00184 Rome
Tel. +39 06 4870270 - Fax +39 06 4827386

ATLANTICO **
Via Cavour 23 - 00184 Rome
Tel. +39 06 485951 - Fax + 39 06 485951

SAN GIORGIO **
Via G. Amendola 61 - 00185 Rome
Tel. +39 06 4827341 - Fax + 39 06 4883191

NORD NUOVA ROMA *
Via G. Amendola 3 - 00185 Rome
Tel. +39 06 4885441 - Fax + 39 06 4817163

RELAIS CERTOSA **
Via Colle Ramole 2 - 50124 Florence
Tel + 39 055 2047171 - Fax +39 055 268575

In Florence

The Hotel Relais Certosa lies 500 meters from the Florence-Certosa exit of the A1 highway, in a park bordering the Certosa di Galluzzo Monastery. 5 km from the historical center, the hotel offers a free shuttle service to and from the Central Station. Equipped with conference halls, restaurants and tennis courts, this hotel is an ideal location for holding meetings and conferences in a relaxed atmosphere, surrounded by the green Tuscan countryside. Only 10 minutes from the city center.

FondazioneAntonioMazzotta

50, Foro Buonaparte, Milan - tel. 02-878197, fax 02-8693046
www.milanoweb.com/mazzotta/   email mazzotta@iol.it
Guided visits (reservations): tel./fax 02-86912297
Visiting hours: 10-19.30, Tues. and Thurs. 10-22.30, closed on Mon.
Tickets: L. 12.000 full price, L. 8.000/6.000 reduced price
Public transport: MM2 Lanza, MM1 Cairoli; Tram 3-4-12-14
Buses 43-57-70

MAN RAY

September 13 1998 - January 24 1999
The greatest Italian retrospective devoted to Man Ray who was one
of the most radical and many-faceted representatives of surrealism
and dadaism. Over 500 works make part of a thorough path examining
all the artistic phases and genres to which Man Ray dedicated himself.

Gustav Klimt and the Viennese Sezession 1897-1905

February - April 1999
Over 300 works of the first years of the Viennese Sezession, founded in
1897 are included in this exhibition together with Klimt's masterpieces,
from his symbolist naturalism to the so called "golden style".
Other European artists' works such as Gauguin, Klinger, Munch and
Segantini, reproduced in the Sezession's review "Ver Sacrum", will be
on display, as well.

COME TO THE

Maggiore, Garda and

*Where the blue water
stretches out endlessly
beneath the blue sky.*

- Ferry service on the 3 lakes approximately every 20 minutes.
- 20% discount from Monday to Friday for senior E.U. citizens over 60 years of age.
- Fast hydrofoil runs for reaching any location in a short time.
- Restaurant and bar on board.
- Evening cruises with dinner and dancing.

INFORMATION OFFICE
NAVIGAZIONE LAGHI MANAGEMENT
20145 Milano - Via L. Ariosto, 21 - Tel. 02 4812086-4816230
Fax 02 4980628

LAKES!

Como

Come to the Lakes, for a day out with a difference. Relax on the boats of the Navigazione Laghi and enjoy the peace and quiet of the beautiful surroundings. Have lunch on board, visit the islands, admire the villages, share a drink and a chat with the other passengers. Just step aboard and we will take you to the most beautiful villages and show you the most spectacular scenery of Lakes MAGGIORE, GARDA and COMO.

Your daily starting point for an
enjoyable holiday in Tuscany

Looking over the countryside just a few
steps from the historic centre.

★ ★ ★ ★

Relais Santa Chiara

Via Matteotti 15
53037 San Gimignano (Siena)
Tel: +39 0577 940701 - Fax +39 0577 942096
Internet: cybermarket.it/rsc
Email: rsc@cyber.dada.it

THINKING ABOUT ITALY?

*D*o you have any thoughts about this new Touring Club guidebook?
Or do you want to know about any other TCI services or products?
If so we want to know. Please photocopy this page (to leave the book intact), and write your comments, criticisms, and suggestions below.
Then mail it (or fax it - Italy 39/2/8526331) to:
**Touring Club of Italy,
Segreteria Soci - Corso Italia, 10
20122 Milano**

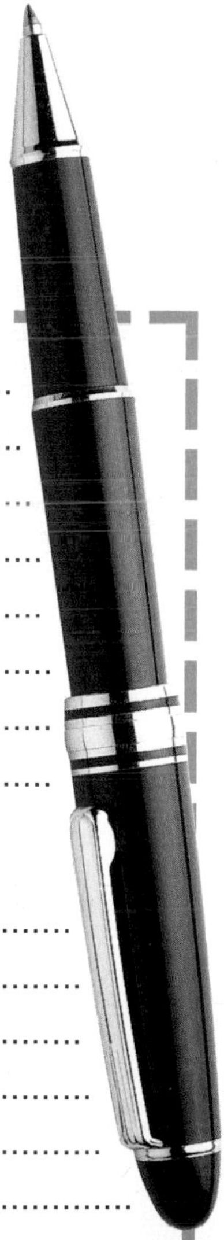

Name

Surname

Address

City

Country

Telephone